THE NIV
HANDY
CONCORDANCE

THE
NIV HANDY
CONCORDANCE

Over 35,000 entries from the
New International Version

Anglicised Edition

Edward W. Goodrick
John R. Kohlenberger III

Hodder & Stoughton
LONDON SYDNEY AUCKLAND

The NIV Handy Concordance
Copyright © 1982 by The Zondervan Corporation
First published in Great Britain 1985
This edition 1996
Reprinted 1999.

The Holy Bible, New International Version
Copyright © 1973, 1978, 1984 by International Bible Society
Published by Hodder & Stoughton,
a member of the Hodder Headline Group.

NIV is a trademark of International Bible Society.
UK trademark number 1448790.

British Library Cataloguing in Publication Data

A record is available for this title

INTRODUCTION

This Concordance to the New International Version is an abridgement of *The NIV Complete Concordance*, taking over 35,000 references from the latter's 250,000. These 35,000 references have been selected as the most helpful for the average Bible reader.

When determining whether or not to include a verse reference, we gave careful consideration to the passage in which the verse is located. We also encourage you to always consider the larger context of the passage, giving special attention to the flow of the thought from beginning to end. Whenever you look up a verse, your goal should be to discover the intended meaning of the verse in context. Do not use this concordance, or any concordance, merely as a *verse-finder*; it should also be used as a *passage-finder*. The contexts surrounding each entry are helpful; but even so, the context excerpts are too brief for study purposes. They serve only to help you locate familiar verses.

In some cases the usual short contextual phrases are ineffective in helping you locate a passage. This is especially true in studying key events in a Bible character's life. Therefore, we have incorporated 260 "block entries" in which we use descriptive phrases that mark the breadth of a passage containing episodes of that person's life. The descriptive phrases replace the brief context surrounding each occurrence of the name.

Often more than one Bible character has the same name. For example, there are more than thirty Zechariahs in the Bible. In these cases we have given the name a block entry, assigning each person a number (1), (2), etc., and have included a descriptive phrase to distinguish each. Less significant names are not included.

In a few instances, where two words with the same spelling have widely divergent meanings, two entries are made in the concordance, and the words are distinguished by a number in square brackets. For example, BEAR [1] indexes all occurrences of BEAR where it means "carry". The creature, BEAR, is indexed under BEAR [2].

In this concordance there are 1,239 key word entries that have an exhaustive list of every appearance of that word. When this occurs, the word or block entry is marked with an asterisk (*). Note that the asterisk for the entry *LORD has a different significance, explained in a footnote.

Since this concordance can only serve one translation—the New International Version—it is difficult for readers familiar with the Authorised Version to make the transition from its older, more archaic language to that of the NIV. We have tried, therefore, to make this transition a bit easier by including some forty-four prominent Authorised Version words and linking them to NIV words that have taken their place. We wish to thank Dr. Daniel E. Sauerwein of Multnomah School of the Bible for supplying the data for these additional words.

We pray that this concordance will be used by NIV readers to introduce them to the full scope of God's truth in every book of the Bible.

John R. Kohlenberger III
Edward W. Goodrick

ABBREVIATIONS FOR THE BOOKS OF THE BIBLE

Genesis	Ge	Nahum	Na
Exodus	Ex	Habakkuk	Hab
Leviticus	Lev	Zephaniah	Zep
Numbers	Nu	Haggai	Hag
Deuteronomy	Dt	Zechariah	Zec
Joshua	Jos	Malachi	Mal
Judges	Jdg	Matthew	Mt
Ruth	Ru	Mark	Mk
1 Samuel	1Sa	Luke	Lk
2 Samuel	2Sa	John	Jn
1 Kings	1Ki	Acts	Ac
2 Kings	2Ki	Romans	Ro
1 Chronicles	1Ch	1 Corinthians	1Co
2 Chronicles	2Ch	2 Corinthians	2Co
Ezra	Ezr	Galatians	Gal
Nehemiah	Ne	Ephesians	Eph
Esther	Est	Philippians	Php
Job	Job	Colossians	Col
Psalms	Ps	1 Thessalonians	1Th
Proverbs	Pr	2 Thessalonians	2Th
Ecclesiastes	Ecc	1 Timothy	1Ti
Song of Songs	SS	2 Timothy	2Ti
Isaiah	Isa	Titus	Tit
Jeremiah	Jer	Philemon	Phm
Lamentations	La	Hebrews	Heb
Ezekiel	Eze	James	Jas
Daniel	Da	1 Peter	1Pe
Hosea	Hos	2 Peter	2Pe
Joel	Joel	1 John	1Jn
Amos	Am	2 John	2Jn
Obadiah	Ob	3 John	3Jn
Jonah	Jnh	Jude	Jude
Micah	Mic	Revelation	Rev

AARON

Genealogy of (Ex 6:16-20; Jos 21:4, 10; 1Ch 6:3-15).

Priesthood of (Ex 28:1; Nu 17; Heb 5:1-4; 7), garments (Ex 28; 39), consecration (Ex 29), ordination (Lev 8).

Spokesman for Moses (Ex 4:14-16, 27-31; 7:1-2). Supported Moses' hands in battle (Ex 17:8-13). Built golden calf (Ex 32; Dt 9:20). Talked against Moses (Nu 12). Priesthood opposed (Nu 16); staff budded (Nu 17). Forbidden to enter land (Nu 20:1-12). Death (Nu 20:22-29; 33:38-39).

ABADDON*

Rev 9: 11 whose name in Hebrew is *A*,

ABANDON (ABANDONED)

Dt   4: 31 he will not *a* or destroy you
1Ki   6: 13 and will not *a* my people Israel."
Ne   9: 19 compassion you did not *a* them
      9: 31 an end to them or *a* them,
Ps   16: 10 you will not *a* me to the grave,
Ac   2: 27 you will not *a* me to the grave,
1Ti   4: 1 in later times some will *a* the faith

ABANDONED (ABANDON)

Ge   24: 27 who has not *a* his kindness
2Co   4: 9 persecuted, but not *a*; struck down,

ABBA*

Mk   14: 36 "*A*, Father," he said, "everything is
Ro   8: 15 And by him we cry, "*A*, Father."
Gal   4: 6 the Spirit who calls out, "*A*, Father

ABEDNEGO

Deported to Babylon with Daniel (Da 1:1-6). Name changed from Azariah (Da 1:7). Refused defilement by food (Da 1:8-20). Refused idol worship (Da 3:1-12); saved from furnace (Da 3:13-30).

ABEL

Second son of Adam (Ge 4:2). Offered proper sacrifice (Ge 4:4; Heb 11:4). Murdered by Cain (Ge 4:8; Mt 23:35; Lk 11:51; 1Jn 3:12).

ABHOR (ABHORS)

Lev 26: 30 of your idols, and I will *a* you.
Dt   7: 26 Utterly *a* and detest it,
Ps   26: 5 I *a* the assembly of evildoers
     119: 163 I hate and *a* falsehood
     139: 21 and *a* those who rise up against you
Am   6: 8 "I *a* the pride of Jacob
Ro   2: 22 You who *a* idols, do you rob

ABHORS (ABHOR)

Pr   11: 1 The LORD *a* dishonest scales,

ABIATHAR

High priest in days of Saul and David (1Sa 22; 2Sa 15; 1Ki 1-2; Mk 2:26). Escaped Saul's slaughter of priests (1Sa 22:18-23). Supported David in Absalom's revolt (2Sa 15:24-29). Supported Adonijah (1Ki 1:7-32); deposed by Solomon (1Ki 2:22-35; cf. 1Sa 2:31-35).

ABIDE see REMAIN

ABIGAIL

1. Sister of David (1Ch 2:16-17).

2. Wife of Nabal (1Sa 25:30); pleaded for his life with David (1Sa 25:14-35). Became David's wife after Nabal's death (1Sa 25:36-42); bore him Kileab (2Sa 3:3) also known as Daniel (1Ch 3:1).

ABIHU

Son of Aaron (Ex 6:23; 24:1, 9); killed for offering unauthorised fire (Lev 10; Nu 3:2-4; 1Ch 24:1-2).

ABIJAH

1. Second son of Samuel (1Ch 6:28); a corrupt judge (1Sa 8:1-5).

2. An Aaronic priest (1Ch 24:10; Lk 1:5).

3. Son of Jeroboam I of Israel; died as prophesied by Ahijah (1Ki 14:1-18).

4. Son of Rehoboam; king of Judah who fought Jeroboam I attempting to reunite the kingdom (1Ki 14:31-15:8; 2Ch 12:16-14:1; Mt 1:7).

ABILITY (ABLE)

Ex   35: 34 tribe of Dan, the *a* to teach others.
Dt   8: 18 for it is he who gives you the *a*
Ezr   2: 69 According to their *a* they gave
Mt   25: 15 one talent, each according to his *a*.
Ac   11: 29 disciples, each according to his *a*,
2Co   1: 8 far beyond our *a* to endure,
      8: 3 were able, and even beyond their *a*.

ABIMELECH

1. King of Gerar who took Abraham's wife Sarah, believing her to be his sister (Ge 20). Later made a covenant with Abraham (Ge 21:22-33).

2. King of Gerar who took Isaac's wife Rebekah, believing her to be his sister (Ge 26:1-11). Later made a covenant with Isaac (Ge 26:12-31).

3. Son of Gideon (Jdg 8:31). Attempted to make himself king (Jdg 9).

ABISHAG*

Shunammite virgin; attendant of David in his old age (1Ki 1:1-15; 2:17-22).

ABISHAI

Son of Zeruiah, David's sister (1Sa 26:6; 1Ch 2:16). One of David's chief warriors (1Ch 11:15-21): against Edom (1Ch 18:12-13), Ammon (2Sa 10), Absalom (2Sa 18), Sheba (2Sa 20). Wanted to kill Saul (1Sa 26), killed Abner (2Sa 2:18-27; 3:22-39), wanted to kill Shimei (2Sa 16:5-13; 19:16-23).

ABLE (ABILITY ENABLE ENABLED ENABLES ENABLING)

Nu   14: 16 'The LORD was not *a*
1Ch 29: 14 that we should be *a* to give
2Ch   2: 6 who is *a* to build a temple for him,
Eze   7: 19 and gold will not be *a* to save them
Da   3: 17 the God we serve is *a* to save us
      4: 37 walk in pride he is *a* to humble.
Mt   9: 28 "Do you believe that I am *a*
Lk   13: 24 will try to enter and will not be *a* to
     14: 30 to build and was not *a* to finish.'
     21: 15 none of your adversaries will be *a*
     21: 36 and that you may be *a* to stand
Ac   5: 39 you will not be *a* to stop these men;
Ro   8: 39 will be *a* to separate us

Ro　14: 4 for the Lord is *a* to make him stand
　　16:25 to him who is *a* to establish you
2Co　9: 8 God is *a* to make all grace abound
Eph　3:20 him who is *a* to do immeasurably
　　6:13 you may be *a* to stand your ground,
1Ti　3: 2 respectable, hospitable, *a* to teach,
2Ti　1:12 and am convinced that he is *a*
　　2:24 kind to everyone, *a* to teach,
　　3:15 which are *a* to make you wise
Heb　2:18 he is *a* to help those who are being
　　7:25 he is *a* to save completely
Jas　3: 2 *a* to keep his whole body in check.
Jude　:24 To him who is *a* to keep you
Rev　5: 5 He is *a* to open the scroll

ABNER

Cousin of Saul and commander of his army (1Sa 14:50; 17:55-57; 26). Made Ish-Bosheth king after Saul (2Sa 2:8-10), but later defected to David (2Sa 3:6-21). Killed Asahel (2Sa 2:18-32), for which he was killed by Joab and Abishai (2Sa 3:22-39).

ABOLISH (ABOLISHED ABOLISHING)

Hos　2:18 I will *a* from the land,
Mt　5:17 that I have come to *a* the Law

ABOLISHED (ABOLISH)

Gal　5:11 the offence of the cross has been *a*.

ABOLISHING* (ABOLISH)

Eph　2:15 by *a* in his flesh the law

ABOMINATION* (ABOMINATIONS)

Da　11:31 set up the *a* that causes desolation.
　　12:11 *a* that causes desolation is set up,
Mt　24:15 the holy place 'the *a* that causes
Mk　13:14 you see 'the *a* that causes

ABOMINATIONS (ABOMINATION)

Da　9:27 who causes desolation will place *a*

ABOUND (ABOUNDING)

2Co　9: 8 able to make all grace *a* to you,
　　9: 8 you will *a* in every good work.
Php　1: 9 that your love may *a* more

ABOUNDING (ABOUND)

Ex　34: 6 slow to anger, *a* in love
Nu　14:18 *a* in love and forgiving sin
Ne　9:17 slow to anger and *a* in love.
Ps　86: 5 *a* in love to all who call to you.
　　86:15 slow to anger, *a* in love
　　103: 8 slow to anger, *a* in love.
Joel　2:13 slow to anger and *a* in love,
Jnh　4: 2 slow to anger and *a* in love,

ABRAHAM

Abram, son of Terah (Ge 11:26-27), husband of Sarah (Ge 11:29).
Covenant relation with the LORD (Ge 12:1-3; 13:14-17; 15; 17; 22:15-18; Ex 2:24; Ne 9:8; Ps 105; Mic 7:20; Lk 1:68-75; Ro 4; Heb 6:13-15).
Called from Ur, via Haran, to Canaan (Ge 12:1; Ac 7:2-4; Heb 11:8-10). Moved to Egypt, nearly lost Sarah to Pharaoh (Ge 12:10-20). Divided the land with Lot; settled in Hebron (Ge 13). Saved Lot from four kings (Ge 14:1-16); blessed by Melchizedek (Ge 14:17-20; Heb 7:1-20). Declared righteous by faith (Ge 15:6; Ro 4:3; Gal 3:6-9). Fathered Ishmael by Hagar (Ge 16).

Name changed from Abram (Ge 17:5; Ne 9:7). Circumcised (Ge 17; Ro 4:9-12). Entertained three visitors (Ge 18); promised a son by Sarah (Ge 18:9-15; 17:16). Questioned destruction of Sodom and Gomorrah (Ge 18:16-33). Moved to Gerar; nearly lost Sarah to Abimelech (Ge 20). Fathered Isaac by Sarah (Ge 21:1-7; Ac 7:8; Heb 11:11-12); sent away Hagar and Ishmael (Ge 21:8-21; Gal 4:22-30). Covenant with Abimelech (Ge 21:22-32). Tested by offering Isaac (Ge 22; Heb 11:17-19; Jas 2:21-24). Sarah died; bought field of Ephron for burial (Ge 23). Secured wife for Isaac (Ge 24). Fathered children by Keturah (Ge 25:1-6; 1Ch 1:32-33). Death (Ge 25:7-11).
Called servant of God (Ge 26:24), friend of God (2Ch 20:7; Isa 41:8; Jas 2:23), prophet (Ge 20:7), father of Israel (Ex 3:15; Isa 51:2; Mt 3:9; Jn 8:39-58).

ABRAM see ABRAHAM

ABSALOM

Son of David by Maacah (2Sa 3:3; 1Ch 3:2). Killed Amnon for rape of his sister Tamar; banished by David (2Sa 13). Returned to Jerusalem; received by David (2Sa 14). Rebelled against David; seized kingdom (2Sa 15-17). Killed (2Sa 18).

ABSENT

Col　2: 5 though I am *a* from you in body,

ABSOLUTE*

1Ti　5: 2 women as sisters, with *a* purity.

ABSTAIN (ABSTAINS)

Ex　19:15 *A* from sexual relations."
Nu　6: 3 he must *a* from wine and other
Ac　15:20 them to *a* from food polluted
1Pe　2:11 to *a* from sinful desires,

ABSTAINS* (ABSTAIN)

Ro　14: 6 thanks to God; and he who *a*,

ABUNDANCE (ABUNDANT)

Ge　41:29 Seven years of great *a* are coming
Job　36:31 and provides food in *a*.
Ps　66:12 but you brought us to a place of *a*.
Ecc　5:12 but the *a* of a rich man
Isa　66:11 and delight in her overflowing *a*."
Jer　2:22 and use an *a* of soap,
Mt　13:12 given more, and he will have an *a*.
　　25:29 given more, and he will have an *a*.
Lk　12:15 consist in the *a* of his possessions."
1Pe　1: 2 Grace and peace be yours in *a*.
2Pe　1: 2 yours in *a* through the knowledge
Jude　:2 peace and love be yours in *a*.

ABUNDANT (ABUNDANCE)

Dt　28:11 will grant you *a* prosperity—
　　32: 2 like *a* rain on tender plants.
Job　36:28 and *a* showers fall on mankind.
Ps　68: 9 You gave *a* showers, O God;
　　78:15 gave them water as *a* as the seas;
　　132:15 I will bless her with *a* provisions;
　　145: 7 will celebrate your *a* goodness
Pr　12:11 works his land will have *a* food,
　　28:19 works his land will have *a* food,
Jer　33: 9 and will tremble at the *a* prosperity
Ro　5:17 who receive God's *a* provision

ABUSIVE

2Ti 3: 2 *a*, disobedient to their parents,

ABYSS*

Lk 8: 31 not to order them to go into the *A.*
Rev 9: 1 the key to the shaft of the *A.*
    9: 2 When he opened the *A*, smoke rose
    9: 2 darkened by the smoke from the *A.*
    9: 11 king over them the angel of the *A*,
    11: 7 up from the *A* will attack them,
    17: 8 and will come up out of the *A*
    20: 1 having the key to the *A*
    20: 3 He threw him into the *A*,

ACCEPT (ACCEPTABLE ACCEPTANCE ACCEPTED ACCEPTS)

Ex 23: 8 "Do not *a* a bribe,
Dt 16: 19 Do not *a* a bribe, for a bribe blinds
Job 42: 8 and I will *a* his prayer and not deal
Pr 10: 8 The wise in heart *a* commands,
    19: 20 Listen to advice and *a* instruction,
Ro 15: 7 *A* one another, then, just
Jas 1: 21 humbly *a* the word planted in you,

ACCEPTABLE (ACCEPT)

Pr 21: 3 is more *a* to the LORD

ACCEPTANCE* (ACCEPT)

Ro 11: 15 what will their *a* be but life
1Ti 1: 15 saying that deserves full *a*:
    4: 9 saying that deserves full *a*

ACCEPTED (ACCEPT)

Ge 4: 7 will you not be *a*? But if you do not
Job 42: 9 and the LORD *a* Job's prayer.
Lk 4: 24 "no prophet is *a* in his home town.
Gal 1: 9 you *a* gospel other than what you *a*,

ACCEPTS (ACCEPT)

Ps 6: 9 the LORD *a* my prayer.
Jn 13: 20 whoever *a* anyone I send *a* me;
    13: 20 whoever *a* me *a* the one who sent

ACCESS

Ro 5: 2 through whom we have gained *a*
Eph 2: 18 For through him we both have *a*

ACCOMPANIED (ACCOMPANY)

1Co 10: 4 from the spiritual rock that *a* them,
Jas 2: 17 if it is not *a* by action, is dead.

ACCOMPANIES (ACCOMPANY)

2Co 9: 13 obedience that *a* your confession

ACCOMPANY (ACCOMPANIED ACCOMPANIES)

Dt 28: 2 *a* you if you obey the LORD your
Mk 16: 17 these signs will *a* those who believe
Heb 6: 9 your case—things that *a* salvation.

ACCOMPLISH

Ecc 2: 2 And what does pleasure *a*?"
Isa 44: 28 and will *a* all that I please;
    55: 11 but will *a* what I desire

ACCORD

Nu 24: 13 not do anything of my own *a*,
Jn 10: 18 but I lay it down of my own *a*.
    12: 49 For I did not speak of my own *a*,

ACCOUNT (ACCOUNTABLE)

Ge 2: 4 This is the *a* of the heavens
    5: 1 This is the written *a* of Adam's line
    6: 9 This is the *a* of Noah.
    10: 1 This is the *a* of Shem, Ham
    11: 10 This is the *a* of Shem.
    11: 27 This is the *a* of Terah.
    25: 12 This is the *a* of Abraham's son
    25: 19 This is the *a* of Abraham's son
    36: 1 This is the *a* of Esau (that is, Edom
    36: 9 This is the *a* of Esau the father
    37: 2 This is the *a* of Jacob.
Mt 12: 36 to give *a* on the day of judgment
Lk 16: 2 Give an *a* of your management,
Ro 14: 12 each of us will give an *a* of himself
Heb 4: 13 of him to whom we must give *a*.

ACCOUNTABLE* (ACCOUNT)

Eze 3: 18 and I will hold you *a* for his blood.
    3: 20 and I will hold you *a* for his blood.
    33: 6 but I will hold the watchman *a*
    33: 8 and I will hold you *a* for his blood.
    34: 10 and will hold them *a* for my flock.
Da 6: 2 The satraps were made *a* to them
Jnh 1: 14 Do not hold us *a* for killing
Ro 3: 19 and the whole world held *a* to God.

ACCURATE

Dt 25: 15 You must have *a* and honest
Pr 11: 1 but *a* weights are his delight.

ACCURSED (CURSE)

2Pe 2: 14 experts in greed—an *a* brood!

ACCUSATION (ACCUSE)

1Ti 5: 19 Do not entertain an *a*

ACCUSATIONS (ACCUSE)

2Pe 2: 11 do not bring slanderous *a*

ACCUSE (ACCUSATION ACCUSATIONS ACCUSER ACCUSES ACCUSING)

Pr 3: 30 Do not *a* a man for no reason—
Lk 3: 14 and don't *a* people falsely—

ACCUSER (ACCUSE)

Jn 5: 45 Your *a* is Moses, on whom your
Rev 12: 10 For the *a* of our brothers,

ACCUSES (ACCUSE)

Job 40: 2 Let him who *a* God answer him!"
Rev 12: 10 who *a* them before our God day

ACCUSING (ACCUSE)

Ro 2: 15 and their thoughts now *a*,

ACHAN*

Sin at Jericho caused defeat at Ai; stoned (Jos 7; 22:20; 1Ch 2:7).

ACHE*

Pr 14: 13 Even in laughter the heart may *a*,

ACHIEVE

Isa 55: 11 *a* the purpose for which I sent it.

ACHISH

King of Gath before whom David feigned insanity (1Sa 21:10-15). Later "ally" of David (2Sa 27-29).

ACKNOWLEDGE (ACKNOWLEDGED ACKNOWLEDGES)

Pr   3: 6   in all your ways *a* him,
Jer   3: 13   Only *a* your guilt—
Hos   6: 3   let us press on to *a* him.
Mt   10: 32   *a* him before my Father in heaven.
Lk   12: 8   *a* him before the angels of God.
1Jn   4: 3   spirit that does not *a* Jesus is not

ACKNOWLEDGED (ACKNOWLEDGE)

Lk   7: 29   *a* that God's way was right,

ACKNOWLEDGES* (ACKNOWLEDGE)

Ps   91: 14   for he *a* my name.
Mt   10: 32   "Whoever *a* me before men,
Lk   12: 8   whoever *a* me before men,
1Jn   2: 23   whoever *a* the Son has the Father
       4: 2   Every spirit that *a* that Jesus Christ
       4: 15   If anyone *a* that Jesus is the Son

ACQUIRES (ACQUIRING)

Pr   18: 15   of the discerning *a* knowledge;

ACQUIRING* (ACQUIRES)

Pr   1: 3   for *a* a disciplined and prudent life,

ACQUIT (ACQUITTING)

Ex   23: 7   to death, for I will not *a* the guilty.

ACQUITTING* (ACQUIT)

Dt   25: 1   *a* the innocent and condemning
Pr   17: 15   *A* the guilty and condemning

ACT (ACTION ACTIONS ACTIVE ACTIVITY ACTS)

Ps   119: 126   It is time for you to *a*, O LORD;

ACTION (ACT)

2Co   9: 2   has stirred most of them to *a*.
Jas   2: 17   if it is not accompanied by *a*,
1Pe   1: 13   minds for *a*; be self-controlled;

ACTIONS (ACT)

Mt   11: 19   wisdom is proved right by her *a*."
Gal   6: 4   Each one should test his own *a*.
Tit   1: 16   but by their *a* they deny him.

ACTIVE* (ACT)

Phm   : 6   I pray that you may be *a*
Heb   4: 12   For the word of God is living and *a*

ACTIVITY (ACT)

Ecc   3: 1   a season for every *a* under heaven:
       3: 17   for there will be a time for every *a*,

ACTS (ACT)

1Ch   16: 9   tell of all his wonderful *a*.
Ps   71: 16   proclaim your mighty *a*,
       71: 24   tell of your righteous *a*
      105: 2   tell of all his wonderful *a*.
      106: 2   Who can proclaim the mighty *a*
      145: 4   they will tell of your mighty *a*
      145: 12   all men may know of your mighty *a*
      150: 2   Praise him for his *a* of power;
Isa   64: 6   all our righteous *a* are like filthy
Mt   6: 1   not to do your '*a* of righteousness'

ADAM

1. First man (Ge 1:26-2:25; Ro 5:14; 1Ti 2:13). Sin of (Ge 3; Hos 6:7; Ro 5:12-21). Children of

(Ge 4:1-5:5). Death of (Ge 5:5; Ro 5:12-21; 1Co 15:22).
2. City (Jos 3:16).

ADD (ADDED)

Dt   4: 2   Do not *a* to what I command you
    12: 32   do not *a* to it or take away from it.
Pr   1: 5   let the wise listen and *a*
     9: 9   he will *a* to his learning.
   30: 6   Do not *a* to his words,
Mt   6: 27   by worrying can *a* a single hour
Lk   12: 25   by worrying can *a* a single hour
Rev   22: 18   God will *a* to him the plagues

ADDED (ADD)

Ecc   3: 14   nothing can be *a* to it and nothing
Ac   2: 47   Lord *a* to their number daily those
Ro   5: 20   The law was *a* so that the trespass
Gal   3: 19   It was *a* because of transgressions

ADDICTED*

Tit   2: 3   to be slanderers or *a* to much wine,

ADMINISTRATION*

1Co   12: 28   with gifts of *a*, and those speaking
Eph   3: 2   Surely you have heard about the *a*
     3: 9   to everyone the *a* of this mystery,

ADMIRABLE*

Php   4: 8   whatever is lovely, whatever is *a*—

ADMIT

Hos   5: 15   until they *a* their guilt.

ADMONISH* (ADMONISHING)

Col   3: 16   and *a* one another with all wisdom,
1Th   5: 12   you in the Lord and who *a* you.

ADMONISHING* (ADMONISH)

Col   1: 28   *a* and teaching everyone

ADONIJAH

1. Son of David by Haggith (2Sa 3:4; 1Ch 3:2). Attempted to be king after David; killed by Solomon's order (1Ki 1-2).
2. Levite; teacher of the Law (2Ch 17:8).

ADOPTED (ADOPTION)

Eph   1: 5   In love he predestined us to be *a*

ADOPTION* (ADOPTED)

Ro   8: 23   as we wait eagerly for our *a* as sons,
     9: 4   Theirs is the *a* as sons; theirs

ADORE*

SS   1: 4   How right they are to *a* you!

ADORNMENT* (ADORNS)

1Pe   3: 3   should not come from outward *a*,

ADORNS* (ADORNMENT)

Ps   93: 5   holiness *a* your house
Isa   61: 10   as a bride *a* herself with her jewels.
   61: 10   bridegroom *a* his head like a priest,

ADULTERER (ADULTERY)

Lev   20: 10   both the *a* and the adulteress must
Heb   13: 4   for God will judge the *a*

ADULTERERS (ADULTERY)

1Co	6: 9	idolaters nor *a* nor male prostitutes
1Ti	1: 10	for murderers, for *a* and perverts,

ADULTERESS (ADULTERY)

Hos	3: 1	she is loved by another and is an *a*.
Mt	5: 32	causes her to become an *a*.

ADULTERIES (ADULTERY)

Jer	3: 8	sent her away because of all her *a*.

ADULTEROUS (ADULTERY)

Mk	8: 38	in this *a* and sinful generation,
Jas	4: 4	You *a* people, don't you know that

ADULTERY (ADULTERER ADULTERERS ADULTERESS ADULTERIES ADULTEROUS)

Ex	20: 14	"You shall not commit *a*.
Dt	5: 18	"You shall not commit *a*.
Mt	5: 27	that it was said, 'Do not commit *a*.'
	5: 28	lustfully has already committed *a*
	5: 32	a woman so divorced commits *a*.
	15: 19	murder, *a*, sexual immorality, theft
	19: 9	marries another woman commits *a*
	19: 18	do not commit *a*, do not steal,
Mk	7: 21	theft, murder, *a*, greed, malice,
	10: 11	marries another woman commits *a*
	10: 12	another man, she commits *a*."
	10: 19	do not commit *a*, do not steal,
Lk	16: 18	a divorced woman commits *a*.
	16: 18	marries another woman commits *a*
	18: 20	'Do not commit *a*, do not murder,
Jn	8: 4	woman was caught in the act of *a*.
Rev	18: 3	of the earth committed *a* with her,

ADULTS*

1Co	14: 20	but in your thinking be *a*.

ADVANCE (ADVANCED)

Ps	18: 29	With your help I can *a*
Php	1: 12	has really served to *a* the gospel.

ADVANCED (ADVANCE)

Job	32: 7	*a* years should teach wisdom.'

ADVANTAGE

Ex	22: 22	"Do not take *a* of a widow
Dt	24: 14	Do not take *a* of a hired man who is
Ro	3: 1	What *a*, then, is there
2Co	11: 20	or exploits you or takes *a* of you
1Th	4: 6	should wrong his brother or take *a*

ADVERSITY*

Pr	17: 17	and a brother is born for *a*.
Isa	30: 20	the Lord gives you the bread of *a*

ADVICE (ADVISERS)

1Ki	12: 8	rejected the *a* the elders
	12: 14	he followed the *a* of the young men
2Ch	10: 8	rejected the *a* the elders
Pr	12: 5	but the *a* of the wicked is deceitful.
	12: 15	but a wise man listens to *a*.
	19: 20	Listen to *a* and accept instruction,
	20: 18	Make plans by seeking *a*;

ADVISERS (ADVICE)

Pr	11: 14	but many *a* make victory sure.

ADVOCATE*

Job	16: 19	my *a* is on high.

AFFLICTED (AFFLICTION)

Job	2: 7	and *a* Job with painful sores
	36: 6	but gives the *a* their rights.
Ps	9: 12	he does not ignore the cry of the *a*.
	9: 18	nor the hope of the *a* ever perish.
	119: 67	Before I was *a* I went astray,
	119: 71	It was good for me to be *a*
	119: 75	and in faithfulness you have *a* me.
Isa	49: 13	will have compassion on his *a* ones.
	53: 4	smitten by him, and *a*.
	53: 7	He was oppressed and *a*,
Na	1: 12	Although I have *a* you, ⌐O Judah,⌐

AFFLICTION (AFFLICTED AFFLICTIONS)

Dt	16: 3	bread of *a*, because you left Egypt
Ps	107: 41	he lifted the needy out of their *a*
Isa	30: 20	of adversity and the water of *a*,
	48: 10	in the furnace of *a*.
La	3: 33	For he does not willingly bring *a*
Ro	12: 12	patient in *a*, faithful in prayer.

AFFLICTIONS (AFFLICTION)

Col	1: 24	lacking in regard to Christ's *a*,

AFRAID (FEAR)

Ge	3: 10	and I was *a* because I was naked;
	26: 24	Do not be *a*, for I am with you;
Ex	2: 14	Then Moses was *a* and thought,
	3: 6	because he was *a* to look at God.
Dt	1: 21	Do not be *a*; do not be discouraged
	1: 29	"Do not be terrified; do not be *a*
	20: 1	do not be *a* of them,
	20: 3	Do not be faint-hearted or *a*;
2Ki	25: 24	"Do not be *a* of the Babylonian
1Ch	13: 12	David was *a* of God that day
Ps	27: 1	of whom shall I be *a*?
	56: 3	When I am *a*,/I will trust in you.
	56: 4	in God I trust; I will not be *a*.
Pr	3: 24	lie down, you will not be *a*;
Isa	10: 24	do not be *a* of the Assyrians,
	12: 2	I will trust and not be *a*.
	44: 8	Do not tremble, do not be *a*.
Jer	1: 8	Do not be *a* of them, for I am
Mt	8: 26	You of little faith, why are you so *a*
	10: 28	be *a* of the one who can destroy
	10: 31	So don't be *a*; you are worth more
Mk	5: 36	"Don't be *a*; just believe."
Lk	9: 34	and they were *a* as they entered
Jn	14: 27	hearts be troubled and do not be *a*.
Ac	27: 24	beside me and said, 'Do not be *a*,
Ro	11: 20	Do not be arrogant, but be *a*.
Heb	13: 6	Lord is my helper; I will not be *a*.

AGAG (AGAGITE)

King of Amalekites not killed by Saul (1Sa 15).

AGAGITE (AGAG)

Est	8: 3	to the evil plan of Haman the *A*,

AGED (AGES)

Job	12: 12	Is not wisdom found among the *a*?
Pr	17: 6	children are a crown to the *a*,

AGES (AGED)

Ro	16: 25	the mystery hidden for long *a* past,
Eph	2: 7	that in the coming *a* he might show
	3: 9	which for *a* past was kept hidden
Col	1: 26	that has been kept hidden for *a*
Rev	15: 3	King of the *a*.

AGONY

Lk 16: 24 because I am in *a* in this fire.'
Rev 16: 10 Men gnawed their tongues in *a*

AGREE (AGREEMENT AGREES)

Mt 18: 19 on earth *a* about anything you ask
Ro 7: 16 want to do, I *a* that the law is good.
Php 4: 2 with Syntyche to *a* with each other

AGREEMENT (AGREE)

2Co 6: 16 What *a* is there between the temple

AGREES* (AGREE)

Ac 7: 42 This *a* with what is written
24: 14 I believe anything that *a*
1Co 4: 17 which *a* with what I teach

AGRIPPA*

Descendant of Herod; king before whom Paul pleaded his case in Caesarea (Ac 25:13-26:32).

AHAB

1. Son of Omri; king of Israel (1Ki 16:28-22:40), husband of Jezebel (1Ki 16:31). Promoted Baal worship (1Ki 16:31-33); opposed by Elijah (1Ki 17:1; 18; 21), a prophet (1Ki 20:35-43), Micaiah (1Ki 22:1-28). Defeated Ben-Hadad (1Ki 20). Killed for failing to kill Ben-Hadad and for murder of Naboth (1Ki 20:35-21:40).
2. A false prophet (Jer 29:21-22).

AHAZ

1. Son of Jotham; king of Judah, (2Ki 16; 2Ch 28). Idolatry of (2Ki 16:3-4, 10-18; 2Ch 28:1-4, 22-25). Defeated by Aram and Israel (2Ki 16:5-6; 2Ch 28:5-15). Sought help from Assyria rather than the LORD (2Ki 16:7-9; 2Ch 28:16-21; Isa 7).
2. Benjamite, descendant of Saul (1Ch 8:35-36).

AHAZIAH

1. Son of Ahab; king of Israel (1Ki 22:51-2Ki 1:18; 2Ch 20:35-37). Made an unsuccessful alliance with Jehoshaphat of Judah (2Ch 20:35-37). Died for seeking Baal rather than the LORD (1Ki 1).
2. Son of Jehoram; king of Judah (2Ki 8:25-29; 9:14-29), also called Jehoahaz (2Ch 21:17-22:9; 25:23). Killed by Jehu while visiting Joram (2Ki 9:14-29; 2Ch 22:1-9).

AHIJAH

1Sa 14: 18 Saul said to *A*, "Bring the ark
1Ki 14: 2 *A* the prophet is there—the one

AHIMELECH

1. Priest who helped David in his flight from Saul (1Sa 21-22).
2. One of David's warriors (1Sa 26:6).

AHITHOPHEL

One of David's counsellors who sided with Absalom (2Sa 15:12, 31-37; 1Ch 27:33-34); committed suicide when his advice was ignored (2Sa 16:15-17:23).

AI

Jos 7: 4 they were routed by the men of *A*,
8: 28 So Joshua burned *A* and made it

AID

Isa 38: 14 troubled; O Lord, come to my *a*!"
Php 4: 16 you sent me *a* again and again

AIM

1Co 7: 34 Her *a* is to be devoted to the Lord
2Co 13: 11 *A* for perfection, listen

AIR

Mt 8: 20 and birds of the *a* have nests,
Lk 9: 58 and birds of the *a* have nests,
1Co 9: 26 not fight like a man beating the *a*.
14: 9 You will just be speaking into the *a*
Eph 2: 2 of the ruler of the kingdom of the *a*,
1Th 4: 17 clouds to meet the Lord in the *a*.

ALABASTER*

Mt 26: 7 came to him with an *a* jar
Mk 14: 3 a woman came with an *a* jar
Lk 7: 37 she brought an *a* jar of perfume,

ALARM (ALARMED)

2Co 7: 11 indignation, what *a*, what longing,

ALARMED (ALARM)

Mk 13: 7 and rumours of wars, do not be *a*.
2Th 2: 2 not to become easily unsettled or *a*

ALERT*

Jos 8: 4 All of you be on the *a*.
Ps 17: 11 with eyes *a*, to throw me
Isa 21: 7 let him be *a*, / fully *a*."
Mk 13: 33 Be *a*! You do not know
Eph 6: 18 be *a* and always keep on praying
1Th 5: 6 but let us be *a* and self-controlled.
1Pe 5: 8 Be self-controlled and *a*.

ALIEN (ALIENATED ALIENS)

Ex 22: 21 "Do not ill-treat an *a*
Lev 24: 22 are to have the same law for the *a*
Ps 146: 9 The LORD watches over the *a*

ALIENATED (ALIEN)

Gal 5: 4 by law have been *a* from Christ;
Col 1: 21 Once you were *a* from God

ALIENS (ALIEN)

Ex 23: 9 know how it feels to be *a*,
1Pe 2: 11 as *a* and strangers in the world,

ALIVE (LIVE)

1Sa 2: 6 LORD brings death and makes *a*;
Lk 24: 23 vision of angels, who said he was *a*.
Ac 1: 3 convincing proofs that he was *a*.
Ro 6: 11 but *a* to God in Christ Jesus.
1Co 15: 22 so in Christ all will be made *a*.
Eph 2: 5 made us *a* with Christ

ALMIGHTY (MIGHT)

Ge 17: 1 "I am God *A*; walk before me
Ex 6: 3 to Isaac and to Jacob as God *A*,
Ru 1: 20 the *A* has made my life very bitter.
Job 11: 7 Can you probe the limits of the *A*?
33: 4 the breath of the *A* gives me life.
Ps 89: 8 O LORD God *A*, who is like you?
91: 1 will rest in the shadow of the *A*.
Isa 6: 3 "Holy, holy, holy is the LORD *A*;
45: 13 says the LORD *A*."
47: 4 the LORD *A* is his name—
48: 2 the LORD *A* is his name:

Isa 51: 15 the LORD *A* is his name.
54: 5 the LORD *A* is his name—
Am 5: 14 the LORD God *A* will be with you,
5: 15 the LORD God *A* will have mercy
Rev 4: 8 holy is the Lord God *A*, who was,
19: 6 For our Lord God *A* reigns.

ALMS see GIVING, (acts of) RIGHTEOUSNESS

ALPHA*

Rev 1: 8 "I am the *A* and the Omega,"
21: 6 I am the *A* and the Omega,
22: 13 I am the *A* and the Omega,

ALTAR

Ge 8: 20 Then Noah built an *a* to the LORD
12: 7 So he built an *a* there to the LORD
13: 18 where he built an *a* to the LORD.
22: 9 Abraham built an *a* there
22: 9 his son Isaac and laid him on the *a*;
26: 25 Isaac built an *a* there and called
35: 1 and build an *a* there to God,
Ex 17: 15 Moses built an *a* and called it
27: 1 "Build an *a* of acacia wood,
30: 1 "Make an *a* of acacia wood
37: 25 They made the *a* of incense out
Dt 27: 5 an *a* to the LORD your God, an *a*
Jos 8: 30 on Mount Ebal an *a* to the LORD,
22: 10 built an imposing *a* there
Jdg 6: 24 So Gideon built an *a* to the LORD
21: 4 the next day the people built an *a*
1Sa 7: 17 he built an *a* there to the LORD.
14: 35 Then Saul built an *a* to the LORD;
2Sa 24: 25 David built an *a* to the LORD
1Ki 12: 33 sacrifices on the *a* he had built
13: 2 "O *a*, *a*! This is what the LORD
16: 32 He set up an *a* for Baal
18: 30 and he repaired the *a* of the LORD
2Ki 16: 11 So Uriah the priest built an *a*
1Ch 21: 26 David built an *a* to the LORD
2Ch 4: 1 made a bronze *a* twenty cubits
4: 19 the golden *a*; the tables
15: 8 He repaired the *a* of the LORD
32: 12 'You must worship before one *a*
33: 16 he restored the *a* of the LORD
Ezr 3: 2 to build the *a* of the God of Israel
Isa 6: 6 taken with tongs from the *a*.
Eze 40: 47 the *a* was in front of the temple.
Mt 5: 23 if you are offering your gift at the *a*
Ac 17: 23 found an *a* with this inscription:
Heb 13: 10 We have an *a* from which those
Rev 6: 9 I saw under the *a* the souls

ALTER*

Ps 89: 34 or *a* what my lips have uttered.

ALWAYS

Dt 15: 11 There will *a* be poor people
Ps 16: 8 I have set the LORD *a* before me.
51: 3 and my sin is *a* before me.
Pr 23: 7 who is *a* thinking about the cost.
Mt 26: 11 The poor you will *a* have with you,
28: 20 And surely I will be with you *a*,
Mk 14: 7 The poor you will *a* have with you,
Jn 12: 8 You will *a* have the poor
1Co 13: 7 *a* protects, *a* trusts, *a* hopes, *a*
Php 4: 4 Rejoice in the Lord *a*.
1Pe 3: 15 *A* be prepared to give an answer

AMALEKITES

Ex 17: 8 *A* came and attacked the Israelites
1Sa 15: 2 'I will punish the *A*

AMASA

Nephew of David (1Ch 2:17). Commander of
Absalom's forces (2Sa 17:24-27). Returned to
David (2Sa 19:13). Killed by Joab (2Sa 20:4-13).

AMASSES*

Pr 28: 8 *a* it for another, who will be kind

AMAZED

Mt 7: 28 the crowds were *a* at his teaching,
Mk 6: 6 And he was *a* at their lack of faith.
10: 24 The disciples were *a* at his words.
Ac 2: 7 Utterly *a*, they asked: "Are not all
13: 12 for he was *a* at the teaching about

AMAZIAH

1. Son of Joash; king of Judah (2Ki 14; 2Ch 25).
Defeated Edom (2Ki 14:7; 2Ch 25:5-13); defeated
by Israel for worshipping Edom's gods (2Ki
14:8-14; 2Ch 25:14-24).
2. Idolatrous priest who opposed Amos (Am
7:10-17).

AMBASSADOR* (AMBASSADORS)

Eph 6: 20 for which I am an *a* in chains.

AMBASSADORS (AMBASSADOR)

2Co 5: 20 We are therefore Christ's *a*,

AMBITION*

Ro 15: 20 It has always been my *a*
Gal 5: 20 fits of rage, selfish *a*, dissensions,
Php 1: 17 preach Christ out of selfish *a*,
2: 3 Do nothing out of selfish *a*
1Th 4: 11 Make it your *a* to lead a quiet life,
Jas 3: 14 and selfish *a* in your hearts,
3: 16 where you have envy and selfish *a*,

AMENDS

Pr 14: 9 Fools mock at making *a* for sin,

AMNON

Firstborn of David (2Sa 3:2; 1Ch 3:1). Killed by
Absalom for raping his sister Tamar (2Sa 13).

AMON

1. Son of Manasseh; king of Judah (2Ki
21:18-26; 1Ch 3:14; 2Ch 33:21-25).
2. Ruler of Samaria under Ahab (1Ki 22:26;
2Ch 18:25).

AMOS

1. Prophet from Tekoa (Am 1:1; 7:10-17).
2. Ancestor of Jesus (Lk 3:25).

ANAK (ANAKITES)

Nu 13: 28 even saw descendants of *A* there.

ANAKITES (ANAK)

Dt 1: 28 We even saw the *A* there.'"
2: 10 and numerous, and as tall as the *A*.
9: 2 "Who can stand up against the *A*?"

ANANIAS

1. Husband of Sapphira; died for lying to God
(Ac 5:1-11).

2. Disciple who baptised Saul (Ac 9:10-19).
3. High priest at Paul's arrest (Ac 22:30-24:1).

ANCESTORS (ANCESTRY)

1Ki 19: 4 I am no better than my *a*."

ANCESTRY (ANCESTORS)

Ro 9: 5 from them is traced the human *a*

ANCHOR

Heb 6:19 We have this hope as an *a*

ANCIENT

Da 7: 9 and the *A* of Days took his seat.
7:13 He approached the *A* of Days
7:22 until the *A* of Days came

ANDREW*

Apostle; brother of Simon Peter (Mt 4:18; 10:2; Mk 1:16-18, 29; 3:18; 13:3; Lk 6:14; Jn 1:35-44; 6:8-9; 12:22; Ac 1:13).

ANGEL (ANGELS ARCHANGEL)

Ge 16: 7 The *a* of the LORD found Hagar
22:11 But the *a* of the LORD called out
Ex 23:20 I am sending an *a* ahead of you
Nu 22:23 When the donkey saw the *a*
Jdg 2: 1 The *a* of the LORD went up
6:22 Gideon realised that it was the *a*
13:15 Manoah said to the *a* of the LORD
2Sa 24:16 The *a* of the LORD was then
1Ki 19: 7 The *a* of the LORD came back
2Ki 19:35 That night the *a* of the LORD went
Ps 34: 7 The *a* of the LORD encamps
Hos 12: 4 He struggled with the *a*
Mt 2:13 an *a* of the Lord appeared
28: 2 for an *a* of the Lord came
Lk 1:26 God sent the *a* Gabriel
2: 9 An *a* of the Lord appeared to them,
22:43 An *a* from heaven appeared to him
Ac 6:15 his face was like the face of an *a*.
12: 7 Suddenly an *a* of the Lord
2Co 11:14 Satan himself masquerades as an *a*
Gal 1: 8 or an *a* from heaven should preach

ANGELS (ANGEL)

Ps 91:11 command his *a* concerning you
Mt 4: 6 command his *a* concerning you,
13:39 of the age, and the harvesters are *a*.
13:49 The *a* will come and separate
18:10 For I tell you that their *a*
25:41 prepared for the devil and his *a*.
Lk 4:10 command his *a* concerning you
20:36 for they are like the *a*.
1Co 6: 3 you not know that we will judge *a*?
13: 1 in the tongues of men and of *a*,
Col 2:18 and the worship of *a* disqualify you
Heb 1: 4 as much superior to the *a*
1: 6 "Let all God's *a* worship him."
1: 7 "He makes his *a* winds,
1:14 Are not all *a* ministering spirits
2: 7 made him a little lower than the *a*;
2: 9 was made a little lower than the *a*,
13: 2 some people have entertained *a*
1Pe 1:12 Even *a* long to look
2Pe 2: 4 For if God did not spare *a*
Jude : 6 *a* who did not keep their positions

ANGER (ANGERED ANGRY)

Ex 15: 7 You unleashed your burning *a*;

Ex 22:24 My *a* will be aroused, and I will kill
32:10 alone so that my *a* may burn
32:11 "why should your *a* burn
32:12 Turn from your fierce *a*; relent
32:19 his *a* burned and he threw
34: 6 slow to *a*, abounding in love
Lev 26:28 then in my *a* I will be hostile
Nu 14:18 slow to *a*, abounding in love
25:11 has turned my *a* away
32:10 LORD's *a* was aroused that day
32:13 The LORD's *a* burned
Dt 9:19 I feared the *a* and wrath
29:28 In furious *a* and in great wrath
Jdg 14:19 Burning with *a*, he went up
2Sa 12: 5 David burned with a *a*
2Ki 22:13 Great is the LORD's *a* that burns
Ne 9:17 slow to *a* and abounding in love.
Ps 30: 5 For his *a* lasts only a moment,
78:38 Time after time he restrained his *a*
86:15 slow to *a*, abounding in love
90: 7 We are consumed by your *a*
103: 8 slow to *a*, abounding in love.
Pr 15: 1 but a harsh word stirs up *a*.
29:11 A fool gives full vent to his *a*,
30:33 so stirring up *a* produces strife."
Jnh 4: 2 slow to *a* and abounding in love,
Eph 4:26 "In your *a* do not sin": Do not let
Jas 1:20 for man's *a* does not bring about

ANGERED (ANGER)

Pr 22:24 do not associate with one easily *a*,
1Co 13: 5 it is not easily *a*, it keeps no record

ANGRY (ANGER)

Ps 2:12 Kiss the Son, lest he be *a*
95:10 For forty years I was *a*
Pr 29:22 An *a* man stirs up dissension,
Mt 5:22 But I tell you that anyone who is *a*
Jas 1:19 slow to speak and slow to become *a*

ANGUISH

Ps 118: 5 In my *a* I cried to the LORD,
Jer 4:19 Oh, my *a*, my *a*!
Zep 1:15 a day of distress and *a*,
Lk 21:25 nations will be in *a* and perplexity
22:24 in *a*, he prayed more earnestly,
Ro 9: 2 and unceasing *a* in my heart.

ANIMALS

Ge 1:24 wild *a*, each according to its kind."
7:16 The *a* going in were male
Dt 14: 4 These are the *a* you may eat: the ox
Job 12: 7 ask the *a*, and they will teach you,
Isa 43:20 The wild *a* honour me,

ANNOUNCE (ANNOUNCED)

Mt 6: 2 give to the needy, do not *a* it

ANNOUNCED (ANNOUNCE)

Isa 48: 5 before they happened I *a* them
Gal 3: 8 and *a* the gospel in advance

ANNOYANCE*

Pr 12:16 A fool shows his *a* at once,

ANNUAL*

Ex 30:10 This *a* atonement must be made
Jdg 21:19 there is the *a* festival of the LORD
1Sa 1:21 family to offer the *a* sacrifice.
2:19 husband to offer the *a* sacrifice.

1Sa 20: 6 an a sacrifice is being made there
2Ch 8: 13 New Moons and the three a feasts
Heb 10: 3 those sacrifices are an a reminder

ANOINT (ANOINTED ANOINTING)

Ex 30: 26 use it to a the Tent of Meeting,
30: 30 "A Aaron and his sons
1Sa 9: 16 A him leader over my people Israel
15: 1 to a you king over his people Israel;
2Ki 9: 3 what the LORD says: I a you king
Ps 23: 5 You a my head with oil;
Da 9: 24 prophecy and to a the most holy.
Jas 5: 14 and a him with oil in the name

ANOINTED (ANOINT)

1Ch 16: 22 "Do not touch my a ones;
Ps 105: 15 "Do not touch my a ones;
Isa 61: 1 because the LORD has a me
Da 9: 26 the A One will be cut off
Lk 4: 18 because he has a me
Ac 10: 38 how God a Jesus of Nazareth

ANOINTING (ANOINT)

Lev 8: 12 some of the a oil on Aaron's head
1Ch 29: 22 a him before the LORD to be ruler
Ps 45: 7 by a you with the oil of joy.
Heb 1: 9 by a you with the oil of joy."
1Jn 2: 20 you have an a from the Holy One,
2: 27 about all things and as that a is real,

ANT* (ANTS)

Pr 6: 6 Go to the a, you sluggard;

ANTICHRIST* (ANTICHRISTS)

1Jn 2: 18 have heard that the a is coming,
2: 22 a man is the a—he denies
4: 3 of the a, which you have heard is
2Jn : 7 person is the deceiver and the a.

ANTICHRISTS* (ANTICHRIST)

1Jn 2: 18 even now many a have come.

ANTIOCH

Ac 11: 26 were first called Christians at A.

ANTS* (ANT)

Pr 30: 25 A are creatures of little strength,

ANXIETIES* (ANXIOUS)

Lk 21: 34 drunkenness and the a of life,

ANXIETY (ANXIOUS)

1Pe 5: 7 Cast all your a on him

ANXIOUS (ANXIETIES ANXIETY)

Pr 12: 25 An a heart weighs a man down,
Php 4: 6 Do not be a about anything,

APOLLOS*

Christian from Alexandria, learned in the Scriptures; instructed by Aquila and Priscilla (Ac 18:24-28). Ministered with Paul at Corinth (Ac 19:1; 1Co 1:12; 3; Tit 3:13).

APOLLYON*

Rev 9: 11 is Abaddon, and in Greek, A.

APOSTLE (APOSTLES APOSTLES')

Ro 11: 13 as I am the a to the Gentiles,
1Co 9: 1 Am I not an a? Have I not seen

2Co 12: 12 The things that mark an a—signs,
Gal 2: 8 of Peter as an a to the Jews,
1Ti 2: 7 was appointed a herald and an a—
2Ti 1: 11 I was appointed a herald and an a
Heb 3: 1 a and high priest whom we confess.

APOSTLES (APOSTLE)

See also Andrew, Bartholomew, James, John, Judas, Matthew, Matthias, Nathanael, Paul, Peter, Philip, Simon, Thaddaeus, Thomas.
Mk 3: 14 twelve—designating them a—
Lk 11: 49 'I will send them prophets and a,
Ac 1: 26 so he was added to the eleven a.
2: 43 signs were done by the a.
1Co 12: 28 God has appointed first of all a,
15: 9 For I am the least of the a
2Co 11: 13 masquerading as a of Christ.
Eph 2: 20 built on the foundation of the a
4: 11 It was he who gave some to be a,
Rev 21: 14 names of the twelve a of the Lamb.

APOSTLES' (APOSTLE)

Ac 5: 2 the rest and put it at the a feet.
8: 18 at the laying on of the a hands,

APPEAL

Ac 25: 11 I a to Caesar!" After Festus had
Phm : 9 yet I a to you on the basis of love.

APPEAR (APPEARANCE APPEARANCES APPEARED APPEARING APPEARS)

Ge 1: 9 to one place, and let dry ground a."
Lev 16: 2 I a in the cloud over the atonement
Mt 24: 30 of the Son of Man will a in the sky,
Mk 13: 22 false prophets will a and perform
Lk 19: 11 of God was going to a at once.
2Co 5: 10 we must all a before the judgment
Col 3: 4 also will a with him in glory.
Heb 9: 24 now to a for us in God's presence.
9: 28 and he will a a second time,

APPEARANCE (APPEAR)

1Sa 16: 7 Man looks at the outward a,
Isa 52: 14 his a was so disfigured beyond that
53: 2 in his a that we should desire him.
Gal 2: 6 God does not judge by external a—

APPEARANCES* (APPEAR)

Jn 7: 24 Stop judging by mere a,

APPEARED (APPEAR)

Nu 14: 10 glory of the LORD a at the Tent
Mt 1: 20 an angel of the Lord a to him
Lk 2: 9 An angel of the Lord a to them,
1Co 15: 5 and that he a to Peter,
Heb 9: 26 now he has a once for all at the end

APPEARING (APPEAR)

1Ti 6: 14 until the a of our Lord Jesus Christ,
2Ti 1: 10 through the a of our Saviour,
4: 8 to all who have longed for his a.
Tit 2: 13 the glorious a of our great God

APPEARS (APPEAR)

Mal 3: 2 Who can stand when he a?
Col 3: 4 When Christ, who is your life, a,
1Pe 5: 4 And when the Chief Shepherd a,
1Jn 3: 2 But we know that when he a,

APPETITE

Pr 16: 26 The labourer's *a* works for him;
Ecc 6: 7 yet his *a* is never satisfied.
Jer 50: 19 his *a* will be satisfied

APPLES

Pr 25: 11 is like *a* of gold in settings of silver.

APPLY (APPLYING)

Pr 22: 17 *a* your heart to what I teach,
     23: 12 *A* your heart to instruction

APPLYING (APPLY)

Pr 2: 2 and *a* your heart to understanding,

APPOINT (APPOINTED)

Ps 61: 7 *a* your love and faithfulness
1Th 5: 9 For God did not *a* us
Tit 1: 5 and *a* elders in every town,

APPOINTED (APPOINT)

Dt 1: 15 *a* them to have authority over you
Pr 8: 23 I was *a* from eternity,
Da 11: 27 an end will still come at the *a* time.
Hab 2: 3 For the revelation awaits an *a* time;
Ro 9: 9 "At the *a* time I will return,

APPROACH (APPROACHING)

Ex 24: 2 but Moses alone is to *a* the LORD;
Eph 3: 12 in him we may *a* God with freedom
Heb 4: 16 Let us then *a* the throne of grace

APPROACHING (APPROACH)

Heb 10: 25 all the more as you see the Day *a*.
1Jn 5: 14 is the confidence we have in *a* God:

APPROPRIATE

1Ti 2: 10 *a* for women who profess

APPROVAL (APPROVE)

Jdg 18: 6 Your journey has the LORD's *a*."
Jn 6: 27 the Father has placed his seal of *a*."
1Co 11: 19 to show which of you have God's *a*
Gal 1: 10 trying to win the *a* of men,

APPROVE (APPROVAL APPROVED APPROVES)

Ro 2: 18 if you know his will and *a*
     12: 2 and *a* what God's will is—

APPROVED* (APPROVE)

Ro 14: 18 pleasing to God and *a* by men.
     16: 10 Greet Apelles, tested and *a*
2Co 10: 18 who commends himself who is *a*,
1Ti 2: 4 as men *a* by God to be entrusted
2Ti 2: 15 to present yourself to God as one *a*,

APPROVES* (APPROVE)

Ro 14: 22 not condemn himself by what he *a*.

APT*

Pr 15: 23 A man finds joy in giving an *a* reply

AQUILA*

Husband of Priscilla; co-worker with Paul, instructor of Apollos (Ac 18; Ro 16:3; 1Co 16:19; 2Ti 4:19).

ARABIA

Gal 1: 17 but I went immediately into *A*

Gal 4: 25 Hagar stands for Mount Sinai in *A*

ARARAT

Ge 8: 4 came to rest on the mountains of *A*.

ARAUNAH

2Sa 24: 16 threshing-floor of *A* the Jebusite.

ARBITER* (ARBITRATE)

Lk 12: 14 who appointed me a judge or an *a*

ARBITRATE* (ARBITER)

Job 9: 33 If only there were someone to *a*

ARCHANGEL* (ANGEL)

1Th 4: 16 with the voice of the *a*
Jude : 9 *a* Michael, when he was disputing

ARCHER

Pr 26: 10 Like an *a* who wounds at random

ARCHIPPUS*

Col 4: 17 Tell *A*: "See to it that you complete
Phm : 2 to *A* our fellow soldier

ARCHITECT*

Heb 11: 10 whose *a* and builder is God.

AREOPAGUS*

Ac 17: 19 brought him to a meeting of the *A*,
     17: 22 up in the meeting of the *A*
     17: 34 of the *A*, also a woman named

ARGUE (ARGUMENT ARGUMENTS)

Job 13: 3 and to *a* my case with God.
     13: 8 Will you *a* the case for God?
Pr 25: 9 If you *a* your case with a neighbour,

ARGUMENT (ARGUE)

Heb 6: 16 is said and puts an end to all *a*.

ARGUMENTS (ARGUE)

Isa 41: 21 "Set forth your *a*," says Jacob's
Col 2: 4 you by fine-sounding *a*.
2Ti 2: 23 to do with foolish and stupid *a*,
Tit 3: 9 and *a* and quarrels about the law,

ARK [1]

Ge 6: 14 So make yourself an *a*

ARK [2]

Ex 25: 21 and put in the *a* the Testimony,
Dt 10: 5 put the tablets in the *a* I had made,
1Sa 4: 11 The *a* of God was captured,
     7: 2 that the *a* remained at Kiriath
2Sa 6: 17 They brought the *a* of the LORD
1Ki 8: 9 There was nothing in the *a*
1Ch 13: 9 out his hand to steady the *a*,
2Ch 35: 3 "Put the sacred *a* in the temple that
Heb 9: 4 This *a* contained the gold jar
     11: 7 in holy fear built an *a*
Rev 11: 19 within his temple was seen the *a*

ARM [1] (ARMS)

Nu 11: 23 "Is the LORD's *a* too short?
Dt 4: 34 hand and an outstretched *a*,
     7: 19 mighty hand and outstretched *a*,
Ps 44: 3 it was your right hand, your *a*,
     98: 1 his right hand and his holy *a*
Jer 27: 5 outstretched *a* I made the earth

ARM [2] (ARMY)

1Pe   4: 1 *a* yourselves also with the same

ARMAGEDDON*

Rev 16: 16 that in Hebrew is called *A.*

ARMIES (ARMY)

1Sa 17: 26 Philistine that he should defy the *a*
Rev 19: 14 *a* of heaven were following him,

ARMOUR (ARMY)

1Ki 20: 11 on his *a* should not boast like one
Jer 46: 4 put on your *a!*
Ro   13: 12 deeds of darkness and put on the *a*
Eph   6: 11 Put on the full *a* of God
       6: 13 Therefore put on the full *a* of God,

ARMS [1] (ARM)

Dt   33: 27 underneath are the everlasting *a.*
Pr   31: 17 her *a* are strong for her tasks.
      31: 20 She opens her *a* to the poor
Isa 40: 11 He gathers the lambs in his *a*
Mk   10: 16 And he took the children in his *a,*
Heb 12: 12 strengthen your feeble *a*

ARMS [2] (ARMY)

Ps   18: 32 It is God who *a* me with strength

ARMY (ARM ARMIES ARMOUR ARMS)

Ps   33: 16 No king is saved by the size of his *a*
Joel 2: 2 a large and mighty *a* comes,
       2: 5 like a mighty *a* drawn up for battle.
       2: 11 thunders at the head of his *a;*
Rev 19: 19 the rider on the horse and his *a.*

AROMA

Ge   8: 21 The LORD smelled the pleasing *a*
Ex   29: 18 a pleasing *a,* an offering made
Lev   3: 16 made by fire, a pleasing *a.*
2Co   2: 15 For we are to God the *a* of Christ

AROUSE (AROUSED)

Ro   11: 14 I may somehow *a* my own people

AROUSED (AROUSE)

Ps   78: 58 they *a* his jealousy with their idols.

ARRANGED

1Co 12: 18 But in fact God has *a* the parts

ARRAYED*

Ps   110: 3 *A* in holy majesty,
Isa 61: 10 and *a* me in a robe of righteousness

ARREST

Mt   10: 19 But when they *a* you, do not worry

ARROGANCE (ARROGANT)

1Sa   2: 3 or let your mouth speak such *a,*
Pr   8: 13 I hate pride and *a,*
Mk   7: 22 lewdness, envy, slander, *a* and folly
2Co 12: 20 slander, gossip, *a* and disorder.

ARROGANT (ARROGANCE)

Ps   5: 5 The *a* cannot stand
      119: 78 May the *a* be put to shame
Pr   17: 7 *A* lips are unsuited to a fool—
      21: 24 *a* man—"Mocker" is his name;
Ro   1: 30 God-haters, insolent, *a*
      11: 20 Do not be *a,* but afraid.

ARM [2] (ARMY)

1Ti   6: 17 in this present world not to be *a*

ARROW (ARROWS)

Ps   91: 5 nor the *a* that flies by day,
Pr   25: 18 Like a club or a sword or a sharp *a*

ARROWS (ARROW)

Ps   64: 3 and aim their words like deadly *a.*
      64: 7 But God will shoot them with *a;*
      127: 4 Like *a* in the hands of a warrior
Pr   26: 18 firebrands or deadly *a*
Eph   6: 16 you can extinguish all the flaming *a*

ARTAXERXES

King of Persia; allowed rebuilding of temple under Ezra (Ezr 4; 7), and of walls of Jerusalem under his cupbearer Nehemiah (Ne 2; 5:14; 13:6).

ARTEMIS

Ac   19: 28 "Great is *A* of the Ephesians!"

ASA

King of Judah (1Ki 15:8-24; 1Ch 3:10; 2Ch 14-16). Godly reformer (2Ch 15); in later years defeated Israel with help of Aram, not the LORD (1Ki 15:16-22; 2Ch 16).

ASAHEL

1. Nephew of David, one of his warriors (2Sa 23:24; 1Ch 2:16; 11:26; 27:7). Killed by Abner (2Sa 2); avenged by Joab (2Sa 3:22-39).
2. Levite; teacher (2Ch 17:8).

ASAPH

1. Recorder to Hezekiah (2Ki 18:18, 37; Isa 36:3, 22).
2. Levitical musician (1Ch 6:39; 15:17-19; 16:4-7, 37). Sons of (1Ch 25; 2Ch 5:12; 20:14; 29:13; 35:15; Ezr 2:41; 3:10; Ne 7:44; 11:17; 12:27-47). Psalms of (2Ch 29:30; Ps 50; 73-83).

ASCEND* (ASCENDED ASCENDING)

Dt   30: 12 "Who will *a* into heaven to get it
Ps   24: 3 Who may *a* the hill of the LORD?
Isa 14: 13 "I will *a* to heaven;
      14: 14 I will *a* above the tops of the clouds
Jn   6: 62 of Man *a* to where he was before!
Ac   2: 34 For David did not *a* to heaven,
Ro   10: 6 'Who will *a* into heaven?' " (that is,

ASCENDED (ASCEND)

Ps   68: 18 When you *a* on high,
Eph   4: 8 "When he *a* on high,

ASCENDING (ASCEND)

Ge   28: 12 and the angels of God were *a*
Jn   1: 51 and the angels of God *a*

ASCRIBE*

1Ch 16: 28 *A* to the LORD, O families
      16: 28 *a* to the LORD glory and strength,
      16: 29 *a* to the LORD the glory due his
Job 36: 3 I will *a* justice to my Maker.
Ps   29: 1 *A* to the LORD, O mighty ones,
      29: 1 *a* to the LORD glory and strength.
      29: 2 *A* to the LORD the glory due his
      96: 7 *A* to the LORD, O families
      96: 7 *a* to the LORD glory and strength.
      96: 8 *A* to the LORD the glory due his

ASHAMED (SHAME)

Mk 8: 38 If anyone is *a* of me and my words
Lk 9: 26 If anyone is *a* of me and my words,
Ro 1: 16 I am not *a* of the gospel,
2Ti 1: 8 So do not be *a* to testify about our
2: 15 who does not need to be *a*

ASHER

Son of Jacob by Zilpah (Ge 30:13; 35:26; 46:17; Ex 1:4; 1Ch 2:2). Tribe of blessed (Ge 49:20; Dt 33:24-25), numbered (Nu 1:40-41; 26:44-47), allotted land (Jos 10:24-31; Eze 48:2), failed to fully possess (Jdg 1:31-32), failed to support Deborah (Jdg 5:17), supported Gideon (Jdg 6:35; 7:23) and David (1Ch 12:36), 12,000 from (Rev 7:6).

ASHERAH (ASHERAHS)

Ex 34: 13 and cut down their *A* poles.
1Ki 18: 19 the four hundred prophets of *A*,

ASHERAHS* (ASHERAH)

Jdg 3: 7 and served the Baals and the *A*.

ASHES

Job 42: 6 and repent in dust and *a*."
Mt 11: 21 ago in sackcloth and *a*.

ASHTORETHS

Jdg 2: 13 and served Baal and the *A*.
1Sa 7: 4 put away their Baals and *A*,

ASLEEP (SLEEP)

1Co 15: 18 who have fallen *a* in Christ are lost.
1Th 4: 13 be ignorant about those who fall *a*,

ASSEMBLY

Ps 1: 5 nor sinners in the *a* of the righteous
35: 18 I will give you thanks in the great *a*
82: 1 God presides in the great *a*;
149: 1 his praise in the *a* of the saints.

ASSIGNED

1Ki 7: 14 and did all the work *a* to him.
Mk 13: 34 with his *a* task, and tells the one
1Co 3: 5 as the Lord has *a* to each his task.
7: 17 place in life that the Lord *a* to him
2Co 10: 13 to the field God has *a* to us,

ASSOCIATE

Pr 22: 24 do not *a* with one easily angered,
Jn 4: 9 (For Jews do not *a* with Samaritans
Ac 10: 28 law for a Jew to *a* with a Gentile
Ro 12: 16 but be willing to *a* with people
1Co 5: 9 to *a* with sexually immoral people
5: 11 am writing to you that you must not *a*
2Th 3: 14 Do not *a* with him,

ASSURANCE (ASSURED)

Heb 10: 22 with a sincere heart in full *a* of faith

ASSURED (ASSURANCE)

Col 4: 12 the will of God, mature and fully *a*.

ASTRAY

Ps 119: 67 Before I was afflicted I went *a*,
Pr 10: 17 ignores correction leads others *a*.
20: 1 whoever is led *a* by them is not
Isa 53: 6 We all, like sheep, have gone *a*,

Jer 50: 6 their shepherds have led them *a*
Jn 16: 1 you so that you will not go *a*.
1Pe 2: 25 For you were like sheep going *a*,
1Jn 3: 7 do not let anyone lead you *a*.

ASTROLOGERS

Isa 47: 13 Let your *a* come forward,
Da 2: 2 *a* to tell him what he had dreamed.

ATE (EAT)

Ge 3: 6 wisdom, she took some and *a* it.
27: 25 Jacob brought it to him and he *a*;
2Sa 9: 11 Mephibosheth *a* at David's table
Ps 78: 25 Men *a* the bread of angels;
Jer 15: 16 When your words came, I *a* them;
Eze 3: 3 So I *a* it, and it tasted as sweet
Mt 14: 20 They all *a* and were satisfied,
15: 37 They all *a* and were satisfied.
Mk 6: 42 They all *a* and were satisfied,
Lk 9: 17 They all *a* and were satisfied,

ATHALIAH

Granddaughter of Omri; wife of Jehoram and mother of Ahaziah; encouraged their evil ways (2Ki 8:18, 27; 2Ch 22:2). At death of Ahaziah she made herself queen, killing all his sons but Joash (2Ki 11:1-3; 2Ch 22:10-12); killed six years later when Joash was revealed (2Ki 11:4-16; 2Ch 23:1-15).

ATHLETE*

2Ti 2: 5 if anyone competes as an *a*,

ATONE* (ATONEMENT)

Ex 30: 15 to the LORD to *a* for your lives.
2Ch 29: 24 for a sin offering to *a* for all Israel,
Da 9: 24 an end to sin, to *a* for wickedness,

ATONED* (ATONEMENT)

Dt 21: 8 And the bloodshed will be *a* for.
1Sa 3: 14 guilt of Eli's house will never be *a*
Pr 16: 6 faithfulness sin is *a* for;
Isa 6: 7 guilt is taken away and your sin *a*
22: 14 your dying day this sin will not be *a*
27: 9 then, will Jacob's guilt be *a* for,

ATONEMENT (ATONE ATONED)

Ex 25: 17 "Make an *a* cover of pure gold—
30: 10 Once a year Aaron shall make *a*
Lev 17: 11 it is the blood that makes *a*
23: 27 this seventh month is the Day of *A*.
Nu 25: 13 and made *a* for the Israelites."
Ro 3: 25 presented him as a sacrifice of *a*,
Heb 2: 17 that he might make *a* for the sins

ATTACK

Ps 109: 3 they *a* me without cause.

ATTAINED

Php 3: 16 up to what we have already *a*.
Heb 7: 11 If perfection could have been *a*

ATTENTION (ATTENTIVE)

Pr 4: 1 pay *a* and gain understanding.
4: 20 My son, pay *a* to what I say;
5: 1 My son, pay *a* to my wisdom,
7: 24 pay *a* to what I say.
22: 17 Pay *a* and listen to the sayings
Ecc 7: 21 Do not pay *a* to every word people
Isa 42: 20 many things, but have paid no *a*;

Tit 1:14 and will pay no *a* to Jewish myths
Heb 2: 1 We must pay more careful *a*,

ATTENTIVE (ATTENTION)

Ne 1:11 let your ear be *a* to the prayer
1Pe 3:12 and his ears are *a* to their prayer,

ATTITUDE (ATTITUDES)

Eph 4:23 new in the *a* of your minds;
Php 2: 5 Your *a* should be the same
1Pe 4: 1 yourselves also with the same *a*,

ATTITUDES (ATTITUDE)

Heb 4:12 it judges the thoughts and *a*

ATTRACTIVE

Tit 2:10 teaching about God our Saviour *a*.

AUDIENCE

Pr 29:26 Many seek an *a* with a ruler,

AUTHORITIES (AUTHORITY)

Ro 13: 1 *a* that exist have been established
13: 5 it is necessary to submit to the *a*,
13: 6 for the *a* are God's servants,
Eph 3:10 and *a* in the heavenly realms,
6:12 but against the rulers, against the *a*,
Col 1:16 thrones or powers or rulers or *a*;
2:15 having disarmed the powers and *a*,
Tit 3: 1 people to be subject to rulers and *a*,
1Pe 3:22 *a* and powers in submission to him.

AUTHORITY (AUTHORITIES)

Mt 7:29 because he taught as one who had *a*
9: 6 the Son of Man has *a* on earth
28:18 "All *a* in heaven and on earth has
Mk 1:22 he taught them as one who had *a*,
2:10 the Son of Man has *a* on earth
Lk 4:32 because his message had *a*.
5:24 the Son of Man has *a* on earth
Jn 10:18 *a* to lay it down and *a*
Ac 1: 7 the Father has set by his own *a*.
Ro 7: 1 that the law has *a* over a man only
13: 1 for there is no *a* except that which
13: 2 rebels against the *a* is rebelling
1Co 11:10 to have a sign of *a* on her head.
15:24 he has destroyed all dominion, *a*
1Ti 2: 2 for kings and all those in *a*,
2:12 to teach or to have *a* over a man;
Tit 2:15 Encourage and rebuke with all *a*.
Heb 13:17 your leaders and submit to their *a*.

AUTUMN*

Dt 11:14 both *a* and spring rains,
Ps 84: 6 the *a* rains also cover it with pools.
Jer 5:24 who gives *a* and spring rains
Joel 2:23 both *a* and spring rains, as before.
Jas 5: 7 and how patient he is for the *a*
Jude :12 blown along by the wind; *a* trees,

AVENGE (VENGEANCE)

Lev 26:25 sword upon you to *a* the breaking
Dt 32:35 It is mine to *a*; I will repay.
32:43 for he will *a* the blood
Ro 12:19 "It is mine to *a*; I will repay,"
Heb 10:30 "It is mine to *a*; I will repay,"
Rev 6:10 of the earth and *a* our blood?"

AVENGER (VENGEANCE)

Nu 35:27 the *a* of blood may kill the accused

Jos 20: 3 find protection from the *a* of blood.
Ps 8: 2 to silence the foe and the *a*.

AVENGES (VENGEANCE)

Ps 94: 1 O LORD, the God who *a*,

AVENGING (VENGEANCE)

1Sa 25:26 and from *a* yourself with your own
Na 1: 2 The LORD is a jealous and *a* God;

AVOID (AVOIDS)

Pr 4:15 *A* it, do not travel on it;
20: 3 It is to a man's honour to *a* strife,
20:19 so *a* a man who talks too much.
Ecc 7:18 who fears God will *a* all extremes.
1Th 4: 3 you should *a* sexual immorality;
5:22 *A* every kind of evil.
2Ti 2:16 *A* godless chatter, because those
Tit 3: 9 But *a* foolish controversies

AVOIDS* (AVOID)

Pr 16: 6 of the LORD a man *a* evil.
16:17 The highway of the upright *a* evil;

AWAITS (WAIT)

Pr 15:10 Stern discipline *a* him who leaves
28:22 and is unaware that poverty *a* him.

AWAKE (WAKE)

Ps 17:15 when I *a*, I will be satisfied
Pr 6:22 when you *a*, they will speak to you.

AWARD*

2Ti 4: 8 will *a* to me on that day—

AWARE

Ex 34:29 he was not *a* that his face was
Mt 24:50 and at an hour he is not *a* of.
Lk 12:46 and at an hour he is not *a* of.

AWE* (AWESOME OVERAWED)

1Sa 12:18 So all the people stood in *a*
1Ki 3:28 they held the king in *a*,
Job 25: 2 "Dominion and *a* belong to God;
Ps 119:120 I stand in *a* of your laws.
Ecc 5: 7 Therefore stand in *a* of God.
Isa 29:23 will stand in *a* of the God of Israel.
Jer 2:19 and have no *a* of me,"
33: 9 they will be in *a* and will tremble
Hab 3: 2 I stand in *a* of your deeds,
Mal 2: 5 and stood in *a* of my name.
Mt 9: 8 they were filled with *a*;
Lk 1:65 The neighbours were all filled with *a*
5:26 They were filled with *a* and said,
7:16 They were all filled with *a*
Ac 2:43 Everyone was filled with *a*,
Heb 12:28 acceptably with reverence and *a*,

AWESOME* (AWE)

Ge 28:17 and said, "How *a* is this place!
Ex 15:11 *a* in glory,
34:10 among will see how *a* is the work
Dt 4:34 or by great and *a* deeds,
7:21 is among you, is a great and *a* God.
10:17 the great God, mighty and *a*,
10:21 and *a* wonders you saw
28:58 revere this glorious and *a* name—
34:12 performed the *a* deeds that Moses
Jdg 13: 6 like an angel of God, very *a*.
2Sa 7:23 *a* wonders by driving out nations

1Ch 17: 21 *a* wonders by driving out nations
Ne 1: 5 of heaven, the great and *a* God,
 4: 14 and *a*, and fight for your brothers,
 9: 32 the great, mighty and *a* God,
Job 10: 16 again display your *a* power
 37: 22 God comes in *a* majesty.
Ps 45: 4 let your right hand display *a* deeds.
 47: 2 How *a* is the LORD Most High,
 65: 5 us with *a* deeds of righteousness,
 66: 3 to God, "How *a* are your deeds!
 66: 5 how *a* his works on man's behalf!
 68: 35 You are *a*, O God,
 89: 7 he is more *a* than all who surround
 99: 3 praise your great and *a* name—
 106: 22 and *a* deeds by the Red Sea.
 111: 9 holy and *a* is his name.
 145: 6 of the power of your *a* works,
Isa 64: 3 when you did *a* things that we did
Eze 1: 18 Their rims were high and *a*,
 1: 22 expanse, sparkling like ice and *a*.
Da 2: 31 dazzling statue, *a* in appearance.
 9: 4 "O Lord, the great and *a* God,
Zep 2: 11 The LORD will be *a* to them

AXE

Mt 3: 10 The *a* is already at the root
Lk 3: 9 The *a* is already at the root

BAAL

Jdg 6: 25 Tear down your father's altar to *B*
1Ki 16: 32 *B* in the temple of *B* that he built
 18: 25 Elijah said to the prophets of *B*,
 19: 18 knees have not bowed down to *B*
2Ki 10: 28 Jehu destroyed *B* worship in Israel.
Jer 19: 5 places of *B* to burn their sons
Ro 11: 4 have not bowed the knee to *B*."

BAASHA

King of Israel (1Ki 15:16-16:7; 2Ch 16:1-6).

BABBLER* (BABBLING)

Ac 17: 18 "What is this *b* trying to say?"

BABBLING* (BABBLER)

Mt 6: 7 do not keep on *b* like pagans,

BABIES* (BABY)

Ge 25: 22 The *b* jostled each other within her
Ex 2: 6 "This is one of the Hebrew *b*,"
Lk 18: 15 also bringing *b* to Jesus
Ac 7: 19 them to throw out their newborn *b*
1Pe 2: 2 Like newborn *b*, crave pure

BABY* (BABIES BABY'S)

Ex 2: 6 She opened it and saw the *b*.
 2: 7 women to nurse the *b* for you?"
 2: 9 So the woman took the *b*
 2: 9 "Take this *b* and nurse him for me,
1Ki 3: 17 I had a *b* while she was there
 3: 18 was born, this woman also had a *b*.
 3: 26 give her the living *b*! Don't kill him
 3: 27 Give the living *b* to the first woman
Isa 49: 15 "Can a mother forget the *b*
Lk 1: 41 the *b* leaped in her womb,
 1: 44 the *b* in my womb leaped for joy.
 1: 57 time for Elizabeth to have her *b*,
 2: 6 the time came for the *b* to be born,
 2: 12 You will find a *b* wrapped in cloths
 2: 16 the *b*, who was lying in the manger.
Jn 16: 21 but when her *b* is born she forgets

BABY'S* (BABY)

Ex 2: 8 the girl went and got the *b* mother.

BABYLON

Ps 137: 1 By the rivers of *B* we sat and wept
Jer 29: 10 seventy years are completed for *B*,
 51: 37 *B* will be a heap of ruins,
Rev 14: 8 "Fallen! Fallen is *B* the Great,
 17: 5 MYSTERY *B* THE GREAT

BACKS

2Pe 2: 21 and then to turn their *b*

BACKSLIDING* (BACKSLIDINGS)

Jer 2: 19 your *b* will rebuke you.
 3: 22 I will cure you of *b*."
 14: 7 For our *b* is great;
 15: 6 "You keep on *b*.
Eze 37: 23 them from all their sinful *b*,

BACKSLIDINGS* (BACKSLIDING)

Jer 5: 6 and their *b* many.

BALAAM

Prophet who attempted to curse Israel (Nu 22-24; Dt 23:4-5; 2Pe 2:15; Jude 11). Killed in Israel's vengeance on Midianites (Nu 31:8; Jos 13:22).

BALAK

Moabite king who hired Balaam to curse Israel (Nu 22-24; Jos 24:9).

BALDHEAD

2Ki 2: 23 "Go on up, you *b*!" they said.

BALM

Jer 8: 22 Is there no *b* in Gilead?

BANISH (BANISHED)

Jer 25: 10 I will *b* from them the sounds of joy

BANISHED (BANISH)

Dt 30: 4 Even if you have been *b*

BANNER

Ex 17: 15 and called it The LORD is my *B*.
SS 2: 4 and his *b* over me is love.
Isa 11: 10 the Root of Jesse will stand as a *b*

BANQUET

SS 2: 4 He has taken me to the *b* hall,
Lk 14: 13 when you give a *b*, invite the poor,

BAPTISE* (BAPTISED BAPTISING BAPTISM BAPTISMS)

Mt 3: 11 He will *b* you with the Holy Spirit
 3: 11 "I *b* you with water for repentance.
Mk 1: 8 I *b* you with water, but he will
 1: 8 he will *b* you with the Holy Spirit."
Lk 3: 16 He will *b* you with the Holy Spirit
 3: 16 John answered them all, "I *b* you
Jn 1: 25 "Why then do you *b*
 1: 26 nor the Prophet?" "I *b* with water,"
 1: 33 and remain is he who will *b*
 1: 33 me to *b* with water told me,
1Co 1: 14 I am thankful that I did not *b* any
 1: 17 For Christ did not send me to *b*,

BAPTISED* (BAPTISE)

Mt   3: 6 they were *b* by him in the Jordan
      3: 13 to the Jordan to be *b* by John.
      3: 14 saying, "I need to be *b* by you,
      3: 16 as Jesus was *b*, he went up out
Mk 1: 5 they were *b* by him in the Jordan
      1: 9 and was *b* by John in the Jordan.
      10: 38 or be *b* with the baptism I am
      10: 38 with the baptism I am *b* with?"
      10: 39 and be *b* with the baptism I am
      10: 39 with the baptism I am *b* with,
      16: 16 believes and is *b* will be saved,
Lk   3: 7 to the crowds coming out to be *b*
      3: 12 Tax collectors also came to be *b*.
      3: 21 were being *b*, Jesus was *b* too.
      7: 29 because they had been *b* by John.
      7: 30 they had not been *b* by John.)
Jn   3: 22 spent some time with them, and *b*.
      3: 23 were constantly coming to be *b*.
      4: 2 in fact it was not Jesus who *b*,
Ac   1: 5 For John *b* with water,
      1: 5 but in a few days you will be *b*
      2: 38 Repent and be *b*, every one of you,
      2: 41 who accepted his message were *b*,
      8: 12 they were *b*, both men and women.
      8: 13 Simon himself believed and was *b*.
      8: 16 they had simply been *b*
      8: 36 Why shouldn't I be *b*?"
      8: 38 into the water and Philip *b* him.
      9: 18 was *b*, and after taking some food,
      10: 47 people from being *b* with water?
      10: 48 So he ordered that they be *b*
      11: 16 what the Lord had said, 'John *b*
      11: 16 you will be *b* with the Holy Spirit.'
      16: 15 members of her household were *b*,
      16: 33 he and all his family were *b*.
      18: 8 heard him believed and were *b*.
      19: 5 they were *b* into the name
      22: 16 be *b* and wash your sins away,
Ro   6: 3 *b* into Christ Jesus were *b*
1Co 1: 13 Were you *b* into the name of Paul?
      1: 15 so no-one can say that you were *b*
      1: 16 I also *b* the household of Stephanas
      1: 16 I don't remember if I *b* anyone else
      10: 2 They were all *b* into Moses
      12: 13 For we were all *b* by one Spirit
      15: 29 what will those do who are *b*
      15: 29 why are people *b* for them?
Gal 3: 27 all of you who were *b*

BAPTISING* (BAPTISE)

Mt   3: 7 coming to where he was *b*,
    28: 19 *b* them in the name of the Father
Mk 1: 4 *b* in the desert region
Jn   1: 28 of the Jordan, where John was *b*.
      1: 31 but the reason I came *b*
      3: 23 also was *b* at Aenon near Salim,
      3: 26 he is *b*, and everyone is going
      4: 1 and *b* more disciples than John,
      10: 40 to the place where John had been *b*

BAPTISM* (BAPTISE)

Mt 21: 25 John's *b*—where did it come from?
Mk 1: 4 and preaching a *b* of repentance
      10: 38 baptised with the *b* I am baptised
      10: 39 baptised with the *b* I am baptised
      11: 30 John's *b*—was it from heaven,
Lk   3: 3 preaching a *b* of repentance
    12: 50 But I have a *b* to undergo,

Lk 20: 4 John's *b*—was it from heaven,
Ac   1: 22 beginning from John's *b*
      10: 37 after the *b* that John preached—
      13: 24 and *b* to all the people of Israel.
      18: 25 though he knew only the *b* of John.
      19: 3 did you receive?" "John's *b*,"
      19: 3 "Then what *b* did you receive?"
      19: 4 "John's *b* was a *b* of repentance.
Ro   6: 4 with him through *b* into death
Eph 4: 5 one Lord, one faith, one *b*;
Col   2: 12 having been buried with him in *b*
1Pe 3: 21 this water symbolises *b* that now

BAPTISMS* (BAPTISE)

Heb 6: 2 instruction about *b*, the laying

BAR-JESUS*

Ac 13: 6 and false prophet named *B*,

BARABBAS

Mt 27: 26 Then he released *B* to them.

BARAK*

Judge who fought with Deborah against
Canaanites (Jdg 4-5; 1Sa 12:11; Heb 11:32).

BARBARIAN*

Col   3: 11 circumcised or uncircumcised, *b*,

BARBS*

Nu 33: 55 allow to remain will become *b*

BARE

Hos 2: 3 as *b* as on the day she was born;
Heb 4: 13 and laid *b* before the eyes of him

BARNABAS*

Disciple, originally Joseph (Ac 4:36), prophet
(Ac 13:1), apostle (Ac 14:14). Brought Paul to
apostles (Ac 9:27), Antioch (Ac 11:22-29; Gal 2:
1-13), on the first missionary journey (Ac 13-14).
Together at Jerusalem Council, they separated
over John Mark (Ac 15). Later co-workers (1Co
9:6; Col 4:10).

BARREN

Ge 11: 30 Sarai was *b*; she had no children.
      29: 31 her womb, but Rachel was *b*.
Ps 113: 9 He settles the *b* woman
Isa 54: 1 "Sing, O *b* woman,
Lk   1: 7 children, because Elizabeth was *b*;
Gal 4: 27 "Be glad, O *b* woman,
Heb 11: 11 and Sarah herself was *b*—

BARTHOLOMEW*

Apostle (Mt 10:3; Mk 3:18; Lk 6:14; Ac 1:13).
Possibly also known as Nathanael (Jn 1:45-49;
21:2).

BARUCH

Jeremiah's secretary (Jer 32:12-16; 36; 43:1-6;
45:1-2).

BARZILLAI

1. Gileadite who aided David during Absalom's
revolt (2Sa 17:27; 19:31-39).
2. Son-in-law of 1. (Ezr 2:61; Ne 7:63).

BASHAN

Jos 22: 7 Moses had given land in *B*,

Ps 22:12 strong bulls of *B* encircle me.

BASIN

Ex 30:18 "Make a bronze *b*,

BASKET

Ex 2: 3 she got a papyrus *b* for him
Ac 9:25 him in a *b* through an opening
2Co 11:33 I was lowered in a *b* from a window

BATCH*

Ro 11:16 then the whole *b* is holy;
1Co 5: 6 through the whole *b* of dough?
    5: 7 old yeast that you may be a new *b*
Gal 5: 9 through the whole *b* of dough."

BATH (BATHING)

Jn 13:10 person who has had a *b* needs only

BATHING (BATH)

2Sa 11: 2 From the roof he saw a woman *b*.

BATHSHEBA*

Wife of Uriah who committed adultery with and
became wife of David (2Sa 11), mother of
Solomon (2Sa 12:24; 1Ki 1-2; 1Ch 3:5).

BATTLE (BATTLES)

1Sa 17:47 for the *b* is the LORD's,
2Ch 20:15 For the *b* is not yours, but God's.
Ps 24: 8 the LORD mighty in *b*.
Ecc 9:11 or the *b* to the strong,
Isa 31: 4 down to do *b* on Mount Zion
Eze 13: 5 in the *b* on the day of the LORD.
Rev 16:14 them for the *b* on the great day
    20: 8 and Magog—to gather them for *b*.

BATTLES* (BATTLE)

1Sa 8:20 to go out before us and fight our *b*."
    18:17 and fight the *b* of the LORD."
    25:28 because he fights the LORD's *b*.
2Ch 32: 8 God to help us and to fight our *b*."

**BEAR [1] (BEARING BEARS BIRTH
BIRTHRIGHT BORE BORN CHILDBEARING
CHILDBIRTH FIRSTBORN NEWBORN
REBIRTH)**

Ge 4:13 punishment is more than I can *b*.
Ps 38: 4 like a burden too heavy to *b*.
Isa 53:11 and he will *b* their iniquities.
Mt 7:18 A good tree cannot *b* bad fruit,
Jn 15: 2 branch that does *b* fruit he trims
    15: 8 glory, that you *b* much fruit,
    15:16 but I chose you to go and *b* fruit—
Ro 7: 4 in order that we might *b* fruit
    15: 1 ought to *b* with the failings
1Co 10:13 tempted beyond what you can *b*.
Col 3:13 *B* with each other and forgive

BEAR [2]

Isa 11: 7 The cow will feed with the *b*,
Da 7: 5 beast, which looked like a *b*.

BEARD

Lev 19:27 or clip off the edges of your *b*.
Isa 50: 6 to those who pulled out my *B*;

BEARING (BEAR)

Eph 4: 2 *b* with one another in love.
Col 1: 6 *b* fruit and growing,

Col 1:10 *b* fruit in every good work,
Heb 13:13 outside the camp, *b* the disgrace he

BEARS (BEAR [1])

1Ki 8:43 house I have built *b* your Name.
Ps 68:19 who daily *b* our burdens.

BEAST (BEASTS)

Rev 13:18 him calculate the number of the *b*,
    16: 2 people who had the mark of the *b*
    19:20 who had received the mark of the *b*

BEASTS (BEAST)

Da 7: 3 Four great *b*, each different
1Co 15:32 If I fought wild *b* in Ephesus

BEAT (BEATEN BEATING BEATINGS)

Isa 2: 4 They will *b* their swords
Joel 3:10 *B* your ploughshares into swords
Mic 4: 3 They will *b* their swords
1Co 9:27 I *b* my body and make it my slave

BEATEN (BEAT)

Lk 12:47 do what his master wants will be *b*
    12:48 deserving punishment will be *b*
2Co 11:25 Three times I was *b* with rods,

BEATING (BEAT)

1Co 9:26 I do not fight like a man *b* the air.
1Pe 2:20 if you receive a *b* for doing wrong

BEATINGS (BEAT)

Pr 19:29 and *b* for the backs of fools.

BEAUTIFUL* (BEAUTY)

Ge 6: 2 that the daughters of men were *b*,
    12:11 "I know what a *b* woman you are.
    12:14 saw that she was a very *b* woman.
    24:16 The girl was very *b*, a virgin;
    26: 7 of Rebekah, because she is *b*."
    29:17 Rachel was lovely in form, and *b*.
    49:21 that bears *b* fawns.
Nu 24: 5 "How *b* are your tents, O Jacob,
Dt 21:11 among the captives a *b* woman
Jos 7:21 saw in the plunder a *b* robe
1Sa 25: 3 was an intelligent and *b* woman,
2Sa 11: 2 The woman was very *b*,
    13: 1 the *b* sister of Absalom son
    14:27 and she became a *b* woman.
1Ki 1: 3 throughout Israel for a *b* girl
    1: 4 The girl was very *b*; she took care
Est 2: 2 for *b* young virgins for the king.
    2: 3 realm to bring all these *b* girls
Job 38:31 "Can you bind the *b* Pleiades?
    42:15 land were there found women as *b*
Ps 48: 2 It is *b* in its loftiness,
Pr 11:22 is a *b* woman who shows no
    24: 4 filled with rare and *b* treasures.
Ecc 3:11 He has made everything *b*
SS 1: 8 If you do not know, most *b*
    1:10 Your cheeks are *b* with earrings,
    1:15 Oh, how *b*!
    1:15 How *b* you are, my darling!
    2:10 my *b* one, and come with me.
    2:13 my *b* one, come with me."
    4: 1 How *b* you are, my darling!
    4: 1 Oh, how *b*!
    4: 7 All *b* you are, my darling;
    5: 9 most *b* of women?
    6: 1 most *b* of women?

SS   6: 4   You are *b*, my darling,
     7: 1   How *b* your sandalled feet,
     7: 6   How *b* you are and how pleasing,
Isa   4: 2   of the LORD will be *b*
   28: 5   a *b* wreath
   52: 7   How *b* on the mountains
Jer   3: 19   the most *b* inheritance
     6: 2   so *b* and delicate.
   11: 16   with fruit *b* in form.
   46: 20   "Egypt is a *b* heifer,
Eze   7: 20   They were proud of their *b* jewellery
   16: 7   and became the most *b* of jewels.
   16: 12   and a *b* crown on your head.
   16: 13   You became very *b* and rose
   20: 6   and honey, the most *b* of all lands.
   20: 15   and honey, most *b* of all lands—
   23: 42   and *b* crowns on their heads
   27: 24   traded with you *b* garments,
   31: 3   with *b* branches overshadowing
   31: 9   I made it *b*
   33: 32   who sings love songs with a *b* voice
Da   4: 12   Its leaves were *b*, its fruit abundant
   4: 21   with *b* leaves and abundant fruit,
   8: 9   to the east and towards the *B* Land.
   11: 16   will establish himself in the *B* Land
   11: 41   He will also invade the *B* Land.
   11: 45   the seas at the *b* holy mountain.
Zec   9: 17   How attractive and *b* they will be!
Mt   23: 27   which look *b* on the outside
   26: 10   She has done a *b* thing to me.
Mk   14: 6   She has done a *b* thing to me.
Lk   21: 5   temple was adorned with *b* stones
Ac   3: 2   carried to the temple gate called *B*,
   3: 10   at the temple gate called *B*,
Ro   10: 15   "How *b* are the feet
1Pe   3: 5   in God used to make themselves *b*.

BEAUTY* (BEAUTIFUL)

Est   1: 11   order to display her *b* to the people
     2: 3   let *b* treatments be given to them.
     2: 9   her with her *b* treatments
     2: 12   months of *b* treatments prescribed
Ps   27: 4   to gaze upon the *b* of the LORD
   37: 20   LORD's enemies will be like the *b*
   45: 11   The king is enthralled by your *b*;
   50: 2   From Zion, perfect in *b*,
Pr   6: 25   lust in your heart after her *b*
   31: 30   is deceptive, and *b* is fleeting;
Isa   3: 24   instead of *b*, branding.
   28: 1   to the fading flower, his glorious *b*,
   28: 4   That fading flower, his glorious *b*,
   33: 17   Your eyes will see the king in his *b*
   53: 2   He had no *b* or majesty
   61: 3   to bestow on them a crown of *b*
La   2: 15   the perfection of *b*,
Eze   16: 14   had given you made your *b* perfect,
   16: 14   the nations on account of your *b*,
   16: 15   passed by and your *b* became his.
   16: 15   "'But you trusted in your *b*
   16: 25   lofty shrines and degraded your *b*,
   27: 3   "I am perfect in *b*."
   27: 4   your builders brought your *b*
   27: 11   they brought your *b* to perfection.
   28: 7   draw their swords against your *b*
   28: 12   full of wisdom and perfect in *b*.
   28: 17   proud on account of your *b*,
   31: 7   It was majestic in *b*,
   31: 8   could match its *b*.
Jas   1: 11   blossom falls and its *b* is destroyed.
1Pe   3: 3   Your *b* should not come

1Pe   3: 4   the unfading *b* of a gentle

BED (SICKBED)

Isa   28: 20   The *b* is too short to stretch out on,
Lk   11: 7   and my children are with me in *b*.
   17: 34   night two people will be in one *b*;
Heb   13: 4   and the marriage *b* kept pure,

BEELZEBUB*

Mt   10: 25   of the house has been called *B*,
   12: 24   "It is only by *B*, the prince
   12: 27   And if I drive out demons by *B*,
Mk   3: 22   possessed by *B*! By the prince
Lk   11: 15   "By *B*, the prince of demons,
   11: 18   claim that I drive out demons by *B*.
   11: 19   Now if I drive out demons by *B*,

BEER

Pr   20: 1   Wine is a mocker and *b* a brawler;

BEERSHEBA

Ge   21: 14   and wandered in the desert of *B*.
Jdg   20: 1   all the Israelites from Dan to *B*
1Sa   3: 20   to *B* recognised that Samuel was
2Sa   3: 10   and Judah from Dan to *B*"
   17: 11   Let all Israel, from Dan to *B*—
   24: 2   the tribes of Israel from Dan to *B*
   24: 15   of the people from Dan to *B* died.
1Ki   4: 25   from Dan to *B*, lived in safety,
1Ch   21: 2   count the Israelites from *B* to Dan.
2Ch   30: 5   throughout Israel, from *B* to Dan,

BEFALLS*

Pr   12: 21   No harm *b* the righteous,

BEGGING

Ps   37: 25   or their children *b* bread.
Ac   16: 9   of Macedonia standing and *b* him,

BEGINNING

Ge   1: 1   In the *b* God created the heavens
Ps   102: 25   In the *b* you laid the foundations
   111: 10   of the LORD is the *b* of wisdom;
Pr   1: 7   of the LORD is the *b* of knowledge
   9: 10   of the LORD is the *b* of wisdom,
Ecc   3: 11   fathom what God has done from *b*
Isa   40: 21   Has it not been told you from the *b*
   46: 10   I make known the end from the *b*,
Mt   24: 8   All these are the *b* of birth-pains.
Lk   1: 3   investigated everything from the *b*,
Jn   1: 1   In the *b* was the Word,
1Jn   1: 1   That which was from the *b*,
Rev   21: 6   and the Omega, the *B* and the End.
   22: 13   and the Last, the *B* and the End.

BEHAVE (BEHAVIOUR)

Ro   13: 13   Let us *b* decently, as in the daytime

BEHAVIOUR (BEHAVE)

1Pe   3: 1   without talk by the *b* of their wives,
   3: 16   maliciously against your good *b*

BEHEMOTH*

Job   40: 15   "Look at the *b*,

BELIEVE (BELIEVED BELIEVER BELIEVERS BELIEVES BELIEVING)

Ex   4: 1   "What if they do not *b* me
1Ki   10: 7   I did not *b* these things until I came
2Ch   9: 6   But I did not *b* what they said

Ps 78:32 of his wonders, they did not *b*.
Hab 1: 5 that you would not *b*,
Mt 18: 6 one of these little ones who *b* in me
21:22 If you *b*, you will receive whatever
27:42 the cross, and we will *b* in him
Mk 1:15 Repent and *b* the good news!"
5:36 ruler, "Don't be afraid; just *b*."
9:24 "I do *b*; help me overcome my
9:42 one of these little ones who *b* in me
11:24 *b* that you have received it,
15:32 the cross, that we may see and *b*."
16:16 but whoever does not *b* will be
16:17 signs will accompany those who *b*:
Lk 8:12 so that they may not *b* and be saved.
8:13 They *b* for a while, but in the time
8:50 just *b*, and she will be healed."
22:67 you will not *b* me,
24:25 to *b* all that the prophets have
Jn 1: 7 that through him all men might *b*.
3:18 does not *b* stands condemned
4:42 "We no longer *b* just
5:38 for you do not *b* the one he sent.
5:46 believed Moses, you would *b* me,
6:29 to *b* in the one he has sent."
6:69 We *b* and know that you are
7: 5 his own brothers did not *b* in him.
8:24 if you do not *b* that I am ,the one I
9:35 "Do you *b* in the Son of Man?"
9:36 "Tell me so that I may *b* in him."
9:38 "Lord, I *b*," and he worshipped him.
10:26 you do not *b* because you are not
10:37 Do not *b* me unless I do what my
10:38 you do not *b* me, *b* the miracles,
11:27 "I *b* that you are the Christ,
12:37 they still would not *b* in him.
12:39 For this reason they could not *b*,
12:44 in me, he does not *b* in me only,
13:19 does happen you will *b* that I am
14:10 Don't you *b* that I am in the Father
14:11 *B* me when I say that I am
14:11 or at least *b* on the evidence
16:30 This makes us *b* that you came
16:31 "You *b* at last!" Jesus answered.
17:21 that the world may *b* that you have
19:35 he testifies so that you also may *b*.
20:27 Stop doubting and *b*."
20:31 written that you may *b* that Jesus is
Ac 16:31 They replied, "*B* in the Lord Jesus,
19: 4 the people to *b* in the one coming
24:14 I *b* everything that agrees
26:27 Agrippa, do you *b* the prophets?
Ro 3:22 faith in Jesus Christ to all who *b*.
4:11 he is the father of all who *b*
10: 9 *b* in your heart that God raised him
10:10 For it is with your heart that you *b*
10:14 And how can they *b* in the one
16:26 so that all nations might *b*
1Co 1:21 preached to save those who *b*.
Gal 3:22 might be given to those who *b*.
Php 1:29 of Christ not only to *b* on him,
1Th 4:14 We *b* that Jesus died and rose again
2Th 2:11 delusion so that they will *b* the lie
1Ti 4:10 and especially of those who *b*.
Tit 1: 6 a man whose children *b*
Heb 11: 6 comes to him must *b* that he exists
Jas 1: 6 But when he asks, he must *b*
2:19 Even the demons *b* that—
2:19 You *b* that there is one God.
1Pe 2: 7 to you who *b*, this stone is precious
1Jn 3:23 to *b* in the name of his Son,

1Jn 4: 1 Dear friends, do not *b* every spirit,
5:13 things to you who *b* in the name

BELIEVED (BELIEVE)
Ge 15: 6 Abram *b* the LORD, and he
Ex 4:31 signs before the people, and they *b*.
Isa 53: 1 Who has *b* our message
Jnh 3: 5 The Ninevites *b* God.
Lk 1:45 is she who has *b* that what the Lord
Jn 1:12 to those who *b* in his name,
2:22 Then they *b* the Scripture
3:18 because he has not *b* in the name
5:46 If you *b* Moses, you would believe
7:39 whom those who *b*
11:40 "Did I not tell you that if you *b*,
12:38 "Lord, who has *b* our message
20: 8 He saw and *b*.
20:29 who have not seen and yet have *b*."
Ac 13:48 were appointed for eternal life *b*.
19: 2 the Holy Spirit when you *b*?"
Ro 4: 3 Scripture say? "Abraham *b* God,
10:14 call on the one they have not *b* in?
10:16 "Lord, who has *b* our message?"
1Co 15: 2 Otherwise, you have *b* in vain.
Gal 3: 6 Consider Abraham: "He *b* God,
2Th 2:12 who have not *b* the truth
1Ti 3:16 was *b* on in the world,
2Ti 1:12 because I know whom I have *b*,
Jas 2:23 that says, "Abraham *b* God,

BELIEVER* (BELIEVE)
1Ki 18: 3 (Obadiah was a devout *b*
Ac 16: 1 whose mother was a Jewess and a *b*
16:15 "If you consider me a *b* in the Lord
1Co 7:12 brother has a wife who is not a *b*
7:13 has a husband who is not a *b*
2Co 6:15 What does a *b* have in common
1Ti 5:16 any woman who is a *b* has widows

BELIEVERS* (BELIEVE)
Jn 4:41 of his words many more became *b*.
Ac 1:15 among the *b* (a group numbering
2:44 All the *b* were together
4:32 All the *b* were one in heart
5:12 And all the *b* used to meet together
9:41 he called the *b* and the widows
10:45 The circumcised *b* who had come
11: 2 the circumcised *b* criticised him
15: 2 along with some other *b*,
15: 5 Then some of the *b* who belonged
15:23 To the Gentile *b* in Antioch,
21:25 for the Gentile *b*, we have written
1Co 6: 5 to judge a dispute between *b*?
14:22 is for *b*, not for unbelievers.
14:22 not for *b* but for unbelievers;
Gal 6:10 who belong to the family of *b*.
1Th 1: 7 a model to all the *b* in Macedonia
1Ti 4:12 set an example for the *b* in speech,
6: 2 benefit from their service are *b*,
Jas 2: 1 in our glorious Lord Jesus Christ,
1Pe 2:17 Love the brotherhood of *b*,

BELIEVES* (BELIEVE)
Pr 14:15 A simple man *b* anything,
Mk 9:23 is possible for him who *b*."
11:23 but what he says will happen,
16:16 Whoever *b* and is baptised will be
Jn 3:15 that everyone who *b*
3:16 that whoever *b* in him shall not
3:18 Whoever *b* in him is not

Jn   3: 36 Whoever *b* in the Son has eternal
      5: 24 *b* him who sent me has eternal life
      6: 35 and he who *b* in me will never be
      6: 40 and *b* in him shall have eternal life,
      6: 47 he who *b* has everlasting life.
      7: 38 Whoever *b* in me, as the Scripture
     11: 25 He who *b* in me will live, even
     11: 26 and *b* in me will never die.
     12: 44 Jesus cried out, "When a man *b*
     12: 46 so that no-one who *b*
Ac   10: 43 about him that everyone who *b*
     13: 39 him everyone who *b* is justified
Ro   1: 16 for the salvation of everyone who *b*
     10: 4 righteousness for everyone who *b*.
1Jn   5: 1 Everyone who *b* that Jesus is
      5: 5 Only he who *b* that Jesus is the Son
      5: 10 Anyone who *b* in the Son

BELIEVING* (BELIEVE)

Jn   20: 31 and that by *b* you may have life
Ac   9: 26 not *b* that he really was a disciple.
1Co   7: 14 sanctified through her *b* husband.
      7: 15 A *b* man or woman is not bound
      9: 5 right to take a *b* wife along with us,
Gal   3: 2 or by *b* what you heard? Are you
1Ti   6: 2 Those who have *b* masters are not

BELLY

Ge   3: 14 You will crawl on your *b*
Da   2: 32 its *b* and thighs of bronze,
Mt   12: 40 three nights in the *b* of a huge fish,

BELONG (BELONGING BELONGS)

Ge   40: 8 "Do not interpretations *b* to God?
Lev 25: 55 for the Israelites *b* to me
Dt   10: 14 LORD your God *b* the heavens,
     29: 29 The secret things *b*
Job 12: 13 "To God *b* wisdom and power;
     12: 16 to him *b* strength and victory;
     25: 2 "Dominion and awe *b* to God;
Ps   47: 9 for the kings of the earth *b* to God;
    ·95: 4 and the mountain peaks *b* to him.
    115: 16 The highest heavens *b*
Jer   5: 10 for these people do not *b*
Jn   8: 44 You *b* to your father, the devil,
     15: 19 As it is, you do not *b* to the world,
Ro   1: 6 called to *b* to Jesus Christ.
      7: 4 that you might *b* to another,
      8: 9 of Christ, he does not *b* to Christ.
     14: 8 we live or die, we *b* to the Lord.
1Co   7: 39 but he must *b* to the Lord.
     15: 23 when he comes, those who *b*
Gal   3: 29 If you *b* to Christ, then you are
      5: 24 Those who *b* to Christ Jesus have
1Th   5: 5 We do not *b* to the night
      5: 8 But since we *b* to the day, let us be
1Jn   3: 19 then is how we know that we *b*

BELONGING (BELONG)

1Pe   2: 9 a holy nation, a people *b* to God,

BELONGS (BELONG)

Lev 27: 30 *b* to the LORD; it is holy
Dt   1: 17 of any man, for judgment *b* to God.
Job 41: 11 Everything under heaven *b* to me.
Ps   22: 28 for dominion *b* to the LORD
     89: 18 Indeed, our shield *b* to the LORD,
    111: 10 To him *b* eternal praise.
Eze 18: 4 For every living soul *b* to me,
Jn   8: 47 He who *b* to God hears what God

Ro   12: 5 each member *b* to all the others.
Rev   7: 10 "Salvation *b* to our God,

BELOVED* (LOVE)

Dt   33: 12 "Let the *b* of the LORD rest secure
SS   5: 9 How is your *b* better than others,
      5: 9 How is your *b* better
Jer 11: 15 "What is my *b* doing in my temple

BELSHAZZAR

King of Babylon in days of Daniel (Da 5).

BELT

Ex   12: 11 with your cloak tucked into your *b*,
1Ki 18: 46 and, tucking his cloak into his *b*,
2Ki   4: 29 "Tuck your cloak into your *b*,
      9: 1 "Tuck your cloak into your *b*,
Isa 11: 5 Righteousness will be his *b*
Eph   6: 14 with the *b* of truth buckled

BENEFICIAL* (BENEFIT)

1Co   6: 12 for me"—but not everything is *b*.
     10: 23 but not everything is *b*.

BENEFIT (BENEFICIAL BENEFITS)

Job 22: 2 "Can a man be of *b* to God?
Isa 38: 17 Surely it was for my *b*
Ro   6: 22 the *b* you reap leads to holiness,
2Co   4: 15 All this is for your *b*,

BENEFITS (BENEFIT)

Ps   103: 2 and forget not all his *b*.
Jn   4: 38 you have reaped the *b* of their labour

BENJAMIN

Twelfth son of Jacob by Rachel (Ge 35:16-24;
46:19-21; 1Ch 2:2). Jacob refused to send him to
Egypt, but relented (Ge 42-45). Tribe of blessed
(Ge 49:27; Dt 33:12), numbered (Nu 1:37; 26:41),
allotted land (Jos 18:11-28; Eze 48:23), failed to
fully possess (Jdg 1:21), nearly obliterated (Jdg
20-21), sided with Ish-Bosheth (2Sa 2), but turned
to David (1Ch 12:2, 29). 12,000 from (Rev 7:8).

BEREANS*

Ac   17: 11 the *B* were of more noble character

BESTOWING* (BESTOWS)

Pr   8: 21 *b* wealth on those who love me

BESTOWS (BESTOWING)

Ps   84: 11 the LORD *b* favour and honour;

BETHANY

Mk   11: 1 and *B* at the Mount of Olives,

BETHEL

Ge   28: 19 He called that place *B*,

BETHLEHEM

Ru   1: 19 went on until they came to *B*.
1Sa 16: 1 I am sending you to Jesse of *B*.
2Sa 23: 15 from the well near the gate of *B*!"
Mic   5: 2 "But you, *B* Ephrathah,
Mt   2: 1 After Jesus was born in *B* in Judea,
      2: 6 "'But you, *B*, in the land of Judah,

BETHPHAGE

Mt   21: 1 came to *B* on the Mount of Olives,

BETHSAIDA

Jn   12: 21 who was from *B* in Galilee,

BETRAY (BETRAYED BETRAYS)

Ps   89: 33 nor will I ever *b* my faithfulness.
Pr   25: 9 do not *b* another man's confidence,
Mt   10: 21 "Brother will *b* brother to death,
     26: 21 the truth, one of you will *b* me."

BETRAYED (BETRAY)

Mt   27: 4 "for I have *b* innocent blood."

BETRAYS (BETRAY)

Pr   11: 13 A gossip *b* a confidence,
     20: 19 A gossip *b* a confidence;

BEULAH*

Isa 62: 4 and your land *B*;

BEWITCHED*

Gal   3: 1 foolish Galatians! Who has *b* you?

BEZALEL

Judahite craftsman in charge of building the
tabernacle (Ex 31:1-11; 35:30-39:31).

BIDDING*

Ps   103: 20 you mighty ones who do his *b*,
     148: 8 stormy winds that do his *b*,

BILDAD

One of Job's friends (Job 8; 18; 25).

BILHAH

Servant of Rachel, mother of Jacob's sons Dan
and Naphtali (Ge 30:1-7; 35:25; 46:23-25).

BIND (BINDS BOUND)

Dt   6: 8 and *b* them on your foreheads.
Pr   3: 3 *b* them around your neck,
      6: 21 *B* them upon your heart for ever;
      7: 3 *B* them on your fingers;
Isa 61: 1 me to *b* up the broken-hearted,
Mt   16: 19 whatever you *b* on earth will be

BINDS (BIND)

Ps   147: 3 and *b* up their wounds.
Isa 30: 26 when the LORD *b* up the bruises

BIRD (BIRDS)

Pr   27: 8 Like a *b* that strays from its nest
Ecc 10: 20 a *b* of the air may carry your words,

BIRDS (BIRD)

Mt   8: 20 and *b* of the air have nests,
Lk   9: 58 and *b* of the air have nests,

BIRTH (BEAR [1])

Ps   51: 5 Surely I have been a sinner from *b*,
     58: 3 Even from *b* the wicked go astray;
Isa 26: 18 but we gave *b* to wind.
Mt   1: 18 This is how the *b* of Jesus Christ
     24: 8 these are the beginning of *b*-pains.
Jn   3: 6 Flesh gives *b* to flesh, but the Spirit
1Pe   1: 3 great mercy he has given us new *b*

BIRTHRIGHT (BEAR [1])

Ge   25: 34 So Esau despised his *b*.

BISHOP see OVERSEER

BITTEN

Nu   21: 8 anyone who is *b* can look at it

BITTER (BITTERNESS EMBITTER)

Ex   12: 8 along with *b* herbs, and bread made
Pr   27: 7 what is *b* tastes sweet.

BITTERNESS (BITTER)

Pr   14: 10 Each heart knows its own *b*,
     17: 25 and *b* to the one who bore him.
Ro   3: 14 full of cursing and *b*."
Eph   4: 31 Get rid of all *b*, rage and anger,

BLACK

Zec   6: 6 The one with the *b* horses is going
Rev   6: 5 and there before me was a *b* horse!

BLAMELESS* (BLAMELESSLY)

Ge   6: 9 *b* among the people of his time,
     17: 1 walk before me and be *b*.
Dt   18: 13 You must be *b* before the LORD
2Sa 22: 24 I have been *b* before him
     22: 26 to the *b* you show yourself *b*,
Job   1: 1 This man was *b* and upright;
      1: 8 one on earth like him; he is *b*
      2: 3 one on earth like him; he is *b*
      4: 6 and your *b* ways your hope?
      8: 20 God does not reject a *b* man
      9: 20 if I were *b*, it would pronounce me
      9: 21 "Although I am *b*,
      9: 22 'He destroys both the *b*
     12: 4 though righteous and *b*!
     22: 3 gain if your ways were *b*?
     31: 6 and he will know that I am *b*—
Ps   15: 2 He whose walk is *b*
     18: 23 I have been *b* before him
     18: 25 to the *b* you show yourself *b*,
     19: 13 Then will I be *b*,
     26: 1 for I have led a *b* life;
     26: 11 But I lead a *b* life;
     37: 18 The days of the *b* are known
     37: 37 Consider the *b*, observe the upright
     84: 11 from those whose walk is *b*.
    101: 2 I will be careful to lead a *b* life—
    101: 2 house with *b* heart.
    101: 6 he whose walk is *b*
    119: 1 Blessed are they whose ways are *b*,
    119: 80 May my heart be *b*
Pr   2: 7 a shield to those whose walk is *b*,
      2: 21 and the *b* will remain in it;
     11: 5 of the *b* makes a straight way
     11: 20 in those whose ways are *b*.
     19: 1 Better a poor man whose walk is *b*
     20: 7 The righteous man leads a *b* life;
     28: 6 Better a poor man whose walk is *b*
     28: 10 *b* will receive a good inheritance.
     28: 18 He whose walk is *b* is kept safe,
Eze 28: 15 You were *b* in your ways
1Co   1: 8 so that you will be *b* on the day
Eph   1: 4 world to be holy and *b* in his sight.
      5: 27 any other blemish, but holy and *b*.
Php   1: 10 and *b* until the day of Christ,
      2: 15 so that you may become *b* and pure
1Th   2: 10 and *b* we were among you who
      3: 13 hearts so that you will be *b*
      5: 23 and body be kept *b* at the coming
Tit   1: 6 An elder must be *b*, the husband of
      1: 7 he must be *b*— not overbearing,
Heb   7: 26 *b*, pure, set apart from sinners,
2Pe   3: 14 effort to be found spotless, *b*

Rev 14: 5 found in their mouths; they are *b*.

BLAMELESSLY* (BLAMELESS)

Lk 1: 6 commandments and regulations *b*.

BLASPHEME* (BLASPHEMED BLASPHEMER BLASPHEMES BLASPHEMIES BLASPHEMING BLASPHEMOUS BLASPHEMY)

Ex 22: 28 "Do not *b* God or curse the ruler
Ac 26: 11 and I tried to force them to *b*.
1Ti 1: 20 over to Satan to be taught not to *b*.
2Pe 2: 12 these men *b* in matters they do not
Rev 13: 6 He opened his mouth to *b* God,

BLASPHEMED* (BLASPHEME)

Lev 24: 11 of the Israelite woman *b* the name
2Ki 19: 6 of the king of Assyria have *b* me.
19: 22 Who is it you have insulted and *b*?
Isa 37: 6 of the king of Assyria have *b* me.
37: 23 Who is it you have insulted and *b*?
52: 5 my name is constantly *b*.
Eze 20: 27 your fathers *b* me by forsaking me:
Ac 19: 37 robbed temples nor *b* our goddess.
Ro 2: 24 name is *b* among the Gentiles

BLASPHEMER* (BLASPHEME)

Lev 24: 14 "Take the *b* outside the camp.
24: 23 they took the *b* outside the camp
1Ti 1: 31 I was once a *b* and a persecutor

BLASPHEMES* (BLASPHEME)

Lev 24: 16 anyone who *b* the name
24: 16 native-born, when he *b* the Name,
Nu 15: 30 native-born or alien, *b* the LORD,
Mk 3: 29 whoever *b* against the Holy Spirit
Lk 12: 10 but anyone who *b* against the Holy

BLASPHEMIES* (BLASPHEME)

Ne 9: 18 or when they committed awful *b*.
9: 26 to you; they committed awful *b*.
Mk 3: 28 and *b* of men will be forgiven them.
Rev 13: 5 and *b* and to exercise his authority

BLASPHEMING* (BLASPHEME)

Mt 9: 3 "This fellow is *b*!" Knowing their
Mk 2: 7 He's *b*! Who can forgive sins

BLASPHEMOUS* (BLASPHEME)

Rev 13: 1 and on each head a *b* name.
17: 3 that was covered with *b* names

BLASPHEMY* (BLASPHEME)

Mt 12: 31 and *b* will be forgiven men,
12: 31 the *b* against the Spirit will not be
26: 65 Look, now you have heard the *b*.
26: 65 "He has spoken *b*! Why do we,
Mk 14: 64 "You have heard the *b*.
Lk 5: 21 "Who is this fellow who speaks *b*?
Jn 10: 33 replied the Jews, "but for *b*,
10: 36 Why then do you accuse me of *b*
Ac 6: 11 words of *b* against Moses

BLAST*

Ex 15: 8 By the *b* of your nostrils
19: 13 horn sounds a long *b* may they go
19: 16 and a very loud trumpet *b*.
Nu 10: 5 When a trumpet *b* is sounded,
10: 6 At the sounding of a second *b*,
10: 6 The *b* will be the signal

Nu 10: 9 sound a *b* on the trumpets.
Jos 6: 5 you hear them sound a long *b*
6: 16 the priests sounded the trumpet *b*,
2Sa 22: 16 at the *b* of breath from his nostrils
Job 4: 9 at the *b* of his anger they perish.
39: 25 At the *b* of the trumpet he snorts,
Ps 18: 15 the *b* of breath from your nostrils.
98: 6 and the *b* of the ram's horn—
147: 17 Who can withstand his icy *b*?
Isa 27: 8 with his fierce *b* he drives her out,
Eze 22: 20 a furnace to melt it with a fiery *b*,
Am 2: 2 tumult amid war cries and the *b*
Heb 12: 19 to a trumpet *b* or to such a voice

BLEATING*

1Sa 15: 14 "What then is this *b* of sheep

BLEMISH (BLEMISHES)

Lev 22: 21 be without defect or *b*
Eph 5: 27 or wrinkle or any other *b*,
Col 1: 22 without *b* and free from accusation
1Pe 1: 19 a lamb without *b* or defect.

BLEMISHES* (BLEMISH)

2Pe 2: 13 and *b*, revelling in their pleasures
Jude : 12 These men are *b* at your love feasts

BLESS (BLESSED BLESSES BLESSING BLESSINGS)

Ge 12: 3 I will *b* those who *b* you,
32: 26 not let you go unless you *b* me."
Dt 7: 13 He will love you and *b* you
33: 11 *B* all his skills, O LORD,
Ps 72: 15 and *b* him all day long.
Ro 12: 14 *B* those who persecute you; *b*

BLESSED (BLESS)

Ge 1: 22 God *b* them and said, "Be fruitful
2: 3 And God *b* the seventh day
22: 18 nations on earth will be *b*,
Nu 24: 9 "May those who bless you be *b*
1Ch 17: 27 have *b* it, and it will be *b* for ever."
Ps 1: 1 *B* is the man
2: 12 *B* are all who take refuge in him.
32: 2 *B* is the man
33: 12 *B* is the nation whose God is
40: 4 *B* is the man
41: 1 *B* is he who has regard for the weak
84: 5 *B* are those whose strength is
89: 15 *B* are those who have learned
94: 12 *B* is the man you discipline,
106: 3 *B* are they who maintain justice,
112: 1 *B* is the man who fears the LORD,
118: 26 *B* is he who comes in the name
119: 1 *B* are they whose ways are
119: 2 *B* are they who keep his statutes
127: 5 *B* is the man
Pr 3: 13 *B* is the man who finds wisdom,
8: 34 *B* is the man who listens to me,
28: 20 A faithful man will be richly *b*,
29: 18 but *b* is he who keeps the law.
31: 28 Her children arise and call her *b*;
Isa 30: 18 *B* are all who wait for him!
Mal 3: 12 Then all the nations will call you *b*,
3: 15 But now we call the arrogant *b*.
Mt 5: 3 saying: "*B* are the poor in spirit,
5: 4 *B* are those who mourn,
5: 5 *B* are the meek,
5: 6 *B* are those who hunger
5: 7 *B* are the merciful,

Mt   5: 8   *B* are the pure in heart,
        5: 9   *B* are the peacemakers,
        5: 10 *B* are those who are persecuted
        5: 11 "*B* are you when people insult you,
Lk   1: 48 on all generations will call me *b*,
Jn   12: 13 "*B* is he who comes in the name
Ac   20: 35 'It is more *b* to give than to receive
Tit   2: 13 while we wait for the *b* hope—
Jas   1: 12 *B* is the man who perseveres
Rev   1: 3   *B* is the one who reads the words
        22: 7 *B* is he who keeps the words
        22: 14 "*B* are those who wash their robes,

BLESSES (BLESS)

Ps   29: 11 the LORD *b* his people with peace.
Ro   10: 12 and richly *b* all who call on him,

BLESSING (BLESS)

Ge   27: 4 so that I may give you my *b*
Dt   23: 5 turned the curse into a *b* for you,
        33: 1 This is the *b* that Moses the man
Pr   10: 22 The *b* of the LORD brings wealth,
Eze   34: 26 there will be showers of *b*.

BLESSINGS (BLESS)

Dt   11: 29 proclaim on Mount Gerizim the *b*,
Jos   8: 34 all the words of the law—the *b*
Pr   10: 6 *B* crown the head of the righteous,
Ro   15: 27 shared in the Jews' spiritual *b*,

BLIND (BLINDED)

Mt   15: 14 a *b* man leads a *b* man, both will fall
        23: 16 "Woe to you, *b* guides! You say,
Mk   10: 46 a *b* man, Bartimaeus (that is,
Lk   6: 39 "Can a *b* man lead a *b* man?
Jn   9: 25 I was *b* but now I see!"

BLINDED (BLIND)

Jn   12: 40 elsewhere: "He has *b* their eyes
2Co   4: 4   The god of this age has *b* the minds

BLOOD (BLOODSHED BLOODTHIRSTY)

Ge   4: 10 Your brother's *b* cries out to me
        9: 6   "Whoever sheds the *b* of man,
Ex   12: 13 and when I see the *b*, I will pass
        24: 8 "This is the *b* of the covenant that
Lev   16: 15 and take its *b* behind the curtain
        17: 11 For the life of a creature is in the *b*,
Dt   12: 23 eat the *b*, because the *b* is the life,
Ps   72: 14 for precious is their *b* in his sight.
Pr   6: 17 hands that shed innocent *b*,
Isa   1: 11 pleasure in the *b* of bulls and lambs
Mt   26: 28 This is my *b* of the covenant,
        27: 24 "I am innocent of this man's *b*,"
Mk   14: 24 "This is my *b* of the covenant,
Lk   22: 44 drops of *b* falling to the ground.
Jn   6: 53 of the Son of Man and drink his *b*,
Ac   15: 20 of strangled animals and from *b*.
        20: 26 innocent of the *b* of all men.
Ro   3: 25 of atonement, through faith in his *b*
        5: 9   have now been justified by his *b*,
1Co   11: 25 cup is the new covenant in my *b*;
Eph   1: 7   we have redemption through his *b*,
        2: 13 near through the *b* of Christ.
Col   1: 20 by making peace through his *b*,
Heb   9: 7   once a year, and never without *b*,
        9: 12 once for all by his own *b*,
        9: 20 "This is the *b* of the covenant,
        9: 22 of *b* there is no forgiveness.
        12: 24 word than the *b* of Abel.

1Pe   1: 19 but with the precious *b* of Christ,
1Jn   1: 7   and the *b* of Jesus, his Son,
Rev   1: 5   has freed us from our sins by his *b*,
        5: 9   with your *b* you purchased men
        7: 14 white in the *b* of the Lamb.
        12: 11 him by the *b* of the Lamb
        19: 13 He is dressed in a robe dipped in *b*,

BLOODSHED (BLOOD)

Jer   48: 10 on him who keeps his sword from *b*
Ezc   35: 6 did not hate *b*, *b* will pursue you.
Hab   2: 12 to him who builds a city with *b*

BLOODTHIRSTY* (BLOOD)

Ps   5: 6   *b* and deceitful men
        26: 9 or my life with *b* men,
        55: 23 *b* and deceitful men
        59: 2 and save me from *b* men.
        139: 19 Away from me, you *b* men!
Pr   29: 10 *B* men hate a man of integrity

BLOSSOM

Isa   35: 1 the wilderness will rejoice and *b*.

BLOT (BLOTS)

Ex   32: 32 then *b* me out of the book you have
Ps   51: 1 *b* out my transgressions.
Rev   3: 5   I will never *b* out his name

BLOTS (BLOT)

Isa   43: 25 "I, even I, am he who *b* out

BLOWN

Eph   4: 14 and *b* here and there by every wind
Jas   1: 6   doubts is like a wave of the sea, *b*
Jude   : 12   without rain, *b* along by the wind;

BLUSH

Jer   6: 15 they do not even know how to *b*.

BOAST (BOASTS)

1Ki   20: 11 armour should not *b* like one who
Ps   34: 2 My soul will *b* in the LORD;
        44: 8 In God we make our *b* all day long,
Pr   27: 1 Do not *b* about tomorrow,
Jer   9: 23 or the rich man *b* of his riches,
1Co   1: 31 Let him who boasts *b* in the Lord."
2Co   10: 17 Let him who boasts *b* in the Lord."
        11: 30 I do not inwardly burn? If I must *b*,
Gal   6: 14 May I never *b* except in the cross
Eph   2: 9   not by works, so that no-one can *b*.

BOASTS (BOAST)

Jer   9: 24 but let him who *b* boast about this:

BOAZ

Wealthy Bethlehemite who showed favour to Ruth (Ru 2), married her (Ru 4). Ancestor of David (Ru 4:18-22; 1Ch 2:12-15), Jesus (Mt 1:5-16; Lk 3:23-32).

BODIES (BODY)

Isa   26: 19 their *b* will rise.
Ro   12: 1 to offer your *b* as living sacrifices,
1Co   6: 15 not know that your *b* are members
Eph   5: 28 to love their wives as their own *b*.

BODILY (BODY)

Col   2: 9   of the Deity lives in *b* form.

BODY (BODIES BODILY EMBODIMENT)

Zec 13: 6 What are these wounds on your *b*?'
Mt 10: 28 afraid of those who kill the *b*
26: 26 saying, "Take and eat; this is my *b*
26: 41 spirit is willing, but the *b* is weak."
Mk 14: 22 saying, "Take it; this is my *b*."
Lk 22: 19 saying, "This is my *b* given for you;
Jn 13: 10 wash his feet; his whole *b* is clean.
Ro 6: 13 Do not offer the parts of your *b*
12: 4 us has one *b* with many members,
1Co 6: 19 not know that your *b* is a temple
6: 20 Therefore honour God with your *b*.
11: 24 "This is my *b*, which is for you;
12: 12 The *b* is a unit, though it is made up
12: 13 baptised by one Spirit into one *b*—
15: 44 a natural *b*, it is raised a spiritual *b*.
Eph 1: 23 which is his *b*, the fulness
4: 25 for we are all members of one *b*.
5: 30 for we are members of his *b*.
Php 1: 20 Christ will be exalted in my *b*,
Col 1: 24 sake of his *b*, which is the church.

BOLD (BOLDNESS)

Ps 138: 3 you made me *b* and stout-hearted.
Pr 21: 29 A wicked man puts up a *b* front,
28: 1 but the righteous are as *b* as a lion.

BOLDNESS* (BOLD)

Lk 11: 8 because of the man's *b*
Ac 4: 29 to speak your word with great *b*.

BONDAGE

Ezr 9: 9 God has not deserted us in our *b*.

BONES

Ge 2: 23 "This is now bone of my *b*
Ps 22: 14 and all my *b* are out of joint.
22: 17 I can count all my *b*;
Eze 37: 1 middle of a valley; it was full of *b*.
Jn 19: 36 "Not one of his *b* will be broken,"

BOOK (BOOKS)

Ex 32: 33 against me I will blot out of my *b*.
Jos 1: 8 Do not let this *B* of the Law depart
2Ki 22: 8 "I have found the *B* of the Law
2Ch 34: 15 "I have found the *B* of the Law
Ne 8: 8 They read from the *B* of the Law
Ps 69: 28 May they be blotted out of the *b*
Da 12: 1 name is found written in the *b*—
Jn 20: 30 which are not recorded in this *b*.
Php 4: 3 whose names are in the *b* of life.
Rev 3: 5 never erase his name from the *b*
20: 12 *b* was opened, which is the *b*
20: 15 was not found written in the *b*
21: 27 written in the Lamb's *b* of life.
22: 18 him the plagues described in this *b*.

BOOKS* (BOOK)

Ecc 12: 12 Of making many *b* there is no end,
Da 7: 10 and the *b* were opened.
Jn 21: 25 for the *b* that would be written.
Rev 20: 12 the throne, and *b* were opened.
20: 12 they had done as recorded in the *b*.

BORE (BEAR [1])

Isa 53: 12 For he *b* the sin of many,
1Pe 2: 24 He himself *b* our sins in his body

BORN (BEAR [1])

Ecc 3: 2 a time to be *b* and a time to die,

Isa 9: 6 For to us a child is *b*,
66: 8 Can a country be *b* in a day
Lk 2: 11 of David a Saviour has been *b* to you
Jn 3: 3 a man is *b* again, he cannot see
3: 4 How can a man be *b* when he is old
3: 5 unless a man is *b* of water
3: 7 at my saying, 'You must be *b* again
3: 8 it is with everyone *b* of the Spirit."
1Pe 1: 23 For you have been *b* again,
1Jn 3: 9 because he has been *b* of God.
4: 7 Everyone who loves has been *b*
5: 1 believes that Jesus is the Christ is *b*
5: 4 for everyone *b* of God overcomes
5: 18 We know that anyone *b*

BORROWER

Pr 22: 7 and the *b* is servant to the lender.

BOTHER (BOTHERING)

Lk 11: 7 one inside answers, 'Don't *b* me.

BOTHERING (BOTHER)

Lk 18: 5 yet because this widow keeps *b* me,

BOUGHT (BUY)

Ac 20: 28 which he *b* with his own blood.
1Co 6: 20 You are not your own; you were *b*
7: 23 You were *b* at a price; do not
2Pe 2: 1 the sovereign Lord who *b* them—

BOUND (BIND)

Isa 56: 3 Let no foreigner who has *b* himself
Mt 16: 19 bind on earth will be *b* in heaven,
18: 18 bind on earth will be *b* in heaven,
Ro 7: 2 by law a married woman is *b*
1Co 7: 39 A woman is *b* to her husband
Jude : 6 *b* with everlasting chains
Rev 20: 2 and *b* him for a thousand years.

BOUNDARY (BOUNDS)

Nu 34: 3 your southern *b* will start
Pr 23: 10 Do not move an ancient *b* stone
Hos 5: 10 who move *b* stones.

BOUNDS (BOUNDARY)

2Co 7: 4 all our troubles my joy knows no *b*.

BOUNTY*

Ge 49: 26 than the *b* of the age-old hills.
Dt 28: 12 heavens, the storehouse of his *b*,
1Ki 10: 13 he had given her out of his royal *b*.
Ps 65: 11 You crown the year with your *b*,
68: 10 from your *b*, O God, you provided
Jer 31: 12 rejoice in the *b* of the LORD—
31: 14 my people will be filled with my *b*

BOW [1]

1Ki 22: 34 But someone drew his *b* at random
Ps 44: 6 I do not trust in my *b*,

BOW [2] (BOWED BOWS)

Dt 5: 9 You shall not *b* down to them
Ps 5: 7 in reverence will I *b* down
95: 6 Come, let us *b* down in worship,
138: 2 I will *b* down towards your holy
Isa 44: 19 Shall I *b* down to a block of wood?"
45: 23 Before me every knee will *b*;
Ro 14: 11 'Every knee will *b* before me;
Php 2: 10 name of Jesus every knee should *b*,

BOWED (BOW [2])

Ps 145: 14 and lifts up all who are *b* down.
146: 8 the LORD lifts up those who are *b*

BOWS (BOW [2])

Isa 44: 15 he makes an idol and *b* down to it.
44: 17 he *b* down to it and worships.

BOY (BOY'S BOYS)

Ge 21: 17 God heard the *b* crying,
22: 12 not lay a hand on the *b*
Jdg 13: 5 *b* is to be a Nazirite,
1Sa 2: 11 *b* ministered before the LORD.
3: 8 the LORD was calling the *b*.
Isa 7: 16 before the *b* knows enough
Mt 17: 18 demon, and it came out of the *b*
Lk 2: 43 the *b* Jesus stayed behind

BOY'S (BOY)

1Ki 17: 22 the *b* life returned to him
2Ki 4: 34 the *b* body grew warm

BOYS (BOY)

Ge 25: 24 twin *b* in her womb
Ex 1: 18 they let the *b* live.

BRACE*

Job 38: 3 *B* yourself like a man;
40: 7 out of the storm: "*B* yourself like
Na 2: 1 *b* yourselves,

BRAG*

Am 4: 5 and *b* about your freewill offerings
Ro 2: 17 *b* about your relationship to God;
2: 23 temples? You who *b* about the law,
Jas 4: 16 As it is, you boast and *b*.

BRAIDED

1Ti 2: 9 not with *b* hair or gold or pearls
1Pe 3: 3 as *b* hair and the wearing

BRANCH (BRANCHES)

Isa 4: 2 In that day the *B* of the LORD will
Jer 23: 5 up to David a righteous *B*,
33: 15 I will make a righteous *B* sprout
Zec 3: 8 going to bring my servant, the *B*.
6: 12 is the man whose name is the *B*.
Jn 15: 2 while every *b* that does bear fruit
15: 4 No *b* can bear fruit by itself;

BRANCHES (BRANCH)

Jn 15: 5 "I am the vine; you are the *b*.
Ro 11: 21 if God did not spare the natural *b*,

BRAVE

2Sa 2: 7 Now then, be strong and *b*,
13: 28 you this order? Be strong and *b*."

BREACH (BREAK)

Ps 106: 23 stood in the *b* before him

BREACHING (BREAK)

Pr 17: 14 Starting a quarrel is like *b* a dam;

BREAD

Ex 12: 8 and *b* made without yeast.
23: 15 the Feast of Unleavened *B*;
25: 30 Put the *b* of the Presence
Dt 8: 3 that man does not live on *b* alone
Ps 78: 25 Men ate the *b* of angels;

Pr 30: 8 but give me only my daily *b*.
Ecc 11: 1 Cast your *b* upon the waters,
Isa 55: 2 Why spend money on what is not *b*
Mt 4: 3 tell these stones to become *b*."
4: 4 'Man does not live on *b* alone,
6: 11 Give us today our daily *b*.
26: 26 Jesus took *b*, gave thanks
Mk 14: 22 Jesus took *b*, gave thanks
Lk 4: 3 tell this stone to become *b*."
4: 4 'Man does not live on *b* alone.'"
9: 13 "We have only five loaves of *b*
11: 3 Give us each day our daily *b*.
22: 19 And he took *b*, gave thanks
Jn 6: 33 For the *b* of God is he who comes
6: 35 Jesus declared, "I am the *b* of life.
6: 41 "I am the *b* that came
6: 48 I am the *b* of life.
6: 51 I am the living *b* that came
6: 51 This *b* is my flesh, which I will give
21: 13 took the *b* and gave it to them,
1Co 10: 16 And is not the *b* that we break
11: 23 took *b*, and when he had given
11: 26 For whenever you eat this *b*

BREAK (BREACH BREACHING BREAKERS BREAKING BREAKS BROKE BROKEN BROKENNESS)

Nu 30: 2 he must not *b* his word
Jdg 2: 1 'I will never *b* my covenant
Pr 25: 15 and a gentle tongue can *b* a bone.
Isa 42: 3 A bruised reed he will not *b*,
Mal 2: 15 and do not *b* faith with the wife
Mt 12: 20 A bruised reed he will not *b*,
Ac 20: 7 week we came together to *b* bread.
1Co 10: 16 the bread that we *b* a participation
Rev 5: 2 "Who is worthy to *b* the seals

BREAKERS* (BREAK)

Ps 42: 7 all your waves and *b*
93: 4 mightier than the *b* of the sea—
Jnh 2: 3 all your waves and *b*

BREAKING (BREAK)

Jos 9: 20 fall on us for *b* the oath we swore
Eze 16: 59 oath by *b* the covenant.
17: 18 the oath by *b* the covenant.
Ac 2: 42 to the *b* of bread and to prayer.
Jas 2: 10 at just one point is guilty of *b* all

BREAKS (BREAK)

Jer 23: 29 "and like a hammer that *b* a rock
1Jn 3: 4 Everyone who sins *b* the law;

BREASTPIECE (BREASTPLATE)

Ex 28: 15 Fashion a *b* for making decisions—

BREASTPLATE* (BREASTPIECE)

Isa 59: 17 He put on righteousness as his *b*,
Eph 6: 14 with the *b* of righteousness in place
1Th 5: 8 putting on faith and love as a *b*,

BREASTS

La 4: 3 Even jackals offer their *b*

BREATH (BREATHED GOD-BREATHED)

Ge 2: 7 into his nostrils the *b* of life,

BREATHED (BREATH)

Ge 2: 7 *b* into his nostrils the breath of life,
Mk 15: 37 With a loud cry, Jesus *b* his last.

Jn   20: 22 And with that he *b* on them

BREEDS*

Pr   13: 10 Pride only *b* quarrels,

BRIBE

Ex   23: 8 "Do not accept a *b*,
Dt   16: 19 for a *b* blinds the eyes of the wise
     27: 25 "Cursed is the man who accepts a *b*
Pr   6: 35 will refuse the *b*, however great it

BRIDE

Isa   62: 5 as a bridegroom rejoices over his *b*,
Rev   19: 7 and his *b* has made herself ready.
     21: 2 as a *b* beautifully dressed
     21: 9 I will show you the *b*, the wife
     22: 17 The Spirit and the *b* say, "Come!"

BRIDEGROOM

Ps   19: 5 which is like a *b* coming forth
Mt   25: 1 and went out to meet the *b*.
     25: 5 The *b* was a long time in coming,

BRIGHTENS* (BRIGHTNESS)

Pr   16: 15 When a king's face *b*, it means life;
Ecc   8: 1 Wisdom *b* a man's face

BRIGHTER (BRIGHTNESS)

Pr   4: 18 shining ever *b* till the full light

BRIGHTNESS* (BRIGHTENS BRIGHTER)

2Sa   22: 13 Out of the *b* of his presence
     23: 4 like the *b* after rain
Ps   18: 12 of the *b* of his presence clouds
Isa   59: 9 for *b*, but we walk in deep shadows.
     60: 3 and kings to the *b* of your dawn.
     60: 19 will the *b* of the moon shine on you
Da   12: 3 who are wise will shine like the *b*
Am   5: 20 pitch-dark, without a ray of *b*?

BRILLIANCE* (BRILLIANT)

Ac   22: 11 the *b* of the light had blinded me.
Rev   1: 16 was like the sun shining in all its *b*.
     21: 11 its *b* was like that of a very precious

BRILLIANT* (BRILLIANCE)

Ecc   9: 11 or wealth to the *b*
Eze   1: 4 and surrounded by *b* light.
     1: 27 and *b* light surrounded him.

BRINK*

Pr   5: 14 I have come to the *b* of utter ruin

BRITTLE

Da   2: 42 will be partly strong and partly *b*.

BROAD

Mt   7: 13 and *b* is the road that leads

BROKE (BREAK)

Mt   26: 26 took bread, gave thanks and *b* it,
Mk   14: 22 took bread, gave thanks and *b* it,
Ac   2: 46 They *b* bread in their homes
     20: 11 he went upstairs again and *b* bread
1Co   11: 24 when he had given thanks, he *b* it

BROKEN (BREAK)

Ps   34: 20 not one of them will be *b*.
     51: 17 The sacrifices of God are a *b* spirit;
Ecc   4: 12 of three strands is not quickly *b*.

Lk   20: 18 on that stone will be *b* to pieces,
Jn   7: 23 the law of Moses may not be *b*,
     10: 35 and the Scripture cannot be *b*—
     19: 36 "Not one of his bones will be *b*,"
Ro   11: 20 they were *b* off because of unbelief,

BROKEN-HEARTED* (HEART)

Ps   34: 18 The Lord is close to the *b*
     109: 16 and the needy and the *b*.
     147: 3 He heals the *b*
Isa   61: 1 He has sent me to bind up the *b*,

BROKENNESS* (BREAK)

Isa   65: 14 and wail in *b* of spirit.

BRONZE

Ex   27: 2 and overlay the altar with *b*.
     30: 18 "Make a *b* basin, with its *b* stand,
Nu   21: 9 So Moses made a *b* snake
Da   2: 32 and thighs of *b*, its legs of iron,
     10: 6 legs like the gleam of burnished *b*,
Rev   1: 15 His feet were like *b* glowing
     2: 18 whose feet are like burnished *b*.

BROTHER (BROTHER'S BROTHERHOOD BROTHERLY BROTHERS)

Pr   17: 17 and a *b* is born for adversity.
     18: 24 a friend who sticks closer than a *b*.
     27: 10 neighbour nearby than a *b* far away.
Mt   5: 24 and be reconciled to your *b*;
     18: 15 "If your *b* sins against you,
Mk   3: 35 Whoever does God's will is my *b*
Lk   17: 3 "If your *b* sins, rebuke him,
Ro   14: 15 not by your eating destroy your *b*
     14: 21 anything else that will cause your *b*
1Co   8: 13 if what I eat causes my *b* to fall
2Th   3: 6 away from every *b* who is idle
     3: 15 as an enemy, but warn him as a *b*.
Phm   : 16 but better than a slave, as a dear *b*.
Jas   2: 15 Suppose a *b* or sister is
     4: 11 Anyone who speaks against his *b*
1Jn   2: 9 hates his *b* is still in the darkness.
     2: 10 Whoever loves his *b* lives
     2: 11 But whoever hates his *b* is
     3: 10 is anyone who does not love his *b*.
     3: 15 who hates his *b* is a murderer,
     3: 17 material possessions and sees his *b*
     4: 20 For anyone who does not love his *b*
     4: 20 yet hates his *b*, he is a liar.
     4: 21 loves God must also love his *b*.
     5: 16 If anyone sees his *b* commit a sin

BROTHER'S (BROTHER)

Ge   4: 9 "Am I my *b* keeper?" The Lord
Mt   7: 5 remove the speck from your *b* eye.
Ro   14: 13 or obstacle in your *b* way.

BROTHERHOOD (BROTHER)

1Pe   2: 17 Love the *b* of believers, fear God,

BROTHERLY* (BROTHER)

Ro   12: 10 devoted to one another in *b* love.
1Th   4: 9 Now about *b* love we do not need
2Pe   1: 7 and to godliness, *b* kindness;
     1: 7 kindness; and to *b* kindness,

BROTHERS (BROTHER)

Jos   1: 14 You are to help your *b*
Ps   133: 1 is when *b* live together in unity!
Pr   6: 19 who stirs up dissension among *b*.

Mt 12: 49 "Here are my mother and my *b*.
19: 29 everyone who has left houses or *b*
25: 40 one of the least of these *b* of mine,
Mk 3: 33 "Who are my mother and my *b*?"
10: 29 or *b* or sisters or mother or father
Lk 21: 16 You will be betrayed by parents, *b*,
22: 32 turned back, strengthen your *b*."
Jn 7: 5 his own *b* did not believe in him.
Ac 15: 32 to encourage and strengthen the *b*.
Ro 9: 3 off from Christ for the sake of my *b*
1Co 8: 12 sin against your *b* in this way
2Co 11: 26 and in danger from false *b*.
Gal 2: 4 some false *b* had infiltrated our
1Th 4: 10 you do love all the *b*
5: 26 Greet all the *b* with a holy kiss.
1Ti 6: 2 for them because they are *b*.
Heb 2: 11 Jesus is not ashamed to call them *b*,
2: 17 to be made like his *b* in every way,
13: 1 Keep on loving each other as *b*.
1Pe 1: 22 you have sincere love for your *b*,
3: 8 be sympathetic, love as *b*,
1Jn 3: 14 death to life, because we love our *b*.
3: 16 to lay down our lives for our *b*.
3Jn : 10 he refuses to welcome the *b*.
Rev 12: 10 For the accuser of our *b*,

BROW

Ge 3: 19 By the sweat of your *b*

BRUISED (BRUISES)

Isa 42: 3 A *b* reed he will not break,
Mt 12: 20 A *b* reed he will not break,

BRUISES (BRUISED)

Isa 30: 26 when the LORD binds up the *b*

BRUTAL (BRUTE)

2Ti 3: 3 slanderous, without self-control, *b*,

BRUTE* (BRUTAL)

Ps 73: 22 I was a *b* beast before you.
2Pe 2: 12 They are like *b* beasts, creatures

BUBBLING*

Pr 18: 4 the fountain of wisdom is a *b* brook
Isa 35: 7 the thirsty ground *b* springs.

BUCKET*

Isa 40: 15 the nations are like a drop in a *b*;

BUCKLED* (BUCKLER)

Eph 6: 14 belt of truth *b* around your waist,

BUCKLER* (BUCKLED)

Ps 35: 2 Take up shield and *b*;

BUD (BUDDED)

Isa 27: 6 Israel will *b* and blossom

BUDDED (BUD)

Heb 9: 4 Aaron's staff that had *b*,

**BUILD (BUILDER BUILDERS BUILDING
BUILDS BUILT REBUILD REBUILT)**

2Sa 7: 5 Are you the one to *b* me a house
1Ki 6: 1 he began to *b* the temple
Ecc 3: 3 a time to tear down and a time to *b*,
Mt 16: 18 and on this rock I will *b* my church,
Ac 20: 32 which can *b* you up and give you
Ro 15: 2 neighbour for his good, to *b* him up.

1Co 14: 12 excel in gifts that *b* up the church.
1Th 5: 11 one another and *b* each other up,
Jude : 20 *b* yourselves up in your most holy

BUILDER* (BUILD)

1Co 3: 10 I laid a foundation as an expert *b*,
Heb 3: 3 the *b* of a house has greater honour
3: 4 but God is the *b* of everything.
11: 10 whose architect and *b* is God.

BUILDERS (BUILD)

Ps 118: 22 The stone the *b* rejected
Mt 21: 42 " 'The stone the *b* rejected
Mk 12: 10 " 'The stone the *b* rejected
Lk 20: 17 " 'The stone the *b* rejected
Ac 4: 11 " 'the stone you *b* rejected,
1Pe 2: 7 "The stone the *b* rejected

BUILDING (BUILD)

Ezr 3: 8 to supervise the *b* of the house
Ne 4: 17 of Judah who were *b* the wall.
Ro 15: 20 so that I would not be *b*
1Co 3: 9 you are God's field, God's *b*.
2Co 5: 1 we have a *b* from God, an eternal
10: 8 us for *b* you up rather
13: 10 the Lord gave me for *b* you up,
Eph 2: 21 him the whole *b* is joined together
4: 29 helpful for *b* others up according

BUILDS (BUILD)

Ps 127: 1 Unless the LORD *b* the house,
Pr 14: 1 The wise woman *b* her house,
1Co 3: 10 one should be careful how he *b*.
3: 12 If any man *b* on this foundation
8: 1 Knowledge puffs up, but love *b* up.
Eph 4: 16 grows and *b* itself up in love,

BUILT (BUILD)

1Ki 6: 14 So Solomon *b* the temple
Mt 7: 24 is like a wise man who *b* his house
Lk 6: 49 is like a man who *b* a house
Ac 17: 24 does not live in temples *b* by hands.
1Co 3: 14 If what he has *b* survives, he will.
2Co 5: 1 in heaven, not *b* by human hands.
Eph 2: 20 *b* on the foundation of the apostles
4: 12 the body of Christ may be *b* up
Col 2: 7 live in him, rooted and *b* up in him,
1Pe 2: 5 are being *b* into a spiritual house

BULL (BULLS)

Lev 4: 3 bring to the LORD a young *b*

BULLS (BULL)

1Ki 7: 25 The Sea stood on twelve *b*,
Heb 10: 4 it is impossible for the blood of *b*

**BURDEN (BURDENED BURDENS
BURDENSOME)**

Ps 38: 4 like a *b* too heavy to bear.
Ecc 1: 13 What a heavy *b* God has laid
Mt 11: 30 my yoke is easy and my *b* is light."
Ac 15: 28 to us not to *b* you with anything
2Co 11: 9 from being a *b* to you in any way,
12: 14 and I will not be a *b* to you,
1Th 2: 9 day in order not to be a *b* to anyone
2Th 3: 8 so that we would not be a *b* to any
Heb 13: 17 not a *b*, for that would be

BURDENED* (BURDEN)

Isa 43: 23 have not *b* you with grain offerings

Isa 43:24 But you have *b* me with your sins
Mic 6: 3 How have I *b* you? Answer me.
Mt 11:28 all you who are weary and *b*,
2Co 5: 4 are in this tent, we groan and are *b*,
Gal 5: 1 do not let yourselves be *b* again
1Ti 5:16 not let the church be *b* with them,

BURDENS (BURDEN)

Ps 68:19 who daily bears our *b*.
Lk 11:46 down with *b* they can hardly carry,
Gal 6: 2 Carry each other's *b*,

BURDENSOME (BURDEN)

1Jn 5: 3 And his commands are not *b*,

BURIED (BURY)

Ru 1:17 die I will die, and there I will be *b*.
Ro 6: 4 *b* with him through baptism
1Co 15: 4 that he was *b*, that he was raised
Col 2:12 having been *b* with him in baptism

BURN (BURNING BURNT)

Dt 7: 5 and *b* their idols in the fire.
Ps 79: 5 long will your jealousy *b* like fire?
1Co 7: 9 to marry than to *b* with passion.

BURNING (BURN)

Ex 27:20 so that the lamps may be kept *b*.
Lev 6: 9 the fire must be kept *b* on the altar.
Ps 18:28 You, O LORD, keep my lamp *b*;
Pr 25:22 you will heap *b* coals on his head,
Ro 12:20 you will heap *b* coals on his head."
Rev 19:20 alive into the fiery lake of *b* sulphur.

BURNISHED*

1Ki 7:45 of the LORD were of *b* bronze.
Eze 1: 7 and gleamed like *b* bronze.
Da 10: 6 and legs like the gleam of *b* bronze,
Rev 2:18 and whose feet are like *b* bronze.

BURNT (BURN)

Ge 8:20 he sacrificed *b* offerings on it.
22: 2 as a *b* offering on one
Ex 10:25 and *b* offerings to present
18:12 brought a *b* offering and other
40: 6 Place the altar of *b* offering in front
Lev 1: 3 "'If the offering is a *b* offering
Jos 8:31 offered to the LORD *b* offerings
Jdg 6:26 offer the second bull as a *b* offering
13:16 But if you prepare a *b* offering,
1Ki 3: 4 offered a thousand *b* offerings
9:25 year Solomon sacrificed *b* offerings
10: 5 and the *b* offerings he made
Ezr 3: 2 Israel to sacrifice *b* offerings on it,
Eze 43:18 for sacrificing *b* offerings

BURST

Ps 98: 4 *b* into jubilant song with music;
Isa 44:23 *B* into song, you mountains,
49:13 *b* into song, O mountains!
52: 9 *B* into songs of joy together,
54: 1 *b* into song, shout for joy,
55:12 will *b* into song before you,

BURY (BURIED)

Mt 8:22 and let the dead *b* their own dead."
Lk 9:60 "Let the dead *b* their own dead,

BUSH

Ex 3: 2 the *b* was on fire it did not burn up.

Mk 12:26 the account of the *b*, how God said
Lk 20:37 But in the account of the *b*,
Ac 7:35 who appeared to him in the *b*.

BUSINESS

Ecc 4: 8 a miserable *b*!
Da 8:27 and went about the king's *b*.
1Co 5:12 What *b* is it of mine to judge those
1Th 4:11 to mind your own *b* and to work
Jas 1:11 even while he goes about his *b*.

BUSY*

1Ki 18:27 Perhaps he is deep in thought, or *b*,
20:40 While your servant was *b* here
Isa 32: 6 his mind is *b* with evil:
Hag 1: 9 of you is *b* with his own house.
2Th 3:11 They are not *b*; they are
Tit 2: 5 to be *b* at home, to be kind,

BUSYBODIES*

2Th 3:11 They are not busy; they are *b*.
1Ti 5:13 *b*, saying things they ought not to.

BUY (BOUGHT BUYS)

Pr 23:23 *B* the truth and do not sell it;
Isa 55: 1 Come, *b* wine and milk
Rev 13:17 so that no-one could *b* or sell

BUYS (BUY)

Pr 31:16 She considers a field and *b* it;

BYWORD (WORD)

1Ki 9: 7 Israel will then become a *b*
Ps 44:14 You have made us a *b*
Joel 2:17 a *b* among the nations.

CAESAR

Mt 22:21 "Give to *C* what is Caesar's,

CAIN

Firstborn of Adam (Ge 4:1), murdered brother Abel (Ge 4:1-16; 1Jn 3:12).

CAKE

Hos 7: 8 Ephraim is a flat *c* not turned over.

CALEB

Judahite who spied out Canaan (Nu 13:6); allowed to enter land because of faith (Nu 13:30-14:38; Dt 1:36). Possessed Hebron (Jos 14:6; 15:19).

CALF

Ex 32: 4 into an idol cast in the shape of a *c*,
Pr 15:17 than a fattened *c* with hatred.
Lk 15:23 Bring the fattened *c* and kill it.
Ac 7:41 made an idol in the form of a *c*.

CALL (CALLED CALLING CALLS)

1Ki 18:24 I will *c* on the name of the LORD.
2Ki 5:11 *c* on the name of the LORD his name;
1Ch 16: 8 to the LORD, *c* on his name;
Ps 105: 1 to the LORD, *c* on his name;
116:13 and *c* on the name of the LORD.
116:17 and *c* on the name of the LORD.
145:18 near to all who *c* on him,
Pr 31:28 children arise and *c* her blessed;
Isa 5:20 Woe to those who *c* evil good
12: 4 to the LORD, *c* on his name;
55: 6 *c* on him while he is near.

Isa	65: 24	Before they *c* I will answer;
Jer	33: 3	'C to me and I will answer you
Zep	3: 9	that all of them may *c* on the name
Zec	13: 9	They will *c* on my name
Mt	9: 13	come to *c* the righteous,
Mk	2: 17	I have not come to *c* the righteous,
Lk	5: 32	I have not come to *c* the righteous,
Ac	2: 39	all whom the Lord our God will *c*."
	9: 14	to arrest all who *c* on your name."
	9: 21	among those who *c* on this name?
Ro	10: 12	and richly blesses all who *c* on him,
	11: 29	gifts and his *c* are irrevocable.
1Co	1: 2	with all those everywhere who *c*
1Th	4: 7	For God did not *c* us to be impure,
2Ti	2: 22	along with those who *c*

CALLED (CALL)

Ge	2: 23	she shall be *c* 'woman,'
	5: 2	he blessed them and *c* them "man
	12: 8	and *c* on the name of the LORD.
	21: 33	and there he *c* upon the name
	26: 25	and *c* on the name of the LORD.
1Sa	3: 5	and said, "Here I am; you *c* me."
2Ch	7: 14	if my people, who are *c*
Ps	34: 6	This poor man *c*, and the LORD
	116: 4	Then I *c* on the name of the LORD
Isa	56: 7	for my house will be *c*
La	3: 55	I *c* on your name, O LORD,
Hos	11: 1	and out of Egypt I *c* my son.
Mt	1: 16	was born Jesus, who is *c* Christ.
	2: 15	"Out of Egypt I *c* my son."
	21: 13	" 'My house will be *c* a house
Mk	11: 17	" 'My house will be *c*
Lk	1: 32	will be *c* the Son of the Most High.
	1: 35	to be born will be *c* the Son of God.
Ro	1: 1	*c* to be an apostle and set apart
	1: 6	among those who are *c* to belong
	1: 7	loved by God and *c* to be saints:
	8: 28	who have been *c* according
	8: 30	And those he predestined, he also *c*
1Co	1: 1	*c* to be an apostle of Christ Jesus
	1: 2	in Christ Jesus and *c* to be holy,
	1: 24	but to those whom God has *c*,
	1: 26	of what you were when you were *c*.
	7: 15	God has *c* us to live in peace.
	7: 17	and to which God has *c* him.
Gal	1: 6	deserting the one who *c* you
	1: 15	from birth and *c* me by his grace,
	5: 13	You, my brothers, were *c* to be free
Eph	1: 18	the hope to which he has *c* you,
	4: 4	as you were *c* to one hope
Col	3: 15	of one body you were *c* to peace.
2Th	2: 14	He *c* you to this through our gospel
1Ti	6: 12	life to which you were *c*
2Ti	1: 9	who has saved us and *c* us
Heb	9: 15	that those who are *c* may receive
1Pe	1: 15	But just as he who *c* you is holy,
	2: 9	of him who *c* you out of darkness
	3: 9	to this you were *c* so that you may
	5: 10	who *c* you to his eternal glory
2Pe	1: 3	of him who *c* us by his own glory
Jude	: 1	To those who have been *c*,

CALLING (CALL)

Isa	40: 3	A voice of one *c*:
Mt	3: 3	"A voice of one *c* in the desert,
Mk	1: 3	"a voice of one *c* in the desert,
	10: 49	Cheer up! On your feet! He's *c* you
Lk	3: 4	"A voice of one *c* in the desert,
Jn	1: 23	I am the voice of one *c* in the desert

Ac	22: 16	wash your sins away, *c* on his name
Eph	4: 1	worthy of the *c* you have received.
2Th	1: 11	may count you worthy of his *c*,
2Pe	1: 10	all the more eager to make your *c*

CALLOUS* (CALLOUSED)

Ps	17: 10	They close up their *c* hearts,
	73: 7	From their *c* hearts comes iniquity;
	119: 70	Their hearts are *c* and unfeeling,

CALLOUSED* (CALLOUS)

Isa	6: 10	Make the heart of this people *c*;
Mt	13: 15	this people's heart has become *c*;
Ac	28: 27	this people's heart has become *c*;

CALLS (CALL)

Ps	147: 4	and *c* them each by name.
Isa	40: 26	and *c* them each by name.
Joel	2: 32	And everyone who *c*
Mt	22: 43	speaking by the Spirit, *c* him 'Lord
Jn	10: 3	He *c* his own sheep by name
Ac	2: 21	And everyone who *c*
Ro	10: 13	"Everyone who *c* on the name
1Th	2: 12	who *c* you into his kingdom
	5: 24	The one who *c* you is faithful

CALM (CALMS)

Ps	107: 30	They were glad when it grew *c*,
Isa	7: 4	keep *c* and don't be afraid.
Eze	16: 42	I will be *c* and no longer angry.

CALMS* (CALM)

Pr	15: 18	but a patient man *c* a quarrel.

CAMEL

Mt	19: 24	it is easier for a *c* to go
	23: 24	strain out a gnat but swallow a *c*.
Mk	10: 25	It is easier for a *c* to go
Lk	18: 25	it is easier for a *c* to go

CAMP (ENCAMPS)

Heb	13: 13	outside the *c*, bearing the disgrace

CANAAN (CANAANITE CANAANITES)

Ge	10: 15	*C* was the father of Sidon his
Lev	14: 34	"When you enter the land of *C*,
	25: 38	of Egypt to give you the land of *C*
Nu	13: 2	men to explore the land of *C*,
	33: 51	'When you cross the Jordan into *C*,
Jdg	4: 2	a king of *C*, who reigned in Hazor.
1Ch	16: 18	"To you I will give the land of *C*
Ps	105: 11	"To you I will give the land of *C*
Ac	13: 19	He overthrew seven nations in *C*

CANAANITE (CANAAN)

Ge	10: 18	Later the *C* clans scattered
	28: 1	"Do not marry a *C* woman.
Jos	5: 1	all the *C* kings along the coast
Jdg	1: 32	lived among the *C* inhabitants

CANAANITES (CANAAN)

Ex	33: 2	before you and drive out the *C*,

CANCEL (CANCELLED)

Dt	15: 1	seven years you must *c* debts.

CANCELLED (CANCEL)

Mt	18: 27	pity on him, *c* the debt
Lk	7: 42	so he *c* the debts of both.
Col	2: 14	having *c* the written code,

CANDLESTICKS see LAMPSTANDS

CANOPY*

2Sa	22: 12	He made darkness his *c*
2Ki	16: 18	away the Sabbath *c* that had been
Ps	18: 11	made darkness his covering, his *c*
Isa	4: 5	over all the glory will be a *c*.
	40: 22	stretches out the heavens like a *c*,
Jer	43: 10	he will spread his royal *c*

CAPERNAUM

Mt	4: 13	Nazareth, he went and lived in *C*,
Jn	6: 59	teaching in the synagogue in *C*.

CAPITAL

Dt	21: 22	guilty of a *c* offence is put to death

CAPSTONE* (STONE)

Ps	118: 22	has become the *c*;
Zec	4: 7	he will bring out the *c* to shouts
Mt	21: 42	has become the *c*;
Mk	12: 10	has become the *c*;
Lk	20: 17	has become the *c*'?
Ac	4: 11	which has become the *c*.'
1Pe	2: 7	has become the *c*,"

CAPTIVATE* (CAPTIVE)

Pr	6: 25	or let her *c* you with her eyes,

CAPTIVATED* (CAPTIVE)

Pr	5: 19	may you ever be *c* by her love.
	5: 20	Why be *c*, my son, by an adulteress

CAPTIVE (CAPTIVATE CAPTIVATED CAPTIVES CAPTIVITY CAPTURED)

Ac	8: 23	full of bitterness and *c* to sin."
2Co	10: 5	and we take *c* every thought
Col	2: 8	See to it that no-one takes you *c*
2Ti	2: 26	who has taken them *c* to do his will.

CAPTIVES (CAPTIVE)

Ps	68: 18	you led *c* in your train;
Isa	61: 1	to proclaim freedom for the *c*
Eph	4: 8	he led *c* in his train

CAPTIVITY (CAPTIVE)

Dt	28: 41	because they will go into *c*.
2Ki	25: 21	So Judah went into *c*, away
Jer	30: 3	Israel and Judah back from *c*
	52: 27	So Judah went into *c*, away
Eze	29: 14	I will bring them back from *c*

CAPTURED (CAPTIVE)

1Sa	4: 11	The ark of God was *c*,
2Sa	5: 7	David *c* the fortress of Zion,
2Ki	17: 6	the king of Assyria *c* Samaria

CARCASS

Jdg	14: 9	taken the honey from the lion's *c*.
Mt	24: 28	there is a *c*, there the vultures

CARE (CAREFUL CARES CARING)

Ps	8: 4	the son of man that you *c* for him?
	65: 9	You *c* for the land and water it;
	144: 3	what is man that you *c* for him,
Pr	29: 7	The righteous *c* about justice
Mk	5: 26	deal under the *c* of many doctors
Lk	10: 34	him to an inn and took *c* of him.
	18: 4	I don't fear God or *c* about men,

Jn	21: 16	Jesus said, "Take *c* of my sheep."
1Ti	3: 5	how can he take *c* of God's church
	6: 20	what has been entrusted to your *c*.
Heb	2: 6	the son of man that you *c* for him?
1Pe	5: 2	of God's flock that is under your *c*,

CAREFUL* (CARE)

Ge	31: 24	"Be *c* not to say anything to Jacob,
	31: 29	'Be *c* not to say anything to Jacob,
Ex	19: 12	'Be *c* that you do not go up
	23: 13	"Be *c* to do everything I have said
	34: 12	Be *c* not to make a treaty
	34: 15	"Be *c* not to make a treaty
Lev	18: 4	and be *c* to follow my decrees.
	25: 18	" 'Follow my decrees and be *c*
	26: 3	and are *c* to obey my commands,
Dt	2: 4	afraid of you, but be very *c*.
	4: 9	before you today? Only be *c*,
	4: 23	Be *c* not to forget the covenant
	5: 32	So be *c* to do what the LORD your
	6: 3	be *c* to obey so that it may go well
	6: 12	be *c* that you do not forget
	6: 25	And if we are *c* to obey all this law
	7: 12	attention to these laws and are *c*
	8: 1	Be *c* to follow every command I am
	8: 11	Be *c* that you do not forget
	11: 16	Be *c*, or you will be enticed
	12: 1	and laws you must be *c* to follow
	12: 13	Be *c* not to sacrifice your burnt
	12: 19	Be *c* not to neglect the Levites
	12: 28	Be *c* to obey all these regulations I
	12: 30	be *c* not to be ensnared
	15: 5	are *c* to follow all these commands
	15: 9	Be *c* not to harbour this wicked
	17: 10	Be *c* to do everything they direct
	24: 8	cases of leprous diseases be very *c*
Jos	1: 7	Be *c* to obey all the law my servant
	1: 8	so that you may be *c*
	22: 5	But be very *c* to keep
	23: 6	be *c* to obey all that is written
	23: 11	be very *c* to love the LORD your
1Ki	8: 25	if only your sons are *c* in all they do
2Ki	10: 31	Yet Jehu was not *c* to keep the law
	17: 37	You must always be *c*
	21: 8	if only they will be *c*
1Ch	22: 13	if you are *c* to observe the decrees
	28: 8	Be *c* to follow all the commands
2Ch	6: 16	if only your sons are *c* in all they do
	33: 8	if only they will be *c*
Ezr	4: 22	Be *c* not to neglect this matter.
Job	36: 18	Be *c* that no-one entices you
Ps	101: 2	I will be *c* to lead a blameless life—
Pr	13: 24	he who loves him is *c*
	27: 23	give *c* attention to your herds;
Isa	7: 4	Be *c*, keep calm and don't be afraid.
Jer	17: 21	Be *c* not to carry a load
	17: 24	But if you are *c* to obey me,
	22: 4	For if you are *c* to carry out these
Eze	11: 20	will follow my decrees and be *c*
	18: 19	has been *c* to keep all my decrees,
	20: 19	follow my decrees and be *c*
	20: 21	they were not *c* to keep my laws—
	36: 27	you to follow my decrees and be *c*
	37: 24	and be *c* to keep my decrees.
Mic	7: 5	be *c* of your words.
Hag	1: 5	"Give *c* thought to your ways.
	1: 7	"Give *c* thought to your ways.
	2: 15	give *c* thought to this from this day
	2: 18	Give *c* thought: Is there yet any
	2: 18	give *c* thought to the day

Mt 2: 8 and make a *c* search for the child.
6: 1 "Be *c* not to do your 'acts
16: 6 "Be *c*," Jesus said to them.
Mk 8: 15 "Be *c*," Jesus warned them.
Lk 21: 34 Be *c*, or your hearts will be weighed
Ro 12: 17 Be *c* to do what is right in the eyes
1Co 3: 10 each one should be *c* how he builds
8: 9 Be *c*, however, that the exercise
10: 12 standing firm, be *c* that you don't
Eph 5: 15 Be very *c*, then, how you live—
2Ti 4: 2 great patience and *c* instruction.
Tit 3: 8 may be *c* to devote themselves
Heb 2: 1 We must pay more *c* attention,
4: 1 let us be *c* that none

CARELESS*

Mt 12: 36 for every *c* word they have spoken.

CARES* (CARE)

Dt 11: 12 It is a land the LORD your God *c*
Job 39: 16 she *c* not that her labour was in vain,
Ps 55: 22 Cast your *c* on the LORD
142: 4 no-one *c* for my life.
Pr 12: 10 A righteous man *c* for the needs
Ecc 5: 3 when there are many *c*,
Jer 12: 11 because there is no-one who *c*.
30: 17 Zion for whom no-one *c*.'
Na 1: 7 He *c* for those who trust in him,
Jn 10: 13 and *c* nothing for the sheep.
Eph 5: 29 but he feeds and *c* for it, just
1Pe 5: 7 on him because he *c* for you.

CARING* (CARE)

1Th 2: 7 like a mother *c* for her little
1Ti 5: 4 practice by *c* for their own family

CARNAL see SINFUL, UNSPIRITUAL, WORLDLY

CARPENTER (CARPENTER'S)

Mk 6: 3 does miracles! Isn't this the *c*?

CARPENTER'S* (CARPENTER)

Mt 13: 55 "Isn't this the *c* son? Isn't his

CARRIED (CARRY)

Ex 19: 4 and how I *c* you on eagles' wings
Dt 1: 31 How the LORD your God *c* you,
Isa 53: 4 and *c* our sorrows,
63: 9 he lifted them up and *c* them
Mt 8: 17 and *c* our diseases."
Heb 13: 9 Do not be *c* away by all kinds
2Pe 1: 21 as they were *c* along by the Holy
3: 17 so that you may not be *c* away

CARRIES (CARRY)

Dt 32: 11 and *c* them on its pinions.
Isa 40: 11 and *c* them close to his heart;

CARRY (CARRIED CARRIES CARRYING)

Lev 16: 22 goat will *c* on itself all their sins
26: 15 and fail to *c* out all my commands
Isa 46: 4 I have made you and I will *c* you;
Lk 14: 27 anyone who does not *c* his cross
Gal 6: 2 *C* each other's burdens,
6: 5 for each one should *c* his own load.

CARRYING (CARRY)

Jn 19: 17 *C* his own cross, he went out
1Jn 5: 2 loving God and *c* out his

CARVED (CARVES)

Ne 33: 52 Destroy all their *c* images
Mic 5: 13 I will destroy your *c* images

CARVES* (CARVED)

Dt 27: 15 "Cursed is the man who *c* an image

CASE

Pr 18: 17 to present his *c* seems right,
22: 23 for the LORD will take up their *c*
23: 11 he will take up their *c* against you.

CAST (CASTING)

Ex 34: 17 "Do not make *c* idols.
Lev 16: 8 He is to *c* lots for the two goats—
Ps 22: 18 and *c* lots for my clothing.
55: 22 *C* your cares on the LORD
Pr 16: 33 The lot is *c* into the lap,
Ecc 11: 1 *C* your bread upon the waters,
Jn 19: 24 and *c* lots for my clothing."
1Pe 5: 7 *C* all your anxiety on him

CASTING (CAST)

Pr 18: 18 *C* the lot settles disputes
Mt 27: 35 divided up his clothes by *c* lots.

CATCH (CATCHES CAUGHT)

Lk 5: 4 and let down the nets for a *c*."
5: 10 from now on you will *c* men."

CATCHES (CATCH)

Job 5: 13 He *c* the wise in their craftiness,
1Co 3: 19 "He *c* the wise in their craftiness";

CATTLE

Ps 50: 10 and the *c* on a thousand hills.

CAUGHT (CATCH)

Ge 22: 13 there in a thicket he saw a ram *c*
2Co 12: 2 who fourteen years ago was *c* up
1Th 4: 17 and are left will be *c* up with them

CAUSE (CAUSES)

Pr 24: 28 against your neighbour without *c*,
Ecc 8: 3 Do not stand up for a bad *c*,
Mt 18: 7 of the things that *c* people to sin!
Ro 14: 21 else that will *c* your brother
1Co 10: 32 Do not *c* anyone to stumble,

CAUSES (CAUSE)

Ps 7: 16 The trouble he *c* recoils on himself;
Isa 8: 14 a stone that *c* men to stumble
Mt 5: 29 If your right eye *c* you to sin,
5: 30 And if your right hand *c* you to sin,
18: 6 if anyone *c* one of these little ones
18: 8 or your foot *c* you to sin,
Ro 14: 20 to eat anything that *c* someone else
1Co 8: 13 if what I eat *c* my brother to fall
1Pe 2: 8 "A stone that *c* men to stumble

CAUTIOUS*

Pr 12: 26 A righteous man is *c* in friendship,

CEASE

Ps 46: 9 He makes wars *c* to the ends

CELEBRATE*

Ex 10: 9 we are to *c* a festival to the LORD
12: 14 generations to come you shall *c* it

Ex	12: 17	*C* this day as a lasting ordinance
	12: 17	"*C* the Feast of Unleavened Bread,
	12: 47	community of Israel must *c* it.
	12: 48	to *c* the LORD's Passover must
	23: 14	are to *c* a festival to me.
	23: 15	"*C* the Feast of Unleavened Bread;
	23: 16	"*C* the Feast of Harvest
	23: 16	"*C* the Feast of Ingathering
	34: 18	"*C* the Feast of Unleavened Bread.
	34: 22	"*C* the Feast of Weeks
Lev	23: 39	*c* the festival to the LORD
	23: 41	*C* this as a festival to the LORD
	23: 41	for the generations to come; *c* it
Nu	9: 2	"Have the Israelites *c* the Passover
	9: 3	*C* it at the appointed time,
	9: 4	told the Israelites to *c* the Passover,
	9: 6	of them could not *c* the Passover
	9: 10	they may still *c* the LORD's
	9: 11	are to *c* it on the fourteenth day
	9: 12	When they *c* the Passover,
	9: 13	on a journey fails to *c* the Passover,
	9: 14	to *c* the LORD's Passover must do
	29: 12	*C* a festival to the LORD
Dt	16: 1	*c* the Passover of the LORD your
	16: 10	Then *c* the Feast of Weeks
	16: 13	*C* the Feast of Tabernacles
	16: 15	For seven days *c* the Feast
Jdg	16: 23	to Dagon their god and to *c*,
2Sa	6: 21	the LORD's people Israel—I will *c*
2Ki	23: 21	"*C* the Passover to the LORD your
2Ch	30: 1	and *c* the Passover to the LORD,
	30: 2	decided to *c* the Passover
	30: 3	able to *c* it at the regular time
	30: 5	and *c* the Passover to the LORD,
	30: 13	in Jerusalem to *c* the Feast
	30: 23	to *c* the festival seven more days;
Ne	8: 12	of food and to *c* with great joy,
	12: 27	to *c* joyfully the dedication
Est	9: 21	to have them *c* annually
Ps	145: 7	They will *c* your abundant
Isa	30: 29	as on the night you *c* a holy festival
Na	1: 15	*C* your festivals, O Judah,
Zec	14: 16	and to *c* the Feast of Tabernacles.
	14: 18	up to *c* the Feast of Tabernacles.
	14: 19	up to *c* the Feast of Tabernacles.
Mt	26: 18	I am going to *c* the Passover
Lk	15: 23	Let's have a feast and *c*.
	15: 24	So they began to *c*.
	15: 29	goat so I could *c* with my friends.
	15: 32	But we had to *c* and be glad,
Rev	11: 10	will *c* by sending each other gifts,

CELESTIAL*

2Pe	2: 10	afraid to slander *c* beings;
Jude	: 8	authority and slander *c* beings.

CENSER (CENSERS)

Lev	16: 12	is to take a *c* full of burning coals
Rev	8: 3	Another angel, who had a golden *c*,

CENSERS (CENSER)

Nu	16: 6	Take *c* and tomorrow put fire

CENTURION

Mt	8: 5	had entered Capernaum, a *c* came
	27: 54	When the *c* and those
Mk	15: 39	And when the *c*, who stood there
Lk	7: 3	The *c* heard of Jesus and sent some
	23: 47	The *c*, seeing what had happened,
Ac	10: 1	a *c* in what was known

Ac	27: 1	handed over to a *c* named Julius,

CEPHAS* (PETER)

Jn	1: 42	You will be called *C*" (which,
1Co	1: 12	another, "I follow *C*"; still another,
	3: 22	Paul or Apollos or *C* or the world
	9: 5	and the Lord's brothers and *C*?

CEREMONIAL* (CEREMONY)

Lev	14: 2	at the time of his *c* cleansing,
	15: 13	off seven days for his *c* cleansing;
Mk	7: 3	they give their hands a *c* washing,
Jn	2: 6	used by the Jews for *c* washing,
	3: 25	Jew over the matter of *c* washing.
	11: 55	to Jerusalem for their *c* cleansing
	18: 28	to avoid *c* uncleanness the Jews did
Heb	9: 10	drink and various *c* washings—
	13: 9	not by *c* foods, which are

CEREMONIALLY* (CEREMONY)

Lev	4: 12	outside the camp to a place *c* clean,
	5: 2	touches anything *c* unclean—
	6: 11	the camp to a place that is *c* clean.
	7: 19	anyone *c* clean may eat it.
	7: 19	touches anything *c* unclean must
	10: 14	Eat them in a *c* clean place;
	11: 4	not have a split hoof; it is *c* unclean
	12: 2	birth to a son will be *c* unclean
	12: 7	and then she will be *c* clean
	13: 3	he shall pronounce him *c* unclean.
	14: 8	with water; then he will be *c* clean.
	15: 28	and after that she will be *c* clean.
	15: 33	lies with a woman who is *c* unclean.
	21: 1	must not make himself *c* unclean
	22: 3	of your descendants is *c* unclean
	27: 11	he vowed is a *c* unclean animal—
Nu	5: 2	who is *c* unclean because of a dead
	6: 7	must not make himself *c* unclean
	8: 6	Israelites and make them *c* clean.
	9: 6	they were *c* unclean on account
	9: 13	But if a man who is *c* clean
	18: 11	household who is *c* clean may eat
	18: 13	household who is *c* clean may eat
	19: 7	but he will be *c* unclean till evening
	19: 9	and put them in a *c* clean place
	19: 18	Then a man who is *c* clean is
Dt	12: 15	Both the *c* unclean and the clean
	12: 22	Both the *c* unclean and the clean
	14: 7	they are *c* unclean for you.
	15: 22	Both the *c* unclean and the clean
1Sa	20: 26	to David to make him *c* unclean—
2Ch	13: 11	the bread on the *c* clean table
	30: 17	for all those who were not *c* clean
Ezr	6: 20	themselves and were all *c* clean.
Ne	12: 30	Levites had purified themselves *c*,
Isa	66: 20	of the LORD in *c* clean vessels.
Eze	22: 10	period when they are *c* unclean.
Mk	7: 2	that is, *c* unwashed—hands.
Ac	24: 18	I was *c* clean when they found me
Heb	9: 13	those who are *c* unclean sanctify

**CEREMONY* (CEREMONIAL
CEREMONIALLY)**

Ge	50: 11	Egyptians are holding a solemn *c*
Ex	12: 25	as he promised, observe this *c*.
	12: 26	'What does this *c* mean to you?'
	13: 5	are to observe this *c* in this month:

CERTAIN (CERTAINTY)

2Pe	1: 19	word of the prophets made more *c*,

CERTAINTY* (CERTAIN)

Lk 1: 4 so that you may know the c
Jn 17: 8 They knew with c that I came

CERTIFICATE* (CERTIFIED)

Dt 24: 1 and he writes her a c of divorce,
24: 3 and writes her a c of divorce,
Isa 50: 1 "Where is your mother's c
Jer 3: 8 I gave faithless Israel her c
Mt 5:31 divorces his wife must give her a c
19: 7 that a man give his wife a c
Mk 10: 4 a man to write a c of divorce

CERTIFIED* (CERTIFICATE)

Jn 3:33 has accepted it has c that God is

CHAFF

Ps 1: 4 They are like c
35: 5 May they be like c before the wind,
Da 2:35 became like c on a threshing floor
Mt 3:12 up the c with unquenchable fire."

CHAINED (CHAINS)

2Ti 2: 9 But God's word is not c.

CHAINS (CHAINED)

Eph 6:20 for which I am an ambassador in c.
Col 4:18 Remember my c.
2Ti 1:16 and was not ashamed of my c.
Jude : 6 with everlasting c for judgment

CHAMPION

Ps 19: 5 like a c rejoicing to run his course.

CHANCE

Ecc 9:11 but time and c happen to them all.

CHANGE (CHANGED)

1Sa 15:29 of Israel does not lie or c his mind;
Ps 110: 4 and will not c his mind:
Jer 7: 5 If you really c your ways
Mal 3: 6 "I the LORD do not c.
Mt 18: 3 unless you c and become like little
Heb 7:21 and will not c his mind:
Jas 1:17 who does not c like shifting

CHANGED (CHANGE)

1Sa 10: 6 you will be c into a different person
Hos 11: 8 My heart is c within me;
1Co 15:51 but we will all be c—in a flash,

CHARACTER*

Ru 3:11 that you are a woman of noble c.
Pr 12: 4 of noble c is her husband's crown,
31:10 A wife of noble c who can find?
Ac 17:11 noble c than the Thessalonians,
Ro 5: 4 perseverance, c; and c, hope.
1Co 15:33 "Bad company corrupts good c."

CHARGE (CHARGES)

Job 34:13 him in c of the whole world?
Ro 8:33 Who will bring any c
1Co 9:18 the gospel I may offer it free of c,
2Co 11: 7 the gospel of God to you free of c?
2Ti 4: 1 I give you this c: Preach the Word;
Phm : 18 or owes you anything, c it to me.

CHARGES (CHARGE)

Isa 50: 8 Who then will bring c against me?

CHARIOT (CHARIOTS)

2Ki 2:11 suddenly a c of fire and horses
Ps 104: 3 He makes the clouds his c
Ac 8:28 sitting in his c reading the book

CHARIOTS (CHARIOT)

2Ki 6:17 and c of fire all around Elisha.
Ps 20: 7 Some trust in c and some in horses,
68:17 The c of God are tens of thousands

CHARITY see LOVE

CHARM* (CHARMING)

Pr 17: 8 bribe is a c to the one who gives it;
31:30 C is deceptive, and beauty is

CHARMING* (CHARM)

Pr 26:25 his speech is c, do not believe
SS 1:16 Oh, how c!

CHASE (CHASES)

Lev 26: 8 Five of you will c a hundred,

CHASES* (CHASE)

Pr 12:11 he who c fantasies lacks judgment.
28:19 one who c fantasies will have his

CHASM*

Lk 16:26 and you a great c has been fixed,

CHATTER* (CHATTERING)

1Ti 6:20 Turn away from godless c
2Ti 2:16 Avoid godless c, because those

CHATTERING* (CHATTER)

Pr 10: 8 but a c fool comes to ruin.
10:10 and a c fool comes to ruin.

CHEAT* (CHEATED CHEATING CHEATS)

Mal 1:14 "Cursed is the c who has
1Co 6: 8 you yourselves c and do wrong,

CHEATED* (CHEAT)

Ge 31: 7 yet your father has c me
1Sa 12: 3 Whom have I c? Whom have I
12: 4 "You have not c or oppressed us,"
Lk 19: 8 if I have c anybody out of anything,
1Co 6: 7 Why not rather be c? Instead,

CHEATING* (CHEAT)

Am 8: 5 and c with dishonest scales,

CHEATS* (CHEAT)

Lev 6: 2 or if he c him, or if he finds lost

CHEEK (CHEEKS)

Mt 5:39 someone strikes you on the right c,
Lk 6:29 If someone strikes you on one c,

CHEEKS (CHEEK)

Isa 50: 6 my c to those who pulled out my

CHEERFUL* (CHEERS)

Pr 15:13 A happy heart makes the face c,
15:15 but the c heart has a continual feast
15:30 A c look brings joy to the heart,
17:22 A c heart is good medicine,
2Co 9: 7 for God loves a c giver.

CHEERS (CHEERFUL)
Pr   12: 25 but a kind word c him up.

CHEMOSH
2Ki   23: 13 for C the vile god of Moab,

CHERISH (CHERISHED CHERISHES)
Ps   17: 14 You still the hunger of those you c;

CHERISHED (CHERISH)
Ps   66: 18 If I had c sin in my heart,

CHERISHES* (CHERISH)
Pr   19: 8 he who c understanding prospers.

CHERUB (CHERUBIM)
Ex   25: 19 Make one c on one end
Eze   28: 14 You were anointed as a guardian c,

CHERUBIM (CHERUB)
Ge   3: 24 side of the Garden of Eden c
1Sa   4: 4 who is enthroned between the c.
2Sa   6: 2 enthroned between the c that are
      22: 11 He mounted the c and flew;
1Ki   6: 23 a pair of c of olive wood,
2Ki   19: 15 of Israel, enthroned between the c,
1Ch   13: 6 who is enthroned between the c—
Ps   18: 10 He mounted the c and flew;
      80: 1 who sit enthroned between the c,
      99: 1 he sits enthroned between the c,
Isa   37: 16 of Israel, enthroned between the c,
Eze   10: 1 was over the heads of the c.

CHEST
Ex   25: 10 "Have them make a c
2Ki   12: 9 Jehoiada the priest took a c
Da   2: 32 its c and arms of silver, its belly
Rev   1: 13 with a golden sash around his c.

CHEWS
Lev   11: 3 divided and that c the cud.

CHIEF
1Pe   5: 4 And when the C Shepherd appears,

CHILD (CHILDISH CHILDREN CHILDREN'S GRANDCHILDREN)
Pr   20: 11 Even a c is known by his actions,
      22: 6 Train a c in the way he should go,
      22: 15 Folly is bound up in the heart of a c
      23: 13 not withhold discipline from a c;
      29: 15 c left to itself disgraces his mother.
Isa   7: 14 The virgin will be with c
       9: 6 For to us a c is born,
      11: 6 and a little c will lead them.
      66: 13 As a mother comforts her c,
Mt   1: 23 "The virgin will be with c
      18: 2 He called a little c and had him
Lk   1: 42 and blessed is the c you will bear!
       1: 80 And the c grew and became strong
1Co   13: 11 When I was a c, I talked like a c,
1Jn   5: 1 who loves the father loves his c

CHILDBEARING (BEAR [1])
Ge   3: 16 greatly increase your pains in c;

CHILDBIRTH (BEAR [1])
Gal   4: 19 the pains of c until Christ is formed

CHILDISH* (CHILD)
1Co   13: 11 When I became a man, I put c ways

CHILDREN (CHILD)
Ex   20: 5 punishing the c for the sin
Dt   4: 9 Teach them to your c
       6: 7 Impress them on your c.
      11: 19 them to your c, talking about them
      14: 1 You are the c of the LORD your
      24: 16 nor c put to death for their fathers;
      30: 19 so that you and your c may live
      32: 46 so that you may command your c
Job   1: 5 "Perhaps my c have sinned
Ps   8: 2 From the lips of c and infants
      78: 5 forefathers to teach their c,
Pr   17: 6 Children's c are a crown
      20: 7 blessed are his c after him.
      31: 28 Her c arise and call her blessed;
Joel   1: 3 Tell it to your c,
Mal   4: 6 the hearts of the fathers to their c,
Mt   7: 11 how to give good gifts to your c,
      11: 25 and revealed them to little c.
      18: 3 you change and become like little c
      19: 14 "Let the little c come to me,
      21: 16 "'From the lips of c and infants
Mk   9: 37 one of these little c in my name
      10: 14 "Let the little c come to me,
      10: 16 And he took the c in his arms,
      13: 12 C will rebel against their parents
Lk   10: 21 and revealed them to little c.
      18: 16 "Let the little c come to me,
Jn   1: 12 the right to become c of God—
Ac   2: 39 The promise is for you and your c
Ro   8: 16 with our spirit that we are God's c.
1Co   14: 20 Brothers, stop thinking like c.
2Co   12: 14 parents, but parents for their c.
Eph   6: 1 C, obey your parents in the Lord,
       6: 4 do not exasperate your c; instead,
Col   3: 20 C, obey your parents in everything,
       3: 21 Fathers, do not embitter your c,
1Ti   3: 4 and see that his c obey him
       3: 12 and must manage his c and his
       5: 10 bringing up c, showing hospitality,
Heb   2: 13 and the c God has given me."
1Jn   3: 1 that we should be called c of God!

CHILDREN'S (CHILD)
Isa   54: 13 and great will be your c peace.

CHOKE
Mk   4: 19 come in and c the word,

CHOOSE (CHOOSES CHOSE CHOSEN)
Dt   30: 19 Now c life, so that you
Jos   24: 15 then c for yourselves this day
Pr   8: 10 C my instruction instead of silver,
      16: 16 to c understanding rather
Jn   15: 16 You did not c me, but I chose you

CHOOSES (CHOOSE)
Mt   11: 27 to whom the Son c to reveal him.
Lk   10: 22 to whom the Son c to reveal him."
Jn   7: 17 If anyone c to do God's Will,

CHOSE (CHOOSE)
Ge   13: 11 So Lot c for himself the whole plain
Ps   33: 12 the people he c for his inheritance.
Jn   15: 16 but I c you and appointed you to go
1Co   1: 27 But God c the foolish things

Eph	1: 4	he *c* us in him before the creation
2Th	2: 13	from the beginning God *c* you

CHOSEN (CHOOSE)

Isa	41: 8	Jacob, whom I have *c*,
Mt	22: 14	For many are invited, but few are *c*
Lk	10: 42	Mary has *c* what is better,
	23: 35	the Christ of God, the *C* One."
Jn	15: 19	but I have *c* you out of the world.
1Pe	1: 20	He was *c* before the creation
	2: 9	But you are a *c* people, a royal

CHRIST (CHRIST'S CHRISTIAN CHRISTIANS CHRISTS)

Mt	1: 16	was born Jesus, who is called *C*.
	16: 16	Peter answered, "You are the *C*,
	22: 42	"What do you think about the *C*?
Mk	1: 1	of the gospel about Jesus *C*,
	8: 29	Peter answered, "You are the *C*."
	14: 61	"Are you the *C*, the Son
Lk	9: 20	Peter answered, "The *C* of God."
Jn	1: 41	found the Messiah" (that is, the *C*).
	20: 31	you may believe that Jesus is the *C*,
Ac	2: 36	you crucified, both Lord and *C*."
	5: 42	the good news that Jesus is the *C*.
	9: 22	by proving that Jesus is the *C*.
	9: 34	said to him, "Jesus *C* heals you.
	17: 3	proving that the *C* had to suffer
	18: 28	the Scriptures that Jesus was the *C*.
	26: 23	that the *C* would suffer and,
Ro	1: 4	from the dead: Jesus *C* our Lord.
	3: 22	comes through faith in Jesus *C*
	5: 1	God through our Lord Jesus *C*,
	5: 6	we were still powerless, *C* died
	5: 8	While we were still sinners, *C* died
	5: 11	in God through our Lord Jesus *C*,
	5: 17	life through the one man, Jesus *C*.
	6: 4	as *C* was raised from the dead
	6: 9	that since *C* was raised
	6: 23	life in *C* Jesus our Lord.
	7: 4	to the law through the body of *C*,
	8: 1	for those who are in *C* Jesus,
	8: 9	Spirit of *C*, he does not belong to *C*.
	8: 17	heirs of God and co-heirs with *C*,
	8: 34	Who is he that condemns? *C* Jesus,
	8: 35	us from the love of *C*?
	9: 5	is traced the human ancestry of *C*,
	10: 4	*C* is the end of the law
	12: 5	so in *C* we who are many form one
	13: 14	yourselves with the Lord Jesus *C*,
	14: 9	*C* died and returned to life
	15: 3	For even *C* did not please himself
	15: 5	yourselves as you follow *C* Jesus,
	15: 7	then, just as *C* accepted you,
	16: 18	people are not serving our Lord *C*,
1Co	1: 2	to those sanctified in *C* Jesus
	1: 7	for our Lord Jesus *C* to be revealed.
	1: 13	Is *C* divided? Was Paul crucified
	1: 17	For *C* did not send me to baptise,
	1: 23	but we preach *C* crucified:
	1: 30	of him that you are in *C* Jesus,
	2: 2	except Jesus *C* and him crucified.
	3: 11	one already laid, which is Jesus *C*.
	5: 7	For *C*, our Passover lamb,
	6: 15	bodies are members of *C* himself?
	8: 6	and there is but one Lord, Jesus *C*,
	8: 12	conscience, you sin against *C*.
	10: 4	them, and that rock was *C*.
	11: 1	as I follow the example of *C*.
	11: 3	the head of every man is *C*,

1Co	12: 27	Now you are the body of *C*,
	15: 3	that *C* died for our sins according
	15: 14	And if *C* has not been raised,
	15: 22	so in *C* all will be made alive.
	15: 57	victory through our Lord Jesus *C*.
2Co	1: 5	as the sufferings of *C* flow
	2: 14	us in triumphal procession in *C*
	3: 3	show that you are a letter from *C*,
	3: 14	because only in *C* is it taken away.
	4: 4	light of the gospel of the glory of *C*,
	4: 5	not preach ourselves, but Jesus *C*
	4: 6	of the glory of God in the face of *C*.
	5: 10	before the judgment seat of *C*,
	5: 17	Therefore, if anyone is in *C*,
	6: 15	What harmony is there between *C*
	10: 1	the meekness and gentleness of *C*,
	11: 2	you to one husband, to *C*,
Gal	1: 7	are trying to pervert the gospel of *C*
	2: 4	on the freedom we have in *C* Jesus
	2: 16	but by faith in Jesus *C*.
	2: 17	does that mean that *C* promotes sin
	2: 20	I have been crucified with *C*
	2: 21	*C* died for nothing!" You foolish
	3: 13	*C* redeemed us from the curse
	3: 16	meaning one person, who is *C*.
	3: 26	of God through faith in *C* Jesus,
	4: 19	of childbirth until *C* is formed
	5: 1	for freedom that *C* has set us free.
	5: 4	by law have been alienated from *C*;
	5: 24	to *C* Jesus have crucified the sinful
	6: 14	in the cross of our Lord Jesus *C*,
Eph	1: 3	with every spiritual blessing in *C*.
	1: 10	together under one head, even *C*.
	1: 20	which he exerted in *C*
	2: 5	made us alive with *C*
	2: 10	created in *C* Jesus
	2: 12	time you were separate from *C*,
	2: 20	with *C* Jesus himself as the chief
	3: 8	the unsearchable riches of *C*,
	3: 17	so that *C* may dwell in your hearts
	4: 7	has been given as *C* apportioned it.
	4: 13	measure of the fulness of *C*.
	4: 15	into him who is the Head, that is, *C*
	4: 32	just as in *C* God forgave you.
	5: 2	as *C* loved us and gave himself up
	5: 21	out of reverence for *C*.
	5: 23	as *C* is the head of the church,
	5: 25	just as *C* loved the church
Php	1: 18	motives or true, *C* is preached.
	1: 21	to live is *C* and to die is gain.
	1: 23	I desire to depart and be with *C*,
	1: 27	worthy of the gospel of *C*.
	1: 29	on behalf of *C* not only to believe
	2: 5	be the same as that of *C* Jesus:
	3: 7	now consider loss for the sake of *C*.
	3: 10	I want to know *C* and the power
	3: 18	as enemies of the cross of *C*.
	4: 19	to his glorious riches in *C* Jesus.
Col	1: 4	heard of your faith in *C* Jesus
	1: 27	which is *C* in you, the hope of glory
	1: 28	may present everyone perfect in *C*.
	2: 2	the mystery of God, namely, *C*,
	2: 6	as you received *C* Jesus as Lord,
	2: 9	For in *C* all the fulness
	2: 13	God made you alive with *C*,
	2: 17	the reality, however, is found in *C*.
	3: 1	then, you have been raised with *C*,
	3: 3	and your life is now hidden with *C*
	3: 15	Let the peace of *C* rule
1Th	5: 9	through our Lord Jesus *C*.

2Th 2: 1 the coming of our Lord Jesus *C*
     2:14 in the glory of our Lord Jesus *C.*
1Ti 1:12 I thank *C* Jesus our Lord, who has
     1:15 *C* Jesus came into the world
     1:16 *C* Jesus might display his unlimited
     2: 5 the man *C* Jesus, who gave himself
2Ti 1: 9 us in *C* Jesus before the beginning
     1:10 appearing of our Saviour, *C* Jesus,
     2: 1 in the grace that is in *C* Jesus.
     2: 3 us like a good soldier of *C* Jesus.
     2: 8 Remember Jesus *C*, raised
     2:10 the salvation that is *C* Jesus,
     3:12 life in *C* Jesus will be persecuted,
     3:15 salvation through faith in *C* Jesus.
     4: 1 presence of God and of *C* Jesus,
Tit 2:13 our great God and Saviour, Jesus *C*,
Heb 3: 6 But *C* is faithful as a son
     3:14 to share in *C* if we hold firmly
     5: 5 So *C* also did not take
     6: 1 the elementary teachings about *C*
     9:11 When *C* came as high priest
     9:14 more, then, will the blood of *C*,
     9:15 For this reason *C* is the mediator
     9:24 For *C* did not enter a man-made
     9:26 Then *C* would have had
     9:28 so *C* was sacrificed once
    10:10 of the body of Jesus *C* once for all.
    13: 8 Jesus *C* is the same yesterday
1Pe 1: 2 for obedience to Jesus *C*
     1: 3 of Jesus *C* from the dead,
     1:11 he predicted the sufferings of *C*
     1:19 but with the precious blood of *C*,
     2:21 because *C* suffered for you,
     3:15 in your hearts set apart *C* as Lord.
     3:18 For *C* died for sins once for all,
     3:21 you by the resurrection of Jesus *C*,
     4:13 participate in the sufferings of *C*,
     4:14 insulted because of the name of *C*,
2Pe 1: 1 and Saviour Jesus *C* have received
     1:16 and coming of our Lord Jesus *C*,
1Jn 2: 1 Jesus *C*, the Righteous One.
     2:22 man who denies that Jesus is the *C.*
     3:16 Jesus *C* laid down his life for us.
     3:23 in the name of his Son, Jesus *C*,
     4: 2 that Jesus *C* has come
     5: 1 believes that Jesus is the *C* is born
     5:20 even in his Son Jesus *C.*
2Jn   : 9 teaching of *C* does not have God;
Jude : 4 deny Jesus *C* our only Sovereign
Rev 1: 1 The revelation of Jesus *C*,
     1: 5 from Jesus *C*, who is the faithful
    11:15 kingdom of our Lord and of his *C*,
    20: 4 reigned with *C* a thousand years.
    20: 6 they will be priests of God and of *C*

CHRIST'S (CHRIST)

1Co 9:21 from God's law but am under *C* law
2Co 5:14 For *C* love compels us,
     5:20 We are therefore *C* ambassadors,
    12: 9 so that *C* power may rest on me.
Col 1:22 by *C* physical body through death

CHRISTIAN* (CHRIST)

Ac 26:28 you can persuade me to be a *C*?"
1Pe 4:16 as a *C*, do not be ashamed,

CHRISTIANS* (CHRIST)

Ac 11:26 The disciples were first called *C*

CHRISTS* (CHRIST)

Mt 24:24 For false *C* and false prophets will
Mk 13:22 For false *C* and false prophets will

CHURCH

Mt 16:18 and on this rock I will build my *c*,
    18:17 if he refuses to listen even to the *c*,
Ac 20:28 Be shepherds of the *c* of God,
1Co 5:12 of mine to judge those outside the *c*
    14: 4 but he who prophesies edifies the *c*.
    14:12 to excel in gifts that build up the *c*.
    14:26 done for the strengthening of the *c*.
    15: 9 because I persecuted the *c* of God.
Gal 1:13 how intensely I persecuted the *c*
Eph 5:23 as Christ is the head of the *c*,
Col 1:18 he is the head of the body, the *c*;
     1:24 the sake of his body, which is the *c*.

CHURNING

Pr 30:33 For as *c* the milk produces butter,

CIRCLE

Isa 40:22 enthroned above the *c* of the earth,

CIRCUMCISE (CIRCUMCISED CIRCUMCISION)

Dt 10:16 *C* your hearts, therefore,

CIRCUMCISED (CIRCUMCISE)

Ge 17:10 Every male among you shall be *c*.
    17:12 who is eight days old must be *c*,
Jos 5: 3 and *c* the Israelites at Gibeath
Gal 5: 2 that if you let yourselves be *c*,

CIRCUMCISION (CIRCUMCISE)

Ro 2:25 *C* has value if you observe the law,
    2:29 and *c* is *c* of the heart, by the Spirit,
1Co 7:19 *C* is nothing and uncircumcision is

CIRCUMSTANCES

Php 4:11 to be content whatever the *c*.
1Th 5:18 continually; give thanks in all *c*,

CITIES (CITY)

Lk 19:17 small matter, take charge of ten *c*.'
    19:19 'You take charge of five *c*.'

CITIZENSHIP* (FELLOW-CITIZENS)

Ac 22:28 "I had to pay a big price for my *c*."
Eph 2:12 excluded from *c* in Israel
Php 3:20 But our *c* is in heaven.

CITY (CITIES)

Mt 5:14 A *c* on a hill cannot be hidden.
Ac 18:10 I have many people in this *c*."
Heb 13:14 here we do not have an enduring *c*,
Rev 21: 2 saw the Holy *C*, the new

CIVILIAN*

2Ti 2: 4 a soldier gets involved in *c* affairs—

CLAIM (CLAIMS RECLAIM)

Pr 25: 6 do not *c* a place among great men;
1Jn 1: 6 If we *c* to have fellowship
     1: 8 If we *c* to be without sin, we
     1:10 If we *c* we have not sinned,

CLAIMS (CLAIM)

Jas 2:14 if a man *c* to have faith

1Jn　2: 6　Whoever *c* to live in him must walk
　　　2: 9　Anyone who *c* to be in the light

CLANGING*

1Co　13: 1　a resounding gong or a *c* cymbal.

CLAP* (CLAPPED CLAPS)

Job　21: 5　*c* your hand over your mouth.
Ps　47: 1　*C* your hands, all you nations;
　　　98: 8　Let the rivers *c* their hands,
Pr　30: 32　*c* your hand over your mouth!
Isa　55: 12　will *c* their hands.
La　2: 15　*c* their hands at you;

CLAPPED* (CLAP)

2Ki　11: 12　and the people *c* their hands
Eze　25: 6　Because you have *c* your hands

CLAPS* (CLAP)

Job　27: 23　It *c* its hands in derision
　　　34: 37　scornfully he *c* his hands among us
Na　3: 19　*c* his hands at your fall,

CLASSIFY*

2Co　10: 12　dare to *c* or compare ourselves

CLAUDIUS

Ac　11: 28　happened during the reign of *C*.)
　　　18: 2　because *C* had ordered all the Jews

CLAY

Isa　45: 9　Does the *c* say to the potter,
　　　64: 8　We are the *c*, you are the potter;
Jer　18: 6　"Like *c* in the hand of the potter,
La　4: 2　are now considered as pots of *c*,
Da　2: 33　partly of iron and partly of baked *c*.
Ro　9: 21　of the same lump of *c* some pottery
2Co　4: 7　we have this treasure in jars of *c*
2Ti　2: 20　and *c*; some are for noble purposes

CLEAN (CLEANNESS CLEANSE CLEANSED CLEANSES CLEANSING)

Ge　7: 2　seven of every kind of *c* animal,
Lev　4: 12　the camp to a place ceremonially *c*,
　　　16: 30　you will be *c* from all your sins.
Ps　24: 4　He who has *c* hands and a pure
　　　51: 7　with hyssop, and I will be *c*;
Pr　20: 9　I am *c* and without sin"?
Eze　36: 25　I will sprinkle *c* water on you,
Mt　8: 2　are willing, you can make me *c*."
　　　12: 44　the house unoccupied, swept *c*
　　　23: 25　You *c* the outside of the cup
Mk　7: 19　Jesus declared all foods "*c*.")
Jn　13: 10　to wash his feet; his whole body is *c*
　　　15: 3　are already *c* because of the word
Ac　10: 15　impure that God has made *c*."
Ro　14: 20　All food is *c*, but it is wrong

CLEANNESS (CLEAN)

2Sa　22: 25　according to my *c* in his sight.

CLEANSE (CLEAN)

Ps　51: 2　and *c* me from my sin.
　　　51: 7　*C* me with hyssop, and will be
Pr　20: 30　Blows and wounds *c* away evil,
Heb　9: 14　*c* our consciences from acts that
　　　10: 22　having our hearts sprinkled to *c* us

CLEANSED (CLEAN)

Heb　9: 22　requires that nearly everything be *c*

2Pe　1: 9　has forgotten that he has been *c*

CLEANSES* (CLEAN)

2Ti　2: 21　If a man *c* himself from the latter,

CLEANSING (CLEAN)

Eph　5: 26　*c* her by the washing with water

CLEFT*

Ex　33: 22　I will put you in a *c* in the rock

CLEVER

Isa　5: 21　and *c* in their own sight.

CLING

Ro　12: 9　Hate what is evil; *c* to what is good.

CLOAK

Ex　12: 11　with your *c* tucked into your belt,
2Ki　4: 29　"Tuck your *c* into your belt,
　　　9: 1　"Tuck your *c* into your belt,
Mt　5: 40　let him have your *c* as well.

CLOSE (CLOSER)

2Ki　11: 8　Stay *c* to the king wherever he goes
2Ch　23: 7　Stay *c* to the king wherever he goes
Ps　34: 18　LORD is *c* to the broken-hearted
　　　148: 14　of Israel, the people *c* to his heart.
Isa　40: 11　and carries them *c* to his heart;
Jer　30: 21　himself to be *c* to me?'

CLOSER (CLOSE)

Ex　3: 5　"Do not come any *c*," God said.
Pr　18: 24　there is a friend who sticks *c*

CLOSES

Pr　28: 27　he who *c* his eyes to them receives

CLOTHE (CLOTHED CLOTHES CLOTHING CLOTHS)

Ps　45: 3　*c* yourself with splendour
Isa　52: 1　*c* yourself with strength.
Ro　13: 14　*c* yourselves with the Lord Jesus
Col　3: 12　*c* yourselves with compassion,
1Pe　5: 5　*C* yourselves with humility

CLOTHED (CLOTHE)

Ps　30: 11　removed my sackcloth and *c* me
　　　104: 1　you are *c* with splendour
Pr　31: 22　she is *c* in fine linen and purple.
　　　31: 25　She is *c* with strength and dignity;
Isa　61: 10　For he has *c* me with garments
Lk　24: 49　until you have been *c* with power
Gal　3: 27　into Christ have *c* yourselves

CLOTHES (CLOTHE)

Dt　8: 4　Your *c* did not wear out
Mt　6: 25　the body more important than *c*?
　　　6: 28　"And why do you worry about *c*?
　　　27: 35　they divided up his *c* by casting lots
Jn　11: 44　Take off the grave *c* and let him go

CLOTHING (CLOTHE)

Dt　22: 5　A woman must not wear men's *c*,
Job　29: 14　I put on righteousness as my *c*;
Ps　22: 18　and cast lots for my *c*.
Mt　7: 15　They come to you in sheep's *c*,
1Ti　6: 8　But if we have food and *c*,

CLOTHS (CLOTH)

Lk   2: 12   You will find a baby wrapped in *c*

CLOUD (CLOUDS)

Ex   13: 21   them in a pillar of *c* to guide them
1Ki   18: 44   *c* as small as a man's hand is rising
Pr   16: 15   his favour is like a rain *c* in spring.
Isa   19: 1   See, the LORD rides on a swift *c*
Lk   21: 27   of Man coming in a *c* with power
Heb   12: 1   by such a great *c* of witnesses,
Rev   14: 14   seated on the *c* was one "like a son

CLOUDS (CLOUD)

Dt   33: 26   and on the *c* in his majesty.
Ps   68: 4   extol him who rides on the *c*—
      104: 3   He makes the *c* his chariot
Pr   25: 14   Like *c* and wind without rain
Da   7: 13   coming with the *c* of heaven.
Mt   24: 30   of Man coming on the *c* of the sky,
     26: 64   and coming on the *c* of heaven."
Mk   13: 26   coming in a *c* with great power
1Th   4: 17   with them in the *c* to meet the Lord
Rev   1: 7   Look, he is coming with the *c*,

CLUB

Pr   25: 18   Like a *c* or a sword or a sharp arrow

CO-HEIRS* (INHERIT)

Ro   8: 17   heirs of God and *c* with Christ,

COALS

Pr   25: 22   you will heap burning *c* on his head
Ro   12: 20   you will heap burning *c* on his head

COARSE*

Eph   5: 4   or *c* joking, which are out of place,

COCK

Mt   26: 34   this very night, before the *c* crows,

CODE*

Ro   2: 27   even though you have the written *c*
      2: 29   by the Spirit, not by the written *c*.
      7: 6   not in the old way of the written *c*.
Col   2: 14   having cancelled the written *c*,

COINS

Mt   26: 15   out for him thirty silver *c*.
Lk   15: 8   suppose a woman has ten silver *c*

COLD

Pr   25: 25   Like *c* water to a weary soul
Mt   10: 42   if anyone gives a cup of *c* water
     24: 12   the love of most will grow *c*,

COLLECTION

1Co   16: 1   Now about the *c* for God's people:

COLT

Zec   9: 9   on a *c*, the foal of a donkey.
Mt   21: 5   on a *c*, the foal of a donkey.'"

COMB

Ps   19: 10   than honey from the *c*.

COMFORT* (COMFORTED COMFORTER COMFORTERS COMFORTING COMFORTS)

Ge   5: 29   "He will *c* us in the labour
     37: 35   and daughters came to *c* him,

Ru   2: 13   "You have given me *c*
1Ch   7: 22   and his relatives came to *c* him.
Job   2: 11   sympathise with him and *c* him.
      7: 13   When I think my bed will *c* me
     16: 5   *c* from my lips would bring you
     36: 16   to the *c* of your table laden
Ps   23: 4   rod and your staff, they *c* me.
     71: 21   and *c* me once again.
    119: 50   My *c* in my suffering is this:
    119: 52   and I find *c* in them.
    119: 76   May your unfailing love be my *c*,
    119: 82   I say, "When will you *c* me?"
Isa   40: 1   *C*, *c* my people,
     51: 3   The LORD will surely *c* Zion
     51: 19   who can *c* you?—
     57: 18   I will guide him and restore *c*
     61: 2   to *c* all who mourn,
     66: 13   so will I *c* you;
Jer   16: 7   food to *c* those who mourn
     31: 13   I will give them *c* and joy instead
La   1: 2   there is none to *c* her.
     1: 9   there was none to *c* her.
     1: 16   No-one is near to *c* me,
     1: 17   but there is no-one to *c* her.
     1: 21   but there is no-one to *c* me.
     2: 13   that I may *c* you,
Eze   16: 54   all you have done in giving them *c*.
Na   3: 7   Where can I find anyone to *c* you?"
Zec   1: 17   and the LORD will again *c* Zion
     10: 2   they give *c* in vain.
Lk   6: 24   you have already received your *c*.
Jn   11: 19   and Mary to *c* them in the loss
1Co   14: 3   encouragement and *c*.
2Co   1: 3   of compassion and the God of all *c*,
     1: 4   so that we can *c* those
     1: 4   with the *c* we ourselves have
     1: 5   through Christ our *c* overflows.
     1: 6   if we are comforted, it is for your *c*,
     1: 6   it is for your *c* and salvation;
     1: 7   so also you share in our *c*.
     2: 7   you ought to forgive and *c* him,
     7: 7   also by the *c* you had given him.
Php   2: 1   if any *c* from his love,
Col   4: 11   and they have proved a *c* to me.

COMFORTED* (COMFORT)

Ge   24: 67   Isaac was *c* after his mother's death
     37: 35   comfort him, but he refused to be *c*.
2Sa   12: 24   Then David *c* his wife Bathsheba,
Job   42: 11   They *c* and consoled him
Ps   77: 2   and my soul refused to be *c*.
     86: 17   have helped me and *c* me.
Isa   12: 1   and you have *c* me.
     52: 9   for the LORD has *c* his people,
     54: 11   lashed by storms and not *c*,
     66: 13   and you will be *c* over Jerusalem."
Jer   31: 15   and refusing to be *c*,
Mt   2: 18   and refusing to be *c*,
     5: 4   for they will be *c*.
Lk   16: 25   but now he is *c* here and you are
Ac   20: 12   man home alive and were greatly *c*.
2Co   1: 6   if we are *c*, it is for your comfort,
     7: 6   *c* us by the coming of Titus,

COMFORTER* (COMFORT)

Ecc   4: 1   and they have no *c*;
Jer   8: 18   O my *C* in sorrow,

COMFORTERS* (COMFORT)

Job   16: 2   miserable *c* are you all!

Ps   69: 20 for *c*, but I found none.

COMFORTING* (COMFORT)

Isa   66: 11 satisfied at her *c* breasts;
Zec   1: 13 *c* words to the angel who talked
Jn   11: 31 *c* her, noticed how quickly she got
1Th   2: 12 *c* and urging you to live lives

COMFORTS* (COMFORT)

Job   29: 25 I was like one who *c* mourners.
Isa   49: 13 For the LORD *c* his people
      51: 12 "I, even I, am he who *c* you.
      66: 13 As a mother *c* her child,
2Co   1: 4 who *c* us in all our troubles,
       7: 6 But God, who *c* the downcast,

COMMAND (COMMANDED COMMANDING COMMANDMENT COMMANDMENTS COMMANDS)

Ex   7: 2 You are to say everything I *c* you,
Nu   14: 41 are you disobeying the LORD's *c*?
      24: 13 to go beyond the *c* of the LORD—
Dt   4: 2 Do not add to what I *c* you
       8: 1 To follow every *c* I am giving you
      12: 32 See that you do all I *c* you;
      15: 11 *c* you to be open-handed
      30: 16 For I *c* you today to love
      32: 46 so that you may *c* your children
Ps   91: 11 For he will *c* his angels concerning
Pr   13: 13 but he who respects a *c* is rewarded
Ecc   8: 2 Obey the king's *c*, I say,
Jer   1: 7 you to and say whatever I *c* you.
       1: 17 and say to them whatever I *c* you.
       7: 23 Walk in all the ways I *c* you,
      11: 4 Obey me and do everything I *c* you
      26: 2 Tell them everything I *c* you;
Joel   2: 11 mighty are those who obey his *c*.
Mt   4: 6 He will *c* his angels concerning you
      15: 3 why do you break the *c* of God
Lk   4: 10 "'He will *c* his angels concerning
Jn   13: 34 "A new *c* I give you: Love one
      14: 15 love me, you will obey what I *c*.
      15: 12 My *c* is this: Love each other
      15: 14 friends if you do what I *c*.
      15: 17 This is my *c*: Love each other.
1Co   14: 37 writing to you is the Lord's *c*.
Gal   5: 14 law is summed up in a single *c*:
1Ti   1: 5 goal of this *c* is love, which comes
       6: 14 you to keep this *c* without spot
       6: 17 *C* those who are rich
Heb   11: 3 universe was formed at God's *c*,
2Pe   2: 21 on the sacred *c* that was passed
       3: 2 and the *c* given by our Lord
1Jn   2: 7 I am not writing you a new *c*
       3: 23 this is his *c*: to believe in the name
       4: 21 And he has given us this *c*:
2Jn   : 6 his *c* is that you walk in love.

COMMANDED (COMMAND)

Ge   2: 16 And the LORD God *c* the man,
       7: 5 Noah did all that the LORD *c* him.
      50: 12 Jacob's sons did as he had *c* them:
Ex   7: 6 did just as the LORD *c* them.
      19: 7 all the words the LORD had *c* him
Dt   4: 5 laws as the LORD my God *c* me,
       6: 24 The LORD *c* us to obey all these
Jos   1: 9 Have I not *c* you? Be strong
       1: 16 Whatever you have *c* us we will do,
2Sa   5: 25 So David did as the LORD *c* him,
2Ki   17: 13 the entire Law that I *c* your fathers

2Ki   21: 8 careful to do everything I *c* them
2Ch   33: 8 do everything I *c* them concerning
Ps   33: 9 he *c*, and it stood firm.
      78: 5 which he *c* our forefathers
     148: 5 for he *c* and they were created.
Mt   28: 20 to obey everything I have *c* you.
1Co   9: 14 Lord has *c* that those who preach
1Jn   3: 23 and to love one another as he *c* us.
2Jn   : 4 in the truth, just as the Father *c* us.

COMMANDING (COMMAND)

2Ti   2: 4 he wants to please his *c* officer.

COMMANDMENT* (COMMAND)

Jos   22: 5 But be very careful to keep the *c*
Mt   22: 36 which is the greatest *c* in the Law?"
      22: 38 This is the first and greatest *c*.
Mk   12: 31 There is no *c* greater than these."
Lk   23: 56 the Sabbath in obedience to the *c*.
Ro   7: 8 the opportunity afforded by the *c*,
       7: 9 when the *c* came, sin sprang to life
       7: 10 that the very *c* that was intended
       7: 11 and through the *c* put me to death.
       7: 11 the opportunity afforded by the *c*,
       7: 12 and the *c* is holy, righteous
       7: 13 through the *c* sin might become
      13: 9 and whatever other *c* there may be,
Eph   6: 2 which is the first *c* with a promise
Heb   9: 19 Moses had proclaimed every *c*

COMMANDMENTS* (COMMAND)

Ex   20: 6 who love me and keep my *c*.
      34: 28 of the covenant—the Ten *C*.
Dt   4: 13 to you his covenant, the Ten *C*,
       5: 10 who love me and keep my *c*.
       5: 22 These are the LORD
       6: 6 These *c* that I give you today are
       9: 10 were all the *c* the LORD
      10: 4 The Ten *C* he had proclaimed
Ecc   12: 13 Fear God and keep his *c*,
Mt   5: 19 one of the least of these *c*
      19: 17 If you want to enter life, obey the *c*
      22: 40 the Prophets hang on these two *c*."
Mk   10: 19 You know the *c*: 'Do not murder,
      12: 28 "Of all the *c*, which is the most
Lk   1: 6 observing all the Lord's *c*
      18: 20 You know the *c*: 'Do not commit
Ro   13: 9 The *c*, "Do not commit adultery,"
Eph   2: 15 in his flesh the law with its *c*
Rev   12: 17 those who obey God's *c*
      14: 12 part of the saints who obey God's *c*

COMMANDS (COMMAND)

Ex   24: 12 and *c* I have written for their
      25: 22 give you all my *c* for the Israelites.
      34: 32 gave them all the *c* the LORD had
Lev   22: 31 "Keep my *c* and follow them.
Nu   15: 39 and so you will remember all the *c*
Dt   7: 9 those who love him and keep his *c*.
       7: 11 Therefore, take care to follow the *c*
      11: 1 decrees, his laws and his *c* always.
      11: 27 the blessing if you obey the *c*
      28: 1 carefully follow all his *c* I give you
      30: 10 LORD your God and keep his *c*
Jos   22: 5 to walk in all his ways, to obey his *c*
1Ki   2: 3 and keep his decrees and *c*,
       8: 58 in all his ways and to keep the *c*,
       8: 61 to live by his decrees and obey his *c*
1Ch   28: 7 unswerving in carrying out my *c*
      29: 19 devotion to keep your *c*,

2Ch 31: 21 in obedience to the law and the *c*,
Ne   1: 5 those who love him and obey his *c*,
Ps   78: 7 but would keep his *c*.
     112: 1 who finds great delight in his *c*.
     119: 10 do not let me stray for your *c*;
     119: 32 I run in the path of your *c*,
     119: 35 Direct me in the path of your *c*,
     119: 47 for I delight in your *c*
     119: 48 lift up my hands to your *c*,
     119: 73 me understanding to learn your *c*.
     119: 86 All your *c* are trustworthy;
     119: 96 but your *c* are boundless.
     119: 98 Your *c* make me wiser
     119: 115 that I may keep the *c* of my God!
     119: 127 Because I love your *c*
     119: 131 longing for your *c*.
     119: 143 but your *c* are my delight.
     119: 151 and all your *c* are true.
     119: 172 for all your *c* are righteous.
     119: 176 for I have not forgotten your *c*.
Pr   2: 1 and store up my *c* within you,
      3: 1 but keep my *c* in your heart,
      6: 23 For these *c* are a lamp,
     10: 8 The wise in heart accept *c*,
Isa 48: 18 you had paid attention to my *c*,
Da   9: 4 all who love him and obey his *c*,
Mt   5: 19 teaches these *c* will be called great
Mk   7: 8 You have let go of the *c* of God
      7: 9 way of setting aside the *c* of God
Jn   14: 21 Whoever has my *c* and obeys them,
     15: 10 If you obey my *c*, you will remain
Ac   17: 30 but now he *c* all people everywhere
1Co   7: 19 Keeping God's *c* is what counts.
1Jn   2: 3 come to know him if we obey his *c*.
      2: 4 but does not do what he *c* is a liar,
      3: 22 we obey his *c* and do what pleases
      3: 24 Those who obey his *c* live in him,
      5: 2 loving God and carrying out his *c*.
      5: 3 And his *c* are not burdensome,
      5: 3 This is love for God: to obey his *c*.
2Jn   : 6 that we walk in obedience to his *c*.

COMMEMORATE

Ex   12: 14 "This is a day you are to *c*;

COMMEND* (COMMENDABLE COMMENDED COMMENDS)

Ps 145: 4 One generation will *c* your works
Ecc   8: 15 So I *c* the enjoyment of life,
Ro   13: 3 do what is right and he will *c* you.
     16: 1 I *c* to you our sister Phoebe,
2Co   3: 1 beginning to *c* ourselves again?
      4: 2 the truth plainly we *c* ourselves
      5: 12 trying to *c* ourselves to you again,
      6: 4 as servants of God we *c* ourselves
     10: 12 with some who *c* themselves
1Pe   2: 14 and to *c* those who do right.

COMMENDABLE* (COMMEND)

1Pe   2: 19 For it is *c* if a man bears up
      2: 20 you endure it, this is *c* before God.

COMMENDED* (COMMEND)

Ne   11: 2 The people *c* all the men who
Job 29: 11 and those who saw me *c* me,
Lk   16: 8 master *c* the dishonest manager
Ac   15: 40 *c* by the brothers to the grace
2Co 12: 11 I ought to have been *c* by you,
Heb 11: 2 This is what the ancients were *c* for

Heb 11: 4 By faith he was *c* as a righteous
     11: 5 he was *c* as one who pleased God.
     11: 39 These were all *c* for their faith,

COMMENDS* (COMMEND)

Pr   15: 2 of the wise *c* knowledge,
2Co 10: 18 but the one whom the Lord *c*.
     10: 18 not the one who *c* himself who is

COMMIT (COMMITS COMMITTED)

Ex   20: 14 "You shall not *c* adultery.
Dt   5: 18 "You shall not *c* adultery.
1Sa   7: 3 and *c* yourselves to the LORD
Ps   31: 5 Into your hands I *c* my spirit;
     37: 5 *C* your way to the LORD;
Pr   16: 3 *C* to the LORD whatever you do,
Mt   5: 27 that it was said, 'Do not *c* adultery.'
      5: 32 causes her to *c* adultery,
     19: 18 do not *c* adultery, do not steal,
Mk   10: 19 do not *c* adultery, do not steal,
Lk   18: 20 'Do not *c* adultery, do not murder,
     23: 46 into your hands I *c* my spirit."
Ac   20: 32 I *c* you to God and to the word
Ro   2: 22 do you *c* adultery? You who abhor
      2: 22 that people should not *c* adultery,
     13: 9 "Do not *c* adultery,"
1Co   6: 8 We should not *c* sexual immorality,
Jas   2: 11 do not *c* adultery but do *c* murder,
1Pe   4: 19 to God's will should *c* themselves
Rev   2: 22 I will make those who *c* adultery

COMMITS (COMMIT)

Pr   6: 32 man who *c* adultery lacks
     29: 22 a hot-tempered one *c* many sins.
Ecc   8: 12 a wicked man *c* a hundred crimes
Eze 18: 12 He *c* robbery.
     18: 14 who sees all the sins his father *c*,
     18: 24 from his righteousness and *c* sin
     18: 26 from his righteousness and *c* sin,
     22: 11 you one man *c* a detestable offence
Mt   5: 32 a woman so divorced *c* adultery.
     19: 9 marries another woman *c* adultery
Mk   10: 11 marries another woman *c* adultery
     10: 12 another man, she *c* adultery."
Lk   16: 18 a divorced woman *c* adultery.
     16: 18 marries another woman *c* adultery,

COMMITTED (COMMIT)

Nu   5: 7 and must confess the sin he has *c*.
1Ki   8: 61 But your hearts must be fully *c*
     15: 14 Asa's heart was fully *c*
2Ch 16: 9 those whose hearts are fully *c*
Mt   5: 28 lustfully has already *c* adultery
     11: 27 "All things have been *c* to me
Lk   10: 22 "All things have been *c* to me
Ac   14: 23 *c* them to the Lord
     14: 26 where they had been *c* to the grace
1Co   9: 17 I am simply discharging the trust *c*
2Co   5: 19 And he has *c* to us the message
1Pe   2: 22 "He *c* no sin,
Rev 17: 2 the kings of the earth *c* adultery
     18: 3 of the earth *c* adultery with her,
     18: 9 kings of the earth who *c* adultery

COMMON

Ge   11: 1 had one language and a *c* speech.
Lev 10: 10 distinguish between the holy and the *c*,
Pr   22: 2 Rich and poor have this in *c*:
     29: 13 the oppressor have this in *c*:
Ac   2: 44 together and had everything in *c*.

1Co 10: 13 has seized you except what is c
2Co 6: 14 and wickedness have in c?

COMPANION (COMPANIONS)

Ps 55: 13 my c, my close friend,
55: 20 My c attacks his friends;
Pr 13: 20 but a c of fools suffers harm.
28: 7 a c of gluttons disgraces his father.
29: 3 c of prostitutes squanders his
Rev 1: 9 your brother and c in the suffering

COMPANIONS (COMPANION)

Ps 45: 7 your God, has set you above your c
Pr 18: 24 A man of many c may come to ruin
Heb 1: 9 your God, has set you above your c

COMPANY

Ps 14: 5 present in the c of the righteous.
Pr 21: 16 comes to rest in the c of the dead.
24: 1 do not desire their c;
Jer 15: 17 I never sat in the c of revellers,
1Co 15: 33 "Bad c corrupts good character."

COMPARE* (COMPARED COMPARING COMPARISON)

Job 28: 17 Neither gold nor crystal can c
28: 19 The topaz of Cush cannot c with it;
39: 13 but they cannot c with the pinions
Ps 86: 8 no deeds can c with yours.
89: 6 skies above can c with the LORD?
Pr 3: 15 nothing you desire can c with her.
8: 11 nothing you desire can c with her.
Isa 40: 18 To whom, then, will you c God?
40: 18 What image will you c him to?
40: 25 "To whom will you c me?
46: 5 "To whom will you c me
La 2: 13 With what can I c you,
Eze 31: 8 c with its branches—
Da 1: 13 Then c our appearance with that
Mt 11: 16 "To what can I c this generation?
Lk 7: 31 I c the people of this generation?
13: 18 What shall I c it to? It is like
13: 20 What shall I c the kingdom of God
2Co 10: 12 and c themselves with themselves,
10: 12 or c ourselves with some who

COMPARED* (COMPARE)

Jdg 8: 2 What have I accomplished c to you
8: 3 What was I able to do c to you?"
Isa 46: 5 you liken me that we may be c?
Eze 31: 2 Who can be c with you in majesty?
31: 18 the trees of Eden can be c with you
Php 3: 8 I consider everything a loss c

COMPARING* (COMPARE)

Ro 8: 18 present sufferings are not worth c
2Co 8: 8 the sincerity of your love by c it
Gal 6: 4 without c himself to somebody else

COMPARISON* (COMPARE)

2Co 3: 10 now in c with the surpassing glory.

COMPASSION* (COMPASSIONATE COMPASSIONS)

Ex 33: 19 I will have c on whom I will have c.
Dt 13: 17 he will show you mercy, have c
28: 54 man among you will have no c
30: 3 restore your fortunes and have c
32: 36 and have c on his servants

Jdg 2: 18 for the LORD had c on them
1Ki 3: 26 son was alive was filled with c
2Ki 13: 23 and had c and showed concern
2Ch 30: 9 and your children will be shown c
Ne 9: 19 of your great c you did not
9: 27 and in your great c you gave them
9: 28 in your c you delivered them time
Ps 51: 1 according to your great c
77: 9 Has he in anger withheld his c?"
90: 13 Have c on your servants.
102: 13 You will arise and have c on Zion,
103: 4 and crowns me with love and c.
103: 13 As a father has c on his children,
103: 13 so the LORD has c
116: 5 our God is full of c.
119: 77 Let your c come to me that I may
119: 156 Your c is great, O LORD;
135: 14 and have c on his servants.
145: 9 he has c on all he has made.
Isa 13: 18 will they look with c on children.
14: 1 The LORD will have c on Jacob;
27: 11 so their Maker has no c on them,
30: 18 he rises to show you c.
49: 10 He who has c on them will guide
49: 13 and will have c on his afflicted ones
49: 15 and have no c on the child she has
51: 3 and will look with c on all her ruins
54: 7 with deep c I will bring you back.
54: 8 I will have c on you,"
54: 10 says the LORD, who has c on you.
60: 10 in favour I will show you c.
63: 7 to his c and many kindnesses.
63: 15 and c are withheld from us.
Jer 12: 15 I will again have c and will bring
13: 14 c to keep me from destroying them
15: 6 I can no longer show c.
21: 7 show them no mercy or pity or c.'
30: 18 and have c on his dwellings;
31: 20 I have great c for him,"
33: 26 restore their fortunes and have c
42: 12 I will show you c so that he will
42: 12 so that he will have c on you
La 3: 32 he brings grief, he will show c,
Eze 9: 5 without showing pity or c.
16: 5 or had c enough to do any
39: 25 and will have c on all the people
Hos 2: 19 in love and c.
11: 8 all my c is aroused.
13: 14 "I will have no c,
14: 3 for in you the fatherless find c."
Am 1: 11 stifling all c,
Jnh 3: 9 with c turn from his fierce anger
3: 10 he had c and did not bring
Mic 7: 19 You will again have c on us;
Zec 7: 9 show mercy and c to one another.
10: 6 because I have c on them.
Mal 3: 17 as in c a man spares his son who
Mt 9: 36 When he saw the crowds, he had c
14: 14 he had c on them and healed their
15: 32 "I have c for these people;
20: 34 Jesus had c on them and touched
Mk 1: 41 with c, Jesus reached out his hand
6: 34 and saw a large crowd, he had c
8: 2 "I have c for these people;
Lk 15: 20 and was filled with c for him;
Ro 9: 15 and I will have c on whom I have c
2Co 1: 3 the Father of c and the God
Php 2: 1 and c, then make my joy complete
Col 3: 12 clothe yourselves with c, kindness,
Jas 5: 11 The Lord is full of c and mercy.

COMPASSIONATE* (COMPASSION)

Ex   22: 27 out to me, I will hear, for I am *c*.
      34: 6 the LORD, the *c* and gracious God
2Ch 30: 9 LORD your God is gracious and *c*.
Ne   9: 17 gracious and *c*, slow to anger
Ps   86: 15 O Lord, are a *c* and gracious God,
     103: 8 The LORD is *c* and gracious,
     111: 4 the LORD is gracious and *c*.
     112: 4 the gracious and *c* and righteous
     145: 8 The LORD is gracious and *c*,
La   4: 10 With their own hands *c* women
Joel   2: 13 for he is gracious and *c*,
Jnh   4: 2 that you are a gracious and *c* God,
Eph   4: 32 Be kind and *c* to one another,
1Pe   3: 8 love as brothers, be *c* and humble.

COMPASSIONS* (COMPASSION)

La   3: 22 for his *c* never fail.

COMPELLED (COMPULSION)

Ac   20: 22 "And now, *c* by the Spirit,
1Co   9: 16 I cannot boast, for I am *c* to preach.

COMPELS (COMPULSION)

Job 32: 18 and the spirit within me *c* me;
2Co   5: 14 For Christ's love *c* us, because we

COMPETENCE* (COMPETENT)

2Co   3: 5 but our *c* comes from God.

COMPETENT* (COMPETENCE)

Ro   15: 14 and *c* to instruct one another.
1Co   6: 2 are you not *c* to judge trivial cases?
2Co   3: 5 Not that we are *c* to claim anything
      3: 6 He has made us *c* as ministers

COMPETES*

1Co   9: 25 Everyone who *c* in the games goes
2Ti   2: 5 Similarly, if anyone *c* as an athlete,
      2: 5 unless he *c* according to the rules.

COMPLACENCY* (COMPLACENT)

Pr   1: 32 and the *c* of fools will destroy them
Eze 30: 9 ships to frighten Cush out of her *c*.

COMPLACENT* (COMPLACENCY)

Isa   32: 9 You women who are so *c*,
     32: 11 Tremble, you *c* women;
Am   6: 1 Woe to you who are *c* in Zion,
Zep   1: 12 and punish those who are *c*,

COMPLAINING*

Php   2: 14 Do everything without *c* or arguing

COMPLETE

Dt   16: 15 your hands, and your joy will be *c*.
Jn   3: 29 That joy is mine, and it is now *c*.
     15: 11 and that your joy may be *c*.
     16: 24 will receive, and your joy will be *c*.
     17: 23 May they be brought to *c* unity
Ac   20: 24 *c* the task the Lord Jesus has given
Php   2: 2 then make my joy *c*
Col   4: 17 to it that you *c* the work you have
Jas   1: 4 so that you may be mature and *c*,
      2: 22 his faith was made *c* by what he did
1Jn   1: 4 We write this to make our joy *c*.
      2: 5 God's love is truly made *c* in him.
      4: 12 and his love is made *c* in us.
      4: 17 Love is made *c* among us
2Jn   : 12 to face, so that our joy may be *c*.

COMPLIMENTS*

Pr   23: 8 and will have wasted your *c*.

COMPREHEND* (COMPREHENDED)

Job 28: 13 Man does not *c* its worth;
Ecc   8: 17 No-one can *c* what goes
      8: 17 he knows, he cannot really *c* it.

COMPREHENDED* (COMPREHEND)

Job 38: 18 Have you *c* the vast expanses

COMPULSION (COMPELLED COMPELS)

2Co   9: 7 not reluctantly or under *c*,

CONCEAL (CONCEALED CONCEALS)

Ps   40: 10 I do not *c* your love and your truth
Pr   25: 2 It is the glory of God to *c* a matter;

CONCEALED (CONCEAL)

Jer   16: 17 nor is their sin *c* from my eyes.
Mt   10: 26 There is nothing *c* that will not be
Mk   4: 22 and whatever is *c* is meant
Lk   8: 17 nothing *c* that will not be known
     12: 2 There is nothing *c* that will not be

CONCEALS* (CONCEAL)

Pr   10: 18 He who *c* his hatred has lying lips,
     28: 13 He who *c* his sins does not prosper,

CONCEIT* (CONCEITED CONCEITS)

Isa   16: 6 her overweening pride and *c*,
Jer   48: 29 her overweening pride and *c*,
Php   2: 3 out of selfish ambition or vain *c*,

CONCEITED* (CONCEIT)

1Sa 17: 28 I know how *c* you are and how
Ro   11: 25 brothers, so that you may not be *c*:
     12: 16 Do not be *c*.
2Co   12: 7 To keep me from becoming *c*
Gal   5: 26 Let us not become *c*, provoking
1Ti   3: 6 or he may become *c* and fall
      6: 4 he is *c* and understands nothing.
2Ti   3: 4 of the good, treacherous, rash, *c*,

CONCEITS* (CONCEIT)

Ps   73: 7 evil *c* of their minds know no

CONCEIVED (CONCEIVES)

Ps   51: 5 from the time my mother *c* me.
Mt   1: 20 what is *c* in her is from the Holy
1Co   2: 9 no mind has *c*
Jas   1: 15 after desire has *c*, it gives birth

CONCEIVES* (CONCEIVED)

Ps   7: 14 *c* trouble gives birth

CONCERN* (CONCERNED)

Ge   39: 6 he did not *c* himself with anything
     39: 8 "my master does not *c* himself
1Sa 23: 21 "The LORD bless you for your *c*
2Ki 13: 23 and had compassion and showed *c*
Job   9: 21 have no *c* for myself;
     19: 4 my error remains my *c* alone.
Ps 131: 1 I do not *c* myself with great matters
Pr   29: 7 but the wicked have no such *c*.
Eze 36: 21 I had *c* for my holy name, which
Ac   15: 14 God at first showed his *c* by taking
     18: 17 But Gallio showed no *c* whatever.
1Co   7: 32 I would like you to be free from *c*.
     12: 25 that its parts should have equal *c*

2Co	7: 7	your deep sorrow, your ardent c
	7: 11	what alarm, what longing, what c,
	8: 16	of Titus the same c I have for you.
	11: 28	of my c for all the churches.
Php	4: 10	at last you have renewed your c

CONCERNED (CONCERN)

Ex	2: 25	Israelites and was c about them.
Ps	142: 4	no-one is c for me.
Jnh	4: 10	"You have been c about this vine,
	4: 11	Should I not be c about that great
1Co	7: 32	An unmarried man is c about
	9: 9	Is it about oxen that God is c?
Php	4: 10	you have been c, but you had no

CONCESSION*

1Co	7: 6	I say this as a c, not as a command.

CONDEMN* (CONDEMNATION CONDEMNED CONDEMNING CONDEMNS)

Job	9: 20	innocent, my mouth would c me;
	10: 2	I will say to God: Do not c me,
	34: 17	Will you c the just and mighty One
	34: 29	if he remains silent, who can c him?
	40: 8	Would you c me to justify yourself?
Ps	94: 21	and c the innocent to death.
	109: 7	and may his prayers c him.
	109: 31	from those who c him.
Isa	50: 9	Who is he that will c me?
Mt	12: 41	with this generation and c it;
	12: 42	with this generation and c it;
	20: 18	They will c him to death
Mk	10: 33	They will c him to death
Lk	6: 37	Do not c, and you will not be
	11: 31	men of this generation and c them,
	11: 32	this generation and c it,
Jn	3: 17	Son into the world to c the world,
	7: 51	"Does our law c a man
	8: 11	"Then neither do I c you,"
	12: 48	very word which I spoke will c him
Ro	2: 27	yet obeys the law will c you who,
	14: 3	everything must not c the man who
	14: 22	is the man who does not c himself
2Co	7: 3	this to c you; I have said
1Jn	3: 20	presence whenever our hearts c us.
	3: 21	if our hearts do not c us,

CONDEMNATION* (CONDEMN)

Jer	42: 18	of c and reproach; you will never
	44: 12	and horror, of c and reproach.
Ro	3: 8	may result"? Their c is deserved.
	5: 16	followed one sin and brought c,
	5: 18	of one trespass was c for all men,
	8: 1	there is now no c for those who are
2Pe	2: 3	Their c has long been hanging
Jude	: 4	certain men whose c was written

CONDEMNED* (CONDEMN)

Dt	13: 17	of those c things shall be found
Job	32: 3	to refute Job, and yet had c him.
Ps	34: 21	the foes of the righteous will be c.
	34: 22	who takes refuge in him will be c.
	37: 33	let them be c when brought to trial.
	79: 11	preserve those c to die.
	102: 20	and release those c to death."
Mt	12: 7	you would not have c the innocent.
	12: 37	and by your words you will be c."
	23: 33	How will you escape being c to hell
	27: 3	betrayed him, saw that Jesus was c,
Mk	14: 64	They all c him as worthy of death.

Mk	16: 16	whoever does not believe will be c.
Lk	6: 37	condemn, and you will not be c.
Jn	3: 18	Whoever believes in him is not c,
	3: 18	does not believe stands c already
	5: 24	has eternal life and will not be c;
	5: 29	who have done evil will rise to be c.
	8: 10	Has no-one c you?" "No-one, sir,"
	16: 11	prince of this world now stands c.
Ac	25: 15	against him and asked that he be c.
Ro	3: 7	why am I still c as a sinner?"
	8: 3	And so he c sin in sinful man,
	14: 23	But the man who has doubts is c
1Co	4: 9	like men c to die in the arena.
	11: 32	disciplined so that we will not be c
Gal	1: 8	let him be eternally c! As we have
	1: 9	let him be eternally c! Am I now
2Th	2: 12	that all will be c who have not
Tit	2: 8	of speech that cannot be c,
Heb	11: 7	By his faith he c the world
Jas	5: 6	You have c and murdered innocent
	5: 12	and your "No," no, or you will be c
2Pe	2: 6	if he c the cities of Sodom
Rev	19: 2	He has c the great prostitute

CONDEMNING* (CONDEMN)

Dt	25: 1	the innocent and c the guilty.
1Ki	8: 32	c the guilty and bringing
Pr	17: 15	the guilty and c the innocent—
Ac	13: 27	yet in c him they fulfilled the words
Ro	2: 1	judge the other, you are c yourself,

CONDEMNS* (CONDEMN)

Job	15: 6	Your own mouth c you, not mine;
Pr	12: 2	but the LORD c a crafty man.
Ro	8: 34	Who is he that c? Christ Jesus,
2Co	3: 9	the ministry that c men is glorious,

CONDITION

Pr	27: 23	Be sure you know the c

CONDUCT (CONDUCTED CONDUCTS)

Pr	10: 23	A fool finds pleasure in evil c,
	20: 11	by whether his c is pure and right.
	21: 8	but the c of the innocent is upright.
Ecc	6: 8	how to c himself before others?
Jer	4: 18	"Your own c and actions
	17: 10	to reward a man according to his c,
Eze	7: 3	I will judge you according to your c
Php	1: 27	c yourselves in a manner worthy
1Ti	3: 15	to c themselves in God's household

CONDUCTED* (CONDUCT)

2Co	1: 12	testifies that we have c ourselves

CONDUCTS* (CONDUCT)

Ps	112: 5	who c his affairs with justice.

CONFESS* (CONFESSED CONFESSES CONFESSING CONFESSION)

Lev	5: 5	he must c in what way he has
	16: 21	and c over it all the wickedness
	26: 40	"'But if they will c their sins
Nu	5: 7	must c the sin he has committed.
1Ki	8: 33	back to you and c your name,
	8: 35	towards this place and c your name
2Ch	6: 24	they turn back and c your name,
	6: 26	towards this place and c your name
Ne	1: 6	I c the sins we Israelites, including
Ps	32: 5	I said, "I will c
	38: 18	I c my iniquity;

Jn	1: 20	fail to c, but confessed freely,
	12: 42	they would not c their faith
Ro	10: 9	That if you c with your mouth,
	10: 10	it is with your mouth that you c
	14: 11	every tongue will c to God.'"
Php	2: 11	every tongue c that Jesus Christ is
Heb	3: 1	and high priest whom we c.
	13: 15	the fruit of lips that c his name.
Jas	5: 16	Therefore c your sins to each other
1Jn	1: 9	if we c our sins, he is faithful

CONFESSED* (CONFESS)

1Sa	7: 6	day they fasted and there they c,
Ne	9: 2	in their places and c their sins
Da	9: 4	to the LORD my God and c:
Jn	1: 20	but c freely, "I am not the Christ."
Ac	19: 18	and openly c their evil deeds.

CONFESSES* (CONFESS)

Pr	28: 13	whoever c and renounces them
2Ti	2: 19	and, "Everyone who c the name

CONFESSING* (CONFESS)

Ezr	10: 1	While Ezra was praying and c,
Da	9: 20	c my sin and the sin
Mt	3: 6	C their sins, they were baptised
Mk	1: 5	C their sins, they were baptised

CONFESSION* (CONFESS)

Ezr	10: 11	Now make c to the LORD,
Ne	9: 3	and spent another fourth in c
2Co	9: 13	obedience that accompanies your c
1Ti	6: 12	called when you made your good c
	6: 13	Pontius Pilate made the good c,

CONFIDENCE* (CONFIDENT)

Jdg	9: 26	and its citizens put their c in him.
2Ki	18: 19	On what are you basing this c
2Ch	32: 8	And the people gained c
	32: 10	On what are you basing your c,
Job	4: 6	Should not your piety be your c
Ps	71: 5	my c since my youth.
Pr	3: 26	for the LORD will be your c
	3: 32	but takes the upright into his c.
	11: 13	A gossip betrays a c,
	20: 19	A gossip betrays a c;
	25: 9	do not betray another man's c,
	31: 11	Her husband has full c in her
Isa	32: 17	will be quietness and c for ever.
	36: 4	On what are you basing this c
Jer	17: 7	whose c is in him.
	49: 31	which lives in c,"
Eze	29: 16	a source of c for the people of Israel
Mic	7: 5	put no c in a friend.
2Co	2: 3	I had c in all of you, that you would
	3: 4	Such c as this is ours
	7: 4	I have great c in you; I take great
	7: 16	I am glad I can have complete c
	8: 22	so because of his great c in you.
Eph	3: 12	God with freedom and c.
Php	3: 3	and who put no c in the flesh—
	3: 4	I myself have reasons for such c.
	3: 4	reasons to put c in the flesh,
2Th	3: 4	We have c in the Lord that you are
Heb	3: 14	till the end the c we had at first.
	4: 16	the throne of grace with c,
	10: 19	since we have c to enter the Most
	10: 35	So do not throw away your c;
	13: 6	So we say with c,
1Jn	3: 21	we have c before God and receive

1Jn	4: 17	us so that we will have c on the day
	5: 14	the c we have in approaching God:

CONFIDENT* (CONFIDENCE)

Job	6: 20	because they had been c;
Ps	27: 3	even then will I be c.
	27: 13	I am still c of this:
Lk	18: 9	To some who were c
2Co	1: 15	Because I was c of this, I planned
	5: 6	Therefore we are always c
	5: 8	We are c, I say, and would prefer
	9: 4	ashamed of having been so c.
	10: 7	If anyone is c that he belongs
Gal	5: 10	I am c in the Lord that you will
Php	1: 6	day until now, being c of this,
	2: 24	I am c in the Lord that I myself will
Phm	: 21	C of your obedience, I write to you,
Heb	6: 9	we are c of better things
1Jn	2: 28	that when he appears we may be c

CONFIDES*

Ps	25: 14	The LORD c in those who fear him

CONFORM* (CONFORMED CONFORMITY CONFORMS)

Ro	12: 2	Do not c any longer to the pattern
1Pe	1: 14	do not c to the evil desires you had

CONFORMED* (CONFORM)

Eze	5: 7	c to the standards of the nations
	11: 12	but have c to the standards
Ro	8: 29	predestined to be c to the likeness

CONFORMITY* (CONFORM)

Eph	1: 11	in c with the purpose of his will,

CONFORMS* (CONFORM)

1Ti	1: 11	to the sound doctrine that c

CONQUEROR* (CONQUERORS)

Mic	1: 15	I will bring a c against you
Rev	6: 2	he rode out as a c bent on conquest.

CONQUERORS (CONQUEROR)

Ro	8: 37	than c through him who loved us.

CONSCIENCE* (CONSCIENCE-STRICKEN CONSCIENCES CONSCIENTIOUS)

Ge	20: 5	I have done this with a clear c
	20: 6	I know you did this with a clear c,
1Sa	25: 31	have on his c the staggering burden
Job	27: 6	my c will not reproach me as long
Ac	23: 1	to God in all good c to this day."
	24: 16	to keep my c clear before God
Ro	9: 1	my c confirms it in the Holy Spirit
	13: 5	punishment but also because of c.
1Co	4: 4	My c is clear, but that does not
	8: 7	since their c is weak, it is defiled.
	8: 10	with a weak c sees you who have
	8: 12	in this way and wound their weak c
	10: 25	without raising questions of c,
	10: 27	you without raising questions of c.
	10: 28	man who told you and for c' sake—
	10: 29	freedom be judged by another's c?
	10: 29	the other man's c, I mean,
2Co	1: 12	Our c testifies that we have
	4: 2	to every man's c in the sight of God
	5: 11	and I hope it is also plain to your c.
1Ti	1: 5	and a good c and a sincere faith.
	1: 19	holding on to faith and a good c.

1Ti 　3: 9 truths of the faith with a clear *c*.
2Ti 　1: 3 as my forefathers did, with a clear *c*
Heb 　9: 9 able to clear the *c* of the worshipper.
　　 10: 22 to cleanse us from a guilty *c*
　　 13: 18 We are sure that we have a clear *c*
Pe 　3: 16 and respect, keeping a clear *c*,
　　 3: 21 the pledge of a good *c* towards God.

CONSCIENCE-STRICKEN* (CONSCIENCE)

1Sa 24: 5 David was *c* for having cut
2Sa 24: 10 David was *c* after he had counted

CONSCIENCES* (CONSCIENCE)

Ro 　2: 15 their *c* also bearing witness,
1Ti 　4: 2 whose *c* have been seared
Tit 　1: 15 their minds and *c* are corrupted.
Heb 　9: 14 cleanse our *c* from acts that lead

CONSCIENTIOUS* (CONSCIENCE)

2Ch 29: 34 for the Levites had been more *c*

CONSCIOUS*

Ro 　3: 20 through the law we become *c* of sin
1Pe 　2: 19 of unjust suffering because he is *c*

CONSECRATE (CONSECRATED)

Ex 　13: 2 "*C* to me every firstborn male.
　　 40: 9 *c* it and all its furnishings,
Lev 20: 7 "'*C* yourselves and be holy,
　　 25: 10 *C* the fiftieth year and proclaim
1Ch 15: 12 fellow Levites are to *c* yourselves

CONSECRATED (CONSECRATE)

Ex 　29: 43 and the place will be *c* by my glory.
Lev 　8: 30 So he *c* Aaron and his garments
2Ch 　7: 16 *c* this temple so that my Name may
Lk 　2: 23 is to be *c* to the Lord"),
1Ti 　4: 5 because it is *c* by the word of God

CONSENT

1Co 　7: 5 except by mutual *c* and for a time,

CONSIDER (CONSIDERATE CONSIDERED CONSIDERS)

1Sa 12: 24 *c* what great things he has done
　　 16: 7 "Do not *c* his appearance
2Ch 19: 6 "*C* carefully what you do,
Job 37: 14 stop and *c* God's wonders.
Ps 　8: 3 When I *c* your heavens,
　　 77: 12 and *c* all your mighty deeds.
　　 107: 43 and *c* the great love of the LORD.
　　 143: 5 and *c* what your hands have done.
Pr 　6: 6 *c* its ways and be wise!
　　 20: 25 and only later to *c* his vows.
Ecc 　7: 13 *C* what God has done:
Lk 12: 24 *C* the ravens: They do not sow
　　 12: 27 about the rest? "*C* how the lilies
Php 　2: 3 but in humility *c* others better
　　 3: 8 I *c* everything a loss compared
Heb 10: 24 And let us *c* how we may spur one
Jas 　1: 2 *C* it pure joy, my brothers,

CONSIDERATE* (CONSIDER)

Tit 　3: 2 to be peaceable and *c*,
Jas 　3: 17 then peace loving, *c*, submissive,
1Pe 　2: 18 only to those who are good and *c*,
　　 3: 7 in the same way be *c* as you live

CONSIDERED (CONSIDER)

Job 　1: 8 "Have you *c* my servant Job?

Job 　2: 3 "Have you *c* my servant Job?
Ps 　44: 22 we are *c* as sheep to be slaughtered.
Isa 53: 4 yet we *c* him stricken by God,
Ro 　8: 36 we are *c* as sheep to be slaughtered

CONSIDERS (CONSIDER)

Pr 　31: 16 She *c* a field and buys it;
Ro 　14: 5 One man *c* one day more sacred
Jas 　1: 26 If anyone *c* himself religious

CONSIST (CONSISTS)

Lk 12: 15 a man's life does not *c*

CONSISTS (CONSIST)

Eph 　5: 9 fruit of the light *c* in all goodness,

CONSOLATION

Ps 94: 19 your *c* brought joy to my soul.

CONSPIRE

Ps 　2: 1 Why do the nations *c*

CONSTANT

Dt 　28: 66 You will live in *c* suspense,
Pr 　19: 13 wife is like a *c* dripping.
　　 27: 15 a *c* dripping on a rainy day;
Ac 27: 33 "you have been in *c* suspense
Heb 　5: 14 by *c* use have trained themselves

CONSTRUCTIVE*

1Co 10: 23 but not everything is *c*.

CONSULT

Pr 　15: 12 he will not *c* the wise.
Gal 　1: 16 I did not *c* any man, nor did I go up

CONSUME (CONSUMES CONSUMING)

Jn 　2: 17 "Zeal for your house will *c* me."

CONSUMES (CONSUME)

Ps 69: 9 for zeal for your house *c* me,

CONSUMING (CONSUME)

Dt 　4: 24 For the LORD your God is a *c* fire,
Heb 12: 29 and awe, for our God is a *c* fire.

CONTAIN* (CONTAINED CONTAINS)

1Ki 　8: 27 the highest heaven, cannot *c* you.
2Ch 　2: 6 the highest heavens, cannot *c* him?
　　 6: 18 the highest heavens, cannot *c* you.
Ecc 　8: 8 power over the wind to *c* it;
2Pe 　3: 16 His letters *c* some things that are

CONTAINED (CONTAIN)

Heb 　9: 4 This ark *c* the gold jar of manna,

CONTAINS (CONTAIN)

Pr 15: 6 of the righteous *c* great treasure,

CONTAMINATES*

2Co 　7: 1 from everything that *c* body

CONTEMPT

Pr 14: 31 He who oppresses the poor shows *c*
　　 17: 5 He who mocks the poor shows *c*
　　 18: 3 When wickedness comes, so does *c*
Da 12: 2 others to shame and everlasting *c*.
Mal 　1: 6 O priests, who show *c* for my name.
Ro 　2: 4 Or do you show *c* for the riches
Gal 　4: 14 you did not treat me with *c*

1Th 5: 20 do not treat prophecies with c.

CONTEND (CONTENDED CONTENDING CONTENTIOUS)

Ge 6: 3 "My Spirit will not c
Ps 35: 1 C, O LORD, with those who
Isa 49: 25 I will c with those who c with you,
Jude : 3 you to c for the faith that was once

CONTENDED (CONTEND)

Php 4: 3 help these women who have c

CONTENDING* (CONTEND)

Php 1: 27 c as one man for the faith

CONTENT* (CONTENTMENT)

Jos 7: 7 If only we had been c to stay
Pr 13: 25 The righteous eat to their hearts' c,
19: 23 one rests c, untouched by trouble.
Ecc 4: 8 yet his eyes were not c
Lk 3: 14 don't accuse people falsely—be c
Php 4: 11 to be c whatever the circumstances
4: 12 I have learned the secret of being c
1Ti 6: 8 and clothing, we will be c with that.
Heb 13: 5 and be c with what you have,

CONTENTIOUS* (CONTEND)

1Co 11: 16 If anyone wants to be c about this,

CONTENTMENT* (CONTENT)

Job 36: 11 and their years in c.
SS 8: 10 like one bringing c.
1Ti 6: 6 But godliness with c is great gain.

CONTEST*

Heb 10: 32 in a great c in the face of suffering.

CONTINUAL (CONTINUE)

Pr 15: 15 but the cheerful heart has a c feast.
Eph 4: 19 of impurity, with a c lust for more.

CONTINUE (CONTINUAL CONTINUES CONTINUING)

1Ki 8: 23 servants who c wholeheartedly
2Ch 6: 14 servants who c wholeheartedly
Ps 36: 10 C your love to those who know you
Ac 13: 43 urged them to c in the grace of God
Ro 11: 22 provided that you c in his kindness.
Gal 3: 10 Cursed is everyone who does not c
Php 2: 12 c to work out your salvation
Col 1: 23 if you c in your faith, established
2: 6 received Christ Jesus as Lord, c
1Ti 2: 15 if they c in faith, love and holiness
2Ti 3: 14 c in what you have learned
1Jn 2: 28 And now, dear children, c in him,
3: 9 born of God will c to sin,
5: 18 born of God does not c to sin;
2Jn : 9 and does not c in the teaching
Rev 22: 11 and let him who is holy c to be holy
22: 11 let him who does right c to do right;

CONTINUES (CONTINUE)

Ps 100: 5 c through all generations.
119: 90 Your faithfulness c
2Co 10: 15 Our hope is that, as your faith c
1Jn 3: 6 No-one who c to sin has

CONTINUING (CONTINUE)

Ro 13: 8 the c debt to love one another,

CONTRIBUTION (CONTRIBUTIONS)

Ro 15: 26 pleased to make a c for the poor

CONTRIBUTIONS (CONTRIBUTION)

2Ch 24: 10 all the people brought their c gladly
31: 12 they faithfully brought in the c,

CONTRITE*

Ps 51: 17 a broken and c heart,
Isa 57: 15 also with him who is c and lowly
57: 15 and to revive the heart of the c.
66: 2 he who is humble and c in spirit,

CONTROL (CONTROLLED CONTROLS SELF-CONTROL SELF-CONTROLLED)

Pr 29: 11 a wise man keeps himself under c.
1Co 7: 9 But if they cannot c themselves,
7: 37 but has c over his own will,
1Th 4: 4 you should learn to c his own body

CONTROLLED (CONTROL)

Ps 32: 9 but must be c by bit and bridle
Ro 8: 6 but the mind c by the Spirit is life
8: 8 Those c by the sinful nature cannot

CONTROLS* (CONTROL)

Job 37: 15 you know how God c the clouds
Pr 16: 32 a man who c his temper

CONTROVERSIES*

Ac 26: 3 with all the Jewish customs and c.
1Ti 1: 4 These promote c rather
6: 4 He has an unhealthy interest in c
Tit 3: 9 But avoid foolish c and genealogies

CONVERSATION

Col 4: 6 Let your c be always full of grace,

CONVERT

1Ti 3: 6 He must not be a recent c,

CONVICT (CONVICTION)

Pr 24: 25 with those who c the guilty,
Jn 16: 8 he will c the world of guilt in regard
Jude : 15 and to c all the ungodly

CONVICTION* (CONVICT)

1Th 1: 5 the Holy Spirit and with deep c.

CONVINCE* (CONVINCED CONVINCING)

Ac 28: 23 and tried to c them about Jesus

CONVINCED* (CONVINCE)

Ge 45: 28 "I'm c! My son Joseph is still alive.
Lk 16: 31 will not be c even if someone rises
Ac 19: 26 and hear how this fellow Paul has c
26: 9 "I too was c that I ought
26: 26 I am c that none of this has escaped
28: 24 Some were c by what he said,
Ro 2: 19 if you are c that you are a guide
8: 38 For I am c that neither death
14: 5 Each one should be fully c
14: 14 I am fully c that no food is unclean
15: 14 I myself am c, my brothers,
1Co 14: 24 he will be c by all that he is a sinner
2Co 5: 14 we are c that one died for all,
Php 1: 25 C of this, I know that I will remain,
2Ti 1: 12 and am c that he is able
3: 14 have learned and have become c

CONVINCING* (CONVINCE)

Ac 1: 3 and gave many *c* proofs that he was

COOLNESS*

Pr 25: 13 Like the *c* of snow at harvest time

COPIES (COPY)

Heb 9: 23 for the *c* of the heavenly things

COPY (COPIES)

Dt 17: 18 for himself on a scroll a *c* of this law
Heb 8: 5 They serve at a sanctuary that is a *c*
9: 24 sanctuary that was only a *c*

CORBAN*

Mk 7: 11 received from me is *C* (that is,

CORD (CORDS)

Jos 2: 18 you have tied this scarlet *c*
Ecc 4: 12 *c* of three strands is not quickly

CORDS (CORD)

Pr 5: 22 the *c* of his sin hold him fast.
Isa 54: 2 lengthen your *c*,
Hos 11: 4 them with *c* of human kindness,

CORINTH

Ac 18: 1 Paul left Athens and went to C.
1Co 1: 2 To the church of God in C,
2Co 1: 1 To the church of God in C,

CORNELIUS*

Roman to whom Peter preached; first Gentile
Christian (Ac 10).

CORNER (CORNERS)

Ru 3: 9 "Spread the *c* of your garment
Pr 21: 9 Better to live on a *c* of the roof
25: 24 Better to live on a *c* of the roof
Ac 26: 26 because it was not done in a *c*.

CORNERS (CORNER)

Mt 6: 5 on the street *c* to be seen by men.
22: 9 Go to the street *c* and invite

CORNERSTONE* (STONE)

Job 38: 6 or who laid its *c*—
Isa 28: 16 a precious *c* for a sure foundation;
Jer 51: 26 rock will be taken from you for a *c*,
Zec 10: 4 From Judah will come the *c*,
Eph 2: 20 Christ Jesus himself as the chief *c*.
1Pe 2: 6 a chosen and precious *c*,

CORRECT* (CORRECTED CORRECTING CORRECTION CORRECTIONS CORRECTS)

Job 6: 26 Do you mean to *c* what I say,
40: 2 Contends with the Almighty *c* him?
Jer 10: 24 C me, LORD, but only with justice
2Ti 4: 2 *c*, rebuke and encourage—

CORRECTED* (CORRECT)

Pr 29: 19 A servant cannot be *c*

CORRECTING* (CORRECT)

2Ti 3: 16 *c* and training in righteousness,

CORRECTION* (CORRECT)

Lev 26: 23 things you do not accept my *c*
Job 36: 10 He makes them listen to *c*

Pr 5: 12 How my heart spurned *c*!
10: 17 whoever ignores *c* leads others
12: 1 but he who hates *c* is stupid.
13: 18 but whoever heeds *c* is honoured.
15: 5 whoever heeds *c* shows prudence.
15: 10 he who hates *c* will die.
15: 12 A mocker resents *c*;
15: 32 whoever heeds *c* gains
29: 15 The rod of *c* imparts wisdom,
Jer 2: 30 they did not respond to *c*.
5: 3 crushed them, but they refused *c*.
7: 28 LORD its God or responded to *c*.
Zep 3: 2 she accepts no *c*.
3: 7 you will fear me / and accept *c*!'

CORRECTIONS* (CORRECT)

Pr 6: 23 and the *c* of discipline

CORRECTS* (CORRECT)

Job 5: 17 "Blessed is the man whom God *c*;
Pr 9: 7 Whoever *c* a mocker invites insult;

CORRUPT (CORRUPTED CORRUPTION CORRUPTS)

Ge 6: 11 Now the earth was *c* in God's sight
Ps 14: 1 They are *c*, their deeds are vile;
14: 3 they have together become *c*;
Pr 4: 24 keep *c* talk far from your lips.
6: 12 who goes about with a *c* mouth,
19: 28 A *c* witness mocks at justice,

CORRUPTED (CORRUPT)

2Co 7: 2 wronged no-one, we have *c* no-one,
Tit 1: 15 but to those who are *c* and do not

CORRUPTION (CORRUPT)

2Pe 1: 4 escape the *c* in the world caused
2: 20 If they have escaped the *c*

CORRUPTS* (CORRUPT)

Ecc 7: 7 and a bribe *c* the heart.
1Co 15: 33 "Bad company *c* good character."
Jas 3: 6 It *c* the whole person, sets

COST (COSTS)

Nu 16: 38 sinned at the *c* of their lives.
Pr 4: 7 Though it *c* all you have, get
7: 23 little knowing it will *c* him his life.
Isa 55: 1 milk without money and without *c*.
Lk 14: 28 and estimate the *c* to see
Rev 21: 6 to drink without *c* from the spring

COSTS (COST)

Pr 6: 31 it *c* him all the wealth of his house.

COUNCIL

Ps 89: 7 In the *c* of the holy ones God is
107: 32 and praise him in the *c* of the elders

COUNSEL (COUNSELLOR COUNSELS)

1Ki 22: 5 "First seek the *c* of the LORD."
2Ch 18: 4 "First seek the *c* of the LORD."
Job 38: 2 "Who is this that darkens my *c*
42: 3 'Who is this that obscures my *c*
Ps 1: 1 walk in the *c* of the wicked
73: 24 You guide me with your *c*,
107: 11 despised the *c* of the Most High.
Pr 8: 14 C and sound judgment are mine;
15: 22 Plans fail for lack of *c*,
27: 9 from his earnest *c*.

Isa 28:29 wonderful in *c* and magnificent
1Ti 5:14 So I *c* younger widows to marry,
Rev 3:18 I *c* you to buy from me gold refined

COUNSELLOR (COUNSEL)

Isa 9: 6 Wonderful *C*, Mighty God,
Jn 14:16 he will give you another *C* to be
14:26 But the *C*, the Holy Spirit,
15:26 "When the *C* comes, whom I will
16: 7 the *C* will not come to you;
Ro 11:34 Or who has been his *c*?"

COUNSELS (COUNSEL)

Ps 16: 7 I will praise the LORD, who *c* me;

COUNT (COUNTED COUNTING COUNTS)

Ps 22:17 I can *c* all my bones;
Ro 4: 8 whose sin the Lord will never *c*
6:11 *c* yourselves dead to sin
2Th 1:11 that our God may *c* you worthy

COUNTED (COUNT)

Ac 5:41 because they had been *c* worthy
2Th 1: 5 and as a result you will be *c* worthy

COUNTERFEIT*

2Th 2: 9 displayed in all kinds of *c* miracles,
1Jn 2:27 not *c*—just as it has taught you,

COUNTING (COUNT)

2Co 5:19 not *c* men's sins against them.

COUNTRY

Pr 28: 2 When a *c* is rebellious, it has many
29: 4 By justice a king gives a *c* stability,
Isa 66: 8 Can a *c* be born in a day
Lk 15:13 off for a distant *c* and there
Jn 4:44 prophet has no honour in his own *c*.)
2Co 11:26 in danger in the *c*, in danger at sea;
Heb 11:14 looking for a *c* of their own.

COUNTRYMEN

2Co 11:26 danger from my own *c*, in danger

COUNTS (COUNT)

Jn 6:63 The Spirit gives life; the flesh *c*
1Co 7:19 God's commands is what *c*.
Gal 5: 6 only thing that *c* is faith expressing

COURAGE* (COURAGEOUS)

Jos 2:11 everyone's *c* failed because of you,
5: 1 and they no longer had the *c*
2Sa 4: 1 he lost *c*, and all Israel became
7:27 So your servant has found *c*
1Ch 17:25 So your servant has found *c* to pray
2Ch 15: 8 son of Oded the prophet, he took *c*.
19:11 Act with *c*, and may the LORD be
Ezr 7:28 I took *c* and gathered leading men
10: 4 We will support you, so take *c*
Ps 107:26 in their peril their *c* melted away.
Eze 22:14 Will your *c* endure or your hands
Da 11:25 and *c* against the king of the South.
Mt 14:27 said to them: "Take *c*!
Mk 6:50 spoke to them and said, "Take *c*!
Ac 4:13 When they saw the *c* of Peter
23:11 "Take *c*! As you have testified
27:22 now I urge you to keep up your *c*,
27:25 So keep up your *c*, men,
1Co 16:13 stand firm in the faith; be men of *c*;
Php 1:20 will have sufficient *c* so that now

Heb 3: 6 if we hold on to our *c* and the hope

COURAGEOUS* (COURAGE)

Dt 31: 6 Be strong and *c*.
31: 7 of all Israel, "Be strong and *c*,
31:23 son of Nun: "Be strong and *c*,
Jos 1: 6 and *c*, because you will lead these
1: 7 Be strong and very *c*.
1: 9 commanded you? Be strong and *c*.
1:18 Only be strong and *c*!"
10:25 Be strong and *c*.
1Ch 22:13 Be strong and *c*.
28:20 "Be strong and *c*, and do the work.
2Ch 26:17 priest with eighty other *c* priests
32: 7 with these words: "Be strong and *c*.

COURSE

Ps 19: 5 a champion rejoicing to run his *c*.
Pr 2: 8 for he guards the *c* of the just
15:21 of understanding keeps a straight *c*.
16: 9 In his heart a man plans his *c*,
17:23 to pervert the *c* of justice.
Jas 3: 6 sets the whole *c* of his life on fire,

COURT (COURTS)

Pr 22:22 and do not crush the needy in *c*,
25: 8 do not bring hastily to *c*,
Mt 5:25 adversary who is taking you to *c*.
1Co 4: 3 judged by you or by any human *c*;

COURTS (COURT)

Ps 84:10 Better is one day in your *c*
100: 4 and his *c* with praise;
Am 5:15 maintain justice in the *c*.
Zec 8:16 and sound judgment in your *c*;

COURTYARD

Ex 27: 9 "Make a *c* for the tabernacle.

COUSIN

Col 4:10 as does Mark, the *c* of Barnabas.

COVENANT (COVENANTS)

Ge 9: 9 "I now establish my *c* with you
17: 2 I will confirm my *c* between me
Ex 19: 5 if you obey me fully and keep my *c*,
24: 7 Then he took the Book of the *C*
Dt 4:13 declared to you his *c*, the Ten
29: 1 in addition to the *c* he had made
Jdg 2: 1 'I will never break my *c* with you,
1Sa 23:18 of them made a *c* before the LORD
1Ki 8:21 in which is the *c* of the LORD that
8:23 you who keep your *c* of love
2Ki 23: 2 the words of the Book of the *C*,
1Ch 16:15 He remembers his *c* for ever,
2Ch 6:14 you who keep your *c* of love
34:30 the words of the Book of the *C*,
Ne 1: 5 who keeps his *c* of love
Job 31: 1 "I made a *c* with my eyes
Ps 105: 8 He remembers his *c* for ever,
Pr 2:17 ignored the *c* she made before God
Isa 42: 6 you to be a *c* for the people
61: 8 make an everlasting *c* with them.
Jer 11: 2 "Listen to the terms of this *c*
31:31 "when I will make a new *c*
31:32 It will not be like the *c*
31:33 "This is the *c* I will make
Eze 37:26 I will make a *c* of peace with them;
Da 9:27 He will confirm a *c* with many
Hos 6: 7 Like Adam, they have broken the *c*

Mal 2: 14 the wife of your marriage c.
3: 1 of the c, whom you desire,
Mt 26: 28 blood of the c, which is poured out
Mk 14: 24 "This is my blood of the c,
Lk 22: 20 "This cup is the new c in my blood,
1Co 11: 25 "This cup is the new c in my blood;
2Co 3: 6 as ministers of a new c—
Gal 4: 24 One c is from Mount Sinai
Heb 8: 6 as the c of which he is mediator is
8: 8 when I will make a new c
9: 15 Christ is the mediator of a new c,
12: 24 to Jesus the mediator of a new c,

COVENANTS (COVENANT)

Ro 9: 4 theirs the divine glory, the c,
Gal 4: 24 for the women represent two c.

COVER (COVER-UP COVERED COVERING COVERINGS COVERS)

Ex 25: 17 "Make an atonement c of pure gold
25: 21 Place the c on top of the ark
33: 22 and c you with my hand
Lev 16: 2 in the cloud over the atonement c.
Ps 32: 5 and did not c up my iniquity.
91: 4 He will c you with his feathers,
Hos 10: 8 say to the mountains, "C us!"
Lk 23: 30 and to the hills, "C us!"'
1Co 11: 6 If a woman does not c her head,
11: 6 shaved off, she should c her head.
11: 7 A man ought not to c his head,
Jas 5: 20 and c over a multitude of sins.

COVER-UP* (COVER)

1Pe 2: 16 but do not use your freedom as a c

COVERED (COVER)

Ps 32: 1 whose sins are c.
85: 2 and c all their sins.
Isa 6: 2 With two wings they c their faces,
51: 16 c you with the shadow of my hand
Ro 4: 7 whose sins are c.
1Co 11: 4 with his head c dishonours his head.

COVERING (COVER)

1Co 11: 15 For long hair is given to her as a c.

COVERINGS (COVER)

Ge 3: 7 and made c for themselves.
Pr 31: 22 She makes c for her bed;

COVERS (COVER)

Pr 10: 12 but love c over all wrongs.
17: 9 He who c over an offence promotes
2Co 3: 15 Moses is read, a veil c their hearts.
1Pe 4: 8 love c over a multitude of sins.

COVET* (COVETED COVETOUS)

Ex 20: 17 You shall not c your neighbour's
20: 17 "You shall not c your neighbour's
34: 24 and no-one will c your land
Dt 5: 21 "You shall not c your neighbour's
7: 25 Do not c the silver and gold
Mic 2: 2 They c fields and seize them,
Ro 7: 7 if the law had not said. "Do not c."
7: 7 was to c if the law had not said,
13: 9 "Do not steal," "Do not c,"
Jas 4: 2 c, but you cannot have what you

COVETED* (COVET)

Jos 7: 21 weighing fifty shekels, I c them

Ac 20: 33 I have not c anyone's silver or gold

COVETOUS* (COVET)

Ro 7: 8 in me every kind of c desire.

COWARDLY*

Rev 21: 8 But the c, the unbelieving, the vile,

COWS

Ge 41: 2 of the river there came up seven c,
Ex 25: 5 skins dyed red and hides of sea c;
Nu 4: 6 are to cover this with hides of sea c,
1Sa 6: 7 Hitch the c to the cart,

CRAFTINESS* (CRAFTY)

Job 5: 13 He catches the wise in their c,
1Co 3: 19 "He catches the wise in their c";
Eph 4: 14 and c of men in their deceitful

CRAFTSMAN

Pr 8: 30 Then I was the c at his side.

CRAFTY* (CRAFTINESS)

Ge 3: 1 the serpent was more c than any
1Sa 23: 22 They tell me he is very c.
Job 5: 12 He thwarts the plans of the c,
15: 5 you adopt the tongue of the c.
Pr 7: 10 like a prostitute and with c intent.
12: 2 but the LORD condemns a c man.
14: 17 and a c man is hated.
2Co 12: 16 c fellow that I am, I caught you

CRAVE* (CRAVED CRAVES CRAVING CRAVINGS)

Nu 11: 4 with them began to c other food,
Dt 12: 20 you c meat and say, "I would like
Pr 23: 3 Do not c his delicacies;
23: 6 do not c his delicacies;
31: 4 not for rulers to c beer;
Mic 7: 1 none of the early figs that I c.
1Pe 2: 2 newborn babies, c pure spiritual

CRAVED* (CRAVE)

Nu 11: 34 the people who had c other food.
Ps 78: 18 by demanding the food they c.
78: 29 for he had given them what they c.
78: 30 turned from the food they c,

CRAVES* (CRAVE)

Pr 13: 4 The sluggard c and gets nothing,
21: 10 The wicked man c evil;
21: 26 All day long he c for more,

CRAVING* (CRAVE)

Job 20: 20 he will have no respite from his c;
Ps 106: 14 In the desert they gave in to their c;
Pr 10: 3 but he thwarts the c of the wicked.
13: 2 the unfaithful have a c for violence.
21: 25 The sluggard's c will be the death
Jer 2: 24 sniffing the wind in her c—

CRAVINGS* (CRAVE)

Ps 10: 3 He boasts of the c of his heart;
Eph 2: 3 gratifying the c of our sinful nature
1Jn 2: 16 in the world—the c of sinful man,

CRAWL

Ge 3: 14 You will c on your belly

CREATE* (CREATED CREATES CREATING CREATION CREATOR)

Ps	51:10	*C* in me a pure heart, O God,
Isa	4: 5	Then the LORD will *c* over all
	45: 7	I bring prosperity and *c* disaster;
	45: 7	I form the light and *c* darkness,
	45:18	he did not *c* it to be empty,
	65:17	"Behold, I will *c* / new heavens
	65:18	for I will *c* Jerusalem to be a delight
	65:18	for ever in what I will *c*,
Jer	31:22	The LORD will *c* a new thing
Mal	2:10	one Father? Did not one God *c* us?
Eph	2:15	His purpose was to *c*

CREATED* (CREATE)

Ge	1: 1	In the beginning God *c* the heavens
	1:21	God *c* the great creatures of the sea
	1:27	So God *c* man in his own image,
	1:27	in the image of God he *c* him;
	1:27	male and female he *c* them.
	2: 4	and the earth when they were *c*.
	5: 1	When God *c* man, he made him
	5: 2	He *c* them male and female;
	5: 2	when they were *c*, he called them
	6: 7	whom I have *c*, from the face
Dt	4:32	from the day God *c* man
Ps	89:12	You *c* the north and the south;
	89:47	what futility you have *c* all men!
	102:18	a people not yet *c* may praise
	104:30	you send your Spirit, / they are *c*,
	139:13	For you *c* my inmost being;
	148: 5	for he commanded and they were *c*
Isa	40:26	Who *c* all these?
	41:20	that the Holy One of Israel has *c* it.
	42: 5	he who *c* the heavens and stretched
	43: 1	he who *c* you, O Jacob,
	43: 7	whom I *c* for my glory,
	45: 8	I, the LORD, have *c* it.
	45:12	and *c* mankind upon it.
	45:18	he who *c* the heavens,
	48: 7	They are *c* now, and not long ago;
	54:16	And it is I who have *c* the destroyer
	54:16	"See, it is I who *c* the blacksmith
	57:16	the breath of man that I have *c*.
Eze	21:30	In the place where you were *c*,
	28:13	the day you were *c* they were
	28:15	ways from the day you were *c*
Mk	13:19	when God *c* the world, until now—
Ro	1:25	and served *c* things rather
1Co	11: 9	neither was man *c* for woman,
Eph	2:10	*c* in Christ Jesus to do good works,
	3: 9	hidden in God, who *c* all things.
	4:24	*c* to be like God in true
Col	1:16	For by him all things were *c*:
	1:16	all things were *c* by him
1Ti	4: 3	which God *c* to be received
	4: 4	For everything God *c* is good,
Heb	12:27	*c* things—so that what cannot be
Jas	1:18	a kind of firstfruits of all he *c*.
Rev	4:11	and by your will they were *c*
	4:11	for you *c* all things,
	10: 6	who *c* the heavens and all that is

CREATES* (CREATE)

Am	4:13	*c* the wind,

CREATING* (CREATE)

Ge	2: 3	the work of *c* that he had done.
Isa	57:19	*c* praise on the lips of the mourners

CREATION* (CREATE)

Hab	2:18	he who makes it trusts in his own *c*;
Mt	13:35	hidden since the *c* of the world."
	25:34	for you since the *c* of the world.
Mk	10: 6	of *c* God 'made them male
	16:15	and preach the good news to all *c*.
Jn	17:24	me before the *c* of the world.
Ro	1:20	For since the *c* of the world God's
	8:19	The *c* waits in eager expectation
	8:20	For the *c* was subjected
	8:21	in hope that the *c* itself will be
	8:22	that the whole *c* has been groaning
	8:39	depth, nor anything else in all *c*,
2Co	5:17	he is a new *c*; the old has gone,
Gal	6:15	anything; what counts is a new *c*.
Eph	1: 4	us in him before the *c* of the world
Col	1:15	God, the firstborn over all *c*.
Heb	4: 3	finished since the *c* of the world.
	4:13	Nothing in all *c* is hidden
	9:11	that is to say, not a part of this *c*.
	9:26	times since the *c* of the world.
1Pe	1:20	chosen before the *c* of the world,
2Pe	3: 4	as it has since the beginning of *c*."
Rev	3:14	true witness, the ruler of God's *c*.
	13: 8	slain from the *c* of the world.
	17: 8	life from the *c* of the world will be

CREATOR* (CREATE)

Ge	14:19	*C* of heaven and earth.
	14:22	God Most High, *C* of heaven
Dt	32: 6	Is he not your Father, your *C*,
Ecc	12: 1	Remember your *C*
Isa	27:11	and their *C* shows them no favour.
	40:28	the *C* of the ends of the earth.
	43:15	Israel's *C*, your King."
Mt	19: 4	the beginning the *C* 'made them
Ro	1:25	created things rather than the *C*—
Col	3:10	in knowledge in the image of its *C*.
1Pe	4:19	themselves to their faithful *C*

CREATURE (CREATURES)

Lev	17:11	For the life of a *c* is in the blood,
	17:14	the life of every *c* is its blood.
Ps	136:25	and who gives food to every *c*.
Eze	1:15	beside each *c* with its four faces.
Rev	4: 7	The first living *c* was like a lion,

CREATURES (CREATURE)

Ge	6:19	bring into the ark two of all living *c*,
	8:21	again will I destroy all living *c*,
Ps	104:24	the earth is full of your *c*.
Eze	1: 5	was what looked like four living *c*.

CREDIT (CREDITED CREDITOR CREDITS)

Lk	6:33	what *c* is that to you? Even
Ro	4:24	to whom God will *c* righteousness
1Pe	2:20	it to your *c* if you receive a beating

CREDITED (CREDIT)

Ge	15: 6	and he *c* it to him as righteousness.
Ps	106:31	This was *c* to him as righteousness
Eze	18:20	of the righteous man will be *c*
Ro	4: 3	and it was *c* to him as righteousness
	4: 4	his wages are not *c* to him as a gift,
	4: 5	his faith is *c* as righteousness.
	4: 9	saying that Abraham's faith was *c*
	4:23	The words "it was *c*
Gal	3: 6	and it was *c* to him as righteousness
Php	4:17	for what may be *c* to your account.

Jas   2: 23 and it was c to him as righteousness

CREDITOR (CREDIT)
Dt   15: 2 Every c shall cancel the loan he has

CREDITS (CREDIT)
Ro   4: 6 whom God c righteousness apart

CRETANS (CRETE)
Tit   1: 12 "C are always liars, evil brutes,

CRETE (CRETANS)
Ac   27: 12 harbour in C, facing both south-west

CRIED (CRY)
Ex   2: 23 groaned in their slavery and c out,
       14: 10 They were terrified and c out
Nu   20: 16 but when we c out to the LORD,
Jos   24: 7 But they c to the LORD for help,
Jdg   3: 9 But when they c out to the LORD,
        3: 15 Again the Israelites c out
        4: 3 they c to the LORD for help.
        6: 6 the Israelites that they c out
       10: 12 Maonites oppressed you and you c
1Sa   7: 9 He c out to the LORD
       12: 8 they c to the LORD for help,
       12: 10 they c out to the LORD and said,
Ps   18: 6 I c to my God for help.

CRIMINALS
Lk   23: 32 both c, were also led out with him

CRIMSON
Isa   1: 18 though they are red as c,
       63: 1 with his garments stained c?

CRIPPLED
2Sa   9: 3 of Jonathan; he is c in both feet."
Mk   9: 45 better for you to enter life c

CRISIS*
1Co   7: 26 of the present c, I think that it is

CRITICISM*
2Co   8: 20 We want to avoid any c

CROOKED*
Dt   32: 5 but a warped and c generation.
2Sa   22: 27 to the c you show yourself shrewd.
Ps   18: 26 to the c you show yourself shrewd.
      125: 5 But those who turn to c ways
Pr   2: 15 whose paths are c
        5: 6 her paths are c, but she knows it
        8: 8 none of them is c or perverse.
       10: 9 he who takes c paths will be found
Ecc   7: 13 what he has made c?
Isa   59: 8 have turned them into c roads;
La   3: 9 he has made my paths c.
Lk   3: 5 The c roads shall become straight,
Php   2: 15 children of God without fault in a c

CROP (CROPS)
Mt   13: 8 where it produced a c—a hundred,
       21: 41 share of the c at harvest time."

CROPS (CROP)
Pr   3: 9 with the firstfruits of all your c;
       10: 5 He who gathers c in summer is
       28: 3 like a driving rain that leaves no c.
2Ti   2: 6 the first to receive a share of the c.

CROSS [1] (CROSSED CROSSING)
Dt   4: 21 Swore that I would not c the Jordan
       12: 10 But you will c the Jordan

CROSS [2]
Mt   10: 38 and anyone who does not take his c
       16: 24 and take up his c and follow me.
Mk   8: 34 and take up his c and follow me.
Lk   9: 23 take up his c daily and follow me.
       14: 27 anyone who does not carry his c
Jn   19: 17 Carrying his own c, he went out
Ac   2: 23 to death by nailing him to the c.
1Co   1: 17 lest the c of Christ be emptied
        1: 18 the message of the c is foolishness
Gal   5: 11 offence of the c has been abolished.
        6: 12 persecuted for the c of Christ.
        6: 14 in the c of our Lord Jesus Christ,
Eph   2: 16 both of them to God through the c,
Php   2: 8 even death on a c!
        3: 18 as enemies of the c of Christ.
Col   1: 20 through his blood, shed on the c.
        2: 14 he took it away, nailing it to the c.
        2: 15 triumphing over them by the c.
Heb   12: 2 set before him endured the c,

CROSSED (CROSS [1])
Jos   4: 7 When it c the Jordan, the waters
Jn   5: 24 he has c over from death to life.

CROSSING (CROSS [1])
Ge   48: 14 he was the younger, and c his arms,

CROSSROADS (ROAD)
Jer   6: 16 "Stand at the c and look;

CROUCHING
Ge   4: 7 sin is c at your door; it desires

CROWD (CROWDS)
Ex   23: 2 Do not follow the c in doing wrong.

CROWDS (CROWD)
Mt   9: 36 he saw the c, he had compassion

CROWED (CROWS)
Mt   26: 74 the man!" Immediately a cock c.

CROWN (CROWNED CROWNS)
Pr   4: 9 present you with a c of splendour."
       10: 6 Blessings c the head
       12: 4 noble character is her husband's c,
       16: 31 Grey hair is a c of splendour;
       17: 6 Children's children are a c
Isa   35: 10 everlasting joy will c their heads.
       51: 11 everlasting joy will c their heads.
       61: 3 to bestow on them a c of beauty
       62: 3 You will be a c of splendour
Eze   16: 12 and a beautiful c on your head.
Zec   9: 16 like jewels in a c.
Mt   27: 29 and then twisted together a c of thorns
Mk   15: 17 then twisted together a c of thorns
Jn   19: 2 The soldiers twisted together a c
       19: 5 When Jesus came out wearing the c
1Co   9: 25 it to get a c that will last for ever.
        9: 25 it to get a c that will not last;
Php   4: 1 and long for, my joy and c,
1Th   2: 19 or the c in which we will glory
2Ti   2: 5 he does not receive the victor's c
        4: 8 store for me the c of righteousness,
Jas   1: 12 he will receive the c

1Pe	5: 4	you will receive the *c*
Rev	2: 10	and I will give you the *c* of life.
	3: 11	so that no-one will take your *c*.
	14: 14	a son of man" with a *c* of gold

CROWNED* (CROWN)

Ps	8: 5	and *c* him with glory and honour.
Pr	14: 18	the prudent are *c* with knowledge.
SS	3: 11	crown with which his mother *c* him
Heb	2: 7	you *c* him with glory and honour
	2: 9	now *c* with glory and honour

CROWNS (CROWN)

Ps	103: 4	and *c* me with love and compassion
	149: 4	he *c* the humble with salvation.
Pr	11: 26	blessing *c* him who is willing to sell.
Rev	4: 4	and had *c* of gold on their heads.
	4: 10	They lay their *c* before the throne
	12: 3	ten horns and seven *c* on his heads.
	19: 12	and on his head are many *c*.

CROWS (CROWED)

Mt	26: 34	this very night, before the cock *c*

CRUCIFIED* (CRUCIFY)

Mt	20: 19	to be mocked and flogged and *c*.
	26: 2	of Man will be handed over to be *c*
	27: 26	and handed him over to be *c*.
	27: 35	When they had *c* him, they divided
	27: 38	Two robbers were *c* with him,
	27: 44	same way the robbers who were *c*
	28: 5	looking for Jesus, who was *c*.
Mk	15: 15	and handed him over to be *c*.
	15: 24	And they *c* him.
	15: 25	the third hour when they *c* him.
	15: 27	They *c* two robbers with him,
	15: 32	Those *c* with him also heaped
	16: 6	for Jesus the Nazarene, who was *c*.
Lk	23: 23	insistently demanded that he be *c*,
	23: 33	*c* him, along with the criminals—
	24: 7	be *c* and on the third day be raised
	24: 20	sentenced to death, and they *c* him;
Jn	19: 16	him over to them to be *c*.
	19: 18	Here they *c* him, and with him two
	19: 20	for the place where Jesus was *c* was
	19: 23	When the soldiers *c* Jesus,
	19: 32	of the first man who had been *c*
	19: 41	At the place where Jesus was *c*,
Ac	2: 36	whom you *c*, both Lord and Christ
	4: 10	whom you *c* but whom God raised
Ro	6: 6	For we know that our old self was *c*
1Co	1: 13	Is Christ divided? Was Paul *c*
	1: 23	but we preach Christ *c*: a stumbling
	2: 2	except Jesus Christ and him *c*.
	2: 8	they would not have *c* the Lord
2Co	13: 4	to be sure, he was *c* in weakness,
Gal	2: 20	I have been *c* with Christ
	3: 1	Christ was clearly portrayed as *c*.
	5: 24	Christ Jesus have *c* the sinful
	6: 14	which the world has been *c*
Rev	11: 8	where also their Lord was *c*.

CRUCIFY* (CRUCIFIED CRUCIFYING)

Mt	23: 34	Some of them you will kill and *c*;
	27: 22	They all answered, "*C* him!" "Why
	27: 23	they shouted all the louder, "*C* him
	27: 31	Then they led him away to *c* him.
Mk	15: 13	"*C* him!" they shouted.
	15: 14	they shouted all the louder, "*C* him
	15: 20	Then they led him out to *c* him.

Lk	23: 21	they kept shouting, "*C* him! *C* him
Jn	19: 6	they shouted, "*C*! *C*!"
	19: 6	"You take him and *c* him.
	19: 10	either to free you or to *c* you?"
	19: 15	*C* him!" "Shall I *c* your king
	19: 15	away! Take him away! *C* him!"

CRUCIFYING* (CRUCIFY)

Heb	6: 6	to their loss they are *c* the Son

CRUSH (CRUSHED)

Ge	3: 15	he will *c* your head,
Isa	53: 10	it was the LORD's will to *c* him
Ro	16: 20	The God of peace will soon *c* Satan

CRUSHED (CRUSH)

Ps	34: 18	and saves those who are *c* in spirit.
Pr	17: 22	but a *c* spirit dries up the bones.
	18: 14	but a *c* spirit who can bear?
Isa	53: 5	he was *c* for our iniquities;
2Co	4: 8	not *c*; perplexed, but not in despair;

CRY (CRIED)

Ex	2: 23	*c* for help because of their slavery
Ps	5: 2	Listen to my *c* for help,
	34: 15	and his ears are attentive to their *c*;
	40: 1	he turned to me and heard my *c*.
	130: 1	Out of the depths I *c* to you,
Pr	21: 13	to the *c* of the poor,
La	2: 18	*c* out to the Lord.
Hab	2: 11	The stones of the wall will *c* out,
Lk	19: 40	keep quiet, the stones will *c* out."

CUNNING

2Co	11: 3	deceived by the serpent's *c*,
Eph	4: 14	and by the *c* and craftiness of men

CUP

Ps	23: 5	my *c* overflows.
Isa	51: 22	from that *c*, the goblet of my wrath,
	51: 22	the *c* that made you stagger;
Mt	10: 42	if anyone gives a *c* of cold water
	20: 22	"Can you drink the *c* I am going
	23: 25	You clean the outside of the *c*
	23: 26	First clean the inside of the *c*
	26: 27	Then he took the *c*, gave thanks
	26: 39	may this *c* be taken from me.
	26: 42	possible for this *c* to be taken away
Mk	9: 41	anyone who gives you a *c* of water
	10: 38	"Can you drink the *c* I drink
	10: 39	"You will drink the *c* I drink
	14: 23	Then he took the *c*, gave thanks
	14: 36	Take this *c* from me.
Lk	11: 39	Pharisees clean the outside of the *c*
	22: 17	After taking the *c*, he gave thanks
	22: 20	after the supper he took the *c*,
	22: 20	"This *c* is the new covenant
	22: 42	if you are willing, take this *c*
Jn	18: 11	I not drink the *c* the Father has
1Co	10: 16	Is not the *c* of thanksgiving
	10: 21	the *c* of the Lord and the *c*
	11: 25	after supper he took the *c*, saying,
	11: 25	"This *c* is the new covenant

CUPBEARER

Ge	40: 1	the *c* and the baker of the king
Ne	1: 11	I was *c* to the king.

CURE (CURED)

Jer	17: 9	and beyond *c*.

Jer 30: 15 your pain that has no c?
Hos 5: 13 But he is not able to c you,
Lk 9: 1 out all demons and to c diseases,

CURED (CURE)

Mt 11: 5 those who have leprosy are c,
Lk 6: 18 troubled by evil spirits were c,

CURSE (ACCURSED CURSED CURSES CURSING)

Ge 4: 11 Now you are under a c
8: 21 "Never again will I c the ground
12: 3 and whoever curses you I will c;
Dt 11: 26 before you today a blessing and a c
11: 28 the c if you disobey the commands
21: 23 hung on a tree is under God's c.
23: 5 turned the c into a blessing for you,
Job 1: 11 he will surely c you to your face."
2: 5 he will surely c you to your face."
2: 9 C God and die!" He replied,
Ps 109: 28 They may c, but you will bless;
Pr 3: 33 The LORD's c is on the house
24: 24 peoples will c him and nations
Mal 2: 2 and I will c your blessings.
Lk 6: 28 bless those who c you, pray
Ro 12: 14 persecute you; bless and do not c.
Gal 3: 10 on observing the law are under a c,
3: 13 of the law by becoming a c for us,
Jas 3: 9 with it we c men, who have been
Rev 22: 3 No longer will there be any c.

CURSED (CURSE)

Ge 3: 17 "C is the ground because of you;
Dt 27: 15 "C is the man who carves an image
27: 16 "C is the man who dishonours his
27: 17 "C is the man who moves his
27: 18 "C is the man who leads the blind
27: 19 C is the man who withholds justice
27: 20 "C is the man who sleeps
27: 21 "C is the man who has sexual
27: 22 "C is the man who sleeps
27: 23 "C is the man who sleeps
27: 24 "C is the man who kills his
27: 25 "C is the man who accepts a bribe
27: 26 "C is the man who does not uphold
Jer 17: 5 "C is the one who trusts in man,
Mal 1: 14 "C is the cheat who has
Ro 9: 3 I could wish that I myself were c
1Co 4: 12 When we are c, we bless;
12: 3 "Jesus be c," and no-one can say,
Gal 3: 10 "C is everyone who does not
3: 13 C is everyone who is hung on a tree

CURSES (CURSE)

Ex 21: 17 "Anyone who c his father
Lev 20: 9 "'If anyone c his father or mother,
Nu 5: 23 is to write these c on a scroll
Jos 8: 34 the blessings and the c—just
Pr 20: 20 If a man c his father or mother,
28: 27 to them receives many c.
Mt 15: 4 and 'Anyone who c his father
Mk 7: 10 and, 'Anyone who c his father

CURSING (CURSE)

Ps 109: 18 He wore c as his garment;
Ro 3: 14 "Their mouths are full of c
Jas 3: 10 the same mouth come praise and c.

CURTAIN

Ex 26: 31 "Make a c of blue, purple

Ex 26: 33 The c will separate the Holy Place
Mt 27: 51 At that moment the c
Mk 15: 38 The c of the temple was torn in two
Lk 23: 45 the c of the temple was torn in two.
Heb 6: 19 the inner sanctuary behind the c,
9: 3 Behind the second c was a room
10: 20 opened for us through the c,

CUSTOM

Job 1: 5 This was Job's regular c.
Mk 10: 1 and as was his c, he taught them.
Lk 4: 16 into the synagogue, as was his c.
Ac 17: 2 As his c was, Paul went

CUT

Lev 19: 27 "'Do not c the hair at the sides
21: 5 of their beards or c their bodies.
1Ki 3: 25 "C the living child in two
Isa 51: 1 to the rock from which you were c
53: 8 For he was c off from the land
Da 2: 45 of the rock c out of a mountain,
9: 26 the Anointed One will be c off
Mt 3: 10 not produce good fruit will be c
24: 22 If those days had not been c short,
1Co 11: 6 for a woman to have her hair c

CYMBAL* (CYMBALS)

1Co 13: 1 a resounding gong or a clanging c.

CYMBALS (CYMBAL)

1Ch 15: 16 instruments: lyres, harps and c.
2Ch 5: 12 dressed in fine linen and playing c,
Ps 150: 5 praise him with resounding c.

CYRUS

Persian king who allowed exiles to return (2Ch 36:22-Ezr 1:8), to rebuild temple (Ezr 5:13-6:14), as appointed by the LORD (Isa 44:28-45:13).

DAGON

Jdg 16: 23 offer a great sacrifice to D their god
1Sa 5: 2 D's temple and set it beside D.

DAMASCUS

Ac 9: 3 As he neared D on his journey,

DAN

1. Son of Jacob by Bilhah (Ge 30:4-6; 35:25; 46:23). Tribe of blessed (Ge 49:16-17; Dt 33:22), numbered (Nu 1:39; 26:43), allotted land (Jos 19:40-48; Eze 48:1), failed to fully possess (Jdg 1:34-35), failed to support Deborah (Jdg 5:17), possessed Laish/Dan (Jdg 18).
2. Northernmost city in Israel (Ge 14:14; Jdg 18; 20:1).

DANCE (DANCED DANCING)

Ecc 3: 4 a time to mourn and a time to d,
Mt 11: 17 and you did not d;

DANCED (DANCE)

2Sa 6: 14 d before the LORD
Mk 6: 22 of Herodias came in and d,

DANCING (DANCE)

Ps 30: 11 You turned my wailing into d;
149: 3 Let them praise his name with d

DANGER

Pr 22: 3 A prudent man sees d

Pr   27: 12 The prudent see *d* and take refuge,
Mt   5: 22   will be in *d* of the fire of hell.
Ro   8: 35   famine or nakedness or *d* or sword?
2Co   11: 26 I have been in *d* from rivers,

DANIEL

1. Hebrew exile to Babylon, name changed to Belteshazzar (Da 1:6-7). Refused to eat unclean food (Da 1:8-21). Interpreted Nebuchadnezzar's dreams (Da 2; 4), writing on the wall (Da 5). Thrown into lions' den (Da 6). Visions of (Da 7-12).
2. Son of David (1Ch 3:1).

DARIUS

1. King of Persia (Ezr 4:5), allowed rebuilding of temple (Ezr 5-6).
2. Mede who conquered Babylon (Da 5:31).

DARK (DARKENED DARKENS DARKNESS)

Job   34: 22 There is no *d* place, no deep
Ps   18: 9   *d* clouds were under his feet.
Pr   31: 15 She gets up while it is still *d*;
SS   1: 6   Do not stare at me because I am *d*,
Jn   12: 35 in the *d* does not know where he is
Ro   2: 19   a light for those who are in the *d*,
2Pe   1: 19   as to a light shining in a *d* place,

DARKENED (DARK)

Joel 2: 10   the sun and moon are *d*,
Mt   24: 29 " 'the sun will be *d*,
Ro   1: 21   and their foolish hearts were *d*.
Eph   4: 18   They are *d* in their understanding

DARKENS (DARK)

Job   38: 2   "Who is this that *d* my counsel

DARKNESS (DARK)

Ge   1: 2   *d* was over the surface of the deep,
      1: 4   he separated the light from the *d*.
Ex   10: 22 and total *d* covered all Egypt
      20: 21 approached the thick *d* where God
2Sa   22: 29 the LORD turns my *d* into light.
Ps   18: 28 my God turns my *d* into light.
      91: 6   the pestilence that stalks in the *d*,
      112: 4 Even in *d* light dawns
      139: 12 even the *d* will not be dark to you;
Pr   4: 19   the way of the wicked is like deep *d*
Isa   5: 20   and light for *d*,
      42: 16 I will turn the *d* into light
      45: 7   I form the light and create *d*,
      58: 10 then your light will rise in the *d*,
      61: 1   release from *d* for the prisoners,
Joel 2: 31   The sun will be turned to *d*
Mt   4: 16   the people living in *d*
      6: 23   how great is that *d*! "No-one can
Lk   11: 34 are bad, your body also is full of *d*.
      23: 44 and *d* came over the whole land
Jn   1: 5   The light shines in the *d*,
      3: 19   but men loved *d* instead of light
Ac   2: 20   The sun will be turned to *d*
2Co   4: 6   who said, "Let light shine out of *d*
      6: 14   fellowship can light have with *d*?
Eph   5: 8   For you were once *d*, but now you
      5: 11   to do with the fruitless deeds of *d*,
1Pe   2: 9   out of *d* into his wonderful light.
2Pe   2: 17   Blackest *d* is reserved for them.
1Jn   1: 5   in him there is no *d* at all.
      2: 9   but hates his brother is still in the *d*.
Jude : 6   in *d*, bound with everlasting chains

Jude : 13   for whom blackest *d* has been

DASH

Ps   2: 9   you will *d* them to pieces like

DAUGHTER (DAUGHTERS)

Ex   1: 10   she took him to Pharaoh's *d*
Jdg   11: 48 to commemorate the *d* of Jephthah
Est   2: 7   Mordecai had taken her as his own *d*
Ps   9: 14   praises in the gates of the *D* of Zion
      137: 8 O *D* of Babylon, doomed
Isa   62: 11 "Say to the *D* of Zion
Zec   9: 9   Shout, *D* of Jerusalem!
Mk   5: 34   "*D*, your faith has healed you.
      7: 29   the demon has left your *d*.

DAUGHTERS (DAUGHTER)

Ge   6: 2   the *d* of men were beautiful,
      19: 36 Lot's *d* became pregnant
Nu   36: 10 Zelophehad's *d* did as the LORD
Joel 2: 28   sons and *d* will prophesy,

DAVID

Son of Jesse (Ru 4:17-22; 1Ch 2:13-15), ancestor of Jesus (Mt 1:1-17; Lk 3:31). Wives and children (1Sa 18; 25:39-44; 2Sa 3:2-5; 5:13-16; 11:27; 1Ch 3:1-9).
Anointed king by Samuel (1Sa 16:1-13). Musician to Saul (1Sa 16:14-23; 18:10). Killed Goliath (1Sa 17). Relation with Jonathan (1Sa 18:1-4; 19-20; 23:16-18; 2Sa 1). Disfavour of Saul (1Sa 18:6-23:29). Spared Saul's life (1Sa 24; 26). Among Philistines (1Sa 21:10-14; 27-30). Lament for Saul and Jonathan (2Sa 1).
Anointed king of Judah (2Sa 2:1-11). Conflict with house of Saul (2Sa 2-4). Anointed king of Israel (2Sa 5:1-4; 1Ch 11:1-3). Conquered Jerusalem (2Sa 6; 1Ch 13; 15-16). The LORD promised eternal dynasty (2Sa 7; 1Ch 17; Ps 132). Showed kindness to Mephibosheth (2Sa 9). Adultery with Bathsheba, murder of Uriah (2Sa 11-12). Son Amnon raped daughter Tamar; killed by Absalom (2Sa 13). Absalom's revolt (2Sa 14-17); death (2Sa 18). Sheba's revolt (2Sa 20). Victories: Philistines (2Sa 5:17-25; 1Ch 14:8-17; 2Sa 21:15-22; 1Ch 20:4-8), Ammonites (2Sa 10; 1Ch 19; 2Sa 8; 1Ch 18). Mighty men (2Sa 23:8-39; 1Ch 11-12). Punished for numbering army (2Sa 24; 1Ch 21). Appointed Solomon king (1Ki 1:28-2:9). Prepared for building of temple (1Ch 22-29). Last words (2Sa 23:1-7). Death (1Ki 2:10-12; 1Ch 29:28).
Psalmist (Mt 22:43-45), musician (Am 6:5), prophet (2Sa 23:2-7; Ac 1:16; 2:30).
Psalms of: 2 (Ac 4:25), 3-32, 34-41, 51-65, 68-70, 86, 95 (Heb 4:7), 101, 103, 108-110, 122, 124, 131, 133, 138-145.

DAWN (DAWNED DAWNS)

Ps   37: 6   your righteousness shine like the *d*,
Pr   4: 18   is like the first gleam of *d*,
Isa   14: 12 O morning star, son of the *d*!
Am   4: 13   he who turns *d* to darkness,
      5: 8   who turns blackness into *d*

DAWNED (DAWN)

Isa   9: 2   a light has *d*.
Mt   4: 16   a light has *d*."

DAWNS* (DAWN)

Ps	65: 8	where morning *d* and evening
	112: 4	in darkness light *d* for the upright,
Hos	10: 15	When that day *d*,
2Pe	1: 19	until the day *d* and the morning

DAY (DAYS)

Ge	1: 5	God called the light "*d*"
	1: 5	and there was morning—the first *d*
	1: 8	there was morning—the second *d*.
	1: 13	there was morning—the third *d*.
	1: 19	there was morning—the fourth *d*.
	1: 23	there was morning—the fifth *d*.
	1: 31	there was morning—the sixth *d*.
	2: 2	so on the seventh *d* he rested
	8: 22	*d* and night
Ex	16: 30	the people rested on the seventh *d*.
	20: 8	"Remember the Sabbath *d*
Lev	16: 30	on this *d* atonement will be made
	23: 28	because it is the *D* of Atonement,
Nu	14: 14	before them in a pillar of cloud by *d*
Jos	1: 8	meditate on it *d* and night,
2Ki	7: 9	This is a *d* of good news
	25: 30	*D* by *d* the king gave Jehoiachin
1Ch	16: 23	proclaim his salvation *d* after *d*.
Ne	8: 18	*D* after *d*, from the first *d*
Ps	84: 10	Better is one *d* in your courts
	96: 2	proclaim his salvation *d* after *d*.
	118: 24	This is the *d* the LORD has made;
Pr	27: 1	not know what a *d* may bring forth.
Isa	13: 9	a cruel *d*, with wrath and fierce
Jer	46: 10	But that *d* belongs to the LORD,
	50: 31	"for your *d* has come,
Eze	30: 2	"Alas for that *d*!"
Joel	2: 31	and dreadful *d* of the LORD.
Am	3: 14	On the *d* I punish Israel for her sins
	5: 20	Will not the *d* of the LORD be
Ob	: 15	"The *d* of the LORD is near
Zep	1: 14	The great *d* of the LORD is near—
Zec	2: 11	joined with the LORD in that *d*
	14: 1	A *d* of the LORD is coming
	14: 7	It will be a unique *d*,
Mal	4: 5	dreadful *d* of the LORD comes.
Mt	24: 38	up to the *d* Noah entered the ark;
Lk	11: 3	Give us each *d* our daily bread.
	17: 24	in his *d* will be like the lightning,
Ac	5: 42	*D* after *d*, in the temple courts
	17: 11	examined the Scriptures every *d*
	17: 17	as in the market-place *d* by *d*
Ro	14: 5	man considers every *d* alike.
1Co	5: 5	his spirit saved on the *d* of the Lord
2Co	4: 16	we are being renewed *d* by *d*.
	11: 25	I spent a night and a *d*
1Th	5: 2	for you know very well that the *d*
	5: 4	so that this *d* should surprise you
2Th	2: 2	saying that the *d* of the Lord has
Heb	7: 27	need to offer sacrifices *d* after *d*,
2Pe	3: 8	With the Lord a *d* is like
	3: 10	*d* of the Lord will come like a thief.
Rev	6: 17	For the great *d* of their wrath has
	16: 14	on the great *d* of God Almighty.

DAYS (DAY)

Dt	17: 19	he is to read it all the *d* of his life
	32: 7	Remember the *d* of old;
Ps	23: 6	all the *d* of my life,
	34: 12	and desires to see many good *d*,
	39: 5	have made my *d* a mere
	90: 10	The length of our *d* is seventy years
	90: 12	Teach us to number our *d* aright,

Ps	103: 15	As for man, his *d* are like grass,
	128: 5	all the *d* of your life;
Pr	31: 12	all the *d* of her life.
Ecc	9: 9	all the *d* of this meaningless life
	12: 1	Creator in the *d* of your youth,
Isa	38: 20	all the *d* of our lives
Da	7: 9	and the Ancient of *D* took his seat.
	7: 13	He approached the Ancient of *D*
	7: 22	until the Ancient of *D* came
Hos	3: 5	and to his blessings in the last *d*.
Joel	2: 29	I will pour out my Spirit in those *d*.
Mic	4: 1	In the last *d*
Lk	19: 43	The *d* will come upon you
Ac	2: 17	by the prophet Joel: "'In the last *d*,
2Ti	3: 1	will be terrible times in the last *d*.
Heb	1: 2	in these last *d* he has spoken to us
2Pe	3: 3	that in the last *d* scoffers will come,

DAZZLING*

Da	2: 31	*d* statue, awesome in appearance.
Mk	9: 3	His clothes became *d* white,

DEACON* (DEACONS)

1Ti	3: 12	A *d* must be the husband of

DEACONS* (DEACON)

Php	1: 1	together with the overseers and *d*:
1Ti	3: 8	*D*, likewise, are to be men worthy
	3: 10	against them, let them serve as *d*.

DEAD (DIE)

Lev	17: 15	who eats anything found *d*
Dt	18: 11	or spiritist or who consults the *d*.
Isa	8: 19	Why consult the *d* on behalf
Mt	8: 22	and let the *d* bury their own *d*."
	28: 7	'He has risen from the *d*
Lk	15: 24	For this son of mine was *d*
	24: 46	rise from the *d* on the third day,
Ro	6: 11	count yourselves *d* to sin
1Co	15: 29	do who are baptised for the *d*?
Eph	2: 1	you were *d* in your transgressions
1Th	4: 16	and the *d* in Christ will rise first.
Jas	2: 17	is not accompanied by action, is *d*.
	2: 26	so faith without deeds is *d*.
Rev	14: 13	Blessed are the *d* who die
	20: 12	And I saw the *d*, great and small,

DEADENED* (DIE)

Jn	12: 40	and *d* their hearts,

DEAR* (DEARER)

2Sa	1: 26	you were very *d* to me.
Ps	102: 14	For her stones are *d*
Jer	31: 20	Is not Ephraim my *d* son,
Jn	2: 4	"*D* woman, why do you involve me
	19: 26	he said to his mother, "*D* woman,
Ac	15: 25	to you with our *d* friends Barnabas
Ro	16: 5	Greet my *d* friend Epenetus.
	16: 9	in Christ, and my *d* friend Stachys.
	16: 12	Greet my *d* friend Persis, another
1Co	4: 14	but to warn you, as my *d* children.
	10: 14	my *d* friends, flee from idolatry.
	15: 58	Therefore, my *d* brothers,
2Co	7: 1	we have these promises, *d* friends,
	12: 19	and everything we do, *d* friends,
Gal	4: 19	My *d* children, for whom I am
Eph	6: 21	the *d* brother and faithful servant
Php	2: 12	my *d* friends, as you have always
	4: 1	firm in the Lord, *d* friends!
Col	1: 7	Epaphras, our *d* fellow-servant,

Col	4: 7	He is a *d* brother, a faithful
	4: 9	our faithful and *d* brother,
	4:14	Our *d* friend Luke, the doctor,
1Th	2: 8	because you had become so *d* to us.
1Ti	6: 2	their service are believers, and *d*
2Ti	1: 2	To Timothy, my *d* son: Grace,
Phm	: 1	To Philemon our *d* friend
	:16	He is very *d* to me but
	:16	better than a slave, as a *d* brother.
Heb	6: 9	we speak like this, *d* friends,
Jas	1:16	Don't be deceived, my *d* brothers.
	1:19	My *d* brothers, take note of this:
	2: 5	thoughts? Listen, my *d* brothers:
1Pe	2:11	*D* friends, I urge you, as aliens
	4:12	*D* friends, do not be surprised
2Pe	3: 1	*D* friends, this is now my second
	3: 8	not forget this one thing, *d* friends:
	3:14	*d* friends, since you are looking
	3:15	just as our *d* brother Paul
	3:17	*d* friends, since you already know
1Jn	2: 1	My *d* children, I write this to you
	2: 7	*D* friends, I am not writing you
	2:12	I write to you, *d* children,
	2:13	I write to you, *d* children,
	2:18	*D* children, this is the last hour;
	2:28	*d* children, continue in him,
	3: 2	*D* friends, now we are children
	3: 7	*D* children, do not let anyone lead
	3:18	love of God be in him? *D* children,
	3:21	*D* friends, if our hearts do not
	4: 1	*D* friends, do not believe every
	4: 4	*d* children, are from God
	4: 7	*D* friends, let us love one another,
	4:11	*D* friends, since God so loved us,
	5:21	*D* children, keep yourselves
2Jn	: 5	*d* lady, I am not writing you a new
3Jn	: 1	The elder, To my *d* friend Gaius,
	: 2	*D* friend, I pray that you may enjoy
	: 5	*D* friend, you are faithful
	:11	*D* friend, do not imitate what is evil
Jude	: 3	*D* friends, although I was very
	:17	But, *d* friends, remember what
	:20	*d* friends, build yourselves up

DEARER* (DEAR)

Phm	:16	dear to me but even *d* to you,

DEATH (DIE)

Ex	21:12	kills him shall surely be put to *d*.
Nu	35:16	the murderer shall be put to *d*.
Dt	30:19	set before you life and *d*,
Ru	1:17	if anything but *d* separates you
2Ki	4:40	O man of God, there is *d* in the pot
Job	26: 6	*D* is naked before God;
Ps	23: 4	the valley of the shadow of *d*,
	44:22	for your sake we face *d* all day long
	89:48	What man can live and not see *d*,
	116:15	is the *d* of his saints.
Pr	8:36	all who hate me love *d*."
	11:19	he who pursues evil goes to his *d*.
	14:12	but in the end it leads to *d*.
	15:11	*D* and Destruction lie open
	16:25	but in the end it leads to *d*.
	18:21	tongue has the power of life and *d*,
	19:18	do not be a willing party to his *d*.
	23:14	and save his soul from *d*.
Ecc	7: 2	for *d* is the destiny of every man;
Isa	25: 8	he will swallow up *d* for ever.
	53:12	he poured out his life unto *d*,
Eze	18:23	pleasure in the *d* of the wicked?

Eze	18:32	pleasure in the *d* of anyone,
	33:11	pleasure in the *d* of the wicked,
Hos	13:14	Where, O *d*, are your plagues?
Jn	5:24	he has crossed over from *d* to life.
Ro	4:25	delivered over to *d* for our sins
	5:12	and in this way *d* came to all men,
	5:14	*d* reigned from the time of Adam
	6: 3	Jesus were baptised into his *d*?
	6:23	For the wages of sin is *d*,
	7:24	me from this body of *d*?
	8:13	put to *d* the misdeeds of the body,
	8:36	your sake we face *d* all day long;
1Co	15:21	For since *d* came through a man,
	15:26	The last enemy to be destroyed is *d*
	15:55	Where, O *d*, is your sting?"
2Ti	1:10	who has destroyed *d* and has
Heb	2:14	him who holds the power of *d*—
1Jn	5:16	There is a sin that leads to *d*.
Rev	1:18	And I hold the keys of *d* and Hades
	2:11	hurt at all by the second *d*.
	20: 6	The second *d* has no power
	20:14	The lake of fire is the second *d*.
	20:14	Then *d* and Hades were thrown
	21: 4	There will be no more *d*
	21: 8	This is the second *d*."

DEBAUCHERY*

Ro	13:13	not in sexual immorality and *d*,
2Co	12:21	and *d* in which they have indulged.
Gal	5:19	impurity and *d*; idolatry
Eph	5:18	drunk on wine, which leads to *d*.
1Pe	4: 3	living in *d*, lust, drunkenness,

DEBORAH*

1. Prophetess who led Israel to victory over Canaanites (Jdg 4-5).
2. Rebekah's nurse (Ge 35:8).

DEBT* (DEBTOR DEBTORS DEBTS)

Dt	15: 3	must cancel any *d* your brother
	24: 6	the upper one—as security for a *d*,
1Sa	22: 2	or in *d* or discontented gathered
Job	24: 9	of the poor is seized for a *d*.
Mt	18:25	that he had been sold to repay the *d*.
	18:27	cancelled the *d* and let him go.
	18:30	into prison until he could pay the *d*.
	18:32	'I cancelled all that *d* of yours
Lk	7:43	who had the bigger *d* cancelled."
Ro	13: 8	Let no *d* remain outstanding,
	13: 8	continuing to love one another,

DEBTOR* (DEBT)

Isa	24: 2	for *d* as for creditor.

DEBTORS* (DEBT)

Hab	2: 7	Will not your *d* suddenly rise?
Mt	6:12	as we also have forgiven our *d*.
Lk	16: 5	called in each one of his master's *d*.

DEBTS* (DEBT)

Dt	15: 1	seven years you must cancel *d*.
	15: 2	time for cancelling *d* has been
	15: 9	the year for cancelling *d*, is near,"
	31:10	in the year for cancelling *d*,
2Ki	4: 7	"Go, sell the oil and pay your *d*.
Ne	10:31	the land and will cancel all *d*.
Pr	22:26	or puts up security for *d*;
Mt	6:12	Forgive us our *d*,
Lk	7:42	so he cancelled the *d* of both.

DECAY*

Ps	16: 10	will you let your Holy One see *d*.
	49: 9	and not see *d*.
	49: 14	their forms will *d* in the grave,
Pr	12: 4	a disgraceful wife is like *d*
Isa	5: 24	so their roots will *d*
Hab	3: 16	*d* crept into my bones,
Ac	2: 27	will you let your Holy One see *d*,
	2: 31	to the grave, nor did his body see *d*.
	13: 34	never to *d*, is stated in these words:
	13: 35	will not let your Holy One see *d*.'
	13: 37	raised from the dead did not see *d*.
Ro	8: 21	liberated from its bondage to *d*

DECEIT (DECEIVE)

Ps	5: 9	with their tongue they speak *d*.
Isa	53: 9	nor was any *d* in his mouth.
Da	8: 25	He will cause *d* to prosper,
Zep	3: 13	nor will *d* be found in their mouths.
Mk	7: 22	greed, malice, *d*, lewdness, envy,
Ac	13: 10	You are full of all kinds of *d*
Ro	1: 29	murder, strife, *d* and malice.
	3: 13	their tongues practise *d*."
1Pe	2: 1	yourselves of all malice and all *d*,
	2: 22	and no *d* was found in his mouth."

DECEITFUL (DECEIVE)

Jer	17: 9	The heart is *d* above all things
Hos	10: 2	Their heart is *d*,
2Co	11: 13	men are false apostles, *d* workmen,
Eph	4: 14	of men in their *d* scheming.
	4: 22	is being corrupted by its *d* desires;
1Pe	3: 10	and his lips from *d* speech.
Rev	21: 27	who does what is shameful or *d*,

DECEITFULNESS* (DECEIVE)

Ps	119: 118	for their *d* is in vain.
Mt	13: 22	and the *d* of wealth choke it,
Mk	4: 19	the *d* of wealth and the desires
Heb	3: 13	of you may be hardened by sin's *d*.

DECEIVE (DECEIT DECEITFUL DECEITFULNESS DECEIVED DECEIVER DECEIVERS DECEIVES DECEIVING DECEPTION DECEPTIVE)

Lev	19: 11	"'Do not *d* one another.
Pr	14: 5	A truthful witness does not *d*,
	24: 28	or use your lips to *d*.
Jer	37: 9	Do not *d* yourselves, thinking,
Zec	13: 4	garment of hair in order to *d*.
Mt	24: 5	'I am the Christ,' and will *d* many.
	24: 11	will appear and *d* many people.
	24: 24	and miracles to *d* even the elect—
Mk	13: 6	'I am he,' and will *d* many.
	13: 22	and miracles to *d* the elect—
Ro	16: 18	and flattery they *d* the minds
1Co	3: 18	Do not *d* yourselves.
Eph	5: 6	Let no-one *d* you with empty words
Col	2: 4	this so that no-one may *d* you
2Th	2: 3	Don't let anyone *d* you in any way,
Jas	1: 22	to the word, and so *d* yourselves.
1Jn	1: 8	we *d* ourselves and the truth is not
Rev	20: 8	and will go out to *d* the nations

DECEIVED (DECEIVE)

Ge	3: 13	"The serpent *d* me, and I ate."
Lk	21: 8	"Watch out that you are not *d*.
1Co	6: 9	the kingdom of God? Do not be *d*:
2Co	11: 3	Eve was *d* by the serpent's cunning

Gal	6: 7	Do not be *d*: God cannot be
1Ti	2: 14	And Adam was not the one *d*;
2Ti	3: 13	to worse, deceiving and being *d*.
Tit	3: 3	*d* and enslaved by all kinds
Jas	1: 16	Don't be *d*, my dear brothers.
Rev	13: 14	he *d* the inhabitants of the earth.
	20: 10	And the devil, who *d* them,

DECEIVER (DECEIVE)

Mt	27: 63	while he was still alive that *d* said,
2Jn	: 7	Any such person is the *d*

DECEIVERS* (DECEIVE)

Ps	49: 5	when wicked *d* surround me—
Tit	1: 10	and *d*, especially those
2Jn	: 7	Many *d*, who do not acknowledge

DECEIVES (DECEIVE)

Pr	26: 19	is a man who *d* his neighbour
Mt	24: 4	"Watch out that no-one *d* you.
Mk	13: 5	"Watch out that no-one *d* you.
Gal	6: 3	when he is nothing, he *d* himself.
2Th	2: 10	sort of evil that *d* those who are
Jas	1: 26	he *d* himself and his religion is

DECEIVING* (DECEIVE)

Lev	6: 2	by *d* his neighbour about something
1Ti	4: 1	follow *d* spirits and things taught
2Ti	3: 13	go from bad to worse, *d*
Rev	20: 3	him from *d* the nations any more

DECENCY* (DECENTLY)

1Ti	2: 9	women to dress modestly, with *d*

DECENTLY* (DECENCY)

Ro	13: 13	Let us behave *d*, as in the daytime,

DECEPTION (DECEIVE)

Pr	14: 8	but the folly of fools is *d*.
	26: 26	His malice may be concealed by *d*,
Mt	27: 64	This last *d* will be worse
2Co	4: 2	we do not use *d*, nor do we distort

DECEPTIVE (DECEIVE)

Pr	11: 18	The wicked man earns *d* wages,
	31: 30	Charm is *d*, and beauty is fleeting;
Jer	7: 4	Do not trust in *d* words and say,
Col	2: 8	through hollow and *d* philosophy,

DECIDED (DECISION)

2Co	9: 7	man should give what he has *d*

DECISION (DECIDED)

Ex	28: 29	heart on the breastpiece of *d*
Joel	3: 14	multitudes in the valley of *d*!

DECLARE (DECLARED DECLARING)

1Ch	16: 24	*D* his glory among the nations,
Ps	19: 1	The heavens *d* the glory of God;
	96: 3	*D* his glory among the nations,
Isa	42: 9	and new things I *d*;

DECLARED (DECLARE)

Mk	7: 19	Jesus *d* all foods "clean".)
Ro	2: 13	the law who will be *d* righteous.
	3: 20	no-one will be *d* righteous

DECLARING (DECLARE)

Ps	71: 8	*d* your splendour all day long.
Ac	2: 11	we hear them *d* the wonders

DECREE (DECREED DECREES)

Ex	15: 25	There the LORD made a *d*
1Ch	16: 17	He confirmed it to Jacob as a *d*,
Ps	2: 7	I will proclaim the *d* of the LORD:
	7: 6	Awake, my God; *d* justice.
	81: 4	this is a *d* for Israel,
	148: 6	he gave a *d* that will never pass
Da	4: 24	and this is the *d* the Most High has
Lk	2: 1	Augustus issued a *d* that a census
Ro	1: 32	know God's righteous *d* that those

DECREED (DECREE)

Ps	78: 5	He *d* statutes for Jacob
Jer	40: 2	LORD your God *d* this disaster
La	3: 37	happen if the Lord has not *d* it?
Da	9: 24	"Seventy 'sevens' are *d*
	9: 26	and desolations have been *d*.
Lk	22: 22	Son of Man will go as it has been *d*,

DECREES (DECREE)

Ge	26: 5	my commands, my *d* and my laws
Ex	15: 26	to his commands and keep all his *d*,
	18: 16	inform them of God's *d* and laws."
	18: 20	Teach them the *d* and laws,
Lev	10: 11	Israelites all the *d* the LORD has
	18: 4	and be careful to follow my *d*.
	18: 5	Keep my *d* and laws,
	18: 26	you must keep my *d* and my laws.
Ps	119: 12	teach me your *d*.
	119: 16	I delight in your *d*;
	119: 48	and I meditate on your *d*.
	119: 112	My heart is set on keeping your *d*

DEDICATE (DEDICATED DEDICATION)

Nu	6: 12	He must *d* himself to the LORD
Pr	20: 25	for a man to *d* something rashly

DEDICATED (DEDICATE)

Lev	21: 12	he has been *d* by the anointing oil
Nu	6: 9	thus defiling the hair he has *d*,
	6: 18	shave off the hair that he *d*.
	18: 6	*d* to the LORD to do the work
1Ki	8: 63	and all the Israelites *d* the temple
2Ch	29: 31	"You have now *d* yourselves
Ne	3: 1	They *d* it and set its doors in place,

DEDICATION (DEDICATE)

Nu	6: 19	shaved off the hair of his *d*,
Jn	10: 22	came the Feast of *D* at Jerusalem.
1Ti	5: 11	sensual desires overcome their *d*

DEED [1]

Jer	32: 10	and sealed the *d*, had it witnessed,
	32: 16	After I had given the *d* of purchase

DEED [2] (DEEDS)

Col	3: 17	you do, whether in word or *d*,
2Th	2: 17	and strengthen you in every good *d*

DEEDS (DEED [2])

Dt	3: 24	or on earth who can do the *d*
	4: 34	or by great and awesome *d*,
	34: 12	the awesome *d* that Moses
1Sa	2: 3	and by him *d* are weighed.
1Ch	16: 24	his marvellous *d* among all peoples.
Job	34: 25	Because he takes note of their *d*,
Ps	26: 7	and telling of all your wonderful *d*.
	45: 4	right hand display awesome.
	65: 5	with awesome *d* of righteousness,
	66: 3	"How awesome are your *d*!

Ps	71: 17	day I declare your marvellous *d*.
	72: 18	who alone does marvellous *d*.
	73: 28	I will tell of all your *d*.
	75: 1	men tell of your wonderful *d*.
	77: 11	I will remember the *d* of the LORD
	77: 12	and consider all your mighty *d*.
	78: 4	the praiseworthy *d* of the LORD,
	78: 7	and would not forget his *d*
	86: 8	no *d* can compare with yours.
	86: 10	you are great and do marvellous *d*;
	88: 12	or your righteous *d* in the land
	90: 16	May your *d* be shown
	92: 4	For you make me glad by your *d*,
	96: 3	his marvellous *d* among all peoples.
	107: 8	and his wonderful *d* for men,
	107: 15	and his wonderful *d* for men,
	107: 21	and his wonderful *d* for men.
	107: 24	his wonderful *d* in the deep.
	107: 31	and his wonderful *d* for men.
	111: 3	Glorious and majestic are his *d*,
	145: 6	and I will proclaim your great *d*.
Jer	32: 19	purposes and mighty are your *d*.
Hab	3: 2	I stand in awe of your *d*, O LORD.
Mt	5: 16	that they may see your good *d*
Lk	1: 51	He has performed mighty *d*
	23: 41	we are getting what our *d* deserve.
Ac	26: 20	prove their repentance by their *d*.
1Ti	6: 18	rich in good *d*, and to be generous
Heb	10: 24	on towards love and good *d*.
Jas	2: 14	claims to have faith but has no *d*?
	2: 18	Show me your faith without *d*,
	2: 20	faith without *d* is useless?
	2: 26	so faith without *d* is dead.
1Pe	2: 12	they may see your good *d*
Rev	2: 19	I know your *d*, your love and faith,
	2: 23	each of you according to your *d*.
	3: 1	I know your *d*; you have
	3: 2	I have not found your *d* complete
	3: 8	I know your *d*.
	3: 15	I know your *d*, that you are neither
	14: 13	for their *d* will follow them."
	15: 3	"Great and marvellous are your *d*,

DEEP (DEPTH DEPTHS)

Ge	1: 2	was over the surface of the *d*,
	8: 2	Now the springs of the *d*
Ps	42: 7	*D* calls to *d*
Lk	5: 4	to Simon, "Put out into *d* water,
1Co	2: 10	all things, even the *d* things
1Ti	3: 9	hold of the *d* truths of the faith

DEER

Ps	42: 1	As the *d* pants for streams of water,

DEFAMED*

Isa	48: 11	How can I let myself be *d*?

DEFEATED

1Co	6: 7	have been completely *d* already.

DEFENCE (DEFEND)

Ps	35: 23	Awake, and rise to my *d*!
Php	1: 16	here for the *d* of the gospel.
1Jn	2: 1	speaks to the Father in our *d*—

DEFEND (DEFENCE DEFENDED DEFENDER DEFENDING DEFENDS)

Ps	72: 4	He will *d* the afflicted
	74: 22	Rise up, O God, and *d* your cause;
	82: 2	"How long will you *d* the unjust

Ps 82: 3 *D* the cause of the weak
119:154 *D* my cause and redeem me;
Pr 31: 9 *d* the rights of the poor and needy
Isa 1: 17 *D* the cause of the fatherless,
1: 23 They do not *d* the cause
Jer 5: 28 they do not *d* the rights of the poor.
50: 34 He will vigorously *d* their cause

DEFENDED (DEFEND)

Jer 22: 16 He *d* the cause of the poor

DEFENDER (DEFEND)

Ex 22: 2 the *d* is not guilty of bloodshed,
Ps 68: 5 to the fatherless, a *d* of widows,
Pr 23: 11 for their *D* is strong;

DEFENDING (DEFEND)

Ps 10: 18 *d* the fatherless and the oppressed,
Ro 2: 15 now accusing, now even *d* them.)
Php 1: 7 or *d* and confirming the gospel,

DEFENDS* (DEFEND)

Dt 10: 18 He *d* the cause of the fatherless
33: 7 With his own hands he *d* his cause.
Isa 51: 22 your God, who *d* his people:

DEFERRED*

Pr 13: 12 Hope *d* makes the heart sick,

DEFIED

1Sa 17: 45 armies of Israel, whom you have *d*.
1Ki 13: 26 the man of God who *d* the word

DEFILE (DEFILED)

Da 1: 8 Daniel resolved not to *d* himself
Rev 14: 4 are those who did not *d* themselves

DEFILED (DEFILE)

Isa 24: 5 The earth is *d* by its people;

DEFRAUD

Lev 19: 13 Do not *d* your neighbour or rob him.
Mk 10: 19 do not *d*, honour your father

DEITY*

Col 2: 9 of the *D* lives in bodily form,

DELAY

Ecc 5: 4 vow to God, do not *d* in fulfilling it.
Isa 48: 9 my own name's sake I *d* my wrath;
Heb 10: 37 is coming will come and will not *d*.
Rev 10: 6 and said, "There will be no more *d*!

DELICACIES

Ps 141: 4 let me not eat of their *d*.
Pr 23: 3 Do not crave his *d*,
23: 6 do not crave his *d*;

DELICIOUS*

Pr 9: 17 food eaten in secret is *d*!"

DELIGHT* (DELIGHTED DELIGHTFUL DELIGHTING DELIGHTS)

Lev 26: 31 and I will take no *d* in the pleasing
Dt 30: 9 The Lord will again *d* in you
1Sa 2: 1 for I *d* in your deliverance.
15: 22 "Does the Lord *d*
Ne 1: 11 the prayer of your servants who *d*
Job 22: 26 Surely then you will find *d*
27: 10 Will he find *d* in the Almighty?

Ps 1: 2 But his *d* is in the law of the Lord
16: 3 in whom is all my *d*.
35: 9 and *d* in his salvation.
35: 27 those who *d* in my vindication
37: 4 *D* yourself in the Lord
43: 4 to God, my joy and my *d*.
51: 16 You do not *d* in sacrifice,
51: 19 whole burnt offerings to *d* you;
62: 4 they take *d* in lies.
68: 30 Scatter the nations who *d* in war.
111: 2 by all who *d* in them.
112: 1 who finds great *d* in his commands.
119: 16 I *d* in your decrees;
119: 24 Your statutes are my *d*;
119: 35 for there I find *d*.
119: 47 for I *d* in your commands
119: 70 but I *d* in your law.
119: 77 for your law is my *d*.
119: 92 If your law had not been my *d*,
119: 143 but your commands are my *d*.
119: 174 and your law is my *d*.
147: 10 nor his *d* in the legs of a man;
149: 4 For the Lord takes *d*
Pr 1: 22 How long will mockers *d*
2: 14 who *d* in doing wrong
8: 30 I was filled with *d* day after day,
11: 1 but accurate weights are his *d*.
29: 17 he will bring *d* to your soul.
Ecc 2: 10 My heart took *d* in all my work,
SS 1: 4 We rejoice and *d* in you;
2: 3 I *d* to sit in his shade,
Isa 5: 7 are the garden of his *d*.
11: 3 he will *d* in the fear of the Lord.
13: 17 and have no *d* in gold.
32: 14 the *d* of donkeys, a pasture
42: 1 my chosen one in whom I *d*;
55: 2 and your soul will *d* in the richest
58: 13 if you call the Sabbath a *d*
61: 10 I *d* greatly in the Lord;
62: 4 for the Lord will take *d* in you,
65: 18 for I will create Jerusalem to be a *d*
65: 19 and take *d* in my people;
66: 3 their souls *d* in their abominations;
66: 11 *d* in her overflowing abundance."
Jer 9: 24 for in these I *d*,"
15: 16 they were my joy and my heart's *d*,
31: 20 the child in whom I *d*?
49: 25 the town in which I *d*?
Eze 24: 16 away from you the *d* of your eyes.
24: 21 in which you take pride, the *d*
24: 25 and glory, the *d* of their eyes,
Hos 7: 3 *d* the king with their wickedness,
Mic 1: 16 for the children in whom you *d*;
7: 18 but *d* to show mercy.
Zep 3: 17 He will take great *d* in you,
Mt 12: 18 the one I love, in whom I *d*;
Mk 12: 37 large crowd listened to him with *d*.
Lk 1: 14 He will be a joy and *d* to you,
Ro 7: 22 in my inner being I *d* in God's law;
1Co 13: 6 Love does not *d* in evil
2Co 12: 10 for Christ's sake, I *d* in weaknesses,
Col 2: 5 and *d* to see how orderly you are

DELIGHTED (DELIGHT)

2Sa 22: 20 he rescued me because he *d* in me.
1Ki 10: 9 who has *d* in you and placed you
2Ch 9: 8 who has *d* in you and placed you
Ps 18: 19 he rescued me because he *d* in me.
Lk 13: 17 but the people were *d* with all

DELIGHTFUL* (DELIGHT)
Ps   16: 6 surely I have a *d* inheritance.
SS   1: 2 for your love is more *d* than wine.
    4: 10 How *d* is your love, my sister,
Mal 3: 12 for yours will be a *d* land,"

DELIGHTING* (DELIGHT)
Pr   8: 31 and *d* in mankind.

DELIGHTS (DELIGHT)
Est   6: 6 for the man the king *d* to honour?"
Ps 22: 8 since he *d* in him."
   35: 27 who *d* in the well-being
   36: 8 from your river of *d*.
   37: 23 The LORD *d* in the way of the man
 147: 11 the LORD *d* in those who fear him,
Pr   3: 12 as a father the son he *d* in.
   10: 23 of understanding *d* in wisdom.
   11: 20 he *d* in those whose ways are
   12: 22 but he *d* in men who are truthful.
   14: 35 A king *d* in a wise servant,
   18: 2 but *d* in airing his own opinions.
   23: 24 he who has a wise son *d* in him.
Col 2: 18 Do not let anyone who *d*

DELILAH*
Woman who betrayed Samson (Jdg 16:4-22).

DELIVER (DELIVERANCE DELIVERED DELIVERER DELIVERS)
Dt 32: 39 and no-one can *d* out of my hand.
Ps 22: 8 Let him *d* him,
   72: 12 For he will *d* the needy who cry out
   79: 9 *d* us and atone for our sins
 109: 21 of the goodness of your love, *d* me.
 119: 170 *d* me according to your promise.
Mt   6: 13 but *d* us from the evil one.'
2Co 1: 10 hope that he will continue to *d* us,

DELIVERANCE (DELIVER)
1Sa 2: 1 for I delight in your *d*.
Ps   3: 8 From the LORD comes *d*.
   32: 7 and surround me with songs of *d*.
   33: 17 A horse is a vain hope for *d*;
Ob   : 17 But on Mount Zion will be *d*;

DELIVERED (DELIVER)
Ps 34: 4 he *d* me from all my fears.
 107: 6 and he *d* them from their distress.
 116: 8 have *d* my soul from death,
Da 12: 1 written in the book—will be *d*.
Ro   4: 25 He was *d* over to death for our sins

DELIVERER* (DELIVER)
Jdg 3: 9 for them a *d*, Othniel son of Kenaz,
   3: 15 he gave them a *d*—Ehud,
2Sa 22: 2 is my rock, my fortress and my *d*;
2Ki 13: 5 The LORD provided a *d* for Israel,
Ps 18: 2 is my rock, my fortress and my *d*;
   40: 17 You are my help and my *d*;
   70: 5 You are my help and my *d*;
 140: 7 O Sovereign LORD, my strong *d*,
 144: 2 my stronghold and my *d*,
Ac   7: 35 sent to be their ruler and *d*
Ro 11: 26 "The *d* will come from Zion;

DELIVERS (DELIVER)
Ps 34: 17 he *d* them from all their troubles.
   34: 19 but the LORD *d* him from them all

Ps 37: 40 The LORD helps them and *d* them
   37: 40 he *d* them from the wicked

DELUSION*
2Th 2: 11 God sends them a powerful *d*

DEMAND (DEMANDED)
Lk   6: 30 belongs to you, do not *d* it back.

DEMANDED (DEMAND)
Lk 12: 20 This very night your life will be *d*
   12: 48 been given much, much will be *d*;

DEMETRIUS
Ac 19: 24 A silversmith named *D*, who made

DEMON* (DEMONS)
Mt   9: 33 And when the *d* was driven out,
   11: 18 and they say, 'He has a *d*.'
   17: 18 Jesus rebuked the *d*, and it came
Mk   7: 26 to drive the *d* out of her daughter.
   7: 29 the *d* has left your daughter."
   7: 30 lying on the bed, and the *d* gone.
Lk   4: 33 there was a man possessed by a *d*,
   4: 35 Then the *d* threw the man
   7: 33 wine, and you say, 'He has a *d*.'
   8: 29 driven by the *d* into solitary places.
   9: 42 the *d* threw him to the ground
   11: 14 When the *d* left, the man who had
   11: 14 was driving out a *d* that was mute.
Jn   8: 49 "I am not possessed by a *d*,"
   10: 21 Can a *d* open the eyes of the blind
   10: 21 sayings of a man possessed by a *d*.

DEMON-POSSESSED* (DEMON-POSSESSION)
Mt   4: 24 those suffering severe pain, the *d*,
   8: 16 many who were *d* were brought
   8: 28 two *d* men coming
   8: 33 what had happened to the *d* men.
   9: 32 man who was *d* and could not talk
   12: 22 they brought him a *d* man who was
Mk   1: 32 brought to Jesus all the sick and *d*,
   5: 16 what had happened to the *d* man—
   5: 18 the man who had been *d* begged
Lk   8: 27 met by a *d* man from the town.
   8: 36 the people how the *d* man had been
Jn   7: 20 "You are *d*," the crowd answered.
   8: 48 that you are a Samaritan and *d*?"
   8: 52 "Now we know that you are *d*!
   10: 20 Many of them said, "He is *d*
Ac 19: 13 Jesus over those who were *d*.

DEMON-POSSESSION* (DEMON-POSSESSED)
Mt 15: 22 is suffering terribly from *d*."

DEMONS* (DEMON)
Dt 32: 17 to *d*, which are not God—
Ps 106: 37 and their daughters to *d*.
Mt   7: 22 and in your name drive out *d*
   8: 31 *d* begged Jesus, "If you drive us
   9: 34 prince of *d* that he drives out *d*."
   10: 8 who have leprosy, drive out *d*.
   12: 24 of *d*, that this fellow drives out
   12: 24 that this fellow drives out *d*."
   12: 27 And if I drive out *d* by Beelzebub,
   12: 28 if I drive out *d* by the Spirit of God,
Mk   1: 34 He also drove out many *d*,
   1: 34 but he would not let the *d* speak
   1: 39 their synagogues and driving out *d*.
   3: 15 to have authority to drive out *d*.

Mk 3: 22 the prince of *d* he is driving out *d*."
   5: 12 The *d* begged Jesus, "Send us
   5: 15 possessed by the legion of *d*,
   6: 13 They drove out many *d*
   9: 38 "we saw a man driving out *d*
   16: 9 out of whom he had driven seven *d*
   16: 17 In my name they will drive out *d*;
Lk 4: 41 *d* came out of many people,
   8: 2 from whom seven *d* had come out;
   8: 30 because many *d* had gone into him.
   8: 32 The *d* begged Jesus to let them go
   8: 33 When the *d* came out of the man,
   8: 35 from whom the *d* had gone out,
   8: 38 from whom the *d* had gone out
   9: 1 and authority to drive out all *d*
   9: 49 "we saw a man driving out *d*
   10: 17 the *d* submit to us in your name."
   11: 15 the prince of *d*, he is driving out *d*."
   11: 18 you claim that I drive out *d*
   11: 19 Now if I drive out *d* by Beelzebub,
   11: 20 if I drive out *d* by the finger of God,
   13: 32 'I will drive out *d* and heal people
Ro 8: 38 neither angels nor *d*, neither
1Co 10: 20 of pagans are offered to *d*,
   10: 20 you to be participants with *d*.
   10: 21 of the Lord and the cup of *d* too;
   10: 21 the Lord's table and the table of *d*.
1Ti 4: 1 spirits and things taught by *d*.
Jas 2: 19 Good! Even the *d* believe that—
Rev 9: 20 they did not stop worshipping *d*,
   16: 14 of *d* performing miraculous signs,
   18: 2 She has become a home for *d*

DEMONSTRATE* (DEMONSTRATES DEMONSTRATION)

Ro 3: 25 He did this to *d* his justice,
   3: 26 he did it to *d* his justice

DEMONSTRATES* (DEMONSTRATE)

Ro 5: 8 God *d* his own love for us in this:

DEMONSTRATION* (DEMONSTRATE)

1Co 2: 4 but with a *d* of the Spirit's power,

DEN

Da 6: 16 and threw him into the lions' *d*.
Mt 21: 13 you are making it a '*d* of robbers.' "
Mk 11: 17 you have made it 'a *d* of robbers.' "
Lk 19: 46 but you have made it 'a *d* of robbers

DENARII* (DENARIUS)

Mt 18: 28 who owed him a hundred *d*.
Lk 7: 41 One owed him five hundred *d*,

DENARIUS (DENARII)

Mt 20: 2 agreed to pay them a *d* for the day
Mk 12: 15 Bring me a *d* and let me look at it."

DENIED (DENY)

Mt 26: 70 But he *d* it before them all.
Mk 14: 68 But he *d* it.
Lk 22: 57 But he *d* it.
Jn 18: 25 He *d* it, saying, "I am not."
1Ti 5: 8 he has *d* the faith and is worse
Rev 3: 8 my word and have not *d* my name.

DENIES (DENY)

1Jn 2: 22 It is the man who *d* that Jesus is
   2: 23 No-one who *d* the Son has

DENY (DENIED DENIES DENYING)

Ex 23: 6 "Do not *d* justice to your poor
Job 27: 5 till I die, I will not *d* my integrity.
Isa 5: 23 but *d* justice to the innocent.
La 3: 35 to *d* a man his rights
Am 2: 7 and *d* justice to the oppressed.
Mt 16: 24 he must *d* himself and take up his
Mk 8: 34 he must *d* himself and take up his
Lk 9: 23 he must *d* himself and take up his
   22: 34 you will *d* three times that you
Ac 4: 16 miracle, and we cannot *d* it.
Tit 1: 16 but by their actions they *d* him.
Jas 3: 14 do not boast about it or *d* the truth.
Jude : 4 *d* Jesus Christ our only Sovereign

DENYING* (DENY)

Eze 22: 29 mistreat the alien, *d* them justice.
2Ti 3: 5 a form of godliness but *d* its power.
2Pe 2: 1 the sovereign Lord who bought

DEPART (DEPARTED DEPARTS DEPARTURE)

Ge 49: 10 The sceptre will not *d* from Judah,
Job 1: 21 and naked I will *d*.
Mt 25: 41 '*D* from me, you who are cursed,
Php 1: 23 I desire to *d* and be with Christ,

DEPARTED (DEPART)

1Sa 4: 21 "The glory has *d* from Israel"—
Ps 119: 102 I have not *d* from your laws,

DEPARTS (DEPART)

Ecc 5: 15 and as he comes, so he *d*.

DEPARTURE (DEPART)

Lk 9: 31 spoke about his *d*, which he was
2Ti 4: 6 and the time has come for my *d*.
2Pe 1: 15 after my *d* you will always be able

DEPEND

Ps 62: 7 My salvation and my honour *d*

DEPOSES*

Da 2: 21 he sets up kings and *d* them.

DEPOSIT

Mt 25: 27 money on *d* with the bankers,
Lk 19: 23 didn't you put my money on *d*,
2Co 1: 22 put his Spirit in our hearts as a *d*,
   5: 5 and has given us the Spirit as a *d*,
Eph 1: 14 who is a *d* guaranteeing our
2Ti 1: 14 Guard the good *d* that was

DEPRAVED* (DEPRAVITY)

Eze 16: 47 ways you soon became more *d*
   23: 11 and prostitution she was more *d*
Ro 1: 28 he gave them over to a *d* mind,
Php 2: 15 fault in a crooked and *d* generation,
2Ti 3: 8 oppose the truth—men of *d* minds,

DEPRAVITY* (DEPRAVED)

Ro 1: 29 of wickedness, evil, greed and *d*.
2Pe 2: 19 they themselves are slaves of *d*—

DEPRIVE

Dt 24: 17 Do not *d* the alien or the fatherless
Pr 18: 5 or to *d* the innocent of justice.
   31: 5 *d* all the oppressed of their rights.
Isa 10: 2 to *d* the poor of their rights

Isa 29: 21 with false testimony *d* the innocent
La 3: 36 to *d* a man of justice—
1Co 7: 5 Do not *d* each other
 9: 15 die than have anyone *d* me

DEPTH (DEEP)

Ro 8: 39 any powers, neither height nor *d*,
 11: 33 the *d* of the riches of the wisdom

DEPTHS (DEEP)

Ps 130: 1 Out of the *d* I cry to you, O LORD;

DERIDES*

Pr 11: 12 who lacks judgment *d* his neighbour,

DERIVES*

Eph 3: 15 in heaven and on earth *d* its name.

DESCEND (DESCENDED DESCENDING)

Ro 10: 7 "or 'Who will *d* into the deep?'"

DESCENDED (DESCEND)

Eph 4: 9 except that he also *d* to the lower,
Heb 7: 14 For it is clear that our Lord *d*

DESCENDING (DESCEND)

Ge 28: 12 of God were ascending and *d* on it.
Mt 3: 16 the Spirit of God *d* like a dove
Mk 1: 10 and the Spirit *d* on him like a dove.
Jn 1: 51 and *d* on the Son of Man."

DESECRATING*

Ne 13: 17 you are doing—*d* the Sabbath day?
 13: 18 against Israel by *d* the Sabbath.
Isa 56: 2 who keeps the Sabbath without *d* it
 56: 6 who keep the Sabbath without *d* it
Eze 44: 7 *d* my temple while you offered me

DESERT

Nu 32: 13 wander in the *d* forty years,
Dt 8: 16 He gave you manna to eat in the *d*,
 29: 5 years that I led you through the *d*,
Ne 9: 19 you did not abandon them in the *d*.
Ps 78: 19 "Can God spread a table in the *d*?
 78: 52 led them like sheep through the *d*.
Pr 21: 19 Better to live in a *d*
Isa 32: 2 like streams of water in the *d*
 32: 15 and the *d* becomes a fertile field,
 35: 6 and streams in the *d*.
 43: 20 because I provide water in the *d*
Mk 1: 3 "a voice of one calling in the *d*,
 1: 13 and he was in the *d* forty days,
Rev 12: 6 fled into the *d* to a place prepared

DESERTED (DESERTS)

Ezr 9: 9 our God has not *d* us
Mt 26: 56 all the disciples *d* him and fled.
2Ti 1: 15 in the province of Asia has *d* me,

DESERTING (DESERTS)

Gal 1: 6 are so quickly *d* the one who called

DESERTS (DESERTED DESERTING)

Zec 11: 17 who *d* the flock!

DESERVE* (DESERVED DESERVES)

Ge 40: 15 to *d* being put in a dungeon."
Lev 26: 21 times over, as your sins *d*
Jdg 20: 10 it can give them what they *d*
1Sa 26: 16 you and your men *d* to die,

1Ki 2: 26 You *d* to die, but I will not put you
Ps 28: 4 bring back upon them what they *d*.
 94: 2 pay back to the proud what they *d*.
 103: 10 he does not treat us as our sins *d*
Pr 3: 27 from those who *d* it,
Ecc 8: 14 men who get what the righteous *d*.
 8: 14 men who get what the wicked *d*,
Isa 66: 6 repaying his enemies all they *d*.
Jer 14: 16 out on them the calamity they *d*.
 17: 10 according to what his deeds *d*."
 21: 14 I will punish you as your deeds *d*,
 32: 19 to his conduct and as his deeds *d*.
 49: 12 "If those who do not *d*
La 3: 64 Pay them back what they *d*,
Eze 16: 59 I will deal with you as you *d*,
Zec 1: 6 to us what our ways and practices *d*
Mt 8: 8 I do not *d* to have you come
 22: 8 those I invited did not *d* to come.
Lk 7: 6 for I do not *d* to have you come
 23: 15 he has done nothing to *d* death.
 23: 41 for we are getting what our deeds *d*
Ro 1: 32 those who do such things *d* death,
1Co 15: 9 even *d* to be called an apostle,
 16: 18 Such men *d* recognition.
2Co 11: 15 end will be what their actions *d*.
Rev 16: 6 blood to drink as they *d*."

DESERVED* (DESERVE)

2Sa 19: 28 descendants *d* nothing
Ezr 9: 13 less than our sins have *d*
Job 33: 27 but I did not get what I *d*.
Ac 23: 29 charge against him that *d* death
Ro 3: 8 Their condemnation is *d*.

DESERVES* (DESERVE)

Nu 35: 31 the life of a murderer, who *d* to die.
Dt 25: 2 If the guilty man *d* to be beaten,
 25: 2 the number of lashes his crime *d*,
Jdg 9: 16 and if you have treated him as he *d*
2Sa 12: 5 the man who did this *d* to die!
Job 34: 11 upon him what his conduct *d*.
Jer 51: 6 he will pay her what she *d*.
Lk 7: 4 "This man *d* to have you do this,
 10: 7 for the worker *d* his wages.
Ac 26: 31 is not doing anything that *d* death
1Ti 1: 15 saying that *d* full acceptance:
 4: 9 saying that *d* full acceptance
 5: 18 and "The worker *d* his wages."
Heb 10: 29 severely do you think a man *d*

DESIGNATED

Lk 6: 13 also *d* apostles: Simon (whom he
Heb 5: 10 and was *d* by God to be high priest

DESIRABLE* (DESIRE)

Ge 3: 6 and also *d* for gaining wisdom,
Pr 22: 1 A good name is more *d*
Jer 3: 19 and give you a *d* land,

DESIRE* (DESIRABLE DESIRED DESIRES)

Ge 3: 16 Your *d* will be for your husband,
Dt 5: 21 You shall not set your *d*
1Sa 9: 20 to whom is all the *d* of Israel turned
2Sa 19: 38 anything you *d* from me I will do
 23: 5 and grant me my every *d*?
1Ch 29: 18 keep this *d* in their hearts
2Ch 1: 11 "Since this is your heart's *d*
 9: 8 and his *d* to uphold them for ever,
Job 13: 3 But I *d* to speak to the Almighty
 21: 14 We have no *d* to know your ways.

Ps	10: 17	O Lord, the *d* of the afflicted;
	20: 4	May he give you the *d*
	21: 2	You have granted him the *d*
	27: 12	me over to the *d* of my foes,
	40: 6	Sacrifice and offering you did not *d*
	40: 8	I *d* to do your will, O my God;
	40: 14	may all who *d* my ruin
	41: 2	him to the *d* of his foes.
	51: 6	Surely you *d* truth
	70: 2	may all who *d* my ruin
	73: 25	being with you, I *d* nothing
Pr	3: 15	nothing you *d* can compare
	8: 11	and nothing you *d* can compare
	10: 24	what the righteous *d* will be
	11: 23	The *d* of the righteous ends only
	12: 12	The wicked *d* the plunder
	17: 16	since he has no *d* to get wisdom?
	24: 1	do not *d* their company;
Ecc	12: 5	and *d* no longer is stirred.
SS	6: 12	my *d* set me among the royal
	7: 10	and his *d* is for me.
Isa	26: 8	are the *d* of our hearts.
	53: 2	appearance that we should *d* him.
	55: 11	but will accomplish what I *d*
Eze	24: 25	delight of their eyes, their heart's *d*,
Hos	6: 6	For I *d* mercy, not sacrifice,
Mic	7: 3	the powerful dictate what they *d*—
Mal	3: 1	whom you *d*, will come," says
Mt	9: 13	learn what this means: 'I *d* mercy,
	12: 7	what these words mean, 'I *d* mercy,
Jn	8: 44	want to carry out your father's *d*.
Ro	7: 8	in me every kind of covetous *d*.
	7: 18	For I have the *d* to do what is good,
	9: 16	depend on man's *d* or effort,
	10: 1	my heart's *d* and prayer to God
1Co	12: 31	But eagerly *d* the greater gifts.
	14: 1	and eagerly *d* spiritual gifts,
2Co	8: 10	but also to have the *d* to do so.
	8: 13	Our *d* is not that others might be
Php	1: 23	I *d* to depart and be with Christ,
Heb	10: 5	Sacrifice and offering you did not *d*
	10: 8	and sin offerings you did not *d*,
	13: 18	*d* to live honourably in every way.
Jas	1: 14	by his own evil *d*, he is dragged
	1: 15	Then, after *d* has conceived,
2Pe	2: 10	of those who follow the corrupt *d*

DESIRED (DESIRE)

Hag	2: 7	and the *d* of all nations will come,
Lk	22: 15	"I have eagerly *d* to eat this

DESIRES* (DESIRE)

Ge	4: 7	at your door; it *d* to have you,
	41: 16	will give Pharaoh the answer he *d*."
2Sa	3: 21	rule over all that your heart *d*."
1Ki	11: 37	rule over all that your heart *d*;
Job	17: 11	and so are the *d* of my heart.
	31: 16	"If I have denied the *d* of the poor
Ps	34: 12	and *d* to see many good days,
	37: 4	he will give you the *d* of your heart.
	103: 5	He satisfies my *d* with good things,
	140: 8	do not grant the wicked their *d*,
	145: 16	satisfy the *d* of every living thing.
	145: 19	He fulfils the *d* of those who fear
Pr	11: 6	the unfaithful are trapped by evil *d*.
	13: 4	*d* of the diligent are fully satisfied.
	19: 22	What a man *d* is unfailing love;
Ecc	6: 2	so that he lacks nothing his heart *d*,
SS	2: 7	or awaken love/until it so *d*.
	3: 5	or awaken love/until it so *d*.

SS	8: 4	or awaken love/until it so *d*.
Hab	2: 4	his *d* are not upright—
Mk	4: 19	and the *d* for other things come in
Ro	1: 24	over in the sinful *d* of their hearts
	6: 12	body so that you obey its evil *d*.
	8: 5	set on what that nature *d*;
	8: 5	set on what the Spirit *d*.
	13: 14	to gratify the *d* of the sinful nature.
Gal	5: 16	and you will not gratify the *d*
	5: 17	the sinful nature *d* what is contrary
	5: 24	nature with its passions and *d*.
Eph	2: 3	and following its *d* and thoughts.
	4: 22	being corrupted by its deceitful *d*;
Col	3: 5	impurity, lust, evil *d* and greed,
1Ti	3: 1	an overseer, he *d* a noble task.
	5: 11	their sensual *d* overcome their
	6: 9	and harmful *d* that plunge men
2Ti	2: 22	Flee the evil *d* of youth,
	3: 6	are swayed by all kinds of evil *d*,
	4: 3	Instead, to suit their own *d*,
Jas	1: 20	about the righteous life that God *d*.
	4: 1	from your *d* that battle within you?
1Pe	1: 14	conform to the evil *d* you had
	2: 11	to abstain from sinful *d*, which war
	4: 2	of his earthly life for evil human *d*,
2Pe	1: 4	in the world caused by evil *d*.
	2: 18	to the lustful *d* of sinful human
	3: 3	and following their own evil *d*.
1Jn	2: 17	The world and its *d* pass away,
Jude	: 16	they follow their own evil *d*;
	: 18	will follow their own ungodly *d*."

DESOLATE (DESOLATION)

Isa	54: 1	are the children of the *d* woman
Gal	4: 27	are the children of the *d* woman

DESOLATION (DESOLATE)

Da	11: 31	up the abomination that causes *d*.
	12: 11	abomination that causes *d* is set up,
Mt	24: 15	'the abomination that causes *d*,'

DESPAIR (DESPAIRED)

Isa	61: 3	instead of a spirit of *d*.
2Co	4: 8	perplexed, but not in *d*; persecuted,

DESPAIRED* (DESPAIR)

2Co	1: 8	ability to endure, so that we *d*

DESPERATE*

2Sa	12: 18	He may do something *d*."
Ps	60: 3	have shown your people *d* times;
	79: 8	for we are in *d* need.
	142: 6	for I am in *d* need;

DESPISE (DESPISED DESPISES)

2Sa	12: 9	Why did you *d* the word
Job	5: 17	so do not *d* the discipline
	36: 5	God is mighty, but does not *d* men;
	42: 6	Therefore I *d* myself
Ps	51: 17	O God, you will not *d*.
	102: 17	he will not *d* their plea.
Pr	1: 7	but fools *d* wisdom and discipline.
	3: 11	do not *d* the Lord's discipline
	6: 30	Men do not *d* a thief if he steals
	23: 22	do not *d* your mother
Jer	14: 21	of your name do not *d* us;
Am	5: 10	and *d* him who tells the truth.
	5: 21	"I hate, I *d* your religious feasts;
Mt	6: 24	devoted to the one and *d* the other.
Lk	16: 13	devoted to the one and *d* the other.

1Co 11: 22 Or do you *d* the church of God
Tit 2: 15 Do not let anyone *d* you.
2Pe 2: 10 of the sinful nature and *d* authority.

DESPISED (DESPISE)

Ge 25: 34 So Esau *d* his birthright.
Ps 22: 6 by men and *d* by the people.
Pr 12: 8 but men with warped minds are *d*.
Isa 53: 3 He was *d* and rejected by men,
53: 3 he was *d*, and we esteemed him not
1Co 1: 28 of this world and the *d* things—

DESPISES (DESPISE)

Pr 14: 21 He who *d* his neighbour sins,
15: 20 but a foolish man *d* his mother.
15: 32 who ignores discipline *d* himself,
Zec 4: 10 "Who *d* the day of small things?

DESTINED (DESTINY)

Lk 2: 34 "This child is *d* to cause the falling
1Co 2: 7 and that God *d* for our glory
Col 2: 22 These are all *d* to perish with use,
1Th 3: 3 know quite well that we were *d*
Heb 9: 27 Just as man is *d* to die once,
1Pe 2: 8 which is also what they were *d* for.

DESTINY* (DESTINED PREDESTINED)

Job 8: 13 Such is the *d* of all who forget God;
Ps 73: 17 then I understood their final *d*.
Ecc 7: 2 for death is the *d* of every man;
9: 2 share a common *d*—the righteous
9: 3 the sun: The same *d* overtakes all.
Isa 65: 11 and fill bowls of mixed wine for *D*,
Php 3: 19 Their *d* is destruction, their god is

DESTITUTE

Ps 102: 17 to the prayer of the *d*;
Pr 31: 8 for the rights of all who are *d*.
Heb 11: 37 *d*, persecuted and ill-treated—

**DESTROY (DESTROYED DESTROYING
DESTROYS DESTRUCTION DESTRUCTIVE)**

Ge 6: 17 floodwaters on the earth to *d* all life
9: 11 will there be a flood to *d* the earth."
Pr 1: 32 complacency of fools will *d* them;
Mt 10: 28 of the one who can *d* both soul
Mk 14: 58 'I will *d* this man-made temple
Lk 4: 34 to *d* us? I know who you are—
Jn 10: 10 only to steal and kill and *d*;
Ac 8: 3 But Saul began to *d* the church.
Rev 11: 18 destroying those who *d* the earth."

DESTROYED (DESTROY)

Dt 8: 19 you today that you will surely be *d*.
Job 19: 26 And after my skin has been *d*,
Pr 6: 15 he will suddenly be *d*—
11: 3 the unfaithful are *d*
21: 28 listens to him will be *d* for ever.
29: 1 will suddenly be *d*—
Isa 55: 13 which will not be *d*."
Da 2: 44 up a kingdom that will never be *d*,
6: 26 his kingdom will not be *d*,
1Co 5: 5 so that the sinful nature may be *d*
8: 11 for whom Christ died, is *d*
15: 24 Father after he has *d* all dominion,
15: 26 The last enemy to be *d* is death.
2Co 4: 9 abandoned; struck down, but not *d*.
5: 1 if the earthly tent we live in is *d*,
Gal 5: 15 or you will be *d* by each other.
Eph 2: 14 the two one and has *d* the barrier,

2Ti 1: 10 who has *d* death and has brought
Heb 10: 39 of those who shrink back and are *d*,
2Pe 2: 12 born only to be caught and *d*,
3: 10 the elements will be *d* by fire,
3: 11 Since everything will be *d*
Jude : 5 later *d* those who did not believe.
: 11 have been *d* in Korah's rebellion.

DESTROYING (DESTROY)

Jer 23: 1 "Woe to the shepherds who are *d*

DESTROYS (DESTROY)

Pr 6: 32 whoever does so *d* himself.
11: 9 mouth the godless *d* his neighbour,
18: 9 is brother to one who *d*.
28: 24 he is partner to him who *d*.
Ecc 9: 18 but one sinner *d* much good.
1Co 3: 17 If anyone *d* God's temple,

DESTRUCTION (DESTROY)

Nu 32: 15 and you will be the cause of their *d*
Pr 16: 18 Pride goes before *d*,
17: 19 he who builds a high gate invites *d*.
24: 22 for those two will send sudden *d*
Hos 13: 14 Where, O grave, is your *d*?
Mt 7: 13 broad is the road that leads to *d*,
Lk 6: 49 it collapsed and its *d* was complete
Jn 17: 12 except the one doomed to *d*
Ro 9: 22 of his wrath—prepared for *d*?
Gal 6: 8 from that nature will reap *d*;
Php 3: 19 Their destiny is *d*, their god is their
1Th 5: 3 *d* will come on them suddenly,
2Th 1: 9 punished with everlasting *d*
2: 3 is revealed, the man doomed to *d*.
1Ti 6: 9 that plunge men into ruin and *d*.
2Pe 2: 1 bringing swift *d* on themselves.
2: 3 and their *d* has not been sleeping.
3: 7 of judgment and *d* of ungodly men.
3: 12 That day will bring about the *d*
3: 16 other Scriptures, to their own *d*.
Rev 17: 8 out of the Abyss and go to his *d*.
17: 11 to the seven and is going to his *d*.

DESTRUCTIVE (DESTROY)

2Pe 2: 1 will secretly introduce *d* heresies,

DETERMINED (DETERMINES)

Job 14: 5 Man's days are *d*;
Isa 14: 26 This is the plan *d* for the whole
Da 11: 36 for what has been *d* must take place
Ac 17: 26 and he *d* the times set for them

DETERMINES* (DETERMINED)

Ps 147: 4 He *d* the number of the stars
Pr 16: 9 but the LORD *d* his steps.
1Co 12: 11 them to each one, just as he *d*.

**DETEST (DETESTABLE DETESTED
DETESTS)**

Lev 11: 10 in the water—you are to *d*.
Pr 8: 7 for my lips *d* wickedness.
13: 19 but fools *d* turning from evil.
16: 12 Kings *d* wrongdoing,
24: 9 and men *d* a mocker.
29: 27 The righteous *d* the dishonest;
29: 27 the wicked *d* the upright.

DETESTABLE (DETEST)

Pr 6: 16 seven that are *d* to him:
21: 27 The sacrifice of the wicked is *d*—

Pr 28: 9 even his prayers are *d*.
Isa 1: 13 Your incense is *d* to me.
    41: 24 he who chooses you is *d*.
    44: 19 Shall I make a *d* thing
Jer 44: 4 'Do not do this *d* thing that I hate!'
Eze 8: 13 doing things that are even more *d*."
Lk 16: 15 among men is *d* in God's sight.
Tit 1: 16 They are *d*, disobedient
1Pe 4: 3 orgies, carousing and *d* idolatry.

DETESTED* (DETEST)

Zec 11: 8 The flock *d* me, and I grew weary

DETESTS* (DETEST)

Dt 22: 5 LORD your God *d* anyone who
    23: 18 the LORD your God *d* them both.
    25: 16 LORD your God *d* anyone who
Pr 3: 32 for the LORD *d* a perverse man
    11: 20 The LORD *d* men
    12: 22 The LORD *d* lying lips,
    15: 8 The LORD *d* the sacrifice
    15: 9 The LORD *d* the way
    15: 26 The LORD *d* the thoughts
    16: 5 The LORD *d* all the proud of heart
    17: 15 the LORD *d* them both.
    20: 10 the LORD *d* them both.
    20: 23 The LORD *d* differing weights,

DEVIATE*

2Ch 8: 15 They did not *d* from the king's

DEVICES*

Ps 81: 12 to follow their own *d*.

DEVIL* (DEVIL'S)

Mt 4: 1 the desert to be tempted by the *d*.
    4: 5 the *d* took him to the holy city
    4: 8 *d* took him to a very high mountain
    4: 11 the *d* left him, and angels came
    13: 39 the enemy who sows them is the *d*.
    25: 41 the eternal fire prepared for the *d*
Lk 4: 2 forty days he was tempted by the *d*.
    4: 3 *d* said to him, "If you are the Son
    4: 5 The *d* led him up to a high place
    4: 9 The *d* led him to Jerusalem
    4: 13 When the *d* had finished all this
    8: 12 then the *d* comes and takes away
Jn 6: 70 of you is a *d*!" (He meant Judas,
    8: 44 You belong to your father, the *d*,
    13: 2 the *d* had already prompted Judas
Ac 10: 38 were under the power of the *d*,
    13: 10 "You are a child of the *d*
Eph 4: 27 and do not give the *d* a foothold.
1Ti 3: 6 under the same judgment as the *d*.
2Ti 2: 26 and escape from the trap of the *d*,
Heb 2: 14 the *d*—and free those who all their
Jas 3: 15 but is earthly, unspiritual, of the *d*.
    4: 7 Resist the *d*, and he will flee
1Pe 5: 8 Your enemy the *d* prowls
1Jn 3: 8 because the *d* has been sinning
    3: 8 who does what is sinful is of the *d*,
    3: 10 and who the children of the *d* are:
Jude : 9 with the *d* about the body of Moses
Rev 2: 10 the *d* will put some of you in prison
    12: 9 that ancient serpent called the *d*
    12: 12 has gone down to you!
    20: 2 that ancient serpent, who is the *d*,
    20: 10 And the *d*, who deceived them,

DEVIL'S* (DEVIL)

Eph 6: 11 stand against the *d* schemes.
1Ti 3: 7 into disgrace and into the *d* trap.
1Jn 3: 8 was to destroy the *d* work.

DEVILS see DEMONS

DEVIOUS*

Pr 2: 15 and who are *d* in their ways.
    14: 2 he whose ways are *d* despises him.
    21: 8 The way of the guilty is *d*,

DEVOTE* (DEVOTED DEVOTING DEVOTION DEVOUT)

1Ch 22: 19 Now *d* your heart and soul
2Ch 31: 4 Levites so they could *d* themselves
Job 11: 13 "Yet if you *d* your heart to him
Jer 30: 21 for who is he who will *d* himself
Mic 4: 13 You will *d* their ill-gotten gains
1Co 7: 5 so that you may *d* yourselves
Col 4: 2 *D* yourselves to prayer, being
1Ti 1: 4 nor to *d* themselves to myths
    4: 13 *d* yourself to the public reading
Tit 3: 8 may be careful to *d* themselves
    3: 14 people must learn to *d* themselves

DEVOTED (DEVOTE)

1Ki 11: 4 and his heart was not fully *d*
Ezr 7: 10 For Ezra had *d* himself to the study
Ps 86: 2 Guard my life, for I am *d* to you.
Mt 6: 24 or he will be *d* to the one
Mk 7: 11 from me is Corban' (that is, a gift *d*
Ac 2: 42 They *d* themselves
    18: 5 Paul *d* himself exclusively
Ro 12: 10 Be *d* to one another
1Co 7: 34 Her aim is to be *d* to the Lord
    16: 15 and they have *d* themselves
2Co 7: 12 for yourselves how *d* to us you are.

DEVOTING* (DEVOTE)

1Ti 5: 10 *d* herself to all kinds of good deeds.

DEVOTION* (DEVOTE)

2Ki 20: 3 and with wholehearted *d* and have
1Ch 28: 9 and serve him with wholehearted *d*
    29: 3 in my *d* to the temple
    29: 19 son Solomon the wholehearted *d*
2Ch 32: 32 and his acts of *d* are written
    35: 26 of Josiah's reign and his acts of *d*,
Job 6: 14 despairing man should have the *d*
    15: 4 and hinder *d* to God.
Isa 38: 3 and with wholehearted *d* and have
Jer 2: 2 "'I remember the *d* of your youth,
Eze 33: 31 With their mouths they express *d*,
1Co 7: 35 way in undivided *d* to the Lord.
2Co 11: 3 from your sincere and pure *d*

DEVOUR (DEVOURED DEVOURING DEVOURS)

2Sa 2: 26 "Must the sword *d* for ever?
Mk 12: 40 They *d* widows' houses
1Pe 5: 8 lion looking for someone to *d*.

DEVOURED (DEVOUR)

Jer 30: 16 But all who devour you will be *d*;

DEVOURING (DEVOUR)

Gal 5: 15 keep on biting and *d* each other,

DEVOURS (DEVOUR)

2Sa 11: 25 the sword *d* one as well as another.
Pr 21: 20 but a foolish man *d* all he has.

DEVOUT* (DEVOTE)

1Ki 18: 3 (Obadiah was a *d* believer
Isa 57: 1 *d* men are taken away,
Lk 2: 25 Simeon, who was righteous and *d*.
Ac 10: 2 his family were *d* and God-fearing;
10: 7 a *d* soldier who was one
13: 43 and *d* converts to Judaism followed
22: 12 He was a *d* observer of the law

DEW

Jdg 6: 37 If there is *d* only on the fleece

DICTATED

Jer 36: 4 and while Jeremiah *d* all the words

DIE (DEAD DEADENED DEATH DIED DIES DYING)

Ge 2: 17 when you eat of it you will surely *d*
3: 3 you must not touch it, or you will *d*
3: 4 will not surely *d*," the serpent said
Ex 11: 5 Every firstborn son in Egypt will *d*,
Ru 1: 17 Where you *d* I will *d*, and there I
2Ki 14: 6 each is to *d* for his own sins."
Job 2: 9 Curse God and *d*!" He replied,
Pr 5: 23 He will *d* for lack of discipline,
10: 21 but fools *d* for lack of judgment.
15: 10 he who hates correction will *d*.
23: 13 with the rod, he will not *d*.
Ecc 3: 2 a time to be born and a time to *d*,
Isa 22: 13 "for tomorrow we *d*!"
66: 24 their worm will not *d*, nor will their
Jer 31: 30 everyone will *d* for his own sin;
Eze 3: 18 that wicked man will *d* for his sin,
3: 19 he will *d* for his sin; but you will
3: 20 block before him, he will *d*.
18: 4 soul who sins is the one who will *d*.
18: 20 soul who sins is the one who will *d*.
18: 31 Why will you *d*, O house of Israel?
33: 8 'O wicked man, you will surely *d*,'
Mt 26: 52 "for all who draw the sword will *d*
Mk 9: 48 "'their worm does not *d*,
Jn 8: 21 and you will *d* in your sin.
11: 26 and believes in me will never *d*.
Ro 5: 7 Very rarely will anyone *d*
14: 8 and if we *d*, we *d* to the Lord.
1Co 15: 22 in Adam all *d*, so in Christ all will
15: 31 I *d* every day—I mean that,
15: 32 for tomorrow we *d*."
Php 1: 21 to live is Christ and to *d* is gain.
Heb 9: 27 Just as man is destined to *d* once,
1Pe 2: 24 so that we might *d* to sins
Rev 14: 13 Blessed are the dead who *d*

DIED (DIE)

1Ki 16: 18 So he *d*, because of the sins he had
1Ch 1: 51 Hadad also *d*.
10: 13 Saul *d* because he was unfaithful
Lk 16: 22 "The time came when the beggar *d*
Ro 5: 6 we were still powerless, Christ *d*
5: 8 we were still sinners, Christ *d*
6: 2 By no means! We *d* to sin;
6: 7 anyone who has *d* has been freed
6: 8 if we *d* with Christ, we believe that
6: 10 The death he *d*, he *d* to sin once
14: 9 Christ *d* and returned to life
14: 15 brother for whom Christ *d*.

1Co 8: 11 for whom Christ *d*, is destroyed
15: 3 that Christ *d* for our sins according
2Co 5: 14 *d* for all, and therefore all *d*.
5: 15 he *d* for all, that those who live
Col 2: 20 Since you *d* with Christ
3: 3 For you *d*, and your life is now
1Th 4: 14 We believe that Jesus *d*
5: 10 He *d* for us so that, whether we are
2Ti 2: 11 If we *d* with him,
Heb 9: 15 now that he has *d* as a ransom
9: 17 in force only when somebody has *d*
1Pe 3: 18 For Christ *d* for sins once for all,
Rev 2: 8 who *d* and came to life again.

DIES (DIE)

Job 14: 14 If a man *d*, will he live again?
Pr 11: 7 a wicked man *d*, his hope perishes;
26: 20 without gossip a quarrel *d* down.
Jn 11: 25 in me will live, even though he *d*;
12: 24 But if it *d*, it produces many seeds.
Ro 7: 2 but if her husband *d*, she is released
14: 7 and none of us *d* to himself alone.
1Co 7: 39 But if her husband *d*, she is free
15: 36 does not come to life unless it *d*.

DIFFERENCE* (DIFFERENT)

2Sa 19: 35 Can I tell the *d* between what is
2Ch 12: 8 so that they may learn the *d*
Eze 22: 26 they teach that there is no *d*
44: 23 are to teach my people the *d*
Ro 3: 22 There is no *d*, for all have sinned
10: 12 For there is no *d* between Jew
Gal 2: 6 whatever they were makes no *d*

DIFFERENCES* (DIFFERENT)

1Co 11: 19 to be *d* among you to show which

DIFFERENT* (DIFFERENCE DIFFERENCES DIFFERING DIFFERS)

Lev 19: 19 "'Do not mate *d* kinds of animals.
Nu 14: 24 my servant Caleb has a *d* spirit
1Sa 10: 6 you will be changed into a *d* person
Est 1: 7 each one *d* from the other,
3: 8 Their customs are *d* from those
Da 7: 3 Four great beasts, each *d*
7: 7 It was *d* from all the former beasts,
7: 19 which was *d* from all the others
7: 23 It will be *d* from all the other
7: 24 them another king will arise, *d*
11: 29 but this time the outcome will be *d*
Mk 16: 12 Jesus appeared in a *d* form
Ro 12: 6 We have *d* gifts, according
1Co 4: 7 For who makes you *d*
12: 4 There are *d* kinds of gifts,
12: 5 There are *d* kinds of service,
12: 6 There are *d* kinds of working.
12: 10 to speak in *d* kinds of tongues,
12: 28 and then those speaking in *d* kinds
2Co 11: 4 or a *d* gospel from the one you
11: 4 or if you receive a *d* spirit
Gal 1: 6 and are turning to a *d* gospel—
4: 1 he is no *d* from a slave,
Heb 7: 13 are said belonged to a *d* tribe,
Jas 2: 25 and sent them off in a *d* direction?

DIFFERING* (DIFFERENT)

Dt 25: 13 Do not have two *d* weights
25: 14 Do not have two *d* measures
Pr 20: 10 *D* weights and *d* measures

Pr 20: 23 The Lord detests *d* weights,

DIFFERS* (DIFFERENT)

1Co 15: 41 and star *d* from star in splendour.

DIFFICULT (DIFFICULTIES)

Ex 18: 22 but have them bring every *d* case
Dt 30: 11 commanding you today is not too *d*
2Ki 2: 10 "You have asked a *d* thing,"
Eze 3: 5 of obscure speech and *d* language,
Ac 15: 19 that we should not make it *d*

DIFFICULTIES* (DIFFICULT)

Dt 31: 17 and *d* will come upon them,
31: 21 when many disasters and *d* come
2Co 12: 10 in hardships, in persecutions, in *d*.

DIGNITY

Pr 31: 25 She is clothed with strength and *d*;

DIGS

Pr 26: 27 If a man *d* a pit, he will fall into it;

DILIGENCE (DILIGENT)

Ezr 5: 8 The work is being carried on with *d*
Heb 6: 11 to show this same *d* to the very end

DILIGENT (DILIGENCE)

Pr 10: 4 but *d* hands bring wealth.
12: 24 *D* hands will rule,
12: 27 the *d* man prizes his possessions.
13: 4 of the *d* are fully satisfied.
21: 5 The plans of the *d* lead to profit
1Ti 4: 15 Be *d* in these matters; give yourself

DINAH*

Only daughter of Jacob, by Leah (Ge 30:21; 46:15). Raped by Shechem; avenged by Simeon and Levi (Ge 34).

DINE

Pr 23: 1 When you sit to *d* with a ruler,

DIOTREPHES*

3Jn : 9 but *D*, who loves to be first,

DIRECT (DIRECTED DIRECTIVES DIRECTS)

Ge 18: 19 so that he will *d* his children
Dt 17: 10 to do everything they *d* you to do.
Ps 119: 35 *D* me in the path of your
119: 133 *D* my footsteps according
Jer 10: 23 it is not for man to *d* his steps.
2Th 3: 5 May the Lord *d* your hearts
1Ti 5: 17 The elders who *d* the affairs

DIRECTED (DIRECT)

Ge 24: 51 master's son, as the Lord has *d*."
Nu 16: 40 as the Lord *d* him through Moses
Dt 2: 1 Sea, as the Lord had *d* me.
6: 1 laws the Lord your God *d* me
Jos 11: 9 did to them as the Lord had *d*:
11: 23 just as the Lord had *d* Moses,
Pr 20: 24 A man's steps are *d* by the Lord.
Jer 13: 2 as the Lord *d*, and put it
Ac 7: 44 It had been made as God *d* Moses,
Tit 1: 5 elders in every town, as I *d* you.

DIRECTIVES* (DIRECT)

1Co 11: 17 In the following *d* I have no praise

DIRECTS (DIRECT)

Ps 42: 8 By day the Lord *d* his love,
Isa 48: 17 who *d* you in the way you should

DIRGE*

Mt 11: 17 we sang a *d*,
Lk 7: 32 we sang a *d*,

DISABLED*

Jn 5: 3 number of *d* people used to lie—
Heb 12: 13 so that the lame may not be *d*,

DISAGREEMENT*

Ac 15: 39 had such a sharp *d* that they parted

DISAPPEAR (DISAPPEARED DISAPPEARS)

Mt 5: 18 will by any means *d* from the Law
Lk 16: 17 earth to *d* than for the least stroke
Heb 8: 13 is obsolete and aging will soon *d*.
2Pe 3: 10 The heavens will *d* with a roar;

DISAPPEARED (DISAPPEAR)

1Ki 20: 40 busy here and there, the man *d*."

DISAPPEARS (DISAPPEAR)

1Co 13: 10 perfection comes, the imperfect *d*.

DISAPPOINT* (DISAPPOINTED)

Ro 5: 5 And hope does not *d* us,

DISAPPOINTED (DISAPPOINT)

Ps 22: 5 in you they trusted and were not *d*.

DISAPPROVE*

Pr 24: 18 or the Lord will see and *d*

DISARMED*

Col 2: 15 And having *d* the powers

DISASTER

Ex 32: 12 and do not bring *d* on your people.
Ps 57: 1 wings until the *d* has passed.
Pr 1: 26 I in turn will laugh at your *d*;
3: 25 Have no fear of sudden *d*
6: 15 Therefore *d* will overtake him
16: 4 even the wicked for a day of *d*.
17: 5 over *d* will not go unpunished.
27: 10 house when *d* strikes you—
Isa 45: 7 I bring prosperity and create *d*;
Jer 17: 17 you are my refuge in the day of *d*.
Eze 7: 5 An unheard-of *d* is coming.

DISCERN (DISCERNED DISCERNING DISCERNMENT)

Ps 19: 12 Who can *d* his errors?
139: 3 You *d* my going out and my lying
Php 1: 10 you may be able to *d* what is best

DISCERNED (DISCERN)

1Co 2: 14 because they are spiritually *d*.

DISCERNING (DISCERN)

1Ki 3: 9 So give your servant a *d* heart
3: 12 I will give you a wise and *d* heart,
Pr 1: 5 and let the *d* get guidance—
8: 9 To the *d* all of them are right;
10: 13 on the lips of the *d*,
14: 6 knowledge comes easily to the *d*.
14: 33 in the heart of the *d*

DISCERNMENT

Pr	15: 14	The *d* heart seeks knowledge,
	16: 21	The wise in heart are called *d*,
	17: 24	A *d* man keeps wisdom in view.
	17: 28	and *d* if he holds his tongue.
	18: 15	heart of the *d* acquires knowledge;
	19: 25	rebuke a *d* man, and he will gain
	28: 7	He who keeps the law is a *d* son,

DISCERNMENT (DISCERN)

Ps	119: 125	I am your servant; give me *d*
Pr	3: 21	preserve sound judgment and *d*,
	17: 10	A rebuke impresses a man of *d*
	28: 11	a poor man who has *d* sees

DISCHARGED* (DISCHARGING)

Ecc	8: 8	As no-one is *d* in time of war,

DISCHARGING* (DISCHARGED)

1Co	9: 17	I am simply *d* the trust committed

DISCIPLE (DISCIPLES DISCIPLES')

Mt	10: 42	these little ones because he is my *d*,
Lk	14: 26	his own life—he cannot be my *d*.
	14: 27	and follow me cannot be my *d*.
	14: 33	everything he has cannot be my *d*.
Jn	13: 23	of them, the *d* whom Jesus loved,
	19: 26	and the *d* whom he loved standing
	21: 7	Then the *d* whom Jesus loved said
	21: 20	saw that the *d* whom Jesus loved

DISCIPLES (DISCIPLE)

Mt	10: 1	He called his twelve *d* to him
	26: 56	Then all the *d* deserted him
	28: 19	Therefore go and make *d*
Mk	3: 7	withdrew with his *d* to the lake,
	16: 20	Then the *d* went out and preached
Lk	6: 13	he called his *d* to him and chose
Jn	2: 11	and his *d* put their faith in him.
	6: 66	many of his *d* turned back
	8: 31	to my teaching, you are really my *d*
	12: 16	At first his *d* did not understand all
	13: 35	men will know that you are my *d*
	15: 8	showing yourselves to be my *d*.
	20: 20	The *d* were overjoyed
Ac	6: 1	the number of *d* was increasing,
	11: 26	The *d* were first called Christians
	14: 22	strengthening the *d*
	18: 23	Phrygia, strengthening all the *d*.

DISCIPLES' (DISCIPLE)

Jn	13: 5	and began to wash his *d* feet,

DISCIPLINE* (DISCIPLINED DISCIPLINES SELF-DISCIPLINE)

Dt	4: 36	made you hear his voice to *d* you.
	11: 2	and experienced the *d*
	21: 18	listen to them when they *d* him,
Job	5: 17	so do not despise the *d*
Ps	6: 1	or *d* me in your wrath.
	38: 1	or *d* me in your wrath.
	39: 11	You rebuke and *d* men for their sin;
	94: 12	Blessed is the man you *d*, O LORD
Pr	1: 2	for attaining wisdom and *d*;
	1: 7	but fools despise wisdom and *d*.
	3: 11	do not despise the LORD's *d*
	5: 12	You will say, "How I hated *d*!
	5: 23	He will die for lack of *d*,
	6: 23	and the corrections of *d*
	10: 17	He who heeds *d* shows the way
	12: 1	Whoever loves *d* loves knowledge,

DISCIPLINED* (DISCIPLINE)

Pr	1: 3	for acquiring a *d* and prudent life,
Isa	26: 16	when you *d* them,
Jer	31: 18	and I have been *d*.
	31: 18	'You *d* me like an unruly calf,
1Co	11: 32	we are being *d* so that we will not
Tit	1: 8	upright, holy and *d*.
Heb	12: 7	For what son is not *d* by his father?
	12: 8	you are not *d* (and everyone
	12: 9	all had human fathers who *d* us
	12: 10	Our fathers *d* us for a little while

DISCIPLINES* (DISCIPLINE)

Dt	8: 5	so the LORD your God *d* you.
	8: 5	your heart that as a man *d* his son,
Ps	94: 10	Does he who *d* nations not punish?
Pr	3: 12	the LORD *d* those he loves,
Heb	12: 6	because the Lord *d* those he loves,
	12: 10	but God *d* us for our good,

DISCLOSED

Lk	8: 17	is nothing hidden that will not be *d*,
Col	1: 26	and generations, but is now *d*
Heb	9: 8	Holy Place had not yet been *d*

DISCORD

Gal	5: 20	idolatry and witchcraft; hatred, *d*,

DISCOURAGED* (DISCOURAGEMENT)

Nu	32: 9	they *d* the Israelites
Dt	1: 21	Do not be afraid; do not be *d*."
Dt	31: 8	Do not be afraid; do not be *d*."
Jos	1: 9	Do not be terrified; do not be *d*,
	8: 1	"Do not be afraid; do not be *d*.
	10: 25	"Do not be afraid; do not be *d*.
1Ch	22: 13	Do not be afraid or *d*.
	28: 20	or *d*, for the LORD God,
2Ch	20: 15	or *d* because of this vast army.
	20: 17	Do not be afraid; do not be *d*.
	32: 7	or *d* because of the king of Assyria
Job	4: 5	to you, and you are *d*;
Isa	42: 4	he will not falter or be *d*
Eph	3: 13	to be *d* because of my sufferings
Col	3: 21	children, or they will become *d*.

DISCOURAGEMENT* (DISCOURAGED)

Ex	6: 9	of their *d* and cruel bondage.

DISCOURAGEMENT

Pr	13: 18	He who ignores *d* comes to poverty
	13: 24	who loves him is careful to *d* him.
	15: 5	A fool spurns his father's *d*,
	15: 10	Stern *d* awaits him who leaves
	15: 32	He who ignores *d* despises himself,
	19: 18	*D* your son, for in that there is hope
	22: 15	the rod of *d* will drive it far
	23: 13	Do not withhold *d* from a child;
	23: 23	get wisdom, *d* and understanding.
	29: 17	*D* your son, and he will give you
Jer	17: 23	would not listen or respond to *d*.
	30: 11	I will *d* you but only with justice;
	32: 33	would not listen or respond to *d*.
	46: 28	I will *d* you but only with justice;
Hos	5: 2	I will *d* all of them.
Heb	12: 5	do not make light of the Lord's *d*.
	12: 7	as *d*; God is treating you
	12: 8	(and everyone undergoes *d*),
	12: 11	No *d* seems pleasant at the time,
Rev	3: 19	Those whom I love I rebuke and *d*.

DISCOVERED

2Ki   23: 24 book that Hilkiah the priest had *d*

DISCREDIT* (DISCREDITED)

Ne   6: 13 would give me a bad name to *d* me.
Job   40: 8 "Would you *d* my justice?

DISCREDITED (DISCREDIT)

2Co   6: 3 so that our ministry will not be *d*.

DISCRETION*

1Ch 22: 12 May the LORD give you *d*
Pr   1: 4 knowledge and *d* to the young—
      2: 11 *D* will protect you,
      5: 2 that you may maintain *d*
      8: 12 I possess knowledge and *d*.
     11: 22 a beautiful woman who shows no *d*.

DISCRIMINATED*

Jas   2: 4 have you not *d* among yourselves

DISEASE (DISEASES)

Mt   4: 23 and healing every *d* and sickness
      9: 35 and healing every *d* and sickness.
     10: 1 and to heal every *d* and sickness.

DISEASES (DISEASE)

Ps   103: 3 and heals all my *d*;
Mt   8: 17 and carried our *d*."
Mk   3: 10 those with *d* were pushing forward
Lk   9: 1 drive out all demons and to cure *d*,

DISFIGURE* (DISFIGURED)

Mt   6: 16 for they *d* their faces

DISFIGURED (DISFIGURE)

Isa   52: 14 his appearance was so *d*

DISGRACE (DISGRACEFUL DISGRACES)

Ps   44: 15 My *d* is before me all day long,
     52: 1 you who are a *d* in the eyes of God?
     74: 21 not let the oppressed retreat in *d*;
Pr   6: 33 Blows and *d* are his lot,
     11: 2 When pride comes, then comes *d*,
     14: 34 but sin is a *d* to any people.
     19: 26 is a son who brings shame and *d*.
Mt   1: 19 want to expose her to public *d*,
Ac   5: 41 of suffering *d* for the Name.
1Co 11: 6 and if it is a *d* for a woman
     11: 14 it is a *d* to him, but that
1Ti   3: 7 so that he will not fall into *d*
Heb   6: 6 and subjecting him to public *d*.
     11: 26 He regarded *d* for the sake
     13: 13 the camp, bearing the *d* he bore.

DISGRACEFUL (DISGRACE)

Pr   10: 5 during harvest is a *d* son.
     12: 4 a *d* wife is like decay in his bones.
     17: 2 wise servant will rule over a *d* son,
1Co 14: 35 for it is *d* for a woman to speak

DISGRACES (DISGRACE)

Pr   28: 7 of gluttons *d* his father.
     29: 15 but a child left to itself *d* his mother

DISGUISES*

Pr   26: 24 A malicious man *d* himself

DISH

Pr   19: 24 sluggard buries his hand in the *d*;
Mt   23: 25 the outside of the cup and *d*,

DISHONEST*

Ex   18: 21 trustworthy men who hate *d* gain
Lev 19: 35 "'Do not use *d* standards
1Sa   8: 3 They turned aside after *d* gain
Pr   11: 1 The LORD abhors *d* scales,
     13: 11 *D* money dwindles away,
     20: 23 and *d* scales do not please him.
     29: 27 The righteous detest the *d*;
Jer 22: 17 are set only on *d* gain,
Eze 28: 18 By your many sins and *d* trade
Hos 12: 7 The merchant uses *d* scales;
Am   8: 5 and cheating with *d* scales,
Mic   6: 11 Shall I acquit a man with *d* scales,
Lk   16: 8 master commended the *d* manager
     16: 10 whoever is *d* with very little will
     16: 10 with very little will also be *d*
1Ti   3: 8 wine, and not pursuing *d* gain.
Tit   1: 7 not violent, not pursuing *d* gain.
      1: 11 and that for the sake of *d* gain.

DISHONOUR* (DISHONOURED DISHONOURS)

Lev 18: 7 "'Do not *d* your father
     18: 8 wife; that would *d* your father.
     18: 10 daughter; that would *d* you.
     18: 14 "'Do not *d* your father's brother
     18: 16 that would *d* your brother.
     20: 19 for that would *d* a close relative;
Dt   22: 30 he must not *d* his father's bed.
Pr   30: 9 and so *d* the name of my God.
Jer 14: 21 do not *d* your glorious throne.
     20: 11 their *d* will never be forgotten.
La   2: 2 princes down to the ground in *d*.
Eze 22: 10 are those who *d* their fathers' bed;
Jn   8: 49 I honour my Father and you *d* me.
Ro   2: 23 do you *d* God by breaking the law?
1Co 15: 43 it is sown in *d*, it is raised in glory;
2Co   6: 8 through glory and *d*, bad report

DISHONOURED* (DISHONOUR)

Lev 20: 11 father's wife, he has *d* his father.
     20: 17 He has *d* his sister and will be held
     20: 20 with his aunt, he has *d* his uncle.
     20: 21 of impurity; he has *d* his brother.
Dt   21: 14 as a slave, since you have *d* her.
Ezr   4: 14 proper for us to see the king *d*,
1Co   4: 10 You are honoured, we are *d*!

DISHONOURS* (DISHONOUR)

Dt   27: 16 Cursed is the man who *d* his father
     27: 20 for he *d* his father's bed."
Job 20: 3 I hear a rebuke that *d* me,
Mic   7: 6 For a son *d* his father,
1Co 11: 4 with his head covered *d* his head.
     11: 5 her head uncovered *d* her head—

DISILLUSIONMENT*

Ps   7: 14 conceives trouble gives birth to *d*.

DISMAYED

Isa 28: 16 the one who trusts will never be *d*.
     41: 10 do not be *d*, for I am your God.

DISOBEDIENCE* (DISOBEY)

Jos 22: 22 in rebellion or *d* to the LORD,

Jer 43: 7 So they entered Egypt in *d*
Ro 5: 19 as through the *d* of the one man
11: 30 mercy as a result of their *d*,
11: 32 to *d* so that he may have mercy
2Co 10: 6 ready to punish every act of *d*,
Heb 2: 2 and *d* received its just punishment,
4: 6 go in, because of their *d*.
4: 11 fall by following their example of *d*.

DISOBEDIENT* (DISOBEY)

Ne 9: 26 "But they were *d* and rebelled
Lk 1: 17 and the *d* to the wisdom
Ac 26: 19 I was not *d* to the vision
Ro 10: 21 hands to a *d* and obstinate people."
11: 30 as you who were at one time *d*
11: 31 so they too have now become *d*
Eph 2: 2 now at work in those who are *d*.
5: 6 comes on those who are *d*.
5: 12 to mention what the *d* do in secret.
2Ti 3: 2 proud, abusive, *d* to their parents,
Tit 1: 6 to the charge of being wild and *d*.
1: 16 *d* and unfit for doing anything
3: 3 At one time we too were foolish, *d*,
Heb 11: 31 killed with those who were *d*.

DISOBEY* (DISOBEDIENCE DISOBEDIENT DISOBEYED DISOBEYING DISOBEYS)

Dt 11: 28 the curse if you *d* the commands
2Ch 24: 20 'Why do you *d* the LORD's
Est 3: 3 Why do you *d* the king's command
Jer 42: 13 and so *d* the LORD your God,
Ro 1: 30 they *d* their parents; they are
1Pe 2: 8 because they *d* the message—

DISOBEYED* (DISOBEY)

Nu 14: 22 and in the desert but who *d* me
27: 14 both of you *d* my command
Jdg 2: 2 Yet you have *d* me.
Ne 9: 29 arrogant and *d* your commands.
Isa 24: 5 they have *d* the laws,
Jer 43: 4 and all the people *d* the LORD's
Lk 15: 29 for you and never *d* your orders.
Heb 3: 18 rest if not to those who *d*?
1Pe 3: 20 the spirits in prison who *d* long ago

DISOBEYING* (DISOBEY)

Nu 14: 41 "Why are you *d* the LORD's

DISOBEYS* (DISOBEY)

Eze 33: 12 man will not save him when he *d*,

DISORDER

1Co 14: 33 For God is not a God of *d*
2Co 12: 20 slander, gossip, arrogance and *d*.
Jas 3: 16 there you find *d* and every evil

DISOWN (DISOWNS)

Pr 30: 9 I may have too much and *d* you
Mt 10: 33 I will *d* him before my Father
26: 35 to die with you, I will never *d* you."
2Ti 2: 12 If we *d* him,

DISOWNS (DISOWN)

Lk 12: 9 he who *d* me before men will be

DISPENSATION see ADMINISTRATION, TRUST

DISPLACES

Pr 30: 23 a maidservant who *d* her mistress.

DISPLAY (DISPLAYED DISPLAYS)

Ps 45: 4 your right hand *d* awesome deeds.
Eze 39: 21 I will *d* my glory among the nations
Ro 9: 17 that I might *d* my power in you
1Co 4: 9 on *d* at the end of the procession,
1Ti 1: 16 Christ Jesus might *d* his unlimited

DISPLAYED (DISPLAY)

Jn 9: 3 work of God might be *d* in his life.
2Th 2: 9 the work of Satan *d* in all kinds

DISPLAYS (DISPLAY)

Isa 44: 23 he *d* his glory in Israel.

DISPLEASE (DISPLEASED)

1Th 2: 15 They *d* God and are hostile

DISPLEASED (DISPLEASE)

2Sa 11: 27 David had done *d* the LORD.

DISPUTABLE* (DISPUTE)

Ro 14: 1 passing judgment on *d* matters.

DISPUTE (DISPUTABLE DISPUTES DISPUTING)

Pr 17: 14 before a *d* breaks out.
1Co 6: 1 If any of you has a *d* with another,

DISPUTES (DISPUTE)

Pr 18: 18 Casting the lot settles *d*

DISPUTING (DISPUTE)

1Ti 2: 8 in prayer, without anger or *d*.

DISQUALIFIED*

1Co 9: 27 I myself will not be *d* for the prize.

DISREPUTE*

2Pe 2: 2 will bring the way of truth into *d*.

DISSENSION* (DISSENSIONS)

Pr 6: 14 he always stirs up *d*.
6: 19 and a man who stirs up *d*
10: 12 Hatred stirs up *d*,
15: 18 A hot-tempered man stirs up *d*,
16: 28 A perverse man stirs up *d*,
28: 25 A greedy man stirs up *d*,
29: 22 An angry man stirs up *d*,
Ro 13: 13 debauchery, not in *d* and jealousy.

DISSENSIONS* (DISSENSION)

Gal 5: 20 selfish ambition, *d*, factions

DISSIPATION*

Lk 21: 34 will be weighed down with *d*,
1Pe 4: 4 with them into the same flood of *d*,

DISTINCTION

Ac 15: 9 He made no *d* between us

DISTINGUISH

1Ki 3: 9 and to *d* between right and wrong.
1Co 12: 10 the ability to *d* between spirits,
Heb 5: 14 themselves to *d* good from evil.

DISTORT

Ac 20: 30 and *d* the truth in order
2Co 4: 2 nor do we *d* the word of God.
2Pe 3: 16 ignorant and unstable people *d*,

DISTRACTED*

Lk   10: 40   But Martha was *d* by all

DISTRESS (DISTRESSED)

2Ch   15: 4   in their *d* they turned to the LORD
Ps   18: 6   In my *d* I called to the LORD;
       81: 7   In your *d* you called and I rescued
    120: 1   I call on the LORD in my *d*,
Jnh   2: 2   "In my *d* I called to the LORD,
Mt   24: 21   For then there will be great *d*,
Jas   1: 27   after orphans and widows in their *d*

DISTRESSED (DISTRESS)

Lk   12: 50   how *d* I am until it is completed!
Ro   14: 15   If your brother is *d*

DIVIDE (DIVIDED DIVIDING DIVISION DIVISIONS DIVISIVE)

Ps   22: 18   They *d* my garments among them

DIVIDED (DIVIDE)

Mt   12: 25   household *d* against itself will not
Lk   23: 34   they *d* up his clothes by casting lots
1Co   1: 13   Is Christ *d*? Was Paul crucified

DIVIDING (DIVIDE)

Eph   2: 14   destroyed the barrier, the *d* wall
Heb   4: 12   it penetrates even to *d* soul

DIVINATION

Lev   19: 26   "'Do not practise *d* or sorcery.

DIVINE

Ro   1: 20   his eternal power and *d* nature—
2Co   10: 4   they have *d* power
2Pe   1: 4   you may participate in the *d* nature

DIVISION (DIVIDE)

Lk   12: 51   on earth? No, I tell you, but *d*.
1Co   12: 25   so that there should be no *d*

DIVISIONS (DIVIDE)

Ro   16: 17   to watch out for those who cause *d*
1Co   1: 10   another so that there may be no *d*
    11: 18   there are *d* among you,

DIVISIVE* (DIVIDE)

Tit   3: 10   Warn a *d* person once,

DIVORCE* (DIVORCED DIVORCES)

Dt   22: 19   he must not *d* her as long as he lives
    22: 29   He can never *d* her as long
    24: 1   and he writes her a certificate of *d*,
    24: 3   and writes her a certificate of *d*,
Isa   50: 1   is your mother's certificate of *d*
Jer   3: 8   faithless Israel her certificate of *d*
Mal   2: 16   "I hate *d*," says the LORD God
Mt   1: 19   he had in mind to *d* her quietly.
     5: 31   must give her a certificate of *d*.'
    19: 3   for a man to *d* his wife for any
    19: 7   man give his wife a certificate of *d*
    19: 8   permitted you to *d* your wives
Mk   10: 2   Is it lawful for a man to *d* his wife?"
    10: 4   a man to write a certificate of *d*
1Co   7: 11   And a husband must not *d* his wife.
     7: 12   to live with him, he must not *d* her.
     7: 13   to live with her, she must not *d* him
     7: 27   Are you married? Do not seek a *d*.

DIVORCED* (DIVORCE)

Lev   21: 7   or *d* from their husbands,
    21: 14   not marry a widow, a *d* woman,
    22: 13   daughter becomes a widow or is *d*,
Nu   30: 9   or *d* woman will be binding on her.
Dt   24: 4   then her first husband, who *d* her,
1Ch   8: 8   after he had *d* his wives Hushim
Eze   44: 22   not marry widows or *d* women;
Mt   5: 32   a woman so *d* commits adultery.
Lk   16: 18   who marries a *d* woman commits

DIVORCES* (DIVORCE)

Jer   3: 1   "If a man *d* his wife
Mt   5: 31   'Anyone who *d* his wife must give
     5: 32   tell you that anyone who *d* his wife,
    19: 9   tell you that anyone who *d* his wife,
Mk   10: 11   "Anyone who *d* his wife
    10: 12   And if she *d* her husband
Lk   16: 18   "Anyone who *d* his wife

DOCTOR

Mt   9: 12   "It is not the healthy who need a *d*,

DOCTRINE* (DOCTRINES)

1Ti   1: 10   to the sound *d* that conforms
     4: 16   Watch your life and *d* closely.
2Ti   4: 3   men will not put up with sound *d*.
Tit   1: 9   can encourage others by sound *d*
     2: 1   is in accord with sound *d*.

DOCTRINES* (DOCTRINE)

1Ti   1: 3   not to teach false *d* any longer
     6: 3   If anyone teaches false *d*

DOEG*

Edomite; Saul's head shepherd; responsible for murder of priests at Nob (1Sa 21:7; 22:6-23; Ps 52).

DOG (DOGS)

Pr   26: 11   As a *d* returns to its vomit,
Ecc   9: 4   a live *d* is better off than a dead lion
2Pe   2: 22   "A *d* returns to its vomit," and,

DOGS (DOG)

Mt   7: 6   "Do not give *d* what is sacred;
    15: 26   bread and toss it to their *d*."

DOMINION

Job   25: 2   "*D* and awe belong to God;
Ps   22: 28   for *d* belongs to the LORD

DONKEY

Nu   22: 30   *d* said to Balaam, "Am I not your
Zec   9: 9   gentle and riding on a *d*,
Mt   21: 5   gentle and riding on a *d*,
2Pe   2: 16   for his wrongdoing by a *d*—

DOOR (DOORS)

Job   31: 32   for my *d* was always open
Ps   141: 3   keep watch over the *d* of my lips.
Mt   6: 6   close the *d* and pray to your Father
     7: 7   and the *d* will be opened to you.
Ac   14: 27   how he had opened the *d* of faith
1Co   16: 9   a great *d* for effective work has
2Co   2: 12   found that the LORD had opened a *d*
Rev   3: 20   I stand at the *d* and knock.

DOOR-FRAMES

Dt   6: 9   Write them on the *d* of your houses

DOORKEEPER

Ps 84: 10 I would rather be a *d* in the house

DOORS (DOOR)

Ps 24: 7 be lifted up, you ancient *d*,

DORCAS

Ac 9: 36 is *D*), who was always doing good

DOUBLE

2Ki 2: 9 "Let me inherit a *d* portion
1Ti 5: 17 church well are worthy of *d* honour,

DOUBLE-EDGED (EDGE)

Heb 4: 12 Sharper than any *d* sword,
Rev 1: 16 of his mouth came a sharp *d* sword.
        2: 12 of him who has the sharp, *d* sword.

DOUBLE-MINDED* (MIND)

Ps 119: 113 I hate *d* men,
Jas 1: 8 he is a *d* man, unstable
      4: 8 and purify your hearts, you *d*.

DOUBT (DOUBTING DOUBTS)

Mt 14: 31 he said, "why did you *d*?"
      21: 21 if you have faith and do not *d*,
Mk 11: 23 and does not *d* in his heart
Jas 1: 6 he must believe and not *d*,
Jude   : 22 Be merciful to those who *d*;

DOUBTING* (DOUBT)

Jn 20: 27 Stop *d* and believe."

DOUBTS* (DOUBT)

Lk 24: 38 and why do *d* rise in your minds?
Ro 14: 23 the man who has *d* is condemned
Jas 1: 6 he who *d* is like a wave of the sea,

DOVE (DOVES)

Ge 8: 8 Then he sent out a *d* to see
Mt 3: 16 Spirit of God descending like a *d*

DOVES (DOVE)

Lev 12: 8 is to bring two *d* or two young
Mt 10: 16 as snakes and as innocent as *d*.
Lk 2: 24 "a pair of *d* or two young pigeons."

DOWNCAST

Ps 42: 5 Why are you *d*, O my soul?
2Co 7: 6 But God, who comforts the *d*,

DOWNFALL

Hos 14: 1 Your sins have been your *d*!

DRAGON

Rev 12: 7 and his angels fought against the *d*,
      13: 2 The *d* gave the beast his power
      20: 2 He seized the *d*, that ancient

DRAW (DRAWING DRAWS)

Mt 26: 52 "for all who *d* the sword will die
Jn 12: 32 up from the earth, will *d* all men
Heb 10: 22 let us *d* near to God

DRAWING (DRAW)

Lk 21: 28 because your redemption is *d* near

DRAWS (DRAW)

Jn 6: 44 the Father who sent me *d* him,

DREAD (DREADFUL)

Ps 53: 5 they were, overwhelmed with *d*,

DREADFUL (DREAD)

Mt 24: 19 How *d* it will be in those days
Heb 10: 31 It is a *d* thing to fall into the hands

DREAM

Joel 2: 28 your old men will *d* dreams,
Ac 2: 17 your old men will *d* dreams.

DRESS

1Ti 2: 9 I also want women to *d* modestly,

DRIFT*

Heb 2: 1 so that we do not *d* away.

**DRINK (DRINKING DRINKS DRUNK
DRUNKARD DRUNKARD'S DRUNKARDS
DRUNKENNESS)**

Ex 29: 40 of a hin of wine as a *d* offering.
Nu 6: 3 He must not *d* grape juice
Jdg 7: 5 from those who kneel down to *d*."
2Sa 23: 15 that someone would get me a *d*
Pr 5: 15 *D* water from your own cistern,
Mt 20: 22 "Can you *d* the cup I am going to *d*
      26: 27 saying, "*D* from it, all of you.
Mk 16: 18 and when they *d* deadly poison,
Lk 12: 19 Take life easy; eat, *d* and be merry
Jn 7: 37 let him come to me and *d*.
      18: 11 Shall I not *d* the cup the Father has
1Co 10: 4 and drank the same spiritual *d*;
      12: 13 were all given the one Spirit to *d*.
Php 2: 17 being poured out like a *d* offering
2Ti 4: 6 being poured out like a *d* offering,
Rev 14: 10 too, will *d* of the wine of God's fury
      21: 6 to *d* without cost from the spring

DRINKING (DRINK)

Ro 14: 17 God is not a matter of eating and *d*,

DRINKS (DRINK)

Isa 5: 22 and champions at mixing *d*,
Jn 4: 13 "Everyone who *d* this water will be
      6: 54 and *d* my blood has eternal life,
1Co 11: 27 or *d* the cup of the Lord

DRIPPING

Pr 19: 13 wife is like a constant *d*.
      27: 15 a constant *d* on a rainy day;

DRIVE (DRIVES)

Ex 23: 30 Little by little I will *d* them out
Nu 33: 52 *d* out all the inhabitants of the land
Jos 13: 13 Israelites did not *d* out the people
      23: 13 will no longer *d* out these nations
Pr 22: 10 *D* out the mocker, and out goes
Mt 10: 1 authority to *d* out evil spirits
Jn 6: 37 comes to me I will never *d* away.

DRIVES (DRIVE)

Mt 12: 26 If Satan *d* out Satan, he is divided
1Jn 4: 18 But perfect love *d* out fear,

DROP (DROPS)

Pr 17: 14 so *d* the matter before a dispute
Isa 40: 15 Surely the nations are like a *d*

DROPS (DROP)

Lk 22: 44 his sweat was like *d* of blood falling

DROSS

Ps 119: 119 of the earth you discard like *d*;
Pr 25: 4 Remove the *d* from the silver,

DROUGHT

Jer 17: 8 It has no worries in a year of *d*

DROWNED

Ex 15: 4 are *d* in the Red Sea.
Mt 18: 6 and to be *d* in the depths of the sea.
Heb 11: 29 tried to do so, they were *d*.

DROWSINESS*

Pr 23: 21 and *d* clothes them in rags.

DRUNK (DRINK)

1Sa 1: 13 Eli thought she was *d* and said
Ac 2: 15 men are not *d*, as you suppose.
Eph 5: 18 Do not get *d* on wine, which leads

DRUNKARD (DRINK)

Mt 11: 19 and a *d*, a friend of tax collectors
1Co 5: 11 or a slanderer, a *d* or a swindler.

DRUNKARD'S* (DRINK)

Pr 26: 9 Like a thornbush in a *d* hand

DRUNKARDS (DRINK)

Pr 23: 21 for *d* and gluttons become poor,
1Co 6: 10 nor the greedy nor *d* nor slanderers

DRUNKENNESS (DRINK)

Lk 21: 34 weighed down with dissipation, *d*
Ro 13: 13 and *d*, not in sexual immorality
Gal 5: 21 factions and envy; *d*, orgies,
1Ti 3: 3 not given to *d*,
Tit 1: 7 not given to *d*,
1Pe 4: 3 living in debauchery, lust, *d*, orgies,

DRY

Ge 1: 9 place, and let *d* ground appear."
Ex 14: 16 go through the sea on *d* ground.
Jos 3: 17 the crossing on *d* ground.
Isa 53: 2 and like a root out of *d* ground.
Eze 37: 4 '*D* bones, hear the word

DULL

Isa 6: 10 make their ears *d*
2Co 3: 14 But their minds were made *d*,

DUST

Ge 2: 7 man from the *d* of the ground
3: 19 for *d* you are
Job 42: 6 and repent in *d* and ashes."
Ps 22: 15 you lay me in the *d* of death.
103: 14 he remembers that we are *d*.
Ecc 3: 20 all come from *d*, and to *d* all return.
Mt 10: 14 shake the *d* off your feet
1Co 15: 47 was of the *d* of the earth,

DUTIES (DUTY)

2Ti 4: 5 discharge all the *d* of your ministry

DUTY (DUTIES)

Ecc 12: 13 for this is the whole *d* of man.
Ac 23: 1 I have fulfilled my *d* to God
1Co 7: 3 husband should fulfil his marital *d*

DWELL (DWELLING DWELLINGS DWELLS DWELT)

Ex 25: 8 for me, and I will *d* among them.
2Sa 7: 5 the one to build me a house to *d* in?
1Ki 8: 27 "But will God really *d* on earth?
Ps 23: 6 I will *d* in the house of the LORD
37: 3 *d* in the land and enjoy safe pasture
61: 4 I long to *d* in your tent for ever
Pr 8: 12 wisdom, *d* together with prudence;
Isa 33: 14 of us can *d* with the consuming fire
43: 18 do not *d* on the past.
Jn 5: 38 nor does his word *d* in you,
Eph 3: 17 so that Christ may *d* in your hearts
Col 1: 19 to have all his fulness *d* in him,
3: 16 the word of Christ *d* in you richly

DWELLING (DWELL)

2Co 5: 2 to be clothed with our heavenly *d*,
Eph 2: 22 to become a *d* in which God lives

DWELLING-PLACE

Lev 26: 11 I will put my *d* among you
Dt 26: 15 from heaven, your holy *d*,
Ps 90: 1 Lord, you have been our *d*

DWELLINGS (DWELL)

Lk 16: 9 will be welcomed into eternal *d*.

DWELLS (DWELL)

Ps 46: 4 holy place where the Most High *d*.
91: 1 He who *d* in the shelter

DWELT (DWELL)

Dt 33: 16 of him who *d* in the burning bush.

DYING (DIE)

Ro 7: 6 by *d* to what once bound us,
2Co 6: 9 yet regarded as unknown; *d*,

EAGER

Pr 31: 13 and works with *e* hands
Ro 8: 19 The creation waits in *e* expectation
1Co 14: 12 Since you are *e* to have spiritual
14: 39 my brothers, be *e* to prophesy,
Tit 2: 14 a people that are his very own, *e*
1Pe 5: 2 greedy for money, but *e* to serve;

EAGLE (EAGLE'S EAGLES)

Dt 32: 11 like an *e* that stirs up its nest
Eze 1: 10 each also had the face of an *e*.
Rev 4: 7 the fourth was like a flying *e*.
12: 14 given the two wings of a great *e*,

EAGLE'S (EAGLE)

Ps 103: 5 my youth is renewed like the *e*.

EAGLES (EAGLE)

Isa 40: 31 They will soar on wings like *e*;

EAR (EARS)

Ex 21: 6 and pierce his *e* with an awl.
Ps 5: 1 Give *e* to my words, O LORD,
Pr 2: 2 turning your *e* to wisdom
1Co 2: 9 no *e* has heard,
12: 16 if the *e* should say, "Because I am
Rev 2: 7 He who has an *e*, let him hear what

EAR-RING (EAR-RINGS)

Pr 25: 12 Like an *e* of gold or an ornament

EAR-RINGS (EAR-RING)

Ex 32: 2 Take off the gold *e* that your wives,

EARN (EARNED EARNINGS)

2Th 3:12 down and *e* the bread they eat.

EARNED (EARN)

Pr 31:31 Give her the reward she has *e,*

EARNEST see DEPOSIT

EARNESTNESS

2Co 7:11 what *e,* what eagerness
8: 7 in complete *e* and in your love

EARNINGS (EARN)

Pr 31:16 out of her *e* she plants a vineyard.

EARS (EAR)

Job 42: 5 My *e* had heard of you
Ps 34:15 and his *e* are attentive to their cry;
Pr 21:13 If a man shuts his *e* to the cry
26:17 Like one who seizes a dog by the *e*
Isa 6:10 hear with their *e,*
Mt 11:15 He who has *e,* let him hear.
2Ti 4: 3 to say what their itching *e* want
1Pe 3:12 his *e* are attentive to their prayer,

EARTH (EARTH'S EARTHLY)

Ge 1: 1 God created the heavens and the *e.*
1: 2 Now the *e* was formless and empty,
7:24 The waters flooded the *e*
14:19 Creator of heaven and *e.*
1Ki 8:27 "But will God really dwell on *e?*
Job 26: 7 he suspends the *e* over nothing.
Ps 24: 1 *e* is the LORD's, and everything
46: 6 he lifts his voice, the *e* melts.
90: 2 or you brought forth the *e*
97: 5 before the Lord of all the *e.*
102:25 you laid the foundations of the *e,*
108: 5 and let your glory be over all the *e.*
Pr 8:26 before he made the *e* or its fields
Isa 6: 3 the whole *e* is full of his glory."
24:20 The *e* reels like a drunkard,
37:16 You have made heaven and *e,*
40:22 enthroned above the circle of the *e,*
51: 6 the *e* will wear out like a garment
54: 5 he is called the God of all the *e.*
55: 9 the heavens are higher than the *e,*
65:17 new heavens and a new *e.*
66: 1 and the *e* is my footstool.
Jer 10:10 When he is angry, the *e* trembles;
23:24 "Do not I fill heaven and *e?*"
33:25 and the fixed laws of heaven and *e,*
Hab 2:20 let all the *e* be silent before him."
Mt 5: 5 for they will inherit the *e.*
5:35 or by the *e,* for it is his footstool;
6:10 done on *e* as it is in heaven.
16:19 bind on *e* will be bound
24:35 Heaven and *e* will pass away,
28:18 and on *e* has been given to me.
Lk 2:14 on *e* peace to men
Jn 12:32 when I am lifted up from the *e,*
Ac 4:24 "you made the heaven and the *e*
7:49 and the *e* is my footstool.
1Co 10:26 The *e* is the Lord's, and everything
Eph 3:15 in heaven and on *e* derives its name
Php 2:10 in heaven and on *e* and under the *e,*
Heb 1:10 you laid the foundations of the *e,*
2Pe 3:13 to a new heaven and a new *e,*

Rev 8: 7 A third of the *e* was burned up,
12:12 But woe to the *e* and the sea,
20:11 *E* and sky fled from his presence,
21: 1 I saw a new heaven and a new *e,*
21: 1 and the first *e* had passed away,

EARTH'S (EARTH)

Job 38: 4 when I laid the *e* foundation?

EARTHENWARE

Pr 26:23 Like a coating of glaze over *e*

EARTHLY (EARTH)

Eph 4: 9 descended to the lower, *e* regions?
Php 3:19 Their mind is on *e* things.
Col 3: 2 on things above, not on *e* things.
3: 5 whatever belongs to your *e* nature:

EARTHQUAKE (EARTHQUAKES)

Eze 38:19 at that time there shall be a great *e*
Mt 28: 2 There was a violent *e,* for an angel
Rev 6:12 There was a great *e.*

EARTHQUAKES (EARTHQUAKE)

Mt 24: 7 There will be famines and *e*

EASE

Pr 1:33 and be at *e,* without fear of harm."

EASIER (EASY)

Lk 16:17 It is *e* for heaven and earth
18:25 it is *e* for a camel to go

EAST

Ge 2: 8 God had planted a garden in the *e,*
Ps 103:12 as far as the *e* is from the west,
Eze 43: 2 God of Israel coming from the *e.*
Mt 2: 1 Magi from the *e* came to Jerusalem
2: 2 We saw his star in the *e*

EASY (EASIER)

Mt 11:30 For my yoke is *e* and my burden is

EAT (ATE EATEN EATER EATING EATS)

Ge 2:16 "You are free to *e* from any tree
2:17 but you must not *e* from the tree
3:19 you will *e* your food
Ex 12:11 *E* it in haste; it is the LORD's
Lev 11: 2 these are the ones you may *e:*
17:12 "None of you may *e* blood,
Dt 8:16 He gave you manna to *e*
14: 4 These are the animals you may *e:*
Jdg 14:14 "Out of the eater, something to *e;*
2Sa 9: 7 and you will always *e* at my table."
Pr 31:27 and does not *e* the bread of idleness
Isa 55: 1 come, buy and *e!*
65:25 and the lion will *e* straw like the ox,
Eze 3: 1 *e* what is before you, *e* this scroll;
Mt 14:16 You give them something to *e.*"
15: 2 wash their hands before they *e!*"
26:26 "Take and *e;* this is my body."
Mk 14:14 where I may *e* the Passover
Lk 10: 8 and are welcomed, *e* what is set
12:19 Take life easy; *e,* drink
12:22 what you will *e;* or about your body
Jn 4:32 to *e* that you know nothing about."
6:31 bread from heaven to *e.*'"
6:52 can this man give us his flesh to *e?*"
Ac 10:13 Kill and *e.*"
Ro 14: 2 faith allows him to *e* everything,

Ro	14: 15	is distressed because of what you *e*,
	14: 20	to *e* anything that causes someone
	14: 21	It is better not to *e* meat
1Co	5: 11	With such a man do not even *e*.
	8: 13	if what I *e* causes my brother to fall
	10: 25	*E* anything sold in the meat market
	10: 27	*e* whatever is put before you
	10: 31	So whether you *e* or drink
	11: 26	For whenever you *e* this bread
2Th	3: 10	man will not work, he shall not *e*."
Rev	2: 7	the right to *e* from the tree of life,
	3: 20	I will come in and *e* with him,

EATEN (EAT)

Ge	3: 11	Have you *e* from the tree that I
Ac	10: 14	"I have never *e* anything impure
Rev	10: 10	when I had *e* it, my stomach turned

EATER (EAT)

Isa	55: 10	for the sower and bread for the *e*,

EATING (EAT)

Ex	34: 28	and forty nights without *e* bread
Ro	14: 15	not by your *e* destroy your brother
	14: 17	kingdom of God is not a matter of *e*
	14: 23	because his *e* is not from faith;
1Co	8: 4	about *e* food sacrificed to idols:
	8: 10	you who have this knowledge *e*
Jude	: 12	*e* with you without the slightest

EATS (EAT)

1Sa	14: 24	"Cursed be any man who *e* food
Lk	15: 2	"This man welcomes sinners and *e*
Jn	6: 51	If a man *e* of this bread, he will live
	6: 54	Whoever *e* my flesh and drinks my
Ro	14: 2	faith is weak, *e* only vegetables.
	14: 3	man who *e* everything must not
	14: 6	He who *e* meat, *e* to the Lord,
	14: 23	has doubts is condemned if he *e*,
1Co	11: 27	whoever *e* the bread or drinks

EBAL

Dt	11: 29	and on Mount *E* the curses.
Jos	8: 30	Joshua built on Mount *E* an altar

EBENEZER

1Sa	7: 12	He named it *E*, saying, "Thus far

EDEN

Ge	2: 8	in *E*; and there he put the man
Eze	28: 13	You were in *E*,

EDGE (DOUBLE-EDGED)

Mt	9: 20	and touched the *e* of his cloak.

EDICT

Heb	11: 23	they were not afraid of the king's *e*.

EDIFICATION (EDIFIED EDIFIES)

Ro	14: 19	leads to peace and to mutual *e*.

EDIFIED* (EDIFICATION)

1Co	14: 5	so that the church may be *e*.
	14: 17	but the other man is not *e*.

EDIFIES* (EDIFICATION)

1Co	14: 4	but he who prophesies *e* the church
	14: 4	speaks in a tongue *e* himself,

EDOM

Ge	36: 1	the account of Esau (that is, *E*).
	36: 8	*E*) settled in the hill country of Seir
Isa	63: 1	Who is this coming from *E*,
Ob	: 1	Sovereign LORD says about *E*—

EDUCATED*

Ac	7: 22	Moses was *e* in all the wisdom

EFFECT* (EFFECTIVE)

Job	41: 26	sword that reaches him has no *e*,
Isa	32: 17	*e* of righteousness will be quietness
Ac	7: 53	put into *e* through angels
1Co	15: 10	his grace to me was not without *e*.
Gal	3: 19	put into *e* through angels
Eph	1: 10	put into *e* when the times will have
Heb	9: 17	it never takes *e* while the one who
	9: 18	put into *e* without blood.

EFFECTIVE* (EFFECT)

1Co	16: 9	a great door for *e* work has opened
Jas	5: 16	a righteous man is powerful and *e*.

EFFORT*

Ecc	2: 19	into which I have poured my *e*
Da	6: 14	and made every *e* until sundown
Lk	13: 24	"Make every *e* to enter
Jn	5: 44	yet make no *e* to obtain the praise
Ro	9: 16	depend on man's desire or *e*,
	14: 19	make every *e* to do what leads
Gal	3: 3	to attain your goal by human *e*?
Eph	4: 3	Make every *e* to keep the unity
1Th	2: 16	to all men in their *e* to keep us
	2: 17	intense longing we made every *e*
Heb	4: 11	make every *e* to enter that rest,
	12: 14	Make every *e* to live in peace
2Pe	1: 5	make every *e* to add
	1: 15	And I will make every *e* to see that
	3: 14	make every *e* to be found spotless,

EGG

Lk	11: 12	for an *e*, will give him a scorpion?

EGLON

1. Fat king of Moab killed by Ehud (Jdg 3:12-30).
2. City in Canaan (Jos 10).

EGYPT (EGYPTIANS)

Ge	12: 10	went down to *E* to live there
	37: 28	Ishmaelites, who took him to *E*.
	42: 3	went down to buy grain from *E*.
	45: 20	the best of all *E* will be yours.'"
	46: 6	and all his offspring went to *E*.
	47: 27	Now the Israelites settled in *E*
Ex	3: 11	and bring the Israelites out of *E*?"
	12: 40	lived in *E* was 430 years.
	12: 41	all the LORD's divisions left *E*.
	32: 1	Moses who brought us up out of *E*,
Nu	11: 18	We were better off in *E*!"
	14: 4	choose a leader and go back to *E*."
	24: 8	"God brought them out of *E*;
Dt	6: 21	"We were slaves of Pharaoh in *E*,
1Ki	4: 30	greater than all the wisdom of *E*.
	10: 28	horses were imported from *E*
	11: 40	but Jeroboam fled to *E*,
	14: 25	king of *E* attacked Jerusalem.
2Ch	35: 20	Neco king of *E* went up to fight
	36: 3	The king of *E* dethroned him
Isa	19: 23	a highway from *E* to Assyria.

Hos 11: 1 and out of *E* I called my son.
Mt   2: 15 "Out of *E* I called my son."
Heb 11: 27 By faith he left *E*, not fearing
Rev 11: 8 is figuratively called Sodom and *E*,

EGYPTIANS (EGYPT)

Nu   14: 13 "Then the *E* will hear about it!

EHUD

Left-handed judge who delivered Israel from
Moabite king, Eglon (Jdg 3:12-30).

EKRON

1Sa   5: 10 So they sent the ark of God to *E*.

ELAH

Son of Baasha; king of Israel (1Ki 16:6-14).

ELATION

Pr   28: 12 righteous triumph, there is great *e*;

**ELDER* (ELDERLY ELDERS
FELLOW-ELDER)**

Isa   3: 2 the soothsayer and *e*,
1Ti   5: 19 an accusation against an *e*
Tit   1: 6 *e* must be blameless, the husband
2Jn   : 1 The *e*, To the chosen lady
3Jn   : 1 The *e*, To my dear friend Gaius,

ELDERLY* (ELDER)

Lev 19: 32 show respect for the *e*

ELDERS (ELDER)

1Ki   12: 8 rejected the advice the *e* gave him
Mt   15: 2 break the tradition of the *e*?
Mk   7: 3 holding to the tradition of the *e*.
        7: 5 to the tradition of the *e* instead
Ac   11: 30 gift to the *e* by Barnabas
        14: 23 and Barnabas appointed *e* for them
        15: 2 the apostles and *e* about this
        15: 4 the church and the apostles and *e*,
        15: 6 and *e* met to consider this question.
        15: 22 and *e*, with the whole church,
        15: 23 The apostles and *e*, your brothers,
        16: 4 and *e* in Jerusalem for the people
        20: 17 to Ephesus for the *e* of the church.
        21: 18 and all the *e* were present.
        23: 14 They went to the chief priests and *e*
        24: 1 to Caesarea with some of the *e*
1Ti   4: 14 when the body of *e* laid their hands
        5: 17 The *e* who direct the affairs
Tit   1: 5 and appoint *e* in every town,
Jas   5: 14 He should call the *e* of the church
1Pe   5: 1 To the *e* among you, I appeal
Rev   4: 4 seated on them were twenty-four *e*.
        4: 10 the twenty-four *e* fall

ELEAZAR

Third son of Aaron (Ex 6:23-25). Succeeded
Aaron as high priest (Nu 20:26; Dt 10:6). Allotted
land to tribes (Jos 14:1). Death (Jos 24:33).

ELECT* (ELECTION)

Mt   24: 22 the sake of the *e* those days will be
        24: 24 miracles to deceive even the *e*—
        24: 31 and they will gather his *e*
Mk   13: 20 sake of the *e*, whom he has chosen,
        13: 22 and miracles to deceive the *e*—
        13: 27 gather his *e* from the four winds,
Ro   11: 7 it did not obtain, but the *e* did.

1Ti   5: 21 and Christ Jesus and the *e* angels,
2Ti   2: 10 everything for the sake of the *e*,
Tit   1: 1 Christ for the faith of God's *e*
1Pe   1: 1 To God's *e*, strangers in the world,

ELECTION* (ELECT)

Ro   9: 11 God's purpose in *e* might stand:
        11: 28 but as far as *e* is concerned,
2Pe   1: 10 to make your calling and *e* sure.

ELEMENTARY* (ELEMENTS)

Heb   5: 12 someone to teach you the *e* truths
        6: 1 us leave the *e* teachings about

ELEMENTS* (ELEMENTARY)

2Pe   3: 10 the *e* will be destroyed by fire,
        3: 12 and the *e* will melt in the heat.

ELEVATE*

2Co   11: 7 to *e* you by preaching the gospel

ELI

High priest in youth of Samuel (1Sa 1-4).
Blessed Hannah (1Sa 1:12-18); raised Samuel (1Sa
2:11-26). Prophesied against because of wicked
sons (1Sa 2:27-36). Death of Eli and sons (1Sa
4:11-22).

ELIHU

One of Job's friends (Job 32-37).

ELIJAH

Prophet; predicted famine in Israel (1Ki 17:1;
Jas 5:17). Fed by ravens (1Ki 17:2-6). Raised
Sidonian widow's son (1Ki 17:7-24). Defeated
prophets of Baal at Carmel (1Ki 18:16-46). Ran
from Jezebel (1Ki 19:1-9). Prophesied death of
Azariah (2Ki 1). Succeeded by Elisha (1Ki
19:19-21; 2Ki 2:1-18). Taken to heaven in
whirlwind (2Ki 2:11-12).
Return prophesied (Mal 4:5-6); equated with
John the Baptist (Mt 17:9-13; Mk 9:9-13; Lk 1:17).
Appeared with Moses in transfiguration of Jesus
(Mt 17:1-8; Mk 9:1-8).

ELIMELECH

Ru   1: 3 Now *E*, Naomi's husband, died,

ELIPHAZ

1. Firstborn of Esau (Ge 36).
2. One of Job's friends (Job 4-5; 15; 22).

ELISHA

Prophet; successor of Elijah (1Ki 19:16-21);
inherited his cloak (2Ki 2:1-18). Purified bad water
(2Ki 2:19-22). Cursed young men (2Ki 2:23-25).
Aided Israel's defeat of Moab (2Ki 3). Provided
widow with oil (2Ki 4:1-7). Raised Shunammite
woman's son (2Ki 4:8-37). Purified food (2Ki
4:38-41). Fed 100 men (2Ki 4:42-44). Healed
Naaman's leprosy (2Ki 5). Made axe-head float
(2Ki 6:1-7). Captured Arameans (2Ki 6:8-23).
Political adviser to Israel (2Ki 6:24-8:6; 9:1-3;
13:14-19), Damascus (2Ki 8:7-15). Death (2Ki
13:20).

ELIZABETH*

Mother of John the Baptist, relative of Mary (Lk
1:5-58).

ELKANAH
Husband of Hannah, father of Samuel (1Sa 1-2).

ELOI*
Mt   27: 46 "E, E, *lama sabachthani?*"—
Mk   15: 34 "E, E, *lama sabachthani?*"—

ELOQUENCE* (ELOQUENT)
1Co   2: 1 come with e or superior wisdom

ELOQUENT* (ELOQUENCE)
Ex   4: 10 "O Lord, I have never been e,

ELYMAS
Ac   13: 8 E the sorcerer (for that is what his

EMBEDDED*
Ecc   12: 11 sayings like firmly e nails—

EMBERS
Pr   26: 21 As charcoal to e and as wood to fire

EMBITTER* (BITTER)
Col   3: 21 Fathers, do not e your children,

EMBODIMENT* (BODY)
Ro   2: 20 have in the law the e of knowledge

EMPTIED (EMPTY)
1Co   1: 17 the cross of Christ be e of its power.

EMPTY (EMPTIED)
Ge   1: 2 Now the earth was formless and e,
Job 26: 7 the northern ⌞skies⌟ over e space;
Isa 45: 18 he did not create it to be e,
     55: 11 It will not return to me e,
Jer   4: 23 and it was formless and e;
Lk   1: 53 but has sent the rich away e.
Eph   5: 6 no-one deceive you with e words,
1Pe   1: 18 from the e way of life handed
2Pe   2: 18 For they mouth e, boastful words

ENABLE (ABLE)
Lk   1: 74 to e us to serve him without fear
Ac   4: 29 e your servants to speak your word

ENABLED* (ABLE)
Lev 26: 13 e you to walk with heads held high.
Ru   4: 13 And the LORD e her to conceive,
Jn   6: 65 unless the Father has e him."
Ac   2: 4 other tongues as the Spirit e them.
      7: 10 and e him to gain the goodwill
Heb 11: 11 was e to become a father

ENABLES (ABLE)
Php   3: 21 by the power that e him

ENABLING* (ABLE)
Ac   14: 3 the message of his grace by e them

ENCAMPS* (CAMP)
Ps   34: 7 The angel of the LORD e

ENCOURAGE* (ENCOURAGED
ENCOURAGEMENT ENCOURAGES
ENCOURAGING)
Dt   1: 38 E him, because he will lead Israel
      3: 28 and e and strengthen him,
2Sa 11: 25 Say this to e Joab."
     19: 7 Now go out and e your men.

Job 16: 5 But my mouth would e you;
Ps   10: 17 you e them, and you listen
     64: 5 They e each other in evil plans,
Isa   1: 17 e the oppressed.
Jer 29: 8 to the dreams you e them to have.
Ac   15: 32 to e and strengthen the brothers.
Ro   12: 8 if it is encouraging, let him e;
Eph   6: 22 how we are, and that he may e you.
Col   4: 8 and that he may e your hearts.
1Th   3: 2 to strengthen and e you
      4: 18 Therefore e each other
      5: 11 Therefore e one another
      5: 14 those who are idle, e the timid,
2Th   2: 17 e your hearts and strengthen you
2Ti   4: 2 rebuke and e—with great patience
Tit   1: 9 so that he can e others
      2: 6 e the young men to be
      2: 15 E and rebuke with all authority.
Heb   3: 13 But e one another daily, as long
     10: 25 but let us e one another—

ENCOURAGED* (ENCOURAGE)
Jdg   7: 11 you will be e to attack the camp."
     20: 22 But the men of Israel e one another
2Ch 22: 3 for his mother e him
     32: 6 and e them with these words:
     35: 2 and e them in the service
Eze 13: 22 you e the wicked not to turn
Ac   9: 31 It was strengthened; and e
     11: 23 and e them all to remain true
     16: 40 met with the brothers and e them.
     18: 27 the brothers e him and wrote
     27: 36 They were all e and ate some food
     28: 15 men Paul thanked God and was e.
Ro   1: 12 and I may be mutually e
1Co 14: 31 everyone may be instructed and e.
2Co   7: 4 I am greatly e; in all our troubles
      7: 13 By all this we are e.
Php   1: 14 brothers in the Lord have been e
Col   2: 2 My purpose is that they may be e
1Th   3: 7 persecution we were e about you
Heb   6: 18 offered to us may be greatly e.

ENCOURAGEMENT* (ENCOURAGE)
Ac   4: 36 Barnabas (which means Son of E),
     13: 15 a message of e for the people,
     20: 2 speaking many words of e
Ro   15: 4 e of the Scriptures we might have
     15: 5 and e give you a spirit of unity
1Co 14: 3 to men for their strengthening, e
2Co   7: 13 to our own e, we were especially
Php   2: 1 If you have any e from being united
2Th   2: 16 and by his grace gave us eternal e
Phm   : 7 love has given me great joy and e,
Heb 12: 5 word of e that addresses you

ENCOURAGES* (ENCOURAGE)
Isa 41: 7 The craftsman e the goldsmith,

ENCOURAGING* (ENCOURAGE)
Ac   14: 22 e them to remain true to the faith.
     15: 31 and were glad for its e message.
     20: 1 for the disciples and, after e them,
Ro   12: 8 if it is e, let him encourage;
1Th   2: 12 e, comforting and urging you
1Pe   5: 12 e you and testifying that this is

ENCROACH
Pr   23: 10 or e on the fields of the fatherless,

END (ENDS)

Ps 119: 33 then I will keep them to the *e.*
119: 112 to the very *e.*
Pr 1: 19 Such is the *e* of all who go
5: 4 but in the *e* she is bitter as gall,
5: 11 At the *e* of your life you will groan,
14: 12 but in the *e* it leads to death.
14: 13 and joy may *e* in grief.
16: 25 but in the *e* it leads to death.
19: 20 and in the *e* you will be wise.
20: 21 will not be blessed at the *e.*
23: 32 In the *e* it bites like a snake
25: 8 for what will you do in the *e*
28: 23 in the *e* gain more favour
29: 21 he will bring grief in the *e.*
Ecc 3: 11 done from beginning to *e.*
7: 8 The *e* of a matter is better
12: 12 making many books there is no *e,*
Eze 7: 2 The *e!* The *e* has come
Mt 10: 22 firm to the *e* will be saved.
24: 13 firm to the *e* will be saved.
24: 14 nations, and then the *e* will come.
Lk 21: 9 but the *e* will not come right away
Ro 10: 4 Christ is the *e* of the law
1Co 15: 24 the *e* will come, when he hands
Rev 21: 6 Omega, the Beginning and the *E.*
22: 13 the Last, the Beginning and the *E.*

ENDS (END)

Ps 19: 4 their words to the *e* of the world.
Pr 20: 17 he *e* up with a mouth full of gravel.
Isa 49: 6 salvation to the *e* of the earth."
62: 11 proclamation to the *e* of the earth:
Ac 13: 47 salvation to the *e* of the earth.'"
Ro 10: 18 their words to the *e* of the world."

ENDURANCE* (ENDURE)

Ro 15: 4 through *e* and the encouragement
15: 5 May the God who gives *e*
2Co 1: 6 which produces in you patient *e*
6: 4 in great *e;* in troubles, hardships
Col 1: 11 might so that you may have great *e*
1Th 1: 3 and your *e* inspired by hope
1Ti 6: 11 faith, love, *e* and gentleness.
2Ti 3: 10 patience, love, *e,* persecutions,
Tit 2: 2 and sound in faith, in love and in *e.*
Rev 1: 9 and patient *e* that are ours in Jesus,
13: 10 This calls for patient *e*
14: 12 This calls for patient *e* on the part

ENDURE (ENDURANCE ENDURED ENDURES ENDURING)

Ps 72: 17 May his name *e* for ever;
Pr 12: 19 Truthful lips *e* for ever,
27: 24 for riches do not *e* for ever,
Ecc 3: 14 everything God does will *e* for ever;
Da 2: 44 to an end, but it will itself *e* for ever.
Mal 3: 2 who can *e* the day of his coming?
1Co 4: 12 when we are persecuted, we *e* it;
2Co 1: 8 far beyond our ability to *e,*
2Ti 2: 3 *E* hardship with us like a good
2: 10 Therefore I *e* everything
2: 12 if we *e,* / we will also reign
4: 5 head in all situations, *e* hardship,
Heb 12: 7 *E* hardship as discipline; God is
1Pe 2: 20 a beating for doing wrong and *e* it?
2: 20 suffer for doing good and you *e* it,
Rev 3: 10 kept my command to *e* patiently,

ENDURED* (ENDURE)

Ps 123: 3 for we have *e* much contempt.
123: 4 We have *e* much ridicule
132: 1 and all the hardships he *e.*
Ac 13: 18 and *e* their conduct forty years
2Ti 3: 11 and Lystra, the persecutions I *e.*
Heb 12: 2 set before him *e* the cross,
12: 3 him who *e* such opposition
Rev 2: 3 and have *e* hardships for my name,

ENDURES (ENDURE)

Ps 102: 12 renown *e* through all generations.
112: 9 his righteousness *e* for ever;
136: 1 *His love e for ever.*
Da 9: 15 made for yourself a name that *e*
2Co 9: 9 his righteousness *e* for ever."

ENDURING (ENDURE)

2Th 1: 4 persecutions and trials you are *e.*
1Pe 1: 23 through the living and *e* word

ENEMIES (ENEMY)

Ps 23: 5 in the presence of my *e.*
110: 1 hand until I make your *e*
Pr 16: 7 his *e* live at peace with him.
Isa 59: 18 wrath to his *e*
Mic 7: 6 a man's *e* are the members
Mt 5: 44 Love your *e* and pray
10: 36 a man's *e* will be the members
Lk 6: 27 Love your *e,* do good
6: 35 But love your *e,* do good to them,
20: 43 hand until I make your *e*
Ro 5: 10 For if, when we were God's *e,*
1Co 15: 25 reign until he has put all his *e*
Php 3: 18 many live as *e* of the cross of Christ
Heb 1: 13 hand until I make your *e*
10: 13 for his *e* to be made his footstool,

ENEMY (ENEMIES ENMITY)

Pr 24: 17 Do not gloat when your *e* falls;
25: 21 If your *e* is hungry, give him food
27: 6 but an *e* multiplies kisses.
29: 24 of a thief is his own *e;*
Lk 10: 19 to overcome all the power of the *e;*
Ro 12: 20 "If your *e* is hungry, feed him;
1Co 15: 26 The last *e* to be destroyed is death.
1Ti 5: 14 and to give the *e* no opportunity
1Pe 5: 8 Your *e* the devil prowls

ENERGY*

Col 1: 29 struggling with all his *e,* which

ENGRAVED

Isa 49: 16 I have *e* you on the palms
2Co 3: 7 which was *e* in letters on stone,

ENHANCES*

Ro 3: 7 my falsehood *e* God's truthfulness

ENJOY (JOY)

Dt 6: 2 and so that you may *e* long life.
Ps 37: 3 dwell in the land and *e* safe pasture.
Pr 28: 16 ill-gotten gain will *e* a long life.
Ecc 3: 22 better for a man than to *e* his work,
Eph 6: 3 and that you may *e* long life
Heb 11: 25 rather than to *e* the pleasures of sin
3Jn : 2 I pray that you may *e* good health

ENJOYMENT (JOY)

Ecc 5: 8 and why am I depriving myself of *e*

1Ti 6: 17 us with everything for our *e*.

ENLARGE (ENLARGES)
2Co 9: 10 *e* the harvest of your righteousness.

ENLARGES (ENLARGE)
Dt 33: 20 Blessed is he who *e* Gad's domain!

ENLIGHTENED* (LIGHT [2])
Eph 1: 18 that the eyes of your heart may be *e*
Heb 6: 4 for those who have once been *e*,

ENMITY* (ENEMY)
Ge 3: 15 And I will put *e*

ENOCH
1. Son of Cain (Ge 4:17-18).
2. Descendant of Seth; walked with God and taken by him (Ge 5:18-24; Heb 11:5). Prophet (Jude 14).

ENQUIRE
Isa 8: 19 should not a people *e* of their God?

ENSLAVED (SLAVE)
Gal 4: 9 Do you wish to be *e* by them all
Tit 3: 3 and *e* by all kinds of passions

ENSNARE (SNARE)
Pr 5: 22 of a wicked man *e* him;
Ecc 7: 26 but the sinner she will *e*.

ENSNARED* (SNARE)
Dt 7: 25 for yourselves, or you will be *e* by it
12: 30 be careful not to be *e*
Ps 9: 16 the wicked are *e* by the work
Pr 6: 2 *e* by the words of your mouth,
22: 25 and get yourself *e*.

ENTANGLED (ENTANGLES)
2Pe 2: 20 and are again *e* in it and overcome,

ENTANGLES* (ENTANGLED)
Heb 12: 1 and the sin that so easily *e*,

ENTER (ENTERED ENTERING ENTERS ENTRANCE)
Ps 95: 11 "They shall never *e* my rest."
100: 4 *E* his gates with thanksgiving
Pr 2: 10 For wisdom will *e* your heart,
Mt 5: 20 will certainly not *e* the kingdom
7: 13 "*E* through the narrow gate.
7: 21 Lord,' will *e* the kingdom of heaven
18: 3 you will never *e* the kingdom
18: 8 It is better for you to *e* life maimed
19: 17 to *e* life, obey the commandments
19: 23 men to *e* the kingdom of heaven.
Mk 9: 43 It is better for you to *e* life maimed
9: 45 It is better for you to *e* life crippled
9: 47 for you to *e* the kingdom of God
10: 15 like a little child will never *e* it."
10: 23 is for the rich to *e* the kingdom
Lk 13: 24 will try to *e* and will not be able to.
13: 24 "Make every effort to *e*
18: 17 like a little child will never *e* it."
18: 24 is for the rich to *e* the kingdom
Jn 3: 5 he cannot *e* the kingdom of God.
Heb 3: 11 'They shall never *e* my rest.'"
4: 11 make every effort to *e* that rest,

ENTERED (ENTER)
Ps 73: 17 me till I *e* the sanctuary of God;
Eze 4: 14 meat has ever *e* my mouth."
Ac 11: 8 or unclean has ever *e* my mouth.'
Ro 5: 12 as sin *e* the world through one man,
Heb 9: 12 but he *e* the Most Holy Place once

ENTERING (ENTER)
Mt 21: 31 the prostitutes are *e* the kingdom
Lk 11: 52 have hindered those who were *e*."
Heb 4: 1 the promise of *e* his rest still stands,

ENTERS (ENTER)
Mk 7: 18 you see that nothing that *e* a man
Jn 10: 2 The man who *e* by the gate is

ENTERTAIN* (ENTERTAINED ENTERTAINMENT)
Jdg 16: 25 "Bring out Samson to *e* us."
Mt 9: 4 "Why do you *e* evil thoughts
1Ti 5: 19 Do not *e* an accusation
Heb 13: 2 Do not forget to *e* strangers,

ENTERTAINED* (ENTERTAIN)
Ac 28: 7 and for three days *e* us hospitably.
Heb 13: 2 so doing some people have *e* angels

ENTERTAINMENT* (ENTERTAIN)
Da 6: 18 without any *e* being brought to him

ENTHRALLED*
Ps 45: 11 The king is *e* by your beauty;

ENTHRONED* (THRONE)
1Sa 4: 4 who is *e* between the cherubim.
2Sa 6: 2 who is *e* between the cherubim that
2Ki 19: 15 of Israel, *e* between the cherubim,
1Ch 13: 6 who is *e* between the cherubim—
Ps 2: 4 The One *e* in heaven laughs;
9: 11 to the LORD; *e* in Zion;
22: 3 Yet you are *e* as the Holy One;
29: 10 The LORD sits *e* over the flood;
29: 10 the LORD is *e* as King for ever.
55: 19 God, who is *e* for ever,
61: 7 May he be *e* in God's presence
80: 1 who sit *e* between the cherubim,
99: 1 he sits *e* between the cherubim,
102: 12 But you, O LORD, sit *e* for ever;
113: 5 the One who sits *e* on high,
132: 14 here I will sit *e*, for I have desired it
Isa 14: 13 I will sit *e* on the mount
37: 16 of Israel, *e* between the cherubim,
40: 22 He sits *e* above the circle
52: 2 rise up, sit *e*, O Jerusalem.

ENTHRONES* (THRONE)
Job 36: 7 he *e* them with kings

ENTHUSIASM*
2Co 8: 17 he is coming to you with much *e*
9: 2 and your *e* has stirred most of them

ENTICE* (ENTICED ENTICES)
Pr 1: 10 My son, if sinners *e* you,
2Pe 2: 18 they *e* people who are just escaping
Rev 2: 14 who taught Balak to *e* the Israelites

ENTICED* (ENTICE)
Dt 4: 19 do not be *e* into bowing
11: 16 or you will be *e* to turn away

2Ki 17: 21 Jeroboam e Israel away
Job 31: 9 If my heart has been e by a woman,
     31: 27 so that my heart was secretly e
Jas   1: 14 desire, he is dragged away and e.

ENTICES* (ENTICE)

Dt   13: 6 your closest friend secretly e you,
Job 36: 18 Be careful that no-one e you
Pr   16: 29 A violent man e his neighbour

ENTIRE

Gal   5: 14 The e law is summed up

ENTRANCE (ENTER)

Mt   27: 60 stone in front of the e to the tomb
Mk   15: 46 a stone against the e of the tomb.
     16: 3 away from the e of the tomb?"
Jn   11: 38 cave with a stone laid across the e.
     20: 1 had been removed from the e.

ENTRUST (TRUST)

Jn   2: 24 Jesus would not e himself to them,
2Ti   2: 2 the presence of many witnesses e

ENTRUSTED (TRUST)

Jer 13: 20 Where is the flock that was e to you
Jn   5: 22 but has e all judgment to the Son,
Ro   3: 2 they have been e with the very
      6: 17 of teaching to which you were e.
1Co   4: 1 as those e with the secret things
Gal   2: 7 I had been e with the task
1Th   2: 4 by God to be e with the gospel.
1Ti   1: 11 of the blessed God, which he e
      6: 20 guard what has been e to your care.
2Ti   1: 12 able to guard what I have e to him
      1: 14 Guard the good deposit that was e
Tit   1: 3 light through the preaching e to me
      1: 7 Since an overseer is e
1Pe   2: 23 he e himself to him who judges
      5: 3 not lording it over those e to you,
Jude   : 3 once for all e to the saints.

ENVIES (ENVY)

Jas   4: 5 he caused to live in us e intensely?

ENVIOUS (ENVY)

Dt   32: 21 I will make them e
Pr   24: 19 or be e of the wicked,
Ro   10: 19 "I will make you e

ENVOY

Pr   13: 17 but a trustworthy e brings healing.

ENVY (ENVIES ENVIOUS ENVYING)

Pr   3: 31 Do not e a violent man
     14: 30 but e rots the bones.
     23: 17 Do not let your heart e sinners,
     24: 1 Do not e wicked men,
Mk   7: 22 malice, deceit, lewdness, e, slander
Ro   1: 29 They are full of e, murder, strife,
     11: 14 arouse my own people to e
1Co 13: 4 It does not e, it does not boast,
Gal   5: 21 factions and e; drunkenness, orgies
Php   1: 15 that some preach Christ out of e
1Ti   6: 4 quarrels about words that result in e,
Tit   3: 3 lived in malice and e, being hated
Jas   3: 14 But if you harbour bitter e
      3: 16 where you have e and selfish
1Pe   2: 1 e, and slander of every kind.

ENVYING* (ENVY)

Gal   5: 26 provoking and e each other.

EPHAH

Eze 45: 11 The e and the bath are

EPHESUS

Ac   8: 19 at E, where Paul left Priscilla
     19: 1 the interior and arrived at E.
Eph   1: 1 To the saints in E, the faithful
Rev   2: 1 the angel of the church in E write:

EPHRAIM

1. Second son of Joseph (Ge 41:52; 46:20).
Blessed as firstborn by Jacob (Ge 48). Tribe of
numbered (Nu 1:33; 26:37), blessed (Dt 33:17),
allotted land (Jos 16:4-9; Eze 48:5), failed to fully
possess (Jos 16:10; Jdg 1:29).
2. Synonymous with Northern Kingdom (Isa
7:17; Hos 5).

EQUAL (EQUALITY EQUITY)

Dt   33: 25 and your strength will e your days.
1Sa   9: 2 without e among the Israelites—
Isa 40: 25 who is my e?" says the Holy One.
     46: 5 you compare me or count me e?
Da   1: 19 and he found none e to Daniel,
Jn   5: 18 making himself e with God.
1Co 12: 25 that its parts should have e concern
2Co   2: 16 And who is e to such a task?

EQUALITY* (EQUAL)

2Co   8: 13 pressed, but that there might be e.
      8: 14 Then there will be e, as it is written:
Php   2: 6 did not consider e

EQUIP* (EQUIPPED)

Heb 13: 21 e you with everything good

EQUIPPED (EQUIP)

2Ti   3: 17 man of God may be thoroughly e

EQUITY* (EQUAL)

Ps   96: 10 he will judge the peoples with e.
     98: 9 and the peoples with e.
     99: 4 you have established e;

ERODES*

Job 14: 18 "But as a mountain e and crumbles

ERROR (ERRORS)

Jas   5: 20 Whoever turns a sinner from the e
2Pe   2: 18 escaping from those who live in e.

ERRORS* (ERROR)

Ps   19: 12 Who can discern his e?
Ecc 10: 4 calmness can lay great e to rest.

ESAU

Firstborn of Isaac, twin of Jacob (Ge 25:21-
26). Also called Edom (Ge 25:30). Sold Jacob his
birthright (Ge 25:29-34); lost blessing (Ge 27).
Married Hittites (Ge 26:34), Ishmaelites (Ge
28:6-9). Reconciled to Jacob (Ge 22). Genealogy
(Ge 36). The LORD chose Jacob over Esau (Mal
1:2-3), but gave Esau land (Dt 2:2-12).
Descendants eventually obliterated (Ob 1-21; Jer
49:7-22).

ESCAPE (ESCAPED ESCAPES ESCAPING)

Ps	68: 20	from the Sovereign LORD comes e
Pr	11: 9	through knowledge the righteous e.
Ro	2: 3	think you will e God's judgment?
1Th	5: 3	woman, and they will not e.
2Ti	2: 26	and e from the trap of the devil,
Heb	2: 3	how shall we e if we ignore such
	12: 25	If they did not e when they refused
2Pe	1: 4	and e the corruption in the world

ESCAPED (ESCAPE)

2Pe	2: 20	If they have e the corruption

ESCAPES (ESCAPE)

Pr	12: 13	but a righteous man e trouble.

ESCAPING (ESCAPE)

1Co	3: 15	only as one e through the flames.
2Pe	2: 18	they entice people who are just e

ESTABLISH (ESTABLISHED ESTABLISHES)

Ge	6: 18	But I will e my covenant with you,
	17: 21	But my covenant I will e with Isaac
2Sa	7: 11	the LORD himself will e a house
1Ki	9: 5	I will e your royal throne
1Ch	28: 7	I will e his kingdom for ever
Ps	90: 17	e the work of our hands for us—
Isa	26: 12	LORD, you e peace for us;
Ro	10: 3	God and sought to e their own,
	16: 25	able to e you by my gospel
Heb	10: 9	sets aside the first to e the second.

ESTABLISHED (ESTABLISH)

Ge	9: 17	the sign of the covenant I have e
Ex	6: 4	also e my covenant with them
Pr	16: 12	a throne is e through righteousness.

ESTABLISHES (ESTABLISH)

Job	25: 2	he e order in the heights of heaven.
Isa	42: 4	till he e justice on earth.

ESTATE

Ps	136: 23	who remembered us in our low e

ESTEEMED

Pr	22: 1	to be e is better than silver or gold.
Isa	53: 3	he was despised, and we e him not.

ESTHER

Jewess, originally named Hadassah, who lived in
Persia; cousin of Mordecai (Est 2:7). Chosen
queen of Xerxes (Est 2:8-18). Persuaded by
Mordecai to foil Haman's plan to exterminate the
Jews (Est 3-4). Revealed Haman's plans to
Xerxes, resulting in Haman's death (Est 7), the
Jews' preservation (Est 8-9), Mordecai's exaltation
(Est 8:15; 9:4; 10). Decreed celebration of Purim
(Est 9:18-32).

ETERNAL* (ETERNALLY ETERNITY)

Ge	21: 33	the name of the LORD, the E God.
Dt	33: 27	The e God is your refuge,
1Ki	10: 9	of the LORD's e love for Israel,
Ps	16: 11	with e pleasures at your right hand.
	21: 6	you have granted him e blessings
	111: 10	To him belongs e praise.
	119: 89	Your word, O LORD, is e;
	119: 160	all your righteous laws are e.
Ecc	12: 5	Then man goes to his e home

Isa	26: 4	LORD, the LORD, is the Rock e.
	47: 7	the e queen!'
Jer	10: 10	he is the living God, the e King.
Da	4: 3	His kingdom is an e kingdom;
	4: 34	His dominion is an e dominion;
Hab	3: 6	His ways are e.
Mt	18: 8	two feet and be thrown into e fire.
	19: 16	good thing must I do to get e life?"
	19: 29	as much and will inherit e life.
	25: 41	into the e fire prepared for the devil
	25: 46	but the righteous to e life."
	25: 46	they will go away to e punishment,
Mk	3: 29	be forgiven; he is guilty of an e sin."
	10: 17	"what must I do to inherit e life?"
	10: 30	and in the age to come, e life.
Lk	10: 25	"what must I do to inherit e life?"
	16: 9	will be welcomed into e dwellings.
	18: 18	what must I do to inherit e life?"
	18: 30	and, in the age to come, e life."
Jn	3: 15	believes in him may have e life.
	3: 16	him shall not perish but have e life.
	3: 36	believes in the Son has e life,
	4: 14	spring of water welling up to e life."
	4: 36	now he harvests the crop for e life,
	5: 24	believes him who sent me has e life
	5: 39	that by them you possess e life.
	6: 27	but for food that endures to e life,
	6: 40	believes in him shall have e life,
	6: 54	and drinks my blood has e life,
	6: 68	You have the words of e life.
	10: 28	I give them e life, and they shall
	12: 25	in this world will keep it for e life.
	12: 50	that his command leads to e life.
	17: 2	all people that he might give e life
	17: 3	this is e life: that they may know
Ac	13: 46	yourselves worthy of e life,
	13: 48	were appointed for e life believed.
Ro	1: 20	his e power and divine nature—
	2: 7	and immortality, he will give e life.
	5: 21	righteousness to bring e life
	6: 22	to holiness, and the result is e life.
	6: 23	but the gift of God is e life
	16: 26	by the command of the e God,
2Co	4: 17	for us an e glory that far outweighs
	4: 18	temporary, but what is unseen is e.
	5: 1	from God, an e house in heaven,
Gal	6: 8	from the Spirit will reap e life.
Eph	3: 11	to his e purpose which he
2Th	2: 16	his grace gave us e encouragement
1Ti	1: 16	believe on him and receive e life.
	1: 17	Now to the King e, immortal,
	6: 12	Take hold of the e life
2Ti	2: 10	is in Christ Jesus, with e glory.
Tit	1: 2	resting on the hope of e life,
	3: 7	heirs having the hope of e life.
Heb	5: 9	he became the source of salvation
	6: 2	of the dead, and e judgment.
	9: 12	having obtained e redemption.
	9: 14	through the e Spirit offered himself
	9: 15	the promised e inheritance—
	13: 20	of the e covenant brought back
1Pe	5: 10	you to his e glory in Christ,
2Pe	1: 11	into the e kingdom of our Lord
1Jn	1: 2	and we proclaim to you the e life,
	2: 25	what he promised us—even e life.
	3: 15	know that no murderer has e life
	5: 11	God has given us e life,
	5: 13	you may know that you have e life,
	5: 20	He is the true God and e life.
Jude	: 7	who suffer the punishment of e fire.

Jude : 21 Christ to bring you to e life.
Rev 14: 6 and he had the e gospel to proclaim

ETERNALLY* (ETERNAL)

Gal 1: 8 let him be e condemned! As we
1: 9 let him be e condemned! Am I now

ETERNITY* (ETERNAL)

Ps 93: 2 you are from all e.
Pr 8: 23 I was appointed from e,
Ecc 3: 11 also set e in the hearts of men;

ETHIOPIAN*

Jer 13: 23 Can the E change his skin
Ac 8: 27 and on his way he met an E eunuch

EUNUCH (EUNUCHS)

Ac 8: 27 on his way he met an Ethiopian e,

EUNUCHS (EUNUCH)

Isa 56: 4 "To the e who keep my Sabbaths,
Mt 19: 12 For some are e because they were

EUTYCHUS*

Ac 20: 9 was a young man named E,

EVANGELIST* (EVANGELISTS)

Ac 21: 8 stayed at the house of Philip the e,
2Ti 4: 5 hardship, do the work of an e,

EVANGELISTS* (EVANGELIST)

Eph 4: 11 some to be prophets, some to be e,

EVE*

Ge 3: 20 Adam named his wife E,
4: 1 Adam lay with his wife E,
2Co 11: 3 as E was deceived by the serpent's
1Ti 2: 13 For Adam was formed first, then E

EVEN-TEMPERED* (TEMPER)

Pr 17: 27 and a man of understanding is e.

EVENING

Ge 1: 5 there was e, and there was morning

EVER (EVERLASTING EVERMORE)

Ge 3: 22 the tree of life and eat, and live for e.
6: 3 Spirit will not contend with man for e,
Ex 3: 15 This is my name for e, the name
15: 18 Lord will reign for e and e.
Dt 8: 19 If you e forget the Lord your
2Sa 7: 26 so that your name will be great for e.
1Ki 2: 33 may there be the LORD's peace for e.
3: 12 anyone like you, nor will there e be.
9: 3 by putting my Name there for e.
1Ch 16: 15 He remembers his covenant for e,
16: 34 his love endures for e.
16: 41 "for his love endures for e."
17: 24 and that your name will be great for e.
2Ch 5: 13 his love endures for e.
20: 21 for his love endures for e.
Job 4: 7 were the upright e destroyed?
Ps 5: 11 let them e sing for joy.
9: 7 The LORD reigns for e
10: 16 The LORD is King for e and e.
21: 4 length of days, for e and e
23: 6 dwell in the house of the LORD for e
25: 3 will e be put to shame
25: 15 My eyes are e on the LORD,
26: 3 for your Love is e before me,

Ps 28: 9 be their shepherd and carry them for e
29: 10 The Lord is enthroned as King for e.
33: 11 the plans of the LORD stand firm for e
37: 28 They will be protected for e
44: 8 and we will praise your name for e
45: 6 O God, will last for e and e
45: 17 nations will praise you for e and e.
46: 1 an e present help in trouble
48: 14 For this God is our God for e and e.
52: 8 God's unfailing love for e and e
61: 4 I long to dwell in your tent for e
61: 8 will I e sing praise to your name
71: 6 I will e praise your
72: 19 Praise be to his glorious name for e
73: 26 and my portion for e
77: 8 Has his unfailing love vanished for e?
79: 13 will praise you for e;
81: 15 and their punishment would last for e.
84: 4 they are e praising you
86: 12 I will glorify your name for e
89: 1 of the LORD's great love for e
89: 33 nor will I e betray my faithfulness.
92: 8 But you, O LORD, are exalted for e.
100: 5 is good and his love endures for e.
102: 12 But you, O LORD, sit enthroned for e
104: 31 of the LORD endure for e
107: 1 his love endures for e
110: 4 "You are a priest for e
111: 3 and his righteousness endures for e.
111: 8 They are steadfast for e and e
112: 6 man will be remembered for e.
117: 2 of the LORD endures for e
118: 1 his love endures for e
119: 44 your law, for e and e
119: 98 for they are e with me
119: 111 Your statutes are my heritage for e
119: 152 that you established them to last for e
132: 12 sit on your throne for e and e
136: 1 *His love endures for e*
145: 1 I will praise your name for e and e
145: 2 and extol your name for e and e
145: 21 his holy name for e and e
146: 6 the LORD, who remains faithful for e
Pr 4: 18 shining & brighter till the full light
5: 19 may you e be captivated
10: 25 but the righteous stand firm for e.
27: 24 for riches do not endure for e
Isa 25: 8 he will swallow up death for e
26: 4 Trust in the LORD for e,
32: 17 will be quietness and confidence for e
40: 8 but the word of our God stands for e
51: 6 But my salvation will last for e
51: 8 But my righteousness will last for e
57: 15 he who lives for e, whose name is holy:
59: 21 from this time on and for e
66: 8 Who has e heard of such a thing?
66: 8 Who has e seen such things?
Jer 7: 7 I gave your forefathers for e and e.
25: 5 and your fathers for e and e
31: 36 the descendants of Israel e cease
33: 11 his love endures for e
Eze 37: 26 put my sanctuary among them for e
Da 2: 20 be to the name of God for e and e
2: 44 to an end, but it will itself endure for e
3: 9 live for e! You have issued a decree,
7: 18 for e—yes, for e and e
12: 3 like the stars for e and e
Mic 4: 5 our God for e and e
Mt 13: 14 you will be e seeing but never
13: 14 you will be e hearing

Mk	4: 12	*e* hearing but never understanding
Jn	1: 18	No-one has *e* seen God
	6: 51	eats of this bread, he will live for *e*
	14: 16	Counsellor to be with you for *e*—
Ro	9: 5	who is God over all, for *e* praised!
	16: 27	to the only wise God be glory for *e*
1Co	9: 25	to get a crown that will last for *e*
Gal	1: 5	to whom be glory for *e* and *e*
Eph	3: 21	all generations, for *e* and *e*!
Phi	4: 20	and Father be glory for *e* and *e*
1Th	4: 17	And so we will be with the Lord for *e*
1Ti	1: 17	be honour and glory for *e* and *e*
2Ti	4: 18	To him be glory for *e* and *e*
Heb	1: 8	O God, will last for *e* and *e*
	5: 6	You are a priest for *e*
	7: 17	You are a priest for *e*
	7: 24	Jesus lives for *e*, he has a permanent
	13: 8	same yesterday and today and for *e*
	13: 21	to whom be glory for *e* and *e*
1Pe	1: 25	but the word of the Lord stands for *e*
	4: 11	the glory and the power for *e* and *e*
	5: 11	To him be the power for *e* and *e*
Jn	2: 17	who does the will of God lives for *e*
	4: 12	No-one has *e* seen God;
2Jn	: 2	lives in us and will be with us for *e*
Rev	1: 6	him be glory and power for *e* and *e*!
	1: 18	and behold I am alive for *e* and *e*!
	21: 27	Nothing impure will *e* enter it
	22: 5	And they will reign for *e* and *e*

EVER-INCREASING* (INCREASE)

Ro	6: 19	to impurity and to *e* wickedness,
2Co	3: 18	into his likeness with *e* glory,

EVERLASTING* (EVER)

Ge	9: 16	and remember the *e* covenant
	17: 7	an *e* covenant between me and you
	17: 8	I will give as an *e* possession to you
	17: 13	in your flesh is to be an *e* covenant.
	17: 19	an *e* covenant for his descendants
	48: 4	*e* possession to your descendants
Nu	18: 19	It is an *e* covenant of salt
Dt	33: 15	and the fruitfulness of the *e* hills;
	33: 27	and underneath are the *e* arms.
2Sa	23: 5	made with me an *e* covenant,
1Ch	16: 17	to Israel as an *e* covenant:
	16: 36	from *e* to *e*.
	29: 10	from *e* to *e*.
Ezr	9: 12	to your children as an *e* inheritance
Ne	9: 5	your God, who is from *e* to *e*."
Ps	41: 13	from *e* to *e*.
	52: 5	God will bring you down to *e* ruin:
	74: 3	through these *e* ruins,
	78: 66	he put them to *e* shame.
	90: 2	from *e* to *e* you are God.
	103: 17	But from *e* to *e*
	105: 10	to Israel as an *e* covenant:
	106: 48	from *e* to *e*.
	119: 142	Your righteousness is *e*
	139: 24	and lead me in the way *e*.
	145: 13	Your kingdom is an *e* kingdom,
Isa	9: 6	*E* Father, Prince of Peace.
	24: 5	and broken the *e* covenant.
	30: 8	it may be an *e* witness.
	33: 14	Who of us can dwell with *e* burning
	35: 10	*e* joy will crown their heads.
	40: 28	The LORD is the *e* God,
	45: 17	the LORD with an *e* salvation;
	45: 17	to ages *e*.
	51: 11	*e* joy will crown their heads.

Isa	54: 8	but with *e* kindness
	55: 3	I will make an *e* covenant with you,
	55: 13	for an *e* sign,
	56: 5	I will give them an *e* name
	60: 15	I will make you the *e* pride
	60: 19	for the LORD will be your *e* light,
	60: 20	the LORD will be your *e* light,
	61: 7	and *e* joy will be theirs.
	61: 8	and make an *e* covenant with them.
	63: 12	to gain for himself *e* renown,
Jer	5: 22	an *e* barrier it cannot cross.
	23: 40	I will bring upon you *e* disgrace—
	23: 40	*e* shame that will not be forgotten."
	25: 9	of horror and scorn, and an *e* ruin.
	31: 3	"I have loved you with an *e* love;
	32: 40	I will make you an *e* covenant
	50: 5	the LORD in an *e* covenant
Eze	16: 60	and I will establish an *e* covenant
	37: 26	with them; it will be an *e* covenant.
Da	7: 14	dominion is an *e* dominion that will
	7: 27	His kingdom will be an *e* kingdom,
	9: 24	to bring in *e* righteousness,
	12: 2	others to shame and *e* contempt.
	12: 2	some to *e* life, others to shame
Mic	6: 2	you *e* foundations of the earth.
Hab	1: 12	O LORD, are you not from *e*?
Jn	6: 47	the truth, he who believes has *e* life.
2Th	1: 9	punished with *e* destruction
Jude	: 6	bound with *e* chains for judgment

EVERMORE

Ps	113: 2	both now and for *e*.

EVIDENCE (EVIDENT)

Jn	14: 11	on the *e* of the miracles themselves.
Ac	11: 23	and saw the *e* of the grace of God,
2Th	1: 5	All this is *e* that God's judgment is
Jas	2: 20	do you want *e* that faith

EVIDENT (EVIDENCE)

Php	4: 5	Let your gentleness be *e* to all.

EVIL (EVILDOER EVILDOERS EVILS)

Ge	2: 9	of the knowledge of good and *e*.
	3: 5	be like God, knowing good and *e*."
	6: 5	of his heart was only *e* all the time.
Ex	32: 22	how prone these people are to *e*,
Jdg	2: 11	Then the Israelites did *e* in the eyes
	3: 7	The Israelites did *e* in the eyes
	3: 12	Once again the Israelites did *e*
	4: 1	the Israelites once again did *e*
	6: 1	Again the Israelites did *e*
	10: 6	Again the Israelites did *e*
	13: 1	Again the Israelites did *e*
1Ki	11: 6	So Solomon did *e* in the eyes
	16: 25	But Omri did *e* in the eyes
2Ki	15: 24	Pekahiah did *e* in the eyes
Job	1: 1	he feared God and shunned *e*.
	1: 8	a man who fears God and shuns *e*."
	34: 10	Far be it from God to do *e*,
	36: 21	Beware of turning to *e*,
Ps	5: 4	not a God who takes pleasure in *e*;
	23: 4	I will fear no *e*,
	34: 13	keep your tongue from *e*
	34: 14	Turn from *e* and do good;
	34: 16	is against those who do *e*,
	37: 1	Do not fret because of *e* men
	37: 8	do not fret—it leads only to *e*.
	37: 27	Turn from *e* and do good;
	49: 5	fear when *e* days come,

Ps	51: 4	and done what is *e* in your sight,
	97: 10	those who love the LORD hate *e*,
	101: 4	I will have nothing to do with *e*.
	141: 4	not my heart be drawn to what is *e*,
Pr	4: 27	keep your foot from *e*.
	8: 13	To fear the LORD is to hate *e*;
	10: 23	A fool finds pleasure in *e* conduct,
	11: 19	he who pursues *e* goes to his death.
	11: 27	*e* comes to him who searches for it.
	14: 16	man fears the LORD and shuns *e*,
	17: 13	If a man pays back *e* for good,
	20: 30	Blows and wounds cleanse away *e*,
	24: 19	Do not fret because of *e* men
	24: 20	for the *e* man has no future hope,
	26: 23	are fervent lips with an *e* heart.
	28: 5	*E* men do not understand justice,
	29: 6	An *e* man is snared by his own sin,
Ecc	12: 14	whether it is good or *e*.
Isa	5: 20	Woe to those who call *e* good
	13: 11	I will punish the world for its *e*,
	55: 7	and the *e* man his thoughts.
Jer	4: 14	wash the *e* from your heart
	18: 8	nation I warned repents of its *e*,
	18: 11	So turn from your *e* ways,
Eze	33: 11	Turn! Turn from your *e* ways!
	33: 13	he will die for the *e* he has done.
	33: 15	and does no *e*, he will surely live;
Am	5: 13	for the times are *e*.
Hab	1: 13	Your eyes are too pure to look on *e*;
Zec	8: 17	do not plot *e* against your neighbour,
Mt	5: 45	He causes his sun to rise on the *e*
	6: 13	but deliver us from the *e* one.'
	7: 11	If you, then, though you are *e*,
	12: 34	you who are *e* say anything good?
	12: 35	and the *e* man brings *e* things out
	12: 35	out of the *e* stored up in him.
	12: 43	"When an *e* spirit comes out
	15: 19	out of the heart come *e* thoughts,
Mk	7: 21	come *e* thoughts, sexual
Lk	6: 45	and the *e* man brings *e* things out
	11: 13	If you then, though you are *e*,
Jn	3: 19	of light because their deeds were *e*.
	3: 20	Everyone who does *e* hates
	17: 15	you protect them from the *e* one.
Ro	1: 30	they invent ways of doing *e*;
	2: 8	who reject the truth and follow *e*,
	2: 9	for every human being who does *e*:
	3: 8	"Let us do *e* that good may result"?
	6: 12	body so that you obey its *e* desires.
	7: 19	no, the *e* I do not want to do—
	7: 21	to do good, *e* is right there with me.
	12: 9	Hate what is *e*; cling
	12: 17	Do not repay anyone *e* for *e*.
	12: 21	Do not be overcome by *e*,
	14: 16	good to be spoken of as *e*.
	16: 19	and innocent about what is *e*.
1Co	13: 6	Love does not delight in *e*
	14: 20	In regard to *e* be infants,
Eph	5: 16	because the days are *e*.
	6: 12	forces of *e* in the heavenly realms.
	6: 16	all the flaming arrows of the *e* one.
Col	3: 5	impurity, lust, *e* desires and greed,
1Th	5: 22	Avoid every kind of *e*.
2Th	3: 3	and protect you from the *e* one.
1Ti	6: 10	of money is a root of all kinds of *e*.
2Ti	2: 22	Flee the *e* desires of youth,
	3: 6	are swayed by all kinds of *e* desires,
	3: 13	while *e* men and impostors will go
Heb	5: 14	to distinguish good from *e*.
Jas	1: 13	For God cannot be tempted by *e*,

Jas	1: 21	and the *e* that is so prevalent,
	3: 6	a world of *e* among the parts
	3: 8	It is a restless *e*, full
1Pe	2: 16	your freedom as a cover-up for *e*;
	3: 9	Do not repay *e* with *e* or insult
	3: 10	must keep his tongue from *e*
	3: 17	for doing good than for doing *e*.
1Jn	2: 13	you have overcome the *e* one.
	2: 14	and you have overcome the *e* one.
	3: 12	who belonged to the *e* one
	5: 18	and the *e* one cannot harm him.
	5: 19	is under the control of the *e* one.
3Jn	: 11	do not imitate what is *e*

EVILDOER* (EVIL)

2Sa	3: 39	the LORD repay the *e* according
Ps	101: 8	I will cut off every *e*
Mal	4: 1	and every *e* will be stubble,

EVILDOERS* (EVIL)

1Sa	24: 13	saying goes, 'From *e* come evil
Job	8: 20	or strengthen the hands of *e*.
	34: 8	He keeps company with *e*;
	34: 22	where *e* can hide.
Ps	14: 4	Will *e* never learn—
	14: 6	You *e* frustrate the plans
	26: 5	I abhor the assembly of *e*
	36: 12	See how the *e* lie fallen—
	53: 4	Will the *e* never learn—
	59: 2	Deliver me from *e*
	64: 2	from that noisy crowd of *e*,
	92: 7	and all *e* flourish,
	92: 9	all *e* will be scattered.
	94: 4	all the *e* are full of boasting.
	94: 16	will take a stand for me against *e*?
	119: 115	Away from me, you *e*,
	125: 5	the LORD will banish with the *e*.
	141: 4	deeds with men who are *e*;
	141: 5	ever against the deeds of *e*;
	141: 9	from the traps set by *e*.
Pr	21: 15	but terror to *e*.
Isa	1: 4	a brood of *e*,
	31: 2	against those who help *e*.
Jer	23: 14	They strengthen the hands of *e*,
Hos	10: 9	the *e* in Gibeah?
Mal	3: 15	Certainly the *e* prosper, and
Mt	7: 23	you *e*!' "Therefore everyone who
Lk	13: 27	Away from me, all you *e*!'
	18: 11	*e*, adulterers—or even like this tax

EVILS* (EVIL)

Mk	7: 23	All these *e* come from inside

EWE

2Sa	12: 3	one little *e* lamb he had bought.

EXACT*

Ge	43: 21	the *e* weight—in the mouth
Est	4: 7	including the *e* amount
Mt	2: 7	from them the *e* time the star had
Jn	4: 53	realised that this was the *e* time
Ac	17: 26	the places where they should live.
Heb	1: 3	the *e* representation of his being,

EXALT* (EXALTED EXALTS)

Ex	15: 2	my father's God, and I will *e* him.
Jos	3: 7	begin to *e* you in the eyes
1Sa	2: 10	and the horn of his anointed."
1Ch	25: 5	the promises of God to *e* him.
	29: 12	power to *e* and give strength to all.

Job 19: 5 If indeed you would *e* yourselves
Ps 30: 1 I will *e* you, O LORD,
34: 3 let us *e* his name together.
35: 26 may all who *e* themselves over me
37: 34 He will *e* you to inherit the land;
38: 16 *e* themselves over me
75: 6 or from the desert can *e* a man.
89: 17 and by your favour you *e* our horn.
99: 5 *E* the LORD our God
99: 9 *E* the LORD our God
107: 32 Let them *e* him in the assembly
118: 28 you are my God, and I will *e* you.
145: 1 I will *e* you, my God the King;
Pr 4: 8 Esteem her, and she will *e* you;
25: 6 Do not *e* yourself in the king's
Isa 24: 15 *e* the name of the LORD, the God
25: 1 I will *e* you and praise your name,
Eze 29: 15 and will never again *e* itself
Da 4: 37 *e* and glorify the King of heaven,
11: 36 He will *e* and magnify himself
11: 37 but will *e* himself above them all.
Hos 11: 7 he will by no means *e* them.

EXALTED* (EXALT)

Ex 15: 1 for he is highly *e*.
15: 21 for he is highly *e*.
Nu 24: 7 their kingdom will be *e*.
Jos 4: 14 That day the LORD *e* Joshua
2Sa 5: 12 and had *e* his kingdom for the sake
22: 47 *E* be God, the Rock, my Saviour!
22: 49 You *e* me above my foes;
23: 1 of the man *e* by the Most High,
1Ch 14: 2 that his kingdom had been highly *e*
17: 17 as though I were the most *e* of men,
29: 11 you are *e* as head over all.
29: 25 The LORD highly *e* Solomon
Ne 9: 5 and may it be *e* above all blessing
Job 24: 24 For a little while they are *e*,
36: 22 "God is *e* in his power.
37: 23 beyond our reach and *e* in power;
Ps 18: 46 *E* be God my Saviour!
18: 48 You *e* me above my foes;
21: 13 Be *e*, O LORD, in your strength;
27: 6 Then my head will be *e*
35: 27 they always say, "The LORD be *e*,
40: 16 "The LORD be *e*!"
46: 10 I will be *e* among the nations,
46: 10 I will be *e* in the earth."
47: 9 he is greatly *e*.
57: 5 Be *e*, O God, above the heavens;
57: 11 Be *e*, O God, above the heavens;
70: 4 "Let God be *e*!"
89: 13 hand is strong, your right hand *e*.
89: 19 I have *e* a young man
89: 24 through my name his horn will be *e*
89: 27 the most *e* of the kings of the earth.
89: 42 You have *e* the right hand
92: 8 But you, O LORD, are *e* for ever.
92: 10 You have *e* my horn like that
97: 9 you are *e* far above all gods.
99: 2 he is *e* over all the nations.
108: 5 Be *e*, O God, above the heavens,
113: 4 The LORD is *e* over all the nations
138: 2 for you have *e* above all things
148: 13 for his name alone is *e*;
Pr 11: 11 of the upright a city is *e*,
30: 32 have played the fool and *e* yourself,
Isa 2: 11 the LORD alone will be *e*
2: 12 for all that is *e*
2: 17 the LORD alone will be *e*

Isa 5: 16 the LORD Almighty will be *e*
6: 1 *e*, and the train of his robe filled
12: 4 and proclaim that his name is *e*.
24: 4 the *e* of the earth languish.
33: 5 The LORD is *e*, for he dwells
33: 10 "Now will I be *e*;
52: 13 be raised and lifted up and highly *e*.
Jer 17: 12 A glorious throne, *e*
La 2: 17 he has *e* the horn of your foes.
Eze 21: 26 The lowly will be *e* and the *e* will be
Hos 13: 1 he was *e* in Israel.
Mic 6: 6 and bow down before the *e* God?
Mt 23: 12 whoever humbles himself will be *e*.
Lk 14: 11 he who humbles himself will be *e*."
18: 14 he who humbles himself will be *e*."
Ac 2: 33 *E* to the right hand of God,
5: 31 God *e* him to his own right hand
Php 1: 20 always Christ will be *e* in my body,
2: 9 Therefore God *e* him
Heb 7: 26 from sinners, *e* above the heavens.

EXALTS* (EXALT)

1Sa 2: 7 he humbles and he *e*.
Job 36: 7 and *e* them for ever.
Ps 75: 7 He brings one down, he *e* another.
Pr 14: 34 Righteousness *e* a nation,
Mt 23: 12 For whoever *e* himself will be
Lk 14: 11 For everyone who *e* himself will be
18: 14 For everyone who *e* himself will be
2Th 2: 4 *e* himself over everything that is

EXAMINE (EXAMINED EXAMINES)

Ps 11: 4 his eyes *e* them.
17: 3 you probe my heart and *e* me
26: 2 *e* my heart and my mind;
Jer 17: 10 and *e* the mind,
20: 12 Almighty, you who *e* the righteous
La 3: 40 Let us *e* our ways and test them,
1Co 11: 28 A man ought to *e* himself
2Co 13: 5 *E* yourselves to see whether you

EXAMINED (EXAMINE)

Job 13: 9 Would it turn out well if he *e* you?
Ac 17: 11 *e* the Scriptures every day to see

EXAMINES (EXAMINE)

Ps 11: 5 The LORD *e* the righteous,
Pr 5: 21 and he *e* all his paths.

EXAMPLE* (EXAMPLES)

2Ki 14: 3 In everything he followed the *e*
Ecc 9: 13 also saw under the sun this *e*
Eze 14: 8 and make him an *e* and a byword.
Jn 13: 15 have set you an *e* that you should
Ro 7: 2 as long as he lives? For *e*,
1Co 11: 1 Follow my *e*, as I follow
11: 1 as I follow the *e* of Christ.
Gal 3: 15 let me take an *e* from everyday life.
Php 3: 17 Join with others in following my *e*,
2Th 3: 7 how you ought to follow our *e*.
1Ti 1: 16 as an *e* for those who would believe
4: 12 set an *e* for the believers in speech,
Tit 2: 7 In everything set them an *e*
Heb 4: 11 fall by following their *e*
Jas 3: 4 Or take ships as an *e*.
5: 10 as an *e* of patience in the face
1Pe 2: 21 leaving you an *e*, that you should
2Pe 2: 6 made them an *e* of what is going
Jude : 7 as an *e* of those who suffer

EXAMPLES* (EXAMPLE)

1Co 10: 6 Now these things occurred as *e*,
10: 11 as *e* and were written down
1Pe 5: 3 to you, but being *e* to the flock.

EXASPERATE*

Eph 6: 4 Fathers, do not *e* your children;

EXCEL* (EXCELLENT)

Ge 49: 4 as the waters, you will no longer *e*,
1Co 14: 12 to *e* in gifts that build up the church
2Co 8: 7 But just as you *e* in everything—
8: 7 also *e* in this grace of giving.

EXCELLENT (EXCEL)

1Co 12: 31 now I will show you the most *e* way
Php 4: 8 if anything is *e* or praiseworthy—
1Ti 3: 13 have served well gain an *e* standing
Tit 3: 8 These things are *e* and profitable

EXCESSIVE

Eze 18: 8 or take *e* interest.
2Co 2: 7 not be overwhelmed by *e* sorrow.

EXCHANGE (EXCHANGED)

Mt 16: 26 Or what can a man give in *e*
Mk 8: 37 Or what can a man give in *e*
2Co 6: 13 As a fair *e*—I speak

EXCHANGED (EXCHANGE)

Ps 106: 20 They *e* their Glory
Jer 2: 11 But my people have *e* their Glory
Hos 4: 7 they *e* their Glory
Ro 1: 23 *e* the glory of the immortal God
1: 25 They *e* the truth of God for a lie,
1: 26 their women *e* natural relations

EXCLAIM

Ps 35: 10 My whole being will *e*,

EXCUSE* (EXCUSES)

Ps 25: 3 who are treacherous without *e*.
Lk 14: 18 Please *e* me.'
14: 19 Please *e* me.'
Jn 15: 22 they have no *e* for their sin.
Ro 1: 20 so that men are without *e*.
2: 1 You, therefore, have no *e*,

EXCUSES* (EXCUSE)

Lk 14: 18 "But they all alike began to make *e*.

EXERTED*

Eph 1: 20 which he *e* in Christ

EXHORT*

1Ti 5: 1 but *e* him as if he were your father.

EXILE

2Ki 17: 23 taken from their homeland into *e*
25: 11 into *e* the people who remained

EXISTED* (EXISTS)

2Pe 3: 5 ago by God's word the heavens *e*

EXISTS (EXISTED)

Heb 2: 10 and through whom everything *e*,
11: 6 to him must believe that he *e*

EXPANSE

Ge 1: 7 So God made the *e* and separated

Ge 1: 8 God called the *e* "sky."

EXPECT (EXPECTATION EXPECTED EXPECTING)

Mt 24: 44 at an hour when you do not *e* him.
Lk 12: 40 at an hour when you do not *e* him."
Php 1: 20 I eagerly *e* and hope that I will

EXPECTATION (EXPECT)

Ro 8: 19 waits in eager *e* for the sons
Heb 10: 27 but only a fearful *e* of judgment

EXPECTED (EXPECT)

Pr 11: 7 all he *e* from his power comes
Hag 1: 9 "You *e* much, but see, it turned out

EXPECTING (EXPECT)

Lk 6: 35 and lend to them without *e*

EXPEL* (EXPELLED)

1Co 5: 13 *E* the wicked man from among you

EXPELLED (EXPEL)

Eze 28: 16 and I *e* you, O guardian cherub,

EXPENSE (EXPENSIVE)

1Co 9: 7 Who serves as a soldier at his own *e*

EXPENSIVE* (EXPENSE)

Mt 26: 7 jar of very *e* perfume,
Mk 14: 3 jar of very *e* perfume,
Lk 7: 25 those who wear *e* clothes
Jn 12: 3 a pint of pure nard, an *e* perfume;
1Ti 2: 9 or gold or pearls or *e* clothes,

EXPERT

1Co 3: 10 I laid a foundation as an *e* builder,

EXPLAINING (EXPLAINS)

Ac 17: 3 *e* and proving that the Christ had

EXPLAINS* (EXPLAINING)

Ac 8: 31 he said, "unless someone *e* it to me

EXPLOIT* (EXPLOITED EXPLOITING EXPLOITS)

Pr 22: 22 Do not *e* the poor because they are
Isa 58: 3 and *e* all your workers.
2Co 12: 17 Did I *e* you through any
12: 18 Titus did not *e* you, did he?
2Pe 2: 3 greed these teachers will *e* you

EXPLOITED* (EXPLOIT)

2Co 7: 2 no-one, we have *e* no-one.

EXPLOITING* (EXPLOIT)

Jas 2: 6 Is it not the rich who are *e* you?

EXPLOITS (EXPLOIT)

2Co 11: 20 or *e* you or takes advantage of you

EXPLORE

Nu 13: 2 "Send some men to *e* the land

EXPOSE (EXPOSED)

1Co 4: 5 will *e* the motives of men's hearts.
Eph 5: 11 of darkness, but rather *e* them.

EXPOSED (EXPOSE)

Jn 3: 20 for fear that his deeds will be *e*.

Eph　5:13 everything *e* by the light becomes

EXPRESS (EXPRESSING)
Ro　8:26 us with groans that words cannot *e.*

EXPRESSING* (EXPRESS)
1Co　2:13 *e* spiritual truths in spiritual words.
Gal　5: 6 thing that counts is faith *e* itself

EXTENDS (EXTENT)
Pr　31:20 and *e* her hands to the needy.
Lk　1:50 His mercy *e* to those who fear him,

EXTENT (EXTENDS)
Jn　13: 1 he now showed them the full *e*

EXTERNAL
Gal　2: 6 judge by *e* appearance—

EXTINGUISH (EXTINGUISHED)
Eph　6:16 which you can *e* all the flaming

EXTINGUISHED (EXTINGUISH)
2Sa　21:17 the lamp of Israel will not be *e.*"

EXTOL*
Job　36:24 Remember to *e* his work,
Ps　34: 1 I will *e* the LORD at all times;
　　68: 4 *e* him who rides on the clouds—
　　95: 2 and *e* him with music and song.
　109:30 mouth I will greatly *e* the LORD;
　111: 1 I will *e* the LORD with all my heart
　115:18 it is we who *e* the LORD,
　117: 1 *e* him, all you peoples.
　145: 2 and *e* your name for ever and ever.
　145:10 your saints will *e* you.
　147:12 *E* the LORD, O Jerusalem;

EXTORT*
Lk　3:14 "Don't *e* money and don't accuse

EXTRAORDINARY*
Ac　19:11 God did *e* miracles through Paul.

EXTREME (EXTREMES)
2Co　8: 2 and their *e* poverty welled up

EXTREMES* (EXTREME)
Ecc　7:18 who fears God will avoid all ˌ*e*ˌ.

EXULT
Ps　89:16 they *e* in your righteousness.
Isa　45:25 will be found righteous and will *e.*

EYE (EYES)
Ge　3: 6 good for food and pleasing to the *e,*
Ex　21:24 you are to take life for life, *e* for *e,*
Dt　19:21 life for life, *e* for *e,* tooth for tooth,
Ps　94: 9 Does he who formed the *e* not see?
Mt　5:29 If your right *e* causes you to sin,
　　5:38 '*E* for *e,* and tooth for tooth.'
　　6:22 "The *e* is the lamp of the body.
　　7: 3 of sawdust in your brother's *e*
1Co　2: 9 "No *e* has seen,
　12:16 I am not an *e,* I do not belong
　15:52 of an *e,* at the last trumpet.
Eph　6: 6 favour when their *e* is on you,
Col　3:22 not only when their *e* is on you
Rev　1: 7 and every *e* will see him,

EYE-WITNESSES* (WITNESS)
Lk　1: 2 by those who from the first were *e*
2Pe　1:16 but we were *e* of his majesty.

EYES (EYE)
Nu　15:39 the lusts of your own hearts and *e.*
　　33:55 remain will become barbs in your *e*
Dt　11:12 the *e* of the LORD your God are
　　12:25 right in the *e* of the LORD.
　　16:19 of a bribe blinds the *e* of the wise
Jos　23:13 on your backs and thorns in your *e,*
1Sa　15:17 you were once small in your own *e,*
1Ki　10: 7 I came and saw with my own *e.*
2Ki　9:30 heard about it, she painted her *e,*
2Ch　16: 9 For the *e* of the LORD range
Job　31: 1 "I made a covenant with my *e*
　　36: 7 He does not take his *e*
Ps　25:15 My *e* are ever on the LORD,
　　36: 1 God before his *e.*
　101: 6 My *e* will be on the faithful
　118:23 and it is marvellous in our *e.*
　119:18 Open my *e* that I may see
　119:37 my *e* away from worthless things;
　121: 1 I lift up my *e* to the hills—
　123: 1 I lift up my *e* to you,
　139:16 your *e* saw my unformed body.
　141: 8 But my *e* are fixed on you,
Pr　3: 7 Do not be wise in your own *e;*
　　4:25 Let your *e* look straight ahead,
　　15: 3 The *e* of the LORD are everywhere
　　17:24 a fool's *e* wander to the ends
Isa　6: 5 and my *e* have seen the King,
　　33:17 Your *e* will see the king
　　42: 7 to open *e* that are blind,
Jer　24: 6 My *e* will watch over them
Hab　1:13 Your *e* are too pure to look on evil;
Mt　6:22 If your *e* are good, your whole
　　21:42 and it is marvellous in our *e'*?
Lk　16:15 ones who justify yourselves in the *e*
　　24:31 Then their *e* were opened
Jn　4:35 open your *e* and look at the fields!
Ac　1: 9 he was taken up before their very *e,*
2Co　4:18 So we fix our *e* not on what is seen,
　　8:21 not only in the *e* of the Lord but
Eph　1:18 also that the *e* of your heart may be
Heb　12: 2 Let us fix our *e* on Jesus, the author
Jas　2: 5 poor in the *e* of the world to be rich
1Pe　3:12 For the *e* of the Lord are
Rev　7:17 wipe away every tear from their *e.*"
　　21: 4 He will wipe every tear from their *e*

EZEKIEL*
Priest called to be prophet to the exiles (Eze 1-3). Symbolically acted out destruction of Jerusalem (Eze 4-5; 12; 24).

EZRA*
Priest and teacher of the Law who led a return of exiles to Israel to re-establish temple and worship (Ezr 7-8). Corrected intermarriage of priests (Ezr 9-10). Read Law at celebration of Feast of Tabernacles (Ne 8). Participated in dedication of Jerusalem's walls (Ne 12).

FACE (FACES)
Ge　32:30 "It is because I saw God *f* to *f,*
Ex　3: 6 Moses hid his *f,* because he was
　　33:11 would speak to Moses *f* to *f,*
　　33:20 But," he said, "you cannot see my *f*
　　34:29 was not aware that his *f* was radiant

Nu	6: 25	the LORD make his *f* shine
	12: 8	With him I speak *f* to *f*,
	14: 14	O LORD, have been seen *f* to *f*,
Dt	5: 4	The LORD spoke to you *f* to *f* out
	31: 17	I will hide my *f* from them,
	34: 10	whom the LORD knew *f* to *f*,
Jdg	6: 22	the angel of the LORD *f* to *f*!"
2Ki	14: 8	challenge: "Come, meet me *f* to *f*."
1Ch	16: 11	seek his *f* always.
2Ch	7: 14	and seek my *f* and turn
	25: 17	of Israel: "Come, meet me *f* to *f*."
Ezr	9: 6	and disgraced to lift up my *f* to you,
Ps	4: 6	Let the light of your *f* shine upon us
	27: 8	Your *f*, LORD, I will seek.
	31: 16	Let your *f* shine on your servant;
	44: 3	and the light of your *f*,
	44: 22	Yet for your sake we *f* death all day
	51: 9	Hide your *f* from my sins
	67: 1	and make his *f* shine upon us; *Selah*
	80: 3	make your *f* shine upon us,
	105: 4	seek his *f* always.
	119: 135	Make your *f* shine
SS	2: 14	and your *f* is lovely.
Isa	50: 7	Therefore have I set my *f* like flint,
	50: 8	Let us *f* each other!
	54: 8	I hid my *f* from you for a moment,
Jer	32: 4	and will speak with him *f* to *f*
	34: 3	and he will speak with you *f* to *f*.
Eze	1: 10	Each of the four had the *f* of a man,
	20: 35	*f* to *f*, I will execute judgment
Mt	17: 2	His *f* shone like the sun,
	18: 10	angels in heaven always see the *f*
Lk	9: 29	the appearance of his *f* changed,
Ro	8: 36	"For your sake we *f* death all day
1Co	13: 12	reflection; then we shall see *f* to *f*.
2Co	3: 7	could not look steadily at the *f*
	4: 6	the glory of God in the *f* of Christ.
	10: 1	who am "timid" when *f* to *f*
1Pe	3: 12	but the *f* of the Lord is
2Jn	: 12	to visit you and talk with you *f* to *f*,
3Jn	: 14	see you soon, and we will talk *f* to *f*.
Rev	1: 16	His *f* was like the sun shining
	22: 4	They will see his *f*, and his name

FACES (FACE)

2Co	3: 18	who with unveiled *f* all reflect

FACTIONS

2Co	12: 20	outbursts of anger, *f*, slander,
Gal	5: 20	selfish ambition, dissensions, *f*

FADE (FADING)

Jas	1: 11	the rich man will *f* away
1Pe	5: 4	of glory that will never *f* away.

FADING (FADE)

2Co	3: 7	*f* though it was, will not
	3: 11	if what was *f* away came with glory,
	3: 13	at it while the radiance was *f* away.

FAIL (FAILED FAILING FAILINGS FAILS FAILURE)

Lev	26: 15	and *f* to carry out all my commands
1Ki	2: 4	you will never *f* to have a man
1Ch	28: 20	He will not *f* you or forsake you
2Ch	34: 33	they did not *f* to follow the LORD,
Ps	89: 28	my covenant with him will never *f*.
Pr	15: 22	Plans *f* for lack of counsel,
Isa	51: 6	my righteousness will never *f*.
La	3: 22	for his compassions never *f*.

Lk	22: 32	Simon, that your faith may not *f*.
2Co	13: 5	unless, of course, you *f* the test?

FAILED (FAIL)

Jos	23: 14	has been fulfilled; not one has *f*.
1Ki	8: 56	Not one word has *f*
Ps	77: 8	Has his promise *f* for all time?
Ro	9: 6	as though God's word had *f*.
2Co	13: 6	discover that we have not *f* the test.

FAILING (FAIL)

1Sa	12: 23	sin against the LORD by *f* to pray

FAILINGS (FAIL)

Ro	15: 1	ought to bear with the *f* of the weak

FAILS (FAIL)

Jer	14: 6	their eyesight *f*
Joel	1: 10	the oil *f*.
1Co	13: 8	Love never *f*.

FAILURE* (FAIL)

1Th	2: 1	that our visit to you was not a *f*.

FAINT

Isa	40: 31	they will walk and not be *f*.

FAINT-HEARTED* (HEART)

Dt	20: 3	Do not be *f* or afraid; do not be
	20: 8	shall add, "Is any man afraid or *f*?

FAIR (FAIRNESS)

Pr	1: 3	doing what is right and just and *f*;
Col	4: 1	slaves with what is right and *f*,

FAIRNESS* (FAIR)

Pr	29: 14	If a king judges the poor with *f*,

FAITH* (FAITHFUL FAITHFULLY FAITHFULNESS FAITHLESS)

Ex	21: 8	because he has broken *f* with her.
Dt	32: 51	both of you broke *f* with me
Jos	22: 16	'How could you break *f*
Jdg	9: 16	and in good *f* when you made
	9: 19	and in good *f* towards Jerub-Baal
1Sa	14: 33	"You have broken *f*," he said.
2Ch	20: 20	Have *f* in the LORD your God
	20: 20	have *f* in his prophets and you will
Isa	7: 9	If you do not stand firm in your *f*,
	26: 2	the nation that keeps *f*.
Hab	2: 4	but the righteous will live by his *f*—
Mal	2: 10	by breaking *f* with one another?
	2: 11	one another? Judah has broken *f*.
	2: 14	because you have broken *f* with her
	2: 15	and do not break *f* with the wife
	2: 16	in your spirit, and do not break *f*.
Mt	6: 30	O you of little *f*? So do not worry,
	8: 10	anyone in Israel with such great *f*.
	8: 26	He replied, "You of little *f*,
	9: 2	When Jesus saw their *f*, he said
	9: 22	he said, "your *f* has healed you."
	9: 29	According to your *f* will it be done
	13: 58	there because of their lack of *f*.
	14: 31	of little *f*," he said, "why did you
	15: 28	"Woman, you have great *f*!
	16: 8	Jesus asked, "You of little *f*,
	17: 20	if you have *f* as small as a mustard
	17: 20	"Because you have so little *f*.
	21: 21	if you have *f* and do not doubt,
	24: 10	many will turn away from the *f*

Mk	2: 5	When Jesus saw their *f*, he said
	4: 40	still have no *f*?" They were
	5: 34	"Daughter, your *f* has healed you.
	6: 6	he was amazed at their lack of *f*.
	10: 52	said Jesus, "your *f* has healed you."
	11: 22	"Have *f* in God," Jesus answered.
	16: 14	he rebuked them for their lack of *f*
Lk	5: 20	When Jesus saw their *f*, he said,
	7: 9	I have not found such great *f*
	7: 50	the woman, "Your *f* has saved you;
	8: 25	"Where is your *f*?" he asked his
	8: 48	"Daughter, your *f* has healed you.
	12: 28	will he clothe you, O you of little *f*!
	17: 5	"Increase our *f*!" He replied,
	17: 6	"If you have *f* as small
	17: 19	your *f* has made you well."
	18: 8	will he find *f* on the earth?"
	18: 42	your sight; your *f* has healed you."
	22: 32	Simon, that your *f* may not fail.
Jn	2: 11	and his disciples put their *f* in him.
	7: 31	in the crowd put their *f* in him.
	8: 30	he spoke, many put their *f* in him.
	11: 45	had seen what Jesus did, put their *f*
	12: 11	to Jesus and putting their *f* in him.
	12: 42	they would not confess their *f*
	14: 12	anyone who has *f* in me will do
Ac	3: 16	By *f* in the name of Jesus, this man
	3: 16	*f* that comes through him that has
	6: 5	full of *f* and of the Holy Spirit;
	6: 7	of priests became obedient to the *f*.
	11: 24	full of the Holy Spirit and *f*,
	13: 8	to turn the proconsul from the *f*.
	14: 9	saw that he had *f* to be healed
	14: 22	them to remain true to the *f*.
	14: 27	the door of *f* to the Gentiles.
	15: 9	for he purified their hearts by *f*.
	16: 5	were strengthened in the *f*
	20: 21	and have *f* in our Lord Jesus.
	24: 24	as he spoke about *f* in Christ Jesus.
	26: 18	those who are sanctified by *f*
	27: 25	for I have *f* in God that it will
Ro	1: 5	to the obedience that comes from *f*.
	1: 8	because your *f* is being reported all
	1: 12	encouraged by each other's *f*.
	1: 17	is by *f* from first to last,
	1: 17	"The righteous will live by *f*."
	3: 3	What if some did not have *f*?
	3: 3	lack of *f* nullify God's faithfulness?
	3: 22	comes through *f* in Jesus Christ
	3: 25	a sacrifice of atonement, through *f*
	3: 26	one who justifies those who have *f*
	3: 27	the law? No, but on that of *f*.
	3: 28	by *f* apart from observing the law.
	3: 30	through that same *f*.
	3: 30	will justify the circumcised by *f*
	3: 31	nullify the law by this *f*? Not at all!
	4: 5	his *f* is credited as righteousness.
	4: 9	that Abraham's *f* was credited
	4: 11	had by *f* while he was still
	4: 12	of the *f* that our father Abraham
	4: 13	the righteousness that comes by *f*.
	4: 14	*f* has no value and the promise is
	4: 16	Therefore, the promise comes by *f*,
	4: 16	are of the *f* of Abraham.
	4: 19	Without weakening in his *f*,
	4: 20	but was strengthened in his *f*
	5: 1	we have been justified through *f*,
	5: 2	access by *f* into this grace
	9: 30	a righteousness that is by *f*;
	9: 32	Because they pursued it not by *f*

Ro	10: 6	the righteousness that is by *f* says:
	10: 8	the word of *f* we are proclaiming:
	10: 17	*f* comes from hearing the message,
	11: 20	of unbelief, and you stand by *f*.
	12: 3	measure of *f* God has given you.
	12: 6	let him use it in proportion to his *f*.
	14: 1	Accept him whose *f* is weak,
	14: 2	One man's *f* allows him
	14: 2	but another man, whose *f* is weak,
	14: 23	because his eating is not from *f*;
	14: 23	that does not come from *f* is sin.
1Co	2: 5	so that your *f* might not rest
	12: 9	to another *f* by the same Spirit,
	13: 2	and if I have a *f* that can move
	13: 13	And now these three remain: *f*,
	15: 14	is useless and so is your *f*.
	15: 17	has not been raised, your *f* is futile;
	16: 13	stand firm in the *f*; be men
2Co	1: 24	Not that we lord it over your *f*,
	1: 24	because it is by *f* you stand firm.
	4: 13	With that same spirit of *f* we
	5: 7	We live by *f*, not by sight.
	8: 7	in *f*, in speech, in knowledge,
	10: 15	as your *f* continues to grow,
	13: 5	to see whether you are in the *f*;
Gal	1: 23	now preaching the *f* he once tried
	2: 16	Jesus that we may be justified by *f*
	2: 16	but by *f* in Jesus Christ.
	2: 16	have put our *f* in Christ Jesus that
	2: 20	I live by *f* in the Son of God,
	3: 8	would justify the Gentiles by *f*,
	3: 9	So those who have *f* are blessed
	3: 9	along with Abraham, the man of *f*.
	3: 11	"The righteous will live by *f*."
	3: 12	based on *f*; on the contrary,
	3: 14	by *f* we might receive the promise.
	3: 22	being given through *f*
	3: 23	Before this *f* came, we were held
	3: 23	up until *f* should be revealed.
	3: 24	that we might be justified by *f*.
	3: 25	that *f* has come, we are no longer
	3: 26	of God through *f* in Christ Jesus,
	5: 5	But by *f* we eagerly await
	5: 6	that counts is *f* expressing itself
Eph	1: 15	ever since I heard about your *f*
	2: 8	through *f*—and this not
	3: 12	through *f* in him we may approach
	3: 17	dwell in your hearts through *f*.
	4: 5	one Lord, one *f*, one baptism;
	4: 13	up until we all reach unity in the *f*
	6: 16	to all this, take up the shield of *f*,
	6: 23	love with *f* from God the Father
Php	1: 25	for your progress and joy in the *f*,
	1: 27	as one man for the *f* of the gospel
	2: 17	and service coming from your *f*,
	3: 9	comes from God and is by *f*.
	3: 9	that which is through *f* in Christ—
Col	1: 4	heard of your *f* in Christ Jesus
	1: 5	the *f* and love that spring
	1: 23	continue in your *f*, established
	2: 5	and how firm your *f* in Christ is.
	2: 7	in the *f* as you were taught,
	2: 12	him through your *f* in the power
1Th	1: 3	Father your work produced by *f*,
	1: 8	your *f* in God has become known
	3: 2	and encourage you in your *f*,
	3: 5	I sent to find out about your *f*.
	3: 6	brought good news about your *f*.
	3: 7	about you because of your *f*.
	3: 10	supply what is lacking in your *f*.

1Th	5: 8	on *f* and love as a breastplate,
2Th	1: 3	because your *f* is growing more
	1: 4	and *f* in all the persecutions
	1:11	and every act prompted by your *f.*
	3: 2	evil men, for not everyone has *f.*
1Ti	1: 2	To Timothy my true son in the *f:*
	1: 4	than God's work—which is by *f.*
	1: 5	a good conscience and a sincere *f.*
	1:14	along with the *f* and love that are
	1:19	and so have shipwrecked their *f.*
	1:19	on to *f* and a good conscience.
	2: 7	of the true *f* to the Gentiles.
	2:15	if they continue in *f,* love
	3: 9	of the *f* with a clear conscience.
	3:13	assurance in their *f* in Christ Jesus.
	4: 1	later times some will abandon the *f*
	4: 6	brought up in the truths of the *f*
	4:12	in life, in love, in *f* and in purity.
	5: 8	he has denied the *f* and is worse
	6:10	have wandered from the *f*
	6:11	pursue righteousness, godliness, *f,*
	6:12	Fight the good fight of the *f.*
	6:21	so doing have wandered from the *f.*
2Ti	1: 5	been reminded of your sincere *f,*
	1:13	with *f* and love in Christ Jesus.
	2:18	and they destroy the *f* of some.
	2:22	and pursue righteousness, *f,*
	3: 8	as far as the *f* is concerned,
	3:10	my purpose, *f,* patience, love,
	3:15	wise for salvation through *f*
	4: 7	finished the race, I have kept the *f.*
Tit	1: 1	Christ for the *f* of God's elect
	1: 2	a *f* and knowledge resting
	1: 4	my true son in our common *f:*
	1:13	so that they will be sound in the *f*
	2: 2	self-controlled, and sound in *f,*
	3:15	Greet those who love us in the *f.*
Phm	: 5	because I hear about your *f*
	: 6	may be active in sharing your *f,*
Heb	4: 2	heard did not combine it with *f.*
	4:14	firmly to the *f* we profess.
	6: 1	and of *f* in God, instruction about
	6:12	but to imitate those who through *f*
	10:22	heart in full assurance of *f,*
	10:38	But my righteous one will live by *f.*
	11: 1	*f* is being sure of what we hope for
	11: 3	By *f* we understand that
	11: 4	And by *f* he still speaks, even
	11: 4	By *f* Abel offered God a better
	11: 4	By *f* he was commended
	11: 5	By *f* Enoch was taken from this life
	11: 6	And without *f* it is impossible
	11: 7	By his *f* he condemned the world
	11: 7	By *f* Noah, when warned about
	11: 7	the righteousness that comes by *f.*
	11: 8	By *f* Abraham, when called to go
	11: 9	By *f* he made his home
	11:11	By *f* Abraham, even though he was
	11:13	living by *f* when they died.
	11:17	By *f* Abraham, when God tested
	11:20	By *f* Isaac blessed Jacob
	11:21	By *f* Jacob, when he was dying,
	11:22	By *f* Joseph, when his end was near
	11:23	By *f* Moses' parents hid him
	11:24	By *f* Moses, when he had grown up
	11:27	By *f* he left Egypt, not fearing
	11:28	By *f* he kept the Passover
	11:29	By *f* the people passed
	11:30	By *f* the walls of Jericho fell,
	11:31	By *f* the prostitute Rahab,

Heb	11:33	through *f* conquered kingdoms,
	11:39	were all commended for their *f,*
	12: 2	the author and perfecter of our *f,*
	13: 7	way of life and imitate their *f.*
Jas	1: 3	of your *f* develops perseverance.
	2: 5	the eyes of the world to be rich in *f*
	2:14	has no deeds? Can such *f* save him?
	2:14	if a man claims to have *f*
	2:17	In the same way, *f* by itself,
	2:18	I will show you my *f* by what I do.
	2:18	Show me your *f* without deeds,
	2:18	"You have *f;* I have deeds."
	2:20	do you want evidence that *f*
	2:22	You see that his *f* and his actions
	2:22	and his *f* was made complete
	2:24	by what he does and not by *f* alone.
	2:26	so *f* without deeds is dead.
	5:15	in *f* will make the sick person well;
1Pe	1: 5	who through *f* are shielded
	1: 7	These have come so that your *f*—
	1: 9	you are receiving the goal of your *f,*
	1:21	and so your *f* and hope are in God.
	5: 9	Resist him, standing firm in the *f,*
2Pe	1: 1	Jesus Christ have received a *f*
	1: 5	effort to add to your *f* goodness;
1Jn	5: 4	overcome the world, even our *f.*
Jude	: 3	to contend for the *f* that was once
	: 20	up in your most holy *f*
Rev	2:13	You did not renounce your *f* in me,
	2:19	your love and *f,* your service

FAITHFUL* (FAITH)

Nu	12: 7	he is *f* in all my house.
Dt	7: 9	your God is God; he is the *f* God,
	32: 4	A *f* God who does no wrong,
1Sa	2:35	I will raise up for myself a *f* priest,
2Sa	20:19	We are the peaceful and *f* in Israel.
	22:26	"To the *f* you show yourself *f,*
1Ki	3: 6	because he was *f* to you
2Ch	31:18	were *f* in consecrating themselves.
	31:20	and *f* before the LORD his God.
Ne	9: 8	You found his heart *f* to you,
Ps	12: 1	the *f* have vanished
	18:25	To the *f* you show yourself *f,*
	25:10	of the LORD are loving and *f*
	31:23	The LORD preserves the *f,*
	33: 4	he is *f* in all he does.
	37:28	and will not forsake his *f* ones.
	78: 8	whose spirits were not *f* to him.
	78:37	they were not *f* to his covenant.
	89:19	to your *f* people you said:
	89:24	My *f* love will be with him,
	89:37	the *f* witness in the sky."
	97:10	for he guards the lives of his *f* ones
	101: 6	My eyes will be on the *f* in the land,
	111: 7	The works of his hands are *f*
	145:13	The LORD is *f* to all his promises
	146: 6	the LORD, who remains *f* for ever.
Pr	2: 8	and protects the way of his *f* ones.
	20: 6	but a *f* man who can find?
	27: 6	but *f* are the wounds of a friend.
	28:20	A *f* man will be richly blessed,
	31:26	and *f* instruction is on her tongue.
Isa	1:21	See how the *f* city has become
	1:26	The *F* City."
	49: 7	because of the LORD, who is *f,*
	55: 3	my *f* love promised to David.
Jer	42: 5	*f* witness against us if we do not act
Eze	43:11	so that they may be *f* to its design
	48:11	who were *f* in serving me

Hos 11: 12 even against the *f* Holy One.
Zec 8: 8 I will be *f* and righteous to them
Mt 24: 45 Who then is the *f* and wise servant,
    25: 21 'Well done, good and *f* servant!
    25: 21 You have been *f* with a few things;
    25: 23 You have been *f* with a few things;
    25: 23 'Well done, good and *f* servant!
Lk 12: 42 then is the *f* and wise manager,
Ro 12: 12 patient in affliction, *f* in prayer.
1Co 1: 9 his Son Jesus Christ our Lord, is *f*.
     4: 2 been given a trust must prove *f*.
     4: 17 my son whom I love, who is *f*
    10: 13 And God is *f*; he will not let you be
2Co 1: 18 no"? But as surely as God is *f*,
Eph 1: 1 in Ephesus, the *f* in Christ Jesus:
     6: 21 the dear brother and *f* servant
Col 1: 2 and *f* brothers in Christ at Colosse:
     1: 7 who is a *f* minister of Christ
     4: 7 a *f* minister and fellow-servant
     4: 9 He is coming with Onesimus, our *f*
1Th 5: 24 The one who calls you is *f*
2Th 3: 3 the Lord is *f*, and he will strengthen
1Ti 1: 12 he considered me *f*, appointing me
     5: 9 has been *f* to her husband,
2Ti 2: 13 he will remain *f*,
Heb 2: 17 and *f* high priest in service to God,
     3: 2 He was *f* to the one who appointed
     3: 2 as Moses was *f* in all God's house.
     3: 5 Moses was *f* as a servant
     3: 6 But Christ is *f* as a son
     8: 9 because they did not remain *f*
    10: 23 for he who promised is *f*.
    11: 11 he considered him *f* who had made
1Pe 4: 19 themselves to their *f* Creator
     5: 12 whom I regard as a *f* brother,
1Jn 1: 9 he is *f* and just and will forgive us
3Jn   : 5 you are *f* in what you are doing
Rev 1: 5 who is the *f* witness, the firstborn
     2: 10 Be *f*, even to the point of death,
     2: 13 the days of Antipas, my *f* witness,
     3: 14 the words of the Amen, the *f*
    14: 12 commandments and remain *f*
    17: 14 his called, chosen and *f* followers."
    19: 11 whose rider is called *F* and True.

FAITHFULLY* (FAITH)

Dt 11: 13 if you *f* obey the commands I am
Jos 2: 14 *f* when the LORD gives us the land
1Sa 12: 24 and serve him *f* with all your heart;
1Ki 2: 4 and if they walk *f* before me
2Ki 20: 3 how I have walked before you *f*
    22: 7 because they are acting *f*."
2Ch 19: 9 must serve *f* and wholeheartedly
    31: 12 they *f* brought in the contributions,
    31: 15 and Shecaniah assisted him *f*
    32: 1 all that Hezekiah had so *f* done,
    34: 12 The men did the work *f*.
Ne   9: 33 you have acted *f*, while we did
    13: 14 so *f* done for the house of my God
Isa 38: 3 how I have walked before you *f*
Jer 23: 28 one who has my word speak it *f*.
Eze 18: 9 and *f* keeps my laws.
    44: 15 and who *f* carried out the duties
1Pe 4: 10 *f* administering God's grace

FAITHFULNESS* (FAITH)

Ge 24: 27 not abandoned his kindness and *f*
    24: 49 if you will show kindness and *f*
    32: 10 and *f* you have shown your servant.
    47: 29 you will show me kindness and *f*.

Ex 34: 6 *f*, maintaining love to thousands,
Jos 24: 14 the LORD and serve him with all *f*.
1Sa 26: 23 man for his righteousness and *f*.
2Sa 2: 6 now show you kindness and *f*,
    15: 20 May kindness and *f* be with you."
Ps 30: 9 Will it proclaim your *f*?
    36: 5 your *f* to the skies.
    40: 10 I speak of your *f* and salvation.
    54: 5 in your *f* destroy them.
    57: 3 God sends his love and his *f*.
    57: 10 your *f* reaches to the skies.
    61: 7 appoint your love and *f*
    71: 22 the harp for your *f*, O my God;
    85: 10 Love and *f* meet together;
    85: 11 *F* springs forth from the earth,
    86: 15 to anger, abounding in love and *f*.
    88: 11 your *f* in Destruction?
    89: 1 mouth I will make your *f* known
    89: 2 that you established your *f*
    89: 5 your *f* too, in the assembly
    89: 8 and your *f* surrounds you.
    89: 14 love and *f* go before you.
    89: 33 nor will I ever betray my *f*.
    89: 49 which in your *f* you swore to David
    91: 4 his *f* will be your shield
    92: 2 and your *f* at night,
    98: 3 and his *f* to the house of Israel;
   100: 5 *f* continues through all
   108: 4 your *f* reaches to the skies.
   111: 8 done in *f* and uprightness.
   115: 1 because of your love and *f*.
   117: 2 the *f* of the LORD endures for ever.
   119: 75 and in *f* you have afflicted me.
   119: 90 *f* continues through all
   138: 2 name for your love and your *f*,
   143: 1 in your *f* and righteousness
Pr   3: 3 Let love and *f* never leave you;
    14: 22 plan what is good find love and *f*.
    16: 6 Through love and *f* sin is atoned for
    20: 28 Love and *f* keep a king safe;
Isa 11: 5 and *f* the sash around his waist.
    16: 5 in *f* a man will sit on it—
    25: 1 for in perfect *f*
    38: 18 cannot hope for your *f*.
    38: 19 about your *f*.
    42: 3 In *f* he will bring forth justice;
    61: 8 In my *f* I will reward them
La   3: 23 great is your *f*.
Hos 2: 20 I will betroth you in *f*,
     4: 1 "There is no *f*, no love,
Mt 23: 23 of the law—justice, mercy and *f*.
Ro   3: 3 lack of faith nullify God's *f*?
Gal 5: 22 patience, kindness, goodness, *f*,
3Jn   : 3 and tell about your *f* to the truth
Rev 13: 10 and *f* on the part of the saints.

FAITHLESS* (FAITH)

Ps 78: 57 fathers they were disloyal and *f*,
   101: 3 The deeds of *f* men I hate;
   119: 158 I look on the *f* with loathing,
Pr 14: 14 The *f* will be fully repaid
Jer 3: 6 you seen what *f* Israel has done?
     3: 8 I gave *f* Israel her certificate
     3: 11 "*F* Israel is more righteous
     3: 12 *f* Israel,' declares the LORD,
     3: 14 *f* people," declares the LORD,
     3: 22 "Return, *f* people;
    12: 1 Why do all the *f* live at ease?
Ro   1: 31 they are senseless, *f*, heartless,
2Ti 2: 13 if we are *f*,

FALL (FALLEN FALLING FALLS)

Ps	37: 24	though he stumble, he will not *f*,
	55: 22	he will never let the righteous *f*.
	69: 9	of those who insult you *f* on me.
	145: 14	The LORD upholds all those who *f*
Pr	11: 28	Whoever trusts in his riches will *f*,
Isa	40: 7	The grass withers and the flowers *f*,
Mt	7: 25	yet it did not *f*, because it had its
Lk	10: 18	"I saw Satan *f* like lightning
	11: 17	a house divided against itself will *f*.
	23: 30	say to the mountains, "*F* on us!"
Ro	3: 23	and *f* short of the glory of God,
Heb	6: 6	if they *f* away, to be brought back

FALLEN (FALL)

2Sa	1: 19	How the mighty have *f*!
Isa	14: 12	How you have *f* from heaven,
1Co	11: 30	and a number of you have *f* asleep.
	15: 6	though some have *f* asleep.
	15: 18	who have *f* asleep in Christ are lost.
	15: 20	of those who have *f* asleep.
Gal	5: 4	you have *f* away from grace.
1Th	4: 15	precede those who have *f* asleep.

FALLING (FALL)

Jude	: 24	able to keep you from *f*

FALLS (FALL)

Pr	11: 14	For lack of guidance a nation *f*,
	24: 17	Do not gloat when your enemy *f*;
	28: 14	he who hardens his heart *f*
Mt	13: 21	of the word, he quickly *f* away.
	21: 44	He who *f* on this stone will be
Jn	12: 24	a grain of wheat *f* to the ground
Ro	14: 4	To his own master he stands or *f*.

FALSE (FALSEHOOD FALSELY)

Ex	20: 16	"You shall not give *f* testimony
	23: 1	"Do not spread *f* reports.
	23: 7	Have nothing to do with a *f* charge
Dt	5: 20	"You shall not give *f* testimony
Pr	12: 17	but a *f* witness tells lies.
	13: 5	The righteous hate what is *f*,
	14: 5	but a *f* witness pours out lies.
	14: 25	but a *f* witness is deceitful.
	19: 5	A *f* witness will not go unpunished,
	19: 9	A *f* witness will not go unpunished,
	21: 28	A *f* witness will perish,
	25: 18	is the man who gives *f* testimony
Isa	44: 25	who foils the signs of *f* prophets
Jer	23: 16	they fill you with *f* hopes.
Mt	7: 15	"Watch out for *f* prophets.
	15: 19	theft, *f* testimony, slander.
	19: 18	not steal, do not give *f* testimony,
	24: 11	and many *f* prophets will appear
	24: 24	For *f* Christs and *f* prophets will
Mk	10: 19	do not give *f* testimony, do not
	13: 22	For *f* Christs and *f* prophets will
Lk	6: 26	their fathers treated the *f* prophets.
	18: 20	not steal, do not give *f* testimony,
Jn	1: 47	in whom there is nothing *f*."
1Co	15: 15	found to be *f* witnesses about God,
2Co	11: 13	For such men are *f* apostles,
	11: 26	and in danger from *f* brothers.
Gal	2: 4	some *f* brothers had infiltrated our
Php	1: 18	whether from *f* motives or true,
Col	2: 18	anyone who delights in *f* humility
	2: 23	their *f* humility and their harsh
1Ti	1: 3	not to teach *f* doctrines any longer
	6: 3	If anyone teaches *f* doctrines

2Pe	2: 1	also *f* prophets among the people,
	2: 1	there will be *f* teachers among you.
1Jn	4: 1	many *f* prophets have gone out
Rev	16: 13	out of the mouth of the *f* prophet,
	19: 20	with him the *f* prophet who had
	20: 10	and the *f* prophet had been thrown.

FALSEHOOD* (FALSE)

Job	21: 34	left of your answers but *f*!"
	31: 5	"If I have walked in *f*
Ps	52: 3	*f* rather than speaking the truth.
	119: 163	I hate and abhor *f*
Pr	30: 8	Keep *f* and lies far from me;
Isa	28: 15	and *f* our hiding place."
Ro	3: 7	"If my *f* enhances God's
Eph	4: 25	each of you must put off *f*
1Jn	4: 6	Spirit of truth and the spirit of *f*.
Rev	22: 15	everyone who loves and practises *f*

FALSELY (FALSE)

Lev	19: 12	"'Do not swear *f* by my name
Mt	5: 11	*f* say all kinds of evil against you
Lk	3: 14	and don't accuse people *f*—
1Ti	6: 20	ideas of what is *f* called knowledge,

FALTER*

Pr	24: 10	If you *f* in times of trouble,
Isa	42: 4	he will not *f* or be discouraged

FAME

Jos	9: 9	of the *f* of the LORD your God.
Isa	66: 19	islands that have not heard of my *f*
Hab	3: 2	LORD, I have heard of your *f*;

FAMILIES (FAMILY)

Ps	68: 6	God sets the lonely in *f*,

FAMILY (FAMILIES)

Pr	15: 27	greedy man brings trouble to his *f*,
	31: 15	she provides food for her *f*
Mk	5: 19	to your *f* and tell them how much
Lk	9: 61	go back and say good-bye to my *f*."
	12: 52	in one *f* divided against each other,
Ac	10: 2	He and all his *f* were devout
	16: 33	and all his *f* were baptised.
	16: 34	and the whole *f* was filled with joy,
1Ti	3: 4	He must manage his own *f* well
	3: 5	how to manage his own *f*,
	5: 4	practice by caring for their own *f*
	5: 8	and especially for his immediate *f*,

FAMINE

Ge	12: 10	Now there was a *f* in the land,
	26: 1	Now there was a *f* in the land—
	41: 30	seven years of *f* will follow them.
Ru	1: 1	the judges ruled, there was a *f*
1Ki	18: 2	Now the *f* was severe in Samaria,
Am	8: 11	but a *f* of hearing the words
Ro	8: 35	or persecution or *f* or nakedness

FAN*

2Ti	1: 6	you to *f* into flame the gift of God,

FANTASIES*

Ps	73: 20	you will despise them as *f*.
Pr	12: 11	but he who chases *f* lacks judgment
	28: 19	one who chases *f* will have his fill

FAST [1]

Dt	10: 20	Hold *f* to him and take your oaths
	11: 22	in all his ways and to hold *f* to him

Dt	13: 4	serve him and hold *f* to him.
	30: 20	to his voice, and hold *f* to him.
Jos	22: 5	to hold *f* to him and to serve him
	23: 8	to hold *f* to the LORD your God,
2Ki	18: 6	He held *f* to the LORD
Ps	119: 31	I hold *f* to your statutes, O LORD;
	139: 10	your right hand will hold me *f*.
1Pe	5: 12	Stand *f* in it.

FAST [2] (FASTING)

Mt	6: 16	"When you *f*, do not look sombre

FASTING (FAST)

Ps	35: 13	and humbled myself with *f*.
Ac	13: 2	were worshipping the Lord and *f*,
	14: 23	and *f*, committed them to the Lord

**FATHER (FATHER'S FATHERED
FATHERLESS FATHERS FOREFATHERS)**

Ge	2: 24	this reason a man will leave his *f*
	17: 4	You will be the *f* of many nations.
Ex	20: 12	"Honour your *f* and your mother,
	21: 15	"Anyone who attacks his *f*
	21: 17	"Anyone who curses his *f*
Lev	18: 7	" 'Do not dishonour your *f*
	19: 3	you must respect his mother and *f*,
	20: 9	" 'If anyone curses his *f* or mother,
Dt	1: 31	carried you, as a *f* carries his son,
	5: 16	"Honour your *f* and your mother,
	21: 18	son who does not obey his *f*
	32: 6	Is he not your *F*, your Creator,
2Sa	7: 14	I will be his *f*, and he will be my son
1Ch	17: 13	I will be his *f*, and he will be my son
	22: 10	will be my son, and I will be his *f*.
	28: 6	to be my son, and I will be his *f*.
Job	38: 28	Does the rain have a *f*?
Ps	2: 7	today I have become your *F*.
	27: 10	Though my *f* and mother forsake
	68: 5	A *f* to the fatherless, a defender
	89: 26	to me, 'You are my *F*,
	103: 13	As a *f* has compassion
Pr	3: 12	as a *f* the son he delights in.
	10: 1	A wise son brings joy to his *f*,
	17: 21	there is no joy for the *f* of a fool.
	17: 25	A foolish son brings grief to his *f*
	23: 22	Listen to your *f*, who gave you life,
	23: 24	*f* of a righteous man has great joy;
	28: 7	of gluttons disgraces his *f*.
	28: 24	He who robs his *f* or mother
	29: 3	loves wisdom brings joy to his *f*,
Isa	9: 6	Everlasting *F*, Prince of Peace.
	45: 10	Woe to him who says to his *f*,
	63: 16	But you are our *F*,
Jer	2: 27	They say to wood, 'You are my *f*,'
	3: 19	I thought you would call me '*F*'
	31: 9	because I am Israel's *f*,
Eze	18: 19	the son not share the guilt of his *f*?'
Mic	7: 6	For a son dishonours his *f*,
Mal	1: 6	If I am a *f*, where is the honour due
	2: 10	we not all one *F*? Did not one God
Mt	3: 9	'We have Abraham as our *f*.'
	5: 16	and praise your *F* in heaven.
	6: 9	" 'Our *F* in heaven,
	6: 26	yet your heavenly *F* feeds them.
	10: 37	"Anyone who loves his *f*
	11: 27	no-one knows the *F* except the Son
	15: 4	'Honour your *f* and mother'
	18: 10	the face of my *F* in heaven.
	19: 5	this reason a man will leave his *f*
	19: 19	honour your *f* and mother,'
Mt	19: 29	or brothers or sisters or *f* or mother
	23: 9	And do not call anyone on earth '*f*,'
Mk	7: 10	'Honour your *f* and mother,' and,
Lk	9: 59	"Lord, first let me go and bury my *f*
	12: 53	*f* against son and son against *f*,
	14: 26	and does not hate his *f* and mother,
	18: 20	honour your *f* and mother.' "
	23: 34	Jesus said, "*F*, forgive them,
Jn	3: 35	The *F* loves the Son and has placed
	4: 21	you will worship the *F* neither
	5: 17	"My *F* is always at his work
	5: 18	he was even calling God his own *F*,
	5: 20	For the *F* loves the Son
	6: 44	the *F* who sent me draws him,
	6: 46	No-one has seen the *F*
	8: 19	"You do not know me or my *F*,"
	8: 28	speak just what the *F* has taught me
	8: 41	The only *F* we have is God himself
	8: 42	God were your *F*, you would love
	8: 44	You belong to your *f*, the devil,
	10: 17	reason my *F* loves me is that I lay
	10: 30	I and the *F* are one."
	10: 38	and understand that the *F* is in me,
	14: 6	No-one comes to the *F*
	14: 9	who has seen me has seen the *F*.
	14: 28	for the *F* is greater than I.
	15: 9	"As the *F* has loved me,
	15: 23	He who hates me hates my *F*
	20: 17	'I am returning to my *F* and your *F*,
Ac	13: 33	today I have become your *F*.'
Ro	4: 11	he is the *f* of all who believe
	4: 16	He is the *f* of us all.
	8: 15	And by him we cry, "*Abba, F*."
1Co	4: 15	for in Christ Jesus I became your *f*
2Co	6: 18	"I will be a *F* to you,
Eph	5: 31	this reason a man will leave his *f*
	6: 2	"Honour your *f* and mother"—
Php	2: 11	to the glory of God the *F*.
Heb	1: 5	today I have become your *F*"?
	12: 7	what son is not disciplined by his *f*?
1Jn	1: 3	And our fellowship is with the *F*
	2: 15	the love of the *F* is not in him.
	2: 22	he denies the *F* and the Son.

FATHER'S (FATHER)

Pr	13: 1	A wise son heeds his *f* instruction,
	15: 5	A fool spurns his *f* discipline,
	19: 13	A foolish son is his *f* ruin,
Mt	16: 27	going to come in his *F* glory
Lk	2: 49	had to be in my *F* house?"
Jn	2: 16	How dare you turn my *F* house
	10: 29	can snatch them out of my *F* hand.
	14: 2	In my *F* house are many rooms;
	15: 8	to my *F* glory, that you bear much

FATHERED (FATHER)

Dt	32: 18	You deserted the Rock, who *f* you;

FATHERLESS (FATHER)

Dt	10: 18	He defends the cause of the *f*
	14: 29	the *f* and the widows who live
	24: 17	Do not deprive the alien or the *f*
	24: 19	Leave it for the alien, the *f*
	26: 12	the alien, the *f* and the widow,
Ps	68: 5	A father to the *f*, a defender
	82: 3	Defend the cause of the weak and *f*
Pr	23: 10	or encroach on the fields of the *f*,

FATHERS (FATHER)

Ex	20: 5	for the sin of the *f* to the third

Jer	31: 29	'The *f* have eaten sour grapes,
Mal	4: 6	the hearts of the children to their *f*;
Lk	1: 17	the hearts of the *f* to their children
	11: 11	"Which of you *f*, if your son asks
Jn	4: 20	Our *f* worshipped on this mountain,
1Co	4: 15	you do not have many *f*,
Eph	6: 4	*F*, do not exasperate your children;
Col	3: 21	*F*, do not embitter your children,
Heb	12: 9	all had human *f* who disciplined us

FATHOM* (FATHOMED)

Job	11: 7	"Can you *f* the mysteries of God?
Ps	145: 3	his greatness no-one can *f*.
Ecc	3: 11	yet they cannot *f* what God has
Isa	40: 28	and his understanding no-one can *f*
1Co	13: 2	and can *f* all mysteries and all

FATHOMED* (FATHOM)

Job	5: 9	performs wonders that cannot be *f*,
	9: 10	performs wonders that cannot be *f*,

FATTENED

Pr	15: 17	than a *f* calf with hatred.
Lk	15: 23	Bring the *f* calf and kill it.

FAULT (FAULTS)

1Sa	29: 3	I have found no *f* in him."
Mt	18: 15	and show him his *f*, just
Php	2: 15	of God without *f* in a crooked
Jas	1: 5	generously to all without finding *f*,
Jude	: 24	his glorious presence without *f*

FAULT-FINDERS*

Jude	: 16	These men are grumblers and *f*;

FAULTLESS*

Pr	8: 9	they are *f* to those who have
Php	3: 6	as for legalistic righteousness, *f*.
Jas	1: 27	Father accepts as pure and *f* is this:

FAULTS* (FAULT)

Job	10: 6	that you must search out my *f*
Ps	19: 12	Forgive my hidden *f*.

FAVOUR (FAVOURITISM)

Ge	4: 4	The Lord looked with *f* on Abel
	6: 8	But Noah found *f* in the eyes
Ex	33: 12	and you have found *f* with me.'
	34: 9	if I have found *f* in your eyes,"
Lev	26: 9	"'I will look on you with *f*
Nu	11: 15	if I have found *f* in your eyes—
Jdg	6: 17	"If now I have found *f* in your eyes,
1Sa	2: 26	in *f* with the Lord and with men.
2Sa	2: 6	and I too will show you the same *f*
2Ki	13: 4	Jehoahaz sought the Lord's *f*,
2Ch	33: 12	In his distress he sought the *f*
Est	7: 3	"If I have found *f* with you, O king,
Ps	90: 17	May the *f* of the Lord our God rest
Pr	8: 35	and receives *f* from the Lord.
	18: 22	and receives *f* from the Lord.
	19: 6	Many curry *f* with a ruler,
Isa	61: 2	proclaim the year of the Lord's *f*
Zec	11: 7	called one *F* and the other Union,
Lk	1: 30	Mary, you have found *f* with God.
	2: 14	to men on whom his *f* rests."
	2: 52	and in *f* with God and men.
	4: 19	to proclaim the year of the Lord's *f*
2Co	6: 2	now is the time of God's *f*,

FAVOURITISM* (FAVOUR)

Ex	23: 3	and do not show *f* to a poor man

Lev	19: 15	to the poor or *f* to the great,
Ac	10: 34	true it is that God does not show *f*
Ro	2: 11	For God does not show *f*.
Eph	6: 9	and there is no *f* with him.
Col	3: 25	for his wrong, and there is no *f*.
1Ti	5: 21	and to do nothing out of *f*.
Jas	2: 1	Lord Jesus Christ, don't show *f*.
	2: 9	But if you show *f*, you sin

FEAR (AFRAID FEARED FEARS
FRIGHTENED GOD-FEARING)

Dt	6: 13	*F* the Lord your God, serve him
	10: 12	but to *f* the Lord your God,
	31: 12	and learn to *f* the Lord your God
	31: 13	and learn to *f* the Lord your God
Jos	4: 24	you might always *f* the Lord
	24: 14	"Now *f* the Lord and serve him
1Sa	12: 14	If you *f* the Lord and serve
	12: 24	But be sure to *f* the Lord
2Sa	23: 3	when he rules in the *f* of God,
2Ch	19: 7	let the *f* of the Lord be upon you.
	26: 5	who instructed him in the *f* of God.
Job	1: 9	"Does Job *f* God for nothing?"
Ps	2: 11	Serve the Lord with *f*
	19: 9	The *f* of the Lord is pure,
	23: 4	I will *f* no evil,
	27: 1	whom shall I *f*?
	33: 8	Let all the earth *f* the Lord;
	34: 7	around those who *f* him,
	34: 9	*F* the Lord, you his saints,
	46: 2	Therefore we will not *f*,
	86: 11	that I may *f* your name.
	90: 11	great as the *f* that is due you.
	91: 5	You will not *f* the terror of night,
	111: 10	*f* of the Lord is the beginning
	118: 4	Let those who *f* the Lord say:
	128: 1	Blessed are all who *f* the Lord,
	145: 19	of those who *f* him;
	147: 11	delights in those who *f* him,
Pr	1: 7	*f* of the Lord is the beginning
	1: 33	and be at ease, without *f* of harm."
	8: 13	To *f* the Lord is to hate evil;
	9: 10	*f* of the Lord is the beginning
	10: 27	The *f* of the Lord adds length
	14: 27	The *f* of the Lord is a fountain
	15: 33	*f* of the Lord teaches a man
	16: 6	through the *f* of the Lord a man
	19: 23	The *f* of the Lord leads to life:
	22: 4	Humility and the *f* of the Lord
	29: 25	*F* of man will prove to be a snare,
	31: 21	she has no *f* for her household;
Ecc	12: 13	*F* God and keep his
Isa	11: 3	delight in the *f* of the Lord.
	33: 6	the *f* of the Lord is the key
	35: 4	"Be strong, do not *f*;
	41: 10	So do not *f*, for I am with you;
	41: 13	and says to you, Do not *f*;
	43: 1	"F not, for I have redeemed you;
	51: 7	Do not *f* the reproach of men
	54: 14	you will have nothing to *f*.
Jer	17: 8	It does not *f* when heat comes;
Lk	12: 5	I will show you whom you should *f*:
2Co	5: 11	we know what it is to *f* the Lord,
Php	2: 12	to work out your salvation with *f*
1Jn	4: 18	But perfect love drives out *f*,
Jude	: 23	to others show mercy, mixed with *f*
Rev	14: 7	"F God and give him glory,

FEARED (FEAR)

Job	1: 1	he *f* God and shunned evil.

Ps 76: 7 You alone are to be *f*.
Mal 3: 16 those who *f* the LORD talked

FEARS (FEAR)

Job 1: 8 a man who *f* God and shuns evil."
     2: 3 a man who *f* God and shuns evil.
Ps 34: 4 he delivered me from all my *f*.
    112: 1 is the man who *f* the LORD,
Pr 14: 16 A wise man *f* the LORD
    14: 26 He who *f* the LORD has a secure
    31: 30 a woman who *f* the LORD is
2Co 7: 5 conflicts on the outside, *f* within.
1Jn 4: 18 The one who *f* is not made perfect

FEAST (FEASTING FEASTS)

Pr 15: 15 the cheerful heart has a continual *f*.
2Pe 2: 13 pleasures while they *f* with you.

FEASTING (FEAST)

Pr 17: 1 than a house full of *f*, with strife.

FEASTS (FEAST)

Am 5: 21 "I hate, I despise your religious *f*;
Jude : 12 men are blemishes at your love *f*,

FEATHERS

Ps 91: 4 He will cover you with his *f*,

FEEBLE

Job 4: 3 you have strengthened *f* hands.
Isa 35: 3 Strengthen the *f* hands,
Heb 12: 12 strengthen your *f* arms

FEED (FEEDS)

Jn 21: 15 Jesus said, "*F* my lambs."
    21: 17 Jesus said, "*F* my sheep.
Ro 12: 20 "If your enemy is hungry, *f* him;
Jude : 12 shepherds who *f* only themselves.

FEEDS (FEED)

Pr 15: 14 but the mouth of a fool *f* on folly.
Mt 6: 26 yet your heavenly Father *f* them.
Jn 6: 57 so the one who *f* on me will live

FEEL

Jdg 16: 26 me where I can *f* the pillars that
Ps 115: 7 they have hands, but cannot *f*,

FEET (FOOT)

Ru 3: 8 discovered a woman lying at his *f*.
Ps 8: 6 you put everything under his *f*:
    22: 16 have pierced my hands and my *f*.
    40: 2 he set my *f* on a rock
    56: 13 and my *f* from stumbling,
    66: 9 and kept our *f* from slipping.
    73: 2 as for me, my *f* had almost slipped;
   110: 1 a footstool for your *f*."
   119: 105 Your word is a lamp to my *f*
Pr 4: 26 Make level paths for your *f*
Isa 52: 7 are the *f* of those who bring good
Da 2: 33 its *f* partly of iron and partly
Na 1: 15 the *f* of one who brings good news,
Mt 10: 14 shake the dust off your *f*
    22: 44 enemies under your *f*.' "
Lk 1: 79 to guide our *f* into the path of peace
    20: 43 a footstool for your *f*.' "
    24: 39 Look at my hands and my *f*.
Jn 13: 5 and began to wash his disciples' *f*,
    13: 14 also should wash one another's *f*.
Ro 3: 15 "Their *f* are swift to shed blood;

Ro 10: 15 "How beautiful are the *f*
    16: 20 will soon crush Satan under your *f*.
1Co 12: 21 And the head cannot say to the *f*,
    15: 25 has put all his enemies under his *f*.
Eph 1: 22 God placed all things under his *f*
1Ti 5: 10 washing the *f* of the saints,
Heb 1: 13 a footstool for your *f*"?
    2: 8 and put everything under his *f*."
    12: 13 "Make level paths for your *f*,"
Rev 1: 15 His *f* were like bronze glowing

FELIX

Governor before whom Paul was tried (Ac 23:23-24:27).

FELLOW-CITIZENS (CITIZENSHIP)

Eph 2: 19 but *F* with God's people

FELLOW-ELDER (ELDER)

1Pe 5: 1 among you, I appeal as a *f*

FELLOW-WORKERS (WORK)

1Co 3: 9 For we are God's *f*

FELLOWSHIP

Ex 20: 24 burnt offerings and *f* offerings,
Lev 3: 1 If someone's offering is a *f* offering,
1Co 1: 9 who has called you into *f*
    5: 2 out of your *f* the man who did this?
2Co 6: 14 what *f* can light have with darkness
    13: 14 and the *f* of the Holy Spirit be
Gal 2: 9 and Barnabas the right hand of *f*
Php 2: 1 if any *f* with the Spirit,
    3: 10 the *f* of sharing in his sufferings,
1Jn 1: 3 And our *f* is with the Father
    1: 3 so that you also may have *f* with us.
    1: 6 claim to have *f* with him yet walk
    1: 7 we have *f* with one another,

FEMALE

Ge 1: 27 male and *f* he created them.
    5: 2 He created them male and *f*;
Mt 19: 4 Creator 'made them male and *f*,'
Mk 10: 6 God 'made them male and *f*.'
Gal 3: 28 *f*, for you are all one in Christ Jesus

FEROCIOUS

Mt 7: 15 but inwardly they are *f* wolves.

FERTILE (FERTILISE)

Isa 32: 15 and the desert becomes a *f* field,
Jer 2: 7 I brought you into a *f* land

FERTILISE* (FERTILE)

Lk 13: 8 and I'll dig around it and *f* it.

FERVOUR*

Ac 18: 25 and he spoke with great *f*
Ro 12: 11 but keep your spiritual *f*, serving

FESTIVAL

1Co 5: 8 Therefore let us keep the *F*,
Col 2: 16 or with regard to a religious *f*.

FESTUS

Successor of Felix; sent Paul to Caesar (Ac 25-26).

FEVER

Job 30: 30 my body burns with *f*.

Mt	8: 14	mother-in-law lying in bed with a *f*.
Lk	4: 38	was suffering from a high *f*,
Jn	4: 52	"The *f* left him yesterday
Ac	28: 8	suffering from *f* and dysentery.

FIELD (FIELDS)

Ge	4: 8	Abel, "Let's go out to the *f*."
Lev	19: 9	reap to the very edges of your *f*
	19: 19	Do not plant your *f* with two kinds
Pr	31: 16	She considers a *f* and buys it;
Isa	40: 6	glory is like the flowers of the *f*.
Mt	6: 28	See how the lilies of the *f* grow.
	6: 30	how God clothes the grass of the *f*,
	13: 38	*f* is the world, and the good seed
	13: 44	is like treasure hidden in a *f*.
Lk	14: 18	I have just bought a *f*, and I must go
1Co	3: 9	you are God's *f*, God's building.
1Pe	1: 24	glory is like the flowers of the *f*;

FIELDS (FIELD)

Ru	2: 2	go to the *f* and pick up the leftover
Lk	2: 8	were shepherds living out in the *f*
Jn	4: 35	open your eyes and look at the *f*!

FIG (FIG-TREE FIGS SYCAMORE-FIG)

Ge	3: 7	so they sewed *f* leaves together

FIG-TREE (FIG)

Jdg	9: 10	"Next, the trees said to the *f*,
1Ki	4: 25	man under his own vine and *f*.
Pr	27: 18	He who tends a *f* will eat its
Mic	4: 4	and under his own *f*,
Zec	3: 10	to sit under his vine and *f*,'
Mt	21: 19	Seeing a *f* by the road,
Lk	13: 6	"A man had a *f*, planted
Jas	3: 12	brothers, can a *f* bear olives,
Rev	6: 13	drop from a *f* when shaken

FIGHT (FIGHTING FIGHTS FOUGHT)

Ex	14: 14	The LORD will *f* for you; you need
Dt	1: 30	going before you, will *f* for you,
	3: 22	the LORD your God himself will *f*
Ne	4: 20	Our God will *f* for us!"
Ps	35: 1	*f* against those who *f* against me.
Jn	18: 36	my servants would *f*
1Co	9: 26	I do not *f* like a man beating the air.
2Co	10: 4	The weapons we *f*
1Ti	1: 18	them you may *f* the good *f*,
	6: 12	*F* the good *f* of the faith.
2Ti	4: 7	fought the good *f*, I have finished

FIGHTING (FIGHT)

Jos	10: 14	Surely the LORD was *f* for Israel!

FIGHTS (FIGHT)

Jos	23: 10	the LORD your God *f* for you,
1Sa	25: 28	because he *f* the LORD's battles.
Jas	4: 1	What causes *f* and quarrels

FIGS (FIG)

Lk	6: 44	People do not pick *f*
Jas	3: 12	grapevine bear *f*? Neither can a salt

FILL (FILLED FILLING FILLS FULL FULLY FULNESS)

Ge	1: 28	and increase in number; *f* the earth
Ps	16: 11	you will *f* me with joy
	81: 10	wide your mouth and I will *f* it.
Pr	28: 19	who chases fantasies will have his *f*
Hag	2: 7	and I will *f* this house with glory,'

Jn	6: 26	you ate the loaves and had your *f*.
Ac	2: 28	you will *f* me with joy
Ro	15: 13	the God of hope *f* you with all joy

FILLED (FILL)

Ex	31: 3	I have *f* him with the Spirit of God,
	35: 31	he has *f* him with the Spirit of God,
Dt	34: 9	son of Nun was *f* with the spirit
1Ki	8: 10	the cloud *f* the temple
	8: 11	glory of the LORD *f* his temple.
2Ch	5: 14	of the LORD *f* the temple of God.
	7: 1	the glory of the LORD *f* the temple
Ps	72: 19	may the whole earth be *f*
	119: 64	The earth is *f* with your love,
Isa	6: 4	and the temple was *f* with smoke.
Eze	10: 3	and a cloud *f* the inner court.
	10: 4	The cloud *f* the temple,
	43: 5	the glory of the LORD *f* the temple
Hab	2: 14	For the earth will be *f*
	3: 3	and his praise *f* the earth.
Mt	5: 6	for they will be *f*.
Lk	1: 15	and he will be *f* with the Holy Spirit
	1: 41	and Elizabeth was *f* with the Holy
	1: 67	His father Zechariah was *f*
	2: 40	and became strong; he was *f*
Jn	12: 3	the house was *f* with the fragrance
Ac	2: 2	*f* the whole house where they were
	2: 4	All of them were *f*
	4: 8	Then Peter, *f* with the Holy Spirit,
	4: 31	they were all *f* with the Holy Spirit
	9: 17	and be *f* with the Holy Spirit."
	13: 9	called Paul, *f* with the Holy Spirit,
Eph	5: 18	Instead, be *f* with the Spirit.
Php	1: 11	*f* with the fruit of righteousness
Rev	15: 8	And the temple was *f* with smoke

FILLING (FILL)

Eze	44: 4	the glory of the LORD *f* the temple

FILLS (FILL)

Nu	14: 21	of the LORD *f* the whole earth,
Ps	107: 9	and *f* the hungry with good things.
Eph	1: 23	fulness of him who *f* everything

FILTH (FILTHY)

Isa	4: 4	The LORD will wash away the *f*
Jas	1: 21	rid of all moral *f* and the evil that is

FILTHY (FILTH)

Isa	64: 6	all our righteous acts are like *f* rags;
Col	3: 8	and *f* language from your lips.
2Pe	2: 7	by the *f* lives of lawless men

FINAL (FINALITY)

Ps	73: 17	then I understood their *f* destiny.

FINALITY* (FINAL)

Ro	9: 28	on earth with speed and *f*."

FINANCIAL*

1Ti	6: 5	that godliness is a means to *f* gain.

FIND (FINDS FOUND)

Nu	32: 23	be sure that your sin will *f* you out.
Dt	4: 29	you will *f* him if you look for him
1Sa	23: 16	and helped him *f* strength in God.
Job	23: 3	If only I knew where to *f* him;
Ps	36: 7	*f* refuge in the shadow
	62: 5	*F* rest, O my soul, in God alone;
	91: 4	under his wings you will *f* refuge;

Pr	8: 17	and those who seek me *f* me.
	14: 22	those who plan what is good *f* love
	20: 6	but a faithful man who can *f*?
	24: 14	if you *f* it, there is a future hope
	31: 10	A wife of noble character who can *f*
Jer	6: 16	and you will *f* rest for your souls.
	29: 13	and *f* me when you seek me
Mt	7: 7	seek and you will *f*; knock
	11: 29	and you will *f* rest for your souls.
	16: 25	loses his life for me will *f* it.
	22: 9	invite to the banquet anyone you *f*.'
Lk	11: 9	seek and you will *f*; knock
	18: 8	will he *f* faith on the earth?"
Jn	10: 9	come in and go out, and *f* pasture.

FINDS (FIND)

Ps	62: 1	My soul *f* rest in God alone;
	112: 1	who *f* great delight
	119: 162	like one who *f* great spoil.
Pr	3: 13	Blessed is the man who *f* wisdom.
	8: 35	For whoever *f* me *f* life
	11: 27	He who seeks good *f* good will,
	18: 22	He who *f* a wife *f* what is good
Mt	7: 8	he who seeks *f*; and to him who
	10: 39	Whoever *f* his life will lose it,
Lk	11: 10	he who seeks *f*, and to him who
	12: 37	whose master *f* them watching
	12: 43	servant whom the master *f* doing
	15: 4	go after the lost sheep until he *f* it?
	15: 8	and search carefully until she *f* it?

FINE-SOUNDING* (SOUND)

Col	2: 4	may deceive you by *f* arguments.

FINGER

Ex	8: 19	to Pharaoh, "This is the *f* of God,"
	31: 18	of stone inscribed by the *f* of God.
Dt	9: 10	two stone tablets inscribed by the *f*
Lk	11: 20	But if I drive out demons by the *f*
	16: 24	to dip the tip of his *f* in water
Jn	8: 6	to write on the ground with his *f*.
	20: 25	and put my *f* where the nails were,

FINISH (FINISHED)

Jn	4: 34	him who sent me and to *f* his work.
	5: 36	that the Father has given me to *f*,
Ac	20: 24	if only I may *f* the race
2Co	8: 11	Now *f* the work, so that your eager
Jas	1: 4	Perseverance must *f* its work

FINISHED (FINISH)

Ge	2: 2	seventh day God had *f* the work he
Jn	19: 30	the drink, Jesus said, "It is *f*."
2Ti	4: 7	I have *f* the race, I have kept

FIRE

Ex	3: 2	in flames of *f* from within a bush.
	13: 21	in a pillar of *f* to give them light,
Lev	6: 12	*f* on the altar must be kept burning;
	9: 24	*F* came out from the presence
1Ki	18: 38	Then the *f* of the LORD fell
2Ki	2: 11	suddenly a chariot of *f*
Isa	5: 24	as tongues of *f* lick up straw
	30: 27	and his tongue is a consuming *f*.
Jer	23: 29	my word like *f*," declares
Da	3: 25	four men walking around in the *f*,
Zec	3: 2	stick snatched from the *f*?"
Mal	3: 2	For he will be like a refiner's *f*
Mt	3: 11	you with the Holy Spirit and with *f*.
	3: 12	the chaff with unquenchable *f*."

Mt	5: 22	will be in danger of the *f* of hell.
	18: 8	and be thrown into eternal *f*.
	25: 41	into the eternal *f* prepared
Mk	9: 43	where the *f* never goes out.
	9: 48	and the *f* is not quenched.'
	9: 49	Everyone will be salted with *f*.
Lk	3: 16	you with the Holy Spirit and with *f*.
	12: 49	I have come to bring *f* on the earth,
Ac	2: 3	to be tongues of *f* that separated
1Co	3: 13	It will be revealed with *f*,
1Th	5: 19	Do not put out the Spirit's *f*;
Heb	12: 29	for our God is a consuming *f*.
Jas	3: 5	set on *f* by a small spark.
	3: 6	also is a *f*, a world of evil
2Pe	3: 10	the elements will be destroyed by *f*,
Jude	: 7	suffer the punishment of eternal *f*.
	: 23	snatch others from the *f*
Rev	1: 14	and his eyes were like blazing *f*.
	20: 14	The lake of *f* is the second death.

FIRM*

Ex	14: 13	Stand *f* and you will see
	15: 8	surging waters stood *f* like a wall;
Jos	3: 17	the covenant of the LORD stood *f*
2Ch	20: 17	stand *f* and see the deliverance
Ezr	9: 8	giving us a *f* place in his sanctuary,
Job	11: 15	you will stand *f* and without fear.
	36: 5	he is mighty, and *f* in his purpose.
	41: 23	they are *f* and immovable.
Ps	20: 8	but we rise up and stand *f*.
	30: 7	you made my mountain stand *f*;
	33: 9	he commanded, and it stood *f*.
	33: 11	of the LORD stand *f* for ever,
	37: 23	whose steps he has made *f*;
	40: 2	and gave me a *f* place to stand.
	75: 3	it is I who hold its pillars *f*.
	78: 13	made the water stand *f* like a wall.
	89: 2	that your love stands *f* for ever,
	89: 4	and make your throne *f*
	93: 5	Your statutes stand *f*;
	119: 89	it stands *f* in the heavens.
Pr	4: 26	and take only ways that are *f*.
	10: 25	but the righteous stand *f* for ever.
	12: 7	the house of the righteous stands *f*.
Isa	7: 9	If you do not stand *f* in your faith,
	22: 17	about to take *f* hold of you
	22: 23	drive him like a peg into a *f* place;
	22: 25	into the *f* place will give way;
Eze	13: 5	so that it will stand *f* in the battle
Zec	8: 23	nations will take *f* hold of one Jew
Mt	10: 22	he who stands *f* to the end will be
	24: 13	he who stands *f* to the end will be
Mk	13: 13	he who stands *f* to the end will be
Lk	21: 19	By standing *f* you will gain life.
1Co	10: 12	So, if you think you are standing *f*,
	15: 58	my dear brothers, stand *f*.
	16: 13	on your guard; stand *f* in the faith;
2Co	1: 7	for you is *f*, because we know that
	1: 21	who makes both us and you stand *f*
	1: 24	because it is by faith you stand *f*.
Gal	5: 1	Stand *f*, then, and do not let
Eph	6: 14	Stand *f* then, with the belt
Php	1: 27	I will know that you stand *f*
	4: 1	that is how you should stand *f*
Col	1: 23	in your faith, established and *f*,
	2: 5	and how *f* your faith in Christ is.
	4: 12	that you may stand *f* in all the will
1Th	3: 8	since you are standing *f* in the Lord
2Th	2: 15	stand *f* and hold to the teachings
1Ti	6: 19	a *f* foundation for the coming age,

2Ti	2: 19	God's solid foundation stands *f*,
Heb	6: 19	an anchor for the soul, *f* and secure
Jas	5: 8	You too, be patient and stand *f*,
1Pe	5: 9	Resist him, standing *f* in the faith,
	5: 10	make you strong, *f* and steadfast.

FIRMAMENT see EXPANSE, HEAVENS, SKIES

FIRST

Ge	1: 5	and there was morning—the *f* day.
	13: 4	and where he had *f* built an altar.
Ex	34: 19	*f* offspring of every womb belongs
1Ki	22: 5	"*F* seek the counsel of the LORD."
Pr	18: 17	*f* to present his case seems right,
Isa	44: 6	I am the *f* and I am the last;
	48: 12	I am the *f* and I am the last.
Mt	5: 24	*F* go and be reconciled
	6: 33	But seek *f* his kingdom
	7: 5	*f* take the plank out
	19: 30	But many who are *f* will be last,
	20: 16	last will be *f*, and the *f* will be last."
	20: 27	wants to be *f* must be your slave—
	22: 38	This is the *f* and greatest
	23: 26	*F* clean the inside of the cup
Mk	9: 35	to be *f*, he must be the very last,
	10: 31	are *f* will be last, and the last *f*."
	10: 44	wants to be *f* must be slave
	13: 10	And the gospel must *f* be preached
Lk	13: 30	will be *f*, and *f* who will be last."
Jn	8: 7	let him be the *f* to throw a stone
Ac	11: 26	disciples were *f* called Christians
Ro	1: 16	*f* for the Jew, then for the Gentile.
	1: 17	is by faith from *f* to last,
	2: 9	*f* for the Jew, then for the Gentile;
	2: 10	*f* for the Jew, then for the Gentile.
1Co	12: 28	in the church God has appointed *f*
	15: 45	"The *f* man Adam became a living
2Co	8: 5	they gave themselves *f* to the Lord
Eph	6: 2	which is the *f* commandment
1Th	4: 16	and the dead in Christ will rise *f*.
1Ti	2: 13	For Adam was formed *f*, then Eve.
Heb	10: 9	He sets aside the *f*
Jas	3: 17	comes from heaven is *f* of all pure;
1Jn	4: 19	We love because he *f* loved us.
3Jn	: 9	but Diotrephes, who loves to be *f*,
Rev	1: 17	I am the *F* and the Last.
	2: 4	You have forsaken your *f* love.
	22: 13	and the Omega, the *F* and the Last,

FIRSTBORN (BEAR [1])

Ex	11: 5	Every *f* son in Egypt will die,
	34: 20	Redeem all your *f* sons.
Ps	89: 27	I will also appoint him my *f*,
Lk	2: 7	and she gave birth to her *f*, a son.
Ro	8: 29	that he might be the *f*
Col	1: 15	image of the invisible God, the *f*
	1: 18	and the *f* from among the dead,
Heb	1: 6	when God brings his *f*
	12: 23	of the *f*, whose names are written
Rev	1: 5	who is the faithful witness, the *f*

FIRSTFRUITS

Ex	23: 16	the Feast of Harvest with the *f*
	23: 19	"Bring the best of the *f* of your soil
Ro	8: 23	who have the *f* of the Spirit,
1Co	15: 23	Christ, the *f*; then, when he comes,
Rev	14: 4	offered as *f* to God and the Lamb.

FISH (FISHERS)

Ge	1: 26	let them rule over the *f* of the sea

Jnh	1: 17	But the LORD provided a great *f*
Mt	7: 10	asks for a *f*, will give him a snake?
	12: 40	three nights in the belly of a huge *f*,
	14: 17	loaves of bread and two *f*,"
Mk	6: 38	they said, "Five—and two *f*."
Lk	5: 6	of *f* that their nets began to break.
	9: 13	loaves of bread and two *f*—
Jn	6: 9	small barley loaves and two small *f*,
	21: 5	haven't you any *f*?" "No,"
	21: 11	It was full of large *f*, 153, but

FISH-HOOK*

Job	41: 1	pull in the leviathan with a *f*

FISHERMEN

Mk	1: 16	a net into the lake, for they were *f*.

FISHERS (FISH)

Mt	4: 19	"and I will make you *f* of men."
Mk	1: 17	"and I will make you *f* of men."

FISTS

Mt	26: 67	and struck him with their *f*.

FIT (FITTING)

Jdg	17: 6	no king; everyone did as he saw *f*.
	21: 25	no king; everyone did as he saw *f*.

FITTING* (FIT)

Ps	33: 1	it is *f* for the upright to praise him.
	147: 1	how pleasant and *f* to praise him!
Pr	10: 32	of the righteous know what is *f*,
	19: 10	It is not *f* for a fool to live in luxury
	26: 1	honour is not *f* for a fool.
1Co	14: 40	everything should be done in a *f*
Col	3: 18	to your husbands, as is *f* in the Lord
Heb	2: 10	sons to glory, it was *f* that God,

FIX* (FIXED)

Dt	11: 18	*F* these words of mine
Job	14: 3	Do you *f* your eye on such a one?
Pr	4: 25	*f* your gaze directly before you.
Isa	46: 8	"Remember this, *f* it in mind,
Am	9: 4	I will *f* my eyes upon them
2Co	4: 18	we *f* our eyes not on what is seen,
Heb	3: 1	heavenly calling, *f* your thoughts
	12: 2	Let us *f* our eyes on Jesus,

FIXED* (FIX)

2Ki	8: 11	stared at him with a *f* gaze
Job	38: 10	when I *f* limits for it
Ps	141: 8	my eyes are *f* on you, O Sovereign
Pr	8: 28	*f* securely the fountains of the deep
Jer	33: 25	and night and the *f* laws of heaven
Lk	16: 26	and you a great chasm has been *f*,

FLAME (FLAMES FLAMING)

2Ti	1: 6	you to fan into *f* the gift of God,

FLAMES (FLAME)

1Co	3: 15	only as one escaping through the *f*.
	13: 3	and surrender my body to the *f*,

FLAMING (FLAME)

Eph	6: 16	you can extinguish all the *f* arrows

FLANK

Eze	34: 21	Because you shove with *f*

FLASH

1Co	15: 52	in a *f*, in the twinkling of an eye,

FLATTER* (FLATTERING FLATTERS FLATTERY)

Job 32: 21 nor will I f any man;
Ps 78: 36 But then they would f him
Jude : 16 f others for their own advantage.

FLATTERING* (FLATTER)

Ps 12: 2 their f lips speak with deception.
12: 3 May the LORD cut off all f lips
Pr 26: 28 and a f mouth works ruin.
28: 23 than he who has a f tongue.
Eze 12: 24 or f divinations among the people

FLATTERS* (FLATTER)

Ps 36: 2 For in his own eyes he f himself
Pr 29: 5 Whoever f his neighbour

FLATTERY* (FLATTER)

Job 32: 22 for if I were skilled in f,
Da 11: 32 With f he will corrupt those who
Ro 16: 18 and f they deceive the minds
1Th 2: 5 You know we never used f,

FLAWLESS*

2Sa 22: 31 the word of the LORD is f.
Job 11: 4 You say to God, 'My beliefs are f
Ps 12: 6 And the words of the LORD are f,
18: 30 the word of the LORD is f.
Pr 30: 5 "Every word of God is f;
SS 5: 2 my dove, my f one.

FLEE (FLEES)

Ps 139: 7 Where can I f from your presence?
1Co 6: 18 F from sexual immorality.
10: 14 my dear friends, f from idolatry.
1Ti 6: 11 But you, man of God, f from all this
2Ti 2: 22 F the evil desires of youth,
Jas 4: 7 Resist the devil, and he will f

FLEECE

Jdg 6: 37 I will place a wool f

FLEES (FLEE)

Pr 28: 1 The wicked man f though no-one

FLEETING*

Job 14: 2 like a f shadow, he does not endure
Ps 39: 4 let me know how f is my life.
89: 47 Remember how f is my life.
144: 4 his days are like a f shadow.
Pr 21: 6 is a f vapour and a deadly snare.
31: 30 Charm is deceptive, and beauty is f

FLESH see also BODY, MANKIND, PEOPLE, SINFUL (nature)

Ge 2: 23 and f of my f;
2: 24 and they will become one f.
2Ch 32: 8 With him is only the arm of f,
Job 19: 26 yet in my f I will see God;
Eze 11: 19 of stone and give them a heart of f.
36: 26 of stone and give you a heart of f.
Mt 19: 5 and the two will become one f'?
Mk 10: 8 and the two will become one f.'
Jn 1: 14 The Word became f and made his
6: 51 This bread is my f, which I will give
1Co 6: 16 "The two will become one f."
15: 39 All f is not the same: Men have one
Eph 5: 31 and the two will become one f."
6: 12 For our struggle is not against f
Php 3: 2 do evil, those mutilators of the f.

1Jn 4: 2 come in the f is from God,
Jude : 23 the clothing stained by corrupted f.

FLIGHT

Dt 32: 30 or two put ten thousand to f,

FLINT

Isa 50: 7 Therefore have I set my face like f,
Zec 7: 12 They made their hearts as hard as f

FLIRTING*

Isa 3: 16 f with their eyes,

FLOCK (FLOCKS)

Ps 77: 20 You led your people like a f
78: 52 he brought his people out like a f;
95: 7 the f under his care.
Isa 40: 11 He tends his f like a shepherd:
Jer 10: 21 and all their f is scattered.
23: 2 "Because you have scattered my f
31: 10 watch over his f like a shepherd.'
Eze 34: 2 not shepherds take care of the f?
Zec 11: 17 who deserts the f!
Mt 26: 31 the sheep of the f will be scattered.'
Lk 12: 32 little f, for your Father has been
Jn 10: 16 shall be one f and one shepherd.
Ac 20: 28 all the f of which the Holy Spirit
1Co 9: 7 Who tends a f and does not drink
1Pe 5: 2 Be shepherds of God's f that is
5: 3 but being examples to the f.

FLOCKS (FLOCK)

Lk 2: 8 keeping watch over their f at night.

FLOG (FLOGGED FLOGGING)

Pr 19: 25 F a mocker, and the simple will
Ac 22: 25 to f a Roman citizen who hasn't

FLOGGED (FLOG)

Jn 19: 1 Pilate took Jesus and had him f.
Ac 5: 40 the apostles in and had them f.
16: 23 After they had been severely f,
2Co 11: 23 frequently, been f more severely,

FLOGGING (FLOG)

Heb 11: 36 f, while still others were chained

FLOOD (FLOODGATES)

Ge 7: 7 ark to escape the waters of the f.
Mal 2: 13 You f the LORD's altar with tears.
Mt 24: 38 For in the days before the f,
2Pe 2: 5 world when he brought the f

FLOODGATES (FLOOD)

Ge 7: 11 the f of the heavens were opened.
Mal 3: 10 see if I will not throw open the f

FLOOR

Jas 2: 3 or "Sit on the f by my feet,"

FLOUR

Lev 2: 1 his offering is to be of fine f.
Nu 7: 13 filled with fine f mixed with oil
28: 9 of an ephah of fine f mixed with oil.

FLOURISH (FLOURISHES FLOURISHING)

Ps 72: 7 In his days the righteous will f;
92: 7 and all evildoers f,
92: 12 The righteous will f like a palm tree
Pr 14: 11 but the tent of the upright will f.

FLOURISHES (FLOURISH)
Pr　12: 12　but the root of the righteous *f*.

FLOURISHING (FLOURISH)
Ps　52: 8　*f* in the house of God;

FLOW (FLOWING)
Nu　13: 27　and it does *f* with milk and honey!
Jn　7: 38　streams of living water will *f*

FLOWER (FLOWERS)
Job　14: 2　up like a *f* and withers away;
Ps　103: 15　he flourishes like a *f* of the field;
Jas　1: 10　he will pass away like a wild *f*.

FLOWERS (FLOWER)
Isa　40: 6　and all their glory is like the *f*
　　　40: 7　The grass withers and the *f* fall,
1Pe　1: 24　and all their glory is like the *f*

FLOWING (FLOW)
Ex　3: 8　a land *f* with milk and honey—
　　　33: 3　Go up to the land *f* with milk
Nu　16: 14　us into a land *f* with milk
Jos　5: 6　a land *f* with milk and honey.
Ps　107: 33　*f* springs into thirsty ground,
　　　107: 35　the parched ground into *f* springs;
Jer　32: 22　a land *f* with milk and honey.
Eze　20: 6　a land *f* with milk and honey,
Rev　22: 1　*f* from the throne of God

FLUTE
Ps　150: 4　praise him with the strings and *f*,
Mt　11: 17　"'We played the *f* for you,
1Co　14: 7　that make sounds, such as the *f*

FOAL*
Zec　9: 9　on a colt, the *f* of a donkey.
Mt　21: 5　on a colt, the *f* of a donkey.'"

FOILS*
Ps　33: 10　The Lord *f* the plans
Isa　44: 25　who *f* the signs of false prophets

FOLDING* (FOLDS)
Pr　6: 10　a little *f* of the hands to rest—
　　　24: 33　a little *f* of the hands to rest—

FOLDS (FOLDING)
Ecc　4: 5　The fool *f* his hands

FOLLOW (FOLLOWED FOLLOWING FOLLOWS)
Ex　23: 2　Do not *f* the crowd in doing wrong.
Lev　18: 4　and be careful to *f* my decrees.
Dt　5: 1　Learn them and be sure to *f* them.
　　　17: 19　*f* carefully all the words of this law
1Ki　11: 6　he did not *f* the Lord completely,
2Ch　34: 33　they did not fail to *f* the Lord.
Ps　23: 6　Surely goodness and love will *f* me
　　　119: 166　and I *f* your commands.
Mt　4: 19　*f* me," Jesus said, "and I will make
　　　8: 19　I will *f* you wherever you go."
　　　8: 22　But Jesus told him, "*F* me,
　　　16: 24　and take up his cross and *f* me.
　　　19: 27　"We have left everything to *f* you!
Lk　9: 23　take up his cross daily and *f* me.
　　　9: 61　Still another said, "I will *f* you,
Jn　10: 4　his sheep *f* him because they know

Jn　10: 5　But they will never *f* a stranger;
　　　10: 27　I know them, and they *f* me.
　　　12: 26　Whoever serves me must *f* me;
　　　21: 19　Then he said to him, "*F* me!"
1Co　1: 12　One of you says, "I *f* Paul";
　　　11: 1　*F* my example, as I *f*
　　　14: 1　*F* the way of love and eagerly
2Th　3: 9　ourselves a model for you to *f*.
1Pe　2: 21　that you should *f* in his steps.
Rev　14: 4　They *f* the Lamb wherever he goes.

FOLLOWED (FOLLOW)
Nu　32: 11　they have not *f* me wholeheartedly,
Dt　1: 36　he *f* the Lord wholeheartedly."
Jos　14: 14　he *f* the Lord, the God of Israel,
2Ch　10: 14　he *f* the advice of the young men
Mt　4: 20　once they left their nets and *f* him.
　　　9: 9　and Matthew got up and *f* him.
　　　26: 58　But Peter *f* him at a distance,
Lk　18: 43　he received his sight and *f* Jesus,

FOLLOWING (FOLLOW)
Ps　119: 14　I rejoice in *f* your statutes
Php　3: 17　Join with others in *f* my example,
1Ti　1: 18　by *f* them you may fight the good

FOLLOWS (FOLLOW)
Jn　8: 12　Whoever *f* me will never walk

FOLLY (FOOL)
Pr　14: 29　a quick-tempered man displays *f*.
　　　19: 3　A man's own *f* ruins his life,
Ecc　10: 1　so a little *f* outweighs wisdom
Mk　7: 22　envy, slander, arrogance and *f*.
2Ti　3: 9　their *f* will be clear to everyone.

FOOD (FOODS)
Ge　1: 30　I give every green plant for *f*."
Pr　12: 9　to be somebody and have no *f*.
　　　12: 11　his land will have abundant *f*,
　　　20: 13　you will have *f* to spare.
　　　20: 17　*F* gained by fraud tastes sweet
　　　21: 20　of the wise are stores of choice *f*
　　　22: 9　for he shares his *f* with the poor.
　　　23: 3　for that *f* is deceptive.
　　　23: 6　Do not eat the *f* of a stingy man,
　　　25: 21　If your enemy is hungry, give him *f*
　　　31: 14　bringing her *f* from afar.
　　　31: 15　she provides *f* for her family
Isa　58: 7　not to share your *f* with the hungry
Eze　18: 7　but gives his *f* to the hungry
Da　1: 8　to defile himself with the royal *f*
Mt　3: 4　His *f* was locusts and wild honey.
　　　6: 25　Is not life more important than *f*,
Jn　4: 32　"I have *f* to eat that you know
　　　4: 34　have brought him *f*?" "My *f*,"
　　　6: 27　Do not work for *f* that spoils,
　　　6: 55　my flesh is real *f* and my blood is
Ac　15: 20　to abstain from *f* polluted by idols,
Ro　14: 14　fully convinced that no *f* is unclean
1Co　8: 1　Now about *f* sacrificed to idols:
　　　8: 8　But *f* does not bring us near to God
2Co　11: 27　and have often gone without *f*;
1Ti　6: 8　But if we have *f* and clothing,
Heb　5: 14　But solid *f* is for the mature,
Jas　2: 15　sister is without clothes and daily *f*.

FOODS (FOOD)
Mk　7: 19　Jesus declared all *f* "clean".)

FOOL (FOLLY FOOL'S FOOLISH FOOLISHNESS FOOLS)

1Sa	25: 25	his name is *F*, and folly goes
Ps	14: 1	The *f* says in his heart,
Pr	10: 10	and a chattering *f* comes to ruin.
	10: 18	and whoever spreads slander is a *f*.
	12: 15	The way of a *f* seems right to him,
	12: 16	A *f* shows his annoyance at once,
	14: 16	but a *f* is hotheaded and reckless.
	15: 5	A *f* spurns his father's discipline,
	17: 12	than a *f* in his folly.
	17: 16	use is money in the hand of a *f*,
	17: 21	To have a *f* for a son brings grief;
	17: 28	Even a *f* is thought wise
	18: 2	A *f* finds no pleasure
	20: 3	but every *f* is quick to quarrel.
	23: 9	Do not speak to a *f*,
	24: 7	Wisdom is too high for a *f*;
	26: 4	Do not answer a *f* according
	26: 5	Answer a *f* according to his folly,
	26: 7	is a proverb in the mouth of a *f*.
	26: 11	so a *f* repeats his folly.
	26: 12	for a *f* than for him.
	27: 22	Though you grind a *f* in a mortar,
	28: 26	He who trusts in himself is a *f*,
	29: 11	A *f* gives full vent to his anger,
	29: 20	for a *f* than for him.
Mt	5: 22	But anyone who says, 'You *f* !'
Lk	12: 20	"But God said to him, 'You *f* !
1Co	3: 18	he should become a "*f*"
2Co	11: 21	I am speaking as a *f*—I

FOOL'S (FOOL)

Pr	14: 3	A *f* talk brings a rod to his back,
	18: 7	A *f* mouth is his undoing,

FOOLISH (FOOL)

Pr	10: 1	but a *f* son grief to his mother.
	14: 1	her own hands the *f* one tears hers
	15: 20	but a *f* man despises his mother.
	17: 25	A *f* son brings grief to his father
	19: 13	A *f* son is his father's ruin,
Mt	7: 26	practice is like a *f* man who built
	25: 2	of them were *f* and five were wise.
Lk	11: 40	You *f* people! Did not the one who
	24: 25	He said to them, "How *f* you are,
1Co	1: 20	Has not God made *f* the wisdom
	1: 27	God chose the *f* things of the world
Gal	3: 1	died for nothing!" You *f* Galatians!
Eph	5: 4	should there be obscenity, *f* talk
	5: 17	Therefore do not be *f*,
Tit	3: 9	But avoid *f* controversies

FOOLISHNESS (FOOL)

1Co	1: 18	of the cross is *f* to those who are
	1: 21	through the *f* of what was preached
	1: 23	block to Jews and *f* to Gentiles,
	1: 25	For the *f* of God is wiser
	2: 14	for they are *f* to him, and he cannot
	3: 19	of this world is *f* in God's sight.

FOOLS (FOOL)

Pr	1: 7	but *f* despise wisdom and discipline
	3: 35	but *f* he holds up to shame.
	12: 23	but the heart of *f* blurts out folly.
	13: 19	but *f* detest turning from evil.
	13: 20	but a companion of *f* suffers harm.
	14: 9	*F* mock at making amends for sin,
	14: 24	but the folly of *f* yields folly.

Ecc	7: 5	than to listen to the song of *f*.
	7: 6	so is the laughter of *f*.
	10: 6	*F* are put in many high positions,
Mt	23: 17	You blind *f* ! Which is greater:
Ro	1: 22	they became *f* and exchanged
1Co	4: 10	We are *f* for Christ, but you are

FOOT (FEET FOOTHOLD)

Jos	1: 3	every place where you set your *f*,
Ps	121: 3	He will not let your *f* slip—
Pr	3: 23	and your *f* will not stumble;
	4: 27	keep your *f* from evil.
	25: 17	Seldom set *f* in your neighbour's
Isa	1: 6	From the sole of your *f* to the top
Mt	18: 8	or your *f* causes you to sin,
Lk	4: 11	so that you will not strike your *f*
1Co	12: 15	If the *f* should say, "Because I am
Rev	10: 2	He planted his right *f* on the sea

FOOTHOLD* (FOOT)

Ps	69: 2	where there is no *f*.
	73: 2	I had nearly lost my *f*.
Eph	4: 27	and do not give the devil a *f*.

FOOTSTEPS (STEP)

Ps	119: 133	Direct my *f* according

FOOTSTOOL

Ps	99: 5	and worship at his *f*;
	110: 1	a *f* for your feet."
Isa	66: 1	and the earth is my *f*.
Mt	5: 35	for it is his *f*; or by Jerusalem,
Ac	7: 49	and the earth is my *f*.
Heb	1: 13	a *f* for your feet"?
	10: 13	for his enemies to be made his *f*,

FORBEARANCE*

Ro	3: 25	because in his *f* he had left the sins

FORBID

1Co	14: 39	and do not *f* speaking in tongues.
1Ti	4: 3	They *f* people to marry

FORCE (FORCED FORCEFUL FORCES FORCING)

Jn	6: 15	to come and make him king by *f*,
Ac	26: 11	and I tried to *f* them to blaspheme.
Gal	2: 14	that you *f* Gentiles

FORCED (FORCE)

Mt	27: 32	and they *f* him to carry the cross.
Phm	: 14	do will be spontaneous and not *f*.

FORCEFUL* (FORCE)

Mt	11: 12	forcefully advancing, and *f* men lay
2Co	10: 10	"His letters are weighty and *f*,

FORCES [1] (FORCE)

Mt	5: 41	If someone *f* you to go one mile,

FORCES [2] (FORCE)

Eph	6: 12	and against the spiritual *f* of evil

FORCING (FORCE)

Lk	16: 16	and everyone is *f* his way into it.

FOREFATHERS (FATHER)

Heb	1: 1	spoke to our *f* through the prophets
1Pe	1: 18	handed down to you from your *f*,

FOREHEAD (FOREHEADS)

Ex   13: 9 a reminder on your *f* that the law
        13:16 on your *f* that the LORD brought
1Sa 17:49 and struck the Philistine on the *f.*
Rev 13:16 a mark on his right hand or on his *f,*

FOREHEADS (FOREHEAD)

Dt   6: 8 hands and bind them on your *f.*
Rev   9: 4 not have the seal of God on their *f.*
      14: 1 his Father's name written on their *f*

FOREIGN (FOREIGNER FOREIGNERS)

Ge 35: 2 "Get rid of the *f* gods you have
2Ch 14: 3 He removed the *f* altars
     33:15 He got rid of the *f* gods
Isa 28:11 with *f* lips and strange tongues

FOREIGNER (FOREIGN)

Lk   17:18 give praise to God except this *f?*"
1Co 14:11 I am a *f* to the speaker,

FOREIGNERS (FOREIGN)

Eph 2:12 *f* to the covenants of the promise,
      2:19 you are no longer *f* and aliens,

FOREKNEW* (KNOWN)

Ro   8:29 For those God *f* he
      11: 2 not reject his people, whom he *f.*

FOREKNOWLEDGE* (KNOW)

Ac   2:23 to you by God's set purpose and *f;*
1Pe   1: 2 to the *f* of God the Father,

FORESAW*

Gal   3: 8 Scripture *f* that God would justify

FOREST

Jas   3: 5 Consider what a great *f* is set

FORFEIT

Mk   8:36 the whole world, yet *f* his soul?
Lk   9:25 and yet lose or *f* his very self?

FORGAVE (FORGIVE)

Ps   32: 5 and you *f,*
     65: 3 you *f* our transgressions
     78: 3 he *f* their iniquities
Eph 4:32 just as in Christ God *f* you.
Col   2:13 He *f* us all our sins, having
      3:13 Forgive as the Lord *f* you.

FORGET (FORGETS FORGETTING FORGOT FORGOTTEN)

Dt   4:23 Be careful not to *f* the covenant
      6:12 that you do not *f* the LORD,
2Ki 17:38 Do not *f* the covenant I have made
Ps   9:17 all the nations that *f* God.
     10:12 Do not *f* the helpless.
     50:22 "Consider this, you who *f* God,
     78: 7 and would not *f* his deeds
   103: 2 and *f* not all his benefits.
   119:93 I will never *f* your precepts,
   137: 5 may my right hand *f* its skill .
Pr   3: 1 My son, do not *f* my teaching,
      4: 5 do not *f* my words or swerve
Isa 49:15 "Can a mother *f* the baby
     51:13 that you *f* the LORD your Maker,
Jer   2:32 Does a maiden *f* her jewellery,
     23:39 I will surely *f* you and cast you out
Heb 6:10 he will not *f* your work

Heb 13: 2 Do not *f* to entertain strangers,
     13:16 And do not *f* to do good
2Pe   3: 8 But do not *f* this one thing,

FORGETS (FORGET)

Jn   16:21 her baby is born she *f* the anguish
Jas   1:24 immediately *f* what he looks like.

FORGETTING* (FORGET)

Php 3:13 *F* what is behind and straining
Jas   1:25 to do this, not *f* what he has heard,

FORGIVE* (FORGAVE FORGIVENESS FORGIVES FORGIVING)

Ge 50:17 I ask you to *f* your brothers the sins
     50:17 please *f* the sins of the servants
Ex   10:17 Now *f* my sin once more
     23:21 he will not *f* your rebellion,
     32:32 But now, please *f* their sin—
     34: 9 *f* our wickedness and our sin,
Nu 14:19 with your great love, *f* the sin
Dt 29:20 will never be willing to *f* him;
Jos 24:19 He will not *f* your rebellion
1Sa 15:25 *f* my sin and come back with me,
     25:28 Please *f* your servant's offence,
1Ki 8:30 place, and when you hear, *f.*
      8:34 and *f* the sin of your people Israel
      8:36 and *f* the sin of your servants,
      8:39 *F* and act; deal with each man
      8:50 *f* all the offences they have
      8:50 *f* your people, who have sinned
2Ki 5:18 But may the LORD *f* your servant
      5:18 may the LORD *f* your servant
     24: 4 and the LORD was not willing to *f.*
2Ch 6:21 place; and when you hear, *f.*
      6:25 and *f* the sin of your people Israel
      6:27 and *f* the sin of your servants,
      6:30 *F,* and deal with each man
      6:39 *f* your people, who have sinned
      7:14 will *f* their sin and will heal their
Job   7:21 and *f* my sins?
Ps 19:12 *F* my hidden faults.
     25:11 *f* my iniquity, though it is great.
     79: 9 deliver us and *f* our sins
Isa   2: 9 do not *f* them.
Jer   5: 1 I will *f* this city.
      5: 7 "Why should I *f* you?
     18:23 Do not *f* their crimes
     31:34 "For I will *f* their wickedness
     33: 8 and will *f* all their sins of rebellion
     36: 3 then I will *f* their wickedness
     50:20 for I will *f* the remnant I spare.
Da   9:19 O Lord, listen! O Lord, *f!* O Lord,
Hos 1: 6 that I should at all *f* them.
     14: 2 "*F* all our sins
Am   7: 2 *f!* How can Jacob survive?
Mt   6:12 *F* us our debts,
      6:14 For if you *f* men when they sin
      6:14 heavenly Father will also *f* you.
      6:15 But if you do not *f* men their sins,
      6:15 your Father will not *f* your sins.
      9: 6 authority on earth to *f* sins . . .
     18:21 many times shall I *f* my brother
     18:35 you *f* your brother from your heart
Mk   2: 7 Who can *f* sins but God alone?"
      2:10 authority on earth to *f* sins
     11:25 anything against anyone, *f* him,
     11:25 in heaven may *f* you your sins."
Lk   5:21 Who can *f* sins but God alone?"
      5:24 authority on earth to *f* sins. . .

Lk	6: 37	*F*, and you will be forgiven.
	11: 4	*F* us our sins,
	11: 4	*f* everyone who sins against us.
	17: 3	rebuke him, and if he repents, *f* him
	17: 4	and says, 'I repent,' *f* him."
	23: 34	Jesus said, "Father, *f* them,
Jn	20: 23	If you *f* anyone his sins, they are
	20: 23	if you do not *f* them, they are not
Ac	8: 22	Perhaps he will *f* you
2Co	2: 7	you ought to *f* and comfort him,
	2: 10	If you *f* anyone, I also *f* him.
	2: 10	if there was anything to *f*—
	12: 13	a burden to you? *F* me this wrong!
Col	3: 13	and *f* whatever grievances you may
	3: 13	*F* as the Lord forgave you.
Heb	8: 12	For I will *f* their wickedness
1Jn	1: 9	and just and will *f* us our sins

FORGIVENESS* (FORGIVE)

Ps	130: 4	But with you there is *f*;
Mt	26: 28	out for many for the *f* of sins.
Mk	1: 4	of repentance for the *f* of sins.
Lk	1: 77	salvation through the *f* of their sins,
	3: 3	of repentance for the *f* of sins.
	24: 47	and *f* of sins will be preached
Ac	5: 31	that he might give repentance and *f*
	10: 43	believes in him receives *f* of sins
	13: 38	that through Jesus the *f*
	26: 18	so that they may receive *f* of sins
Eph	1: 7	through his blood, the *f* of sins,
Col	1: 14	in whom we have redemption, the *f*
Heb	9: 22	the shedding of blood there is no *f*.

FORGIVES* (FORGIVE)

Ps	103: 3	He *f* all my sins
Mic	7: 18	pardons sin and *f* the transgression
Lk	7: 49	"Who is this who even *f* sins?"

FORGIVING* (FORGIVE)

Ex	34: 7	and *f* wickedness, rebellion and sin.
Nu	14: 18	abounding in love and *f* sin
Ne	9: 17	But you are a *f* God, gracious
Ps	86: 5	You are *f* and good, O Lord,
	99: 8	you were to Israel a *f* God,
Da	9: 9	The Lord our God is merciful and *f*
Eph	4: 32	to one another, *f* each other,

FORGOT (FORGET)

Dt	32: 18	you *f* the God who gave you birth.
Ps	78: 11	They *f* what he had done,
	106: 13	But they soon *f* what he had done

FORGOTTEN (FORGET)

Job	11: 6	God has even *f* some of your sin.
Ps	44: 20	If we had *f* the name of our God
Isa	17: 10	You have *f* God your Saviour;
Hos	8: 14	Israel has *f* his Maker.
Lk	12: 6	Yet not one of them is *f* by God.
2Pe	1: 9	and has *f* that he has been cleansed

FORM (FORMED)

Isa	52: 14	*f* marred beyond human likeness—
2Ti	3: 5	having a *f* of godliness

FORMED (FORM)

Ge	2: 7	the Lord God *f* man
	2: 19	Now the Lord God had *f* out
Ps	103: 14	for he knows how we are *f*,
Ecc	11: 5	or how the body is *f* in a mother's
Isa	29: 16	Shall what is *f* say to him who *f* it,

Isa	45: 18	but *f* it to be inhabited—
	49: 5	he who *f* me in the womb
Jer	1: 5	"Before I *f* you in the womb I knew
Ro	9: 20	"Shall what is *f* say to him who *f* it,
Gal	4: 19	of childbirth until Christ is *f* in you,
1Ti	2: 13	For Adam was *f* first, then Eve.
Heb	11: 3	understand that the universe was *f*
2Pe	3: 5	and the earth was *f* out of water

FORMLESS*

Ge	1: 2	Now the earth was *f* and empty,
Jer	4: 23	and it was *f* and empty;

FORNICATION see IMMORALITY, UNFAITHFULNESS

FORSAKE (FORSAKEN)

Dt	31: 6	he will never leave you nor *f* you."
Jos	1: 5	I will never leave you or *f* you.
	24: 16	"Far be it from us to *f* the Lord
2Ch	15: 2	but if you *f* him, he will *f* you.
Ps	27: 10	Though my father and mother *f* me
	94: 14	he will never *f* his inheritance.
Isa	55: 7	Let the wicked *f* his way
Heb	13: 5	never will I *f* you."

FORSAKEN (FORSAKE)

Ps	22: 1	my God, why have you *f* me?
	37: 25	I have never seen the righteous *f*
Mt	27: 46	my God, why have you *f* me?"
Rev	2: 4	You have *f* your first love.

FORTRESS

2Sa	22: 2	"The Lord is my rock, my *f*
Ps	18: 2	The Lord is my rock, my *f*
	31: 2	a strong *f* to save me.
	59: 16	for you are my *f*,
	71: 3	for you are my rock and my *f*.
Pr	14: 26	who fears the Lord has a secure *f*,

FORTUNE-TELLING*

Ac	16: 16	deal of money for her owners by *f*.

FORTY

Ge	7: 4	on the earth for *f* days and *f* nights,
	18: 29	"What if only *f* are found there?"
Ex	16: 35	The Israelites ate manna *f* years,
	24: 18	on the mountain *f* days and *f* nights
Nu	14: 34	For *f* years—one year for each
Jos	14: 7	I was *f* years old when Moses
1Sa	4: 18	He had led Israel *f* years.
2Sa	5: 4	king, and he reigned *f* years.
1Ki	19: 8	he travelled *f* days and *f* nights
2Ki	12: 1	and he reigned in Jerusalem *f* years
2Ch	9: 30	in Jerusalem over all Israel *f* years.
Eze	29: 12	her cities will lie desolate *f* years
Jnh	3: 4	"*F* more days and Nineveh will be
Mt	4: 2	After fasting *f* days and *f* nights,

FOUGHT (FIGHT)

1Co	15: 32	If I *f* wild beasts in Ephesus
2Ti	4: 7	I have *f* the good fight, I have

FOUND (FIND)

2Ki	22: 8	"I have *f* the Book of the Law
1Ch	28: 9	If you seek him, he will be *f* by you;
2Ch	15: 15	sought God eagerly, and he was *f*
Isa	55: 6	Seek the Lord while he may be *f*;
	65: 1	I was *f* by those who did not seek
Da	5: 27	on the scales and *f* wanting.
Mt	1: 18	she was *f* to be with child

Lk 15: 6 with me; I have *f* my lost sheep.'
15: 9 with me; I have *f* my lost coin.'
15: 24 is alive again; he was lost and is *f*.'
Ac 4: 12 Salvation is *f* in no-one else,
Ro 10: 20 "I was *f* by those who did not seek
Jas 2: 8 If you really keep the royal law *f*
Rev 5: 4 no one was *f* who was worthy

FOUNDATION (FOUNDATIONS FOUNDED)

Isa 28: 16 a precious cornerstone for a sure *f*;
Mt 7: 25 because it had its *f* on the rock.
Lk 14: 29 For if he lays the *f* and is not able
Ro 15: 20 building on someone else's *f*.
1Co 3: 10 I laid a *f* as an expert builder,
3: 11 For no-one can lay any *f* other
Eph 2: 20 built on the *f* of the apostles
1Ti 3: 15 the pillar and *f* of the truth.
2Ti 2: 19 God's solid *f* stands firm,
Heb 6: 1 not laying again the *f* of repentance

FOUNDATIONS (FOUNDATION)

Ps 102: 25 In the beginning you laid the *f*
Heb 1: 10 O Lord, you laid the *f* of the earth,

FOUNDED (FOUNDATION)

Jer 10: 12 he *f* the world by his wisdom
Heb 8: 6 and it is *f* on better promises.

FOUNTAIN

Ps 36: 9 For with you is the *f* of life;
Pr 14: 27 The fear of the LORD is a *f* of life,
18: 4 the *f* of wisdom is a bubbling brook.
Zec 13: 1 "On that day a *f* will be opened

FOX (FOXES)

Lk 13: 32 He replied, "Go tell that *f*,

FOXES (FOX)

SS 2: 15 the little *f*
Mt 8: 20 "*F* have holes and birds

FRAGRANCE (FRAGRANT)

Ex 30: 38 it to enjoy its *f* must be cut
Jn 12: 3 filled with the *f* of the perfume.
2Co 2: 14 us spreads everywhere the *f*
2: 16 of death; to the other, the *f* of life.

FRAGRANT (FRAGRANCE)

Eph 5: 2 as a *f* offering and sacrifice to God.
Php 4: 18 They are a *f* offering, an acceptable

FREE (FREED FREEDOM FREELY)

Ge 2: 16 "You are *f* to eat from any tree
Ps 118: 5 and he answered by setting me *f*.
119: 32 for you have set my heart *f*.
146: 7 The LORD sets prisoners *f*,
Pr 6: 3 then do this, my son, to *f* yourself,
Jn 8: 32 and the truth will set you *f*."
8: 36 if the Son sets you *f*, you will be *f*
Ro 6: 18 You have been set *f* from sin
8: 2 of life set me *f* from the law of sin
1Co 12: 13 whether Jews or Greeks, slave or *f*
Gal 3: 28 slave nor *f*, male nor female,
5: 1 for freedom that Christ has set us *f*.
1Pe 2: 16 *f* men, but do not use your freedom

FREED (FREE)

Ps 116: 16 you have *f* me from my chains.
Ro 6: 7 anyone who has died has been *f*

Rev 1: 5 has *f* us from our sins by his blood,

FREEDOM (FREE)

Ps 119: 45 I will walk about in *f*,
Isa 61: 1 to proclaim *f* for the captives
Lk 4: 18 me to proclaim *f* for the prisoners
Ro 8: 21 into the glorious *f* of the children
1Co 7: 21 although if you can gain your *f*,
2Co 3: 17 the Spirit of the Lord is, there is *f*.
Gal 2: 4 ranks to spy on the *f* we have
5: 13 But do not use your *f* to indulge
Jas 1: 25 into the perfect law that gives *f*,
1Pe 2: 16 but do not use your *f* as a cover-up

FREELY (FREE)

Isa 55: 7 and to our God, for he will *f* pardon
Mt 10: 8 *F* you have received, *f* give.
Ro 3: 24 and are justified *f* by his grace
Eph 1: 6 which he has *f* given us

FRESH

Jas 3: 11 Can both *f* water and salt water

FRET*

Ps 37: 1 Do not *f* because of evil men
37: 7 do not *f* when men succeed
37: 8 do not *f*—it leads only to evil.
Pr 24: 19 Do not *f* because of evil men

FRICTION

1Ti 6: 5 and constant *f* between men

FRIEND (FRIENDS FRIENDSHIP)

Ex 33: 11 as a man speaks with his *f*.
2Ch 20: 7 descendants of Abraham your *f*?
Pr 17: 17 A *f* loves at all times,
18: 24 there is a *f* who sticks closer
27: 6 wounds from a *f* can be trusted,
27: 10 Do not forsake your *f* and the *f*
Isa 41: 8 you descendants of Abraham my *f*,
Mt 11: 19 a *f* of tax collectors and "sinners".'
Lk 11: 8 him the bread because he is his *f*,
Jn 19: 12 "If you let this man go, you are no *f*
Jas 2: 23 and he was called God's *f*.
4: 4 Anyone who chooses to be a *f*

FRIENDS (FRIEND)

Pr 16: 28 and a gossip separates close *f*.
17: 9 the matter separates close *f*.
Zec 13: 6 given at the house of my *f*.'
Jn 15: 13 that one lay down his life for his *f*.
15: 14 You are my *f* if you do what I

FRIENDSHIP (FRIEND)

Jas 4: 4 don't you know that *f*

FRIGHTENED (FEAR)

Php 1: 28 gospel without being *f* in any way
1Pe 3: 14 fear what they fear; do not be *f*."

FROGS

Ex 8: 2 plague your whole country with *f*.
Rev 16: 13 three evil spirits that looked like *f*;

FRUIT (FRUITFUL)

Jdg 9: 11 'Should I give up my *f*, so good
Ps 1: 3 which yields its *f* in season
Pr 11: 30 The *f* of the righteous is a tree
12: 14 From the *f* of his lips a man is filled
27: 18 He who tends a fig-tree will eat its *f*

Isa   11: 1 from his roots a Branch will bear *f*.
       27: 6 and fill all the world with *f*.
       32: 17 The *f* of righteousness will be peace
Jer   17: 8 and never fails to bear *f*."
Hos   10: 12 reap the *f* of unfailing love,
       14: 2 that we may offer the *f* of our lips.
Am   8: 1 showed me: a basket of ripe *f*.
Mt   3: 8 Produce *f* in keeping
       3: 10 does not produce good *f* will be cut
       7: 16 By their *f* you will recognise them.
       7: 17 good *f*, but a bad tree bears bad *f*.
       7: 20 by their *f* you will recognise them.
       12: 33 a tree gives and its *f* will be good,
Lk   3: 9 does not produce good *f* will be cut
       6: 43 nor does a bad tree bear good *f*.
       13: 6 and he went to look for *f* on it,
Jn   15: 2 branch in me that bears no *f*,
       15: 16 and bear *f*—*f* that will last.
Ro   7: 4 in order that we might bear *f*
Gal   5: 22 But the *f* of the Spirit is love, joy,
Php   1: 11 with the *f* of righteousness that
Col   1: 10 bearing *f* in every good work,
Heb   13: 15 the *f* of lips that confess his name.
Jas   3: 17 and good *f*, impartial and sincere.
Jude   : 12 autumn trees, without *f*
Rev   22: 2 of *f*, yielding its *f* every month.

FRUITFUL (FRUIT)

Ge   1: 22 "Be *f* and increase in number
       9: 1 "Be *f* and increase in number
       35: 11 be *f* and increase in number.
Ex   1: 7 the Israelites were *f* and multiplied
Ps   128: 3 Your wife will be like a *f* vine
Jn   15: 2 clean so that it will be even more *f*.
Php   1: 22 this will mean *f* labour for me.

FRUITLESS*

Eph   5: 11 to do with the *f* deeds of darkness,

FRUSTRATION

Ro   8: 20 For the creation was subjected to *f*,

FUEL

Isa   44: 19 "Half of it I used for *f*;

FULFIL (FULFILLED FULFILMENT FULFILS)

Nu   23: 19 Does he promise and not *f*?
Ps   61: 8 and *f* my vows day after day.
      116: 14 I will *f* my vows to the LORD
      138: 8 The LORD will *f* his purpose﹐
Ecc   5: 5 than to make a vow and not *f* it.
Isa   46: 11 far-off land, a man to *f* my purpose.
Jer   33: 14 'when I will *f* the gracious promise
Mt   1: 22 place to *f* what the Lord had said
       3: 15 us to do this to *f* all righteousness."
       4: 14 *f* what was said
       5: 17 come to abolish them but to *f* them.
       8: 17 This was to *f* what was spoken
       12: 17 This was to *f* what was spoken
       21: 4 place to *f* what was spoken
Jn   12: 38 This was to *f* the word
       13: 18 But this is to *f* the scripture:
       15: 25 But this is to *f* what is written
1Co   7: 3 husband should *f* his marital duty

FULFILLED (FULFIL)

Jos   21: 45 of Israel failed; every one was *f*.
       23: 14 Every promise has been *f*;
Pr   13: 12 but a longing *f* is a tree of life.
       13: 19 A longing *f* is sweet to the soul,
Mt   2: 15 so was *f* what the Lord had said

Mt   2: 17 the prophet Jeremiah was *f*:
       2: 23 So was *f* what was said
       13: 14 In them is *f* the prophecy of Isaiah:
       13: 35 So was *f* what was spoken
       26: 54 would the Scriptures be *f* that say it
       26: 56 of the prophets might be *f*."
       27: 9 by Jeremiah the prophet was *f*:
Mk   13: 4 that they are all about to be *f*?"
       14: 49 But the Scriptures must be *f*."
Lk   4: 21 "Today this scripture is *f*
       18: 31 about the Son of Man will be *f*.
       24: 44 Everything must be *f* that is
Jn   18: 9 words he had spoken would be *f*:
       19: 24 the Scripture might be *f* which said,
       19: 28 and so that the Scripture would be *f*
       19: 36 so that the Scripture would be *f*:
Ac   1: 16 to be *f* which the Holy Spirit spoke
Ro   13: 8 loves his fellow-man has *f* the law.
Jas   2: 23 And the scripture was *f* that says,

FULFILMENT (FULFIL)

Ro   13: 10 Therefore love is the *f* of the law.

FULFILS (FULFIL)

Ps   57: 2 to God, who *f* his purpose﹐ for me.
      145: 19 He *f* the desires of those who fear

FULL (FILL)

2Ch   24: 10 them into the chest until it was *f*.
Ps   127: 5 whose quiver is *f* of them.
Pr   27: 7 He who is *f* loathes honey,
       31: 11 Her husband has *f* confidence
Isa   6: 3 the whole earth is *f* of his glory."
       11: 9 for the earth will be *f*
Lk   1: 1 Jesus, *f* of the Holy Spirit,
Jn   10: 10 may have life, and have it to the *f*.
Ac   6: 3 known to be *f* of the Spirit
       6: 5 a man *f* of faith and of the Holy
       7: 55 But Stephen, *f* of the Holy Spirit,
       11: 24 *f* of the Holy Spirit and faith,

FULL-GROWN* (GROW)

Jas   1: 15 when it is *f*, gives birth to death.

FULLY (FILL)

1Ki   8: 61 your hearts must be *f* committed
2Ch   16: 9 whose hearts are *f* committed
Ps   119: 4 that are to be *f* obeyed.
      119: 138 they are *f* trustworthy.
Pr   13: 4 of the diligent are *f* satisfied.
Lk   6: 40 everyone who is *f* trained will be
Ro   4: 21 being *f* persuaded that God had
       14: 5 Each one should be *f* convinced
1Co   13: 12 shall know *f*, even as I am *f* known.
       15: 58 Always give yourselves *f*
2Ti   4: 17 the message might be *f* proclaimed

FULNESS* (FILL)

Dt   33: 16 gifts of the earth and its *f*
Jn   1: 16 From the *f* of his grace we have all
Ro   11: 12 greater riches will their *f* bring!
Eph   1: 23 the *f* of him who fills everything
       3: 19 to the measure of all the *f* of God.
       4: 13 to the whole measure of the *f*
Col   1: 19 to have all his *f* dwell in him,
       1: 25 to you the word of God in its *f*—
       2: 9 in Christ all the *f* of the Deity lives
       2: 10 and you have been given *f* in Christ

FURIOUS (FURY)

Dt   29: 28 In *f* anger and in great wrath

Jer 32: 37 where I banish them in my *f* anger

FURNACE
Isa 48: 10 in the *f* of affliction.
Da 3: 6 be thrown into a blazing *f*."
Mt 13: 42 will throw them into the fiery *f*,

FURY (FURIOUS)
Isa 14: 6 and in *f* subdued nations
Jer 21: 5 and a mighty arm in anger and *f*
Rev 14: 10 will drink of the wine of God's *f*,
16: 19 with the wine of the *f* of his wrath.
19: 15 the winepress of the *f* of the wrath

FUTILE (FUTILITY)
Mal 3: 14 You have said, 'It is *f* to serve God.
1Co 3: 20 that the thoughts of the wise are *f*."

FUTILITY (FUTILE)
Eph 4: 17 in the *f* of their thinking.

FUTURE
Ps 37: 37 there is a *f* for the man of peace.
Pr 23: 18 There is surely a *f* hope for you,
Ecc 7: 14 anything about his *f*.
8: 7 Since no man knows the *f*,
Jer 29: 11 plans to give you hope and a *f*.
31: 17 So there is hope for your *f*,"
Ro 8: 38 neither the present nor the *f*,
1Co 3: 22 life or death or the present or the *f*

GABRIEL*
Angel who interpreted Daniel's visions (Da 8:16-26; 9:20-27); announced births of John (Lk 1:11-20), Jesus (Lk 1:26-38).

GAD
1. Son of Jacob by Zilpah (Ge 30:9-11; 35:26; 1Ch 2:2). Tribe of blessed (Ge 49:19; Dt 33:20-21), numbered (Nu 1:25; 26:18), allotted land east of the Jordan (Nu 32; 34:14; Jos 18:7; 22), west (Eze 48:27-28), 12,000 from (Rev 7:5).
2. Prophet; seer of David (1Sa 22:5; 2Sa 24:11-19; 1Ch 29:29).

GAIN (GAINED GAINS)
Ex 14: 17 And I will *g* glory through Pharaoh
Ps 60: 12 With God we will *g* the victory,
Pr 4: 1 pay attention and *g* understanding.
8: 5 You who are simple, *g* prudence;
28: 16 he who hates ill-gotten *g* will enjoy
28: 23 in the end *g* more favour
Isa 63: 12 to *g* for himself everlasting renown
Da 2: 8 that you are trying to *g* time,
Mk 8: 36 it for a man to *g* the whole world,
Lk 9: 25 it for a man to *g* the whole world,
1Co 13: 3 but have not love, I *g* nothing.
Php 1: 21 to live is Christ and to die is *g*.
3: 8 that I may *g* Christ and be found
1Ti 3: 13 have served well *g* an excellent
6: 5 godliness is a means to financial *g*.
6: 6 with contentment is great *g*.

GAINED (GAIN)
Jer 32: 20 have *g* the renown that is still yours
Ro 5: 2 through whom we have *g* access

GAINS (GAIN)
Pr 3: 13 the man who *g* understanding,
11: 16 A kindhearted woman *g* respect,

Pr 15: 32 heeds correction *g* understanding.
29: 23 but a man of lowly spirit *g* honour.
Mt 16: 26 for a man if he *g* the whole world,

GALILEE
Isa 9: 1 but in the future he will honour *G*
Mt 4: 15 *G* of the Gentiles—
26: 32 I will go ahead of you into *G*."
28: 10 Go and tell my brothers to go to *G*;

GALL
Mt 27: 34 mixed with *g*; but after tasting it,

GALLIO
Ac 18: 12 While *G* was proconsul of Achaia,

GALLOWS
Est 7: 10 Haman on the *g* he had prepared

GAMALIEL
Ac 5: 34 But a Pharisee named *G*, a teacher

GAMES
1Co 9: 25 in the *g* goes into strict training.

GAP
Eze 22: 30 stand before me in the *g* on behalf

GAPE*
Ps 35: 21 They *g* at me and say, "Aha! Aha!

GARDEN (GARDENER)
Ge 2: 8 the LORD God had planted a *g*
2: 15 put him in the *G* of Eden to work it
SS 4: 12 You are a *g* locked up, my sister,
Isa 58: 11 You will be like a well-watered *g*,
Jer 31: 12 They will be like a well-watered *g*,
Eze 28: 13 the *g* of God;
31: 9 Eden in the *g* of God.

GARDENER (GARDEN)
Jn 15: 1 true vine and my Father is the *g*.

GARLAND*
Pr 1: 9 They will be a *g* to grace your head
4: 9 She will set a *g* of grace

GARMENT (GARMENTS)
Ps 102: 26 they will all wear out like a *g*.
Isa 50: 9 They will all wear out like a *g*;
51: 6 the earth will wear out like a *g*
61: 3 and a *g* of praise
Mt 9: 16 of unshrunk cloth on an old *g*,
Jn 19: 23 This *g* was seamless, woven
Heb 1: 11 They will all wear out like a *g*.

GARMENTS (GARMENT)
Ge 3: 21 The LORD God made *g* of skin
Ex 28: 2 Make sacred *g* for your brother
Lev 16: 23 and take off the linen *g* he put
16: 24 holy place and put on his regular *g*.
Isa 61: 10 me with *g* of salvation
63: 1 with his *g* stained crimson?
Joel 2: 13 and not your *g*.
Zec 3: 4 and I will put rich *g* on you."
Jn 19: 24 "They divided my *g* among them

GATE (GATES)
Ps 118: 20 This is the *g* of the LORD
Pr 31: 23 husband is respected at the city *g*,

Pr   31: 31   works bring her praise at the city *g*.
Mt   7: 13   For wide is the *g* and broad is
      7: 13   "Enter through the narrow *g*.
Jn   10: 1   not enter the sheep pen by the *g*,
      10: 2   enters by the *g* is the shepherd
      10: 7   "I tell you the truth, I am the *g*
      10: 9   I am the *g*; whoever enters
Heb   13: 12   also suffered outside the city *g*
Rev   21: 21   each *g* made of a single pearl.

GATES (GATE)

Ps   24: 7   Lift up your heads, O you *g*;
      24: 9   Lift up your heads, O you *g*;
      100: 4   Enter his *g* with thanksgiving
      118: 19   Open for me the *g* of righteousness
Isa   60: 11   Your *g* will always stand open,
      60: 18   and your *g* Praise.
      62: 10   Pass through, pass through the *g*!
Mt   16: 18   the *g* of Hades will not overcome it
Rev   21: 12   On the *g* were written the names
      21: 21   The twelve *g* were twelve pearls,
      21: 25   On no day will its *g* ever be shut,
      22: 14   may go through the *g* into the city.

GATH

1Sa   17: 23   the Philistine champion from *G*,
2Sa   1: 20   "Tell it not in *G*,
Mic   1: 10   Tell it not in *G*;

GATHER (GATHERED GATHERS)

Ps   106: 47   and *g* us from the nations,
Isa   11: 12   and *g* the exiles of Israel;
Jer   3: 17   and all nations will *g* in Jerusalem
      23: 3   "I myself will *g* the remnant
      31: 10   who scattered Israel will *g* them
Zep   2: 1   *G* together, *g* together,
      3: 20   At that time I will *g* you;
Zec   14: 2   I will *g* all the nations to Jerusalem
Mt   12: 30   he who does not *g* with me scatters
      13: 30   then *g* the wheat and bring it
      23: 37   longed to *g* your children together,
      24: 31   and they will *g* his elect
      25: 26   *g* where I have not scattered seed?
Mk   13: 27   and *g* his elect from the four winds,
Lk   3: 17   and to *g* the wheat into his barn,
      11: 23   and he who does not *g* with me,
      13: 34   longed to *g* your children together,

GATHERED (GATHER)

Ex   16: 18   and he who *g* little did not have too
Pr   30: 4   Who has *g* up the wind
Mt   25: 32   All the nations will be *g* before him
2Co   8: 15   and he that *g* little did not have too
2Th   2: 1   Lord Jesus Christ and our being *g*
Rev   16: 16   Then they *g* the kings together

GATHERS (GATHER)

Ps   147: 2   he *g* the exiles of Israel.
Pr   10: 5   He who *g* crops in summer is a wise
Isa   40: 11   He *g* the lambs in his arms
Mt   23: 37   a hen *g* her chicks under her wings,

GAVE (GIVE)

Ge   2: 20   man *g* names to all the livestock,
      3: 6   She also *g* some to her husband,
      14: 20   Abram *g* him a tenth of everything.
      28: 4   the land God *g* to Abraham."
      35: 12   The land I *g* to Abraham
      39: 23   *g* him success in whatever he did.
      47: 11   *g* them property in the best part

Ex   4: 11   to him, "Who *g* man his mouth?
      31: 18   he *g* him the two tablets
Dt   2: 12   did in the land the LORD *g* them
      2: 36   The LORD our God *g* us all
      3: 12   I *g* the Reubenites and the Gadites
      3: 13   I *g* to the half tribe of Manasseh.
      3: 15   And I *g* Gilead to Makir.
      3: 16   Gadites I *g* the territory extending
      8: 16   He *g* you manna to eat in the desert
      26: 9   us to this place and *g* us this land,
      32: 8   the Most High *g* the nations their
Jos   11: 23   and he *g* it as an inheritance
      13: 14   tribe of Levi he *g* no inheritance,
      14: 13   *g* him Hebron as his inheritance.
      21: 44   The LORD *g* them rest
      24: 13   I *g* you a land on which you did not
1Sa   27: 6   So on that day Achish *g* him Ziklag
2Sa   12: 8   I *g* you the house of Israel
1Ki   4: 29   God *g* Solomon wisdom
      5: 12   The LORD *g* Solomon wisdom,
Ezr   2: 69   According to their ability they *g*
Ne   9: 15   In their hunger you *g* them bread
      9: 20   You *g* your good Spirit
      9: 22   You *g* them kingdoms and nations,
      9: 27   compassion you *g* them deliverers,
Job   1: 21   LORD *g* and the LORD has taken
      42: 10   prosperous again and *g* him twice
Ps   69: 21   and *g* me vinegar for my thirst.
      135: 12   he *g* their land as an inheritance,
Ecc   12: 7   the spirit returns to God who *g* it.
Eze   3: 2   and he *g* me the scroll to eat.
Mt   1: 25   And he *g* him the name Jesus.
      25: 35   and you *g* me something to drink,
      25: 42   and you *g* me nothing to drink,
      26: 26   Jesus took bread, *g* thanks
      27: 50   in a loud voice, he *g* up his spirit.
Mk   6: 7   *g* them authority over evil spirits.
Jn   1: 12   he *g* the right to become children
      3: 16   so loved the world that he *g* his one
      17: 4   by completing the work you *g* me
      17: 6   you *g* them to me and they have
      19: 30   bowed his head and *g* up his spirit.
Ac   1: 3   *g* many convincing proofs that he
      2: 45   they *g* to anyone as he had need.
      11: 17   *g* them the same gift as he *g* us,
Ro   1: 24   Therefore God *g* them
      1: 26   God *g* them over to shameful lusts.
      1: 28   he *g* them over to a depraved mind,
      8: 32   not spare his own Son, but *g* him up
2Co   5: 18   *g* us the ministry of reconciliation:
      8: 3   For I testify that they *g* as much
      8: 5   they *g* themselves first to the Lord
Gal   1: 4   who *g* himself for our sins
      2: 20   who loved me and *g* himself for me
Eph   4: 8   and *g* gifts to men."
      5: 2   as Christ loved us and *g* himself up
      5: 25   and *g* himself up for her
2Th   2: 16   and by his grace *g* us eternal
1Ti   2: 6   who *g* himself as a ransom
Tit   2: 14   who *g* himself for us to redeem us
1Jn   3: 24   We know it by the Spirit he *g* us.

GAZE

Ps   27: 4   to *g* upon the beauty of the LORD
Pr   4: 25   fix your *g* directly before you.

GEDALIAH

Governor of Judah appointed by
Nebuchadnezzar (2Ki 25:22-26; Jer 39-41).

GEHAZI*
Servant of Elisha (2Ki 4:12-5:27; 8:4-5).

GENEALOGIES
1Ti 1: 4 themselves to myths and endless *g*.
Tit 3: 9 avoid foolish controversies and *g*

GENERATION (GENERATIONS)
Ex 3:15 am to be remembered from *g* to *g*.
Nu 32:13 until the whole *g* of those who had
Dt 1:35 of this evil *g* shall see the good land
Jdg 2:10 After that whole *g* had been
Ps 24: 6 Such is the *g* of those who seek him
48:13 tell of them to the next *g*.
71:18 I declare your power to the next *g*,
78: 4 we will tell the next *g*
102:18 Let this be written for a future *g*,
112: 2 each *g* of the upright will be blessed
145: 4 One *g* will commend your works
La 5:19 your throne endures from *g* to *g*.
Da 4: 3 his dominion endures from *g* to *g*.
4:34 his kingdom endures from *g* to *g*.
Joel 1: 3 and their children to the next *g*.
Mt 12:39 adulterous *g* asks for a miraculous
17:17 "O unbelieving and perverse *g*,"
23:36 all this will come upon this *g*.
24:34 this *g* will certainly not pass away
Mk 9:19 "O unbelieving *g*," Jesus replied,
13:30 this *g* will certainly not pass away
Lk 1:50 who fear him, from *g* to *g*.
11:29 Jesus said, "This is a wicked *g*.
11:30 will the Son of Man be to this *g*.
11:50 Therefore this *g* will be held
21:32 this *g* will certainly not pass away
Ac 2:40 Save yourselves from this corrupt *g*
Php 2:15 fault in a crooked and depraved *g*,

GENERATIONS (GENERATION)
Ge 9:12 a covenant for all *g* to come:
17: 7 after you for the *g* to come,
17: 9 after you for the *g* to come.
Ex 31:13 and you for the *g* to come,
Dt 7: 9 covenant of love to a thousand *g*
32: 7 consider the *g* long past.
1Ch 16:15 he commanded, for a thousand *g*,
Job 8: 8 "Ask the former *g*
Ps 22:30 future *g* will be told about the Lord
33:11 of his heart through all *g*.
45:17 your memory through all *g*;
89: 1 faithfulness known through all *g*.
90: 1 throughout all *g*.
100: 5 continues through all *g*.
102:12 your renown endures through all *g*.
105: 8 he commanded, for a thousand *g*,
119:90 continues through all *g*;
135:13 renown, O LORD, through all *g*.
145:13 dominion endures through all *g*.
146:10 your God, O Zion, for all *g*.
Pr 27:24 and a crown is not secure for all *g*.
Isa 41: 4 forth the *g* from the beginning?
51: 8 my salvation through all *g*."
Lk 1:48 now on all *g* will call me blessed,
Eph 3: 5 not made known to men in other *g*
3:21 in Christ Jesus throughout all *g*,
Col 1:26 been kept hidden for ages and *g*,

GENEROSITY* (GENEROUS)
2Co 8: 2 poverty welled up in rich *g*.
9:11 and through us your *g* will result
9:13 and for your *g* in sharing with them

GENEROUS* (GENEROSITY)
Ps 37:26 They are always *g* and lend freely;
112: 5 Good will come to him who is *g*
Pr 11:25 A *g* man will prosper;
22: 9 A *g* man will himself be blessed,
Mt 20:15 Or are you envious because I am *g*
2Co 9: 5 Then it will be ready as a *g* gift,
9: 5 for the *g* gift you had promised.
9:11 way so that you can be *g*
1Ti 6:18 and to be *g* and willing to share.

GENTILE (GENTILES)
Ac 21:25 As for the *G* believers, we have
Ro 1:16 first for the Jew, then for the *G*.
2: 9 first for the Jew, then for the *G*;
2:10 first for the Jew, then for the *G*.
10:12 difference between Jew and *G*—

GENTILES (GENTILE)
Isa 42: 6 and a light for the *G*,
49: 6 also make you a light for the *G*,
49:22 "See, I will beckon to the *G*,
Lk 2:32 a light for revelation to the *G*
21:24 on by the *G* until the times
Ac 9:15 to carry my name before the *G*
10:45 been poured out even on the *G*.
11:18 granted the *G* repentance unto life
13:16 and you *G* who worship God,
13:46 of eternal life, we now turn to the *G*
13:47 I have made you a light for the *G*,
14:27 opened the door of faith to the *G*.
15:14 by taking from the *G* a people
18: 6 From now on I will go to the *G*."
22:21 I will send you far away to the *G*.'"
26:20 and in all Judea, and to the *G* also,
28:28 salvation has been sent to the *G*,
Ro 2:14 when *G*, who do not have the law,
3: 9 and *G* alike are all under sin.
3:29 Is he not the God of *G* too? Yes,
9:24 from the Jews but also from the *G*?
11:11 to the *G* to make Israel envious.
11:12 their loss means riches for the *G*,
11:13 as I am the apostle to the *G*,
15: 9 I will praise you among the *G*;
15: 9 so that the *G* may glorify God
1Co 1:23 block to Jews and foolishness to *G*,
Gal 1:16 I might preach him among the *G*,
2: 2 gospel that I preach among the *G*.
2: 8 my ministry as an apostle to the *G*,
2: 9 agreed that we should go to the *G*,
3: 8 that God would justify the *G*
3:14 to the *G* through Christ Jesus,
Eph 3: 6 the gospel the *G* are heirs together
3: 8 to the *G* the unsearchable riches
Col 1:27 among the *G* the glorious riches
1Ti 2: 7 a teacher of the true faith to the *G*.
2Ti 4:17 and all the *G* might hear it.

GENTLE* (GENTLENESS)
Dt 28:54 Even the most *g* and sensitive man
28:56 The most *g* and sensitive woman
28:56 and *g* that she would not venture
2Sa 18: 5 Be *g* with the young man Absalom
1Ki 19:12 And after the fire came a *g* whisper
Job 41: 3 Will he speak to you with *g* words?
Pr 15: 1 A *g* answer turns away wrath,
25:15 and a *g* tongue can break a bone.
Jer 11:19 I had been like a *g* lamb led
Zec 9: 9 *g* and riding on a donkey,
Mt 11:29 for I am *g* and humble in heart,

Mt 21: 5 *g* and riding on a donkey,
Ac 27: 13 When a *g* south wind began
1Co 4: 21 or in love and with a *g* spirit?
Eph 4: 2 Be completely humble and *g*;
1Th 2: 7 but we were *g* among you,
1Ti 3: 3 not violent but *g*, not quarrelsome,
1Pe 3: 4 the unfading beauty of a *g*

GENTLENESS* (GENTLE)

2Co 10: 1 By the meekness and *g* of Christ,
Gal 5: 23 faithfulness, *g* and self-control.
Php 4: 5 Let your *g* be evident to all.
Col 3: 12 kindness, humility, *g* and patience.
1Ti 6: 11 faith, love, endurance and *g*.
1Pe 3: 15 But do this with *g* and respect,

GENUINE*

2Co 6: 8 *g*, yet regarded as impostors;
Php 2: 20 who takes a *g* interest
1Pe 1: 7 may be proved *g* and may result

GERIZIM

Dt 27: 12 on Mount *G* to bless the people:

GERSHOM

Ex 2: 22 and Moses named him *G*, saying,

GETHSEMANE*

Mt 26: 36 disciples to a place called *G*,
Mk 14: 32 They went to a place called *G*,

GHOST see also SPIRIT

Lk 24: 39 a *g* does not have flesh and bones,

GIBEON

Jos 10: 12 "O sun, stand still over *G*,

GIDEON*

Judge, also called Jerub-Baal; freed Israel from Midianites (Jdg 6-8; Heb 11:32). Given sign of fleece (Jdg 6:36-40).

GIFT (GIFTED GIFTS)

Pr 18: 16 A *g* opens the way for the giver
21: 14 A *g* given in secret soothes anger,
Ecc 3: 13 in all his toil—this is the *g* of God.
Mt 5: 23 if you are offering your *g*
Jn 4: 10 "If you knew the *g* of God
Ac 1: 4 wait for the *g* my Father promised,
2: 38 And you will receive the *g*
11: 17 So if God gave them the same *g*
Ro 6: 23 but the *g* of God is eternal life
12: 6 If a man's *g* is prophesying,
1Co 7: 7 each man has his own *g* from God;
2Co 8: 12 the *g* is acceptable according
9: 15 be to God for his indescribable *g*!
Eph 2: 8 it is the *g* of God—not by works,
1Ti 4: 14 not neglect your *g*, which was
2Ti 1: 6 you to fan into flame the *g* of God,
Heb 6: 4 who have tasted the heavenly *g*,
Jas 1: 17 and perfect *g* is from above,
1Pe 3: 7 with you of the gracious *g* of life,
4: 10 should use whatever *g* he has
Rev 22: 17 let him take the free *g* of the water

GIFTED* (GIFT)

1Co 14: 37 he is a prophet or spiritually *g*,

GIFTS (GIFT)

Ps 76: 11 bring *g* to the One to be feared.

Ps 112: 9 He has scattered abroad his *g*
Pr 25: 14 of *g* he does not give.
Mt 2: 11 and presented him with *g* of gold
7: 11 Father in heaven give good *g*
7: 11 to give good *g* to your children,
Lk 11: 13 to give good *g* to your children,
Ac 10: 4 and *g* to the poor have come up
Ro 11: 29 for God's *g* and his call are
12: 6 We have different *g*, according
1Co 12: 1 Now about spiritual *g*, brothers,
12: 4 There are different kinds of *g*,
12: 28 those with *g* of administration,
12: 30 all work miracles? Do all have *g*
12: 31 But eagerly desire the greater *g*.
14: 1 and eagerly desire spiritual *g*,
14: 12 eager to have spiritual *g*,
14: 12 excel in *g* that build up the church.
2Co 9: 9 "He has scattered abroad his *g*
Eph 4: 8 and gave *g* to men."
Heb 2: 4 and *g* of the Holy Spirit distributed
9: 9 indicating that the *g* and sacrifices

GILEAD

1Ch 27: 21 the half-tribe of Manasseh in *G*:
Jer 8: 22 Is there no balm in *G*?
46: 11 "Go up to *G* and get balm,

GILGAL

Jos 5: 9 So the place has been called *G*

GIRD*

Ps 45: 3 *G* your sword upon your side,

GIRL

Ge 24: 16 *g* was very beautiful, a virgin;
2Ki 5: 2 a young *g* from Israel.
Mk 5: 41 Little *g*, I say to you, get up!

GIVE (GAVE GIVEN GIVER GIVES GIVING LIFE-GIVING)

Ge 28: 22 that you *g* me I will *g* you a tenth."
Ex 20: 16 "You shall not *g* false testimony
30: 15 The rich are not to *g* more
Nu 6: 26 and *g* you peace."'
Dt 5: 20 "You shall not *g* false testimony
15: 10 *G* generously to him and do
15: 14 *G* to him as the Lord your God
1Sa 1: 11 then I will *g* him to the Lord
1: 28 So now I *g* him to the Lord.
2Ch 15: 7 be strong and do not *g* up,
Pr 21: 26 but the righteous *g* without sparing
23: 26 My son, *g* me your heart
25: 21 if he is thirsty, *g* him water to drink
30: 8 but *g* me only my daily bread.
31: 31 *G* her the reward she has earned,
Ecc 3: 6 a time to search and a time to *g* up,
Isa 42: 8 I will not *g* my glory to another
Eze 36: 26 I will *g* you a new heart
Mt 6: 11 *G* us today our daily bread.
7: 11 know how to *g* good gifts
10: 8 Freely you have received, freely *g*.
16: 19 I will *g* you the keys
22: 21 "*G* to Caesar what is Caesar's,
Mk 8: 37 Or what can a man *g* in exchange
10: 19 not steal, do not *g* false testimony,
Lk 6: 38 *G*, and it will be given to you.
11: 3 *G* us each day our daily bread.
11: 13 Father in heaven *g* the Holy Spirit
14: 33 who does not *g* up everything he
Jn 10: 28 I *g* them eternal life, and they shall

Jn	13:34	"A new commandment I *g* you:
	14:16	he will *g* you another Counsellor
	14:27	I do not *g* to you as the world gives.
	14:27	leave with you; my peace I *g* you.
	17:2	people that he might *g* eternal life
Ac	20:35	blessed to *g* than to receive.'"
Ro	2:7	immortality, he will *g* eternal life.
	8:32	with him, graciously *g* us all things
	12:8	let him *g* generously;
	13:7	*G* everyone what you owe him:
	14:12	each of us will *g* an account
2Co	9:7	Each man should *g* what he has
Gal	2:5	We did not *g* in to them
	6:9	reap a harvest if we do not *g* up.
Heb	10:25	Let us not *g* up meeting together,
Rev	14:7	"Fear God and *g* him glory,

GIVEN (GIVE)

Nu	8:16	are to be *g* wholly to me.
Dt	26:11	things the LORD your God has *g*
Job	3:23	Why is life *g* to a man
Ps	115:16	but the earth he has *g* to man.
Isa	9:6	to us a son is *g*,
Mt	6:33	and all these things will be *g* to you
	7:7	"Ask and it will be *g* to you;
	13:12	Whoever has will be *g* more,
	22:30	people will neither marry nor be *g*
	25:29	everyone who has will be *g* more,
Lk	6:38	Give, and it will be *g* to you.
	8:10	kingdom of God has been *g* to you,
	11:9	Ask and it will be *g* to you;
	22:19	saying, "This is my body *g* for you;
Jn	3:27	man can receive only what is *g* him
	15:7	you wish, and it will be *g* you.
	17:24	I want those you have *g* me to be
	17:24	the glory you have *g* me
	18:11	the cup the Father has *g* me?"
Ac	5:32	whom God has *g* to those who
	20:24	the task the Lord Jesus has *g* me—
Ro	5:5	the Holy Spirit, whom he has *g* us.
1Co	4:2	those who have been *g* a trust must
	11:24	and when he had *g* thanks,
	12:13	we were all *g* the one Spirit to drink
2Co	5:5	and has *g* us the Spirit as a deposit,
Eph	1:6	which he has freely *g* us
	4:7	to each one of us grace has been *g*
1Ti	4:14	was *g* you through a prophetic
1Jn	4:13	because he has *g* us of his Spirit.

GIVER* (GIVE)

Pr	18:16	A gift opens the way for the *g*
2Co	9:7	for God loves a cheerful *g*.

GIVES (GIVE)

Job	35:10	who *g* songs in the night,
Ps	119:130	The entrance of your words *g* light;
Pr	3:34	but *g* grace to the humble.
	11:24	One man *g* freely, yet gains
	14:30	A heart at peace *g* life to the body,
	15:30	good news *g* health to the bones.
	19:6	of a man who *g* gifts.
	25:26	is a righteous man who *g* way
	28:27	He who *g* to the poor will lack
	29:4	justice a king *g* a country stability,
Isa	40:29	He *g* strength to the weary
Hab	2:15	"Woe to him who *g* drink
Mt	10:42	And if anyone *g* a cup of cold water
Jn	5:21	even so the Son *g* life to whom he is
	6:63	The Spirit *g* life; the flesh counts
1Co	15:57	He *g* us the victory

2Co	3:6	the letter kills, but the Spirit *g* life.
1Th	4:8	who *g* you his Holy Spirit.
Jas	1:25	into the perfect law that *g* freedom,
	4:6	but *g* grace to the humble."
1Pe	5:5	but *g* grace to the humble."

GIVING (GIVE)

Ne	8:8	*g* the meaning so that the people
Est	9:19	a day for *g* presents to each other.
Ps	19:8	*g* joy to the heart.
Pr	15:23	A man finds joy in *g* an apt reply—
Mt	6:4	so that your *g* may be in secret.
	24:38	marrying and *g* in marriage,
Ac	15:8	them by *g* the Holy Spirit to them,
2Co	8:7	also excel in this grace of *g*.
Php	4:15	shared with me in the matter of *g*

GLAD* (GLADDENS GLADNESS)

Ex	4:14	his heart will be *g* when he sees you
Jos	22:33	They were *g* to hear the report
Jdg	8:25	"We'll be *g* to give them."
	18:20	household?" Then the priest was *g*.
1Sa	19:5	and you saw it and were *g*.
2Sa	1:20	daughters of the Philistines be *g*,
1Ki	8:66	and *g* in heart for all the good
1Ch	16:31	heavens rejoice, let the earth be *g*;
2Ch	7:10	and *g* in heart for the good things
Ps	5:11	let all who take refuge in you be *g*;
	9:2	I will be *g* and rejoice in you;
	14:7	let Jacob rejoice and Israel be *g*!
	16:9	Therefore my heart is *g*
	21:6	made him *g* with the joy
	31:7	I will be *g* and rejoice in your love,
	32:11	Rejoice in the LORD and be *g*,
	40:16	rejoice and be *g* in you;
	45:8	music of the strings makes you *g*.
	46:4	whose streams make *g* the city
	48:11	the villages of Judah are *g*
	53:6	let Jacob rejoice and Israel be *g*!
	58:10	The righteous will be *g*
	67:4	May the nations be *g* and sing
	68:3	But may the righteous be *g*
	69:32	The poor will see and be *g*—
	70:4	rejoice and be *g* in you;
	90:14	for joy and be *g* all our days.
	90:15	Make us *g* for as many days
	92:4	For you make me *g* by your deeds,
	96:11	heavens rejoice, let the earth be *g*;
	97:1	LORD reigns, let the earth be *g*;
	97:8	and the villages of Judah are *g*
	105:38	Egypt was *g* when they left,
	107:30	They were *g* when it grew calm,
	118:24	let us rejoice and be *g* in it.
	149:2	of Zion be *g* in their King.
Pr	23:15	then my heart will be *g*;
	23:25	May your father and mother be *g*;
	29:6	a righteous one can sing and be *g*.
Ecc	8:15	sun than to eat and drink and be *g*.
Isa	25:9	let us rejoice and be *g*
	35:1	and the parched land will be *g*;
	65:18	But be *g* and rejoice for ever
	66:10	with Jerusalem and be *g* for her,
Jer	20:15	who made him very *g*, saying,
	31:13	Then maidens will dance and be *g*,
	41:13	were with him, they were *g*.
	50:11	"Because you rejoice and are *g*,
La	4:21	be *g*, O Daughter of Edom,
Joel	2:21	be *g* and rejoice.
	2:23	Be *g*, O people of Zion,
Hab	1:15	and so he rejoices and is *g*.

Zep	3: 14	Be *g* and rejoice with all your heart
Zec	2: 10	and be *g*, O Daughter of Zion.
	8: 19	will become joyful and *g* occasions
	10: 7	their hearts will be *g* as with wine.
Mt	5: 12	be *g*, because great is your reward
Lk	15: 32	But we had to celebrate and be *g*,
Jn	4: 36	and the reaper may be *g* together.
	8: 56	my day; he saw it and was *g*."
	11: 15	for your sake I am *g* I was not there
	14: 28	you would be *g* that I am going
Ac	2: 26	Therefore my heart is *g*
	2: 46	together with *g* and sincere hearts,
	11: 23	he was *g* and encouraged them all
	13: 48	they were *g* and honoured the word
	15: 3	news made all the brothers very *g*.
	15: 31	were *g* for its encouraging message.
1Co	16: 17	was *g* when Stephanas, Fortunatus
2Co	2: 2	who is left to make me *g*
	7: 16	I am *g* I can have complete
	13: 9	We are *g* whenever we are weak
Gal	4: 27	"Be *g*, O barren woman,
Php	2: 17	I am *g* and rejoice with all of you.
	2: 18	So you too should be *g* and rejoice
	2: 28	you see him again you may be *g*
Rev	19: 7	Let us rejoice and be *g*

GLADDENS* (GLAD)

Ps	104: 15	wine that *g* the heart of man,

GLADNESS* (GLAD)

2Ch	29: 30	So they sang praises with *g*
Est	8: 16	a time of happiness and joy, *g*
	8: 17	there was joy and *g*
Job	3: 22	who are filled with *g*
Ps	35: 27	shout for joy and *g*;
	45: 15	They are led in with joy and *g*;
	51: 8	Let me hear joy and *g*;
	65: 12	the hills are clothed with *g*.
	100: 2	Worship the LORD with *g*;
Ecc	5: 20	God keeps him occupied with *g*
	9: 7	Go, eat your food with *g*,
Isa	16: 10	*g* are taken away from the orchards
	35: 10	*G* and joy will overtake them,
	51: 3	Joy and *g* will be found in her,
	51: 11	*G* and joy will overtake them,
	61: 3	the oil of *g* / instead of mourning,
Jer	7: 34	and *g* and to the voices of bride
	16: 9	and *g* and to the voices of bride
	25: 10	from them the sounds of joy and *g*,
	31: 13	I will turn their mourning into *g*;
	33: 11	once more the sounds of joy and *g*,
	48: 33	Joy and *g* are gone
Joel	1: 16	joy and *g*

GLAZE*

Pr	26: 23	of *g* over earthenware

GLEAM*

Pr	4: 18	of the righteous is like the first *g*
Da	10: 6	legs like the *g* of burnished bronze,

GLOAT (GLOATS)

Pr	24: 17	Do not *g* when your enemy falls;

GLOATS* (GLOAT)

Pr	17: 5	whoever *g* over disaster will not go

GLORIES* (GLORY)

1Pe	1: 11	and the *g* that would follow.

GLORIFIED* (GLORY)

Isa	66: 5	'Let the LORD be *g*,
Eze	39: 13	day I am *g* will be a memorable day
Da	4: 34	and *g* him who lives for ever.
Jn	7: 39	since Jesus had not yet been *g*.
	11: 4	glory so that God's Son may be *g*
	12: 16	after Jesus was *g* did they realise
	12: 23	come for the Son of Man to be *g*.
	12: 28	"I have *g* it, and will glorify it again
	13: 31	Son of Man *g* and God is *g* in him.
	13: 32	If God is *g* in him, God will glorify
Ac	3: 13	our fathers, has *g* his servant Jesus.
Ro	1: 21	they neither *g* him as God
	8: 30	those he justified, he also *g*.
2Th	1: 10	comes to be *g* in his holy people
	1: 12	of our Lord Jesus may be *g* in you,
1Pe	1: 21	him from the dead and *g* him,

GLORIFIES* (GLORY)

Lk	1: 46	My soul *g* the Lord
Jn	8: 54	as your God, is the one who *g* me.

GLORIFY* (GLORY)

Ps	34: 3	*G* the LORD with me;
	63: 3	my lips will *g* you.
	69: 30	and *g* him with thanksgiving.
	86: 12	I will *g* your name for ever.
Isa	60: 13	and I will *g* the place of my feet.
Da	4: 37	and exalt and *g* the King of heaven,
Jn	8: 54	Jesus replied, "If I *g* myself,
	12: 28	glorified it, and will *g* it again."
	12: 28	*g* your name!" Then a voice came
	13: 32	God will *g* the Son in himself,
	13: 32	in himself, and will *g* him at once.
	17: 1	*G* your Son, that your Son may
	17: 1	your Son, that your Son may *g* you.
	17: 5	*g* me in your presence
	21: 19	death by which Peter would *g* God.
Ro	15: 6	and mouth you may *g* the God
	15: 9	so that the Gentiles may *g* God
1Pe	2: 12	and *g* God on the day he visits us.
Rev	16: 9	they refused to repent and *g* him.

GLORIFYING* (GLORY)

Lk	2: 20	*g* and praising God

GLORIOUS* (GLORY)

Dt	28: 58	not revere this *g* and awesome
	33: 29	and your *g* sword.
1Ch	29: 13	and praise your *g* name.
Ne	9: 5	"Blessed be your *g* name,
Ps	3: 3	my *G* One, who lifts up my head.
	16: 3	they are the *g* ones
	45: 13	All *g* is the princess
	72: 19	Praise be to his *g* name for ever;
	87: 3	*G* things are said of you,
	111: 3	*G* and majestic are his deeds,
	145: 5	of the *g* splendour of your majesty,
	145: 12	the *g* splendour of your kingdom.
Isa	3: 8	defying his *g* presence.
	4: 2	the LORD will be beautiful and *g*,
	11: 10	and his place of rest will be *g*.
	12: 5	for he has done *g* things;
	28: 1	to the fading flower, his *g* beauty,
	28: 4	That fading flower, his *g* beauty,
	28: 5	will be a *g* crown,
	42: 21	to make his law great and *g*.
	60: 7	and I will adorn my *g* temple.
	63: 12	who sent his *g* arm of power
	63: 14	to make for yourself a *g* name.

Isa	63: 15	from your lofty throne, holy and *g*.
	64: 11	*g* temple, where our fathers praised
Jer	13: 18	for your *g* crowns
	14: 21	do not dishonour your *g* throne.
	17: 12	A *g* throne, exalted
	48: 17	how broken the *g* staff!'
Mt	19: 28	the Son of Man sits on his *g* throne,
Lk	9: 31	appeared in *g* splendour, talking
Ac	2: 20	of the great and *g* day of the Lord.
Ro	8: 21	and brought into the *g* freedom
2Co	3: 8	of the Spirit be even more *g*?
	3: 9	how much more *g* is the ministry
	3: 9	ministry that condemns men is *g*,
	3: 10	for what was *g* has no glory now
Eph	1: 6	to the praise of his *g* grace,
	1: 17	*g* Father, may give you the Spirit
	1: 18	the riches of his *g* inheritance
	3: 16	of his *g* riches he may strengthen
Php	3: 21	so that they will be like his *g* body.
	4: 19	to his *g* riches in Christ Jesus.
Col	1: 11	all power according to his *g* might
	1: 27	among the Gentiles the *g* riches
1Ti	1: 11	to the *g* gospel of the blessed God,
Tit	2: 13	the *g* appearing of our great God
Jas	2: 1	believers in our *g* Lord Jesus Christ
1Pe	1: 8	with an inexpressible and *g* joy,
Jude	: 24	before his *g* presence without fault

GLORIOUSLY* (GLORY)

Isa	24: 23	and before its elders, *g*.

GLORY (GLORIES GLORIFIED GLORIFIES GLORIFY GLORIFYING GLORIOUS GLORIOUSLY)

Ex	14: 4	But I will gain *g* for myself
	14: 17	And I will gain *g* through Pharaoh
	15: 11	awesome in *g*,
	16: 10	and there was the *g* of the Lord
	24: 16	and the *g* of the Lord settled
	33: 18	Moses said, "Now show me your *g*
	40: 34	and the *g* of the Lord filled
Nu	14: 21	the *g* of the Lord fills the whole
Dt	5: 24	Lord our God has shown us his *g*
Jos	7: 19	"My son, give *g* to the Lord,
1Sa	4: 21	"The *g* has departed from Israel"—
1Ch	16: 10	*G* in his holy name;
	16: 24	Declare his *g* among the nations,
	16: 28	ascribe to the Lord *g*
	29: 11	and the *g* and the majesty
Ps	8: 1	You have set your *g*
	8: 5	and crowned him with *g* and honour
	19: 1	The heavens declare the *g* of God;
	24: 7	that the King of *g* may come in.
	26: 8	the place where your *g* dwells.
	29: 1	ascribe to the Lord *g*
	29: 9	And in his temple all cry, "*G*!"
	57: 5	let your *g* be over all the earth.
	66: 2	Sing the *g* of his name;
	72: 19	the whole earth be filled with his *g*.
	96: 3	Declare his *g* among the nations,
	102: 15	of the earth will revere your *g*.
	108: 5	and let your *g* be over all the earth.
	149: 9	This is the *g* of all his saints.
Pr	19: 11	it is to his *g* to overlook an offence.
	25: 2	It is the *g* of God to conceal
Isa	4: 5	over all the *g* will be a canopy.
	6: 3	the whole earth is full of his *g*."
	24: 16	"*G* to the Righteous One."
	26: 15	You have gained *g* for yourself;
	35: 2	they will see the *g* of the Lord,

Isa	40: 5	the *g* of the Lord will be revealed
	42: 8	I will not give my *g* to another
	42: 12	Let them give *g* to the Lord
	43: 7	whom I created for my *g*,
	44: 23	he displays his *g* in Israel.
	48: 11	I will not yield my *g* to another.
	66: 18	and they will come and see my *g*.
	66: 19	They will proclaim my *g*
Eze	1: 28	the likeness of the *g* of the Lord.
	10: 4	the radiance of the *g* of the Lord.
	43: 2	and the land was radiant with his *g*.
	44: 4	and saw the *g* of the Lord filling
Hab	2: 14	knowledge of the *g* of the Lord,
	3: 3	His *g* covered the heavens
Zec	2: 5	'and I will be its *g* within.'
Mt	16: 27	in his Father's *g* with his angels,
	24: 30	of the sky, with power and great *g*.
	25: 31	sit on his throne in heavenly *g*.
	25: 31	the Son of Man comes in his *g*,
Mk	8: 38	in his Father's *g* with the holy
	13: 26	in clouds with great power and *g*.
Lk	2: 9	and the *g* of the Lord shone
	2: 14	saying, "*G* to God in the highest,
	9: 26	and in the *g* of the Father
	9: 26	of him when he comes in his *g*
	9: 32	they saw his *g* and the two men
	19: 38	in heaven and *g* in the highest!"
	21: 27	in a cloud with power and great *g*.
	24: 26	these things and then enter his *g*?"
Jn	1: 14	We have seen his *g*, the *g* of the one
	2: 11	He thus revealed his *g*,
	8: 50	I am not seeking *g* for myself;
	8: 54	myself, my *g* means nothing.
	11: 4	for God's *g* so that God's Son may
	11: 40	you would see the *g* of God?"
	12: 41	he saw Jesus' *g* and spoke about
	14: 13	so that the Son may bring *g*
	15: 8	is to my Father's *g*, that you bear
	16: 14	He will bring *g* to me by taking
	17: 4	I have brought you *g* on earth
	17: 5	presence with the *g* I had with you
	17: 10	*g* has come to me through them.
	17: 22	given them the *g* that you gave
	17: 24	to see my *g*, the *g* you have given
Ac	7: 2	The God of *g* appeared
	7: 55	up to heaven and saw the *g* of God,
Ro	1: 23	exchanged the *g* of the immortal
	2: 7	by persistence in doing good seek *g*
	2: 10	then for the Gentile; but *g*,
	3: 7	truthfulness and so increases his *g*,
	3: 23	and fall short of the *g* of God,
	4: 20	in his faith and gave *g* to God,
	8: 17	that we may also share in his *g*.
	8: 18	with the *g* that will be revealed
	9: 4	theirs the divine *g*, the covenants,
	9: 23	riches of his *g* known to the objects
	9: 23	whom he prepared in advance for *g*
	11: 36	To him be the *g* for ever! Amen.
	15: 17	Therefore I *g* in Christ Jesus
	16: 27	to the only wise God be *g* for ever
1Co	2: 7	for our *g* before time began
	10: 31	whatever you do, do it all for the *g*
	11: 7	but the woman is the *g* of man.
	11: 7	since he is the image and *g* of God;
	11: 15	it is her *g*? For long hair is given
	15: 43	it is raised in *g*; it is sown
2Co	1: 20	spoken by us to the *g* of God.
	3: 7	in letters on stone, came with *g*,
	3: 7	the face of Moses because of its *g*,
	3: 10	comparison with the surpassing *g*.

2Co	3:10	what was glorious has no *g* now
	3:11	how much greater is the *g*
	3:11	what was fading away came with *g*,
	3:18	faces all reflect the Lord's *g*,
	3:18	likeness with ever-increasing *g*,
	4: 4	of the gospel of the *g* of Christ,
	4: 6	of the knowledge of the *g* of God
	4:15	to overflow to the *g* of God.
	4:17	us an eternal *g* that far outweighs
Gal	1: 5	to whom be *g* for ever and ever.
Eph	1:12	might be for the praise of his *g*.
	1:14	to the praise of his *g*.
	3:13	for you, which are your *g*.
	3:21	to him be *g* in the church
Php	1:11	to the *g* and praise of God.
	2:11	to the *g* of God the Father.
	3: 3	of God, who *g* in Christ Jesus,
	4:20	and Father be *g* for ever and ever.
Col	1:27	Christ in you, the hope of *g*.
	3: 4	also will appear with him in *g*.
1Th	2:12	you into his kingdom and *g*.
	2:19	in which we will *g* in the presence
	2:20	Indeed, you are our *g* and joy.
2Th	2:14	in the *g* of our Lord Jesus Christ.
1Ti	1:17	be honour and *g* for ever and ever.
	3:16	was taken up in *g*.
2Ti	2:10	is in Christ Jesus, with eternal *g*.
	4:18	To him be *g* for ever and ever.
Heb	1: 3	The Son is the radiance of God's *g*
	2: 7	you crowned him with *g* and honour
	2: 9	now crowned with *g* and honour
	2:10	In bringing many sons to *g*,
	5: 5	take upon himself the *g*
	9: 5	the ark were the cherubim of the *G*,
	13:21	to whom be *g* for ever and ever.
1Pe	1: 7	*g* and honour when Jesus Christ is
	1:24	and all their *g* is like the flowers
	4:11	To him be the *g* and the power
	4:13	overjoyed when his *g* is revealed.
	4:14	for the Spirit of *g* and of God rests
	5: 1	will share in the *g* to be revealed:
	5: 4	of *g* that will never fade away.
	5:10	you to his eternal *g* in Christ,
2Pe	1: 3	of him who called us by his own *g*
	1:17	and *g* from God the Father
	1:17	came to him from the Majestic *G*,
	3:18	To him be *g* both now and for ever!
Jude	:25	to the only God our Saviour be *g*,
Rev	1: 6	to him be *g* and power for ever
	4: 9	the living creatures give *g*,
	4:11	to receive *g* and honour and power,
	5:12	and honour and *g* and praise!''
	5:13	and honour and *g* and power,
	7:12	Praise and *g*
	11:13	and gave *g* to the God of heaven.
	14: 7	''Fear God and give him *g*,
	15: 4	and bring *g* to your name?
	15: 8	with smoke from the *g* of God
	19: 1	*g* and power belong to our God,
	19: 7	and give him *g*!
	21:11	It shone with the *g* of God,
	21:23	for the *g* of God gives it light,
	21:26	*g* and honour of the nations will be

GLOWING

Eze	8: 2	was as bright as *g* metal.
Rev	1:15	His feet were like bronze *g*

GLUTTONS* (GLUTTONY)

Pr	23:21	for drunkards and *g* become poor,

Pr	28: 7	of *g* disgraces his father.
Tit	1:12	always liars, evil brutes, lazy *g*.''

GLUTTONY* (GLUTTONS)

Pr	23: 2	throat if you are given to *g*.

GNASHING

Mt	8:12	where there will be weeping and *g*

GNAT* (GNATS)

Mt	23:24	You strain out a *g* but swallow

GNATS (GNAT)

Ex	8:16	of Egypt the dust will become *g*.''

GOADS

Ecc	12:11	The words of the wise are like *g*,
Ac	26:14	hard for you to kick against the *g*.'

GOAL*

Lk	13:32	on the third day I will reach my *g*.'
2Co	5: 9	So we make it our *g* to please him,
Gal	3: 3	to attain your *g* by human effort?
Php	3:14	on towards the *g* to win the prize
1Ti	1: 5	The *g* of this command is love,
1Pe	1: 9	for you are receiving the *g*

GOAT (GOATS SCAPEGOAT)

Ge	15: 9	''Bring me a heifer, a *g* and a ram,
	30:32	and every spotted or speckled *g*.
	37:31	slaughtered a *g* and dipped
Ex	26: 7	Make curtains of *g* hair for the tent
Lev	16: 9	shall bring the *g* whose lot falls
Nu	7:16	one male *g* for a sin offering;
Isa	11: 6	the leopard will lie down with the *g*
Da	8: 5	suddenly a *g* with a prominent

GOATS (GOAT)

Nu	7:17	five male *g* and five male lambs
Mt	25:32	separates the sheep from the *g*.
Heb	10: 4	of bulls and *g* to take away sins.

GOD (GOD'S GODLINESS GODLY GODS)

Ge	1: 1	In the beginning *G* created
	1: 2	and the Spirit of *G* was hovering
	1: 3	And *G* said, ''Let there be light,''
	1: 7	So *G* made the expanse
	1: 9	And *G* said, ''Let the water
	1:11	Then *G* said, ''Let the land produce
	1:20	And *G* said, ''Let the water teem
	1:21	So *G* created the great creatures
	1:25	*G* made the wild animals according
	1:26	Then *G* said, ''Let us make man
	1:27	So *G* created man in his own image
	1:31	*G* saw all that he had made,
	2: 3	And *G* blessed the seventh day
	2: 7	And the LORD *G* formed man
	2: 8	the LORD *G* had planted a garden
	2:18	The LORD *G* said, ''It is not good
	2:22	Then the LORD *G* made a woman
	3: 1	to the woman, ''Did *G* really say,
	3: 5	you will be like *G*, knowing good
	3: 8	from the LORD *G* among the trees
	3: 9	But the LORD *G* called to the man
	3:21	The LORD *G* made garments
	3:22	LORD *G* said, ''The man has now
	3:23	So the LORD *G* banished him
	5: 1	When *G* created man, he made him
	5:22	Enoch walked with *G* 300 years
	5:24	because *G* took him away.

Ge	6: 2	sons of *G* saw that the daughters
	6: 9	of his time, and he walked with *G*.
	6:12	*G* saw how corrupt the earth had
	8: 1	But *G* remembered Noah
	9: 1	Then *G* blessed Noah and his sons,
	9: 6	for in the image of *G*
	9:16	everlasting covenant between *G*
	14:18	He was priest of *G* Most High,
	14:19	Blessed be Abram by *G* Most High,
	16:13	"You are the *G* who sees me,"
	17: 1	"I am *G* Almighty; walk before me
	17: 7	to be your *G* and the *G*
	21: 4	him, as *G* commanded him.
	21: 6	"*G* has brought me laughter,
	21:20	*G* was with the boy as he grew up.
	21:22	*G* is with you in everything you do.
	21:33	name of the LORD, the Eternal *G*.
	22: 1	Some time later *G* tested Abraham.
	22: 8	"*G* himself will provide the lamb
	22:12	Now I know that you fear *G*,
	25:11	Abraham's death, *G* blessed his
	28:12	and the angels of *G* were ascending
	28:17	other than the house of *G*;
	31:42	But *G* has seen my hardship
	31:50	remember that *G* is a witness
	32: 1	and the angels of *G* met him.
	32:28	because you have struggled with *G*
	32:30	"It is because I saw *G* face to face,
	33:11	for *G* has been gracious to me
	35: 1	and build an altar there to *G*,
	35: 5	and the terror of *G* fell
	35:10	*G* said to him, "Your name is Jacob
	35:11	*G* said to him, "I am *G* Almighty;
	41:51	*G* has made me forget all my
	41:52	*G* has made me fruitful in the land
	50:20	but *G* intended it for good
	50:24	But *G* will surely come to your aid
Ex	2:24	*G* heard their groaning
	3: 5	"Do not come any closer," *G* said.
	3: 6	because he was afraid to look at *G*.
	3:12	And *G* said, "I will be with you.
	3:14	what shall I tell them?" *G* said
	4:27	he met Moses at the mountain of *G*
	6: 7	own people, and I will be your *G*.
	8:10	is no-one like the LORD our *G*.
	10:16	sinned against the LORD your *G*
	13:18	So *G* led the people
	15: 2	He is my *G*, and I will praise him,
	16:12	that I am the LORD your *G*.'"
	17: 9	with the staff of *G* in my hands."
	18: 5	camped near the mountain of *G*.
	19: 3	Then Moses went up to *G*,
	20: 1	And *G* spoke all these words:
	20: 2	the LORD your *G*, who brought
	20: 5	the LORD your *G*, am a jealous *G*,
	20: 7	the name of the LORD your *G*,
	20:10	a Sabbath to the LORD your *G*.
	20:12	the LORD your *G* is giving you.
	20:19	But do not have *G* speak to us
	20:20	the fear of *G* will be with you
	22:20	"Whoever sacrifices to any *g* other
	22:28	"Do not blaspheme *G*
	23:19	to the house of the LORD your *G*.
	31:18	inscribed by the finger of *G*.
	34: 6	the compassionate and gracious *G*,
	34:14	name is Jealous, is a jealous *G*.
Lev	2:13	salt of the covenant of your *G* out
	11:44	the LORD your *G*; consecrate
	18:21	not profane the name of your *G*.
	19: 2	the LORD your *G*, am holy.
Lev	20: 7	because I am the LORD your *G*.
	21: 6	They must be holy to their *G*
	22:33	out of Egypt to be your *G*.
	26:12	walk among you and be your *G*,
Nu	15:40	and will be consecrated to your *G*.
	22:18	the command of the LORD my *G*.
	22:38	I must speak only what *G* puts
	23:19	*G* is not a man, that he should lie,
	25:13	zealous for the honour of his *G*
Dt	1:17	for judgment belongs to *G*.
	1:21	the LORD your *G* has given you
	1:30	The LORD your *G*, who is going
	3:22	LORD your *G* himself will fight
	3:24	For what *g* is there in heaven
	4:24	is a consuming fire, a jealous *G*.
	4:29	there you seek the LORD your *G*,
	4:31	the LORD your *G* is a merciful *G*;
	4:39	heart this day that the LORD is *G*
	5: 9	the LORD your *G*, am a jealous *G*,
	5:11	the name of the LORD your *G*,
	5:12	the LORD your *G* has commanded
	5:14	a Sabbath to the LORD your *G*.
	5:15	the LORD your *G* brought you out
	5:16	the LORD your *G* has commanded
	5:16	the LORD your *G* is giving you.
	5:24	LORD our *G* has shown us his
	5:26	of the living *G* speaking out of fire,
	6: 2	them may fear the LORD your *G*
	6: 4	LORD our *G*, the LORD is one.
	6: 5	Love the LORD your *G*
	6:13	the LORD your *G*, serve him only
	6:16	Do not test the LORD your *G*
	7: 6	holy to the LORD your *G*.
	7: 9	your *G* is *G*; he is the faithful *G*,
	7:12	the LORD your *G* will keep his
	7:19	LORD your *G* will do the same
	7:21	is a great and awesome *G*.
	8: 5	the LORD your *G* disciplines you.
	8:11	do not forget the LORD your *G*,
	8:18	But remember the LORD your *G*,
	9:10	inscribed by the finger of *G*.
	10:12	but to fear the LORD your *G*,
	10:14	the LORD your *G* belong
	10:17	For the LORD your *G* is *G* of gods
	10:21	He is your praise; he is your *G*,
	11: 1	Love the LORD your *G*
	11:13	to love the LORD your *G*
	12:12	rejoice before the LORD your *G*,
	12:28	in the eyes of the LORD your *G*.
	13: 3	The LORD your *G* is testing you
	13: 4	the LORD your *G* you must
	15: 6	the LORD your *G* will bless you
	15:19	the LORD your *G* every firstborn
	16:11	rejoice before the LORD your *G*
	16:17	the LORD your *G* has blessed you.
	18:13	before the LORD your *G*.
	18:15	The LORD your *G* will raise up
	19: 9	to love the LORD your *G*
	22: 5	the LORD your *G* detests anyone
	23: 5	the LORD your *G* loves you.
	23:14	the LORD your *G* moves about
	23:21	a vow to the LORD your *G*,
	25:16	the LORD your *G* detests anyone
	26: 5	declare before the LORD your *G*:
	29:13	that he may be your *G*
	29:29	belong to the LORD our *G*,
	30: 2	return to the LORD your *G*
	30: 4	the LORD your *G* will gather you
	30: 6	The LORD your *G* will circumcise
	30:16	today to love the LORD your *G*,

Dt   30: 20 you may love the LORD your *G*,
      31: 6 for the LORD your *G* goes
      32: 3 Oh, praise the greatness of our *G*!
      32: 4 A faithful *G* who does no wrong,
      33: 27 The eternal *G* is your refuge,
Jos   1: 9 for the LORD your *G* will be
      14: 8 the LORD my *G* wholeheartedly.
      14: 9 the LORD my *G* wholeheartedly.'
      14: 14 the *G* of Israel, wholeheartedly.
      22: 5 to love the LORD your *G*,
      22: 22 The Mighty One, *G*, the LORD!
      22: 34 BETWEEN US THAT THE LORD IS *G*.
      23: 8 to hold fast to the LORD your *G*,
      23: 11 careful to love the LORD your *G*,
      23: 14 the LORD your *G* gave you has
      23: 15 of the LORD your *G* has come true
      24: 19 He is a holy *G*; he is a jealous *G*.
      24: 23 to the LORD, the *G* of Israel."
Jdg   5: 3 to the LORD, the *G* of Israel.
      16: 28 O *G*, please strengthen me just
Ru   1: 16 be my people and your *G* my *G*.
       2: 12 by the LORD, the *G* of Israel,
1Sa   2: 2 there is no Rock like our *G*.
       2: 3 for the LORD is a *G* who knows,
       2: 25 another man, *G* may mediate
      10: 26 men whose hearts *G* had touched.
      12: 12 the LORD your *G* was your king.
      16: 15 spirit from *G* is tormenting you.
      17: 26 defy the armies of the living *G*?"
      17: 36 defied the armies of the living *G*.
      17: 45 the *G* of the armies of Israel,
      17: 46 world will know that there is a *G*
      23: 16 and helped him find strength in *G*.
      28: 15 and *G* has turned away from me.
      30: 6 strength in the LORD his *G*.
2Sa   7: 22 and there is no *G* but you,
       7: 23 on earth that *G* went out to redeem
      14: 14 But *G* does not take away life;
      21: 14 *G* answered prayer on behalf
      22: 3 my *G* is my rock, in whom I take
      22: 31 "As for *G*, his way is perfect;
      22: 32 And who is the Rock except our *G*
      22: 33 It is *G* who arms me with strength
      22: 47 Exalted be *G*, the Rock, my Saviour!
1Ki   2: 3 what the LORD your *G* requires:
       4: 29 *G* gave Solomon wisdom
       5: 5 for the Name of the LORD my *G*,
       8: 23 there is no *G* like you in heaven
       8: 27 "But will *G* really dwell on earth?
       8: 60 may know that the LORD is *G*
       8: 61 committed to the LORD our *G*,
      10: 24 to hear the wisdom *G* had put
      15: 30 he provoked the LORD, the *G*
      18: 21 If the LORD is *G*, follow him;
      18: 36 it be known today that you are *G*
      18: 37 are *G*, and that you are turning
      20: 28 a *g* of the hills and not a *g*
2Ki   5: 15 "Now I know that there is no *G*
      18: 5 in the LORD, the *G* of Israel.
      19: 15 *G* of Israel, enthroned
      19: 19 Now, O LORD our *G*, deliver us
1Ch   12: 18 for your *G* will help you."
      13: 2 if it is the will of the LORD our *G*,
      16: 35 Cry out, "Save us, O *G* our Saviour;
      17: 20 and there is no *G* but you,
      17: 24 the *G* over Israel, is Israel's *G*!'
      21: 8 said to *G*, "I have sinned greatly
      22: 1 house of the LORD *G* is to be here,
      22: 19 soul to seeking the LORD your *G*.
      28: 2 for the footstool of our *G*,

1Ch   28: 9 acknowledge the *G* of your father,
      28: 20 for the LORD *G*, my *G*, is with you
      29: 1 not for man but for the LORD *G*.
      29: 2 provided for the temple of my *G*—
      29: 3 of my *G* I now give my personal
      29: 10 *G* of our father Israel,
      29: 13 Now, our *G*, we give you thanks,
      29: 16 O LORD our *G*, as for all this
      29: 17 my *G*, that you test the heart
      29: 18 *G* of our fathers Abraham,
2Ch   2: 4 for the Name of the LORD my *G*
       5: 14 of the LORD filled the temple of *G*
       6: 4 be to the LORD, the *G* of Israel,
       6: 14 there is no *G* like you in heaven
       6: 18 "But will *G* really dwell on earth
      10: 15 for this turn of events was from *G*,
      13: 12 *G* is with us; he is our leader.
      15: 3 was without the true *G*,
      15: 12 the *G* of their fathers,
      15: 15 They sought *G* eagerly,
      18: 13 I can tell him only what my *G* says
      19: 3 have set your heart on seeking *G*."
      19: 7 with the LORD our *G* there is no
      20: 6 are you not the *G* who is in heaven?
      20: 20 Have faith in the LORD your *G*
      25: 8 for *G* has the power to help
      26: 5 sought the LORD, *G* gave him
      30: 9 for the LORD your *G* is gracious
      30: 19 who sets his heart on seeking *G*—
      31: 21 he sought his *G* and worked
      32: 31 *G* left him to test him
      33: 12 the favour of the LORD his *G*
      34: 33 fail to follow the LORD, the *G*
Ezr   6: 21 to seek the LORD, the *G* of Israel.
       7: 18 accordance with the will of your *G*.
       7: 23 Whatever the *G* of heaven has
       8: 22 "The gracious hand of our *G* is
       8: 31 The hand of our *G* was on us,
       9: 6 "O my *G*, I am too ashamed
       9: 9 our *G* has not deserted us
       9: 13 our *G*, you have punished us less
       9: 15 *G* of Israel, you are righteous!
Ne   1: 5 the great and awesome *G*,
       5: 9 fear of our *G* to avoid the reproach
       5: 15 for *G* I did not act like that.
       7: 2 feared *G* more than most men do.
       8: 8 from the Book of the Law of *G*,
       8: 18 from the Book of the Law of *G*,
       9: 5 and praise the LORD your *G*,
       9: 17 But you are a forgiving *G*,
       9: 31 you are a gracious and merciful *G*.
       9: 32 the great, mighty and awesome *G*,
      10: 29 oath to follow the Law of *G* given
      10: 39 not neglect the house of our *G*."
      12: 43 *G* had given them great joy.
      13: 11 Why is the house of *G* neglected?"
      13: 26 He was loved by his *G*,
      13: 31 Remember me with favour, O my *G*
Job   1: 1 he feared *G* and shunned evil.
       1: 22 by charging *G* with wrongdoing.
       2: 10 Shall we accept good from *G*,
       4: 17 a mortal be more righteous than *G*?
       5: 17 is the man whom *G* corrects;
       8: 3 Does *G* pervert justice?
       8: 20 "Surely *G* does not reject
       9: 2 a mortal be righteous before *G*?
      11: 7 Can you fathom the mysteries of *G*
      12: 13 "To *G* belong wisdom and power;
      16: 7 Surely, O *G*, you have worn me out
      19: 26 yet in my flesh I will see *G*;

Job 21: 19 'G stores up a man's punishment
21: 22 Can anyone teach knowledge to G,
22: 12 "Is not G in the heights of heaven?
22: 13 Yet you say, 'What does G know?
22: 21 "Submit to G and be at peace
25: 2 "Dominion and awe belong to G;
25: 4 can a man be righteous before G?
26: 6 Death is naked before G;
30: 20 O G, but you do not answer;
31: 6 let G weigh me in honest scales
31: 14 do when G confronts me?
32: 13 let G refute him, not man.'
33: 6 I am just like you before G;
33: 14 For G does speak—now one way,
33: 26 He prays to G and finds favour
34: 10 Far be it from G to do evil,
34: 12 is unthinkable that G would do
34: 23 G has no need to examine men
34: 33 Should G then reward you
36: 5 "G is mighty, but does not despise
36: 26 is G—beyond our understanding!
37: 22 G comes in awesome majesty.

Ps 5: 4 You are not a G who takes pleasure
7: 11 G is a righteous judge,
10: 14 O G, do see trouble and grief;
14: 5 for G is present in the company
18: 2 my G is my rock, in whom I take
18: 28 my G turns my darkness into light.
18: 30 As for G, his way is perfect;
18: 31 And who is the Rock except our G
18: 32 It is G who arms me with strength
18: 46 Exalted be G my Saviour!
19: 1 The heavens declare the glory of G;
22: 1 G, my G, why have you forsaken
22: 10 womb you have been my G.
27: 9 O G my Saviour.
29: 3 The G of glory thunders,
31: 5 redeem me, O Lord, the G
31: 14 I say, "You are my G."
33: 12 the nation whose G is the Lord,
35: 24 righteousness, O Lord my G;
37: 31 The law of his G is in his heart;
40: 3 a hymn of praise to our G.
40: 8 I desire to do your will, O my G;
42: 1 so my soul pants for you, O G.
42: 2 thirsts for G, for the living G.
42: 5 Put your hope in G,
42: 8 a prayer to the G of my life.
42: 11 Put your hope in G,
43: 4 to G, my joy and my delight.
44: 8 In G we make our boast all day
45: 6 O G, will last for ever and ever;
45: 7 therefore G, your G, has set you
46: 1 G is our refuge and strength,
46: 5 G will help her at break of day.
46: 10 "Be still, and know that I am G;
47: 1 shout to G with cries of joy.
47: 6 Sing praises to G, sing praises;
47: 7 For G is the King of all the earth;
48: 9 Within your temple, O G,
49: 7 or give to G a ransom for him—
50: 2 G shines forth.
50: 3 Our G comes and will not be silent;
51: 1 Have mercy on me, O G,
51: 10 Create in me a pure heart, O G,
51: 17 O G, you will not despise.
53: 2 any who seek G.
54: 4 Surely G is my help;
55: 19 G, who is enthroned for ever,
56: 4 In G, whose word I praise,

Ps 56: 10 In G, whose word I praise,
56: 13 that I may walk before G
57: 3 G sends his love and his
57: 7 My heart is steadfast, O G,
59: 17 are my fortress, my loving G.
62: 1 My soul finds rest in G alone;
62: 7 my honour depend on G;
62: 8 for G is our refuge.
62: 11 One thing G has spoken,
63: 1 O G, you are my G,
65: 5 O G our Saviour,
66: 1 Shout with joy to G, all the earth!
66: 3 Say to G, "How awesome are your
66: 5 Come and see what G has done,
66: 16 listen, all you who fear G;
66: 20 Praise be to G,
68: 4 Sing to G, sing praise to his name,
68: 6 G sets the lonely in families,
68: 20 Our G is a G who saves;
68: 24 has come into view, O G,
68: 35 You are awesome, O G,
69: 5 You know my folly, O G;
70: 1 Hasten, O G, to save me;
70: 4 "Let G be exalted!"
70: 5 come quickly to me, O G.
71: 17 my youth, O G, you have taught
71: 18 do not forsake me, O G,
71: 19 reaches to the skies, O G,
71: 22 harp for your faithfulness, O my G;
73: 17 me till I entered the sanctuary of G;
73: 26 but G is the strength of my heart
76: 11 Make vows to the Lord your G
77: 13 What g is so great as our G?
77: 14 You are the G who performs
78: 19 Can G spread a table in the desert?
79: 9 Help us, O G our Saviour,
81: 1 Sing for joy to G our strength;
82: 1 G presides in the great assembly;
84: 2 out for the living G.
84: 10 a doorkeeper in the house of my G
84: 11 For the Lord G is a sun
86: 12 O Lord my G, with all my heart;
86: 15 a compassionate and gracious G,
87: 3 O city of G: Selah
89: 7 of the holy ones G is greatly feared;
90: 2 to everlasting you are G.
91: 2 my G, in whom I trust."
94: 22 my G the rock in whom I take
95: 7 for he is our G
99: 8 you were to Israel a forgiving G,
99: 9 Exalt the Lord our G
100: 3 Know that the Lord is G.
108: 1 My heart is steadfast, O G;
113: 5 Who is like the Lord our G,
115: 3 Our G is in heaven;
116: 5 our G is full of compassion.
123: 2 look to the Lord our G,
136: 2 Give thanks to the G of gods.
136: 26 Give thanks to the G of heaven.
139: 17 to me are your thoughts, O G!
139: 23 Search me, O G, and know my
143: 10 for you are my G;
144: 2 He is my loving G and my fortress,
147: 1 is to sing praises to our G,

Pr 3: 4 in the sight of G and man.
14: 31 to the needy honours G—
25: 2 of G to conceal a matter;
30: 5 "Every word of G is flawless;

Ecc 2: 26 G gives wisdom, knowledge
3: 11 cannot fathom what G has done

Ecc 3: 13 in all his toil—this is the gift of *G*.
3: 14 *G* does it, so men will revere him.
5: 4 When you make a vow to *G*,
5: 19 in his work—this is a gift of *G*.
8: 12 who are reverent before *G*.
11: 5 cannot understand the work of *G*,
12: 7 the spirit returns to *G* who gave it.
12: 13 Fear *G* and keep his

Isa 5: 16 the holy *G* will show himself holy
9: 6 Wonderful Counsellor, Mighty *G*,
12: 2 Surely *G* is my salvation;
25: 9 "Surely this is our *G*;
28: 11 *G* will speak to this people,
29: 23 will stand in awe of the *G* of Israel.
30: 18 For the LORD is a *G* of justice.
35: 4 your *G* will come,
37: 16 you alone are *G* over all
40: 1 says your *G*.
40: 3 a highway for our *G*.
40: 8 the word of our *G* stands for ever."
40: 18 then, will you compare *G*?
40: 28 The LORD is the everlasting *G*,
41: 10 not be dismayed, for I am your *G*.
41: 13 For I am the LORD, your *G*,
43: 10 Before me no *g* was formed,
44: 6 apart from me there is no *G*.
44: 15 he also fashions a *g* and worships it;
45: 18 he is *G*;
48: 17 "I am the LORD your *G*,
52: 7 "Your *G* reigns!"
52: 12 *G* of Israel will be your rear guard.
55: 7 to our *G*, for he will freely pardon.
57: 21 says my *G*, "for the wicked."
59: 2 you from your *G*;
60: 19 and your *G* will be your glory.
61: 2 and the day of vengeance of our *G*,
61: 10 my soul rejoices in my *G*.
62: 5 so will your *G* rejoice over you.

Jer 7: 23 I will be your *G* and you will be my
10: 10 But the LORD is the true *G*;
10: 12 But *G* made the earth by his power;
23: 23 "Am I only a *G* nearby,
23: 36 distort the words of the living *G*,
31: 33 I will be their *G*,
32: 27 "I am the LORD, the *G*
42: 6 for we will obey the LORD our *G*."
51: 10 what the LORD our *G* has done.'
51: 56 For the LORD is a *G* of retribution

Eze 28: 13 the garden of *G*;
34: 31 and I am your *G*, declares

Da 2: 28 there is a *G* in heaven who reveals
3: 17 the *G* we serve is able to save us
3: 29 for no other *g* can save in this way
6: 16 "May your *G*, whom you serve
9: 4 O Lord, the great and awesome *G*,
10: 12 to humble yourself before your *G*,
11: 36 things against the *G* of gods.

Hos 1: 9 my people, and I am not your *G*.
1: 10 will be called 'sons of the living *G*'.
4: 6 you have ignored the law of your *G*
6: 6 acknowledgment of *G* rather
9: 8 The prophet, along with my *G*,
12: 6 and wait for your *G* always.

Joel 2: 13 Return to the LORD your *G*,
2: 23 rejoice in the LORD your *G*,

Am 4: 12 prepare to meet your *G*, O Israel."
4: 13 the LORD *G* Almighty is his name

Jnh 1: 6 Get up and call on your *g*!
4: 2 a gracious and compassionate *G*,

Mic 6: 8 and to walk humbly with your *G*.

Mic 7: 7 I wait for *G* my Saviour;
7: 18 Who is a *G* like you,

Na 1: 2 LORD is a jealous and avenging *G*;

Hab 3: 18 I will be joyful in *G* my Saviour.

Zep 3: 17 The LORD your *G* is with you,

Zec 14: 5 Then the LORD my *G* will come,

Mal 2: 10 Father? Did not one *G* create us?
2: 16 says the LORD *G* of Israel,
3: 8 Will a man rob *G*? Yet you rob me.

Mt 1: 23 which means, "*G* with us."
4: 4 comes from the mouth of *G*.'"
4: 7 'Do not put the Lord your *G*
4: 10 'Worship the Lord your *G*,
5: 8 for they will see *G*.
6: 24 You cannot serve both *G*
19: 6 Therefore what *G* has joined
19: 26 but with *G* all things are possible."
22: 21 and to *G* what is God's."
22: 32 He is not the *G* of the dead
22: 37 "'Love the Lord your *G*
27: 46 which means, "My *G*, my *G*,

Mk 2: 7 Who can forgive sins but *G* alone?"
7: 13 Thus you nullify the word of *G*
10: 6 of creation *G* 'made them male
10: 9 Therefore what *G* has joined
10: 18 "No-one is good—except *G* alone.
10: 27 all things are possible with *G*."
11: 22 "Have faith in *G*," Jesus answered.
12: 17 and to *G* what is God's."
12: 29 the Lord our *G*, the Lord is one.
12: 30 Love the Lord your *G*
15: 34 which means, "My *G*, my *G*,
16: 19 and he sat at the right hand of *G*.

Lk 1: 30 Mary, you have found favour with *G*
1: 37 For nothing is impossible with *G*."
1: 47 my spirit rejoices in *G* my Saviour.
2: 14 "Glory to *G* in the highest,
2: 52 and in favour with *G* and men.
4: 8 'Worship the Lord your *G*
5: 21 Who can forgive sins but *G* alone?"
8: 39 tell how much *G* has done for you."
10: 9 'The kingdom of *G* is near you.'
10: 27 "'Love the Lord your *G*
13: 18 "What is the kingdom of *G* like?
18: 19 "No-one is good—except *G* alone.
18: 27 with men is possible with *G*."
20: 25 and to *G* what is God's."
20: 38 He is not the *G* of the dead,
22: 69 at the right hand of the mighty *G*."

Jn 1: 1 was with *G*, and the Word was *G*.
1: 18 ever seen *G*, but *G* the only ˏSonˌˌ
1: 29 Lamb of *G*, who takes away the sin
3: 16 "For *G* so loved the world that he
3: 34 the one whom *G* has sent speaks
4: 24 *G* is spirit, and his worshippers must
5: 44 praise that comes from the only *G*?
6: 29 answered, "The work of *G* is this:
7: 17 my teaching comes from *G* or
8: 42 to them, "If *G* were your Father,
8: 47 belongs to *G* hears what *G* says.
11: 40 you would see the glory of *G*?"
13: 3 from *G* and was returning to *G*;
13: 31 of Man glorified and *G* is glorified
14: 1 Trust in *G*; trust also in me.
17: 3 the only true *G*, and Jesus Christ,
20: 17 your Father, to my *G* and your *G*
20: 28 "My Lord and my *G*!"
20: 31 the Son of *G*, and that

Ac 2: 11 wonders of *G* in our own tongues!"
2: 24 But *G* raised him from the dead,

Ac   2: 33 Exalted to the right hand of *G*,
      2: 36 *G* has made this Jesus, whom you
      3: 15 but *G* raised him from the dead.
      3: 19 Repent, then, and turn to *G*,
      4: 31 and spoke the word of *G* boldly.
      5: 4 You have not lied to men but to *G*
      5: 29 "We must obey *G* rather than men!
      5: 31 *G* exalted him to his own right
      5: 32 whom *G* has given
      7: 55 to heaven and saw the glory of *G*,
      8: 21 your heart is not right before *G*.
   11: 9 anything impure that *G* has made
   12: 24 But the word of *G* continued
   13: 32 What *G* promised our fathers he
   15: 10 to test *G* by putting on the necks
   17: 23 TO AN UNKNOWN *G*.
   17: 30 In the past *G* overlooked such
   20: 27 to you the whole will of *G*.
   20: 32 "Now I commit you to *G*
   24: 16 keep my conscience clear before *G*
Ro   1: 16 the power of *G* for the salvation
      1: 17 a righteousness from *G* is revealed,
      1: 18 The wrath of *G* is being revealed
      1: 24 Therefore *G* gave them
      1: 26 *G* gave them over to shameful lusts
      2: 11 For *G* does not show favouritism.
      2: 16 when *G* will judge men's secrets
      3: 4 Let *G* be true, and every man a liar.
      3: 19 world held accountable to *G*.
      3: 23 and fall short of the glory of *G*,
      3: 29 Is *G* the *G* of Jews only? Is he not
      4: 3 say? "Abraham believed *G*,
      4: 6 to whom *G* credits righteousness
      4: 17 the *G* who gives life to the dead
      4: 24 to whom *G* will credit
      5: 1 we have peace with *G*
      5: 5 because *G* has poured out his love
      5: 8 *G* demonstrates his own love for us
      6: 22 and have become slaves to *G*,
      6: 23 but the gift of *G* is eternal life
      8: 7 the sinful mind is hostile to *G*.
      8: 17 heirs of *G* and co-heirs with Christ,
      8: 28 in all things *G* works for the good
      9: 14 What then shall we say? Is *G* unjust
      9: 18 Therefore *G* has mercy
   10: 9 in your heart that *G* raised him
   11: 2 *G* did not reject his people,
   11: 22 the kindness and sternness of *G*:
   11: 32 For *G* has bound all men
   13: 1 exist have been established by *G*.
   14: 12 give an account of himself to *G*.
   16: 20 *G* of peace will soon crush Satan
1Co 1: 18 are being saved it is the power of *G*.
      1: 20 Has not *G* made foolish
      1: 25 For the foolishness of *G* is wiser
      1: 27 But *G* chose the foolish things
      2: 9 what *G* has prepared
      2: 11 of *G* except the Spirit of *G*.
      3: 6 watered it, but *G* made it grow.
      3: 17 God's temple, *G* will destroy
      6: 20 Therefore honour *G* with your body.
      7: 7 each man has his own gift from *G*;
      7: 15 *G* has called us to live in peace.
      7: 20 was in when *G* called him.
      7: 24 each man, as responsible to *G*,
      8: 3 man who loves *G* is known by *G*.
      8: 8 food does not bring us near to *G*;
   10: 13 *G* is faithful; he will not let you be
   10: 31 do it all for the glory of *G*.
   12: 24 But *G* has combined the members

1Co 14: 33 For *G* is not a *G* of disorder
   15: 24 over the kingdom to *G* the Father
   15: 28 so that *G* may be all in all.
   15: 34 are some who are ignorant of *G*—
   15: 57 be to *G*! He gives us the victory
2Co 1: 9 rely on ourselves but on *G*,
      2: 14 be to *G*, who always leads us
      2: 15 For we are to *G* the aroma of Christ
      2: 17 we do not peddle the word of *G*
      3: 5 but our competence comes from *G*.
      4: 2 nor do we distort the word of *G*.
      4: 7 this all-surpassing power is from *G*
      5: 5 Now it is *G* who has made us
      5: 19 that *G* was reconciling the world
      5: 20 though *G* were making his appeal
      5: 21 *G* made him who had no sin
      6: 16 we are the temple of the living *G*.
      9: 7 for *G* loves a cheerful giver.
      9: 8 *G* is able to make all grace abound
   10: 13 to the field *G* has assigned to us,
Gal 2: 6 *G* does not judge by external
      3: 5 Does *G* give you his Spirit
      3: 6 Abraham: "He believed *G*,
      3: 11 justified before *G* by the law,
      3: 26 You are all sons of *G* through faith
      6: 7 not be deceived: *G* cannot be
Eph 1: 22 *G* placed all things under his feet
      2: 8 it is the gift of *G*—not by works,
      2: 10 which *G* prepared in advance for us
      2: 22 in which *G* lives by his Spirit.
      4: 6 one baptism; one *G* and Father
      4: 24 to be like *G* in true righteousness
      5: 1 Be imitators of *G*, therefore,
      6: 6 doing the will of *G* from your heart.
Php 2: 6 Who, being in very nature *G*,
      2: 9 Therefore *G* exalted him
      2: 13 for it is *G* who works in you to will
      4: 7 peace of *G*, which transcends all
      4: 19 And my *G* will meet all your needs
Col 1: 19 For *G* was pleased
      2: 13 *G* made you alive with Christ.
1Th 2: 4 trying to please men but *G*.
      2: 13 but as it actually is, the word of *G*,
      3: 9 How can we thank *G* enough
      4: 7 For *G* did not call us to be impure,
      4: 9 taught by *G* to love each other.
      5: 9 For *G* did not appoint us
1Ti 2: 5 one mediator between *G* and men,
      4: 4 For everything *G* created is good,
      5: 4 for this is pleasing to *G*.
2Ti 1: 6 you to fan into flame the gift of *G*,
Tit   1: 2 which *G*, who does not lie,
      2: 13 glorious appearing of our great *G*
Heb 1: 1 In the past *G* spoke
      3: 4 but *G* is the builder of everything.
      4: 4 "And on the seventh day *G* rested
      4: 12 For the word of *G* is living
      6: 10 *G* is not unjust; he will not forget
      6: 18 in which it is impossible for *G* to lie
      7: 19 by which we draw near to *G*.
      7: 25 come to *G* through him,
   10: 22 draw near to *G* with a sincere heart
   10: 31 to fall into the hands of the living *G*
   11: 5 commended as one who pleased *G*.
   11: 6 faith it is impossible to please *G*,
   12: 7 as discipline; *G* is treating you
   12: 10 but *G* disciplines us for our good,
   12: 29 for our *G* is a consuming fire.
   13: 15 offer to *G* a sacrifice of praise—
Jas 1: 12 crown of life that *G* has promised

Jas 1: 13 For *G* cannot be tempted by evil,
1: 27 religion that *G* our Father accepts
2: 19 You believe that there is one *G*.
2: 23 "Abraham believed *G*,
4: 4 the world becomes an enemy of *G*.
4: 6 "*G* opposes the proud
4: 8 Come near to *G* and he will come
1Pe 1: 23 the living and enduring word of *G*.
2: 20 this is commendable before *G*.
3: 18 the unrighteous, to bring you to *G*.
4: 11 it with the strength *G* provides,
5: 5 because, "*G* opposes the proud
2Pe 1: 21 but men spoke from *G*
2: 4 For if *G* did not spare angels
1Jn 1: 5 *G* is light; in him there is no
2: 17 the will of *G* lives for ever.
3: 1 we should be called children of *G*!
3: 9 born of *G* will continue to sin,
3: 10 we know who the children of *G* are
3: 20 For *G* is greater than our hearts,
4: 7 for love comes from *G*.
4: 8 not know *G*, because *G* is love.
4: 9 This is how *G* showed his love
4: 11 Dear friends, since *G* so loved us,
4: 12 No-one has ever seen *G*;
4: 15 *G* lives in him and he in *G*.
4: 16 *G* is love.
4: 20 "I love *G*," yet hates his brother,
4: 21 Whoever loves *G* must
5: 2 that we love the children of *G*:
5: 3 love for *G*: to obey his commands.
5: 4 born of *G* overcomes the world.
5: 10 does not believe *G* has made him
5: 14 have in approaching *G*:
5: 18 born of *G* does not continue to sin;
Rev 4: 8 holy is the Lord *G* Almighty,
7: 12 be to our *G* for ever and ever.
7: 17 *G* will wipe away every tear
11: 16 fell on their faces and worshipped *G*,
15: 3 Lord *G* Almighty.
17: 17 For *G* has put it into their hearts
19: 6 For our Lord *G* Almighty reigns.
21: 3 Now the dwelling of *G* is with men,
21: 23 for the glory of *G* gives it light,

GOD-BREATHED* (BREATH)

2Ti 3: 16 All Scripture is *G* and is useful

GOD-FEARING* (FEAR)

Ecc 8: 12 that it will go better with *G* men,
Ac 2: 5 staying in Jerusalem *G* Jews
10: 2 all his family were devout and *G*;
10: 22 He is a righteous and *G* man,
13: 26 of Abraham, and you *G* Gentiles.
13: 50 But the Jews incited the *G* women
17: 4 as did a large number of *G* Greeks
17: 17 with the Jews and the *G* Greeks,

GOD-HATERS* (HATE)

Ro 1: 30 They are gossips, slanderers, *G*,

GOD'S (GOD)

2Ch 20: 15 For the battle is not yours, but *G*.
Job 37: 14 stop and consider *G* wonders.
Ps 52: 8 I trust in *G* unfailing love
69: 30 I will praise *G* name in song
Mk 3: 35 Whoever does *G* will is my brother
Jn 7: 17 If anyone chooses to do *G* will,
10: 36 'I am *G* Son'? Do not believe me
Ro 2: 3 think you will escape *G* judgment?

Ro 2: 4 not realising that *G* kindness leads
3: 3 lack of faith nullify *G* faithfulness?
7: 22 in my inner being I delight in *G* law
9: 16 or effort, but on *G* mercy.
11: 29 for *G* gifts and his call are
12: 2 and approve what *G* will is—
12: 13 Share with *G* people who are
13: 6 for the authorities are *G* servants,
1Co 7: 19 Keeping *G* commands is what
2Co 6: 2 now is the time of *G* favour,
Eph 1: 7 riches of *G* grace that he lavished
1Th 4: 3 *G* will that you should be sanctified:
5: 18 for this is *G* will for you
1Ti 6: 1 so that *G* name and our teaching
2Ti 2: 19 *G* solid foundation stands firm,
Tit 1: 7 overseer is entrusted with *G* work,
Heb 1: 3 The Son is the radiance of *G* glory
9: 24 now to appear for us in *G* presence,
11: 3 was formed at *G* command,
1Pe 2: 15 For it is *G* will that
3: 4 which is of great worth in *G* sight.
1Jn 2: 5 *G* love is truly made complete

GODLESS

Job 20: 5 the joy of the *g* lasts but a moment.
1Ti 6: 20 Turn away from *g* chatter

GODLINESS (GOD)

1Ti 2: 2 and quiet lives in all *g* and holiness.
4: 8 but *g* has value for all things,
6: 5 and who think that *g* is a means
6: 6 with contentment is great gain.
6: 11 and pursue righteousness, *g*, faith,
2Pe 1: 6 and to perseverance, *g*;

GODLY (GOD)

Ps 4: 3 that the LORD has set apart the *g*
2Co 7: 10 *G* sorrow brings repentance that
11: 2 jealous for you with a *g* jealousy.
2Ti 3: 12 everyone who wants to live a *g* life
2Pe 3: 11 You ought to live holy and *g* lives

GODS (GOD)

Ex 20: 3 "You shall have no other *g*
Dt 5: 7 "You shall have no other *g*
1Ch 16: 26 For all the *g* of the nations are idols
Ps 82: 6 "I said, 'You are "*g*";
Jn 10: 34 have said you are *g*'? If he called
Ac 19: 26 He says that man-made *g* are no *g*

GOG

Eze 38: 18 When *G* attacks the land of Israel,
Rev 20: 8 *G* and Magog—to gather them

GOLD

1Ki 20: 3 'Your silver and *g* are mine,
Job 22: 25 then the Almighty will be your *g*,
23: 10 tested me, I will come forth as *g*.
28: 15 cannot be bought with the finest *g*,
31: 24 "If I have put my trust in *g*
Ps 19: 10 They are more precious than *g*,
119: 127 more than *g*, more than pure *g*,
Pr 3: 14 and yields better returns than *g*.
22: 1 esteemed is better than silver or *g*.
Hag 2: 8 The silver is mine and the *g* is mine
Mt 2: 11 and presented him with gifts of *g*
Rev 3: 18 to buy from me *g* refined in the fire,

GOLGOTHA*

Mt 27: 33 to a place called *G* (which means
Mk 15: 22 to the place called *G* (which means

Jn   19: 17 (which in Aramaic is called *G*).

GOLIATH

Philistine giant killed by David (1Sa 17; 21:9).

GOMORRAH

Ge   19: 24 sulphur on Sodom and *G*—
Mt   10: 15 and *G* on the day of judgment
2Pe   2: 6 and *G* by burning them to ashes,
Jude   : 7 *G* and the surrounding towns gave

GOOD

Ge   1: 4 God saw that the light was *g*,
       1: 10 And God saw that it was *g*.
       1: 12 And God saw that it was *g*.
       1: 18 And God saw that it was *g*.
       1: 21 And God saw that it was *g*.
       1: 25 And God saw that it was *g*.
       1: 31 he had made, and it was very *g*.
       2: 9 and the tree of the knowledge of *g*
       2: 9 pleasing to the eye and *g* for food.
       2: 18 "It is not *g* for the man to be alone.
       3: 22 become like one of us, knowing *g*
      50: 20 but God intended it for *g*
2Ch   7: 3 "He is *g*; / his love endures
      31: 20 doing what was *g* and right
Job   2: 10 Shall we accept *g* from God,
Ps   14: 1 there is no-one who does *g*.
      34: 8 Taste and see that the LORD is *g*;
      34: 14 Turn from evil and do *g*;
      37: 3 Trust in the LORD and do *g*;
      37: 27 Turn from evil and do *g*;
      52: 9 for your name is *g*.
      53: 3 there is no-one who does *g*,
      84: 11 no *g* thing does he withhold
     100: 5 For the LORD is *g* and his love
     103: 5 satisfies my desires with *g* things,
     112: 5 *G* will come to him who is
     119: 68 You are *g*, and what you do is *g*;
     133: 1 How *g* and pleasant it is
     145: 9 The LORD is *g* to all;
     147: 1 How *g* it is to sing praises
Pr   3: 4 you will win favour and a *g* name
       3: 27 Do not withhold *g*
      11: 27 He who seeks *g* finds goodwill,
      13: 22 A *g* man leaves an inheritance
      14: 22 those who plan what is *g* find love
      15: 3 on the wicked and the *g*.
      15: 23 and how *g* is a timely word!
      15: 30 *g* news gives health to the bones.
      17: 22 A cheerful heart is *g* medicine,
      18: 22 He who finds a wife finds what is *g*
      19: 2 It is not *g* to have zeal
      22: 1 A *g* name is more desirable
      31: 12 She brings him *g*, not harm,
Ecc   12: 14 whether it is *g* or evil.
Isa   5: 20 Woe to those who call evil *g*
      40: 9 You who bring *g* tidings
      52: 7 the feet of those who bring *g* news,
      61: 1 me to preach *g* news to the poor.
Jer   6: 16 ask where the *g* way is,
      13: 23 Neither can you do *g*
      32: 39 the *g* of their children after them.
Eze   34: 14 I will tend them in a *g* pasture,
Mic   6: 8 has showed you, O man, what is *g*.
Na   1: 15 the feet of one who brings *g* news,
Mt   5: 45 sun to rise on the evil and the *g*,
       7: 11 Father in heaven give *g* gifts
       7: 17 Likewise every *g* tree bears *g* fruit,
       7: 18 A *g* tree cannot bear bad fruit,

Mt   12: 35 The *g* man brings *g* things out
      13: 8 Still other seed fell on *g* soil,
      13: 24 is like a man who sowed *g* seed
      13: 48 and collected the *g* fish in baskets,
      19: 17 "There is only One who is *g*.
      22: 10 both *g* and bad, and the wedding
      25: 21 'Well done, *g* and faithful servant!
Mk   1: 15 Repent and believe the *g* news!'
       3: 4 lawful on the Sabbath: to do *g*
       4: 8 Still other seed fell on *g* soil.
       8: 36 What *g* is it for a man
      10: 18 "No-one is *g*—except God alone.
      16: 15 preach the *g* news to all creation.
Lk   2: 10 I bring you *g* news
       3: 9 does not produce *g* fruit will be
       6: 27 do *g* to those who hate you,
       6: 43 nor does a bad tree bear *g* fruit.
       6: 45 The *g* man brings *g* things out
       8: 8 Still other seed fell on *g* soil.
       9: 25 What *g* is it for a man
      14: 34 "Salt is *g* but if it loses its saltiness,
      18: 19 "No-one is *g*—except God alone.
      19: 17 "'Well done, my *g* servant!'
Jn   10: 11 "I am the *g* shepherd.
Ro   3: 12 there is no-one who does *g*,
       7: 12 is holy, righteous and *g*.
       7: 16 want to do, I agree that the law is *g*.
       7: 18 I have the desire to do what is *g*,
       8: 28 for the *g* of those who love him,
      10: 15 feet of those who bring *g* news!"
      12: 2 his *g*, pleasing and perfect will.
      12: 9 Hate what is evil; cling to what is *g*.
      13: 4 For he is God's servant to do you *g*
      16: 19 you to be wise about what is *g*,
1Co   7: 1 It is *g* for a man not to marry.
      10: 24 should seek his own *g*, but the *g*
      15: 33 Bad company corrupts *g* character
2Co   9: 8 you will abound in every *g* work.
Gal   4: 18 provided the purpose is *g*,
       6: 9 us not become weary in doing *g*,
       6: 10 as we have opportunity, let us do *g*
Eph   2: 10 in Christ Jesus to do *g* works,
       6: 8 everyone for whatever *g* he does,
Php   1: 6 that he who began a *g* work
Col   1: 10 bearing fruit in every *g* work,
1Th   5: 21 Hold on to the *g*.
1Ti   3: 7 have a *g* reputation with outsiders,
       4: 4 For everything God created is *g*,
       6: 12 Fight the *g* fight of the faith.
       6: 18 them to do *g*, to be rich in *g* deeds,
2Ti   3: 17 equipped for every *g* work.
       4: 7 I have fought the *g* fight, I have
Tit   1: 8 loves what is *g*, who is
       2: 7 an example by doing what is *g*.
       2: 14 his very own, eager to do what is *g*.
Heb   5: 14 to distinguish *g* from evil.
      10: 24 on towards love and *g* deeds.
      12: 10 but God disciplines us for our *g*,
      13: 16 do not forget to do *g* and to share
Jas   4: 17 who knows the *g* he ought to do
1Pe   2: 3 you have tasted that the Lord is *g*.
       2: 12 Live such *g* lives among the pagans
       2: 18 not only to those who are *g*
       3: 17 to suffer for doing *g*

GOODS

Ecc   5: 11 As *g* increase,

GORGE

Pr   23: 20 or *g* themselves on meat,

GOSHEN

Ge 45: 10 You shall live in the region of G
Ex   8: 22 differently with the land of G,

GOSPEL

Ro   1: 16 I am not ashamed of the g,
      15: 16 duty of proclaiming the g of God,
      15: 20 to preach the g where Christ was
1Co   1: 17 to preach the g—not with words
       9: 12 rather than hinder the g of Christ.
       9: 14 who preach the g should receive
       9: 16 Woe to me if I do not preach the g!
      15: 1 you of the g I preached to you,
      15: 2 By this g you are saved,
2Co   4: 4 light of the g of the glory of Christ,
       9: 13 your confession of the g
Gal   1: 7 a different g—which is really no g
Eph   6: 15 comes from the g of peace.
Php   1: 27 in a manner worthy of the g
Col   1: 23 This is the g that you heard
1Th   2: 4 by God to be entrusted with the g.
2Th   1: 8 do not obey the g of our Lord Jesus
2Ti   1: 10 immortality to light through the g.
Rev 14: 6 he had the eternal g to proclaim

GOSSIP*

Pr   11: 13 A g betrays a confidence,
    16: 28 and a g separates close friends.
    18: 8 of a g are like choice morsels;
    20: 19 A g betrays a confidence;
    26: 20 without g a quarrel dies down.
    26: 22 of a g are like choice morsels;
2Co 12: 20 slander, g, arrogance and disorder.

GOVERN (GOVERNMENT)

Ge   1: 16 the greater light to g the day
Job 34: 17 Can he who hates justice g?
Ro   12: 8 it is leadership, let him g diligently;

GOVERNMENT (GOVERN)

Isa   9: 6 and the g will be on his shoulders.

GRACE* (GRACIOUS)

Ps   45: 2 lips have been anointed with g,
Pr   1: 9 will be a garland to g your head
    3: 22 an ornament to g your neck.
    3: 34 but gives g to the humble.
    4: 9 She will set a garland of g
Isa 26: 10 Though g is shown to the wicked,
Jnh   2: 8 forfeit the g that could be theirs.
Zec 12: 10 of Jerusalem a spirit of g
Lk   2: 40 and the g of God was upon him.
Jn   1: 14 who came from the Father, full of g
    1: 16 of his g we have all received one
    1: 17 g and truth came through Jesus
Ac   4: 33 and much g was upon them all.
    6: 8 a man full of God's g and power,
  11: 23 saw the evidence of the g of God.
  13: 43 them to continue in the g of God.
  14: 3 message of his g by enabling them
  14: 26 they had been committed to the g
  15: 11 We believe it is through the g
  15: 40 by the brothers to the g of the Lord
  18: 27 to those who by g had believed.
  20: 24 testifying to the gospel of God's g.
  20: 32 to God and to the word of his g,
Ro   1: 5 we received g and apostleship
    1: 7 G and peace to you
    3: 24 and are justified freely by his g
    4: 16 be by g and may be guaranteed

Ro   5: 2 access by faith into this g
    5: 15 came by the g of the one man,
    5: 15 how much more did God's g
    5: 17 God's abundant provision of g
    5: 20 where sin increased, g increased all
    5: 21 also g might reign
    6: 1 on sinning so that g may increase?
    6: 14 you are not under law, but under g.
    6: 15 we are not under law but under g?
  11: 5 there is a remnant chosen by g.
  11: 6 if by g, then it is no longer by works
  11: 6 if it were, g would no longer be g.
  12: 3 For by the g given me I say
  12: 6 according to the g given us.
  15: 15 because of the g God gave me
  16: 20 The g of our Lord Jesus be
1Co   1: 3 G and peace to you
    1: 4 of his g given you in Christ Jesus.
    3: 10 By the g God has given me,
  15: 10 But by the g of God I am what I am
  15: 10 but the g of God that was with me.
  15: 10 his g to me was not without effect.
  16: 23 The g of the Lord Jesus be with you
2Co   1: 2 G and peace to you
    1: 12 wisdom but according to God's g.
    4: 15 so that the g that is reaching more
    6: 1 not to receive God's g in vain.
    8: 1 to know about the g that God has
    8: 6 also to completion this act of g
    8: 7 also excel in this g of giving.
    8: 9 For you know the g
    9: 8 able to make all g abound to you,
    9: 14 of the surpassing g God has given
  12: 9 "My g is sufficient for you,
  13: 14 May the g of the Lord Jesus Christ,
Gal   1: 3 G and peace to you
    1: 6 the one who called you by the g
    1: 15 from birth and called me by his g,
    2: 9 when they recognised the g given
    2: 21 I do not set aside the g of God,
    3: 18 God in his g gave it to Abraham
    5: 4 you have fallen away from g.
    6: 18 The g of our Lord Jesus Christ be
Eph   1: 2 G and peace to you
    1: 6 to the praise of his glorious g,
    1: 7 riches of God's g that he lavished
    2: 5 it is by g you have been saved.
    2: 7 the incomparable riches of his g,
    2: 8 For it is by g you have been saved,
    3: 2 of God's g that was given to me
    3: 7 by the gift of God's g given me
    3: 8 God's people, this g was given me:
    4: 7 to each one of us g has been given
    6: 24 G to all who love our Lord Jesus
Php   1: 2 G and peace to you
    1: 7 all of you share in God's g with me.
    4: 23 The g of the Lord Jesus Christ be
Col   1: 2 G and peace to you
    1: 6 understood God's g in all its truth.
    4: 6 conversation be always full of g,
    4: 18 G be with you.
1Th   1: 1 and the Lord Jesus Christ: G
    5: 28 The g of our Lord Jesus Christ be
2Th   1: 2 G and peace to you
    1: 12 according to the g of our God
    2: 16 and by his g gave us eternal
    3: 18 The g of our Lord Jesus Christ be
1Ti   1: 2 my true son in the faith: G,
    1: 14 The g of our Lord was poured out
    6: 21 G be with you.

2Ti   1: 2 To Timothy, my dear son: G,
       1: 9 This g was given us in Christ Jesus
       1: 9 because of his own purpose and g.
       2: 1 be strong in the g that is
       4: 22 G be with you.
Tit   1: 4 G and peace from God the Father
       2: 11 For the g of God that brings
       3: 7 having been justified by his g,
       3: 15 G be with you all.
Phm   : 3 G to you and peace
        : 25 The g of the Lord Jesus Christ be
Heb   2: 9 that by the g of God he might taste
       4: 16 find g to help us in our time of need
       4: 16 the throne of g with confidence,
      10: 29 and who has insulted the Spirit of g
      12: 15 See to it that no-one misses the g
      13: 9 hearts to be strengthened by g,
      13: 25 G be with you all.
Jas   4: 6 but gives g to the humble."
       4: 6 But he gives us more g. That is why
1Pe   1: 2 G and peace be yours in abundance
       1: 10 who spoke of the g that was
       1: 13 fully on the g to be given you
       4: 10 faithfully administering God's g
       5: 5 but gives g to the humble."
       5: 10 the God of all g, who called you
       5: 12 and testifying that this is the true g
2Pe   1: 2 G and peace be yours in abundance
       3: 18 But grow in the g and knowledge
2Jn   : 3 and will be with us for ever: G,
Jude   : 4 who change the g of our God
Rev   1: 4 G and peace to you
      22: 21 The g of the Lord Jesus be

GRACIOUS (GRACE)

Ex   34: 6 the compassionate and g God,
Nu   6: 25 and be g to you;
Ne   9: 17 But you are a forgiving God, g
Ps   67: 1 May God be g to us and bless us
Pr   22: 11 a pure heart and whose speech is g
Isa   30: 18 Yet the LORD longs to be g to you

GRAIN

Lev   2: 1 When someone brings a g offering
Mk   4: 28 then the full g in the ear.
Lk   17: 35 women will be grinding g together;
Jn   12: 24 a g of wheat falls to the ground
1Co   9: 9 ox while it is treading out the g."

GRANDCHILDREN (CHILD)

1Ti   5: 4 But if a widow has children or g,

GRANDMOTHER (MOTHER)

2Ti   1: 5 which first lived in your g Lois

GRANT (GRANTED)

Ps   20: 5 May the LORD g all your requests
      51: 12 g me a willing spirit, to sustain me.

GRANTED (GRANT)

Pr   10: 24 what the righteous desire will be g.
Mt   15: 28 great faith! Your request is g."
Php   1: 29 For it has been g to you on behalf

GRAPES

Nu   13: 23 branch bearing a single cluster of g
Jer   31: 29 'The fathers have eaten sour g,
Eze   18: 2 "'The fathers eat sour g,
Mt   7: 16 Do people pick g from thornbushes
Rev   14: 18 and gather the clusters of g

GRASPED

Php   2: 6 with God something to be g,

GRASS

Ps   103: 15 As for man, his days are like g,
Isa   40: 6 "All men are like g,
Mt   6: 30 If that is how God clothes the g
1Pe   1: 24 "All men are like g,

GRASSHOPPERS

Nu   13: 33 We seemed like g in our own eyes,

GRATIFY* (GRATITUDE)

Ro   13: 14 think about how to g the desires
Gal   5: 16 and you will not g the desires

GRATITUDE (GRATIFY)

Col   3: 16 and spiritual songs with g

GRAVE (GRAVES)

Nu   19: 16 who touches a human bone or a g,
Dt   34: 6 day no-one knows where his g is.
Ps   5: 9 Their throat is an open g;
      49: 15 will redeem my soul from the g;
Pr   7: 27 Her house is a highway to the g,
Hos   13: 14 Where, O g, is your destruction?
Jn   11: 44 "Take off the g clothes
Ac   2: 27 you will not abandon me to the g,

GRAVES (GRAVE)

Eze   37: 12 I am going to open your g
Jn   5: 28 are in their g will hear his voice
Ro   3: 13 "Their throats are open g;

GREAT (GREATER GREATEST GREATNESS)

Ge   12: 2 I will make your name g,
      12: 2 "I will make you into a g nation
Ex   32: 11 out of Egypt with g power
Nu   14: 19 In accordance with your g love,
Dt   4: 32 so g as this ever happened,
      10: 17 the g God, mighty and awesome,
      29: 28 in g wrath the LORD uprooted
Jos   7: 9 do for your own g name?'
Jdg   16: 5 you the secret of his g strength
2Sa   7: 22 "How g you are, O Sovereign
      22: 36 you stoop down to make me g.
      24: 14 for his mercy is g; but do not let me
1Ch   17: 19 made known all these g promises.
Ps   18: 35 you stoop down to make me g.
      19: 11 in keeping them there is g reward.
      47: 2 the g King over all the earth!
      57: 10 For g is your love, reaching
      68: 11 and g was the company
      89: 1 of the LORD's g love for ever;
     103: 11 so g is his love for those who fear
     107: 43 consider the g love of the LORD.
     108: 4 For g is your love, higher
     117: 2 For g is his love towards us.
     119: 165 G peace have they who love your
     145: 3 G is the LORD and most worthy
Pr   22: 1 is more desirable than g riches;
      23: 24 of a righteous man has g joy;
Isa   42: 21 to make his law g and glorious.
Jer   27: 5 With my g power and outstretched
      32: 19 g are your purposes and mighty are
La   3: 23 g is your faithfulness.
Da   9: 4 "O Lord, the g and awesome God,
Joel   2: 11 The day of the LORD is g;
       2: 20 Surely he has done g things.
Zep   1: 14 "The g day of the LORD is near—

Mal   1: 11   My name will be *g*
     4: 5   the prophet Elijah before that *g*
Mt   20: 26   Whoever wants to become *g*
Mk   10: 43   whoever wants to become *g*
Lk   6: 23   because *g* is your reward in heaven.
     6: 35   Then your reward will be *g*,
     21: 27   in a cloud with power and *g* glory.
Eph   1: 19   and his incomparably *g* power
     2: 4   But because of his *g* love for us,
1Ti   6: 6   with contentment is *g* gain.
Tit   2: 13   glorious appearing of our *g* God
Heb   2: 3   if we ignore such a *g* salvation?
1Jn   3: 1   How *g* is the love the Father has
Rev   6: 17   For the *g* day of their wrath has
     20: 11   Then I saw a *g* white throne

GREATER (GREAT)

Mt   11: 11   there has not risen anyone *g*
     12: 6   I tell you that one *g*
     12: 41   and now one *g* than Jonah is here.
     12: 42   now one *g* than Solomon is here.
Mk   12: 31   There is no commandment *g*
Jn   1: 50   You shall see *g* things than that."
     3: 30   He must become *g*; I must become
     14: 12   He will do even *g* things than these
     15: 13   *G* love has no-one than this,
1Co   12: 31   But eagerly desire the *g* gifts.
2Co   3: 11   how much *g* is the glory
Heb   3: 3   the builder of a house has *g* honour
     3: 3   worthy of *g* honour than Moses,
     7: 7   lesser person is blessed by the *g*.
     11: 26   as of *g* value than the treasures
1Jn   3: 20   For God is *g* than our hearts,
     4: 4   is in you is *g* than the one who is

GREATEST (GREAT)

Mt   22: 38   is the first and *g* commandment.
     23: 11   *g* among you will be your servant.
Lk   9: 48   least among you all—he is the *g*."
1Co   13: 13   But the *g* of these is love.

GREATNESS* (GREAT)

Ex   15: 7   In the *g* of your majesty
Dt   3: 24   to show to your servant your *g*
     32: 3   Oh, praise the *g* of our God!
1Ch   29: 11   O LORD, is the *g* and the power
2Ch   9: 6   half the *g* of your wisdom was told
Est   10: 2   account of the *g* of Mordecai
Ps   145: 3   his *g* no-one can fathom.
     150: 2   praise him for his surpassing *g*.
Isa   63: 1   forward in the *g* of his strength?
Eze   38: 23   I will show my *g* and my holiness,
Da   4: 22   your *g* has grown until it reaches
     5: 18   and *g* and glory and splendour.
     7: 27   and *g* of the kingdoms
Mic   5: 4   will live securely, for then his *g*
Lk   9: 43   And they were all amazed at the *g*
Php   3: 8   compared to the surpassing *g*

GREED (GREEDY)

Lk   12: 15   on your guard against all kinds of *g*
Ro   1: 29   kind of wickedness, evil, *g*
Eph   5: 3   or of any kind of impurity, or of *g*,
Col   3: 5   evil desires and *g*, which is idolatry
2Pe   2: 14   experts in *g*—an accursed brood!

GREEDY (GREED)

Pr   15: 27   A *g* man brings trouble
1Co   6: 10   nor thieves nor the *g* nor drunkards
Eph   5: 5   No immoral, impure or *g* person—

1Pe   5: 2   not *g* for money, but eager to serve;

GREEK (GREEKS)

Gal   3: 28   There is neither Jew nor *G*,
Col   3: 11   Here there is no *G* or Jew,

GREEKS (GREEK)

1Co   1: 22   miraculous signs and *G* look

GREEN

Ps   23: 2   makes me lie down in *g* pastures,

GREW (GROW)

Lk   1: 80   And the child *g* and became strong
     2: 52   And Jesus *g* in wisdom and stature,
Ac   9: 31   by the Holy Spirit, it *g* in numbers,
     16: 5   in the faith and *g* daily in numbers.

GREY

Pr   16: 31   *G* hair is a crown of splendour;
     20: 29   *g* hair the splendour of the old.

GRIEF (GRIEFS GRIEVANCES GRIEVE GRIEVED)

Ps   10: 14   O God, do see trouble and *g*;
Pr   10: 1   but a foolish son *g* to his mother.
     14: 13   and joy may end in *g*.
     17: 21   To have a fool for a son brings *g*;
Ecc   1: 18   the more knowledge, the more *g*.
La   3: 32   Though he brings *g*, he will show
Jn   16: 20   but your *g* will turn to joy.
1Pe   1: 6   had to suffer *g* in all kinds of trials.

GRIEFS* (GRIEF)

1Ti   6: 10   pierced themselves with many *g*.

GRIEVANCES* (GRIEF)

Col   3: 13   forgive whatever *g* you may have

GRIEVE (GRIEF)

Eph   4: 30   do not *g* the Holy Spirit of God,
1Th   4: 13   or to *g* like the rest of men,

GRIEVED (GRIEF)

Isa   63: 10   and *g* his Holy Spirit.

GRINDING

Lk   17: 35   women will be *g* grain together;

GROAN (GROANING GROANS)

Ro   8: 23   *g* inwardly as we wait eagerly
2Co   5: 4   For while we are in this tent, we *g*

GROANING (GROAN)

Ex   2: 24   God heard their *g* and he
Eze   21: 7   'Why are you *g*?' you shall say,
Ro   8: 22   that the whole creation has been *g*

GROANS (GROAN)

Ro   8: 26   with *g* that words cannot express.

GROUND

Ge   1: 10   God called the dry *g* "land",
     3: 17   "Cursed is the *g* because of you;
     4: 10   blood cries out to me from the *g*.
Ex   3: 5   where you are standing is holy *g*."
     15: 19   walked through the sea on dry *g*.
Isa   53: 2   and like a root out of dry *g*.
Mt   10: 29   fall to the *g* apart from the will
     25: 25   and hid your talent in the *g*.

Jn 8: 6 to write on the *g* with his finger.
Eph 6: 13 you may be able to stand your *g*,

GROW (FULL-GROWN GREW GROWING GROWS)

Pr 13: 11 by little makes it *g*.
20: 13 not love sleep or you will *g* poor;
Isa 40: 31 they will run and not *g* weary,
Mt 6: 28 See how the lilies of the field *g*.
1Co 3: 6 watered it, but God made it *g*.
2Pe 3: 18 But *g* in the grace and knowledge

GROWING (GROW)

Col 1: 6 this gospel is bearing fruit and *g*,
1: 10 *g* in the knowledge of God,
2Th 1: 3 your faith is *g* more and more,

GROWS (GROW)

Eph 4: 16 *g* and builds itself up in love,
Col 2: 19 *g* as God causes it to grow.

GRUMBLE (GRUMBLED GRUMBLERS GRUMBLING)

1Co 10: 10 And do not *g*, as some of them did
Jas 5: 9 Don't *g* against each other,

GRUMBLED (GRUMBLE)

Ex 15: 24 So the people *g* against Moses,
Nu 14: 29 and who has *g* against me.

GRUMBLERS* (GRUMBLE)

Jude : 16 These men are *g* and fault-finders;

GRUMBLING (GRUMBLE)

Jn 6: 43 "Stop *g* among yourselves,"
1Pe 4: 9 to one another without *g*.

GUARANTEE (GUARANTEEING)

Heb 7: 22 Jesus has become the *g*

GUARANTEEING* (GUARANTEE)

2Co 1: 22 as a deposit, *g* what is to come.
5: 5 as a deposit, *g* what is to come.
Eph 1: 14 who is a deposit *g* our inheritance

GUARD (GUARDS)

1Sa 2: 9 He will *g* the feet of his saints,
Ps 141: 3 Set a *g* over my mouth, O LORD;
Pr 2: 11 and understanding will *g* you.
4: 13 *g* it well, for it is your life.
4: 23 Above all else, *g* your heart,
7: 2 *g* my teachings as the apple
Isa 52: 12 the God of Israel will be your rear *g*
Mk 13: 33 Be on *g*! Be alert! You do not know
Lk 12: 1 "Be on your *g* against the yeast
12: 15 Be on your *g* against all kinds
Ac 20: 31 So be on your *g*! Remember that
1Co 16: 13 Be on your *g*; stand firm in the faith
Php 4: 7 will *g* your hearts and your minds
1Ti 6: 20 *g* what has been entrusted
2Ti 1: 14 *G* the good deposit that was

GUARDS (GUARD)

Pr 13: 3 He who *g* his lips *g* his life,
19: 16 who obeys instructions *g* his life,
21: 23 He who *g* his mouth and his tongue
22: 5 he who *g* his soul stays far

GUIDANCE (GUIDE)

Pr 1: 5 and let the discerning get *g*—
11: 14 For lack of *g* a nation falls,

Pr 24: 6 for waging war you need *g*,

GUIDE (GUIDANCE GUIDED GUIDES)

Ex 13: 21 of cloud to *g* them on their way
15: 13 In your strength you will *g* them
Ne 9: 19 cease to *g* them on their path,
Ps 25: 5 *g* me in your truth and teach me,
43: 3 let them *g* me;
48: 14 he will be our *g* even to the end.
67: 4 and *g* the nations of the earth.
73: 24 You *g* me with your counsel,
139: 10 even there your hand will *g* me,
Pr 4: 11 I *g* you in the way of wisdom
6: 22 When you walk, they will *g* you;
Isa 58: 11 The LORD will *g* you always;
Jn 16: 13 comes, he will *g* you into all truth.

GUIDED (GUIDE)

Ps 107: 30 he *g* them to their desired haven.

GUIDES (GUIDE)

Ps 23: 3 He *g* me in paths of righteousness
25: 9 He *g* the humble in what is right
Pr 11: 3 The integrity of the upright *g* them,
16: 23 A wise man's heart *g* his mouth,
Mt 23: 16 "Woe to you, blind *g*! You say,
23: 24 You blind *g*! You strain out a gnat

GUILT (GUILTY)

Lev 5: 15 It is a *g* offering.
Ps 32: 5 the *g* of my sin.
38: 4 My *g* has overwhelmed me
Isa 6: 7 your *g* is taken away and your sin
Jer 2: 22 the stain of your *g* is still before me
Eze 18: 19 'Why does the son not share the *g*

GUILTY (GUILT)

Ex 34: 7 does not leave the *g* unpunished;
Mk 3: 29 Spirit will never be forgiven; he is *g*
Jn 8: 46 Can any of you prove me *g* of sin?
1Co 11: 27 in an unworthy manner will be *g*
Heb 10: 2 and would no longer have felt *g*
10: 22 to cleanse us from a *g* conscience
Jas 2: 10 at just one point is *g* of breaking all

HABAKKUK*

Prophet to Judah (Hab 1:1; 3:1).

HABIT

1Ti 5: 13 they get into the *h* of being idle
Heb 10: 25 as some are in the *h* of doing,

HADAD

Edomite adversary of Solomon (1Ki 11:14-25).

HADES*

Mt 16: 18 the gates of *H* will not overcome it.
Rev 1: 18 And I hold the keys of death and *H*
6: 8 *H* was following close behind him.
20: 13 and *H* gave up the dead that were
20: 14 *H* were thrown into the lake of fire.

HAGAR

Servant of Sarah, wife of Abraham, mother of Ishmael (Ge 16:1-6; 25:12). Driven away by Sarah while pregnant (Ge 16:5-16); after birth of Isaac (Ge 21:9-21; Gal 4:21-31).

HAGGAI*

Post-exilic prophet who encouraged rebuilding of the temple (Ezr 5:1; 6:14; Hag 1-2).

HAIL

Ex	9: 19	the *h* will fall on every man
Rev	8: 7	and there came *h* and fire mixed

HAIR (HAIRS HAIRY)

Lev	19: 27	" 'Do not cut the *h* at the sides
Nu	6: 5	he must let the *h* of his head grow
Pr	16: 31	Grey *h* is a crown of splendour;
	20: 29	grey *h* the splendour of the old.
Lk	7: 44	and wiped them with her *h*.
	21: 18	But not a *h* of your head will perish
Jn	11: 2	and wiped his feet with her *h*.
	12: 3	and wiped his feet with her *h*.
1Co	11: 6	for a woman to have her *h* cut
	11: 6	she should have her *h* cut off;
	11: 14	that if a man has long *h*,
	11: 15	For long *h* is given to her
	11: 15	but that if a woman has long *h*,
1Ti	2: 9	not with braided *h* or gold or pearls
1Pe	3: 3	as braided *h* and the wearing
Rev	1: 14	and *h* were white like wool,

HAIRS (HAIR)

Mt	10: 30	even the very *h* of your head are all
Lk	12: 7	the very *h* of your head are all

HAIRY (HAIR)

Ge	27: 11	"But my brother Esau is a *h* man,

HALF

Ex	30: 13	This *h* shekel is an offering
Jos	8: 33	*H* of the people stood in front
1Ki	3: 25	give *h* to one and *h* to the other."
	10: 7	Indeed, not even *h* was told me;
Est	5: 3	Even up to *h* the kingdom,
Da	7: 25	him for a time, times and *h* a time.
Mk	6: 23	up to *h* my kingdom."

HALF-TRIBE (TRIBE)

Nu	32: 33	and the *h* of Manasseh son

HALLELUJAH*

Rev 19: 1, 3, 4, 6.

HALLOWED* (HOLY)

Mt	6: 9	*h* be your name,
Lk	11: 2	*h* be your name,

HALT

Job	38: 11	here is where your proud waves *h*'?

HALTER*

Pr	26: 3	for the horse, a *h* for the donkey,

HAM

Son of Noah (Ge 5:32; 1Ch 1:4), father of Canaan (Ge 9:18; 10:6-20; 1Ch 1:8-16). Saw Noah's nakedness (Ge 9:20-27).

HAMAN

Agagite nobleman honoured by Xerxes (Est 3:1-2). Plotted to exterminate the Jews because of Mordecai (Est 3:3-15). Forced to honour Mordecai (Est 5-6). Plot exposed by Esther (Est 5:1-8; 7:1-8). Hanged (Est 7:9-10).

HAMPERED*

Pr	4: 12	you walk, your steps will not be *h*;

HAND (HANDED HANDFUL HANDS OPEN-HANDED)

Ge	24: 2	"Put your *h* under my thigh.
	47: 29	put your *h* under my thigh
Ex	13: 3	out of it with a mighty *h*.
	15: 6	Your right *h*, O LORD,
	33: 22	and cover you with my *h*
Dt	12: 7	in everything you have put your *h*
1Ki	8: 42	and your mighty *h* and your
	13: 4	But the *h* he stretched out
1Ch	29: 14	you only what comes from your *h*.
	29: 16	it comes from your *h*, and all
2Ch	6: 15	with your *h* you have fulfilled it—
Ne	4: 17	materials did their work with one *h*
Job	40: 4	I put my *h* over my mouth.
Ps	16: 8	Because he is at my right *h*,
	32: 4	your *h* was heavy upon me;
	37: 24	the LORD upholds him with his *h*.
	44: 3	it was your right *h*, your arm,
	45: 9	at your right *h* is the royal bride
	63: 8	your right *h* upholds me.
	75: 8	In the *h* of the LORD is a cup
	91: 7	ten thousand at your right *h*,
	98: 1	his right *h* and his holy arm
	109: 31	at the right *h* of the needy one,
	110: 1	"Sit at my right *h*
	137: 5	may my right *h* forget ˎits skillˏ.
	139: 10	even there your *h* will guide me,
	145: 16	You open your *h*
Pr	27: 16	or grasping oil with the *h*.
Ecc	5: 15	that he can carry in his *h*.
	9: 10	Whatever your *h* finds to do,
Isa	11: 8	the young child put his *h*
	40: 12	the waters in the hollow of his *h*,
	41: 13	who takes hold of your right *h*
	44: 5	still another will write on his *h*,
	48: 13	My own *h* laid the foundations
	64: 8	we are all the work of your *h*.
La	3: 3	he has turned his *h* against me
Da	10: 10	*h* touched me and set me trembling
Jnh	4: 11	people who cannot tell their right *h*
Hab	3: 4	rays flashed from his *h*,
Mt	5: 30	if your right *h* causes you to sin,
	6: 3	know what your right *h* is doing,
	12: 10	a man with a shrivelled *h* was there.
	18: 8	If your *h* or your foot causes you
	22: 44	"Sit at my right *h*
	26: 64	at the right *h* of the Mighty One
Mk	3: 1	a man with a shrivelled *h* was there.
	9: 43	If your *h* causes you to sin, cut it off
	12: 36	"Sit at my right *h*
	16: 19	and he sat at the right *h* of God.
Lk	6: 6	there whose right *h* was shrivelled.
	20: 42	"Sit at my right *h*
	22: 69	at the right *h* of the mighty God."
Jn	10: 28	one can snatch them out of my *h*.
	20: 27	Reach out your *h* and put it
Ac	7: 55	Jesus standing at the right *h* of God
1Co	12: 15	I am not a *h*, I do not belong
Heb	1: 13	"Sit at my right *h*
Rev	13: 16	to receive a mark on his right *h*

HANDED (HAND)

Da	7: 25	The saints will be *h* over to him
1Ti	1: 20	whom I have *h* over to Satan

HANDFUL (HAND)

Ecc	4: 6	Better one *h* with tranquillity

HANDLE (HANDLES)

Col 2:21 "Do not *h*! Do not taste! Do not

HANDLES (HANDLE)

2Ti 2:15 who correctly *h* the word of truth.

HANDS (HAND)

Ge 27:22 but the *h* are the *h* of Esau."
Ex 17:11 As long as Moses held up his *h*,
     29:10 his sons shall lay their *h* on its head
Dt 6:8 Tie them as symbols on your *h*
Jdg 7:6 lapped with their *h* to their mouths.
2Ki 11:12 and the people clapped their *h*
2Ch 6:4 who with his *h* has fulfilled what he
Ps 22:16 they have pierced my *h*
     24:4 He who has clean *h* and a pure
     31:5 Into your *h* I commit my spirit;
     31:15 My times are in your *h*;
     47:1 Clap your *h*, all you nations;
     63:4 and in your name I will lift up my *h*
Pr 10:4 Lazy *h* make a man poor,
     21:25 because his *h* refuse to work.
     31:13 and works with eager *h*.
     31:20 and extends her *h* to the needy.
Ecc 10:18 if his *h* are idle, the house leaks.
Isa 35:3 Strengthen the feeble *h*,
     49:16 you on the palms of my *h*;
     55:12 will clap their *h*.
     65:2 All day long I have held out my *h*
La 3:41 Let us lift up our hearts and our *h*
Lk 23:46 into your *h* I commit my spirit."
Ac 6:6 who prayed and laid their *h*
     8:18 at the laying on of the apostles' *h*,
     13:3 they placed their *h* on them
     19:6 When Paul placed his *h* on them,
     28:8 placed his *h* on him and healed him
1Th 4:11 and to work with your *h*,
1Ti 2:8 to lift up holy *h* in prayer,
     4:14 body of elders laid their *h* on you.
     5:22 hasty in the laying on of *h*,
2Ti 1:6 you through the laying on of my *h*.
Heb 6:2 the laying on of *h*, the resurrection

HANDSOME*

Ge 39:6 Now Joseph was well-built and *h*,
1Sa 16:12 a fine appearance and *h* features.
     17:42 ruddy and *h*, and he despised him.
2Sa 14:25 praised for his *h* appearance
1Ki 1:6 also very *h* and was born next
SS 1:16 How *h* you are, my lover!
Eze 23:6 all of them *h* young men,
     23:12 horsemen, all *h* young men.
     23:23 with them, *h* young men,
Da 1:4 without any physical defect, *h*,
Zec 11:13 the *h* price at which they priced me

HANG (HANGED HANGING HUNG)

Mt 22:40 and the Prophets *h* on these two

HANGED (HANG)

Mt 27:5 Then he went away and *h* himself.

HANGING (HANG)

Ac 10:39 They killed him by *h* him on a tree,

HANNAH*

Wife of Elkanah, mother of Samuel (1Sa 1).
Prayer at dedication of Samuel (1Sa 2:1-10).
Blessed (1Sa 2:18-21).

HAPPIER (HAPPY)

Mt 18:13 he is *h* about that one sheep
1Co 7:40 she is *h* if she stays as she is—

HAPPINESS* (HAPPY)

Dt 24:5 bring *h* to the wife he has married.
Est 8:16 For the Jews it was a time of *h*
Job 7:7 my eyes will never see *h* again.
Ecc 2:26 gives wisdom, knowledge and *h*,
Mt 25:21 Come and share your master's *h*!'
     25:23 Come and share your master's *h*!'

HAPPY* (HAPPIER HAPPINESS)

Ge 30:13 The women will call me *h*."
     30:13 Then Leah said, "How *h* I am!
1Ki 4:20 they drank and they were *h*.
     10:8 How *h* your men must be!
     10:8 men must be! How *h* your officials,
2Ch 9:7 How *h* your men must be!
     9:7 men must be! How *h* your officials,
Est 5:9 Haman went out that day *h*
     5:14 the king to the dinner and be *h*."
Ps 10:6 I'll always be *h* and never have
     68:3 may they be *h* and joyful.
     113:9 as a *h* mother of children.
     137:8 *h* is he who repays you
Pr 15:13 A *h* heart makes the face cheerful,
Ecc 3:12 better for men than to be *h*
     5:19 to accept his lot and be *h*
     7:14 When times are good, be *h*;
     11:9 Be *h*, young man, while you are
Jnh 4:6 Jonah was very *h* about the vine.
Zec 8:19 and glad occasions and *h* festivals
1Co 7:30 those who are *h*, as if they were not
2Co 7:9 yet now I am *h*, not because you
     7:13 delighted to see how *h* Titus was,
Jas 5:13 Is anyone *h*? Let him sing songs

HARD (HARDEN HARDENED HARDENING
HARDENS HARDER HARDSHIP HARDSHIPS)

Ge 18:14 Is anything too *h* for the LORD?
1Ki 10:1 came to test him with *h* questions.
Pr 14:23 All *h* work brings a profit,
Jer 32:17 Nothing is too *h* for you.
Zec 7:12 They made their hearts as *h* as flint
Mt 19:23 it is *h* for a rich man
Mk 10:5 your hearts were *h* that Moses
Jn 6:60 disciples said, "This is a *h* teaching.
Ac 20:35 of *h* work we must help the weak,
     26:14 It is *h* for you to kick
Ro 16:12 woman who has worked very *h*
1Co 4:12 We work *h* with our own hands.
2Co 6:5 imprisonments and riots; in *h* work
1Th 5:12 to respect those who work *h*
Rev 2:2 your *h* work and your

HARD-HEARTED* (HEART)

Dt 15:7 do not be *h* or tight-fisted

HARDEN (HARD)

Ex 4:21 I will *h* his heart so that he will not
Ps 95:8 do not *h* your hearts as you did
Ro 9:18 he hardens whom he wants to *h*.
Heb 3:8 do not *h* your hearts

HARDENED (HARD)

Ex 10:20 But the LORD *h* Pharaoh's heart,

HARDENING* (HARD)

Ro 11:25 Israel has experienced a *h* in part

Eph   4:18 in them due to the *h* of their hearts.

HARDENS* (HARD)

Pr   28:14 he who *h* his heart falls into trouble
Ro   9:18 and he *h* whom he wants to harden.

HARDER (HARD)

1Co   15:10 No, I worked *h* than all of them—
2Co   11:23 I have worked much *h*, been

HARDSHIP (HARD)

Ro   8:35 Shall trouble or *h* or persecution
2Ti   2: 3 Endure *h* with us like a good
        4: 5 endure *h*, do the work
Heb   12: 7 Endure *h* as discipline; God is

HARDSHIPS (HARD)

Ac   14:22 go through many *h* to enter
2Co   6: 4 in troubles, *h* and distresses;
       12:10 in insults, in *h*, in persecutions,
Rev   2: 3 and have endured *h* for my name,

HARLOT see PROSTITUTE

HARM (HARMS)

1Ch   16:22 do my prophets no *h*."
Ps   105:15 do my prophets no *h*."
      121: 6 the sun will not *h* you by day,
Pr   3:29 not plot *h* against your neighbour,
      12:21 No *h* befalls the righteous,
      31:12 She brings him good, not *h*,
Jer   10: 5 they can do no *h*
      29:11 to prosper you and not to *h* you,
Ro   13:10 Love does no *h* to its neighbour.
1Co   11:17 for your meetings do more *h*
1Jn   5:18 the evil one cannot *h* him.

HARMONY*

Zec   6:13 there will be *h* between the two.'
Ro   12:16 Live in *h* with one another.
2Co   6:15 What *h* is there between Christ
1Pe   3: 8 live in *h* with one another;

HARMS* (HARM)

Pr   8:36 whoever fails to find me *h* himself;

HARP (HARPS)

Ge   4:21 the father of all who play the *h*
1Sa   16:23 David would take his *h* and play.
Ps   33: 2 Praise the LORD with the *h*;
      98: 5 with the *h* and the sound of singing
     150: 3 praise him with the *h* and lyre,
Rev   5: 8 Each one had a *h* and they were

HARPS (HARP)

Ps   137: 2 we hung our *h*,

HARSH

Pr   15: 1 but a *h* word stirs up anger.
Col   2:23 and their *h* treatment of the body,
        3:19 and do not be *h* with them.
1Pe   2: 8 but also to those who are *h*.
Jude   :15 of all the *h* words ungodly sinners

HARVEST (HARVESTERS)

Ge   8:22 seedtime and *h*,
Ex   23:16 the Feast of *H* with the firstfruits
Dt   16:15 God will bless you in all your *h*
Pr   10: 5 during *h* is a disgraceful son.

Jer   8:20 "The *h* is past,
Joel   3:13 for the *h* is ripe.
Mt   9:37 *h* is plentiful but the workers are
Lk   10: 2 He told them, "The *h* is plentiful,
Jn   4:35 at the fields! They are ripe for *h*.
1Co   9:11 if we reap a material *h* from you?
2Co   9:10 the *h* of your righteousness.
Gal   6: 9 at the proper time we will reap a *h*
Heb   12:11 it produces a *h* of righteousness
Jas   3:18 in peace raise a *h* of righteousness.
Rev   14:15 for the *h* of the earth is ripe."

HARVESTERS (HARVEST)

Ru   2: 3 to glean in the fields behind the *h*.

HASTE (HASTEN HASTY)

Ex   12:11 it in *h*; it is the LORD's Passover.
Pr   21: 5 as surely as *h* leads to poverty.
      29:20 Do you see a man who speaks in *h*?

HASTEN (HASTE)

Ps   70: 1 *H*, O God, to save me;
     119:60 I will *h* and not delay

HASTY* (HASTE)

Pr   19: 2 nor to be *h* and miss the way.
Ecc   5: 2 do not be *h* in your heart
1Ti   5:22 Do not be *h* in the laying

**HATE (GOD-HATERS HATED HATES
HATING HATRED)**

Lev   19:17 "'Do not *h* your brother
Ps   5: 5 you *h* all who do wrong.
      36: 2 too much to detect or *h* his sin.
      45: 7 righteousness and *h* wickedness;
      97:10 those who love the LORD *h* evil,
     119:104 therefore I *h* every wrong path.
     119:163 I *h* and abhor falsehood
     139:21 Do I not *h* those who *h* you,
Pr   8:13 To fear the LORD is to *h* evil;
       9: 8 rebuke a mocker or he will *h* you;
      13: 5 The righteous *h* what is false,
      25:17 too much of you, and he will *h* you.
      29:10 Bloodthirsty men *h* a man
Ecc   3: 8 a time to love and a time to *h*,
Isa   61: 8 I *h* robbery and iniquity.
Eze   35: 6 Since you did not *h* bloodshed,
Am   5:15 *H* evil, love good;
Mal   2:16 "I *h* divorce," says the LORD God
Mt   5:43 your neighbour and *h* your enemy.'
      10:22 All men will *h* you because of me,
Lk   6:22 Blessed are you when men *h* you,
       6:27 do good to those who *h* you,
      14:26 does not *h* his father and mother,
Ro   12: 9 *H* what is evil; cling to what is good

HATED (HATE)

Mal   1: 3 loved Jacob, but Esau I have *h*,
Jn   15:18 keep in mind that it *h* me first.
Ro   9:13 "Jacob I loved, but Esau I *h*."
Eph   5:29 no-one ever *h* his own body,
Heb   1: 9 righteousness and *h* wickedness;

HATES (HATE)

Pr   6:16 There are six things the LORD *h*,
      13:24 He who spares the rod *h* his son,
      15:27 but he who *h* bribes will live.
      26:28 A lying tongue *h* those it hurts,
Jn   3:20 Everyone who does evil *h* the light,
      12:25 while the man who *h* his life

HATING

1Jn 2: 9 *h* his brother is still in the darkness.
4: 20 "I love God," yet *h* his brother,

HATING (HATE)

Jude : 23 *h* even the clothing stained

HATRED (HATE)

Pr 10: 12 *H* stirs up dissension,
15: 17 than a fattened calf with *h*.
Jas 4: 4 with the world is *h* towards God?

HAUGHTY

Pr 6: 17 detestable to him: / *h* eyes,
16: 18 a *h* spirit before a fall.

HAVEN

Ps 107: 30 he guided them to their desired *h*.

HAY

1Co 3: 12 costly stones, wood, *h* or straw,

HEAD (HEADS HOTHEADED)

Ge 3: 15 he will crush your *h*,
Nu 6: 5 no razor may be used on his *h*.
Jdg 16: 17 If my *h* were shaved, my strength
1Sa 9: 2 a *h* taller than any of the others.
2Sa 18: 9 Absalom's *h* got caught in the tree.
Ps 23: 5 You anoint my *h* with oil;
133: 2 is like precious oil poured on the *h*,
Pr 10: 6 Blessings crown the *h*
25: 22 will heap burning coals on his *h*,
Isa 59: 17 and the helmet of salvation on his *h*
Eze 33: 4 his blood will be on his own *h*.
Mt 8: 20 of Man has nowhere to lay his *h*."
Jn 19: 2 crown of thorns and put it on his *h*.
Ro 12: 20 will heap burning coals on his *h*."
1Co 11: 3 and the *h* of Christ is God.
11: 5 her *h* uncovered dishonours her *h*—
12: 21 And the *h* cannot say to the feet,
Eph 1: 22 him to be *h* over everything
5: 23 For the husband is the *h* of the wife
Col 1: 18 And he is the *h* of the body,
2Ti 4: 5 keep your *h* in all situations,
Rev 14: 14 with a crown of gold on his *h*
19: 12 and on his *h* are many crowns.

HEADS (HEAD)

Lev 26: 13 you to walk with *h* held high.
Ps 22: 7 they hurl insults, shaking their *h*:
24: 7 Lift up your *h*, O you gates;
Isa 35: 10 everlasting joy will crown their *h*.
51: 11 everlasting joy will crown their *h*.
Mt 27: 39 shaking their *h* and saying,
Lk 21: 28 stand up and lift up your *h*,
Ac 18: 6 "Your blood be on your own *h*!
Rev 4: 4 and had crowns of gold on their *h*.

HEAL* (HEALED HEALING HEALS)

Nu 12: 13 please *h* her!" The LORD replied
Dt 32: 39 I have wounded and I will *h*,
2Ki 20: 5 and seen your tears; I will *h* you.
20: 8 the sign that the LORD will *h* me
2Ch 7: 14 their sin and will *h* their land.
Job 5: 18 he injures, but his hands also *h*.
Ps 6: 2 *h* me, for my bones are in agony.
41: 4 *h* me, for I have sinned against you
Ecc 3: 3 a time to kill and a time to *h*,
Isa 19: 22 he will strike them and *h* them.
19: 22 respond to their pleas and *h* them.
57: 18 seen his ways, but I will *h* him;

Isa 57: 19 "And I will *h* them."
Jer 17: 14 *H* me, O LORD, and I will be
30: 17 and *h* your wounds,'
33: 6 I will *h* my people and will let them
La 2: 13 Who can *h* you?
Hos 5: 13 not able to *h* your sores.
6: 1 but he will *h* us;
7: 1 whenever I would *h* Israel,
14: 4 "I will *h* their waywardness
Na 3: 19 Nothing can *h* your wound;
Zec 11: 16 or seek the young, or *h* the injured,
Mt 8: 7 said to him, "I will go and *h* him."
10: 1 to *h* every disease and sickness.
10: 8 *H* the sick, raise the dead,
12: 10 "Is it lawful to *h* on the Sabbath?"
13: 15 and turn, and I would *h* them.'
17: 16 but they could not *h* him."
Mk 3: 2 if he would *h* him on the Sabbath.
6: 5 on a few sick people and *h* them.
Lk 4: 23 to me: 'Physician, *h* yourself!
5: 17 present for him to *h* the sick.
6: 7 to see if he would *h* on the Sabbath.
7: 3 him to come and *h* his servant,
8: 43 years, but no-one could *h* her.
9: 2 kingdom of God and to *h* the sick.
10: 9 *H* the sick who are there
13: 32 and *h* people today and tomorrow,
14: 3 "Is it lawful to *h* on the Sabbath
Jn 4: 47 begged him to come and *h* his son,
12: 40 nor turn—and I would *h* them."
Ac 4: 30 Stretch out your hand to *h*
28: 27 and turn and I would *h* them.'

HEALED* (HEAL)

Ge 20: 17 to God, and God *h* Abimelech,
Ex 21: 19 and see that he is completely *h*.
Lev 13: 37 hair has grown in it, the itch is *h*.
14: 3 If the person has been *h*
Jos 5: 8 were in camp until they were *h*.
1Sa 3: 9 you will be *h*, and you will know
2Ki 2: 21 LORD says: "I have *h* this water.
2Ch 30: 20 heard Hezekiah and *h* the people.
Ps 30: 2 and you *h* me.
107: 20 He sent forth his word and *h* them;
Isa 6: 10 and turn and be *h*."
53: 5 and by his wounds we are *h*.
Jer 14: 19 us so that we cannot be *h*?
17: 14 Heal me, O LORD, and I will be *h*;
51: 8 perhaps she can be *h*.
51: 9 but she cannot be *h*;
51: 9 "'We would have *h* Babylon,
Eze 34: 4 the weak or *h* the sick
Hos 11: 3 it was I who *h* them.
Mt 4: 24 and the paralytics, and he *h* them.
8: 8 the word, and my servant will be *h*.
8: 13 his servant was *h* at that very hour.
8: 16 with a word and *h* all the sick.
9: 21 If I only touch his cloak, I will be *h*
9: 22 he said, "your faith has *h* you."
9: 22 woman was *h* from that moment.
12: 15 him, and he *h* all their sick,
12: 22 Jesus *h* him, so that he could both
14: 14 on them and *h* their sick.
14: 36 and all who touched him were *h*.
15: 28 And her daughter was *h*
15: 30 laid them at his feet; and he *h* them
17: 18 and he was *h* from that moment.
19: 2 followed him, and he *h* them there.
21: 14 to him at the temple, and he *h* them
Mk 1: 34 and Jesus *h* many who had various

Mk	3: 10	For he had *h* many, so that those
	5: 23	hands on her so that she will be *h*
	5: 28	If I just touch his clothes, I will be *h*
	5: 34	"Daughter, your faith has *h* you.
	6: 13	people with oil and *h* them.
	6: 56	and all who touched him were *h*.
	10: 52	said Jesus, "your faith has *h* you."
Lk	4: 40	hands on each one, he *h* them.
	5: 15	and to be *h* of their sicknesses.
	6: 18	and to be *h* of their diseases.
	7: 7	the word, and my servant will be *h*.
	8: 47	and how she had been instantly *h*.
	8: 48	"Daughter, your faith has *h* you.
	8: 50	just believe, and she will be *h*."
	9: 11	and *h* those who needed healing.
	9: 42	*h* the boy and gave him back
	13: 14	Jesus had *h* on the Sabbath,
	13: 14	So come and be *h* on those days,
	14: 4	he *h* him and sent him away.
	17: 15	when he saw he was *h*, came back,
	18: 42	your sight; your faith has *h* you."
	22: 51	touched the man's ear and *h* him.
Jn	5: 10	said to the man who had been *h*,
	5: 13	man who was *h* had no idea who it
Ac	4: 9	and are asked how he was *h*,
	4: 10	stands before you *h*.
	4: 14	who had been *h* standing there
	4: 22	man who was miraculously *h* was
	5: 16	evil spirits, and all of them were *h*.
	8: 7	paralytics and cripples were *h*.
	14: 9	saw that he had faith to be *h*
	28: 8	placed his hands on him and *h* him.
Heb	12: 13	may not be disabled, but rather *h*.
Jas	5: 16	for each other so that you may be *h*
1Pe	2: 24	by his wounds you have been *h*.
Rev	13: 3	but the fatal wound had been *h*.
	13: 12	whose fatal wound had been *h*.

HEALING* (HEAL)

2Ch	28: 15	food and drink, and *h* balm.
Pr	12: 18	but the tongue of the wise brings *h*.
	13: 17	but a trustworthy envoy brings *h*.
	15: 4	The tongue that brings *h* is a tree
	16: 24	sweet to the soul and *h* to the bones
Isa	58: 8	and your *h* will quickly appear;
Jer	8: 15	for a time of *h*
	8: 22	Why then is there no *h*
	14: 19	for a time of *h*
	30: 12	your injury beyond *h*.
	30: 13	no *h* for you.
	33: 6	I will bring health and *h* to it;
	46: 11	there is no *h* for you.
Eze	30: 21	It has not been bound up for *h*
	47: 12	for food and their leaves for *h*."
Mal	4: 2	rise with *h* in its wings.
Mt	4: 23	and *h* every disease and sickness
	9: 35	and *h* every disease and sickness.
Lk	6: 19	coming from him and *h* them all.
	9: 6	gospel and *h* people everywhere.
	9: 11	and healed those who needed *h*.
Jn	7: 23	angry with me for *h* the whole man
Ac	3: 16	him that has given this complete *h*
	10: 38	*h* all who were under the power
1Co	12: 9	to another gifts of *h*
	12: 28	also those having gifts of *h*,
	12: 30	Do all have gifts of *h*? Do all speak
Rev	22: 2	are for the *h* of the nations.

HEALS* (HEAL)

Ex	15: 26	for I am the LORD who *h* you."

Lev	13: 18	a boil on his skin and it *h*,
Ps	103: 3	and *h* all my diseases;
	147: 3	He *h* the broken-hearted
Isa	30: 26	and *h* the wounds he inflicted.
Ac	9: 34	said to him, "Jesus Christ *h* you.

HEALTH* (HEALTHIER HEALTHY)

1Sa	25: 6	And good *h* to all that is yours!
	25: 6	Good *h* to you and your household
Ps	38: 3	of your wrath there is no *h*
	38: 7	there is no *h* in my body.
Pr	3: 8	This will bring *h* to your body
	4: 22	and *h* to a man's whole body.
	15: 30	and good news gives *h* to the bones
Isa	38: 16	You restored me to *h*
Jer	30: 17	But I will restore you to *h*
	33: 6	I will bring *h* and healing to it;
3Jn	: 2	I pray that you may enjoy good *h*

HEALTHIER* (HEALTH)

Da	1: 15	end of the ten days they looked *h*

HEALTHY* (HEALTH)

Ge	41: 5	Seven heads of grain, *h* and good,
	41: 7	of grain swallowed up the seven *h*,
Ps	73: 4	their bodies are *h* and strong.
Zec	11: 16	or heal the injured, or feed the *h*,
Mt	9: 12	"It is not the *h* who need a doctor,
Mk	2: 17	"It is not the *h* who need a doctor,
Lk	5: 31	"It is not the *h* who need a doctor,

HEAP

Pr	25: 22	you will *h* burning coals
Ro	12: 20	you will *h* burning coals

HEAR (HEARD HEARING HEARS)

Ex	15: 14	The nations will *h* and tremble;
	22: 27	I will *h*, for I am compassionate.
Nu	14: 13	Then the Egyptians will *h* about it!
Dt	1: 16	*H* the disputes between your
	4: 36	heaven he made you *h* his voice
	6: 4	*H*, O Israel: The LORD our God,
	19: 20	The rest of the people will *h* of this
	31: 13	must *h* it and learn
Jos	7: 9	of the country will *h* about this
1Ki	8: 30	*H* the supplication of your servant
2Ki	19: 16	O LORD, and *h*; open your eyes,
2Ch	7: 14	then will I *h* from heaven
Job	31: 35	("Oh, that I had someone to *h* me!
Ps	94: 9	he who implanted the ear not *h*?
	95: 7	Today, if you *h* his voice,
Ecc	7: 21	or you may *h* your servant cursing
Isa	21: 3	I am staggered by what I *h*,
	29: 18	that day the deaf will *h* the words
	39: 21	your ears will *h* a voice behind you,
	51: 7	*H* me, you who know what is right,
	59: 1	nor his ear too dull to *h*.
	65: 24	while they are still speaking I will *h*
Jer	5: 21	who have ears but do not *h*:
Eze	33: 7	so *h* the word I speak and give
	37: 4	'Dry bones, *h* the word
Mt	11: 5	the deaf *h*, the dead are raised,
	11: 15	He who has ears, let him *h*.
	13: 17	and to *h* what you *h* but did not *h* it
Mk	12: 29	answered Jesus, "is this: '*H*,
Lk	7: 22	the deaf *h*, the dead are raised
Jn	8: 47	reason you do not *h* is that you do
Ac	13: 7	he wanted to *h* the word of God.
	13: 44	gathered to *h* the word of the Lord.
	17: 32	"We want to *h* you again

Ro	2: 13	is not those who *h* the law who are
	10: 14	they *h* without someone preaching
2Ti	4: 3	what their itching ears want to *h*.
Heb	3: 7	"Today, if you *h* his voice,
Rev	1: 3	and blessed are those who *h* it

HEARD (HEAR)

Ex	2: 24	God *h* their groaning and he
Dt	4: 32	has anything like it ever been *h* of?
2Sa	7: 22	as we have *h* with our own ears.
Job	42: 5	My ears had *h* of you
Isa	40: 21	Have you not *h*?
	40: 28	Have you not *h*?
	66: 8	Who has ever *h* of such a thing?
Jer	18: 13	Who has ever *h* anything like this?
Da	10: 12	your words were *h*, and I have
	12: 8	I *h*, but I did not understand.
Hab	3: 16	I *h* and my heart pounded,
Mt	5: 21	"You have *h* that it was said
	5: 27	"You have *h* that it was said,
	5: 33	you have *h* that it was said
	5: 38	"You have *h* that it was said,
	5: 43	"You have *h* that it was said,
Lk	12: 3	in the dark will be *h* in the daylight,
Jn	8: 26	and what I have *h* from him I tell
Ac	2: 6	because each one *h* them speaking
1Co	2: 9	no ear has *h*,
2Co	12: 4	He *h* inexpressible things,
1Th	2: 13	word of God, which you *h* from us,
2Ti	1: 13	What you *h* from me, keep
Jas	1: 25	not forgetting what he has *h*,
Rev	22: 8	am the one who *h* and saw these

HEARING (HEAR)

Isa	6: 9	Be ever *h*, but never understanding
Mt	13: 14	will be ever *h* but never
Mk	4: 12	ever *h* but never understanding;
Ac	28: 26	will be ever *h* but never
Ro	10: 17	faith comes from *h* the message,
1Co	12: 17	where would the sense of *h* be?

HEARS (HEAR)

Jn	5: 24	whoever *h* my word and believes
1Jn	5: 14	according to his will, he *h* us.
Rev	3: 20	If anyone *h* my voice and opens

HEART (BROKEN-HEARTED
FAINT-HEARTED HARD-HEARTED HEART'S
HEARTACHE HEARTS KIND-HEARTED
SIMPLE-HEARTED STOUT-HEARTED
WHOLEHEARTED WHOLEHEARTEDLY)

Ge	6: 5	of his *h* was only evil all the time.
Ex	4: 21	But I will harden his *h*
	25: 2	each man whose *h* prompts him
	35: 21	and whose *h* moved him came
Lev	19: 17	Do not hate your brother in your *h*.
Dt	4: 9	or let them slip from your *h* as long
	4: 29	if you look for him with all your *h*
	6: 5	LORD your God with all your *h*
	10: 12	LORD your God with all your *h*
	11: 13	and to serve him with all your *h*
	13: 3	you love him with all your *h*
	15: 10	and do so without a grudging *h*;
	26: 16	observe them with all your *h*
	29: 18	you today whose *h* turns away
	30: 2	and obey him with all your *h*
	30: 6	you may love him with all your *h*
	30: 10	LORD your God with all your *h*
Jos	22: 5	and to serve him with all your *h*
	23: 14	You know with all your *h*

1Sa	10: 9	God changed Saul's *h*,
	12: 20	serve the LORD with all your *h*.
	12: 24	serve him faithfully with all your *h*;
	13: 14	sought out a man after his own *h*
	14: 7	I am with you *h* and soul."
	16: 7	but the LORD looks at the *h*."
	17: 32	"Let no-one lose *h* on account
1Ki	2: 4	faithfully before me with all their *h*
	3: 9	So give your servant a discerning *h*
	3: 12	give you a wise and discerning *h*,
	8: 48	back to you with all their *h*
	9: 3	and my *h* will always be there.
	9: 4	walk before me in integrity of *h*
	10: 24	the wisdom God had put in his *h*.
	11: 4	and his *h* was not fully devoted
	14: 8	and followed me with all his *h*,
	15: 14	Asa's *h* was fully committed
2Ki	22: 19	Because your *h* was responsive
	23: 3	with all his *h* and all his soul,
1Ch	28: 9	for the LORD searches every *h*
2Ch	6: 38	back to you with all their *h*
	7: 16	and my *h* will always be there.
	15: 12	of their fathers, with all their *h*
	15: 17	Asa's *h* was fully committed
	17: 6	His *h* was devoted to the ways
	22: 9	sought the LORD with all his *h*."
	34: 31	with all his *h* and all his soul,
	36: 13	stiff-necked and hardened his *h*
Ezr	1: 5	everyone whose *h* God had moved
Ne	4: 6	the people worked with all their *h*.
Job	19: 27	How my *h* yearns within me!
	22: 22	and lay up his words in your *h*.
	37: 1	"At this my *h* pounds
Ps	9: 1	you, O LORD, with all my *h*;
	14: 1	The fool says in his *h*,
	16: 9	Therefore my *h* is glad
	19: 14	and the meditation of my *h*
	20: 4	he give you the desire of your *h*
	24: 4	who has clean hands and a pure *h*,
	26: 2	examine my *h* and my mind;
	37: 4	will give you the desires of your *h*.
	37: 31	The law of his God is in his *h*;
	44: 21	since he knows the secrets of the *h*
	45: 1	My *h* is stirred by a noble theme
	51: 10	Create in me a pure *h*, O God,
	51: 17	a broken and contrite *h*,
	53: 1	The fool says in his *h*,
	66: 18	If I had cherished sin in my *h*,
	73: 1	to those who are pure in *h*.
	73: 26	My flesh and my *h* may fail,
	86: 11	give me an undivided *h*,
	90: 12	that we may gain a *h* of wisdom.
	97: 11	and joy on the upright in *h*.
	108: 1	My *h* is steadfast, O God;
	109: 22	and my *h* is wounded within me.
	111: 1	will extol the LORD with all my *h*
	112: 7	his *h* is steadfast, trusting
	112: 8	His *h* is secure, he will have no fear
	119: 2	and seek him with all their *h*.
	119: 10	I seek you with all my *h*;
	119: 11	I have hidden your word in my *h*
	119: 30	I have set my *h* on your laws.
	119: 32	for you have set my *h* free.
	119: 34	and obey it with all my *h*.
	119: 36	Turn my *h* towards your statutes
	119: 58	sought your face with all my *h*;
	119: 69	I keep your precepts with all my *h*.
	119: 111	they are the joy of my *h*.
	119: 112	My *h* is set on keeping your
	119: 145	I call with all my *h*; answer me,

Ps 125: 4 to those who are upright in *h.*
    138: 1 you, O Lord, with all my *h;*
    139: 23 Search me, O God, and know my *h*
Pr   2: 2 applying your *h* to understanding,
      3: 1 but keep my commands in your *h,*
      3: 3 write them on the tablet of your *h.*
      3: 5 Trust in the Lord with all your *h*
      4: 4 hold of my words with all your *h;*
      4: 21 keep them within your *h;*
      4: 23 Above all else, guard your *h,*
      6: 21 Bind them upon your *h* for ever;
      7: 3 write them on the tablet of your *h.*
     10: 8 The wise in *h* accept commands,
     13: 12 Hope deferred makes the *h* sick,
     14: 13 Even in laughter the *h* may ache,
     14: 30 A *h* at peace gives life to the body,
     15: 13 A happy *h* makes the face cheerful,
     15: 15 the cheerful *h* has a continual feast,
     15: 28 *h* of the righteous weighs its
     15: 30 A cheerful look brings joy to the *h,*
     16: 23 A wise man's *h* guides his mouth,
     17: 22 A cheerful *h* is good medicine,
     20: 9 can say, "I have kept my *h* pure;
     22: 11 He who loves a pure *h*
     22: 17 apply your *h* to what I teach,
     22: 18 when you keep them in your *h*
     23: 15 My son, if your *h* is wise,
     23: 19 and keep your *h* on the right path.
     23: 26 My son, give me your *h*
     24: 17 stumbles, do not let your *h* rejoice,
     27: 19 so a man's *h* reflects the man.
Ecc   5: 2 do not be hasty in your *h*
      8: 5 wise *h* will know the proper time
     11: 10 banish anxiety from your *h*
SS   3: 1 I looked for the one my *h* loves;
      4: 9 You have stolen my *h,* my sister,
      5: 2 I slept but my *h* was awake
      5: 4 my *h* began to pound for him.
      8: 6 Place me like a seal over your *h,*
Isa   6: 10 Make the *h* of this people calloused
     40: 11 and carries them close to his *h;*
     57: 15 and to revive the *h* of the contrite.
     66: 14 you see this, your *h* will rejoice
Jer   3: 15 give you shepherds after my own *h,*
      4: 14 wash the evil from your *h*
      9: 26 of Israel is uncircumcised in *h."*
     17: 9 The *h* is deceitful above all things
     20: 9 is in my *h* like a fire,
     24: 7 I will give them a *h* to know me,
     29: 13 when you seek me with all your *h.*
     32: 39 I will give them singleness of *h*
     32: 41 them in this land with all my *h*
     51: 46 Do not lose *h* or be afraid
Eze 11: 19 I will give them an undivided *h*
     18: 31 and get a new *h* and a new spirit.
     36: 26 I will give you a new *h*
     44: 7 foreigners uncircumcised in *h*
Da   7: 4 and the *h* of a man was given to it.
Joel 2: 12 "return to me with all your *h,*
      2: 13 Rend your *h*
Zep   3: 14 Be glad and rejoice with all your *h,*
Mt   5: 8 Blessed are the pure in *h,*
      5: 28 adultery with her in his *h.*
      6: 21 treasure is, there your *h* will be
     11: 29 for I am gentle and humble in *h,*
     12: 34 of the *h* the mouth speaks.
     13: 15 For this people's *h* has become
     15: 18 out of the mouth come from the *h,*
     15: 19 For out of the *h* come evil thoughts
     18: 35 forgive your brother from your *h."*

Mt   22: 37 the Lord your God with all your *h*
Mk   11: 23 and does not doubt in his *h*
     12: 30 the Lord your God with all your *h*
     12: 33 To love him with all your *h,*
Lk   2: 19 and pondered them in her *h.*
      2: 51 treasured all these things in her *h.*
      6: 45 out of the good stored up in his *h,*
      6: 45 overflow of his *h* his mouth speaks.
      8: 15 for those with a noble and good *h,*
     10: 27 the Lord your God with all your *h*
     12: 34 treasure is, there your *h* will be
Jn   12: 27 "Now my *h* is troubled,
Ac   1: 24 "Lord, you know everyone's *h.*
      2: 37 they were cut to the *h*
      4: 32 All the believers were one in *h*
      8: 21 your *h* is not right before God.
     15: 8 who knows the *h,* showed that he
     16: 14 The Lord opened her *h* to respond
     28: 27 For this people's *h* has become
Ro   1: 9 with my whole *h* in preaching
      2: 29 in circumcision of the *h,*
     10: 9 in your *h* that God raised him
     10: 10 is with your *h* that you believe
     15: 6 with one *h* and mouth you may
1Co 14: 25 the secrets of his *h* will be laid bare.
2Co   2: 4 anguish of *h* and with many tears,
      4: 1 this ministry, we do not lose *h.*
      4: 16 Therefore we do not lose *h.*
      9: 7 give what he has decided in his *h*
Eph   1: 18 eyes of your *h* may be enlightened
      5: 19 make music in your *h* to the Lord,
      6: 5 and with sincerity of *h,* just
      6: 6 doing the will of God from your *h.*
Php   1: 7 since I have you in my *h;* for
Col   2: 2 is that they may be encouraged in *h*
      3: 22 but with sincerity of *h*
      3: 23 work at it with all your *h,*
1Ti   1: 5 which comes from a pure *h*
      3: 1 If anyone sets his *h*
2Ti   2: 22 call on the Lord out of a pure *h.*
Phm   : 12 who is my very *h*—back to you.
       : 20 in the Lord; refresh my *h* in Christ.
Heb   4: 12 the thoughts and attitudes of the *h.*
1Pe   1: 22 one another deeply, from the *h.*

HEART'S* (HEART)

2Ch   1: 11 "Since this is your *h* desire
Jer 15: 16 they were my joy and my *h* delight,
Eze 24: 25 delight of their eyes, their *h* desire,
Ro   10: 1 my *h* desire and prayer to God

HEARTACHE* (HEART)

Pr   15: 13 but *h* crushes the spirit.

HEARTLESS*

La   4: 3 but my people have become *h*
Ro   1: 31 they are senseless, faithless, *h,*

HEARTS (HEART)

Lev 26: 41 their uncircumcised *h* are humbled
Dt   6: 6 are to be upon your *h.*
     10: 16 Circumcise your *h,* therefore,
     11: 18 Fix these words of mine in your *h*
     30: 6 your God will circumcise your *h*
Jos 11: 20 himself who hardened their *h*
     24: 23 and yield your *h* to the Lord,
1Sa   7: 3 to the Lord with all your *h,*
     10: 26 valiant men whose *h* God had
2Sa 15: 6 and so he stole the *h* of the men
1Ki   8: 39 for you alone know the *h* of all men

1Ki 8: 61 your *h* must be fully committed
18: 37 are turning their *h* back again."
1Ch 29: 18 and keep their *h* loyal to you.
2Ch 6: 30 (for you alone know the *h* of men),
11: 16 tribe of Israel who set their *h*
29: 31 all whose *h* were willing brought
Ps 7: 9 who searches minds and *h*,
33: 21 In him our *h* rejoice,
62: 8 pour out your *h* to him,
95: 8 do not harden your *h* as you did
Ecc 3: 11 also set eternity in the *h* of men;
Isa 26: 8 are the desire of our *h*.
29: 13 but their *h* are far from me.
35: 4 say to those with fearful *h*,
51: 7 people who have my law in your *h*:
63: 17 harden our *h* so we do not revere
65: 14 out of the joy of their *h*,
Jer 4: 4 circumcise your *h*,
12: 2 but far from their *h*.
17: 1 on the tablets of their *h*
31: 33 and write it on their *h*.
Mal 4: 6 He will turn the *h* of the fathers
Mt 15: 8 but their *h* are far from me.
Mk 6: 52 the loaves; their *h* were hardened.
7: 6 but their *h* are far from me.
7: 21 out of men's *h*, come evil thoughts,
Lk 1: 17 to turn the *h* of the fathers
16: 15 of men, but God knows your *h*.
24: 32 "Were not our *h* burning within us
Jn 5: 42 not have the love of God in your *h*.
14: 1 "Do not let your *h* be troubled
14: 27 Do not let your *h* be troubled
Ac 7: 51 with uncircumcised *h* and ears!
11: 23 true to the Lord with all their *h*.
15: 9 for he purified their *h* by faith.
28: 27 understand with their *h*
Ro 1: 21 and their foolish *h* were darkened.
2: 15 of the law are written on their *h*,
5: 5 love into our *h* by the Holy Spirit,
8: 27 who searches our *h* knows
1Co 4: 5 will expose the motives of men's *h*.
2Co 1: 22 put his Spirit in our *h* as a deposit,
3: 2 written in our *h*, known
3: 3 but on tablets of human *h*.
4: 6 shine in our *h* to give us the light
6: 11 and opened wide our *h* to you.
6: 13 to my children—open wide your *h*
7: 2 Make room for us in your *h*.
Gal 4: 6 the Spirit of his Son into our *h*,
Eph 3: 17 dwell in your *h* through faith.
Php 4: 7 will guard your *h* and your minds
Col 3: 1 set your *h* on things above,
3: 15 the peace of Christ rule in your *h*,
3: 16 with gratitude in your *h* to God.
1Th 2: 4 men but God, who tests our *h*.
3: 13 May he strengthen your *h*
2Th 2: 17 encourage your *h* and strengthen
Phm : 7 have refreshed the *h* of the saints.
Heb 3: 8 do not harden their *h*.
8: 10 and write them on their *h*.
10: 16 I will put my laws in their *h*,
10: 22 having our *h* sprinkled
Jas 4: 8 purify your *h*, you double-minded.
2Pe 1: 19 the morning star rises in your *h*.
1Jn 3: 20 For God is greater than our *h*,

HEAT

Ps 19: 6 nothing is hidden from its *h*.
2Pe 3: 12 and the elements will melt in the *h*.

HEATHEN see GENTILES, NATIONS

HEAVEN (HEAVENLY HEAVENS HEAVENWARDS)

Ge 14: 19 Creator of *h* and earth.
28: 12 with its top reaching to *h*,
Ex 16: 4 rain down bread from *h* for you.
20: 22 that I have spoken to you from *h*:
Dt 26: 15 from *h*, your holy dwelling-place,
30: 12 "Who will ascend into *h* to get it
1Ki 8: 27 the highest *h*, cannot contain you.
8: 30 Hear from *h*, your dwelling-place,
22: 19 the host of *h* standing round him
2Ki 2: 1 up to *h* in a whirlwind,
19: 15 You have made *h* and earth.
2Ch 7: 14 then will I hear from *h*
Isa 14: 12 How you have fallen from *h*,
66: 1 "*H* is my throne
Da 7: 13 coming with the clouds of *h*.
Mt 3: 2 for the kingdom of *h* is near."
3: 16 At that moment *h* was opened,
4: 17 for the kingdom of *h* is near."
5: 12 because great is your reward in *h*,
5: 19 great in the kingdom of *h*.
6: 9 "'Our Father in *h*,
6: 10 done on earth as it is in *h*.
6: 20 up for yourselves treasures in *h*,
7: 21 Lord,' will enter the kingdom of *h*,
16: 19 bind on earth will be bound in *h*,
18: 3 will never enter the kingdom of *h*.
18: 18 bind on earth will be bound in *h*,
19: 14 the kingdom of *h* belongs to such
19: 21 and you will have treasure in *h*.
19: 23 man to enter the kingdom of *h*.
23: 13 the kingdom of *h* in men's faces.
24: 35 *H* and earth will pass away,
26: 64 and coming on the clouds of *h*."
28: 18 "All authority in *h*
Mk 1: 10 he saw *h* being torn open
10: 21 and you will have treasure in *h*.
13: 31 *H* and earth will pass away,
14: 62 and coming on the clouds of *h*."
16: 19 he was taken up into *h*
Lk 3: 21 *h* was opened and the Holy Spirit
10: 18 saw Satan fall like lightning from *h*.
10: 20 that your names are written in *h*."
12: 33 in *h* that will not be exhausted,
15: 7 in *h* over one sinner who repents
18: 22 and you will have treasure in *h*.
21: 33 *H* and earth will pass away,
24: 51 left them and was taken up into *h*.
Jn 3: 13 No-one has ever gone into *h*
6: 38 down from *h* not to do my will
12: 28 Then a voice came from *h*,
Ac 1: 11 has been taken from you into *h*,
7: 49 the prophet says: "'*H* is my
7: 55 looked up to *h* and saw the glory
9: 3 a light from *h* flashed around him.
26: 19 disobedient to the vision from *h*.
Ro 10: 6 'Who will ascend into *h*?'" (that is,
1Co 15: 47 the earth, the second man from *h*.
2Co 5: 1 an eternal house in *h*, not built
12: 2 ago was caught up to the third *h*.
Eph 1: 10 to bring all things in *h*
Php 2: 10 *h* and on earth and under the earth,
3: 20 But our citizenship is in *h*.
Col 1: 16 things in *h* and on earth, visible
4: 1 that you also have a Master in *h*.
1Th 1: 10 and to wait for his Son from *h*,
4: 16 himself will come down from *h*,
Heb 1: 3 hand of the Majesty in *h*.
8: 5 and shadow of what is in *h*.

Heb   9: 24 he entered *h* itself, now to appear
        12: 23 whose names are written in *h*.
1Pe   1: 4 spoil or fade—kept in *h* for you,
         3: 22 who has gone into *h* and is
2Pe   3: 13 we are looking forward to a new *h*
Rev   5: 13 Then I heard every creature in *h*
        11: 19 God's temple in *h* was opened,
        12: 7 And there was war in *h*.
        15: 5 this I looked and in *h* the temple,
        19: 1 of a great multitude in *h* shouting:
        19: 11 I saw *h* standing open and there
        21: 1 Then I saw a new *h* and a new earth
        21: 10 coming down out of *h* from God.

HEAVENLY (HEAVEN)

Ps   8: 5 him a little lower than the *h* beings
2Co   5: 2 to be clothed with our *h* dwelling,
Eph   1: 3 in the *h* realms with every spiritual
        1: 20 at his right hand in the *h* realms,
2Ti   4: 18 bring me safely to his *h* kingdom.
Heb   12: 22 to the *h* Jerusalem, the city

HEAVENS (HEAVEN)

Ge   1: 1 In the beginning God created the *h*
        11: 4 with a tower that reaches to the *h*,
Dt   33: 26 who rides on the *h* to help you
1Ki   8: 27 The *h*, even the highest heaven,
2Ch   2: 6 since the *h*, even the highest
Ezr   9: 6 and our guilt has reached to the *h*.
Ne   9: 6 You made the *h*, even the highest
Job   11: 8 They are higher than the *h*—
        38: 33 Do you know the laws of the *h*?
Ps   8: 3 When I consider your *h*,
        19: 1 The *h* declare the glory of God;
        33: 6 of the LORD were the *h* made,
        57: 5 Be exalted, O God, above the *h*;
       102: 25 the *h* are the work of your hands.
       103: 11 as high as the *h* are above the earth,
       108: 4 is your love, higher than the *h*,
       115: 16 The highest *h* belong to the LORD
       119: 89 it stands firm in the *h*.
       135: 6 in the *h* and on the earth,
       139: 8 If I go up to the *h*, you are there;
       148: 1 Praise the LORD from the *h*,
Isa   40: 26 Lift your eyes and look to the *h*:
        45: 8 "You *h* above, rain
        51: 6 Lift up your eyes to the *h*,
        55: 9 "As the *h* are higher than the earth,
        65: 17 new *h* and a new earth.
Jer   31: 37 if the *h* above can be measured
        32: 17 you have made the *h* and the earth
Eze   1: 1 *h* were opened and I saw visions
Da   12: 3 shine like the brightness of the *h*,
Joel   2: 30 I will show wonders in the *h*
Mt   24: 31 from one end of the *h* to the other.
Mk   13: 27 of the earth to the ends of the *h*.
Eph   4: 10 who ascended higher than all the *h*,
Heb   4: 14 priest who has gone through the *h*,
        7: 26 from sinners, exalted above the *h*.
2Pe   3: 5 ago by God's word the *h* existed
        3: 10 The *h* will disappear with a roar;

HEAVENWARDS (HEAVEN)

Php   3: 14 for which God has called me *h*

HEAVIER (HEAVY)

Pr   27: 3 provocation by a fool is *h* than both

HEAVY (HEAVIER)

1Ki   12: 4 and the *h* yoke he put on us,

Ecc   1: 13 What a *h* burden God has laid
Isa   47: 6 you laid a very *h* yoke.
Mt   23: 4 They tie up *h* loads and put them

HEBREW (HEBREWS)

Ge   14: 13 and reported this to Abram the *H*.
2Ki   18: 26 speak to us in *H* in the hearing
Php   3: 5 tribe of Benjamin, a *H* of Hebrews;

HEBREWS (HEBREW)

Ex   9: 1 of the *H*, says: "Let my people go,
2Co   11: 22 Are they *H*? So am I.

HEBRON

Ge   13: 18 near the great trees of Mamre at *H*,
        23: 2 died at Kiriath Arba (that is, *H*)
Jos   14: 13 and gave him *H* as his inheritance.
        20: 7 *H*) in the hill country of Judah.
        21: 13 the priest they gave *H* (a city
2Sa   2: 11 king in *H* over the house

HEDGE

Job   1: 10 "Have you not put a *h* around him

HEED (HEEDS)

Ecc   7: 5 It is better to *h* a wise man's rebuke

HEEDS (HEED)

Pr   13: 1 wise son *h* his father's instruction,
        13: 18 whoever *h* correction is honoured.
        15: 5 whoever *h* correction shows
        15: 32 whoever *h* correction gains

HEEL

Ge   3: 15 and you will strike his *h*."

HEIR (INHERIT)

Gal   4: 7 God has made you also an *h*.
Heb   1: 2 whom he appointed *h* of all things,

HEIRS (INHERIT)

Ro   8: 17 then we are *h*—*h* of God
Gal   3: 29 and *h* according to the promise.
Eph   3: 6 gospel the Gentiles are *h* together
1Pe   3: 7 as *h* with you of the gracious gift

HELD (HOLD)

Ex   17: 11 As long as Moses *h* up his hands,
Dt   4: 4 but all of you who *h* fast
2Ki   18: 6 He *h* fast to the LORD
SS   3: 4 I *h* him and would not let him go
Isa   65: 2 All day long I have *h* out my hands
Ro   10: 21 day long I have *h* out my hands
Col   2: 19 and *h* together by its ligaments

HELL*

Mt   5: 22 will be in danger of the fire of *h*.
        5: 29 body to be thrown into *h*.
        5: 30 for your whole body to go into *h*.
        10: 28 destroy both soul and body in *h*.
        18: 9 and be thrown into the fire of *h*.
        23: 15 as much a son of *h* as you are.
        23: 33 you escape being condemned to *h*?
Mk   9: 43 than with two hands to go into *h*,
        9: 45 have two feet and be thrown into *h*.
        9: 47 two eyes and be thrown into *h*,
Lk   12: 5 has power to throw you into *h*.
        16: 23 In *h*, where he was in torment,
Jas   3: 6 and is itself set on fire by *h*.
2Pe   2: 4 but sent them to *h*, putting them

HELMET

Isa 59: 17 and the *h* of salvation on his head;
Eph 6: 17 Take the *h* of salvation
1Th 5: 8 and the hope of salvation as a *h*.

HELP (HELPED HELPER HELPFUL HELPING HELPLESS HELPS)

Ex   23: 5 leave it there; be sure you *h* him
Lev 25: 35 *h* him as you would an alien
Dt   33: 26 who rides on the heavens to *h* you
2Ch 16: 12 even in his illness he did not seek *h*
Ps   18: 6 I cried to my God for *h*.
     30: 2 my God, I called to you for *h*
     33: 20 he is our *h* and our shield.
     46: 1 an ever-present *h* in trouble.
     72: 12 the afflicted who have no-one to *h*.
     79: 9 *H* us, O God our Saviour,
    108: 12 for the *h* of man is worthless.
    115: 9 he is their *h* and shield.
    121: 1 where does my *h* come from?
Ecc   4: 10 his friend can *h* him up.
Isa 41: 10 I will strengthen you and *h* you;
Jnh   2: 2 depths of the grave I called for *h*,
Mk   9: 24 *h* me overcome my unbelief!"
Lk   11: 46 will not lift one finger to *h* them.
Ac   16: 9 Come over to Macedonia and *h* us
     18: 27 he was a great *h* to those who
     20: 35 of hard work we must *h* the weak,
     26: 22 I have had God's *h* to this very day,
1Co 12: 28 those able to *h* others, those
2Co   9: 2 For I know your eagerness to *h*,
1Ti   5: 16 she should *h* them and not let

HELPED (HELP)

1Sa   7: 12 "Thus far has the LORD *h* us."

HELPER (HELP)

Ge   2: 18 I will make a *h* suitable for him."
Ps   10: 14 you are the *h* of the fatherless.
Heb 13: 6 Lord is my *h*; I will not be afraid.

HELPFUL (HELP)

Eph   4: 29 only what is *h* for building others

HELPING (HELP)

Ac   9: 36 always doing good and *h* the poor.
1Ti   5: 10 *h* those in trouble and devoting

HELPLESS (HELP)

Ps   10: 12 Do not forget the *h*.
Mt   9: 36 because they were harassed and *h*,

HELPS (HELP)

Ro   8: 26 the Spirit *h* us in our weakness.

HEN

Mt   23: 37 as a *h* gathers her chicks
Lk   13: 34 as a *h* gathers her chicks

HERALD

1Ti   2: 7 for this purpose I was appointed a *h*
2Ti   1: 11 of this gospel I was appointed a *h*

HERBS

Ex   12: 8 with bitter *h*, and bread made

HERITAGE (INHERIT)

Ps   61: 5 you have given me the *h*
    119: 111 Your statutes are my *h* for ever;
    127: 3 Sons are a *h* from the LORD,

HEROD

1. King of Judea who tried to kill Jesus (Mt 2; Lk 1:5).
2. Son of 1. Tetrarch of Galilee who arrested and beheaded John the Baptist (Mt 14:1-12; Mk 6:14-29; Lk 3:1, 19-20; 9:7-9); tried Jesus (Lk 23:6-15).
3. Grandson of 1. King of Judea who killed James (Ac 12:2); arrested Peter (Ac 12:3-19). Death (Ac 12:19-23).

HERODIAS

Wife of Herod the Tetrarch who persuaded her daughter to ask for John the Baptist's head (Mt 14:1-12; Mk 6:14-29).

HEWN

Isa 51: 1 the quarry from which you were *h*;

HEZEKIAH

King of Judah. Restored the temple and worship (2Ch 29-31). Sought the LORD for help against Assyria (2Ki 18-19; 2Ch 32:1-23; Isa 36-37). Illness healed (2Ki 20:1-11; 2Ch 32:24-26; Isa 38). Judged for showing Babylonians his treasures (2Ki 20:12-21; 2Ch 32:31; Isa 39).

HID (HIDE)

Ge   3: 8 and they *h* from the LORD God
Ex   2: 2 she *h* him for three months.
Jos   6: 17 because she *h* the spies we sent.
1Ki 18: 13 I *h* a hundred of the LORD's
2Ch 22: 11 she *h* the child from Athaliah
Isa 54: 8 I *h* my face from you for a moment,
Mt   13: 44 When a man found it, he *h* it again,
     25: 25 and *h* your talent in the ground.
Heb 11: 23 By faith Moses' parents *h* him

HIDDEN (HIDE)

1Sa 10: 22 has *h* himself among the baggage."
Job 28: 11 and brings *h* things to light.
Ps   19: 12 Forgive my *h* faults.
     78: 2 I will utter things *h* from of old—
    119: 11 I have *h* your word in my heart
Pr   2: 4 and search for it as for *h* treasure,
     27: 5 rebuke than *h* love.
Isa 59: 2 your sins have *h* his face from you,
Da   2: 22 He reveals deep and *h* things;
Mt   5: 14 A city on a hill cannot be *h*.
     10: 26 or *h* that will not be made known.
     11: 25 because you have *h* these things
     13: 35 I will utter things *h*
     13: 44 of heaven is like treasure *h*
Mk   4: 22 For whatever is *h* is meant
Ro   16: 25 of the mystery *h* for long ages past,
1Co   2: 7 a wisdom that has been *h*
Eph   3: 9 for ages past was kept *h* in God,
Col   1: 26 the mystery that has been kept *h*
      2: 3 in whom are *h* all the treasures
      3: 3 and your life is now *h* with Christ

HIDE (HID HIDDEN HIDING HIDING-PLACE)

Dt   31: 17 I will *h* my face from them,
Ps   17: 8 *h* me in the shadow of your wings
     27: 5 he will *h* me in the shelter
    143: 9 for I *h* myself in you.
Isa 53: 3 one from whom men *h* their faces

HIDING (HIDE)

Pr   28: 12 to power, men go into *h*.

HIDING-PLACE (HIDE)

Ps 32: 7 You are my *h*

HIGH

Ge 14: 18 He was priest of God Most *H*,
14: 22 God Most *H*, Creator of heaven
Ps 21: 7 the unfailing love of the Most *H*
82: 6 you are all sons of the Most *H*.'
Isa 14: 14 I will make myself like the Most *H*
Da 4: 17 know that the Most *H* is sovereign
Mk 5: 7 Jesus, Son of the Most *H* God?
Heb 7: 1 and priest of God Most *H*.

HIGHWAY

Isa 40: 3 a *h* for our God.

HILL (HILLS)

Ps 24: 3 ascend the *h* of the LORD?
Isa 40: 4 every mountain and *h* made low;
Mt 5: 14 A city on a *h* cannot be hidden.
Lk 3: 5 every mountain and *h* made low.

HILLS (HILL)

1Ki 20: 23 "Their gods are gods of the *h*.
Ps 50: 10 and the cattle on a thousand *h*.
121: 1 I lift up my eyes to the *h*—
Hos 10: 8 and to the *h*, "Fall on us!"
Lk 23: 30 and to the *h*, "Cover us!"'
Rev 17: 9 The seven heads are seven *h*

HINDER (HINDERED HINDERS)

1Sa 14: 6 Nothing can *h* the LORD
Mt 19: 14 come to me, and do not *h* them,
1Co 9: 12 anything rather than *h* the gospel
1Pe 3: 7 so that nothing will *h* your prayers.

HINDERED (HINDER)

Lk 11: 52 and you have *h* those who were

HINDERS (HINDER)

Heb 12: 1 let us throw off everything that *h*

HINT*

Eph 5: 3 even a *h* of sexual immorality,

HIP

Ge 32: 32 socket of Jacob's *h* was touched

HIRAM

King of Tyre; helped David build his palace (2Sa 5:11-12; 1Ch 14:1); helped Solomon build the temple (1Ki 5; 2Ch 2) and his navy (1Ki 9:10-27; 2Ch 8).

HIRED

Lk 15: 15 and *h* himself out to a citizen
Jn 10: 12 *h* hand is not the shepherd who

HOARDED (HOARDS)

Ecc 5: 13 wealth *h* to the harm of its owner,
Jas 5: 3 You have *h* wealth in the last days.

HOARDS (HOARDED)

Pr 11: 26 People curse the man who *h* grain,

HOLD (HELD HOLDS)

Ex 20: 7 LORD will not *h* anyone guiltless
Lev 19: 13 "'Do not *h* back the wages
Dt 5: 11 LORD will not *h* anyone guiltless
11: 22 in all his ways and to *h* fast to him

Dt 13: 4 serve him and *h* fast to him.
30: 20 listen to his voice, and *h* fast to him
Jos 22: 5 to *h* fast to him and to serve him
2Ki 4: 16 "you will *h* a son in your arms."
Ps 18: 16 from on high and took *h* of me;
73: 23 you *h* me by my right hand.
Pr 4: 4 "Lay *h* of my words
Isa 41: 13 who takes *h* of your right hand
54: 2 do not *h* back;
Eze 3: 18 and I will *h* you accountable
3: 20 and I will *h* you accountable
33: 6 I will *h* the watchman accountable
Zec 8: 23 nations will take firm *h* of one Jew
Mk 11: 25 if you *h* anything against anyone,
Jn 20: 17 Jesus said, "Do not *h* on to me,
Php 2: 16 as you *h* out the word of life—
3: 12 but I press on to take *h* of that
Col 1: 17 and in him all things *h* together.
1Th 5: 21 *H* on to the good.
1Ti 6: 12 Take *h* of the eternal life
Heb 10: 23 Let us *h* unswervingly

HOLDS (HOLD)

Pr 10: 19 but he who *h* his tongue is wise.
17: 28 and discerning if he *h* his tongue.

HOLES

Hag 1: 6 to put them in a purse with *h* in it."
Mt 8: 20 "Foxes have *h* and birds

HOLINESS* (HOLY)

Ex 15: 11 majestic in *h*,
Dt 32: 51 because you did not uphold my *h*
1Ch 16: 29 the LORD in the splendour of his *h*.
2Ch 20: 21 him for the splendour of his *h*
Ps 29: 2 in the splendour of his *h*.
89: 35 Once for all, I have sworn by my *h*
93: 5 *h* adorns your house
96: 9 in the splendour of his *h*;
Isa 29: 23 they will acknowledge the *h*
35: 8 it will be called the Way of *H*.
Eze 36: 23 I will show the *h* of my great name,
38: 23 I will show my greatness and my *h*,
Am 4: 2 LORD has sworn by his *h*:
Lk 1: 75 fear in *h* and righteousness
Ro 1: 4 the Spirit of *h* was declared
6: 19 to righteousness leading to *h*.
6: 22 the benefit you reap leads to *h*,
1Co 1: 30 our righteousness, *h*
2Co 1: 12 in the *h* and sincerity that are
7: 1 perfecting *h* out of reverence
Eph 4: 24 God in true righteousness and *h*.
1Ti 2: 2 quiet lives in all godliness and *h*.
2: 15 love and *h* with propriety.
Heb 12: 10 that we may share in his *h*.
12: 14 without *h* no-one will see the Lord.

HOLY (HALLOWED HOLINESS)

Ge 2: 3 the seventh day and made it *h*,
Ex 3: 5 you are standing is *h* ground."
16: 23 a *h* Sabbath to the LORD.
19: 6 kingdom of priests and a *h* nation.'
20: 8 the Sabbath day by keeping it *h*.
26: 33 Place from the Most *H* Place.
26: 33 curtain will separate the *H* Place
28: 36 seal: *H* TO THE LORD.
29: 37 Then the altar will be most *h*,
30: 10 It is most *h* to the LORD."
30: 29 them so they will be most *h*,
31: 13 I am the LORD, who makes you *h*.

Ex	40: 9	all its furnishings, and it will be *h*.
Lev	10: 3	I will show myself *h*;
	10: 10	must distinguish between the *h*
	10: 13	in a *h* place, because it is your share
	11: 44	and be *h*, because I am *h*.
	11: 45	therefore be *h*, because I am *h*.
	19: 2	'Be *h* because I, the LORD your
	19: 8	he has desecrated what is *h*
	19: 24	the fourth year all its fruit will be *h*,
	20: 3	and profaned my *h* name.
	20: 7	" 'Consecrate yourselves and be *h*,
	20: 8	I am the LORD, who makes you *h*.
	20: 26	You are to be *h* to me because I,
	21: 6	They must be *h* to their God
	21: 8	Consider them *h*, because I
	22: 9	am the LORD, who makes them *h*.
	22: 32	Do not profane my *h* name.
	25: 12	For it is a jubilee and is to be *h*
	27: 9	given to the LORD becomes *h*.
Nu	4: 15	they must not touch the *h* things
	6: 5	He must be *h* until the period
	20: 12	as *h* in the sight of the Israelites,
	20: 13	and where he showed himself *h*
Dt	5: 12	the Sabbath day by keeping it *h*,
	23: 14	Your camp must be *h*,
	26: 15	from heaven, your *h* dwelling-place
	33: 2	He came with myriads of *h* ones
Jos	5: 15	place where you are standing is *h*."
	24: 19	He is a *h* God; he is a jealous God.
1Sa	2: 2	"There is no-one *h* like the LORD;
	6: 20	of the LORD, this *h* God?
	21: 5	even on missions that are not *h*.
2Ki	4: 9	often comes our way is a *h* man
1Ch	16: 10	Glory in his *h* name;
	16: 35	may give thanks to your *h* name,
	29: 3	I have provided for this *h* temple:
2Ch	30: 27	heaven, his *h* dwelling-place.
Ezr	9: 2	and have mingled the *h* race
Ne	11: 1	the *h* city, while the remaining nine
Job	6: 10	not denied the words of the *H* One.
Ps	2: 6	King on Zion, my *h* hill."
	11: 4	The LORD is in his *h* temple;
	16: 10	will you let your *H* One see decay.
	22: 3	you are enthroned as the *H* One;
	24: 3	Who may stand in his *h* place?
	30: 4	praise his *h* name.
	77: 13	Your ways, O God, are *h*.
	78: 54	to the border of his *h* land,
	99: 3	he is *h*.
	99: 5	he is *h*.
	99: 9	for the LORD our God is *h*.
	105: 3	Glory in his *h* name;
	111: 9	*h* and awesome is his name.
Pr	9: 10	of the *H* One is understanding.
Isa	5: 16	the *h* God will show himself *h*
	6: 3	*H*, *h*, *h* is the LORD Almighty;
	8: 13	is the one you are to regard as *h*,
	29: 23	they will keep my name *h*;
	40: 25	who is my equal?" says the *H* One.
	43: 3	the *H* One of Israel, your Saviour;
	54: 5	*H* One of Israel is your Redeemer;
	57: 15	who lives for ever, whose name is *h*:
	58: 13	and the LORD's *h* day honourable,
Jer	17: 22	but keep the Sabbath day *h*,
Eze	20: 41	I will show myself *h* among you
	22: 26	to my law and profane my *h* things;
	28: 25	I will show myself *h* among them
	36: 20	nations they profaned my *h* name,
	38: 16	when I show myself *h* through you
	44: 23	the difference between the *h*

Da	9: 24	prophecy and to anoint the most *h*.
Hab	2: 20	But the LORD is in his *h* temple;
Zec	14: 5	and all the *h* ones with him.
	14: 20	On that day *H* TO THE LORD
Mt	24: 15	in the *h* place 'the abomination
Mk	1: 24	the *H* One of God!" "Be quiet!"
Lk	1: 35	the *h* one to be born will be called
	1: 49	*h* is his name.
	4: 34	the *H* One of God!" "Be quiet!"
Jn	6: 69	and know that you are the *H* One
Ac	2: 27	will you let your *H* One see decay.
	13: 35	will not let your *H* One see decay.'
Ro	1: 2	prophets in the *H* Scriptures
	7: 12	and the commandment is *h*,
	11: 16	if the root is *h*, so are the branches.
	12: 1	as living sacrifices, *h* and pleasing
1Co	1: 2	in Christ Jesus and called to be *h*,
	7: 14	be unclean, but as it is, they are *h*.
Eph	1: 4	the creation of the world to be *h*
	2: 21	and rises to become a *h* temple
	3: 5	by the Spirit to God's *h* apostles
	5: 3	improper for God's *h* people.
	5: 26	up for her to make her *h*,
Col.	1: 22	death to present you *h* in his sight,
1Th	2: 10	and so is God, of how *h*,
	3: 13	and *h* in the presence of our God
	4: 7	us to be impure, but to live a *h* life.
2Th	1: 10	to be glorified in his *h* people
1Ti	2: 8	to lift up *h* hands in prayer,
2Ti	1: 9	saved us and called us to a *h* life—
	2: 21	for noble purposes, made *h*,
	3: 15	you have known the *h* Scriptures,
Tit	1: 8	upright, *h* and disciplined.
Heb	2: 11	Both the one who makes men *h*
	7: 26	one who is *h*, blameless, pure,
	10: 10	we have been made *h*
	10: 14	those who are being made *h*.
	10: 19	to enter the Most *H* Place
	12: 14	in peace with all men and to be *h*;
	13: 12	gate to make the people *h*
1Pe	1: 15	But just as he who called you is *h*,
	1: 16	is written: "Be *h*, because I am *h*."
	2: 5	house to be a *h* priesthood,
	2: 9	a royal priesthood, a *h* nation,
	3: 5	For this is the way the *h* women
2Pe	3: 11	You ought to live *h* and godly lives
Jude	: 14	upon thousands of his *h* ones
Rev	3: 7	are the words of him who is *h*
	4: 8	"*H*, *h*, *h* is the Lord God
	15: 4	For you alone are *h*.
	20: 6	and *h* are those who have part
	22: 11	let him who is *h* continue to be *h*."

HOLY SPIRIT see SPIRIT

HOME (HOMES)

Dt	6: 7	Talk about them when you sit at *h*
	11: 19	about them when you sit at *h*
	20: 5	Let him go *h*, or he may die
	25: 5	is to be free to stay at *h*
Ru	1: 11	"Return *h*, my daughters.
2Sa	7: 10	them so that they can have a *h*
1Ch	16: 43	and David returned *h* to bless his
Ps	84: 3	Even the sparrow has found a *h*,
	113: 9	settles the barren woman in her *h*
Pr	3: 33	but he blesses the *h* of the righteous
	27: 8	is a man who strays from his *h*.
Ecc	12: 5	Then man goes to his eternal *h*
Eze	36: 8	for they will soon come *h*.
Mic	2: 2	They defraud a man of his *h*,

Mt   1: 24 and took Mary *h* as his wife.
       13: 57 "Only in his *h* town
Mk   10: 29 "no-one who has left *h* or brothers
Lk   10: 38 named Martha opened her *h*
Jn   14: 23 to him and make our *h* with him.
       19: 27 this disciple took her into his *h*.
Ac   16: 15 baptised, she invited us to her *h*.
Tit   2: 5 to be busy at *h*, to be kind,

HOMELESS*

1Co   4: 11 we are brutally treated, we are *h*.

HOMES (HOME)

Ne   4: 14 daughters, your wives and your *h*."
Isa   32: 18 in secure *h*,
Mk   10: 30 as much in this present age (*h*,
1Ti   5: 14 to manage their *h* and to give

HOMOSEXUAL*

1Co   6: 9 male prostitutes nor *h* offenders

HONEST (HONESTY)

Lev   19: 36 Use *h* scales and *h* weights,
Dt   25: 15 and *h* weights and measures,
Job   31: 6 let God weigh me in *h* scales
Pr   12: 17 truthful witness gives *h* testimony,

HONESTY (HONEST)

2Ki   12: 15 they acted with complete *h*.

HONEY (HONEYCOMB)

Ex   3: 8 a land flowing with milk and *h*—
Jdg   14: 8 a swarm of bees and some *h*,
1Sa   14: 26 they saw the *h* oozing out,
Ps   19: 10 than *h* from the comb.
      119: 103 sweeter than *h* to my mouth!
Pr   25: 16 If you find *h*, eat just enough—
SS   4: 11 milk and *h* are under your tongue.
Isa   7: 15 and *h* when he knows enough
Eze   3: 3 it tasted as sweet as *h* in my mouth.
Mt   3: 4 His food was locusts and wild *h*.
Rev   10: 9 mouth it will be as sweet as *h*."

HONEYCOMB (HONEY)

SS   4: 11 Your lips drop sweetness as the *h*,
        5: 1 I have eaten my *h* and my honey;

HONOUR (HONOURABLE HONOURABLY HONOURED HONOURS)

Ex   20: 12 "*H* your father and your mother,
Nu   20: 12 trust in me enough to *h* me
       25: 13 he was zealous for the *h* of his God
Dt   5: 16 "*H* your father and your mother,
Jdg   4: 9 going about this, the *h* will not be
1Sa   2: 8 and has them inherit a throne of *h*.
        2: 30 Those who *h* me I will *h*,
1Ch   29: 12 Wealth and *h* come from you;
2Ch   1: 11 or *h*, nor for the death
       18: 1 had great wealth and *h*,
Est   6: 6 for the man the king delights to *h*
Ps   8: 5 and crowned him with glory and *h*.
       45: 11 *h* him, for he is your lord.
       84: 11 the Lord bestows favour and *h*;
Pr   3: 9 *H* the Lord with your wealth,
        3: 35 The wise inherit *h*,
       15: 33 and humility comes before *h*.
       18: 12 but humility comes before *h*.
       20: 3 It is to a man's *h* to avoid strife,
       25: 27 is it honourable to seek one's own *h*.
Isa   29: 13 and *h* me with their lips.

Jer   33: 9 and *h* before all nations
Mt   13: 57 own house is a prophet without *h*."
       15: 4 '*H* your father and mother'
       15: 8 These people *h* me with their lips,
       19: 19 *h* your father and mother,'
       23: 6 they love the place of *h* at banquets
Mk   6: 4 own house is a prophet without *h*."
Lk   14: 8 do not take the place of *h*,
Jn   5: 23 that all may *h* the Son just
        7: 18 does so to gain *h* for himself,
       12: 26 My Father will *h* the one who
Ro   12: 10 *H* one another above yourselves.
1Co   6: 20 Therefore *h* God with your body.
Eph   6: 2 "*H* your father and mother"—
1Ti   5: 17 well are worthy of double *h*,
Heb   2: 7 you crowned him with glory and *h*
Rev   4: 9 *h* and thanks to him who sits

HONOURABLE (HONOUR)

1Th   4: 4 body in a way that is holy and *h*,

HONOURABLY (HONOUR)

Heb   13: 18 and desire to live *h* in every way.

HONOURED (HONOUR)

Ps   12: 8 when what is vile is *h* among men.
Pr   13: 18 but whoever heeds correction is *h*.
Da   4: 34 I *h* and glorified him who lives
1Co   12: 26 if one part is *h*, every part rejoices
Heb   13: 4 Marriage should be *h* by all,

HONOURS (HONOUR)

Ps   15: 4 but *h* those who fear the Lord,
Pr   14: 31 to the needy *h* God.

HOOF

Ex   10: 26 not a *h* is to be left behind.

HOOKS

Isa   2: 4 and their spears into pruning *h*.
Joel   3: 10 and your pruning *h* into spears.
Mic   4: 3 and their spears into pruning *h*.

HOPE (HOPES)

Job   13: 15 Though he slay me, yet will I *h*
Ps   25: 3 No-one whose *h* is in you
       33: 17 A horse is a vain *h* for deliverance;
       33: 18 on those whose *h* is
       42: 5 Put your *h* in God,
       62: 5 my *h* comes from him.
      119: 74 for I have put my *h* in your word.
      130: 5 and in his word I put my *h*.
      130: 7 O Israel, put your *h* in the Lord,
      146: 5 whose *h* is in the Lord his God,
      147: 11 who put their *h* in his unfailing love
Pr   13: 12 *H* deferred makes the heart sick,
       23: 18 There is surely a future *h* for you,
Isa   40: 31 but those who *h* in the Lord
Jer   29: 11 plans to give you *h* and a future.
La   3: 21 and therefore I have *h*:
Zec   9: 12 to your fortress, O prisoners of *h*;
Ro   5: 4 character; and character, *h*.
        8: 20 in *h* that the creation itself will be
        8: 24 But *h* that is seen is no *h* at all.
        8: 25 if we *h* for what we do not yet have,
       12: 12 Be joyful in *h*, patient in affliction,
       15: 4 of the Scriptures we might have *h*.
       15: 13 May the God of *h* fill you
1Co   13: 13 now these three remain: faith, *h*
       15: 19 for this life we have *h* in Christ,

Eph	2:12	without *h* and without God
Col	1:27	Christ in you, the *h* of glory.
1Th	1: 3	and your endurance inspired by *h*
	5: 8	and the *h* of salvation as a helmet.
1Ti	4:10	that we have put our *h*
	6:17	but to put their *h* in God,
Tit	1: 2	resting on the *h* of eternal life,
	2:13	while we wait for the blessed *h*—
Heb	6:19	We have this *h* as an anchor
	10:23	unswervingly to the *h* we profess,
	11: 1	faith is being sure of what we *h* for
1Jn	3: 3	Everyone who has this *h*

HOPES (HOPE)

1Co	13: 7	always *h*, always perseveres.

HORN (HORNS)

Ex	19:13	when the ram's *h* sounds a long
	27: 2	Make a *h* at each of the four
Da	7: 8	This *h* had eyes like the eyes

HORNS (HORN)

Da	7:24	ten *h* are ten kings who will come
Rev	5: 6	He had seven *h* and seven eyes,
	12: 3	and ten *h* and seven crowns
	13: 1	He had ten *h* and seven heads,
	17: 3	and had seven heads and ten *h*.

HORRIBLE (HORROR)

Jer	5:30	"A *h* and shocking thing

HORROR (HORRIBLE)

Jer	2:12	and shudder with great *h*,"

HORSE

Ps	147:10	not in the strength of the *h*,
Pr	26: 3	A whip for the *h*, a halter
Zec	1: 8	before me was a man riding a red *h*
Rev	6: 2	and there before me was a white *h*!
	6: 4	Come!" Then another *h* came out,
	6: 5	and there before me was a black *h*!
	6: 8	and there before me was a pale *h*!
	19:11	and there before me was a white *h*,

HOSANNA

Mt	21: 9	"*H* in the highest!"
Mk	11: 9	"*H*!"
Jn	12:13	"*H*!"

HOSEA

Prophet whose wife and family pictured the unfaithfulness of Israel (Hos 1-3).

HOSHEA (JOSHUA)

1. Original name of Joshua (Nu 13:16).
2. Last king of Israel (2Ki 15: 30; 17:1-6).

HOSPITABLE* (HOSPITALITY)

1Ti	3: 2	self-controlled, respectable, *h*,
Tit	1: 8	Rather he must be *h*, one who loves

HOSPITABLY* (HOSPITALITY)

Ac	28: 7	and for three days entertained us *h*.

HOSPITALITY* (HOSPITABLE HOSPITABLY)

Ro	12:13	Practise *h*.
	16:23	whose *h* I and the whole church
1Ti	5:10	as bringing up children, showing *h*,
1Pe	4: 9	Offer *h* to one another
3Jn	: 8	therefore to show *h* to such men

HOSTILE (HOSTILITY)

Ro	8: 7	the sinful mind is *h* to God.

HOSTILITY (HOSTILE)

Eph	2:14	wall of *h*, by abolishing
	2:16	by which he put to death their *h*.

HOT

1Ti	4: 2	have been seared as with a *h* iron.
Rev	3:15	that you are neither cold nor *h*.

HOT-TEMPERED (TEMPER)

Pr	15:18	A *h* man stirs up dissension,
	19:19	A *h* man must pay the penalty;
	22:24	Do not make friends with a *h* man,
	29:22	and a *h* one commits many sins.

HOTHEADED (HEAD)

Pr	14:16	but a fool is *h* and reckless.

HOUR

Ecc	9:12	knows when his *h* will come:
Mt	6:27	you by worrying can add a single *h*
Lk	12:40	the Son of Man will come at an *h*
Jn	12:23	The *h* has come for the Son of Man
	12:27	for this very reason I came to this *h*

HOUSE (HOUSEHOLD HOUSEHOLDS HOUSES STOREHOUSE)

Ex	12:22	the door of his *h* until morning.
	20:17	shall not covet your neighbour's *h*.
Nu	12: 7	he is faithful in all my *h*.
Dt	5:21	desire on your neighbour's *h*
2Sa	7:11	LORD himself will establish a *h*
1Ch	17:23	and his *h* be established for ever.
Ne	10:39	"We will not neglect the *h*
Ps	23: 6	I will dwell in the *h* of the LORD
	27: 4	dwell in the *h* of the LORD
	69: 9	for zeal for your *h* consumes me,
	84:10	a doorkeeper in the *h* of my God
	122: 1	"Let us go to the *h* of the LORD."
	127: 1	Unless the LORD builds the *h*,
Pr	7:27	Her *h* is a highway to the grave,
	21: 9	than share a *h* with a quarrelsome
Isa	56: 7	a *h* of prayer for all nations."
Jer	7:11	Has this *h*, which bears my Name,
	18: 2	"Go down to the potter's *h*,
Eze	33: 7	made you a watchman for the *h*
Joel	3:18	will flow out of the LORD's *h*
Zec	13: 6	given at the *h* of my friends.'
Mt	7:24	is like a wise man who built his *h*
	10:11	and stay at his *h* until you leave.
	12:29	can anyone enter a strong man's *h*
	21:13	My *h* will be called a *h* of prayer,'
Mk	3:25	If a *h* is divided against itself,
	11:17	"'My *h* will be called
Lk	6:48	He is like a man building a *h*,
	10: 7	Do not move around from *h* to *h*.
	11:17	a *h* divided against itself will fall.
	11:24	'I will return to the *h* I left.'
	15: 8	sweep the *h* and search carefully
	19: 9	Today salvation has come to this *h*,
Jn	2:16	How dare you turn my Father's *h*
	2:17	"Zeal for your *h* will consume me."
	12: 3	the *h* was filled with the fragrance
	14: 2	In my Father's *h* are many rooms;
Ac	20:20	you publicly and from *h* to *h*.
Ro	16: 5	the church that meets at their *h*.
Heb	3: 3	the builder of a *h* has greater honour
1Pe	2: 5	built into a spiritual *h* to be a holy

HOUSEHOLD (HOUSE)

Ex   12: 3 lamb for his family, one for each *h*.
Jos 24: 15 my *h*, we will serve the LORD."
Pr   31: 21 it snows, she has no fear for her *h*;
     31: 27 over the affairs of her *h*
Mic   7: 6 are the members of his own *h*.
Mt   10: 36 will be the members of his own *h*.'
     12: 25 or *h* divided against itself will not
Ac   16: 31 you will be saved—you and your *h*
Eph   2: 19 people and members of God's *h*,
1Ti   3: 12 manage his children and his *h* well.
      3: 15 to conduct themselves in God's *h*,

HOUSEHOLDS (HOUSE)

Tit   1: 11 because they are ruining whole *h*

HOUSES (HOUSE)

Ex   12: 27 passed over the *h* of the Israelites
Mt   19: 29 everyone who has left *h* or brothers

HOVERING* (HOVERS)

Ge   1: 2 of God was *h* over the waters.
Isa 31: 5 Like birds *h* overhead,

HOVERS* (HOVERING)

Dt   32: 11 and *h* over its young,

HULDAH*

Prophetess enquired of by Hilkiah for Josiah
(2Ki 22; 2Ch 34:14-28).

HUMAN (HUMANITY)

Lev 24: 17 If anyone takes the life of a *h* being,
Isa 52: 14 his form marred beyond *h* likeness
Jn   8: 15 You judge by *h* standards;
Ro   1: 3 as to his *h* nature was a descendant
      9: 5 from them is traced the *h* ancestry
1Co   1: 17 not with words of *h* wisdom,
      1: 26 of you were wise by *h* standards,
      2: 13 not in words taught us by *h* wisdom
2Co   3: 3 of stone but on tablets of *h* hearts.
Gal   3: 3 to attain your goal by *h* effort?
2Pe   2: 18 lustful desires of sinful *h* nature,

HUMANITY* (HUMAN)

Heb   2: 14 he too shared in their *h* so that

HUMBLE (HUMBLED HUMBLES HUMILIATE HUMILIATED HUMILITY)

Nu   12: 3 (Now Moses was a very *h* man,
2Ch   7: 14 will *h* themselves and pray
Ps   18: 27 You save the *h*
     25: 9 He guides the *h* in what is right
    149: 4 he crowns the *h* with salvation.
Pr   3: 34 but gives grace to the *h*.
Isa 66: 2 he who is *h* and contrite in spirit,
Mt   11: 29 for I am gentle and *h* in heart,
Eph   4: 2 Be completely *h* and gentle;
Jas   4: 6 but gives grace to the *h*."
      4: 10 *H* yourselves before the Lord,
1Pe   5: 5 but gives grace to the *h*."
      5: 6 *H* yourselves,

HUMBLED (HUMBLE)

Mt   23: 12 whoever exalts himself will be *h*,
Lk   14: 11 who exalts himself will be *h*,
Php   2: 8 he *h* himself

HUMBLES* (HUMBLE)

1Sa   2: 7 he *h* and he exalts.

Isa 26: 5 He *h* those who dwell on high,
Mt   18: 4 whoever *h* himself like this child is
     23: 12 whoever *h* himself will be exalted.
Lk   14: 11 he who *h* himself will be exalted."
     18: 14 he who *h* himself will be exalted."

HUMILIATE* (HUMBLE)

Pr   25: 7 than for him to *h* you
1Co 11: 22 and *h* those who have nothing?

HUMILIATED (HUMBLE)

Jer 31: 19 I was ashamed and *h*
Lk   14: 9 *h*, you will have to take the least

HUMILITY* (HUMBLE)

Ps   45: 4 of truth, *h* and righteousness;
Pr   11: 2 but with *h* comes wisdom.
     15: 33 and *h* comes before honour.
     18: 12 but *h* comes before honour.
     22: 4 *H* and the fear of the LORD
Zep   2: 3 Seek righteousness, seek *h*;
Ac   20: 19 I served the Lord with great *h*
Php   2: 3 but in *h* consider others better
Col   2: 18 let anyone who delights in false *h*
      2: 23 their false *h* and their harsh
      3: 12 *h*, gentleness and patience.
Tit   3: 2 and to show true *h* towards all men.
Jas   3: 13 in the *h* that comes from wisdom.
1Pe   5: 5 Clothe yourselves with *h*

HUNG (HANG)

Dt   21: 23 anyone who is *h* on a tree is
Mt   18: 6 him to have a large millstone *h*
Lk   19: 48 all the people *h* on his words.
Gal   3: 13 "Cursed is everyone who is *h*

HUNGER (HUNGRY)

Ne   9: 15 In their *h* you gave them bread
Pr   6: 30 to satisfy his *h* when he is starving.
Mt   5: 6 Blessed are those who *h*
Lk   6: 21 Blessed are you who *h* now,
2Co   6: 5 sleepless nights and *h*; in purity,
     11: 27 I have known *h* and thirst
Rev   7: 16 Never again will they *h*;

HUNGRY (HUNGER)

Job 24: 10 carry the sheaves, but still go *h*.
Ps 107: 9 and fills the *h* with good things.
    146: 7 and gives food to the *h*.
Pr   19: 15 and the shiftless man goes *h*.
     25: 21 If your enemy is *h*, give him food
     27: 7 to the *h* even what is bitter tastes
Isa 58: 7 not to share your food with the *h*
     58: 10 spend yourselves on behalf of the *h*
Eze 18: 7 but gives his food to the *h*
     18: 16 but gives his food to the *h*
Mt   15: 32 I do not want to send them away *h*,
     25: 35 For I was *h* and you gave me
     25: 42 For I was *h* and you gave me
Lk   1: 53 He has filled the *h* with good things
Jn   6: 35 comes to me will never go *h*,
Ro   12: 20 "If your enemy is *h*, feed him;
1Co   4: 11 To this very hour we go *h*
Php   4: 12 whether well fed or *h*,

HUR

Ex   17: 12 Aaron and *H* held his hands up—

HURL

Mic   7: 19 *h* all our iniquities into the depths

HURT (HURTS)

Ecc	8: 9	it over others to his own *h*.
Mk	16: 18	deadly poison, it will not *h* them
Rev	2: 11	He who overcomes will not be *h*

HURTS* (HURT)

Ps	15: 4	even when it *h*,
Pr	26: 28	A lying tongue hates those it *h*,

HUSBAND (HUSBAND'S HUSBANDS)

Pr	31: 11	Her *h* has full confidence in her
	31: 23	Her *h* is respected at the city gate,
	31: 28	her *h* also, and he praises her:
Isa	54: 5	For your Maker is your *h*—
Jer	3: 14	the LORD, "for I am your *h*.
	3: 20	like a woman unfaithful to her *h*,
Jn	4: 17	"I have no *h*," she replied.
Ro	7: 2	a married woman is bound to her *h*
1Co	7: 2	and each woman her own *h*.
	7: 3	The *h* should fulfil his marital duty
	7: 10	wife must not separate from her *h*.
	7: 11	And a *h* must not divorce his wife.
	7: 13	And if a woman has a *h* who is not
	7: 14	For the unbelieving *h* has been
	7: 39	A woman is bound to her *h* as long
	7: 39	But if her *h* dies, she is free
2Co	11: 2	I promised you to one *h*, to Christ,
Gal	4: 27	woman than of her who has a *h*."
Eph	5: 23	For the *h* is the head of the wife
	5: 33	and the wife must respect her *h*.
1Ti	3: 2	the *h* of but one wife, temperate,
	3: 12	A deacon must be the *h* of
	5: 9	has been faithful to her *h*,
Tit	1: 6	An elder must be blameless, the *h*

HUSBANDMAN see GARDENER

HUSBAND'S (HUSBAND)

Dt	25: 5	Her *h* brother shall take her
Pr	12: 4	of noble character is her *h* crown,
1Co	7: 4	the *h* body does not belong

HUSBANDS (HUSBAND)

Eph	5: 22	submit to your *h* as to the Lord.
	5: 25	*H*, love your wives, just
	5: 28	*h* ought to love their wives
Col	3: 18	submit to your *h*, as is fitting
	3: 19	*H*, love your wives and do not be
Tit	2: 4	the younger women to love their *h*
	2: 5	and to be subject to their *h*,
1Pe	3: 1	same way be submissive to your *h*
	3: 7	*H*, in the same way be considerate

HUSHAI

Wise man of David who frustrated Ahithophel's advice and foiled Absalom's revolt (2Sa 15:32-37; 16:15-17:16; 1Ch 27:33).

HYMN* (HYMNS)

Ps	40: 3	a *h* of praise to our God.
Mt	26: 30	they had sung a *h*, they went out
Mk	14: 26	they had sung a *h*, they went out
1Co	14: 26	everyone has a *h*, or a word

HYMNS* (HYMN)

Ac	16: 25	Silas were praying and singing *h*
Ro	15: 9	I will sing *h* to your name."
Eph	5: 19	to one another with psalms, *h*
Col	3: 16	*h* and spiritual songs with gratitude

HYPOCRISY* (HYPOCRITE HYPOCRITES HYPOCRITICAL)

Mt	23: 28	but on the inside you are full of *h*
Mk	12: 15	we?" But Jesus knew their *h*.
Lk	12: 1	yeast of the Pharisees, which is *h*.
Gal	2: 13	The other Jews joined him in his *h*,
	2: 13	by their *h* even Barnabas was led
1Pe	2: 1	*h*, envy, and slander of every kind.

HYPOCRITE* (HYPOCRISY)

Mt	7: 5	You *h*, first take the plank out
Lk	6: 42	You *h*, first take the plank out

HYPOCRITES* (HYPOCRISY)

Ps	26: 4	nor do I consort with *h*;
Mt	6: 2	as the *h* do in the synagogues
	6: 5	when you pray, do not be like the *h*
	6: 16	do not look sombre as the *h* do,
	15: 7	You *h*! Isaiah was right
	22: 18	their evil intent, said, "You *h*,
	23: 13	of the law and Pharisees, you *h*!
	23: 15	of the law and Pharisees, you *h*!
	23: 23	of the law and Pharisees, you *h*!
	23: 25	of the law and Pharisees, you *h*!
	23: 27	you *h*! You are like whitewashed
	23: 29	of the law and Pharisees, you *h*!
	24: 51	and assign him a place with the *h*,
Mk	7: 6	when he prophesied about you *h*;
Lk	12: 56	*H*! You know how
	13: 15	The Lord answered him, "You *h*!

HYPOCRITICAL* (HYPOCRISY)

1Ti	4: 2	teaching come through *h* liars,

HYSSOP

Ex	12: 22	Take a bunch of *h*, dip it
Ps	51: 7	with *h*, and I will be clean;
Jn	19: 29	the sponge on a stalk of the *h* plant,

ICHABOD

1Sa	4: 21	She named the boy *I*, saying,

IDLE* (IDLENESS IDLERS)

Dt	32: 47	They are not just *i* words for you—
Job	11: 3	Will your *i* talk reduce men
Ecc	10: 18	if his hands are *i*, the house leaks.
	11: 6	at evening let not your hands be *i*,
Isa	58: 13	as you please or speaking *i* words,
Col	2: 18	mind puffs him up with *i* notions.
1Th	5: 14	those who are *i*, encourage
2Th	3: 6	away from every brother who is *i*
	3: 7	We were not *i* when we were
	3: 11	We hear that some among you are *i*
1Ti	5: 13	they get into the habit of being *i*

IDLENESS* (IDLE)

Pr	31: 27	and does not eat the bread of *i*.

IDLERS* (IDLE)

1Ti	5: 13	And not only do they become *i*,

IDOL (IDOLATER IDOLATERS IDOLATRY IDOLS)

Ex	20: 4	make for yourself an *i* in the form
	32: 4	made it into an *i* cast in the shape
Isa	40: 19	As for an *i*, a craftsman casts it,
	41: 7	He nails down the *i*
	44: 15	he makes an *i* and bows down to it.
	44: 17	From the rest he makes a god, his *i*;

Hab   2:18 "Of what value is an *i*,
1Co   8: 4 We know that an *i* is nothing at all

IDOLATER* (IDOL)

1Co   5:11 an *i* or a slanderer, a drunkard
Eph   5: 5 greedy person—such a man is an *i*

IDOLATERS (IDOL)

1Co   5:10 or the greedy and swindlers, or *i*.
      6: 9 Neither the sexually immoral nor *i*

IDOLATRY (IDOL)

1Sa   15:23 and arrogance like the evil of *i*.
1Co   10:14 my dear friends, flee from *i*.
Gal   5:20 and debauchery; *i* and witchcraft;
Col   3: 5 evil desires and greed, which is *i*.
1Pe   4: 3 orgies, carousing and detestable *i*.

IDOLS (IDOL)

Dt   32:16 angered him with their detestable *i*.
Ps   78:58 aroused his jealousy with their *i*.
Isa   44: 9 All who make *i* are nothing,
Ez   23:39 sacrificed their children to their *i*,
Ac   15:20 to abstain from food polluted by *i*,
      21:25 abstain from food sacrificed to *i*,
1Co   8: 1 Now about food sacrificed to *i*:
1Jn   5:21 children, keep yourselves from *i*.
Rev   2:14 to sin by eating food sacrificed to *i*

IGNORANT (IGNORE)

1Co   15:34 for there are some who are *i* of God
Heb   5: 2 to deal gently with those who are *i*
1Pe   2:15 good you should silence the *i* talk
2Pe   3:16 which *i* and unstable people distort

IGNORE (IGNORANT IGNORED IGNORES)

Dt   22: 1 do not *i* it but be sure
Ps   9:12 he does not *i* the cry of the afflicted
Heb   2: 3 if we *i* such a great salvation?

IGNORED (IGNORE)

Hos   4: 6 you have *i* the law of your God,
1Co   14:38 he ignores this, he himself will be *i*.

IGNORES* (IGNORE)

Pr   10:17 whoever *i* correction leads others
      13:18 He who *i* discipline comes
      15:32 He who *i* discipline despises
1Co   14:38 If he *i* this, he himself will be

ILL (ILLNESS)

Mt   4:24 brought to him all who were *i*

ILL-GOTTEN

Pr   1:19 the end of all who go after *i* gain;
      10: 2 *I* treasures are of no value,

ILL-TEMPERED* (TEMPER)

Pr   21:19 than with a quarrelsome and *i* wife.

ILL-TREAT (ILL-TREATED)

Ex   22:21 "Do not *i* an alien or oppress him,
Eze   22:29 and needy and *i* the alien,
Lk   6:28 pray for those who *i* you.

ILL-TREATED (ILL-TREAT)

Eze   22: 7 *i* the fatherless and the widow.
Heb   11:25 to be *i* along with the people
      11:37 destitute, persecuted and *i*—
      13: 3 who are *i* as if you yourselves

ILLEGITIMATE

Heb   12: 8 then you are *i* children

ILLNESS (ILL)

2Ki   8: 9 'Will I recover from this *i*?' "
2Ch   16:12 even in his *i* he did not seek help
Ps   41: 3 and restore him from his bed of *i*.
Isa   38: 9 king of Judah after his *i*

ILLUMINATED*

Rev   18: 1 and the earth was *i* by his splendour.

IMAGE (IMAGES)

Ge   1:26 "Let us make man in our *i*,
      1:27 So God created man in his own *i*,
      9: 6 for in the *i* of God
Dt   27:15 "Cursed is the man who carves an *i*
Isa   40:18 What *i* will you compare him to?
Da   3: 1 King Nebuchadnezzar made an *i*
1Co   11: 7 since he is the *i* and glory of God;
2Co   4: 4 glory of Christ, who is the *i* of God.
Col   1:15 He is the *i* of the invisible God,
      3:10 in knowledge in the *i* of its Creator.
Rev   13:14 them to set up an *i* in honour

IMAGES (IMAGE)

Ps   97: 7 All who worship *i* are put to shame,
Jer   10:14 His *i* are a fraud;
Ro   1:23 of the immortal God for *i* made

IMAGINATION (IMAGINE)

Eze   13: 2 who prophesy out of their own *i*:

IMAGINE (IMAGINATION)

Eph   3:20 more than all we ask or *i*,

IMITATE (IMITATORS)

1Co   4:16 Therefore I urge you to *i* me.
Heb   6:12 but to *i* those who through faith
      13: 7 of their way of life and *i* their faith.
3Jn   :11 do not *i* what is evil but what is

IMITATORS* (IMITATE)

Eph   5: 1 Be *i* of God, therefore,
1Th   1: 6 You became *i* of us and of the Lord
      2:14 became *i* of God's churches

IMMANUEL*

Isa   7:14 birth to a son, and will call him *I*.
      8: 8 O *I*!"
Mt   1:23 and they will call him *I*"—

IMMORAL* (IMMORALITY)

Pr   6:24 keeping you from the *i* woman,
1Co   5: 9 to associate with sexually *i* people
      5:10 the people of this world who are *i*,
      5:11 but is sexually *i* or greedy,
      6: 9 Neither the sexually *i* nor idolaters
Eph   5: 5 No *i*, impure or greedy person—
Heb   12:16 See that no-one is sexually *i*,
      13: 4 the adulterer and all the sexually *i*.
Rev   21: 8 the murderers, the sexually *i*,
      22:15 the sexually *i*, the murderers,

IMMORALITY* (IMMORAL)

Nu   25: 1 in sexual *i* with Moabite women,
Jer   3: 9 Because Israel's *i* mattered so little
Mt   15:19 murder, adultery, sexual *i*, theft,
Mk   7:21 sexual *i*, theft, murder, adultery,
Ac   15:20 from sexual *i*, from the meat

Ac 15: 29 animals and from sexual *i.*
21: 25 animals and from sexual *i.*"
Ro 13: 13 not in sexual *i* and debauchery,
1Co 5: 1 reported that there is sexual *i*
6: 13 The body is not meant for sexual *i,*
6: 18 Flee from sexual *i.*
7: 2 But since there is so much *i,*
10: 8 We should not commit sexual *i,*
Gal 5: 19 sexual *i,* impurity and debauchery;
Eph 5: 3 must not be even a hint of sexual *i,*
Col 3: 5 sexual *i,* impurity, lust, evil desires
1Th 4: 3 that you should avoid sexual *i;*
Jude : 4 grace of our God into a licence for *i*
: 7 gave themselves up to sexual *i*
Rev 2: 14 and by committing sexual *i.*
2: 20 misleads my servants into sexual *i*
2: 21 given her time to repent of her *i,*
9: 21 their sexual *i* or their thefts.

IMMORTAL* (IMMORTALITY)

Ro 1: 23 glory of the *i* God for images made
1Ti 1: 17 Now to the King eternal, *i,*
6: 16 who alone is *i* and who lives

IMMORTALITY* (IMMORTAL)

Pr 12: 28 along that path is *i.*
Ro 2: 7 honour and *i,* he will give eternal life
1Co 15: 53 and the mortal with *i.*
15: 54 with *i,* then the saying that is
2Ti 1: 10 and *i* to light through the gospel.

IMPARTIAL*

Jas 3: 17 and good fruit, *i* and sincere.

IMPARTS*

Pr 29: 15 The rod of correction *i* wisdom,

IMPERFECT*

1Co 13: 10 perfection comes, the *i* disappears.

IMPERISHABLE

1Co 15: 42 it is raised *i;* it is sown in dishonour,
15: 50 nor does the perishable inherit the *i*
1Pe 1: 23 not of perishable seed, but of *i,*

IMPLANTED*

Ps 94: 9 Does he who *i* the ear not hear?

IMPLORE*

Mal 1: 9 "Now *i* God to be gracious to us.
2Co 5: 20 We *i* you on Christ's behalf:

IMPORTANCE* (IMPORTANT)

1Co 15: 3 passed on to you as of first *i:*

IMPORTANT (IMPORTANCE)

Mt 6: 25 Is not life more *i* than food,
23: 23 have neglected the more *i* matters
Mk 12: 29 "The most *i* one," answered Jesus,
12: 33 as yourself is more *i* than all burnt
Php 1: 18 The *i* thing is that in every way,

IMPOSSIBLE

Mt 17: 20 Nothing will be *i* for you."
19: 26 "With man this is *i,*
Mk 10: 27 "With man this is *i,* but not
Lk 1: 37 For nothing is *i* with God."
18: 27 "What is *i* with men is possible
Ac 2: 24 it was *i* for death to keep its hold
Heb 6: 4 It is *i* for those who have once been

Heb 6: 18 things in which it is *i* for God to lie,
10: 4 because it is *i* for the blood of bulls
11: 6 without faith it is *i* to please God,

IMPOSTORS

2Ti 3: 13 and *i* will go from bad to worse,

IMPRESS* (IMPRESSES)

Dt 6: 7 *I* them on your children.

IMPRESSES* (IMPRESS)

Pr 17: 10 A rebuke *i* a man of discernment

IMPROPER*

Eph 5: 3 these are *i* for God's holy people.

IMPURE (IMPURITY)

Ac 10: 15 not call anything *i* that God has
Eph 5: 5 No immoral, *i* or greedy person—
1Th 2: 3 spring from error or *i* motives,
4: 7 For God did not call us to be *i,*
Rev 21: 27 Nothing *i* will ever enter it,

IMPURITY (IMPURE)

Ro 1: 24 hearts to sexual *i* for the degrading
Gal 5: 19 sexual immorality, *i*
Eph 4: 19 as to indulge in every kind of *i,*
5: 3 or of any kind of *i,* or of greed,
Col 3: 5 *i,* lust, evil desires and greed,

INCENSE

Ex 30: 1 altar of acacia wood for burning *i.*
40: 5 Place the gold altar of *i* in front
Ps 141: 2 my prayer be set before you like *i;*
Mt 2: 11 him with gifts of gold and of *i*
Heb 9: 4 which had the golden altar of *i*
Rev 5: 8 were holding golden bowls full of *i,*
8: 4 The smoke of the *i,* together

INCLINATION (INCLINES)

Ge 6: 5 and that every *i* of the thoughts

INCLINES* (INCLINATION)

Ecc 10: 2 The heart of the wise *i* to the right,

INCOME

Ecc 5: 10 wealth is never satisfied with his *i.*
1Co 16: 2 sum of money in keeping with his *i,*

INCOMPARABLE*

Eph 2: 7 ages he might show the *i* riches

INCREASE (EVER-INCREASING INCREASED INCREASES INCREASING)

Ge 1: 22 "Be fruitful and *i* in number
3: 16 "I will greatly *i* your pains
8: 17 be fruitful and *i* in number upon it
Ps 62: 10 though your riches *i,*
Pr 22: 16 oppresses the poor to *i* his wealth
Isa 9: 7 Of the *i* of his government
Mt 24: 12 Because of the *i* of wickedness,
Lk 17: 5 said to the Lord, "*I* our faith!"
Ac 12: 24 But the word of God continued to *i*
Ro 5: 20 added so that the trespass might *i.*
1Th 3: 12 May the Lord make your love *i*

INCREASED (INCREASE)

Ac 6: 7 of disciples in Jerusalem *i* rapidly,
Ro 5: 20 But where sin *i,* grace *i* all the more

INCREASES (INCREASE)

Pr 24: 5 and a man of knowledge *i* strength;

INCREASING (INCREASE)

Ac 6: 1 when the number of disciples was *i*,
2Th 1: 3 one of you has for each other is *i*.
2Pe 1: 8 these qualities in *i* measure,

INCREDIBLE*

Ac 26: 8 of you consider it *i* that God raises

INDECENT

Ro 1: 27 Men committed *i* acts

INDEPENDENT*

1Co 11: 11 however, woman is not *i* of man,
11: 11 of man, nor is man *i* of woman.

INDESCRIBABLE*

2Co 9: 15 Thanks be to God for his *i* gift!

INDESTRUCTIBLE*

Heb 7: 16 on the basis of the power of an *i* life

INDIGNANT

Mk 10: 14 When Jesus saw this, he was *i*.

INDISPENSABLE*

1Co 12: 22 seem to be weaker are *i*,

INEFFECTIVE*

2Pe 1: 8 they will keep you from being *i*

INEXPRESSIBLE*

2Co 12: 4 He heard *i* things, things that man
1Pe 1: 8 are filled with an *i* and glorious joy,

INFANCY* (INFANTS)

2Ti 3: 15 from *i* you have known the holy

INFANTS (INFANCY)

Ps 8: 2 From the lips of children and *i*
Mt 21: 16 "'From the lips of children and *i*
1Co 3: 1 but as worldly—mere *i* in Christ.
14: 20 In regard to evil be *i*,
Eph 4: 14 Then we will no longer be *i*,

INFIRMITIES*

Isa 53: 4 Surely he took up our *i*
Mt 8: 17 "He took up our *i*

INFLAMED

Ro 1: 27 were *i* with lust for one another.

INFLUENTIAL*

1Co 1: 26 not many were *i*; not many were

INHABITANTS (INHABITED)

Nu 33: 55 "'But if you do not drive out the *i*
Rev 8: 13 Woe! Woe to the *i* of the earth,

INHABITED (INHABITANTS)

Isa 45: 18 but formed it to be *i*—

INHERIT (CO-HEIRS HEIR HEIRS HERITAGE INHERITANCE)

Dt 1: 38 because he will lead Israel to *i* it.
Jos 1: 6 people to *i* the land I swore
Ps 37: 11 But the meek will *i* the land
37: 29 the righteous will *i* the land

Zec 2: 12 The LORD will *i* Judah
Mt 5: 5 for they will *i* the earth.
19: 29 as much and will *i* eternal life.
Mk 10: 17 "what must I do to *i* eternal life?"
Lk 10: 25 "what must I do to *i* eternal life?"
18: 18 what must I do to *i* eternal life?"
1Co 6: 9 the wicked will not *i* the kingdom
15: 50 blood cannot *i* the kingdom of God
Rev 21: 7 He who overcomes will *i* all this,

INHERITANCE (INHERIT)

Lev 20: 24 I will give it to you as an *i*,
Dt 4: 20 to be the people of his *i*,
10: 9 the LORD is their *i*, as the LORD
Jos 14: 3 two-and-a-half tribes their *i* east
Ps 16: 6 surely I have a delightful *i*.
33: 12 the people he chose for his *i*.
136: 21 and gave their land as an *i*,
Pr 13: 22 A good man leaves an *i*
Mt 25: 34 blessed by my Father; take your *i*,
Eph 1: 14 who is a deposit guaranteeing our *i*
5: 5 has any *i* in the kingdom of Christ
Col 1: 12 you to share in the *i* of the saints
3: 24 you know that you will receive an *i*
Heb 9: 15 receive the promised eternal *i*—
1Pe 1: 4 and into an *i* that can never perish,

INIQUITIES (INIQUITY)

Ps 78: 38 he forgave their *i*
103: 10 or repay us according to our *i*.
Isa 53: 5 he was crushed for our *i*;
53: 11 and he will bear their *i*.
59: 2 But your *i* have separated
Mic 7: 19 and hurl all our *i* into the depths

INIQUITY (INIQUITIES)

Ps 25: 11 forgive my *i*, though it is great.
32: 5 and did not cover up my *i*.
51: 2 Wash away all my *i*
51: 9 and blot out all my *i*.
Isa 53: 6 the *i* of us all.

INJURED

Eze 34: 16 will bind up the *i* and strengthen
Zec 11: 16 or heal the *i*, or feed the healthy,

INJUSTICE

2Ch 19: 7 the LORD our God there is no *i*

INK

2Co 3: 3 not with *i* but with the Spirit

INN*

Lk 2: 7 there was no room for them in the *i*
10: 34 took him to an *i* and took care

INNOCENT

Ex 23: 7 do not put an *i* or honest person
Dt 25: 1 acquitting the *i* and condemning
Pr 6: 17 hands that shed *i* blood,
17: 26 It is not good to punish an *i* man,
Mt 10: 16 shrewd as snakes and as *i* as doves.
27: 4 "for I have betrayed *i* blood."
27: 24 I am *i* of this man's blood," he said.
Ac 20: 26 declare to you today that I am *i*
Ro 16: 19 what is good, and *i* about what is
1Co 4: 4 but that does not make me *i*.

INSCRIPTION

Mt 22: 20 And whose *i*?" "Caesar's,"
2Ti 2: 19 with this *i*: "The Lord knows those

INSIGHT

1Ki	4: 29	Solomon wisdom and very great *i*,
Ps	119: 99	I have more *i* than all my teachers,
Pr	5: 1	listen well to my words of *i*,
	21: 30	There is no wisdom, no *i*, no plan
Php	1: 9	more in knowledge and depth of *i*,
2Ti	2: 7	for the Lord will give you *i*

INSOLENT

Ro	1: 30	God-haters, *i*, arrogant

INSPIRED*

Hos	9: 7	the *i* man a maniac.
1Th	1: 3	and your endurance *i* by hope

INSTALLED

Ps	2: 6	"I have *i* my King

INSTINCT* (INSTINCTS)

2Pe	2: 12	are like brute beasts, creatures of *i*,
Jude	: 10	things they do understand by *i*,

INSTINCTS* (INSTINCT)

Jude	: 19	who follow mere natural *i*

INSTITUTED

Ro	13: 2	rebelling against what God has *i*,
1Pe	2: 13	to every authority *i* among men:

INSTRUCT (INSTRUCTED INSTRUCTION INSTRUCTIONS INSTRUCTOR)

Ps	32: 8	I will *i* you and teach you
	105: 22	to *i* his princes as he pleased
Pr	9: 9	*I* a wise man and he will be wiser
Ro	15: 14	and competent to *i* one another.
1Co	2: 16	that he may *i* him?"
	14: 19	to *i* others than ten thousand words
2Ti	2: 25	who oppose him must gently *i*,

INSTRUCTED (INSTRUCT)

2Ch	26: 5	who *i* him in the fear of God.
Pr	21: 11	a wise man is *i*, he gets knowledge.
Isa	50: 4	LORD has given me an *i* tongue,
Mt	13: 52	who has been *i* about the kingdom
1Co	14: 31	in turn so that everyone may be *i*

INSTRUCTION (INSTRUCT)

Pr	1: 8	Listen, my son, to your father's *i*
	4: 1	Listen, my sons, to a father's *i*;
	4: 13	Hold on to *i*, do not let it go;
	8: 10	Choose my *i* instead of silver,
	8: 33	Listen to my *i* and be wise;
	13: 1	A wise son heeds his father's *i*,
	13: 13	He who scorns *i* will pay for it,
	16: 20	Whoever gives heed to *i* prospers,
	16: 21	and pleasant words promote *i*.
	19: 20	Listen to advice and accept *i*,
	23: 12	Apply your heart to *i*
1Co	14: 6	or prophecy or word of *i*?
	14: 26	or a word of *i*, a revelation,
Eph	6: 4	up in the training and *i* of the Lord.
1Th	4: 8	he who rejects this *i* does not reject
2Th	3: 14	If anyone does not obey our *i*
1Ti	1: 18	I give you this *i* in keeping
	6: 3	to the sound *i* of our Lord Jesus
2Ti	4: 2	with great patience and careful *i*.

INSTRUCTIONS (INSTRUCT)

1Ti	3: 14	I am writing you these *i* so that,

INSTRUCTOR (INSTRUCT)

Gal	6: 6	share all good things with his *i*.

INSTRUMENT* (INSTRUMENTS)

Eze	33: 32	beautiful voice and plays an *i* well,
Ac	9: 15	This man is my chosen *i*
2Ti	2: 21	he will be an *i* for noble purposes,

INSTRUMENTS (INSTRUMENT)

Ro	6: 13	as *i* of wickedness, but rather offer

INSULT (INSULTED INSULTS)

Pr	9: 7	corrects a mocker invites *i*;
	12: 16	but a prudent man overlooks an *i*.
Mt	5: 11	Blessed are you when people *i* you,
Lk	6: 22	when they exclude you and *i* you
1Pe	3: 9	evil with evil or *i* with *i*,

INSULTED (INSULT)

Heb	10: 29	and who has *i* the Spirit of grace?
Jas	2: 6	love him? But you have *i* the poor.
1Pe	4: 14	If you are *i* because of the name

INSULTS (INSULT)

Ps	22: 7	they hurl *i*, shaking their heads:
	69: 9	the *i* of those who insult you fall
Pr	22: 10	quarrels and *i* are ended.
Mk	15: 29	passed by hurled *i* at him,
Jn	9: 28	Then they hurled *i* at him and said,
Ro	15: 3	"The *i* of those who insult you have
2Co	12: 10	in *i*, in hardships, in persecutions,
1Pe	2: 23	When they hurled their *i* at him,

INTEGRITY*

Dt	9: 5	or your *i* that you are going
1Ki	9: 4	if you walk before me in *i* of heart
1Ch	29: 17	the heart and are pleased with *i*.
Ne	7: 2	because he was a man of *i*
Job	2: 3	And he still maintains his *i*,
	2: 9	"Are you still holding on to your *i*?
	6: 29	reconsider, for my *i* is at stake.
	27: 5	till I die, I will not deny my *i*.
Ps	7: 8	according to my *i*, O Most High.
	25: 21	May *i* and uprightness protect me,
	41: 12	In my *i* you uphold me
	78: 72	David shepherded them with *i*
Pr	10: 9	The man of *i* walks securely,
	11: 3	The *i* of the upright guides them,
	13: 6	Righteousness guards the man of *i*,
	17: 26	or to flog officials for their *i*.
	29: 10	Bloodthirsty men hate a man of *i*
Isa	45: 23	my mouth has uttered in all *i*
	59: 4	no-one pleads his case with *i*.
Mt	22: 16	"we know you are a man of *i*
Mk	12: 14	we know you are a man of *i*.
Tit	2: 7	your teaching show *i*, seriousness

INTELLIGENCE (INTELLIGENT)

Isa	29: 14	the *i* of the intelligent will vanish."
1Co	1: 19	*i* of the intelligent I will frustrate."

INTELLIGENT (INTELLIGENCE)

Isa	29: 14	the intelligence of the *i* will vanish

INTELLIGIBLE

1Co	14: 19	I would rather speak five *i* words

INTENDED

Ge	50: 20	place of God? You *i* to harm me,

INTENSE

1Th   2: 17 out of our *i* longing we made every
Rev 16: 9 They were seared by the *i* heat

INTERCEDE (INTERCEDES INTERCEDING INTERCESSION INTERCESSOR)

Heb   7: 25 he always lives to *i* for them.

INTERCEDES* (INTERCEDE)

Ro   8: 26 but the Spirit himself *i* for us
       8: 27 because the Spirit *i* for the saints

INTERCEDING* (INTERCEDE)

Ro   8: 34 hand of God and is also *i* for us.

INTERCESSION* (INTERCEDE)

Isa 53: 12 and made *i* for the transgressors.
1Ti   2: 1 *i* and thanksgiving be made

INTERCESSOR* (INTERCEDE)

Job 16: 20 My *i* is my friend

INTEREST [1]

Lev 25: 36 Do not take *i* of any kind from him,
Dt   23: 20 You may charge a foreigner *i*,
Mt   25: 27 would have received it back with *i*.

INTEREST [2] (INTERESTS)

Php   2: 20 who takes a genuine *i*

INTERESTS (INTEREST [2])

1Co   7: 34 his wife—and his *i* are divided.
Php   2: 4 only to your own *i*, but also to the *i*
       2: 21 everyone looks out for his own *i*,

INTERFERE*

Ezr   6: 7 Do not *i* with the work

INTERMARRY (MARRY)

Dt   7: 3 Do not *i* with them.
Ezr   9: 14 and *i* with the peoples who commit

INTERPRET (INTERPRETATION INTERPRETER INTERPRETS)

Ge   41: 15 "I had a dream, and no-one can *i* it.
Mt   16: 3 you cannot *i* the signs of the times.
1Co 12: 30 Do all *i*? But eagerly desire
     14: 13 pray that he may *i* what he says.
     14: 27 one at a time, and someone must *i*.

INTERPRETATION (INTERPRET)

1Co 12: 10 and to still another the *i* of tongues.
     14: 26 a revelation, a tongue or an *i*.
2Pe   1: 20 about by the prophet's own *i*.

INTERPRETER (INTERPRET)

1Co 14: 28 If there is no *i*, the speaker should

INTERPRETS (INTERPRET)

1Co 14: 5 he *i*, so that the church may be

INVADED

2Ki 17: 5 king of Assyria *i* the entire land,
     24: 1 king of Babylon *i* the land,

INVENT* (INVENTED)

Ro   1: 30 boastful; they *i* ways of doing evil;

INVENTED* (INVENT)

2Pe   1: 16 We did not follow cleverly *i* stories

INVESTIGATED

Lk   1: 3 I myself have carefully *i* everything

INVISIBLE*

Ro   1: 20 of the world God's *i* qualities—
Col   1: 15 He is the image of the *i* God,
      1: 16 and on earth, visible and *i*,
1Ti   1: 17 immortal, *i*, the only God,
Heb 11: 27 because he saw him who is *i*.

INVITE (INVITED INVITES)

Mt   22: 9 *i* to the banquet anyone you find.'
     25: 38 did we see you a stranger and *i* you
Lk   14: 12 do not *i* your friends, your brothers
     14: 13 you give a banquet, *i* the poor,

INVITED (INVITE)

Zep   1: 7 he has consecrated those he has *i*.
Mt   22: 14 For many are *i*, but few are chosen
     25: 35 I was a stranger and you *i* me in,
Lk   14: 10 But when you are *i*, take the lowest
Rev 19: 9 'Blessed are those who are *i*

INVITES (INVITE)

Pr   18: 6 and his mouth *i* a beating.
1Co 10: 27 If some unbeliever *i* you to a meal

INVOLVED

2Ti   2: 4 a soldier gets *i* in civilian affairs—

IRON

2Ki   6: 6 threw it there, and made the *i* float.
Ps   2: 9 will rule them with an *i* sceptre;
Pr   27: 17 As *i* sharpens *i*,
Da   2: 33 and thighs of bronze, its legs of *i*,
1Ti   4: 2 have been seared as with a hot *i*.
Rev   2: 27 He will rule them with an *i* sceptre;
     12: 5 all the nations with an *i* sceptre.
     19: 15 He will rule them with an *i* sceptre

IRRELIGIOUS*

1Ti   1: 9 and sinful, the unholy and *i*;

IRREVOCABLE*

Ro   11: 29 for God's gifts and his call are *i*.

ISAAC

Son of Abraham by Sarah (Ge 17:19; 21:1-7; 1Ch 1:28). Abrahamic covenant perpetuated through (Ge 17:21; 26:2-5). Offered up by Abraham (Ge 22; Heb 11:17-19). Rebekah taken as wife (Ge 24). Inherited Abraham's estate (Ge 25:5). Fathered Esau and Jacob (Ge 25:19-26; 1Ch 1:34). Nearly lost Rebekah to Abimelech (Ge 26:1-11). Covenant with Abimelech (Ge 26:12-31). Tricked into blessing Jacob (Ge 27). Death (Ge 35:27-29). Father of Israel (Ex 3:6; Dt 29:13; Ro 9:10).

ISAIAH

Prophet to Judah (Isa 1:1). Called by the LORD (Isa 6). Announced judgment to Ahaz (Isa 7), deliverance from Assyria to Hezekiah (2Ki 19; Isa 36-37), deliverance from death to Hezekiah (2Ki 20:1-11; Isa 38). Chronicler of Judah's history (2Ch 26:22; 32:32).

ISCARIOT see JUDAS

ISH-BOSHETH*

Son of Saul who attempted to succeed him as king (2Sa 2:8-4:12; 1Ch 8:33).

ISHMAEL

Son of Abraham by Hagar (Ge 16; 1Ch 1:28). Blessed, but not son of covenant (Ge 17:18-21; Gal 4:21-31). Sent away by Sarah (Ge 21:8-21). Children (Ge 25:12-18; 1Ch 1:29-31). Death (Ge 25:17).

ISLAND

Rev   1: 9 was on the *i* of Patmos
      16: 20 Every *i* fled away

ISRAEL (ISRAEL'S ISRAELITE ISRAELITES)

1. Name given to Jacob (see JACOB).
2. Corporate name of Jacob's descendants; often specifically Northern Kingdom.

Ex   28: 11 Engrave the names of the sons of *I*
      28: 29 of the sons of *I* over his heart
Nu   24: 17 a sceptre will rise out of *I*.
Dt   6: 4 Hear, O *I*: The LORD our God,
      10: 12 O *I*, what does the LORD your
Jos   4: 22 *I* crossed the Jordan on dry ground
Jdg 17: 6 In those days *I* had no king;
Ru   2: 12 of *I*, under whose wings you have
1Sa   3: 20 *I* from Dan to Beersheba
      4: 21 "The glory has departed from *I*"—
    14: 23 So the LORD rescued *I* that day,
    15: 26 has rejected you as king over *I*!"
    17: 46 will know that there is a God in *I*.
    18: 16 But all *I* and Judah loved David,
2Sa   5: 2 'You will shepherd my people *I*,
      5: 3 they anointed David king over *I*.
    14: 25 In all *I* there was not a man
1Ki   1: 35 I have appointed him ruler over *I*
    10: 9 of the LORD's eternal love for *I*,
    18: 17 "Is that you, you troubler of *I*?"
    19: 18 Yet I reserve seven thousand in *I*—
2Ki   5: 8 know that there is a prophet in *I*."
1Ch 17: 22 made your people *I* your very own
    21: 1 incited David to take a census of *I*.
    29: 25 Solomon in the sight of all *I*
2Ch 9: 8 of the love of your God for *I*
Ps   73: 1 Surely God is good to *I*,
    81: 8 if you would but listen to me, O *I*!
    98: 3 his faithfulness to the house of *I*;
    99: 8 you were to *I* a forgiving God,
Isa 11: 12 and gather the exiles of *I*;
    27: 6 *I* will bud and blossom
    44: 21 O *I*, I will not forget you.
    46: 13 my splendour to *I*.
Jer   2: 3 *I* was holy to the LORD,
    23: 6 and *I* will live in safety.
    31: 2 I will come to give rest to *I*."
    31: 10 'He who scattered *I* will gather
    31: 31 covenant with the house of *I*
    33: 17 sit on the throne of the house of *I*,
Eze   3: 17 you a watchman for the house of *I*;
    33: 7 you a watchman for the house of *I*;
    34: 2 prophesy against the shepherds of *I*
    37: 28 that I the LORD make *I* holy,
    39: 23 of *I* went into exile for their sin,
Da   9: 20 my sin and the sin of my people *I*
Hos 11: 1 "When *I* was a child, I loved him,
Am   4: 12 prepare to meet your God, O *I*."
     7: 11 and *I* will surely go into exile,
     8: 2 "The time is ripe for my people *I*;
     9: 14 I will bring back my exiled people *I*

Mic   5: 2 one who will be ruler over *I*,
Zep   3: 13 The remnant of *I* will do no wrong;
Zec 11: 14 brotherhood between Judah and *I*.
Mal   1: 5 even beyond the borders of *I*!'
Mt   2: 6 be the shepherd of my people *I*.' "
    10: 6 Go rather to the lost sheep of *I*.
    15: 24 only to the lost sheep of *I*."
Mk 12: 29 'Hear, O *I*, the Lord our God,
Lk   22: 30 judging the twelve tribes of *I*.
Ac   1: 6 going to restore the kingdom to *I*?"
     9: 15 and before the people of *I*.
Ro   9: 4 of my own race, the people of *I*.
     9: 6 all who are descended from *I* are *I*.
     9: 31 but *I*, who pursued a law
    11: 7 What *I* sought so earnestly it did
    11: 26 And so all *I* will be saved,
Gal   6: 16 who follow this rule, even to the *I*
Eph 2: 12 excluded from citizenship in *I*
     3: 6 Gentiles are heirs together with *I*,
Heb 8: 8 covenant with the house of *I*
Rev   7: 4 144,000 from all the tribes of *I*.
    21: 12 the names of the twelve tribes of *I*.

ISRAEL'S (ISRAEL)

Jdg 10: 16 he could bear *I* misery no longer.
2Sa 23: 1 *I* singer of songs:
Isa 44: 6 *I* King and Redeemer, the LORD
Jer   3: 9 Because *I* immorality mattered
    31: 9 because I am *I* father,
Jn   3: 10 "You are *I* teacher," said Jesus,

ISRAELITE (ISRAEL)

Ex   16: 1 The whole *I* community set out
    35: 29 All the *I* men and women who
Nu   8: 16 offspring from every *I* woman.
    20: 1 the whole *I* community arrived
    20: 22 The whole *I* community set out
Jn   1: 47 "Here is a true *I*, in whom there is
Ro   11: 1 I am an *I* myself, a descendant

ISRAELITES (ISRAEL)

Ex   1: 7 the *I* were fruitful and multiplied
    2: 23 The *I* groaned in their slavery
    3: 9 the cry of the *I* has reached me,
    12: 35 The *I* did as Moses instructed
    12: 37 The *I* journeyed from Rameses
    14: 22 and the *I* went through the sea
    16: 12 I have heard the grumbling of the *I*.
    16: 35 The *I* ate manna forty years,
    24: 17 To the *I* the glory of the LORD
    28: 30 decisions for the *I* over his heart
    29: 45 Then I will dwell among the *I*
    31: 16 The *I* are to observe the Sabbath,
    33: 5 "Tell the *I*, 'You are a stiff-necked
    39: 42 The *I* had done all the work just
Lev 22: 32 be acknowledged as holy by the *I*.
    25: 46 rule over your fellow *I* ruthlessly.
    25: 55 for the *I* belong to me as servants.
Nu   2: 32 These are the *I*, counted according
    6: 23 'This is how you are to bless the *I*.
    9: 2 "Have the *I* celebrate the Passover
    9: 17 the *I* set out; wherever the cloud
    10: 12 Then the *I* set out from the Desert
    14: 2 All the *I* grumbled against Moses
    20: 12 as holy in the sight of the *I*,
    21: 6 they bit the people and many *I* died
    26: 65 had told those *I* they would surely
    27: 12 and see the land I have given the *I*.
    33: 3 The *I* set out from Rameses
    35: 10 "Speak to the *I* and say to them:

Dt 33: 1 on the *I* before his death.
Jos 1: 2 about to give to them—to the *I*.
5: 6 The *I* had moved about
7: 1 the *I* acted unfaithfully in regard
8: 32 There in the presence of the *I*,
18: 1 of the *I* gathered at Shiloh
21: 3 the *I* gave the Levites the following
22: 9 of Manasseh left the *I* at Shiloh
Jdg 2: 11 Then the *I* did evil in the eyes
3: 12 Once again the *I* did evil
4: 1 the *I* once again did evil in the eyes
6: 1 Again the *I* did evil in the eyes
10: 6 Again the *I* did evil in the eyes
13: 1 Again the *I* did evil in the eyes
1Sa 17: 2 Saul and the *I* assembled
1Ki 8: 63 and all the *I* dedicated the temple
9: 22 did not make slaves of any of the *I*;
12: 1 for all the *I* had gone there
12: 17 But as for the *I* who were living
2Ki 17: 24 towns of Samaria to replace the *I*.
1Ch 9: 2 in their own towns were some *I*,
10: 1 fought against Israel; the *I* fled
11: 4 and all the *I* marched to Jerusalem,
2Ch 7: 6 and all the *I* were standing.
Ne 1: 6 the sins we *I*, including myself
Jer 16: 14 who brought the *I* up out of Egypt,'
Hos 1: 10 "Yet the *I* will be like the sand
3: 1 Love her as the LORD loves the *I*,
Am 4: 5 boast about them, you *I*,
Mic 5: 3 return to join the *I*.
Ro 9: 27 the number of the *I* be like the sand
10: 1 for the *I* is that they may be saved.
10: 16 But not all the *I* accepted the good
2Co 11: 22 Are they *I*? So am I.

ISSACHAR

Son of Jacob by Leah (Ge 30:18; 35:23; 1Ch 2:1). Tribe of blessed (Ge 49:14-15; Dt 33:18-19), numbered (Nu 1:29; 26:25), allotted land (Jos 19:17-23; Eze 48:25), assisted Deborah (Jdg 5:15), 12,000 from (Rev 7:7).

ISSUING*

Da 9: 25 From the *i* of the decree to restore

ITALY

Ac 27: 1 decided that we would sail for *I*,
Heb 13: 24 from *I* send you their greetings.

ITCHING*

2Ti 4: 3 to say what their *i* ears want to hear

ITHAMAR

Son of Aaron (Ex 6:23; 1Ch 6:3). Duties at tabernacle (Ex 38:21; Nu 4:21-33; 7:8).

ITTAI

2Sa 15: 19 The king said to *I* the Gittite,

IVORY

1Ki 10: 22 silver and *i*, and apes and baboons.
22: 39 the palace he built and inlaid with *i*

JABBOK

Ge 32: 22 and crossed the ford of the *J*.
Dt 3: 16 and out to the *J* River,

JABESH

1Sa 11: 1 And all the men of *J* said to him,
31: 12 wall of Beth Shan and went to *J*,

1Ch 10: 12 and his sons and brought them to *J*.

JABESH GILEAD

Jdg 21: 8 that no-one from *J* had come to
2Sa 2: 4 the men of *J* who had buried Saul,
1Ch 10: 11 the inhabitants of *J* heard

JACOB

Second son of Isaac, twin of Esau (Ge 26:21-26; 1Ch 1:34). Bought Esau's birthright (Ge 26:29-34); tricked Isaac into blessing him (Ge 27:1-37). Fled to Haran (Ge 28:1-5). Abrahamic covenant perpetuated through (Ge 28:13-15; Mal 1:2). Vision at Bethel (Ge 28:10-22). Served Laban for Rachel and Leah (Ge 29:1-30). Children (Ge 29:31-30:24; 35:16-26; 1Ch 2-9). Flocks increased (Ge 30:25-43). Returned to Canaan (Ge 31). Wrestled with God; name changed to Israel (Ge 32:22-32). Reconciled to Esau (Ge 33). Returned to Bethel (Ge 35:1-15). Favoured Joseph (Ge 37:3). Sent sons to Egypt during famine (Ge 42-43). Settled in Egypt (Ge 46). Blessed Ephraim and Manasseh (Ge 48). Blessed sons (Ge 49:1-28; Heb 11:21). Death (Ge 49:29-33). Burial (Ge 50:1-14).

JAEL*

Woman who killed Canaanite general, Sisera (Jdg 4:17-22; 5:24-27).

JAIR

Judge from Gilead (Jdg 10:3-5).

JAIRUS*

Synagogue ruler whose daughter Jesus raised (Mk 5:22-43; Lk 8:41-56).

JAMES

1. Apostle; brother of John (Mt 4:21-22; 10:2; Mk 3:17; Lk 5:1-10). At transfiguration (Mt 17:1-13; Mk 9:1-13; Lk 9:28-36). Killed by Herod (Ac 12:2).

2. Apostle; son of Alphaeus (Mt 10:3; Mk 3:18; Lk 6:15).

3. Brother of Jesus (Mt 13:55; Mk 6:3; Lk 24:10; Gal 1:19) and Judas (Jude 1). With believers before Pentecost (Ac 1:13). Leader of church at Jerusalem (Ac 12:17; 15; 21:18; Gal 2:9, 12). Author of epistle (Jas 1:1).

JAPHETH

Son of Noah (Ge 5:32; 1Ch 1:4-5). Blessed (Ge 9:18-28). Sons of (Ge 10:2-5).

JAR (JARS)

Ge 24: 14 let down your *j* that I may have
1Ki 17: 14 'The *j* of flour will not be used up
Jer 19: 1 "Go and buy a clay *j* from a potter.
Lk 8: 16 hides it in a *j* or puts it under a bed.

JARS (JAR)

Jn 2: 6 Nearby stood six stone water *j*,
2Co 4: 7 we have this treasure in *j* of clay

JASPER

Ex 28: 20 row a chrysolite, an onyx and a *j*.
Eze 28: 13 chrysolite, onyx and *j*,
Rev 4: 3 sat there had the appearance of *j*
21: 19 The first foundation was *j*,

JAVELIN

1Sa 17: 45 me with sword and spear and *j*,

JAWBONE

Jdg 15: 15 Finding a fresh *j* of a donkey,

JEALOUS (JEALOUSY)

Ex 20: 5 the LORD your God, am a *j* God,
34: 14 whose name is *J*, is a *j* God.
Dt 4: 24 God is a consuming fire, a *j* God.
6: 15 is a *j* God and his anger will burn
32: 21 They made me *j* by what is no god
Jos 24: 19 He is a holy God; he is a *j* God.
Eze 16: 38 of my wrath and *j* anger.
16: 42 my *j* anger will turn away from you
23: 25 I will direct my *j* anger against you,
36: 6 in my *j* wrath because you have
Joel 2: 18 the LORD will be *j* for his land
Na 1: 2 LORD is a *j* and avenging God;
Zep 3: 8 consumed by the fire of my *j* anger.
Zec 1: 14 I am very *j* for Jerusalem and Zion,
8: 2 "I am very *j* for Zion; I am burning
2Co 11: 2 I am *j* for you with a godly jealousy

JEALOUSY (JEALOUS)

Ps 79: 5 How long will your *j* burn like fire?
Pr 6: 34 for *j* arouses a husband's fury,
27: 4 but who can stand before *j*?
SS 8: 6 its *j* unyielding as the grave.
Zep 1: 18 In the fire of his *j*
Zec 8: 2 I am burning with *j* for her."
Ro 13: 13 debauchery, not in dissension and *j*
1Co 3: 3 For since there is *j* and quarrelling
10: 22 trying to arouse the Lord's *j*?
2Co 11: 2 I am jealous for you with a godly *j*.
12: 20 *j*, outbursts of anger, factions,
Gal 5: 20 hatred, discord, *j*, fits of rage,

JECONIAH see JEHOIACHIN

JEERS*

Heb 11: 36 Some faced *j* and flogging,

JEHOAHAZ

1. Son of Jehu; king of Israel (2Ki 13:1-9).
2. Son of Josiah; king of Judah (2Ki 23:31-34; 2Ch 36:1-4).

JEHOASH

1. See JOASH.
2. Son of Jehoahaz; king of Israel. Defeat of Aram prophesied by Elisha (2Ki 13:10-25). Defeated Amaziah in Jerusalem (2Ki 14:1-16; 2Ch 25:17-24).

JEHOIACHIN

Son of Jehoiakim; king of Judah exiled by Nebuchadnezzar (2Ki 24:8-17; 2Ch 36:8-10; Jer 22:24-30; 24:1). Raised from prisoner status (2Ki 25:27-30; Jer 52:31-34).

JEHOIADA

Priest who sheltered Joash from Athaliah (2Ki 11-12; 2Ch 22:11-24:16).

JEHOIAKIM

Son of Jehoahaz; made king of Judah by Pharaoh Neco (2Ki 23:34-24:6; 2Ch 36:4-8; Jer 22:18-23). Burned scroll of Jeremiah's prophecies (Jer 36).

JEHORAM

1. Son of Jehoshaphat; king of Judah (2Ki 8:16-24). Prophesied against by Elijah; killed by the LORD (2Ch 21).
2. See JORAM.

JEHOSHAPHAT

Son of Asa; king of Judah. Strengthened his kingdom (2Ch 17). Joined with Ahab against Aram (2Ki 22; 2Ch 18). Established judges (2Ch 19). Joined with Joram against Moab (2Ki 3; 2Ch 20).

JEHOVAH see †LORD

JEHU

1. Prophet against Baasha (2Ki 16:1-7).
2. King of Israel. Anointed by Elijah to obliterate house of Ahab (1Ki 19:16-17); anointed by servant of Elisha (2Ki 9:1-13). Killed Joram and Ahaziah (2Ki 9:14-29; 2Ch 22:7-9), Jezebel (2Ki 9:30-37), relatives of Ahab (2Ki 10:1-17), ministers of Baal (2Ki 10:18-29). Death (2Ki 10:30-36).

JEPHTHAH

Judge from Gilead who delivered Israel from Ammon (Jdg 10:6-12:7). Made rash vow concerning his daughter (Jdg 11:30-40).

JEREMIAH

Prophet to Judah (Jer 1:1-3). Called by the LORD (Jer 1). Put in stocks (Jer 20:1-3). Threatened for prophesying (Jer 11:18-23; 26). Opposed by Hananiah (Jer 28). Scroll burned (Jer 36). Imprisoned (Jer 37). Thrown into cistern (Jer 38). Forced to Egypt with those fleeing Babylonians (Jer 43).

JERICHO

Nu 22: 1 along the Jordan across from *J*.
Jos 3: 16 the people crossed over opposite *J*.
5: 10 camped at Gilgal on the plains of *J*,
Lk 10: 30 going down from Jerusalem to *J*,
Heb 11: 30 By faith the walls of *J* fell,

JEROBOAM

1. Official of Solomon; rebelled to become first king of Israel (1Ki 11:26-40; 12:1-20; 2Ch 10). Idolatry (1Ki 12:25-33); judgment for (1Ki 13-14; 2Ch 13).
2. Son of Jehoash; king of Israel (1Ki 14:23-29).

JERUB-BAAL see GIDEON

JERUSALEM

Jos 10: 1 of *J* heard that Joshua had taken Ai
15: 8 of the Jebusite city (that is, *J*).
Jdg 1: 8 The men of Judah attacked *J* also
1Sa 17: 54 head and brought it to *J*,
2Sa 5: 5 and in *J* he reigned over all Israel
5: 6 and his men marched to *J*
9: 13 And Mephibosheth lived in *J*,
11: 1 But David remained in *J*.
15: 29 took the ark of God back to *J*
24: 16 stretched out his hand to destroy *J*,
1Ki 3: 1 the LORD, and the wall around *J*.
9: 15 the wall of *J*, and Hazor, Megiddo
9: 19 whatever he desired to build in *J*,
10: 26 cities and also with him in *J*.
10: 27 as common in *J* as stones,
11: 7 of *J*, Solomon built a high place

1Ki	11: 13	my servant and for the sake of *J*,
	11: 36	always have a lamp before me in *J*,
	11: 42	Solomon reigned in *J*
	12: 27	at the temple of the LORD in *J*,
	14: 21	and he reigned seventeen years in *J*
	14: 25	Shishak king of Egypt attacked *J*.
	15: 2	and he reigned in *J* three years.
	15: 10	and he reigned in *J* forty-one years.
	22: 42	he reigned in *J* twenty-five years.
2Ki	8: 17	and he reigned in *J* eight years.
	8: 26	and he reigned in *J* one year.
	12: 1	and he reigned in *J* forty years.
	12: 17	Then he turned to attack *J*.
	14: 2	he reigned in *J* twenty-nine years.
	14: 13	Then Jehoash went to *J*
	15: 2	and he reigned in *J* fifty-two years.
	15: 33	and he reigned in *J* sixteen years.
	16: 2	and he reigned in *J* sixteen years.
	16: 5	Israel marched up to fight against *J*
	18: 2	he reigned in *J* twenty-nine years.
	18: 17	Lachish to King Hezekiah at *J*.
	19: 31	For out of *J* will come a remnant,
	21: 1	and he reigned in *J* fifty-five years.
	21: 12	going to bring such disaster on *J*
	21: 19	and he reigned in *J* two years.
	22: 1	he reigned in *J* thirty-one years.
	23: 27	and I will reject *J*, the city I chose,
	23: 31	and he reigned in *J* three months.
	23: 36	and he reigned in *J* eleven years.
	24: 8	and he reigned in *J* three months.
	24: 10	king of Babylon advanced on *J*
	24: 14	He carried into exile all *J*:
	24: 18	and he reigned in *J* eleven years.
	24: 20	anger that all this happened to *J*
	25: 1	king of Babylon marched against *J*
	25: 9	royal palace and all the houses of *J*.
1Ch	11: 4	and all the Israelites marched to *J*,
	21: 16	sword in his hand extended over *J*.
2Ch	1: 4	he had pitched a tent for it in *J*.
	3: 1	the LORD in *J* on Mount Moriah,
	6: 6	now I have chosen *J* for my Name
	9: 1	she came to *J* to test him
	20: 15	and all who live in Judah and *J*!
	20: 27	and *J* returned joyfully to *J*,
	29: 8	LORD has fallen on Judah and *J*;
	36: 19	and broke down the wall of *J*;
Ezr	1: 2	a temple for him at *J* in Judah.
	2: 1	to Babylon (they returned to *J*
	3: 1	people assembled as one man in *J*.
	4: 12	up to us from you have gone to *J*
	4: 24	of God in *J* came to a standstill
	6: 12	or to destroy this temple in *J*.
	7: 8	Ezra arrived in *J* in the fifth month
	9: 9	a wall of protection in Judah and *J*.
	10: 7	for all the exiles to assemble in *J*.
Ne	1: 2	the exile, and also about *J*.
	1: 3	The wall of *J* is broken down,
	2: 11	to *J*, and after staying there three
	2: 17	Come, let us rebuild the wall of *J*,
	2: 20	you have no share in *J* or any claim
	3: 8	They restored *J* as far as the Broad
	4: 8	fight against *J* and stir up trouble
	11: 1	leaders of the people settled in *J*,
	12: 27	At the dedication of the wall of *J*,
	12: 43	in *J* could be heard far away.
Ps	51: 18	build up the walls of *J*.
	79: 1	they have reduced *J* to rubble.
	122: 2	in your gates, O *J*.
	122: 3	*J* is built like a city
	122: 6	Pray for the peace of *J*:

Ps	125: 2	As the mountains surround *J*,
	128: 5	may you see the prosperity of *J*,
	137: 5	If I forget you, O *J*,
	147: 2	The LORD builds up *J*;
	147: 12	Extol the LORD, O *J*;
SS	6: 4	lovely as *J*,
Isa	1: 1	and *J* that Isaiah son of Amoz saw
	2: 1	saw concerning Judah and *J*:
	3: 1	is about to take from *J* and Judah
	3: 8	*J* staggers,
	4: 3	recorded among the living in *J*.
	8: 14	And for the people of *J* he will be
	27: 13	LORD on the holy mountain in *J*.
	31: 5	the LORD Almighty will shield *J*;
	33: 20	your eyes will see *J*,
	40: 2	Speak tenderly to *J*,
	40: 9	You who bring good tidings to *J*,
	52: 1	O *J*, the holy city.
	52: 2	rise up, sit enthroned, O *J*.
	62: 6	on your walls, O *J*,
	62: 7	give him no rest till he establishes *J*
	65: 18	for I will create *J* to be a delight
Jer	2: 2	and proclaim in the hearing of *J*:
	3: 17	time they will call *J* The Throne
	4: 5	and proclaim in *J* and say:
	4: 14	O *J*, wash the evil from your heart
	5: 1	"Go up and down the streets of *J*,
	6: 6	and build siege ramps against *J*.
	8: 5	Why does *J* always turn away?
	9: 11	"I will make *J* a heap of ruins,
	13: 27	Woe to you, O *J*!
	23: 14	And among the prophets of *J*
	24: 1	into exile from *J* to Babylon
	26: 18	*J* will become a heap of rubble,
	32: 2	of Babylon was then besieging *J*,
	33: 10	the streets of *J* that are deserted,
	39: 1	This is how *J* was taken: In
	51: 50	and think on *J*."
	52: 14	broke down all the walls around *J*.
La	1: 7	*J* remembers all the treasures
Eze	14: 21	send against *J* my four dreadful
	16: 2	confront *J* with her detestable
Da	6: 10	the windows opened towards *J*.
	9: 2	of *J* would last seventy years.
	9: 12	done like what has been done to *J*.
	9: 25	and rebuild *J* until the Anointed
Joel	3: 1	restore the fortunes of Judah and *J*,
	3: 16	and thunder from *J*;
	3: 17	*J* will be holy;
Am	2: 5	will consume the fortresses of *J*."
Ob	: 11	and cast lots for *J*,
Mic	1: 5	Is it not *J*?
	4: 2	the word of the LORD from *J*.
Zep	3: 16	On that day they will say to *J*,
Zec	1: 14	'I am very jealous for *J* and Zion,
	1: 17	comfort Zion and choose *J*.'"
	2: 2	He answered me, "To measure *J*,
	2: 4	'*J* will be a city without walls
	8: 3	I will return to Zion and dwell in *J*.
	8: 8	I will bring them back to live in *J*;
	8: 15	determined to do good again to *J*
	8: 22	powerful nations will come to *J*
	9: 9	Shout, Daughter of *J*!
	9: 10	and the war-horses from *J*,
	12: 3	I will make *J* an immovable rock
	12: 10	the inhabitants of *J* a spirit of grace
	14: 2	the nations of *J* to fight against it;
	14: 8	living water will flow out from *J*,
	14: 16	that have attacked *J* will go up
Mt	16: 21	to his disciples that he must go to *J*

Mt 20: 18 said to them, "We are going up to *J*
21: 10 When Jesus entered *J*, the whole
23: 37 "O *J*, *J*, you who kill the prophets
Mk 10: 33 "We are going up to *J*," he said,
Lk 2: 22 Mary took him to *J* to present him
2: 41 Every year his parents went to *J*
2: 43 the boy Jesus stayed behind in *J*,
4: 9 The devil led him to *J*
9: 31 about to bring to fulfilment at *J*.
9: 51 Jesus resolutely set out for *J*,
13: 34 die outside *J*! "O *J*, *J*,
18: 31 told them, "We are going up to *J*,
19: 41 As he approached *J* and saw
21: 20 "When you see *J* surrounded
21: 24 *J* will be trampled
24: 47 name to all nations, beginning at *J*.
Jn 4: 20 where we must worship is in *J*."
Ac 1: 4 this command: "Do not leave *J*,
1: 8 and you will be my witnesses in *J*,
6: 7 of disciples in *J* increased rapidly,
20: 22 by the Spirit, I am going to *J*,
23: 11 As you have testified about me in *J*
Ro 15: 19 So from *J* all the way
Gal 4: 25 corresponds to the present city of *J*
4: 26 But the *J* that is above is free,
Heb 12: 22 to the heavenly *J*, the city
Rev 3: 12 the new *J*, which is coming
21: 2 I saw the Holy City, the new *J*,
21: 10 and showed me the Holy City, *J*,

JESSE

Father of David (Ru 4:17-22; 1Sa 16; 1Ch 2:12-17).

JESUS

LIFE: Genealogy (Mt 1:1-17; Lk 3:21-37). Birth announced (Mt 1:18-25; Lk 1:26-45). Birth (Mt 2:1-12; Lk 2:1-40). Escape to Egypt (Mt 2:13-23). As a boy in the temple (Lk 2:41-52). Baptism (Mt 3:13-17; Mk 1:9-11; Lk 3:21-22; Jn 1:32-34). Temptation (Mt 4:1-11; Mk 1:12-13; Lk 4:1-13). Ministry in Galilee (Mt 4:12-18:35; Mk 1:14-9:50; Lk 4:14-13:9; Jn 1:35-2:11; 4; 6), Transfiguration (Mt 17:1-8; Mk 9:2-8; Lk 9:28-36), on the way to Jerusalem (Mt 19-20; Mk 10; Lk 13:10-19:27), in Jerusalem (Mt 21-25; Mk 11-13; Lk 19:28-21:38; Jn 2:12-3:36; 5; 7-12). Last supper (Mt 26:17-35; Mk 14:12-31; Lk 22:1-38; Jn 13-17). Arrest and trial (Mt 26:36-27:31; Mk 14:43-15:20; Lk 22:39-23:25; Jn 18:1-19:16). Crucifixion (Mt 27:32-66; Mk 15:21-47; Lk 23:26-55; Jn 19:28-42). Resurrection and appearances (Mt 28; Mk 16; Lk 24; Jn 20-21; Ac 1:1-11; 7:56; 9:3-6; 1Co 15:1-8; Rev 1:1-20).

MIRACLES. Healings: official's son (Jn 4:43-54), demoniac in Capernaum (Mk 1:23-26; Lk 4:33-35), Peter's mother-in-law (Mt 8:14-17; Mk 1:29-31; Lk 4:38-39), leper (Mt 8:2-4; Mk 1:40-45; Lk 5:12-16), paralytic (Mt 9:1-8; Mk 2:1-12; Lk 5:17-26), cripple (Jn 5:1-9), shrivelled hand (Mt 12:10-13; Mk 3:1-5; Lk 6:6-11), centurion's servant (Mt 8:5-13; Lk 7:1-10), widow's son raised (Lk 7:11-17), demoniac (Mt 12:22-23; Lk 11:14), Gadarene demoniacs (Mt 8:28-34; Mk 5:1-20; Lk 8:26-39), woman's bleeding and Jairus' daughter (Mt 9:18-26; Mk 5:21-43; Lk 8:40-56), blind man (Mt 9:27-31), mute man (Mt 9:32-33), Canaanite woman's daughter (Mt 15:21-28; Mk 7:24-30), deaf man (Mk 7:31-37), blind man (Mk 8:22-26), demoniac boy (Mt 17:14-18; Mk 9:14-29; Lk 9:37-43), ten lepers (Lk 17:11-19), man born blind

(Jn 9:1-7), Lazarus raised (Jn 11), crippled woman (Lk 13:11-17), man with dropsy (Lk 14:1-6), two blind men (Mt 20:29-34; Mk 10:46-52; Lk 18:35-43), Malchus' ear (Lk 22:50-51). Other Miracles: water to wine (Jn 2:1-11), catch of fish (Lk 5:1-11), storm stilled (Mt 8:23-27; Mk 4:37-41; Lk 8:22-25), 5,000 fed (Mt 14:15-21; Mk 6:35-44; Lk 9:10-17; Jn 6:1-14), walking on water (Mt 14:25-33; Mk 6:48-52; Jn 6:15-21), 4,000 fed (Mt 15:32-39; Mk 8:1-9), money from fish (Mt 17:24-27), fig-tree cursed (Mt 21:18-22; Mk 11:12-14), catch of fish (Jn 21:1-14).

MAJOR TEACHING: Sermon on the Mount (Mt 5-7; Lk 6:17-49), to Nicodemus (Jn 3), to Samaritan woman (Jn 4), Bread of Life (Jn 6:22-59), at Feast of Tabernacles (Jn 7-8), woes to Pharisees (Mt 23; Lk 11:37-54), Good Shepherd (Jn 10:1-18), Mt of Olives Discourse (Mt 24-25; Mk 13; Lk 21:5-36), Upper Room Discourse (Jn 13-16).

PARABLES: Sower (Mt 13:3-23; Mk 4:3-25; Lk 8:5-18), seed's growth (Mk 4:26-29), wheat and weeds (Mt 13:24-30, 36-43), mustard seed (Mt 13:31-32; Mk 4:30-32), yeast (Mt 13:33-35; Mk 4:33-34), hidden treasure (Mt 13:44), valuable pearl (Mt 13:45-46), net (Mt 13:47-51), house owner (Mt 13:52), good Samaritan (Lk 10:25-37), unmerciful servant (Mt 18:15-35), lost sheep (Mt 18:10-14; Lk 15:4-7), lost coin (Lk 15:8-10), prodigal son (Lk 15:11-32), dishonest manager (Lk 16:1-13), rich man and Lazarus (Lk 16:19-31), persistent widow (Lk 18:1-8), Pharisee and tax collector (Lk 18:9-14), payment of workers (Mt 20:1-16), tenants and the vineyard (Mt 21:28-46; Mt 12:1-12; Lk 20:9-19), wedding banquet (Mt 22:1-14), faithful servant (Mt 24:45-51), ten virgins (Mt 25:1-13), talents (Mt 25:1-30; Lk 19:12-27).

DISCIPLES see APOSTLES. Call of (Jn 1:35-51; Mt 4:18-22; 9:9; Mk 1:16-20; 2:13-14; Lk 5:1-11, 27-28). Named Apostles (Mk 3:13-19; Lk 6:12-16). Twelve sent out (Mt 10; Mk 6:7-11; Lk 9:1-5). Seventy sent out (Lk 10:1-24). Defection of (Jn 6:60-71; Mt 26:56; Mk 14:50-52). Final commission (Mt 28:16-20; Jn 21:15-23; Ac 1:3-8).

Ac 2: 32 God has raised this *J* to life,
9: 5 "I am *J*, whom you are persecuting
9: 34 said to him, "*J* Christ heals you.
15: 11 of our Lord *J* that we are saved,
16: 31 "Believe in the Lord *J*,
20: 24 the task the Lord *J* has given me—
Ro 3: 24 redemption that came by Christ *J*.
5: 17 life through the one man, *J* Christ.
8: 1 for those who are in Christ *J*,
1Co 1: 7 for our Lord *J* Christ to be revealed
2: 2 except *J* Christ and him crucified.
6: 11 in the name of the Lord *J* Christ
8: 6 and there is but one Lord, *J* Christ,
12: 3 and no-one can say, "*J* is Lord,"
2Co 4: 5 not preach ourselves, but *J* Christ
13: 5 Do you not realise that Christ *J* is
Gal 2: 16 but by faith in *J* Christ.
3: 28 for you are all one in Christ *J*.
5: 6 in Christ *J* neither circumcision
6: 17 bear on my body the marks of *J*.
Eph 1: 5 as his sons through *J* Christ,
2: 10 created in Christ *J*
2: 20 with Christ *J* himself as the chief
Php 1: 6 until the day of Christ *J*.
2: 5 be the same as that of Christ *J*:
2: 10 name of *J* every knee should bow,

Col	3: 17	do it all in the name of the Lord *J*,
1Th	1: 10	whom he raised from the dead—*J*,
	4: 14	We believe that *J* died
	5: 23	at the coming of our Lord *J* Christ.
2Th	1: 7	when the Lord *J* is revealed
	2: 1	the coming of our Lord *J* Christ
1Ti	1: 15	Christ *J* came into the world
2Ti	1: 10	appearing of our Saviour, Christ *J*,
	2: 3	us like a good soldier of Christ *J*.
	3: 12	life in Christ *J* will be persecuted,
Tit	2: 13	our great God and Saviour, *J* Christ,
Heb	2: 9	But we see *J*, who was made a little
	2: 11	So *J* is not ashamed to call them
	3: 1	fix your thoughts on *J*, the apostle
	3: 3	*J* has been found worthy
	4: 14	through the heavens, *J* the Son
	6: 20	where *J*, who went before us,
	7: 22	*J* has become the guarantee
	7: 24	but because *J* lives for ever,
	8: 6	But the ministry *J* has received is
	12: 2	Let us fix our eyes on *J*, the author
	12: 24	to *J* the mediator of a new
1Pe	1: 3	the resurrection of *J* Christ
2Pe	1: 16	and coming of our Lord *J* Christ,
1Jn	1: 7	and the blood of *J*, his Son,
	2: 1	*J* Christ, the Righteous One.
	2: 6	to live in him must walk as *J* did.
	4: 15	anyone acknowledges that *J* is
Rev	1: 1	The revelation of *J* Christ,
	22: 16	*J*, have sent my angel
	22: 20	Come, Lord *J*.

JETHRO

Father-in-law and adviser of Moses (Ex 3:1; 18). Also known as Reuel (Ex 2:18).

JEW (JEWS JEWS' JUDAISM)

Est	2: 5	of Susa a *J* of the tribe of Benjamin,
Zec	8: 23	of one *J* by the edge of his robe
Ac	21: 39	"I am a *J*, from Tarsus in Cilicia,
Ro	1: 16	first for the *J*, then for the Gentile.
	2: 28	A man is not a *J* if he is only one
	10: 12	there is no difference between *J*
1Co	9: 20	To the Jews I became like a *J*,
Gal	2: 14	"You are a *J*, yet you live like
	3: 28	There is neither *J* nor Greek,
Col	3: 11	Here there is no Greek or *J*,

JEWEL (JEWELLERY JEWELS)

Pr	20: 15	that speak knowledge are a rare *j*.
SS	4: 9	with one *j* of your necklace.
Rev	21: 11	that of a very precious *j*,

JEWELLERY (JEWEL)

Ex	35: 22	and brought gold *j* of all kinds:
Jer	2: 32	Does a maiden forget her *j*,
Eze	16: 11	you with *j*: I put bracelets
1Pe	3: 3	wearing of gold *j* and fine clothes.

JEWELS (JEWEL)

Isa	54: 12	your gates of sparkling *j*,
	61: 10	as a bride adorns herself with her *j*.
Zec	9: 16	like *j* in a crown.

JEWS (JEW)

Ne	4: 1	He ridiculed the *J*,
Est	3: 13	kill and annihilate all the *J*—
	4: 14	and deliverance for the *J* will arise
Mt	2: 2	who has been born king of the *J*?
	27: 11	"Are you the king of the *J*?" "Yes,

Jn	4: 9	(For *J* do not associate
	4: 22	for salvation is from the *J*.
	19: 3	saying, "Hail, O king of the *J*!"
Ac	20: 21	I have declared to both *J*
Ro	3: 29	Is God the God of *J* only?
	9: 24	not only from the *J* but
	15: 27	they owe it to the *J* to share
1Co	1: 22	*J* demand miraculous signs
	9: 20	To the *J* I became like a Jew,
	12: 13	whether *J* or Greeks, slave or free
Gal	2: 8	of Peter as an apostle to the *J*,
Rev	2: 9	slander of those who say they are *J*
	3: 9	claim to be *J* though they are not,

JEWS' (JEW)

Ro	15: 27	shared in the *J* spiritual blessings,

JEZEBEL

Sidonian wife of Ahab (1Ki 16:31). Promoted Baal worship (1Ki 16:32-33). Killed prophets of the LORD (1Ki 18:4, 13). Opposed Elijah (1 Ki 19:1-2). Had Naboth killed (1Ki 21). Death prophesied (1Ki 21:17-24). Killed by Jehu (2Ki 9:30-37).

JEZREEL

2Ki	9: 36	at *J* dogs will devour Jezebel's flesh
	10: 7	and sent them to Jehu in *J*.
Hos	1: 4	house of Jehu for the massacre at *J*,

JOAB

Nephew of David (1Ch 2:16). Commander of his army (2Sa 8:16). Victorious over Ammon (2Sa 10; 1Ch 19), Rabbah (2Sa 11; 1Ch 20), Jerusalem (1Ch 11:6), Absalom (2Sa 18), Sheba (2Sa 20). Killed Abner (2Sa 3:22-39), Amasa (2Sa 20:1-13). Numbered David's army (2Sa 24; 1Ch 21). Sided with Adonijah (1Ki 1:17, 19). Killed by Benaiah (1Ki 2:5-6, 28-35).

JOASH

Son of Ahaziah; king of Judah. Sheltered from Athaliah by Jehoiada (2 Ki 11; 2Ch 22:10-23:21). Repaired temple (2Ki 12; 2Ch 24).

JOB

Wealthy man from Uz; feared God (Job 1:1-5). Righteousness tested by disaster (Job 1:6-22), personal affliction (Job 2). Maintained innocence in debate with three friends (Job 3-31), Elihu (Job 32-37). Rebuked by the LORD (Job 38-41). Vindicated and restored to greater stature by the LORD (Job 42). Example of righteousness (Eze 14:14, 20).

JOCHEBED*

Mother of Moses and Aaron (Ex 6:20; Nu 26:59).

JOEL

Prophet (Joel 1:1; Ac 2:16).

JOHN

1. Son of Zechariah and Elizabeth (Lk 1). Called the Baptist (Mt 3:1-12; Mk 1:2-8). Witness to Jesus (Mt 3:11-12; Mk 1:7-8; Lk 3:15-18; Jn 1:6-35; 3:27-30; 5:33-36). Doubts about Jesus (Mt 11:2-6; Lk 7:18-23). Arrest (Mt 4:12; Mk 1:14). Execution (Mt 14:1-12; Mk 6:14-29; Lk 9:7-9).

Ministry compared to Elijah (Mt 11:7-19; Mk 9:11-13; Lk 7:24-35).

2. Apostle; brother of James (Mt 4:21-22; 10:2; Mk 3:17; Lk 5:1-10). At transfiguration (Mt 17:1-13; Mk 9:1-13; Lk 9:28-36). Desire to be greatest (Mk 10:35-45). Leader of church at Jerusalem (Ac 4:1-3; Gal 2:9). Elder who wrote epistles (2Jn 1; 3Jn 1). Prophet who wrote Revelation (Rev 1:1; 22:8).

3. Cousin of Barnabas, co-worker with Paul, (Ac 12:12-13:13; 15:37), see MARK.

JOIN (JOINED JOINS)

Ne	10: 29	all these now *j* their brothers
Pr	23: 20	Do not *j* those who drink too much
	24: 21	and do not *j* with the rebellious,
Jer	3: 18	of Judah will *j* the house of Israel,
Eze	37: 17	*J* them together into one stick
Da	11: 34	who are not sincere will *j* them.
Ro	15: 30	to *j* me in my struggle by praying
2Ti	1: 8	*j* with me in suffering for the gospel

JOINED (JOIN)

Zec	2: 11	"Many nations will be *j*
Mt	19: 6	Therefore what God has *j* together,
Mk	10: 9	Therefore what God has *j* together,
Ac	1: 14	They all *j* together constantly
Eph	2: 21	him the whole building is *j* together
	4: 16	*j* and held together

JOINS (JOIN)

1Co	16: 16	and to everyone who *j* in the work,

JOINT (JOINTS)

Ps	22: 14	and all my bones are out of *j*.

JOINTS (JOINT)

Heb	4: 12	even to dividing soul and spirit, *j*

JOKING*

Ge	19: 14	his sons-in-law thought he was *j*.
Pr	26: 19	and says, "I was only *j*!"
Eph	5: 4	or coarse *j*, which are out of place.

JONAH

Prophet in days of Jeroboam II (2Ki 14:25). Called to Nineveh; fled to Tarshish (Jnh 1:1-3). Cause of storm; thrown into sea (Jnh 1:4-16). Swallowed by fish (Jnh 1:17). Prayer (Jnh 2). Preached to Nineveh (Jnh 3). Attitude reproved by the LORD (Jnh 4). Sign of (Mt 12:39-41; Lk 11:29-32).

JONATHAN

Son of Saul (1Sa 13:16; 1Ch 8:33). Valiant warrior (1Sa 13-14). Relation to David (1Sa 18:1-4; 19-20; 23:16-18). Killed at Gilboa (1Sa 31). Mourned by David (2Sa 1).

JOPPA

Ezr	3: 7	logs by sea from Lebanon to *J*,
Jnh	1: 3	to *J*, where he found a ship bound
Ac	9: 43	Peter stayed in *J* for some time

JORAM

1. Son of Ahab; king of Israel. Fought with Jehoshaphat against Moab (2Ki 3). Killed with Ahaziah by Jehu (2Ki 8:25-29; 9:14-26; 2Ch 22:5-9).

2. See JEHORAM.

JORDAN

Ge	13: 10	plain of the *J* was well watered,
Nu	22: 1	and camped along the *J*
	34: 12	boundary will go down along the *J*
Dt	3: 27	you are not going to cross this *J*.
Jos	1: 2	get ready to cross the *J* River
	3: 11	go into the *J* ahead of you.
	3: 17	ground in the middle of the *J*,
	4: 22	Israel crossed the *J* on dry ground.'
2Ki	2: 7	and Elisha had stopped at the *J*.
	2: 13	and stood on the bank of the *J*.
	5: 10	wash yourself seven times in the *J*,
	6: 4	They went to the *J* and began
Ps	114: 3	the *J* turned back;
Isa	9: 1	along the *J*—The people walking
Jer	12: 5	manage in the thickets by the *J*?
Mt	3: 6	baptised by him in the *J* River.
	4: 15	the way to the sea, along the *J*,
Mk	1: 9	and was baptised by John in the *J*.

JOSEPH

1. Son of Jacob by Rachel (Ge 30:24; 1Ch 2:2). Favoured by Jacob, hated by brothers (Ge 37:3-4). Dreams (Ge 37:5-11). Sold by brothers (Ge 37:12-36). Served Potiphar; imprisoned by false accusation (Ge 39). Interpreted dreams of Pharaoh's servants (Ge 40), of Pharaoh (Ge 41:4-40). Made greatest in Egypt (Ge 41:41-57). Sold grain to brothers (Ge 42-45). Brought Jacob and sons to Egypt (Ge 46-47). Sons Ephraim and Manasseh blessed (Ge 48). Blessed (Ge 49:22-26; Dt 33:13-17). Death (Ge 50:22-26; Ex 13:19; Heb 11:22). 12,000 from (Rev 7:8).

2. Husband of Mary, mother of Jesus (Mt 1:16-24; 2:13-19; Lk 1:27; 2; Jn 1:45).

3. Disciple from Arimathea, who gave his tomb for Jesus' burial (Mt 27:57-61; Mk 15:43-47; Lk 24:50-52).

4. Original name of Barnabas (Ac 4:36).

JOSHUA (HOSHEA)

1. Son of Nun; name changed from Hoshea (Nu 13:8, 16; 1Ch 7:27). Fought Amalekites under Moses (Ex 17:9-14). Servant of Moses on Sinai (Ex 24:13; 32:17). Spied Canaan (Nu 13). With Caleb, allowed to enter land (Nu 14:6, 30). Succeeded Moses (Dt 1:38; 31:1-18; 33:9). Charged Israel to conquer Canaan (Jos 1). Crossed Jordan (Jos 3-4). Circumcised sons of wilderness wanderings (Jos 5). Conquered Jericho (Jos 6), Ai (Jos 7-8), five kings at Gibeon (Jos 10:1-28), southern Canaan (Jos 10:29-43), northern Canaan (Jos 11-12). Defeated at Ai (Jos 7). Deceived by Gibeonites (Jos 9). Renewed covenant (Jos 8:30-35; 24:1-27). Divided land among tribes (Jos 13-22). Last words (Jos 23). Death (Jos 24:28-31).

2. High priest during rebuilding of temple (Hag 1-2; Zec 3:1-9; 6:11).

JOSIAH

Son of Amon; king of Judah (2Ki 21:26; 1Ch 3:14). Prophesied (1Ki 13:2). Book of Law discovered during his reign (2Ki 22; 2Ch 34:14-31). Reforms (2Ki 23:1-25; 2Ch 34:1-13; 35:1-19). Killed by Pharaoh Neco (2Ki 23:29-30; 2Ch 35:20-27).

JOTHAM

1. Son of Gideon (Jdg 9).

2. Son of Azariah (Uzziah); king of Judah (2Ki 15:32-38; 2Ch 26:21-27:9).

JOURNEY

Dt	1: 33	who went ahead of you on your *j*,
	2: 7	over your *j* through this vast desert
Jdg	18: 6	Your *j* has the LORD's approval."
Ezr	8: 21	and ask him for a safe *j* for us
Job	16: 22	before I go on the *j* of no return.
Isa	35: 8	The unclean will not *j* on it;
Mt	25: 14	it will be like a man going on a *j*,
Ro	15: 24	to have you assist me on my *j* there

JOY* (ENJOY ENJOYMENT JOYFUL JOYOUS OVERJOYED REJOICE REJOICES REJOICING)

Ge	31: 27	so I could send you away with *j*
Lev	9: 24	shouted for *j* and fell face down.
Dt	16: 15	and your *j* will be complete.
Jdg	9: 19	may Abimelech be your *j*,
1Ch	12: 40	and sheep, for there was *j* in Israel.
	16: 27	strength and *j* in his dwelling-place.
	16: 33	sing for *j* before the LORD,
	29: 17	with *j* how willingly your people
	29: 22	drank with great *j* in the presence
2Ch	30: 26	There was great *j* in Jerusalem,
Ezr	3: 12	while many others shouted for *j*.
	3: 13	of the shouts of *j* from the sound
	6: 16	of the house of God with *j*.
	6: 22	with *j* by changing the attitude
	6: 22	*j* the Feast of Unleavened Bread,
Ne	8: 10	for the *j* of the LORD is your
	8: 12	and to celebrate with great *j*,
	8: 17	And their *j* was very great.
	12: 43	God had given them great *j*.
Est	8: 16	a time of happiness and *j*,
	8: 17	there was *j* and gladness
	9: 17	and made it a day of feasting and *j*.
	9: 18	and made it a day of feasting and *j*.
	9: 19	as a day of *j* and feasting,
	9: 22	and *j* and giving presents of food
	9: 22	their sorrow was turned into *j*
Job	3: 7	may no shout of *j* be heard in it.
	6: 10	my *j* in unrelenting pain—
	8: 21	and your lips with shouts of *j*.
	9: 25	they fly away without a glimpse of *j*
	10: 20	from me so I can have a moment's *j*
	20: 5	the *j* of the godless lasts
	33: 26	he sees God's face and shouts for *j*;
	38: 7	and all the angels shouted for *j*?
Ps	4: 7	have filled my heart with greater *j*
	5: 11	let them ever sing for *j*.
	16: 11	me with *j* in your presence,
	19: 8	giving *j* to the heart.
	20: 5	We will shout for *j*
	21: 1	How great is his *j* in the victories
	21: 6	with the *j* of your presence.
	27: 6	will I sacrifice with shouts of *j*;
	28: 7	My heart leaps for *j*
	30: 11	sackcloth and clothed me with *j*,
	33: 3	play skilfully, and shout for *j*.
	35: 27	shout for *j* and gladness;
	42: 4	with shouts of *j* and thanksgiving
	43: 4	to God, my *j* and my delight.
	45: 7	by anointing you with the oil of *j*.
	45: 15	They are led in with *j* and gladness;
	47: 1	shout to God with cries of *j*.
	47: 5	God has ascended amid shouts of *j*,
	48: 2	the *j* of the whole earth.

Ps	51: 8	Let me hear *j* and gladness;
	51: 12	to me the *j* of your salvation
	65: 8	you call forth songs of *j*.
	65: 13	they shout for *j* and sing.
	66: 1	Shout with *j* to God, all the earth!
	67: 4	the nations be glad and sing for *j*,
	71: 23	My lips will shout for *j*
	81: 1	Sing for *j* to God our strength;
	86: 4	Bring *j* to your servant,
	89: 12	Hermon sing for *j* at your name.
	90: 14	for *j* and be glad all our days.
	92: 4	I sing for *j* at the works
	94: 19	your consolation brought *j*
	95: 1	let us sing for *j* to the LORD;
	96: 12	the trees of the forest will sing for *j*;
	97: 11	and *j* on the upright in heart.
	98: 4	for *j* to the LORD, all the earth,
	98: 6	shout for *j* before the LORD,
	98: 8	the mountains sing together for *j*;
	100: 1	for *j* to the LORD, all the earth.
	105: 43	his chosen ones with shouts of *j*;
	106: 5	share in the *j* of your nation
	107: 22	and tell of his works with songs of *j*
	118: 15	Shouts of *j* and victory
	119: 111	they are the *j* of my heart.
	126: 2	our tongues with songs of *j*.
	126: 3	and we are filled with *j*.
	126: 5	will reap with songs of *j*.
	126: 6	will return with songs of *j*,
	132: 9	may your saints sing for *j*."
	132: 16	and her saints will ever sing for *j*.
	137: 3	tormentors demanded songs of *j*;
	137: 6	my highest *j*.
	149: 5	and sing for *j* on their beds.
Pr	10: 1	A wise son brings *j* to his father,
	10: 28	The prospect of the righteous is *j*,
	11: 10	wicked perish, there are shouts of *j*.
	12: 20	but *j* for those who promote peace.
	14: 10	and no-one else can share its *j*.
	14: 13	and *j* may end in grief.
	15: 20	A wise son brings *j* to his father,
	15: 23	A man finds *j* in giving an apt reply
	15: 30	A cheerful look brings *j*
	17: 21	there is no *j* for the father of a fool.
	21: 15	it brings *j* to the righteous
	23: 24	of a righteous man has great *j*;
	27: 9	incense bring *j* to the heart,
	27: 11	my son, and bring *j* to my heart;
	29: 3	A man who loves wisdom brings *j*
Ecc	8: 15	Then *j* will accompany him
	11: 9	let your heart give you *j* in the days
Isa	9: 3	and increased their *j*;
	12: 3	With *j* you will draw water
	12: 6	Shout aloud and sing for *j*,
	16: 9	shouts of *j* over your ripened fruit
	16: 10	*J* and gladness are taken away
	22: 13	But see, there is *j* and revelry,
	24: 11	all *j* turns to gloom,
	24: 14	raise their voices, they shout for *j*;
	26: 19	wake up and shout for *j*.
	35: 2	will rejoice greatly and shout for *j*.
	35: 6	the mute tongue shout for *j*.
	35: 10	Gladness and *j* will overtake them,
	35: 10	everlasting *j* will crown their heads
	42: 11	Let the people of Sela sing for *j*;
	44: 23	Sing for *j*, O heavens,
	48: 20	Announce this with shouts of *j*
	49: 13	Shout for *j*, O heavens;
	51: 3	*J* and gladness will be found in her,
	51: 11	Gladness and *j* will overtake them,

Isa   51: 11 everlasting *j* will crown their heads
       52: 8 together they shout for *j*.
       52: 9 Burst into songs of *j* together,
       54: 1 burst into song, shout for *j*,
       55: 12 You will go out in *j*
       56: 7 give them *j* in my house of prayer.
       58: 14 then you will find your *j*
       60: 5 heart will throb and swell with *j*;
       60: 15 and the *j* of all generations.
       61: 7 and everlasting *j* will be theirs.
       65: 14 out of the *j* of their hearts,
       65: 18 and its people a *j*.
       66: 5 that we may see your *j*!'
Jer   7: 34 will bring an end to the sounds of *j*
       15: 16 they were my *j* and my heart's
       16: 9 will bring an end to the sounds of *j*
       25: 10 banish from them the sounds of *j*
       31: 7 "Sing with *j* for Jacob;
       31: 12 shout for *j* on the heights of Zion;
       31: 13 give them comfort and *j* instead
       33: 9 this city will bring me renown, *j*,
       33: 11 be heard once more the sounds of *j*
       48: 33 *J* and gladness are gone
       48: 33 no-one treads them with shouts of *j*
       48: 33 they are not shouts of *j*.
       51: 48 will shout for *j* over Babylon,
La   2: 15 the *j* of the whole earth?"
        5: 15 *J* is gone from our hearts;
Eze   7: 7 not *j*, upon the mountains.
       24: 25 their *j* and glory, the delight
Joel   1: 12 Surely the *j* of mankind
        1: 16 *j* and gladness
Mt   13: 20 and at once receives it with *j*.
       13: 44 in his *j* went and sold all he had
       28: 8 afraid yet filled with *j*,
Mk   4: 16 and at once receive it with *j*.
Lk   1: 14 He will be a *j* and delight to you,
        1: 44 the baby in my womb leaped for *j*.
        1: 58 great mercy, and they shared her *j*.
        2: 10 news of great *j* that will be
        6: 23 "Rejoice in that day and leap for *j*,
        8: 13 the word with *j* when they hear it,
       10: 17 The seventy-two returned with *j*
       10: 21 full of *j* through the Holy Spirit,
       24: 41 still did not believe it because of *j*
       24: 52 returned to Jerusalem with great *j*.
Jn   3: 29 That *j* is mine, and it is now
        3: 29 full of *j* when he hears
       15: 11 and that your *j* may be complete.
       15: 11 this so that my *j* may be in you
       16: 20 but your grief will turn to *j*.
       16: 21 because of her *j* that a child is born
       16: 22 and no-one will take away your *j*.
       16: 24 and your *j* will be complete.
       17: 13 measure of my *j* within them.
Ac   2: 28 with *j* in your presence.'
        8: 8 So there was great *j* in that city.
       13: 52 And the disciples were filled with *j*
       14: 17 and fills your hearts with *j*."
       16: 34 the whole family was filled with *j*,
Ro   14: 17 peace and *j* in the Holy Spirit,
       15: 13 the God of hope fill you with all *j*
       15: 32 will I may come to you with *j*
       16: 19 so I am full of *j* over you;
2Co   1: 24 but we work with you for your *j*,
        2: 3 that you would all share my *j*.
        7: 4 our troubles my *j* knows no
        7: 7 so that my *j* was greater than ever.
        8: 2 their overflowing *j* and their
Gal   4: 15 What has happened to all your *j*?

Gal   5: 22 *j*, peace, patience, kindness,
Php   1: 4 I always pray with *j*
        1: 25 for your progress and *j* in the faith,
        1: 26 being with you again your *j*
        2: 2 then make my *j* complete
        2: 29 him in the Lord with great *j*,
        4: 1 and long for, my *j* and crown,
1Th   1: 6 with the *j* given by the Holy Spirit.
        2: 19 For what is our hope, our *j*,
        2: 20 Indeed, you are our glory and *j*.
        3: 9 you in return for all the *j* we have
2Ti   1: 4 so that I may be filled with *j*.
Phm   : 7 Your love has given me great *j*
Heb   1: 9 by anointing you with the oil of *j*."
       12: 2 for the *j* set before him endured
       13: 17 them so that their work will be a *j*,
Jas   1: 2 Consider it pure *j*, my brothers,
        4: 9 to mourning and your *j* to gloom.
1Pe   1: 8 with an inexpressible and glorious *j*
1Jn   1: 4 this to make our *j* complete.
2Jn   : 4 It has given me great *j* to find some
        : 12 so that our *j* may be complete.
3Jn   : 3 It gave me great *j* to have some
        : 4 I have no greater *j*
Jude   : 24 without fault and with great *j*—

JOYFUL* (JOY)

Dt   16: 14 Be *j* at your Feast—you, your sons
1Sa   18: 6 with *j* songs and with tambourines
1Ki   8: 66 *j* and glad in heart
1Ch   15: 16 as singers to sing *j* songs,
2Ch   7: 10 *j* and glad in heart
Ps   68: 3 may they be happy and *j*.
      100: 2 come before him with *j* songs.
Ecc   9: 7 and drink your wine with a *j* heart,
Isa   24: 8 the *j* harp is silent.
Jer   31: 4 and go out to dance with the *j*.
Hab   3: 18 I will be *j* in God my Saviour.
Zec   8: 19 and tenth months will become *j*
       10: 7 Their children will see it and be *j*;
Ro   12: 12 Be *j* in hope, patient in affliction,
1Th   5: 16 Be *j* always; pray continually;
Heb   12: 22 thousands of angels in *j* assembly,

JOYOUS* (JOY)

Est   8: 15 the city of Susa held a *j* celebration.

JUBILANT

Ps   96: 12 let the fields be *j*, and everything
       98: 4 burst into *j* song with music;

JUBILEE

Lev   25: 11 The fiftieth year shall be a *j* for you;

JUDAH (JUDEA)

1. Son of Jacob by Leah (Ge 29:35; 35:23; 1Ch 2:1). Did not want to kill Joseph (Ge 37:26-27). Among Canaanites, fathered Perez by Tamar (Ge 38). Tribe of blessed as ruling tribe (Ge 49:8-12; Dt 33:7), numbered (Nu 1:27; 26:22), allotted land (Jos 15; Eze 48:7), failed to fully possess (Jos 15:63; Jdg 1:1-20).
2. Name used for people and land of Southern Kingdom.

Ru   1: 7 take them back to the land of *J*.
2Sa   2: 4 king over the house of *J*.
Isa   1: 1 The vision concerning *J*
        3: 8 *J* is falling;
Jer   13: 19 All *J* will be carried into exile,
       30: 3 bring my people Israel and *J* back

Hos 1: 7 I will show love to the house of *J*;
Zec 10: 4 From *J* will come the cornerstone,
Mt 2: 6 least among the rulers of *J*;
Heb 7: 14 that our Lord descended from *J*,
8: 8 and with the house of *J*.
Rev 5: 5 of the tribe of *J*, the Root of David,

JUDAISM (JEW)

Ac 13: 43 devout converts to *J* followed Paul
Gal 1: 13 of my previous way of life in *J*,
1: 14 advancing in *J* beyond many Jews

JUDAS

1. Apostle; son of James (Lk 6:16; Jn 14:22; Ac 1:13). Probably also called Thaddaeus (Mt 10:3; Mk 3:18).
2. Brother of James and Jesus (Mt 13:55; Mk 6:3), also called Jude (Jude 1).
3. Christian prophet (Ac 15:22-32).
4. Apostle, also called Iscariot, who betrayed Jesus (Mt 10:4; 26:14-56; Mk 3:19; 14:10-50; Lk 6:16; 22:3-53; Jn 6:71; 12:4; 13:2-30; 18:2-11). Suicide of (Mt 27:3-5; Ac 1:16-25).

JUDE see JUDAS

JUDEA (JUDAH)

Mt 2: 1 born in Bethlehem in *J*,
24: 16 are in *J* flee to the mountains.
Lk 3: 1 Pontius Pilate was governor of *J*,
Ac 1: 8 and in all *J* and Samaria,
9: 31 Then the church throughout *J*,
1Th 2: 14 imitators of God's churches in *J*,

JUDGE (JUDGED JUDGES JUDGING JUDGMENT JUDGMENTS)

Ge 16: 5 May the LORD *j* between you
18: 25 Will not the *J* of all the earth do
Lev 19: 15 but *j* your neighbour fairly.
Dt 1: 16 between your brothers and *j* fairly,
17: 12 man who shows contempt for the *j*
32: 36 The LORD will *j* his people
Jdg 2: 18 Whenever the LORD raised up a *j*
1Sa 2: 10 the LORD will *j* the ends
3: 13 that I would *j* his family for ever
7: 15 *j* over Israel all the days of his life.
24: 12 May the LORD *j* between you
1Ki 8: 32 *J* between your servants,
1Ch 16: 33 for he comes to *j* the earth.
2Ch 6: 23 *J* between your servants, repaying
19: 7 *J* carefully, for with the LORD our
Job 9: 15 plead with my *J* for mercy.
Ps 7: 8 *J* me, O LORD, according
7: 8 let the LORD *j* the peoples.
7: 11 God is a righteous *j*,
9: 8 He will *j* the world in righteousness
50: 6 for God himself is *j*.
51: 4 and justified when you *j*.
75: 2 it is I who *j* uprightly.
76: 9 when you, O God, rose up to *j*,
82: 8 Rise up, O God, *j* the earth,
94: 2 Rise up, O *J* of the earth;
96: 10 he will *j* the peoples with equity.
96: 13 He will *j* the world in righteousness
98: 9 He will *j* the world in righteousness
110: 6 He will *j* the nations, heaping up
Pr 31: 9 Speak up and *j* fairly;
Isa 2: 4 He will *j* between the nations
3: 13 he rises to *j* the people.
11: 3 He will not *j* by what he sees

Isa 33: 22 For the LORD is our *j*,
Jer 11: 20 Almighty, you who *j* righteously
Eze 7: 3 I will *j* you according
7: 27 by their own standards I will *j* them
18: 30 O house of Israel, I will *j* you,
20: 36 so I will *j* you, declares
22: 2 "Son of man, will you *j* her?
34: 17 I will *j* between one sheep
Joel 3: 12 sit to *j* all the nations on every side.
Mic 3: 11 Her leaders *j* for a bribe,
4: 3 He will *j* between many peoples
Mt 7: 1 Do not *j*, or you too will be judged.
Lk 6: 37 "Do not *j*, and you will not be
18: 2 there was a *j* who neither feared
Jn 5: 27 And he has given him authority to *j*
5: 30 By myself I can do nothing; I *j* only
8: 16 But if I do *j*, my decisions are right,
12: 47 For I did not come to *j* the world,
12: 48 There is a *j* for the one who rejects
Ac 10: 42 as *j* of the living and the dead.
17: 31 a day when he will *j* the world
Ro 2: 16 day when God will *j* men's secrets
3: 6 how could God *j* the world?
14: 10 then, why do you *j* your brother?
1Co 4: 3 Indeed, I do not even *j* myself.
4: 5 Therefore *j* nothing
6: 2 And if you are to *j* the world,
6: 2 that the saints will *j* the world?
Gal 2: 6 not *j* by external appearance—
Col 2: 16 Therefore do not let anyone *j* you
2Ti 4: 1 who will *j* the living and the dead,
4: 8 which the Lord, the righteous *J*,
Heb 10: 30 "The Lord will *j* his people."
12: 23 come to God, the *j* of all men,
13: 4 for God will *j* the adulterer
Jas 4: 12 There is only one Lawgiver and *J*,
4: 12 who are you to *j* your neighbour?
1Pe 4: 5 to him who is ready to *j* the living
Rev 20: 4 who had been given authority to *j*.

JUDGED (JUDGE)

Mt 7: 1 "Do not judge, or you too will be *j*.
1Co 4: 3 I care very little if I am *j* by you
10: 29 For why should my freedom be *j*
11: 31 But if we *j* ourselves, we would not
14: 24 all that he is a sinner and will be *j*
Jas 3: 1 who teach will be *j* more strictly.
Rev 20: 12 The dead were *j* according

JUDGES (JUDGE)

Jdg 2: 16 Then the LORD raised up *j*,
Job 9: 24 he blindfolds its *j*.
Ps 58: 11 there is a God who *j* the earth."
75: 7 But it is God who *j*:
Pr 29: 14 If a king *j* the poor with fairness,
Jn 5: 22 Moreover, the Father *j* no-one,
1Co 4: 4 It is the Lord who *j* me.
Heb 4: 12 it *j* the thoughts and attitudes
1Pe 1: 17 on a Father who *j* each man's work
2: 23 himself to him who *j* justly.
Rev 19: 11 With justice he *j* and makes war.

JUDGING (JUDGE)

Ps 9: 4 on your throne, *j* righteously.
Pr 24: 23 To show partiality in *j* is not good:
Isa 16: 5 one who in *j* seeks justice
Mt 19: 28 *j* the twelve tribes of Israel.
Jn 7: 24 Stop *j* by mere appearances,

JUDGMENT (JUDGE)

Nu	33: 4	for the LORD had brought *j*
Dt	1: 17	of any man, for *j* belongs to God.
	32: 41	and my hand grasps it in *j*,
1Sa	25: 33	May you be blessed for your good *j*
Ps	1: 5	the wicked will not stand in the *j*,
	9: 7	he has established his throne for *j*.
	76: 8	From heaven you pronounced *j*,
	82: 1	he gives *j* among the "gods":
	119: 66	Teach me knowledge and good *j*,
	143: 2	Do not bring your servant into *j*,
Pr	3: 21	preserve sound *j* and discernment,
	6: 32	man who commits adultery lacks *j*;
	8: 14	Counsel and sound *j* are mine;
	10: 21	but fools die for lack of *j*.
	11: 12	man who lacks *j* derides his
	12: 11	but he who chases fantasies lacks *j*.
	17: 18	A man lacking in *j* strikes hands
	18: 1	he defies all sound *j*.
	28: 16	A tyrannical ruler lacks *j*,
Ecc	12: 14	God will bring every deed into *j*,
Isa	3: 14	The LORD enters into *j*
	28: 6	justice to him who sits in *j*,
	53: 8	By oppression and *j*, he was taken
	66: 16	the LORD will execute *j*
Jer	2: 35	But I will pass *j* on you
	25: 31	he will bring *j* on all mankind
	51: 18	when their *j* comes, they will
Eze	11: 10	and I will execute *j* on you
Da	7: 22	pronounced *j* in favour of the saints
Am	7: 4	Sovereign LORD was calling for *j*
Zec	8: 16	and sound *j* in your courts;
Mal	3: 5	"So I will come near to you for *j*.
Mt	5: 21	who murders will be subject to *j*.'
	5: 22	with his brother will be subject to *j*.
	10: 15	on the day of *j* than for that town.
	11: 24	on the day of *j* than for you."
	12: 36	have to give account on the day of *j*
	12: 41	up at the *j* with this generation
Jn	5: 22	but has entrusted all *j* to the Son,
	5: 30	as I hear, and my *j* is just,
	7: 24	appearances, and make a right *j*."
	8: 26	"I have much to say in *j* of you.
	9: 39	"For *j* I have come into this world,
	12: 31	Now is the time for *j* on this world;
	16: 8	to sin and righteousness and *j*:
	16: 11	in regard to *j*, because the prince
Ac	24: 25	self-control and the *j* to come,
Ro	2: 1	you who pass *j* on someone else,
	2: 2	Now we know that God's *j*
	5: 16	The *j* followed one sin
	12: 3	rather think of yourself with sober *j*
	14: 10	stand before God's *j* seat.
	14: 13	Therefore let us stop passing *j*
1Co	7: 40	In my *j*, she is happier if she stays
	11: 29	body of the Lord eats and drinks *j*
2Co	5: 10	appear before the *j* seat of Christ,
2Th	1: 5	is evidence that God's *j* is right,
1Ti	3: 6	fall under the same *j* as the devil.
	5: 12	Thus they bring *j* on themselves,
Heb	6: 2	of the dead, and eternal *j*.
	9: 27	to die once, and after that to face *j*,
	10: 27	but only a fearful expectation of *j*
Jas	2: 13	*j* without mercy will be shown
	4: 11	are not keeping it, but sitting in *j*
1Pe	4: 17	For it is time for *j* to begin
2Pe	2: 9	the unrighteous for the day of *j*,
	3: 7	being kept for the day of *j*
1Jn	4: 17	have confidence on the day of *j*,
Jude	: 6	bound with everlasting chains for *j*

Rev	14: 7	because the hour of his *j* has come.

JUDGMENTS (JUDGE)

Jer	1: 16	I will pronounce my *j* on my people
Da	9: 11	and sworn *j* written in the Law
Hos	6: 5	my *j* flashed like lightning
Ro	11: 33	How unsearchable his *j*,
1Co	2: 15	spiritual man makes *j* about all
Rev	16: 7	true and just are your *j*."

JUG

1Sa	26: 12	and water *j* near Saul's head,
1Ki	17: 12	of flour in a jar and a little oil in a *j*.

JUST* (JUSTICE JUSTIFICATION JUSTIFIED JUSTIFIES JUSTIFY JUSTIFYING JUSTLY)

Ge	18: 19	LORD by doing what is right and *j*,
Dt	32: 4	and all his ways are *j*.
	32: 4	upright and *j* is he.
2Sa	8: 15	doing what was *j* and right
1Ch	18: 14	doing what was *j* and right
2Ch	12: 6	and said, "The LORD is *j*."
Ne	9: 13	and laws that are *j* and right,
	9: 33	you have been *j*; you have acted
Job	34: 17	Will you condemn the *j*
	35: 2	Elihu said: "Do you think this is *j*?
Ps	37: 28	For the LORD loves the *j*
	37: 30	and his tongue speaks what is *j*.
	99: 4	what is *j* and right.
	111: 7	of his hands are faithful and *j*;
	119: 121	I have done what is righteous and *j*;
Pr	1: 3	doing what is right and *j* and fair;
	2: 8	for he guards the course of the *j*
	2: 9	will understand what is right and *j*
	8: 8	All the words of my mouth are *j*;
	8: 15	and rulers make laws that are *j*;
	12: 5	The plans of the righteous are *j*,
	21: 3	To do what is right and *j*
Isa	32: 7	even when the plea of the needy is *j*
	58: 2	They ask me for *j* decisions
Jer	4: 2	if in a truthful, *j* and righteous way
	22: 3	what the LORD says: Do what is *j*
	22: 15	He did what was right and *j*,
	23: 5	do what is *j* and right in the land.
	33: 15	he will do what is *j* and right
Eze	18: 5	who does what is *j* and right.
	18: 19	Since the son has done what is *j*
	18: 21	and does what is *j* and right,
	18: 25	The way of the Lord is not *j*.'
	18: 27	and does what is *j* and right,
	18: 29	'The way of the Lord is not *j*.'
	33: 14	and does what is *j* and right—
	33: 16	He has done what is *j* and right;
	33: 17	But it is their way that is not *j*.
	33: 17	'The way of the Lord is not *j*.'
	33: 19	and does what is *j* and right,
	33: 20	'The way of the Lord is not *j*.'
	45: 9	and oppression and do what is *j*
Da	4: 37	does is right and all his ways are *j*.
Jn	5: 30	as I hear, and my judgment is *j*,
Ro	3: 26	as to be *j* and the one who justifies
2Th	1: 6	God is *j*: He will pay back trouble.
Heb	2: 2	received its *j* punishment,
1Jn	1: 9	and *j* and will forgive us our sins
Rev	15: 3	*J* and true are your ways,
	16: 5	"You are *j* in these judgments,

Rev 16: 7 true and *j* are your judgments."
19: 2 for true and *j* are his judgments.

JUSTICE* (JUST)

Ge 49: 16 "Dan will provide *j* for his people
Ex 23: 2 do not pervert *j* by siding
23: 6 "Do not deny *j* to your poor people
Lev 19: 15 " 'Do not pervert *j*; do not show
Dt 16: 19 Do not pervert *j* or show partiality.
16: 20 Follow *j* and *j* alone,
24: 17 the alien or the fatherless of *j*,
27: 19 Cursed is the man who withholds *j*
1Sa 8: 3 accepted bribes and perverted *j*.
2Sa 15: 4 and I would see that he gets *j*."
15: 6 came to the king asking for *j*,
1Ki 3: 11 for discernment in administering *j*,
3: 28 wisdom from God to administer *j*.
7: 7 the Hall of *J*, where he was to judge
10: 9 to maintain *j* and righteousness."
2Ch 9: 8 to maintain *j* and righteousness."
Ezr 7: 25 and judges to administer *j*
Est 1: 13 experts in matters of law and *j*,
Job 8: 3 Does God pervert *j*?
9: 19 matter of *j*, who will summon him?
19: 7 though I call for help, there is no *j*.
27: 2 as God lives, who has denied me *j*,
29: 14 *j* was my robe and my turban.
31: 13 "If I have denied *j*
34: 5 but God denies me *j*.
34: 12 that the Almighty would pervert *j*.
34: 17 Can he who hates *j* govern?
36: 3 I will ascribe *j* to my Maker.
36: 17 *j* have taken hold of you.
37: 23 in his *j* and great righteousness,
40: 8 "Would you discredit my *j*?
Ps 7: 6 Awake, my God; decree *j*.
9: 8 he will govern the peoples with *j*.
9: 16 The LORD is known by his *j*;
11: 7 he loves *j*;
33: 5 LORD loves righteousness and *j*;
36: 6 your *j* like the great deep.
37: 6 *j* of your cause like the noonday
45: 6 a sceptre of *j* will be the sceptre
72: 1 Endow the king with your *j*, O God
72: 2 your afflicted ones with *j*
89: 14 *j* are the foundation of your throne;
97: 2 *j* are the foundation of his throne.
99: 4 The King is mighty, he loves *j*—
101: 1 I will sing of your love and *j*;
103: 6 and *j* for all the oppressed.
106: 3 Blessed are they who maintain *j*,
112: 5 who conducts his affairs with *j*.
140: 12 I know that the LORD secures *j*
Pr 8: 20 along the paths of *j*,
16: 10 and his mouth should not betray *j*.
17: 23 to pervert the course of *j*.
18: 5 or to deprive the innocent of *j*.
19: 28 A corrupt witness mocks at *j*,
21: 15 When *j* is done, it brings joy
28: 5 Evil men do not understand *j*,
29: 4 By *j* a king gives a country stability
29: 7 The righteous care about *j*
29: 26 from the LORD that man gets *j*.
Ecc 3: 16 place of *j*—wickedness was there.
5: 8 poor oppressed in a district, and *j*
Isa 1: 17 Seek *j*,
1: 21 She once was full of *j*;
1: 27 Zion will be redeemed with *j*,
5: 7 he looked for *j*, but saw bloodshed;
5: 16 Almighty will be exalted by his *j*,

Isa 5: 23 but deny *j* to the innocent.
9: 7 it with *j* and righteousness
10: 2 and withhold *j* from the oppressed
11: 4 with *j* he will give decisions
16: 5 one who in judging seeks *j*
28: 6 He will be a spirit of *j*
28: 17 I will make *j* the measuring line
29: 21 deprive the innocent of *j*.
30: 18 For the LORD is a God of *j*.
32: 1 and rulers will rule with *j*.
32: 16 *J* will dwell in the desert
33: 5 with *j* and righteousness.
42: 1 and he will bring *j* to the nations.
42: 3 In faithfulness he will bring forth *j*;
42: 4 till he establishes *j* on earth.
51: 4 my *j* will become a light
51: 5 my arm will bring *j* to the nations.
56: 1 "Maintain *j*
59: 4 No-one calls for *j*;
59: 8 there is no *j* in their paths.
59: 9 So *j* is far from us,
59: 11 We look for *j*, but find none;
59: 14 So *j* is driven back,
59: 15 that there was no *j*.
61: 8 "For I, the LORD, love *j*;
Jer 9: 24 *j* and righteousness on earth,
10: 24 Correct me, LORD, but only with *j*
12: 1 speak with you about your *j*:
21: 12 " 'Administer *j* every morning;
30: 11 I will discipline you but only with *j*;
46: 28 I will discipline you but only with *j*;
La 3: 36 to deprive a man of *j*—
Eze 22: 29 ill-treat the alien, denying them *j*.
34: 16 I will shepherd the flock with *j*.
Hos 2: 19 you in righteousness and *j*,
12: 6 maintain love and *j*,
Am 2: 7 and deny *j* to the oppressed.
5: 7 You who turn *j* into bitterness
5: 12 and you deprive the poor of *j*
5: 15 maintain *j* in the courts.
5: 24 But let *j* roll on like a river,
6: 12 But you have turned *j* into poison
Mic 3: 1 Should you not know *j*,
3: 8 and with *j* and might,
3: 9 who despise *j*
Hab 1: 4 and *j* never prevails.
1: 4 so that *j* is perverted.
Zep 3: 5 by morning he dispenses his *j*,
Zec 7: 9 'Administer true *j*; show mercy
Mal 2: 17 or "Where is the God of *j*?"
3: 5 and deprive aliens of *j*,
Mt 12: 18 he will proclaim *j* to the nations.
12: 20 till he leads *j* to victory.
23: 23 important matters of the law—*j*,
Lk 11: 42 you neglect *j* and the love of God.
18: 3 'Grant me *j* against my adversary.'
18: 5 I will see that she gets *j*,
18: 7 And will not God bring about *j*
18: 8 he will see that they get *j*,
Ac 8: 33 humiliation he was deprived of *j*.
17: 31 with *j* by the man he has appointed.
28: 4 *J* has not allowed him to live."
Ro 3: 25 He did this to demonstrate his *j*,
3: 26 it to demonstrate his *j*
2Co 7: 11 what readiness to see *j* done.
Heb 11: 33 administered *j*, and gained what
Rev 19: 11 With *j* he judges and makes war.

JUSTIFICATION* (JUST)

Eze 16: 52 for you have furnished some *j*

Ro   4: 25 and was raised to life for our *j*.
        5: 16 many trespasses and brought *j*.
        5: 18 of righteousness was *j* that brings

JUSTIFIED* (JUST)

Ps   51: 4 and *j* when you judge.
Lk   18: 14 rather than the other, went home *j*
Ac   13: 39 from everything you could not be *j*
       13: 39 him everyone who believes is *j*
Ro   3: 24 and are *j* freely by his grace
        3: 28 For we maintain that a man is *j*
        4: 2 If, in fact, Abraham was *j* by works,
        5: 1 since we have been *j* through faith,
        5: 9 Since we have now been *j*
        8: 30 those he called, he also *j*; those he *j*,
       10: 10 heart that you believe and are *j*,
1Co   6: 11 you were *j* in the name
Gal   2: 16 in Christ Jesus that we may be *j*
        2: 16 observing the law no-one will be *j*.
        2: 16 sinners' know that a man is not *j*
        2: 17 "If, while we seek to be *j* in Christ,
        3: 11 Clearly no-one is *j* before God
        3: 24 to Christ that we might be *j* by faith
        5: 4 to be *j* by law have been alienated
Tit   3: 7 so that, having been *j* by his grace,
Jas   2: 24 You see that a person is *j*

JUSTIFIES* (JUST)

Ro   3: 26 one who *j* those who have faith
        4: 5 but trusts God who *j* the wicked,
        8: 33 God has chosen? It is God who *j*.

JUSTIFY* (JUST)

Est   7: 4 such distress would *j* disturbing
Job   40: 8 you condemn me to *j* yourself?
Isa   53: 11 my righteous servant will *j* many,
Lk   10: 29 But he wanted to *j* himself,
       16: 15 "You are the ones who *j* yourselves
Ro   3: 30 who will *j* the circumcised by faith
Gal   3: 8 that God would *j* the Gentiles

JUSTIFYING* (JUST)

Job   32: 2 angry with Job for *j* himself rather

JUSTLY* (JUST)

Ps   58: 1 Do you rulers indeed speak *j*?
       67: 4 for you rule the peoples *j*
Jer   7: 5 and deal with each other *j*,
Mic   6: 8 To act *j* and to love mercy
Lk   23: 41 We are punished *j*,
1Pe   2: 23 himself to him who judges *j*.

KADESH

Nu   20: 1 of Zin, and they stayed at *K*.
Dt   1: 46 And so you stayed in *K* many days

KADESH BARNEA

Nu   32: 8 I sent them from *K* to look over

KEBAR

Eze   1: 1 among the exiles by the *K* River,

KEDORLAOMER

Ge   14: 17 Abram returned from defeating *K*

KEEP (KEEPER KEEPING KEEPS KEPT)

Ge   31: 49 "May the LORD *k* watch
Ex   15: 26 his commands and *k* all his
       20: 6 and *k* my commandments.
Lev   15: 31 You must *k* the Israelites separate

Nu   6: 24 and *k* you;
Dt   4: 2 but *k* the commands of the LORD
        6: 17 Be sure to *k* the commands
        7: 9 who love him and *k* his commands.
        7: 12 your God will *k* his covenant
       11: 1 your God and *k* his requirements,
       13: 4 *K* his commands and obey him;
       30: 10 your God and *k* his commands
       30: 16 and to *k* his commands, decrees
Jos   22: 5 careful to *k* the commandment
1Ki   8: 58 and to *k* the commands,
2Ki   17: 19 Judah did not *k* the commands
       23: 3 the LORD and *k* his commands,
1Ch   29: 18 and *k* their hearts loyal to you.
2Ch   6: 14 you who *k* your covenant of love
       34: 31 the LORD and *k* his commands,
Job   14: 16 but not *k* track of my sin.
Ps   18: 28 You, O LORD, *k* my lamp burning
       19: 13 *K* your servant also from wilful
       78: 10 they did not *k* God's covenant
      119: 2 Blessed are they who *k* his statutes
      119: 9 can a young man *k* his way pure?
      121: 7 The LORD will *k* you
      141: 3 *k* watch over the door of my lips.
Pr   4: 21 *k* them within your heart;
        4: 24 *k* corrupt talk far from your lips.
       30: 8 *K* falsehood and lies far from me;
Ecc   3: 6 a time to *k* and a time
       12: 13 and *k* his commandments,
Isa   26: 3 You will *k* in perfect peace
       42: 6 I will *k* you and will make you
       58: 13 "If you *k* your feet
Jer   16: 11 forsook me and did not *k* my law.
Eze   20: 19 and be careful to *k* my laws.
Mt   10: 10 for the worker is worth his *k*.
Lk   12: 35 and *k* your lamps burning,
       17: 33 tries to *k* his life will lose it,
Jn   10: 24 How long will you *k* us in suspense
       12: 25 in this world will *k* it for eternal life
Ac   2: 24 for death to *k* its hold on him,
       18: 9 "Do not be afraid; *k* on speaking,
Ro   7: 19 want to do—this I *k* on doing.
       12: 11 but *k* your spiritual fervour,
       14: 22 you believe about these things *k*
       16: 17 *K* away from them.
1Co   1: 8 He will *k* you strong to the end,
2Co   12: 7 To *k* me from becoming conceited
Gal   5: 25 let us *k* in step with the Spirit.
Eph   4: 3 Make every effort to *k* the unity
2Th   3: 6 to *k* away from every brother who
1Ti   5: 22 *K* yourself pure.
2Ti   4: 5 *k* your head in all situations,
Heb   9: 20 God has commanded you to *k*."
       13: 5 *K* your lives free from the love
Jas   1: 26 and yet does not *k* a tight rein
        2: 8 If you really *k* the royal law found
        3: 2 able to *k* his whole body in check.
2Pe   1: 8 will *k* you from being ineffective
Jude   : 21 *K* yourselves in God's love
         : 24 able to *k* you from falling
Rev   3: 10 also *k* you from the hour
       22: 9 of all who *k* the words of this book.

KEEPER (KEEP)

Ge   4: 9 I my brother's *k*?" The LORD

KEEPING (KEEP)

Ex   20: 8 the Sabbath day by *k* it holy.
Dt   5: 12 the Sabbath day by *k* it holy,
       13: 18 *k* all his commands that I am

Ps   19: 11 in *k* them there is great reward.
      119: 112 My heart is set on *k* your decrees
Pr   15: 3 *k* watch on the wicked
Mt   3: 8 Produce fruit in *k* with repentance.
Lk   2: 8 *k* watch over their flocks at night.
1Co   7: 19 *K* God's commands is what counts.
2Co   8: 5 and then to us in *k* with God's will.
Jas   4: 11 you are not *k* it, but sitting
1Pe   3: 16 and respect, *k* a clear conscience,
2Pe   3: 9 Lord is not slow in *k* his promise,

KEEPS (KEEP)

Ne   1: 5 who *k* his covenant of love
Ps   15: 4 who *k* his oath
Pr   12: 23 A prudent man *k* his knowledge
      15: 21 of understanding *k* a straight
      17: 28 a fool is thought wise if he *k* silent,
      29: 11 a wise man *k* himself under control
Isa   56: 2 who *k* the Sabbath
Da   9: 4 who *k* his covenant of love
Am   5: 13 Therefore the prudent man *k* quiet
Jn   7: 19 Yet not one of you *k* the law.
       8: 51 if anyone *k* my word, he will never
1Co   13: 5 is not easily angered, it *k* no record
Jas   2: 10 For whoever *k* the whole law
Rev   22: 7 Blessed is he who *k* the words

KEILAH

1Sa   23: 13 that David had escaped from *K*,

KEPT (KEEP)

Ex   12: 42 Because the LORD *k* vigil that
Dt   7: 8 and *k* the oath he swore
2Ki   18: 6 he *k* the commands the LORD had
Ne   9: 8 You have *k* your promise
Ps   130: 3 If you, O LORD, *k* a record of sins,
Isa   38: 17 In your love you *k* me
Mt   19: 20 these I have *k*," the young man
2Co   11: 9 I have *k* myself from being
2Ti   4: 7 finished the race, I have *k* the faith.
1Pe   1: 4 spoil or fade—*k* in heaven for you,

KEY (KEYS)

Isa   33: 6 the fear of the LORD is the *k*
Rev   20: 1 having the *k* to the Abyss

KEYS* (KEY)

Mt   16: 19 I will give you the *k* of the kingdom
Rev   1: 18 And I hold the *k* of death

KICK*

Ac   26: 14 for you to *k* against the goads.'

KILL (KILLED KILLS)

Ecc   3: 3 a time to *k* and a time to heal,
Mt   10: 28 *k* the body but cannot *k* the soul.
      17: 23 They will *k* him, and on the third
Mk   9: 31 will *k* him, and after three days
      10: 34 spit on him, flog him and *k* him.

KILLED (KILL)

Ge   4: 8 his brother Abel and *k* him.
Ex   2: 12 he *k* the Egyptian and hid him
      13: 15 the LORD *k* every firstborn
Nu   35: 11 who has *k* someone accidentally
1Sa   17: 50 down the Philistine and *k* him.
Ne   9: 26 They *k* your prophets, who had
Hos   6: 5 I *k* you with the words
Lk   11: 48 they *k* the prophets, and you build
Ac   3: 15 You *k* the author of life,

KILLS (KILL)

Ex   21: 12 *k* him shall surely be put to death.
Lev   24: 21 but whoever *k* a man must be put
2Co   3: 6 for the letter *k*, but the Spirit gives

KIND [1] (KINDS)

Ge   1: 24 animals, each according to its *k*."
1Co   15: 35 With what *k* of body will they

KIND [2] (KINDNESS KINDNESSES)

2Ch   10: 7 "If you will be *k* to these people
Ps   86: 5 You are *k* and forgiving, O Lord,
Pr   11: 17 A *k* man benefits himself,
      12: 25 but a *k* word cheers him up.
      14: 21 blessed is he who is *k* to the needy.
      14: 31 whoever is *k* to the needy honours
      19: 17 He who is *k* to the poor lends
Da   4: 27 by being *k* to the oppressed.
Lk   6: 35 because he is *k* to the ungrateful
1Co   13: 4 Love is patient, love is *k*.
Eph   4: 32 Be *k* and compassionate
1Th   5: 15 but always try to be *k* to each other
2Ti   2: 24 instead, he must be *k* to everyone,
Tit   2: 5 to be busy at home, to be *k*,

KIND-HEARTED* (HEART)

Pr   11: 16 A *k* woman gains respect,

KINDNESS (KIND [2])

Ge   24: 12 and show *k* to my master Abraham
      32: 10 I am unworthy of all the *k*
      39: 21 he showed him *k* and granted him
Jdg   8: 35 also failed to show *k* to the family
Ru   2: 20 has not stopped showing his *k*
2Sa   9: 3 to whom I can show God's *k*?"
      22: 51 he shows unfailing *k*
Ps   18: 50 he shows unfailing *k*
      141: 5 righteous man strike me—it is a *k*;
Isa   54: 8 but with everlasting *k*
Jer   9: 24 I am the LORD, who exercises *k*,
Hos   11: 4 I led them with cords of human *k*,
Ac   14: 17 He has shown *k* by giving you rain
Ro   11: 22 Consider therefore the *k*
2Co   6: 6 understanding, patience and *k*;
Gal   5: 22 peace, patience, *k*, goodness,
Eph   2: 7 expressed in his *k* to us
Col   3: 12 yourselves with compassion, *k*,
Tit   3: 4 But when the *k* and love
2Pe   1: 7 brotherly *k*; and to brotherly *k*,

KINDNESSES* (KIND [2])

Ps   106: 7 did not remember your many *k*,
Isa   63: 7 I will tell of the *k* of the LORD,
      63: 7 to his compassion and many *k*.

KINDS (KIND [1])

Ge   1: 12 bearing seed according to their *k*
1Co   12: 4 There are different *k* of gifts,
1Ti   6: 10 of money is a root of all *k* of evil.
1Pe   1: 6 had to suffer grief in all *k* of trials.

KING (KING'S KINGDOM KINGDOMS KINGS)

1. Kings of Judah and Israel: see Saul, David, Solomon.

2. Kings of Judah: see Rehoboam, Abijah, Asa, Jehoshaphat, Jehoram, Ahaziah, Athaliah (Queen), Joash, Amaziah, Azariah (Uzziah), Jotham, Ahaz, Hezekiah, Manasseh, Amon, Josiah, Jehoahaz, Jehoiakim, Jehoiachin, Zedekiah.

3. Kings of Israel: see Jeroboam I, Nadab, Baasha, Elah, Zimri, Tibni, Omri, Ahab, Ahaziah, Joram, Jehu, Jehoahaz, Jehoash, Jeroboam II, Zechariah, Shallum, Menahem, Pekah, Pekahiah, Hoshea.

Ex	1: 8	a new *k*, who did not know about
Dt	17: 14	"Let us set a *k* over us like all
Jdg	17: 6	In those days Israel had no *k*;
1Sa	8: 5	now appoint a *k* to lead us,
	11: 15	as *k* in the presence of the LORD.
	12: 12	the LORD your God was your *k*.
2Sa	2: 4	and there they anointed David *k*
1Ki	1: 30	Solomon your son shall be *k*
Ps	2: 6	"I have installed my *K*
	24: 7	that the *K* of glory may come in.
	44: 4	You are my *K* and my God,
	47: 7	For God is the *K* of all the earth;
Isa	32: 1	See, a *k* will reign in righteousness
Jer	30: 9	and David their *k*,
Hos	3: 5	their God and David their *k*.
Mic	2: 13	*k* will pass through before them,
Zec	9: 9	See, your *k* comes to you,
Mt	2: 2	is the one who has been born *k*
	27: 11	"Are you the *k* of the Jews?" "Yes,
Lk	19: 38	"Blessed is the *k* who comes
	23: 3	"Are you the *k* of the Jews?" "Yes,
	23: 38	THE *K* OF THE JEWS.
Jn	1: 49	of God; you are the *K* of Israel."
	12: 13	"Blessed is the *K* of Israel!"
Ac	17: 7	saying that there is another *k*,
1Ti	1: 17	Now to the *K* eternal, immortal,
	6: 15	the *K* of kings and Lord of lords,
Heb	7: 1	This Melchizedek was *k* of Salem
1Pe	2: 13	to the *k*, as the supreme authority,
	2: 17	of believers, fear God, honour the *k*.
Rev	15: 3	*K* of the ages.
	17: 14	he is Lord of lords and *K* of kings—
	19: 16	*K* OF KINGS AND LORD

KING'S (KING)

Pr	21: 1	The *k* heart is in the hand
Ecc	8: 3	in a hurry to leave the *k* presence.

KINGDOM (KING)

Ex	19: 6	you will be for me a *k* of priests
Dt	17: 18	When he takes the throne of his *k*,
2Sa	7: 12	body, and I will establish his *k*.
1Ki	11: 31	to tear the *k* out of Solomon's hand
1Ch	17: 11	own sons, and I will establish his *k*.
	29: 11	Yours, O LORD, is the *k*;
Ps	45: 6	justice will be the sceptre of your *k*.
	103: 19	and his *k* rules over all.
	145: 11	They will tell of the glory of your *k*
Eze	29: 14	There they will be a lowly *k*.
Da	2: 39	"After you, another *k* will rise,
	4: 3	His *k* is an eternal *k*;
	7: 27	His *k* will be an everlasting *k*,
Ob	: 21	And the *k* will be the LORD's.
Mt	3: 2	Repent, for the *k* of heaven is near
	4: 17	Repent, for the *k* of heaven is near
	4: 23	preaching the good news of the *k*,
	5: 3	for theirs is the *k* of heaven.
	5: 10	for theirs is the *k* of heaven.
	5: 19	great in the *k* of heaven.
	5: 19	least in the *k* of heaven,
	5: 20	you will certainly not enter the *k*
	6: 10	your *k* come,
	6: 33	But seek first his *k* and his
	7: 21	Lord,' will enter the *k* of heaven,
	8: 11	Isaac and Jacob in the *k* of heaven.

Mt	8: 12	the subjects of the *k* will be thrown
	9: 35	preaching the good news of the *k*
	10: 7	preach this message: 'The *k*
	11: 11	least in the *k* of heaven is greater
	11: 12	the *k* of heaven has been forcefully
	12: 25	"Every *k* divided against itself will
	12: 26	How then can his *k* stand?
	12: 28	then the *k* of God has come
	13: 11	knowledge of the secrets of the *k*
	13: 19	hears the message about the *k*
	13: 24	"The *k* of heaven is like a man who
	13: 31	*k* of heaven is like a mustard seed,
	13: 33	"The *k* of heaven is like yeast that
	13: 38	stands for the sons of the *k*.
	13: 41	of his *k* everything that causes sin
	13: 43	the sun in the *k* of their Father.
	13: 44	*k* of heaven is like treasure hidden
	13: 45	the *k* of heaven is like a merchant
	13: 47	*k* of heaven is like a net that was let
	13: 52	has been instructed about the *k*
	16: 19	the keys of the *k* of heaven;
	16: 28	the Son of Man coming in his *k*."
	18: 1	the greatest in the *k* of heaven?"
	18: 3	you will never enter the *k*
	18: 4	the greatest in the *k* of heaven.
	18: 23	the *k* of heaven is like a king who
	19: 12	because of the *k* of heaven.
	19: 14	for the *k* of heaven belongs to such
	19: 23	man to enter the *k* of heaven.
	19: 24	for a rich man to enter the *k* of God
	20: 1	"For the *k* of heaven is like
	20: 21	the other at your left in your *k*."
	21: 31	the prostitutes are entering the *k*
	21: 43	"Therefore I tell you that the *k*
	22: 2	"The *k* of heaven is like a king who
	23: 13	You shut the *k* of heaven
	24: 7	rise against nation, and *k* against *k*.
	24: 14	gospel of the *k* will be preached
	25: 1	"At that time the *k*
	25: 34	the *k* prepared for you
	26: 29	anew with you in my Father's *k*."
Mk	1: 15	"The *k* of God is near.
	3: 24	If a *k* is divided against itself,
	3: 24	against itself, that *k* cannot stand.
	4: 11	"The secret of the *k*
	4: 26	"This is what the *k* of God is like.
	4: 30	"What shall we say the *k*
	6: 23	I will give you, up to half my *k*."
	9: 1	before they see the *k* of God come
	9: 47	better for you to enter the *k* of God
	10: 14	for the *k* of God belongs to such
	10: 15	anyone who will not receive the *k*
	10: 23	for the rich to enter the *k* of God!"
	10: 24	how hard it is to enter the *k* of God
	10: 25	for a rich man to enter the *k* of God
	11: 10	"Blessed is the coming *k*
	12: 34	"You are not far from the *k* of God
	13: 8	rise against nation, and *k* against *k*.
	14: 25	day when I drink it anew in the *k*
	15: 43	who was himself waiting for the *k*
Lk	1: 33	Jacob for ever; his *k* will never
	4: 43	of the *k* of God to the other towns
	6: 20	for yours is the *k* of God.
	7: 28	in the *k* of God is greater than he."
	8: 1	proclaiming the good news of the *k*
	8: 10	knowledge of the secrets of the *k*
	9: 2	out to preach the *k* of God
	9: 11	spoke to them about the *k* of God,
	9: 27	before they see the *k* of God."
	9: 60	you go and proclaim the *k* of God

Lk	9: 62	fit for service in the *k* of God."
	10: 9	'The *k* of God is near you.'
	10: 11	sure of this: The *k* of God is near.'
	11: 2	your *k* come.
	11: 17	"Any *k* divided against itself will
	11: 18	himself, how can his *k* stand?
	11: 20	then the *k* of God has come to you.
	12: 31	seek his *k*, and these things will be
	12: 32	has been pleased to give you the *k*.
	13: 18	"What is the *k* of God like?
	13: 20	What shall I compare the *k* of God
	13: 28	all the prophets in the *k* of God,
	13: 29	places at the feast in the *k* of God.
	14: 15	eat at the feast in the *k* of God."
	16: 16	the good news of the *k*
	17: 20	when the *k* of God would come,
	17: 20	*k* of God does not come with your
	17: 21	because the *k* of God is within you
	18: 16	for the *k* of God belongs to such
	18: 17	anyone who will not receive the *k*
	18: 24	for the rich to enter the *k* of God!
	18: 25	for a rich man to enter the *k* of God
	18: 29	for the sake of the *k* of God will fail
	19: 11	and the people thought that the *k*
	21: 10	rise against nation, and *k* against *k*.
	21: 31	you know that the *k* of God is near.
	22: 16	until it finds fulfilment in the *k*
	22: 18	the vine until the *k* of God comes."
	22: 29	And I confer on you a *k*, just
	22: 30	and drink at my table in my *k*
	23: 42	me when you come into your *k*."
	23: 51	he was waiting for the *k* of God.
Jn	3: 3	he cannot see the *k* of God."
	3: 5	he cannot enter the *k* of God.
	18: 36	now my *k* is from another place."
	18: 36	"My *k* is not of this world.
Ac	1: 3	and spoke about the *k* of God.
	1: 6	going to restore the *k* to Israel?"
	8: 12	he preached the good news of the *k*
	14: 22	hardships to enter the *k* of God,"
	19: 8	arguing persuasively about the *k*
	20: 25	about preaching the *k* will ever see
	28: 23	and declared to them the *k* of God
	28: 31	hindrance he preached the *k*
Ro	14: 17	For the *k* of God is not a matter
1Co	4: 20	For the *k* of God is not a matter
	6: 9	the wicked will not inherit the *k*
	6: 10	swindlers will inherit the *k* of God.
	15: 24	hands over the *k* to God the Father
	15: 50	blood cannot inherit the *k* of God,
Gal	5: 21	live like this will not inherit the *k*
Eph	2: 2	and of the ruler of the *k* of the air,
	5: 5	has any inheritance in the *k*
Col	1: 12	of the saints in the *k* of light.
	1: 13	and brought us into the *k*
	4: 11	among my fellow-workers for the *k*
1Th	2: 12	who calls you into his *k* and glory.
2Th	1: 5	will be counted worthy of the *k*
2Ti	4: 1	in view of his appearing and his *k*,
	4: 18	bring me safely to his heavenly *k*.
Heb	1: 8	will be the sceptre of your *k*.
	12: 28	we are receiving a *k* that cannot be
Jas	2: 5	to inherit the *k* he promised those
2Pe	1: 11	into the eternal *k* of our Lord
Rev	1: 6	has made us to be a *k* and priests
	1: 9	companion in the suffering and *k*
	5: 10	You have made them to be a *k*
	11: 15	of the world has become the *k*
	11: 15	"The *k* of the world has become
	12: 10	the power and the *k* of our God,

Rev	16: 10	his *k* was plunged into darkness.
	17: 12	who have not yet received a *k*,

KINGDOMS (KING)

2Ki	19: 15	God over all the *k* of the earth.
	19: 19	so that all *k* on earth may know
2Ch	20: 6	rule over all the *k* of the nations.
Ps	68: 32	Sing to God, O *k* of the earth,
Isa	37: 16	God over all the *k* of the earth.
	37: 20	so that all *k* on earth may know
Eze	29: 15	It will be the lowliest of *k*
	37: 22	or be divided into two *k*.
Da	4: 17	Most High is sovereign over the *k*
	7: 17	great beasts are four *k* that will rise
Zep	3: 8	to gather the *k*

KINGS (KING)

Ps	2: 2	The *k* of the earth take their stand
	47: 9	for the *k* of the earth belong to God
	68: 29	*k* will bring you gifts.
	72: 11	All *k* will bow down to him
	110: 5	he will crush *k* on the day
	149: 8	to bind their *k* with fetters,
Pr	16: 12	*K* detest wrongdoing,
Isa	24: 21	and the *k* on the earth below.
	52: 15	and *k* will shut their mouths
	60: 11	their *k* led in triumphal procession.
Da	2: 21	he sets up *k* and deposes them.
	7: 24	ten horns are ten *k* who will come
Lk	21: 12	and you will be brought before *k*
1Co	4: 8	You have become *k*—
1Ti	2: 2	for *k* and all those in authority,
	6: 15	the King of *k* and Lord of lords,
Rev	1: 5	and the ruler of the *k* of the earth.
	17: 14	he is Lord of lords and King of *k*—
	19: 16	KING OF *K* AND LORD

KINSMAN-REDEEMER (REDEEM)

Ru	3: 9	over me, since you are a *k*."
	4: 14	day has not left you without a *k*.

KISS (KISSED KISSES)

Ps	2: 12	*K* the Son, lest he be angry
Pr	24: 26	is like a *k* on the lips.
SS	1: 2	Let him *k* me
	8: 1	I would *k* you,
Lk	22: 48	the Son of Man with a *k*?"
Ro	16: 16	Greet one another with a holy *k*.
1Co	16: 20	Greet one another with a holy *k*.
2Co	13: 12	Greet one another with a holy *k*.
1Th	5: 26	Greet all the brothers with a holy *k*
1Pe	5: 14	Greet one another with a *k* of love.

KISSED (KISS)

Mk	14: 45	Judas said, "Rabbi!" and *k* him.
Lk	7: 38	*k* them and poured perfume

KISSES* (KISS)

Pr	27: 6	but an enemy multiplies *k*.
SS	1: 2	with the *k* of his mouth—

KNEE (KNEES)

Isa	45: 23	Before me every *k* will bow;
Ro	14: 11	'Every *k* will bow before me;
Php	2: 10	name of Jesus every *k* should bow,

KNEEL (KNELT)

Est	3: 2	But Mordecai would not *k* down
Ps	95: 6	let us *k* before the LORD our
Eph	3: 14	For this reason I *k*

KNEES (KNEE)

1Ki	19: 18	all whose *k* have not bowed
Isa	35: 3	steady the *k* that give way;
Da	6: 10	times a day he got down on his *k*
Lk	5: 8	he fell at Jesus' *k* and said,
Heb	12: 12	your feeble arms and weak *k*.

KNELT* (KNEEL)

1Ki	1: 16	Bathsheba bowed low and *k*
2Ch	6: 13	and then *k* down before the whole
	7: 3	they *k* on the pavement
	29: 29	everyone present with him *k* down
Est	3: 2	officials at the king's gate *k* down
Mt	8: 2	and *k* before him and said,
	9: 18	a ruler came and *k* before him
	15: 25	The woman came and *k* before him
	17: 14	a man approached Jesus and *k*
	27: 29	*k* in front of him and mocked him.
Lk	22: 41	*k* down and prayed, "Father,
Ac	20: 36	he *k* down with all of them
	21: 5	there on the beach we *k* to pray.

KNEW (KNOW)

2Ch	33: 13	Manasseh *k* that the LORD is God
Job	23: 3	If only I *k* where to find him;
Pr	24: 12	"But we *k* nothing about this,"
Jer	1: 5	you in the womb I *k* you,
Jnh	4: 2	I *k* that you are a gracious
Mt	7: 23	tell them plainly, 'I never *k* you.
	12: 25	Jesus *k* their thoughts
Jn	2: 24	himself to them, for he *k* all men.
	14: 7	If you really *k* me, you would know

KNIFE

Ge	22: 10	and took the *k* to slay his son.
Pr	23: 2	and put a *k* to your throat

KNOCK* (KNOCKS)

Mt	7: 7	*k* and the door will be opened
Lk	11: 9	*k* and the door will be opened
Rev	3: 20	I am! I stand at the door and *k*.

KNOCKS (KNOCK)

Mt	7: 8	and to him who *k*, the door will be

KNOW (FOREKNEW FOREKNOWLEDGE KNEW KNOWING KNOWLEDGE KNOWN KNOWS)

Ge	22: 12	Now I *k* that you fear God,
Ex	6: 7	you will *k* that I am the LORD
	14: 4	and the Egyptians will *k* that I am
	33: 13	teach me your ways so I may *k* you
Dt	7: 9	*K* therefore that the LORD your
	18: 21	"How can we *k* when a message
Jos	4: 24	of the earth might *k* that the hand
	23: 14	You *k* with all your heart
1Sa	17: 46	the whole world will *k* that there is
1Ki	8: 39	heart (for you alone *k* the hearts
Job	11: 6	*K* this: God has even forgotten
	19: 25	I *k* that my Redeemer lives,
	42: 3	things too wonderful for me to *k*.
Ps	9: 10	Those who *k* your name will trust
	46: 10	"Be still, and *k* that I am God;
	100: 3	*K* that the LORD is God.
	139: 1	and you *k* me.
	139: 23	Search me, O God, and *k* my heart;
	145: 12	so that all men may *k*
Pr	27: 1	for you do not *k* what a day may
	30: 4	Tell me if you *k*!

Ecc	8: 5	wise heart will *k* the proper time
Isa	29: 15	"Who sees us? Who will *k*?"
	40: 21	Do you not *k*?
Jer	6: 15	they do not even *k* how to blush.
	22: 16	Is that not what it means to *k* me?"
	24: 7	I will give them a heart to *k* me,
	31: 34	his brother, saying, '*K* the LORD,'
	33: 3	unsearchable things you do not *k*.'
Eze	2: 5	they will *k* that a prophet has been
	6: 10	they will *k* that I am the LORD;
Da	11: 32	people who *k* their God will firmly
Mt	6: 3	let your left hand *k* what your right
	7: 11	*k* how to give good gifts
	9: 6	But so that you may *k* that the Son
	22: 29	you do not *k* the Scriptures
	24: 42	you do not *k* on what day your
	26: 74	"I don't *k* the man!" Immediately
Mk	12: 24	you do not *k* the Scriptures
Lk	1: 4	so that you may *k* the certainty
	11: 13	*k* how to give good gifts
	12: 48	But the one who does not *k*
	13: 25	'I don't *k* you or where you come
	21: 31	you *k* that the kingdom of God is
	23: 34	for they do not *k* what they are
Jn	1: 26	among you stands one you do not *k*
	3: 11	we speak of what we *k*,
	4: 22	we worship what we do *k*,
	4: 42	and we *k* that this man really is
	6: 69	and *k* that you are the Holy One
	7: 28	You do not *k* him, but I *k* him
	8: 14	for I *k* where I came from
	8: 19	"You do not *k* me or my Father,"
	8: 32	Then you will *k* the truth,
	8: 55	Though you do not *k* him, I *k* him.
	9: 25	One thing I do *k*.
	10: 4	him because they *k* his voice.
	10: 14	I *k* my sheep and my sheep *k* me—
	10: 27	I *k* them, and they follow me.
	12: 35	the dark does not *k* where he is
	13: 17	Now that you *k* these things,
	13: 35	All men will *k* that you are my
	14: 17	you *k* him, for he lives with you
	15: 21	for they do not *k* the One who sent
	16: 30	we can see that you *k* all things
	17: 3	that they may *k* you, the only true
	17: 23	to let the world *k* that you sent me
	21: 15	he said, "you *k* that I love you."
	21: 24	We *k* that his testimony is true.
Ac	1: 7	"It is not for you to *k* the times
	1: 24	"Lord, you *k* everyone's heart.
Ro	3: 17	and the way of peace they do not *k*
	6: 3	Or don't you *k* that all
	6: 6	For we *k* that our old self was
	6: 16	Don't you *k* that when you offer
	7: 14	We *k* that the law is spiritual;
	7: 18	I *k* that nothing good lives in me,
	8: 22	We *k* that the whole creation has
	8: 26	We do not *k* what we ought to pray
	8: 28	we *k* that in all things God works
1Co	1: 21	through its wisdom did not *k* him,
	2: 2	For I resolved to *k* nothing
	3: 16	Don't you *k* that you yourselves
	5: 6	Don't you *k* that a little yeast
	6: 2	Do you not *k* that the saints will
	6: 15	Do you not *k* that your bodies are
	6: 16	Do you not *k* that he who unites
	6: 19	Do you not *k* that your body is
	7: 16	How do you *k*, wife, whether you
	8: 2	does not yet *k* as he ought to *k*.
	9: 13	Don't you *k* that those who work

1Co	9: 24	Do you not *k* that
	13: 9	For we *k* in part and we prophesy
	13: 12	Now I *k* in part; then I shall *k* fully,
	15: 58	because you *k* that your labour
2Co	5: 1	we *k* that if the earthly tent we live
	5: 11	we *k* what it is to fear the Lord,
	8: 9	For you *k* the grace
Gal	1: 11	you to *k*, brothers, that the gospel I
	2: 16	not 'Gentile sinners' *k* that a man
Eph	1: 17	so that you may *k* him better.
	1: 18	in order that you may *k* the hope
	6: 8	you *k* that the Lord will reward
	6: 9	since you *k* that he who is both
Php	3: 10	I want to *k* Christ and the power
	4: 12	I *k* what it is to be in need,
Col	2: 2	order that they may *k* the mystery
	4: 1	because you *k* that you
	4: 6	so that you may *k* how
1Th	3: 3	You *k* quite well that we were
	5: 2	for you *k* very well that the day
2Th	1: 8	punish those who do not *k* God
1Ti	1: 7	they do not *k* what they are talking
	3: 5	(If anyone does not *k* how
	3: 15	you will *k* how people ought
2Ti	1: 12	because I *k* whom I have believed,
	2: 23	you *k* they produce quarrels.
	3: 14	you *k* those from whom you
Heb	8: 11	because they will all *k* me,
	11: 8	he did not *k* where he was going.
Jas	1: 3	because you *k* that the testing
	3: 1	you *k* that we who teach will be
	4: 4	don't you *k* that friendship
	4: 14	*k* what will happen tomorrow.
1Pe	1: 18	For you *k* that it was not
2Pe	1: 12	even though you *k* them
1Jn	2: 3	We *k* that we have come
	2: 4	The man who says, "I *k* him,"
	2: 5	This is how we *k* we are in him:
	2: 11	he does not *k* where he is going,
	2: 20	and all of you *k* the truth.
	2: 29	you *k* that everyone who does
	3: 1	not *k* us is that it did not *k* him.
	3: 2	But we *k* that when he appears,
	3: 10	This is how we *k* who the children
	3: 14	We *k* that we have passed
	3: 16	This is how we *k* what love is:
	3: 19	then is how we *k* that we belong
	3: 24	We *k* it by the Spirit he gave us.
	4: 8	does not love does not *k* God,
	4: 13	We *k* that we live in him
	4: 16	so we *k* and rely on the love God
	5: 2	This is how we *k* that we love
	5: 13	so that you may *k* that you have
	5: 15	And if we *k* that he hears us—
	5: 18	We *k* that anyone born
	5: 20	We *k* also that the Son
Rev	2: 2	I *k* your deeds, your hard work
	2: 9	I *k* your afflictions and your
	2: 19	I *k* your deeds, your love and faith,
	3: 3	you will not *k* at what time I will
	3: 15	I *k* your deeds, that you are neither

KNOWING (KNOW)

Ge	3: 5	and you will be like God, *k* good
	3: 22	now become like one of us, *k* good
Jn	19: 28	*k* that all was now completed,
Php	3: 8	of *k* Christ Jesus my Lord,
Phm	: 21	*k* that you will do even more
Heb	13: 2	entertained angels without *k* it.

KNOWLEDGE (KNOW)

Ge	2: 9	the tree of the *k* of good and evil.
	2: 17	eat from the tree of the *k* of good
2Ch	1: 10	and *k*, that I may lead this people,
Job	21: 22	"Can anyone teach *k* to God,
	38: 2	counsel with words without *k*?
	42: 3	obscures my counsel without *k*?'
Ps	19: 2	night after night they display *k*.
	73: 11	Does the Most High have *k*?"
	94: 10	Does he who teaches man lack *k*?
	119: 66	Teach me *k* and good judgment,
	139: 6	Such *k* is too wonderful for me,
Pr	1: 4	*k* and discretion to the young—
	1: 7	of the LORD is the beginning of *k*,
	2: 5	and find the *k* of God.
	2: 6	from his mouth come *k*
	2: 10	and *k* will be pleasant to your soul.
	3: 20	by his *k* the deeps were divided,
	8: 10	*k* rather than choice gold,
	8: 12	I possess *k* and discretion.
	9: 10	*k* of the Holy One is understanding
	10: 14	Wise men store up *k*,
	12: 1	Whoever loves discipline loves *k*,
	12: 23	A prudent man keeps his *k*
	13: 16	Every prudent man acts out of *k*,
	14: 6	*k* comes easily to the discerning.
	15: 7	The lips of the wise spread *k*;
	15: 14	The discerning heart seeks *k*,
	17: 27	A man of *k* uses words
	18: 15	heart of the discerning acquires *k*;
	19: 2	to have zeal without *k*,
	19: 25	discerning man, and he will gain *k*.
	20: 15	lips that speak *k* are a rare jewel.
	23: 12	and your ears to words of *k*.
	24: 4	through *k* its rooms are filled
Ecc	7: 12	but the advantage of *k* is this:
Isa	11: 2	the Spirit of *k* and of the fear
	11: 9	full of the *k* of the LORD
	40: 14	Who was it that taught him *k*
Jer	3: 15	who will lead you with *k*
Hos	4: 6	are destroyed from lack of *k*.
Hab	2: 14	filled with the *k* of the glory
Mal	2: 7	lips of a priest ought to preserve *k*,
Mt	13: 11	The *k* of the secrets of the kingdom
Lk	8: 10	The *k* of the secrets of the kingdom
	11: 52	you have taken away the key to *k*.
Ac	18: 24	with a thorough *k* of the Scriptures
Ro	1: 28	worth while to retain the *k* of God,
	10: 2	but their zeal is not based on *k*.
	11: 33	riches of the wisdom and *k* of God!
1Co	8: 1	*K* puffs up, but love builds up.
	8: 11	Christ died, is destroyed by your *k*.
	12: 8	to another the message of *k*
	13: 2	can fathom all mysteries and all *k*,
	13: 8	where there is *k*, it will pass away.
2Co	2: 14	everywhere the fragrance of the *k*
	4: 6	light of the *k* of the glory of God
	8: 7	in *k*, in complete earnestness
	11: 6	a trained speaker, but I do have *k*.
Eph	3: 19	to know this love that surpasses *k*
	4: 13	and in the *k* of the Son of God
Php	1: 9	and more in *k* and depth of insight,
Col	1: 9	God to fill you with the *k* of his will
	1: 10	every good work, growing in the *k*
	2: 3	all the treasures of wisdom and *k*.
	3: 10	which is being renewed in *k*
1Ti	2: 4	and to come to a *k* of the truth.
	6: 20	ideas of what is falsely called *k*,
Tit	1: 1	and the *k* of the truth that leads
Heb	10: 26	after we have received the *k*

2Pe 1: 5 and to goodness, *k*; and to *k*,
3: 18 grow in the grace and *k* of our Lord

KNOWN (KNOW)

Ex 6: 3 the LORD I did not make myself *k*
Ps 16: 11 You have made *k* to me the path
89: 1 I will make your faithfulness *k*
98: 2 LORD has made his salvation *k*
105: 1 make *k* among the nations what he
119: 168 for all my ways are *k* to you.
Pr 20: 11 Even a child is *k* by his actions,
Isa 12: 4 make *k* among the nations what he
46: 10 *k* the end from the beginning,
61: 9 Their descendants will be *k*
Eze 38: 23 I will make myself *k* in the sight
39: 7 " 'I will make *k* my holy name
Mt 10: 26 or hidden that will not be made *k*.
24: 43 of the house had *k* at what time
Lk 19: 42 had only *k* on this day what would
Jn 15: 15 from my Father I have made *k*
16: 14 from what is mine and making it *k*
17: 26 I have made you *k* to them,
Ac 2: 28 You have made *k* to me the paths
Ro 1: 19 since what may be *k* about God is
3: 21 apart from law, has been made *k*,
9: 22 his wrath and make his power *k*,
11: 34 "Who has *k* the mind of the Lord?
15: 20 the gospel where Christ was not *k*,
16: 26 and made *k* through the prophetic
1Co 2: 16 "For who has *k* the mind
8: 3 But the man who loves God is *k*
13: 12 know fully, even as I am fully *k*.
2Co 3: 2 written on our hearts, *k*
Gal 4: 9 or rather are *k* by God—
Eph 3: 5 which was not made *k* to men
6: 19 will fearlessly make *k* the mystery
2Ti 3: 15 infancy you have *k* the holy
2Pe 2: 21 than to have *k* it and then

KNOWS (KNOW)

1Sa 2: 3 for the LORD is a God who *k*,
Est 4: 14 And who *k* but that you have come
Job 23: 10 But he *k* the way that I take;
Ps 44: 21 since he *k* the secrets of the heart?
94: 11 The LORD *k* the thoughts of man;
103: 14 for he *k* how we are formed,
Ecc 8: 7 Since no man *k* the future,
8: 17 Even if a wise man claims he *k*,
9: 12 no man *k* when his hour will come:
Isa 29: 16 "He *k* nothing"?
Jer 9: 24 that he understands and *k* me,
Mt 6: 8 for your Father *k* what you need
11: 27 No-one *k* the Son
24: 36 "No-one *k* about that day or hour,
Lk 12: 47 "That servant who *k* his master's
16: 15 of men, but God *k* your hearts.
Ac 15: 8 who *k* the heart, showed that he
Ro 8: 27 who searches our hearts *k* the mind
1Co 2: 11 who among men *k* the thoughts
8: 2 who thinks he *k* something does
2Ti 2: 19 The Lord *k* those who are his," and
Jas 4: 17 who *k* the good he ought to do
1Jn 4: 6 and whoever *k* God listens to us;
4: 7 born of God and *k* God.

KOHATHITE (KOHATHITES)

Nu 3: 29 The *K* clans were to camp

KOHATHITES (KOHATHITE)

Nu 3: 28 The *K* were responsible

Nu 4: 15 *K* are to carry those things that are

KORAH

Levite who led rebellion against Moses and Aaron (Nu 16; Jude 11).

KORAZIN

Mt 11: 21 "Woe to you, *K*! Woe to you,

LABAN

Brother of Rebekah (Ge 24:29), father of Rachel and Leah (Ge 29:16). Received Abraham's servant (Ge 24:29-51). Provided daughters as wives for Jacob in exchange for Jacob's service (Ge 29:1-30). Provided flocks for Jacob's service (Ge 30:25-43). After Jacob's departure, pursued and covenanted with him (Ge 31).

LABOUR (LABOURING)

Ex 1: 11 to oppress them with forced *l*,
20: 9 Six days you shall *l* and do all your
Dt 5: 13 Six days you shall *l* and do all your
Ps 127: 1 its builders *l* in vain.
128: 2 You will eat the fruit of your *l*;
Pr 12: 24 but laziness ends in slave *l*.
Isa 54: 1 you who were never in *l*;
55: 2 and your *l* on what does not satisfy
Mt 6: 28 They do not *l* or spin.
Jn 4: 38 have reaped the benefits of their *l*."
1Co 3: 8 rewarded according to his own *l*.
15: 58 because you know that your *l*
Gal 4: 27 you who have no *l* pains;
Php 2: 16 day of Christ that I did not run or *l*
Rev 14: 13 "they will rest from their *l*,

LABOURING* (LABOUR)

2Th 3: 8 *l* and toiling so that we would not

LACK (LACKED LACKING LACKS)

Ps 34: 9 for those who fear him *l* nothing.
Pr 5: 23 He will die for *l* of discipline,
10: 21 but fools die for *l* of judgment.
11: 14 For *l* of guidance a nation falls,
15: 22 Plans fail for *l* of counsel,
28: 27 to the poor will *l* nothing,
Mk 6: 6 he was amazed at their *l* of faith.
16: 14 he rebuked them for their *l* of faith
Ro 3: 3 Will their *l* of faith nullify God's
1Co 1: 7 you do not *l* any spiritual gift
7: 5 because of your *l* of self-control.
Col 2: 23 *l* any value in restraining sensual

LACKED (LACK)

Dt 2: 7 and you have not *l* anything.
Ne 9: 21 them in the desert; they *l* nothing,
1Co 12: 24 honour to the parts that *l* it,

LACKING (LACK)

Pr 17: 18 A man *l* in judgment strikes hands
Ro 12: 11 Never be *l* in zeal, but keep your
Jas 1: 4 and complete, not *l* anything.

LACKS (LACK)

Pr 6: 32 who commits adultery *l* judgment;
11: 12 man who *l* judgment derides his
12: 11 he who chases fantasies *l* judgment
15: 21 delights a man who *l* judgment,
24: 30 of the man who *l* judgment;
25: 28 is a man who *l* self-control.
28: 16 A tyrannical ruler *l* judgment,
31: 11 and *l* nothing of value.

Eze 34: 8 because my flock *l* a shepherd
Jas 1: 5 any of you *l* wisdom, he should ask

LAID (LAY)

Isa 53: 6 and the LORD has *l* on him
Mk 6: 29 took his body and *l* it in a tomb.
Lk 6: 48 and *l* the foundation on rock.
Ac 6: 6 and *l* their hands on them.
1Co 3: 11 other than the one already *l*,
1Ti 4: 14 body of elders *l* their hands on you.
1Jn 3: 16 Jesus Christ *l* down his life for us.

LAKE

Mt 8: 24 a furious storm came up on the *l*,
14: 25 out to them, walking on the *l*.
Mk 4: 1 into a boat and sat in it out on the *l*,
Lk 8: 33 down the steep bank into the *l*
Jn 6: 25 him on the other side of the *l*,
Rev 19: 20 into the fiery *l* of burning sulphur.
20: 14 The *l* of fire is the second death.

LAMB (LAMB'S LAMBS)

Ge 22: 8 "God himself will provide the *l*
Ex 12: 21 and slaughter the Passover *l*.
Nu 9: 11 are to eat the *l*, together
2Sa 12: 4 he took the ewe *l* that belonged
Isa 11: 6 The wolf will live with the *l*,
53: 7 he was led like a *l* to the slaughter,
Mk 14: 12 to sacrifice the Passover *l*,
Jn 1: 29 *L* of God, who takes away the sin
Ac 8: 32 as a *l* before the shearer is silent,
1Co 5: 7 our Passover *l*, has been sacrificed.
1Pe 1: 19 a *l* without blemish or defect.
Rev 5: 6 Then I saw a *L*, looking
5: 12 "Worthy is the *L*, who was slain,
7: 14 white in the blood of the *L*.
14: 4 They follow the *L* wherever he
15: 3 of God and the song of the *L*:
17: 14 but the *L* will overcome them
19: 9 to the wedding supper of the *L*!'"
21: 23 gives it light, and the *L* is its lamp.

LAMB'S (LAMB)

Rev 21: 27 written in the *L* book of life.

LAMBS (LAMB)

Lk 10: 3 I am sending you out like *l*
Jn 21: 15 Jesus said, "Feed my *l*."

LAME

Isa 33: 23 even the *l* will carry off plunder.
35: 6 Then will the *l* leap like a deer,
Mt 11: 5 The blind receive sight, the *l* walk,
15: 31 the *l* walking and the blind seeing.
Lk 14: 21 the crippled, the blind and the *l*.'

LAMENT

2Sa 1: 17 took up this *l* concerning Saul
Eze 19: 1 Take up a *l* concerning the princes

LAMP (LAMPS LAMPSTAND LAMPSTANDS)

2Sa 22: 29 You are my *l*, O LORD;
Ps 18: 28 You, O LORD, keep my *l* burning;
119: 105 Your word is a *l* to my feet
132: 17 and set up a *l* for my anointed one.
Pr 6: 23 For these commands are a *l*,
20: 27 *l* of the LORD searches the spirit
31: 18 and her *l* does not go out at night.
Mt 6: 22 "The eye is the *l* of the body.
Lk 8: 16 "No-one lights a *l* and hides it

Rev 21: 23 gives it light, and the Lamb is its *l*.
22: 5 They will not need the light of a *l*

LAMPS (LAMP)

Mt 25: 1 be like ten virgins who took their *l*
Lk 12: 35 for service and keep your *l* burning,
Rev 4: 5 the throne, seven *l* were blazing.

LAMPSTAND (LAMP)

Ex 25: 31 "Make a *l* of pure gold
Zec 4: 2 "I see a solid gold *l* with a bowl
4: 11 on the right and the left of the *l*?"
Heb 9: 2 In its first room were the *l*,
Rev 2: 5 and remove your *l* from its place.

LAMPSTANDS (LAMP)

2Ch 4: 7 He made ten gold *l* according
Rev 1: 12 when I turned I saw seven golden *l*,
1: 20 and of the seven golden *l* is this:

LAND (LANDS)

Ge 1: 10 God called the dry ground "*l*",
1: 11 "Let the *l* produce vegetation:
1: 24 "Let the *l* produce living creatures
12: 1 and go to the *l* I will show you.
12: 7 To your offspring I will give this *l*."
13: 15 All the *l* that you see I will give
15: 18 "To your descendants I give this *l*,
50: 24 out of this *l* to the *l* he promised
Ex 3: 8 a *l* flowing with milk and honey—
6: 8 to the *l* I swore with uplifted hand
33: 3 Go up to the *l* flowing with milk
Lev 25: 23 *l* must not be sold permanently,
Nu 14: 8 us into that *l*, a *l* flowing with milk
35: 33 Do not pollute the *l* where you are.
Dt 1: 8 See, I have given you this *l*.
8: 7 God is bringing you into a good *l*—
11: 10 The *l* you are entering to take
28: 21 you from the *l* you are entering
29: 19 will bring disaster on the watered *l*
34: 1 LORD showed him the whole *l*—
Jos 13: 2 "This is the *l* that remains:
14: 4 Levites received no share of the *l*
14: 9 *l* on which your feet have walked
2Sa 21: 14 answered prayer on behalf of the *l*.
2Ki 17: 5 of Assyria invaded the entire *l*,
24: 1 king of Babylon invaded the *l*,
25: 21 into captivity, away from her *l*.
2Ch 7: 14 their sin and will heal their *l*.
7: 20 then I will uproot Israel from my *l*,
36: 21 The *l* enjoyed its Sabbath rests;
Ezr 9: 11 entering to possess is a *l* polluted
Ne 9: 36 in the *l* you gave our forefathers
Ps 37: 11 But the meek will inherit the *l*
37: 29 the righteous will inherit the *l*,
136: 21 and gave their *l* as an inheritance,
142: 5 my portion in the *l* of the living."
Pr 2: 21 For the upright will live in the *l*,
12: 11 who works his *l* will have abundant
Isa 6: 13 though a tenth remains in the *l*,
53: 8 cut off from the *l* of the living;
Jer 2: 7 But you came and defiled my *l*
Eze 36: 24 and bring you back into your own *l*.

LANDS (LAND)

Ps 111: 6 giving them the *l* of other nations.
Eze 20: 6 honey, the most beautiful of all *l*.
Zec 10: 9 in distant *l* they will remember me.

LANGUAGE (LANGUAGES)

Ge	11: 1	Now the whole world had one *l*
	11: 9	there the Lord confused the *l*
Ps	19: 3	There is no speech or *l*
Jn	8: 44	When he lies, he speaks his native *l*
Ac	2: 6	heard them speaking in his own *l.*
Col	3: 8	slander, and filthy *l* from your lips.
Rev	5: 9	from every tribe and *l* and people
	7: 9	every nation, tribe, people and *l,*
	14: 6	to every nation, tribe, *l* and people.

LANGUAGES (LANGUAGE)

Zec	8: 23	"In those days ten men from all *l*

LAODICEA

Rev	3: 14	the angel of the church in *L* write:

LAP

Jdg	7: 5	"Separate those who *l* the water

LASHES

Pr	17: 10	more than a hundred *l* a fool.
2Co	11: 24	from the Jews the forty *l* minus one

LAST [1] (LATTER)

2Sa	23: 1	These are the *l* words of David:
Isa	2: 2	and Jerusalem: In the *l* days
	41: 4	and with the *l*—I am he."
	44: 6	I am the first and I am the *l*;
	48: 12	I am the first and I am the *l.*
Hos	3: 5	and to his blessings in the *l* days.
Mic	4: 1	In the *l* days
Mt	19: 30	But many who are first will be *l,*
	20: 8	beginning with the *l* ones hired
	21: 37	*L* of all, he sent his son to them.
Mk	9: 35	must be the very *l,* and the servant
	10: 31	are first will be *l,* and the *l* first."
	15: 37	a loud cry, Jesus breathed his *l.*
Jn	6: 40	and I will raise him up at the *l* day."
Ac	2: 17	"'In the *l* days, God says,
Ro	1: 17	is by faith from first to *l,*
1Co	15: 26	*l* enemy to be destroyed is death.
	15: 52	of an eye, at the *l* trumpet.
2Ti	3: 1	will be terrible times in the *l* days.
2Pe	3: 3	in the *l* days scoffers will come,
Jude	: 18	"In the *l* times there will be
Rev	1: 17	I am the First and the *L.*
	22: 13	the First and the *L,* the Beginning

LAST [2] (LASTING LASTS)

Jn	15: 16	and bear fruit—fruit that will *l.*

LASTING (LAST [2])

Ex	12: 14	to the Lord—a *l* ordinance.
Lev	24: 8	of the Israelites, as a *l* covenant.
Nu	25: 13	have a covenant of a *l* priesthood,
Heb	10: 34	had better and *l* possessions.

LASTS (LAST [2])

Ps	30: 5	For his anger *l* only a moment,
2Co	3: 11	greater is the glory of that which *l!*

LATTER (LAST [1])

Job	42: 12	The Lord blessed the *l* part
Mt	23: 23	You should have practised the *l,*
Php	1: 16	I do so in love, knowing that I am

LAUGH (LAUGHED LAUGHS LAUGHTER)

Ps	59: 8	But you, O Lord, *l* at them;
Pr	31: 25	she can *l* at the days to come.

Ecc	3: 4	a time to weep and a time to *l,*
Lk	6: 21	for you will *l.*
	6: 25	Woe to you who *l* now,

LAUGHED (LAUGH)

Ge	17: 17	Abraham fell face down; he *l*
	18: 12	So Sarah *l* to herself as she thought,

LAUGHS (LAUGH)

Ps	2: 4	The One enthroned in heaven *l*;
	37: 13	but the Lord *l* at the wicked,

LAUGHTER (LAUGH)

Ge	21: 6	Sarah said, "God has brought me *l,*
Ps	126: 2	Our mouths were filled with *l,*
Pr	14: 13	Even in *l* the heart may ache,
Jas	4: 9	Change your *l* to mourning

LAVISHED

Eph	1: 8	of God's grace that he *l* on us
1Jn	3: 1	great is the love the Father has *l*

LAW (LAWFUL LAWGIVER LAWS)

Lev	24: 22	are to have the same *l* for the alien
Nu	6: 13	"'Now this is the *l* for the Nazirite
Dt	1: 5	Moses began to expound this *l,*
	6: 25	to obey all this *l* before the Lord
	27: 26	of this *l* by carrying them out."
	31: 11	you shall read this *l* before them
	31: 26	"Take this Book of the *L*
Jos	1: 7	to obey all the *l* my servant Moses
	1: 8	of the *L* depart from your mouth;
	22: 5	and the *l* that Moses the servant
2Ki	22: 8	of the *L* in the temple of the Lord
2Ch	6: 16	walk before me according to my *l,*
	17: 9	the Book of the *L* of the Lord;
	34: 14	of the *L* of the Lord that had
Ezr	7: 6	versed in the *L* of Moses,
Ne	8: 2	Ezra the priest brought the *L*
	8: 8	from the Book of the *L* of God,
Ps	1: 2	and on his *l* he meditates day
	19: 7	The *l* of the Lord is perfect,
	37: 31	The *l* of his God is in his heart;
	40: 8	your *l* is within my heart."
	119: 18	wonderful things in your *l.*
	119: 70	but I delight in your *l.*
	119: 72	*l* from your mouth is more precious
	119: 77	for your *l* is my delight.
	119: 97	Oh, how I love your *l!*
	119: 163	but I love your *l.*
	119: 165	peace have they who love your *l,*
Pr	28: 9	If anyone turns a deaf ear to the *l,*
	29: 18	but blessed is he who keeps the *l.*
Isa	2: 3	The *l* will go out from Zion,
	8: 20	To the *l* and to the testimony!
	42: 21	to make his *l* great and glorious.
Jer	2: 8	deal with the *l* did not know me;
	8: 8	for we have the *l* of the Lord,"
	31: 33	"I will put my *l* in their minds
Mic	4: 2	The *l* will go out from Zion,
Hab	1: 7	they are a *l* to themselves
Zec	7: 12	as flint and would not listen to the *l*
Mt	5: 17	that I have come to abolish the *L*
	7: 12	sums up the *L* and the Prophets.
	22: 36	greatest commandment in the *L*?"
	22: 40	All the *L* and the Prophets hang
	23: 23	more important matters of the *l*—
Lk	11: 52	"Woe to you experts in the *l,*
	16: 17	stroke of a pen to drop out of the *L.*
	24: 44	me in the *L* of Moses,

Jn	1: 17	For the *l* was given through Moses;
Ac	13: 39	justified from by the *l* of Moses.
Ro	2: 12	All who sin apart from the *l* will
	2: 15	of the *l* are written on their hearts,
	2: 20	you have in the *l* the embodiment
	2: 25	value if you observe the *l*,
	3: 19	we know that whatever the *l* says,
	3: 20	in his sight by observing the *l*;
	3: 21	apart from *l*, has been made known
	3: 28	by faith apart from observing the *l*.
	3: 31	Not at all! Rather, we uphold the *l*.
	4: 13	It was not through *l* that Abraham
	4: 15	worthless, because *l* brings wrath.
	4: 16	not only to those who are of the *l*
	5: 13	for before the *l* was given,
	5: 20	*l* was added so that the trespass
	6: 14	because you are not under *l*,
	6: 15	we are not under *l* but under grace?
	7: 1	that the *l* has authority
	7: 4	also died to the *l* through the body
	7: 5	aroused by the *l* were at work
	7: 6	released from the *l* so that we serve
	7: 7	then? Is the *l* sin? Certainly not!
	7: 8	For apart from *l*, sin is dead.
	7: 12	*l* is holy, and the commandment is
	7: 14	We know that the *l* is spiritual;
	7: 22	my inner being I delight in God's *l*;
	7: 25	in my mind am a slave to God's *l*,
	8: 2	because through Christ Jesus the *l*
	8: 3	For what the *l* was powerless to do
	8: 4	of the *l* might be fully met in us,
	8: 7	It does not submit to God's *l*,
	9: 4	covenants, the receiving of the *l*,
	9: 31	who pursued a *l* of righteousness,
	10: 4	Christ is the end of the *l*
	13: 8	his fellow-man has fulfilled the *l*.
	13: 10	love is the fulfilment of the *l*.
1Co	6: 6	goes to *l* against another—
	9: 9	For it is written in the *L* of Moses:
	9: 20	the *l* I became like one under the *l*
	9: 21	I became like one not having the *l*
	15: 56	and the power of sin is the *l*.
Gal	2: 16	justified by observing the *l*,
	2: 19	For through the *l* I died to the *l*
	3: 2	the Spirit by observing the *l*,
	3: 5	you because you observe the *l*,
	3: 10	on observing the *l* are under a curse
	3: 11	justified before God by the *l*,
	3: 13	curse of the *l* by becoming a curse
	3: 17	The *l*, introduced 430 years later,
	3: 19	then, was the purpose of the *l*?
	3: 21	Is the *l*, therefore, opposed
	3: 23	we were held prisoners by the *l*,
	3: 24	So the *l* was put in charge to lead us
	4: 21	you who want to be under the *l*,
	5: 3	obligated to obey the whole *l*.
	5: 4	justified by *l* have been alienated
	5: 14	The entire *l* is summed up
	5: 18	by the Spirit, you are not under *l*.
	6: 2	and in this way you will fulfil the *l*
Eph	2: 15	flesh the *l* with its commandments
Php	3: 9	of my own that comes from the *l*,
1Ti	1: 8	We know that the *l* is good
Heb	7: 12	there must also be a change of the *l*.
	7: 19	(for the *l* made nothing perfect),
	10: 1	The *l* is only a shadow
Jas	1: 25	intently into the perfect *l* that gives
	2: 8	If you really keep the royal *l* found
	2: 10	For whoever keeps the whole *l*
	4: 11	or judges him speaks against the *l*

1Jn	3: 4	Everyone who sins breaks the *l*;

LAWFUL (LAW)

Mt	12: 12	Therefore it is *l* to do good

LAWGIVER* (LAW)

Isa	33: 22	the LORD is our *l*,
Jas	4: 12	There is only one *L* and Judge,

LAWLESS (LAWLESSNESS)

2Th	2: 8	And then the *l* one will be revealed
Heb	10: 17	"Their sins and *l* acts

LAWLESSNESS* (LAWLESS)

2Th	2: 3	and the man of *l* is revealed,
	2: 7	power of *l* is already at work;
1Jn	3: 4	sins breaks the law; in fact, sin is *l*.

LAWS (LAW)

Ex	21: 1	"These are the *l* you are to set
Lev	25: 18	and be careful to obey my *l*,
Dt	4: 1	and *l* I am about to teach you.
	30: 16	decrees and *l*; then you will live
Ps	119: 30	I have set my heart on your *l*.
	119: 43	for I have put my hope in your *l*.
	119: 120	I stand in awe of your *l*.
	119: 164	for your righteous *l*.
	119: 175	and may your *l* sustain me.
Eze	36: 27	and be careful to keep my *l*.
Heb	8: 10	I will put my *l* in their minds
	10: 16	I will put my *l* in their hearts,

LAWSUITS

Hos	10: 4	therefore *l* spring up
1Co	6: 7	The very fact that you have *l*

LAY (LAID LAYING LAYS)

Ex	29: 10	and his sons shall *l* their hands
Lev	1: 4	He is to *l* his hand on the head
	4: 15	the community are to *l* their hands
Nu	8: 10	the Israelites are to *l* their hands
	27: 18	whom is the spirit, and *l* your hand
1Sa	26: 9	Who can *l* a hand on the LORD's
Job	1: 12	on the man himself do not *l* a finger
	22: 22	and *l* up his words in your heart.
Ecc	10: 4	calmness can *l* great errors to rest.
Isa	28: 16	"See, I *l* a stone in Zion,
Mt	8: 20	of Man has nowhere to *l* his head."
	28: 6	Come and see the place where he *l*.
Mk	6: 5	*l* his hands on a few sick people
Lk	9: 58	of Man has nowhere to *l* his head."
Jn	10: 15	and I *l* down my life for the sheep.
	10: 18	but I *l* it down of my own accord.
	15: 13	that one *l* down his life
Ac	8: 19	on whom I *l* my hands may receive
Ro	9: 33	I *l* in Zion a stone that causes men
1Co	3: 11	no-one can *l* any foundation other
1Pe	2: 6	"See, I *l* a stone in Zion,
1Jn	3: 16	And we ought to *l* down our lives
Rev	4: 10	They *l* their crowns

LAYING (LAY)

Lk	4: 40	and *l* his hands on each one,
Ac	8: 18	at the *l* on of the apostles' hands,
1Ti	5: 22	Do not be hasty in the *l* on of hands
2Ti	1: 6	is in you through the *l*
Heb	6: 1	not *l* again the foundation
	6: 2	instruction about baptisms, the *l*

LAYS (LAY)

Jn	10: 11	The good shepherd *l* down his life

LAZARUS

1. Poor man in Jesus' parable (Lk 16:19-31).
2. Brother of Mary and Martha whom Jesus raised from the dead (Jn 11:1-12:19).

LAZINESS* (LAZY)

Pr 12: 24 but *l* ends in slave labour.
    19: 15 *L* brings on deep sleep,

LAZY* (LAZINESS)

Ex 5: 8 They are *l*; that is why they are
    5: 17 "*L*, that's what you are—*l*!
Pr 10: 4 *L* hands make a man poor,
    12: 27 The *l* man does not roast his game,
    26: 15 he is too *l* to bring it back
Ecc 10: 18 If a man is *l*, the rafters sag;
Mt 25: 26 replied, 'You wicked, *l* servant!
Tit 1: 12 liars, evil brutes, *l* gluttons."
Heb 6: 12 We do not want you to become *l*,

LEAD (LEADER LEADERS LEADERSHIP LEADS LED)

Ex 15: 13 "In your unfailing love you will *l*
Nu 14: 8 with us, he will *l* us into that land,
Dt 31: 2 and I am no longer able to *l* you.
Jos 1: 6 because you will *l* these people
1Sa 8: 5 now appoint a king to *l* us,
2Ch 1: 10 knowledge, that I may *l* this people
Ps 27: 11 *l* me in a straight path
    61: 2 *l* me to the rock that is higher
    139: 24 and *l* me in the way everlasting.
    143: 10 *l* me on level ground.
Pr 4: 11 and *l* you along straight paths.
Ecc 5: 6 Do not let your mouth *l* you
Isa 11: 6 and a little child will *l* them.
    49: 10 and *l* them beside springs of water.
Da 12: 3 those who *l* many to righteousness,
Mt 6: 13 And *l* us not into temptation,
Lk 11: 4 And *l* us not into temptation.' "
Gal 3: 24 So the law was put in charge to *l* us
1Th 4: 11 it your ambition to *l* a quiet life,
1Jn 3: 7 do not let anyone *l* you astray.
Rev 7: 17 he will *l* them to springs

LEADER (LEAD)

1Sa 7: 6 Samuel was *l* of Israel at Mizpah.
    10: 1 Has not the LORD anointed you *l*
    12: 2 I have been your *l* from my youth
    13: 14 and appointed him *l* of his people,

LEADERS (LEAD)

Heb 13: 7 Remember your *l*, who spoke
    13: 17 Obey your *l* and submit

LEADERSHIP* (LEAD)

Nu 33: 1 by divisions under the *l* of Moses
Ps 109: 8 may another take his place of *l*.
Ac 1: 20 " 'May another take his place of *l*.'
Ro 12: 8 if it is *l*, let him govern diligently;

LEADS (LEAD)

Dt 27: 18 is the man who *l* the blind astray
Ps 23: 2 he *l* me beside quiet waters,
    37: 8 do not fret—it *l* only to evil.
    68: 6 he *l* forth the prisoners
Pr 2: 18 For her house *l* down to death
    10: 17 ignores correction *l* others astray.
    14: 23 but mere talk *l* only to poverty.
    16: 25 but in the end it *l* to death.

Pr 19: 23 The fear of the LORD *l* to life:
    20: 7 righteous man *l* a blameless life;
    21: 5 as surely as haste *l* to poverty.
Isa 40: 11 he gently *l* those that have young.
Mt 7: 13 and broad is the road that *l*
    12: 20 till he *l* justice to victory.
    15: 14 If a blind man *l* a blind man,
Jn 10: 3 sheep by name and *l* them out.
Ro 6: 16 which *l* to death, or to obedience,
    6: 22 the benefit you reap *l* to holiness,
    14: 19 effort to do what *l* to peace
2Co 2: 14 always *l* us in triumphal procession
    7: 10 sorrow brings repentance that *l*
Tit 1: 1 of the truth that *l* to godliness—

LEAH

Wife of Jacob (Ge 29:16-30); bore six sons and one daughter (Ge 29:31-30:21; 34:1; 35:23).

LEAN (LEANED)

Pr 3: 5 *l* not on your own understanding;

LEANED (LEAN)

Ge 47: 31 as he *l* on the top of his staff.
Jn 21: 20 (This was the one who had *l* back
Heb 11: 21 as he *l* on the top of his staff.

LEAP (LEAPED LEAPS)

Isa 35: 6 Then will the lame *l* like a deer,
Mal 4: 2 *l* like calves released from the stall.
Lk 6: 23 "Rejoice in that day and *l* for joy,

LEAPED (LEAP)

Lk 1: 41 heard Mary's greeting, the baby *l*

LEAPS (LEAP)

Ps 28: 7 My heart *l* for joy

LEARN (LEARNED LEARNING LEARNS)

Dt 4: 10 so that they may *l* to revere me
    5: 1 *L* them and be sure to follow them.
    31: 12 and *l* to fear the LORD your God
Ps 119: 7 as I *l* your righteous laws.
Isa 1: 17 *l* to do right!
    26: 9 of the world *l* righteousness.
Mt 11: 29 yoke upon you and *l* from me,
Jn 14: 31 world must *l* that I love the Father
1Th 4: 4 that each of you should *l*
1Ti 2: 11 A woman should *l* in quietness
    5: 4 these should *l* first of all

LEARNED (LEARN)

Ps 119: 152 Long ago I *l* from your statutes
Mt 11: 25 things from the wise and *l*,
Php 4: 9 Whatever you have *l* or received
    4: 11 for I have *l* to be content whatever
2Ti 3: 14 continue in what you have *l*
Heb 5: 8 he *l* obedience from what he

LEARNING (LEARN)

Pr 1: 5 let the wise listen and add to their *l*,
    9: 9 man and he will add to his *l*.
Isa 44: 25 who overthrows the *l* of the wise
Jn 7: 15 "How did this man get such *l*
2Ti 3: 7 always *l* but never able

LEARNS (LEARN)

Jn 6: 45 and *l* from him comes to me.

LEATHER

2Ki 1: 8 and a *l* belt round his waist."

Mt   3: 4 and he had a *l* belt round his waist

LEAVES

Ge   3: 7 so they sewed fig *l* together
Eze 47:12 for food and their *l* for healing."
Rev 22: 2 the *l* of the tree are for the healing

LEBANON

Dt   11:24 from the desert to *L*,
1Ki   4:33 from the cedar of *L*

LED (LEAD)

Ex   3: 1 and he *l* the flock to the far side
Dt   8: 2 the LORD your God *l* you all
1Ki 11: 3 and his wives *l* him astray.
2Ch 26:16 his pride *l* to his downfall.
Ne   13:26 he was *l* into sin by foreign women.
Ps   68:18 you *l* captives in your train;
     78:52 he *l* them like sheep
Pr   7:21 persuasive words she *l* him astray;
     20: 1 whoever is *l* astray
Isa 53: 7 he was *l* like a lamb to the slaughter
Jer 11:19 I had been like a gentle lamb *l*
Am   2:10 and I *l* you forty years in the desert
Mt   4: 1 Then Jesus was *l* by the Spirit
     27:31 they *l* him away to crucify him.
Lk   4: 1 was *l* by the Spirit in the desert,
Ac   8:32 "He was *l* like a sheep
Ro   8:14 those who are *l* by the Spirit
2Co   7: 9 your sorrow *l* you to repentance.
Gal   5:18 But if you are *l* by the Spirit,
Eph   4: 8 he *l* captives in his train

LEEKS*

Nu   11: 5 melons, *l*, onions and garlic.

LEFT

Dt   28:14 or to the *l*, following other gods
Jos   1: 7 turn from it to the right or to the *l*,
     23: 6 aside to the right or to the *l*.
2Ki 22: 2 aside to the right or to the *l*.
Pr   4:27 Do not swerve to the right or the *l*;
Isa 30:21 turn to the right or to the *l*,
Mt   6: 3 do not let your *l* hand know what
     25:33 on his right and the goats on his *l*.

LEGALISTIC*

Php   3: 6 as for *l* righteousness, faultless.

LEGION

Mk   5: 9 "My name is *L*," he replied,

LEND (LENDER LENDS MONEY-LENDER)

Lev 25:37 You must not *l* him money
Dt   15: 8 freely *l* him whatever he needs.
Ps   37:26 are always generous and *l* freely;
Eze 18: 8 He does not *l* at usury
Lk   6:34 if you *l* to those from whom you

LENDER (LEND)

Pr   22: 7 and the borrower is servant to the *l*.
Isa 24: 2 for borrower as for *l*,

LENDS (LEND)

Ps   15: 5 who *l* his money without usury
    112: 5 to him who is generous and *l* freely,
Pr   19:17 to the poor *l* to the LORD,

LENGTH (LONG [1])

Ps   90:10 The *l* of our days is seventy years—

Pr   10:27 The fear of the LORD adds *l* to life

LENGTHY* (LONG [1])

Mk   12:40 and for a show make *l* prayers.
Lk   20:47 and for a show make *l* prayers.

LEOPARD

Isa 11: 6 the *l* will lie down with the goat,
Da   7: 6 beast, one that looked like a *l*.
Rev 13: 2 The beast I saw resembled a *l*,

LEPROSY (LEPROUS)

Nu   12:10 towards her and saw that she had *l*;
2Ki   5: 1 was a valiant soldier, but he had *l*.
      7: 3 men with *l* at the entrance
2Ch 26:21 King Uzziah had *l*
Mt   11: 5 those who have *l* are cured,
Lk   17:12 ten men who had *l* met him.

LEPROUS (LEPROSY)

Ex   4: 6 and when he took it out, it was *l*,

LETTER (LETTERS)

Mt   5:18 not the smallest *l*, not the least
2Co   3: 2 You yourselves are our *l*, written
      3: 6 for the *l* kills, but the Spirit gives
2Th   3:14 not obey our instruction in this *l*,

LETTERS (LETTER)

2Co   3: 7 which was engraved in *l* on stone,
     10:10 "His *l* are weighty and forceful,
2Pe   3:16 His *l* contain some things that are

LEVEL

Ps 143:10 lead me on *l* ground.
Pr   4:26 Make *l* paths for your feet
Isa 26: 7 The path of the righteous is *l*;
     40: 4 the rough ground shall become *l*,
Jer 31: 9 on a *l* path where they will not
Heb 12:13 "Make *l* paths for your feet,"

LEVI (LEVITE LEVITES LEVITICAL)

1. Son of Jacob by Leah (Ge 29:34; 46:11; 1Ch 2:1). With Simeon avenged rape of Dinah (Ge 34). Tribe of blessed (Ge 49:5-7; Dt 33:8-11), chosen as priests (Nu 3-4), numbered (Nu 3:39; 26:62), allotted cities, but not land (Nu 18; 35; Dt 10:9; Jos 13:14; 21), land (Eze 48:8-22), 12,000 from (Rev 7:7).
2. See MATTHEW.

LEVIATHAN

Job 41: 1 pull in the *l* with a fish-hook
Ps   74:14 you who crushed the heads of *L*
Isa 27: 1 *L* the gliding serpent,

LEVITE (LEVI)

Dt   26:12 you shall give it to the *L*, the alien,
Jdg 19: 1 a *L* who lived in a remote area

LEVITES (LEVI)

Nu   1:53 The *L* are to be responsible
      3:12 "I have taken the *L*
      8: 6 "Take the *L* from among the other
     18:21 I give to the *L* all the tithes in Israel
     35: 7 must give the *L* forty-eight towns,
2Ch 31: 2 assigned the priests and *L*
Mal   3: 3 he will purify the *L* and refine them

LEVITICAL (LEVI)

Heb   7:11 attained through the *L* priesthood

LEWDNESS

Mk 7:22 malice, deceit, *l*, envy, slander,

LIAR* (LIE [2])

Dt 19:18 and if the witness proves to be a *l*,
Job 34:6 I am considered a *l*;
Pr 17:4 *l* pays attention to a malicious
19:22 better to be poor than a *l*.
30:6 will rebuke you and prove you a *l*.
Mic 2:11 If a *l* and deceiver comes and says,
Jn 8:44 for he is a *l* and the father of lies.
8:55 I did not, I would be a *l* like you,
Ro 3:4 Let God be true, and every man a *l*.
1Jn 1:10 we make him out to be a *l*
2:4 not do what he commands is a *l*,
2:22 Who is the *l*? It is the man who
4:20 yet hates his brother, he is a *l*.
5:10 God had made him out to be a *l*,

LIARS* (LIE [2])

Ps 63:11 the mouths of *l* will be silenced.
116:11 "All men are *l*."
Isa 57:4 the offspring of *l*?
Mic 6:12 her people are *l*
1Ti 1:10 for slave traders and *l* and perjurers
4:2 come through hypocritical *l*,
Tit 1:12 "Cretans are always *l*, evil brutes,
Rev 3:9 though they are not, but are *l*—
21:8 magic arts, the idolaters and all *l*—

LIBERATED*

Ro 8:21 that the creation itself will be *l*

LICENCE

Jude 4 of our God into a *l* for immorality

LICK

Ps 72:9 and his enemies will *l* the dust.
Isa 49:23 they will *l* the dust at your feet.
Mic 7:17 They will *l* dust like a snake,

LIE [1]

Lev 18:22 "'Do not *l* with a man
Dt 6:7 when you *l* down and when you get
25:2 the judge shall make him *l* down
Ps 4:8 I will *l* down and sleep in peace,
23:2 me *l* down in green pastures,
Pr 3:24 when you *l* down, you will not be
Isa 11:6 leopard will *l* down with the goat,
Eze 34:14 they will *l* down in good grazing

LIE [2] (LIAR LIARS LIED LIES LYING)

Lev 19:11 "'do not *l*.
Nu 23:19 God is not a man, that he should *l*,
1Sa 15:29 the Glory of Israel does not *l*
Ps 89:35 and I will not *l* to David
Isa 28:15 for we have made a *l* our refuge
Jer 9:5 They have taught their tongues to *l*
23:14 They commit adultery and live a *l*.
Eze 13:6 are false and their divinations a *l*,
Ro 1:25 exchanged the truth of God for a *l*,
Col 3:9 Do not *l* to each other
2Th 2:11 so that they will believe the *l*
Tit 1:2 which God, who does not *l*,
Heb 6:18 it is impossible for God to *l*,
1Jn 2:21 because no *l* comes from the truth.
Rev 14:5 No *l* was found in their mouths; .

LIED* (LIE [2])

Ac 5:4 You have not *l* to men but to God."

LIES* (LIE [2])

Lev 6:3 finds lost property and *l* about it,
Ps 5:6 You destroy those who tell *l*;
10:7 His mouth is full of curses and *l*
12:2 Everyone *l* to his neighbour;
34:13 and your lips from speaking *l*.
58:3 they are wayward and speak *l*.
144:8 whose mouths are full of *l*,
Pr 6:19 a false witness who pours out *l*
12:17 but a false witness tells *l*.
19:5 he who pours out *l* will not go free.
19:9 and he who pours out *l* will perish.
29:12 If a ruler listens to *l*,
30:8 Keep falsehood and *l* far from me;
Isa 59:3 Your lips have spoken *l*,
Jer 5:31 The prophets prophesy *l*,
9:3 like a bow, to shoot *l*;
14:14 "The prophets are prophesying *l*
Hos 11:12 Ephraim has surrounded me with *l*,
Jn 8:44 for he is a liar and the father of *l*.

LIFE (LIVE)

Ge 1:30 everything that has the breath of *l*
2:7 into his nostrils the breath of *l*,
2:9 of the garden were the tree of *l*
6:17 to destroy all *l* under the heavens,
9:5 for the *l* of his fellow-man.
9:11 Never again will all *l* be cut
Ex 21:6 Then he will be his servant for *l*.
21:23 you are to take *l* for *l*, eye for eye,
23:26 I will give you a full *l* span.
Lev 17:14 the *l* of every creature is its blood.
24:17 "'If anyone takes the *l*
24:18 must make restitution—*l* for *l*.
Nu 35:31 a ransom for the *l* of a murderer.
Dt 4:42 one of these cities and save his *l*.
12:23 because the blood is the *l*,
19:21 Show no pity: *l* for *l*, eye for eye,
30:15 I set before you today *l*
30:19 Now choose *l*, so that you
30:20 For the LORD is your *l*,
32:39 I put to death and I bring to *l*,
32:47 words for you—they are your *l*.
1Sa 19:5 He took his *l* in his hands
Job 2:6 hands; but you must spare his *l*."
33:4 of the Almighty gives me *l*.
33:30 that the light of *l* may shine on him.
Ps 16:11 known to me the path of *l*;
17:14 this world whose reward is in this *l*.
23:6 all the days of my *l*,
27:1 LORD is the stronghold of my *l*—
34:12 Whoever of you loves *l*
36:9 For with you is the fountain of *l*;
39:4 let me know how fleeting is my *l*.
41:2 will protect him and preserve his *l*;
49:7 No man can redeem the *l*
49:8 the ransom for a *l* is costly,
49:15 God will redeem my *l*
63:3 Because your love is better than *l*,
69:28 they be blotted out of the book of *l*
91:16 With long *l* will I satisfy him
104:33 I will sing to the LORD all my *l*;
119:25 preserve my *l* according to your word
Pr 1:3 a disciplined and prudent *l*,
3:2 will prolong your *l* many years

Pr	3: 18	of *l* to those who embrace her;
	4: 23	for it is the wellspring of *l*.
	6: 23	are the way to *l*,
	6: 26	adulteress preys upon your very *l*.
	7: 23	little knowing it will cost him his *l*.
	8: 35	For whoever finds me finds *l*
	10: 11	of the righteous is a fountain of *l*,
	10: 27	of the LORD adds length to *l*,
	11: 30	of the righteous is a tree of *l*,
	13: 3	He who guards his lips guards his *l*,
	13: 12	but a longing fulfilled is a tree of *l*.
	13: 14	of the wise is a fountain of *l*,
	14: 27	of the LORD is a fountain of *l*,
	15: 4	that brings healing is a tree of *l*,
	16: 22	Understanding is a fountain of *l*
	19: 3	A man's own folly ruins his *l*,
	19: 23	The fear of the LORD leads to *l*:
	21: 21	finds *l*, prosperity and honour.
Isa	53: 10	LORD makes his *l* a guilt offering,
	53: 11	he will see the light ͺof *l*ͺ
	53: 12	he poured out his *l* unto death,
Jer	10: 23	that a man's *l* is not his own;
La	3: 58	you redeemed my *l*.
Eze	18: 27	and right, he will save his *l*.
	37: 5	enter you, and you will come to *l*.
Da	12: 2	some to everlasting *l*, others
Jnh	2: 6	you brought my *l* up from the pit,
Mal	2: 5	a covenant of *l* and peace,
Mt	6: 25	Is not *l* more important than food,
	7: 14	and narrow the road that leads to *l*,
	10: 39	Whoever finds his *l* will lose it,
	16: 21	and on the third day be raised to *l*.
	16: 25	wants to save his *l* will lose it,
	18: 8	better for you to enter *l* maimed
	19: 16	thing must I do to get eternal *l*?"
	19: 29	as much and will inherit eternal *l*.
	20: 28	to give his *l* as a ransom for many."
	25: 46	but the righteous to eternal *l*."
Mk	8: 35	but whoever loses his *l* for me
	9: 43	better for you to enter *l* maimed
	10: 17	"what must I do to inherit eternal *l*
	10: 30	and in the age to come, eternal *l*.
	10: 45	to give his *l* as a ransom for many."
Lk	6: 9	to save *l* or to destroy it?"
	9: 22	and on the third day be raised to *l*."
	9: 24	wants to save his *l* will lose it,
	12: 15	a man's *l* does not consist
	12: 22	do not worry about your *l*,
	12: 25	can add a single hour to his *l*?
	14: 26	even his own *l*—he cannot be my
	17: 33	tries to keep his *l* will lose it,
	21: 19	standing firm you will gain *l*.
Jn	1: 4	In him was *l*, and that *l* was
	3: 15	believes in him may have eternal *l*.
	3: 36	believes in the Son has eternal *l*,
	4: 14	of water welling up to eternal *l*."
	5: 21	raises the dead and gives them *l*,
	5: 24	him who sent me has eternal *l*
	5: 26	For as the Father has *l* in himself,
	5: 39	that by them you possess eternal *l*.
	5: 40	refuse to come to me to have *l*.
	6: 27	for food that endures to eternal *l*,
	6: 33	down from heaven and gives *l*
	6: 35	Jesus declared, "I am the bread of *l*
	6: 40	believes in him shall have eternal *l*,
	6: 47	he who believes has everlasting *l*.
	6: 48	I am the bread of *l*.
	6: 51	give for the *l* of the world."
	6: 53	and drink his blood, you have no *l*
	6: 63	The Spirit gives *l*; the flesh counts

Jn	6: 68	You have the words of eternal *l*.
	8: 12	but will have the light of *l*."
	10: 10	I have come that they may have *l*,
	10: 15	and I lay down my *l* for the sheep.
	10: 17	loves me is that I lay down my *l*—
	10: 28	I give them eternal *l*, and they shall
	11: 25	"I am the resurrection and the *l*.
	12: 25	The man who loves his *l* will lose it,
	12: 50	his command leads to eternal *l*.
	13: 37	I will lay down my *l* for you."
	14: 6	am the way and the truth and the *l*.
	15: 13	lay down his *l* for his friends.
	17: 2	people that he might give eternal *l*
	17: 3	Now this is eternal *l*: that they may
	20: 31	that by believing you may have *l*
Ac	2: 32	God has raised this Jesus to *l*,
	3: 15	You killed the author of *l*,
	11: 18	the Gentiles repentance unto *l*."
	13: 48	appointed for eternal *l* believed.
Ro	2: 7	immortality, he will give eternal *l*.
	4: 25	was raised to *l* for our justification.
	5: 10	shall we be saved through his *l*!
	5: 18	was justification that brings *l*
	5: 21	righteousness to bring eternal *l*
	6: 4	the Father, we too may live a new *l*.
	6: 13	have been brought from death to *l*;
	6: 22	holiness, and the result is eternal *l*.
	6: 23	but the gift of God is eternal *l*
	8: 6	mind controlled by the Spirit is *l*
	8: 11	also give *l* to your mortal bodies
	8: 38	convinced that neither death nor *l*,
1Co	15: 19	If only for this *l* we have hope
	15: 36	What you sow does not come to *l*
2Co	2: 16	to the other, the fragrance of *l*.
	3: 6	letter kills, but the Spirit gives *l*.
	4: 10	so that the *l* of Jesus may
	5: 4	is mortal may be swallowed up by *l*.
Gal	2: 20	The *l* I live in the body, I live
	3: 21	had been given that could impart *l*,
	6: 8	from the Spirit will reap eternal *l*.
Eph	4: 1	I urge you to live a *l* worthy
Php	2: 16	as you hold out the word of *l*—
	4: 3	whose names are in the book of *l*.
Col	1: 10	order that you may live a *l* worthy
	3: 3	your *l* is now hidden with Christ
1Th	4: 12	so that your daily *l* may win
1Ti	1: 16	on him and receive eternal *l*.
	4: 8	for both the present *l* and the *l*
	4: 12	in *l*, in love, in faith and in purity.
	4: 16	Watch your *l* and doctrine closely.
	6: 12	Take hold of the eternal *l*
	6: 19	hold of the *l* that is truly *l*.
2Ti	1: 9	saved us and called us to a holy *l*—
	1: 10	destroyed death and has brought *l*
	3: 12	to live a godly *l* in Christ Jesus will
Tit	1: 2	resting on the hope of eternal *l*,
	3: 7	heirs having the hope of eternal *l*.
Heb	7: 16	of the power of an indestructible *l*.
Jas	1: 12	crown of *l* that God has promised
	3: 13	Let him show it by his good *l*,
1Pe	3: 7	with you of the gracious gift of *l*,
	3: 10	"Whoever would love *l*
	4: 2	rest of his earthly *l* for evil human
2Pe	1: 3	given us everything we need for *l*
1Jn	1: 1	proclaim concerning the Word of *l*.
	2: 25	he promised us—even eternal *l*.
	3: 14	we have passed from death to *l*,
	3: 16	Jesus Christ laid down his *l* for us.
	5: 11	has given us eternal *l*, and this *l* is
	5: 20	He is the true God and eternal *l*.

Jude : 21 Christ to bring you to eternal *l*.
Rev   2: 7 the right to eat from the tree of *l*,
      2: 8 who died and came to *l* again.
      2: 10 and I will give you the crown of *l*.
      3: 5 name from the book of *l*,
      13: 8 written in the book of *l* belonging
      17: 8 in the book of *l* from the creation
      20: 12 was opened, which is the book of *l*.
      20: 15 not found written in the book of *l*,
      21: 6 from the spring of the water of *l*.
      21: 27 written in the Lamb's book of *l*.
      22: 1 me the river of the water of *l*,
      22: 2 side of the river stood the tree of *l*,
      22: 14 may have the right to the tree of *l*
      22: 17 take the free gift of the water of *l*.
      22: 19 from him his share in the tree of *l*

LIFE-GIVING (GIVE)

Pr   15: 31 He who listens to a *l* rebuke
1Co   15: 45 being"; the last Adam, a *l* spirit.

LIFETIME (LIVE)

Ps   30: 5 but his favour lasts a *l*;
Lk   16: 25 in your *l* you received your good

LIFT (LIFTED LIFTING LIFTS)

Ps   28: 2 as I *l* up my hands
      63: 4 in your name I will *l* up my hands.
      91: 12 they will *l* you up in their hands,
      121: 1 I *l* up my eyes to the hills—
      123: 1 I *l* up my eyes to you,
      134: 2 *L* up your hands in the sanctuary
      143: 8 for to you I *l* up my soul.
Isa   40: 9 *l* up your voice with a shout,
La   2: 19 *L* up your hands to him
      3: 41 Let us *l* up our hearts and our
Mt   4: 6 they will *l* you up in their hands,
Lk   21: 28 stand up and *l* up your heads,
1Ti   2: 8 everywhere to *l* up holy hands
Jas   4: 10 the Lord, and he will *l* you up.
1Pe   5: 6 that he may *l* you up in due time.

LIFTED (LIFT)

Ne   8: 6 and all the people *l* their hands
Ps   24: 7 be *l* up, you ancient doors,
      40: 2 He *l* me out of the slimy pit,
      41: 9 has *l* up his heel against me.
Isa   52: 13 *l* up and highly exalted.
      63: 9 he *l* them up and carried them
Jn   3: 14 Moses *l* up the snake in the desert,
      8: 28 "When you have *l* up the Son
      12: 32 when I am *l* up from the earth,
      12: 34 'The Son of Man must be *l* up'?
      13: 18 shares my bread has *l* up his heel

LIFTING (LIFT)

Ps   141: 2 may the *l* up of my hands be like

LIFTS (LIFT)

Ps   3: 3 Glorious One, who *l* up my head.
      113: 7 and *l* the needy from the ash heap;

LIGAMENT* (LIGAMENTS)

Eph   4: 16 held together by every supporting *l*

LIGAMENTS* (LIGAMENT)

Col   2: 19 held together by its *l* and sinews,

LIGHT [1]

Mt   11: 30 yoke is easy and my burden is *l*."

LIGHT [2] (ENLIGHTENED LIGHTS)

Ge   1: 3 "Let there be *l*," and there was *l*.
Ex   13: 21 in a pillar of fire to give them *l*,
      25: 37 it so that they *l* the space in front
2Sa   22: 29 LORD turns my darkness into *l*.
Job   38: 19 "What is the way to the abode of *l*?
Ps   4: 6 Let the *l* of your face shine upon us
      18: 28 my God turns my darkness into *l*.
      19: 8 giving *l* to the eyes.
      27: 1 LORD is my *l* and my salvation—
      36: 9 in your *l* we see *l*.
      56: 13 God in the *l* of life.
      76: 4 You are resplendent with *l*,
      89: 15 who walk in the *l* of your presence,
      104: 2 He wraps himself in *l*
      119: 105 and a *l* for my path.
      119: 130 The unfolding of your words gives *l*;
      139: 12 for darkness is as *l* to you.
Pr   4: 18 till the full *l* of day.
Isa   2: 5 let us walk in the *l* of the LORD.
      9: 2 have seen a great *l*;
      42: 6 and a *l* for the Gentiles,
      45: 7 I form the *l* and create darkness,
      49: 6 also make you a *l* for the Gentiles,
      53: 11 he will see the *l* of life」
      60: 1 "Arise, shine, for your *l* has come,
      60: 19 LORD will be your everlasting *l*,
Eze   1: 27 and brilliant *l* surrounded him.
Mic   7: 8 the LORD will be my *l*.
Mt   4: 16 have seen a great *l*;
      5: 14 "You are the *l* of the world.
      5: 15 it gives *l* to everyone in the house.
      5: 16 let your *l* shine before men,
      6: 22 your whole body will be full of *l*.
      17: 2 his clothes became as white as the *l*
      24: 29 and the moon will not give its *l*;
Mk   13: 24 and the moon will not give its *l*;
Lk   2: 32 a *l* for revelation to the Gentiles
      8: 16 those who come in can see the *l*.
      11: 33 those who come in may see the *l*.
Jn   1: 4 and that life was the *l* of men.
      1: 5 The *l* shines in the darkness,
      1: 7 witness to testify concerning that *l*,
      1: 9 The true *l* that gives *l*
      3: 19 but men loved darkness instead of *l*
      3: 20 Everyone who does evil hates the *l*,
      8: 12 he said, "I am the *l* of the world.
      9: 5 in the world, I am the *l* of the world
      12: 35 Walk while you have the *l*,
      12: 46 I have come into the world as a *l*,
Ac   13: 47 "'I have made you a *l*
Ro   13: 12 darkness and put on the armour of *l*.
2Co   4: 6 made his *l* shine in our hearts
      6: 14 Or what fellowship can *l* have
      11: 14 masquerades as an angel of *l*.
Eph   5: 8 but now you are *l* in the Lord.
1Th   5: 5 You are all sons of the *l*
1Ti   6: 16 and who lives in unapproachable *l*,
1Pe   2: 9 of darkness into his wonderful *l*.
2Pe   1: 19 as to a *l* shining in a dark place,
1Jn   1: 5 God is *l*; in him there is no
      1: 7 But if we walk in the *l*,
      2: 9 Anyone who claims to be in the *l*
Rev   21: 23 for the glory of God gives it *l*,
      22: 5 for the Lord God will give them *l*.

LIGHTNING

Ex   9: 23 and *l* flashed down to the ground.

Ex	20: 18	and *l* and heard the trumpet
Ps	18: 12	with hailstones and bolts of *l*.
Eze	1: 13	it was bright, and *l* flashed out of it.
Da	10: 6	his face like *l*, his eyes like flaming
Mt	24: 27	For as the *l* comes from the east
	28: 3	His appearance was like *l*,
Lk	10: 18	"I saw Satan fall like *l* from heaven.
Rev	4: 5	From the throne came flashes of *l*,

LIGHTS (LIGHT [2])

Ge	1: 14	"Let there be *l* in the expanse
Lk	8: 16	No-one *l* a lamp and hides it in a jar

LIKE-MINDED* (MIND)

Php	2: 2	make my joy complete by being *l*,

LIKENESS

Ge	1: 26	man in our image, in our *l*,
Ps	17: 15	I will be satisfied with seeing your *l*
Isa	52: 14	his form marred beyond human *l*—
Ro	8: 3	Son in the *l* of sinful man
	8: 29	to be conformed to the *l* of his Son,
2Co	3: 18	his *l* with ever-increasing glory,
Php	2: 7	being made in human *l*.
Jas	3: 9	who have been made in God's *l*.

LILIES (LILY)

Lk	12: 27	"Consider how the *l* grow.

LILY (LILIES)

SS	2: 1	a *l* of the valleys.
	2: 2	Like a *l* among thorns

LIMIT

Ps	147: 5	his understanding has no *l*.
Jn	3: 34	him God gives the Spirit without *l*.

LINEN

Lev	16: 4	He is to put on the sacred *l* tunic,
Pr	31: 22	she is clothed in fine *l* and purple.
	31: 24	She makes *l* garments
Mk	15: 46	So Joseph bought some *l* cloth,
Jn	20: 6	He saw the strips of *l* lying there,
Rev	15: 6	shining *l* and wore golden sashes
	19: 8	Fine *l*, bright and clean,

LINGER

Hab	2: 3	Though it *l*, wait for it;

LION (LION'S LIONS')

Jdg	14: 6	power so that he tore the *l* apart
1Sa	17: 34	When a *l* or a bear came
Isa	11: 7	and the *l* will eat straw like the ox.
	65: 25	and the *l* will eat straw like the ox,
Eze	1: 10	right side each had the face of a *l*,
	10: 14	the third the face of a *l*,
Da	7: 4	"The first was like a *l*,
1Pe	5: 8	around like a roaring *l* looking
Rev	4: 7	The first living creature was like a *l*
	5: 5	See, the *L* of the tribe of Judah,

LION'S (LION)

Ge	49: 9	You are a *l* cub, O Judah;

LIONS' (LION)

Da	6: 7	shall be thrown into the *l* den.

LIPS

Ps	8: 2	From the *l* of children and infants
	34: 1	his praise will always be on my *l*.

Ps	40: 9	I do not seal my *l*,
	63: 3	my *l* will glorify you.
	119: 171	May my *l* overflow with praise,
	140: 3	the poison of vipers is on their *l*.
	141: 3	keep watch over the door of my *l*.
Pr	10: 13	on the *l* of the discerning,
	10: 18	who conceals his hatred has lying *l*,
	10: 32	*l* of the righteous know what is
	12: 22	The LORD detests lying *l*,
	13: 3	He who guards his *l* guards his life
	14: 7	will not find knowledge on his *l*.
	24: 26	is like a kiss on the *l*.
	26: 23	are fervent *l* with an evil heart.
	27: 2	someone else, and not your own *l*.
Isa	6: 5	For I am a man of unclean *l*,
	28: 11	with foreign *l* and strange tongues
	29: 13	and honour me with their *l*,
Mal	2: 7	"For the *l* of a priest ought
Mt	15: 8	These people honour me with their *l*
	21: 16	"'From the *l* of children
Lk	4: 22	words that came from his *l*.
Ro	3: 13	"The poison of vipers is on their *l*."
Col	3: 8	and filthy language from your *l*.
Heb	13: 15	the fruit of *l* that confess his name.
1Pe	3: 10	and his *l* from deceitful speech.

LISTEN (LISTENED LISTENING LISTENS)

Dt	18: 15	You must *l* to him.
	30: 20	*l* to his voice, and hold fast to him.
1Ki	4: 34	came to *l* to Solomon's wisdom,
2Ki	21: 9	But the people did not *l*.
Pr	1: 5	let the wise *l* and add
Ecc	5: 1	Go near to *l* rather
Eze	2: 5	And whether they *l* or fail to *l*—
Mt	12: 42	earth to *l* to Solomon's wisdom,
Mk	9: 7	*L* to him!" Suddenly,
Jn	10: 27	My sheep *l* to my voice; I know
Ac	3: 22	you must *l* to everything he tells
Jas	1: 19	Everyone should be quick to *l*,
	1: 22	Do not merely *l* to the word,
1Jn	4: 6	not from God does not *l* to us.

LISTENED (LISTEN)

Ne	8: 3	And all the people *l* attentively
Isa	66: 4	when I spoke, no-one *l*.
Da	9: 6	We have not *l* to your servants

LISTENING (LISTEN)

1Sa	3: 9	Speak, LORD, for your servant is *l*
Pr	18: 13	He who answers before *l*—
Lk	10: 39	at the Lord's feet *l* to what he said.

LISTENS (LISTEN)

Pr	12: 15	but a wise man *l* to advice.
Lk	10: 16	"He who *l* to you *l*
1Jn	4: 6	and whoever knows God *l* to us;

LIVE (ALIVE LIFE LIFETIME LIVES LIVING)

Ge	3: 22	tree of life and eat, and *l* for ever."
Ex	20: 12	so that you may *l* long
	33: 20	for no-one may see me and *l*."
Nu	21: 8	who is bitten can look at it and *l*."
Dt	5: 24	we have seen that a man can *l*
	6: 2	as you *l* by keeping all his decrees
	8: 3	to teach you that man does not *l*
Job	14: 14	If a man dies, will he *l* again?
Ps	15: 1	Who may *l* on your holy hill?
	24: 1	the world, and all who *l* in it;
	26: 8	I love the house where you *l*,
	119: 175	Let me *l* that I may praise you,

Pr   21: 9   Better to *l* on a corner of the roof
    21: 19   Better to *l* in a desert
Ecc   9: 4   a *l* dog is better off than a dead lion
Isa   26: 19   But your dead will *l*;
    55: 3   hear me, that your soul may *l*.
Eze   17: 19   LORD says: As surely as I *l*,
    20: 11   for the man who obeys them will *l*
    37: 3   can these bones *l*?" I said,
Am   5: 6   Seek the LORD and *l*,
Hab   2: 4   but the righteous will *l* by his faith
Zec   2: 11   I will *l* among you and you will
Mt   4: 4   'Man does not *l* on bread alone,
Lk   4: 4   'Man does not *l* on bread alone.' "
Jn   14: 19   Because I *l*, you also will *l*.
Ac   17: 24   does not *l* in temples built by hands
    17: 28   'For in him we *l* and move
Ro   1: 17   "The righteous will *l* by faith."
2Co   5: 7   We *l* by faith, not by sight.
    6: 16   "I will *l* with them and walk
Gal   2: 20   The life I *l* in the body, I *l* by faith
    3: 11   "The righteous will *l* by faith."
    5: 25   Since we *l* by the Spirit, let us keep
Eph   4: 17   that you must no longer *l*
Php   1: 21   to *l* is Christ and to die is gain.
Col   1: 10   order that you may *l* a life worthy
1Th   4: 1   we instructed you how to *l* in order
    5: 13   *L* in peace with each other.
1Ti   2: 2   that we may *l* peaceful
2Ti   3: 12   who wants to *l* a godly life
Tit   2: 12   and to *l* self-controlled, upright
Heb   10: 38   But my righteous one will *l* by faith
    12: 14   Make every effort to *l* in peace
1Pe   1: 17   *l* your lives as strangers here
    3: 8   *l* in harmony with one another;

LIVES (LIVE)

Ge   45: 7   and to save your *l* by a great
Job   19: 25   I know that my Redeemer *l*,
Pr   1: 19   it takes away the *l*
Isa   57: 15   he who *l* for ever, whose name is
Da   3: 28   to give up their *l* rather than serve
Jn   14: 17   for he *l* with you and will be in you.
Ro   6: 10   but the life he *l*, he *l* to God.
    7: 18   I know that nothing good *l* in me,
    8: 9   if the Spirit of God *l* in you.
    14: 7   For none of us *l* to himself alone
1Co   3: 16   and that God's Spirit *l* in you?
Gal   2: 20   I no longer live, but Christ *l* in me.
1Th   2: 8   only the gospel of God but our *l*
1Ti   2: 2   quiet *l* in all godliness and holiness.
Tit   2: 12   and godly *l* in this present age,
Heb   7: 24   but because Jesus *l* for ever,
    13: 5   Keep your *l* free from the love
1Pe   3: 2   the purity and reverence of your *l*.
2Pe   3: 11   You ought to live holy and godly *l*
1Jn   3: 16   to lay down our *l* for our brothers.
    4: 16   Whoever *l* in love *l* in God,

LIVING (LIVE)

Ge   2: 7   and man became a *l* being.
1Sa   17: 26   defy the armies of the *l* God?"
Isa   53: 8   cut off from the land of the *l*;
Jer   2: 13   the spring of *l* water,
Eze   1: 5   what looked like four *l* creatures.
Zec   14: 8   On that day *l* water will flow out
Mt   22: 32   the God of the dead but of the *l*."
Jn   4: 10   he would have given you *l* water."
    6: 51   I am the *l* bread that came
    7: 38   streams of *l* water will flow
Ro   8: 11   Jesus from the dead is *l* in you,

Ro   12: 1   to offer your bodies as *l* sacrifices,
1Co   9: 14   the gospel should receive their *l*
Heb   4: 12   For the word of God is *l* and active.
    10: 20   and *l* way opened for us
    10: 31   to fall into the hands of the *l* God.
1Pe   1: 23   through the *l* and enduring word
Rev   1: 18   I am the *L* One; I was dead,
    4: 6   the throne, were four *l* creatures,
    7: 17   to springs of *l* water.

LOAD (LOADS)

Gal   6: 5   for each one should carry his own *l*.

LOADS (LOAD)

Mt   23: 4   They tie up heavy *l* and put them

LOAF (LOAVES)

1Co   10: 17   for we all partake of the one *l*.

LOAVES (LOAF)

Mk   6: 41   Taking the five *l* and the two fish
    8: 6   When he had taken the seven *l*
Lk   11: 5   'Friend, lend me three *l* of bread,

LOCKED

Jn   20: 26   the doors were *l*, Jesus came
Gal   3: 23   *l* up until faith should be revealed.

LOCUSTS

Ex   10: 4   I will bring *l* into your country
Joel   2: 25   you for the years the *l* have eaten—
Mt   3: 4   His food was *l* and wild honey.
Rev   9: 3   And out of the smoke *l* came

LOFTY

Ps   139: 6   too *l* for me to attain.
Isa   57: 15   is what the high and *l* One says—

LONELY

Ps   68: 6   God sets the *l* in families,
Lk   5: 16   Jesus often withdrew to *l* places

LONG [1] (LENGTH LENGTHY)

Ex   17: 11   As *l* as Moses held up his hands,
Nu   6: 5   the hair of his head grow *l*.
1Ki   18: 21   "How *l* will you waver
Ps   119: 97   I meditate on it all day *l*.
Mt   25: 5   The bridegroom was a *l* time
Jn   9: 4   As *l* as it is day, we must do
1Co   11: 14   that if a man has *l* hair,
Eph   3: 18   to grasp how wide and *l* and high

LONG [2] (LONGED LONGING LONGINGS LONGS)

Ps   119: 174   I *l* for your salvation, O Lord,
Hos   7: 13   I *l* to redeem them
Am   5: 18   Why do you *l* for the day
Php   1: 8   God can testify how I *l* for all
1Pe   1: 12   Even angels *l* to look

LONGED (LONG [2])

Mt   13: 17   righteous men *l* to see what you see
    23: 37   how often I have *l*
Lk   13: 34   how often I have *l*
2Ti   4: 8   to all who have *l* for his appearing.

LONGING* (LONG [2])

Dt   28: 65   with *l*, and a despairing heart.
Job   7: 2   Like a slave *l* for the evening
Ps   119: 20   My soul is consumed with *l*

Ps	119: 81	with *l* for your salvation,
	119: 131	*l* for your commands.
	143: 7	my spirit faints with *l*.
Pr	13: 12	but a *l* fulfilled is a tree of life.
	13: 19	A *l* fulfilled is sweet to the soul,
Eze	23: 27	look on these things with *l*
Lk	16: 21	and *l* to eat what fell from the rich
Ro	15: 23	since I have been *l* for many years
2Co	5: 2	*l* to be clothed with our heavenly
	7: 7	He told us about your *l* for me,
	7: 11	what alarm, what *l*, what concern,
1Th	2: 17	out of our intense *l* we made every
Heb	11: 16	they were *l* for a better country—

LONGINGS* (LONG [2])

Ps	38: 9	All my *l* lie open before you,
	112: 10	the *l* of the wicked will come

LONGS* (LONG [2])

Ps	63: 1	my body *l* for you,
Isa	26: 9	in the morning my spirit *l* for you.
	30: 18	Yet the Lord *l* to be gracious
Php	2: 26	For he *l* for all of you and is

LOOK (LOOKED LOOKING LOOKS)

Ge	19: 17	"Flee for your lives! Don't *l* back,
Ex	3: 6	because he was afraid to *l* at God.
Nu	21: 8	anyone who is bitten can *l* at it
	32: 8	Kadesh Barnea to *l* over the land.
Dt	4: 29	you will find him if you *l* for him
1Sa	16: 7	The Lord does not *l*
Job	31: 1	not to *l* lustfully at a girl.
Ps	34: 5	Those who *l* to him are radiant;
	105: 4	*L* to the Lord and his strength;
	113: 6	who stoops down to *l*
	123: 2	As the eyes of slaves *l* to the hand
Pr	1: 28	they will *l* for me but will not find
	4: 25	Let your eyes *l* straight ahead,
	15: 30	A cheerful *l* brings joy to the heart,
Isa	17: 7	In that day men will *l*
	31: 1	do not *l* to the Holy One of Israel,
	40: 26	Lift your eyes and *l* to the heavens;
	60: 5	Then you will *l* and be radiant,
Jer	3: 3	Yet you have the brazen *l*
	6: 16	"Stand at the crossroads and *l*;
Eze	34: 11	for my sheep and *l* after them.
Hab	1: 13	Your eyes are too pure to *l* on evil;
Zec	12: 10	They will *l* on me, the one they
Mt	18: 10	"See that you do not *l* down on one
	18: 12	go to *l* for the one that wandered
	23: 27	which *l* beautiful on the outside
Mk	13: 21	'*L*, here is the Christ!' or, '*L*,
Lk	6: 41	"Why do you *l* at the speck
	24: 39	*L* at my hands and my feet.
Jn	1: 36	he said, "*L*, the Lamb of God!"
	4: 35	open your eyes and *l* at the fields!
	19: 37	"They will *l* on the one they have
Ro	14: 10	why do you *l* down on your brother
Php	2: 4	Each of you should *l* not only
1Ti	4: 12	Don't let anyone *l* down on you
Jas	1: 27	to *l* after orphans and widows
1Pe	1: 12	long to *l* into these things.
2Pe	3: 12	as you *l* forward to the day of God

LOOKED (LOOK)

Ge	19: 26	Lot's wife *l* back and she became
Ex	2: 25	So God *l* on the Israelites
1Sa	6: 19	because they had *l* into the ark
SS	3: 1	I *l* for the one my heart loves;
Eze	22: 30	"I *l* for a man among them who

Eze	34: 6	and no-one searched or *l* for them.
	44: 4	I *l* and saw the glory
Da	7: 9	"As I *l*,
	10: 5	I *l* up and there before me was
Hab	3: 6	he *l*, and made the nations tremble.
Mt	25: 36	I was sick and you *l* after me,
Lk	18: 9	and *l* down on everybody else,
	22: 61	The Lord turned and *l* straight
1Jn	1: 1	which we have *l* at and our hands

LOOKING (LOOK)

Ps	69: 3	*l* for my God.
	119: 82	My eyes fail, *l* for your promise;
	119: 123	My eyes fail, *l* for your salvation,
Mk	16: 6	"You are *l* for Jesus the Nazarene,
2Co	10: 7	You are *l* only on the surface
Php	4: 17	Not that I am *l* for a gift,
1Th	2: 6	We were not *l* for praise from men,
2Pe	3: 13	with his promise we are *l* forward
Rev	5: 6	I saw a Lamb, *l* as if it had been

LOOKS (LOOK)

1Sa	16: 7	Man *l* at the outward appearance,
Ezr	8: 22	is on everyone who *l* to him,
Ps	104: 32	He *l* at the earth, and it trembles;
	138: 6	on high, he *l* upon the lowly,
Pr	27: 18	he who *l* after his master will be
Eze	34: 12	As a shepherd *l* after his scattered
Mt	5: 28	But I tell you that anyone who *l*
	16: 4	and adulterous generation *l*
Lk	9: 62	and *l* back is fit for service
Jn	6: 40	Father's will is that everyone who *l*
	12: 45	When he *l* at me, he sees the one
Php	2: 21	For everyone *l* out
Jas	1: 25	But the man who *l* intently

LOOSE

Isa	33: 23	Your rigging hangs *l*:
Mt	16: 19	and whatever you *l* on earth will be
	18: 18	and whatever you *l* on earth will be

*LORD (LORD'S LORDED LORDING)

Ge	18: 27	been so bold as to speak to the *L*,
Ex	15: 17	O *L*, your hands established.
Nu	16: 13	now you also want to *l* it over us?
Dt	10: 17	God of gods and *L* of lords,
Jos	3: 13	the *L* of all the earth—set foot
1Ki	3: 10	*L* was pleased that Solomon had
Ne	4: 14	Remember the *L*, who is great
Job	28: 28	'The fear of the *L*—that is wisdom
Ps	37: 13	but the *L* laughs at the wicked,
	38: 22	O *L* my Saviour.
	54: 4	the *L* is the one who sustains me.
	62: 12	and that you, O *L*, are loving.
	69: 6	O *L*, the Lord Almighty;
	86: 5	You are forgiving and good, O *L*,
	86: 8	gods there is none like you, O *L*;
	89: 49	O *L*, where is your former great
	110: 1	The Lord says to my *L*:
	110: 5	The *L* is at your right hand;
	130: 3	O *L*, who could stand?
	135: 5	that our *L* is greater than all gods.
	136: 3	Give thanks to the *L* of lords:
	147: 5	Great is our *L* and mighty in power
Isa	6: 1	I saw the *L* seated on a throne,
Da	2: 47	and the *L* of kings and a revealer
	9: 4	"O *L*, the great and awesome God,

*See also †Lord, †Lord's.

Da 9: 7 "*L*, you are righteous,
9: 9 The *L* our God is merciful
9: 19 O *L*, listen! O *L*, forgive! O *L*,
Mt 3: 3 'Prepare the way for the *L*,
4: 7 'Do not put the *L* your God
4: 10 'Worship the *L* your God,
7: 21 "Not everyone who says to me, '*L*,
9: 38 Ask the *L* of the harvest, therefore,
12: 8 Son of Man is *L* of the Sabbath."
20: 25 of the Gentiles *l* it over them,
21: 9 comes in the name of the *L*!"
22: 37 "'Love the *L* your God
22: 44 For he says, "'The *L* said to my *L*:
23: 39 comes in the name of the *L*.'"
Mk 1: 3 'Prepare the way for the *L*,
12: 11 the *L* has done this,
12: 29 the *L* our God, the *L* is one.
12: 30 Love the *L* your God
Lk 2: 9 glory of the *L* shone around them,
6: 5 The Son of Man is *L* of the Sabbath
6: 46 "Why do you call me, '*L*, *L*,'
10: 27 "'Love the *L* your God
11: 1 one of his disciples said to him, "*L*,
24: 34 The *L* has risen and has appeared
Jn 1: 23 'Make straight the way for the *L*.'"
Ac 2: 21 on the name of the *L* will be saved.'
2: 25 "'I saw the *L* always before me.
2: 34 "'The *L* said to my *L*:
8: 16 into the name of the *L* Jesus.
9: 5 "Who are you, *L*?" Saul asked.
10: 36 through Jesus Christ, who is *L*
11: 23 true to the *L* with all their hearts.
16: 31 replied, "Believe in the *L* Jesus,
Ro 4: 24 in him who raised Jesus our *L*
5: 11 in God through our *L* Jesus Christ,
6: 23 life in Christ Jesus our *L*.
8: 39 of God that is in Christ Jesus our *L*.
10: 9 with your mouth, "Jesus is *L*,"
10: 13 on the name of the *L* will be saved
10: 16 *L*, who has believed our message?"
11: 34 Who has known the mind of the *L*?
12: 11 your spiritual fervour, serving the *L*.
13: 14 yourselves with the *L* Jesus Christ,
14: 4 for the *L* is able to make him stand.
14: 8 we live to the *L*; and if we die,
1Co 1: 31 Let him who boasts boast in the *L*."
3: 5 the *L* has assigned to each his task.
4: 5 time; wait till the *L* comes.
6: 13 for the *L*, and the *L* for the body.
6: 14 By his power God raised the *L*
7: 32 affairs—how he can please the *L*.
7: 34 to be devoted to the *L* in both body
7: 35 in undivided devotion to the *L*.
7: 39 but he must belong to the *L*.
8: 6 and there is but one *L*, Jesus Christ,
10: 9 We should not test the *L*,
11: 23 For I received from the *L* what I
12: 3 "Jesus is *L*," except by the Holy
15: 57 victory through our *L* Jesus Christ.
15: 58 fully to the work of the *L*,
16: 22 If anyone does not love the *L*—
2Co 1: 24 Not that we *l* it over your faith,
2: 12 found that the *L* had opened a door
3: 17 Now the *L* is the Spirit,
4: 5 but Jesus Christ as *L*, and ourselves
5: 6 in the body we are away from the *L*
8: 5 they gave themselves first to the *L*
8: 21 not only in the eyes of the *L* but
10: 17 Let him who boasts boast in the *L*."
10: 18 but the one whom the *L* commends

2Co 13: 10 the authority the *L* gave me
Gal 6: 14 in the cross of our *L* Jesus Christ,
Eph 4: 5 one *L*, one faith, one baptism;
5: 8 but now you are light in the *L*.
5: 10 and find out what pleases the *L*.
5: 19 make music in your heart to the *L*,
5: 22 submit to your husbands as to the *L*
6: 1 obey your parents in the *L*,
6: 7 as if you were serving the *L*,
6: 8 know that the *L* will reward
6: 10 in the *L* and in his mighty power.
Php 2: 11 confess that Jesus Christ is *L*,
3: 1 my brothers, rejoice in the *L*!
3: 8 of knowing Christ Jesus my *L*,
4: 1 you should stand firm in the *L*,
4: 4 Rejoice in the *L* always.
4: 5 The *L* is near.
Col 1: 10 you may live a life worthy of the *L*
2: 6 as you received Christ Jesus as *L*,
3: 13 Forgive as the *L* forgave you.
3: 17 do it all in the name of the *L* Jesus,
3: 18 your husbands, as is fitting in the *L*.
3: 20 in everything, for this pleases the *L*
3: 23 as working for the *L*, not for men,
3: 24 It is the *L* Christ you are serving.
3: 24 receive an inheritance from the *L*
4: 17 work you have received in the *L*."
1Th 3: 8 since you are standing firm in the *L*
3: 12 May the *L* make your love increase
4: 1 and urge you in the *L* Jesus
4: 6 The *L* will punish men
4: 15 who are left till the coming of the *L*
5: 2 day of the *L* will come like a thief
5: 23 at the coming of our *L* Jesus Christ.
2Th 1: 7 when the *L* Jesus is revealed
1: 12 of our *L* Jesus may be glorified
2: 1 the coming of our *L* Jesus Christ
2: 8 whom the *L* Jesus will overthrow
3: 3 *L* is faithful, and he will strengthen
3: 5 May the *L* direct your hearts
1Ti 6: 15 the King of kings and *L* of lords,
2Ti 1: 8 ashamed to testify about our *L*,
2: 19 "The *L* knows those who are his,"
4: 8 which the *L*, the righteous Judge,
4: 17 the *L* stood at my side
Heb 1: 10 O *L*, you laid the foundations
10: 30 "The *L* will judge his people."
12: 14 holiness no-one will see the *L*.
13: 6 *L* is my helper; I will not be afraid.
Jas 3: 9 With the tongue we praise our *L*
4: 10 Humble yourselves before the *L*,
5: 11 The *L* is full of compassion
1Pe 1: 25 the word of the *L* stands for ever."
2: 3 you have tasted that the *L* is good.
3: 12 eyes of the *L* are on the righteous
3: 15 in your hearts set apart Christ as *L*.
2Pe 1: 11 into the eternal kingdom of our *L*
1: 16 and coming of our *L* Jesus Christ,
2: 1 the sovereign *L* who bought
2: 9 then the *L* knows how
3: 9 The *L* is not slow in keeping his
3: 18 and knowledge of our *L* and Saviour
Jude : 14 the *L* is coming with thousands
Rev 4: 8 holy, holy is the *L* God Almighty,
4: 11 "You are worthy, our *L* and God,
11: 15 has become the kingdom of our *L*
17: 14 he is *L* of lords and King of kings—
19: 16 KINGS AND *L* OF LORDS.
22: 5 for the *L* God will give them light.
22: 20 Come, *L* Jesus.

*LORD'S (*LORD)

Lk	1: 38	"I am the *L* servant," Mary
Ac	11: 21	The *L* hand was with them,
	21: 14	and said, "The *L* will be done."
1Co	7: 32	is concerned about the *L* affairs—
	10: 26	"The earth is the *L*, and everything
	11: 26	you proclaim the *L* death
2Co	3: 18	faces all reflect the *L* glory,
Eph	5: 17	but understand what the *L* will is.
2Ti	2: 24	And the *L* servant must not quarrel
Heb	12: 5	light of the *L* discipline,
Jas	4: 15	you ought to say, "If it is the *L* will,
	5: 8	because the *L* coming is near.
1Pe	2: 13	Submit yourselves for the *L* sake

LORDED (*LORD)

Ne	5: 15	Their assistants also *l* it

LORDING (*LORD)

1Pe	5: 3	not *l* it over those entrusted to you,

†LORD (†LORD'S)

Ge	2: 4	When the *L* God made the earth
	2: 7	And the *L* God formed man
	2: 22	Then the *L* God made a woman
	3: 21	The *L* God made garments of skin
	3: 23	So the *L* God banished him
	4: 4	The *L* looked with favour on Abel
	4: 26	began to call on the name of the *L*.
	6: 7	So the *L* said, "I will wipe mankind
	7: 16	Then the *L* shut him in.
	9: 26	Blessed be the *L*, the God of Shem!
	11: 9	there the *L* confused the language
	12: 1	*L* had said to Abram, "Leave your
	15: 6	Abram believed the *L*,
	15: 18	On that day the *L* made a covenant
	17: 1	the *L* appeared to him and said,
	18: 1	The *L* appeared to Abraham
	18: 14	Is anything too hard for the *L*?
	18: 19	way of the *L* by doing what is right
	21: 1	Now the *L* was gracious to Sarah
	22: 14	that place "The *L* will provide."
	24: 1	the *L* had blessed him in every way
	26: 2	The *L* appeared to Isaac and said,
	28: 13	There above it stood the *L*,
	31: 49	"May the *L* keep watch
	39: 2	The *L* was with Joseph
	39: 21	in the prison, the *L* was with him;
Ex	3: 2	the angel of the *L* appeared to him
	4: 11	Is it not I, the *L*? Now go;
	4: 31	heard that the *L* was concerned
	6: 2	also said to Moses, "I am the *L*.
	9: 12	the *L* hardened Pharaoh's heart
	12: 27	'It is the Passover sacrifice to the *L*,
	12: 43	The *L* said to Moses and Aaron,
	13: 9	For the *L* brought you out of Egypt
	13: 21	By day the *L* went ahead of them
	14: 13	the deliverance the *L* will bring
	14: 30	That day the *L* saved Israel
	15: 3	The *L* is a warrior;
	15: 11	among the gods is like you, O *L*?
	15: 26	for I am the *L* who heals you."
	16: 12	know that I am the *L* your God.'"
	16: 23	day of rest, a holy Sabbath to the *L*.
	17: 15	and called it The *L* is my Banner.
	19: 8	will do everything the *L* has said."

†This entry represents the translation of the Hebrew name for God, *Yahweh*, always indicated in the NIV by LORD. For Lord, see the concordance entries *LORD and *LORD's.

Ex	19: 20	The *L* descended to the top
	20: 2	"I am the *L* your God, who
	20: 5	the *L* your God, am a jealous God,
	20: 7	for the *L* will not hold anyone
	20: 10	a Sabbath to the *L* your God.
	20: 11	in six days the *L* made the heavens
	20: 12	in the land the *L* your God is giving
	23: 25	Worship the *L* your God,
	24: 3	"Everything the *L* has said we will
	24: 12	The *L* said to Moses, "Come up
	24: 16	and the glory of the *L* settled
	25: 1	The *L* said to Moses, "Tell
	28: 36	HOLY TO THE *L*.
	30: 11	Then the *L* said to Moses,
	31: 13	so you may know that I am the *L*,
	31: 18	When the *L* finished speaking
	33: 11	The *L* would speak to Moses face
	33: 19	And the *L* said, "I will cause all my
	34: 1	*L* said to Moses, "Chisel out two
	34: 6	proclaiming, "The *L*, the *L*,
	34: 10	awesome is the work that I, the *L*,
	34: 29	because he had spoken with the *L*.
	40: 34	glory of the *L* filled the tabernacle.
	40: 38	So the cloud of the *L* was
Lev	8: 36	did everything the *L* commanded
	9: 23	and the glory of the *L* appeared
	10: 2	and they died before the *L*.
	19: 2	'Be holy because I, the *L* your God,
	20: 8	I am the *L*, who makes you holy.
	20: 26	to be holy to me because I, the *L*,
	23: 40	and rejoice before the *L* your God
	24: 11	the name of the *L* with a curse;
Nu	6: 24	Say to them: " '"The *L* bless you
	8: 5	*L* said to Moses: "Take the Levites
	11: 1	hardships in the hearing of the *L*,
	14: 14	O *L*, have been seen face to face,
	14: 18	you have declared: 'The *L* is slow
	14: 21	glory of the *L* fills the whole earth,
	21: 6	Then the *L* sent venomous snakes
	22: 31	Then the *L* opened Balaam's eyes,
	23: 12	"Must I not speak what the *L* puts
	30: 2	When a man makes a vow to the *L*
	32: 12	followed the *L* wholeheartedly.'
Dt	1: 21	and take possession of it as the *L*,
	2: 7	forty years the *L* your God has
	4: 29	there you seek the *L* your God,
	5: 6	And he said: "I am the *L* your God,
	5: 9	the *L* your God, am a jealous God,
	6: 4	The *L* our God, the *L* is one.
	6: 5	Love the *L* your God
	6: 16	Do not test the *L* your God
	6: 25	law before the *L* our God,
	7: 1	When the *L* your God brings you
	7: 6	holy to the *L* your God.
	7: 8	But it was because the *L* loved you
	7: 9	that the *L* your God is God;
	7: 12	then the *L* your God will keep his
	8: 5	so the *L* your God disciplines you.
	9: 10	The *L* gave me two stone tablets
	10: 12	but to fear the *L* your God,
	10: 14	To the *L* your God belong
	10: 17	For the *L* your God is God of gods
	10: 20	Fear the *L* your God and serve him
	10: 22	now the *L* your God has made you
	11: 1	Love the *L* your God and keep his
	11: 13	to love the *L* your God
	16: 1	the Passover of the *L* your God,
	17: 15	the king the *L* your God chooses.
	28: 1	If you fully obey the *L* your God
	28: 15	if you do not obey the *L* your God

Dt	29: 1	covenant the L commanded Moses
	29: 29	things belong to the L our God,
	30: 4	from there the L your God will
	30: 6	L your God will circumcise your
	30: 10	if you obey the L your God
	30: 16	today to love the L your God,
	30: 20	For the L is your life, and he will
	31: 6	for the L your God goes with you;
	34: 5	of the L died there in Moab,
Jos	10: 14	a day when the L listened to a man.
	22: 5	to love the L your God, to walk
	23: 11	careful to love the L your God.
	24: 15	my household, we will serve the L
	24: 18	We too will serve the L,
Jdg	2: 12	They forsook the L, the God
Ru	1: 8	May the L show kindness to you,
	4: 13	And the L enabled her to conceive,
1Sa	1: 11	him to the L for all the days
	1: 15	I was pouring out my soul to the L.
	1: 28	So now I give him to the L.
	2: 2	"There is no-one holy like the L;
	2: 25	but if a man sins against the L,
	2: 26	in favour with the L and with men.
	3: 9	L, for your servant is listening.'"
	3: 19	The L was with Samuel
	7: 12	"Thus far has the L helped us."
	9: 17	sight of Saul, the L said to him,
	11: 15	as king in the presence of the L.
	12: 18	all the people stood in awe of the L
	12: 22	his great name the L will not reject
	12: 24	But be sure to fear the L
	13: 14	the L has sought out a man
	14: 6	Nothing can hinder the L
	15: 22	"Does the L delight
	16: 13	Spirit of the L came upon David
	17: 45	you in the name of the L Almighty,
2Sa	6: 14	danced before the L
	7: 22	How great you are, O Sovereign L!
	8: 6	L gave David victory everywhere
	12: 7	This is what the L, the God
	22: 2	"The L is my rock, my fortress
	22: 29	You are my lamp, O L;
	22: 31	the word of the L is flawless.
1Ki	1: 30	today what I swore to you by the L,
	2: 3	and observe what the L your God
	3: 7	O L my God, you have made your
	5: 5	for the Name of the L my God,
	5: 12	The L gave Solomon wisdom,
	8: 11	the glory of the L filled his temple.
	8: 23	towards heaven and said: "O L,
	8: 61	fully committed to the L our God,
	9: 3	The L said to him: "I have heard
	10: 9	Praise be to the L your God,
	15: 14	committed to the L all his life.
	18: 21	If the L is God, follow him;
	18: 36	"O L, God of Abraham, Isaac
	18: 39	"The L—he is God! The L—
	21: 23	also concerning Jezebel the L says:
2Ki	13: 23	But the L was gracious to them
	17: 18	So the L was very angry with Israel
	18: 5	Hezekiah trusted in the L,
	19: 1	and went into the temple of the L.
	20: 11	L made the shadow go back the ten
	21: 12	Therefore this is what the L,
	22: 2	right in the eyes of the L
	22: 8	of the Law in the temple of the L."
	23: 3	to follow the L and keep his
	23: 21	the Passover to the L your God,
	23: 25	a king like him who turned to the L
	24: 2	The L sent Babylonian, Aramean,

2Ki	24: 4	and the L was not willing to forgive
1Ch	10: 13	because he was unfaithful to the L;
	11: 3	with them at Hebron before the L,
	11: 9	the L Almighty was with him.
	13: 6	from there the ark of God the L, who
	16: 8	Give thanks to the L, call
	16: 11	Look to the L and his strength;
	16: 14	He is the L our God;
	16: 23	Sing to the L, all the earth;
	17: 1	covenant of the L is under a tent."
	21: 24	take for the L what is yours,
	22: 5	to be built for the L should be
	22: 11	build the house of the L your God,
	22: 13	and laws that the L gave Moses
	22: 16	Now begin the work, and the L be
	22: 19	soul to seeking the L your God.
	25: 7	and skilled in music for the L—
	28: 9	for the L searches every heart
	28: 20	for the L God, my God, is with you
	29: 1	not for man but for the L God.
	29: 11	O L, is the greatness and the power
	29: 18	O L, God of our fathers Abraham,
	29: 25	The L highly exalted Solomon
2Ch	1: 1	for the L his God was with him
	5: 13	to give praise and thanks to the L.
	5: 14	the glory of the L filled the temple
	6: 16	"Now L, God of Israel, keep
	6: 41	O L God, and come
	6: 42	O L God, do not reject your
	7: 1	the glory of the L filled the temple.
	7: 12	the L appeared to him at night
	7: 21	'Why has the L done such a thing
	9: 8	as king to rule for the L your God.
	13: 12	do not fight against the L,
	14: 2	right in the eyes of the L his God.
	15: 14	to the L with loud acclamation,
	16: 9	of the L range throughout the earth
	17: 9	the Book of the Law of the L;
	18: 13	said, "As surely as the L lives,
	19: 6	judging for man but for the L,
	19: 9	wholeheartedly in the fear of the L.
	20: 15	This is what the L says to you:
	20: 20	Have faith in the L your God
	20: 21	appointed men to sing to the L
	26: 5	As long as he sought the L,
	26: 16	He was unfaithful to the L his God,
	29: 30	to praise the L with the words
	30: 9	for the L your God is gracious
	31: 20	and faithful before the L his God.
	32: 8	with us is the L our God to help us
	34: 14	Law of the L that had been given
	34: 31	to follow the L and keep his
Ezr	3: 10	foundation of the temple of the L,
	7: 6	for the hand of the L his God was
	7: 10	observance of the Law of the L,
	9: 5	hands spread out to the L my God
	9: 8	the L our God has been gracious
	9: 15	O L, God of Israel, you are
Ne	1: 5	Then I said: "O L, God of heaven,
	8: 1	which the L had commanded
	9: 6	You alone are the L.
Job	1: 6	to present themselves before the L,
	1: 21	L gave and the L has taken away;
	38: 1	the L answered Job out
	42: 9	and the L accepted Job's prayer.
	42: 12	The L blessed the latter part
Ps	1: 2	But his delight is in the law of the L
	1: 6	For the L watches over the way
	4: 6	of your face shine upon us, O L.
	4: 8	for you alone, O L,

Ps 5: 3 Morning by morning, O *L*,
6: 1 O *L*, do not rebuke me
8: 1 O *L*, our Lord,
9: 9 The *L* is a refuge for the oppressed,
9: 19 Arise, O *L*, let not man triumph;
10: 16 The *L* is King for ever and ever;
12: 6 And the words of the *L* are flawless
16: 5 *L*, you have assigned me my
16: 8 I have set the *L* always before me.
18: 1 I love you, O *L*, my strength.
18: 6 In my distress I called to the *L*;
18: 30 the word of the *L* is flawless.
19: 7 The law of the *L* is perfect,
19: 14 O *L*, my Rock and my Redeemer.
20: 5 May the *L* grant all your requests.
20: 7 in the name of the *L* our God.
22: 8 let the *L* rescue him.
23: 1 The *L* is my shepherd, I shall not
23: 6 I will dwell in the house of the *L*
24: 3 Who may ascend the hill of the *L*?
24: 8 The *L* strong and mighty,
25: 10 All the ways of the *L* are loving
27: 1 The *L* is my light and my salvation
27: 4 to gaze upon the beauty of the *L*
27: 6 I will sing and make music to the *L*.
29: 1 Ascribe to the *L*, O mighty ones,
29: 4 The voice of the *L* is powerful;
30: 4 Sing to the *L*, you saints of his;
31: 5 redeem me, O *L*, the God of truth.
32: 2 whose sin the *L* does not count
33: 1 joyfully to the *L*, you righteous;
33: 6 of the *L* were the heavens made,
33: 12 is the nation whose God is the *L*,
33: 18 But the eyes of the *L* are
34: 1 I will extol the *L* at all times;
34: 3 Glorify the *L* with me;
34: 4 I sought the *L*, and he answered me
34: 7 The angel of the *L* encamps
34: 8 Taste and see that the *L* is good;
34: 9 Fear the *L*, you his saints,
34: 15 The eyes of the *L* are
34: 18 The *L* is close to the broken-hearted
37: 4 Delight yourself in the *L*
37: 5 Commit your way to the *L*;
39: 4 "Show me, O *L*, my life's end
40: 1 I waited patiently for the *L*;
40: 5 Many, O *L* my God,
46: 8 Come and see the works of the *L*,
47: 2 How awesome is the *L* Most High,
48: 1 Great is the *L*, and most worthy
50: 1 The Mighty One, God, the *L*,
55: 22 Cast your cares on the *L*
59: 8 But you, O *L*, laugh at them;
68: 4 his name is the *L*—
68: 18 O *L* God, might dwell there.
68: 20 from the Sovereign *L* comes escape
69: 31 This will please the *L* more
72: 18 Praise be to the *L* God, the God
75: 8 In the hand of the *L* is a cup
78: 4 the praiseworthy deeds of the *L*,
84: 8 my prayer, O *L* God Almighty;
84: 11 For the *L* God is a sun and shield;
85: 7 Show us your unfailing love, O *L*,
86: 11 Teach me your way, O *L*,
87: 2 the *L* loves the gates of Zion
89: 5 heavens praise your wonders, O *L*,
89: 8 O *L* God Almighty, who is like you
91: 2 I will say of the *L*, "He is my refuge
92: 1 It is good to praise the *L*
92: 4 by your deeds, O *L*;

Ps 92: 13 planted in the house of the *L*,
93: 1 The *L* reigns, he is robed in majesty
93: 5 house for endless days, O *L*.
94: 1 O *L*, the God who avenges,
94: 12 is the man you discipline, O *L*,
94: 18 your love, O *L*, supported me.
95: 1 Come, let us sing for joy to the *L*;
95: 3 For the *L* is the great God,
95: 6 let us kneel before the *L* our Maker
96: 1 Sing to the *L* a new song;
96: 5 but the *L* made the heavens.
96: 8 to the *L* the glory due his name;
96: 9 Worship the *L* in the splendour
96: 13 they will sing before the *L*,
97: 1 The *L* reigns, let the earth be glad;
97: 9 O *L*, are the Most High
98: 1 Sing to the *L* a new song,
98: 2 *L* has made his salvation known
98: 4 Shout for joy to the *L*, all the earth,
99: 1 The *L* reigns,
99: 2 Great is the *L* in Zion;
99: 5 Exalt the *L* our God
99: 9 Exalt the *L* our God
100: 1 Shout for joy to the *L*, all the earth.
100: 2 Worship the *L* with gladness;
100: 3 Know that the *L* is God.
100: 5 For the *L* is good and his love
101: 1 to you, O *L*, I will sing praise.
102: 12 But you, O *L*, sit enthroned for ever
103: 1 Praise the *L*, O my soul;
103: 8 The *L* is compassionate
103: 19 The *L* has established his throne
104: 1 O *L* my God, you are very great;
104: 24 How many are your works, O *L*!
104: 33 I will sing to the *L* all my life;
105: 4 Look to the *L* and his strength;
105: 7 He is the *L* our God;
106: 2 proclaim the mighty acts of the *L*
107: 1 Give thanks to the *L*, for he is good
107: 8 to the *L* for his unfailing love
107: 21 to the *L* for his unfailing love
107: 43 and consider the great love of the *L*
108: 3 I will praise you, O *L*,
109: 26 Help me, O *L* my God;
110: 1 The *L* says to my Lord:
110: 4 The *L* has sworn
111: 2 Great are the works of the *L*;
111: 4 *L* is gracious and compassionate.
111: 10 The fear of the *L* is the beginning
112: 1 Blessed is the man who fears the *L*,
113: 1 Praise, O servants of the *L*,
113: 2 Let the name of the *L* be praised,
113: 4 *L* is exalted over all the nations,
113: 5 Who is like the *L* our God,
115: 1 Not to us, O *L*, not to us
115: 18 it is we who extol the *L*,
116: 12 How can I repay the *L*
116: 15 Precious in the sight of the *L*
117: 1 Praise the *L*, all you nations;
118: 1 Give thanks to the *L*, for he is good
118: 5 In my anguish I cried to the *L*,
118: 8 It is better to take refuge in the *L*
118: 18 The *L* has chastened me severely,
118: 23 the *L* has done this,
118: 24 This is the day the *L* has made;
118: 26 comes in the name of the *L*.
119: 1 to the law of the *L*.
119: 64 with your love, O *L*;
119: 89 Your word, O *L*, is eternal;
119: 126 It is time for you to act, O *L*;

Ps 119: 159 O L, according to your love.
120: 1 I call on the L in my distress,
121: 2 My help comes from the L,
121: 5 The L watches over you—
121: 8 the L will watch over your coming
122: 1 "Let us go to the house of the L."
123: 2 so our eyes look to the L our God,
124: 1 If the L had not been on our side—
124: 8 Our help is in the name of the L,
125: 2 so the L surrounds his people
126: 3 The L has done great things for us,
126: 4 Restore our fortunes, O L,
127: 1 Unless the L builds the house,
127: 3 Sons are a heritage from the L,
128: 1 Blessed are all who fear the L,
130: 1 O L;/O Lord, hear my voice.
130: 3 If you, O L, kept a record of sins,
130: 5 I wait for the L, my soul waits,
131: 3 O Israel, put your hope in the L
132: 1 O L, remember David
132: 13 For the L has chosen Zion,
133: 3 For there the L bestows his
134: 3 May the L, the Maker of heaven
135: 4 For the L has chosen Jacob
135: 6 The L does whatever pleases him,
136: 1 Give thanks to the L, for he is good
137: 4 How can we sing the songs of the L
138: 1 I will praise you, O L,
138: 8 The L will fulfil ‚his purpose‚
139: 1 O L, you have searched me
140: 1 Rescue me, O L, from evil men;
141: 1 O L, I call to you; come quickly
141: 3 Set a guard over my mouth, O L;
142: 5 I cry to you, O L;
143: 9 Rescue me from my enemies, O L,
144: 3 O L, what is man that you care
145: 3 Great is the L and most worthy
145: 8 L is gracious and compassionate,
145: 9 The L is good to all;
145: 17 The L is righteous in all his ways
145: 18 The L is near to all who call on him
146: 5 whose hope is in the L his God,
146: 7 The L sets prisoners free,
147: 2 The L builds up Jerusalem;
147: 7 Sing to the L with thanksgiving;
147: 11 L delights in those who fear him,
147: 12 Extol the L, O Jerusalem;
148: 1 Praise the L from the heavens,
148: 7 Praise the L from the earth,
149: 4 For the L takes delight
150: 1 Praise the L.
150: 6 that has breath praise the L.
Pr 1: 7 The fear of the L is the beginning
1: 29 and did not choose to fear the L,
2: 5 will understand the fear of the L
2: 6 For the L gives wisdom,
3: 5 Trust in the L with all your heart
3: 7 fear the L and shun evil.
3: 9 Honour the L with your wealth,
3: 12 the L disciplines those he loves,
3: 19 By wisdom the L laid the earth's
5: 21 are in full view of the L,
6: 16 There are six things the L hates,
8: 13 To fear the L is to hate evil;
9: 10 "The fear of the L is the beginning
10: 27 The fear of the L adds length to life
11: 1 The L abhors dishonest scales,
12: 22 The L detests lying lips,
14: 2 whose walk is upright fears the L,
14: 26 He who fears the L has a secure

Pr 14: 27 The fear of the L is a fountain
15: 3 The eyes of the L are everywhere,
15: 16 Better a little with the fear of the L
15: 33 of the L teaches a man wisdom,
16: 2 but motives are weighed by the L.
16: 3 Commit to the L whatever you do,
16: 4 The L works out everything
16: 5 The L detests all the proud of heart
16: 9 but the L determines his steps.
16: 33 but its every decision is from the L.
18: 10 The name of the L is a strong tower
18: 22 and receives favour from the L.
19: 14 but a prudent wife is from the L.
19: 17 to the poor lends to the L,
19: 23 The fear of the L leads to life:
20: 10 the L detests them both.
21: 2 but the L weighs the heart.
21: 3 to the L than sacrifice.
21: 30 that can succeed against the L.
21: 31 but victory rests with the L.
22: 2 The L is the Maker of them all.
22: 23 for the L will take up their case
23: 17 for the fear of the L.
24: 18 or the L will see and disapprove
24: 21 Fear the L and the king, my son,
25: 22 and the L will reward you.
28: 14 is the man who always fears the L,
29: 26 from the L that man gets justice.
30: 7 "Two things I ask of you, O L;
31: 30 a woman who fears the L is
Isa 2: 3 up to the mountain of the L,
2: 10 the ground from dread of the L
3: 17 the L will make their scalps bald."
4: 2 of the L will be beautiful
5: 16 the L Almighty will be exalted
6: 3 holy, holy is the L Almighty;
9: 7 The zeal of the L Almighty
11: 2 The Spirit of the L will rest on him
11: 9 full of the knowledge of the L
12: 2 The L, the L, is my strength
18: 7 of the Name of the L Almighty.
24: 1 the L is going to lay waste the earth
25: 1 O L, you are my God;
25: 6 this mountain the L Almighty will
25: 8 The Sovereign L will wipe away
26: 4 Trust in the L for ever,
26: 8 L, walking in the way of your laws,
26: 13 O L, our God, other lords
26: 21 the L is coming out of his dwelling
27: 1 the L will punish with his sword,
27: 12 In that day the L will thresh
28: 5 In that day the L Almighty
29: 6 the L Almighty will come
29: 15 to hide their plans from the L,
30: 18 For the L is a God of justice.
30: 26 when the L binds up the bruises
30: 27 the Name of the L comes from afar
30: 30 The L will cause men
33: 2 O L, be gracious to us;
33: 6 the fear of the L is the key
33: 22 For the L is our judge,
34: 2 The L is angry with all nations;
35: 2 they will see the glory of the L,
35: 10 the ransomed of the L will return.
38: 7 to you that the L will do what he
40: 3 the way for the L;
40: 5 the glory of the L will be revealed,
40: 7 the breath of the L blows on them.
40: 10 the Sovereign L comes with power,
40: 14 Whom did the L consult

Isa	40: 28	The *L* is the everlasting God,
	40: 31	but those who hope in the *L*
	41: 14	will help you," declares the *L*,
	41: 20	that the hand of the *L* has done this
	42: 6	the *L*, have called you
	42: 8	"I am the *L*; that is my name!
	42: 13	The *L* will march out like a mighty
	42: 21	It pleased the *L*
	43: 3	For I am the *L*, your God,
	43: 11	I, even I, am the *L*,
	44: 6	"This is what the *L* says—
	44: 24	I am the *L*,
	45: 5	I am the *L*, and there is no other;
	45: 7	I, the *L*, do all these things.
	45: 21	Was it not I, the *L*?
	48: 17	"I am the *L* your God,
	50: 4	Sovereign *L* has given me
	50: 10	Who among you fears the *L*
	51: 1	and who seek the *L*:
	51: 11	The ransomed of the *L* will return.
	51: 15	the *L* Almighty is his name.
	53: 1	the arm of the *L* been revealed?
	53: 6	and the *L* has laid on him
	53: 10	and the will of the *L* will prosper
	54: 5	the *L* Almighty is his name—
	55: 6	Seek the *L* while he may be found;
	55: 7	to the *L*, and he will have mercy
	56: 6	who bind themselves to the *L*
	58: 8	of the *L* will be your rear guard.
	58: 11	The *L* will guide you always;
	59: 1	the arm of the *L* is not too short
	60: 1	the glory of the *L* rises upon you.
	60: 16	Then you will know that I, the *L*,
	60: 20	the *L* will be your everlasting light,
	61: 1	Spirit of the Sovereign *L* is on me,
	61: 3	a planting of the *L*
	61: 10	I delight greatly in the *L*;
	61: 11	so the Sovereign *L* will make
	62: 4	for the *L* will take delight in you,
	63: 7	I will tell of the kindnesses of the *L*,
	64: 8	Yet, O *L*, you are our Father.
	66: 15	See, the *L* is coming with fire,
Jer	1: 9	Then the *L* reached out his hand
	2: 19	when you forsake the *L* your God
	3: 25	sinned against the *L* our God,
	4: 4	Circumcise yourselves to the *L*,
	8: 7	the requirements of the *L*.
	9: 24	I am the *L*, who exercises kindness,
	10: 6	No-one is like you, O *L*;
	10: 10	But the *L* is the true God;
	12: 1	You are always righteous, O *L*,
	14: 7	O *L*, do something for the sake
	14: 20	O *L*, we acknowledge our
	16: 15	will say, 'As surely as the *L* lives,
	16: 19	O *L*, my strength and my fortress,
	17: 7	is the man who trusts in the *L*,
	17: 10	"I the *L* search the heart
	20: 11	*L* is with me like a mighty warrior;
	23: 6	The *L* Our Righteousness.
	24: 7	heart to know me, that I am the *L*.
	28: 9	as one truly sent by the *L* only
	31: 11	For the *L* will ransom Jacob
	31: 22	The *L* will create a new thing
	31: 34	his brother, saying, 'Know the *L*,'
	32: 27	I am the *L*, the God of all mankind.
	33: 16	The *L* Our Righteousness.'
	36: 6	the words of the *L* that you wrote
	40: 3	now the *L* has brought it about;
	42: 3	Pray that the *L* your God will tell
	42: 4	I will tell you everything the *L* says

Jer	42: 6	we will obey the *L* our God,
	50: 4	go in tears to seek the *L* their God.
	51: 10	" 'The *L* has vindicated us;
	51: 56	For the *L* is a God of retribution;
La	3: 24	to myself, "The *L* is my portion;
	3: 25	*L* is good to those whose hope is
	3: 40	and let us return to the *L*.
Eze	1: 3	the word of the *L* came
	1: 28	of the likeness of the glory of the *L*.
	4: 14	Sovereign *L*! I have never defiled
	10: 4	Then the glory of the *L* rose
	15: 7	you will know that I am the *L*.
	30: 3	the day of the *L* is near—
	36: 23	nations will know that I am the *L*,
	37: 4	'Dry bones, hear the word of the *L*!
	43: 4	glory of the *L* entered the temple
	44: 4	LORD filling the temple of the *L*,
Da	9: 2	to the word of the *L* given
Hos	1: 7	horsemen, but by the *L* their God."
	2: 20	and you will acknowledge the *L*.
	3: 1	as the *L* loves the Israelites,
	3: 5	They will come trembling to the *L*
	6: 1	"Come, let us return to the *L*.
	6: 3	Let us acknowledge the *L*;
	10: 12	for it is time to seek the *L*,
	12: 5	the *L* is his name of renown!
	14: 1	O Israel, to the *L* your God.
Joel	1: 1	The word of the *L* that came
	1: 15	For the day of the *L* is near;
	2: 1	for the day of the *L* is coming.
	2: 11	The day of the *L* is great;
	2: 13	Return to the *L* your God,
	2: 23	rejoice in the *L* your God,
	2: 31	the great and dreadful day of the *L*.
	2: 32	on the name of the *L* will be saved;
	3: 14	For the day of the *L* is near
	3: 16	will be a refuge for his people,
Am	4: 13	the *L* God Almighty is his name.
	5: 6	Seek the *L* and live,
	5: 15	Perhaps the *L* God Almighty will
	5: 18	long for the day of the *L*?
	7: 15	*L* took me from tending the flock
	8: 12	searching for the word of the *L*,
	9: 5	The Lord, the *L* Almighty,
Ob	: 15	"The day of the *L* is near
Jnh	1: 3	But Jonah ran away from the *L*
	1: 4	the *L* sent a great wind on the sea,
	1: 17	But the *L* provided a great fish
	2: 9	Salvation comes from the *L*."
	4: 2	He prayed to the *L*, "O *L*,
	4: 6	Then the *L* God provided a vine
Mic	1: 1	The word of the *L* given to Micah
	4: 2	up to the mountain of the *L*,
	5: 4	flock in the strength of the *L*,
	6: 2	For the *L* has a case
	6: 8	And what does the *L* require of you
	7: 7	as for me, I watch in hope for the *L*,
Na	1: 2	The *L* takes vengeance on his foes
	1: 3	The *L* is slow to anger
Hab	2: 14	knowledge of the glory of the *L*,
	2: 20	But the *L* is in his holy temple;
	3: 2	I stand in awe of your deeds, O *L*,
Zep	1: 1	The word of the *L* that came
	1: 7	for the day of the *L* is near.
	3: 17	The *L* your God is with you,
Hag	1: 1	the word of the *L* came
	1: 8	and be honoured," says the *L*.
	2: 23	that day,' declares the *L* Almighty,
Zec	1: 1	the word of the *L* came
	1: 17	and the *L* will again comfort Zion

Zec   3: 1   standing before the angel of the *L*,
     4: 6   by my Spirit,' says the *L* Almighty.
     6: 12   and build the temple of the *L*.
     8: 21   the *L* and seek the *L* Almighty.
     9: 16   The *L* their God will save them
     14: 5   Then the *L* my God will come,
     14: 9   The *L* will be king
     14: 16   the *L* Almighty, and to celebrate
Mal   1: 1   The word of the *L* to Israel
     3: 6   "I the *L* do not change.
     4: 5   and dreadful day of the *L* comes.

†LORD'S (†LORD)

Ex   4: 14   the *L* anger burned against Moses
     12: 11   Eat it in haste; it is the *L* Passover.
     34: 34   he entered the *L* presence
Lev   23: 4   "'These are the *L* appointed feasts,
Nu   9: 23   At the *L* command they encamped
     14: 41   you disobeying the *L* command?
     32: 13   The *L* anger burned against Israel
Dt   6: 18   is right and good in the *L* sight,
     10: 13   and to observe the *L* commands
     32: 9   For the *L* portion is his people,
Jos   21: 45   Not one of all the *L* good promises
1Sa   24: 10   because he is the *L* anointed.'
1Ki   10: 9   Because of the *L* eternal love
Ps   24: 1   The earth is the *L*, and everything
     32: 10   but the *L* unfailing love
     89: 1   of the *L* great love for ever;
     103: 17   *L* love is with those who fear him,
     118: 15   "The *L* right hand has done mighty
Pr   3: 11   do not despise the *L* discipline
     19: 21   but it is the *L* purpose that prevails.
Isa   24: 14   west they acclaim the *L* majesty.
     30: 9   to listen to the *L* instruction.
     49: 4   Yet what is due to me is in the *L*
     53: 10   Yet it was the *L* will to crush him
     55: 13   This will be for the *L* renown,
     61: 2   to proclaim the year of the *L* favour
     62: 3   of splendour in the *L* hand,
Jer   25: 17   So I took the cup from the *L* hand
     48: 10   lax in doing the *L* work!
     51: 7   was a gold cup in the *L* hand;
La   3: 22   of the *L* great love we are not
Eze   7: 19   them in the day of the *L* wrath.
Joel   3: 18   will flow out of the *L* house
Ob   : 21   And the kingdom will be the *L*.
Mic   4: 1   of the *L* temple will be established
     6: 2   O mountains, the *L* accusation;
Hab   2: 16   from the *L* right hand is coming
Zep   2: 3   sheltered on the day of the *L* anger.

LOSE (LOSES LOSS LOST)

Dt   1: 28   Our brothers have made us *l* heart.
1Sa   17: 32   "Let no-one *l* heart on account
Isa   7: 4   Do not *l* heart because of these two
Mt   10: 39   Whoever finds his life will *l* it,
Lk   9: 25   and yet *l* or forfeit his very self?
Jn   6: 39   that I shall *l* none of all that he has
2Co   4: 1   this ministry, we do not *l* heart.
     4: 16   Therefore we do not *l* heart.
Heb   12: 3   will not grow weary and *l* heart.
     12: 5   do not *l* heart when he rebukes you
2Jn   : 8   that you do not *l* what you have

LOSES (LOSE)

Mt   5: 13   But if the salt *l* its saltiness,
Lk   15: 4   you has a hundred sheep and *l* one
     15: 8   has ten silver coins and *l* one.

LOSS (LOSE)

Ro   11: 12   and their *l* means riches
1Co   3: 15   he will suffer *l*; he himself will be
Php   3: 8   I consider everything a *l* compared

LOST (LOSE)

Ps   73: 2   I had nearly *l* my foothold.
Jer   50: 6   "My people have been *l* sheep;
Eze   34: 4   the strays or searched for the *l*.
     34: 16   for the *l* and bring back the strays.
Mt   18: 14   any of these little ones should be *l*.
Lk   15: 4   go after the *l* sheep until he finds it?
     15: 6   with me; I have found my *l* sheep.'
     15: 9   with me; I have found my *l* coin.'
     15: 24   is alive again; he was *l* and is found
     19: 10   to seek and to save what was *l*."
Php   3: 8   for whose sake I have *l* all things.

LOT [1]

Nephew of Abraham (Ge 11:27; 12:5). Chose to live in Sodom (Ge 13). Rescued from four kings (Ge 14). Rescued from Sodom (Ge 19:1-29; 2Pe 2:7). Fathered Moab and Ammon by his daughters (Ge 19: 30-38).

LOT [2] (LOTS)

Est   3: 7   the *l*) in the presence of Haman
     9: 24   the *l*) for their ruin and destruction.
Pr   16: 33   The *l* is cast into the lap,
     18: 18   Casting the *l* settles disputes
Ecc   3: 22   his work, because that is his *l*.
Ac   1: 26   Then they cast lots, and the *l* fell

LOTS (LOT [2])

Jos   18: 10   Joshua then cast *l* for them
Ps   22: 18   and cast *l* for my clothing.
Joel   3: 3   They cast *l* for my people
Ob   : 11   and cast *l* for Jerusalem,
Mt   27: 35   divided up his clothes by casting *l*.
Ac   1: 26   Then they cast *l*, and the lot fell

LOVE* (BELOVED LOVED LOVELY LOVER LOVER'S LOVERS LOVES LOVING LOVING-KINDNESS)

Ge   20: 13   'This is how you can show your *l*
     22: 2   your only son Isaac, whom you *l*,
     29: 18   Jacob was in *l* with Rachel and said
     29: 20   days to him because of his *l* for her.
     29: 32   Surely my husband will *l* me now."
Ex   15: 13   "In your unfailing *l* you will lead
     20: 6   showing *l* to thousands who *l* me
     21: 5   'I *l* my master and my wife
     34: 6   abounding in *l* and faithfulness,
     34: 7   maintaining *l* to thousands,
Lev   19: 18   but *l* your neighbour as yourself.
     19: 34   *L* him as yourself,
Nu   14: 18   abounding in *l* and forgiving sin
     14: 19   In accordance with your great *l*,
Dt   5: 10   showing *l* to thousands who *l* me
     6: 5   *L* the Lord your God
     7: 9   generations of those who *l* him
     7: 9   keeping his covenant of *l*
     7: 12   God will keep his covenant of *l*
     7: 13   He will *l* you and bless you
     10: 12   to walk in all his ways, to *l* him,
     10: 19   you are to *l* those who are aliens,
     11: 1   *L* the Lord your God
     11: 13   to *l* the Lord your God
     11: 22   to *l* the Lord your God,

Dt	13: 3	you *l* him with all your heart
	13: 6	wife you *l*, or your closest friend
	19: 9	to *l* the LORD your God
	21: 15	the son of the wife he does not *l*,
	21: 16	the son of the wife he does not *l*.
	30: 6	so that you may *l* him
	30: 16	today to *l* the LORD your God,
	30: 20	and that you may *l* the LORD your
	33: 3	Surely it is you who *l* the people;
Jos	22: 5	to *l* the LORD your God, to walk
	23: 11	careful to *l* the LORD your God.
Jdg	5: 31	may they who *l* you be like the sun
	14: 16	You hate me! You don't really *l* me
	16: 4	he fell in *l* with a woman
	16: 15	"How can you say, 'I *l* you,'
1Sa	18: 20	Saul's daughter Michal was in *l*
	20: 17	had David reaffirm his oath out of *l*
2Sa	1: 26	Your *l* for me was wonderful,
	7: 15	But my *l* will never be taken away
	13: 1	son of David fell in *l* with Tamar,
	13: 4	said to him, "I'm in *l* with Tamar,
	16: 17	"Is this the *l* you show your friend?
	19: 6	You *l* those who hate you
	19: 6	hate you and hate those who *l* you.
1Ki	3: 3	Solomon showed his *l*
	8: 23	you who keep your covenant of *l*
	10: 9	of the LORD's eternal *l* for Israel,
	11: 2	Solomon held fast to them in *l*.
1Ch	16: 34	his *l* endures for ever.
	16: 41	"for his *l* endures for ever."
	17: 13	I will never take my *l* away
2Ch	5: 13	his *l* endures for ever."
	6: 14	you who keep your covenant of *l*
	6: 42	Remember the great *l* promised
	7: 3	his *l* endures for ever."
	7: 6	saying, "His *l* endures for ever."
	9: 8	Because of the *l* of your God
	19: 2	and *l* those who hate the LORD?
	20: 21	for his *l* endures for ever."
Ezr	3: 11	his *l* to Israel endures for ever."
Ne	1: 5	covenant of *l* with those who *l* him
	9: 17	slow to anger and abounding in *l*.
	9: 32	who keeps his covenant of *l*,
	13: 22	to me according to your great *l*.
Job	15: 34	of those who *l* bribes.
	19: 19	those I *l* have turned against me.
	37: 13	or to water his earth and show his *l*.
Ps	4: 2	How long will you *l* delusions
	5: 11	that those who *l* your name may
	6: 4	save me because of your unfailing *l*.
	11: 5	wicked and those who *l* violence
	13: 5	But I trust in your unfailing *l*;
	17: 7	Show the wonder of your great *l*,
	18: 1	I *l* you, O LORD, my strength.
	21: 7	through the unfailing *l*
	23: 6	Surely goodness and *l* will follow
	25: 6	O LORD, your great mercy and *l*,
	25: 7	according to your *l* remember me,
	26: 3	for your *l* is ever before me,
	26: 8	I *l* the house where you live,
	31: 7	I will be glad and rejoice in your *l*,
	31: 16	save me in your unfailing *l*.
	31: 21	for he showed his wonderful *l*
	31: 23	*L* the LORD, all his saints!
	32: 10	but the LORD's unfailing *l*
	33: 5	the earth is full of his unfailing *l*.
	33: 18	whose hope is in his unfailing *l*,
	33: 22	May your unfailing *l* rest upon us,
	36: 5	Your *l*, O LORD, reaches
	36: 7	How priceless is your unfailing *l*!

Ps	36: 10	Continue your *l* to those who know
	40: 10	I do not conceal your *l*
	40: 11	may your *l* and your truth always
	40: 16	may those who *l* your salvation
	42: 8	By day the LORD directs his *l*,
	44: 26	of your unfailing *l*.
	45: 7	You *l* righteousness and hate
	48: 9	we meditate on your unfailing *l*.
	51: 1	according to your unfailing *l*;
	52: 3	You *l* evil rather than good,
	52: 4	You *l* every harmful word,
	52: 8	I trust in God's unfailing *l*
	57: 3	God sends his *l* and his faithfulness
	57: 10	For great is your *l*, reaching
	59: 16	in the morning I will sing of your *l*;
	60: 5	that those you *l* may be delivered.
	61: 7	appoint your *l* and faithfulness
	63: 3	Because your *l* is better than life,
	66: 20	or withheld his *l* from me!
	69: 13	in your great *l*, O God,
	69: 16	out of the goodness of your *l*;
	69: 36	and those who *l* his name will dwell
	70: 4	may those who *l* your salvation
	77: 8	Has his unfailing *l* vanished for ever
	85: 7	Show us your unfailing *l*, O LORD
	85: 10	*L* and faithfulness meet together;
	86: 5	abounding in *l* to all who call
	86: 13	For great is your *l* towards me;
	86: 15	abounding in *l* and faithfulness.
	88: 11	Is your *l* declared in the grave,
	89: 1	of the LORD's great *l* for ever;
	89: 2	declare that your *l* stands firm
	89: 14	*l* and faithfulness go before you.
	89: 24	My faithful *l* will be with him,
	89: 28	I will maintain my *l* to him for ever,
	89: 33	but I will not take my *l* from him,
	89: 49	where is your former great *l*,
	90: 14	with your unfailing *l*,
	92: 2	to proclaim your *l* in the morning
	94: 18	your *l*, O LORD, supported me.
	97: 10	Let those who *l* the LORD hate
	98: 3	He has remembered his *l*
	100: 5	is good and his *l* endures for ever;
	101: 1	I will sing of your *l* and justice;
	103: 4	crowns me with *l* and compassion.
	103: 8	slow to anger, abounding in *l*.
	103: 11	so great is his *l* for those who fear
	103: 17	LORD's *l* is with those who fear
	106: 1	his *l* endures for ever.
	106: 45	and out of his great *l* he relented.
	107: 1	his *l* endures for ever.
	107: 8	to the LORD for his unfailing *l*
	107: 15	to the LORD for his unfailing *l*
	107: 21	to the LORD for his unfailing *l*
	107: 31	to the LORD for his unfailing *l*
	107: 43	consider the great *l* of the LORD.
	108: 4	For great is your *l*, higher
	108: 6	that those you *l* may be delivered.
	109: 21	out of the goodness of your *l*,
	109: 26	save me in accordance with your *l*.
	115: 1	because of your *l* and faithfulness.
	116: 1	I *l* the LORD, for he heard my
	117: 2	For great is his *l* towards us,
	118: 1	his *l* endures for ever.
	118: 2	"His *l* endures for ever."
	118: 3	"His *l* endures for ever."
	118: 4	"His *l* endures for ever."
	118: 29	his *l* endures for ever.
	119: 41	May your unfailing *l* come to me,
	119: 47	because I *l* them.

Ps 119: 48 for your commandments, which I *l*,
119: 64 The earth is filled with your *l*,
119: 76 May your unfailing *l* be my
119: 88 my life according to your *l*,
119: 97 Oh, how I *l* your law!
119: 113 but I *l* your law.
119: 119 therefore I *l* your statutes.
119: 124 your servant according to your *l*
119: 127 Because I *l* your commands
119: 132 to those who *l* your name.
119: 149 in accordance with your *l*;
119: 159 O LORD, according to your *l*.
119: 159 See how I *l* your precepts;
119: 163 but I *l* your law.
119: 165 peace have they who *l* your law,
119: 167 for I *l* them greatly.
122: 6 "May those who *l* you be secure.
130: 7 for with the LORD is unfailing *l*
136: 1-26 His *l endures for ever.*
138: 2 for your *l* and your faithfulness,
138: 8 your *l*, O LORD, endures for ever
143: 8 of your unfailing *l*,
143: 12 In your unfailing *l*, silence my
145: 8 slow to anger and rich in *l*.
145: 20 over all who *l* him,
147: 11 who put their hope in his unfailing *l*
Pr 1: 22 you simple ones *l* your simple
3: 3 Let *l* and faithfulness never leave
4: 6 *l* her, and she will watch over you.
5: 19 you ever be captivated by her *l*.
7: 18 let's drink deep of *l* till morning;
7: 18 let's enjoy ourselves with *l*!
8: 17 I *l* those who *l* me,
8: 21 wealth on those who *l* me
8: 36 all who hate me *l* death."
9: 8 rebuke a wise man and he will *l* you
10: 12 but *l* covers over all wrongs.
14: 22 those who plan what is good find *l*
15: 17 of vegetables where there is *l*
16: 6 Through *l* and faithfulness sin is
17: 9 over an offence promotes *l*,
18: 21 and those who *l* it will eat its fruit.
19: 22 What a man desires is unfailing *l*;
20: 6 claims to have unfailing *l*,
20: 13 Do not *l* sleep or you will grow
20: 28 *L* and faithfulness keep a king safe;
20: 28 through *l* his throne is made secure
21: 21 who pursues righteousness and *l*
27: 5 rebuke than hidden *l*.
Ecc 3: 8 a time to *l* and a time to hate,
9: 1 but no man knows whether *l*
9: 6 Their *l*, their hate
9: 9 life with your wife, whom you *l*,
SS 1: 2 for your *l* is more delightful
1: 3 No wonder the maidens *l* you!
1: 4 we will praise your *l* more
1: 7 you whom I *l*, where you graze
2: 4 and his banner over me is *l*.
2: 5 for I am faint with *l*.
2: 7 Do not arouse or awaken *l*
3: 5 Do not arouse or awaken *l*
4: 10 How delightful is your *l*, my sister,
4: 10 How much more pleasing is your *l*
5: 8 Tell him I am faint with *l*.
7: 6 O *l*, with your delights!
7: 12 there I will give you my *l*.
8: 4 Do not arouse or awaken *l*
8: 6 for *l* is as strong as death,
8: 7 Many waters cannot quench *l*;
8: 7 all the wealth of his house for *l*,

Isa 1: 23 they all *l* bribes
5: 1 I will sing for the one I *l*
16: 5 In *l* a throne will be established;
38: 17 In your *l* you kept me
43: 4 and because I *l* you,
54: 10 yet my unfailing *l* for you will not
55: 3 my faithful *l* promised to David.
56: 6 to *l* the name of the LORD,
56: 10 they *l* to sleep.
57: 8 a pact with those whose beds you *l*,
61: 8 "For I, the LORD, *l* justice;
63: 9 In his *l* and mercy he redeemed
66: 10 all you who *l* her;
Jer 2: 25 I *l* foreign gods,
2: 33 How skilled you are at pursuing *l*!
5: 31 and my people *l* it this way.
12: 7 I will give the one I *l*
14: 10 "They greatly *l* to wander;
16: 5 my *l* and my pity from this people
31: 3 you with an everlasting *l*;
32: 18 You show *l* to thousands
33: 11 his *l* endures for ever."
La 3: 22 of the LORD's great *l* we are not
3: 32 so great is his unfailing *l*.
Eze 16: 8 saw that you were old enough for *l*,
23: 17 of *l*, and in their lust they defiled
33: 32 more than one who sings *l* songs
Da 9: 4 covenant of *l* with all who *l* him
Hos 1: 6 for I will no longer show *l*
1: 7 Yet I will show *l* to the house
2: 4 I will not show my *l* to her children
2: 19 in *l* and compassion.
2: 23 I will show my *l* to the one I called
3: 1 Go, show your *l* to your wife again,
3: 1 and *l* the sacred raisin cakes."
3: 1 *L* her as the LORD loves
4: 1 "There is no faithfulness, no *l*,
4: 18 their rulers dearly *l* shameful ways.
6: 4 Your *l* is like the morning mist,
9: 1 you *l* the wages of a prostitute
9: 15 I will no longer *l* them;
10: 12 reap the fruit of unfailing *l*,
11: 4 with ties of *l*;
12: 6 maintain *l* and justice,
14: 4 and *l* them freely,
Joel 2: 13 slow to anger and abounding in *l*,
Am 4: 5 for this is what you *l* to do,"
5: 15 Hate evil, *l* good;
Jnh 4: 2 slow to anger and abounding in *l*,
Mic 3: 2 you who hate good and *l* evil;
6: 8 To act justly and to *l* mercy
Zep 3: 17 he will quiet you with his *l*,
Zec 8: 17 and do not *l* to swear falsely.
8: 19 Therefore *l* truth and peace."
Mt 3: 17 "This is my Son, whom I *l*;
5: 43 '*L* your neighbour and hate your
5: 44 *L* your enemies and pray
5: 46 you *l* those who *l* you, what reward
6: 5 for they *l* to pray standing
6: 24 he will hate the one and *l* the other,
12: 18 the one I *l*, in whom I delight;
17: 5 "This is my Son, whom I *l*;
19: 19 and '*l* your neighbour as yourself.'"
22: 37 "'*L* the Lord your God
22: 39 '*L* your neighbour as yourself.'
23: 6 they *l* the place of honour
23: 7 they *l* to be greeted
24: 12 the *l* of most will grow cold,
Mk 1: 11 "You are my Son, whom I *l*;
9: 7 "This is my Son, whom I *l*.

Mk	12: 30	*L* the Lord your God
	12: 31	'*L* your neighbour as yourself.'
	12: 33	To *l* him with all your heart,
	12: 33	and to *l* your neighbour
Lk	3: 22	"You are my Son, whom I *l*;
	6: 27	you who hear me: *L* your enemies,
	6: 32	Even 'sinners' *l* those who *l* them.
	6: 32	you *l* those who *l* you, what credit
	6: 35	*l* your enemies, do good to them,
	7: 42	which of them will *l* him more?"
	10: 27	and, '*L* your neighbour as yourself
	10: 27	"'*L* the Lord your God
	11: 42	you neglect justice and the *l* of God
	11: 43	you *l* the most important seats
	16: 13	he will hate the one and *l* the other,
	20: 13	whom I *l*; perhaps they will respect
	20: 46	*l* to be greeted in the market-places
Jn	5: 42	I know that you do not have the *l*
	8: 42	were your Father, you would *l* me,
	11: 3	"Lord, the one you *l* is sick."
	13: 1	them the full extent of his *l*.
	13: 34	I give you: *L* one another.
	13: 34	so you must *l* one another.
	13: 35	disciples if you *l* one another."
	14: 15	"If you *l* me, you will obey what I
	14: 21	I too will *l* him and show myself
	14: 23	My Father will *l* him, and we will
	14: 24	He who does not *l* me will not obey
	14: 31	world must learn that I *l* the Father
	15: 9	Now remain in my *l*.
	15: 10	commands and remain in his *l*.
	15: 10	you will remain in my *l*,
	15: 12	*L* each other as I have loved you.
	15: 13	Greater *l* has no-one than this,
	15: 17	This is my command: *L* each other.
	15: 19	to the world, it would *l* you
	17: 26	known in order that the *l* you have
	21: 15	do you truly *l* me more than these
	21: 15	he said, "you know that I *l* you."
	21: 16	Yes, Lord, you know that I *l* you."
	21: 16	do you truly *l* me?" He answered,
	21: 17	all things; you know that I *l* you."
	21: 17	"Do you *l* me?" He said, "Lord,
	21: 17	"Simon son of John, do you *l* me?"
Ro	5: 5	because God has poured out his *l*
	5: 8	God demonstrates his own *l* for us
	8: 28	for the good of those who *l* him,
	8: 35	us from the *l* of Christ?
	8: 39	us from the *l* of God that is
	12: 9	*L* must be sincere.
	12: 10	to one another in brotherly *l*.
	13: 8	continuing debt to *l* one another,
	13: 9	"*L* your neighbour as yourself."
	13: 10	Therefore *l* is the fulfilment
	13: 10	*L* does no harm to its neighbour.'
	14: 15	you are no longer acting in *l*.
	15: 30	and by the *l* of the Spirit,
	16: 8	Greet Ampliatus, whom I *l*
1Co	2: 9	prepared for those who *l* him"—
	4: 17	my son whom I *l*, who is faithful
	4: 21	or in *l* and with a gentle spirit?
	8: 1	Knowledge puffs up, but *l* builds up
	13: 1	have not *l*, I am only a resounding
	13: 2	but have not *l*, I am nothing.
	13: 3	but have not *l*, I gain nothing.
	13: 4	*L* is patient, *l* is kind.
	13: 6	*L* does not delight in evil
	13: 8	*L* never fails.
	13: 13	But the greatest of these is *l*.
	13: 13	three remain: faith, hope and *l*.

1Co	14: 1	way of *l* and eagerly desire spiritual
	16: 14	Do everything in *l*.
	16: 22	If anyone does not *l* the Lord—
	16: 24	My *l* to all of you in Christ Jesus.
2Co	2: 4	to let you know the depth of my *l*
	2: 8	therefore, to reaffirm your *l* for him
	5: 14	For Christ's *l* compels us,
	6: 6	in the Holy Spirit and in sincere *l*;
	8: 7	complete earnestness and in your *l*
	8: 8	sincerity of your *l* by comparing it
	8: 24	show these men the proof of your *l*
	11: 11	Why? Because I do not *l* you?
	12: 15	If I *l* you more, will you *l* me less?
	13: 11	And the God of *l* and peace will be
	13: 14	of the Lord Jesus Christ, and the *l*
Gal	5: 6	is faith expressing itself through *l*.
	5: 13	rather, serve one another in *l*.
	5: 14	"*L* your neighbour as yourself."
	5: 22	But the fruit of the Spirit is *l*, joy,
Eph	1: 4	In *l* he predestined us
	1: 15	and your *l* for all the saints,
	2: 4	But because of his great *l* for us,
	3: 17	being rooted and established in *l*,
	3: 18	and high and deep is the *l* of Christ,
	3: 19	and to know this *l* that surpasses
	4: 2	bearing with one another in *l*.
	4: 15	Instead, speaking the truth in *l*,
	4: 16	grows and builds itself up in *l*,
	5: 2	loved children and live a life of *l*,
	5: 25	*l* your wives, just as Christ loved
	5: 28	husbands ought to *l* their wives
	5: 33	each one of you also must *l* his wife
	6: 23	with faith from God the Father
	6: 24	Christ with an undying *l*.
	6: 24	to all who *l* our Lord Jesus Christ
Php	1: 9	that your *l* may abound more
	1: 16	so in *l*, knowing that I am put here
	2: 1	from his *l*, if any fellowship
	2: 2	having the same *l*, being one
	4: 1	you whom I *l* and long for,
Col	1: 4	of the *l* you have for all the saints—
	1: 5	*l* that spring from the hope that is
	1: 8	also told us of your *l* in the Spirit.
	2: 2	in heart and united in *l*,
	3: 14	And over all these virtues put on *l*,
	3: 19	*l* your wives and do not be harsh
1Th	1: 3	your labour prompted by *l*,
	3: 6	good news about your faith and *l*.
	3: 12	May the Lord make your *l* increase
	4: 9	about brotherly *l* we do not need
	4: 9	taught by God to *l* each other.
	4: 10	you do *l* all the brothers
	5: 8	on faith and *l* as a breastplate,
	5: 13	them in the highest regard in *l*
2Th	1: 3	and the *l* every one of you has
	2: 10	because they refused to *l* the truth
	3: 5	direct your hearts into God's *l*
1Ti	1: 5	The goal of this command is *l*,
	1: 14	and *l* that are in Christ Jesus.
	2: 15	*l* and holiness with propriety.
	4: 12	in life, in *l*, in faith and in purity.
	6: 10	For the *l* of money is a root
	6: 11	faith, *l*, endurance and gentleness.
2Ti	1: 7	of power, of *l* and of self-discipline.
	1: 13	with faith and *l* in Christ Jesus.
	2: 22	and pursue righteousness, faith, *l*
	3: 3	unholy, without *l*, unforgiving,
	3: 10	faith, patience, *l*, endurance,
Tit	2: 2	in faith, in *l* and in endurance.
	2: 4	women to *l* their husbands

Tit	3: 4	and *l* of God our Saviour appeared,
	3: 15	Greet those who *l* us in the faith.
Phm	: 5	and your *l* for all the saints.
	: 7	Your *l* has given me great joy
	: 9	yet I appeal to you on the basis of *l*.
Heb	6: 10	and the *l* you have shown him
	10: 24	may spur one another on towards *l*
	13: 5	free from the *l* of money
Jas	1: 12	promised to those who *l* him.
	2: 5	he promised those who *l* him?
	2: 8	"*L* your neighbour as yourself,"
1Pe	1: 8	you have not seen him, you *l* him;
	1: 22	the truth so that you have sincere *l*
	1: 22	*l* one another deeply,
	2: 17	*L* the brotherhood of believers,
	3: 8	be sympathetic, *l* as brothers,
	3: 10	"Whoever would *l* life
	4: 8	Above all, *l* each other deeply,
	4: 8	*l* covers over a multitude of sins.
	5: 14	Greet one another with a kiss of *l*.
2Pe	1: 7	and to brotherly *l*, *l*.
	1: 17	"This is my Son, whom I *l*;
1Jn	2: 5	God's *l* is truly made complete
	2: 15	Do not *l* the world or anything
	2: 15	the *l* of the Father is not in him.
	3: 1	How great is the *l* the Father has
	3: 10	anyone who does not *l* his brother.
	3: 11	We should *l* one another.
	3: 14	Anyone who does not *l* remains
	3: 14	because we *l* our brothers.
	3: 16	This is how we know what *l* is:
	3: 17	how can the *l* of God be in him?
	3: 18	let us not *l* with words or tongue
	3: 23	to *l* one another as he commanded
	4: 7	Dear friends, let us *l* one another,
	4: 7	for *l* comes from God.
	4: 8	Whoever does not *l* does not know
	4: 8	not know God, because God is *l*.
	4: 9	This is how God showed his *l*
	4: 10	This is *l*: not that we loved God,
	4: 11	we also ought to *l* one another.
	4: 12	and his *l* is made complete in us.
	4: 12	seen God; but if we *l* each other,
	4: 16	God is *l*.
	4: 16	Whoever lives in *l* lives in God,
	4: 16	and rely on the *l* God has for us.
	4: 17	*l* is made complete among us
	4: 18	But perfect *l* drives out fear,
	4: 18	There is no fear in *l*.
	4: 18	who fears is not made perfect in *l*.
	4: 19	We *l* because he first loved us.
	4: 20	If anyone says, "I *l* God,"
	4: 20	anyone who does not *l* his brother,
	4: 20	whom he has seen, cannot *l* God,
	4: 21	loves God must also *l* his brother.
	5: 2	we know that we *l* the children
	5: 3	This is *l* for God: to obey his
2Jn	: 1	whom I *l* in the truth—
	: 3	will be with us in truth and *l*.
	: 5	I ask that we *l* one another.
	: 6	his command is that you walk in *l*.
	: 6	this is *l*: that we walk in obedience
3Jn	: 1	To my dear friend Gaius, whom I *l*
	: 6	have told the church about your *l*.
Jude	: 2	peace and *l* be yours in abundance.
	: 12	men are blemishes at your *l* feasts,
	: 21	Keep yourselves in God's *l*
Rev	2: 4	You have forsaken your first *l*.
	2: 19	I know your deeds, your *l* and faith
	3: 19	Those whom I *l* I rebuke

Rev	12: 11	they did not *l* their lives so much

LOVED* (LOVE)

Ge	24: 67	she became his wife, and he *l* her;
	25: 28	*l* Esau, but Rebekah *l* Jacob.
	29: 30	and he *l* Rachel more than Leah.
	29: 31	the LORD saw that Leah was not *l*,
	29: 33	the LORD heard that I am not *l*,
	34: 3	and he *l* the girl and spoke tenderly
	37: 3	Now Israel *l* Joseph more than any
	37: 4	saw that their father *l* him more
Dt	4: 37	Because he *l* your forefathers
	7: 8	But it was because the LORD *l* you
	10: 15	on your forefathers and *l* them,
1Sa	1: 5	a double portion because he *l* her,
	18: 1	in spirit with David, and he *l* him
	18: 3	with David because he *l* him
	18: 16	But all Israel and Judah *l* David,
	18: 28	that his daughter Michal *l* David,
	20: 17	because he *l* him as he *l* himself.
2Sa	1: 23	in life they were *l* and gracious,
	12: 24	The LORD *l* him; and
	12: 25	and because the LORD *l* him,
	13: 15	hated her more than he had *l* her.
1Ki	11: 1	*l* many foreign women
2Ch	11: 21	Rehoboam *l* Maacah daughter
	26: 10	in the fertile lands, for he *l* the soil.
Ne	13: 26	He was *l* by his God, and God
Ps	44: 3	light of your face, for you *l* them.
	47: 4	the pride of Jacob, whom he *l*.
	78: 68	Mount Zion, which he *l*.
	88: 18	taken my companions and *l* ones
	109: 17	He *l* to pronounce a curse—
Isa	5: 1	My *l* one had a vineyard
Jer	2: 2	how as a bride you *l* me
	8: 2	which they have *l* and served
	31: 3	"I have *l* you with an everlasting
Eze	16: 37	those you *l* as well as those you
Hos	2: 1	and of your sisters, 'My *l* one.'
	2: 23	to the one I called 'Not my *l* one.'
	3: 1	though she is *l* by another
	9: 10	became as vile as the thing they *l*.
	11: 1	"When Israel was a child, I *l* him,
Mal	1: 2	"But you ask, 'How have you *l* us?'
	1: 2	"I have *l* you," says the LORD.
	1: 2	"Yet I have *l* Jacob, but Esau I
Mk	10: 21	Jesus looked at him and *l* him.
	12: 6	left to send, a son, whom he *l*.
Lk	7: 47	been forgiven—for she *l* much.
	16: 14	The Pharisees, who *l* money,
Jn	3: 16	so *l* the world that he gave his one
	3: 19	but men *l* darkness instead of light
	11: 5	Jesus *l* Martha and her sister
	11: 36	"See how he *l* him!" But some
	12: 43	for they *l* praise from men more
	13: 1	Having *l* his own who were
	13: 23	the disciple whom Jesus *l*,
	13: 34	As I have *l* you, so you must love
	14: 21	He who loves me will be *l*
	14: 28	If you *l* me, you would be glad that
	15: 9	the Father has *l* me, so have I *l* you.
	15: 12	Love each other as I have *l* you.
	16: 27	loves you because you have *l* me
	17: 23	have *l* them even as you have *l* me.
	17: 24	you *l* me before the creation
	19: 26	the disciple whom he *l* standing
	20: 2	one Jesus *l*, and said, "They have
	21: 7	the disciple whom Jesus *l* said
	21: 20	whom Jesus *l* was following

Ro	1: 7	To all in Rome who are *l* by God
	8: 37	conquerors through him who *l* us.
	9: 13	"Jacob I *l*, but Esau I hated."
	9: 25	her 'my *l* one' who is not my *l* one,"
	11: 28	they are *l* on account
Gal	2: 20	who *l* me and gave himself for me.
Eph	5: 1	as dearly *l* children and live a life
	5: 2	as Christ *l* us and gave himself up
	5: 25	just as Christ *l* the church
Col	3: 12	and dearly *l*, clothe yourselves
1Th	1: 4	Brothers *l* by God, we know that
	2: 8	We *l* you so much that we were
2Th	2: 13	for you, brothers *l* by the Lord,
	2: 16	who *l* us and by his grace gave us
2Ti	4: 10	for Demas, because he *l* this world,
Heb	1: 9	You have *l* righteousness
2Pe	2: 15	who *l* the wages of wickedness.
1Jn	4: 10	This is love: not that we *l* God,
	4: 10	but that he *l* us and sent his Son
	4: 11	Dear friends, since God so *l* us,
	4: 19	We love because he first *l* us.
Jude	: 1	who are *l* by God the Father
Rev	3: 9	and acknowledge that I have *l* you.

LOVELY* (LOVE)

Ge	29: 17	but Rachel was *l* in form,
Est	1: 11	and nobles, for she was *l* to look at.
	2: 7	was *l* in form and features,
Ps	84: 1	How *l* is your dwelling-place,
SS	1: 5	Dark am I, yet *l*,
	2: 14	and your face is *l*.
	4: 3	your mouth is *l*.
	5: 16	he is altogether *l*.
	6: 4	*l* as Jerusalem,
Am	8: 13	*l* young women and strong young
Php	4: 8	whatever is *l*, whatever is

LOVER* (LOVE)

SS	1: 13	My *l* is to me a sachet of myrrh
	1: 14	My *l* is to me a cluster
	1: 16	How handsome you are, my *l*!
	2: 3	is my *l* among the young men.
	2: 8	Listen! My *l*!
	2: 9	My *l* is like a gazelle or a young
	2: 10	My *l* spoke and said to me,
	2: 16	My *l* is mine and I am his;
	2: 17	turn, mý *l*,
	4: 16	Let my *l* come into his garden
	5: 2	Listen! My *l* is knocking:
	5: 4	My *l* thrust his hand
	5: 5	I arose to open for my *l*,
	5: 6	I opened for my *l*,
	5: 6	but my *l* had left; he was gone.
	5: 8	if you find my *l*,
	5: 10	My *l* is radiant and ruddy,
	5: 16	This is my *l*, this my friend,
	6: 1	Where has your *l* gone,
	6: 1	Which way did your *l* turn,
	6: 2	My *l* has gone
	6: 3	I am my lover's and my *l* is mine;
	7: 9	May the wine go straight to my *l*,
	7: 10	I belong to my *l*,
	7: 11	my *l*, let us go to the countryside,
	7: 13	that I have stored up for you, my *l*.
	8: 5	leaning on her *l*?
	8: 14	Come away, my *l*,
1Ti	3: 3	not quarrelsome, not a *l* of money.

LOVER'S* (LOVE)

SS	6: 3	I am my *l* and my lover is mine;

LOVERS* (LOVE)

SS	5: 1	drink your fill, O *l*.
Jer	3: 1	as a prostitute with many *l*—
	3: 2	the roadside you sat waiting for *l*,
	4: 30	Your *l* despise you;
La	1: 2	Among all her *l*
Eze	16: 33	but you give gifts to all your *l*,
	16: 36	in your promiscuity with your *l*,
	16: 37	I am going to gather all your *l*,
	16: 39	Then I will hand you over to your *l*,
	16: 41	and you will no longer pay your *l*.
	23: 5	she lusted after her *l*, the Assyrians
	23: 9	I handed her over to her *l*,
	23: 20	There she lusted after her *l*,
	23: 22	I will stir up your *l* against you,
Hos	2: 5	She said, 'I will go after my *l*,
	2: 7	She will chase after her *l*
	2: 10	lewdness before the eyes of her *l*;
	2: 12	she said were her pay from her *l*;
	2: 13	and went after her *l*,
	8: 9	Ephraim has sold herself to *l*.
2Ti	3: 2	People will be *l* of themselves,
	3: 2	*l* of money, boastful, proud,
	3: 3	without self-control, brutal, not *l*
	3: 4	*l* of pleasure rather than *l* of God—

LOVES* (LOVE)

Ge	44: 20	sons left, and his father *l* him.'
Dt	10: 18	and *l* the alien, giving him food
	15: 16	because he *l* you and your family
	21: 15	and he *l* one but not the other,
	21: 16	son of the wife he *l* in preference
	23: 5	because the LORD your God *l* you
	28: 54	wife he *l* or his surviving children,
	28: 56	will begrudge the husband she *l*
	33: 12	and the one the LORD *l* rests
Ru	4: 15	who *l* you and who is better to you
2Ch	2: 11	"Because the LORD *l* his people,
Ps	11: 7	he *l* justice;
	33: 5	The LORD *l* righteousness
	34: 12	Whoever of you *l* life
	37: 28	For the LORD *l* the just
	87: 2	the LORD *l* the gates of Zion
	91: 14	Because he *l* me," says the LORD,
	99: 4	The King is mighty, he *l* justice—
	119: 140	and your servant *l* them,
	127: 2	for he grants sleep to those he *l*.
	146: 8	the LORD *l* the righteous.
Pr	3: 12	the LORD disciplines those he *l*,
	12: 1	Whoever *l* discipline *l* knowledge,
	13: 24	he who *l* him is careful
	15: 9	he *l* those who pursue
	17: 17	A friend *l* at all times,
	17: 19	He who *l* a quarrel *l* sin;
	19: 8	He who gets wisdom *l* his own soul
	21: 17	He who *l* pleasure will become
	21: 17	whoever *l* wine and oil will never
	22: 11	He who *l* a pure heart and whose
	29: 3	A man who *l* wisdom brings joy
Ecc	5: 10	Whoever *l* money never has
	5: 10	whoever *l* wealth is never satisfied
SS	3: 1	I looked for the one my heart *l*;
	3: 2	I will search for the one my heart *l*.
	3: 3	"Have you seen the one my heart *l*
	3: 4	when I found the one my heart *l*.
Hos	3: 1	as the LORD *l* the Israelites,
	10: 11	that *l* to thresh;
	12: 7	he *l* to defraud.
Mal	2: 11	the sanctuary the LORD *l*,

Mt	10: 37	anyone who *l* his son or daughter
	10: 37	"Anyone who *l* his father
Lk	7: 5	because he *l* our nation
	7: 47	has been forgiven little *l* little."
Jn	3: 35	Father *l* the Son and has placed
	5: 20	For the Father *l* the Son
	10: 17	reason my Father *l* me is that I lay
	12: 25	The man who *l* his life will lose it,
	14: 21	He who *l* me will be loved
	14: 21	obeys them, he is the one who *l* me.
	14: 23	Jesus replied, "If anyone *l* me,
	16: 27	the Father himself *l* you
Ro	13: 8	for he who *l* his fellow-man has
1Co	8: 3	But the man who *l* God is known
2Co	9: 7	for God *l* a cheerful giver.
Eph	1: 6	has freely given us in the One he *l*.
	5: 28	He who *l* his wife *l* himself.
	5: 33	must love his wife as he *l* himself,
Col	1: 13	us into the kingdom of the Son he *l*,
Tit	1: 8	one who *l* what is good, who is
Heb	12: 6	the Lord disciplines those he *l*,
1Jn	2: 10	Whoever *l* his brother lives
	2: 15	If anyone *l* the world, the love
	4: 7	Everyone who *l* has been born
	4: 21	Whoever *l* God must also love his
	5: 1	who *l* the father *l* his child
3Jn	: 9	but Diotrephes, who *l* to be first,
Rev	1: 5	To him who *l* us and has freed us
	20: 9	camp of God's people, the city he *l*.
	22: 15	and everyone who *l* and practises

LOVING* (LOVE)

Ps	25: 10	All the ways of the LORD are *l*
	59: 10	my *l* God.
	59: 17	O God, are my fortress, my *l* God.
	62: 12	and that you, O Lord, are *l*.
	144: 2	He is my *l* God and my fortress,
	145: 13	and *l* towards all he has made.
	145: 17	and *l* towards all he has made.
Pr	5: 19	A *l* doe, a graceful deer—
Heb	13: 1	Keep on *l* each other as brothers.
1Jn	5: 2	by *l* God and carrying out his

LOVING-KINDNESS* (LOVE)

Jer	31: 3	I have drawn you with *l*.

LOWER

Ps	8: 5	You made him a little *l*
1Co	11: 7	a sin for me to *l* myself in order
Heb	2: 7	You made him a little *l*

LOWING

1Sa	15: 14	What is this *l* of cattle that I hear?"

LOWLY

Job	5: 11	The *l* he sets on high,
Ps	138: 6	on high, he looks upon the *l*,
Pr	29: 23	but a man of *l* spirit gains honour.
Isa	57: 15	also with him who is contrite and *l*
Eze	21: 26	*l* will be exalted and the exalted
1Co	1: 28	He chose the *l* things of this world

LOYAL

1Ch	29: 18	and keep their hearts *l* to you.
Ps	78: 8	whose hearts were not *l* to God,

LUKE*

Co-worker with Paul (Col 4:14; 2Ti 4:11; Phm 24).

LUKEWARM*

Rev	3: 16	So, because you are *l*—neither hot

LUST (LUSTED LUSTS)

Pr	6: 25	Do not *l* in your heart
Eze	20: 30	and *l* after their vile images?
Col	3: 5	sexual immorality, impurity, *l*,
1Th	4: 5	not in passionate *l* like the heathen,
1Pe	4: 3	in debauchery, *l*, drunkenness,
1Jn	2: 16	the *l* of his eyes and the boasting

LUSTED (LUST)

Eze	23: 5	she *l* after her lovers, the Assyrians

LUSTS* (LUST)

Nu	15: 39	yourselves by going after the *l*
Ro	1: 26	God gave them over to shameful *l*.

LUXURY

Jas	5: 5	You have lived on earth in *l*

LYDIA'S*

Ac	16: 40	went to *L* house, where they met

LYING (LIE [2])

Pr	6: 17	a *l* tongue,
	12: 22	The LORD detests *l* lips,
	21: 6	A fortune made by a *l* tongue
	26: 28	A *l* tongue hates those it hurts,

MACEDONIA

Ac	16: 9	"Come over to *M* and help us."

MAD

Dt	28: 34	The sights you see will drive you *m*

MADE (MAKE)

Ge	1: 7	So God *m* the expanse
	1: 16	God *m* two great lights—
	1: 16	He also *m* the stars.
	1: 25	God *m* the wild animals according
	1: 31	God saw all that he had *m*,
	2: 22	Then the LORD God *m* a woman
	6: 6	was grieved that he had *m* man
	9: 6	has God *m* man.
	15: 18	that day the LORD *m* a covenant
Ex	20: 11	six days the LORD *m* the heavens
	20: 11	the Sabbath day and *m* it holy.
	24: 8	the covenant that the LORD has *m*
	32: 4	*m* it into an idol cast in the shape
Lev	16: 34	Atonement is to be *m* once a year
Dt	32: 6	who *m* you and formed you?
Jos	24: 25	On that day Joshua *m* a covenant
2Ki	19: 15	You have *m* heaven and earth.
2Ch	2: 12	the God of Israel, who *m* heaven
Ne	9: 6	You *m* the heavens,
	9: 10	You *m* a name for yourself,
Ps	33: 6	of the LORD were the heavens *m*,
	95: 5	The sea is his, for he *m* it,
	96: 5	but the LORD *m* the heavens.
	100: 3	It is he who *m* us, and we are his;
	118: 24	This is the day the LORD has *m*;
	136: 7	who *m* the great lights—
	139: 14	I am fearfully and wonderfully *m*;
Ecc	3: 11	He has *m* everything beautiful
Isa	43: 7	whom I formed and *m*."
	45: 12	It is I who *m* the earth
	45: 18	he who fashioned and *m* the earth,
	66: 2	Has not my hand *m* all these things
Jer	10: 12	But God *m* the earth by his power;

Jer 27: 5 and outstretched arm I *m* the earth
     32: 17 you have *m* the heavens
     33: 2 LORD says, he who *m* the earth,
     51: 15 "He *m* the earth by his power;
Eze   3: 17 I have *m* you a watchman
     33: 7 I have *m* you a watchman
Am   5: 8 (he who *m* the Pleiades and Orion,
Jnh   1: 9 who *m* the sea and the land."
Mk   2: 27 "The Sabbath was *m* for man,
Jn   1: 3 Through him all things were *m*;
Ac   17: 24 "The God who *m* the world
1Co   3: 6 watered it, but God *m* it grow.
Heb   1: 2 through whom he *m* the universe.
Jas   3: 9 who have been *m* in God's likeness
Rev 14: 7 Worship him who *m* the heavens,

MAGDALENE

Lk   8: 2 Mary (called *M*) from whom seven

MAGI

Mt   2: 1 *M* from the east came to Jerusalem

MAGIC (MAGICIANS)

Eze 13: 20 I am against your *m* charms
Rev 21: 8 those who practise *m* arts,
     22: 15 those who practise *m* arts,

MAGICIANS (MAGIC)

Ex   7: 11 the Egyptian *m* also did the same
Da   2: 2 So the king summoned the *m*,

MAGNIFICENCE* (MAGNIFICENT)

1Ch 22: 5 for the LORD should be of great *m*

MAGNIFICENT (MAGNIFICENCE)

1Ki   8: 13 I have indeed built a *m* temple
Isa 28: 29 in counsel and *m* in wisdom.
Mk   13: 1 stones! What *m* buildings!"

MAGOG

Eze 38: 2 of the land of *M*, the chief prince
     39: 6 I will send fire on *M*
Rev 20: 8 and *M*—to gather them for battle.

MAIDEN (MAIDENS)

Pr   30: 19 and the way of a man with a *m*.
Isa 62: 5 As a young man marries a *m*,
Jer   2: 32 Does a *m* forget her jewellery,

MAIDENS (MAIDEN)

SS   1: 3 No wonder the *m* love you!

MAIMED

Mt   18: 8 It is better for you to enter life *m*

MAINTAIN (MAINTAINING)

Ps   82: 3 *m* the rights of the poor
    106: 3 Blessed are they who *m* justice,
Hos 12: 6 *m* love and justice
Am   5: 15 *m* justice in the courts.
Ro   3: 28 For we *m* that a man is justified

MAINTAINING* (MAINTAIN)

Ex   34: 7 faithfulness, *m* love to thousands,

MAJESTIC* (MAJESTY)

Ex   15: 6 was *m* in power.
     15: 11 *m* in holiness,
Job 37: 4 he thunders with his *m* voice.
Ps   8: 1 how *m* is your name in all the earth

Ps   8: 9 how *m* is your name in all the earth
     29: 4 the voice of the LORD is *m*.
     68: 15 of Bashan are *m* mountains;
     76: 4 more *m* than mountains rich
    111: 3 Glorious and *m* are his deeds,
SS   6: 4 *m* as troops with banners.
      6: 10 *m* as the stars in procession?
Isa 30: 30 men to hear his *m* voice
Eze 31: 7 It was *m* in beauty,
2Pe   1: 17 came to him from the *M* Glory,

MAJESTY* (MAJESTIC)

Ex   15: 7 In the greatness of your *m*
Dt   5: 24 has shown us his glory and his *m*,
     11: 2 his *m*, his mighty hand, his
     33: 17 In *m* he is like a firstborn bull;
     33: 26 and on the clouds in his *m*.
1Ch 16: 27 Splendour and *m* are before him;
     29: 11 and the *m* and the splendour,
Est   1: 4 the splendour and glory of his *m*.
      7: 3 if it pleases your *m*, grant me my
Job 37: 22 God comes in awesome *m*.
     40: 10 and clothe yourself in honour and *m*
Ps   21: 5 on him splendour and *m*.
     45: 3 with splendour and *m*.
     45: 4 In your *m* ride forth victoriously
     68: 34 whose *m* is over Israel,
     93: 1 The LORD reigns, he is robed in *m*
     93: 1 the LORD is robed in *m*
     96: 6 Splendour and *m* are before him;
    104: 1 clothed with splendour and *m*.
    110: 3 Arrayed in holy *m*,
    145: 5 of the glorious splendour of your *m*,
Isa   2: 10 and the splendour of his *m*!
      2: 19 and the splendour of his *m*,
      2: 21 and the splendour of his *m*,
     24: 14 west they acclaim the LORD's *m*.
     26: 10 and regard not the *m* of the LORD.
     53: 2 or *m* to attract us to him,
Eze 31: 2 can be compared with you in *m*?
     31: 18 with you in splendour and *m*?
Da   4: 30 and for the glory of my *m*?"
Mic   5: 4 in the *m* of the name
Zec   6: 13 and he will be clothed with *m*
Ac   19: 27 will be robbed of her divine *m*."
     25: 26 to write to His *M* about him.
2Th   1: 9 and from the *m* of his power
Heb   1: 3 hand of the *M* in heaven.
      8: 1 of the throne of the *M* in heaven,
2Pe   1: 16 but we were eye-witnesses of his *m*.
Jude : 25 only God our Saviour be glory, *m*,

**MAKE (MADE MAKER MAKERS MAKES
MAKING MAN-MADE)**

Ge   1: 26 "Let us *m* man in our image,
      2: 18 I will *m* a helper suitable for him."
      6: 14 *m* yourself an ark of cypress wood;
     12: 2 "I will *m* you into a great nation
Ex   22: 3 thief must certainly *m* restitution,
     25: 9 *M* this tabernacle and all its
     25: 40 See that you *m* them according
Nu   6: 25 the LORD *m* his face shine
2Sa   7: 9 Now I will *m* your name great,
Job   7: 17 "What is man that you *m* so much
Ps   4: 8 *m* me dwell in safety.
     20: 7 and *m* all your plans succeed.
    108: 1 *m* music with all my soul.
    110: 1 hand until I *m* your enemies
    119: 165 and nothing can *m* them stumble.
Pr   3: 6 and he will *m* your paths straight.

Pr   4: 26 *M* level paths for your feet
        20: 18 *M* plans by seeking advice;
Isa   14: 14 I will *m* myself like the Most High
        29: 16 "He did not *m* me"?
        55: 3 I will *m* an everlasting covenant
        61: 8 and *m* an everlasting covenant
Jer   31: 31 "when I will *m* a new covenant
Eze   37: 26 I will *m* a covenant of peace
Mt   3: 3 *m* straight paths for him.'"
        28: 19 and *m* disciples of all nations,
Mk   1: 17 "and I will *m* you fishers of men."
Lk   13: 24 "*M* every effort to enter
        14: 23 country lanes and *m* them come in,
Ro   14: 19 *m* every effort to do what leads
2Co   5: 9 So we *m* it our goal to please him,
Eph   4: 3 *M* every effort to keep the unity
Col   4: 5 *m* the most of every opportunity.
1Th   4: 11 *M* it your ambition
Heb   4: 11 *m* every effort to enter that rest,
         8: 5 it that you *m* everything according
        12: 14 *M* every effort to live in peace
2Pe   1: 5 *m* every effort to add
         3: 14 *m* every effort to be found spotless,

MAKER* (MAKE)

Job   4: 17 Can a man be more pure than his *M*
         9: 9 He is the *M* of the Bear and Orion,
        32: 22 my *M* would soon take me away.
        35: 10 no-one says, 'Where is God my *M*,
        36: 3 I will ascribe justice to my *M*.
        40: 19 yet his *M* can approach him
Ps   95: 6 kneel before the LORD our *M*;
       115: 15 the *M* of heaven and earth.
       121: 2 the *M* of heaven and earth.
       124: 8 the *M* of heaven and earth.
       134: 3 the *M* of heaven and earth,
       146: 6 the *M* of heaven and earth,
       149: 2 Let Israel rejoice in their *M*;
Pr   14: 31 poor shows contempt for their *M*,
        17: 5 poor shows contempt for their *M*;
        22: 2 The LORD is the *M* of them all.
Ecc   11: 5 the *M* of all things.
Isa   17: 7 that day men will look to their *M*
        27: 11 so their *M* has no compassion
        45: 9 to him who quarrels with his *M*,
        45: 11 the Holy One of Israel, and its *M*:
        51: 13 that you forget the LORD your *M*,
        54: 5 For your *M* is your husband—
Jer   10: 16 for he is the *M* of all things,
        51: 19 for he is the *M* of all things,
Hos   8: 14 Israel has forgotten his *M*

MAKERS* (MAKE)

Isa   45: 16 All the *m* of idols will be put

MAKES (MAKE)

Ps   23: 2 *m* me lie down in green pastures,
Pr   13: 12 Hope deferred *m* the heart sick,
1Co   3: 7 but only God, who *m* things grow.

MAKING (MAKE)

Ps   19: 7 *m* wise the simple.
Ecc   12: 12 Of many books there is no end,
Jn   5: 18 *m* himself equal with God.
Eph   5: 16 *m* the most of every opportunity,

MALACHI*

Mal   1: 1 of the LORD to Israel through *M*.

MALE

Ge   1: 27 *m* and female he created them.
Ex   13: 2 to me every firstborn *m*.
Nu   8: 16 the first *m* offspring
Mt   19: 4 the Creator 'made them *m*
Gal   3: 28 slave nor free, *m* nor female,

MALICE (MALICIOUS)

Mk   7: 22 adultery, greed, *m*, deceit,
Ro   1: 29 murder, strife, deceit and *m*.
1Co   5: 8 the yeast of *m* and wickedness,
Eph   4: 31 along with every form of *m*.
Col   3: 8 *m*, slander, and filthy language
1Pe   2: 1 rid yourselves of all *m*

MALICIOUS (MALICE)

Pr   26: 24 A *m* man disguises himself
1Ti   3: 11 not *m* talkers but temperate
         6: 4 *m* talk, evil suspicions

MALIGN

Tit   2: 5 so that no-one will *m* the word

MAMMON see MONEY, WEALTH

MAN (MAN'S MANKIND MEN MEN'S WOMAN WOMEN)

Ge   1: 26 "Let us make *m* in our image,
         2: 7 God formed the *m* from the dust
         2: 8 *m* became a living being
         2: 15 God took the *m* and put
         2: 18 for the *m* to be alone
         2: 20 *m* gave names to all the
         2: 23 she was taken out of *m*.
         2: 25 *m* and his wife were both
         3: 9 God called to the *m*,
         3: 22 *m* has now become like
         4: 1 I have brought forth a *m*.
         6: 3 not contend with *m* for ever,
         6: 6 grieved that he had made *m*
         9: 6 Whoever sheds the blood of *m*,
Dt   8: 3 *m* does not live on bread
1Sa   13: 14 a *m* after his own heart
        15: 29 he is not a *m* that he
        16: 7 at the things *m* looks at.
Job   14: 1 *M* born of woman is of few
        14: 14 If a *m* dies, will he live
Ps   1: 1 Blessed is the *m* who does
         8: 4 what is *m* that you are
        32: 2 Blessed is the *m* whose sin
        40: 4 Blessed is the *m* who makes
        84: 12 blessed is the *m* who trusts
       103: 15 As for *m*, his days are
       112: 1 Blessed is the *m* who fears
       119: 9 can a young *m* keep his
       127: 5 Blessed is the *m* whose quiver
       144: 3 what is *m* that you care
Pr   3: 13 Blessed is the *m* who finds
         9: 9 Instruct a wise *m*
        14: 12 that seems right to a *m*,
        30: 19 way of a *m* with a maiden.
Isa   53: 3 a *m* of sorrows,
Jer   17: 5 the one who trusts in *m*,
        17: 7 blessed is the *m* who trusts
Eze   22: 30 I looked for a *m*
Mt   4: 4 *M* does not live on bread
        19: 5 a *m* will leave his father
Mk   8: 36 What good is it for a *m*
Lk   4: 4 '*M* does not live on bread
Ro   5: 12 entered the world through one *m*

1Co   2: 15 spiritual *m* makes judgments
       3: 12 If any *m* builds on this
       7: 1 good for a *m* not to marry.
       7: 2 each *m* should have his own
     11: 3 head of every *m* is Christ,
     11: 3 head of the woman is *m*
     13: 11 When I became a *m*,
     15: 21 death came through a *m*,
     15: 45 first *m* Adam became a
     15: 47 the second *m* from heaven
2Co 12: 2 I know a *m* in Christ
Eph   2: 15 create in himself one new *m*
       5: 31 a *m* will leave his father
Php   2: 8 found in appearance as a *m*,
1Ti   2: 5 the *m* Christ Jesus,
       2: 11 have authority over a *m*;
2Ti   3: 17 that the *m* of God may be
Heb   2: 6 what is *m* that you are
       9: 27 as *m* is destined to die

MAN'S (MAN)

Pr   20: 24 A *m* steps are directed by
Jer   10: 23 a *m* life is not his own;
1Co   1: 25 is wiser than *m* wisdom,

MAN-MADE (MAKE)

Heb   9: 11 perfect tabernacle that is not *m*,
       9: 24 not enter a *m* sanctuary that was

MANAGE (MANAGER)

Jer   12: 5 how will you *m* in the thickets
1Ti   3: 4 He must *m* his own family well
       3: 12 one wife and must *m* his children
       5: 14 to *m* their homes and to give

MANAGER (MANAGE)

Lk   12: 42 Who then is the faithful and wise *m*
     16: 1 a rich man whose *m* was accused

MANASSEH

    1. Firstborn of Joseph (Ge 41:51; 46:20).
Blessed by Jacob but not firstborn (Ge 48). Tribe
of blessed (Dt 33:17), numbered (Nu 1:35; 26:34),
half allotted land east of Jordan (Nu 32; Jos
13:8-33), half west (Jos 16; Eze 48:4), failed to
fully possess (Jos 16:10; Jdg 1:27), 12,000 from
(Rev 7:6).
    2. Son of Hezekiah; king of Judah (2Ki 21:1-18;
2Ch 33:1-20). Judah exiled for his detestable sins
(2Ki 21:10-15). Repentance (2Ch 33:12-19).

MANDRAKES

Ge   30: 14 give me some of your son's *m*."

MANGER

Lk   2: 12 wrapped in cloths and lying in a *m*."

MANIFESTATION*

1Co 12: 7 to each one the *m* of the Spirit is

MANKIND (MAN)

Ge   6: 7 I will wipe *m*, whom I have created
Ps   33: 13 and sees all *m*;
Pr   8: 31 and delighting in *m*.
Ecc   7: 29 God made *m* upright,
Isa   40: 5 and all *m* together will see it.
     45: 12 and created *m* upon it.
Jer   32: 27 "I am the LORD, the God of all *m*.
Zec   2: 13 Be still before the LORD, all *m*,
Lk   3: 6 And all *m* will see God's salvation

MANNA

Ex   16: 31 people of Israel called the bread *m*.
Dt   8: 16 He gave you *m* to eat in the desert,
Jn   6: 49 Your forefathers ate the *m*
Rev   2: 17 I will give some of the hidden *m*.

MANNER

1Co 11: 27 in an unworthy *m* will be guilty
Php   1: 27 conduct yourselves in a *m* worthy

MANSIONS*

Ps   49: 14 far from their princely *m*.
Isa   5: 9 the fine *m* left without occupants.
Am   3: 15 and the *m* will be demolished,"
       5: 11 though you have built stone *m*,

MARCH

Jos   6: 4 *m* around the city seven times,
Isa   42: 13 LORD will *m* out like a mighty

MARITAL* (MARRY)

Ex   21: 10 of her food, clothing and *m* rights.
Mt   5: 32 except for *m* unfaithfulness,
     19: 9 except for *m* unfaithfulness,
1Co   7: 3 husband should fulfil his *m* duty

MARK [1] (MARKS)

Ge   4: 15 Then the LORD put a *m* on Cain
Rev   13: 16 to receive a *m* on his right hand

MARK [2]

    Cousin of Barnabas (Col 4:10; 2Ti 4:11; Phm 24;
1Pe 5:13), see JOHN.

MARKET (MARKET-PLACE
MARKET-PLACES)

Jn   2: 16 turn my Father's house into a *m*!"

MARKET-PLACE (MARKET)

Lk   7: 32 are like children sitting in the *m*

MARKET-PLACES (MARKET)

Mt   23: 7 they love to be greeted in the *m*

MARKS (MARK [1])

Jn   20: 25 Unless I see the nail *m* in his hands
Gal   6: 17 bear on my body the *m* of Jesus.

MARRED

Isa   52: 14 his form *m* beyond human likeness

MARRIAGE (MARRY)

Mt   22: 30 neither marry nor be given in *m*;
     24: 38 marrying and giving in *m*,
Ro   7: 2 she is released from the law of *m*.
Heb 13: 4 by all, and the *m* bed kept pure,

MARRIED (MARRY)

Dt   24: 5 happiness to the wife he has *m*.
Ezr   10: 10 you have *m* foreign women,
Pr   30: 23 an unloved woman who is *m*,
Mt   1: 18 pledged to be *m* to Joseph,
Mk   12: 23 since the seven were *m* to her?"
Ro   7: 2 by law a *m* woman is bound
1Co   7: 27 Are you *m*? Do not seek a divorce.
       7: 33 But a *m* man is concerned about
       7: 36 They should get *m*.

MARRIES (MARRY)

Mt   5: 32 and anyone who *m* a woman

Mt   19: 9 and *m* another woman commits
Lk   16:18 the man who *m* a divorced woman

MARROW

Heb   4:12 joints and *m*; it judges the thoughts

MARRY (INTERMARRY MARITAL MARRIAGE MARRIED MARRIES)

Dt   25: 5 brother shall take her and *m* her
Mt   22:30 resurrection people will neither *m*
1Co   7: 1 It is good for a man not to *m*.
      7: 9 control themselves, they should *m*,
      7:28 if you do *m*, you have not sinned;
1Ti   4: 3 They forbid people to *m*
      5:14 So I counsel younger widows to *m*,

MARTHA*

Sister of Mary and Lazarus (Lk 10:38-42; Jn 11; 12:2).

MARVELLED* (MARVELLOUS)

Lk   2:33 mother *m* at what was said about
2Th   1:10 and to be *m* at among all those who

MARVELLING* (MARVELLOUS)

Lk   9:43 While everyone was *m*

MARVELLOUS* (MARVELLED MARVELLING)

1Ch   16:24 his *m* deeds among all peoples.
Job   37: 5 God's voice thunders in *m* ways;
Ps   71:17 to this day I declare your *m* deeds.
      72:18 who alone does *m* deeds.
      86:10 For you are great and do *m* deeds;
      96: 3 his *m* deeds among all peoples.
      98: 1 for he has done *m* things;
      118:23 and it is *m* in our eyes.
Isa   25: 1 you have done *m* things,
Zec   8: 6 but will it seem *m* to me?"
      8: 6 "It may seem *m* to the remnant
Mt   21:42 and it is *m* in our eyes'?
Mk   12:11 and it is *m* in our eyes'?"
Rev   15: 1 in heaven another great and *m* sign
      15: 3 "Great and *m* are your deeds,

MARY

1. Mother of Jesus (Mt 1:16-25; Lk 1:27-56; 2:1-40). With Jesus at temple (Lk 2:41-52), at the wedding in Cana (Jn 2:1-5), questioning his sanity (Mk 3:21), at the cross (Jn 19:25-27). Among disciples after Ascension (Ac 1:14).
2. Magdalene; former demoniac (Lk 8:2). Helped support Jesus' ministry (Lk 8:1-3). At the cross (Mt 27:56; Mk 15:40; Jn 19:25), burial (Mt 27:61; Mk 15:47). Saw angel after resurrection (Mt 28:1-10; Mk 16:1-9; Lk 24:1-12); also Jesus (Jn 20:1-18).
3. Sister of Martha and Lazarus (Jn 11). Washed Jesus' feet (Jn 12:1-8).

MASQUERADES*

2Co   11:14 for Satan himself *m* as an angel

MASTER (MASTER'S MASTERED MASTERS MASTERY)

Ge   4: 7 to have you, but you must *m* it."
Hos   2:16 you will no longer call me 'my *m*'.
Mal   1: 6 If I am a *m*, where is the respect
Mt   10:24 nor a servant above his *m*.
      23: 8 for you have only one *M*

Mt   24:46 that servant whose *m* finds him
      25:21 "His *m* replied, 'Well done,
      25:23 "His *m* replied, 'Well done,
Ro   6:14 For sin shall not be your *m*,
      14: 4 To his own *m* he stands or falls.
Col   4: 1 you know that you also have a *M*
2Ti   2:21 useful to the *M* and prepared

MASTER'S (MASTER)

Mt   25:21 Come and share your *m* happiness

MASTERED* (MASTER)

1Co   6:12 but I will not be *m* by anything.
2Pe   2:19 a slave to whatever has *m* him.

MASTERS (MASTER)

Pr   25:13 he refreshes the spirit of his *m*.
Mt   6:24 "No-one can serve two *m*.
Lk   16:13 "No servant can serve two *m*.
Eph   6: 5 obey your earthly *m* with respect
      6: 9 And *m*, treat your slaves
Col   3:22 obey your earthly *m* in everything;
      4: 1 *M*, provide your slaves
1Ti   6: 1 should consider their *m* worthy
      6: 2 who have believing *m* are not
Tit   2: 9 subject to their *m* in everything,
1Pe   2:18 to your *m* with all respect,

MASTERY* (MASTER)

Ro   6: 9 death no longer has *m* over him.

MAT

Mk   2: 9 'Get up, take your *m* and walk'?
Ac   9:34 Get up and take care of your *m*."

MATCHED*

2Co   8:11 do it may be *m* by your completion

MATTHEW*

Apostle; former tax collector (Mt 9:9-13; 10:3; Mk 3:18; Lk 6:15; Ac 1:13). Also called Levi (Mk 2:14-17; Lk 5:27-32).

MATTHIAS

Ac   1:26 the lot fell to *M*; so he was added

MATURE* (MATURITY)

Lk   8:14 and pleasures, and they do not *m*.
1Co   2: 6 a message of wisdom among the *m*,
Eph   4:13 of the Son of God and become *m*,
Php   3:15 of us who are *m* should take such
Col   4:12 firm in all the will of God, *m*
Heb   5:14 But solid food is for the *m*,
Jas   1: 4 work so that you may be *m*

MATURITY* (MATURE)

Heb   6: 1 about Christ and go on to *m*,

MEAL

Pr   15:17 Better a *m* of vegetables where
1Co   10:27 some unbeliever invites you to a *m*
Heb   12:16 for a single *m* sold his inheritance

MEANING

Ne   8: 8 and giving the *m* so that the people

MEANINGLESS

Ecc   1: 2 "*M*! *M*!" says the Teacher.
1Ti   1: 6 from these and turned to *m* talk.

MEANS

1Co   9: 22 by all possible *m* I might save some

MEASURE (MEASURED MEASURES)

Ps   71: 15 though I know not its *m*.
Eze   45: 3 In the sacred district, *m*
Zec   2: 2 He answered me, "To *m* Jerusalem
Lk   6: 38 A good *m*, pressed
Eph   3: 19 to the *m* of all the fulness of God.
       4: 13 to the whole *m* of the fulness
Rev   11: 1 "Go and *m* the temple of God

MEASURED (MEASURE)

Isa   40: 12 Who has *m* the waters
Jer   31: 37 if the heavens above can be *m*

MEASURES (MEASURE)

Dt   25: 14 Do not have two differing *m*
Pr   20: 10 Differing weights and differing *m*

MEAT

Pr   23: 20 or gorge themselves on *m*,
Ro   14: 6 He who eats *m*, eats to the Lord,
       14: 21 It is better not to eat *m*
1Co   8: 13 I will never eat *m* again,
       10: 25 *m* market without raising questions

MEDDLER* (MEDDLES)

1Pe   4: 15 kind of criminal, or even as a *m*.

MEDDLES* (MEDDLER)

Pr   26: 17 is a passer-by who *m*

MEDIATOR

1Ti   2: 5 and one *m* between God and men,
Heb   8: 6 of which he is *m* is superior
       9: 15 For this reason Christ is the *m*
      12: 24 to Jesus the *m* of a new covenant,

MEDICINE*

Pr   17: 22 A cheerful heart is good *m*,

MEDITATE* (MEDITATED MEDITATES MEDITATION)

Ge   24: 63 out to the field one evening to *m*,
Jos   1: 8 from your mouth; *m* on it day
Ps   48: 9 we *m* on your unfailing love.
      77: 12 I will *m* on all your works
     119: 15 I *m* on your precepts
     119: 23 your servant will *m*
     119: 27 then I will *m* on your wonders.
     119: 48 and I *m* on your decrees.
     119: 78 but I will *m* on your precepts.
     119: 97 I *m* on it all day long.
     119: 99 for I *m* on your statutes.
     119: 148 that I may *m* on your promises.
     143: 5 I *m* on all your works
     145: 5 I will *m* on your wonderful works.

MEDITATED* (MEDITATE)

Ps   39: 3 and as I *m*, the fire burned;

MEDITATES* (MEDITATE)

Ps   1: 2 and on his law he *m* day and night.

MEDITATION* (MEDITATE)

Ps   19: 14 of my mouth and the *m* of my heart
     104: 34 May my *m* be pleasing to him,

MEDIUM

Lev   20: 27 "'A man or woman who is a *m*

MEEK* (MEEKNESS)

Ps   37: 11 But the *m* will inherit the land
Zep   3: 12 the *m* and humble,
Mt   5: 5 Blessed are the *m*,

MEEKNESS* (MEEK)

2Co   10: 1 By the *m* and gentleness of Christ,

MEET (MEETING MEETINGS MEETS)

Ps   42: 2 When can I go and *m* with God?
      85: 10 Love and faithfulness *m* together;
Am   4: 12 prepare to *m* your God, O Israel."
1Co   11: 34 when you *m* together it may not
1Th   4: 17 them in the clouds to *m* the Lord

MEETING (MEET)

Ex   40: 34 the cloud covered the Tent of *M*,
Heb   10: 25 Let us not give up *m* together,

MEETINGS* (MEET)

1Co   11: 17 for your *m* do more harm

MEETS (MEET)

Heb   7: 26 Such a high priest *m* our need—

MELCHIZEDEK

Ge   14: 18 *M* king of Salem brought out bread
Ps   110: 4 in the order of *M*."
Heb   7: 11 in the order of *M*, not in the order

MELT (MELTS)

2Pe   3: 12 and the elements will *m* in the heat.

MELTS (MELT)

Am   9: 5 he who touches the earth and it *m*,

MEMBER (MEMBERS)

Ro   12: 5 each *m* belongs to all the others.

MEMBERS (MEMBER)

Mic   7: 6 a man's enemies are the *m*
Mt   10: 36 a man's enemies will be the *m*
Ro   7: 23 law at work in the *m* of my body,
      12: 4 of us has one body with many *m*,
1Co   6: 15 not know that your bodies are *m*
      12: 24 But God has combined the *m*
Eph   3: 6 *m* together of one body,
       4: 25 for we are all *m* of one body.
       5: 30 for we are *m* of his body.
Col   3: 15 as *m* of one body you were called

MEMORABLE* (MEMORY)

Eze   39: 13 day I am glorified will be a *m* day

MEMORIES* (MEMORY)

1Th   3: 6 us that you always have pleasant *m*

MEMORY (MEMORABLE MEMORIES)

Pr   10: 7 *m* of the righteous will be
Mt   26: 13 she has done will also be told, in *m*

MEN (MAN)

Ge   6: 2 daughters of *m* were beautiful,
       6: 4 heroes of old, *m* of renown
Ps   9: 20 nations know they are but *m*.
      11: 4 He observes the sons of *m*;
Mt   4: 19 will make you fishers of *m*
       5: 16 your light shine before *m*
       6: 14 if you forgive *m* when

Mt	10: 32	acknowledges me before *m*
	12: 31	blasphemy will be forgiven *m*,
	12: 36	*m* will have to give account
	23: 5	is done for *m* to see:
Mk	7: 7	are but rules taught by *m*.
Lk	6: 22	Blessed are you when *m*
	6: 26	Woe to you when all *m*
Jn	1: 4	life was the light of *m*.
	2: 24	for he knew all *m*.
	3: 19	*m* loved darkness instead
	12: 32	will draw all *m* to myself
	13: 35	all *m* will know that you
Ac	5: 29	obey God rather than *m*!
Ro	1: 18	wickedness of *m*
	1: 27	indecent acts with other *m*,
	5: 12	death came to all *m*,
1Co	2: 11	among *m* knows the thoughts
	3: 3	acting like mere *m*?
	3: 21	no more boasting about *m*!
	9: 22	all things to all *m*
	13: 1	tongues of *m* and of angels
	16: 13	be *m* of courage;
	16: 18	Such *m* deserve recognition.
2Co	5: 11	we try to persuade *m*.
	8: 21	but also in the eyes of *m*.
Gal	1: 1	sent not from *m* nor
	1: 10	to win approval of *m*, or
Eph	4: 8	and gave gifts to *m*.
1Th	2: 4	as *m* approved by God
	2: 13	not as the word of *m*,
1Ti	2: 4	wants all *m* to be saved
	2: 6	as a ransom for all *m*—
	4: 10	the Saviour of all *m*
	5: 2	younger *m* as brothers
2Ti	2: 2	entrust to reliable *m*
Tit	2: 11	has appeared to all *m*.
Heb	5: 1	is selected from among *m*
	7: 28	high priests *m* who are weak;
2Pe	1: 21	but *m* spoke from God
Rev	21: 3	dwelling of God is with *m*,

MEN'S (MAN)

2Ki	19: 18	fashioned by *m* hands.
2Ch	32: 19	the work of *m* hands.
1Co	2: 5	not rest on *m* wisdom,

MENAHEM*

King of Israel (2Ki 15:17-22).

MENE

Da	5: 25	that was written: *M*, *M*,

MEPHIBOSHETH

Son of Jonathan shown kindness by David (2Sa 4:4; 9; 21:7). Accused of siding with Absalom (2Sa 16:1-4; 19:24-30).

MERCHANT

Pr	31: 14	She is like the *m* ships,
Mt	13: 45	of heaven is like a *m* looking

MERCIFUL (MERCY)

Dt	4: 31	the LORD your God is a *m* God;
Ne	9: 31	for you are a gracious and *m* God.
Ps	77: 9	Has God forgotten to be *m*?
	78: 38	Yet he was *m*;
Jer	3: 12	for I am *m*,' declares the LORD,
Da	9: 9	The Lord our God is *m*
Mt	5: 7	Blessed are the *m*,
Lk	1: 54	remembering to be *m*

Lk	6: 36	Be *m*, just as your Father is *m*.
Heb	2: 17	in order that he might become a *m*
Jas	2: 13	to anyone who has not been *m*.
Jude	: 22	Be *m* to those who doubt; snatch

MERCY (MERCIFUL)

Ex	33: 19	*m* on whom I will have *m*,
2Sa	24: 14	of the LORD, for his *m* is great;
1Ch	21: 13	for his *m* is very great;
Ne	9: 31	But in your great *m* you did not put
Ps	25: 6	O LORD, your great *m* and love,
	28: 6	for he has heard my cry for *m*.
	57: 1	Have *m* on me, O God, have *m*
Pr	28: 13	renounces them finds *m*.
Isa	63: 9	and *m* he redeemed them;
Da	9: 18	but because of your great *m*.
Hos	6: 6	for I desire *m*, not sacrifice,
Am	5: 15	LORD God Almighty will have *m*
Mic	6: 8	To act justly and to love *m*
	7: 18	but delight to show *m*.
Hab	3: 2	in wrath remember *m*.
Zec	7: 9	show *m* and compassion
Mt	5: 7	for they will be shown *m*.
	9: 13	learn what this means: 'I desire *m*,
	12: 7	'I desire *m*, not sacrifice,' you
	18: 33	Shouldn't you have had *m*
	23: 23	justice, *m* and faithfulness.
Lk	1: 50	His *m* extends to those who fear
Ro	9: 15	"I will have *m* on whom I have *m*,
	9: 18	Therefore God has *m*
	11: 32	so that he may have *m* on them all.
	12: 1	brothers, in view of God's *m*,
	12: 8	if it is showing *m*, let him do it
Eph	2: 4	who is rich in *m*, made us alive
1Ti	1: 13	I was shown *m* because I acted
	1: 16	for that very reason I was shown *m*
Tit	3: 5	we had done, but because of his *m*.
Heb	4: 16	so that we may receive *m*
Jas	2: 13	judgment without *m* will be shown
	2: 13	*M* triumphs over judgment!
	3: 17	submissive, full of *m* and good fruit
	5: 11	full of compassion and *m*.
1Pe	1: 3	In his great *m* he has given us new
	2: 10	once you had not received *m*,
Jude	: 23	to others show *m*, mixed with fear

MERRY

Lk	12: 19	Take life easy; eat, drink and be *m*

MESHACH

Hebrew exiled to Babylon; name changed from Mishael (Da 1:6-7). Refused defilement by food (Da 1:8-20). Refused to worship idol (Da 3:1-18); saved from furnace (Da 3:19-30).

MESSAGE (MESSENGER)

Isa	53: 1	Who has believed our *m*
Jn	12: 38	"Lord, who has believed our *m*
Ac	5: 20	"and tell the people the full *m*
	10: 36	You know the *m* God sent
	17: 11	for they received the *m*
Ro	10: 16	who has believed our *m*?"
	10: 17	faith comes from hearing the *m*,
1Co	1: 18	For the *m* of the cross is
	2: 4	My *m* and my preaching were not
2Co	5: 19	to us the *m* of reconciliation.
2Th	3: 1	pray for us that the *m*
Tit	1: 9	firmly to the trustworthy *m*
Heb	4: 2	the *m* they heard was of no value
1Pe	2: 8	because they disobey the *m*—

MESSENGER (MESSAGE)

Pr	25: 13	is a trustworthy *m*
Mal	3: 1	I will send my *m*, who will prepare
Mt	11: 10	"'I will send my *m* ahead of you,
2Co	12: 7	a *m* of Satan, to torment me.

MESSIAH*

Jn	1: 41	"We have found the *M*" (that is,
	4: 25	"I know that *M*" (called Christ) "is

METHUSELAH

Ge	5: 27	Altogether, *M* lived 969 years,

MICAH

1. Idolater from Ephraim (Jdg 17-18).
2. Prophet from Moresheth (Jer 26:18-19; Mic 1:1).

MICAIAH

Prophet of the LORD who spoke against Ahab (1Ki 22:1-28; 2Ch 18:1-27).

MICHAEL

Archangel (Jude 9); warrior in angelic realm, protector of Israel (Da 10:13, 21; 12:1; Rev 12:7).

MICHAL

Daughter of Saul, wife of David (1Sa 14:49; 18:20-28). Warned David of Saul's plot (1Sa 19). Saul gave her to Paltiel (1Sa 25:44); David retrieved her (2Sa 3:13-16). Criticised David for dancing before the ark (2Sa 6:16-23; 1Ch 15:29).

MIDIAN

Ex	2: 15	Pharaoh and went to live in *M*,
Jdg	7: 2	me to deliver *M* into their hands.

MIDWIVES

Ex	1: 17	The *m*, however, feared God

MIGHT (ALMIGHTY MIGHTIER MIGHTY)

Jdg	16: 30	Then he pushed with all his *m*,
2Sa	6: 5	with all their *m* before the LORD,
	6: 14	before the LORD with all his *m*,
2Ch	20: 6	Power and *m* are in your hand,
Ps	21: 13	we will sing and praise your *m*.
	54: 1	vindicate me by your *m*.
Isa	63: 15	Where are your zeal and your *m*?
Mic	3: 8	and with justice and *m*,
Zec	4: 6	'Not by *m* nor by power,
Col	1: 11	power according to his glorious *m*
1Ti	6: 16	To him be honour and *m* for ever.

MIGHTIER (MIGHT)

Ps	93: 4	*M* than the thunder

MIGHTY (MIGHT)

Ge	49: 24	of the hand of the *M* One of Jacob,
Ex	6: 1	of my *m* hand he will drive them
	13: 3	out of it with a *m* hand.
Dt	5: 15	out of there with a *m* hand
	7: 8	he brought you out with a *m* hand
	10: 17	the great God, *m* and awesome,
	34: 12	no-one has ever shown the *m* power
2Sa	1: 19	How the *m* have fallen!
	23: 8	the names of David's *m* men:
Ne	9: 32	the great, *m* and awesome God,
Job	36: 5	God is *m*, but does not despise men
Ps	24: 8	The LORD strong and *m*,

Ps	45: 3	upon your side, O *m* one;
	50: 1	The *M* One, God, the LORD,
	62: 7	he is my *m* rock, my refuge.
	68: 33	who thunders with *m* voice.
	71: 16	proclaim your *m* acts,
	77: 12	and consider all your *m* deeds.
	77: 15	With your *m* arm you redeemed
	89: 8	You are *m*, O LORD,
	93: 4	the LORD on high is *m*.
	99: 4	The King is *m*, he loves justice—
	110: 2	LORD will extend your *m* sceptre
	118: 15	right hand has done *m* things!
	136: 12	with a *m* hand and outstretched
	145: 4	they will tell of your *m* acts.
	145: 12	all men may know of your *m* acts
	147: 5	Great is our Lord and *m* in power;
SS	8: 6	like a *m* flame.
Isa	9: 6	Wonderful Counsellor, *M* God,
	60: 16	your Redeemer, the *M* One
	63: 1	*m* to save."
Jer	10: 6	and your name is *m* in power.
	20: 11	with me like a *m* warrior;
	32: 19	your purposes and *m* are your
Eze	20: 33	I will rule over you with a *m* hand
Zep	3: 17	he is *m* to save.
Mt	26: 64	at the right hand of the *M* One
Eph	1: 19	like the working of his *m* strength,
	6: 10	in the Lord and in his *m* power.
1Pe	5: 6	therefore, under God's *m* hand,

MILE*

Mt	5: 41	If someone forces you to go one *m*,

MILK

Ex	3: 8	a land flowing with *m* and honey—
	23: 19	a young goat in its mother's *m*.
Pr	30: 33	as churning the *m* produces butter,
Isa	55: 1	Come, buy wine and *m*
1Co	3: 2	I gave you *m*, not solid food,
Heb	5: 12	You need *m*, not solid food!
1Pe	2: 2	babies, crave pure spiritual *m*,

MILLSTONE (STONE)

Lk	17: 2	sea with a *m* tied round his neck

MIND (DOUBLE-MINDED LIKE-MINDED MINDED MINDFUL MINDS)

Nu	23: 19	that he should change his *m*.
Dt	28: 65	LORD will give you an anxious *m*,
1Sa	15: 29	Israel does not lie or change his *m*;
1Ch	28: 9	devotion and with a willing *m*,
2Ch	30: 12	the people to give them unity of *m*
Ps	26: 2	examine my heart and my *m*;
	110: 4	and will not change his *m*:
Isa	26: 3	him whose *m* is steadfast,
Jer	17: 10	and examine the *m*,
Mt	22: 37	all your soul and with all your *m*.'
Mk	12: 30	with all your *m* and with all your
Lk	10: 27	your strength and with all your *m*';
Ac	4: 32	believers were one in heart and *m*.
Ro	1: 28	he gave them over to a depraved *m*
	7: 25	I myself in my *m* am a slave
	8: 6	The *m* of sinful man is death,
	8: 7	the sinful *m* is hostile to God.
	12: 2	by the renewing of your *m*.
	14: 13	make up your *m* not
1Co	1: 10	you may be perfectly united in *m*
	2: 9	no *m* has conceived
	14: 14	spirit prays, but my *m* is unfruitful.
2Co	13: 11	be of one *m*, live in peace.

Php   3: 19 Their *m* is on earthly things.
Col   2: 18 and his unspiritual *m* puffs him up
1Th   4: 11 to *m* your own business
Heb   7: 21 and will not change his *m*:

MINDED* (MIND)

1Pe   4: 7 be clear *m* and self-controlled

MINDFUL* (MIND)

Ps   8: 4 what is man that you are *m* of him,
Lk   1: 48 God my Saviour, for he has been *m*
Heb   2: 6 What is man that you are *m* of him,

MINDS (MIND)

Dt   11: 18 of mine in your hearts and *m*;
Ps   7: 9 who searches *m* and hearts,
Jer   31: 33 "I will put my law in their *m*
Lk   24: 38 and why do doubts rise in your *m*?
      24: 45 Then he opened their *m*
Ro   8: 5 to the sinful nature have their *m* set
2Co   4: 4 god of this age has blinded the *m*
Eph   4: 23 new in the attitude of your *m*;
Col   3: 2 Set your *m* on things above,
Heb   8: 10 I will put my laws in their *m*
      10: 16 and I will write them on their *m*."
1Pe   1: 13 prepare your *m* for action;
Rev   2: 23 I am he who searches hearts and *m*,

MINISTER (MINISTERING MINISTERS MINISTRY)

Ps   101: 6 will *m* to me.
1Ti   4: 6 you will be a good *m*

MINISTERING (MINISTER)

Heb   1: 14 Are not all angels *m* spirits sent

MINISTERS (MINISTER)

2Co   3: 6 as *m* of a new covenant—

MINISTRY (MINISTER)

Ac   6: 4 to prayer and the *m* of the word."
Ro   11: 13 I make much of my *m*
2Co   4: 1 God's mercy we have this *m*,
       5: 18 gave us the *m* of reconciliation:
       6: 3 so that our *m* will not be
Gal   2: 8 who was at work in the *m* of Peter
2Ti   4: 5 discharge all the duties of your *m*.
Heb   8: 6 But the *m* Jesus has received is

MIRACLE* (MIRACLES MIRACULOUS)

Ex   7: 9 'Perform a *m*,' then say to Aaron,
Mk   9: 39 "No-one who does a *m*
Lk   23: 8 hoped to see him perform some *m*.
Jn   7: 21 "I did one *m*, and you are all
Ac   4: 16 they have done an outstanding *m*,

MIRACLES* (MIRACLE)

1Ch   16: 12 his *m*, and the judgments he
Ne   9: 17 to remember the *m* you performed
Job   5: 9 *m* that cannot be counted.
       9: 10 *m* that cannot be counted.
Ps   77: 11 I will remember your *m* of long ago
      77: 14 You are the God who performs *m*;
      78: 12 He did *m* in the sight
     105: 5 his *m*, and the judgments he
     106: 7 they gave no thought to your *m*;
     106: 22 *m* in the land of Ham
Mt   7: 22 out demons and perform many *m*?'
      11: 20 most of his *m* had been performed,
      11: 21 If the *m* that were performed

Mt   11: 23 If the *m* that were performed
      13: 58 And he did not do many *m* there
      24: 24 and perform great signs and *m*
Mk   6: 2 does *m*! Isn't this the carpenter?
       6: 5 He could not do any *m* there,
      13: 22 and *m* to deceive the elect—
Lk   10: 13 For if the *m* that were performed
      19: 37 for all the *m* they had seen:
Jn   7: 3 disciples may see the *m* you do.
      10: 25 *m* I do in my Father's name speak
      10: 32 "I have shown you many great *m*
      10: 38 do not believe me, believe the *m*,
      14: 11 the evidence of the *m* themselves.
      15: 24 But now they have seen these *m*,
Ac   2: 22 accredited by God to you by *m*,
       8: 13 by the great signs and *m* he saw.
      19: 11 God did extraordinary *m*
Ro   15: 19 by the power of signs and *m*,
1Co   12: 28 third teachers, then workers of *m*,
      12: 29 Are all teachers? Do all work *m*?
2Co   12: 12 and *m*—were done among you
Gal   3: 5 work *m* among you because you
2Th   2: 9 in all kinds of counterfeit *m*,
Heb   2: 4 it by signs, wonders and various *m*,

MIRACULOUS (MIRACLE)

Dt   13: 1 and announces to you a *m* sign
Mt   12: 39 generation asks for a *m* sign!
      13: 54 this wisdom and these *m* powers?"
Jn   2: 11 This, the first of his *m* signs,
       2: 23 people saw the *m* signs he was
       3: 2 could perform the *m* signs you are
       4: 48 "Unless you people see *m* signs
       7: 31 will he do more *m* signs
       9: 16 "How can a sinner do such *m* signs
      12: 37 Jesus had done all these *m* signs
      20: 30 Jesus did many other *m* signs
Ac   2: 43 *m* signs were done by the apostles
       5: 12 apostles performed many *m* signs
1Co   1: 22 Jews demand *m* signs and Greeks
      12: 10 to another *m* powers,

MIRE

Ps   40: 2 out of the mud and *m*;
Isa   57: 20 whose waves cast up *m* and mud.

MIRIAM

Sister of Moses and Aaron (Nu 26:59). Led
dancing at Red Sea (Ex 15:20-21). Struck with
leprosy for criticising Moses (Nu 12). Death (Nu
20:1).

MIRROR

1Co   13: 12 reflection as in a *m*;
Jas   1: 23 a man who looks at his face in a *m*

MISDEEDS*

Ps   99: 8 though you punished their *m*.
Ro   8: 13 put to death the *m* of the body,

MISERY

Ex   3: 7 "I have indeed seen the *m*
Jdg   10: 16 he could bear Israel's *m* no longer.
Hos   5: 15 in their *m* they will earnestly seek
Ro   3: 16 ruin and *m* mark their ways,
Jas   5: 1 of the *m* that is coming upon you.

MISFORTUNE

Ob   : 12 brother in the day of his *m*,

MISLEAD (MISLED)

Isa 47: 10 wisdom and knowledge *m* you

MISLED (MISLEAD)

1Co 15: 33 Do not be *m*: "Bad company

MISS (MISSES)

Pr 19: 2 nor to be hasty and *m* the way.

MISSES (MISS)

Heb 12: 15 See to it that no-one *m* the grace

MIST

Hos 6: 4 Your love is like the morning *m*,
Jas 4: 14 You are a *m* that appears for a little

MISUSE* (MISUSES)

Ex 20: 7 "You shall not *m* the name
Dt 5: 11 "You shall not *m* the name
Ps 139: 20 your adversaries *m* your name.

MISUSES* (MISUSE)

Ex 20: 7 anyone guiltless who *m* his name.
Dt 5: 11 anyone guiltless who *m* his name.

MIXED (MIXING)

Da 2: 41 even as you saw iron *m* with clay.

MIXING (MIXED)

Isa 5: 22 and champions at *m* drinks,

MOAB (MOABITESS)

Ge 19: 37 she named him *M*; he is the father
Dt 34: 6 He buried him in *M*, in the valley
Ru 1: 1 live for a while in the country of *M*.
Isa 15: 1 An oracle concerning *M*:
Jer 48: 16 "The fall of *M* is at hand;
Am 2: 1 "For three sins of *M*,

MOABITESS (MOAB)

Ru 1: 22 accompanied by Ruth the *M*,

MOAN

Ps 90: 9 we finish our years with a *m*.

MOCK (MOCKED MOCKER MOCKERS MOCKING MOCKS)

Ps 22: 7 All who see me *m* me;
119: 51 The arrogant *m* me
Pr 1: 26 I will *m* when calamity overtakes
14: 9 Fools *m* at making amends for sin,
Mk 10: 34 who will *m* him and spit on him,

MOCKED (MOCK)

Ps 89: 51 with which they have *m* every step
Mt 27: 29 knelt in front of him and *m* him.
27: 41 of the law and the elders *m* him.
Gal 6: 7 not be deceived: God cannot be *m*.

MOCKER (MOCK)

Pr 9: 7 corrects a *m* invites insult;
9: 12 if you are a *m*, you alone will suffer
20: 1 Wine is a *m* and beer a brawler;
22: 10 Drive out the *m*, and out goes strife

MOCKERS (MOCK)

Ps 1: 1 or sit in the seat of *m*.
Pr 29: 8 *M* stir up a city,

MOCKING (MOCK)

Isa 50: 6 face from *m* and spitting.

MOCKS (MOCK)

Pr 17: 5 He who *m* the poor shows
30: 17 "The eye that *m* a father,

MODEL*

Eze 28: 12 "'You were the *m* of perfection,
1Th 1: 7 And so you became a *m*
2Th 3: 9 to make ourselves a *m* for you

MODESTY*

1Co 12: 23 are treated with special *m*,

MOLECH

Lev 20: 2 of his children to *M* must be put
1Ki 11: 33 and *M* the god of the Ammonites,

MOMENT (MOMENTARY)

Job 20: 5 the joy of the godless lasts but a *m*.
Ps 2: 12 for his wrath can flare up in a *m*.
30: 5 For his anger lasts only a *m*,
Pr 12: 19 but a lying tongue lasts only a *m*.
Isa 54: 7 "For a brief *m* I abandoned you,
66: 8 or a nation be brought forth in a *m*?
Gal 2: 5 We did not give in to them for a *m*,

MOMENTARY* (MOMENT)

2Co 4: 17 and *m* troubles are achieving

MONEY

Pr 13: 11 Dishonest *m* dwindles away,
Ecc 5: 10 Whoever loves *m* never has *m*
Isa 55: 1 and you who have no *m*,
Mt 6: 24 You cannot serve both God and *M*.
27: 5 Judas threw the *m* into the temple
Lk 3: 14 "Don't extort *m* and don't accuse
9: 3 no bread, no *m*, no extra tunic.
16: 13 You cannot serve both God and *M*
Ac 5: 2 part of the *m* for himself,
1Co 16: 2 set aside a sum of *m* in keeping
1Ti 3: 3 not quarrelsome, not a lover of *m*.
6: 10 For the love of *m* is a root
2Ti 3: 2 lovers of *m*, boastful, proud,
Heb 13: 5 free from the love of *m*
1Pe 5: 2 not greedy for *m*, but eager to serve

MONEY-LENDER* (LEND)

Ex 22: 25 not be like a *m*; charge him no
Lk 7: 41 men owed money to a certain *m*.

MONTH (MONTHS)

Ex 12: 2 "This *m* is to be for you the first
Eze 47: 12 Every *m* they will bear,
Rev 22: 2 of fruit, yielding its fruit every *m*.

MONTHS (MONTH)

Gal 4: 10 and *m* and seasons and years!
Rev 11: 2 trample on the holy city for 42 *m*.
13: 5 his authority for forty-two *m*.

MOON

Jos 10: 13 and the *m* stopped,
Ps 8: 3 the *m* and the stars,
74: 16 you established the sun and *m*.
89: 37 be established for ever like the *m*,
104: 19 The *m* marks off the seasons,
121: 6 nor the *m* by night.

Ps 136: 9 the *m* and stars to govern the night;
148: 3 Praise him, sun and *m*,
SS 6: 10 fair as the *m*, bright as the sun,
Joel 2: 31 and the *m* to blood
Hab 3: 11 and *m* stood still in the heavens
Mt 24: 29 and the *m* will not give its light;
Ac 2: 20 and the *m* to blood
1Co 15: 41 *m* another and the stars another;
Col 2: 16 a New *M* celebration or a Sabbath
Rev 6: 12 the whole *m* turned blood red,
21: 23 city does not need the sun or the *m*

MORAL*

Jas 1: 21 rid of all *m* filth and the evil that is

MORDECAI

Benjamite exile who raised Esther (Est 2:5-15). Exposed plot to kill Xerxes (Est 2:19-23). Refused to honour Haman (Est 3:1-6; 5:9-14). Charged Esther to foil Haman's plot against the Jews (Est 4). Xerxes forced Haman to honour Mordecai (Est 6). Mordecai exalted (Est 8-10). Established Purim (Est 9:18-32).

MORIAH*

Ge 22: 2 and go to the region of *M*.
2Ch 3: 1 LORD in Jerusalem on Mount *M*,

MORNING

Ge 1: 5 and there was *m*—the first day.
Dt 28: 67 In the *m* you will say, "If only it
2Sa 23: 4 he is like the light of *m* at sunrise
Ps 5: 3 *M* by *m*, O LORD,
Pr 27: 14 blesses his neighbour early in the *m*,
Isa 14: 12 O *m* star, son of the dawn!
La 3: 23 They are new every *m*;
2Pe 1: 19 and the *m* star rises in your hearts.
Rev 2: 28 I will also give him the *m* star.
22: 16 of David, and the bright *M* Star."

MORTAL

Ge 6: 3 for he is *m*; his days will be
Job 10: 4 Do you see as a *m* sees?
Ro 8: 11 also give life to your *m* bodies
1Co 15: 53 and the *m* with immortality.
2Co 5: 4 that what is *m* may be swallowed

MOSES

Levite; brother of Aaron (Ex 6:20; 1Ch 6:3). Put in basket into Nile; discovered and raised by Pharaoh's daughter (Ex 2:1-10). Fled to Midian after killing Egyptian (Ex 2:11-15). Married to Zipporah, fathered Gershom (Ex 2:16-22).
Called by the LORD to deliver Israel (Ex 3-4). Pharaoh's resistance (Ex 5). Ten plagues (Ex 7-11). Passover and Exodus (Ex 12-13). Led Israel through Red Sea (Ex 14). Song of deliverance (Ex 15:1-21). Brought water from rock (Ex 17:1-7). Raised hands to defeat Amalekites (Ex 17:8-16). Delegated judges (Ex 18; Dt 1:9-18).
Received Law at Sinai (Ex 19-23; 25-31; Jn 1:17). Announced Law to Israel (Ex 19:7-8; 24; 35). Broke tablets because of golden calf (Ex 32; Dt 9). Saw glory of the LORD (Ex 33-34). Supervised building of tabernacle (Ex 36-40). Set apart Aaron and priests (Lev 8-9). Numbered tribes (Nu 1-4; 26). Opposed by Aaron and Miriam (Nu 12). Sent spies into Canaan (Nu 13). Announced forty years of wandering for failure to enter land (Nu 14). Opposed by Korah (Nu 16).

Forbidden to enter land for striking rock (Nu 20:1-13; Dt 1:37). Lifted bronze snake for healing (Nu 21: 4-9; Jn 3:14). Final address to Israel (Dt 31-33). Succeeded by Joshua (Nu 27:12-23; Dt 34). Death (Dt 34:5-12).
"Law of Moses" (1Ki 2:3; Ezr 3:2; Mk 12:26; Lk 24:44). "Book of Moses" (2Ch 25:12; Ne 13:1). "Song of Moses" (Ex 15:1-21; Rev 15:3). "Prayer of Moses" (Ps 90).

MOTH

Mt 6: 19 where *m* and rust destroy,

MOTHER (GRANDMOTHER MOTHER-IN-LAW MOTHER'S)

Ge 2: 24 and *m* and be united to his wife,
3: 20 because she would become the *m*
Ex 20: 12 "Honour your father and your *m*,
Lev 20: 9 "'If anyone curses his father or *m*,
Dt 5: 16 "Honour your father and your *m*,
21: 18 who does not obey his father and *m*
27: 16 who dishonours his father or his *m*."
Jdg 5: 7 arose a *m* in Israel.
1Sa 2: 19 Each year his *m* made him a little
Ps 113: 9 as a happy *m* of children.
Pr 10: 1 but a foolish son grief to his *m*.
23: 22 do not despise your *m*
23: 25 May your father and *m* be glad;
29: 15 a child left to itself disgraces his *m*.
30: 17 that scorns obedience to a *m*,
31: 1 an oracle his *m* taught him:
Isa 49: 15 "Can a *m* forget the baby
66: 13 As a *m* comforts her child,
Jer 20: 17 with my *m* as my grave,
Mic 7: 6 a daughter rises up against her *m*,
Mt 10: 35 a daughter against her *m*,
10: 37 or *m* more than me is not worthy
12: 48 He replied, "Who is my *m*,
15: 4 'Honour your father and *m*'
19: 5 and *m* and be united to his wife,
19: 19 honour your father and *m*,'
Mk 7: 10 'Honour your father and *m*,' and,
10: 19 honour your father and *m*.'"
Lk 11: 27 "Blessed is the *m* who gave you
12: 53 daughter and daughter against *m*,
18: 20 honour your father and *m*.'"
Jn 19: 27 to the disciple, "Here is your *m*."
Gal 4: 26 is above is free, and she is our *m*.
Eph 5: 31 and *m* and be united to his wife,
6: 2 "Honour your father and *m*"—
1Th 2: 7 like a *m* caring for her little
2Ti 1: 5 and in your *m* Eunice and,

MOTHER-IN-LAW (MOTHER)

Ru 2: 19 Ruth told her *m* about the one
Mt 10: 35 a daughter-in-law against her *m*—

MOTHER'S (MOTHER)

Job 1: 21 "Naked I came from my *m* womb,
Pr 1: 8 and do not forsake your *m* teaching
Ecc 5: 15 from his *m* womb,
11: 5 the body is formed in a *m* womb,
Jn 3: 4 time into his *m* womb to be born!"

MOTIVE* (MOTIVES)

1Ch 28: 9 and understands every *m*

MOTIVES* (MOTIVE)

Pr 16: 2 but *m* are weighed by the LORD.
1Co 4: 5 will expose the *m* of men's hearts.

Php 1: 18 whether from false *m* or true,
1Th 2: 3 spring from error or impure *m*,
Jas 4: 3 because you ask with wrong *m*,

MOULDED*

Job 10: 9 Remember that you *m* me like clay

MOULDY

Jos 9: 5 of their food supply was dry and *m*.

MOUNT (MOUNTAIN MOUNTAINS MOUNTAINTOPS)

Ps 89: 9 when its waves *m* up, you still them
Isa 14: 13 enthroned on the *m* of assembly,
Eze 28: 14 You were on the holy *m* of God;
Zec 14: 4 stand on the *M* of Olives,

MOUNTAIN (MOUNT)

Ge 22: 14 "On the *m* of the LORD it will be
Ex 24: 18 And he stayed on the *m* forty days
Dt 5: 4 face to face out of the fire on the *m*.
Job 14: 18 "But as a *m* erodes and crumbles
Ps 48: 1 in the city of our God, his holy *m*.
Isa 40: 4 every *m* and hill made low;
Mic 4: 2 Let us go up to the *m* of the LORD,
Mt 4: 8 the devil took him to a very high *m*
    17: 20 say to this *m*, 'Move from here
Mk 9: 2 with him and led them up a high *m*,
Lk 3: 5 every *m* and hill made low.
Jn 4: 21 the Father neither on this *m*
2Pe 1: 18 were with him on the sacred *m*.

MOUNTAINS (MOUNT)

Ps 36: 6 righteousness is like the mighty *m*,
    46: 2 the *m* fall into the heart of the sea,
    90: 2 Before the *m* were born
Isa 52: 7 How beautiful on the *m*
    54: 10 Though the *m* be shaken
    55: 12 the *m* and hills
Eze 34: 6 My sheep wandered over all the *m*
Mt 24: 16 are in Judea flee to the *m*.
Lk 23: 30 they will say to the *m*, "Fall on us!"
1Co 13: 2 if I have a faith that can move *m*,
Rev 6: 16 They called to the *m* and the rocks,

MOUNTAINTOPS (MOUNT)

Isa 42: 11 let them shout from the *m*.

MOURN (MOURNING MOURNS)

Ecc 3: 4 a time to *m* and a time to dance,
Isa 61: 2 to comfort all who *m*,
Mt 5: 4 Blessed are those who *m*,
Ro 12: 15 *m* with those who *m*.

MOURNING (MOURN)

Isa 61: 3 instead of *m*,
Jer 31: 13 I will turn their *m* into gladness;
Rev 21: 4 There will be no more death or *m*

MOURNS (MOURN)

Zec 12: 10 as one *m* for an only child,

MOUTH (MOUTHS)

Nu 22: 38 only what God puts in my *m*."
Dt 8: 3 comes from the *m* of the LORD.
    18: 18 I will put my words in his *m*,
    30: 14 it is in your *m* and in your heart
Jos 1: 8 of the Law depart from your *m*;
2Ki 4: 34 *m* to *m*, eyes to eyes, hands
Ps 10: 7 His *m* is full of curses and lies

Ps 17: 3 resolved that my *m* will not sin.
    19: 14 May the words of my *m*
    37: 30 *m* of the righteous man utters
    40: 3 He put a new song in my *m*,
    71: 8 My *m* is filled with your praise,
    119: 103 sweeter than honey to my *m*!
    141: 3 Set a guard over my *m*, O LORD;
Pr 2: 6 and from his *m* come knowledge
    4: 24 Put away perversity from your *m*;
    10: 11 The *m* of the righteous is a fountain
    10: 31 *m* of the righteous brings forth
    16: 23 A wise man's heart guides his *m*,
    26: 28 and a flattering *m* works ruin.
    27: 2 praise you, and not your own *m*;
Ecc 5: 2 Do not be quick with your *m*,
SS 1: 2 with the kisses of his *m*—
    5: 16 His *m* is sweetness itself;
Isa 29: 13 come near to me with their *m*
    40: 5 For the *m* of the LORD has spoken
    45: 23 my *m* has uttered in all integrity
    51: 16 I have put my words in your *m*
    53: 7 so he did not open his *m*.
    55: 11 my word that goes out from my *m*:
    59: 21 *m* will not depart from your *m*,
Eze 3: 2 So I opened my *m*, and he gave me
Mal 2: 7 and from his *m* men should seek
Mt 4: 4 comes from the *m* of God.'"
    12: 34 overflow of the heart the *m* speaks.
    15: 11 into a man's *m* does not make him
    15: 18 out of the *m* come from the heart,
Lk 6: 45 overflow of his heart his *m* speaks.
Ro 10: 9 That if you confess with your *m*,
    15: 6 and *m* you may glorify the God
1Pe 2: 22 and no deceit was found in his *m*."
Rev 1: 16 and out of his *m* came a sharp
    2: 16 them with the sword of my *m*.
    3: 16 I am about to spit you out of my *m*.
    19: 15 Out of his *m* comes a sharp sword

MOUTHS (MOUTH)

Ps 78: 36 would flatter him with their *m*,
Eze 33: 31 With their *m* they express devotion
Ro 3: 14 "Their *m* are full of cursing
Eph 4: 29 talk come out of your *m*,
Jas 3: 3 bits into the *m* of horses

MOVE (MOVED MOVES)

Dt 19: 14 Do not *m* your neighbour's
Pr 23: 10 Do not *m* an ancient boundary
Ac 17: 28 and *m* and have our being.'
1Co 13: 2 have a faith that can *m* mountains,
    15: 58 Let nothing *m* you.

MOVED (MOVE)

Ex 35: 21 and whose heart *m* him came
2Ch 36: 22 the LORD *m* the heart
Ezr 1: 5 everyone whose heart God had *m*
Ps 93: 1 it cannot be *m*.
Jn 11: 33 he was deeply *m* in spirit
Col 1: 23 not *m* from the hope held out

MOVES (MOVE)

Dt 23: 14 For the LORD your God *m* about

MUD (MUDDIED)

Ps 40: 2 out of the *m* and mire;
Isa 57: 20 whose waves cast up mire and *m*.
Jn 9: 6 made some *m* with the saliva,
2Pe 2: 22 back to her wallowing in the *m*."

MUDDIED (MUD)

Pr 25: 26 Like a *m* spring or a polluted well
Eze 32: 13 or *m* by the hoofs of cattle.

MULBERRY*

Lk 17: 6 you can say to this *m* tree,

MULTITUDE (MULTITUDES)

Isa 31: 1 who trust in the *m* of their chariots
Jas 5: 20 and cover over a *m* of sins.
1Pe 4: 8 love covers over a *m* of sins.
Rev 7: 9 me was a great *m* that no-one could
19: 1 of a great *m* in heaven shouting:

MULTITUDES (MULTITUDE)

Ne 9: 6 and the *m* of heaven worship you.
Da 12: 2 *M* who sleep in the dust
Joel 3: 14 *M, m* in the valley of decision!

MURDER (MURDERED MURDERER MURDERERS)

Ex 20: 13 "You shall not *m.*
Dt 5: 17 "You shall not *m.*
Pr 28: 17 A man tormented by the guilt of *m*
Mt 5: 21 'Do not *m,* and anyone who
15: 19 *m,* adultery, sexual immorality,
Ro 1: 29 *m,* strife, deceit and malice.
13: 9 "Do not *m,*" "Do not steal,"
Jas 2: 11 adultery," also said, "Do not *m.*"

MURDERED (MURDER)

Mt 23: 31 of those who *m* the prophets.
Ac 7: 52 now you have betrayed and *m* him
1Jn 3: 12 to the evil one and *m* his brother.

MURDERER (MURDER)

Nu 35: 16 he is a *m;* the *m* shall be put
Jn 8: 44 He was a *m* from the beginning,
1Jn 3: 15 who hates his brother is a *m,*

MURDERERS (MURDER)

1Ti 1: 9 for *m,* for adulterers and perverts,
Rev 21: 8 the *m,* the sexually immoral,
22: 15 the sexually immoral, the *m,*

MUSIC* (MUSICAL MUSICIAN MUSICIANS)

Ge 31: 27 singing to the *m* of tambourines
Jdg 5: 3 I will make *m* to the LORD,
1Ch 6: 31 put in charge of the *m* in the house
6: 32 They ministered with *m*
25: 6 fathers for the *m* of the temple
25: 7 and skilled in *m* for the LORD—
Ne 12: 27 and with the *m* of cymbals,
Job 21: 12 They sing to the *m* of tambourine
Ps 27: 6 and make *m* to the LORD.
33: 2 make *m* to him on the ten-stringed
45: 8 the *m* of the strings makes you glad
57: 7 I will sing and make *m.*
81: 2 Begin the *m,* strike the tambourine,
87: 7 As they make *m* they will sing,
92: 1 and make *m* to your name,
92: 3 to the *m* of the ten-stringed lyre
95: 2 and extol him with *m* and song.
98: 4 burst into jubilant song with *m;*
98: 5 make *m* to the LORD
108: 1 make *m* with all my soul.
144: 9 the ten-stringed lyre I will make *m*
147: 7 make *m* to our God on the harp.
149: 3 make *m* to him with tambourine
Isa 30: 32 will be to the *m* of tambourines

La 5: 14 young men have stopped their *m.*
Eze 26: 13 *m* of your harps will be heard no
Da 3: 5 lyre, harp, pipes and all kinds of *m,*
3: 7 and all kinds of *m,* all the peoples,
3: 10 and all kinds of *m* must fall down
3: 15 lyre, harp, pipes and all kinds of *m,*
Am 5: 23 to the *m* of your harps.
Hab 3: 19 For the director of *m.*
Lk 15: 25 came near the house, he heard *m*
Eph 5: 19 make *m* in your heart to the Lord,
Rev 18: 22 The *m* of harpists and musicians,

MUSICAL* (MUSIC)

1Ch 15: 16 accompanied by *m* instruments:
23: 5 with the *m* instruments I have
2Ch 7: 6 with the LORD's *m* instruments,
23: 13 with *m* instruments were leading
34: 12 skilled in playing *m* instruments—
Ne 12: 36 with *m* instruments prescribed
Am 6: 5 and improvise on *m* instruments.

MUSICIAN* (MUSIC)

1Ch 6: 33 Heman, the *m,* the son of Joel,

MUSICIANS* (MUSIC)

1Ki 10: 12 to make harps and lyres for the *m.*
1Ch 9: 33 Those who were *m,* heads
15: 19 The *m* Heman, Asaph
2Ch 5: 12 All the Levites who were *m—*
9: 11 to make harps and lyres for the *m.*
35: 15 The *m,* the descendants of Asaph,
Ps 68: 25 are the singers, after them the *m;*
Rev 18: 22 The music of harpists and *m,*

MUSTARD

Mt 13: 31 kingdom of heaven is like a *m* seed,
17: 20 you have faith as small as a *m* seed,
Mk 4: 31 It is like a *m* seed, which is

MUTE

Mk 7: 37 the deaf hear and the *m* speak."
1Co 12: 2 and led astray to *m* idols.

MUTILATORS*

Php 3: 2 those men who do evil, those *m*

MUTUAL* (MUTUALLY)

Ro 14: 19 leads to peace and to *m* edification.
1Co 7: 5 by *m* consent and for a time,

MUTUALLY* (MUTUAL)

Ro 1: 12 and I may be *m* encouraged

MUZZLE*

Dt 25: 4 Do not *m* an ox while it is treading
Ps 39: 1 I will put a *m* on my mouth
1Co 9: 9 "Do not *m* an ox while it is
1Ti 5: 18 "Do not *m* the ox while it is

MYRRH

Ps 45: 8 All your robes are fragrant with *m*
SS 1: 13 My lover is to me a sachet of *m*
Mt 2: 11 of gold and of incense and of *m.*
Mk 15: 23 offered him wine mixed with *m,*
Jn 19: 39 Nicodemus brought a mixture of *m*
Rev 18: 13 of incense, *m* and frankincense,

MYSTERIES* (MYSTERY)

Job 11: 7 "Can you fathom the *m* of God?
Da 2: 28 a God in heaven who reveals *m.*

Da   2: 29 of *m* showed you what is going
      2: 47 Lord of kings and a revealer of *m*,
1Co 13: 2 can explain all *m* and all knowledge
     14: 2 he utters *m* with his spirit.

MYSTERY* (MYSTERIES)

Da   2: 18 God of heaven concerning this *m*,
      2: 19 the night the *m* was revealed
      2: 27 to the king the *m* he has asked
      2: 30 this *m* has been revealed to me,
      2: 47 for you were able to reveal this *m*."
      4: 9 and no *m* is too difficult for you.
Ro   11: 25 you to be ignorant of this *m*,
     16: 25 to the revelation of the *m* hidden
1Co 15: 51 I tell you a *m*: We will not all sleep,
Eph   1: 9 to us the *m* of his will according
      3: 3 the *m* made known to me
      3: 4 insight into the *m* of Christ,
      3: 6 This *m* is that through the gospel
      3: 9 the administration of this *m*,
      5: 32 This is a profound *m*—
      6: 19 I will fearlessly make known the *m*
Col   1: 26 the *m* that has been kept hidden
      1: 27 the glorious riches of this *m*,
      2: 2 in order that they may know the *m*
      4: 3 so that we may proclaim the *m*
1Ti   3: 16 the *m* of godliness is great:
Rev   1: 20 *m* of the seven stars that you saw
     10: 7 the *m* of God will be accomplished,
     17: 5 written on her forehead: *M*
     17: 7 explain to you the *m* of the woman

MYTHS*

1Ti   1: 4 nor to devote themselves to *m*
      4: 7 Have nothing to do with godless *m*
2Ti   4: 4 from the truth and turn aside to *m*.
Tit   1: 14 will pay no attention to Jewish *m*

NAAMAN

Aramean general whose leprosy was cleansed by
Elisha (2Ki 5).

NABAL

Wealthy Carmelite the LORD killed for refusing
to help David (1Sa 25). David married Abigail, his
widow (1Sa 25:39–42).

NABOTH*

Jezreelite killed by Jezebel for his vineyard (1Ki
21). Ahab's family destroyed for this (1Ki
21:17-24; 2Ki 9:21-37).

NADAB

1. Firstborn of Aaron (Ex 6:23); killed with
Abihu for offering unauthorised fire (Lev 10; Nu
3:4).
2. Son of Jeroboam I; king of Israel (1Ki
15:25-32).

NAHUM

Prophet against Nineveh (Na 1:1).

NAIL* (NAILING)

Jn   20: 25 "Unless I see the *n* marks

NAILING* (NAIL)

Ac   2: 23 him to death by *n* him to the cross.
Col   2: 14 he took it away, *n* it to the cross.

NAIVE

Ro   16: 18 they deceive the minds of *n* people.

NAKED

Ge   2: 25 The man and his wife were both *n*,
Job   1: 21 *N* I came from my mother's womb,
Isa 58: 7 when you see the *n*, to clothe him,
2Co   5: 3 are clothed, we will not be found *n*.

NAME (NAMES)

Ge   2: 19 man to see what he would *n* them;
      4: 26 to call on the *n* of the LORD.
     11: 4 so that we may make a *n*
     12: 2 I will make your *n* great,
     32: 29 Jacob said, "Please tell me your *n*."
Ex   3: 15 This is my *n* for ever, the *n*
     20: 7 "You shall not misuse the *n*
     34: 14 for the LORD, whose *n* is Jealous,
Lev 24: 11 Israelite woman blasphemed the *N*
Dt   5: 11 "You shall not misuse the *n*
     12: 11 choose as a dwelling for his *N*—
     18: 5 minister in the LORD's *n* always.
     25: 6 carry on the *n* of the dead brother
     28: 58 this glorious and awesome *n*—
Jos   7: 9 do for your own great *n*?"
Jdg 13: 17 "What is your *n*, so that we may
1Sa 12: 22 of his great *n* the LORD will not
2Sa   6: 2 which is called by the *N*, the *n*
      7: 9 Now I will make your *n* great,
1Ki   5: 5 will build the temple for my *N*.'
      8: 29 you said, 'My *N* shall be there,'
1Ch 17: 8 I will make your *n* like the names
2Ch   7: 14 my people, who are called by my *n*,
Ne   9: 10 You made a *n* for yourself,
Ps   8: 1 how majestic is your *n*
      9: 10 Those who know your *n* will trust
     20: 7 in the *n* of the LORD our God.
     29: 2 to the LORD the glory due his *n*;
     34: 3 let us exalt his *n* together.
     44: 20 If we had forgotten the *n*
     66: 2 Sing the glory of his *n*;
     68: 4 Sing to God, sing praise to his *n*,
     79: 9 for the glory of your *n*;
     96: 8 to the LORD the glory due his *n*;
    103: 1 my inmost being, praise his holy *n*.
    115: 1 but to your *n* be the glory,
    138: 2 your *n* and your word.
    145: 1 I will praise your *n* for ever
    147: 4 and calls them each by *n*.
Pr   3: 4 you will win favour and a good *n*
     18: 10 *n* of the LORD is a strong tower,
     22: 1 A good *n* is more desirable
     30: 4 What is his *n*, and the *n* of his son?
Ecc   7: 1 A good *n* is better
SS   1: 3 your *n* is like perfume poured out.
Isa 12: 4 thanks to the LORD, call on his *n*;
     26: 8 your *n* and renown
     40: 26 and calls them each by *n*.
     42: 8 "I am the LORD; that is my *n*!
     56: 5 I will give them an everlasting *n*
     57: 15 who lives for ever, whose *n* is holy:
     63: 14 to make for yourself a glorious *n*.
Jer 14: 7 do something for the sake of your *n*
     15: 16 for I bear your *n*,
Eze 20: 9 of my *n* I did what would keep it
     20: 14 of my *n* I did what would keep it
     20: 22 of my *n* I did what would keep it
Da   12: 1 everyone whose *n* is found written
Hos 12: 5 the LORD is his *n* of renown!

Joel 2:32 on the *n* of the LORD will be saved
Mic 5: 4 in the majesty of the *n*
Zep 3: 9 call on the *n* of the LORD
Zec 6:12 is the man whose *n* is the Branch,
14: 9 one LORD, and his *n* the only *n*.
Mal 1: 6 O priests, who show contempt for my *n*.
Mt 1:21 and you are to give him the *n* Jesus,
6: 9 hallowed be your *n*,
18:20 or three come together in my *n*,
24: 5 For many will come in my *n*,
28:19 them in the *n* of the Father
Mk 9:41 gives you a cup of water in my *n*
Lk 11: 2 hallowed be your *n*,
Jn 10: 3 He calls his own sheep by *n*
14:13 I will do whatever you ask in my *n*,
16:24 asked for anything in my *n*.
Ac 2:21 on the *n* of the Lord will be saved.'
4:12 for there is no other *n*
Ro 10:13 "Everyone who calls on the *n*
Php 2: 9 him the *n* that is above every *n*,
2:10 at the *n* of Jesus every knee should
Col 3:17 do it all in the *n* of the Lord Jesus,
Heb 1: 4 as the *n* he has inherited is superior
Jas 5:14 him with oil in the *n* of the Lord.
1Jn 5:13 believe in the *n* of the Son of God
Rev 2:17 stone with a new *n* written on it,
3: 5 I will never blot out his *n*
3:12 I will also write on him my new *n*.
19:13 and his *n* is the Word of God.
20:15 If anyone's *n* was not found written

NAMES (NAME)

Ex 28: 9 engrave on them the *n* of the sons
Lk 10:20 but rejoice that your *n* are written
Php 4: 3 whose *n* are in the book of life.
Heb 12:23 whose *n* are written in heaven.
Rev 21:27 but only those whose *n* are written

NAOMI

Wife of Elimelech, mother-in-law of Ruth (Ru 1:2, 4). Left Bethlehem for Moab during famine (Ru 1:1). Returned a widow, with Ruth (Ru 1:6-22). Advised Ruth to seek marriage with Boaz (Ru 2:17-3:4). Cared for Ruth's son Obed (Ru 4:13-17).

NAPHTALI

Son of Jacob by Bilhah (Ge 30:8; 35:25; 1Ch 2:2). Tribe of blessed (Ge 49:21; Dt 33:23), numbered (Nu 1:43; 26:50), allotted land (Jos 19:32-39; Eze 48:3), failed to fully possess (Jdg 1:33), supported Deborah (Jdg 4:10; 5:18), David (1Ch 12:34), 12,000 from (Rev 7:6).

NARROW

Mt 7:13 "Enter through the *n* gate.
7:14 and *n* the road that leads to life,

NATHAN

Prophet and chronicler of Israel's history (1Ch 29:29; 2Ch 9:29). Announced the Davidic covenant (2Sa 7; 1Ch 17). Denounced David's sin with Bathsheba (2Sa 12). Supported Solomon (1Ki 1).

NATHANAEL*

Apostle (Jn 1:45-49; 21:2). Probably also called Bartholomew (Mt 10:3).

NATION (NATIONS)

Ge 12: 2 "I will make you into a great *n*

Ex 19: 6 a kingdom of priests and a holy *n*.'
Dt 4: 7 What other *n* is so great
Jos 5: 8 And after the whole *n* had been
2Sa 7:23 one *n* on earth that God went out
Ps 33:12 Blessed is the *n* whose God is
Pr 11:14 For lack of guidance a *n* falls,
14:34 Righteousness exalts a *n*,
Isa 2: 4 *N* will not take up sword
26: 2 that the righteous *n* may enter,
60:12 For the *n* or kingdom that will not
65: 1 To a *n* that did not call on my name
66: 8 a *n* be brought forth in a moment?
Mic 4: 3 *N* will not take up sword
Mt 24: 7 *N* will rise against *n*,
Mk 13: 8 *N* will rise against *n*,
1Pe 2: 9 a royal priesthood, a holy *n*,
Rev 5: 9 and language and people and *n*.
7: 9 from every *n*, tribe, people
14: 6 to every *n*, tribe, language

NATIONS (NATION)

Ge 17: 4 You will be the father of many *n*.
18:18 and all *n* on earth will be blessed
Ex 19: 5 of all *n* you will be my treasured
Lev 20:26 apart from the *n* to be my own.
Dt 7: 1 drives out before you many *n*—
15: 6 You will rule over many *n*
Jdg 3: 1 These are the *n* the LORD left
2Ch 20: 6 rule over all the kingdoms of the *n*.
Ne 1: 8 I will scatter you among the *n*,
Ps 2: 1 Why do the *n* conspire
2: 8 I will make the *n* your inheritance,
9: 5 You have rebuked the *n*
22:28 and he rules over the *n*.
46:10 I will be exalted among the *n*,
47: 8 God reigns over the *n*;
66: 7 his eyes watch the *n*—
67: 2 your salvation among all *n*.
68:30 Scatter the *n* who delight in war.
72:17 All *n* will be blessed through him.
96: 3 Declare his glory among the *n*,
99: 2 he is exalted over all the *n*.
106:35 but they mingled with the *n*
110: 6 He will judge the *n*, heaping up
113: 4 The LORD is exalted over all the *n*
Isa 2: 2 and all *n* will stream to it.
11:10 the *n* will rally to him,
12: 4 among the *n* what he has done,
40:15 Surely the *n* are like a drop
42: 1 and he will bring justice to the *n*.
51: 4 justice will become a light to the *n*.
52:15 so will he sprinkle many *n*,
56: 7 a house of prayer for all *n*."
60: 3 *N* will come to your light,
66:18 and gather all *n* and tongues,
Jer 1: 5 you as a prophet to the *n*."
3:17 and all *n* will gather in Jerusalem
31:10 "Hear the word of the LORD, O *n*;
33: 9 and honour before all *n*
46:28 I completely destroy all the *n*
Eze 22: 4 you an object of scorn to the *n*
34:13 I will bring them out from the *n*
36:23 *n* will know that I am the LORD,
37:22 and they will never again be two *n*
39:21 I will display my glory among the *n*
Hos 7: 8 "Ephraim mixes with the *n*;
Joel 2:17 a byword among the *n*.
3: 2 I will gather all *n*
Am 9:12 and all the *n* that bear my name,"
Zep 3: 8 I have decided to assemble the *n*,

Hag 2: 7 and the desired of all *n* will come,
Zec 8: 13 an object of cursing among the *n*,
8: 23 *n* will take firm hold of one Jew
9: 10 He will proclaim peace to the *n*,
14: 2 I will gather all the *n* to Jerusalem
Mt 12: 18 he will proclaim justice to the *n*.
24: 9 and you will be hated by all *n*
24: 14 whole world as a testimony to all *n*,
25: 32 All the *n* will be gathered
28: 19 and make disciples of all *n*,
Mk 11: 17 a house of prayer for all *n*'?
Ac 4: 25 "'Why do the *n* rage
Ro 15: 12 who will arise to rule over the *n*;
Gal 3: 8 All *n* will be blessed through you."
1Ti 3: 16 was preached among the *n*,
Rev 15: 4 All *n* will come
21: 24 Then *n* will walk by its light,
22: 2 are for the healing of the *n*.

NATURAL (NATURE)

Ro 6: 19 you are weak in your *n* selves.
1Co 15: 44 If there is a *n* body, there is

NATURE (NATURAL)

Ro 1: 20 his eternal power and divine *n*—
7: 18 lives in me, that is, in my sinful *n*.
8: 4 do not live according to the sinful *n*
8: 5 to the sinful *n* have their minds set
8: 8 by the sinful *n* cannot please God.
13: 14 to gratify the desires of the sinful *n*.
Gal 5: 13 freedom to indulge the sinful *n*;
5: 19 The acts of the sinful *n* are obvious:
5: 24 Jesus have crucified the sinful *n*
Php 2: 6 Who, being in very *n* God,
Col 3: 5 whatever belongs to your earthly *n*
2Pe 1: 4 you may participate in the divine *n*

NAZARENE* (NAZARETH)

Mt 2: 23 prophets: "He will be called a *N*."
Mk 14: 67 "You also were with that *N*, Jesus,"
16: 6 "You are looking for Jesus the *N*,
Ac 24: 5 He is a ringleader of the *N* sect and

NAZARETH (NAZARENE)

Mt 4: 13 Leaving *N*, he went and lived
Lk 4: 16 to *N*, where he had been brought
Jn 1: 46 "*N*! Can anything good come

NAZIRITE

Nu 6: 2 of separation to the LORD as a *N*,
Jdg 13: 7 because the boy will be a *N* of God

NEBO

Dt 34: 1 Then Moses climbed Mount *N*

NEBUCHADNEZZAR

Babylonian king. Subdued and exiled Judah (2Ki 24-25; 2Ch 36; Jer 39). Dreams interpreted by Daniel (Da 2; 4). Worshipped God (Da 3:28-29; 4:34-37).

NECESSARY*

Ac 1: 21 Therefore it is *n* to choose one
Ro 13: 5 it is *n* to submit to the authorities,
2Co 9: 5 I thought it *n* to urge the brothers
Php 1: 24 it is more *n* for you that I remain
2: 25 But I think it is *n* to send back
Heb 8: 3 and so it was *n* for this one
9: 16 it is *n* to prove the death
9: 23 It was *n*, then, for the copies

NECK (STIFF-NECKED)

Pr 3: 22 an ornament to grace your *n*.
6: 21 fasten them around your *n*.
Mt 18: 6 a large millstone hung around his *n*

NECO

Pharaoh who killed Josiah (2Ki 23:29-30; 2Ch 35:20-22), deposed Jehoahaz (2Ki 23:33-35; 2Ch 36:3-4).

NEED (NEEDS NEEDY)

1Ki 8: 59 Israel according to each day's *n*,
Ps 79: 8 for we are in desperate *n*.
116: 6 when I was in great *n*, he saved me.
142: 6 for I am in desperate *n*;
Mt 6: 8 for your Father knows what you *n*
Lk 15: 14 country, and he began to be in *n*.
Ac 2: 45 they gave to anyone as he had *n*.
Ro 12: 13 with God's people who are in *n*.
1Co 12: 21 say to the hand, "I don't *n* you!"
Eph 4: 28 something to share with those in *n*.
1Ti 5: 3 to those widows who are really in *n*
Heb 4: 16 grace to help us in our time of *n*.
1Jn 3: 17 sees his brother in *n* but has no pity

NEEDLE

Mt 19: 24 go through the eye of a *n*

NEEDS (NEED)

Isa 58: 11 he will satisfy your *n*
Php 2: 25 sent to take care of my *n*.
4: 19 God will meet all your *n* according
Jas 2: 16 does nothing about his physical *n*,

NEEDY (NEED)

Dt 15: 11 towards the poor and *n* in your land.
1Sa 2: 8 and lifts the *n* from the ash heap;
Ps 35: 10 and *n* from those who rob them.
69: 33 The LORD hears the *n*
72: 12 he will deliver the *n* who cry out,
140: 12 and upholds the cause of the *n*.
Pr 14: 21 blessed is he who is kind to the *n*.
14: 31 to the *n* honours God.
22: 22 and do not crush the *n* in court,
31: 9 defend the rights of the poor and *n*
31: 20 and extends her hands to the *n*.
Mt 6: 2 "So when you give to the *n*,

NEGLECT* (NEGLECTED)

Dt 12: 19 Be careful not to *n* the Levites
14: 27 And do not *n* the Levites living
Ezr 4: 22 Be careful not to *n* this matter.
Ne 10: 39 We will not *n* the house of our God
Est 6: 10 Do not *n* anything you have
Ps 119: 16 I will not *n* your word.
Lk 11: 42 you *n* justice and the love of God.
Ac 6: 2 for us to *n* the ministry of the word
1Ti 4: 14 Do not *n* your gift, which was

NEGLECTED (NEGLECT)

Mt 23: 23 But you have *n* the more important

NEHEMIAH

Cupbearer of Artaxerxes (Ne 2:1); governor of Israel (Ne 8:9). Returned to Jerusalem to rebuild walls (Ne 2-6). With Ezra, re-established worship (Ne 8). Prayer confessing nation's sin (Ne 9). Dedicated wall (Ne 12).

NEIGHBOUR (NEIGHBOUR'S)

Ex 20: 16 give false testimony against your *n*.

Ex   20: 17 or anything that belongs to your *n*
Lev   19: 13 Do not defraud your *n* or rob him.
      19: 17 Rebuke your *n* frankly
      19: 18 but love your *n* as yourself.
Ps   15: 3 who does his *n* no wrong
Pr   3: 29 Do not plot harm against your *n*,
      11: 12 who lacks judgment derides his *n*,
      14: 21 He who despises his *n* sins,
      16: 29 A violent man entices his *n*
      24: 28 against your *n* without cause,
      25: 18 gives false testimony against his *n*.
      27: 10 better a *n* near by than a brother far
      27: 14 If a man loudly blesses his *n*
      29: 5 Whoever flatters his *n*
Jer   31: 34 No longer will a man teach his *n*,
Zec   8: 17 do not plot evil against your *n*,
Mt   5: 43 Love your *n* and hate your enemy.'
      19: 19 and 'love your *n* as yourself.'"
Mk   12: 31 The second is this: 'Love your *n*
Lk   10: 27 and, 'Love your *n* as yourself.'"
      10: 29 who is my *n*?" In reply Jesus said:
Ro   13: 9 "Love your *n* as yourself."
      13: 10 Love does no harm to its *n*.
      15: 2 Each of us should please his *n*
Gal   5: 14 "Love your *n* as yourself."
Eph   4: 25 and speak truthfully to his *n*,
Heb   8: 11 No longer will a man teach his *n*,
Jas   2: 8 "Love your *n* as yourself,"

NEIGHBOUR'S (NEIGHBOUR)

Ex   20: 17 You shall not covet your *n* wife,
Dt   5: 21 not set your desire on your *n* house
      19: 14 not move your *n* boundary stone
      27: 17 who moves his *n* boundary stone."
Pr   25: 17 Seldom set foot in your *n* house—

NESTS

Mt   8: 20 and birds of the air have *n*,

NET (NETS)

Pr   1: 17 How useless to spread a *n*
Hab   1: 15 he catches them in his *n*,
Mt   13: 47 of heaven is like a *n* that was let
Jn   21: 6 "Throw your *n* on the right side

NETS (NET)

Ps   141: 10 Let the wicked fall into their own *n*
Mt   4: 20 At once they left their *n*
Lk   5: 4 and let down the *n* for a catch."

NEVER-FAILING*

Am   5: 24 righteousness like a *n* stream!

NEW

Ps   40: 3 He put a *n* song in my mouth,
      98: 1 Sing to the LORD a *n* song,
Ecc   1: 9 there is nothing *n* under the sun.
Isa   42: 9 and *n* things I declare;
      62: 2 you will be called by a *n* name
      65: 17 *n* heavens and a *n* earth.
      66: 22 "As the *n* heavens and the *n* earth
Jer   31: 31 "when I will make a *n* covenant
La   3: 23 They are *n* every morning;
Eze   11: 19 undivided heart and put a *n* spirit
      18: 31 and get a *n* heart and a *n* spirit.
      36: 26 give you a *n* heart and put a *n* spirit
Zep   3: 5 and every *n* day he does not fail,
Mt   9: 17 Neither do men pour *n* wine
Mk   16: 17 they will speak in *n* tongues;
Lk   5: 39 after drinking old wine wants the *n*

Lk   22: 20 "This cup is the *n* covenant
Jn   13: 34 "A *n* commandment I give you:
Ac   5: 20 the full message of this *n* life."
Ro   6: 4 the Father, we too may live a *n* life.
1Co   5: 7 old yeast that you may be a *n* batch
      11: 25 "This cup is the *n* covenant
2Co   3: 6 as ministers of a *n* covenant—
       5: 17 he is a *n* creation; the old has gone,
Gal   6: 15 what counts is a *n* creation.
Eph   4: 23 to be made *n* in the attitude
       4: 24 and to put on the *n* self, created
Col   3: 10 and have put on the *n* self,
Heb   8: 8 when I will make a *n* covenant
       9: 15 is the mediator of a *n* covenant,
      10: 20 by a *n* and living way opened for us
      12: 24 Jesus the mediator of a *n* covenant,
1Pe   1: 3 great mercy he has given us *n* birth
2Pe   3: 13 to a *n* heaven and a *n* earth,
1Jn   2: 8 Yet I am writing you a *n* command;
Rev   2: 17 stone with a *n* name written on it,
       3: 12 the *n* Jerusalem, which is coming
      21: 1 I saw a *n* heaven and a *n* earth,

NEWBORN (BEAR [1])

1Pe   2: 2 Like *n* babies, crave pure spiritual

NEWS

2Ki   7: 9 This is a day of good *n*
Ps   112: 7 He will have no fear of bad *n*;
Pr   15: 30 good *n* gives health to the bones.
      25: 25 is good *n* from a distant land.
Isa   52: 7 the feet of those who bring good *n*,
      61: 1 me to preach good *n* to the poor.
Na   1: 15 the feet of one who brings good *n*,
Mt   4: 23 preaching the good *n*
       9: 35 preaching the good *n*
      11: 5 the good *n* is preached to the poor.
Mk   1: 15 Repent and believe the good *n*!"
      16: 15 preach the good *n* to all creation.
Lk   1: 19 and to tell you this good *n*.
       2: 10 I bring you good *n*
       3: 18 and preached the good *n* to them.
       4: 43 "I must preach the good *n*
       8: 1 proclaiming the good *n*
      16: 16 the good *n* of the kingdom
Ac   5: 42 proclaiming the good *n* that Jesus
      10: 36 telling the good *n* of peace
      14: 7 continued to preach the good *n*.
      14: 21 They preached the good *n*
      17: 18 preaching the good *n* about Jesus
Ro   10: 15 feet of those who bring good *n*!"

NICODEMUS*

Pharisee who visited Jesus at night (Jn 3).
Argued fair treatment of Jesus (Jn 7:50-52). With
Joseph, prepared Jesus for burial (Jn 19:38-42).

NIGHT (NIGHT-TIME NIGHTS)

Ge   1: 5 and the darkness he called "*n*".
       1: 16 and the lesser light to govern the *n*.
Ex   13: 21 and by *n* in a pillar of fire
Dt   28: 66 filled with dread both *n* and day,
Jos   1: 8 and *n*, so that you may be careful
Job   35: 10 who gives songs in the *n*,
Ps   1: 2 on his law he meditates day and *n*.
      19: 2 *n* after *n* they display knowledge.
      42: 8 at *n* his song is with me—
      63: 6 of you through the watches of the *n*
      77: 6 I remembered my songs in the *n*.
      90: 4 or like a watch in the *n*.

Ps   91: 5 You will not fear the terror of *n*,
      119: 148 through the watches of the *n*,
      121: 6 nor the moon by *n*.
      136: 9 the moon and stars to govern the *n*;
Pr   31: 18 and her lamp does not go out at *n*.
Isa   21: 11 Watchman, what is left of the *n*?"
      58: 10 and your *n* will become like
Jer   33: 20 and my covenant with the *n*,
Lk   2: 8 watch over their flocks at *n*.
       6: 12 and spent the *n* praying to God.
Jn   3: 2 He came to Jesus at *n* and said,
       9: 4 *N* is coming, when no-one can work
1Th   5: 2 Lord will come like a thief in the *n*.
       5: 5 We do not belong to the *n*
Rev   21: 25 for there will be no *n* there.

NIGHT-TIME* (NIGHT)

Zec   14: 7 or *n*—a day known to the LORD.

NIGHTS (NIGHT)

Jnh   1: 17 the fish three days and three *n*.
Mt   4: 2 After fasting forty days and forty *n*
      12: 40 three *n* in the belly of a huge fish,
2Co   6: 5 in hard work, sleepless *n*

NIMROD

Ge   10: 9 "Like *N*, a mighty hunter

NINEVEH

Jnh   1: 2 "Go to the great city of *N*
Na   1: 1 An oracle concerning *N*.
Mt   12: 41 The men of *N* will stand up

NOAH

Righteous man (Eze 14:14, 20) called to build
ark (Ge 6-8; Heb 11:7; 1Pe 3:20; 2Pe 2:5). God's
covenant with (Ge 9:1-17). Drunkenness of (Ge
9:18-23). Blessed sons, cursed Canaan (Ge
9:24-27).

NOBLE

Ru   3: 11 you are a woman of *n* character.
Ps   45: 1 My heart is stirred by a *n* theme
Pr   12: 4 of *n* character is her husband's
      31: 10 A wife of *n* character who can find?
      31: 29 "Many women do *n* things,
Isa   32: 8 But the *n* man makes *n* plans,
Lk   8: 15 good soil stands for those with a *n*
Ro   9: 21 of clay some pottery for *n* purposes
Php   4: 8 whatever is *n*, whatever is right,
2Ti   2: 20 some are for *n* purposes

NOSTRILS

Ge   2: 7 and breathed into his *n* the breath
Ex   15: 8 By the blast of your *n*
Ps   18: 15 at the blast of breath from your *n*.

NOTE

Ac   4: 13 and they took *n* that these men had
Php   3: 17 take *n* of those who live according

NOTHING

2Sa   24: 24 offerings that cost me *n*."
Ne   9: 21 in the desert; they lacked *n*,
Jer   32: 17 *N* is too hard for you
Jn   15: 5 apart from me you can do *n*.

NOURISH

Pr   10: 21 The lips of the righteous *n* many,

NULLIFY

Mt   15: 6 Thus you *n* the word of God
Ro   3: 31 Do we, then, *n* the law by this faith

OATH

Ex   33: 1 up to the land I promised on *o*
Nu   30: 2 or takes an *o* to obligate himself
Dt   6: 18 promised on *o* to your forefathers,
       7: 8 and kept the *o* he swore
      29: 12 you this day and sealing with an *o*,
Ps   95: 11 So I declared on *o* in my anger,
      119: 106 I have taken an *o* and confirmed it,
      132: 11 The LORD swore an *o* to David,
Ecc   8: 2 because you took an *o* before God.
Mt   5: 33 'Do not break your *o*, but keep
Heb   7: 20 And it was not without an *o*!

OBADIAH

1. Believer who sheltered 100 prophets from
Jezebel (1Ki 18:1-16).
2. Prophet against Edom (Ob 1).

OBEDIENCE* (OBEY)

Ge   49: 10 and the *o* of the nations is his.
Jdg   2: 17 of *o* to the LORD's commands.
1Ch   21: 19 So David went up in *o*
2Ch   31: 21 in *o* to the law and the commands,
Pr   30: 17 that scorns *o* to a mother,
Lk   23: 56 Sabbath in *o* to the commandment.
Ac   21: 24 but that you yourself are living in *o*
Ro   1: 5 to the *o* that comes from faith.
       5: 19 also through the *o* of the one man
       6: 16 to *o*, which leads to righteousness?
      16: 19 Everyone has heard about your *o*,
2Co   9: 13 for the *o* that accompanies your
      10: 6 once your *o* is complete.
Phm   : 21 Confident of your *o*, I write to you,
Heb   5: 8 he learned *o* from what he suffered
1Pe   1: 2 for *o* to Jesus Christ and sprinkling
2Jn   : 6 that we walk in *o* to his commands.

OBEDIENT* (OBEY)

Dt   30: 17 heart turns away and you are not *o*,
Isa   1: 19 If you are willing and *o*,
Lk   2: 51 with them and was *o* to them.
Ac   6: 7 of priests became *o* to the faith.
2Co   2: 9 if you would stand the test and be *o*
       7: 15 he remembers that you were all *o*,
      10: 5 thought to make it *o* to Christ.
Php   2: 8 and became *o* to death—
Tit   3: 1 to be *o*, to be ready
1Pe   1: 14 As *o* children, do not conform

OBEY (OBEDIENCE OBEDIENT OBEYED OBEYING OBEYS)

Ex   12: 24 "*O* these instructions as a lasting
      19: 5 Now if you *o* me fully and keep my
      24: 7 the LORD has said; we will *o*."
Lev   18: 4 You must *o* my laws and be careful
      25: 18 and be careful to *o* my laws,
Nu   15: 40 remember to *o* all my commands
Dt   5: 27 We will listen and *o*."
       6: 3 careful to *o* so that it may go well
       6: 24 us to *o* all these decrees
      11: 13 if you faithfully *o* the commands I
      12: 28 to *o* all these regulations I am
      13: 4 Keep his commands and *o* him,
      21: 18 son who does not *o* his father
      28: 1 If you fully *o* the LORD your God
      28: 15 if you do not *o* the LORD your

Dt   30: 2 and *o* him with all your heart
        30: 10 if you *o* the LORD your God
        30: 14 and in your heart so you may *o* it.
        32: 46 children to *o* carefully all the words
Jos   1: 7 to *o* all the law my servant Moses
        22: 5 in all his ways, to *o* his commands,
        24: 24 the LORD our God and *o* him."
1Sa   15: 22 To *o* is better than sacrifice,
1Ki   8: 61 by his decrees and *o* his commands
2Ki   17: 13 that I commanded your fathers to *o*
2Ch   34: 31 and to *o* the words of the covenant
Ne   1: 5 who love him and *o* his commands,
Ps   103: 18 and remember to *o* his precepts.
        103: 20 who *o* his word.
        119: 17 I will *o* your word.
        119: 34 and *o* it with all my heart.
        119: 57 I have promised to *o* your words.
        119: 67 but now I *o* your word.
        119: 100 for I *o* your precepts.
        119: 129 therefore I *o* them.
        119: 167 I *o* your statutes,
Pr   5: 13 I would not *o* my teachers
Jer   7: 23 I gave them this command: *O* me,
        11: 4 '*O* me and do everything I
        11: 7 and again, saying, "*O* me."
        42: 6 we will *o* the LORD our God,
Da   9: 4 who love him and *o* his commands,
Mt   8: 27 the winds and the waves *o* him!"
        19: 17 to enter life, *o* the commandments
        28: 20 to *o* everything I have commanded
Lk   11: 28 hear the word of God and *o* it."
Jn   14: 15 you will *o* what I command.
        14: 23 loves me, he will *o* my teaching.
        14: 24 not love me will not *o* my teaching.
        15: 10 If you *o* my commands, you will
Ac   5: 29 "We must *o* God rather than men!
        5: 32 given to those who *o* him."
Ro   2: 13 it is those who *o* the law who will
        6: 12 body so that you *o* its evil desires.
        6: 16 slaves to the one whom you *o*—
        6: 16 yourselves to someone to *o* him
        15: 18 in leading the Gentiles to *o* God
        16: 26 nations might believe and *o* him—
Gal   5: 3 obligated to *o* the whole law.
Eph   6: 1 *o* your parents in the Lord,
        6: 5 *o* your earthly masters with respect
Col   3: 20 *o* your parents in everything,
        3: 22 *o* your earthly masters
2Th   3: 14 anyone does not *o* our instruction
1Ti   3: 4 and see that his children *o* him
Heb   5: 9 eternal salvation for all who *o* him
        13: 17 *O* your leaders and submit
1Pe   4: 17 for those who do not *o* the gospel
1Jn   3: 24 Those who *o* his commands live
        5: 3 love for God: to *o* his commands.
Rev   12: 17 those who *o* God's commandments
        14: 12 the saints who *o* God's

OBEYED (OBEY)

Ge   22: 18 blessed, because you have *o* me."
Jos   1: 17 we fully *o* Moses, so we will obey
Ps   119: 4 that are to be fully *o*.
Da   9: 10 we have not *o* the LORD our God
Jnh   3: 3 Jonah *o* the word of the LORD
Mic   5: 15 the nations that have not *o* me."
Jn   15: 10 as I have *o* my Father's commands
        15: 20 If they *o* my teaching, they will
        17: 6 and they have *o* your word.
Ac   7: 53 through angels but have not *o* it."
Ro   6: 17 you wholeheartedly *o* the form

Php   2: 12 as you have always *o*—not only
Heb   11: 8 *o* and went, even though he did not
1Pe   3: 6 who *o* Abraham and called him her

OBEYING (OBEY)

1Sa   15: 22 as in *o* the voice of the LORD?
Ps   119: 5 steadfast in *o* your decrees!
Gal   5: 7 and kept you from *o* the truth?
1Pe   1: 22 purified yourselves by *o* the truth

OBEYS (OBEY)

Lev   18: 5 for the man who *o* them will live
Pr   19: 16 He who *o* instructions guards his
Eze   20: 11 for the man who *o* them will live
Jn   14: 21 has my commands and *o* them,
Ro   2: 27 and yet *o* the law will condemn you
1Jn   2: 5 if anyone *o* his word, God's love is

OBLIGATED (OBLIGATION)

Ro   1: 14 I am *o* both to Greeks

OBLIGATION (OBLIGATED)

Ro   8: 12 Therefore, brothers, we have an *o*

OBSCENITY*

Eph   5: 4 Nor should there be *o*, foolish talk

OBSCURES*

Job   42: 3 'Who is this that *o* my counsel

OBSERVE (OBSERVING)

Ex   31: 13 'You must *o* my Sabbaths.
Lev   25: 2 the land itself must *o* a sabbath
Dt   4: 6 *O* them carefully, for this will show
        5: 12 "*O* the Sabbath day
        8: 6 *O* the commands of the LORD
        11: 22 If you carefully *o* all these
        26: 16 carefully *o* them with all your heart
Ps   37: 37 the blameless, *o* the upright;

OBSERVING (OBSERVE)

Ro   3: 27 principle? On that of *o* the law?
Gal   2: 16 a man is not justified by *o* the law,
        3: 2 you receive the Spirit by *o* the law,
        3: 10 All who rely on *o* the law are

OBSOLETE

Heb   8: 13 he has made the first one *o*;

OBSTACLE* (OBSTACLES)

Ro   14: 13 or *o* in your brother's way.

OBSTACLES (OBSTACLE)

Ro   16: 17 put *o* in your way that are contrary

OBSTINATE

Isa   65: 2 hands to an *o* people,
Ro   10: 21 to a disobedient and *o* people."

OBTAIN (OBTAINED OBTAINS)

Ro   11: 7 sought so earnestly it did not *o*,
2Ti   2: 10 they too may *o* the salvation that

OBTAINED (OBTAIN)

Ro   9: 30 not pursue righteousness, have *o* it,
Php   3: 12 Not that I have already *o* all this,
Heb   9: 12 having *o* eternal redemption.

OBTAINS* (OBTAIN)

Pr   12: 2 A good man *o* favour

OBVIOUS*

Mt   6: 18   so that it will not be *o*
Gal   5: 19   The acts of the sinful nature are *o*:
1Ti   5: 24   The sins of some men are *o*,
       5: 25   In the same way, good deeds are *o*,

OCCASIONS

Eph   6: 18   in the Spirit in all *o* with all kinds

OFFENCE (OFFENCES OFFENDED OFFENDERS OFFENSIVE)

Pr   17: 9   over an *o* promotes love,
     19: 11   it is to his glory to overlook an *o*.
Gal   5: 11   In that case the *o* of the cross has

OFFENCES (OFFENCE)

Isa   44: 22   swept away your *o* like a cloud,
     59: 12   For our *o* are many in your sight,
Eze   18: 30   Repent! Turn away from all your *o*;
     33: 10   "Our *o* and sins weigh us down,

OFFENDED (OFFENCE)

Pr   18: 19   An *o* brother is more unyielding

OFFENDERS* (OFFENCE)

1Co   6: 9   nor homosexual *o* nor thieves

OFFENSIVE (OFFENCE)

Ps   139: 24   See if there is any *o* way in me,

OFFER (OFFERED OFFERING OFFERINGS OFFERS)

Ps   4: 5   *O* right sacrifices
     66: 2   *o* him glory and praise!
Ro   6: 13   Do not *o* the parts of your body
     12: 1   to *o* your bodies as living sacrifices,
Heb   9: 25   he enter heaven to *o* himself again
     13: 15   therefore, let us continually *o*

OFFERED (OFFER)

Isa   50: 6   I *o* my back to those who beat me,
1Co   9: 13   share in what is *o* on the altar?
     10: 20   of pagans are *o* to demons,
Heb   7: 27   once for all when he *o* himself.
     9: 14   the eternal Spirit *o* himself
     11: 4   By faith Abel *o* God a better
     11: 17   when God tested him, *o* Isaac
Jas   5: 15   prayer *o* in faith will make the sick

OFFERING (OFFER)

Ge   4: 3   of the soil as an *o* to the LORD.
     22: 2   a burnt *o* on one of the mountains I
     22: 8   provide the lamb for the burnt *o*,
Ex   29: 24   before the LORD as a wave *o*.
     29: 40   fourth of a hin of wine as a drink *o*.
Lev   1: 3   If the *o* is a burnt *o* from the herd,
     2: 4   " 'If you bring a grain *o* baked
     3: 1   " 'If someone's *o* is a fellowship *o*,
     4: 3   a sin *o* for the sin he has committed
     5: 15   It is a guilt *o*.
     7: 37   ordination *o* and the fellowship *o*,
     9: 24   and consumed the burnt *o*
     22: 18   to fulfil a vow or as a freewill *o*,
     22: 21   a special vow or as a freewill *o*,
1Sa   13: 9   And Saul offered up the burnt *o*.
1Ch   21: 26   from heaven on the altar of burnt *o*.
2Ch   7: 1   and consumed the burnt *o*
Ps   40: 6   Sacrifice and *o* you did not desire,
     116: 17   I will sacrifice a thank *o* to you
Isa   53: 10   the LORD makes his life a guilt *o*,

Mt   5: 23   if you are *o* your gift at the altar
Ro   8: 3   likeness of sinful man to be a sin *o*.
Eph   5: 2   as a fragrant *o* and sacrifice to God.
Php   2: 17   I am being poured out like a drink *o*,
     4: 18   are a fragrant *o*, an acceptable
2Ti   4: 6   being poured out like a drink *o*,
Heb   10: 5   "Sacrifice and *o* you did not desire,
1Pe   2: 5   *o* spiritual sacrifices acceptable

OFFERINGS (OFFER)

1Sa   15: 22   Does the LORD delight in burnt *o*
2Ch   35: 7   and goats for the Passover *o*,
Isa   1: 13   Stop bringing meaningless *o*!
Hos   6: 6   of God rather than burnt *o*.
Mal   3: 8   do we rob you?' "In tithes and *o*.
Mk   12: 33   is more important than all burnt *o*
Heb   10: 8   First he said, "Sacrifices and *o*,

OFFERS (OFFER)

Heb   10: 11   and again he *o* the same sacrifices,

OFFICER (OFFICIALS)

2Ti   2: 4   wants to please his commanding *o*.

OFFICIALS (OFFICER)

Pr   17: 26   or to flog *o* for their integrity.
     29: 12   all his *o* become wicked.

OFFSPRING

Ge   3: 15   and between your *o* and hers;
     12: 7   "To your *o* I will give this land."
     13: 16   I will make your *o* like the dust
     26: 4   and through your *o* all nations
     28: 14   blessed through you and your *o*.
Ex   13: 2   The first *o* of every womb
Ru   4: 12   Through the *o* the LORD gives
Isa   44: 3   I will pour out my Spirit on your *o*,
     53: 10   he will see his *o* and prolong his
Ac   3: 25   Through your *o* all peoples
     17: 28   own poets have said, 'We are his *o*.'
     17: 29   "Therefore since we are God's *o*,
Ro   4: 18   said to him, "So shall your *o* be."
     9: 8   who are regarded as Abraham's *o*.

OG

Nu   21: 33   *O* king of Bashan and his whole
Ps   136: 20   and *O* king of Bashan—

OIL

Ex   29: 7   Take the anointing *o* and anoint
     30: 25   It will be the sacred anointing *o*.
Dt   14: 23   tithe of your grain, new wine and *o*,
1Sa   10: 1   Then Samuel took a flask of *o*
     16: 13   So Samuel took the horn of *o*
1Ki   17: 16   and the jug of *o* did not run dry,
2Ki   4: 6   Then the *o* stopped flowing.
Ps   23: 5   You anoint my head with *o*;
     45: 7   by anointing you with the *o* of joy.
     104: 15   *o* to make his face shine,
     133: 2   It is like precious *o* poured
Pr   21: 17   loves wine and *o* will never be
Isa   1: 6   or soothed with *o*.
     61: 3   the *o* of gladness
Mt   25: 3   but did not take any *o* with them.
Heb   1: 9   by anointing you with the *o* of joy."

OLIVE (OLIVES)

Ge   8: 11   beak was a freshly plucked *o* leaf!
Jdg   9: 8   said to the *o* tree, 'Be our king.'
Jer   11: 16   LORD called you a thriving *o* tree

Zec   4: 3 Also there are two *o* trees by it,
Ro   11:17 and you, though a wild *o* shoot,
     11:24 of an *o* tree that is wild by nature,
Rev 11: 4 These are the two *o* trees

OLIVES (OLIVE)

Zec 14: 4 stand on the Mount of *O*,
Mt   24: 3 sitting on the Mount of *O*,
Jas   3:12 a fig-tree bear *o*, or a grapevine bear

OMEGA*

Rev   1: 8 "I am the Alpha and the *O*,"
     21: 6 I am the Alpha and the *O*,
     22:13 I am the Alpha and the *O*,

OMIT*

Jer 26: 2 I command you; do not *o* a word.

OMRI

King of Israel (1Ki 16:21-26).

ONESIMUS*

Col   4: 9 He is coming with *O*, our faithful
Phm   :10 I appeal to you for my son *O*,

ONESIPHORUS*

2Ti   1:16 mercy to the household of *O*,
      4:19 Aquila and the household of *O*.

ONIONS*

Nu   11: 5 melons, leeks, *o* and garlic.

ONYX

Ex   28: 9 "Take two *o* stones and engrave
     28:20 in the fourth row a chrysolite, an *o*

OPEN-HANDED* (HAND)

Dt   15: 8 Rather be *o* and freely lend him
     15:11 you to be *o* towards your brothers

OPINIONS*

1Ki 18:21 will you waver between two *o*?
Pr   18: 2 but delights in airing his own *o*.

OPPONENTS (OPPOSE)

Pr   18:18 and keeps strong *o* apart.

OPPORTUNE (OPPORTUNITY)

Lk   4:13 he left him until an *o* time.

OPPORTUNITY* (OPPORTUNE)

1Sa 18:21 "Now you have a second *o*
Jer 46:17 he has missed his *o*.'
Mt   26:16 watched for an *o* to hand him over.
Mk   14:11 So he watched for an *o* to hand him
Lk   22: 6 and watched for an *o* to hand Jesus
Ac   25:16 and has had an *o* to defend himself
Ro   7: 8 seizing the *o* afforded
      7:11 seizing the *o* afforded
1Co 16:12 but he will go when he has the *o*.
2Co   5:12 are giving you an *o* to take pride
     11:12 from under those who want an *o*
Gal   6:10 as we have *o*, let us do good
Eph   5:16 making the most of every *o*,
Php   4:10 but you had no *o* to show it.
Col   4: 5 make the most of every *o*.
1Ti   5:14 to give the enemy no *o* for slander.
Heb 11:15 they would have had *o* to return.

OPPOSE (OPPONENTS OPPOSED OPPOSES OPPOSING OPPOSITION)

Ex   23:22 and will *o* those who *o* you.
1Sa   2:10 those who *o* the LORD will be
Job 23:13 he stands alone, and who can *o* him
Ac   11:17 I to think that I could *o* God!"
2Ti   2:25 Those who *o* him he must gently
Tit   1: 9 doctrine and refute those who *o* it.
      2: 8 so that those who *o* you may be

OPPOSED (OPPOSE)

Gal   2:11 to Antioch, I *o* him to his face,
      3:21 therefore, *o* to the promises of God

OPPOSES (OPPOSE)

Jas   4: 6 "God *o* the proud
1Pe   5: 5 because, "God *o* the proud

OPPOSING (OPPOSE)

1Ti   6:20 the *o* ideas of what is falsely called

OPPOSITION (OPPOSE)

Heb 12: 3 Consider him who endured such *o*

OPPRESS (OPPRESSED OPPRESSES OPPRESSION OPPRESSOR)

Ex   1:11 masters over them to *o* them
     22:21 "Do not ill-treat an alien or *o* him,
Isa   3: 5 People will *o* each other—
Eze 22:29 they *o* the poor and needy
Da   7:25 the Most High and *o* his saints
Am   5:12 You *o* the righteous and take bribes
Zec   7:10 Do not *o* the widow
Mal   3: 5 who *o* the widows

OPPRESSED (OPPRESS)

Jdg   2:18 as they groaned under those who *o*
Ps   9: 9 The LORD is a refuge for the *o*,
     82: 3 the rights of the poor and *o*.
    146: 7 He upholds the cause of the *o*
Pr   16:19 in spirit and among the *o*
     31: 5 and deprive all the *o* of their rights.
Isa   1:17 encourage the *o*.
     53: 7 He was *o* and afflicted,
     58:10 and satisfy the needs of the *o*,
Zec 10: 2 *o* for lack of a shepherd.
Lk   4:18 to release the *o*,

OPPRESSES (OPPRESS)

Pr   14:31 He who *o* the poor shows contempt
     22:16 He who *o* the poor
Eze 18:12 He *o* the poor and needy.

OPPRESSION (OPPRESS)

Ps   12: 5 "Because of the *o* of the weak
     72:14 He will rescue them from *o*
    119:134 Redeem me from the *o* of men,
Isa 53: 8 By *o* and judgment, he was taken
     58: 9 "If you do away with the yoke of *o*,

OPPRESSOR (OPPRESS)

Ps   72: 4 he will crush the *o*.
Isa 51:13 For where is the wrath of the *o*?
Jer 22: 3 hand of his *o* the one who has been

ORDAINED

Ps   8: 2 you have *o* praise
    111: 9 he *o* his covenant for ever—
    139:16 All the days *o* for me
Eze 28:14 for so I *o* you.

Hab 1: 12 you have *o* them to punish.
Mt   21: 16 you have *o* praise'?''

ORDER (ORDERLY ORDERS)

Nu   9: 23 They obeyed the LORD's *o*,
Ps   110: 4 in the *o* of Melchizedek.''
Heb   5: 10 priest in the *o* of Melchizedek.
      9: 10 until the time of the new *o*.
Rev 21: 4 for the old *o* of things has passed

ORDERLY (ORDER)

1Co 14: 40 done in a fitting and *o* way.
Col   2: 5 and delight to see how *o* you are

ORDERS (ORDER)

Mk   1: 27 He even gives *o* to evil spirits
      3: 12 But he gave them strict *o* not
      9: 9 Jesus gave them *o* not

ORDINARY

Ac   4: 13 that they were unschooled, *o* men,

ORGIES*

Ro   13: 13 not in *o* and drunkenness,
Gal   5: 21 drunkenness, *o*, and the like.
1Pe   4: 3 *o*, carousing and detestable

ORIGIN (ORIGINATE ORIGINS)

2Pe   1: 21 For prophecy never had its *o*

ORIGINATE* (ORIGIN)

1Co 14: 36 Did the word of God *o* with you?

ORIGINS* (ORIGIN)

Mic   5: 2 whose *o* are from of old,

ORNAMENT* (ORNAMENTED)

Pr   3: 22 an *o* to grace your neck.
     25: 12 of gold or an *o* of fine gold

ORNAMENTED (ORNAMENT)

Ge   37: 3 and he made a richly *o* robe for him

ORPHAN* (ORPHANS)

Ex   22: 22 advantage of a widow or an *o*.

ORPHANS (ORPHAN)

Jn   14: 18 will not leave you as *o*; I will come
Jas   1: 27 to look after *o* and widows

OTHNIEL

Nephew of Caleb (Jos 15:15-19; Jdg 1:12-15).
Judge who freed Israel from Aram (Jdg 3:7-11).

OUTBURSTS*

2Co 12: 20 jealousy, *o* of anger, factions,

OUTCOME

Heb 13: 7 Consider the *o* of their way of life
1Pe   4: 17 what will the *o* be for those who do

OUTNUMBER

Ps 139: 18 they would *o* the grains of sand.

OUTSIDERS*

Col   4: 5 wise in the way you act towards *o*;
1Th   4: 12 daily life may win the respect of *o*
1Ti   3: 7 also have a good reputation with *o*,

OUTSTANDING

SS   5: 10 *o* among ten thousand.
Ro   13: 8 no debt remain *o*,

OUTSTRETCHED

Ex   6: 6 and will redeem you with an *o* arm
Dt   4: 34 by a mighty hand and an *o* arm,
      5: 15 with a mighty hand and an *o* arm.
1Ki   8: 42 your mighty hand and your *o* arm
Ps 136: 12 with a mighty hand and *o* arm;
Jer 27: 5 and *o* arm I made the earth
     32: 17 by your great power and *o* arm.
Eze 20: 33 an *o* arm and with outpoured wrath

OUTWEIGHS (WEIGH)

2Co   4: 17 an eternal glory that far *o* them all.

OUTWIT*

2Co   2: 11 in order that Satan might not *o* us.

OVERAWED* (AWE)

Ps   49: 16 Do not be *o* when a man grows rich

OVERBEARING*

Tit   1: 7 not *o*, not quick-tempered,

OVERCAME (OVERCOME)

Rev   3: 21 as I *o* and sat down with my Father
     12: 11 They *o* him

OVERCOME (OVERCAME OVERCOMES)

Mt   16: 18 and the gates of Hades will not *o* it.
Mk   9: 24 I do believe; help me *o* my unbelief
Lk   10: 19 to *o* all the power of the enemy;
Jn   16: 33 But take heart! I have *o* the world.''
Ro   12: 21 Do not be *o* by evil, but *o* evil
2Pe   2: 20 and are again entangled in it and *o*,
1Jn   2: 13 because you have *o* the evil one.
      4: 4 are from God and have *o* them,
      5: 4 is the victory that has *o* the world,
Rev 17: 14 but the Lamb will *o* them

OVERCOMES* (OVERCOME)

1Jn   5: 4 born of God *o* the world.
      5: 5 Who is it that *o* the world?
Rev   2: 7 To him who *o*, I will give the right
      2: 11 He who *o* will not be hurt at all
      2: 17 To him who *o*, I will give some
      2: 26 To him who *o* and does my will
      3: 5 He who *o* will, like them, be
      3: 12 Him who *o* I will make a pillar
      3: 21 To him who *o*, I will give the right
     21: 7 He who *o* will inherit all this,

OVERFLOW (OVERFLOWING OVERFLOWS)

Ps   65: 11 and your carts *o* with abundance.
    119: 171 May my lips *o* with praise,
La   1: 16 and my eyes *o* with tears.
Mt   12: 34 out of the *o* of the heart the mouth
Lk   6: 45 out of the *o* of his heart his mouth
Ro   5: 15 Jesus Christ, *o* to the many! Again,
     15: 13 so that you may *o* with hope
2Co   4: 15 to *o* to the glory of God.
1Th   3: 12 *o* for each other and for everyone

OVERFLOWING (OVERFLOW)

Pr   3: 10 then your barns will be filled to *o*,
2Co   8: 2 their *o* joy and their extreme
      9: 12 *o* in many expressions of thanks
Col   2: 7 as you were taught, and *o*

OVERFLOWS* (OVERFLOW)

Ps 23: 5 my cup *o*.
2Co 1: 5 also through Christ our comfort *o*.

OVERJOYED* (JOY)

Da 6: 23 The king was *o* and gave orders
Mt 2: 10 they saw the star, they were *o*.
Jn 20: 20 The disciples were *o*
Ac 12: 14 she was so *o* she ran back
1Pe 4: 13 so that you may be *o*

OVERLOOK

Pr 19: 11 it is to his glory to *o* an offence.

OVERSEER* (OVERSEERS)

Pr 6: 7 no *o* or ruler,
1Ti 3: 1 anyone sets his heart on being an *o*,
3: 2 Now the *o* must be above reproach,
Tit 1: 7 Since an *o* is entrusted
1Pe 2: 27 returned to the Shepherd and O

OVERSEERS* (OVERSEER)

Ac 20: 28 the Holy Spirit has made you *o*.
Php 1: 1 together with the *o* and deacons:
1Pe 5: 2 as *o*—not because you must,

OVERSHADOW* (OVERSHADOWING)

Lk 1: 35 power of the Most High will *o* you.

OVERSHADOWING (OVERSHADOW)

Ex 25: 20 wings spread upwards, *o* the cover
Heb 9: 5 Glory, *o* the atonement cover

OVERTHROW (OVERTHROWS)

2Th 2: 8 whom the Lord Jesus will *o*

OVERTHROWS (OVERTHROW)

Pr 13: 6 but wickedness *o* the sinner.
Isa 44: 25 who *o* the learning of the wise

OVERWHELMED (OVERWHELMING)

2Sa 22: 5 the torrents of destruction *o* me.
1Ki 10: 5 temple of the LORD, she was *o*.
Ps 38: 4 My guilt has *o* me
65: 3 When we were *o* by sins,
Mt 26: 38 "My soul is *o* with sorrow
Mk 7: 37 People were *o* with amazement.
9: 15 they were *o* with wonder
2Co 2: 7 so that he will not be *o*

OVERWHELMING (OVERWHELMED)

Pr 27: 4 Anger is cruel and fury *o*,
Isa 10: 22 *o* and righteous.
28: 15 When an *o* scourge sweeps by,

OWE

Ro 13: 7 If you *o* taxes, pay taxes; if revenue
Phm : 19 to mention that you *o* me your very

OWNER'S (OWNERSHIP)

Isa 1: 3 the donkey his *o* manger,

OWNERSHIP* (OWNER'S)

2Co 1: 22 He anointed us, set his seal of *o*

OX (OXEN)

Dt 25: 4 Do not muzzle an *o*
Isa 11: 7 and the lion will eat straw like the *o*
Eze 1: 10 and on the left the face of an *o*;

Lk 13: 15 of you on the Sabbath untie his *o*
1Co 9: 9 "Do not muzzle an *o*
1Ti 5: 18 "Do not muzzle the *o*
Rev 4: 7 second was like an *o*, the third had

OXEN (OX)

1Ki 19: 20 Elisha then left his *o* and ran
Lk 14: 19 'I have just bought five yoke of *o*,

PAGAN (PAGANS)

Mt 18: 17 as you would a *p* or a tax collector.
Lk 12: 30 For the *p* world runs

PAGANS* (PAGAN)

Isa 2: 6 and clasp hands with *p*.
Mt 5: 47 Do not even *p* do that? Be perfect,
6: 7 do not keep on babbling like *p*,
6: 32 For the *p* run after all these things,
1Co 5: 1 that does not occur even among *p*:
10: 20 but the sacrifices of *p* are offered
12: 2 You know that when you were *p*,
1Pe 2: 12 such good lives among the *p* that,
4: 3 in the past doing what *p* choose
3Jn : 7 receiving no help from the *p*.

PAID (PAY)

Isa 40: 2 that her sin has been *p* for,
Zec 11: 12 So they *p* me thirty pieces of silver.

PAIN (PAINFUL PAINS)

Ge 3: 16 with *p* you will give birth
6: 6 and his heart was filled with *p*.
Job 6: 10 my joy in unrelenting *p*—
33: 19 may be chastened on a bed of *p*
Jer 4: 19 I writhe in *p*.
15: 18 Why is my *p* unending
Mt 4: 24 suffering severe *p*,
Jn 16: 21 woman giving birth to a child has *p*
1Pe 2: 19 up under the *p* of unjust suffering
Rev 21: 4 or mourning or crying or *p*,

PAINFUL (PAIN)

Ge 3: 17 through *p* toil you will eat of it
5: 29 and *p* toil of our hands caused
Job 6: 25 How *p* are honest words!
Eze 28: 24 neighbours who are *p* briers
2Co 2: 1 I would not make another *p* visit
Heb 12: 11 seems pleasant at the time, but *p*.
1Pe 4: 12 at the *p* trial you are suffering,

PAINS (PAIN)

Ge 3: 16 "I will greatly increase your *p*
Mt 24: 8 these are the beginning of birth-*p*.
Ro 8: 22 as in the *p* of childbirth right up
Gal 4: 19 again in the *p* of childbirth
1Th 5: 3 as labour *p* on a pregnant woman,

PAIRS

Ge 7: 8 *P* of clean and unclean animals,

PALACE (PALACES)

2Sa 7: 2 "Here I am, living in a *p* of cedar,
Jer 22: 6 is what the LORD says about the *p*
22: 13 "Woe to him who builds his *p*

PALACES (PALACE)

Mt 11: 8 wear fine clothes are in kings' *p*.
Lk 7: 25 and indulge in luxury are in *p*.

PALE

Isa	29:22	no longer will their faces grow *p*.
Jer	30: 6	every face turned deathly *p*?
Da	10: 8	my face turned deathly *p*
Rev	6: 8	and there before me was a *p* horse!

PALM (PALMS)

Jn	12:13	They took *p* branches and went out
Rev	7: 9	and were holding *p* branches

PALMS (PALM)

Isa	49:16	you on the *p* of my hands;

PAMPERS*

Pr	29:21	If a man *p* his servant from youth,

PANIC

Dt	20: 3	or give way to *p* before them.
1Sa	14:15	It was a *p* sent by God.
Eze	7: 7	there is *p*, not joy,
Zec	14:13	by the LORD with great *p*.

PANTS

Ps	42: 1	As the deer *p* for streams of water,

PARABLES

See also JESUS: Parables

Ps	78: 2	I will open my mouth in *p*,
Mt	13:35	"I will open my mouth in *p*,
Lk	8:10	but to others I speak in *p*, so that,

PARADISE*

Lk	23:43	today you will be with me in *p*."
2Co	12: 4	God knows—was caught up to *P*.
Rev	2: 7	of life, which is in the *p* of God.

PARALYTIC

Mt	9: 2	Some men brought to him a *p*,
Mk	2: 3	bringing to him a *p*, carried by four
Ac	9:33	a *p* who had been bedridden

PARCHED

Ps	143: 6	my soul thirsts for you like a *p* land.

PARCHMENTS*

2Ti	4:13	and my scrolls, especially the *p*.

PARDON* (PARDONED PARDONS)

2Ch	30:18	*p* everyone who sets his heart
Job	7:21	Why do you not *p* my offences
Isa	55: 7	and to our God, for he will freely *p*.
Joel	3:21	I will *p*."

PARDONED* (PARDON)

Nu	14:19	as you have *p* them from the time
Joel	3:21	bloodguilt, which I have not *p*,

PARDONS* (PARDON)

Mic	7:18	who *p* sin and forgives

PARENTS

Pr	17: 6	and *p* are the pride of their children
Pr	19:14	wealth are inherited from *p*,
Mt	10:21	children will rebel against their *p*
Lk	18:29	left home or wife or brothers or *p*
	21:16	You will be betrayed by *p*, brothers
Jn	9: 3	Neither this man nor his *p* sinned,"
Ro	1:30	they disobey their *p*; they are
2Co	12:14	for their *p*, but *p* for their children.

Eph	6: 1	Children, obey your *p* in the Lord,
Col	3:20	obey your *p* in everything,
1Ti	5: 4	repaying their *p* and grandparents,
2Ti	3: 2	disobedient to their *p*, ungrateful,

PARTAKE*

1Co	10:17	for we all *p* of the one loaf.

PARTIAL* (PARTIALITY)

Pr	18: 5	It is not good to be *p* to the wicked

PARTIALITY (PARTIAL)

Lev	19:15	do not show *p* to the poor
Dt	1:17	Do not show *p* in judging;
	10:17	who shows no *p* and accepts no
	16:19	Do not pervert justice or show *p*.
2Ch	19: 7	our God there is no injustice or *p*
Job	32:21	I will show *p* to no-one,
	34:19	who shows no *p* to princes
Pr	24:23	To show *p* in judging is not good:
Mal	2: 9	have shown *p* in matters of the law
Lk	20:21	and that you do not show *p*
1Ti	5:21	keep these instructions without *p*,

PARTICIPANTS (PARTICIPATE)

1Co	10:20	you to be *p* with demons.

PARTICIPATE (PARTICIPANTS PARTICIPATION)

1Pe	4:13	rejoice that you *p* in the sufferings
2Pe	1: 4	that through them you may *p*

PARTICIPATION (PARTICIPATE)

1Co	10:16	is not the bread that we break a *p*

PARTNER (PARTNERS PARTNERSHIP)

Pr	2:17	who has left the *p* of her youth
Mal	2:14	though she is your *p*, the wife
1Pe	3: 7	them with respect as the weaker *p*

PARTNERS (PARTNER)

Eph	5: 7	Therefore do not be *p* with them.

PARTNERSHIP* (PARTNER)

Php	1: 5	because of your *p* in the gospel

PASS (PASSED PASSER-BY PASSING)

Ex	12:13	and when I see the blood, I will *p*
	33:19	goodness to *p* in front of you,
1Ki	9: 8	all who *p* by will be appalled
	19:11	for the LORD is about to *p* by."
Ps	90:10	for they quickly *p*, and we fly away.
	105:19	till what he foretold came to *p*,
Isa	31: 5	he will '*p* over' it and will rescue it
	43: 2	When you *p* through the waters,
	62:10	*P* through, *p* through the gates!
Jer	22: 8	"People from many nations will *p*
La	1:12	to you, all you who *p* by?
Da	7:14	dominion that will not *p* away,
Am	5:17	for I will *p* through your midst,"
Mt	24:34	will certainly not *p* away
	24:35	Heaven and earth will *p* away,
Mk	13:31	Heaven and earth will *p* away,
Lk	21:33	Heaven and earth will *p* away,
1Co	13: 8	there is knowledge, it will *p* away.
Jas	1:10	he will *p* away like a wild flower.
1Jn	2:17	The world and its desires *p* away,

PASSED (PASS)

Ge	15:17	a blazing torch appeared and *p*

Ex 33:22 you with my hand until I have *p* by.
2Ch 21:20 He *p* away, to no-one's regret,
Ps 57: 1 wings until the disaster has *p*.
Lk 10:32 saw him, *p* by on the other side.
1Co 15: 3 For what I received I *p* on to you
Heb 11:29 By faith the people *p*

PASSER-BY* (PASS)

Pr 26:10 is he who hires a fool or any *p*.
26:17 is a *p* who meddles

PASSING (PASS)

1Co 7:31 world in its present form is *p* away.
1Jn 2: 8 because the darkness is *p*

PASSION* (PASSIONATE PASSIONS)

Hos 7: 6 Their *p* smoulders all night;
1Co 7: 9 better to marry than to burn with *p*.

PASSIONATE* (PASSION)

1Th 4: 5 not in *p* lust like the heathen,

PASSIONS* (PASSION)

Ro 7: 5 the sinful *p* aroused
Gal 5:24 crucified the sinful nature with its *p*
Tit 2:12 to ungodliness and worldly *p*,
3: 3 and enslaved by all kinds of *p*

PASSOVER

Ex 12:11 Eat it in haste; it is the LORD's *P*.
Nu 9: 2 Have the Israelites celebrate the *P*
Dt 16: 1 celebrate the *P* of the LORD your
Jos 5:10 the Israelites celebrated the *P*.
2Ki 23:21 "Celebrate the *P* to the LORD
Ezr 6:19 the exiles celebrated the *P*.
Mk 14:12 customary to sacrifice the *P* lamb,
Lk 22: 1 called the *P*, was approaching,
1Co 5: 7 our *P* lamb, has been sacrificed.
Heb 11:28 he kept the *P* and the sprinkling

PAST

Isa 43:18 do not dwell on the *p*.
65:16 For the *p* troubles will be forgotten
Ro 15: 4 in the *p* was written to teach us,
16:25 the mystery hidden for long ages *p*,
Eph 3: 9 which for ages *p* was kept hidden
Heb 1: 1 In the *p* God spoke

PASTORS*

Eph 4:11 and some to be *p* and teachers,

PASTURE (PASTURES)

Ps 37: 3 dwell in the land and enjoy safe *p*.
95: 7 and we are the people of his *p*,
100: 3 we are his people, the sheep of his *p*
Jer 50: 7 against the LORD, their true *p*,
Eze 34:13 I will *p* them on the mountains
Zec 10: 4 "*P* the flock marked for slaughter.
Jn 10: 9 come in and go out, and find *p*.

PASTURES (PASTURE)

Ps 23: 2 He makes me lie down in green *p*,

PATCH

Jer 10: 5 Like a scarecrow in a melon *p*,
Mt 9:16 No one sews a *p* of unshrunk cloth

PATH (PATHS)

Ps 16:11 known to me the *p* of life;
27:11 lead me in a straight *p*

Ps 119: 32 I run in the *p* of your commands,
119: 105 and a light for my *p*.
Pr 2: 9 and fair—every good *p*.
12:28 along that *p* is immortality.
15:10 awaits him who leaves the *p*;
15:19 the *p* of the upright is a highway.
15:24 The *p* of life leads upwards
21:16 from the *p* of understanding
Isa 26: 7 The *p* of the righteous is level;
Jer 31: 9 on a level *p* where they will not
Mt 13: 4 fell along the *p*, and the birds came
Lk 1:79 to guide our feet into the *p* of peace
2Co 6: 3 no stumbling-block in anyone's *p*,

PATHS (PATH)

Ps 23: 3 He guides me in *p* of righteousness
25: 4 teach me your *p*;
Pr 2:13 who leave the straight *p*
3: 6 and he will make your *p* straight.
4:11 and lead you along straight *p*.
4:26 Make level *p* for your feet
5:21 and he examines all his *p*.
8:20 along the *p* of justice,
22: 5 In the *p* of the wicked lie thorns
Isa 2: 3 so that we may walk in his *p*."
Jer 6:16 ask for the ancient *p*,
Mic 4: 2 so that we may walk in his *p*."
Mt 3: 3 make straight *p* for him.'"
Ac 2:28 to me the *p* of life;
Ro 11:33 and his *p* beyond tracing out!
Heb 12:13 "Make level *p* for your feet,"

PATIENCE* (PATIENT)

Pr 19:11 A man's wisdom gives him *p*;
25:15 Through *p* a ruler can be persuaded
Ecc 7: 8 and *p* is better than pride.
Isa 7:13 Is it not enough to try the *p* of men?
7:13 Will you try the *p* of my God also?
Ro 2: 4 and *p*, not realising that God's
9:22 bore with great *p* the objects
2Co 6: 6 understanding, *p* and kindness;
Gal 5:22 joy, peace, *p*, kindness, goodness,
Col 1:11 may have great endurance and *p*,
3:12 humility, gentleness and *p*.
1Ti 1:16 Jesus might display his unlimited *p*
2Ti 3:10 my purpose, faith, *p*, love,
4: 2 with great *p* and careful instruction
Heb 6:12 *p* inherit what has been promised.
Jas 5:10 as an example of *p* in the face
2Pe 3:15 that our Lord's *p* means salvation,

PATIENT* (PATIENCE PATIENTLY)

Ne 9:30 For many years you were *p*
Job 6:11 What prospects, that I should be *p*?
Pr 14:29 A *p* man has great understanding,
15:18 but a *p* man calms a quarrel.
16:32 Better a *p* man than a warrior,
Mt 18:26 'Be *p* with me,' he begged,
18:29 'Be *p* with me, and I will pay you
Ro 12:12 Be joyful in hope, *p* in affliction,
1Co 13: 4 Love is *p*, love is kind.
2Co 1: 6 produces in you *p* endurance
Eph 4: 2 humble and gentle; be *p*,
1Th 5:14 help the weak, be *p* with everyone.
Jas 5: 7 Be *p*, then, brothers,
5: 7 and how *p* he is for the autumn
5: 8 You too, be *p* and stand firm,
2Pe 3: 9 He is *p* with you, not wanting
Rev 1: 9 *p* endurance that are ours in Jesus,
13:10 This calls for *p* endurance

Rev 14: 12 This calls for *p* endurance

PATIENTLY* (PATIENT)

Ps   37: 7   still before the LORD and wait *p*
      40: 1   I waited *p* for the LORD;
Isa 38: 13   I waited *p* till dawn,
Hab 3: 16   Yet I will wait *p* for the day
Ac 26: 3   I beg you to listen to me *p*.
Ro   8: 25   we do not yet have, we wait for it *p*.
Heb 6: 15   after waiting *p*, Abraham received
1Pe 3: 20   ago when God waited *p* in the days
Rev 3: 10   kept my command to endure *p*,

PATTERN

Ex 25: 40   according to the *p* shown you
Ro   5: 14   who was a *p* of the one to come.
      12: 2   longer to the *p* of this world,
2Ti 1: 13   keep as the *p* of sound teaching,
Heb 8: 5   according to the *p* shown you

PAUL

Also called Saul (Ac 13:9). Pharisee from Tarsus (Ac 9:11; Php 3:5). Apostle (Gal 1). At stoning of Stephen (Ac 8:1). Persecuted Church (Ac 9:1-2; Gal 1:13). Vision of Jesus on road to Damascus (Ac 9:4-9; 26:12-18). In Arabia (Gal 1:17). Preached in Damascus; escaped death through the wall in a basket (Ac 9:19-25). In Jerusalem; sent back to Tarsus (Ac 9:26-30).

Brought to Antioch by Barnabas (Ac 11:22-26). First missionary journey to Cyprus and Galatia (Ac 13-14). Stoned at Lystra (Ac 14:19-20). At Jerusalem council (Ac 15). Split with Barnabas over Mark (Ac 15:36-41).

Second missionary journey with Silas (Ac 16-20). Called to Macedonia (Ac 16:6-10). Freed from prison in Philippi (Ac 16:16-40). In Thessalonica (Ac 17:1-9). Speech in Athens (Ac 17:16-33). In Corinth (Ac 18). In Ephesus (Ac 19). Return to Jerusalem (Ac 20). Farewell to Ephesian elders (Ac 20:13-38). Arrival in Jerusalem (Ac 21:1-26). Arrested (Ac 21:27-36). Addressed crowds (Ac 22), Sanhedrin (Ac 23:1-11). Transferred to Caesarea (Ac 23:12-35). Trial before Felix (Ac 24), Festus (Ac 25:1-12). Before Agrippa (Ac 25:13-26:32). Voyage to Rome; shipwreck (Ac 27). Arrival in Rome (Ac 28).

Epistles: Romans, 1 and 2 Corinthians, Galatians, Ephesians, Philippians, Colossians, 1 and 2 Thessalonians, 1 and 2 Timothy, Titus, Philemon.

PAVEMENT

Jn 19: 13   as The Stone *P* (which

PAY (PAID PAYMENT PAYS REPAID REPAY REPAYING)

Lev 26: 43   They will *p* for their sins
Dt   7: 12   If you *p* attention to these laws
Pr   4: 1   *p* attention and gain understanding
      4: 20   My son, *p* attention to what I say;
      5: 1   My son, *p* attention to my wisdom,
      6: 31   if he is caught, he must *p* sevenfold,
     19: 19   man must *p* the penalty;
     22: 17   *P* attention and listen
     24: 29   I'll *p* that man back for what he did
Eze 40: 4   and *p* attention to everything I am
Zec 11: 12   give me my *p*; but if not, keep it."
Mt 20: 2   He agreed to *p* them a denarius

Mt 22: 16   you *p* no attention to who they are.
     22: 17   Is it right to *p* taxes to Caesar
Lk   3: 14   falsely—be content with your *p*."
     19: 8   I will *p* back four times the amount
Ro 13: 6   This is also why you *p* taxes,
2Pe 1: 19   you will do well to *p* attention to it,

PAYMENT (PAY)

Ps 49: 8   no *p* is ever enough—
Php 4: 18   I have received full *p* and

PAYS (PAY)

Pr 17: 13   If a man *p* back evil for good,
1Th 5: 15   sure that nobody *p* back wrong

PEACE (PEACE-LOVING PEACEABLE PEACEFUL PEACEMAKERS)

Lev 26: 6   "'I will grant *p* in the land,
Nu   6: 26   and give you *p*.'"
     25: 12   him I am making my covenant of *p*
Dt 20: 10   make its people an offer of *p*.
Jdg 3: 11   So the land had *p* for forty years,
     3: 30   and the land had *p* for eighty years.
     5: 31   Then the land had *p* for forty years.
     6: 24   and called it "The LORD is *P*."
     8: 28   the land enjoyed *p* for forty years.
1Sa 7: 14   And there was *p* between Israel
2Sa 10: 19   they made *p* with the Israelites
1Ki 2: 33   may there be the LORD's *p* for ever
     22: 44   also at *p* with the king of Israel.
2Ki 9: 17   come in *p*?'" The horseman rode
1Ch 19: 19   they made *p* with David
     22: 9   and I will grant Israel *p*
2Ch 14: 1   and in his days the country was at *p*
     20: 30   kingdom of Jehoshaphat was at *p*,
Job 3: 26   I have no *p*, no quietness;
     22: 21   to God and be at *p* with him;
Ps 29: 11   LORD blesses his people with *p*.
     34: 14   seek *p* and pursue it.
     37: 11   and enjoy great *p*.
     37: 37   there is a future for the man of *p*.
     85: 10   righteousness and *p* kiss each other
   119: 165   Great *p* have they who love your
   120: 7   I am a man of *p*;
   122: 6   Pray for the *p* of Jerusalem:
   147: 14   He grants *p* to your borders
Pr 12: 20   but joy for those who promote *p*.
     14: 30   A heart at *p* gives life to the body,
     16: 7   his enemies live at *p* with him.
     17: 1   Better a dry crust with *p* and quiet
Ecc 3: 8   a time for war and a time for *p*.
Isa 9: 6   Everlasting Father, Prince of *P*.
     14: 7   All the lands are at rest and at *p*;
     26: 3   You will keep in perfect *p*
     32: 17   The fruit of righteousness will be *p*;
     48: 18   your *p* would have been like a river,
     48: 22   "There is no *p*," says the LORD,
     52: 7   who proclaim *p*,
     53: 5   punishment that brought us *p* was
     54: 10   nor my covenant of *p* be removed,"
     55: 12   and be led forth in *p*;
     57: 2   enter into *p*;
     57: 19   *P*, *p*, to those far and near,"
     57: 21   "There is no *p*," says my God,
     59: 8   The way of *p* they do not know;
Jer 6: 14   '*P*, *p*,' they say,
     8: 11   "*P*, *p*,". . . there is no *p*.
     30: 10   Jacob will again have *p*
     46: 27   Jacob will again have *p*

Eze 13: 10 "*P*," when there is no *p*,
     34: 25 "'I will make a covenant of *p*
     37: 26 I will make a covenant of *p*
Mic   5: 5 And he will be their *p*.
Zec   8: 19 Therefore love truth and *p*."
      9: 10 He will proclaim *p* to the nations.
Mal   2: 5 a covenant of life and *p*,
      2: 6 He walked with me in *p*
Mt   10: 34 I did not come to bring *p*,
Mk   9: 50 and be at *p* with each other."
Lk   1: 79 to guide our feet into the path of *p*
      2: 14 on earth *p* to men on whom his
     19: 38 "*P* in heaven and glory
Jn   14: 27 *P* I leave with you; my *p*
     16: 33 so that in me you may have *p*.
Ro   1: 7 and *p* to you from God our Father
      2: 10 and *p* for everyone who does good:
      5: 1 we have *p* with God
      8: 6 by the Spirit is life and *p*;
     12: 18 on you, live at *p* with everyone.
     14: 19 effort to do what leads to *p*
1Co   7: 15 God has called us to live in *p*.
     14: 33 a God of disorder but of *p*.
2Co 13: 11 be of one mind, live in *p*.
Gal   5: 22 joy, *p*, patience, kindness,
Eph   2: 14 he himself is our *p*, who has made
      2: 15 thus making *p*, and in this one body
      2: 17 and *p* to those who were near.
      6: 15 comes from the gospel of *p*.
Php   4: 7 the *p* of God, which transcends all
Col   1: 20 by making *p* through his blood,
      3: 15 Let the *p* of Christ rule
      3: 15 of one body you were called to *p*.
1Th   5: 3 While people are saying, "*P*
      5: 13 Live in *p* with each other.
      5: 23 the God of *p*, sanctify you through
2Th   3: 16 the Lord of *p* himself give you *p*
2Ti   2: 22 righteousness, faith, love and *p*,
Heb   7: 2 "king of Salem" means "king of *p*."
     12: 11 *p* for those who have been trained
     12: 14 effort to live in *p* with all men
     13: 20 May the God of *p*, who
1Pe   3: 11 he must seek *p* and pursue it.
2Pe   3: 14 blameless and at *p* with him.
Rev   6: 4 power to take *p* from the earth

PEACE-LOVING

Jas   3: 17 then *p*, considerate,

PEACEABLE* (PEACE)

Tit   3: 2 to slander no-one, to be *p*

PEACEFUL (PEACE)

1Ti   2: 2 that we may live *p* and quiet lives

PEACEMAKERS* (PEACE)

Mt   5: 9 Blessed are the *p*,
Jas   3: 18 *P* who sow in peace raise a harvest

PEARL* (PEARLS)

Rev 21: 21 each gate made of a single *p*.

PEARLS (PEARL)

Mt   7: 6 do not throw your *p* to pigs.
     13: 45 like a merchant looking for fine *p*.
1Ti   2: 9 or gold or *p* or expensive clothes,
Rev 21: 21 The twelve gates were twelve *p*,

PEDDLE*

2Co   2: 17 we do not *p* the word of God

PEG

Jdg   4: 21 She drove the *p* through his temple

PEKAH

King of Israel (2Ki 16:25-31; Isa 7:1).

PEKAHIAH*

Son of Menaham; king of Israel (2Ki 16:22-26).

PEN

Ps   45: 1 my tongue is the *p*
Mt   5: 18 letter, not the least stroke of a *p*,
Jn   10: 1 who does not enter the sheep *p*

PENETRATES*

Heb   4: 12 it *p* even to dividing soul and spirit,

PENNIES* (PENNY)

Lk   12: 6 not five sparrows sold for two *p*?

PENNY* (PENNIES)

Mt   5: 26 out until you have paid the last *p*.
     10: 29 Are not two sparrows sold for a *p*?
Mk   12: 42 worth only a fraction of a *p*.
Lk   12: 59 out until you have paid the last *p*."

PENTECOST*

Ac   2: 1 of *P* came, they were all together
     20: 16 if possible, by the day of *P*.
1Co 16: 8 I will stay on at Ephesus until *P*,

PEOPLE (PEOPLES)

Ge   11: 6 as one *p* speaking the same
Ex   5: 1 Let my *p* go,
      6: 7 take you as my own *p*,
      8: 23 between my *p* and your *p*.
     15: 13 the *p* you have redeemed.
     19: 8 The *p* all responded together,
     24: 3 Moses went and told the *p*
     32: 1 When the *p* saw that Moses
     32: 9 they are a stiff-necked *p*.
     33: 13 this nation is your *p*.
Lev   9: 7 for yourself and the *p*:
     16: 24 the burnt offering for the *p*,
     26: 12 and you will be my *p*.
Nu   11: 11 burden of all these *p* on
     14: 11 *p* treat me with contempt?
     14: 19 forgive the sin of these *p*,
     22: 5 A *p* has come out of Egypt
Dt   4: 6 a wise and understanding *p*.
      4: 20 the *p* of his inheritance,
      5: 28 what this *p* said to you.
      7: 6 a *p* holy to the Lord
     26: 18 that you are his *p*,
     31: 7 you must go with this *p*
     31: 16 these *p* will soon prostitute
     32: 9 the Lord's portion is his *p*,
     32: 43 atonement for his land and *p*.
     33: 29 a *p* saved by the Lord?
Jos   1: 6 you will lead this *p*
     24: 24 the *p* said to Joshua,
Jdg   2: 7 *p* served the Lord throughout
Ru   1: 16 Your *p* will be my *p*
1Sa   8: 7 the *p* are saying to you;
     12: 22 Lord will not reject his *p*,
2Sa   5: 2 will shepherd my *p* Israel
      7: 10 provide a place for my *p*
1Ki   3: 8 among the *p* you have chosen,
      8: 30 your *p* Israel when they pray
      8: 56 has given rest to his *p*

1Ki	18: 39	when all the *p* saw this,
2Ki	23: 3	all the *p* pledged themselves
1Ch	17: 21	to redeem *p* for himself
	29: 17	how willingly your *p* who are
2Ch	2: 11	Because the LORD loves his *p*,
	7: 5	*p* dedicated the temple
	7: 14	if my *p*, who are called
	30: 6	"*P* of Israel, return to
	36: 16	was aroused against his *p*
Ezr	2: 1	These are the *p* of the
	3: 1	*p* assembled as one man
Ne	1: 10	your *p*, whom you redeemed
	4: 6	*p* worked with all their heart
	8: 1	*p* assembled as one man
Est	3: 6	to destroy all Mordecai's *p*,
Job	12: 2	Doubtless you are the *p*,
Ps	29: 11	gives strength to his *p*;
	33: 12	*p* he chose for his inheritance
	50: 4	that he may judge his *p*
	53: 6	restores the fortunes of his *p*,
	81: 13	If my *p* would but listen
	94: 14	LORD will not reject his *p*;
	95: 7	we are the *p* of his pasture,
	95: 10	a *p* whose hearts go astray,
	125: 2	the LORD surrounds his *p*
	135: 14	LORD will vindicate his *p*
	144: 15	*p* whose God is the LORD.
Pr	14: 34	sin is a disgrace to any *p*.
	29: 2	righteous thrive, the *p* rejoice
	29: 18	the *p* cast off restraint
Isa	1: 3	my *p* do not understand.
	1: 4	a *p* loaded with guilt,
	5: 13	my *p* will go into exile
	6: 10	the heart of this *p* calloused;
	9: 2	the *p* walking in darkness
	11: 12	will assemble the scattered *p*
	19: 25	Blessed be Egypt my *p*,
	25: 8	remove the disgrace of his *p*
	29: 13	These *p* come near to me
	40: 1	Comfort, comfort my *p*
	40: 7	Surely the *p* are grass.
	42: 6	a covenant for the *p*
	49: 13	the LORD comforts his *p*
	51: 4	"Listen to me, my *p*;
	52: 6	my *p* will know my name;
	53: 8	for the transgression of my *p*
	60: 21	will all your *p* be righteous
	62: 12	will be called the Holy *P*,
	65: 23	they will be a *p* blessed
Jer	2: 11	my *p* have exchanged their
	2: 13	*p* have committed two sins:
	2: 32	my *p* have forgotten me,
	4: 22	My *p* are fools;
	5: 14	Because the *p* have spoken
	5: 31	my *p* love it this way
	7: 16	do not pray for this *p*
	18: 15	my *p* have forgotten me;
	25: 7	They will be my *p*,
	30: 3	I will bring my *p* Israel
Eze	13: 23	I will save my *p* from
	36: 8	fruit for my *p* Israel,
	36: 28	you will be my *p*,
	36: 38	be filled with flocks of *p*.
	37: 13	Then you, my *p*, will know
	38: 14	*p* Israel are living in safety
	39: 7	name among my *p* Israel.
Da	7: 27	saints, the *p* of the Most High.
	8: 24	mighty men and the holy *p*
	9: 19	your *p* bear your name
	9: 24	are decreed for your *p*

Da	9: 26	*p* of the ruler who will come
	10: 14	will happen to your *p*
	11: 32	*p* who know their God will
	12: 1	prince who protects your *p*.
Hos	1: 10	'You are not my *p*,'
	2: 23	'You are my *p*';
	4: 14	a *p* without understanding
Joel	2: 18	and take pity on his *p*.
	3: 16	be a refuge for his *p*,
Am	9: 14	back my exiled *p* Israel;
Mic	6: 2	a case against his *p*;
	7: 14	Shepherd your *p* with
Hag	1: 12	remnant of the *p* obeyed
Zec	2: 11	and will become my *p*.
	8: 7	I will save my *p*
	13: 9	will say, 'They are my *p*,'
Mk	7: 6	*p* honour me with their lips
	8: 27	"Who do *p* say I am?"
Lk	1: 17	make ready a *p* prepared
	1: 68	and has redeemed his *p*.
	2: 10	joy that will be for all the *p*.
	21: 23	and wrath against this *p*.
Jn	11: 50	one man die for the *p*
	18: 14	if one man died for the *p*.
Ac	15: 14	from the Gentiles a *p*.
	18: 10	have many *p* in this city.
Ro	9: 25	will call them 'my *p*.'
	11: 1	Did God reject his *p*?
	15: 10	O Gentiles, with his *p*."
2Co	6: 16	and they will be my *p*."
Tit	2: 14	a *p* that are his very own,
Heb	2: 17	for the sins of the *p*.
	4: 9	a Sabbath-rest for the *p*
	5: 3	for the sins of the *p*.
	10: 30	Lord will judge his *p*.
	11: 25	ill-treated along with the *p*
	13: 12	to make the *p* holy
1Pe	2: 9	you are a chosen *p*,
	2: 10	Once you were not a *p*,
	2: 10	you are the *p* of God;
2Pe	2: 1	false prophets among the *p*,
	3: 11	kind of *p* ought you to be?
Rev	18: 4	"Come out of her, my *p*,
	21: 3	They will be his *p*,

PEOPLES (PEOPLE)

Ge	17: 16	kings of *p* will come from her
	25: 23	two *p* from within you will
	27: 29	and *p* bow down to you
	28: 3	become a community of *p*.
	48: 4	you a community of *p*.
Dt	14: 2	of all the *p* on the face of
	28: 10	Then all the *p* on earth
	32: 8	set up boundaries for the *p*
Jos	4: 24	all the *p* of the earth might
1Ki	8: 43	all the *p* of the earth may
2Ch	7: 20	of ridicule among all *p*.
Ps	9: 8	he will govern the *p*
	67: 5	may all the *p* praise you.
	87: 6	in the register of the *p*:
	96: 10	he will judge the *p*
Isa	2: 4	settle disputes for many *p*.
	17: 12	Oh, the uproar of the *p*—
	25: 6	of rich food for all *p*,
	34: 1	pay attention, you *p*!
	55: 4	him a witness to the *p*,
Jer	10: 3	customs of the *p* are worthless
Da	7: 14	all *p*, nations and men
Mic	4: 1	and *p* will stream to it.
	4: 3	will judge between many *p*

Mic 5: 7 in the midst of many *p*
Zep 3: 9 purify the lips of the *p*,
3: 20 among all the *p* of the
Zec 8: 20 Many *p* and the inhabitants
12: 2 all the surrounding *p* reeling.
Rev 10: 11 prophesy again about many *p*,
17: 15 the prostitute sits, are *p*,

PEOR

Nu 25: 3 joined in worshipping the Baal of *P*.
Dt 4: 3 who followed the Baal of *P*,

PERCEIVE (PERCEIVING)

Ps 139: 2 you *p* my thoughts from afar.
Pr 24: 12 not he who weighs the heart *p* it?

PERCEIVING* (PERCEIVE)

Isa 6: 9 be ever seeing, but never *p*.'
Mt 13: 14 you will be ever seeing but never *p*.
Mk 4: 12 may be ever seeing but never *p*,
Ac 28: 26 you will be ever seeing but never *p*

PERFECT* (PERFECTER PERFECTING PERFECTION)

Dt 32: 4 He is the Rock, his works are *p*,
2Sa 22: 31 "As for God, his way is *p*;
22: 33 and makes my way *p*.
Job 36: 4 one *p* in knowledge is with you.
37: 16 of him who is *p* in knowledge?
Ps 18: 30 As for God, his way is *p*;
18: 32 and makes my way *p*.
19: 7 The law of the LORD is *p*,
50: 2 From Zion, *p* in beauty,
64: 6 "We have devised a *p* plan!"
SS 6: 9 but my dove, my *p* one, is unique,
Isa 25: 1 for in *p* faithfulness
26: 3 You will keep in *p* peace
Eze 16: 14 had given you made your beauty *p*,
27: 3 "I am *p* in beauty."
28: 12 full of wisdom and *p* in beauty.
Mt 5: 48 Do not even pagans do that? Be *p*,
5: 48 as your heavenly Father is *p*.
19: 21 answered, "If you want to be *p*,
Ro 12: 2 his good, pleasing and *p* will.
2Co 12: 9 for my power is made *p*
Php 3: 12 or have already been made *p*,
Col 1: 28 so that we may present everyone *p*
3: 14 binds them all together in *p* unity.
Heb 2: 10 the author of their salvation *p*
5: 9 what he suffered and, once made *p*,
7: 19 useless (for the law made nothing *p*
7: 28 who has been made *p* for ever.
9: 11 and more *p* tabernacle that is not
10: 1 make *p* those who draw
10: 14 he has made *p* for ever those who
11: 40 with us would they be made *p*.
12: 23 spirits of righteous men made *p*,
Jas 1: 17 Every good and *p* gift is from above
1: 25 into the *p* law that gives freedom,
3: 2 he is a *p* man, able
1Jn 4: 18 But *p* love drives out fear,
4: 18 The one who fears is not made *p*

PERFECTER* (PERFECT)

Heb 12: 2 the author and *p* of our faith,

PERFECTING* (PERFECT)

2Co 7: 1 *p* holiness out of reverence for God

PERFECTION* (PERFECT)

Ps 119: 96 To all *p* I see a limit;
La 2: 15 the *p* of beauty,
Eze 27: 4 builders brought your beauty to *p*.
27: 11 they brought your beauty to *p*.
28: 12 "'You were the model of *p*,
1Co 13: 10 but when *p* comes, the imperfect
2Co 13: 9 and our prayer is for your *p*.
13: 11 Aim for *p*, listen to my appeal,
Heb 7: 11 If *p* could have been attained

PERFORM (PERFORMED PERFORMS)

Ex 3: 20 with all the wonders that I will *p*
2Sa 7: 23 to *p* great and awesome wonders
Jn 3: 2 no-one could *p* the miraculous

PERFORMED (PERFORM)

Mt 11: 21 If the miracles that were *p*
Jn 10: 41 John never *p* a miraculous

PERFORMS (PERFORM)

Ps 77: 14 You are the God who *p* miracles;

PERFUME

Ecc 7: 1 A good name is better than fine *p*,
SS 1: 3 your name is like *p* poured out.
Mk 14: 3 jar of very expensive *p*,

PERIL

2Co 1: 10 us from such a deadly *p*,

PERISH (PERISHABLE PERISHED PERISHES PERISHING)

Ge 6: 17 Everything on earth will *p*.
Est 4: 16 And if I *p*, I *p*."
Ps 1: 6 but the way of the wicked will *p*.
37: 20 But the wicked will *p*:
73: 27 Those who are far from you will *p*;
102: 26 They will *p*, but you remain;
Pr 11: 10 when the wicked *p*, there are
19: 9 and he who pours out lies will *p*.
21: 28 A false witness will *p*,
28: 28 when the wicked *p*, the righteous
Isa 1: 28 who forsake the LORD will *p*.
29: 14 the wisdom of the wise will *p*,
60: 12 that will not serve you will *p*;
Zec 11: 9 the dying die, and the perishing *p*.
Lk 13: 3 unless you repent, you too will all *p*
13: 5 unless you repent, you too will all *p*
21: 18 But not a hair of your head will *p*.
Jn 3: 16 whoever believes in him shall not *p*
10: 28 eternal life, and they shall never *p*;
Ro 2: 12 apart from the law will also *p* apart
Col 2: 22 These are all destined to *p* with use,
2Th 2: 10 They *p* because they refused
Heb 1: 11 They will *p*, but you remain;
1Pe 1: 4 into an inheritance that can never *p*
2Pe 3: 9 not wanting anyone to *p*,

PERISHABLE (PERISH)

1Co 15: 42 The body that is sown is *p*,
1Pe 1: 18 not with *p* things such
1: 23 not of *p* seed, but of imperishable,

PERISHED (PERISH)

Ps 119: 92 I would have *p* in my affliction.

PERISHES (PERISH)

Job 8: 13 so *p* the hope of the godless.
1Pe 1: 7 which *p* even though refined by fire

PERISHING (PERISH)

1Co   1: 18 foolishness to those who are *p*,
2Co   2: 15 being saved and those who are *p*.
        4: 3 it is veiled to those who are *p*.

PERJURERS* (PERJURY)

Mal   3: 5 and *p*, against those who defraud
1Ti   1: 10 for slave traders and liars and *p*—

PERJURY* (PERJURERS)

Jer   7: 9 murder, commit adultery and *p*,

PERMANENT

Heb   7: 24 lives for ever, he has a *p* priesthood.

PERMISSIBLE (PERMIT)

1Co   6: 12 "Everything is *p* for me"—
     10: 23 "Everything is *p*"—but not

PERMIT (PERMISSIBLE PERMITTED)

Hos   5: 4 "Their deeds do not *p* them
1Ti   2: 12 I do not *p* a woman to teach

PERMITTED (PERMIT)

Mt   19: 8 Moses *p* you to divorce your wives
2Co 12: 4 things that man is not *p* to tell.

PERSECUTE (PERSECUTED PERSECUTION PERSECUTIONS)

Ps 119: 86 for men *p* me without cause.
Mt   5: 11 *p* you and falsely say all kinds
      5: 44 and pray for those who *p* you,
Jn   15: 20 they persecuted me, they will *p* you
Ac   9: 4 why do you *p* me?" "Who are you,
Ro   12: 14 Bless those who *p* you; bless

PERSECUTED (PERSECUTE)

Mt   5: 10 Blessed are those who are *p*
      5: 12 same way they *p* the prophets who
Jn   15: 20 If they *p* me, they will persecute
1Co   4: 12 when we are *p*, we endure it;
     15: 9 because I *p* the church of God.
2Co   4: 9 in despair; *p* but not abandoned;
1Th   3: 4 kept telling you that we would be *p*.
2Ti   3: 12 life in Christ Jesus will be *p*,
Heb 11: 37 destitute, *p* and ill-treated—

PERSECUTION (PERSECUTE)

Mt   13: 21 When trouble or *p* comes
Ro   8: 35 or hardship or *p* or famine

PERSECUTIONS (PERSECUTE)

Mk   10: 30 and with them *p*) and in the age
2Co 12: 10 in hardships, in *p*, in difficulties.
2Th   1: 4 faith in all the *p* and trials you are
2Ti   3: 11 love, endurance, *p*, sufferings—

PERSEVERANCE* (PERSEVERE)

Ro   5: 3 we know that suffering produces *p*;
      5: 4 *p*, character; and character, hope.
2Co 12: 12 were done among you with great *p*.
2Th   1: 4 churches we boast about your *p*
      3: 5 into God's love and Christ's *p*.
Heb 12: 1 run with *p* the race marked out
Jas   1: 3 the testing of your faith develops *p*.
      1: 4 *P* must finish its work
      5: 11 You have heard of Job's *p*
2Pe   1: 6 *p*; and to *p*, godliness;
Rev   2: 2 your hard work and your *p*.
      2: 19 and faith, your service and *p*,

PERSEVERE* (PERSEVERANCE PERSEVERED PERSEVERES PERSEVERING)

1Ti   4: 16 *P* in them, because if you do,
Heb 10: 36 You need to *p* so that

PERSEVERED* (PERSEVERE)

Heb 11: 27 he *p* because he saw him who is
Jas   5: 11 consider blessed those who have *p*.
Rev   2: 3 You have *p* and have endured

PERSEVERES* (PERSEVERE)

1Co 13: 7 trusts, always hopes, always *p*.
Jas   1: 12 Blessed is the man who *p*

PERSEVERING* (PERSEVERE)

Lk   8: 15 retain it, and by *p* produce a crop.

PERSIANS

Da   6: 15 law of the Medes and *P* no decree

PERSISTENCE*

Ro   2: 7 To those who by *p*

PERSUADE (PERSUADED PERSUASIVE)

Ac   18: 4 trying to *p* Jews and Greeks.
2Co   5: 11 is to fear the Lord, we try to *p* men.

PERSUADED (PERSUADE)

Ro   4: 21 being fully *p* that God had power

PERSUASIVE (PERSUADE)

1Co   2: 4 not with wise and *p* words,

PERVERSION* (PERVERT)

Lev 18: 23 sexual relations with it; that is a *p*.
    20: 12 What they have done is a *p*;
Ro   1: 27 the due penalty for their *p*.
Jude   : 7 up to sexual immorality and *p*.

PERVERT (PERVERSION PERVERTED PERVERTS)

Ex   23: 2 do not *p* justice by siding
Dt   16: 19 Do not *p* justice or show partiality.
Job 34: 12 that the Almighty would *p* justice.
Pr   17: 23 to *p* the course of justice.
Gal   1: 7 are trying to *p* the gospel of Christ.

PERVERTED (PERVERT)

1Sa   8: 3 and accepted bribes and *p* justice.

PERVERTS* (PERVERT)

1Ti   1: 10 for murderers, for adulterers and *p*,

PESTILENCE (PESTILENCES)

Ps   91: 6 nor the *p* that stalks in the darkness

PESTILENCES (PESTILENCE)

Lk   21: 11 famines and *p* in various places,

PETER

    Apostle, brother of Andrew, also called Simon (Mt 10:2; Mk 3:16; Lk 6:14; Ac 1:13), and Cephas (Jn 1:42). Confession of Christ (Mt 16:13-20; Mk 8:27-30; Lk 9:18-27). At transfiguration (Mt 17:1-8; Mk 9:2-8; Lk 9:28-36; 2Pe 1:16-18). Caught fish with coin (Mt 17:24-27). Denial of Jesus predicted (Mt 26:31-35; Mk 14:27-31; Lk 22:31-34; Jn 13:31-38). Denied Jesus (Mt 26:69-75; Mk

14:66-72; Lk 22:54-62; Jn 18: 15-27). Commissioned by Jesus to shepherd his flock (Jn 21:15-23).

Speech at Pentecost (Ac 2). Healed beggar (Ac 3:1-10). Speech at temple (Ac 3:11-26), before Sanhedrin (Ac 4:1-22). In Samaria (Ac 8:14-25). Sent by vision to Cornelius (Ac 10). Announced salvation of Gentiles in Jerusalem (Ac 11; 15). Freed from prison (Ac 12). Inconsistency at Antioch (Gal 2:11-21). At Jerusalem Council (Ac 15).

Epistles: 1-2 Peter.

PETITION (PETITIONS)

1Ch	16: 4	to make *p*, to give thanks,
Php	4: 6	by prayer and *p*, with thanksgiving,

PETITIONS (PETITION)

Heb	5: 7	he offered up prayers and *p*

PHANTOM*

Ps	39: 6	Man is a mere *p* as he goes to

PHARAOH (PHARAOH'S)

Ge	12: 15	her to *P*, and she was taken
	41: 14	So *P* sent for Joseph, and he was
Ex	14: 4	glory for myself through *P*
	14: 17	And I will gain glory through *P*

PHARAOH'S (PHARAOH)

Ex	7: 3	But I will harden *P* heart, and

PHARISEE (PHARISEES)

Ac	23: 6	brothers, I am a *P*, the son of a *P*.
Php	3: 5	in regard to the law, a *P*; as for zeal,

PHARISEES (PHARISEE)

Mt	5: 20	surpasses that of the *P*
	16: 6	guard against the yeast of the *P*
	23: 13	of the law and *P*, you hypocrites!
Jn	3: 1	a man of the *P* named Nicodemus,

PHILADELPHIA

Rev	3: 7	the angel of the church in *P* write:

PHILEMON*

Phm	: 1	To *P* our dear friend and fellow

PHILIP

1. Apostle (Mt 10:3; Mk 3:18; Lk 6:14; Jn 1:43-48; 14:8; Ac 1:13).
2. Deacon (Ac 6:1-7); evangelist in Samaria (Ac 8:4-25), to Ethiopian (Ac 8:26-40).

PHILIPPI

Ac	16: 12	From there we travelled to *P*,
Php	1: 1	To all the saints in Christ Jesus at *P*

PHILISTINE (PHILISTINES)

Jos	13: 3	of the five *P* rulers in Gaza,
1Sa	14: 1	let's go over to the *P* outpost
	17: 26	is this uncircumcised *P* that he
	17: 37	me from the hand of this *P*."

PHILISTINES (PHILISTINE)

Jdg	10: 7	them into the hands of the *P*
	13: 1	the hands of the *P* for forty years.
	16: 5	The rulers of the *P* went to her
1Sa	4: 1	at Ebenezer, and the *P* at Aphek.
	5: 8	together all the rulers of the *P*

1Sa	13: 23	a detachment of *P* had gone out
	17: 1	the *P* gathered their forces for war
	23: 1	the *P* are fighting against Keilah
	27: 1	is to escape to the land of the *P*.
	31: 1	Now the *P* fought against Israel;
2Sa	5: 17	When the *P* heard that David had
	8: 1	David defeated the *P* and subdued
	21: 15	there was a battle between the *P*
2Ki	18: 8	he defeated the *P*, as far as Gaza
Am	1: 8	Ekron till the last of the *P* is dead,"

PHILOSOPHER* (PHILOSOPHY)

1Co	1: 20	Where is the *p* of this age?

PHILOSOPHY* (PHILOSOPHER)

Col	2: 8	through hollow and deceptive *p*,

PHINEHAS

Nu	25: 7	When *P* son of Eleazar, the son
Ps	106: 30	But *P* stood up and intervened,

PHOEBE*

Ro	16: 1	I commend to you our sister *P*,

PHYLACTERIES*

Mt	23: 5	They make their *p* wide

PHYSICAL

Ro	2: 28	merely outward and *p*.
Col	1: 22	by Christ's *p* body through death
1Ti	4: 8	For *p* training is of some value,
Jas	2: 16	but does nothing about his *p* needs,

PICK (PICKED)

Mk	16: 18	they will *p* up snakes

PICKED (PICK)

Lk	14: 7	noticed how the guests *p* the places
Jn	5: 9	he *p* up his mat and walked.

PIECE (PIECES)

Jn	19: 23	woven in one *p* from top to bottom.

PIECES (PIECE)

Ge	15: 17	and passed between the *p*.
Jer	34: 18	and then walked between its *p*.
Zec	11: 12	So they paid me thirty *p* of silver.
Mt	14: 20	of broken *p* that were left over.

PIERCE (PIERCED)

Ex	21: 6	and *p* his ear with an awl.
Pr	12: 18	Reckless words *p* like a sword,
Lk	2: 35	a sword will *p* your own soul too."

PIERCED (PIERCE)

Ps	22: 16	they have *p* my hands and my feet.
	40: 6	but my ears you have *p*;
Isa	53: 5	But he was *p* for our transgressions,
Zec	12: 10	look on me, the one they have *p*,
Jn	19: 37	look on the one they have *p*."
Rev	1: 7	even those who *p* him;

PIG'S (PIGS)

Pr	11: 22	Like a gold ring in a *p* snout

PIGEONS

Lev	5: 11	afford two doves or two young *p*,
Lk	2: 24	"a pair of doves or two young *p*."

PIGS (PIG'S)

Mt   7: 6 do not throw your pearls to *p*.
Mk   5: 11 A large herd of *p* was feeding on

PILATE

Governor of Judea. Questioned Jesus (Mt 27:1-26; Mk 15:15; Lk 22:66-23:25; Jn 18:28-19:16); sent him to Herod (Lk 23:6-12); consented to his crucifixion when crowds chose Barabbas (Mt 27:15-26; Mk 15:6-15; Lk 23:13-25; Jn 19:1-10).

PILLAR (PILLARS)

Ge   19: 26 and she became a *p* of salt.
Ex   13: 21 ahead of them in a *p* of cloud
1Ti   3: 15 the *p* and foundation of the truth.
Rev   3: 12 who overcomes I will make a *p*

PILLARS (PILLAR)

Gal   2: 9 and John, those reputed to be *p*,

PINIONS

Dt   32: 11 and carries them on its *p*.

PISGAH

Dt   3: 27 Go up to the top of *P* and look west

PIT

Ps   7: 15 falls into the *p* he has made.
    40: 2 He lifted me out of the slimy *p*,
   103: 4 he redeems my life from the *p*
Pr   23: 27 for a prostitute is a deep *p*
    26: 27 If a man digs a *p*, he will fall into it;
Isa   24: 17 Terror and *p* and snare await you,
    38: 17 me from the *p* of destruction;
Mt   15: 14 a blind man, both will fall into a *p*."

PITCH

Ge   6: 14 and coat it with *p* inside and out.
Ex   2: 3 and coated it with tar and *p*.

PITIED (PITY)

1Co   15: 19 we are to be *p* more than all men.

PITY (PITIED)

Ps   72: 13 He will take *p* on the weak
Ecc   4: 10 But *p* the man who falls
Lk   10: 33 when he saw him, he took *p* on him

PLAGUE (PLAGUED PLAGUES)

2Ch   6: 28 "When famine or *p* comes
Ps   91: 6 nor the *p* that destroys at midday.

PLAGUED* (PLAGUE)

Ps   73: 5 they are not *p* by human ills.
    73: 14 All day long I have been *p*;

PLAGUES (PLAGUE)

Hos   13: 14 Where, O death, are your *p*?
Rev   21: 9 full of the seven last *p* came
    22: 18 to him the *p* described in this book.

PLAIN [1]

Isa   40: 4 the rugged places a *p*.

PLAIN [2]

Ro   1: 19 what may be known about God is *p*

PLAN (PLANNED PLANS)

Ex   26: 30 according to the *p* shown you

Job   42: 2 no *p* of yours can be thwarted.
Pr   14: 22 those who *p* what is good find love
    21: 30 is no wisdom, no insight, no *p*
Am   3: 7 nothing without revealing his *p*
Eph   1: 11 predestined according to the *p*

PLANK

Mt   7: 3 attention to the *p* in your own eye?
Lk   6: 41 attention to the *p* in your own eye?

PLANNED (PLAN)

Ps   40: 5 The things you *p* for us
Isa   14: 24 "Surely, as I have *p*, so it will be,
    23: 9 The LORD Almighty *p* it,
    46: 11 what I have *p*, that will I do.
Heb   11: 40 God had *p* something better for us

PLANS (PLAN)

Ps   20: 4 and make all your *p* succeed.
    33: 11 *p* of the LORD stand firm for ever,
Pr   15: 22 *P* fail for lack of counsel,
    16: 3 and your *p* will succeed.
    19: 21 Many are the *p* in a man's heart,
    20: 18 Make *p* by seeking advice;
Isa   29: 15 to hide their *p* from the LORD,
    30: 1 those who carry out *p* that are not
    32: 8 But the noble man makes noble *p*,
2Co   1: 17 Or do I make my *p* in a worldly

PLANT (PLANTED PLANTING PLANTS)

Am   9: 15 I will *p* Israel in their own land,
Mt   15: 13 "Every *p* that my heavenly Father

PLANTED (PLANT)

Ge   2: 8 the LORD God had *p* a garden
Ps   1: 3 He is like a tree *p* by streams
Jer   17: 8 He will be like a tree *p* by the water
Mt   15: 13 Father has not *p* will be pulled
    21: 33 was a landowner who *p* a vineyard.
Lk   13: 6 "A man had a fig tree, *p*
1Co   3: 6 I *p* the seed, Apollos watered it,
Jas   1: 21 humbly accept the word *p* in you,

PLANTING (PLANT)

Isa   61: 3 a *p* of the LORD

PLANTS (PLANT)

Pr   31: 16 out of her earnings she *p* a vineyard
1Co   3: 7 So neither he who *p* nor he who
    9: 7 Who *p* a vineyard and does not eat

PLATTER

Mk   6: 25 head of John the Baptist on a *p*."

PLAY (PLAYED)

1Sa   16: 23 David would take his harp and *p*.
Isa   11: 8 The infant will *p* near the hole

PLAYED (PLAY)

Lk   7: 32 "'We *p* the flute for you,
1Co   14: 7 anyone know what tune is being *p*

PLEA (PLEAD PLEADED PLEADS)

1Ki   8: 28 to your servant's prayer and his *p*
Ps   102: 17 he will not despise their *p*.
La   3: 56 You heard my *p*: "Do not close

PLEAD (PLEA)

Isa   1: 17 *p* the case of the widow.

PLEADED (PLEA)

2Co 12: 8 Three times I *p* with the Lord

PLEADS (PLEA)

Job 16:21 on behalf of a man he *p* with God

PLEASANT (PLEASE)

Ge 49:15 and how *p* is his land,
Ps 16: 6 for me in *p* places;
133: 1 How good and *p* it is
135: 3 sing praise to his name, for that is *p*
147: 1 how *p* and fitting to praise him!
Pr 2:10 knowledge will be *p* to your soul.
3:17 Her ways are *p* ways,
16:21 and *p* words promote instruction.
16:24 *P* words are a honeycomb,
Isa 30:10 Tell us *p* things,
1Th 3: 6 that you always have *p* memories
Heb 12:11 No discipline seems *p* at the time,

PLEASANTNESS* (PLEASE)

Pr 27: 9 the *p* of one's friend springs

PLEASE (PLEASANT PLEASANTNESS PLEASED PLEASES PLEASING PLEASURE PLEASURES)

Ps 69:31 This will *p* the Lord more
Pr 20:23 and dishonest scales do not *p* him.
Isa 46:10 and I will do all that I *p*.
Jer 6:20 your sacrifices do not *p* me."
27: 5 and I give it to anyone I *p*.
Jn 5:30 for I seek not to *p* myself
Ro 8: 8 by the sinful nature cannot *p* God.
15: 1 of the weak and not to *p* ourselves.
15: 2 Each of us should *p* his neighbour
1Co 7:32 affairs—how he can *p* the Lord.
10:33 I try to *p* everybody in every way.
2Co 5: 9 So we make it our goal to *p* him,
Gal 1:10 or of God? Or am I trying to *p* men
6: 8 the one who sows to *p* the Spirit,
Col 1:10 and my *p* him in every way:
1Th 2: 4 We are not trying to *p* men
4: 1 how to live in order to *p* God,
2Ti 2: 4 wants to *p* his commanding officer.
Tit 2: 9 to try to *p* them, not to talk back
Heb 11: 6 faith it is impossible to *p* God,

PLEASED (PLEASE)

Dt 28:63 as it *p* the Lord to make you
1Sa 12:22 Lord was *p* to make you his own.
1Ki 3:10 The Lord was *p* that Solomon had
1Ch 29:17 that you test the heart and are *p*
Mic 6: 7 Will the Lord be *p*
Mal 1:10 I am not *p* with you," says
Mt 3:17 whom I love; with him I am well *p*
17: 5 whom I love; with him I am well *p*.
Mk 1:11 whom I love; with you I am well *p*
Lk 3:22 whom I love; with you I am well *p*
1Co 1:21 God was *p* through the foolishness
Col 1:19 For God was *p* to have all his
Heb 10: 6 you were not *p*.
10: 8 nor were you *p* with them"
10:38 I will not be *p* with him."
11: 5 commended as one who *p* God.
13:16 for with such sacrifices God is *p*.
2Pe 1:17 whom I love; with him I am well *p*

PLEASES (PLEASE)

Job 23:13 He does whatever he *p*.
Ps 115: 3 he does whatever *p* him.

Ps 135: 6 The Lord does whatever *p* him,
Pr 15: 8 but the prayer of the upright *p* him.
21: 1 it like a watercourse wherever he *p*.
Ecc 2:26 To the man who *p* him, God gives
7:26 man who *p* God will escape her,
Da 4:35 He does as he *p*
Jn 3: 8 The wind blows wherever it *p*.
8:29 for I always do what *p* him."
Eph 5:10 truth) and find out what *p* the Lord
Col 3:20 in everything, for this *p* the Lord.
1Ti 2: 3 This is good, and *p* God our Saviour,
1Jn 3:22 his commands and do what *p* him.

PLEASING (PLEASE)

Ge 2: 9 trees that were *p* to the eye
Lev 1: 9 an aroma *p* to the Lord.
Ps 19:14 be *p* in your sight,
104:34 May my meditation be *p* to him,
Pr 15:26 but those of the pure are *p* to him.
16: 7 When a man's ways are *p*
SS 1: 3 *P* is the fragrance of your perfumes
4:10 How much more *p* is your love
7: 6 How beautiful you are and how *p*,
Ro 12: 1 *p* to God—which is your spiritual
14:18 Christ in this way is *p* to God
Php 4:18 an acceptable sacrifice, *p* to God.
1Ti 5: 4 grandparents, for this is *p* to God.
Heb 13:21 may he work in us what is *p* to him,

PLEASURE (PLEASE)

Ps 5: 4 You are not a God who takes *p*
51:16 you do not take *p* in burnt offerings
147:10 His *p* is not in the strength
Pr 10:23 A fool finds *p* in evil conduct,
18: 2 A fool finds no *p* in understanding
21:17 He who loves *p* will become poor;
Isa 1:11 I have no *p*
Jer 6:10 they find no *p* in it.
Eze 18:23 Do I take any *p* in the death
18:32 For I take no *p* in the death
33:11 I take no *p* in the death
Lk 10:21 Father, for this was your good *p*.
Eph 1: 5 in accordance with his *p* and will—
1: 9 of his will according to his good *p*,
1Ti 5: 6 the widow who lives for *p* is dead
2Ti 3: 4 lovers of *p* rather than lovers
2Pe 2:13 Their idea of *p* is to carouse

PLEASURES* (PLEASE)

Ps 16:11 with eternal *p* at your right hand.
Lk 8:14 and *p*, and they do not mature.
Tit 3: 3 by all kinds of passions and *p*.
Heb 11:25 rather than to enjoy the *p* of sin
Jas 4: 3 may spend what you get on your *p*.
2Pe 2:13 revelling in their *p* while they feast

PLEDGE

Dt 24:17 take the cloak of the widow as a *p*.
1Pe 3:21 but the *p* of a good conscience

PLEIADES

Job 38:31 "Can you bind the beautiful *P*?
Am 5: 8 (he who made the *P* and Orion,

PLENTIFUL (PLENTY)

Mt 9:37 harvest is *p* but the workers are
Lk 10: 2 harvest is *p*, but the workers are

PLENTY (PLENTIFUL)

2Co 8:14 the present time your *p* will supply

Php   4: 12 whether living in *p* or in want.

PLOT (PLOTS)

Est   2: 22 Mordecai found out about the *p*
Ps   2: 1   and the peoples *p* in vain?
Pr   3: 29 not *p* harm against your neighbour,
Zec   8: 17 do not *p* evil against your neighbour,
Ac   4: 25 and the peoples *p* in vain?

PLOTS (PLOT)

Pr   6: 14 who *p* evil with deceit in his heart

PLOUGH (PLOUGHMAN PLOUGHSHARES)

Lk   9: 62 "No-one who puts his hand to the *p*

PLOUGHMAN (PLOUGH)

1Co   9: 10 because when the *p* ploughs

PLOUGHSHARES (PLOUGH)

1Sa   13: 20 to the Philistines to have their *p*,
Isa   2: 4   They will beat their swords into *p*
Joel   3: 10 Beat your *p* into swords
Mic   4: 3   They will beat their swords into *p*

PLUCK

Mk   9: 47 your eye causes you to sin, *p* it out.

PLUNDER (PLUNDERED)

Ex   3: 22 And so you will *p* the Egyptians."
Est   3: 13 of Adar, and to *p* their goods.
       8: 11 to *p* the property of their enemies.
       9: 10 did not lay their hands on the *p*.
Pr   22: 23 and will *p* those who *p* them.
Isa   3: 14 the *p* from the poor is

PLUNDERED (PLUNDER)

Eze   34: 8   lacks a shepherd and so has been *p*

PLUNGE

1Ti   6: 9   and harmful desires that *p* men
1Pe   4: 4   think it strange that you do not *p*

PODS

Lk   15: 16 with the *p* that the pigs were eating,

POINT

Mt   4: 5   on the highest *p* of the temple.
      26: 38 with sorrow to the *p* of death.
Jas   2: 10 yet stumbles at just one *p* is guilty
Rev   2: 10 Be faithful, even to the *p* of death,

POISON

Ps   140: 3   the *p* of vipers is on their lips.
Mk   16: 18 and when they drink deadly *p*,
Ro   3: 13 "The *p* of vipers is on their lips."
Jas   3: 8   It is a restless evil, full of deadly *p*.

POLE (POLES)

Nu   21: 8   "Make a snake and put it up on a *p*;
Dt   16: 21 not set up any wooden Asherah *p*

POLES (POLE)

Ex   25: 13 Then make *p* of acacia wood

POLISHED

Isa   49: 2   he made me into a *p* arrow

POLLUTE* (POLLUTED POLLUTES)

Nu   35: 33 " 'Do not *p* the land where you are.
Jude   : 8   these dreamers *p* their own bodies,

POLLUTED* (POLLUTE)

Ezr   9: 11 entering to possess is a land *p*
Pr   25: 26 Like a muddied spring or a *p* well
Ac   15: 20 to abstain from food *p* by idols,
Jas   1: 27 oneself from being *p* by the world.

POLLUTES* (POLLUTE)

Nu   35: 33 Bloodshed *p* the land,

PONDER (PONDERED)

Ps   64: 9   and *p* what he has done.
     119: 95 but I will *p* your statutes.

PONDERED (PONDER)

Ps   111: 2   they are *p* by all who delight
Lk   2: 19 up all these things and *p* them

POOR (POVERTY)

Lev   19: 10 Leave them for the *p* and the alien.
      23: 22 Leave them for the *p* and the alien.
      27: 8   If anyone making the vow is too *p*
Dt   15: 4   there should be no *p* among you,
      15: 7   is a *p* man among your brothers
      15: 11 There will always be *p* people
      24: 12 If the man is *p*, do not go to sleep
      24: 14 advantage of a hired man who is *p*
Job   5: 16 So the *p* have hope,
      24: 4   force all the *p* of the land
Ps   14: 6   frustrate the plans of the *p*,
      34: 6   This *p* man called, and the LORD
      35: 10 You rescue the *p* from those too
      40: 17 Yet I am *p* and needy;
      68: 10 O God, you provided for the *p*.
      82: 3   maintain the rights of the *p*
     112: 9   scattered abroad his gifts to the *p*,
     113: 7   He raises the *p* from the dust
     140: 12 the LORD secures justice for the *p*
Pr   10: 4   Lazy hands make a man *p*,
      13: 7   to be *p*, yet has great wealth.
      14: 20 The *p* are shunned
      14: 31 oppresses the *p* shows contempt
      17: 5   who mocks the *p* shows contempt
      19: 1   Better a *p* man whose walk is
      19: 17 to the *p* lends to the LORD,
      19: 22 better to be *p* than a liar.
      20: 13 not love sleep or you will grow *p*;
      21: 13 to the cry of the *p*,
      21: 17 who loves pleasure will become *p*;
      22: 2   Rich and *p* have this in common:
      22: 9   for he shares his food with the *p*.
      22: 22 not exploit the *p* because they are *p*
      28: 6   Better a *p* man whose walk is
      28: 27 to the *p* will lack nothing,
      29: 7   care about justice for the *p*,
      31: 9   defend the rights of the *p*
      31: 20 She opens her arms to the *p*
Ecc   4: 13 Better a *p* but wise youth
Isa   3: 14 the plunder from the *p* is
      10: 2   to deprive the *p* of their rights
      14: 30 of the *p* will find pasture.
      25: 4   You have been a refuge for the *p*,
      32: 7   schemes to destroy the *p* with lies,
      61: 1   me to preach good news to the *p*.
Jer   22: 16 He defended the cause of the *p*
Eze   18: 12 He oppresses the *p* and needy.
Am   2: 7   They trample on the heads of the *p*
       4: 1   you women who oppress the *p*
       5: 11 You trample on the *p*
Zec   7: 10 or the fatherless, the alien or the *p*.
Mt   5: 3   saying: "Blessed are the *p* in spirit,

Mt	11: 5	the good news is preached to the *p*.
	19: 21	your possessions and give to the *p*,
	26: 11	The *p* you will always have
Mk	12: 42	But a *p* widow came and put
	14: 7	The *p* you will always have
Lk	4: 18	me to preach good news to the *p*.
	6: 20	"Blessed are you who are *p*,
	11: 41	is inside the dish, to the *p*,
	14: 13	invite the *p*, the crippled, the lame,
	21: 2	also saw a *p* widow put
Jn	12: 8	You will always have the *p*
Ac	9: 36	doing good and helping the *p*.
	10: 4	and gifts to the *p* have come up
	24: 17	to bring my people gifts for the *p*
Ro	15: 26	for the *p* among the saints
1Co	13: 3	If I give all I possess to the *p*
2Co	6: 10	sorrowful, yet always rejoicing; *p*,
	8: 9	yet for your sakes he became *p*,
Gal	2: 10	continue to remember the *p*,
Jas	2: 2	and a *p* man in shabby clothes
	2: 5	not God chosen those who are *p*
	2: 6	But you have insulted the *p*.

POPULATION*

Pr	14: 28	A large *p* is a king's glory,

PORTION

Nu	18: 29	as the Lord's *p* the best
Dt	32: 9	For the Lord's *p* is his people,
1Sa	1: 5	But to Hannah he gave a double *p*
2Ki	2: 9	"Let me inherit a double *p*
Ps	73: 26	and my *p* for ever.
	119: 57	You are my *p*, O Lord;
Isa	53: 12	Therefore I will give him a *p*
Jer	10: 16	He who is the *P* of Jacob is not like
La	3: 24	to myself, "The Lord is my *p*;
Zec	2: 12	Lord will inherit Judah as his *p*

PORTRAIT

Lk	20: 24	Whose *p* and inscription are on it?"

PORTRAYED

Gal	3: 1	very eyes Jesus Christ was clearly *p*

POSITION (POSITIONS)

Ro	12: 16	to associate with people of low *p*.
Jas	1: 9	ought to take pride in his high *p*.
2Pe	3: 17	and fall from your secure *p*.

POSITIONS (POSITION)

2Ch	20: 17	Take up your *p*; stand firm
Jude	: 6	the angels who did not keep their *p*

POSSESS (POSSESSED POSSESSING POSSESSION POSSESSIONS)

Nu	33: 53	for I have given you the land to *p*.
Dt	4: 14	you are crossing the Jordan to *p*.
Pr	8: 12	I *p* knowledge and discretion.
Jn	5: 39	that by them you *p* eternal life.

POSSESSED (POSSESS)

Jn	10: 21	the sayings of a man *p* by a demon.

POSSESSING* (POSSESS)

2Co	6: 10	nothing, and yet *p* everything.

POSSESSION (POSSESS)

Ge	15: 7	to give you this land to take *p* of it
Ex	6: 8	I will give it to you as a *p*.
	19: 5	nations you will be my treasured *p*.

Nu	13: 30	"We should go up and take *p*
Dt	7: 6	to be his people, his treasured *p*.
Jos	1: 11	take *p* of the land the Lord your
Ps	2: 8	the ends of the earth your *p*.
	135: 4	Israel to be his treasured *p*.
Eph	1: 14	of those who are God's *p*—

POSSESSIONS (POSSESS)

Mt	19: 21	go, sell your *p* and give to the poor,
Lk	11: 21	guards his own house, his *p* are safe
	12: 15	consist in the abundance of his *p*."
	19: 8	now I give half of my *p* to the poor,
Ac	4: 32	any of his *p* was his own,
2Co	12: 14	what I want is not your *p* but you.
Heb	10: 34	yourselves had better and lasting *p*.
1Jn	3: 17	If anyone has material *p*

POSSIBLE

Mt	19: 26	but with God all things are *p*."
	26: 39	if it is *p*, may this cup be taken
Mk	9: 23	"Everything is *p* for him who
	10: 27	all things are *p* with God."
	14: 35	prayed that if *p* the hour might pass
Ro	12: 18	If it is *p*, as far as it depends on you,
1Co	6: 5	Is it *p* that there is nobody
	9: 19	to everyone, to win as many as *p*.
	9: 22	by all *p* means I might save some.

POT (POTSHERD POTTER POTTER'S POTTERY)

2Ki	4: 40	there is death in the *p*!"
Jer	18: 4	But the *p* he was shaping

POTIPHAR*

Egyptian who bought Joseph (Ge 37: 36), set him over his house (Ge 39:1-6), sent him to prison (Ge 39:7-30).

POTSHERD (POT)

Isa	45: 9	a *p* among the potsherds

POTTER (POT)

Isa	29: 16	Can the pot say of the *p*,
	45: 9	Does the clay say to the *p*,
	64: 8	We are the clay, you are the *p*;
Jer	18: 6	"Like clay in the hand of the *p*,
Zec	11: 13	it to the *p*"—the handsome price
Ro	9: 21	Does not the *p* have the right

POTTER'S (POT)

Mt	27: 7	to use the money to buy the *p* field

POTTERY (POT)

Ro	9: 21	of clay some *p* for noble purposes

POUR (POURED POURS)

Ps	62: 8	*p* out your hearts to him,
Isa	44: 3	I will *p* out my Spirit
Eze	20: 8	So I said I would *p* out my wrath
	39: 29	for I will *p* out my Spirit
Joel	2: 28	I will *p* out my Spirit on all people.
Zec	12: 10	I will *p* out on the house of David
Mal	3: 10	*p* out so much blessing that you
Ac	2: 17	I will *p* out my Spirit on all people.

POURED (POUR)

Ps	22: 14	I am *p* out like water,
Isa	32: 15	till the Spirit is *p* upon us
Mt	26: 28	which is *p* out for many
Lk	22: 20	in my blood, which is *p* out for you.

Ac 2: 33 and has *p* out what you now see
    10: 45 of the Holy Spirit had been *p* out
Ro 5: 5 because God has *p* out his love
Php 2: 17 even if I am being *p* out like a drink
2Ti 4: 6 I am already being *p* out like
Tit 3: 6 whom he *p* out on us generously
Rev 16: 2 and *p* out his bowl on the land,

POURS (POUR)

Lk 5: 37 And no-one *p* new wine

POVERTY* (POOR)

Dt 28: 48 and thirst, in nakedness and dire *p*,
1Sa 2: 7 the LORD sends *p* and wealth;
Pr   6: 11 *p* will come on you like a bandit
    10: 15 but *p* is the ruin of the poor.
    11: 24 withholds unduly, but comes to *p*.
    13: 18 who ignores discipline comes to *p*
    14: 23 but mere talk leads only to *p*.
    21: 5 as surely as haste leads to *p*.
    22: 16 to the rich—both come to *p*.
    24: 34 *p* will come on you like a bandit
    28: 19 fantasies will have his fill of *p*.
    28: 22 and is unaware that *p* awaits him.
    30: 8 give me neither *p* nor riches,
    31: 7 let them drink and forget their *p*
Ecc 4: 14 born in *p* within his kingdom.
Mk 12: 44 out of her *p* put in everything—
Lk 21: 4 she out of her *p* put in all she had
2Co 8: 2 and their extreme *p* welled up
     8: 9 through his *p* might become rich.
Rev 2: 9 I know your afflictions and your *p*

POWER (POWERFUL POWERS)

Ex 15: 6 was majestic in *p*.
    32: 11 out of Egypt with great *p*
Dt   8: 17 "My *p* and the strength
    34: 12 no-one has ever shown the mighty *p*
1Sa 10: 6 LORD will come upon you in *p*,
    10: 10 Spirit of God came upon him in *p*,
    11: 6 Spirit of God came upon him in *p*,
    16: 13 the LORD came upon David in *p*
1Ch 29: 11 LORD, is the greatness and the *p*
2Ch 20: 6 *P* and might are in your hand,
    32: 7 for there is a greater *p* with us
Job 9: 4 wisdom is profound, his *p* is vast.
    36: 22 "God is exalted in his *p*.
    37: 23 beyond our reach and exalted in *p*;
Ps 20: 6 with the saving *p* of his right hand.
    63: 2 and beheld your *p* and your glory.
    66: 3 So great is your *p*
    68: 34 Proclaim the *p* of God,
    77: 14 you display your *p*
    89: 13 Your arm is endued with *p*;
   145: 6 of the *p* of your awesome works,
   147: 5 Great is our Lord and mighty in *p*;
   150: 2 Praise him for his acts of *p*;
Pr   3: 27 when it is in your *p* to act.
    18: 21 The tongue has the *p* of life
    24: 5 A wise man has great *p*,
Isa 11: 2 the Spirit of counsel and of *p*,
    40: 10 the Sovereign LORD comes with *p*
    40: 26 of his great *p* and mighty strength,
    63: 12 who sent his glorious arm of *p*
Jer 10: 6 and your name is mighty in *p*
    10: 12 But God made the earth by his *p*;
    27: 5 With my great *p* and outstretched
    32: 17 and the earth by your great *p*
Hos 13: 14 from the *p* of the grave;
Na   1: 3 to anger and great in *p*;

Zec 4: 6 nor by *p*, but by my Spirit,'
Mt 22: 29 do not know the Scriptures or the *p*
    24: 30 on the clouds of the sky, with *p*
Lk   1: 35 and the *p* of the Most High will
     4: 14 to Galilee in the *p* of the Spirit,
     9: 1 he gave them *p* and authority
    10: 19 to overcome all the *p* of the enemy;
    24: 49 clothed with *p* from on high."
Ac   1: 8 you will receive *p* when the Holy
     4: 28 They did what your *p* and will had
     4: 33 With great *p* the apostles
    10: 38 with the Holy Spirit and *p*,
    26: 18 and from the *p* of Satan to God,
Ro   1: 16 it is the *p* of God for the salvation
     1: 20 his eternal *p* and divine nature—
     4: 21 fully persuaded that God had *p*
     9: 17 that I might display my *p* in you
    15: 13 overflow with hope by the *p*
    15: 19 through the *p* of the Spirit.
1Co 1: 17 cross of Christ be emptied of its *p*.
     1: 18 to us who are being saved it is the *p*
     2: 4 a demonstration of the Spirit's *p*,
     6: 14 By his *p* God raised the Lord
    15: 24 all dominion, authority and *p*.
    15: 56 of death is sin, and the *p*
2Co 4: 7 to show that this all-surpassing *p* is
     6: 7 in truthful speech and in the *p*
    10: 4 they have divine *p*
    12: 9 for my *p* is made perfect
    13: 4 weakness, yet he lives by God's *p*.
Eph 1: 19 and his incomparably great *p*
     3: 16 you with *p* through his Spirit
     3: 20 according to his *p* that is at work
     6: 10 in the Lord and in his mighty *p*.
Php 3: 10 and the *p* of his resurrection
     3: 21 by the *p* that enables him
Col 1: 11 strengthened with all *p* according
     2: 10 who is the head over every *p*
1Th 1: 5 also with *p*, with the Holy Spirit
2Ti 1: 7 but a spirit of *p*, of love
     3: 5 form of godliness but denying its *p*.
Heb 2: 14 might destroy him who holds the *p*
     7: 16 of the *p* of an indestructible life.
1Pe 1: 5 by God's *p* until the coming
2Pe 1: 3 His divine *p* has given us
Jude : 25 *p* and authority, through Jesus
Rev 4: 11 to receive glory and honour and *p*,
     5: 12 to receive *p* and wealth
    11: 17 you have taken your great *p*
    19: 1 and glory and *p* belong to our God,
    20: 6 The second death has no *p*

POWERFUL (POWER)

2Ch 27: 6 Jotham grew *p* because he walked
Est 9: 4 and he became more and more *p*.
Ps 29: 4 The voice of the LORD is *p*;
Jer 32: 18 *p* God, whose name is the LORD
Zec 8: 22 *p* nations will come to Jerusalem
Mk   1: 7 "After me will come one more *p*
Lk 24: 19 *p* in word and deed before God
2Th 1: 7 in blazing fire with his *p* angels.
Heb 1: 3 sustaining all things by his *p* word.
Jas 5: 16 The prayer of a righteous man is *p*

POWERLESS

Ro   5: 6 when we were still *p*, Christ died
     8: 3 For what the law was *p* to do

POWERS (POWER)

Da   4: 35 pleases with the *p* of heaven

Ro	8: 38	nor any *p*, neither height nor depth
1Co	12: 10	to another miraculous *p*,
Eph	6: 12	against the *p* of this dark world
Col	1: 16	whether thrones or *p* or rulers
	2: 15	And having disarmed the *p*
Heb	6: 5	and the *p* of the coming age,
1Pe	3: 22	and *p* in submission to him.

PRACTICE (PRACTICES PRACTISE PRACTISED PRACTISES)

Ps	119: 56	This has been my *p*:
Eze	33: 31	but they do not put them into *p*.
Mt	7: 24	into *p* is like a wise man who built
Lk	8: 21	hear God's word and put it into *p*."
Php	4: 9	or seen in me—put it into *p*.
1Ti	5: 4	to put their religion into *p* by caring

PRACTICES (PRACTICE)

Col	3: 9	taken off your old self with its *p*

PRACTISE (PRACTICE)

Lev	19: 26	"'Do not *p* divination or sorcery.
	23: 3	for they do not *p* what they preach.
Ro	12: 13	*P* hospitality.

PRACTISED (PRACTISE)

Mt	23: 23	You should have *p* the latter,

PRACTISES (PRACTICE)

Ps	101: 7	No-one who *p* deceit
Mt	5: 19	but whoever *p* and teaches these

PRAISE (PRAISED PRAISES PRAISEWORTHY PRAISING)

Ex	15: 2	He is my God, and I will *p* him,
Dt	10: 21	He is your *p*; he is your God,
	26: 19	declared that he will set you in *p*,
	32: 3	Oh, *p* the greatness of our God!
Ru	4: 14	said to Naomi: "*P* be to the LORD,
2Sa	22: 4	to the LORD, who is worthy of *p*,
	22: 47	The LORD lives! *P* be to my Rock
1Ch	16: 25	is the LORD and most worthy of *p*;
	16: 35	that we may glory in your *p*."
	23: 5	four thousand are to *p* the LORD
	29: 10	"*P* be to you, O LORD,
2Ch	5: 13	they raised their voices in *p*
	20: 21	and to *p* him for the splendour
	29: 30	to *p* the LORD with the words
Ezr	3: 10	took their places to *p* the LORD,
Ne	9: 5	and *p* the LORD your God,
Ps	8: 2	you have ordained *p*
	9: 1	I will *p* you, O LORD,
	16: 7	I will *p* the LORD, who counsels
	26: 7	proclaiming aloud your *p*
	30: 4	*p* his holy name.
	33: 1	it is fitting for the upright to *p* him.
	34: 1	his *p* will always be on my lips.
	40: 3	a hymn of *p* to our God.
	42: 5	for I will yet *p* him,
	43: 5	for I will yet *p* him,
	45: 17	the nations will *p* you for ever
	47: 7	sing to him a psalm of *p*.
	48: 1	the LORD, and most worthy of *p*,
	51: 15	and my mouth will declare your *p*.
	56: 4	In God, whose word I *p*,
	57: 9	I will *p* you, O Lord,
	63: 4	I will *p* you as long as I live,
	65: 1	*P* awaits you, O God, in Zion;
	66: 2	offer him glory and *p*!
	66: 8	*P* our God, O peoples,

Ps	68: 19	*P* be to the Lord, to God our Saviour
	68: 26	*p* the LORD in the assembly
	69: 30	I will *p* God's name in song
	69: 34	Let heaven and earth *p* him,
	71: 8	My mouth is filled with your *p*,
	71: 14	I will *p* you more and more.
	71: 22	I will *p* you with the harp
	74: 21	the poor and needy *p* your name.
	86: 12	I will *p* you, O Lord my God,
	89: 5	The heavens *p* your wonders,
	92: 1	It is good to *p* the LORD
	96: 2	Sing to the LORD, *p* his name;
	100: 4	and his courts with *p*;
	101: 1	to you, O LORD, I will sing *p*.
	102: 18	not yet created may *p* the LORD:
	103: 1	*P* the LORD, O my soul;
	103: 20	*P* the LORD, you his angels,
	104: 1	*P* the LORD, O my soul.
	105: 2	Sing to him, sing *p* to him;
	106: 1	*P* the LORD.
	108: 3	I will *p* you, O LORD,
	111: 1	*P* the LORD.
	113: 1	*P* the LORD.
	117: 1	*P* the LORD, all you nations;
	119: 175	Let me live that I may *p* you,
	135: 1	*P* the LORD.
	135: 20	you who fear him, *p* the LORD.
	138: 1	I will *p* you, O LORD,
	139: 14	I *p* you because I am fearfully
	144: 1	*P* be to the LORD, my Rock,
	145: 3	is the LORD and most worthy of *p*;
	145: 10	All you have made will *p* you,
	145: 21	Let every creature *p* his holy name
	146: 1	*P* the LORD, O my soul.
	147: 1	how pleasant and fitting to *p* him!
	148: 1	*P* the LORD from the heavens,
	148: 13	Let them *p* the name of the LORD,
	149: 1	his *p* in the assembly of the saints.
	149: 6	May the *p* of God be
	149: 9	*P* the LORD.
	150: 2	*p* him for his surpassing greatness.
	150: 6	that has breath *p* the LORD.
Pr	27: 2	Let another *p* you, and not your
	27: 21	man is tested by the *p* he receives.
	31: 31	let her works bring her *p*
SS	1: 4	we will *p* your love more than wine
Isa	12: 1	"I will *p* you, O LORD.
	42: 10	his *p* from the ends of the earth,
	61: 3	and a garment of *p*
Jer	33: 9	*p* and honour before all nations
Da	2: 20	"*P* be to the name of God for ever
	4: 37	*p* and exalt and glorify the King
Mt	5: 16	and *p* your Father in heaven.
	21: 16	you have ordained *p*'?"
Lk	19: 37	to *p* God in loud voices
Jn	5: 44	effort to obtain the *p* that comes
	12: 43	for they loved *p* from men more
Ro	2: 29	Such a man's *p* is not from men,
	15: 7	in order to bring *p* to God.
2Co	1: 3	*P* be to the God and Father
Eph	1: 3	*P* be to the God and Father
	1: 6	to the *p* of his glorious grace,
	1: 12	might be for the *p* of his glory.
	1: 14	to the *p* of his glory.
1Th	2: 6	We were not looking for *p*
Heb	13: 15	offer to God a sacrifice of *p*—
Jas	3: 9	With the tongue we *p* our Lord
	5: 13	happy? Let him sing songs of *p*.
Rev	5: 13	be *p* and honour and glory
	7: 12	*P* and glory

PRAISED (PRAISE)

1Ch	29: 10	David *p* the LORD in the presence
Ne	8: 6	Ezra *p* the LORD, the great God;
Job	1: 21	may the name of the LORD be *p*."
Ps	113: 2	Let the name of the LORD be *p*,
Pr	31: 30	who fears the LORD is to be *p*.
Isa	63: 7	the deeds for which he is to be *p*,
Da	2: 19	Then Daniel *p* the God of heaven
	4: 34	Then I *p* the Most High; I honoured
Lk	18: 43	the people saw it, they also *p* God
	23: 47	seeing what had happened, *p* God
Ro	9: 5	who is God over all, for ever *p*!
Gal	1: 24	And they *p* God because of me.
1Pe	4: 11	that in all things God may be *p*

PRAISES (PRAISE)

2Sa	22: 50	I will sing *p* to your name.
Ps	18: 49	I will sing *p* to your name.
	47: 6	Sing *p* to God, sing *p*;
	147: 1	How good it is to sing *p* to our God,
Pr	31: 28	her husband also, and he *p* her:
1Pe	2: 9	that you may declare the *p*

PRAISEWORTHY* (PRAISE)

Ps	78: 4	the *p* deeds of the LORD,
Php	4: 8	if anything is excellent or *p*—

PRAISING (PRAISE)

Lk	2: 13	*p* God and saying, "Glory to God
	2: 20	*p* God for all the things they had
Ac	2: 47	*p* God and enjoying the favour
	10: 46	speaking in tongues and *p* God.
1Co	14: 16	If you are *p* God with your spirit,

PRAY (PRAYED PRAYER PRAYERS PRAYING PRAYS)

Dt	4: 7	is near us whenever we *p* to him?
1Sa	12: 23	the LORD by failing to *p* for you.
1Ki	8: 30	when they *p* towards this place.
2Ch	7: 14	will humble themselves and *p*
Ezr	6: 10	and *p* for the well-being of the king
Job	42: 8	My servant Job will *p* for you,
Ps	5: 2	for to you I *p*.
	32: 6	let everyone who is godly *p*
	122: 6	*P* for the peace of Jerusalem:
Jer	29: 7	*P* to the LORD for it,
	29: 12	upon me and come and *p* to me,
	42: 3	*P* that the LORD your God will
Mt	5: 44	and *p* for those who persecute you,
	6: 5	"But when you *p*, do not be like
	6: 9	"This is how you should *p*:
	14: 23	up into the hills by himself to *p*.
	19: 13	hands on them and *p* for them.
	26: 36	Sit here while I go over there and *p*
Lk	6: 28	*p* for those who ill-treat you.
	11: 1	us to *p*, just as John taught his
	18: 1	them that they should always *p*
	22: 40	"*P* that you will not fall
Jn	17: 20	I *p* also for those who will believe
Ro	8: 26	do not know what we ought to *p*,
1Co	14: 13	in a tongue should *p* that he may
Eph	1: 18	I *p* also that the eyes
	3: 16	I *p* that out of his glorious riches he
	6: 18	And *p* in the Spirit on all occasions
Col	1: 10	we *p* this in order that you may live
	4: 3	*p* for us, too, that God may open
1Th	5: 17	Be joyful always; *p* continually;
2Ti	1: 11	in mind, we constantly *p* for you,
Jas	5: 13	one of you in trouble? He should *p*.
	5: 16	*p* for each other so that you may be

1Pe	4: 7	self-controlled so that you can *p*.
Jude	: 20	up in your most holy faith and *p*

PRAYED (PRAY)

1Sa	1: 27	I *p* for this child, and the LORD
1Ki	18: 36	Elijah stepped forward and *p*:
	19: 4	under it and *p* that he might die.
2Ki	6: 17	And Elisha *p*, "O LORD,
2Ch	30: 18	But Hezekiah *p* for them, saying,
Ne	4: 9	we *p* to our God and posted a guard
Job	42: 10	After Job had *p* for his friends,
Da	6: 10	got down on his knees and *p*,
	9: 4	I *p* to the LORD my God
Jnh	2: 1	From inside the fish Jonah *p*
Mt	26: 39	with his face to the ground and *p*,
Mk	1: 35	off to a solitary place, where he *p*.
	14: 35	*p* that if possible the hour might
Lk	22: 41	knelt down and *p*, "Father,
Jn	17: 1	he looked towards heaven and *p*:
Ac	4: 31	After they *p*, the place where they
	6: 6	who *p* and laid their hands on them
	8: 15	they *p* for them that they might
	13: 3	So after they had fasted and *p*,

PRAYER (PRAY)

2Ch	30: 27	for their *p* reached heaven,
Ezr	8: 23	about this, and he answered our *p*.
Ps	4: 1	be merciful to me and hear my *p*.
	6: 9	the LORD accepts my *p*.
	17: 1	Give ear to my *p*—
	17: 6	give ear to me and hear my *p*.
	65: 2	O you who hear *p*,
	66: 20	who has not rejected my *p*
	86: 6	Hear my *p*, O LORD;
Pr	15: 8	but the *p* of the upright pleases him
	15: 29	but he hears the *p* of the righteous.
Isa	56: 7	a house of *p* for all nations."
Mt	21: 13	house will be called a house of *p*,'
Mt	21: 22	receive whatever you ask for in *p*."
Mk	9: 29	This kind can come out only by *p*."
	11: 24	whatever you ask for in *p*,
Jn	17: 15	My *p* is not that you take them out
Ac	1: 14	all joined together constantly in *p*,
	2: 42	to the breaking of bread and to *p*.
	6: 4	and will give our attention to *p*
	10: 31	has heard your *p* and remembered
	16: 13	expected to find a place of *p*.
Ro	12: 12	patient in affliction, faithful in *p*.
1Co	7: 5	you may devote yourselves to *p*.
2Co	13: 9	and our *p* is for your perfection.
Php	1: 9	this is my *p*: that your love may
	4: 6	but in everything, by *p* and petition
Col	4: 2	yourselves to *p*, being watchful
1Ti	2: 8	to lift up holy hands in *p*,
	4: 5	by the word of God and *p*.
Jas	5: 15	*p* offered in faith will make the sick
1Pe	3: 12	and his ears are attentive to their *p*,

PRAYERS (PRAY)

1Ch	5: 20	He answered their *p*, because they
Isa	1: 15	even if you offer many *p*,
Mk	12: 40	and for a show make lengthy *p*.
2Co	1: 11	as you help us by your *p*.
Eph	6: 18	on all occasions with all kinds of *p*
1Ti	2: 1	then, first of all, that requests, *p*,
1Pe	3: 7	so that nothing will hinder your *p*.
Rev	5: 8	which are the *p* of the saints.
	8: 3	with the *p* of all the saints,

PRAYING (PRAY)

Ge 24: 45 "Before I finished *p* in my heart,
1Sa 1: 12 As she kept on *p* to the LORD,
Mk 11: 25 And when you stand *p*,
Lk 3: 21 as he was *p*, heaven was opened
  6: 12 and spent the night *p* to God.
  9: 29 As he was *p*, the appearance
Jn 17: 9 I am not *p* for the world,
Ac 9: 11 from Tarsus named Saul, for he is *p*
  16: 25 and Silas were *p* and singing hymns
Ro 15: 30 in my struggle by *p* to God for me.
Eph 6: 18 always keep on *p* for all the saints.

PRAYS (PRAY)

1Co 14: 14 my spirit *p*, but my mind is

PREACH (PREACHED PREACHING)

Isa 61: 1 me to *p* good news to the poor.
Mt 10: 7 As you go, *p* this message:
  23: 3 they do not practise what they *p*.
Mk 16: 15 and *p* the good news to all creation.
Lk 4: 18 me to *p* good news to the poor.
Ac 9: 20 At once he began to *p*
  16: 10 us to *p* the gospel to them.
Ro 1: 15 am so eager to *p* the gospel
  10: 15 how can they *p* unless they are sent
  15: 20 to *p* the gospel where Christ was
1Co 1: 17 to *p* the gospel—not with words
  1: 23 wisdom, but we *p* Christ crucified:
  9: 14 that those who *p* the gospel should
  9: 16 Woe to me if I do not *p* the gospel!
2Co 4: 5 For we do not *p* ourselves,
  10: 16 so that we can *p* the gospel
Gal 1: 8 from heaven should *p* a gospel
2Ti 4: 2 I give you this charge: *P* the Word;

PREACHED (PREACH)

Mt 24: 14 gospel of the kingdom will be *p*
Mk 6: 12 and *p* that people should repent.
  13: 10 And the gospel must first be *p*
  14: 9 wherever the gospel is *p*
Ac 8: 4 had been scattered *p* the word
  28: 31 hindrance he *p* the kingdom
1Co 9: 27 so that after I have *p* to others,
  15: 1 you of the gospel I *p* to you,
2Co 11: 4 other than the Jesus we *p*,
Gal 1: 8 other than the one we *p* to you,
Eph 2: 17 *p* peace to you who were far away
Php 1: 18 false motives or true, Christ is *p*.
1Ti 3: 16 was *p* among the nations,
1Pe 1: 25 this is the word that was *p* to you.
  3: 19 and *p* to the spirits in prison who

PREACHING (PREACH)

Lk 9: 6 *p* the gospel and healing people
Ac 18: 5 devoted himself exclusively to *p*,
Ro 10: 14 hear without someone *p* to them?
1Co 2: 4 and my *p* were not with wise
  9: 18 in *p* the gospel I may offer it free
Gal 1: 9 If anybody is *p* to you a gospel
1Ti 4: 13 the public reading of Scripture, to *p*
  5: 17 especially those whose work is *p*

PRECEDE*

1Th 4: 15 will certainly not *p* those who have

PRECEPTS*

Dt 33: 10 He teaches your *p* to Jacob
Ps 19: 8 The *p* of the LORD are right,
  103: 18 and remember to obey his *p*.

105: 45 that they might keep his *p*
111: 7 all his *p* are trustworthy.
111: 10 who follow his *p* have good
119: 4 You have laid down *p*
119: 15 I meditate on your *p*
119: 27 understand the teaching of your *p*;
119: 40 How I long for your *p*!
119: 45 for I have sought out your *p*.
119: 56 I obey your *p*.
119: 63 to all who follow your *p*.
119: 69 I keep your *p* with all my heart.
119: 78 but I will meditate on your *p*.
119: 87 but I have not forsaken your *p*.
119: 93 I will never forget your *p*,
119: 94 I have sought out your *p*.
119: 100 for I obey your *p*.
119: 104 I gain understanding from your *p*;
119: 110 but I have not strayed from your *p*.
119: 128 because I consider all your *p* right,
119: 134 that I may obey your *p*.
119: 141 I do not forget your *p*.
119: 159 See how I love your *p*;
119: 168 I obey your *p* and your statutes,
119: 173 for I have chosen your *p*.

PRECIOUS

Ps 19: 10 They are more *p* than gold,
  72: 14 for *p* is their blood in his sight.
  116: 15 *P* in the sight of the LORD
  119: 72 from your mouth is more *p* to me
  139: 17 How *p* to me are your thoughts,
Pr 8: 11 for wisdom is more *p* than rubies,
Isa 28: 16 a *p* cornerstone for a sure
1Pe 1: 19 but with the *p* blood of Christ,
  2: 4 but chosen by God and *p* to him—
  2: 6 a chosen and *p* cornerstone,
2Pe 1: 1 Christ have received a faith as *p*
  1: 4 us his very great and *p* promises,

PREDESTINED* (DESTINY)

Ro 8: 29 *p* to be conformed to the likeness
  8: 30 And those he *p*, he also called;
Eph 1: 5 In love he *p* us to be adopted
  1: 11 having been *p* according

PREDICTED (PREDICTION)

1Sa 28: 17 The LORD has done what he *p*
Ac 7: 52 killed those who *p* the coming
1Pe 1: 11 when he *p* the sufferings of Christ

PREDICTION* (PREDICTED PREDICTIONS)

Jer 28: 9 only if his *p* comes true."

PREDICTIONS (PREDICTION)

Isa 44: 26 and fulfils the *p* of his messengers,

PREGNANT

Ex 21: 22 who are fighting hit a *p* woman
Mt 24: 19 be in those days for *p* women
1Th 5: 3 as labour pains on a *p* woman.

PREPARE (PREPARED)

Ps 23: 5 You *p* a table before me
Isa 25: 6 the LORD Almighty will *p*
  40: 3 "In the desert *p*
Am 4: 12 *p* to meet your God, O Israel."
Mal 3: 1 who will *p* the way before me.
Mt 3: 3 '*P* the way for the Lord,
Jn 14: 2 there to *p* a place for you.
Eph 4: 12 to *p* God's people for works

1Pe 1: 13 Therefore, *p* your minds for action;

PREPARED (PREPARE)

Ex	23: 20	to bring you to the place I have *p*.
Mt	25: 34	the kingdom *p* for you
Ro	9: 22	of his wrath—*p* for destruction?
1Co	2: 9	what God has *p* for those who love
Eph	2: 10	which God *p* in advance for us
2Ti	2: 21	and *p* to do any good work.
	4: 2	be *p* in season and out of season;
1Pe	3: 15	Always be *p* to give an answer

PRESCRIBED

Ezr 7: 23 Whatever the God of heaven has *p*,

PRESENCE (PRESENT [1])

Ex	25: 30	Put the bread of the *P* on this table
	33: 14	The LORD replied, "My *P* will go
Nu	4: 7	"Over the table of the *P* they are
1Sa	6: 20	in the *p* of the LORD, this
	21: 6	of the *P* that had been removed
2Sa	22: 13	Out of the brightness of his *p*
2Ki	17: 23	LORD removed them from his *p*,
	23: 27	also from my *p* as I removed Israel,
Ezr	9: 15	one of us can stand in your *p*."
Ps	16: 11	you will fill me with joy in your *p*,
	21: 6	with the joy of your *p*.
	23: 5	in the *p* of my enemies.
	31: 20	the shelter of your *p* you hide them
	41: 12	and set me in your *p* for ever.
	51: 11	Do not cast me from your *p*
	52: 9	in the *p* of your saints.
	89: 15	who walk in the light of your *p*,
	90: 8	our secret sins in the light of your *p*
	114: 7	O earth, at the *p* of the Lord,
	139: 7	Where can I flee from your *p*?
Isa	26: 17	so were we in your *p*, O LORD.
Jer	5: 22	"Should you not tremble in my *p*?
Eze	38: 20	of the earth will tremble at my *p*.
Hos	6: 2	that we may live in his *p*.
Na	1: 5	The earth trembles at his *p*,
Mal	3: 16	in his *p* concerning those who
Ac	2: 28	you will fill me with joy in your *p*.'
1Th	3: 9	have in the *p* of our God
	3: 13	and holy in the *p* of our God
2Th	1: 9	and shut out from the *p* of the Lord
Heb	9: 24	now to appear for us in God's *p*.
1Jn	3: 19	rest in his *p* whenever our hearts
Jude	: 24	before his glorious *p* without fault

PRESENT [1] (PRESENCE)

Ps	46: 1	an ever *p* help in trouble.
1Co	3: 22	life or death or the *p* or the future—
	7: 26	of the *p* crisis, I think that it is good
1Ti	4: 8	holding promise for both the *p* life

PRESENT [2]

2Co	11: 2	so that I might *p* you as a pure
Eph	5: 27	and to *p* her to himself
2Ti	2: 15	Do your best to *p* yourself to God
Jude	: 24	and to *p* you before his glorious

PRESERVE

Lk 17: 33 and whoever loses his life will *p* it.

PRESS (PRESSED PRESSURE)

Php 3: 12 but I *p* on to take hold of that
     3: 14 I *p* on towards the goal

PRESSED (PRESS)

Lk 6: 38 *p* down, shaken together

PRESSURE (PRESS)

2Co 1: 8 We were under great *p*, far
     11: 28 I face daily the *p* of my concern

PREVAILS

1Sa 2: 9 "It is not by strength that one *p*;
Pr 19: 21 but it is the LORD's purpose that *p*

PRICE (PRICELESS)

Job 28: 18 the *p* of wisdom is beyond rubies.
1Co 6: 20 your own; you were bought at a *p*.
     7: 23 bought at a *p*; do not become slaves

PRICELESS* (PRICE)

Ps 36: 7 How *p* is your unfailing love!

PRIDE (PROUD)

Pr	8: 13	I hate *p* and arrogance,
	11: 2	When *p* comes, then comes
	13: 10	*P* only breeds quarrels,
	16: 18	*P* goes before destruction,
	29: 23	A man's *p* brings him low,
Isa	25: 11	God will bring down their *p*
Da	4: 37	And those who walk in *p* he is able
Am	8: 7	The LORD has sworn by the *P*
2Co	5: 12	giving you an opportunity to take *p*
	7: 4	in you; I take great *p* in you.
	8: 24	and the reason for our *p* in you,
Gal	6: 4	Then he can take *p* in himself,
Jas	1: 9	ought to take *p* in his high position.

PRIEST (PRIESTHOOD PRIESTLY PRIESTS)

Ge	14: 18	He was *p* of God Most High,
Nu	5: 10	to the *p* will belong to the *p*.'"
2Ch	13: 9	and seven rams may become a *p*
Ps	110: 4	"You are a *p* for ever,
Heb	2: 17	faithful high *p* in service to God,
	3: 1	and high *p* whom we confess.
	4: 14	have a great high *p* who has gone
	4: 15	do not have a high *p* who is unable
	5: 6	"You are a *p* for ever,
	6: 20	He has become a high *p* for ever,
	7: 3	Son of God he remains a *p* for ever.
	7: 15	clear if another *p* like Melchizedek
	7: 26	Such a high *p* meets our need—
	8: 1	We do have such a high *p*,
	10: 11	Day after day every *p* stands
	13: 11	The high *p* carries the blood

PRIESTHOOD (PRIEST)

Heb 7: 24 lives for ever, he has a permanent *p*.
1Pe 2: 5 into a spiritual house to be a holy *p*,
     2: 9 you are a chosen people, a royal *p*,

PRIESTLY (PRIEST)

Ro 15: 16 to the Gentiles with the *p* duty.

PRIESTS (PRIEST)

Ex	19: 6	you will be for me a kingdom of *p*
Lev	21: 1	"Speak to the *p*, the sons of Aaron,
Eze	42: 13	where the *p* who approach
	46: 2	*p* are to sacrifice his burnt offering
Rev	5: 10	to be a kingdom and *p*
	20: 6	but they will be *p* of God

PRIME

Isa 38: 10 recovery: I said, "In the *p* of my life

PRINCE (PRINCES PRINCESS)

Isa   9: 6 Everlasting Father, *P* of Peace.
Eze 34: 24 and my servant David will be *p*
     37: 25 my servant will be their *p* for ever.
Da   8: 25 stand against the *P* of princes.
Jn 12: 31 now the *p* of this world will be
Ac   5: 31 as *P* and Saviour that he might give

PRINCES (PRINCE)

Ps 118: 9 than to trust in *p*.
   148: 11 you *p* and all rulers on earth,
Isa 40: 23 He brings *p* to naught

PRINCESS* (PRINCE)

Ps 45: 13 All glorious is the *p*

PRISCILLA*

Wife of Aquila; co-worker with Paul (Ac 18; Ro 16:3; 1Co 16:19; 2Ti 4:19); instructor of Apollos (Ac 18:24-28).

PRISON (PRISONER PRISONERS)

Ps 66: 11 You brought us into *p*
  142: 7 Set me free from my *p*,
Isa 42: 7 to free captives from *p*
Mt 25: 36 I was in *p* and you came to visit me
2Co 11: 23 been in *p* more frequently,
Heb 11: 36 others were chained and put in *p*.
   13: 3 Remember those in *p*
1Pe 3: 19 spirits in *p* who disobeyed long ago
Rev 20: 7 Satan will be released from his *p*

PRISONER (PRISON)

Ro   7: 23 and making me a *p* of the law of sin
Gal 3: 22 declares that the whole world is a *p*
Eph 3: 1 the *p* of Christ Jesus for the sake

PRISONERS (PRISON)

Ps 68: 6 he leads forth the *p* with singing;
  79: 11 groans of the *p* come before you;
 107: 10 *p* suffering in iron chains,
 146: 7 the LORD sets *p* free,
Isa 61: 1 and release from darkness for the *p*,
Zec 9: 12 to your fortress, O *p* of hope;
Lk   4: 18 me to proclaim freedom for the *p*
Gal 3: 23 we were held *p* by the law,

PRIVILEGE*

2Co 8: 4 pleaded with us for the *p* of sharing

PRIZE*

1Co 9: 24 Run in such a way as to get the *p*.
   9: 24 but only one gets the *p*? Run
   9: 27 will not be disqualified for the *p*.
Php 3: 14 on towards the goal to win the *p*
Col 2: 18 of angels disqualify you for the *p*.

PROBE

Job 11: 7 Can you *p* the limits
Ps 17: 3 Though you *p* my heart

PROCEDURE

Ecc 8: 6 For there is a proper time and *p*

PROCESSION

Ps 68: 24 Your *p* has come into view, O God,
 118: 27 boughs in hand, join in the festal *p*
1Co 4: 9 on display at the end of the *p*,
2Co 2: 14 us in triumphal *p* in Christ

PROCLAIM (PROCLAIMED PROCLAIMING PROCLAIMS PROCLAMATION)

Ex 33: 19 and I will *p* my name, the LORD,
Lev 25: 10 and *p* liberty throughout the land
Dt 30: 12 and *p* it to us so we may obey it?"
2Sa 1: 20 *p* it not in the streets of Ashkelon,
1Ch 16: 23 *p* his salvation day after day.
Ne   8: 15 and that they should *p* this word
Ps   2: 7 I will *p* the decree of the LORD:
   9: 11 *p* among the nations what he has
  19: 1 the skies *p* the work of his hands.
  22: 31 They will *p* his righteousness
  40: 9 I *p* righteousness in the great
  50: 6 the heavens *p* his righteousness,
  64: 9 they will *p* the works of God
  68: 34 *P* the power of God,
  71: 16 I will come and *p* your mighty acts,
  92: 2 to *p* your love in the morning
  96: 2 *p* his salvation day after day.
  97: 6 The heavens *p* his righteousness,
 106: 2 Who can *p* the mighty acts
 118: 17 will *p* what the LORD has done.
 145: 6 and I will *p* your great deeds.
Isa 12: 4 and *p* that his name is exalted.
  42: 12 and *p* his praise in the islands.
  52: 7 who *p* salvation,
  61: 1 to *p* freedom for the captives
  66: 19 They will *p* my glory
Jer   7: 2 house and there *p* this message:
  50: 2 lift up a banner and *p* it;
Hos 5: 9 I *p* what is certain.
Zec 9: 10 He will *p* peace to the nations.
Mt 10: 27 in your ear, *p* from the housetops.
  12: 18 and he will *p* justice to the nations.
Lk   4: 18 me to *p* freedom for the prisoners
   9: 60 you go and *p* the kingdom of God."
Ac 17: 23 unknown I am going to *p*
  20: 27 hesitated to *p* to you the whole will
1Co 11: 26 you *p* the Lord's death
Col 1: 28 We *p* him, admonishing
   4: 4 Pray that I may *p* it clearly,
1Jn 1: 1 this we *p* concerning the Word

PROCLAIMED (PROCLAIM)

Ex   9: 16 and that my name might be *p*
  34: 5 there with him and *p* his name,
Ps 68: 11 was the company of those who *p* it:
Ro 15: 19 I have fully *p* the gospel of Christ.
Col 1: 23 that has been *p* to every creature
2Ti 4: 17 me the message might be fully *p*

PROCLAIMING (PROCLAIM)

Ps 26: 7 *p* aloud your praise
  92: 15 *p*, "The LORD is upright;
Ac   5: 42 and *p* the good news that Jesus is
Ro 10: 8 the word of faith we are *p*:

PROCLAIMS (PROCLAIM)

Dt 18: 22 If what a prophet *p* in the name

PROCLAMATION (PROCLAIM)

Isa 62: 11 The LORD has made *p*

PRODUCE (PRODUCES)

Mt   3: 8 *P* fruit in keeping with repentance.
   3: 10 tree that does not *p* good fruit will

PRODUCES (PRODUCE)

Pr 30: 33 so stirring up anger *p* strife."
Ro   5: 3 that suffering *p* perseverance;

Heb 12: 11 it *p* a harvest of righteousness

PROFANE (PROFANED)

Lev 19: 12 and so *p* the name of your God.
  22: 32 Do not *p* my holy name.
Mal 2: 10 Why do we *p* the covenant

PROFANED (PROFANE)

Eze 36: 20 the nations they *p* my holy name,

PROFESS*

1Ti 2: 10 for women who *p* to worship God.
Heb 4: 14 let us hold firmly to the faith we *p*.
  10: 23 unswervingly to the hope we *p*,

PROFIT (PROFITABLE)

Pr 14: 23 All hard work brings a *p*,
  21: 5 The plans of the diligent lead to *p*
Isa 44: 10 which can *p* him nothing?
2Co 2: 17 not peddle the word of God for *p*.
Php 3: 7 was to my *p* I now consider loss

PROFITABLE* (PROFIT)

Pr 3: 14 for she is more *p* than silver
  31: 18 She sees that her trading is *p*,
Tit 3: 8 These things are excellent and *p*

PROFOUND

Job 9: 4 His wisdom is *p*, his power is vast.
Ps 92: 5 how *p* your thoughts!
Eph 5: 32 This is a *p* mystery—but I am

PROGRESS

Php 1: 25 continue with all of you for your *p*
1Ti 4: 15 so that everyone may see your *p*.

PROLONG*

Dt 5: 33 *p* your days in the land that you
Ps 85: 5 Will you *p* your anger
Pr 3: 2 for they will *p* your life many years
Isa 53: 10 will see his offspring and *p* his days,
La 4: 22 he will not *p* your exile.

PROMISE (PROMISED PROMISES)

Nu 23: 19 Does he *p* and not fulfil?
Jos 23: 14 Every *p* has been fulfilled;
2Sa 7: 25 keep for ever the *p* you have made
1Ki 8: 20 The LORD has kept the *p* he made
  8: 24 You have kept your *p*
Ne 5: 13 man who does not keep this *p*.
  9: 8 have kept your *p* because you are
Ps 77: 8 Has his *p* failed for all time?
  119: 41 your salvation according to your *p*;
  119: 50 Your *p* renews my life.
  119: 58 to me according to your *p*.
  119: 162 I rejoice in your *p*
Ac 2: 39 The *p* is for you and your children
Ro 4: 13 offspring received the *p* that he
  4: 20 unbelief regarding the *p* of God,
Gal 3: 14 that by faith we might receive the *p*
Eph 2: 12 foreigners to the covenants of the *p*
1Ti 4: 8 holding *p* for both the present life
Heb 6: 13 When God made his *p* to Abraham
  11: 11 him faithful who had made the *p*.
2Pe 3: 9 Lord is not slow in keeping his *p*,
  3: 13 with his *p* we are looking forward

PROMISED (PROMISE)

Ge 21: 1 did for Sarah what he had *p*.
  24: 7 who spoke to me and *p* me on oath,

Ex 3: 17 And I have *p* to bring you up out
Nu 10: 29 for the LORD has *p* good things
Dt 15: 6 your God will bless you as he has *p*,
  26: 18 his treasured possession as he *p*,
2Sa 7: 28 you have *p* these good things
1Ki 9: 5 I *p* David your father when I said,
2Ch 6: 15 with your mouth you have *p*
Ps 119: 57 I have *p* to obey your words.
Lk 24: 49 to send you what my Father has *p*;
Ac 1: 4 but wait for the gift my Father *p*,
  13: 32 What God *p* our fathers he has
Ro 4: 21 power to do what he had *p*.
Tit 1: 2 *p* before the beginning of time,
Heb 10: 23 for he who *p* is faithful.
  10: 36 you will receive what he has *p*.
Jas 1: 12 the crown of life that God has *p*
  2: 5 the kingdom he *p* those who love
2Pe 3: 4 "Where is this 'coming' he *p*?
1Jn 2: 25 And this is what he *p* us—

PROMISES (PROMISE)

Jos 21: 45 one of all the LORD's good *p*
  23: 14 of all the good *p* the LORD your
1Ki 8: 56 failed of all the good *p* he gave
1Ch 17: 19 and made known all these great *p*.
Ps 85: 8 he *p* peace to his people, his saints
  106: 12 Then they believed his *p*
  119: 140 Your *p* have been thoroughly
  119: 148 that I may meditate on your *p*.
  145: 13 The LORD is faithful to all his *p*
Ro 9: 4 the temple worship and the *p*.
2Co 1: 20 matter how many *p* God has made,
  7: 1 Since we have these *p*, dear friends,
Heb 8: 6 and it is founded on better *p*.
2Pe 1: 4 us his very great and precious *p*,

PROMOTE (PROMOTES)

Pr 12: 20 but joy for those who *p* peace.
  16: 21 and pleasant words *p* instruction.
1Ti 1: 4 These *p* controversies rather

PROMOTES (PROMOTE)

Pr 17: 9 over an offence *p* love,

PROMPTED

1Th 1: 3 your labour *p* by love, and your
2Th 1: 11 and every act *p* by your faith.

PRONOUNCE (PRONOUNCED)

1Ch 23: 13 to *p* blessings in his name for ever.

PRONOUNCED (PRONOUNCE)

1Ch 16: 12 miracles, and the judgments he *p*,

PROOF (PROVE)

Ac 17: 31 He has given *p* of this to all men
2Co 8: 24 Therefore show these men the *p*

PROPER

Ps 104: 27 give them their food at the *p* time.
  145: 15 give them their food at the *p* time.
Ecc 5: 18 Then I realised that it is good and *p*
  8: 5 the wise heart will know the *p* time
Mt 24: 45 give them their food at the *p* time?
Lk 1: 20 which will come true at their *p* time
1Co 11: 13 Is it *p* for a woman to pray to God
Gal 6: 9 at the *p* time we will reap a harvest
1Ti 2: 6 the testimony given in its *p* time.
1Pe 2: 17 Show *p* respect to everyone:

PROPERTY

Heb 10: 34 the confiscation of your *p*,

PROPHECIES (PROPHESY)

1Co 13: 8 where there are *p*, they will cease;
1Th   5: 20 do not treat *p* with contempt.

PROPHECY (PROPHESY)

Da   9: 24 to seal up vision and *p*
1Co 12: 10 miraculous powers, to another *p*,
     13: 2 of *p* and can fathom all mysteries
     14: 1 gifts, especially the gift of *p*.
     14: 6 or *p* or word of instruction?
     14: 22 *p*, however, is for believers,
2Pe   1: 20 you must understand that no *p*
Rev 22: 18 the words of the *p* of this book:

PROPHESIED (PROPHESY)

Nu   11: 25 the Spirit rested on them, they *p*,
1Sa 19: 24 and also *p* in Samuel's presence.
Jn   11: 51 that year he *p* that Jesus would
Ac   19: 6 and they spoke in tongues and *p*.
     21: 9 four unmarried daughters who *p*.

PROPHESIES (PROPHESY)

Jer 28: 9 the prophet who *p* peace will be
Eze 12: 27 and he *p* about the distant future.'
1Ch 11: 4 *p* with his head covered dishonours
     14: 3 But everyone who *p* speaks to men

PROPHESY (PROPHECIES PROPHECY PROPHESIED PROPHESIES PROPHESYING PROPHET PROPHET'S PROPHETESS PROPHETS)

1Sa 10: 6 and you will *p* with them;
Eze 13: 2 Say to those who *p* out
     13: 17 daughters of your people who *p* out
     34: 2 *p* against the shepherds of Israel;
     37: 4 "*P* to these bones and say to them,
Joel 2: 28 Your sons and daughters will *p*,
Mt   7: 22 Lord, did we not *p* in your name,
Ac   2: 17 Your sons and daughters will *p*,
1Co 13: 9 know in part and we *p* in part,
     14: 39 my brothers, be eager to *p*,
Rev 11: 3 and they will *p* for 1,260 days,

PROPHESYING (PROPHESY)

1Ch 25: 1 and Jeduthun for the ministry of *p*,
Ro   12: 6 If a man's gift is *p*, let him use it

PROPHET (PROPHESY)

Ex   7: 1 your brother Aaron will be your *p*.
Nu   12: 6 "When a *p* of the LORD is
Dt   13: 1 If a *p*, or one who foretells
     18: 18 up for them a *p* like you
     18: 22 If what a *p* proclaims in the name
1Sa   3: 20 that Samuel was attested as a *p*
      9: 9 because the *p* of today used
1Ki   1: 8 son of Jehoiada, Nathan the *p*,
     18: 36 the *p* Elijah stepped forward
2Ki   5: 8 and he will know that there is a *p*
      6: 12 "but Elisha, the *p* who is in Israel,
     20: 1 The *p* Isaiah son of Amoz went
2Ch 35: 18 since the days of the *p* Samuel;
     36: 12 himself before Jeremiah the *p*,
Ezr   5: 1 Haggai the *p* and Zechariah the *p*,
Eze   2: 5 they will know that a *p* has been
     33: 33 they will know that a *p* has been
Hos   9: 7 the *p* is considered a fool,

Am   7: 14 "I was neither a *p* nor a prophet's
Hab   1: 1 that Habakkuk the *p* received.
Hag   1: 1 came through the *p* Haggai
Zec   1: 1 to the *p* Zechariah son of Berekiah,
     13: 4 that day every *p* will be ashamed
Mal   4: 5 I will send you the *p* Elijah
Mt   10: 41 Anyone who receives a *p*
     11: 9 what did you go out to see? A *p*?
     12: 39 except the sign of the *p* Jonah.
Lk   1: 76 will be called a *p* of the Most High;
      4: 24 "no *p* is accepted in his home town.
      7: 16 A great *p* has appeared among us,"
     24: 19 "He was a *p*, powerful in word
Jn   1: 21 "Are you the *P*?" He answered,
Ac   7: 37 'God will send you a *p* like me
     21: 10 a *p* named Agabus came
1Co 14: 37 If anybody thinks he is a *p*
Rev 16: 13 and out of the mouth of the false *p*.

PROPHET'S (PROPHESY)

2Pe   1: 20 about by the *p* own interpretation.

PROPHETESS (PROPHESY)

Ex   15: 20 Then Miriam the *p*, Aaron's sister,
Jdg   4: 4 a *p*, the wife of Lappidoth,
Isa   8: 3 I went to the *p*, and she conceived
Lk   2: 36 a *p*, Anna, the daughter of Phanuel,

PROPHETS (PROPHESY)

Nu   11: 29 that all the LORD's people were *p*
1Sa 10: 11 Is Saul also among the *p*?"
     28: 6 him by dreams or Urim or *p*.
1Ki 19: 10 put your *p* to death with the sword.
1Ch 16: 22 do my *p* no harm."
Ps 105: 15 do my *p* no harm."
Jer 23: 9 Concerning the *p*:
     23: 30 "I am against the *p* who steal
Eze 13: 2 prophesy against the *p*
Mt   5: 17 come to abolish the Law or the *P*;
      7: 12 for this sums up the Law and the *P*.
      7: 15 "Watch out for false *p*.
     22: 40 and the *P* hang on these two
     23: 37 you who kill the *p* and stone those
     24: 24 false Christs and false *p* will appear
     26: 56 of the *p* might be fulfilled."
Lk   10: 24 For I tell you that many *p*
     11: 49 'I will send them *p* and apostles,
     24: 25 believe all that the *p* have spoken!
     24: 44 me in the Law of Moses, the *P*
Ac   3: 24 "Indeed, all the *p* from Samuel on,
     10: 43 All the *p* testify about him that
     13: 1 the church at Antioch there were *p*
     26: 22 nothing beyond what the *p*
     28: 23 the Law of Moses and from the *P*.
Ro   1: 2 through his *p* in the Holy
      3: 21 to which the Law and the *P* testify.
     11: 3 they have killed your *p*
1Co 12: 28 second *p*, third teachers, then
     12: 29 Are all *p*? Are all teachers?
     14: 32 The spirits of *p* are subject
Eph   2: 20 foundation of the apostles and *p*,
      3: 5 Spirit to God's holy apostles and *p*.
      4: 11 some to be *p*, some
Heb   1: 1 through the *p* at many times
1Pe   1: 10 Concerning this salvation, the *p*,
2Pe   1: 19 word of the *p* made more certain,
      3: 2 spoken in the past by the holy *p*
1Jn   4: 1 because many false *p* have gone out
Rev 11: 10 these two *p* had tormented those
     18: 20 Rejoice, saints and apostles and *p*!

PROPITIATION see (atoning) SACRIFICE

PROPORTION

Dt 16: 10 by giving a freewill offering in *p*
    16: 17 Each of you must bring a gift in *p*

PROPRIETY*

1Ti 2: 9 with decency and *p*,
     2: 15 in faith, love and holiness with *p*.

PROSPECT*

Pr 10: 28 The *p* of the righteous is joy,

PROSPER (PROSPERED PROSPERITY PROSPEROUS PROSPERS)

Dt   5: 33 so that you may live and *p*
    28: 63 pleased the LORD to make you *p*
    29: 9 that you may *p* in everything you
1Ki 2: 3 so that you may *p* in all you do
Ezr 6: 14 and *p* under the preaching
Pr 11: 10 When the righteous *p*, the city
    11: 25 A generous man will *p*;
    17: 20 A man of perverse heart does not *p*
    28: 13 who conceals his sins does not *p*,
    28: 25 he who trusts in the LORD will *p*.
Isa 53: 10 of the LORD will *p* in his hand.
Jer 12: 1 Why does the way of the wicked *p*?

PROSPERED (PROSPER)

Ge 39: 2 was with Joseph and he *p*,
2Ch 14: 7 So they built and *p*.
    31: 21 And so he *p*.

PROSPERITY (PROSPER)

Dt 28: 11 will grant you abundant *p*—
    30: 15 I set before you today life and *p*,
Job 36: 11 will spend the rest of their days in *p*
Ps 73: 3 when I saw the *p* of the wicked.
    122: 9 I will seek your *p*.
    128: 2 blessings and *p* will be yours.
Pr   3: 2 and bring you *p*.
    13: 21 but *p* is the reward of the righteous.
    21: 21 finds life, *p* and honour.
Isa 45: 7 I bring *p* and create disaster;

PROSPEROUS (PROSPER)

Dt 30: 9 your God will make you most *p*
Jos 1: 8 Then you will be *p* and successful.
Job 42: 10 the LORD made him *p* again

PROSPERS (PROSPER)

Ps   1: 3 Whatever he does *p*.
Pr 16: 20 gives heed to instruction *p*,
    19: 8 he who cherishes understanding *p*.

PROSTITUTE (PROSTITUTES PROSTITUTION)

Lev 20: 6 and spiritists to *p* himself
Nu 15: 39 and not *p* yourselves by going
Jos 2: 1 the house of a *p* named Rahab
Pr   6: 26 for the *p* reduces you to a loaf
     7: 10 like a *p* and with crafty intent.
    23: 27 for a *p* is a deep pit
Eze 16: 15 and used your fame to become a *p*.
    23: 7 a *p* to all the elite of the Assyrians
Hos 3: 3 you must not be a *p* or be intimate
1Co 6: 15 of Christ and unite them with a *p*?
     6: 16 with a *p* is one with her in body?
Rev 17: 1 you the punishment of the great *p*,

PROSTITUTES (PROSTITUTE)

Pr 29: 3 of *p* squanders his wealth.
Mt 21: 31 and the *p* are entering the kingdom
Lk 15: 30 property with *p* comes home,
1Co 6: 9 male *p* nor homosexual offenders

PROSTITUTION (PROSTITUTE)

Eze 16: 16 where you carried on your *p*.
    23: 3 engaging in *p* from their youth.
Hos 4: 10 engage in *p* but not increase,

PROSTRATE

Dt   9: 18 again I fell *p* before the LORD
1Ki 18: 39 they fell *p* and cried, "The LORD

PROTECT (PROTECTED PROTECTION PROTECTS)

Dt 23: 14 about in your camp to *p* you
Ps 25: 21 integrity and uprightness *p* me,
    32: 7 you will *p* me from trouble
    40: 11 your truth always *p* me.
    41: 2 The LORD will *p* him
    91: 14 I will *p* him, for he acknowledges
    140: 1 *p* me from men of violence,
Pr   2: 11 Discretion will *p* you,
     4: 6 forsake wisdom, and she will *p* you;
Jn 17: 11 *p* them by the power of your name
    17: 15 that you *p* them from the evil one.
2Th 3: 3 and *p* you from the evil one.

PROTECTED (PROTECT)

Jos 24: 17 He *p* us on our entire journey
1Sa 30: 23 He has *p* us and handed
Ps 37: 28 They will be *p* for ever,
Jn 17: 12 I *p* them and kept them safe

PROTECTION (PROTECT)

Ezr 9: 9 he has given us a wall of *p* in Judah
Ps   5: 11 Spread your *p* over them,

PROTECTS (PROTECT)

Ps 116: 6 The LORD *p* the simple-hearted;
Pr   2: 8 and *p* the way of his faithful ones.
1Co 13: 7 It always *p*, always trusts,

PROUD (PRIDE)

Ps 31: 23 but the *p* he pays back in full.
    101: 5 has haughty eyes and a *p* heart,
    138: 6 but the *p* he knows from afar.
Pr   3: 34 He mocks *p* mockers
    16: 5 The LORD detests all the *p*
    16: 19 than to share plunder with the *p*.
    18: 12 his downfall a man's heart is *p*,
    21: 4 Haughty eyes and a *p* heart,
Isa 2: 12 store for all the *p* and lofty,
Ro 12: 16 Do not be *p*, but be willing
1Co 13: 4 it does not boast, it is not *p*.
2Ti 3: 2 lovers of money, boastful, *p*,
Jas 4: 6 "God opposes the *p*
1Pe 5: 5 because, "God opposes the *p*

PROVE (PROOF PROVED PROVING)

Pr 29: 25 Fear of man will *p* to be a snare,
Jn   8: 46 Can any of you *p* me guilty of sin?
Ac 26: 20 *p* their repentance by their deeds.
1Co 4: 2 been given a trust must *p* faithful.

PROVED (PROVE)

Ps 51: 4 so that you are *p* right
Mt 11: 19 wisdom is *p* right by her actions."

Ro   3: 4 "So that you may be *p* right
1Pe   1: 7 may be *p* genuine and may result

PROVIDE (PROVIDED PROVIDES PROVISION)

Ge   22: 8 "God himself will *p* the lamb
       22:14 that place "The LORD will *p*."
Isa   43:20 because I *p* water in the desert
       61: 3 and *p* for those who grieve in Zion
1Co   10:13 *p* a way out so that you can stand
1Ti   5: 8 If anyone does not *p*
Tit   3:14 in order that they may *p*

PROVIDED (PROVIDE)

Ps   68:10 O God, you *p* for the poor.
      111: 9 He *p* redemption for his people;
Jnh   1:17 But the LORD *p* a great fish
       4: 6 Then the LORD God *p* a vine
       4: 7 dawn the next day God *p* a worm,
       4: 8 God *p* a scorching east wind,
Gal   4:18 to be zealous, *p* the purpose is good
Heb   1: 3 After he had *p* purification for sins,

PROVIDES (PROVIDE)

Ps   111: 5 He *p* food for those who fear him;
Pr   31:15 she *p* food for her family
Eze   18: 7 and *p* clothing for the naked.
1Ti   6:17 who richly *p* us with everything
1Pe   4:11 it with the strength God *p*,

PROVING* (PROVE)

Ac   9:22 by *p* that Jesus is the Christ.
       17: 3 and *p* that the Christ had to suffer
       18:28 *p* from the Scriptures that Jesus

PROVISION (PROVIDE)

Ro   5:17 who receive God's abundant *p*

PROVOKED

Ecc   7: 9 Do not be quickly *p* in your spirit,
Jer   32:32 Judah have *p* me by all the evil they

PROWLS

1Pe   5: 8 Your enemy the devil *p*

PRUDENCE* (PRUDENT)

Pr   1: 4 for giving *p* to the simple,
        8: 5 You who are simple, gain *p*;
        8:12 "I, wisdom, dwell together with *p*;
       15: 5 whoever heeds correction shows *p*.
       19:25 and the simple will learn *p*;

PRUDENT* (PRUDENCE)

Pr   1: 3 acquiring a disciplined and *p* life,
       12:16 but a *p* man overlooks an insult.
       12:23 A *p* man keeps his knowledge
       13:16 Every *p* man acts out of knowledge
       14: 8 The wisdom of the *p* is
       14:15 a *p* man gives thought to his steps.
       14:18 the *p* are crowned with knowledge.
       19:14 but a *p* wife is from the LORD.
       22: 3 *p* man sees danger and takes
       27:12 The *p* see danger and take refuge,
Jer   49: 7 Has counsel perished from the *p*?
Am   5:13 Therefore the *p* man keeps quiet

PRUNES

Jn   15: 2 branch that does bear fruit he *p*

PRUNING

Isa   2: 4 and their spears into *p* hooks.

Joel   3:10 and your *p* hooks into spears.

PSALMS

Eph   5:19 Speak to one another with *p*,
Col   3:16 and as you sing *p*, hymns

PUBLICLY

Ac   20:20 have taught you *p* and from house
1Ti   5:20 Those who sin are to be rebuked *p*,

PUFFS

1Co   8: 1 Knowledge *p* up, but love builds up

PULLING

2Co   10: 8 building you up rather than *p* you

PUNISH (PUNISHED PUNISHES PUNISHMENT)

Ge   15:14 But I will *p* the nation they serve
Ex   32:34 I will *p* them for their sin."
Pr   17:26 It is not good to *p* an innocent man,
       23:13 if you *p* him with the rod, he will
Isa   13:11 I will *p* the world for its evil,
Jer   2:19 Your wickedness will *p* you;
       21:14 I will *p* you as your deeds deserve,
Zep   1:12 and *p* those who are complacent,
Ac   7: 7 But I will *p* the nation they serve
2Th   1: 8 He will *p* those who do not know
1Pe   2:14 by him to *p* those who do wrong

PUNISHED (PUNISH)

Ezr   9:13 you have *p* us less than our sins
Ps   99: 8 though you *p* their misdeeds.
La   3:39 complain when *p* for his sins?
Mk   12:40 Such men will be *p* most severely."
Lk   23:41 the same sentence? We are *p* justly,
2Th   1: 9 be *p* with everlasting destruction
Heb   10:29 to be *p* who has trampled the Son

PUNISHES (PUNISH)

Heb   12: 6 and he *p* everyone he accepts

PUNISHMENT (PUNISH)

Isa   53: 5 the *p* that brought us peace was
Jer   4:18 This is your *p*.
Mt   25:46 Then they will go away to eternal *p*
Lk   12:48 and does things deserving *p* will be
       21:22 For this is the time of *p*
Ro   13: 4 wrath to bring *p* on the wrongdoer.
Heb   2: 2 disobedience received its just *p*,
2Pe   2: 9 while continuing their *p*.

PURCHASED

Ps   74: 2 Remember the people you *p* of old,
Rev   5: 9 with your blood you *p* men for God

PURE (PURIFICATION PURIFIED PURIFIES PURIFY PURITY)

2Sa   22:27 to the *p* you show yourself *p*,
Job   14: 4 Who can bring what is *p*
Ps   19: 9 The fear of the LORD is *p*,
       24: 4 who has clean hands and a *p* heart,
       51:10 Create in me a *p* heart, O God,
      119: 9 can a young man keep his way *p*?
Pr   15:26 those of the *p* are pleasing to him.
       20: 9 can say, "I have kept my heart *p*;
Isa   52:11 Come out from it and be *p*,
Hab   1:13 Your eyes are too *p* to look on evil;
Mt   5: 8 Blessed are the *p* in heart,
2Co   11: 2 I might present you as a *p* virgin

Php   4: 8 whatever is *p*, whatever is lovely,
1Ti   1: 5 which comes from a *p* heart
       5: 22 Keep yourself *p*.
2Ti   2: 22 call on the Lord out of a *p* heart.
Tit   1: 15 To the *p*, all things are *p*,
       2: 5 to be self-controlled and *p*,
Heb   7: 26 blameless, *p*, set apart from sinners
      13: 4 and the marriage bed kept *p*,
Jas   1: 27 that God our Father accepts as *p*
       3: 17 comes from heaven is first of all *p*;
1Jn   3: 3 him purifies himself, just as he is *p*.

PURGE

Pr   20: 30 and beatings *p* the inmost being.

PURIFICATION (PURE)

Heb   1: 3 After he had provided *p* for sins,

PURIFIED (PURE)

Ac   15: 9 for he *p* their hearts by faith.
1Pe   1: 22 Now that you have *p* yourselves

PURIFIES* (PURE)

1Jn   1: 7 of Jesus, his Son, *p* us from all sin.
       3: 3 who has this hope in him *p* himself,

PURIFY (PURE)

Nu   19: 12 He must *p* himself with the water
2Co   7: 1 us *p* ourselves from everything that
Tit   2: 14 to *p* for himself a people that are
Jas   4: 8 you sinners, and *p* your hearts,
1Jn   1: 9 and *p* us from all unrighteousness.

PURIM

Est   9: 26 Therefore these days were called *P*

PURITY* (PURE)

Hos   8: 5 long will they be incapable of *p*?
2Co   6: 6 in *p*, understanding, patience
1Ti   4: 12 in life, in love, in faith and in *p*.
       5: 2 as sisters, with absolute *p*.
1Pe   3: 2 when they see the *p* and reverence

PURPLE

Pr   31: 22 she is clothed in fine linen and *p*.
Mk   15: 17 They put a *p* robe on him, then

PURPOSE (PURPOSED PURPOSES)

Ex   9: 16 I have raised you up for this very *p*,
Job   36: 5 he is mighty, and firm in his *p*.
Pr   19: 21 but it is the LORD's *p* that prevails
Isa   46: 10 I say: My *p* will stand,
      55: 11 and achieve the *p* for which I sent it
Ac   2: 23 handed over to you by God's set *p*
Ro   8: 28 have been called according to his *p*.
       9: 11 in order that God's *p*
       9: 17 "I raised you up for this very *p*,
1Co   3: 8 the man who waters have one *p*,
2Co   5: 5 who has made us for this very *p*
Gal   4: 18 be zealous, provided the *p* is good,
Eph   1: 11 in conformity with the *p* of his will,
       3: 11 according to his eternal *p* which he
Php   2: 2 love, being one in spirit and *p*.
       2: 13 and to act according to his good *p*.
2Ti   1: 9 but because of his own *p* and grace.

PURPOSED (PURPOSE)

Isa   14: 24 and as I have *p*, so it will stand.
      14: 27 For the LORD Almighty has *p*,
Eph   1: 9 which he *p* in Christ, to be put

PURPOSES (PURPOSE)

Ps   33: 10 he thwarts the *p* of the peoples.
Jer   23: 20 the *p* of his heart.
      32: 19 great are your *p* and mighty are

PURSE (PURSES)

Hag   1: 6 to put them in a *p* with holes in it."
Lk   10: 4 Do not take a *p* or bag or sandals;
      22: 36 "But now if you have a *p*, take it,

PURSES (PURSE)

Lk   12: 33 Provide *p* for yourselves that will

PURSUE (PURSUES)

Ps   34: 14 seek peace and *p* it.
Pr   15: 9 he loves those who *p* righteousness
Ro   9: 30 who did not *p* righteousness,
1Ti   6: 11 and *p* righteousness, godliness,
2Ti   2: 22 and *p* righteousness, faith,
1Pe   3: 11 he must seek peace and *p* it.

PURSUES (PURSUE)

Pr   21: 21 He who *p* righteousness and love
      28: 1 wicked man flees though no-one *p*,

QUAIL

Ex   16: 13 That evening *q* came and covered
Nu   11: 31 and drove *q* in from the sea.

QUALITIES* (QUALITY)

Da   6: 3 by his exceptional *q* that the king
Ro   1: 20 of the world God's invisible *q*—
2Pe   1: 8 For if you possess these *q*

QUALITY (QUALITIES)

1Co   3: 13 and the fire test the *q*

QUARREL (QUARRELLING QUARRELS QUARRELSOME)

Pr   15: 18 but a patient man calms a *q*.
      17: 14 Starting a *q* is like breaching a dam;
      17: 19 He who loves a *q* loves sin;
      20: 3 but every fool is quick to *q*.
      26: 17 in a *q* not his own.
      26: 20 without gossip a *q* dies down.
2Ti   2: 24 And the Lord's servant must not *q*;
Jas   4: 2 You *q* and fight.

QUARRELLING (QUARREL)

1Co   3: 3 For since there is jealousy and *q*
2Ti   2: 14 before God against *q* about words;

QUARRELS (QUARREL)

Pr   13: 10 Pride only breeds *q*,
Isa   45: 9 Woe to him who *q* with his Maker,
1Ti   6: 4 *q* about words that result in envy,
2Ti   2: 23 because you know they produce *q*.
Jas   4: 1 What causes fights and *q*

QUARRELSOME (QUARREL)

Pr   19: 13 a *q* wife is like a constant dripping.
      21: 9 than share a house with a *q* wife.
      26: 21 so is a *q* man for kindling strife.
1Ti   3: 3 not violent but gentle, not *q*.

QUEEN

1Ki   10: 1 When the *q* of Sheba heard about
2Ch   9: 1 When the *q* of Sheba heard
Mt   12: 42 The *Q* of the South will rise

QUENCH (QUENCHED)

SS   8: 7 Many waters cannot *q* love;

QUENCHED (QUENCH)

Isa   66: 24 nor will their fire be *q*,
Mk   9: 48 and the fire is not *q*.'

QUICKEN see (make) ALIVE, (give) LIFE, RESTORE, REVIVE

QUICK-TEMPERED* (TEMPER)

Pr   14: 17 A *q* man does foolish things,
       14: 29 but a *q* man displays folly.
Tit   1: 7 not *q*, not given to much wine,

QUIET (QUIETNESS)

Ps   23: 2 he leads me beside *q* waters,
Pr   17: 1 Better a dry crust with peace and *q*
Ecc   9: 17 The *q* words of the wise are more
Am   5: 13 Therefore the prudent man keeps *q*
Zep   3: 17 he will *q* you with his love,
Lk   19: 40 he replied, "if they keep *q*,
1Th   4: 11 it your ambition to lead a *q* life,
1Ti   2: 2 we may live peaceful and *q* lives
1Pe   3: 4 beauty of a gentle and *q* spirit,

QUIETNESS (QUIET)

Isa   30: 15 in *q* and trust is your strength,
       32: 17 the effect of righteousness will be *q*
1Ti   2: 11 A woman should learn in *q*

QUIVER

Ps   127: 5 whose *q* is full of them.

RACE

Ecc   9: 11 The *r* is not to the swift
Ac   20: 24 if only I may finish the *r*
1Co   9: 24 that in a *r* all the runners run,
Gal   2: 2 that I was running or had run my *r*
        5: 7 You were running a good *r*.
2Ti   4: 7 I have finished the *r*, I have kept
Heb   12: 1 perseverance the *r* marked out

RACHEL

Daughter of Laban (Ge 29:16); wife of Jacob (Ge 29:28); bore two sons (Ge 30:22-24; 35:16-24; 46:19). Stole Laban's gods (Ge 31:19, 32-35). Death (Ge 35:19-20).

RADIANCE (RADIANT)

Eze   1: 28 so was the *r* around him.
Heb   1: 3 The Son is the *r* of God's glory

RADIANT (RADIANCE)

Ex   34: 29 he was not aware that his face was *r*
Ps   34: 5 Those who look to him are *r*;
SS   5: 10 My lover is *r* and ruddy,
Isa   60: 5 Then you will look and be *r*,
Eph   5: 27 her to himself as a *r* church,

RAGE

Ac   4: 25 " 'Why do the nations *r*
Col   3: 8 *r*, malice, slander, and filthy

RAGS

Isa   64: 6 our righteous acts are like filthy *r*;

RAHAB

1. Prostitute of Jericho who hid Israelite spies (Jos 2; 6:22-25; Heb 11:31; Jas 2:25).
2. Mother of Boaz (Mt 1:5).

RAIN (RAINBOW)

Ge   7: 4 from now I will send *r* on the earth
1Ki   17: 1 nor *r* in the next few years
       18: 1 and I will send *r* on the land."
Mt   5: 45 and sends *r* on the righteous
Jas   5: 17 it did not *r* on the land for three
Jude   : 12 They are clouds without *r*,

RAINBOW (RAIN)

Ge   9: 13 I have set my *r* in the clouds,

RAISE (RISE)

Jn   6: 39 but *r* them up at the last day.
1Co   15: 15 he did not *r* him if in fact the dead

RAISED (RISE)

Isa   52: 13 he will be *r* and lifted up
Mt   17: 23 on the third day he will be *r* to life
Lk   7: 22 the deaf hear, the dead are *r*,
Ac   2: 24 But God *r* him from the dead,
Ro   4: 25 was *r* to life for our justification.
        6: 4 as Christ was *r* from the dead
        8: 11 And if the Spirit of him who *r* Jesus
       10: 9 in your heart that God *r* him
1Co   15: 4 that he was *r* on the third day
       15: 20 But Christ has indeed been *r*

RALLY*

Isa   11: 10 the nations will *r* to him,

RAM (RAMS)

Ge   22: 13 there in a thicket he saw a *r* caught
Da   8: 3 before me was a *r* with two horns,

RAMPART*

Ps   91: 4 will be your shield and *r*.

RAMS (RAM)

1Sa   15: 22 to heed is better than the fat of *r*.
Mic   6: 7 pleased with thousands of *r*,

RAN (RUN)

Jnh   1: 3 But Jonah *r* away from the LORD

RANSOM (RANSOMED)

Isa   50: 2 Was my arm too short to *r* you?
Hos   13: 14 "I will *r* them from the power
Mt   20: 28 and to give his life as a *r* for many."
Mk   10: 45 and to give his life as a *r* for many."
1Ti   2: 6 who gave himself as a *r* for all men
Heb   9: 15 as a *r* to set them free

RANSOMED (RANSOM)

Isa   35: 10 and the *r* of the LORD will return.

RARE

Pr   20: 15 that speak knowledge are a *r* jewel.

RAVEN (RAVENS)

Ge   8: 7 made in the ark and sent out a *r*,
Job   38: 41 Who provides food for the *r*

RAVENS (RAVEN)

1Ki   17: 6 The *r* brought him bread
Ps   147: 9 and for the young *r* when they call.
Lk   12: 24 Consider the *r*: They do not sow

READ (READING READS)

Dt   17: 19 he is to *r* it all the days of his life
Jos   8: 34 Joshua *r* all the words of the law—

2Ki 23: 2 He *r* in their hearing all the words
Ne 8: 8 They *r* from the Book of the Law
Jer 36: 6 and *r* to the people from the scroll
2Co 3: 2 known and *r* by everybody.

READING (READ)
1Ti 4: 13 to the public *r* of Scripture,

READS (READ)
Rev 1: 3 Blessed is the one who *r* the words

REAFFIRM
2Co 2: 8 therefore, to *r* your love for him.

REAL* (REALITIES REALITY)
Jn 6: 55 is *r* food and my blood is *r* drink.
1Jn 2: 27 all things and as that anointing is *r*,

REALITIES* (REAL)
Heb 10: 1 are coming—not the *r* themselves.

REALITY* (REAL)
Col 2: 17 the *r*, however, is found in Christ.

REALM (REALMS)
Hab 2: 9 "Woe to him who builds his *r*

REALMS (REALM)
Eph 1: 3 the heavenly *r* with every spiritual
2: 6 in the heavenly *r* in Christ Jesus,

REAP (REAPER REAPS)
Job 4: 8 and those who sow trouble *r* it.
Ps 126: 5 will *r* with songs of joy.
Hos 8: 7 and *r* the whirlwind.
10: 12 *r* the fruit of unfailing love,
Jn 4: 38 you to *r* what you have not worked
Ro 6: 22 the benefit you *r* leads to holiness,
2Co 9: 6 generously will also *r* generously.
Gal 6: 8 from that nature will *r* destruction;

REAPER (REAP)
Jn 4: 36 and the *r* may be glad together.

REAPS (REAP)
Pr 11: 18 who sows righteousness *r* a sure
22: 8 He who sows wickedness *r* trouble,
Gal 6: 7 A man *r* what he sows.

REASON (REASONED)
Ge 2: 24 For this *r* a man will leave his
Isa 1: 18 "Come now, let us *r* together,"
Mt 19: 5 'For this *r* a man will leave his
Jn 12: 27 it was for this very *r* I came
15: 25 'They hated me without *r*.'
1Pe 3: 15 to give the *r* for the hope that you
2Pe 1: 5 For this very *r*, make every effort

REASONED (REASON)
1Co 13: 11 thought like a child, I *r* like a child.

REBEKAH
Sister of Laban, secured as bride for Isaac (Ge 24). Mother of Esau and Jacob (Ge 25:19-26). Taken by Abimelech as sister of Isaac; returned (Ge 26:1-11). Encouraged Jacob to trick Isaac out of blessing (Ge 27:1-17).

REBEL (REBELLED REBELLION REBELS)
Nu 14: 9 Only do not *r* against the LORD.

1Sa 12: 14 and do not *r* against his commands,
Mt 10: 21 children will *r* against their parents

REBELLED (REBEL)
Ps 78: 56 and *r* against the Most High;
Isa 63: 10 Yet they *r*

REBELLION (REBEL)
Ex 34: 7 and forgiving wickedness, *r* and sin
Nu 14: 18 in love and forgiving sin and *r*.
1Sa 15: 23 For *r* is like the sin of divination,
2Th 2: 3 will not come, until the *r* occurs

REBELS (REBEL)
Ro 13: 2 he who *r* against the authority is
1Ti 1: 9 but for lawbreakers and *r*,

REBIRTH* (BEAR [1])
Tit 3: 5 us through the washing of *r*

REBUILD (BUILD)
Ezr 5: 2 set to work to *r* the house of God
Ne 2: 17 let us *r* the wall of Jerusalem,
Ps 102: 16 For the LORD will *r* Zion
Da 9: 25 and *r* Jerusalem until the Anointed
Am 9: 14 they will *r* the ruined cities
Ac 15: 16 Its ruins I will *r*,

REBUILT (BUILD)
Zec 1: 16 and there my house will be *r*.

REBUKE (REBUKED REBUKES REBUKING)
Lev 19: 17 *R* your neighbour frankly
Ps 141: 5 let him *r* me—it is oil on my head.
Pr 3: 11 and do not resent his *r*,
9: 8 *r* a wise man and he will love you.
15: 31 He who listens to a life-giving *r*
17: 10 A *r* impresses a man
19: 25 *r* a discerning man, and he will gain
25: 12 is a wise man's *r* to a listening ear.
27: 5 Better is open *r*
30: 6 or he will *r* you and prove you a liar
Ecc 7: 5 It is better to heed a wise man's *r*
Isa 54: 9 never to *r* you again.
Jer 2: 19 your backsliding will *r* you.
Lk 17: 3 "If your brother sins, *r* him,
1Ti 5: 1 Do not *r* an older man harshly,
2Ti 4: 2 correct, *r* and encourage—
Tit 1: 13 Therefore, *r* them sharply,
2: 15 Encourage and *r* with all authority.
Rev 3: 19 Those whom I love I *r*

REBUKED (REBUKE)
Mk 16: 14 he *r* them for their lack of faith
1Ti 5: 20 Those who sin are to be *r* publicly,

REBUKES (REBUKE)
Job 22: 4 "Is it for your piety that he *r* you
Pr 28: 23 He who *r* a man will
29: 1 remains stiff-necked after many *r*
Heb 12: 5 do not lose heart when he *r* you,

REBUKING (REBUKE)
2Ti 3: 16 *r*, correcting and training

RECEIVE (RECEIVED RECEIVES)
Mt 10: 41 a righteous man will *r* a righteous
Mk 10: 15 anyone who will not *r* the kingdom
Jn 20: 22 and said, "*R* the Holy Spirit.
Ac 1: 8 you will *r* power when the Holy

Ac	2: 38	you will *r* the gift of the Holy Spirit
	19: 2	"Did you *r* the Holy Spirit
	20: 35	'It is more blessed to give than to *r*
1Co	9: 14	the gospel should *r* their living
2Co	6: 17	and I will *r* you."
1Ti	1: 16	believe on him and *r* eternal life.
Jas	1: 7	should not think he will *r* anything
2Pe	1: 11	and you will *r* a rich welcome
1Jn	3: 22	and *r* from him anything we ask,
Rev	4: 11	to *r* glory and honour and power,
	5: 12	to *r* power and wealth and wisdom

RECEIVED (RECEIVE)

Mt	6: 2	they have *r* their reward in full.
	10: 8	Freely you have *r*, freely give.
Mk	11: 24	believe that you have *r* it,
Jn	1: 12	Yet to all who *r* him,
	1: 16	his grace we have all *r* one blessing
Ac	8: 17	and they *r* the Holy Spirit.
	10: 47	They have *r* the Holy Spirit just
Ro	8: 15	but you *r* the Spirit of sonship.
1Co	11: 23	For I *r* from the Lord what I
2Co	1: 4	the comfort we ourselves have *r*
Col	2: 6	just as you *r* Christ Jesus as Lord,
1Pe	4: 10	should use whatever gift he has *r*

RECEIVES (RECEIVE)

Pr	18: 22	and *r* favour from the LORD.
	27: 21	but man is tested by the praise he *r*.
Mt	7: 8	everyone who asks *r*; he who seeks
	10: 40	he who *r* me *r* the one who sent me.
	10: 40	"He who *r* you *r* me, and he who
Ac	10: 43	believes in him *r* forgiveness of sins

RECITE

Ps	45: 1	as I *r* my verses for the king;

RECKLESS

Pr	12: 18	*R* words pierce like a sword,
	14: 16	but a fool is hotheaded and *r*.

RECKONING

Isa	10: 3	What will you do on the day of *r*,
Hos	9: 7	the days of *r* are at hand.

RECLAIM* (CLAIM)

Isa	11: 11	time to *r* the remnant that is left

RECOGNISE (RECOGNISED RECOGNITION)

Mt	7: 16	By their fruit you will *r* them.
1Jn	4: 2	This is how you can *r* the Spirit
	4: 6	This is how we *r* the Spirit of truth

RECOGNISED (RECOGNISE)

Mt	12: 33	for a tree is *r* by its fruit.
Ro	7: 13	in order that sin might be *r* as sin,

RECOGNITION (RECOGNISE)

1Co	16: 18	Such men deserve *r*.
1Ti	5: 3	Give proper *r* to those widows who

RECOMPENSE*

Isa	40: 10	and his *r* accompanies him.
	62: 11	and his *r* accompanies him.'"

**RECONCILE* (RECONCILED
RECONCILIATION RECONCILING)**

Ac	7: 26	He tried to *r* them by saying, 'Men,
Eph	2: 16	in this one body to *r* both of them
Col	1: 20	him to *r* to himself all things,

RECONCILED* (RECONCILE)

Mt	5: 24	First go and be *r* to your brother;
Lk	12: 58	try hard to be *r* to him on the way,
Ro	5: 10	how much more, having been *r*,
	5: 10	we were *r* to him through the death
1Co	7: 11	or else be *r* to her husband.
2Co	5: 18	who *r* us to himself through Christ
	5: 20	you on Christ's behalf: Be *r* to God.
Col	1: 22	he has *r* you by Christ's physical

RECONCILIATION* (RECONCILE)

Ro	5: 11	whom we have now received *r*.
	11: 15	For if their rejection is the *r*
2Co	5: 18	and gave us the ministry of *r*:
	5: 19	committed to us the message of *r*.

RECONCILING* (RECONCILE)

2Co	5: 19	that God was *r* the world to himself

RECORD (RECORDED)

Ps	130: 3	If you, O LORD, kept a *r* of sins,
Hos	13: 12	his sins are kept on *r*.
1Co	13: 5	is not easily angered, it keeps no *r*

RECORDED (RECORD)

Job	19: 23	"Oh, that my words were *r*,
Jn	20: 30	which are not *r* in this book.

RECOUNT*

Ps	40: 5	no-one can *r* to you;
	79: 13	we will *r* your praise.
	119: 13	With my lips I *r*

RED

Ex	15: 4	are drowned in the *R* Sea.
Ps	106: 9	He rebuked the *R* Sea,
Pr	23: 31	Do not gaze at wine when it is *r*,
Isa	1: 18	though they are *r* as crimson,

**REDEEM (KINSMAN-REDEEMER
REDEEMED REDEEMER REDEEMS
REDEMPTION)**

Ex	6: 6	will *r* you with an outstretched arm
2Sa	7: 23	on earth that God went out to *r*
Ps	44: 26	*r* us because of your unfailing love.
	49: 7	No man can *r* the life of another
	49: 15	God will *r* my life from the grave;
	130: 8	He himself will *r* Israel
Hos	13: 14	I will *r* them from death.
Gal	4: 5	under law, to *r* those under law,
Tit	2: 14	for us to *r* us from all wickedness

REDEEMED (REDEEM)

Job	33: 28	He *r* my soul from going
Ps	71: 23	I, whom you have *r*.
	107: 2	Let the *r* of the LORD say this—
Isa	35: 9	But only the *r* will walk there,
	63: 9	In his love and mercy he *r* them;
Gal	3: 13	Christ *r* us from the curse
1Pe	1: 18	or gold that you were *r*

REDEEMER (REDEEM)

Job	19: 25	I know that my *R* lives,
Ps	19: 14	O LORD, my Rock and my *R*.
Isa	44: 6	and *R*, the LORD Almighty:
	48: 17	your *R*, the LORD Almighty:
	59: 20	"The *R* will come to Zion,

REDEEMS (REDEEM)

Ps	34: 22	The LORD *r* his servants;

Ps 103: 4 he *r* my life from the pit

REDEMPTION (REDEEM)

Ps 130: 7 and with him is full *r*.
Lk 21: 28 because your *r* is drawing near."
Ro 3: 24 grace through the *r* that came
8: 23 as sons, the *r* of our bodies.
1Co 1: 30 our righteousness, holiness and *r*.
Eph 1: 7 In him we have *r* through his blood
1: 14 until the *r* of those who are God's
4: 30 you were sealed for the day of *r*.
Col 1: 14 in whom we have *r*, the forgiveness
Heb 9: 12 having obtained eternal *r*.

REED

Isa 42: 3 A bruised *r* he will not break,
Mt 12: 20 A bruised *r* he will not break,

REFINE*

Jer 9: 7 "See, I will *r* and test them,
Zec 13: 9 I will *r* them like silver
Mal 3: 3 and *r* them like gold and silver.

REFLECT (REFLECTS)

2Co 3: 18 unveiled faces all *r* the Lord's

REFLECTS (REFLECT)

Pr 27: 19 As water *r* a face,

REFRESH (REFRESHED REFRESHING)

Phm : 20 in the Lord; *r* my heart in Christ.

REFRESHED (REFRESH)

Pr 11: 25 refreshes others will himself be *r*.

REFRESHING* (REFRESH)

Ac 3: 19 that times of *r* may come

REFUGE

Nu 35: 11 towns to be your cities of *r*,
Dt 33: 27 The eternal God is your *r*,
Jos 20: 2 to designate the cities of *r*,
Ru 2: 12 wings you have come to take *r*."
2Sa 22: 3 God is my rock, in whom I take *r*,
22: 31 a shield for all who take *r* in him.
Ps 2: 12 Blessed are all who take *r* in him.
5: 11 But let all who take *r* in you be glad
9: 9 The Lord is a *r* for the oppressed,
16: 1 for in you I take *r*.
17: 7 those who take *r* in you
18: 2 God is my rock, in whom I take *r*.
31: 2 be my rock of *r*,
34: 8 blessed is the man who takes *r*
36: 7 find *r* in the shadow of your wings.
46: 1 God is our *r* and strength,
62: 8 for God is our *r*.
71: 1 In you, O Lord, I have taken *r*;
91: 2 "He is my *r* and my fortress,
144: 2 my shield, in whom I take *r*,
Pr 14: 26 and for his children it will be a *r*.
30: 5 a shield to those who take *r* in him.
Na 1: 7 a *r* in times of trouble.

REFUSE (REFUSED)

Jn 5: 40 yet you *r* to come to me to have life

REFUSED (REFUSE)

2Th 2: 10 because they *r* to love the truth
Rev 16: 9 but they *r* to repent and glorify him

REGARD (REGARDS)

1Th 5: 13 Hold them in the highest *r* in love

REGARDS (REGARD)

Ro 14: 14 But if anyone *r* something

REGRET

2Co 7: 10 leads to salvation and leaves no *r*,

REHOBOAM

Son of Solomon (1Ki 11:43; 1Ch 3:10). Harsh treatment of subjects caused divided kingdom (1K 12:1-24; 14:21-31; 2Ch 10-12).

REIGN (REIGNED REIGNS)

Ex 15: 18 The Lord will *r*
Ps 68: 16 mountain where God chooses to *r*,
Isa 9: 7 He will *r* on David's throne
24: 23 for the Lord Almighty will *r*
32: 1 See, a king will *r* in righteousness
Jer 23: 5 a King who will *r* wisely
Lk 1: 33 and he will *r* over the house
Ro 6: 12 Therefore do not let sin *r*
1Co 15: 25 For he must *r* until he has put all
2Ti 2: 12 we will also *r* with him.
Rev 11: 15 and he will *r* for ever and ever."
20: 6 will *r* with him for a thousand years
22: 5 And they will *r* for ever and ever.

REIGNED (REIGN)

Ro 5: 21 so that, just as sin *r* in death,
Rev 20: 4 and *r* with Christ a thousand years.

REIGNS (REIGN)

Ps 9: 7 The Lord *r* for ever;
47: 8 God *r* over the nations;
93: 1 The Lord *r*, he is robed
96: 10 among the nations, "The Lord *r*
97: 1 The Lord *r*, let the earth be glad;
99: 1 the Lord *r*, / let the nations tremble;
146: 10 The Lord *r* for ever,
Isa 52: 7 "Your God *r*!"
Rev 19: 6 For our Lord God Almighty *r*.

REIN

Jas 1: 26 and yet does not keep a tight *r*

REJECT (REJECTED REJECTION REJECTS)

Ps 94: 14 For the Lord will not *r* his people
Ro 11: 1 I ask then, Did God *r* his people?

REJECTED (REJECT)

1Sa 8: 7 it is not you they have *r*
1Ki 19: 10 The Israelites have *r* your covenant
2Ki 17: 15 They *r* his decrees
Ps 66: 20 who has not *r* my prayer
118: 22 The stone the builders *r*
Isa 5: 24 for they have *r* the law
41: 9 chosen you and have not *r* you.
53: 3 He was despised and *r* by men,
Jer 8: 9 Since they have *r* the word
Mt 21: 42 " 'The stone the builders *r*
1Ti 4: 4 nothing is to be *r* if it is received
1Pe 2: 4 *r* by men but chosen by God
2: 7 "The stone the builders *r*

REJECTION* (REJECT)

Ro 11: 15 For if their *r* is the reconciliation

REJECTS (REJECT)

Lk	10:16	but he who r me r him who sent me
Jn	3:36	whoever r the Son will not see life,
1Th	4: 8	he who r this instruction does not

REJOICE (JOY)

Dt	12: 7	shall r in everything you have put
1Ch	16:10	of those who seek the LORD r.
	16:31	Let the heavens r, let the earth be
Ps	2:11	and r with trembling.
	5:11	those who love your name may r
	9:14	and there r in your salvation.
	34: 2	let the afflicted hear and r.
	63:11	But the king will r in God;
	66: 6	come, let us r in him.
	68: 3	and r before God;
	105: 3	of those who seek the LORD r.
	118:24	let us r and be glad in it.
	119:14	I r in following your statutes
	119:162	I r in your promise
	149: 2	Let Israel r in their Maker;
Pr	5:18	may you r in the wife of your youth
	23:25	may she who gave you birth r!
	24:17	stumbles, do not let your heart r,
Isa	9: 3	as men r
	35: 1	the wilderness will r and blossom.
	61: 7	they will r in their inheritance;
Isa	62: 5	so will your God r over you.
Jer	31:12	they will r in the bounty
Zep	3:17	he will r over you with singing."
Zec	9: 9	R greatly, O Daughter of Zion!
Lk	6:23	"R in that day and leap for joy,
	10:20	but r that your names are written
	15: 6	'R with me; I have found my lost
	15: 9	'R with me; I have found my lost
Ro	5: 2	And we r in the hope of the glory
	12:15	R with those who r; mourn
Php	2:17	I am glad and r with all of you.
	3: 1	Finally, my brothers, r in the Lord!
	4: 4	R in the Lord always.
1Pe	4:13	But r that you participate
Rev	19: 7	Let us r and be glad

REJOICES (JOY)

Ps	13: 5	my heart r in your salvation.
	16: 9	my heart is glad and my tongue r;
Isa	61:10	my soul r in my God.
	62: 5	as a bridegroom r over his bride,
Lk	1:47	and my spirit r in God my Saviour,
Ac	2:26	my heart is glad and my tongue r;
1Co	12:26	if one part is honoured, every part r
	13: 6	delight in evil but r with the truth.

REJOICING (JOY)

2Sa	6:12	to the City of David with r.
Ne	12:43	r because God had given them
Ps	30: 5	but r comes in the morning.
Lk	15: 7	in the same way there will be more r
Ac	5:41	r because they had been counted
1Co	6:10	sorrowful, yet always r; poor,

RELATIVES

Pr	19: 7	A poor man is shunned by all his r
Mk	6: 4	among his r and in his own house is
Lk	21:16	betrayed by parents, brothers, r
1Ti	5: 8	If anyone does not provide for his r

RELEASE (RELEASED)

Isa	61: 1	and r from darkness for the prisoners,
Lk	4:18	to r the oppressed,

RELEASED (RELEASE)

Ro	7: 6	we have been r from the law
Rev	20: 7	Satan will be r from his prison

RELENTED (RELENTS)

Ex	32:14	the LORD r and did not bring
Ps	106:45	and out of his great love he r.

RELENTS* (RELENTED)

Joel	2:13	and he r from sending calamity.
Jnh	4: 2	a God who r from sending calamity

RELIABLE (RELY)

Pr	22:21	teaching you true and r words,
Jn	8:26	But he who sent me is r,
2Ti	2: 2	witnesses entrust to r men who will

RELIANCE* (RELY)

Pr	25:19	is r on the unfaithful in times

RELIED (RELY)

2Ch	13:18	were victorious because they r
	16: 8	Yet when you r on the LORD,
Ps	71: 6	From birth I have r on you;

RELIEF

Job	35: 9	they plead for r from the arm
Ps	94:13	you grant him r from days
	143: 1	come to my r.
La	3:49	without r,
	3:56	to my cry for r."
2Th	1: 7	and give r to you who are troubled,

RELIGION* (RELIGIOUS)

Ac	25:19	dispute with him about their own r
	26: 5	to the strictest sect of our r,
1Ti	5: 4	all to put their r into practice
Jas	1:26	himself and his r is worthless.
	1:27	R that God our Father accepts

RELIGIOUS (RELIGION)

Jas	1:26	If anyone considers himself r

RELY (RELIABLE RELIANCE RELIED)

Isa	50:10	and r on his God.
Eze	33:26	you then possess the land? Your r
2Co	1: 9	this happened that we might not r
Gal	3:10	All who r on observing the law are
1Jn	4:16	and r on the love God has for us.

REMAIN (REMAINS)

Nu	33:55	allow to r will become barbs
Ps	102:27	But you r the same,
Jn	1:32	from heaven as a dove and r on him
	15: 4	R in me, and I will r in you.
	15: 7	If you r in me and my words
	15: 9	Now r in my love.
Ro	13: 8	Let no debt r outstanding,
1Co	13:13	And now these three r: faith,
2Ti	2:13	he will r faithful,
Heb	1:11	They will perish, but you r;
1Jn	2:27	just as it has taught you, r in him.

REMAINS (REMAIN)

Ps	146: 6	the LORD, who r faithful for ever.
Heb	7: 3	Son of God he r a priest for ever.

REMEDY

Isa	3: 7	"I have no r.

REMEMBER (REMEMBERED REMEMBERS REMEMBRANCE)

Ge	9:15	I will r my covenant between me
Ex	20: 8	"R the Sabbath day
	33:13	R that this nation is your people."
Dt	5:15	R that you were slaves in Egypt
1Ch	16:12	R the wonders he has done,
Job	36:24	R to extol his work,
Ps	25: 6	R, O LORD, your great mercy
	63: 6	On my bed I r you;
	74: 2	R the people you purchased of old,
	77:11	I will r the deeds of the LORD;
Ecc	12: 1	R your Creator
Isa	46: 8	"R this, fix it in mind,
Jer	31:34	and will r their sins no more."
Hab	3: 2	in wrath r mercy.
Lk	1:72	and to r his holy covenant,
Gal	2:10	we should continue to r the poor,
Php	1: 3	I thank my God every time I r you.
2Ti	2: 8	R Jesus Christ, raised
Heb	8:12	and will r their sins no more."

REMEMBERED (REMEMBER)

Ex	2:24	he r his covenant with Abraham,
	3:15	am to be r from generation
Ps	98: 3	He has r his love
	106:45	for their sake he r his covenant
	111: 4	He has caused his wonders to be r;
	136:23	to the One who r us
Isa	65:17	The former things will not be r,
Eze	18:22	offences he has committed will be r
	33:13	things he has done will be r;

REMEMBERS (REMEMBER)

Ps	103:14	he r that we are dust.
	111: 5	he r his covenant for ever.
Isa	43:25	and r your sins no more.

REMEMBRANCE (REMEMBER)

Lk	22:19	given for you; do this in r of me."
1Co	11:24	which is for you; do this in r of me
	11:25	whenever you drink it, in r of me."

REMIND

Jn	14:26	will r you of everything I have said
2Pe	1:12	I will always r you of these things,

REMNANT

Ezr	9: 8	has been gracious in leaving us a r
Isa	11:11	time to reclaim the r that is left
Jer	23: 3	"I myself will gather the r
Zec	8:12	inheritance to the r of this people.
Ro	11: 5	the present time there is a r chosen

REMOVED

Ps	30:11	you r my sackcloth and clothed me
	103:12	so far has he r our transgressions
Jn	20: 1	and saw that the stone had been r

REND

Joel	2:13	R your heart

RENEW (RENEWAL RENEWED RENEWING RENEWS)

Ps	51:10	and r a steadfast spirit within me.
Isa	40:31	will r their strength.

RENEWAL (RENEW)

Isa	57:10	You found r of your strength,
Tit	3: 5	of rebirth and r by the Holy Spirit,

RENEWED (RENEW)

Ps	103: 5	that my youth is r like the eagle's.
2Co	4:16	yet inwardly we are being r day

RENEWING* (RENEW)

Ro	12: 2	transformed by the r of your mind.

RENEWS* (RENEW)

Ps	119:50	Your promise r my life.

RENOUNCE (RENOUNCED RENOUNCES)

Da	4:27	R your sins by doing what is right,

RENOUNCED (RENOUNCE)

2Co	4: 2	we have r secret and shameful

RENOUNCES (RENOUNCE)

Pr	28:13	confesses and r them finds

RENOWN*

Ge	6: 4	were the heroes of old, men of r.
Ps	102:12	r endures through all generations.
	135:13	r, O LORD, through all
Isa	26: 8	your name and r
	55:13	This will be for the LORD's r,
	63:12	to gain for himself everlasting r,
Jer	13:11	to be my people for my r and praise
	32:20	have gained the r that is still yours.
	33: 9	Then this city will bring me r, joy,
	49:25	the city of r not been abandoned,
Eze	26:17	How you are destroyed, O city of r,
Hos	12: 5	the LORD is his name of r!

REPAID (PAY)

Lk	6:34	to 'sinners,' expecting to be r in full
	14:14	you will be r at the resurrection
Col	3:25	Anyone who does wrong will be r

REPAY (PAY)

Dt	7:10	But those who hate him he will r
	32:35	It is mine to avenge; I will r.
Ru	2:12	May the LORD r you
Ps	103:10	or r us according to our iniquities.
	116:12	How can I r the LORD
Jer	25:14	I will r them according
Ro	12:17	Do not r anyone evil for evil.
	12:19	"It is mine to avenge; I will r,"
1Pe	3: 9	Do not r evil with evil

REPAYING (PAY)

2Ch	6:23	r the guilty by bringing
1Ti	5: 4	so r their parents and grandparents

REPEATED

Heb	10: 1	the same sacrifices r endlessly year

REPENT (REPENTANCE REPENTED REPENTS)

1Ki	8:47	r and plead with you in the land
Job	36:10	commands them to r of their evil.
	42: 6	and r in dust and ashes."
Jer	15:19	"If you r, I will restore you
Eze	18:30	R! Turn away from all your
	18:32	R and live! "Take up a lament
Mt	3: 2	"R, for the kingdom of heaven is
	4:17	"R, for the kingdom of heaven is
Mk	6:12	and preached that people should r.
Lk	13: 3	unless you r, you too will all perish.
Ac	2:38	Peter replied, "R and be baptised,
	3:19	R, then, and turn to God,

Ac 17:30 all people everywhere to *r*.
　26:20 also, I preached that they should *r*
Rev 2: 5 *R* and do the things you did at first.

REPENTANCE (REPENT)

Isa 30:15 "In *r* and rest is your salvation,
Mt 3: 8 Produce fruit in keeping with *r*.
Mk 1: 4 a baptism of *r* for the forgiveness
Lk 3: 8 Produce fruit in keeping with *r*.
　5:32 call the righteous, but sinners to *r*."
　24:47 and *r* and forgiveness of sins will be
Ac 20:21 that they must turn to God in *r*
　26:20 and prove their *r* by their deeds.
Ro 2: 4 kindness leads you towards *r*?
2Co 7:10 Godly sorrow brings *r* that leads
2Pe 3: 9 but everyone to come to *r*.

REPENTED (REPENT)

Mt 11:21 they would have *r* long ago

REPENTS (REPENT)

Lk 15: 7 in heaven over one sinner who *r*
　15:10 of God over one sinner who *r*."
　17: 3 rebuke him, and if he *r*, forgive him

REPORTS

Ex 23: 1 "Do not spread false *r*.

REPOSES*

Pr 14:33 Wisdom *r* in the heart

REPRESENTATION*

Heb 1: 3 and the exact *r* of his being,

REPROACH

Job 27: 6 my conscience will not *r* me
Isa 51: 7 Do not fear the *r* of men
1Ti 3: 2 Now the overseer must be above *r*,

REPUTATION

1Ti 3: 7 also have a good *r* with outsiders,

REQUESTS

Ps 20: 5 May the LORD grant all your *r*.
Php 4: 6 with thanksgiving, present your *r*

REQUIRE (REQUIRED REQUIRES)

Mic 6: 8 And what does the LORD *r* of you

REQUIRED (REQUIRE)

1Co 4: 2 it is *r* that those who have been
Gal 5: 3 himself be circumcised that he is *r*

REQUIRES (REQUIRE)

1Ki 2: 3 what the LORD your God *r*:
Heb 9:22 the law *r* that nearly everything be

RESCUE (RESCUED RESCUES)

Ps 22: 8 let the LORD *r* him.
　31: 2 come quickly to my *r*;
　69:14 *R* me from the mire,
　91:14 says the LORD, "I will *r* him;
　143: 9 *R* me from my enemies, O LORD,
Da 6:20 been able to *r* you from the lions?"
Ro 7:24 Who will *r* me from this body
Gal 1: 4 himself for our sins to *r* us
2Pe 2: 9 how to *r* godly men from trials

RESCUED (RESCUE)

Ps 18:17 He *r* me from my powerful enemy,

Pr 11: 8 The righteous man is *r*
Col 1:13 For he has *r* us from the dominion

RESCUES (RESCUE)

Da 6:27 He *r* and he saves;
1Th 1:10 who *r* us from the coming wrath.

RESENT* (RESENTFUL RESENTS)

Pr 3:11 and do not *r* his rebuke,

RESENTFUL* (RESENT)

2Ti 2:24 to everyone, able to teach, not *r*.

RESENTS* (RESENT)

Pr 15:12 A mocker *r* correction;

RESERVE (RESERVED)

1Ki 19:18 Yet I *r* seven thousand in Israel—

RESERVED (RESERVE)

Ro 11: 4 "I have *r* for myself seven

RESIST (RESISTED RESISTS)

Da 11:32 know their God will firmly *r* him.
Mt 5:39 I tell you, Do not *r* an evil person.
Lk 21:15 of your adversaries will be able to *r*
Jas 4: 7 *R* the devil, and he will flee
1Pe 5: 9 *R* him, standing firm in the faith,

RESISTED (RESIST)

Job 9: 4 Who has *r* him and come out

RESISTS* (RESIST)

Ro 9:19 For who *r* his will?" But who are

RESOLVED

Ps 17: 3 I have *r* that my mouth will not sin.
Da 1: 8 But Daniel *r* not to defile himself
1Co 2: 2 For I *r* to know nothing while I was

RESOUNDING*

Ps 150: 5 praise him with *r* cymbals.
1Co 13: 1 I am only a *r* gong or a clanging

RESPECT (RESPECTABLE RESPECTED RESPECTS)

Lev 19: 3 "'Each of you must *r* his mother
　19:32 show *r* for the elderly and revere
Pr 11:16 A kind-hearted woman gains *r*,
Mal 1: 6 where is the *r* due me?" says
Eph 5:33 and the wife must *r* her husband.
　6: 5 obey your earthly masters with *r*
1Th 4:12 so that your daily life may win the *r*
　5:12 to *r* those who work hard
1Ti 3: 4 children obey him with proper *r*.
　3: 8 are to be men worthy of *r*, sincere,
　3:11 are to be women worthy of *r*,
　6: 1 their masters worthy of full *r*,
Tit 2: 2 worthy of *r*, self-controlled,
1Pe 2:17 Show proper *r* to everyone:
　3: 7 them with *r* as the weaker partner
　3:16 But do this with gentleness and *r*,

RESPECTABLE* (RESPECT)

1Ti 3: 2 self-controlled, *r*, hospitable,

RESPECTED (RESPECT)

Pr 31:23 Her husband is *r* at the city gate,

RESPECTS (RESPECT)

Pr 13:13 he who *r* a command is rewarded.

RESPLENDENT*

Ps 76: 4 You are *r* with light,
132: 18 but the crown on his head will be *r*

RESPOND

Ps 102: 17 He will *r* to the prayer
Hos 2: 21 "I will *r* to the skies,

RESPONSIBILITY (RESPONSIBLE)

Ac 18: 6 your own heads! I am clear of my *r*.

RESPONSIBLE (RESPONSIBILITY)

Nu 1: 53 The Levites are to be *r* for the care
1Co 7: 24 Brothers, each man, as *r* to God,

REST (RESTED RESTS SABBATH-REST)

Ex 31: 15 the seventh day is a Sabbath of *r*,
33: 14 go with you, and I will give you *r*."
Lev 25: 5 The land is to have a year of *r*.
Dt 31: 16 going to *r* with your fathers,
Jos 14: 15 Then the land had *r* from war.
21: 44 The LORD gave them *r*
1Ki 5: 4 Lord my God has given me *r*
1Ch 22: 9 who will be a man of peace and *r*,
Job 3: 17 and there the weary are at *r*.
Ps 16: 9 my body also will *r* secure,
33: 22 May your unfailing love *r* upon us,
62: 1 My soul finds *r* in God alone;
62: 5 Find *r*, O my soul, in God alone;
90: 17 of the Lord our God *r* upon us;
91: 1 will *r* in the shadow
95: 11 "They shall never enter my *r*."
Pr 6: 10 a little folding of the hands to *r*—
Isa 11: 2 Spirit of the LORD will *r* on him—
11: 10 and his place of *r* will be glorious.
30: 15 "In repentance and *r* is your
32: 18 in undisturbed places of *r*.
57: 20 which cannot *r*,
Jer 6: 16 and you will find *r* for your souls.
47: 6 'how long till you *r*?
Mt 11: 28 and burdened, and I will give you *r*.
2Co 12: 9 so that Christ's power may *r* on me
Heb 3: 11 "They shall never enter my *r*.'"
4: 3 'They shall never enter my *r*.'"
4: 10 for anyone who enters God's *r*
Rev 14: 13 "they will *r* from their labour,

RESTED (REST)

Ge 2: 2 so on the seventh day he *r*
Heb 4: 4 "And on the seventh day God *r*

RESTITUTION

Ex 22: 3 "A thief must certainly make *r*,
Lev 6: 5 He must make *r* in full, add a fifth
Nu 5: 8 the *r* belongs to the LORD

RESTORE (RESTORES)

Ps 51: 12 *R* to me the joy of your salvation
80: 3 *R* us, O God;
126: 4 *R* our fortunes, O LORD,
Jer 31: 18 *R* me, and I will return,
La 5: 21 *R* us to yourself, O LORD,
Da 9: 25 From the issuing of the decree to *r*
Na 2: 2 The LORD will *r* the splendour
Gal 6: 1 are spiritual should *r* him gently.
1Pe 5: 10 will himself *r* you and make you

RESTORES (RESTORE)

Ps 23: 3 he *r* my soul.

RESTRAINED (RESTRAINT)

Ps 78: 38 Time after time he *r* his anger

RESTRAINING (RESTRAINT)

Pr 27: 16 *r* her is like *r* the wind
Col 2: 23 value in *r* sensual indulgence.

RESTRAINT (RESTRAINED RESTRAINING)

Pr 17: 27 of knowledge uses words with *r*,
23: 4 have the wisdom to show *r*.
29: 18 no revelation, the people cast off *r*;

RESTS (REST)

Dt 33: 12 and the one the LORD loves *r*
Pr 19: 23 one *r* content, untouched
Lk 2: 14 to men on whom his favour *r*."

RESULT

Lk 21: 13 This will *r* in your being witnesses
Ro 6: 22 to holiness, and the *r* is eternal life.
11: 31 as a *r* of God's mercy to you.
2Co 3: 3 from Christ, the *r* of our ministry,
2Th 1: 5 as a *r* you will be counted worthy
1Pe 1: 7 may be proved genuine and may *r*

RESURRECTION*

Mt 22: 23 who say there is no *r*, came to him
22: 28 at the *r*, whose wife will she be
22: 30 At the *r* people will neither marry
22: 31 But about the *r* of the dead—
27: 53 and after Jesus' *r* they went
Mk 12: 18 who say there is no *r*, came to him
12: 23 At the *r* whose wife will she be,
Lk 14: 14 repaid at the *r* of the righteous."
20: 27 who say there is no *r*, came to Jesus
20: 33 at the *r* whose wife will she be,
20: 35 in the *r* from the dead will neither
20: 36 since they are children of the *r*.
Jn 11: 24 again in the *r* at the last day."
11: 25 Jesus said to her, "I am the *r*
Ac 1: 22 become a witness with us of his *r*."
2: 31 he spoke of the *r* of the Christ,
4: 2 in Jesus the *r* of the dead.
4: 33 to testify to the *r* of the Lord Jesus,
17: 18 good news about Jesus and the *r*.
17: 32 When they heard about the *r*
23: 6 of my hope in the *r* of the dead."
23: 8 Sadducees say that there is no *r*,
24: 15 that there will be a *r*
24: 21 "It is concerning the *r*
Ro 1: 4 Son of God by his *r* from the dead:
6: 5 also be united with him in his *r*.
1Co 15: 12 some of you say that there is no *r*
15: 13 If there is no *r* of the dead,
15: 21 the *r* of the dead comes
15: 29 if there is no *r*, what will those do
15: 42 So will it be with the *r* of the dead.
Php 3: 10 power of his *r* and the fellowship
3: 11 to attain to the *r* from the dead.
2Ti 2: 18 say that the *r* has already taken
Heb 6: 2 on of hands, the *r* of the dead,
11: 35 so that they might gain a better *r*.
1Pe 1: 3 hope through the *r* of Jesus Christ
3: 21 It saves you by the *r* of Jesus Christ
Rev 20: 5 This is the first *r*.
20: 6 those who have part in the first *r*.

RETALIATE*

1Pe 2: 23 he did not *r*; when he suffered,

RETRIBUTION

Ps 69: 22 may it become *r* and a trap.
Jer 51: 56 For the Lord is a God of *r*;
Ro 11: 9 a stumbling-block and a *r* for them.

RETURN (RETURNED RETURNS)

Ge 3: 19 and to dust you will *r.*"
2Sa 12: 23 go to him, but he will not *r* to me."
2Ch 30: 9 If you *r* to the Lord, then you
Ne 1: 9 but if you *r* to me and obey my
Job 10: 21 joy before I go to the place of no *r,*
16: 22 before I go on the journey of no *r.*
22: 23 If you *r* to the Almighty, you will
Ps 80: 14 *R* to us, O God Almighty!
126: 6 will *r* with songs of joy,
Isa 10: 21 A remnant will *r*, a remnant
35: 10 the ransomed of the Lord will *r.*
55: 11 It will not *r* to me empty,
Jer 24: 7 for they will *r* to me
31: 8 a great throng will *r.*
La 3: 40 and let us *r* to the Lord.
Hos 6: 1 "Come, let us *r* to the Lord.
12: 6 But you must *r* to your God;
14: 1 *R*, O Israel, to the Lord your
Joel 2: 12 "*r* to me with all your heart,
Zec 1: 3 '*R* to me,' declares the Lord
10: 9 and they will *r.*

RETURNED (RETURN)

Ps 35: 13 When my prayers *r*
Am 4: 6 yet you have not *r* to me,"
1Pe 2: 25 now you have *r* to the Shepherd

RETURNS (RETURN)

Pr 3: 14 and yields better *r* than gold.
Isa 52: 8 When the Lord *r* to Zion,
Mt 24: 46 finds him doing so when he *r.*

REUBEN

Firstborn of Jacob by Leah (Ge 29:32; 46:8;
1Ch 2:1). Attempted to rescue Joseph (Ge
37:21-30). Lost birthright for sleeping with Bilhah
(Ge 35: 22; 49: 4). Tribe of blessed (Ge 49:3-4; Dt
33:6), numbered (Nu 1:21; 26:7), allotted land east
of Jordan (Nu 32; 34:14; Jos 13:15), west (Eze
48:6), failed to help Deborah (Jdg 5:15-16),
supported David (1Ch 12:37), 12,000 from (Rev
7:5).

REVEAL (REVEALED REVEALS REVELATION REVELATIONS)

Mt 11: 27 to whom the Son chooses to *r* him.
Gal 1: 16 was pleased to *r* his Son in me

REVEALED (REVEAL)

Dt 29: 29 but the things *r* belong to us
Isa 40: 5 the glory of the Lord will be *r,*
43: 12 I have *r* and saved and proclaimed
53: 1 the arm of the Lord been *r*?
65: 1 I *r* myself to those who did not ask
Mt 11: 25 and *r* them to little children.
Jn 12: 38 the arm of the Lord been *r*?"
17: 6 "I have *r* you to those whom you
Ro 1: 17 a righteousness from God is *r,*
8: 18 with the glory that will be *r* in us.
10: 20 I *r* myself to those who did not ask
16: 26 but now *r* and made known
1Co 2: 10 but God has *r* it to us by his Spirit.
2Th 1: 7 happen when the Lord Jesus is *r*
2: 3 and the man of lawlessness is *r,*

1Pe 1: 7 and honour when Jesus Christ is *r.*
1: 20 but was *r* in these last times
4: 13 overjoyed when his glory is *r.*

REVEALS* (REVEAL)

Nu 23: 3 Whatever he *r* to me I will tell you
Job 12: 22 He *r* the deep things of darkness
Da 2: 22 He *r* deep and hidden things;
2: 28 a God in heaven who *r* mysteries.
Am 4: 13 and *r* his thoughts to man,

REVELATION* (REVEAL)

2Sa 7: 17 David all the words of this entire *r.*
1Ch 17: 15 David all the words of this entire *r.*
Pr 29: 18 Where there is no *r*, the people cast
Da 10: 1 a *r* was given to Daniel (who was
Hab 2: 2 "Write down the *r*
2: 3 For the *r* awaits an appointed time;
Lk 2: 32 a light for *r* to the Gentiles
Ro 16: 25 according to the *r*
1Co 14: 6 I bring you some *r* or knowledge
14: 26 a *r*, a tongue or an interpretation.
14: 30 And if a *r* comes to someone who is
Gal 1: 12 I received it by *r* from Jesus Christ.
2: 2 I went in response to a *r*
Eph 1: 17 you the Spirit of wisdom and *r,*
3: 3 mystery made known to me by *r,*
Rev 1: 1 *r* of Jesus Christ, which God gave

REVELATIONS* (REVEAL)

2Co 12: 1 on to visions and *r* from the Lord.
12: 7 of these surpassingly great *r,*

REVELLED* (REVELRY)

Ne 9: 25 they *r* in your great goodness.

REVELRY (REVELLED)

Ex 32: 6 drink and got up to indulge in *r.*
1Co 10: 7 and got up to indulge in pagan *r.*"

REVENGE (VENGEANCE)

Lev 19: 18 "'Do not seek *r* or bear a grudge
Ro 12: 19 Do not take *r*, my friends,

REVERE* (REVERENCE REVERENT REVERING)

Lev 19: 32 for the elderly and *r* your God.
Dt 4: 10 so that they may learn to *r* me
13: 4 must follow, and him you must *r.*
14: 23 to *r* the Lord your God always.
17: 19 learn to *r* the Lord his God
28: 58 and do not *r* this glorious
Job 37: 24 Therefore, men *r* him,
Ps 22: 23 *R* him, all you descendants
33: 8 let all the people of the world *r* him
102: 15 of the earth will *r* your glory.
Ecc 3: 14 God does it, so men will *r* him.
Isa 25: 3 cities of ruthless nations will *r* you.
59: 19 of the sun, they will *r* his glory.
63: 17 hearts so we do not *r* you?
Jer 10: 7 Who should not *r* you,
Hos 10: 3 because we did not *r* the Lord.
Mal 4: 2 But for you who *r* my name,

REVERENCE (REVERE)

Lev 19: 30 and have *r* for my sanctuary.
Ne 5: 15 of *r* for God I did not act like that.
Ps 5: 7 in *r* will I bow down
Da 6: 26 people must fear and *r* the God
2Co 7: 1 perfecting holiness out of *r* for God

Eph   5: 21 to one another out of *r* for Christ.
Col   3: 22 of heart and *r* for the Lord.
1Pe   3: 2 when they see the purity and *r*
Rev 11: 18 and those who *r* your name,

REVERENT* (REVERE)

Ecc   8: 12 with God-fearing men, who are *r*
Tit   2: 3 women to be *r* in the way they live,
Heb   5: 7 because of his *r* submission.
1Pe   1: 17 as strangers here in *r* fear.

REVERING* (REVERE)

Dt   8: 6 walking in his ways and *r* him.
Ne   1: 11 who delight in *r* your name.

REVERSE*

Isa   43: 13 When I act, who can *r* it?"

REVIVE* (REVIVING)

Ps   80: 18 *r* us, and we will call on your name.
      85: 6 Will you not *r* us again,
Isa   57: 15 and to *r* the heart of the contrite.
      57: 15 to *r* the spirit of the lowly
Hos   6: 2 After two days he will *r* us;

REVIVING (REVIVE)

Ps   19: 7 *r* the soul.

REVOKED

Isa   45: 23 a word that will not be *r*:

REWARD (REWARDED REWARDING REWARDS)

Ge   15: 1 your very great *r*."
1Sa 24: 19 May the LORD *r* you well
Ps   19: 11 in keeping them there is great *r*.
      62: 12 Surely you will *r* each person
    127: 3 children a *r* from him.
Pr   9: 12 are wise, your wisdom will *r* you;
     11: 18 sows righteousness reaps a sure *r*.
     13: 21 prosperity is the *r* of the righteous.
     19: 17 he will *r* him for what he has done.
     25: 22 and the LORD will *r* you.
     31: 31 Give her the *r* she has earned,
Isa   40: 10 See, his *r* is with him,
     49: 4 and my *r* is with my God."
     61: 8 In my faithfulness I will *r* them
     62: 11 See, his *r* is with him,
Jer   17: 10 to *r* a man according to his conduct
     32: 19 you *r* everyone according
Mt   5: 12 because great is your *r* in heaven,
      6: 1 you will have no *r*
      6: 5 they have received their *r* in full.
     10: 41 a prophet will receive a prophet's *r*,
     16: 27 and then he will *r* each person
Lk   6: 23 because great is your *r* in heaven.
      6: 35 Then your *r* will be great,
1Co   3: 14 built survives, he will receive his *r*.
Eph   6: 8 know that the Lord will *r* everyone
Col   3: 24 an inheritance from the Lord as a *r*.
Heb 11: 26 he was looking ahead to his *r*.
Rev 22: 12 I am coming soon! My *r* is with me

REWARDED (REWARD)

Ru   2: 12 May you be richly *r* by the LORD,
2Sa 22: 21 of my hands he has *r* me.
2Ch 15: 7 for your work will be *r*."
Ps   18: 24 The LORD has *r* me according
Pr   13: 13 he who respects a command is *r*.
     14: 14 and the good man *r* for his.

Jer   31: 16 for your work will be *r*,"
1Co   3: 8 and each will be *r* according
Heb 10: 35 your confidence; it will be richly *r*.
2Jn   : 8 but that you may be *r* fully.

REWARDING* (REWARD)

Rev 11: 18 for *r* your servants the prophets

REWARDS (REWARD)

1Sa 26: 23 The LORD *r* every man
Pr   12: 14 the work of his hands *r* him.
Heb 11: 6 that he *r* those who earnestly seek

RIBS

Ge   2: 21 he took one of the man's *r*

RICH (RICHES RICHEST)

Job 34: 19 does not favour the *r* over the poor,
Ps   49: 16 overawed when a man grows *r*,
    145: 8 slow to anger and *r* in love.
Pr   21: 17 loves wine and oil will never be *r*.
     22: 2 *R* and poor have this in common:
     23: 4 Do not wear yourself out to get *r*;
     28: 6 than a *r* man whose ways are
     28: 20 to get *r* will not go unpunished.
     28: 22 A stingy man is eager to get *r*
Ecc   5: 12 but the abundance of a *r* man
Isa   33: 6 a *r* store of salvation and wisdom
     53: 9 and with the *r* in his death,
Jer   9: 23 or the *r* man boast of his riches,
Zec   3: 4 and I will put *r* garments on you."
Mt   19: 23 it is hard for a *r* man
Lk   1: 53 but has sent the *r* away empty.
      6: 24 "But woe to you who are *r*,
     12: 21 for himself but is not *r* towards God
     16: 1 "There was a *r* man whose
     21: 1 Jesus saw the *r* putting their gifts
2Co   6: 10 yet making many *r*; having nothing
      8: 2 poverty welled up in *r* generosity.
      8: 9 he was *r*, yet for your sakes he
      9: 11 You will be made *r* in every way
Eph   2: 4 love for us, God, who is *r* in mercy,
1Ti   6: 9 want to get *r* fall into temptation
      6: 17 Command those who are *r*
      6: 18 to do good, to be *r* in good deeds,
Jas   1: 10 the one who is *r* should take pride
      2: 5 the eyes of the world to be *r* in faith
      5: 1 you *r* people, weep and wail
Rev   2: 9 and your poverty—yet you are *r*!
      3: 18 you can become *r*; and white

RICHES (RICH)

Job 36: 18 that no-one entices you by *r*;
Ps   49: 6 and boast of their great *r*?
     49: 12 despite his *r*, does not endure;
     62: 10 though your *r* increase,
    119: 14 as one rejoices in great *r*.
Pr   3: 16 in her left hand are *r* and honour.
     11: 28 Whoever trusts in his *r* will fall,
     22: 1 is more desirable than great *r*;
     27: 24 for *r* do not endure for ever,
     30: 8 give me neither poverty nor *r*,
Isa   10: 3 Where will you leave your *r*?
     60: 5 to you the *r* of the nations will
Jer   9: 23 or the *r* man boast of his *r*,
Lk   8: 14 *r* and pleasures, and they do not
Ro   9: 23 to make the *r* of his glory known
     11: 33 the depth of the *r* of the wisdom
Eph   2: 7 he might show the incomparable *r*
      3: 8 to the Gentiles the unsearchable *r*

Col   1: 27 among the Gentiles the glorious *r*
        2: 2 so that they may have the full *r*

RICHEST (RICH)

Isa 55: 2 and your soul will delight in the *r*

RID

Ge 21: 10 "Get *r* of that slave woman
1Co 5: 7 Get *r* of the old yeast that you may
Gal 4: 30 "Get *r* of the slave woman

RIDE (RIDER RIDING)

Ps 45: 4 In your majesty *r* forth victoriously

RIDER (RIDE)

Rev 6: 2 was a white horse! Its *r* held a bow,
    19: 11 whose *r* is called Faithful and True.

RIDING (RIDE)

Zec 9: 9 gentle and *r* on a donkey,
Mt 21: 5 gentle and *r* on a donkey,

RIGGING

Isa 33: 23 Your *r* hangs loose:

RIGHT [1] (RIGHTS)

Ge 4: 7 But if you do not do what is *r*,
    18: 19 of the LORD by doing what is *r*
    18: 25 the Judge of all the earth do *r*?"
Ex 15: 26 and do what is *r* in his eyes,
Dt 6: 18 Do what is *r* and good
    13: 18 and doing what is *r* in his eyes.
1Sa 12: 23 you the way that is good and *r*.
1Ki 3: 9 to distinguish between *r* and wrong
    15: 5 For David had done what was *r*
2Ki 7: 9 to each other, "We're not doing *r*.
Ne 9: 13 and laws that are just and *r*,
Ps 19: 8 The precepts of the LORD are *r*,
    25: 9 He guides the humble in what is *r*
    33: 4 For the word of the LORD is *r*
    51: 4 so that you are proved *r*
  106: 3 who constantly do what is *r*.
  119: 144 Your statutes are for ever *r*;
Pr 1: 3 doing what is *r* and just and fair;
    14: 12 There is a way that seems *r*
    18: 17 The first to present his case seems *r*
Ecc 7: 20 who does what is *r* and never sins.
SS 1: 4 How *r* they are to adore you!
Isa 1: 17 learn to do *r*!
    7: 15 reject the wrong and choose the *r*.
    30: 10 us no more visions of what is *r*!
    64: 5 to the help of those who gladly do *r*
Jer 23: 5 and do what is just and *r* in the land
Eze 18: 5 who does what is just and *r*.
    18: 21 and does what is just and *r*,
    33: 14 and does what is just and *r*—
Hos 14: 9 The ways of the LORD are *r*;
Jn 1: 12 he gave the *r* to become children
Ro 3: 4 "So that you may be proved *r*
    9: 21 Does not the potter have the *r*
    12: 17 careful to do what is *r* in the eyes
1Co 9: 4 Don't we have the *r* to food
2Co 8: 21 we are taking pains to do what is *r*,
Eph 6: 1 parents in the Lord, for this is *r*.
Php 4: 8 whatever is *r*, whatever is pure,
2Th 3: 13 never tire of doing what is *r*.
Jas 2: 8 as yourself," you are doing *r*.
1Pe 3: 14 if you should suffer for what is *r*,
1Jn 2: 29 who does what is *r* has been born
Rev 2: 7 I will give the *r* to eat from the tree

Rev 3: 21 I will give the *r* to sit with me
    22: 11 let him who does *r* continue to do *r*

RIGHT [2]

Ge 48: 13 on his left towards Israel's *r* hand
Ex 15: 6 Your *r* hand, O LORD,
Dt 5: 32 do not turn aside to the *r*
Jos 1: 7 do not turn from it to the *r*
Ps 16: 8 Because he is at my *r* hand,
    16: 11 eternal pleasures at your *r* hand.
    17: 7 you who save by your *r* hand
    18: 35 and your *r* hand sustains me;
    44: 3 it was your *r* hand, your arm,
    45: 4 let your *r* hand display awesome
    63: 8 your *r* hand upholds me.
    73: 23 you hold me by my *r* hand.
    91: 7 ten thousand at your *r* hand,
    98: 1 his *r* hand and his holy arm
  110: 1 "Sit at my *r* hand
  118: 15 LORD's *r* hand has done mighty
  137: 5 may my *r* hand forget ⸤its skill⸥.
  139: 10 your *r* hand will hold me fast.
Pr 4: 27 Do not swerve to the *r* or the left
Isa 30: 21 Whether you turn to the *r*
    41: 10 you with my righteous *r* hand
    41: 13 who takes hold of your *r* hand
    48: 13 my *r* hand spread out the heavens
Mt 5: 29 If your *r* eye causes you to sin,
    6: 3 know what your *r* hand is doing,
    22: 44 "Sit at my *r* hand
    25: 33 He will put the sheep on his *r*
Ac 2: 34 "Sit at my *r* hand
    7: 55 Jesus standing at the *r* hand of God
Ro 8: 34 is at the *r* hand of God and is
Eph 1: 20 and seated him at his *r* hand
Heb 1: 3 down at the *r* hand of the Majesty

RIGHTEOUS (RIGHTEOUSLY RIGHTEOUSNESS)

Ge 6: 9 Noah was a *r* man, blameless
    18: 23 "Will you sweep away the *r*
Nu 23: 10 Let me die the death of the *r*,
Ne 9: 8 your promise because you are *r*.
Job 36: 7 He does not take his eyes off the *r*;
Ps 1: 5 nor sinners in the assembly of the *r*.
    5: 12 O LORD, you bless the *r*;
    11: 7 For the LORD is *r*,
    15: 2 and who does what is *r*,
    34: 15 The eyes of the LORD are on the *r*
    37: 16 Better the little that the *r* have
    37: 21 but the *r* give generously;
    37: 25 yet I have never seen the *r* forsaken
    37: 30 of the *r* man utters wisdom,
    55: 22 he will never let the *r* fall.
    64: 10 Let the *r* rejoice in the LORD
    68: 3 But may the *r* be glad
  112: 4 compassionate and *r* man.
  118: 20 through which the *r* may enter.
  119: 7 as I learn your *r* laws.
  119: 137 *R* are you, O LORD,
  140: 13 Surely the *r* will praise your name
  143: 2 for no-one living is *r* before you.
  145: 17 The LORD is *r* in all his ways
Pr 3: 33 but he blesses the home of the *r*.
    4: 18 of the *r* is like the first gleam
    10: 7 of the *r* will be a blessing,
    10: 11 The mouth of the *r* is a fountain
    10: 16 The wages of the *r* bring them life
    10: 20 The tongue of the *r* is choice silver,
    10: 24 what the *r* desire will be granted.

Pr   10: 28   The prospect of the *r* is joy,
      10: 32   of the *r* know what is fitting,
      11: 23   The desire of the *r* ends only
      11: 30   The fruit of the *r* is a tree of life,
      12: 10   A *r* man cares for the needs
      12: 21   No harm befalls the *r*,
      13:   9   The light of the *r* shines brightly,
      15: 28   of the *r* weighs its answers,
      15: 29   but he hears the prayer of the *r*.
      16: 31   it is attained by a *r* life.
      18: 10   the *r* run to it and are safe.
      20:   7   The *r* man leads a blameless life;
      21: 15   justice is done, it brings joy to the *r*
      23: 24   The father of a *r* man has great joy;
      28:   1   but the *r* are as bold as a lion.
      29:   6   but a *r* one can sing and be glad.
      29:   7   The *r* care about justice
      29: 27   The *r* detest the dishonest;
Ecc   7: 20   There is not a *r* man on earth
Isa   26:   7   The path of the *r* is level;
      41: 10   you with my *r* right hand.
      45: 21   a *r* God and a Saviour;
      53: 11   his knowledge my *r* servant will
      64:   6   and all our *r* acts are like filthy rags
Jer   23:   5   up to David a *r* Branch,
Eze   3: 20   when a *r* man turns
      18:   5   "Suppose there is a *r* man
      18: 20   of the *r* man will be credited
      33: 12   The *r* man, if he sins, will not be
Da   9: 18   requests of you because we are *r*,
Hab   2:   4   but the *r* will live by his faith—
Zec   9:   9   *r* and having salvation,
Mal   3: 18   see the distinction between the *r*
Mt   5: 45   rain on the *r* and the unrighteous.
      9: 13   For I have not come to call the *r*,
      10: 41   and anyone who receives a *r* man
      13: 43   Then the *r* will shine like the sun
      13: 49   and separate the wicked from the *r*
Mt   25: 37   "Then the *r* will answer him, 'Lord,
      25: 46   to eternal punishment, but the *r*
Ac   24: 15   will be a resurrection of both the *r*
Ro   1: 17   as it is written: "The *r* will live
      2:   5   when his *r* judgment will be
      2: 13   the law who will be declared *r*.
      3: 10   "There is no-one *r*, not even one;
      3: 20   Therefore no-one will be declared *r*
      5: 19   one man the many will be made *r*.
Gal   3: 11   because, "The *r* will live by faith."
1Ti   1:   9   law is not made for the *r*
2Ti   4:   8   which the Lord, the *r* Judge,
Tit   3:   5   because of *r* things we had done,
Heb   10: 38   But my *r* one will live by faith.
Jas   5: 16   The prayer of a *r* man is powerful
1Pe   3: 12   the eyes of the Lord are on the *r*
      3: 18   the *r* for the unrighteous,
      4: 18   "If it is hard for the *r* to be saved,
1Jn   2:   1   defence—Jesus Christ, the *R* One.
      3:   7   does what is right is *r*, just as he is *r*.
Rev   19:   8   stands for the *r* acts of the saints.)

RIGHTEOUSLY* (RIGHTEOUS)

Ps   9:   4   on your throne, judging *r*.
Isa   33: 15   He who walks *r*
Jer   11: 20   Lord Almighty, you who judge *r*

RIGHTEOUSNESS (RIGHTEOUS)

Ge   15:   6   and he credited it to him as *r*.
Dt   9:   4   of this land because of my *r*."
1Sa   26: 23   Lord rewards every man for his *r*
1Ki   10:   9   to maintain justice and *r*."

Job   37: 23   great *r*, he does not oppress.
Ps   7: 17   to the Lord because of his *r*
      9:   8   He will judge the world in *r*;
      17: 15   And I—in *r* I will see your face;
      23:   3   He guides me in paths of *r*
      33:   5   The Lord loves *r* and justice;
      35: 28   My tongue will speak of your *r*
      36:   6   Your *r* is like the mighty
      37:   6   He will make your *r* shine like
      40:   9   I proclaim *r* in the great assembly;
      45:   4   on behalf of truth, humility and *r*;
      45:   7   You love *r* and hate wickedness;
      48: 10   your right hand is filled with *r*.
      65:   5   us with awesome deeds of *r*,
      71:   2   Rescue me and deliver me in your *r*
      71: 15   My mouth will tell of your *r*,
      71: 19   Your *r* reaches to the skies, O God,
      85: 10   *r* and peace kiss each other.
      89: 14   *R* and justice are the foundation
      96: 13   He will judge the world in *r*
      98:   9   He will judge the world in *r*
      103:   6   The Lord works *r*
      103: 17   his *r* with their children's children
      106: 31   This was credited to him as *r*
      111:   3   and his *r* endures for ever.
      118: 19   Open for me the gates of *r*;
      132:   9   May your priests be clothed with *r*;
      145:   7   and joyfully sing of your *r*.
Pr   11:   5   *r* of the blameless makes a straight
      11: 18   he who sows *r* reaps a sure reward.
      13:   6   *R* guards the man of integrity,
      14: 34   *R* exalts a nation,
      16:   8   Better a little with *r*
      16: 12   a throne is established through *r*.
      21: 21   He who pursues *r* and love
Isa   5: 16   will show himself holy by his *r*.
      9:   7   it with justice and *r*
      11:   4   but with *r* he will judge the needy,
      16:   5   and speeds the cause of *r*.
      26:   9   the people of the world learn *r*.
      32: 17   The fruit of *r* will be peace;
      42:   6   "I, the Lord, have called you in *r*;
      42: 21   the Lord for the sake of his *r*
      45:   8   "You heavens above, rain down *r*;
      51:   1   "Listen to me, you who pursue *r*
      51:   6   my *r* will never fail.
      51:   8   But my *r* will last for ever,
      58:   8   then your *r* will go before you,
      59: 17   He put on *r* as his breastplate,
      61: 10   and arrayed me in a robe of *r*,
      63:   1   "It is I, speaking in *r*,
Jer   9: 24   justice and *r* on earth,
      23:   6   The Lord Our *R*.
Eze   3: 20   a righteous man turns from his *r*
      14: 20   save only themselves by their *r*.
      18: 20   The *r* of the righteous man will be
      33: 12   *r* of the righteous man will not save
Da   9: 24   to bring in everlasting *r*,
      12:   3   and those who lead many to *r*,
Hos   10: 12   Sow for yourselves *r*,
Am   5: 24   *r* like a never-failing stream!
Mic   7:   9   I will see his *r*.
Zep   2:   3   Seek *r*, seek humility;
Mal   4:   2   the sun of *r* will rise with healing
Mt   5:   6   those who hunger and thirst for *r*,
      5: 10   who are persecuted because of *r*,
      5: 20   unless your *r* surpasses that
      6:   1   to do your 'acts of *r*' before men,
      6: 33   But seek first his kingdom and his *r*
Jn   16:   8   world of guilt in regard to sin and *r*

Ac	24:25	Paul discoursed on *r*, self-control
Ro	1:17	For in the gospel a *r* from God is
	3:5	brings out God's *r* more clearly,
	3:22	This *r* from God comes
	4:3	and it was credited to him as *r*."
	4:5	wicked, his faith is credited as *r*.
	4:6	man to whom God credits *r* apart
	4:9	faith was credited to him as *r*.
	4:13	through the *r* that comes by faith.
	4:22	why "it was credited to him as *r*."
	5:18	of *r* was justification that brings life
	6:13	body to him as instruments of *r*,
	6:16	or to obedience, which leads to *r*?
	6:18	and have become slaves to *r*.
	6:19	in slavery to *r* leading to holiness.
	8:10	yet your spirit is alive because of *r*.
	9:30	did not pursue *r*, have obtained it,
	10:3	they did not know the *r* that comes
	14:17	but of *r*, peace and joy
1Co	1:30	our *r*, holiness and redemption.
2Co	3:9	is the ministry that brings *r*!
	5:21	that in him we might become the *r*
	6:7	with weapons of *r* in the right hand
	6:14	For what do *r* and wickedness have
	9:9	his *r* endures for ever."
Gal	2:21	for if *r* could be gained
	3:6	and it was credited to him as *r*."
	3:21	then *r* would certainly have come
Eph	4:24	created to be like God in true *r*
	5:9	*r* and truth) and find out what
	6:14	with the breastplate of *r* in place,
Php	1:11	filled with the fruit of *r* that comes
	3:6	as for legalistic *r*, faultless.
	3:9	not having a *r* of my own that
1Ti	6:11	and pursue *r*, godliness, faith, love,
2Ti	2:22	and pursue *r*, faith, love and peace,
	3:16	correcting and training in *r*,
	4:8	is in store for me the crown of *r*,
Heb	1:8	and *r* will be the sceptre
	5:13	with the teaching about *r*.
	7:2	his name means "king of *r*";
	11:7	became heir of the *r* that comes
	12:11	it produces a harvest of *r*
Jas	2:23	and it was credited to him as *r*,"
	3:18	sow in peace raise a harvest of *r*.
1Pe	2:24	die to sins and live for *r*;
2Pe	2:21	not to have known the way of *r*,
	3:13	and a new earth, the home of *r*.

RIGHTS (RIGHT [1])

Ps	82:3	maintain the *r* of the poor
Pr	31:8	for the *r* of all who are destitute.
Isa	10:2	to deprive the poor of their *r*
La	3:35	to deny a man his *r*
Gal	4:5	that we might receive the full *r*

RING

Pr	11:22	Like a gold *r* in a pig's snout
Lk	15:22	Put a *r* on his finger and sandals

RIOTS

2Co	6:5	imprisonments and *r*; in hard work,

RIPE

Joel	3:13	for the harvest is *r*.
Am	8:1	showed me: a basket of *r* fruit.
Jn	4:35	at the fields! They are *r* for harvest.
Rev	14:15	for the harvest of the earth is *r*."

RISE (RAISE RAISED RISEN ROSE)

Lev	19:32	" '*R* in the presence of the aged,
Nu	24:17	a sceptre will *r* out of Israel.
Isa	26:19	their bodies will *r*.
Mal	4:2	of righteousness will *r* with healing
Mt	27:63	'After three days I will *r* again.'
Mk	8:31	and after three days *r* again.
Lk	18:33	On the third day he will *r* again.'"
Jn	5:29	those who have done good will *r*
	20:9	had to *r* from the dead.)
Ac	17:3	had to suffer and *r* from the dead.
1Th	4:16	and the dead in Christ will *r* first.

RISEN (RISE)

Mt	28:6	He is not here; he has *r*, just
Mk	16:6	He has *r*! He is not here.
Lk	24:34	The Lord has *r* and has appeared

RIVER (RIVERS)

Ps	46:4	There is a *r* whose streams make
Isa	66:12	"I will extend peace to her like a *r*,
Eze	47:12	grow on both banks of the *r*.
Rev	22:1	Then the angel showed me the *r*

RIVERS (RIVER)

Ps	137:1	By the *r* of Babylon we sat

ROAD (CROSSROADS ROADS)

Mt	7:13	and broad is the *r* that leads

ROADS (ROAD)

Lk	3:5	crooked *r* shall become straight,

ROARING

1Pe	5:8	prowls around like a *r* lion looking

ROB (ROBBERS ROBBERY ROBS)

Mal	3:8	"Will a man *r* God? Yet you *r* me.

ROBBERS (ROB)

Jer	7:11	become a den of *r* to you?
Mk	15:27	They crucified two *r* with him,
Lk	19:46	but you have made it 'a den of *r*.'"
Jn	10:8	came before me were thieves and *r*,

ROBBERY (ROB)

Isa	61:8	I hate *r* and iniquity.

ROBE (ROBED ROBES)

Ge	37:3	and he made a richly ornamented *r*
Isa	6:1	the train of his *r* filled the temple.
	61:10	arrayed me in a *r* of righteousness,
Rev	6:11	each of them was given a white *r*,

ROBED (ROBE)

Ps	93:1	the LORD is *r* in majesty
Isa	63:1	Who is this, *r* in splendour,

ROBES (ROBE)

Ps	45:8	All your *r* are fragrant with myrrh
Rev	7:13	"Those in white *r*—who are they,

ROBS* (ROB)

Pr	19:26	He who *r* his father and drives out
	28:24	He who *r* his father or mother

ROCK

Ge	49:24	of the Shepherd, the *R* of Israel,
Ex	17:6	Strike the *r*, and water will come
Nu	20:8	Speak to that *r* before their eyes

Dt   32: 4   He is the *R*, his works are perfect,
        32:13   him with honey from the *r*,
2Sa   22: 2   "The LORD is my *r*, my fortress
Ps   18: 2   The LORD is my *r*, my fortress
        19:14   O LORD, my *R* and my Redeemer
        40: 2   he set my feet on a *r*
        61: 2   lead me to the *r* that is higher
        92:15   he is my *R*, and there is no
Isa   26: 4   the LORD, is the *R* eternal.
        51: 1   to the *r* from which you were cut
Da   2:34   you were watching, a *r* was cut out,
Mt   7:24   man who built his house on the *r*.
Mt   16:18   and on this *r* I will build my church
Ro   9:33   and a *r* that makes them fall,
1Co   10: 4   the spiritual *r* that accompanied
1Pe   2: 8   and a *r* that makes them fall."

ROD (RODS)

2Sa   7:14   I will punish him with the *r* of men,
Ps   23: 4   your *r* and your staff,
Pr   13:24   He was spares the *r* hates his son,
        22:15   the *r* of discipline will drive it far
        23:13   if you punish him with the *r*,
        29:15   *r* of correction imparts wisdom,
Isa   11: 4   the earth with the *r* of his mouth;

RODS (ROD)

2Co   11:25   Three times I was beaten with *r*,

ROLL (ROLLED)

Mk   16: 3   "Who will *r* the stone away

ROLLED (ROLL)

Lk   24: 2   They found the stone *r* away

ROMAN

Ac   16:37   even though we are *R* citizens,
        22:25   you to flog a *R* citizen who hasn't

ROOF

2Ki   19:26   like grass sprouting on the *r*,
Isa   37:27   like grass sprouting on the *r*,
Pr   21: 9   Better to live on a corner of the *r*

ROOM (ROOMS)

Mt   6: 6   When you pray, go into your *r*,
Mk   14:15   He will show you a large upper *r*,
Lk   2: 7   there was no *r* for them in the inn.
Jn   8:37   because you have no *r* for my word
        21:25   the whole world would not have *r*
2Co   7: 2   Make *r* for us in your hearts.

ROOMS (ROOM)

Jn   14: 2   In my Father's house are many *r*;

ROOT (ROOTED ROOTS)

Isa   11:10   In that day the *R* of Jesse will stand
        53: 2   and like a *r* out of dry ground.
Mt   3:10   already at the *r* of the trees,
        13:21   But since he has no *r*, he lasts only
Ro   11:16   if the *r* is holy, so are the branches.
        15:12   "The *r* of Jesse will spring up,
1Ti   6:10   of money is a *r* of all kinds of evil.
Rev   5: 5   the *R* of David, has triumphed.
        22:16   I am the *R* and the Offspring

ROOTED (ROOT)

Eph   3:17   being *r* and established in love,

ROOTS (ROOT)

Isa   11: 1   from his *r* a Branch will bear fruit.

ROSE [1]

SS   2: 1   I am a *r* of Sharon,

ROSE [2] (RISE)

1Th   4:14   believe that Jesus died and *r* again

ROTS

Pr   14:30   but envy *r* the bones.

ROUGH

Isa   42:16   and make the *r* places smooth.
Lk   3: 5   the *r* ways smooth.

ROUND

Ecc   1: 6   *r* and *r* it goes,

ROYAL

Ps   45: 9   at your right hand is the *r* bride
Da   1: 8   not to defile himself with the *r* food
Jas   2: 8   If you really keep the *r* law found
1Pe   2: 9   a *r* priesthood, a holy nation,

RUBBISH*

Php   3: 8   I consider them *r*, that I may gain

RUBIES

Job   28:18   the price of wisdom is beyond *r*.
Pr   3:15   She is more precious than *r*;
        8:11   for wisdom is more precious than *r*,
        31:10   She is worth far more than *r*.

RUDDER*

Jas   3: 4   by a very small *r* wherever the pilot

RUDDY

1Sa   16:12   He was *r*, with a fine appearance
SS   5:10   My lover is radiant and *r*,

RUDE*

1Co   13: 5   It is not *r*, it is not self-seeking,

RUIN (RUINED RUINING RUINS)

Pr   10: 8   but a chattering fool comes to *r*.
        10:10   and a chattering fool comes to *r*.
        10:14   but the mouth of a fool invites *r*.
        10:29   but it is the *r* of those who do evil.
        18:24   many companions may come to *r*,
        19:13   A foolish son is his father's *r*,
        26:28   and a flattering mouth works *r*.
SS   2:15   that *r* the vineyards,
Eze   21:27   A *r*! A *r*! I will make it a *r*!
1Ti   6: 9   desires that plunge men into *r*

RUINED (RUIN)

Isa   6: 5   "I am *r*! For I am a man
Mt   9:17   and the wineskins will be *r*.
        12:25   divided against itself will be *r*,

RUINING* (RUIN)

Tit   1:11   they are *r* whole households

RUINS (RUIN)

Pr   19: 3   A man's own folly *r* his life,
Ecc   4: 5   and *r* himself.
2Ti   2:14   and only *r* those who listen.

RULE (RULER RULERS RULES)

Ge   1: 26 let them *r* over the fish of the sea
        3: 16 and he will *r* over you."
Jdg 8: 22 said to Gideon, "*R* over us—
1Sa 12: 12 'No, we want a king to *r* over us'—
Ps   2: 9 You will *r* them with an iron
      67: 4 for you *r* the peoples justly
    119: 133 let no sin *r* over me.
Pr   17: 2 A wise servant will *r*
Isa 28: 10 *r* on *r*, *r* on *r*;
Eze 20: 33 I will *r* over you with a mighty
Zec 6: 13 and will sit and *r* on his throne.
      9: 10 His *r* will extend from sea to sea
Ro 13: 9 are summed up in this one *r*:
     15: 12 arise to *r* over the nations;
1Co 7: 17 This is the *r* I lay down in all
Gal 6: 16 and mercy to all who follow this *r*,
Eph 1: 21 far above all *r* and authority,
Col 3: 15 the peace of Christ *r* in your hearts,
2Th 3: 10 we gave you this *r*: "If a man will
Rev 2: 27 He will *r* them with an iron sceptre;
     12: 5 who will *r* all the nations
    19: 15 He will *r* them with an iron sceptre

RULER (RULE)

Ps   8: 6 You made him *r* over the works
Pr   19: 6 Many curry favour with a *r*,
     23: 1 When you sit to dine with a *r*,
    25: 15 Through patience a *r* can be
    29: 26 Many seek an audience with a *r*,
Isa 60: 17 and righteousness your *r*.
Da   9: 25 the *r*, comes, there will be seven
Mic 5: 2 one who will be *r* over Israel,
Mt   2: 6 for out of you will come a *r*
Eph 2: 2 of the *r* of the kingdom of the air,
1Ti   6: 15 God, the blessed and only *R*,
Rev 1: 5 and the *r* of the kings of the earth.

RULERS (RULE)

Ps   2: 2 and the *r* gather together
    119: 161 *R* persecute me without cause,
    119: 23 Though *r* sit together and slander
Isa 40: 23 reduces the *r* of this world
Da   7: 27 and all *r* will worship and obey him
Mt 20: 25 "You know that the *r*
Ac 13: 27 and their *r* did not recognise Jesus,
Ro 13: 3 For *r* hold no terror
1Co 2: 6 of this age or of the *r* of this age,
Eph 3: 10 should be made known to the *r*
     6: 12 the *r*, against the authorities,
Col 1: 16 or powers or *r* or authorities;

RULES (RULE)

Nu 15: 15 is to have the same *r* for you
2Sa 23: 3 when he *r* in the fear of God,
Ps 22: 28 and he *r* over the nations.
     66: 7 He *r* for ever by his power,
    103: 19 and his kingdom *r* over all,
Isa 29: 13 is made up only of *r* taught by men.
    40: 10 and his arm *r* for him.
Mt 15: 9 their teachings are but *r* taught
Lk 22: 26 one who *r* like the one who serves.
2Ti 2: 5 he competes according to the *r*.

RUMOURS

Jer 51: 46 afraid when *r* are heard in the land;
Mt 24: 6 You will hear of wars and *r* of wars,

RUN (RAN RUNNERS RUNNING RUNS)

Ps 19: 5 champion rejoicing to *r* his course.

Pr   4: 12 when you *r*, you will not stumble.
    18: 10 the righteous *r* to it and are safe.
Isa 10: 3 To whom will you *r* for help?
    40: 31 they will *r* and not grow weary,
Joel 3: 18 ravines of Judah will *r* with water.
Hab 2: 2 so that a herald may *r* with it.
1Co 9: 24 *R* in such a way as to get the prize.
Gal 2: 2 that I was running or had *r* my race
Php 2: 16 on the day of Christ that I did not *r*
Heb 12: 1 let us *r* with perseverance the race

RUNNERS* (RUN)

1Co 9: 24 that in a race all the *r* run,

RUNNING (RUN)

Ps 133: 2 *r* down on Aaron's beard,
Lk 17: 23 Do not go *r* off after them.
1Co 9: 26 I do not run like a man *r* aimlessly;
Gal 5: 7 You were *r* a good race.

RUNS (RUN)

Jn 10: 12 he abandons the sheep and *r* away.

RUSH

Pr   1: 16 for their feet *r* into sin,
     6: 18 feet that are quick or *r* into evil,
Isa 59: 7 Their feet *r* into sin;

RUST

Mt 6: 19 where moth and *r* destroy,

RUTH*

Moabitess; widow who went to Bethlehem with
mother-in-law Naomi (Ru 1). Gleaned in field of
Boaz; shown favour (Ru 2). Proposed marriage to
Boaz (Ru 3). Married (Ru 4:1-12); bore Obed,
ancestor of David (Ru 4:13-22), Jesus (Mt 1:5).

RUTHLESS

Pr 11: 16 but *r* men gain only wealth.
Ro 1: 31 are senseless, faithless, heartless, *r*.

SABBATH (SABBATHS)

Ex 20: 8 "Remember the *S* day
    31: 14 "'Observe the *S*, because it is holy
Lev 25: 2 the land itself must observe a *s*
Dt   5: 12 "Observe the *S* day
Isa 56: 2 keeps the *S* without desecrating it,
    56: 6 all who keep the *S*
    58: 13 if you call the *S* a delight
Jer 17: 21 not to carry a load on the *S* day
Mt 12: 1 through the cornfields on the *S*.
Lk 13: 10 On a *S* Jesus was teaching in one
Col 2: 16 a New Moon celebration or a *S* day

SABBATH-REST* (REST)

Heb 4: 9 then, a *S* for the people of God;

SABBATHS (SABBATH)

2Ch 2: 4 evening and on *S* and New Moons
Eze 20: 12 Also I gave them my *S*

SACKCLOTH

Ps 30: 11 you removed my *s* and clothed me
Da   9: 3 in fasting, and in *s* and ashes.
Mt 11: 21 would have repented long ago in *s*

SACRED

Lev 23: 2 are to proclaim as *s* assemblies.
Mt 7: 6 "Do not give dogs what is *s*;

Ro   14: 5 One man considers one day more *s*
1Co   3: 17 for God's temple is *s*, and you are
2Pe   1: 18 were with him on the *s* mountain.
       2: 21 on the *s* command that was

SACRIFICE (SACRIFICED SACRIFICES)

Ge   22: 2 *S* him there as a burnt offering
Ex   12: 27 'It is the Passover *s* to the LORD,
1Sa   15: 22 To obey is better than *s*,
1Ki   18: 38 the LORD fell and burned up the *s*,
1Ch   21: 24 or *s* a burnt offering that costs me
Ps   40: 6 *S* and offering you did not desire,
      50: 14 *S* thank offerings to God,
      51: 16 You do not delight in *s*,
      54: 6 I will *s* a freewill offering to you;
     107: 22 Let them *s* thank-offerings
     141: 2 of my hands be like the evening *s*.
Pr   15: 8 The LORD detests the *s*
      21: 3 to the LORD than *s*.
Da   9: 27 that 'seven' he will put an end to *s*
      12: 11 time that the daily *s* is abolished
Hos   6: 6 For I desire mercy, not *s*,
Mt   9: 13 this means: 'I desire mercy, not *s*.'
Ro   3: 25 God presented him as a *s*
Eph   5: 2 as a fragrant offering and *s* to God.
Php   4: 18 an acceptable *s*, pleasing to God.
Heb   9: 26 away with sin by the *s* of himself.
      10: 5 "*S* and offering you did not desire,
      10: 10 holy through the *s* of the body
      10: 14 by one *s* he has made perfect
      10: 18 there is no longer any *s* for sin.
      11: 4 faith Abel offered God a better *s*
      13: 15 offer to God a *s* of praise—
1Jn   2: 2 He is the atoning *s* for our sins,
       4: 10 as an atoning *s* for our sins.

SACRIFICED (SACRIFICE)

Ac   15: 29 are to abstain from food *s* to idols,
1Co   5: 7 our Passover lamb, has been *s*.
       8: 1 Now about food *s* to idols:
Heb   7: 27 He *s* for their sins once for all
       9: 28 so Christ was *s* once

SACRIFICES (SACRIFICE)

Ps   51: 17 The *s* of God are a broken spirit;
Mk   12: 33 than all burnt offerings and *s*."
Ro   12: 1 to offer your bodies as living *s*,
Heb   9: 23 with better *s* than these.
      13: 16 for with such *s* God is pleased.
1Pe   2: 5 offering spiritual *s* acceptable

SAD

Lk   18: 23 he heard this, he became very *s*,

SADDUCEES

Mt   16: 6 the yeast of the Pharisees and *S*."
Mk   12: 18 *S*, who say there is no resurrection,
Ac   23: 8 *S* say that there is no resurrection,

SAFE (SAVE)

Ps   27: 5 he will keep me *s* in his dwelling;
      37: 3 in the land and enjoy *s* pasture.
Pr   18: 10 the righteous run to it and are *s*.
      28: 26 he who walks in wisdom is kept *s*.
      29: 25 in the LORD is kept *s*.
Jer   12: 5 If you stumble in *s* country,
Jn   17: 12 kept them *s* by that name you gave
1Ti   2: 15 But women will be kept *s*
1Jn   5: 18 born of God keeps him *s*,

SAFETY (SAVE)

Ps   4: 8 make me dwell in *s*.
Hos   2: 18 so that all may lie down in *s*.
1Th   5: 3 people are saying, "Peace and *s*,"

SAINTS

1Sa   2: 9 He will guard the feet of his *s*,
Ps   16: 3 As for the *s* who are in the land.
      30: 4 Sing to the LORD, you *s* of his:
      31: 23 Love the LORD, all his *s*!
      34: 9 Fear the LORD, you his *s*,
     116: 15 is the death of his *s*.
     149: 1 his praise in the assembly of the *s*.
     149: 5 Let the *s* rejoice in this honour
Da   7: 18 the *s* of the Most High will receive
Ro   8: 27 intercedes for the *s* in accordance
1Co   6: 2 not know that the *s* will judge
Eph   1: 15 Jesus and your love for all the *s*,
       1: 18 of his glorious inheritance in the *s*,
       6: 18 always keep on praying for all the *s*
Phm   : 7 have refreshed the hearts of the *s*.
Rev   5: 8 which are the prayers of the *s*.
      19: 8 for the righteous acts of the *s*.)

SAKE (SAKES)

1Sa   12: 22 For the *s* of his great name
Ps   23: 3 righteousness for his name's *s*.
      44: 22 Yet for your *s* we face death all day
     106: 8 Yet he saved them for his name's *s*,
Isa   42: 21 for the *s* of his righteousness
      43: 25 your transgressions, for my own *s*,
      48: 9 For my own name's *s* I delay my
      48: 11 For my own, for my own *s*,
Jer   14: 7 for the *s* of your name.
      14: 21 for the *s* of your name do not
Eze   20: 9 But for the *s* of my name I did what
      20: 14 But for the *s* of my name I did what
      20: 22 and for the *s* of my name I did what
      36: 22 but for the *s* of my holy name,
Da   9: 17 For your *s*, O Lord, look with favour
Mt   10: 39 life for my *s* will find it.
      19: 29 for my *s* will receive a hundred
1Co   9: 23 I do all this for the *s* of the gospel,
2Co   12: 10 for Christ's *s*, I delight
Php   3: 7 loss for the *s* of Christ.
Heb   11: 26 He regarded disgrace for the *s*
1Pe   2: 13 for the Lord's *s* to every authority
3Jn   : 7 was for the *s* of the Name that they

SAKES* (SAKE)

2Co   8: 9 yet for your *s* he became poor,

SALEM

Ge   14: 18 king of *S* brought out bread
Heb   7: 2 "king of *S*" means "king of peace."

SALT

Ge   19: 26 and she became a pillar of *s*.
Nu   18: 19 covenant of *s* before the LORD
Mt   5: 13 "You are the *s* of the earth.
Col   4: 6 with *s*, so that you may know how
Jas   3: 11 *s* water flow from the same spring?

SALVATION* (SAVE)

Ex   15: 2 he has become my *s*.
2Sa   22: 3 my shield and the horn of my *s*.
      23: 5 Will he not bring to fruition my *s*
1Ch   16: 23 proclaim his *s* day after day.
2Ch   6: 41 O LORD God, be clothed with *s*,

Ps	9: 14	and there rejoice in your *s*.
	13: 5	my heart rejoices in your *s*.
	14: 7	that *s* for Israel would come out
	18: 2	is my shield and the horn of my *s*,
	27: 1	The LORD is my light and my *s*—
	28: 8	a fortress of *s* for his anointed one.
	35: 3	"I am your *s*."
	35: 9	and delight in his *s*.
	37: 39	The *s* of the righteous comes
	40: 10	I speak of your faithfulness and *s*.
	40: 16	those who love your *s* always say,
	50: 23	way so that I may show him the *s*
	51: 12	Restore to me the joy of your *s*
	53: 6	that *s* for Israel would come out
	62: 1	my *s* comes from him.
	62: 2	He alone is my rock and my *s*;
	62: 6	He alone is my rock and my *s*;
	62: 7	My *s* and my honour depend
	67: 2	your *s* among all nations.
	69: 13	answer me with your sure *s*.
	69: 27	do not let them share in your *s*.
	69: 29	may your *s*, O God, protect me.
	70: 4	those who love your *s* always say,
	71: 15	of your *s* all day long,
	74: 12	you bring *s* upon the earth.
	85: 7	and grant us your *s*.
	85: 9	Surely his *s* is near those who fear
	91: 16	and show him my *s*."
	95: 1	to the Rock of our *s*.
	96: 2	proclaim his *s* day after day.
	98: 1	have worked *s* for him.
	98: 2	The LORD has made his *s* known
	98: 3	the *s* of our God.
	116: 13	I will lift up the cup of *s*
	118: 14	he has become my *s*.
	118: 21	you have become my *s*.
	119: 41	your *s* according to your promise;
	119: 81	with longing for your *s*,
	119: 123	My eyes fail, looking for your *s*,
	119: 155	*S* is far from the wicked,
	119: 166	I wait for your *s*, O LORD,
	119: 174	I long for your *s*, O LORD,
	132: 16	I will clothe her priests with *s*,
	149: 4	he crowns the humble with *s*.
Isa	12: 2	Surely God is my *s*;
	12: 2	he has become my *s*."
	12: 3	from the wells of *s*.
	25: 9	let us rejoice and be glad in his *s*."
	26: 1	God makes *s*
	26: 18	We have not brought *s* to the earth;
	30: 15	"In repentance and rest is your *s*,
	33: 2	our *s* in time of distress.
	33: 6	a rich store of *s* and wisdom
	45: 8	let *s* spring up,
	45: 17	the LORD with an everlasting *s*;
	46: 13	I will grant *s* to Zion,
	46: 13	and my *s* will not be delayed.
	49: 6	that you may bring my *s*
	49: 8	and in the day of *s* I will help you;
	51: 5	my *s* is on the way,
	51: 6	But my *s* will last for ever,
	51: 8	my *s* through all generations."
	52: 7	who proclaim *s*,
	52: 10	the *s* of our God.
	56: 1	for my *s* is close at hand
	59: 16	so his own arm worked *s* for him,
	59: 17	and the helmet of *s* on his head;
	60: 18	but you will call your walls *S*
	61: 10	me with garments of *s*
	62: 1	her *s* like a blazing torch.

Isa	63: 5	so my own arm worked *s* for me,
Jer	3: 23	is the *s* of Israel.
La	3: 26	quietly for the *s* of the LORD.
Jnh	2: 9	*S* comes from the LORD."
Zec	9: 9	righteous and having *s*,
Lk	1: 69	He has raised up a horn of *s* for us
	1: 71	of long ago), *s* from our enemies
	1: 77	give his people the knowledge of *s*
	2: 30	For my eyes have seen your *s*,
	3: 6	And all mankind will see God's *s*
	19: 9	"Today *s* has come to this house,
Jn	4: 22	for *s* is from the Jews.
Ac	4: 12	*S* is found in no-one else,
	13: 26	message of *s* has been sent.
	13: 47	that you may bring *s* to the ends
	28: 28	to know that God's *s* has been sent
Ro	1: 16	for the *s* of everyone who believes:
	11: 11	*s* has come to the Gentiles
	13: 11	because our *s* is nearer now
2Co	1: 6	it is for your comfort and *s*;
	6: 2	in the day of *s* I helped you."
	6: 2	of God's favour, now is the day of *s*.
	7: 10	brings repentance that leads to *s*
Eph	1: 13	word of truth, the gospel of your *s*.
Eph	6: 17	Take the helmet of *s* and the sword
Php	2: 12	to work out your *s* with fear
1Th	5: 8	and the hope of *s* as a helmet.
	5: 9	to receive *s* through our Lord Jesus
2Ti	2: 10	they too may obtain the *s* that is
	3: 15	wise for *s* through faith
Tit	2: 11	of God that brings *s* has appeared
Heb	1: 14	to serve those who will inherit *s*?
	2: 3	This *s*, which was first announced
	2: 3	escape if we ignore such a great *s*?
	2: 10	of their *s* perfect through suffering.
	5: 9	of eternal *s* for all who obey him
	6: 9	case—things that accompany *s*.
	9: 28	to bring *s* to those who are waiting
1Pe	1: 5	the coming of the *s* that is ready
	1: 9	of your faith, the *s* of your souls.
	1: 10	Concerning this *s*, the prophets,
	2: 2	by it you may grow up in your *s*,
2Pe	3: 15	that our Lord's patience means *s*,
Jude	: 3	to write to you about the *s* we share
Rev	7: 10	"*S* belongs to our God,
	12: 10	have come the *s* and the power
	19: 1	*S* and glory and power belong

SAMARIA (SAMARITAN)

1Ki	16: 24	He bought the hill of *S*
2Ki	17: 6	the king of Assyria captured *S*
Jn	4: 4	Now he had to go through *S*.
	4: 5	came to a town in *S* called Sychar,

SAMARITAN (SAMARIA)

Lk	10: 33	But a *S*, as he travelled, came where
	17: 16	and thanked him—and he was a *S*.
Jn	4: 7	When a *S* woman came

SAMSON

Danite judge. Birth promised (Jdg 13). Married to Philistine, but wife given away (Jdg 14). Vengeance on Philistines (Jdg 15). Betrayed by Delilah (Jdg 16:1-22). Death (Jdg 16:23-31). Feats of strength: killed lion (Jdg 14:6), 30 Philistines (Jdg 14:19), 1,000 Philistines with jaw-bone (Jdg 15:13-17), carried off gates of Gaza (Jdg 16:3), pushed down temple of Dagon (Jdg 16:25-30).

SAMUEL

Ephraimite judge and prophet (Heb 11:32).
Birth prayed for (1Sa 1:10-18). Dedicated to
temple by Hannah (1Sa 1:21-28). Raised by Eli
(1Sa 2:11, 18-26). Called as prophet (1Sa 3). Led
Israel to victory over Philistines (1Sa 7). Asked by
Israel for a king (1Sa 8). Anointed Saul as king
(1Sa 9-10). Farewell speech (1Sa 12). Rebuked
Saul for sacrifice (1Sa 13). Announced rejection of
Saul (2Sa 15). Anointed David as king (1Sa 16).
Protected David from Saul (1Sa 19:18-24). Death
(1Sa 25:1). Returned from dead to condemn Saul
(1Sa 28).

SANBALLAT

Led opposition to Nehemiah's rebuilding of
Jerusalem (Ne 2:10, 19; 4; 6).

SANCTIFIED* (SANCTIFY)

Jn 17: 19 that they too may be truly s.
Ac 20: 32 among all those who are s.
    26: 18 among those who are s by faith
Ro 15: 16 to God, s by the Holy Spirit.
1Co 1: 2 to those s in Christ Jesus
     6: 11 But you were washed, you were s,
     7: 14 and the unbelieving wife has been s
     7: 14 the unbelieving husband has been s
1Th 4: 3 God's will that you should be s:
Heb 10: 29 blood of the covenant that s him,

SANCTIFY* (SANCTIFIED SANCTIFYING)

Jn 17: 17 S them by the truth; your word is
    17: 19 For them I s myself, that they too
1Th 5: 23 s you through and through.
Heb 9: 13 are ceremonially unclean s them

SANCTIFYING* (SANCTIFY)

2Th 2: 13 through the s work of the Spirit
1Pe 1: 2 through the s work of the Spirit,

SANCTUARY

Ex 25: 8 "Then have them make a s for me,
Lev 19: 30 and have reverence for my s.
Ps 15: 1 Lord, who may dwell in your s?
    63: 2 I have seen you in the s
    68: 24 of my God and King into the s.
    68: 35 are awesome, O God, in your s;
    73: 17 me till I entered the s of God;
    102: 19 looked down from his s on high,
    134: 2 Lift up your hands in the s
    150: 1 Praise God in his s;
Eze 37: 26 I will put my s among them for ever
    41: 1 the man brought me to the outer s
Da 9: 26 will destroy the city and the s.
Heb 6: 19 It enters the inner s
    8: 2 in the s, the true tabernacle set up
    8: 5 They serve at a s that is a copy
    9: 24 enter a man-made s that was only

SAND

Ge 22: 17 and as the s on the seashore.
Mt 7: 26 man who built his house on s.

SANDAL (SANDALS)

Ru 4: 7 one party took off his s

SANDALS (SANDAL)

Ex 3: 5 off your s, for the place where you
Dt 25: 9 take off one of his s, spit in his face

Jos 5: 15 off your s, for the place where you
Mt 3: 11 whose s I am not fit to carry.

SANG (SING)

Ex 15: 1 and the Israelites s this song
    15: 21 Miriam s to them:
Nu 21: 17 Then Israel s this song:
Jdg 5: 1 Barak son of Abinoam s this song:
1Sa 18: 7 As they danced, they s:
2Sa 22: 1 David s to the Lord the words
2Ch 5: 13 in praise to the Lord and s:
    29: 30 So they s praises with gladness
Ezr 3: 11 thanksgiving they s to the Lord:
Job 38: 7 while the morning stars s together
Ps 106: 12 and s his praise.
Rev 5: 9 And they s a new song:
    5: 12 In a loud voice they s:
    14: 3 they s a new song before the throne
    15: 3 and s the song of Moses the servant

SAP

Ro 11: 17 share in the nourishing s

SAPPHIRA*

Ac 5: 1 together with his wife S,

SARAH

Wife of Abraham, originally named Sarai;
barren (Ge 11:29-31; 1Pe 3:6). Taken by Pharaoh
as Abraham's sister; returned (Ge 12:10-20). Gave
Hagar to Abraham; sent her away in pregnancy
(Ge 16). Name changed; Isaac promised (Ge
17:15-21; 18:10-15; Heb 11:11). Taken by
Abimelech as Abraham's sister; returned (Ge 20).
Isaac born; Hagar and Ishmael sent away (Ge
21:1-21; Gal 4:21-31). Death (Ge 23).

SARDIS

Rev 3: 1 the angel of the church in S write:

SASH (SASHES)

Rev 1: 13 with a golden s around his chest.

SASHES (SASH)

Rev 15: 6 wore golden s around their chests.

SAT (SIT)

Ps 137: 1 By the rivers of Babylon we s
Mk 16: 19 and he s at the right hand of God.
Lk 10: 39 who s at the Lord's feet listening
Heb 1: 3 he s down at the right hand
    8: 1 who s down at the right hand
    10: 12 he s down at the right hand of God.
Heb 12: 2 and s down at the right hand

SATAN

Job 1: 6 and S also came with them.
Zec 3: 2 said to S, "The Lord rebuke you,
Mt 12: 26 If S drives out S, he is divided
    16: 23 S! You are a stumbling-block to me
Mk 4: 15 S comes and takes away the word
Lk 10: 18 "I saw S fall like lightning
    22: 3 S entered Judas, called Iscariot,
Ro 16: 20 The God of peace will soon crush S
1Co 5: 5 is present, hand this man over to S,
2Co 11: 14 for S himself masquerades
    12: 7 a messenger of S, to torment me.
1Ti 1: 20 handed over to S to be taught not
Rev 12: 9 serpent called the devil or S,
    20: 2 or S, and bound him for a thousand
    20: 7 S will be released from his prison

SATISFIED (SATISFY)

Ps	17: 15	I will be *s* with seeing your likeness
	22: 26	The poor will eat and be *s*;
	63: 5	My soul will be *s* as with the richest
	104: 28	they are *s* with good things.
	105: 40	*s* them with the bread of heaven.
Pr	13: 4	the desires of the diligent are fully *s*
	30: 15	are three things that are never *s*,
Ecc	5: 10	whoever loves wealth is never *s*
Isa	53: 11	he will see the light ˌof lifeˌ and be *s*
Mt	14: 20	They all ate and were *s*,
Lk	6: 21	for you will be *s*.

SATISFIES* (SATISFY)

Ps	103: 5	He *s* my desires with good things,
	107: 9	for he *s* the thirsty
	147: 14	and *s* you with the finest of wheat.

SATISFY (SATISFIED SATISFIES)

Ps	90: 14	*S* us in the morning
	145: 16	*s* the desires of every living thing.
Pr	5: 19	may her breasts *s* you always,
Isa	55: 2	and your labour on what does not *s*?
	58: 10	and *s* the needs of the oppressed,

SAUL

1. Benjamite; anointed by Samuel as first king of Israel (1Sa 9-10). Defeated Ammonites (1Sa 11). Rebuked for offering sacrifice (1Sa 13:1-15). Defeated Philistines (1Sa 14). Rejected as king for failing to annihilate Amalekites (1Sa 15). Soothed from evil spirit by David (1Sa 16:14-23). Sent David against Goliath (1Sa 17). Jealousy and attempted murder of David (1Sa 18:1-11). Gave David Michal as wife (1Sa 18:12-30). Second attempt to kill David (1Sa 19). Anger at Jonathan (1Sa 20:26-34). Pursued David: killed priests at Nob (1Sa 22), went to Keilah and Ziph (1Sa 23), life spared by David at En Gedi (1Sa 24) and in his tent (1Sa 26). Rebuked by Samuel's spirit for consulting witch at Endor (1Sa 28). Wounded by Philistines; took his own life (1Sa 31; 1Ch 10). Lamented by David (2Sa 1:17-27). Children (1Sa 14:49-51; 1Ch 8).

2. See PAUL

SAVAGE

Ac	20: 29	*s* wolves will come in among you

SAVE (SAFE SAFETY SALVATION SAVED SAVES SAVIOUR)

Ge	45: 5	to *s* lives that God sent me ahead
1Ch	16: 35	Cry out, "*S* us, O God our Saviour;
Job	40: 14	that your own right hand can *s* you.
Ps	17: 7	you who *s* by your right hand
	18: 27	You *s* the humble
	28: 9	*S* your people and bless your
	31: 16	*s* me in your unfailing love.
	69: 35	for God will *s* Zion
	71: 2	turn your ear to me and *s* me.
	72: 13	and *s* the needy from death.
	89: 48	or *s* himself from the power
	91: 3	Surely he will *s* you
	109: 31	to *s* his life from those who
	146: 3	in mortal men, who cannot *s*.
Pr	2: 16	will *s* you also from the adulteress,
Isa	35: 4	will come to *s* you."
	38: 20	The LORD will *s* me,
	46: 7	it cannot *s* him from his troubles.
	59: 1	of the LORD is not too short to *s*.

Isa	63: 1	mighty to *s*."
Jer	17: 14	*s* me and I will be saved,
Eze	3: 18	ways in order to *s* his life,
	7: 19	able to *s* them in the day
	14: 14	they could *s* only themselves
	33: 12	of the righteous man will not *s* him
	34: 22	I will *s* my flock, and they will no
Da	3: 17	the God we serve is able to *s* us
Hos	1: 7	and I will *s* them—not by bow,
Zep	3: 18	will be able to *s* them
	3: 17	he is mighty to *s*.
Zec	8: 7	"I will *s* my people
Mt	1: 21	he will *s* his people from their sins
	16: 25	wants to *s* his life will lose it,
Lk	19: 10	to seek and to *s* what was lost."
Jn	3: 17	but to *s* the world through him.
	12: 47	come to judge the world, but to *s* it.
Ro	11: 14	people to envy and *s* some of them.
1Co	7: 16	whether you will *s* your husband?
1Ti	1: 15	came into the world to *s* sinners—
Heb	7: 25	to *s* completely those who come
Jas	5: 20	of his way will *s* him from death
Jude	: 23	others from the fire and *s* them;

SAVED (SAVE)

Ps	22: 5	They cried to you and were *s*;
	33: 16	No king is *s* by the size of his army;
	34: 6	he *s* him out of all his troubles.
	106: 21	They forgot the God who *s* them,
	116: 6	when I was in great need, he *s* me.
Isa	25: 9	we trusted in him, and he *s* us.
	45: 22	"Turn to me and be *s*,
	64: 5	How then can we be *s*?
Jer	4: 14	from your heart and be *s*.
	8: 20	and we are not *s*."
Eze	3: 19	but you will have *s* yourself.
	33: 5	warning, he would have *s* himself.
Joel	2: 32	on the name of the LORD will be *s*;
Mt	10: 22	firm to the end will be *s*.
	24: 13	firm to the end will be *s*.
Mk	13: 13	firm to the end will be *s*.
	16: 16	believes and is baptised will be *s*,
Jn	10: 9	enters through me will be *s*.
Ac	2: 21	on the name of the Lord will be *s*.'
	2: 47	daily those who were being *s*.
	4: 12	to men by which we must be *s*."
	15: 11	of our Lord Jesus that we are *s*,
	16: 30	do to be *s*?" They replied,
Ro	5: 9	how much more shall we be *s*
	9: 27	only the remnant will be *s*.
	10: 1	the Israelites is that they may be *s*.
	10: 9	him from the dead, you will be *s*.
	10: 13	on the name of the Lord will be *s*."
	11: 26	so all Israel will be *s*, as it is written:
1Co	1: 18	to us who are being *s* it is the power
	3: 15	will suffer loss; he himself will be *s*
	5: 5	his spirit *s* on the day of the Lord.
	10: 33	of many, so that they may be *s*.
	15: 2	By this gospel you are *s*,
Eph	2: 5	it is by grace you have been *s*.
	2: 8	For it is by grace you have been *s*,
2Th	2: 13	you to be *s* through the sanctifying
1Ti	2: 4	who wants all men to be *s*
2Ti	1: 9	who has *s* us and called us
Tit	3: 5	He *s* us through the washing
Heb	10: 39	but of those who believe and are *s*.

SAVES (SAVE)

Ps	7: 10	who *s* the upright in heart.
	68: 20	Our God is a God who *s*;

Ps 145:19 he hears their cry and s them.
1Pe 3:21 It s you by the resurrection

SAVIOUR* (SAVE)

Dt 32:15 and rejected the Rock his S.
2Sa 22: 3 stronghold, my refuge and my s—
22:47 Exalted be God, the Rock, my S!
1Ch 16:35 Cry out, "Save us, O God our S;
Ps 18:46 Exalted be God my S!
24: 5 and vindication from God his S.
25: 5 for you are God my S,
27: 9 O God my S.
38:22 O Lord my S.
42: 5 my S and
42:11 my S and my God.
43: 5 my S and my God.
65: 5 O God our S,
68:19 Praise be to the Lord, to God our S,
79: 9 Help us, O God our S,
85: 4 Restore us again, O God our S,
89:26 My God, the Rock my S.'
Isa 17:10 You have forgotten God your S;
19:20 he will send them a s and defender,
43: 3 the Holy One of Israel, your S;
43:11 and apart from me there is no s.
45:15 O God and S of Israel.
45:21 a righteous God and a S;
49:26 that I, the LORD, am your S,
60:16 know that I, the LORD, am your S,
62:11 'See, your S comes!'
63: 8 and so he became their S.
Jer 14: 8 its S in times of distress,
Hos 13: 4 no S except me.
Mic 7: 7 I wait for God my S;
Hab 3:18 I will be joyful in God my S.
Lk 1:47 and my spirit rejoices in God my S,
2:11 of David a S has been born to you;
Jn 4:42 know that this man really is the S
Ac 5:31 S that he might give repentance
13:23 God has brought to Israel the S
Eph 5:23 his body, of which he is the S.
Php 3:20 we eagerly await a S from there,
1Ti 1: 1 by the command of God our S
2: 3 This is good, and pleases God our S
4:10 who is the S of all men,
2Ti 1:10 through the appearing of our S,
Tit 1: 3 me by the command of God our S,
1: 4 the Father and Christ Jesus our S.
2:10 about God our S attractive.
2:13 appearing of our great God and S,
3: 4 and love of God our S appeared,
3: 6 through Jesus Christ our S,
2Pe 1: 1 S Jesus Christ have received a faith
1:11 eternal kingdom of our Lord and S
2:20 and S Jesus Christ and are again
3: 2 and S through your apostles.
3:18 and knowledge of our Lord and S
1Jn 4:14 Son to be the S of the world.
Jude :25 to the only God our S be glory,

SCALE

Ps 18:29 with my God I can s a wall.

SCALES [1]

Lev 11: 9 may eat any that have fins and s.

SCALES [2]

Lev 19:36 Use honest s and honest weights,
Pr 11: 1 The LORD abhors dishonest s,
Da 5:27 You have been weighed on the s

Rev 6: 5 Its rider was holding a pair of s

SCAPEGOAT (GOAT)

Lev 16:10 by sending it into the desert as a s.

SCARECROW*

Jer 10: 5 Like a s in a melon patch,

SCARLET

Jos 2:21 she tied the s cord in the window.
Isa 1:18 "Though your sins are like s,
Mt 27:28 They stripped him and put a s robe

SCATTER (SCATTERED SCATTERS)

Dt 4:27 The LORD will s you
Ne 1: 8 I will s you among the nations,
Jer 9:16 I will s them among nations that
30:11 the nations among which I s you,
Zec 10: 9 I s them among the peoples,

SCATTERED (SCATTER)

Isa 11:12 he will assemble the s people
Jer 31:10 "He who s Israel will gather them
Zec 2: 6 "for I have s you to the four winds
13: 7 and the sheep will be s,
Mt 26:31 and the sheep of the flock will be s.'
Jn 11:52 but also for the s children of God,
Ac 8: 4 who had been s preached the word
Jas 1: 1 To the twelve tribes s
1Pe 1: 1 s throughout Pontus, Galatia,

SCATTERS (SCATTER)

Mt 12:30 he who does not gather with me s.

SCEPTRE

Ge 49:10 The s will not depart from Judah,
Nu 24:17 a s will rise out of Israel.
Ps 2: 9 You will rule them with an iron s;
45: 6 a s of justice will be the s
Heb 1: 8 and righteousness will be the s
Rev 2:27 'He will rule them with an iron s;
12: 5 rule all the nations with an iron s.
19:15 "He will rule them with an iron s.''

SCHEMES

Pr 6:18 a heart that devises wicked s,
24: 9 The s of folly are sin,
2Co 2:11 For we are not unaware of his s.
Eph 6:11 stand against the devil's s.

SCHOLAR*

1Co 1:20 Where is the s? Where is

SCOFFERS

2Pe 3: 3 that in the last days s will come,

SCORN (SCORNED SCORNING SCORNS)

Ps 69: 7 For I endure s for your sake,
69:20 S has broken my heart
89:41 he has become the s
109:25 I am an object of s to my accusers;
119:22 Remove from me s and contempt,
Mic 6:16 you will bear the s of the nations.''

SCORNED (SCORN)

Ps 22: 6 s by men and despised

SCORNING (SCORN)

Heb 12: 2 him endured the cross, s its shame,

SCORNS (SCORN)

Pr   13: 13   He who *s* instruction will pay for it,
       30: 17   that *s* obedience to a mother,

SCORPION

Lk   11: 12   will give him a *s*? If you then,
Rev   9: 5   sting of a *s* when it strikes a man.

SCOUNDREL

Pr   6: 12   A *s* and villain,

SCRIPTURE (SCRIPTURES)

Jn   2: 22   Then they believed the *S*
       7: 42   Does not the *S* say that the Christ
     10: 35   and the *S* cannot be broken—
Ac   8: 32   was reading this passage of *S*:
1Ti   4: 13   yourself to the public reading of *S*,
2Ti   3: 16   All *S* is God-breathed
2Pe   1: 20   that no prophecy of *S* came about

SCRIPTURES (SCRIPTURE)

Mt   22: 29   because you do not know the *S*
Lk   24: 27   said in all the *S* concerning himself.
     24: 45   so they could understand the *S*.
Jn   5: 39   These are the *S* that testify about
Ac   17: 11   examined the *S* every day to see
2Ti   3: 15   you have known the holy *S*,
2Pe   3: 16   as they do the other *S*,

SCROLL

Ps   40: 7   it is written about me in the *s*.
Isa   34: 4   and the sky rolled up like a *s*;
Eze   3: 1   eat what is before you, eat this *s*;
Heb   10: 7   it is written about me in the *s*—
Rev   6: 14   The sky receded like a *s*, rolling up,
     10: 8   take the *s* that lies open in the hand

SCUM

1Co   4: 13   this moment we have become the *s*

SEA (SEASHORE)

Ex   14: 16   go through the *s* on dry ground.
Dt   30: 13   "Who will cross the *s* to get it
1Ki   7: 23   He made the *S* of cast metal,
Job   11: 9   and wider than the *s*.
Ps   93: 4   mightier than the breakers of the *s*
     95: 5   The *s* is his, for he made it,
Ecc   1: 7   All streams flow into the *s*,
Isa   57: 20   the wicked are like the tossing *s*,
Jnh   1: 4   Lord sent a great wind on the *s*,
Mic   7: 19   iniquities into the depths of the *s*.
Hab   2: 14   as the waters cover the *s*.
Zec   9: 10   His rule will extend from *s* to *s*
Mt   18: 6   drowned in the depths of the *s*.
1Co   10: 1   that they all passed through the *s*.
Jas   1: 6   who doubts is like a wave of the *s*,
Jude   : 13   They are wild waves of the *s*,
Rev   10: 2   He planted his right foot on the *s*
     13: 1   I saw a beast coming out of the *s*.
     20: 13   The *s* gave up the dead that were
     21: 1   and there was no longer any *s*.

SEAL (SEALED SEALS)

Ps   40: 9   I do not *s* my lips,
SS   8: 6   Place me like a *s* over your heart,
Da   12: 4   and *s* the words of the scroll
Jn   6: 27   God the Father has placed his *s*
1Co   9: 2   For you are the *s* of my apostleship
2Co   1: 22   set his *s* of ownership on us,

Eph   1: 13   you were marked in him with a *s*,
Rev   6: 3   the Lamb opened the second *s*,
     6: 5   When the Lamb opened the third *s*,
     6: 7   the Lamb opened the fourth *s*,
     6: 9   When he opened the fifth *s*,
     6: 12   I watched as he opened the sixth *s*.
     8: 1   When he opened the seventh *s*,
     9: 4   people who did not have the *s*
     22: 10   "Do not *s* up the words

SEALED (SEAL)

Eph   4: 30   with whom you were *s* for the day
2Ti   2: 19   solid foundation stands firm, *s*
Rev   5: 1   on both sides and *s* with seven seals

SEALS (SEAL)

Rev   5: 2   "Who is worthy to break the *s*
     6: 1   opened the first of the seven *s*.

SEAMLESS*

Jn   19: 23   This garment was *s*, woven

SEARCH (SEARCHED SEARCHES SEARCHING)

Ps   4: 4   *s* your hearts and be silent.
     139: 23   *S* me, O God, and know my heart;
Pr   2: 4   and *s* for it as for hidden treasure,
     25: 2   to *s* out a matter is the glory
SS   3: 2   I will *s* for the one my heart loves.
Jer   17: 10   "I the Lord *s* the heart
Eze   34: 11   I myself will *s* for my sheep
     34: 16   I will *s* for the lost and bring back
Lk   15: 8   and *s* carefully until she finds it?

SEARCHED (SEARCH)

Ps   139: 1   O Lord, you have *s* me
Ecc   12: 10   The Teacher *s* to find just the right
1Pe   1: 10   *s* intently and with the greatest

SEARCHES (SEARCH)

1Ch   28: 9   for the Lord *s* every heart
Ps   7: 9   who *s* minds and hearts,
Pr   11: 27   but evil comes to him who *s* for it.
     20: 27   The lamp of the Lord *s* the spirit
Ro   8: 27   And he who *s* our hearts knows
1Co   2: 10   The Spirit *s* all things,
Rev   2: 23   will know that I am he who *s* hearts

SEARCHING (SEARCH)

Jdg   5: 15   there was much *s* of heart.
Am   8: 12   *s* for the word of the Lord,

SEARED

1Ti   4: 2   whose consciences have been *s*

SEASHORE (SEA)

Jos   11: 4   as numerous as the sand on the *s*.
1Ki   4: 29   as measureless as the sand on the *s*.

SEASON (SEASONS)

Lev   26: 4   I will send you rain in its *s*,
Ps   1: 3   which yields its fruit in *s*
2Ti   4: 2   be prepared in *s* and out of *s*;

SEASONED*

Col   4: 6   full of grace, *s* with salt,

SEASONS (SEASONS)

Ge   1: 14   signs to mark *s* and days and years,
Gal   4: 10   and months and *s* and years!

SEAT (SEATED SEATS)

Ps   1: 1   or sit in the *s* of mockers.
Pr   31:23   where he takes his *s*
Da   7: 9   and the Ancient of Days took his *s*.
Lk   14: 9   say to you, 'Give this man your *s*.'
2Co   5:10   before the judgment *s* of Christ,

SEATED (SEAT)

Ps   47: 8   God is *s* on his holy throne.
Isa   6: 1   I saw the Lord *s* on a throne,
Lk   22:69   of Man will be *s* at the right hand
Eph   1:20   and *s* him at his right hand
      2: 6   and *s* us with him in the heavenly
Col   3: 1   where Christ is *s* at the right hand
Rev 14:14   *s* on the cloud was one "like a son
     20:11   white throne and him who was *s*

SEATS (SEAT)

Lk   11:43   you love the most important *s*

SECLUSION*

Lk   1:24   and for five months remained in *s*.

SECRET (SECRETLY SECRETS)

Dt   29:29   The *s* things belong
Jdg 16: 6   Tell me the *s* of your great strength
Ps   90: 8   our *s* sins in the light
    139:15   when I was made in the *s* place.
Pr   11:13   but a trustworthy man keeps a *s*.
     21:14   A gift given in *s* soothes anger,
Jer 23:24   Can anyone hide in *s* places
Mt   6: 4   so that your giving may be in *s*.
      6:18   who sees what is done in *s*,
Mk   4:11   "The *s* of the kingdom
1Co   2: 7   No, we speak of God's *s* wisdom,
      4: 1   entrusted with the *s* things of God.
2Co   4: 2   we have renounced *s* and shameful
Eph   5:12   what the disobedient do in *s*.
Php   4:12   I have learned the *s*

SECRETLY (SECRET)

2Pe   2: 1   They will *s* introduce destructive
Jude : 4   about long ago have *s* slipped

SECRETS (SECRET)

Ps   44:21   since he knows the *s* of the heart?
Ro   2:16   day when God will judge men's *s*
1Co 14:25   the *s* of his heart will be laid bare.
Rev   2:24   Satan's so-called deep *s* (I will not

SECURE (SECURITY)

Dt   33:12   beloved of the Lord rest *s* in him,
Ps   16: 5   you have made my lot *s*.
     16: 9   my body also will rest *s*,
    112: 8   His heart is *s*, he will have no fear;
Pr   14:26   fears the Lord has a *s* fortress,
Heb   6:19   an anchor for the soul, firm and *s*.
2Pe   3:17   and fall from your *s* position.

SECURITY (SECURE)

Job 31:24   or said to pure gold, 'You are my *s*,'

SEED (SEEDS SEEDTIME)

Ge   1:11   on the land that bear fruit with *s*
Isa 55:10   so that it yields *s* for the sower
Mt   13: 3   "A farmer went out to sow his *s*.
     13:31   of heaven is like a mustard *s*,
     17:20   have faith as small as a mustard *s*,
Lk   8:11   of the parable: The *s* is the word

1Co   3: 6   I planted the *s*, Apollos watered it,
2Co   9:10   he who supplies *s* to the sower
Gal   3:29   then you are Abraham's *s*,
1Pe   1:23   not of perishable *s*,
1Jn   3: 9   because God's *s* remains in him;

SEEDS (SEED)

Jn   12:24   But if it dies, it produces many *s*.
Gal   3:16   Scripture does not say "and to *s*,"

SEEDTIME* (SEED)

Ge   8:22   *s* and harvest,

SEEK (SEEKING SEEKS SELF-SEEKING SOUGHT)

Lev 19:18   Do not *s* revenge or bear a grudge
Dt   4:29   if from there you *s* the Lord your
1Ki 22: 5   "First *s* the counsel of the Lord."
1Ch 28: 9   If you *s* him, he will be found
2Ch   7:14   themselves and pray and *s* my face
     15: 2   If you *s* him, he will be found
Ps   34:10   those who *s* the Lord lack no
    105: 3   of those who *s* the Lord rejoice.
    105: 4   *s* his face always.
    119: 2   and *s* him with all their heart.
    119:10   I *s* you with all my heart;
    119:176   *S* your servant,
Pr   8:17   and those who *s* me find me.
     18:15   the ears of the wise *s* it out.
     25:27   is it honourable to *s* one's own honour
     28: 5   those who *s* the Lord understand
Isa 55: 6   *S* the Lord while he may be
     65: 1   found by those who did not *s* me.
Jer 29:13   You will *s* me and find me
Hos 10:12   for it is time to *s* the Lord,
Am   5: 4   "*S* me and live;
Zep   2: 3   *S* the Lord, all you humble
Mt   6:33   But *s* first his kingdom
      7: 7   and it will be given to you; *s*
Lk   12:31   *s* his kingdom, and these things will
     19:10   For the Son of Man came to *s*
Jn   5:30   for I *s* not to please myself
Ro   10:20   found by those who did not *s* me;
1Co   7:27   you married? Do not *s* a divorce.
     10:24   Nobody should *s* his own good,
Heb 11: 6   rewards those who earnestly *s* him.
1Pe   3:11   he must *s* peace and pursue it.

SEEKING (SEEK)

2Ch 30:19   who sets his heart on *s* God—
Pr   20:18   Make plans by *s* advice;
Mal   3: 1   the Lord you are *s* will come
Jn   8:50   I am not *s* glory for myself;
1Co 10:33   For I am not *s* my own good

SEEKS (SEEK)

Pr   11:27   He who *s* good finds good will,
Mt   7: 8   he who *s* finds; and to him who
Jn   4:23   the kind of worshippers the Father *s*.
Ro   3:11   no-one who *s* God.

SEER

1Sa   9: 9   of today used to be called a *s*.)

SELF-CONTROL* (CONTROL)

Pr   25:28   is a man who lacks *s*.
Ac   24:25   *s* and the judgment to come,
1Co   7: 5   you because of your lack of *s*.
Gal   5:23   faithfulness, gentleness and *s*.
2Ti   3: 3   slanderous, without *s*, brutal,

2Pe   1: 6 and to knowledge, *s*; and to *s*,

SELF-CONTROLLED* (CONTROL)

1Th   5: 6 are asleep, but let us be alert and *s*.
       5: 8 let us be *s*, putting on faith and love
1Ti   3: 2 *s*, respectable, hospitable,
Tit   1: 8 who is *s*, upright, holy
       2: 2 worthy of respect, *s*, and sound
       2: 5 to be *s* and pure, to be busy at home
       2: 6 encourage the young men to be *s*.
       2: 12 to live *s*, upright and godly lives
1Pe   1: 13 prepare your minds for action; be *s*;
       4: 7 and *s* so that you can pray.
       5: 8 Be *s* and alert.

SELF-DISCIPLINE* (DISCIPLINE)

2Ti   1: 7 a spirit of power, of love and of *s*.

SELF-INDULGENCE*

Mt   23: 25 inside they are full of greed and *s*.
Jas   5: 5 lived on earth in luxury and *s*.

SELF-SEEKING* (SEEK)

Ro   2: 8 But for those who are *s*
1Co   13: 5 it is not *s*, it is not easily angered,

SELFISH*

Ps   119: 36 and not towards *s* gain.
Pr   18: 1 An unfriendly man pursues *s* ends;
Gal   5: 20 fits of rage, *s* ambition, dissensions,
Php   1: 17 preach Christ out of *s* ambition,
       2: 3 Do nothing out of *s* ambition
Jas   3: 14 and *s* ambition in your hearts,
       3: 16 you have envy and *s* ambition,

SELL (SELLING SELLS SOLD)

Ge   25: 31 "First *s* me your birthright."
Mk   10: 21 *s* everything you have
Rev   13: 17 or *s* unless he had the mark,

SELLING (SELL)

Lk   17: 28 buying and *s*, planting and building

SELLS (SELL)

Pr   31: 24 makes linen garments and *s* them,

SEND (SENDING SENDS SENT)

Ps   43: 3 *S* forth your light and your truth,
Isa   6: 8 *S* me!" He said, "Go and tell this
Mal   3: 1 "See, I will *s* my messenger.
Mt   9: 38 to *s* out workers into his harvest
       24: 31 And he will *s* his angels
Mk   1: 2 I will *s* my messenger ahead of you,
Lk   20: 13 I will *s* my son, whom I love;
Jn   3: 17 For God did not *s* his Son
       16: 7 but if I go, I will *s* him to you.
1Co   1: 17 For Christ did not *s* me to baptise,

SENDING (SEND)

Mt   :: 16 "I am *s* you out like sheep
Jn   20: 21 Father has sent me, I am *s* you."
Ro   8: 3 God did by *s* his own Son

SENDS (SEND)

Ps   57: 3 God *s* his love and his faithfulness.

SENNACHERIB

Assyrian king whose siege of Jerusalem was overthrown by the LORD following prayer of Hezekiah and Isaiah (2Ki 18:13-19:37; 2Ch 32:1-21; Isa 36-37).

SENSES*

Lk   15: 17 "When he came to his *s*, he said,
1Co   15: 34 Come back to your *s* as you ought,
2Ti   2: 26 and that they will come to their *s*

SENSITIVITY*

Eph   4: 19 Having lost all *s*, they have given

SENSUAL* (SENSUALITY)

Col   2: 23 value in restraining *s* indulgence.
1Ti   5: 11 For when their *s* desires overcome

SENSUALITY* (SENSUAL)

Eph   4: 19 have given themselves over to *s*

SENT (SEND)

Ex   3: 14 to the Israelites: 'I AM has *s* me
Isa   55: 11 achieve the purpose for which I *s* it.
       61: 1 He has *s* me to bind up
Jer   28: 9 as one truly *s* by the LORD only
Mt   10: 40 me receives the one who *s* me.
Mk   6: 7 he *s* them out two by two
Lk   4: 18 He has *s* me to proclaim freedom
       9: 2 and he *s* them out to preach
       10: 16 rejects me rejects him who *s* me."
Jn   1: 6 There came a man who was *s*
       4: 34 "is to do the will of him who *s* me
       5: 24 believes him who *s* me has eternal
       8: 16 I stand with the Father who *s* me.
       9: 4 must do the work of him who *s* me.
       16: 5 "Now I am going to him who *s* me,
       17: 3 and Jesus Christ, whom you have *s*.
       17: 18 As you *s* me into the world,
       20: 21 As the Father has *s* me, I am
Ro   10: 15 can they preach unless they are *s*?
Gal   4: 4 God *s* his Son, born of a woman,
1Jn   4: 10 but that he loved us and *s* his Son

SENTENCE

2Co   1: 9 in our hearts we felt the *s* of death.

SEPARATE (SEPARATED SEPARATES SEPARATION)

Mt   19: 6 has joined together, let man not *s*."
Ro   8: 35 Who shall *s* us from the love
1Co   7: 10 wife must not *s* from her husband.
2Co   6: 17 and be *s*, says the Lord.
Eph   2: 12 at that time you were *s* from Christ,

SEPARATED (SEPARATE)

Isa   59: 2 But your iniquities have *s*
Eph   4: 18 in their understanding and *s*

SEPARATES (SEPARATE)

Pr   16: 28 and a gossip *s* close friends.
       17: 9 repeats the matter *s* close friends.
Mt   25: 32 as a shepherd *s* the sheep

SEPARATION (SEPARATE)

Nu   6: 2 a vow of *s* to the LORD

SERAPHS*

Isa   6: 2 Above him were *s*, each
       6: 6 Then one of the *s* flew to me

SERIOUSNESS*

Tit   2: 7 *s* and soundness of speech that

SERPENT (SERPENT'S)

Ge   3: 1 the *s* was more crafty than any

Isa 27: 1 Leviathan the coiling *s*;
Rev 12: 9 that ancient *s* called the devil
       20: 2 that ancient *s*, who is the devil,

SERPENT'S (SERPENT)

2Co 11: 3 Eve was deceived by the *s* cunning,

SERVANT (SERVANTS)

Ex 14: 31 trust in him and in Moses his *s*.
       21: 2 "If you buy a Hebrew *s*, he is
1Sa 3: 10 "Speak, for your *s* is listening."
2Sa 7: 19 the future of the house of your *s*.
1Ki 20: 40 While your *s* was busy here
Job 1: 8 "Have you considered my *s* Job?
Ps 19: 11 By them is your *s* warned;
       19: 13 Keep your *s* also from wilful sins;
       31: 16 Let your face shine on your *s*;
       89: 3 I have sworn to David my *s*,
Pr 14: 35 A king delights in a wise *s*,
       17: 2 wise *s* will rule over a disgraceful
       22: 7 and the borrower is *s* to the lender.
       31: 15 and portions for her *s* girls.
Isa 41: 8 "But you, O Israel, my *s*,
       49: 3 He said to me, "You are my *s*,
       53: 11 my righteous *s* will justify
Zec 3: 8 going to bring my *s*, the Branch.
Mal 1: 6 his father, and a *s* his master.
Mt 8: 13 his *s* was healed at that very hour.
       20: 26 great among you must be your *s*,
       24: 45 Who then is the faithful and wise *s*,
       25: 21 'Well done, good and faithful *s*!
Lk 1: 38 I am the Lord's *s*," Mary answered.
       16: 13 "No *s* can serve two masters.
Jn 12: 26 and where I am, my *s* also will be.
Ro 1: 1 a *s* of Christ Jesus, called
       13: 4 For he is God's *s* to do you good.
Php 2: 7 taking the very nature of a *s*,
Col 1: 23 of which I, Paul, have become a *s*.
2Ti 2: 24 And the Lord's *s* must not quarrel;

SERVANTS (SERVANT)

Lev 25: 55 for the Israelites belong to me as *s*.
2Ki 17: 13 to you through my *s* the prophets."
Ezr 5: 11 "We are the *s* of the God of heaven
Ps 34: 22 The Lord redeems his *s*;
       103: 21 you his *s* who do his will.
       104: 4 flames of fire his *s*.
Isa 44: 26 who carries out the words of his *s*
       65: 8 so will I do on behalf of my *s*;
       65: 13 my *s* will drink,
Lk 17: 10 should say, 'We are unworthy *s*;
Jn 15: 15 longer call you *s*, because a servant
Ro 13: 6 for the authorities are God's *s*,
1Co 3: 5 And what is Paul? Only *s*,
Heb 1: 7 his *s* flames of fire."

SERVE (SERVED SERVES SERVICE SERVING)

Dt 10: 12 to *s* the Lord your God
       11: 13 and to *s* him with all your heart
       13: 4 *s* him and hold fast to him.
       28: 47 you did not *s* the Lord your
Jos 22: 5 and to *s* him with all your heart
       24: 15 this day whom you will *s*,
       24: 18 We too will *s* the Lord,
1Sa 7: 3 to the Lord and *s* him only,
       12: 20 but *s* the Lord with all your heart
       12: 24 *s* him faithfully with all your heart,
2Ch 19: 9 "You must *s* faithfully
Job 36: 11 If they obey and *s* him,

Ps 2: 11 *S* the Lord with fear
Da 3: 17 the God we *s* is able to save us
Mt 4: 10 Lord your God, and *s* him only.'"
       6: 24 "No-one can *s* two masters.
       20: 28 but to *s*, and to give his life
Ro 12: 7 If it is serving, let him *s*;
Gal 5: 13 rather, *s* one another in love.
Eph 6: 7 *S* wholeheartedly,
1Ti 6: 2 they are to *s* them even better,
Heb 9: 14 so that we may *s* the living God!
1Pe 4: 10 gift he has received to *s* others,
       5: 2 greedy for money, but eager to *s*;
Rev 5: 10 kingdom and priests to *s* our God,

SERVED (SERVE)

Mt 20: 28 Son of Man did not come to be *s*,
Jn 12: 2 Martha *s*, while Lazarus was
Ac 17: 25 And he is not *s* by human hands,
Ro 1: 25 and *s* created things rather
1Ti 3: 13 Those who have *s* well gain

SERVES (SERVE)

Lk 22: 26 one who rules like the one who *s*.
       22: 27 But I am among you as one who *s*.
Jn 12: 26 Whoever *s* me must follow me;
Ro 14: 18 because anyone who *s* Christ
1Pe 4: 11 If anyone *s*, he should do it

SERVICE (SERVE)

Lk 9: 62 fit for *s* in the kingdom
       12: 35 "Be dressed ready for *s*
Ro 15: 17 in Christ Jesus in my *s* to God.
1Co 12: 5 There are different kinds of *s*,
       16: 15 themselves to the *s* of the saints.
2Co 9: 12 This *s* that you perform is not only
Eph 4: 12 God's people for works of *s*,
Rev 2: 19 and faith, your *s* and perseverance,

SERVING (SERVE)

Jos 24: 15 if *s* the Lord seems undesirable
2Ch 12: 8 learn the difference between *s* me
Ro 12: 7 If it is *s*, let him serve;
       12: 11 your spiritual fervour, *s* the Lord.
       16: 18 people are not *s* our Lord Christ,
Eph 6: 7 as if you were *s* the Lord, not men,
Col 3: 24 It is the Lord Christ you are *s*.
2Ti 2: 4 No-one *s* as a soldier gets involved

SETH

Ge 4: 25 birth to a son and named him *s*,

SETTLE

Mt 5: 25 "*S* matters quickly
2Th 3: 12 in the Lord Jesus Christ to *s* down

SEVEN (SEVENS SEVENTH)

Ge 7: 2 Take with you *s* of every kind
Jos 6: 4 march around the city *s* times,
1Ki 19: 18 Yet I reserve *s* thousand in Israel—
Pr 6: 16 *s* that are detestable to him:
       24: 16 a righteous man falls *s* times,
Isa 4: 1 In that day *s* women
Da 9: 25 comes, there will be *s* 'sevens',
Mt 18: 21 Up to *s* times?" Jesus answered,
Lk 11: 26 takes *s* other spirits more wicked
Ro 11: 4 for myself *s* thousand who have not
Rev 1: 4 To the *s* churches in the province
       6: 1 opened the first of the *s* seals.
       8: 2 and to them were given *s* trumpets.
       10: 4 And when the *s* thunders spoke,

Rev 15: 7 to the s angels s golden bowls filled

SEVENS* (SEVEN)

Da   9: 24 "Seventy 's' are decreed
        9: 25 will be seven 's', and sixty-two 's'.
        9: 26 the sixty-two 's', the Anointed

SEVENTH (SEVEN)

Ge   2: 2 By the s day God had finished
Ex   20: 10 but the s day is a Sabbath
       23: 11 but during the s year let the land lie
       23: 12 but on the s day do not work,
Heb   4: 4 "And on the s day God rested

SEVERE

2Co   8: 2 Out of the most s trial, their
1Th   1: 6 of the Lord; in spite of s suffering,

SEWED (SEWS)

Ge   3: 7 so they s fig leaves together

SEWS (SEWED)

Mt   9: 16 No-one s a patch of unshrunk cloth

SEXUAL (SEXUALLY)

Ex   22: 19 "Anyone who has s relations
Lev 18: 6 relative to have s relations.
       18: 7 father by having s relations
       18: 20 s relations with your neighbour's
Mt   15: 19 murder, adultery, s immorality,
Ac   15: 20 by idols, from s immorality,
1Co   5: 1 reported that there is s immorality
        6: 13 body is not meant for s immorality,
        6: 18 Flee from s immorality.
       10: 8 should not commit s immorality,
2Co 12: 21 s sin and debauchery
Gal   5: 19 s immorality, impurity
Eph   5: 3 even a hint of s immorality,
Col   3: 5 s immorality, impurity, lust,
1Th   4: 3 that you should avoid s immorality

SEXUALLY (SEXUAL)

1Co   5: 9 to associate with s immoral people
        6: 9 Neither the s immoral nor idolaters
        6: 18 he who sins s sins against his own
Heb 12: 16 See that no-one is s immoral,
       13: 4 the adulterer and all the s immoral.
Rev 21: 8 the murderers, the s immoral,

SHADE

Ps 121: 5 the Lord is your s
Isa 25: 4 and a s from the heat.

SHADOW

Ps   17: 8 hide me in the s of your wings
       23: 4 through the valley of the s of death,
       36: 7 find refuge in the s of your wings.
       91: 1 will rest in the s of the Almighty.
Isa 51: 16 covered you with the s of my hand
Col   2: 17 These are a s of the things that
Heb   8: 5 and s of what is in heaven.
       10: 1 The law is only a s

SHADRACH

   Hebrew exiled to Babylon; name changed from
Hananiah (Da 1:6-7). Refused defilement by food
(Da 1:8-20). Refused to worship idol (Da 3:1-18);
saved from furnace (Da 3:19-30).

SHAKE (SHAKEN SHAKING)

Ps   64: 8 all who see them will s their heads
       99: 1 let the earth s.
Hag   2: 6 I will once more s the heavens
Heb 12: 26 "Once more I will s not only

SHAKEN (SHAKE)

Ps   16: 8 I will not be s.
       30: 6 "I will never be s."
       62: 2 he is my fortress, I will never be s.
      112: 6 Surely he will never be s;
Isa 54: 10 Though the mountains be s
Mt   24: 29 and the heavenly bodies will be s.'
Lk   6: 38 s together and running over,
Ac   2: 25 I will not be s.
Heb 12: 27 that what cannot be s may remain.

SHAKING* (SHAKE)

Ps   22: 7 they hurl insults, s their heads:
Mt   27: 39 insults at him, s their heads
Mk   15: 29 s their heads and saying, "So!

SHALLUM

   King of Israel (2Ki 15:10-16).

SHAME (ASHAMED SHAMED SHAMEFUL)

Ps   25: 3 will ever be put to s,
       34: 5 their faces are never covered with s
       69: 6 not be put to s because of me,
Pr   13: 18 discipline comes to poverty and s,
       18: 13 that is his folly and his s.
Jer   8: 9 The wise will be put to s;
        8: 12 No, they have no s at all;
Ro   9: 33 trusts in him will never be put to s."
       10: 11 trusts in him will never be put to s."
1Co   1: 27 things of the world to s the wise;
Heb 12: 2 endured the cross, scorning its s,

SHAMED (SHAME)

Jer 10: 14 every goldsmith is s by his idols.
Joel 2: 26 never again will my people be s.

SHAMEFUL (SHAME)

2Co   4: 2 have renounced secret and s ways;
2Pe   2: 2 Many will follow their s ways
Rev 21: 27 nor will anyone who does what is s

SHAMGAR

   Judge; killed 600 Philistines (Jdg 3:31).

SHAPE (SHAPES SHAPING)

Job 38: 14 The earth takes s like clay

SHAPES (SHAPE)

Isa 44: 10 Who s a god and casts an idol,

SHAPING (SHAPE)

Jer 18: 4 the pot he was s from the clay was

**SHARE (SHARED SHARERS SHARES
SHARING)**

Ge   21: 10 that slave woman's son will never s
Lev 19: 17 frankly so you will not s in his guilt.
Dt   10: 9 That is why the Levites have no s
1Sa 30: 24 All will s alike."
Eze 18: 20 The son will not s the guilt
Mt   25: 21 and s your master's happiness!'
Lk   3: 11 "The man with two tunics should s
Ro   8: 17 if indeed we s in his sufferings

Ro	12: 13	*S* with God's people who are
2Co	1: 7	as you *s* in our sufferings,
Gal	4: 30	the slave woman's son will never *s*
	6: 6	in the word must *s* all good things
Eph	4: 28	something to *s* with those in need.
Col	1: 12	you to *s* in the inheritance
2Th	2: 14	that you might *s* in the glory
1Th	5: 22	and do not *s* in the sins of others.
	6: 18	and to be generous and willing to *s*.
2Ti	2: 6	the first to receive a *s* of the crops.
Heb	12: 10	that we may *s* in his holiness.
	13: 16	to do good and to *s* with others,
Rev	22: 19	from him his *s* in the tree of life

SHARED (SHARE)

Ps	41: 9	he who *s* my bread,
Ac	4: 32	but they *s* everything they had.
Heb	2: 14	he too *s* in their humanity so that

SHARERS* (SHARE)

Eph	3: 6	and *s* together in the promise

SHARES (SHARE)

Pr	22: 9	for he *s* his food with the poor.
Jn	13: 18	'He who *s* my bread has lifted up

SHARING (SHARE)

1Co	9: 10	so in the hope of *s* in the harvest.
2Co	9: 13	for your generosity in *s* with them
Php	3: 10	the fellowship of *s* in his sufferings,
Phm	: 6	you may be active in *s* your faith,

SHARON

SS	2: 1	I am a rose of *S*,

SHARP (SHARPENED SHARPENS SHARPER)

Pr	5: 4	*s* as a double-edged sword.
Isa	5: 28	Their arrows are *s*,
Rev	1: 16	came a *s* double-edged sword.
	19: 15	Out of his mouth comes a *s* sword

SHARPENED (SHARP)

Eze	21: 9	*s* and polished—

SHARPENS* (SHARP)

Pr	27: 17	As iron *s* iron,
	27: 17	so one man *s* another.

SHARPER* (SHARP)

Heb	4: 12	*S* than any double-edged sword,

SHATTER (SHATTERED SHATTERS)

Jer	51: 20	with you I *s* nations,

SHATTERED (SHATTER)

1Sa	2: 10	who oppose the Lord will be *s*.
Job	16: 12	All was well with me, but he *s* me;
	17: 11	days have passed, my plans are *s*,
Ecc	12: 6	before the pitcher is *s* at the spring,

SHATTERS (SHATTER)

Ps	46: 9	he breaks the bow and *s* the spear,

SHAVED

Jdg	16: 17	my head were *s*, my strength would
1Co	11: 5	it is just as though her head were *s*.

SHEAF (SHEAVES)

Lev	23: 11	is to wave the *s* before the Lord

SHEARER* (SHEARERS)

Ac	8: 32	and as a lamb before the *s* is silent,

SHEARERS (SHEARER)

Isa	53: 7	and as a sheep before her *s* is silent,

SHEAVES (SHEAF)

Ge	37: 7	while your *s* gathered around mine
Ps	126: 6	carrying *s* with him.

SHEBA

1. Benjamite who rebelled against David (2Sa 20).
2. See QUEEN.

SHECHEM

1. Raped Jacob's daughter Dinah; killed by Simeon and Levi (Ge 34).
2. City where Joshua renewed the covenant (Jos 24).

SHED (SHEDDING SHEDS)

Ge	9: 6	by man shall his blood be *s*;
Pr	6: 17	hands that *s* innocent blood,
Ro	3: 15	"Their feet are swift to *s* blood;
Col	1: 20	through his blood, *s* on the cross.

SHEDDING (SHED)

Heb	9: 22	without the *s* of blood there is no

SHEDS (SHED)

Ge	9: 6	"Whoever *s* the blood of man,

SHEEP (SHEEP'S SHEEPSKINS)

Nu	27: 17	Lord's people will not be like *s*
Dt	17: 1	a *s* that has any defect or flaw in it,
1Sa	15: 14	"What then is this bleating of *s*
Ps	44: 22	we are considered as *s*
	78: 52	led them like *s* through the desert.
	100: 3	we are his people, the *s*
	119: 176	I have strayed like a lost *s*.
SS	4: 2	teeth are like a flock of *s* just shorn,
Isa	53: 6	We all, like *s*, have gone astray,
	53: 7	as a *s* before her shearers is silent,
Jer	50: 6	"My people have been lost *s*;
Eze	34: 11	I myself will search for my *s*
Zec	13: 7	and the *s* will be scattered,
Mt	9: 36	helpless, like *s* without a shepherd.
	10: 16	"I am sending you out like *s*
	12: 11	"If any of you has a *s* and it falls
	18: 13	he is happier about that one *s*
	25: 32	as a shepherd separates the *s*
Jn	10: 1	man who does not enter the *s* pen
	10: 3	He calls his own *s* by name
	10: 7	the truth, I am the gate for the *s*.
	10: 15	and I lay down my life for the *s*.
	10: 27	My *s* listen to my voice; I know
	21: 17	Jesus said, "Feed my *s*.
1Pe	2: 25	or you were like *s* going astray,

SHEEP'S* (SHEEP)

Mt	7: 15	They come to you in *s* clothing,

SHEEPSKINS* (SHEEP)

Heb	11: 37	They went about in *s* and goatskins

SHEKEL

Ex	30: 13	This half *s* is an offering

SHELTER

Ps	27: 5	me in the *s* of his tabernacle
	31: 20	In the *s* of your presence you hide
	55: 8	I would hurry to my place of *s*,
	61: 4	take refuge in the *s* of your wings.
	91: 1	in the *s* of the Most High
Ecc	7: 12	Wisdom is a *s*
Isa	4: 6	It will be a *s* and shade
	25: 4	a *s* from the storm
	32: 2	Each man will be like a *s*
	58: 7	the poor wanderer with *s*—

SHEM

Son of Noah (Ge 5:32; 6:10). Blessed (Ge 9:26). Descendants (Ge 10:21-31; 11:10-32).

SHEPHERD (SHEPHERDS)

Ge	48: 15	the God who has been my *S*
	49: 24	because of the *S*, the Rock of Israel
Nu	27: 17	will not be like sheep without a *s*."
2Sa	7: 7	commanded to *s* my people Israel,
1Ki	22: 17	on the hills like sheep without a *s*,
Ps	23: 1	LORD is my *s*, I shall not be in want.
	28: 9	be their *s* and carry them for ever.
	80: 1	Hear us, O *S* of Israel,
Isa	40: 11	He tends his flock like a *s*:
Jer	31: 10	will watch over his flock like a *s*.'
Eze	34: 5	scattered because there was no *s*,
	34: 12	As a *s* looks after his scattered
Zec	11: 9	and said, "I will not be your *s*.
	11: 17	"Woe to the worthless *s*,
	13: 7	"Strike the *s*,
Mt	2: 6	who will be the *s* of my people
	9: 36	and helpless, like sheep without a *s*.
	26: 31	"'I will strike the *s*,
Jn	10: 11	The good *s* lays down his life
	10: 14	"I am the good *s*; I know my sheep
	10: 16	there shall be one flock and one *s*.
Heb	13: 20	that great *S* of the sheep, equip you
1Pe	5: 4	And when the Chief *S* appears,
Rev	7: 17	of the throne will be their *s*;

SHEPHERDS (SHEPHERD)

Jer	23: 1	"Woe to the *s* who are destroying
	50: 6	their *s* have led them astray
Eze	34: 2	prophesy against the *s* of Israel;
Lk	2: 8	there were *s* living out in the fields
Ac	20: 28	Be *s* of the church of God,
1Pe	5: 2	Be *s* of God's flock that is
Jude	: 12	*s* who feed only themselves.

SHIBBOLETH*

Jdg 12: 6 No," they said, "All right, say '*S*'."

SHIELD (SHIELDED SHIELDS)

Ge	15: 1	I am your *s*,
2Sa	22: 3	my *s* and the horn of my salvation.
	22: 36	You give me your *s* of victory;
Ps	3: 3	But you are a *s* around me,
	5: 12	with your favour as with a *s*.
	7: 10	My *s* is God Most High,
	18: 2	He is my *s* and the horn
	28: 7	LORD is my strength and my *s*;
	33: 20	he is our help and our *s*.
	84: 11	For the LORD God is a sun and *s*;
	91: 4	his faithfulness will be your *s*
	115: 9	he is their help and *s*.
	119: 114	You are my refuge and my *s*;
	144: 2	my *s*, in whom I take refuge,
Pr	2: 7	he is a *s* to those whose walk is

Pr	30: 5	he is a *s* to those who take refuge
Eph	6: 16	to all this, take up the *s* of faith,

SHIELDED (SHIELD)

1Pe 1: 5 through faith are *s* by God's power

SHIELDS (SHIELD)

Dt 33: 12 for he *s* him all day long,

SHIFTLESS*

Pr 19: 15 and the s man goes hungry.

SHIMEI

Cursed David (2Sa 16:5-14); spared (2Sa 19:16-23). Killed by Solomon (1Ki 2:8-9, 36-46).

SHINE (SHINES SHINING SHONE)

Nu	6: 25	the LORD make his face *s*
Job	33: 30	that the light of life may *s* on him.
Ps	4: 6	Let the light of your face *s* upon us,
	37: 6	make your righteousness *s* like
	67: 1	and make his face *s* upon us; *Selah*
	80: 1	between the cherubim, *s* forth
	118: 27	and he has made his light *s* upon us.
Isa	60: 1	"Arise, *s*, for your light has come,
Da	12: 3	are wise will *s* like the brightness
Mt	5: 16	let your light *s* before men,
	13: 43	the righteous will *s* like the sun
2Co	4: 6	made his light *s* in our hearts
Eph	5: 14	and Christ will *s* on you."
Php	2: 15	in which you *s* like stars

SHINES (SHINE)

Ps	50: 2	God *s* forth.
Pr	13: 9	The light of the righteous *s* brightly
Jn	1: 5	The light *s* in the darkness,

SHINING (SHINE)

Pr	4: 18	*s* ever brighter till the full light
2Pe	1: 19	as to a light *s* in a dark place,
Rev	1: 16	His face was like the sun *s*

SHIPS

Pr 31: 14 She is like the merchant *s*,

SHIPWRECKED*

2Co	11: 25	I was stoned, three times I was *s*,
1Ti	1: 19	and so have *s* their faith.

SHISHAK

1Ki	14: 25	*S* king of Egypt attacked Jerusalem
2Ch	12: 2	*S* king of Egypt attacked Jerusalem

SHOCKING*

Jer 5: 30 "A horrible and *s* thing

SHONE (SHINE)

Mt	17: 2	His face *s* like the sun,
Lk	2: 9	glory of the Lord *s* around them,
Rev	21: 11	It *s* with the glory of God,

SHOOT

Isa	53: 2	up before him like a tender *s*,
Ro	11: 17	and you, though a wild olive *s*,

SHORE

Lk 5: 3 asked him to put out a little from s.

SHORT (SHORTENED)

Nu 11: 23 "Is the LORD's arm too *s*?

Isa	50: 2	Was my arm too *s* to ransom you?
	59: 1	of the LORD is not too *s* to save,
Mt	24: 22	If those days had not been cut *s*,
Ro	3: 23	and fall *s* of the glory of God,
1Co	7: 29	brothers, is that the time is *s*.
Heb	4: 1	of you be found to have fallen *s* of it
Rev	20: 3	he must be set free for a *s* time.

SHORTENED (SHORT)

Mt	24: 22	of the elect those days will be *s*.

SHOULDER (SHOULDERS)

Zep	3: 9	and serve him *s* to *s*.

SHOULDERS (SHOULDER)

Dt	33: 12	LORD loves rests between his *s*."
Isa	9: 6	and the government will be on his *s*
Lk	15: 5	he joyfully puts it on his *s*

SHOUT (SHOUTED)

Ps	47: 1	*s* to God with cries of joy.
	66: 1	*S* with joy to God, all the earth!
	95: 1	let us *s* aloud to the Rock
	98: 4	*S* for joy to the LORD, all the earth
	100: 1	*S* for joy to the LORD, all the earth
Isa	12: 6	*S* aloud and sing for joy, people
	26: 19	wake up and *s* for joy.
	35: 6	the mute tongue *s* for joy.
	40: 9	lift up your voice with a *s*,
	42: 2	He will not *s* or cry out,
	44: 23	*s* aloud, O earth beneath.
	54: 1	burst into song, *s* for joy,
Zec	9: 9	*S*, Daughter of Jerusalem!

SHOUTED (SHOUT)

Job	38: 7	and all the angels *s* for joy?

SHOW (SHOWED)

Ex	18: 20	and *s* them the way to live
	33: 18	Moses said, "Now *s* me your glory
2Sa	22: 26	the faithful you *s* yourself faithful,
1Ki	2: 2	"So be strong, *s* yourself a man,
Ps	17: 7	*S* the wonder of your great love,
	25: 4	*S* me your ways, O LORD,
	39: 4	"*S* me, O LORD, my life's end
	85: 7	*S* us your unfailing love, O LORD,
	143: 8	*S* me the way I should go,
Pr	23: 4	have the wisdom to *s* restraint.
SS	2: 14	*s* me your face,
Isa	5: 16	the holy God will *s* himself holy
	30: 18	he rises to *s* you compassion.
Eze	28: 25	I will *s* myself holy among them
Joel	2: 30	I will *s* wonders in the heavens
Zec	7: 9	*s* mercy and compassion
Ac	2: 19	I will *s* wonders in the heaven
	10: 34	it is that God does not *s* favouritism
1Co	12: 31	now I will *s* you the most excellent
Eph	2: 7	ages he might *s* the incomparable
Tit	2: 7	In your teaching *s* integrity,
Jas	2: 18	I will *s* you my faith by what I do.
Jude	: 23	to others *s* mercy, mixed with fear

SHOWED (SHOW)

1Ki	3: 3	Solomon *s* his love for the LORD
Lk	24: 40	he *s* them his hands and feet.
1Jn	4: 9	This is how God *s* his love

SHOWERS

Eze	34: 26	in season; there will be *s* of blessing
Hos	10: 12	and *s* righteousness on you.

SHREWD

2Sa	22: 27	to the crooked you show yourself *s*.
Mt	10: 16	Therefore be as *s* as snakes and

SHRINK (SHRINKS)

Heb	10: 39	But we are not of those who *s* back

SHRINKS* (SHRINK)

Heb	10: 38	And if he *s* back,

SHRIVEL

Isa	64: 6	we all *s* up like a leaf,

SHUDDER

Eze	32: 10	and their kings will *s* with horror

SHUHITE

Job	2: 11	Bildad the *S* and Zophar

SHUN* (SHUNS)

Job	28: 28	and to *s* evil is understanding.'"
Pr	3: 7	fear the LORD and *s* evil.

SHUNS (SHUN)

Job	1: 8	a man who fears God and *s* evil."
Pr	14: 16	man fears the LORD and *s* evil,

SHUT

Ge	7: 16	Then the LORD *s* him in.
Isa	22: 22	what he opens no-one can *s*,
	60: 11	they will never be *s*, day or night,
Da	6: 22	and he *s* the mouths of the lions.
Heb	11: 33	who *s* the mouths of lions,
Rev	3: 7	no-one can *s*; and what he shuts,
	21: 25	On no day will its gates ever be *s*,

SICK (SICKNESS)

Pr	13: 12	Hope deferred makes the heart *s*,
Eze	34: 4	or healed the *s* or bound up
Mt	9: 12	who need a doctor, but the *s*.
	10: 8	Heal the *s*, raise the dead, cleanse
	25: 36	I was *s* and you looked after me,
1Co	11: 30	many among you are weak and *s*,
Jas	5: 14	of you *s*? He should call the elders

SICK-BED* (BED)

Ps	41: 3	LORD will sustain him on his *s*

SICKLE

Joel	3: 13	Swing the *s*,
Rev	14: 14	gold on his head and a sharp *s*

SICKNESS (SICK)

Mt	4: 23	and healing every disease and *s*

SIDE (SIDES)

Ps	91: 7	A thousand may fall at your *s*,
	124: 1	If the LORD had not been on our *s*
Jn	18: 37	Everyone on the *s* of truth listens
	20: 20	he showed them his hands and *s*.
2Ti	4: 17	But the Lord stood at my *s*
Heb	10: 33	at other times you stood *s* by *s*

SIDES (SIDE)

Nu	33: 55	in your eyes and thorns in your *s*.

SIFT

Lk	22: 31	Satan has asked to *s* you as wheat.

SIGHING

Isa 35: 10 and sorrow and s will flee away.

SIGHT

Ps 51: 4 and done what is evil in your s,
     90: 4 For a thousand years in your s
    116: 15 Precious in the s of the LORD
Pr   3: 4 in the s of God and man.
Mt 11: 5 The blind receive s, the lame walk,
Ac   4: 19 right in God's s to obey you rather
1Co 3: 19 this world is foolishness in God's s.
2Co 5: 7 We live by faith, not by s.
1Pe 3: 4 which is of great worth in God's s.

SIGN (SIGNS)

Ge   9: 12 "This is the s of the covenant I am
    17: 11 and it will be the s of the covenant
Isa 7: 14 the Lord himself will give you a s:
    55: 13 for an everlasting s,
Eze 20: 12 I gave them my Sabbaths as a s
Mt 12: 38 to see a miraculous s from you."
    24: 3 what will be the s of your coming
    24: 30 "At that time the s of the Son
Lk   2: 12 This will be a s to you: You will
    11: 29 It asks for a miraculous s,
Ro   4: 11 he received the s of circumcision,
1Co 11: 10 to have a s of authority on her head
    14: 22 are a s, not for believers

SIGNS (SIGN)

Ge   1: 14 let them serve as s to mark seasons
Ps 78: 43 day he displayed his miraculous s
   105: 27 They performed his miraculous s
Da   6: 27 he performs s and wonders
Mt 24: 24 and perform great s and miracles
Mk 16: 17 these s will accompany those who
Jn   3: 2 perform the miraculous s you are
    20: 30 Jesus did many other miraculous s
Ac   2: 19 and s on the earth below,
1Co 1: 22 Jews demand miraculous s
2Co 12: 12 s, wonders and miracles—
2Th 2: 9 s and wonders, and in every sort

SIHON

Nu 21: 21 to say to S king of the Amorites:
Ps 136: 19 S king of the Amorites

SILAS*

Prophet (Ac 15:22-32); co-worker with Paul on second missionary journey (Ac 16-18; 2Co 1:19). Co-writer with Paul (1Th 1:1; 2Th 1:1); Peter (1Pe 5:12).

SILENCE (SILENCED SILENT)

1Pe 2: 15 good you should s the ignorant talk
Rev 8: 1 there was s in heaven

SILENCED (SILENCE)

Ro   3: 19 so that every mouth may be s
Tit 1: 11 They must be s, because they are

SILENT (SILENCE)

Est 4: 14 For if you remain s at this time,
Ps 30: 2 to you and not be s.
    32: 3 When I kept s,
    39: 2 But when I was s and still,
Pr 17: 28 a fool is thought wise if he keeps s,
Ecc 3: 7 a time to be s and a time to speak,
Isa 53: 7 as a sheep before her shearers is s,
    62: 1 For Zion's sake I will not keep s,

Hab 2: 20 let all the earth be s before him."
Ac   8: 32 and as a lamb before the shearer is s
1Co 14: 34 women should remain s
1Ti 2: 12 over a man; she must be s.

SILVER

Ps 12: 6 like s refined in a furnace of clay,
    66: 10 you refined us like s.
Pr   2: 4 and if you look for it as for s
     3: 14 for she is more profitable than s
     8: 10 Choose my instruction instead of s,
    22: 1 to be esteemed is better than s
    25: 4 Remove the dross from the s,
    25: 11 is like apples of gold in settings of s.
Isa 48: 10 I have refined you, though not as s;
Eze 22: 18 They are but the dross of s.
Da   2: 32 its chest and arms of s, its belly
Hag 2: 8 'The s is mine and the gold is mine,'
Zec 13: 9 I will refine them like s
Ac   3: 6 Peter said, "S or gold I do not have,
1Co 3: 12 s, costly stones, wood, hay or straw
1Pe 1: 18 not with perishable things such as s

SILVERSMITH

Ac 19: 24 A s named Demetrius, who made

SIMEON

Son of Jacob by Leah (Ge 29:33; 35:23; 1Ch 2:1). With Levi killed Shechem for rape of Dinah (Ge 34:25-29). Held hostage by Joseph in Egypt (Ge 42:24-43:23). Tribe of blessed (Ge 49:5-7), numbered (Nu 1:23; 26:14), allotted land (Jos 19:1-9; Eze 48:24), 12,000 from (Rev 7:7).

SIMON

1. See PETER.
2. Apostle, called the Zealot (Mt 10:4; Mk 3:18; Lk 6:15; Ac 1:13).
3. Samaritan sorcerer (Ac 8:9-24).

SIMPLE

Ps 19: 7 making wise the s.
   119: 130 it gives understanding to the s.
Pr   8: 5 You who are s, gain prudence;
    14: 15 A s man believes anything,

SIMPLE-HEARTED* (HEART)

Ps 116: 6 The LORD protects the s;

SIN (SINFUL SINNED SINNER SINNERS SINNING SINS)

Ge   4: 7 s is crouching at your door;
Ex 32: 32 please forgive their s—but if not,
Nu   5: 7 and must confess the s he has
    32: 23 be sure that your s will find you
Dt 24: 16 each is to die for his own s.
1Sa 12: 23 it from me that I should s
    15: 23 For rebellion is like the s
1Ki 8: 46 for there is no-one who does not s
2Ch 7: 14 and will forgive their s and will heal
Job 1: 22 Job did not s by charging God
Ps   4: 4 In your anger do not s;
    17: 3 resolved that my mouth will not s.
    32: 2 whose s the LORD does not count
    32: 5 Then I acknowledged my s to you
    36: 2 too much to detect or hate his s.
    38: 18 I am troubled by my s.
    39: 1 and keep my tongue from s;
    51: 2 and cleanse me from my s.
    66: 18 If I had cherished s in my heart,

Ps 119: 11 that I might not s against you.
   119: 133 let no s rule over me.
Pr 5: 22 the cords of his s hold him fast.
   10: 19 words are many, s is not absent,
   14: 9 Fools mock at making amends for s
   16: 6 faithfulness s is atoned for;
   17: 19 He who loves a quarrel loves s;
   20: 9 I am clean and without s"?
Isa 3: 9 they parade their s like Sodom;
   6: 7 is taken away and your s atoned
   64: 5 But when we continued to s
Jer 31: 30 everyone will die for his own s;
Eze 18: 18 that wicked man will die for his s,
   18: 26 his righteousness and commits s,
   33: 8 that wicked man will die for his s,
Am 4: 4 "Go to Bethel and s;
Mic 6: 7 of my body for the s of my soul?
   7: 18 who pardons s and forgives
Zec 3: 4 "See, I have taken away your s,
Mt 18: 6 little ones who believe in me to s,
Mk 3: 29 he is guilty of an eternal s."
   9: 43 If your hand causes you to s,
Lk 17: 1 people to s are bound to come,
Jn 1: 29 who takes away the s of the world!
Jn 8: 7 "If any one of you is without s,
   8: 34 everyone who sins is a slave to s.
   8: 46 Can any of you prove me guilty of s
Ro 2: 12 All who s apart from the law will
   5: 12 as s entered the world
   5: 20 where s increased, grace increased
   6: 2 By no means! We died to s;
   6: 11 count yourselves dead to s
   6: 14 For s shall not be your master,
   6: 23 For the wages of s is death,
   7: 7 I would not have known what s was
   7: 25 sinful nature a slave to the law of s.
   14: 23 that does not come from faith is s.
1Co 8: 12 When you s against your brothers
   15: 56 The sting of death is s,
2Co 5: 21 God made him who had no s to be s
Gal 6: 1 if someone is caught in a s,
1Ti 5: 20 Those who s are to be rebuked
Heb 4: 15 just as we are—yet was without s.
   9: 26 to do away with s by the sacrifice
   11: 25 the pleasures of s for a short time.
   12: 1 and the s that so easily entangles,
Jas 1: 15 it gives birth to s; and s,
1Pe 2: 22 "He committed no s,
1Jn 1: 7 his Son, purifies us from all s.
   1: 8 If we claim to be without s,
   2: 1 But if anybody does s, we have one
   3: 4 in fact, s is lawlessness.
   3: 5 And in him is no s.
   3: 6 No-one who continues to s has
   3: 9 born of God will continue to s,
   5: 16 There is a s that leads to death.
   5: 17 All wrongdoing is s, and there is s
   5: 18 born of God does not continue to s;

SINAI

Ex 19: 20 descended to the top of Mount S
   31: 18 speaking to Moses on Mount S,
Ps 68: 17 from S into his sanctuary.

SINCERE* (SINCERITY)

Da 11: 34 many who are not s will join them.
Ac 2: 46 ate together with glad and s hearts,
Ro 12: 9 Love must be s.
2Co 6: 6 in the Holy Spirit and in s love;
   11: 3 somehow be led astray from your s

1Ti 1: 5 a good conscience and a s faith.
   3: 8 s, not indulging in much wine,
2Ti 1: 5 have been reminded of your s faith,
Heb 10: 22 near to God with a s heart
Jas 3: 17 and good fruit, impartial and s.
1Pe 1: 22 the truth so that you have s love

SINCERITY* (SINCERE)

1Co 5: 8 bread without yeast, the bread of s
2Co 1: 12 in the holiness and s that are
   2: 17 speak before God with s,
   8: 8 but I want to test the s of your love
Eph 6: 5 and with s of heart, just
Col 3: 22 but with s of heart and reverence

SINFUL (SIN)

Ps 51: 5 s at birth, s from the time
Lk 5: 8 from me, Lord; I am a s man!"
Ro 7: 5 we were controlled by the s nature,
   7: 18 lives in me, that is, in my s nature.
   7: 25 but in the s nature a slave to the law
   8: 3 Son in the likeness of s man
   8: 4 not live according to the s nature
   8: 7 the s mind is hostile to God.
   8: 8 by the s nature cannot please God.
   8: 9 are controlled not by the s nature
   8: 13 if you live according to the s nature
   13: 14 to gratify the desires of the s nature
1Co 5: 5 so that the s nature may be
Gal 5: 13 freedom to indulge the s nature;
   5: 16 gratify the desires of the s nature.
   5: 19 The acts of the s nature are obvious
   5: 24 Jesus have crucified the s nature
   6: 8 sows to please his s nature,
Col 2: 11 in the putting off of the s nature,
Heb 3: 12 brothers, that none of you has a s,
1Pe 2: 11 abstain from s desires, which war
1Jn 3: 8 He who does what is s is

SING (SANG SINGER SINGING SINGS SONG SONGS SUNG)

Ex 15: 1 "I will s to the LORD,
Ps 5: 11 let them ever s for joy.
   13: 6 I will s to the LORD,
   30: 4 s to the LORD, you saints of his;
   33: 1 S joyfully to the LORD, you
   47: 6 S praises to God, s praises;
   57: 7 I will s and make music.
   59: 16 But I will s of your strength,
   63: 7 I s in the shadow of your wings.
   66: 2 S the glory of his name;
   89: 1 I will s of the LORD's great love
   95: 1 Come, let us s for joy to the LORD
   96: 1 S to the LORD a new song,
   98: 1 S to the LORD a new song,
   101: 1 I will s of your love and justice;
   108: 1 I will s and make music
   137: 3 "S us one of the songs of Zion!"
   147: 1 is to s praises to our God,
   149: 1 S to the LORD a new song,
Isa 54: 1 "S, O barren woman,
1Co 14: 15 also pray with my mind; I will s
Eph 5: 19 S and make music in your heart
Col 3: 16 and as you s psalms, hymns
Jas 5: 13 Is anyone happy? Let him s songs

SINGER* (SING)

2Sa 23: 1 Israel's s of songs:

SINGING (SING)

Ps 63: 5 with s lips my mouth will praise

Ps	68: 6	he leads forth the prisoners with *s*;
	98: 5	with the harp and the sound of *s*,
Isa	35: 10	They will enter Zion with *s*;
Zep	3: 17	he will rejoice over you with *s*."
Ac	16: 25	Silas were praying and *s* hymns
Rev	5: 13	on the sea, and all that is in them, *s*:

SINGLE

Ex	23: 29	I will not drive them out in a *s* year,
Mt	6: 27	you by worrying can add a *s* hour
Gal	5: 14	law is summed up in a *s* command:

SINGS (SING)

Eze	33: 32	more than one who *s* love songs

SINNED (SIN)

Lev	5: 5	confess in what way he has *s*
1Sa	15: 24	Then Saul said to Samuel, "I have *s*
2Sa	12: 13	"I have *s* against the LORD."
	24: 10	I have *s* greatly in what I have done
2Ch	6: 37	'We have *s*, we have done wrong
Job	1: 5	"Perhaps my children have *s*
	33: 27	'I *s*, and perverted what was right,
Ps	51: 4	Against you, you only, have I *s*
Jer	2: 35	because you say, 'I have not *s*.'
	14: 20	we have indeed *s* against you.
Da	9: 5	we have *s* and done wrong.
Mic	7: 9	Because I have *s* against him,
Mt	27: 4	"I have *s*," he said,
Lk	15: 18	I have *s* against heaven
Ro	3: 23	for all have *s* and fall short
	5: 12	all *s*—for before the law was given,
2Pe	2: 4	did not spare angels when they *s*,
1Jn	1: 10	claim we have not *s*, we make him

SINNER (SIN)

Ps	51: 5	Surely I have been a *s* from birth,
Ecc	9: 18	but one *s* destroys much good.
Lk	15: 7	in heaven over one *s* who repents
	18: 13	'God, have mercy on me, a *s*.'
1Co	14: 24	convinced by all that he is a *s*
Jas	5: 20	Whoever turns a *s* from the error
1Pe	4: 18	become of the ungodly and the *s*?"

SINNERS (SIN)

Ps	1: 1	or stand in the way of *s*
	37: 38	But all *s* will be destroyed;
Pr	1: 10	My son, if *s* entice you,
	23: 17	Do not let your heart envy *s*,
Mt	9: 13	come to call the righteous, but *s*."
Ro	5: 8	While we were still *s*, Christ died
Gal	2: 17	evident that we ourselves are *s*,
1Ti	1: 15	came into the world to save *s*—
Heb	7: 26	set apart from *s*, exalted

SINNING (SIN)

Ex	20: 20	be with you to keep you from *s*."
1Co	15: 34	stop *s*; for there are some who are
Heb	10: 26	If we deliberately keep on *s*
1Jn	3: 6	No-one who lives in him keeps on *s*
	3: 9	go on *s*, because he has been born

SINS (SIN)

Lev	5: 1	"'If a person *s* because he does not
	16: 30	you will be clean from all your *s*.
	26: 40	"'But if they will confess their *s*
Nu	15: 30	"'But anyone who *s* defiantly,
1Sa	2: 25	If a man *s* against another man,
2Ki	14: 6	each is to die for his own *s*."
Ezr	9: 6	our *s* are higher than our heads

Ezr	9: 13	less than our *s* have deserved
Ps	19: 13	your servant also from wilful *s*;
	32: 1	whose *s* are covered.
	51: 9	Hide your face from my *s*
	79: 9	deliver us and forgive our *s*
	85: 2	and covered all their *s*.
	103: 3	He forgives all my *s*
	103: 10	does not treat us as our *s* deserve
	130: 3	O LORD, kept a record of *s*,
Pr	14: 21	He who despises his neighbour *s*,
	28: 13	who conceals his *s* does not
	29: 22	one commits many *s*.
Ecc	7: 20	who does what is right and never *s*.
Isa	1: 18	"Though your *s* are like scarlet,
	38: 17	you have put all my *s*
	43: 25	and remembers your *s* no more.
	59: 2	your *s* have hidden his face
	64: 6	like the wind our *s* sweep us away.
Jer	31: 34	and will remember their *s* no more
La	3: 39	complain when punished for his *s*?
Eze	18: 4	soul who *s* is the one who will die.
	33: 10	Our offences and *s* weigh us down,
	36: 33	day I cleanse you from all your *s*,
Hos	14: 1	Your *s* have been your downfall!
Mt	1: 21	he will save his people from their *s*
	6: 15	if you do not forgive men their *s*,
	9: 6	authority on earth to forgive *s* . . ."
	18: 15	"If your brother *s* against you,
	26: 28	for many for the forgiveness of *s*.
Lk	5: 24	authority on earth to forgive *s* . . ."
	11: 4	Forgive us our *s*,
	17: 3	"If your brother *s*, rebuke him,
Jn	8: 24	you will indeed die in your *s*."
	20: 23	If you forgive anyone his *s*,
Ac	2: 38	for the forgiveness of your *s*.
	3: 19	so that your *s* may be wiped out,
	10: 43	forgiveness of *s* through his name."
	22: 16	be baptised and wash your *s* away,
	26: 18	they may receive forgiveness of *s*
Ro	4: 7	whose *s* are covered.
	4: 25	delivered over to death for our *s*
1Co	15: 3	died for our *s* according
2Co	5: 19	not counting men's *s* against them.
Gal	1: 4	himself for our *s* to rescue us
Eph	2: 1	dead in your transgressions and *s*,
Col	2: 13	us all our *s*, having cancelled
1Ti	5: 22	and do not share in the *s* of others.
Heb	1: 3	he had provided purification for *s*,
	2: 17	atonement for the *s* of the people.
	7: 27	He sacrificed for their *s* once for all
	8: 12	and will remember their *s* no more
	9: 28	to take away the *s* of many people;
	10: 4	of bulls and goats to take away *s*.
	10: 12	for all time one sacrifice for *s*,
	10: 26	of the truth, no sacrifice for *s* is left,
Jas	4: 17	ought to do and doesn't do it, *s*.
	5: 16	Therefore confess your *s*
	5: 20	and cover over a multitude of *s*.
1Pe	2: 24	He himself bore our *s* in his body
	3: 18	For Christ died for *s* once for all,
	4: 8	love covers over a multitude of *s*.
1Jn	1: 9	If we confess our *s*, he is faithful
	2: 2	He is the atoning sacrifice for our *s*,
	3: 5	so that he might take away our *s*.
	4: 10	as an atoning sacrifice for our *s*.
Rev	1: 5	has freed us from our *s* by his blood

SISERA

Jdg	4: 2	The commander of his army was *S*,
	5: 26	She struck *S*, she crushed his head,

SISTER (SISTERS)

Lev 18: 9 have sexual relations with your *s*,
Mk   3: 35 does God's will is my brother and *s*

SISTERS (SISTER)

Mt 19: 29 or brothers or *s* or father or mother
1Ti 5: 2 as *s*, with absolute purity.

SIT (SAT SITS SITTING)

Dt   6: 7 them when you *s* at home
1Ki 8: 25 fail to have a man to *s* before me
Ps   1: 1 or *s* in the seat of mockers.
     26: 5 and refuse to *s* with the wicked.
     80: 1 you who *s* enthroned
    110: 1 "*S* at my right hand
    139: 2 You know when I *s* and when I rise
SS   2: 3 I delight to *s* in his shade,
Isa 16: 5 in faithfulness a man will *s* on it—
Mic   4: 4 Every man will *s* under his own
Mt   20: 23 to *s* at my right or left is not for me
     22: 44 "*S* at my right hand
Lk   22: 30 in my kingdom and *s* on thrones,
Heb   1: 13 "*S* at my right hand
Rev   3: 21 right to *s* with me on my throne,

SITS (SIT)

Ps   99: 1 *s* enthroned between the cherubim,
Isa 40: 22 He *s* enthroned above the circle
Mt   19: 28 of Man *s* on his glorious throne,
Rev   4: 9 thanks to him who *s* on the throne

SITTING (SIT)

Est   2: 19 Mordecai was *s* at the king's gate.
Mt   26: 64 the Son of Man *s* at the right hand
Rev   4: 2 in heaven with someone *s* on it.

SITUATION (SITUATIONS)

1Co 7: 24 remain in the *s* God called him
Php   4: 12 of being content in any and every *s*,

SITUATIONS* (SITUATION)

2Ti   4: 5 head in all *s*, endure hardship,

SKIES (SKY)

Ps   19: 1 the *s* proclaim the work
     71: 19 Your righteousness reaches to the *s*
    108: 4 your faithfulness reaches to the *s*.

SKILFUL (SKILL)

Ps   45: 1 my tongue is the pen of a *s* writer.
     78: 72 with *s* hands he led them.

SKILL (SKILFUL SKILLED)

Ps 137: 5 may my right hand forget ‿its *s*‿.
Ecc 10: 10 but *s* will bring success.

SKILLED (SKILL)

Pr   22: 29 Do you see a man *s* in his work?

SKIN (SKINS)

Job 19: 20 with only the *s* of my teeth.
     19: 26 And after my *s* has been destroyed,
Jer 13: 23 Can the Ethiopian change his *s*

SKINS (SKIN)

Ex   25: 5 ram *s* dyed red and hides
Lk   5: 37 the new wine will burst the *s*,

SKULL

Mt   27: 33 (which means The Place of the *S*).

SKY (SKIES)

Ge   1: 8 God called the expanse "*s*".
Pr   30: 19 the way of an eagle in the *s*,
Isa 34: 4 and the *s* rolled up like a scroll;
Jer 32: 22 stars of the *s* and as measureless
Mt   24: 29 the stars will fall from the *s*,
     24: 30 coming on the clouds of the *s*,
Rev 20: 11 Earth and *s* fled from his presence,

SLACK*

Pr   18: 9 One who is *s* in his work

SLAIN (SLAY)

1Sa 18: 7 "Saul has *s* his thousands,
Eze 37: 9 into these *s*, that they may live.' "
Rev   5: 6 as if it had been *s*, standing
      5: 12 "Worthy is the Lamb, who was *s*,
      6: 9 the souls of those who had been *s*

SLANDER (SLANDERED SLANDERER SLANDERERS SLANDEROUS)

Lev 19: 16 " 'Do not go about spreading *s*
Ps   15: 3 and has no *s* on his tongue,
Pr   10: 18 and whoever spreads *s* is a fool.
2Co 12: 20 outbursts of anger, factions, *s*,
Eph   4: 31 rage and anger, brawling and *s*,
1Ti   5: 14 the enemy no opportunity for *s*.
Tit   3: 2 to *s* no-one, to be peaceable
1Pe   3: 16 in Christ may be ashamed of their *s*
2Pe   2: 10 afraid to *s* celestial beings;

SLANDERED (SLANDER)

1Co 4: 13 when we are *s*, we answer kindly.

SLANDERER (SLANDER)

1Co 5: 11 an idolater or a *s*, a drunkard

SLANDERERS (SLANDER)

Ro   1: 30 They are gossips, *s*, God-haters,
1Co   6: 10 nor the greedy nor drunkards nor *s*
Tit   2: 3 not to be *s* or addicted

SLANDEROUS (SLANDER)

2Ti   3: 3 unforgiving, *s*, without self-control
2Pe   2: 11 do not bring *s* accusations

SLAUGHTER (SLAUGHTERED)

Isa 53: 7 he was led like a lamb to the *s*,
Jer 11: 19 been like a gentle lamb led to the *s*;
Ac   8: 32 "He was led like a sheep to the *s*,

SLAUGHTERED (SLAUGHTER)

Ps   44: 22 we are considered as sheep to be *s*.
Ro   8: 36 we are considered as sheep to be *s*

SLAVE (ENSLAVED SLAVERY SLAVES)

Ge   21: 10 "Get rid of that *s* woman
Mt   20: 27 wants to be first must be your *s*—
Jn   8: 34 everyone who sins is a *s* to sin.
Ro   7: 14 I am unspiritual, sold as a *s* to sin.
1Co   7: 21 Were you a *s* when you were called
     12: 13 whether Jews or Greeks, *s* or free
Gal   3: 28 *s* nor free, male nor female,
      4: 7 So you are no longer a *s*, but a son;
      4: 30 Get rid of the *s* woman and her son
Col   3: 11 barbarian, Scythian, *s* or free,
1Ti   1: 10 for *s* traders and liars and perjurers
Phm   : 16 no longer as a *s*, but better than a *s*,
2Pe   2: 19 a man is a *s* to whatever has

SLAVERY (SLAVE)

Ex	2: 23	The Israelites groaned in their s
Ro	6: 19	parts of your body in s to impurity
Gal	4: 3	were in s under the basic principles
1Ti	6: 1	of s should consider their masters

SLAVES (SLAVE)

Ps	123: 2	As the eyes of s look to the hand
Ecc	10: 7	I have seen s on horseback,
Ro	6: 6	that we should not longer be s to sin
	6: 16	you are s to sin, which leads
	6: 22	and have become s to God,
Gal	2: 4	in Christ Jesus and to make us s.
	4: 8	you were s to those who
Eph	6: 5	S, obey your earthly masters
Col	3: 22	S, obey your earthly masters
	4: 1	provide your s with what is right
Tit	2: 9	Teach s to be subject

SLAY (SLAIN)

Job	13: 15	Though he s me, yet will I hope

SLEEP (ASLEEP SLEEPER SLEEPING SLEEPS)

Ge	2: 21	the man to fall into a deep s;
	15: 12	Abram fell into a deep s,
	28: 11	it under his head and lay down to s.
Ps	4: 8	I will lie down and s in peace,
	121: 4	will neither slumber nor s.
	127: 2	for he grants s to those he loves.
Pr	6: 9	When will you get up from your s?
Ecc	5: 12	The s of a labourer is sweet,
1Co	15: 51	We will not all s, but we will all be
1Th	5: 7	For those who s, s at night,

SLEEPER (SLEEP)

Eph	5: 14	"Wake up, O s,

SLEEPING (SLEEP)

Mk	13: 36	suddenly, do not let him find you s.

SLEEPLESS*

2Co	6: 5	in hard work, s nights and hunger;

SLEEPS (SLEEP)

Pr	10: 5	he who s during harvest is

SLIMY

Ps	40: 2	He lifted me out of the s pit,

SLING

1Sa	17: 50	over the Philistine with a s

SLIP (SLIPPING)

Dt	4: 9	let them s from your heart as long
Ps	121: 3	He will not let your foot s—

SLIPPING (SLIP)

Ps	66: 9	and kept our feet from s.

SLOW

Ex	34: 6	and gracious God, s to anger,
Jas	1: 19	s to speak and s to become angry,
2Pe	3: 9	The Lord is not s in keeping his

SLUGGARD

Pr	6: 6	Go to the ant, you s;
	13: 4	The s craves and gets nothing,
	20: 4	A s does not plough in season;
	26: 15	The s buries his hand in the dish;

SLUMBER

Ps	121: 3	he who watches over you will not s;
Pr	6: 10	A little sleep, a little s,
Ro	13: 11	for you to wake up from your s,

SLUR

Ps	15: 3	and casts no s on his fellow-man,

SMELL

Ecc	10: 1	As dead flies give perfume a bad s,
2Co	2: 16	To the one we are the s of death;

SMITTEN

Isa	53: 4	s by him, and afflicted.

SMOKE

Ex	19: 18	Mount Sinai was covered with s,
Ps	104: 32	touches the mountains, and they s.
Isa	6: 4	and the temple was filled with s.
Joel	2: 30	blood and fire and billows of s.
Ac	2: 19	blood and fire and billows of s.
Rev	15: 8	filled with s from the glory

SMYRNA

Rev	2: 8	the angel of the church in S write:

SNAKE (SNAKES)

Nu	21: 8	"Make a s and put it up on a pole;
Pr	23: 32	In the end it bites like a s
Jn	3: 14	as Moses lifted up the s in the desert,

SNAKES (SNAKE)

Mt	10: 16	as shrewd as s and as innocent
Mk	16: 18	they will pick up s with their hands;

SNARE (ENSNARE ENSNARED SNARED)

Dt	7: 16	for that will be a s to you.
Ps	69: 22	before them become a s;
	91: 3	from the fowler's s
Pr	29: 25	Fear of man will prove to be a s,
Ro	11: 9	"May their table become a s

SNARED (SNARE)

Pr	3: 26	will keep your foot from being s.

SNATCH

Jn	10: 28	no-one can s them out of my hand.
Jude	: 23	s others from the fire and save

SNOUT

Pr	11: 22	Like a gold ring in a pig's s

SNOW

Ps	51: 7	and I will be whiter than s.
Isa	1: 18	they shall be as white as s;

SNUFF (SNUFFED)

Isa	42: 3	a smouldering wick he will not s out.
Mt	12: 20	a smouldering wick he will not s out,

SNUFFED (SNUFF)

Pr	13: 9	but the lamp of the wicked is s out.

SOAP

Mal	3: 2	a refiner's fire or a launderer's s.

SOAR (SOARED)

Isa	40: 31	They will s on wings like eagles;

SOARED (SOAR)

2Sa 22: 11 he *s* on the wings of the wind.

SOBER

Ro 12: 3 think of yourself with *s* judgment,

SODOM

Ge 13: 12 and pitched his tents near *S*.
19: 24 rained down burning sulphur on *S*
Isa 1: 9 we would have become like *S*,
Lk 10: 12 on that day for *S* than for that town
Ro 9: 29 we would have become like *S*,
Rev 11: 8 which is figuratively called *S*

SOIL

Ge 4: 2 kept flocks, and Cain worked the *s*.
Mt 13: 23 on good *s* is the man who hears

SOLD (SELL)

1Ki 21: 25 who *s* himself to do evil in the eyes
Mt 10: 29 Are not two sparrows *s* for a penny
13: 44 then in his joy went and *s* all he had
Ro 7: 14 I am unspiritual, *s* as a slave to sin.

SOLDIER

1Co 9: 7 as a *s* at his own expense?
2Ti 2: 3 with us like a good *s* of Christ Jesus

SOLE

Dt 28: 65 place for the *s* of your foot.
Isa 1: 6 From the *s* of your foot to the top

SOLID

2Ti 2: 19 God's *s* foundation stands firm,
Heb 5: 12 You need milk, not *s* food!

SOLOMON

Son of David by Bathsheba; king of Judah (2Sa 12:24; 1Ch 3:5, 10). Appointed king by David (1Ki 1); adversaries Adonijah, Joab, Shimei killed by Benaiah (1Ki 2). Asked for wisdom (1Ki 3; 2Ch 1). Judged between two prostitutes (1Ki 3:16-28). Built temple (1Ki 5-7; 2Ch 2-5); prayer of dedication (1Ki 8; 2Ch 6). Visited by Queen of Sheba (1Ki 9; 2Ch 9). Wives turned his heart from God (1Ki 11:1-13). Jeroboam rebelled against (1Ki 11:26-40). Death (1Ki 11:41-43; 2Ch 9:29-31). Proverbs of (1Ki 4:32; Pr 1:1; 10:1; 25:1); psalms of (Ps 72; 127); song of (SS 1:1).

SON (SONS SONSHIP)

Ge 17: 19 your wife Sarah will bear you a *s*,
21: 10 rid of that slave woman and her *s*,
22: 2 "Take your *s*, your only *s* Isaac,
Ex 11: 5 Every firstborn *s* in Egypt will die,
Dt 1: 31 father carries his *s*, all the way you
6: 20 In the future, when your *s* asks you,
8: 5 as a man disciplines his *s*,
21: 18 rebellious *s* who does not obey his
2Sa 7: 14 be his father, and he will be my *s*.
1Ki 3: 20 and put her dead *s* by my breast.
Ps 2: 7 He said to me, "You are my *S*;
2: 12 Kiss the *S*, lest he be angry
8: 4 the *s* of man that you care for him?
Pr 3: 12 as a father the *s* he delights in.
6: 20 My *s*, keep your father's
10: 1 A wise *s* brings joy to his father,
13: 24 He who spares the rod hates his *s*,
29: 17 Discipline your *s*, and he will give

Isa 7: 14 with child and will give birth to a *s*,
Eze 18: 20 The *s* will not share the guilt
Da 3: 25 the fourth looks like a *s* of the gods
7: 13 before me was one like a *s* of man,
Hos 11: 1 and out of Egypt I called my *s*.
Am 7: 14 neither a prophet nor a prophet's *s*,
Mt 1: 1 of Jesus Christ the *s* of David,
1: 21 She will give birth to a *s*,
2: 15 "Out of Egypt I called my *s*."
3: 17 "This is my *S*, whom I love;
4: 3 "If you are the *S* of God, tell these
8: 20 but the *S* of Man has nowhere
11: 27 No-one knows the *S* except the Father,
12: 8 For the *S* of Man is Lord
12: 32 a word against the *S* of Man will be
12: 40 so the *S* of Man will be three days
13: 41 *S* of Man will send out his angels,
13: 55 "Isn't this the carpenter's *s*?
14: 33 "Truly you are the *S* of God."
16: 16 "You are the Christ, the *S*
16: 27 For the *S* of Man is going to come
17: 5 "This is my *S*, whom I love;
19: 28 when the *S* of Man sits
20: 18 and the *S* of Man will be betrayed
20: 28 as the *S* of Man did not come
21: 9 "Hosanna to the *S* of David!"
22: 42 Whose *s* is he?" "The *s* of David,"
24: 27 so will be the coming of the *S*
24: 30 They will see the *S* of Man coming
24: 44 the *S* of Man will come at an hour
25: 31 "When the *S* of Man comes
26: 63 if you are the Christ, the *S* of God."
27: 54 "Surely he was the *S* of God!"
28: 19 and of the *S* and of the Holy Spirit,
Mk 1: 11 "You are my *S*, whom I love;
2: 28 So the *S* of Man is Lord
8: 38 the *S* of Man will be ashamed
9: 7 "This is my *S*, whom I love.
10: 45 even the *S* of Man did not come
13: 32 not the *S*, but only the Father.
14: 62 you will see the *S* of Man sitting
Lk 1: 32 and will be called the *S*
2: 7 she gave birth to her firstborn, a *s*.
3: 22 "You are my *S*, whom I love;
9: 35 This is my *S*, whom I have chosen;
9: 58 but the *S* of Man has nowhere
12: 8 the *S* of Man will also acknowledge
15: 20 he ran to his *s*, threw his arms
18: 8 when the *S* of Man comes,
18: 31 written by the prophets about the *S*
19: 10 For the *S* of Man came to seek
Jn 1: 14 the glory of the one and only ⌐*S*⌐,
1: 34 I testify that this is the *S* of God."
3: 14 so the *S* of Man must be lifted up,
3: 16 that he gave his one and only *S*,
3: 36 believes in the *S* has eternal life,
5: 19 the *S* can do nothing by himself;
6: 40 is that everyone who looks to the *S*
11: 4 so that God's *S* may be glorified
17: 1 Glorify your *S*, that your *S* may
Ac 7: 56 and the *S* of Man standing
13: 33 "'You are my *S*;
Ro 1: 4 with power to be the *S* of God
5: 10 to him through the death of his *S*,
8: 3 did by sending his own *S*
8: 29 conformed to the likeness of his *S*,
8: 32 He who did not spare his own *S*,
1Co 15: 28 then the *S* himself will be made
Gal 2: 20 I live by faith in the *S* of God,
4: 4 God sent his *S*, born of a woman,

Gal   4: 30 rid of the slave woman and her *s*,
1Th   1: 10 and to wait for his *S* from heaven,
Heb   1: 2 days he has spoken to us by his *S*,
       1: 5 "You are my *S*;
       2: 6 the *s* of man that you care for him?
       4: 14 Jesus the *S* of God, let us hold
       5: 5 "You are my *S*;
       7: 28 appointed the *S*, who has been
      10: 29 punished who has trampled the *S*
      12: 6 everyone he accepts as a *s*."
2Pe   1: 17 saying, "This is my *S*, whom I love;
1Jn   1: 3 is with the Father and with his *S*,
       1: 7 his *S*, purifies us from all sin.
       2: 23 whoever acknowledges the *S* has
       3: 8 reason the *S* of God appeared was
       4: 9 only *S* into the world that we might
       4: 14 that the Father has sent his *S*
       5: 5 he who believes that Jesus is the *S*
       5: 11 eternal life, and this life is in his *S*.
Rev   1: 13 lampstands was someone "like a *s*
      14: 14 on the cloud was one "like a *s*

SONG (SING)

Ex   15: 2 Lord is my strength and my *s*;
Ps   40: 3 He put a new *s* in my mouth,
      69: 30 I will praise God's name in *s*
      96: 1 Sing to the Lord a new *s*;
      98: 4 burst into jubilant *s* with music;
     119: 54 Your decrees are the theme of my *s*
     149: 1 Sing to the Lord a new *s*,
Isa   49: 13 burst into *s*, O mountains!
      55: 12 will burst into *s* before you,
Rev   5: 9 And they sang a new *s*:
      15: 3 and sang the *s* of Moses the servant

SONGS (SING)

2Sa   23: 1 Israel's singer of *s*:
Job   35: 10 who gives *s* in the night,
Ps   100: 2 come before him with joyful *s*.
     126: 6 will return with *s* of joy,
     137: 3 "Sing us one of the *s* of Zion!"
Eph   5: 19 with psalms, hymns and spiritual *s*.
Jas   5: 13 Is anyone happy? Let him sing *s*

SONS (SON)

Ge   6: 2 the *s* of God saw that the daughters
      10: 20 the *s* of Ham by their clans
Ru   4: 15 who is better to you than seven *s*,
Ps   127: 3 *S* are a heritage from the Lord,
     132: 12 if your *s* keep my covenant
Hos   1: 10 they will be called '*s*
Joel   2: 28 Your *s* and daughters will prophesy
Mt   5: 9 for they will be called *s* of God.
Lk   6: 35 and you will be *s* of the Most High,
Jn   12: 36 so that you may become *s* of light."
Ro   8: 14 by the Spirit of God are *s* of God.
       9: 26 they will be called '*s*
2Co   6: 18 and you will be my *s* and daughters
Gal   3: 26 You are all *s* of God through faith
       4: 5 we might receive the full rights of *s*.
       4: 6 Because you are *s*, God sent
Heb   12: 7 discipline; God is treating you as *s*.

SONSHIP* (SON)

Ro   8: 15 but you received the Spirit of *s*.

SORCERY

Lev   19: 26 " 'Do not practise divination or *s*.

SORROW (SORROWS)

Ps   6: 7 My eyes grow weak with *s*;
     116: 3 I was overcome by trouble and *s*.
Isa   60: 20 and your days of *s* will end.
Jer   31: 12 and they will *s* no more.
Ro   9: 2 I have great *s* and unceasing
2Co   7: 10 Godly *s* brings repentance that

SORROWS (SORROW)

Isa   53: 3 a man of *s*, and familiar

SOUGHT (SEEK)

2Ch   26: 5 As long as he *s* the Lord,
      31: 21 he *s* his God and worked
Ps   34: 4 I *s* the Lord, and he answered me
     119: 58 I have *s* your face with all my heart;

SOUL (SOULS)

Dt   6: 5 with all your *s* and with all your
      10: 12 all your heart and with all your *s*,
      30: 6 all your heart and with all your *s*,
Jos   22: 5 with all your heart and all your *s*."
2Ki   23: 25 and with all his *s* and with all his
Ps   23: 3 he restores my *s*.
      63: 8 my *s* clings to you
      34: 2 My *s* will boast in the Lord;
      42: 1 so my *s* pants for you, O God.
      42: 11 Why are you downcast, O my *s*?
      62: 5 Find rest, O my *s*, in God alone;
      94: 19 consolation brought joy to my *s*.
     103: 1 Praise the Lord, O my *s*;
Pr   13: 19 A longing fulfilled is sweet to the *s*,
      16: 24 sweet to the *s* and healing
      22: 5 he who guards his *s* stays far
Isa   55: 2 your *s* will delight in the richest
La   3: 20 and my *s* is downcast within me.
Eze   18: 4 For every living *s* belongs to me,
Mt   10: 28 kill the body but cannot kill the *s*.
      16: 26 yet forfeits his *s*? Or what can
      22: 37 with all your *s* and with all your
Heb   4: 12 even to dividing *s* and spirit,
3Jn   : 2 even as your *s* is getting along well.

SOULS (SOUL)

Pr   11: 30 and he who wins *s* is wise.
Jer   6: 16 and you will find rest for your *s*.
Mt   11: 29 and you will find rest for your *s*.

SOUND [1] (FINE-SOUNDING)

Ge   3: 8 and his wife heard the *s*
Eze   3: 12 I heard behind me a loud rumbling *s*
Jn   3: 8 You hear its *s*, but you cannot tell
Ac   2: 2 Suddenly a *s* like the blowing
1Co   14: 8 if the trumpet does not *s* a clear call
      15: 52 the trumpet will *s*, the dead will

SOUND [2]

Pr   3: 21 Preserve *s* Judgment
1Ti   1: 10 to the *s* doctrine that conforms
2Ti   4: 3 men will not put up with *s* doctrine
Tit   1: 9 can encourage others by *s* doctrine
       2: 1 is in accord with *s* doctrine.

SOUR

Eze   18: 2 " 'The fathers eat *s* grapes,

SOURCE

Heb   5: 9 became the *s* of eternal salvation

SOVEREIGN (SOVEREIGNTY)

Ge   15: 2 But Abram said, "O *S* LORD,
2Sa   7: 18 O *S* LORD, and what is my family,
Ps   71: 16 your mighty acts, O *S* LORD;
Isa   25: 8 *S* LORD will wipe away the tears
       40: 10 the *S* LORD comes with power,
       50: 4 *S* LORD has given me
       61: 1 The Spirit of the *S* LORD is on me,
       61: 11 so the *S* LORD will make
Jer   32: 17 to the LORD: "Ah, *S* LORD,
Eze   12: 28 fulfilled, declares the *S* LORD.' "
Da   4: 25 that the Most High is *s*
2Pe   2: 1 denying the *s* Lord who bought
Jude   : 4 and deny Jesus Christ our only *S*

SOVEREIGNTY (SOVEREIGN)

Da   7: 27 Then the *s*, power and greatness

SOW [1] (SOWER SOWN SOWS)

Job   4: 8 and those who *s* trouble reap it.
Ps   126: 5 Those who *s* in tears
Hos   8: 7 "They *s* the wind
       10: 12 *S* for yourselves righteousness,
Mt   6: 26 they do not *s* or reap or store away
       13: 3 "A farmer went out to *s* his seed.
1Co   15: 36 What you *s* does not come to life
Jas   3: 18 Peacemakers who *s*

SOW [2]

2Pe   2: 22 and, "A *s* that is washed goes back

SOWER (SOW [1])

Isa   55: 10 so that it yields seed for the *s*
Mt   13: 18 to what the parable of the *s* means:
Jn   4: 36 so that the *s* and the reaper may be
2Co   9: 10 Now he who supplies seed to the *s*

SOWN (SOW [1])

Mt   13: 8 sixty or thirty times what was *s*.
Mk   4: 15 along the path, where the word is *s*.
1Co   15: 42 The body that is *s* is perishable,

SOWS (SOW [1])

Pr   11: 18 he who *s* righteousness reaps a sure
       22: 8 He who *s* wickedness reaps trouble
2Co   9: 6 Whoever *s* sparingly will
Gal   6: 7 A man reaps what he *s*.

SPARE (SPARES SPARING)

Est   7: 3 *s* my people—this is my request.
Ro   8: 32 He who did not *s* his own Son,
       11: 21 natural branches, he will not *s* you
2Pe   2: 4 For if God did not *s* angels
       2: 5 if he did not *s* the ancient world

SPARES (SPARE)

Pr   13: 24 He who *s* the rod hates his son,

SPARING (SPARE)

Pr   21: 26 but the righteous give without *s*.

SPARKLE

Zec   9: 16 They will *s* in his land

SPARROW (SPARROWS)

Ps   84: 3 Even the *s* has found a home,

SPARROWS (SPARROW)

Mt   10: 29 Are not two *s* sold for a penny?

SPAT

Mt   27: 30 They *s* on him, and took the staff

SPEAR (SPEARS)

1Sa   19: 10 as Saul drove the *s* into the wall.
Ps   46: 9 breaks the bow and shatters the *s*,

SPEARS (SPEAR)

Isa   2: 4 and their *s* into pruning hooks.
Joel   3: 10 and your pruning hooks into *s*.
Mic   4: 3 and their *s* into pruning hooks.

SPECIAL

Jas   2: 3 If you show *s* attention

SPECK

Mt   7: 3 Look at the *s* of sawdust

SPECTACLE

1Co   4: 9 We have been made a *s*
Col   2: 15 he made a public *s* of them,

SPEECH

Ps   19: 3 There is no *s* or language
Pr   22: 11 pure heart and whose *s* is gracious
2Co   8: 7 in faith, in *s*, in knowledge,
1Ti   4: 12 set an example for the believers in *s*

SPEND (SPENT)

Pr   31: 3 do not *s* your strength on women,
Isa   55: 2 Why *s* money on what is not bread,
2Co   12: 15 So I will very gladly *s*

SPENT (SPEND)

Mk   5: 26 many doctors and had *s* all she had,
Lk   6: 12 and *s* the night praying to God.
       15: 14 After he had *s* everything,

SPIN

Mt   6: 28 They do not labour or *s*.

SPIRIT (SPIRIT'S SPIRITS SPIRITUAL SPIRITUALLY)

Ge   1: 2 and the S of God was hovering
       6: 3 "My *S* will not contend
Ex   31: 3 I have filled him with the *S* of God,
Nu   11: 25 and put the *S* on the seventy elders.
Dt   34: 9 filled with the *s* of wisdom
Jdg   6: 34 Then the *S* of the LORD came
       11: 29 Then the *S* of the LORD came
       13: 25 and the *S* of the LORD began
1Sa   10: 10 the *S* of God came upon him
       16: 13 day on the *S* of the LORD came
       16: 14 the *S* of the LORD had departed
2Sa   23: 2 "The *S* of the LORD spoke
2Ki   2: 9 inherit a double portion of your *s*,"
Ne   9: 20 You gave your good *S*
       9: 30 By your *S* you admonished them
Job   33: 4 The *S* of God has made me;
Ps   31: 5 Into your hands I commit my *s*;
      34: 18 saves those who are crushed in *s*.
      51: 10 and renew a steadfast *s* within me.
      51: 11 or take your Holy *S* from me.
      51: 17 sacrifices of God are a broken *s*;
      106: 33 rebelled against the *S* of God,
      139: 7 Where can I go from your *S*?
      143: 10 may your good *S*
Isa   11: 2 The *S* of the LORD will rest
      30: 1 an alliance, but not by my *S*,
      32: 15 till the *S* is poured upon us

Isa 44: 3 I will pour out my *S*
57: 15 him who is contrite and lowly in *s*,
61: 1 The *S* of the Sovereign LORD is
63: 10 and grieved his Holy *S*.
Eze 11: 19 an undivided heart and put a new *s*
13: 3 prophets who follow their own *s*
36: 26 you a new heart and put a new *s*
Da 4: 8 and the *s* of the holy gods is in him
Joel 2: 28 I will pour out my *S* on all people.
Zec 4: 6 but by my *S*,' says the LORD
Mt 1: 18 to be with child through the Holy *S*
3: 11 will baptise you with the Holy *S*
3: 16 he saw the *S* of God descending
4: 1 led by the *S* into the desert
5: 3 saying: "Blessed are the poor in *s*,
10: 20 but the *S* of your Father speaking
12: 31 against the *S* will not be forgiven.
26: 41 *s* is willing, but the body is weak."
28: 19 and of the Son and of the Holy *S*,
Mk 1: 8 he will baptise you with the Holy *S*
Lk 1: 35 "The Holy *S* will come upon you,
1: 80 child grew and became strong in *s*;
3: 16 will baptise you with the Holy *S*
4: 18 "The *S* of the Lord is on me,
11: 13 Father in heaven give the Holy *S*
23: 46 into your hands I commit my *s*."
Jn 1: 33 who will baptise with the Holy *S*.'
3: 5 a man is born of water and the *S*,
4: 24 God is *s*, and his worshippers must
6: 63 The *S* gives life; the flesh counts
7: 39 Up to that time the *S* had not been
14: 26 But the Counsellor, the Holy *S*,
16: 13 But when he, the *S* of truth, comes,
20: 22 and said, "Receive the Holy *S*.
Ac 1: 5 will be baptised with the Holy *S*."
1: 8 when the Holy *S* comes on you;
2: 4 of them were filled with the Holy *S*
2: 17 I will pour out my *S* on all people.
2: 38 will receive the gift of the Holy *S*.
4: 31 they were all filled with the Holy *S*
5: 3 that you have lied to the Holy *S*
6: 3 who are known to be full of the *S*
8: 15 that they might receive the Holy *S*,
9: 17 and be filled with the Holy *S*."
11: 16 will be baptised with the Holy *S*.'
13: 2 and fasting, the Holy *S* said,
19: 2 "Did you receive the Holy *S*
Ro 8: 4 nature but according to the *S*.
8: 5 set on what the *S* desires.
8: 9 And if anyone does not have the *S*
8: 13 but if by the *S* you put
8: 16 The *S* himself testifies
8: 23 who have the first-fruits of the *S*,
8: 26 the *S* helps us in our weakness.
1Co 2: 10 God has revealed it to us by his *S*.
2: 14 man without the *S* does not accept
5: 3 present, I am with you in *s*.
6: 19 body is a temple of the Holy *S*,
12: 13 baptised by one *S* into one body—
2Co 1: 22 and put his *S* in our hearts
3: 3 but with the *S* of the living God,
3: 6 the letter kills, but the *S* gives life.
3: 17 Now the Lord is the *S*,
5: 5 and has given us the *S* as a deposit,
7: 1 that contaminates body and *s*,
Gal 3: 2 Did you receive the *S*
5: 16 by the *S*, and you will not gratify
5: 22 But the fruit of the *S* is love, joy,
5: 25 let us keep in step with the *S*.
6: 8 from the *S* will reap eternal life.

Eph 1: 13 with a seal, the promised Holy *S*,
2: 22 in which God lives by his *S*.
4: 4 There is one body and one *S*—
4: 30 do not grieve the Holy *S* of God,
5: 18 Instead, be filled with the *S*.
6: 17 of salvation and the sword of the *S*,
Php 2: 2 being one in *s* and purpose.
1Th 5: 23 May your whole *s*, soul
2Th 2: 13 the sanctifying work of the *S*
1Ti 3: 16 was vindicated by the *S*,
2Ti 1: 7 For God did not give us a *s*
Heb 2: 4 of the Holy *S* distributed according
4: 12 even to dividing soul and *s*,
10: 29 and who has insulted the *S* of grace
1Pe 3: 4 beauty of a gentle and quiet *s*,
2Pe 1: 21 carried along by the Holy *S*.
1Jn 3: 24 We know it by the *S* he gave us.
4: 1 Dear friends, do not believe every *s*
4: 13 because he has given us of his *S*.
Jude : 20 holy faith and pray in the Holy *S*.
Rev 2: 7 let him hear what the *S* says

SPIRIT'S* (SPIRIT)

1Co 2: 4 a demonstration of the *S* power,
1Th 5: 19 not put out the *S* fire; do not treat

SPIRITS (SPIRIT)

1Co 12: 10 the ability to distinguish between *s*,
14: 32 The *s* of prophets are subject
1Jn 4: 1 test the *s* to see whether they are

SPIRITUAL (SPIRIT)

Ro 12: 1 to God—this is your *s* act of
12: 11 but keep your *s* fervour, serving
1Co 2: 13 expressing *s* truths in *s* words.
3: 1 I could not address you as *s* but
12: 1 Now about *s* gifts, brothers,
14: 1 of love and eagerly desire *s* gifts,
15: 44 a natural body, it is raised a *s* body.
Gal 6: 1 you who are *s* should restore him
Eph 1: 3 with every *s* blessing in Christ.
5: 19 with psalms, hymns and *s* songs.
6: 12 and against the *s* forces of evil
1Pe 2: 2 newborn babies, crave pure *s* milk,
2: 5 are being built into a *s* house

SPIRITUALLY (SPIRIT)

1Co 2: 14 because they are *s* discerned.

SPIT

Rev 3: 16 I am about to *s* you out

SPLENDOUR

1Ch 16: 29 the LORD in the *s* of his holiness.
29: 11 the glory and the majesty and the *s*,
Job 37: 22 of the north he comes in golden *s*;
Ps 29: 2 in the *s* of his holiness.
45: 3 clothe yourself with *s* and majesty.
96: 6 *S* and majesty are before him;
96: 9 in the *s* of his holiness;
104: 1 you are clothed with *s* and majesty.
145: 5 of the glorious *s* of your majesty,
145: 12 and the glorious *s* of your kingdom.
148: 13 his *s* is above the earth
Pr 4: 9 and present you with a crown of *s*."
16: 31 Grey hair is a crown of *s*;
20: 29 grey hair the *s* of the old.
Isa 55: 5 for he has endowed you with *s*."
60: 21 for the display of my *s*.
61: 3 the LORD for the display of his *s*.

Isa 63: 1 Who is this, robed in *s*,
Hab 3: 4 His *s* was like the sunrise;
Mt 6: 29 in all his *s* was dressed like one
Lk 9: 31 appeared in glorious *s*, talking
2Th 2: 8 and destroy by the *s* of his coming.

SPOIL (SPOILS)

Ps 119: 162 like one who finds great *s*.

SPOILS (SPOIL)

Isa 53: 12 he will divide the *s* with the strong,
Jn 6: 27 Do not work for food that *s*,

SPONTANEOUS*

Phm : 14 so that any favour you do will be *s*

SPOTLESS

2Pe 3: 14 make every effort to be found *s*,

SPOTS (SPOTTED)

Jer 13: 23 or the leopard its *s*?

SPOTTED (SPOTS)

Ge 30: 32 and every *s* or speckled goat.

SPREAD (SPREADING SPREADS)

Ps 78: 19 "Can God *s* a table in the desert?
Ac 6: 7 So the word of God *s*.
    12: 24 of God continued to increase and *s*.
    13: 49 of the Lord *s* through the whole
    19: 20 the word of the Lord *s* widely
2Th 3: 1 message of the Lord may *s* rapidly

SPREADING (SPREAD)

Pr 29: 5 is *s* a net for his feet.
1Th 3: 2 God's fellow-worker in *s* the gospel

SPREADS (SPREAD)

Pr 10: 18 and whoever *s* slander is a fool.

SPRING (SPRINGS WELLSPRING)

Jer 2: 13 the *s* of living water,
Jn 4: 14 in him a *s* of water welling up
Jas 3: 12 can a salt *s* produce fresh water.

SPRINGS (SPRING)

2Pe 2: 17 These men are *s* without water

SPRINKLE (SPRINKLED SPRINKLING)

Lev 16: 14 and with his finger *s* it on the front

SPRINKLED (SPRINKLE)

Heb 10: 22 having our hearts *s* to cleanse us

SPRINKLING (SPRINKLE)

1Pe 1: 2 to Jesus Christ and *s* by his blood:

SPROUT

Pr 23: 5 for they will surely *s* wings
Jer 33: 15 I will make a righteous Branch *s*

SPUR*

Heb 10: 24 how we may *s* one another

SPURNS*

Pr 15: 5 A fool *s* his father's discipline,

SPY

Gal 2: 4 ranks to *s* on the freedom we have

SQUANDERED (SQUANDERS)

Lk 15: 13 there *s* his wealth in wild living.

SQUANDERS* (SQUANDERED)

Pr 29: 3 of prostitutes *s* his wealth.

SQUARE

Rev 21: 16 The city was laid out like a *s*,

STABILITY*

Pr 29: 4 By justice a king gives a country *s*,

STAFF

Ge 49: 10 the ruler's *s* from between his feet,
Ex 7: 12 Aaron's *s* swallowed up their staffs.
Nu 17: 6 and Aaron's *s* was among them.
Ps 23: 4 your rod and your *s*,
Heb 9: 4 Aaron's *s* that had budded,

STAIN (STAINED)

Eph 5: 27 without *s* or wrinkle or any other

STAINED (STAIN)

Isa 63: 1 with his garments *s* crimson?

STAKES

Isa 54: 2 strengthen your *s*.

STAND (STANDING STANDS STOOD)

Ex 14: 13 *S* firm and you will see
Jos 10: 12 "O sun, *s* still over Gibeon,
2Ch 20: 17 *s* firm and see the deliverance
Job 19: 25 in the end he will *s* upon the earth.
Ps 1: 1 or *s* in the way of sinners
    1: 5 Therefore the wicked will not *s*
    24: 3 Who may *s* in his holy place?
    33: 11 of the LORD *s* firm for ever,
    40: 2 and gave me a firm place to *s*.
    76: 7 Who can *s* before you
    93: 5 Your statutes *s* firm;
    119: 120 I *s* in awe of your laws.
    130: 3 O Lord, who could *s*?
Ecc 5: 7 Therefore *s* in awe of God.
Isa 7: 9 If you do not *s* firm in your faith,
    29: 23 will *s* in awe of the God of Israel.
Eze 22: 30 *s* before me in the gap on behalf
Hab 3: 2 I *s* in awe of your deeds, O LORD.
Zec 14: 4 On that day his feet will *s*
Mal 3: 2 Who can *s* when he appears?
Mt 12: 25 divided against itself will not *s*.
Ro 14: 4 for the Lord is able to make him *s*.
    14: 10 we will all *s* before God's judgment
1Co 10: 13 out so that you can *s* up under it.
    15: 58 Therefore, my dear brothers, *s* firm
    16: 13 Be on your guard; *s* firm in the faith
Gal 5: 1 *S* firm, then, and do not let
Eph 6: 14 *S* firm then, with the belt
2Th 2: 15 *s* firm and hold to the teachings we
Jas 5: 8 You too, be patient and *s* firm,
Rev 3: 20 Here I am! I *s* at the door

STANDING (STAND)

Ex 3: 5 where you are *s* is holy ground."
Jos 5: 15 the place where you are *s* is holy."
Ru 2: 1 a man of *s*, whose name was Boaz.
    4: 11 May you have *s* in Ephrathah
Lk 21: 19 By *s* firm you will save yourselves.
1Ti 3: 13 have served well gain an excellent *s*
1Pe 5: 9 Resist him, *s* firm in the faith,

STANDS (STAND)

Ps	89: 2	that your love *s* firm for ever,
	119: 89	it *s* firm in the heavens.
Pr	12: 7	the house of the righteous *s* firm.
Isa	40: 8	but the word of our God *s* for ever."
Mt	10: 22	but he who *s* firm to the end will be
2Ti	2: 19	God's solid foundation *s* firm,
1Pe	1: 25	but the word of the Lord *s* for ever

STAR (STARS)

Nu	24: 17	A *s* will come out of Jacob;
Isa	14: 12	O morning *s*, son of the dawn!
Mt	2: 2	We saw his *s* in the east
2Pe	1: 19	the morning *s* rises in your hearts.
Rev	2: 28	I will also give him the morning *s*.
	22: 16	and the bright Morning *S*."

STARS (STAR)

Ge	1: 16	He also made the *s*.
Job	38: 7	while the morning *s* sang together
Da	12: 3	like the *s* for ever and ever.
Php	2: 15	in which you shine like *s*

STATURE

1Sa	2: 26	boy Samuel continued to grow in *s*
Lk	2: 52	And Jesus grew in wisdom and *s*,

STATUTES

Ps	19: 7	*s* of the Lord are trustworthy,
	93: 5	Your *s* stand firm;
	119: 2	Blessed are they who keep his *s*
	119: 14	I rejoice in following your *s*
	119: 24	Your *s* are my delight;
	119: 36	Turn my heart towards your *s*
	119: 99	for I meditate on your *s*.
	119: 111	Your *s* are my heritage for ever;
	119: 125	that I may understand your *s*.
	119: 129	Your *s* are wonderful;
	119: 138	The *s* you have laid
	119: 152	Long ago I learned from your *s*
	119: 167	I obey your *s*,

STEADFAST*

Ps	51: 10	and renew a *s* spirit within me.
	57: 7	My heart is *s*, O God,
	57: 7	my heart is *s*;
	108: 1	My heart is *s*, O God;
	111: 8	They are *s* for ever and ever,
	112: 7	his heart is *s*, trusting in the Lord
	119: 5	Oh, that my ways were *s*
Isa	26: 3	him whose mind is *s*,
1Pe	5: 10	and make you strong, firm and *s*.

STEADY

Isa	35: 3	*s* the knees that give way;

STEAL (STOLEN)

Ex	20: 15	"You shall not *s*.
Lev	19: 11	"'Do not *s*.
Dt	5: 19	"You shall not *s*.
Mt	19: 18	do not *s*, do not give false
Ro	13: 9	"Do not *s*," "Do not covet,"
Eph	4: 28	has been stealing must *s* no longer,

STEP (FOOTSTEPS STEPS)

Job	34: 21	he sees their every *s*.
Gal	5: 25	let us keep in *s* with the Spirit.

STEPHEN

Deacon (Ac 6:5). Arrested (Ac 6:8-15). Speech to Sanhedrin (Ac 7). Stoned (Ac 7:54-60; 22:20).

STEPS (STEP)

Ps	37: 23	whose *s* he has made firm;
Pr	14: 15	prudent man gives thought to his *s*.
	16: 9	but the Lord determines his *s*.
	20: 24	A man's *s* are directed
Jer	10: 23	it is not for man to direct his *s*.
1Pe	2: 21	that you should follow in his *s*.

STERN (STERNNESS)

Pr	15: 10	*S* discipline awaits him who leaves

STERNNESS* (STERN)

Ro	11: 22	and *s* of God: *s* to those who fell,

STICKS

Pr	18: 24	there is a friend who *s* closer

STIFF-NECKED (NECK)

Ex	34: 9	Although this is a *s* people,
Pr	29: 1	A man who remains *s*

STILL

Jos	10: 13	So the sun stood *s*,
Ps	37: 7	Be *s* before the Lord
	46: 10	"Be *s*, and know that I am God;
	89: 9	its waves mount up, you *s* them.
Zec	2: 13	Be *s* before the Lord, all mankind
Mk	4: 39	said to the waves, "Quiet! Be *s*!"

STIMULATE*

2Pe	3: 1	as reminders to *s* you

STING

1Co	15: 55	Where, O death, is your *s*?"

STINGY

Pr	28: 22	A *s* man is eager to get rich

STIRRED (STIRS)

Ps	45: 1	My heart is *s* by a noble theme

STIRS (STIRRED)

Pr	6: 19	and a man who *s* up dissension
	10: 12	Hatred *s* up dissension,
	15: 1	but a harsh word *s* up anger.
	15: 18	hot-tempered man *s* up dissension,
	16: 28	A perverse man *s* up dissension,
	28: 25	A greedy man *s* up dissension,
	29: 22	An angry man *s* up dissension,

STOLEN (STEAL)

Lev	6: 4	he must return what he has *s*
SS	4: 9	You have *s* my heart, my sister,

STOMACH

1Co	6: 13	Food for the *s* and the *s* for food"—
Php	3: 19	their god is their *s*, and their glory

STONE (CAPSTONE CORNERSTONE MILLSTONE STONED STONES)

Ex	24: 4	set up twelve *s* pillars representing
	28: 10	on one *s* and the remaining six
	34: 1	"Chisel out two *s* tablets like
Dt	4: 13	then wrote them on two *s* tablets.
	19: 14	your neighbour's boundary *s* set up

1Sa	17: 50	the Philistine with a sling and a s;
Ps	91: 12	will not strike your foot against a s.
	118: 22	The s the builders rejected
Pr	22: 28	not move an ancient boundary s
Isa	8: 14	a s that causes men to stumble
	28: 16	"See, I lay a s in Zion,
Eze	11: 19	remove from them their heart of s
	36: 26	remove from you your heart of s
Mt	7: 9	will give him a s? Or if he asks
	21: 42	" 'The s the builders rejected
	24: 2	not one s here will be left
Mk	16: 3	"Who will roll the s away
Lk	4: 3	tell this s to become bread."
Jn	8: 7	the first to throw a s at her."
Ac	4: 11	" 'the s you builders rejected,
Ro	9: 32	stumbled over the "stumbling- s."
2Co	3: 3	not on tablets of s but on tablets
1Pe	2: 6	"See, I lay a s in Zion,
Rev	2: 17	also give him a white s

STONED (STONE)

2Co	11: 25	once I was s, three times I was
Heb	11: 37	They were s; they were sawed

STONES (STONE)

Ex	28: 21	are to be twelve s, one for each
Jos	4: 3	to take up twelve s from the middle
1Sa	17: 40	chose five smooth s
Mt	3: 9	out of these s God can raise up
1Co	3: 12	silver, costly s, wood, hay or straw,
1Pe	2: 5	also, like living s, are being built

STOOD (STAND)

Jos	10: 13	So the sun s still,
Lk	22: 28	You are those who have s by me
2Ti	4: 17	But the Lord s at my side
Jas	1: 12	because when he has s the test,

STOOP (STOOPS)

2Sa	22: 36	you s down to make me great.

STOOPS (STOOP)

Ps	113: 6	who s down to look

STOP

Job	37: 14	s and consider God's wonders.
Isa	1: 13	S bringing meaningless offerings!
	1: 16	S doing wrong,
	2: 22	S trusting in man,
Jer	32: 40	I will never s doing good to them,
Mk	9: 39	"Do not s him," Jesus said.
Jn	6: 43	"S grumbling among yourselves,"
	7: 24	S judging by mere appearances,
	20: 27	S doubting and believe."
Ro	14: 13	Therefore let us s passing judgment
1Co	14: 20	Brothers, s thinking like children.

STORE (STORED)

Pr	2: 1	and s up my commands within you,
	7: 1	and s up my commands within you.
	10: 14	Wise men s up knowledge,
Isa	33: 6	a rich s of salvation and wisdom
Mt	6: 19	not s up for yourselves treasures
	6: 26	or reap or s away in barns,
2Ti	4: 8	Now there is in s for me the crown

STORED (STORE)

Lk	6: 45	out of the good s up in his heart,
Col	1: 5	from the hope that is s up for you

STOREHOUSE (HOUSE)

Mal	3: 10	Bring the whole tithe into the s,

STORIES*

2Pe	1: 16	did not follow cleverly invented s
	2: 3	you with s they have made up.

STORM

Job	38: 1	LORD answered Job out of the s.
Ps	107: 29	He stilled the s to a whisper;
Lk	8: 24	the s subsided, and all was calm.

STOUT-HEARTED* (HEART)

Ps	138: 3	you made me bold and s.

STRAIGHT

Ps	27: 11	lead me in a s path
	107: 7	He led them by a s way
Pr	2: 13	who leave the s paths
	3: 6	and he will make your paths s.
	4: 11	and lead you along s paths.
	4: 25	Let your eyes look s ahead,
	11: 5	of the blameless makes a s way
	15: 21	of understanding keeps a s course.
Isa	40: 3	make s in the wilderness
Mt	3: 3	make s paths for him.' "
Jn	1: 23	'Make s the way for the Lord.' "
2Pe	2: 15	They have left the s way

STRAIN (STRAINING)

Mt	23: 24	You s out a gnat but swallow

STRAINING (STRAIN)

Php	3: 13	and s towards what is ahead,

STRANGE (STRANGER STRANGERS)

Isa	28: 11	with foreign lips and s tongues
1Co	14: 21	"Through men of s tongues
1Pe	4: 4	They think it s that you do not

STRANGER (STRANGE)

Ps	119: 19	I am a s on earth;
Mt	25: 35	I was a s and you invited me in,
Jn	10: 5	But they will never follow a s;

STRANGERS (STRANGE)

Heb	13: 2	Do not forget to entertain s,
1Pe	2: 11	as aliens and s in the world,

STRAW

Isa	11: 7	and the lion will eat s like the ox.
1Co	3: 12	silver, costly stones, wood, hay or s

STRAYED (STRAYS)

Ps	119: 176	I have s like a lost sheep.
Jer	31: 19	After I s,

STRAYS (STRAYED)

Pr	21: 16	A man who s from the path
Eze	34: 16	for the lost and bring back the s.

STREAM (STREAMS)

Am	5: 24	righteousness like a never-failing s!

STREAMS (STREAM)

Ps	1: 3	He is like a tree planted by s
	46: 4	is a river whose s make glad
Ecc	1: 7	All s flow into the sea,
Jn	7: 38	s of living water will flow

STREET

Mt   6: 5 on the *s* corners to be seen by men.
        22: 9 Go to the *s* corners and invite
Rev 21: 21 The *s* of the city was of pure gold,

STRENGTH (STRONG)

Ex   15: 2 The Lord is my *s* and my song;
Dt   4: 37 by his Presence and his great *s*,
        6: 5 all your soul and with all your *s*.
Jdg 16: 15 told me the secret of your great *s*."
2Sa 22: 33 It is God who arms me with *s*
2Ki 23: 25 with all his soul and with all his *s*,
1Ch 16: 11 Look to the Lord and his *s*;
        16: 28 ascribe to the Lord glory and *s*,
        29: 12 In your hands are *s* and power
Ne   8: 10 for the joy of the Lord is your *s*."
Ps   18: 1 I love you, O Lord, my *s*.
        21: 13 Be exalted, O Lord, in your *s*;
        28: 7 The Lord is my *s* and my shield:
        29: 11 The Lord gives *s* to his people;
        33: 16 no warrior escapes by his great *s*.
        46: 1 God is our refuge and *s*,
        59: 17 O my *S*, I sing praise to you;
        65: 6 having armed yourself with *s*,
        73: 26 but God is the *s* of my heart
        84: 5 Blessed are those whose *s* is in you,
        96: 7 ascribe to the Lord glory and *s*.
        105: 4 Look to the Lord and his *s*;
        118: 14 The Lord is my *s* and my song;
        147: 10 not in the *s* of the horse,
Pr   24: 5 a man of knowledge increases *s*;
        30: 25 Ants are creatures of little *s*,
Isa 12: 2 the Lord, is my *s* and my song;
        31: 1 and in the great *s* of their horsemen
        40: 26 of his great power and mighty *s*,
        40: 31 will renew their *s*.
        63: 1 forward in the greatness of his *s*?
Jer   9: 23 or the strong man boast of his *s*
Mic   5: 4 flock in the *s* of the Lord,
Hab   3: 19 The Sovereign Lord is my *s*;
Mk 12: 30 all your mind and with all your *s*.'
1Co   1: 25 of God is stronger than man's *s*.
Eph   1: 19 is like the working of his mighty *s*,
Php   4: 13 through him who gives me *s*.
Heb 11: 34 whose weakness was turned to *s*;
1Pe   4: 11 it with the *s* God provides,

STRENGTHEN (STRONG)

2Ch 16: 9 to *s* those whose hearts are fully
Ps 119: 28 *s* me according to your word.
Isa 35: 3 *S* the feeble hands,
        41: 10 I will *s* you and help you;
Lk   22: 32 have turned back, *s* your brothers."
Eph   6: 10 of his glorious riches he may *s* you
1Th   3: 13 May he *s* your hearts
2Th   2: 17 and *s* you in every good deed
Heb 12: 12 *s* your feeble arms and weak knees.

STRENGTHENED (STRONG)

Col   1: 11 being *s* with all power according
Heb 13: 9 good for our hearts to be *s* by grace,

STRENGTHENING (STRONG)

1Co 14: 26 done for the *s* of the church.

STRETCHES

Ps 104: 2 he *s* out the heavens like a tent

STRICKEN (STRIKE)

Isa 53: 8 of my people he was *s*.

STRICT

1Co   9: 25 in the games goes into *s* training.

STRIFE (STRIVE)

Pr   17: 1 than a house full of feasting, with *s*.
        20: 3 It is to a man's honour to avoid *s*,
        22: 10 out the mocker, and out goes *s*;
        30: 33 so stirring up anger produces *s*."

STRIKE (STRIKES STROKE)

Ge   3: 15 and you will *s* his heel."
Zec 13: 7 "*S* the shepherd,
Mt   4: 6 so that you will not *s* your foot
        26: 31 "'I will *s* the shepherd,

STRIKES (STRIKE)

Mt   5: 39 If someone *s* you on the right

STRIPS

Jn   20: 5 in at the *s* of linen lying there

STRIVE* (STRIFE)

Ac   24: 16 I *s* always to keep my conscience
1Ti   4: 10 (and for this we labour and *s*),

STROKE (STRIKE)

Mt   5: 18 the smallest letter, not the least *s*

STRONG (STRENGTH STRENGTHEN STRENGTHENED STRENGTHENING STRONGER)

Dt   3: 24 your greatness and your *s* hand.
        31: 6 Be *s* and courageous.
Jos   1: 6 "Be *s* and courageous,
Jdg   5: 21 March on, my soul; be *s*!
2Sa 10: 12 Be *s* and let us fight bravely
1Ki   2: 2 "So be *s*, show yourself a man,
1Ch 28: 20 "Be *s* and courageous,
2Ch 32: 7 them with these words: "Be *s*
Ps   24: 8 The Lord *s* and mighty,
        31: 2 a *s* fortress to save me.
        62: 11 that you, O God, are *s*,
Pr   18: 10 The name of the Lord is a *s* tower
        31: 17 her arms are *s* for her tasks.
Ecc   9: 11 or the battle to the *s*,
SS   8: 6 for love is as *s* as death,
Isa 35: 4 "Be *s*, do not fear;
        53: 12 he will divide the spoils with the *s*,
Jer   9: 23 or the *s* man boast of his strength
        50: 34 Yet their Redeemer is *s*;
Hag   2: 4 Be *s*, all you people of the land,'
Mt   12: 29 can anyone enter a *s* man's house
Lk   2: 40 And the child grew and became *s*;
Ro   15: 1 We who are *s* ought to bear
1Co   1: 8 He will keep you *s* to the end,
        1: 27 things of the world to shame the *s*.
        16: 13 in the faith; be men of courage; be *s*
2Co 12: 10 For when I am weak, then I am *s*.
Eph   6: 10 be *s* in the Lord and in his mighty
2Ti   2: 1 be *s* in the grace that is
1Pe   5: 10 restore you and make you *s*,

STRONGER (STRONG)

Dt   4: 38 before you nations greater and *s*
1Co   1: 25 of God is *s* than man's strength.

STRONGHOLD (STRONGHOLDS)

2Sa 22: 3 He is my *s*, my refuge and my
Ps   9: 9 a *s* in times of trouble.
        18: 2 the horn of my salvation, my *s*.

Ps 27: 1 The Lord is the s of my life—
144: 2 my s and my deliverer,

STRONGHOLDS (STRONGHOLD)

Zep 3: 6 their s are demolished.
2Co 10: 4 have divine power to demolish s.

STRUGGLE (STRUGGLED STRUGGLING)

Ro 15: 30 me in my s by praying to God
Eph 6: 12 For our s is not against flesh
Heb 12: 4 In your s against sin, you have not

STRUGGLED (STRUGGLE)

Ge 32: 28 because you have s with God

STRUGGLING* (STRUGGLE)

Col 1: 29 To this end I labour, s
2: 1 to know how much I am s for you

STUDENT (STUDY)

Mt 10: 24 "A s is not above his teacher,

STUDY (STUDENT)

Ezr 7: 10 Ezra had devoted himself to the s
Ecc 12: 12 and much s wearies the body.
Jn 5: 39 You diligently s the Scriptures

STUMBLE (STUMBLES STUMBLING)

Ps 37: 24 though he s, he will not fall,
119: 165 and nothing can make them s.
Pr 3: 23 and your foot will not s;
Isa 8: 14 a stone that causes men to s
Jer 13: 16 before your feet s
31: 9 a level path where they will not s,
Eze 7: 19 for it has made them s into sin.
Hos 14: 9 but the rebellious s in them.
Mal 2: 8 teaching have caused many to s;
Jn 11: 9 A man who walks by day will not s,
Ro 9: 33 in Zion a stone that causes men to s
14: 20 that causes someone else to s.
1Co 10: 32 Do not cause anyone to s,
Jas 3: 2 We all s in many ways.
1Pe 2: 8 and, "A stone that causes men to s
1Jn 2: 10 nothing in him to make him s.

STUMBLES (STUMBLE)

Pr 24: 17 when he s, do not let your heart
Jn 11: 10 is when he walks by night that he s,
Jas 2: 10 and yet s at just one point is guilty

STUMBLING (STUMBLE)

Ps 56: 13 and my feet from s,

STUMBLING-BLOCK

Lev 19: 14 put a s in front of the blind,
Mt 16: 23 Satan! You are a s to me;
11: 9 a s and a retribution for them
14: 13 up your mind not to put any s
1Co 1: 23 a s to Jews and foolishness
8: 9 freedom does not become a s
2Co 6: 3 We put no s in anyone's path,

STUMBLING-STONE

Ro 9: 32 They stumbled over the "s".

STUMP

Isa 6: 13 so the holy seed will be the s
11: 1 up from the s of Jesse;

STUPID

Pr 12: 1 but he who hates correction is s.
2Ti 2: 23 to do with foolish and s arguments,

STUPOR

Ro 11: 8 "God gave them a spirit of s,

SUBDUE (SUBDUED)

Ge 1: 28 in number; fill the earth and s it.

SUBDUED (SUBDUE)

Jos 10: 40 So Joshua s the whole region,
Ps 47: 3 He s nations under us,

SUBJECT (SUBJECTED)

Mt 5: 22 angry with his brother will be s
1Co 14: 32 of prophets are s to the control
15: 28 then the Son himself will be made s
Tit 2: 5 and to be s to their husbands,
2: 9 slaves to be s to their masters
3: 1 Remind the people to be s to rulers

SUBJECTED (SUBJECT)

Ro 8: 20 For the creation was s

SUBMISSION (SUBMIT)

1Co 14: 34 but must be in s, as the Law says.
1Ti 2: 11 learn in quietness and full s.

SUBMISSIVE (SUBMIT)

Jas 3: 17 then peace-loving, considerate, s,
1Pe 3: 1 in the same way be s
5: 5 in the same way be s

SUBMIT (SUBMISSION SUBMISSIVE SUBMITS)

Ro 13: 1 Everyone must s himself
13: 5 necessary to s to the authorities,
1Co 16: 16 to s to such as these
Eph 5: 21 S to one another out of reverence
Col 3: 18 Wives, s to your husbands,
Heb 12: 9 How much more should we s
13: 17 Obey your leaders and s
Jas 4: 7 S yourselves, then, to God.
1Pe 2: 18 s yourselves to your masters

SUBMITS* (SUBMIT)

Eph 5: 24 Now as the church s to Christ,

SUBTRACT*

Dt 4: 2 what I command you and do not s

SUCCEED (SUCCESS SUCCESSFUL)

Ps 20: 4 and make all your plans s.
Pr 15: 22 but with many advisers they s.
16: 3 and your plans will s.
21: 30 that can s against the Lord.

SUCCESS (SUCCEED)

Ge 39: 23 and gave him s in whatever he did.
1Sa 18: 14 In everything he did he had great s,
1Ch 12: 18 S, s to you, and s
22: 13 you will have s if you are careful
2Ch 26: 5 the Lord, God gave him s.
Ecc 10: 10 but skill will bring s.

SUCCESSFUL (SUCCEED)

Jos 1: 7 that you may be s wherever you go.
2Ki 18: 7 he was s in whatever he undertook.
2Ch 20: 20 in his prophets and you will be s."

SUFFER (SUFFERED SUFFERING SUFFERINGS SUFFERS)

Job 36: 15 those who *s* he delivers
Isa 53: 10 to crush him and cause him to *s*,
Mk 8: 31 the Son of Man must *s* many things
Lk 24: 26 the Christ have to *s* these things
24: 46 The Christ will *s* and rise
2Co 1: 6 of the same sufferings we *s*.
Php 1: 29 to *s* for him, since you are going
Heb 9: 26 would have had to *s* many times
1Pe 3: 17 to *s* for doing good
4: 16 However, if you *s* as a Christian,

SUFFERED (SUFFER)

Heb 2: 9 and honour because he *s* death,
2: 18 Because he himself *s*
1Pe 2: 21 Christ *s* for you, leaving you
4: 1 he who has *s* in his body is done

SUFFERING (SUFFER)

Job 36: 15 who suffer he delivers in their *s*;
Ps 22: 24 the *s* of the afflicted one;
Isa 53: 3 of sorrows, and familiar with *s*.
53: 11 After the *s* of his soul,
La 1: 12 Is any *s* like my *s*
Ac 5: 41 worthy of *s* disgrace for the Name.
Ro 5: 3 know that *s* produces
2Ti 1: 8 But join with me in *s* for the gospel,
He 2: 10 of their salvation perfect through *s*.
13: 3 as if you yourselves were *s*,
1Pe 4: 12 at the painful trial you are *s*,

SUFFERINGS (SUFFER)

Go 5: 3 but we also rejoice in our *s*,
8: 17 share in his *s* in order that we may
8: 18 that our present *s* are not worth
2Co 1: 5 as the *s* of Christ flow
Php 3: 10 the fellowship of sharing in his *s*,
1Pe 4: 13 rejoice that you participate in the *s*
5: 9 are undergoing the same kind of *s*.

SUFFERS (SUFFER)

Pr 13: 20 but a companion of fools *s* harm.
1Co 12: 26 If one part *s*, every part *s* with it;

SUFFICIENT

2Co 12: 9 said to me, "My grace is *s* for you,

SUITABLE

Ge 2: 18 I will make a helper *s* for him."

SUMMED* (SUMS)

Ro 13: 9 there may be, are *s* up
Gal 5: 14 The entire law is *s* up

SUMMONS

Ps 50: 1 speaks and *s* the earth
Isa 45: 3 God of Israel, who *s* you by name.

SUMS* (SUMMED)

Mt 7: 12 for this *s* up the Law

SUN (SUNRISE)

Jos 10: 13 So the *s* stood still,
Jdg 5: 31 may they who love you be like the *s*
Ps 84: 11 For the LORD God is a *s*
121: 6 the *s* will not harm you by day,
136: 8 the *s* to govern the day,
Ecc 1: 9 there is nothing new under the *s*.

Isa 60: 19 The *s* will no more be your light
Mal 4: 2 the *s* of righteousness will rise
Mt 5: 45 He causes his *s* to rise on the evil
13: 43 the righteous will shine like the *s*
17: 2 His face shone like the *s*,
Lk 23: 45 for the *s* stopped shining.
Eph 4: 26 Do not let the *s* go
Rev 1: 16 His face was like the *s* shining
21: 23 The city does not need the *s*

SUNG (SING)

Mt 26: 30 When they had *s* a hymn, they

SUNRISE (SUN)

2Sa 23: 4 he is like the light of morning at *s*
Hab 3: 4 His splendour was like the *s*;

SUPERIOR

Heb 1: 4 he became as much *s* to the angels
8: 6 ministry Jesus has received is as *s*

SUPERVISION

Gal 3: 25 longer under the *s* of the law.

SUPPER

Lk 22: 20 after the *s* he took the cup, saying,
1Co 11: 25 after *s* he took the cup,
Rev 19: 9 to the wedding *s* of the Lamb!' "

SUPPLIED (SUPPLY)

Ac 20: 34 of mine have *s* my own needs
Php 4: 18 and even more; I am amply *s*,

SUPPLY (SUPPLIED SUPPLYING)

2Co 8: 14 your plenty will *s* what they need,
1Th 3: 10 and *s* what is lacking in your faith.

SUPPLYING* (SUPPLY)

2Co 9: 12 you perform is not only *s* the needs

SUPPORT (SUPPORTED SUPPORTING)

Ps 18: 18 but the LORD was my *s*.
Ro 11: 18 consider this: You do not *s* the root
1Co 9: 12 If others have this right of *s*

SUPPORTED (SUPPORT)

Ps 94: 18 your love, O LORD, *s* me.
Col 2: 19 *s* and held together by its ligaments

SUPPORTING (SUPPORT)

Eph 4: 16 held together by every *s* ligament,

SUPPRESS*

Ro 1: 18 wickedness of men who *s* the truth

SUPREMACY* (SUPREME)

Col 1: 18 in everything he might have the *s*.

SUPREME (SUPREMACY)

Pr 4: 7 Wisdom is *s*; therefore get wisdom.

SURE

Nu 28: 31 Be *s* the animals are without defect
32: 23 you may be *s* that your sin will find
Dt 6: 17 Be *s* to keep the commands
14: 22 Be *s* to set aside a tenth
29: 18 make *s* there is no root
Jos 23: 13 then you may be *s* that the LORD
1Sa 12: 24 But be *s* to fear the LORD
Ps 19: 9 The ordinances of the LORD are *s*

SURFACE (continued)

Ps	132: 11	a *s* oath that he will not revoke:
Pr	27: 23	Be *s* you know the condition
Isa	28: 16	cornerstone for a *s* foundation;
Eph	5: 5	of this you can be *s*: No immoral,
Heb	11: 1	faith is being *s* of what we hope for
2Pe	1: 10	to make your calling and election *s*.

SURFACE

2Co	10: 7	You are looking only on the *s*

SURPASS* (SURPASSED SURPASSES SURPASSING)

Pr	31: 29	but you *s* them all."

SURPASSED* (SURPASS)

Jn	1: 15	'He who comes after me has *s* me
	1: 30	man who comes after me has *s* me

SURPASSES* (SURPASS)

Pr	8: 19	what I yield *s* choice silver.
Mt	5: 20	unless your righteousness *s* that
Eph	3: 19	to know this love that *s* knowledge

SURPASSING* (SURPASS)

Ps	150: 2	praise him for his *s* greatness.
2Co	3: 10	in comparison with the *s* glory.
	9: 14	of the *s* grace God has given you.
Php	3: 8	the *s* greatness of knowing Christ

SURPRISE (SURPRISED)

1Th	5: 4	that this day should *s* you like

SURPRISED (SURPRISE)

1Pe	4: 12	do not be *s* at the painful trial you
1Jn	3: 13	Do not be *s*, my brothers,

SURRENDER

1Co	13: 3	and *s* my body to the flames,

SURROUND (SURROUNDED SURROUNDS)

Ps	5: 12	you *s* them with your favour
	32: 7	and *s* me with songs of deliverance.
	89: 7	awesome than all who *s* him.
	125: 2	As the mountains *s* Jerusalem,
Jer	31: 22	a woman will *s* a man."

SURROUNDED (SURROUND)

Heb	12: 1	since we are *s* by such a great cloud

SURROUNDS* (SURROUND)

Ps	32: 10	*s* the man who trusts in him.
	89: 8	and your faithfulness *s* you.
	125: 2	so the LORD *s* his people

SUSA

Ezr	4: 9	and Babylon, the Elamites of *S*,
Ne	1: 1	while I was in the citadel of *S*,

SUSPENDS*

Job	26: 7	he *s* the earth over nothing.

SUSPICIONS*

1Ti	6: 4	evil *s* and constant friction

SUSTAIN (SUSTAINING SUSTAINS)

Ps	55: 22	the will *s* you;
Isa	46: 4	I am he, I am he who will *s* you.

SUSTAINING* (SUSTAIN)

Heb	1: 3	*s* all things by his powerful word.

SUSTAINS (SUSTAIN)

Ps	18: 35	and your right hand *s* me;
	146: 9	and *s* the fatherless and the widow,
	147: 6	The LORD *s* the humble
Isa	50: 4	to know the word that *s* the weary.

SWALLOW (SWALLOWED)

Isa	25: 8	he will *s* up death for ever.
Jnh	1: 17	provided a great fish to *s* Jonah,
Mt	23: 24	You strain out a gnat but *s* a camel.

SWALLOWED (SWALLOW)

1Co	15: 54	"Death has been *s* up in victory."
2Co	5: 4	so that what is mortal may be *s* up

SWAYED

Mt	11: 7	A reed *s* by the wind? If not,
	22: 16	You aren't *s* by men, because you
2Ti	3: 6	are *s* by all kinds of evil desires,

SWEAR (SWORE SWORN)

Lev	19: 12	"'Do not *s* falsely by my name
Ps	24: 4	or *s* by what is false.
Isa	45: 23	by me every tongue will *s*.
Mt	5: 34	Do not *s* at all: either by heaven,
Ja	5: 12	Above all, my brothers, do not *s*—

SWEAT*

Ge	3: 19	By the *s* of your brow
Lk	22: 44	his *s* was like drops of blood falling

SWEET (SWEETER SWEETNESS)

Job	20: 12	"Though evil is *s* in his mouth.
Ps	119: 103	How *s* are your promises
Pr	9: 17	"Stolen water is *s*;
	13: 19	A longing fulfilled is *s* to the soul,
	16: 24	*s* to the soul and healing
	20: 17	by fraud tastes *s* to a man,
	24: 14	also that wisdom is *s* to your soul;
Ecc	5: 12	The sleep of a labourer is *s*,
Isa	5: 20	and *s* for bitter.
Eze	3: 3	it tasted as *s* as honey in my mouth.
Rev	10: 10	It tasted as *s* as honey in my mouth

SWEETER (SWEET)

Pr	19: 10	they are *s* than honey,
	119: 103	*s* than honey to my mouth!

SWEETNESS* (SWEET)

SS	4: 11	Your lips drop *s* as the honeycomb,
	5: 16	His mouth is *s* itself;

SWEPT

Mt	12: 44	finds the house unoccupied, *s* clean

SWERVE*

Pr	4: 5	do not forget my words or *s*
	4: 27	Do not *s* to the right or the left;

SWIFT

Pr	1: 16	they are *s* to shed blood.
Ecc	9: 11	The race is not to the *s*
Isa	59: 7	they are *s* to shed innocent blood.
Ro	3: 15	"Their feet are *s* to shed blood;
2Pe	2: 1	bringing *s* destruction

SWINDLER* (SWINDLERS)

1Co	5: 11	or a slanderer, a drunkard or a *s*.

SWINDLERS* (SWINDLER)

1Co	5: 10	or the greedy and s, or idolaters.
	6: 10	s will inherit the kingdom of God.

SWORD (SWORDS)

Ge	3: 24	and a flaming s flashing back
Dt	32: 41	when I sharpen my flashing s
Jos	5: 13	of him with a drawn s in his hand.
1Sa	17: 45	"You come against me with s
	17: 47	here will know that it is not by s
	31: 4	so Saul took his own s and fell on it.
2Sa	12: 10	therefore , the s will never depart
Ps	44: 6	my s does not bring me victory;
	45: 3	Gird your s upon your side,
Pr	12: 18	Reckless words pierce like a s,
Isa	2: 4	Nation will not take up s
Mic	4: 3	Nation will not take up s
Mt	10: 34	come to bring peace, but a s.
	26: 52	all who draw the s will die by the s.
Lk	2: 34	a s will pierce your own soul too."
Ro	13: 4	for he does not bear the s
Eph	6: 17	of salvation and the s of the Spirit,
Heb	4: 12	Sharper than any double-edged s,
Rev	1: 16	came a sharp double-edged s.
	19: 15	Out of his mouth comes a sharp s

SWORDS (SWORD)

Ps	64: 3	who sharpen their tongues like s
Isa	2: 4	They will beat their s
Joel	3: 10	Beat your ploughshares into s

SWORE (SWEAR)

Heb	6: 13	for him to swear by, he s by himself

SWORN (SWEAR)

Ps	110: 4	The LORD has s
Eze	20: 42	the land I had s with uplifted hand
Heb	7: 21	"The Lord has s

SYCAMORE-FIG (FIG)

Am	7: 14	and I also took care of s trees.
Lk	19: 4	and climbed a s tree to see him,

SYMBOLISES*

1Pe	3: 21	this water s baptism that now saves

SYMPATHETIC* (SYMPATHY)

1Pe	3: 8	in harmony with one another; be s,

SYMPATHISED* (SYMPATHY)

Heb	10: 34	You s with those in prison

SYMPATHY (SYMPATHETIC SYMPATHISED)

Ps	69: 20	I looked for s, but there was none,

SYNAGOGUE

Lk	4: 16	the Sabbath day he went into the s,
Ac	17: 2	custom was, Paul went into the s,

TABERNACLE (TABERNACLES)

Ex	40: 34	the glory of the LORD filled the t.
Heb	8: 2	the true t set up by the Lord,
	9: 11	and more perfect t that is not
	9: 21	sprinkled with the blood both the t
Rev	15: 5	that is, the t of Testimony,

TABERNACLES (TABERNACLE)

Lev	23: 34	the LORD's Feast of T begins,
Dt	16: 16	Feast of Weeks and the Feast of T.
Zec	14: 16	and to celebrate the Feast of T.

TABLE (TABLES)

Ex	25: 23	"Make a t of acacia wood—
Ps	23: 5	You prepare a t before me

TABLES (TABLE)

Jn	2: 15	money-changers and overturned their t.
Ac	6: 2	word of God in order to wait on t.

TABLET (TABLETS)

Pr	3: 3	write them on the t of your heart.
	7: 3	write them on the t of your heart.

TABLETS (TABLET)

Ex	31: 18	he gave him the two t
Dt	10: 5	and put the t in the ark I had made,
2Co	3: 3	not on t of stone but on t

TAKE (TAKEN TAKES TAKING TOOK)

Ge	15: 7	land to t possession of it."
	22: 17	Your descendants will t possession
Ex	3: 5	"T off your sandals,
	21: 23	you are to t life for life, eye for eye,
	22: 22	"Do not t advantage of a widow
Lev	10: 17	given to you to t away the guilt
	25: 14	do not t advantage of each other.
Nu	13: 30	and t possession of the land,
Dt	1: 8	and t possession of the land that
	12: 32	do not add to it or t away from it.
	31: 26	"T this Book of the Law
1Sa	8: 11	He will t your sons and make them
1Ch	17: 13	I will never t my love away
Job	23: 10	But he knows the way that I t;
Ps	2: 12	Blessed are all who t refuge in him.
	25: 18	and t away all my sins.
	27: 14	be strong and t heart
	31: 24	Be strong and t heart,
	49: 17	for he will t nothing with him
	51: 11	or t your Holy Spirit from me.
	73: 24	afterwards you will t me into glory.
	118: 8	It is better to t refuge in the LORD
Pr	22: 23	for the LORD will t up their case
Isa	62: 4	for the LORD will t delight in you,
Eze	3: 10	and t to heart all the words I speak
	33: 11	I t no pleasure in the death
Mt	10: 38	anyone who does not t his cross
	11: 29	T my yoke upon you and learn
	16: 24	deny himself and t up his cross
	26: 26	saying, "T and eat; this is my body
Mk	14: 36	T this cup from me.
1Ti	6: 12	T hold of the eternal life

TAKEN (TAKE)

Ge	2: 23	for she was t out of man."
Lev	6: 4	must return what he has stolen or t
Nu	8: 16	I have t them as my own in place
	19: 3	it is to be t outside the camp
Ecc	3: 14	added to it and nothing t from it.
Isa	6: 7	your guilt is t away and your sin
Zec	3: 4	"See, I have t away your sin,
Mt	13: 12	even what he has will be t from him
	24: 40	one will be t and the other left.
	26: 39	may this cup be t from me.
Mk	16: 19	he was t up into heaven
Ac	1: 9	he was t up before their very eyes,
Ro	5: 13	But sin is not t into account
1Ti	3: 16	was t up in glory.

TAKES (TAKE)

1Ki	20: 11	should not boast like one who t it

Ps   5: 4 You are not a God who *t* pleasure
       34: 8 blessed is the man who *t* refuge
Lk   6: 30 and if anyone *t* what belongs to you
Jn   1: 29 who *t* away the sin of the world!
       10: 18 No-one *t* it from me, but I lay it
Rev   22: 19 And if anyone *t* words away

TAKING (TAKE)

Ac   15: 14 by *t* from the Gentiles a people
Php   2: 7 *t* the very nature of a servant,

TALENT

Mt   25: 15 to another one *t*, each according

TALES*

1Ti   4: 7 with godless myths and old wives' *t*

TALL

1Sa   17: 4 He was over nine feet *t*.
1Ch   11: 23 who was seven and a half feet *t*.

TAMAR

   1. Wife of Judah's sons Er and Onan (Ge
38:1-10). Tricked Judah into fathering children
when he refused her his third son (Ge 38:11-30).
   2. Daughter of David, raped by Amnon (2Sa
13).

TAMBOURINE

Ps   150: 4 praise him with *t* and dancing,

TAME* (TAMED)

Jas   3: 8 but no man can *t* the tongue.

TAMED* (TAME)

Jas   3: 7 the sea are being *t* and have been *t*

TARSHISH

Jnh   1: 3 from the LORD and headed for *T*.

TARSUS

Ac   9: 11 ask for a man from *T* named Saul,

TASK (TASKS)

1Ch   29: 1 The *t* is great, because this palatial
Mk   13: 34 each with his assigned *t*,
Ac   20: 24 complete the *t* the Lord Jesus has
1Co   3: 5 the Lord has assigned to each his *t*.
2Co   2: 16 And who is equal to such a *t*?
1Ti   3: 1 an overseer, he desires a noble *t*.

TASKS (TASK)

Pr   31: 17 her arms are strong for her *t*.

TASTE (TASTED TASTY)

Ps   34: 8 *T* and see that the LORD is good;
      119: 103 sweet are your words to my *t*,
Pr   24: 13 from the comb is sweet to your *t*.
SS   2: 3 and his fruit is sweet to my *t*.
Col   2: 21 Do not *t*! Do not touch!"?
Heb   2: 9 the grace of God he might *t* death

TASTED (TASTE)

Eze   3: 3 it *t* as sweet as honey in my mouth.
1Pe   2: 3 now that you have *t* that the Lord
Rev   10: 10 It *t* as sweet as honey in my mouth,

TASTY (TASTE)

Ge   27: 4 Prepare me the kind of *t* food I like

TATTOO*

Lev   19: 28 or put *t* marks on yourselves.

TAUGHT (TEACH)

1Ki   4: 33 He also *t* about animals and birds,
2Ki   17: 28 *t* them how to worship the LORD.
2Ch   17: 9 They *t* throughout Judah,
Ps   119: 102 for you yourself have *t* me.
Pr   4: 4 he *t* me and said,
       31: 1 an oracle his mother *t* him:
Isa   29: 13 is made up only of rules *t* by men.
       50: 4 ear to listen like one being *t*.
Mt   7: 29 he *t* as one who had authority,
       15: 9 their teachings are but rules *t*
Lk   4: 15 He *t* in their synagogues,
Ac   20: 20 have *t* you publicly and from house
1Co   2: 13 but in words *t* by the Spirit,
Gal   1: 12 nor was I *t* it; rather, I received it
1Ti   1: 20 to Satan to be *t* not to blaspheme.
1Jn   2: 27 just as it has *t* you, remain in him.

TAX (TAXES)

Mt   11: 19 a friend of *t* collectors and "sinners
       17: 24 of the two-drachma *t* came to Peter

TAXES (TAX)

Mt   22: 17 Is it right to pay *t* to Caesar or not
Ro   13: 7 If you owe *t*, pay *t*; if revenue,

TEACH (TAUGHT TEACHER TEACHERS TEACHES TEACHING TEACHINGS)

Ex   4: 12 and will *t* you what to say."
       18: 20 *T* them the decrees and laws,
       33: 13 *t* me your ways so I may know you
Lev   10: 11 and you must *t* the Israelites all
Dt   4: 9 *T* them to your children
        6: 1 me to *t* you to observe
        8: 3 to *t* you that man does not live
       11: 19 *T* them to your children, talking
1Sa   12: 23 I will *t* you the way that is good
1Ki   8: 36 *T* them the right way to live,
Job   12: 7 ask the animals, and they will *t* you
Ps   32: 8 *t* you in the way you should go;
       34: 11 I will *t* you the fear of the LORD.
       51: 13 I will *t* transgressors your ways,
       78: 5 forefathers to *t* their children,
       90: 12 *T* us to number our days aright,
      119: 33 *T* me, O LORD, to follow your
      143: 10 *T* me to do your will,
Pr   9: 9 *t* a righteous man and he will add
Jer   31: 34 No longer will a man *t* his neighbour
Mic   4: 2 He will *t* us his ways,
Lk   11: 1 said to him, "Lord, *t* us to pray,
       12: 12 for the Holy Spirit will *t* you
Jn   14: 26 will *t* you all things and will remind
Ro   2: 21 who *t* others, do you not *t* yourself?
       15: 4 in the past was written to *t* us,
1Ti   2: 12 I do not permit a woman to *t*
        3: 2 respectable, hospitable, able to *t*,
2Ti   2: 2 also be qualified to *t* others.
        2: 24 kind to everyone, able to *t*,
Tit   2: 1 You must *t* what is in accord
        2: 15 then, are the things you should *t*.
Heb   8: 11 No longer will a man *t* his neighbour
Jas   3: 1 know that we who *t* will be judged
1Jn   2: 27 you do not need anyone to *t* you.

TEACHER (TEACH)

Ecc   1: 1 The words of the *T*, son of David,

Mt   10: 24 "A student is not above his *t*,
      13: 52 "Therefore every *t*
      23: 10 Nor are you to be called '*t*,'
Lk   6: 40 A student is not above his *t*,
Jn   3: 2 we know you are a *t* who has come
      13: 14 and *T*, have washed your feet,

TEACHERS (TEACH)

Ps   119: 99 I have more insight than all my *t*,
Pr   5: 13 I would not obey my *t*
Lk   20: 46 "Beware of the *t* of the law.
1Co   12: 28 third *t*, then workers of miracles,
Eph   4: 11 and some to be pastors and *t*,
2Ti   4: 3 around them a great number of *t*
Heb   5: 12 by this time you ought to be *t*,
Jas   3: 1 of you should presume to be *t*,
2Pe   2: 1 as there will be false *t* among you.

TEACHES (TEACH)

Ps   25: 9 and *t* them his way.
      94: 10 Does he who *t* man lack
Pr   15: 33 of the LORD *t* a man wisdom,
Isa   48: 17 who *t* you what is best for you,
Mt   5: 19 *t* these commands will be called
1Ti   6: 3 If anyone *t* false doctrines
Tit   2: 12 It *t* us to say "No" to ungodliness
1Jn   2: 27 his anointing *t* you about all things

TEACHING (TEACH)

Ezr   7: 10 to *t* its decrees and laws in Israel.
Pr   1: 8 and do not forsake your mother's *t*.
       3: 1 My son, do not forget my *t*,
       6: 23 this *t* is a light,
Mt   28: 20 *t* them to obey everything I have
Jn   7: 17 whether my *t* comes from God or
       8: 31 to my *t*, you are really my disciples.
      14: 23 loves me, he will obey my *t*.
Ac   2: 42 themselves to the apostles' *t*
Ro   12: 7 let him serve; if it is *t*, let him teach;
Eph   4: 14 and there by every wind of *t*
2Th   3: 6 to the *t* you received from us.
1Ti   4: 13 of Scripture, to preaching and to *t*.
       5: 17 whose work is preaching and *t*.
       6: 3 Lord Jesus Christ and to godly *t*,
2Ti   3: 16 is God-breathed and is useful for *t*,
Tit   1: 11 by *t* things they ought not
       2: 7 In your *t* show integrity,
Heb   5: 13 with the *t* about righteousness.
2Jn   : 9 and does not continue in the *t*

TEACHINGS (TEACH)

Pr   7: 2 guard my *t* as the apple of your eye.
2Th   2: 15 hold to the *t* we passed on to you,
Heb   6: 1 leave the elementary *t* about Christ

TEAR (TEARS)

Rev   7: 17 God will wipe away every *t*
      21: 4 He will wipe every *t*

TEARS (TEAR)

Ps   126: 5 Those who sow in *t*
Isa   25: 8 LORD will wipe away the *t*
Jer   31: 16 and your eyes from *t*,
      50: 4 in *t* to seek the LORD their God.
Lk   7: 38 she began to wet his feet with her *t*.
2Co   2: 4 anguish of heart and with many *t*,
Php   3: 18 and now say again even with *t*,

TEETH (TOOTH)

Job   19: 20 with only the skin of my *t*.

Ps   35: 16 they gnashed their *t* at me.
Jer   31: 29 and the children's *t* are set on edge
Mt   8: 12 will be weeping and gnashing of *t*."

TEMPER (EVEN-TEMPERED HOT-TEMPERED ILL-TEMPERED QUICK-TEMPERED)

Pr   16: 32 a man who controls his *t*

TEMPERANCE see SELF-CONTROL

TEMPERATE*

1Ti   3: 2 *t*, self-controlled, respectable,
       3: 11 not malicious talkers but *t*
Tit   2: 2 Teach the older men to be *t*,

TEMPEST

Ps   50: 3 and around him a *t* rages.
      55: 8 far from the *t* and storm."

TEMPLE (TEMPLES)

1Ki   6: 1 began to build the *t* of the LORD.
       6: 38 the *t* was finished in all its details
       8: 10 the cloud filled the *t* of the LORD.
       8: 27 How much less this *t* I have built!
2Ch   36: 19 They set fire to God's *t*
      36: 23 me to build a *t* for him at Jerusalem
Ezr   6: 14 finished building the *t* according
Ps   27: 4 and to seek him in his *t*.
Isa   6: 1 and the train of his robe filled the *t*.
Eze   10: 4 cloud filled the *t*, and the court was
      43: 4 glory of the LORD entered the *t*
Hab   2: 20 But the LORD is in his holy *t*;
Mt   12: 6 that one greater than the *t* is here.
      26: 61 'I am able to destroy the *t* of God
      27: 51 of the *t* was torn in two from top
Lk   21: 5 about how the *t* was adorned
Jn   2: 14 In the *t* courts he found men selling
1Co   3: 16 that you yourselves are God's *t*
       6: 19 you not know that your body is a *t*
2Co   6: 16 For we are the *t* of the living God.
Rev   21: 22 I did not see a *t* in the city,

TEMPLES (TEMPLE)

Ac   17: 24 does not live in *t* built by hands.

TEMPORARY

2Co   4: 18 what is seen is *t*, but what is unseen

TEMPT* (TEMPTATION TEMPTED TEMPTER TEMPTING)

1Co   7: 5 again so that Satan will not *t* you
Jas   1: 13 does he *t* anyone; but each one is

TEMPTATION* (TEMPT)

Mt   6: 13 And lead us not into *t*,
      26: 41 pray so that you will not fall into *t*.
Mk   14: 38 pray so that you will not fall into *t*.
Lk   11: 4 And lead us not into *t*.'"
      22: 40 "Pray that you will not fall into *t*."
      22: 46 pray so that you will not fall into *t*
1Co   10: 13 No *t* has seized you except what is
1Ti   6: 9 want to get rich fall into *t*

TEMPTED* (TEMPT)

Mk   4: 1 into the desert to be *t* by the devil.
       1: 13 was in the desert forty days, being *t*
Lk   4: 2 for forty days he was *t* by the devil.
1Co   10: 13 But when you are *t*, he will
      10: 13 he will not let you be *t*

Gal	6: 1	yourself, or you also may be *t*.
1Th	3: 5	way the tempter might have *t* you
Heb	2: 18	able to help those who are being *t*.
	2: 18	he himself suffered when he was *t*,
	4: 15	but we have one who has been *t*
Jas	1: 13	For God cannot be *t* by evil,
	1: 13	When *t*, no-one should say,
	1: 14	each one is *t* when, by his own evil

TEMPTER* (TEMPT)

Mt	4: 3	The *t* came to him and said,
1Th	3: 5	some way the *t* might have

TEMPTING* (TEMPT)

Lk	4: 13	the devil had finished all this *t*,
Jas	1: 13	no-one should say, "God is *t* me."

TEN (TENTH TITHE TITHES)

Ex	34: 28	covenant—the *T* Commandments.
Lev	26: 8	of you will chase *t* thousand,
Dt	4: 13	covenant, the *T* Commandments,
	10: 4	The *T* Commandments he had
Ps	91: 7	*t* thousand at your right hand,
Da	7: 24	*t* horns are *t* kings who will come
Mt	25: 1	will be like *t* virgins who took
	25: 28	it to the one who has the *t* talents.
Lk	15: 8	suppose a woman has *t* silver coins
Rev	12: 3	and *t* horns and seven crowns

TENANTS

Mt	21: 34	servants to the *t* to collect his fruit.

TEND

Jer	23: 2	to the shepherds who *t* my people:
Eze	34: 14	I will *t* them in a good pasture,

TENDERNESS*

Isa	63: 15	Your *t* and compassion are
Php	2: 1	fellowship with the Spirit, if any *t*

TENT (TENTMAKER TENTS)

Ex	27: 21	In the *T* of Meeting,
	40: 2	"Set up the tabernacle, the *T*
Isa	54: 2	"Enlarge the place of your *t*,
2Co	5: 1	that if the earthly *t* we live
2Pe	1: 13	as long as I live in the *t* of this body,

TENTH (TEN)

Ge	14: 20	Abram gave him a *t* of everything.
Nu	18: 26	you must present a *t* of that tithe
Dt	14: 22	Be sure to set aside a *t*
1Sa	8: 15	He will take a *t* of your grain
Lk	11: 42	you give God a *t* of your mint,
	18: 12	I fast twice a week and give a *t*
Heb	7: 4	patriarch Abraham gave him a *t*

TENTMAKER* (TENT)

Ac	18: 3	and because he was a *t* as they were

TENTS (TENT)

Ge	13: 12	and pitched his *t* near Sodom.
Ps	84: 10	than dwell in the *t* of the wicked.

TERAH

Ge	11: 31	*T* took his son Abram, his

TERRIBLE (TERROR)

2Ti	3: 1	There will be *t* times

TERRIFIED (TERROR)

Dt	7: 21	Do not be *t* by them,
	20: 3	do not be *t* or give way to panic
Ps	90: 7	and *t* by your indignation.
Mt	14: 26	walking on the lake, they were *t*.
	17: 6	they fell face down to the ground, *t*.
	27: 54	they were *t*, and exclaimed,
Mk	4: 41	They were *t* and asked each other,

TERRIFYING (TERROR)

Heb	12: 21	The sight was so *t* that Moses said,

TERRITORY

2Co	10: 16	done in another man's *t*.

TERROR (TERRIBLE TERRIFIED TERRIFYING)

Dt	2: 25	very day I will begin to put the *t*
	28: 67	of the *t* that will fill your hearts
Job	9: 34	so that his *t* would frighten me no
Ps	91: 5	You will not fear the *t* of night,
Pr	21: 15	but *t* to evildoers.
Isa	13: 8	*T* will seize them,
	24: 17	*T* and pit and snare await you,
	51: 13	live in constant *t* every day
	54: 14	*T* will be far removed;
Lk	21: 26	Men will faint from *t*, apprehensive
Ro	13: 3	For rulers hold no *t*

TEST (TESTED TESTING TESTS)

Dt	6: 16	Do not *t* the LORD your God
Jdg	3: 1	to *t* all those Israelites who had not
1Ki	10: 1	came to *t* him with hard questions.
1Ch	29: 17	that you *t* the heart and are pleased
Ps	26: 2	*T* me, O LORD, and try me,
	78: 18	They wilfully put God to the *t*
	106: 14	wasteland they put God to the *t*.
	139: 23	*t* me and know my anxious
Jer	11: 20	and *t* the heart and mind,
Lk	4: 12	put the Lord your God to the *t*.' "
Ac	5: 9	How could you agree to *t* the Spirit
Ro	12: 2	Then you will be able to *t*
1Co	3: 13	and the fire will *t* the quality
	10: 9	We should not *t* the Lord,
2Co	13: 5	unless, of course, you fail the *t*?
1Th	5: 21	*T* everything.
Jas	1: 12	because when he has stood the *t*,
1Jn	4: 1	*t* the spirits to see whether they are

TESTAMENT see COVENANT

TESTED (TEST)

Ge	22: 1	Some time later God *t* Abraham.
Job	23: 10	when he has *t* me, I will come forth
	34: 36	that Job might be *t* to the utmost
Ps	66: 10	For you, O God, *t* us;
Pr	27: 21	man is *t* by the praise he receives.
Isa	28: 16	a *t* stone,
	48: 10	I have *t* you in the furnace
1Ti	3: 10	They must first be *t*; and then
Heb	11: 17	By faith Abraham, when God *t* him

TESTIFIES (TESTIFY)

Jn	5: 32	There is another who *t* in my favour,
Ro	8: 16	The Spirit himself *t*

TESTIFY (TESTIFIES TESTIMONY)

Pr	24: 28	Do not *t* against your neighbour
Jn	1: 7	a witness to *t* concerning that light,
	1: 34	and I *t* that this is the Son of God."

Jn 5: 39 are the Scriptures that *t* about me,
7: 7 because I *t* that what it does is evil.
15: 26 he will *t* about me; but you
Ac 4: 33 continued to *t* to the resurrection
10: 43 All the prophets *t* about him that
2Ti 1: 8 ashamed to *t* about our Lord,
1Jn 4: 14 *t* that the Father has sent his Son
5: 7 For there are three that *t*: the Spirit

TESTIMONY (TESTIFY)

Ex 20: 16 "You shall not give false *t*
31: 18 gave him the two tablets of the *T*,
Nu 35: 30 only on the *t* of witnesses.
Dt 19: 18 giving false *t* against his brother,
Pr 12: 17 A truthful witness gives honest *t*,
Isa 8: 20 and to the *t*! If they do not speak
Mt 15: 19 sexual immorality, theft, false *t*,
24: 14 preached in the whole world as a *t*
Lk 18: 20 not give false *t*, honour your father
Jn 2: 25 He did not need man's *t* about man
21: 24 We know that his *t* is true.
1Jn 5: 9 but God's *t* is greater because it is
Rev 12: 11 and by the word of their *t*;

TESTING (TEST)

Lk 8: 13 but in the time of *t* they fall away.
Heb 3: 8 during the time of *t* in the desert,
Jas 1: 3 because you know that the *t*

TESTS (TEST)

Pr 17: 3 but the LORD *t* the heart.
1Th 2: 4 but God, who *t* our hearts.

THADDAEUS

Apostle (Mt 10:3; Mk 3:18); probably also
known as Judas son of James (Lk 6:16; Ac 1:13).

THANK (THANKFUL THANKFULNESS THANKS THANKSGIVING)

Php 1: 3 I *t* my God every time I remember
1Th 3: 9 How can we *t* God enough for you

THANKFUL (THANK)

Col 3: 15 And be *t*.
Heb 12: 28 let us be *t*, and so worship God

THANKFULNESS (THANK)

1Co 10: 30 If I take part in the meal with *t*,
Col 2: 7 taught, and overflowing with *t*.

THANKS (THANK)

1Ch 16: 8 Give *t* to the LORD, call
Ne 12: 31 assigned two large choirs to give *t*.
Ps 7: 17 I will give *t* to the LORD
28: 7 and I will give *t* to him in song.
30: 12 my God, I will give you *t* for ever.
35: 18 I will give you *t* in the great
75: 1 we give *t*, for your Name is near;
100: 4 give *t* to him and praise his name.
107: 1 Give *t* to the LORD, for he is good;
118: 28 are my God, and I will give you *t*;
136: 1 Give *t* to the LORD, for he is good.
Ro 1: 21 as God nor gave *t* to him,
1Co 11: 24 when he had given *t*, he broke it
15: 57 *t* be to God! He gives us the victory
2Co 2: 14 *t* be to God, who always leads us
9: 15 *T* be to God for his indescribable
1Th 5: 18 give *t* in all circumstances,
Rev 4: 9 and *t* to him who sits on the throne

THANKSGIVING (THANK)

Ps 95: 2 Let us come before him with *t*
100: 4 Enter his gates with *t*
1Co 10: 16 cup of *t* for which we give thanks
Php 4: 6 by prayer and petition, with *t*,
1Ti 4: 3 created to be received with *t*

THEFT (THIEF)

Mt 15: 19 sexual immorality, *t*, false

THEFTS* (THIEF)

Rev 9: 21 their sexual immorality or their *t*.

THEME*

Ps 45: 1 My heart is stirred by a noble *t*
119: 54 Your decrees are the *t* of my song

THIEF (THEFT THEFTS THIEVES)

Ex 22: 3 A *t* must certainly make restitution
Pr 6: 30 Men do not despise a *t* if he steals
Lk 12: 39 at what hour the *t* was coming,
1Th 5: 2 day of the Lord will come like a *t*
1Pe 4: 15 or *t* or any other kind of criminal,
Rev 16: 15 I come like a *t*! Blessed is he who

THIEVES (THIEF)

Mt 6: 19 and where *t* break in and steal.
Jn 10: 8 whoever came before me were *t*
1Co 6: 10 nor homosexual offenders nor *t*

THINK (THINKING THOUGHT THOUGHTS)

Ps 63: 6 I *t* of you through the watches
Isa 44: 19 No-one stops to *t*,
Mt 22: 42 "What do you *t* about the Christ?
Ro 12: 3 Do not *t* of yourself more highly
Php 4: 8 praiseworthy—*t* about such things

THINKING (THINK)

Pr 23: 7 who is always *t* about the cost.
1Co 14: 20 Brothers, stop *t* like children.
2Pe 3: 1 to stimulate you to wholesome *t*.

THIRST (THIRSTS THIRSTY)

Ps 69: 21 and gave me vinegar for my *t*.
Mt 5: 6 Blessed are those who hunger and *t*
Jn 4: 14 the water I give him will never *t*.
2Co 11: 27 I have known hunger and *t*
Rev 7: 16 never again will they *t*.

THIRSTS (THIRST)

Ps 42: 2 My soul *t* for God,

THIRSTY (THIRST)

Ps 107: 9 for he satisfies the *t*
Pr 25: 21 if he is *t*, give him water to drink.
Isa 55: 1 "Come, all you who are *t*,
Mt 25: 35 I was *t* and you gave me something
Jn 7: 37 "If anyone is *t*, let him come to me
Ro 12: 20 if he is *t*, give him something
Rev 21: 6 To him who is *t* I will give to drink
22: 17 Whoever is *t*, let him come;

THOMAS

Apostle (Mt 10:3; Mk 3:18; Lk 6:15; Jn 11:16;
14:5; 21:2; Ac 1:13). Doubted resurrection (Jn
20:24-28).

THONGS

Mk 1: 7 *t* of whose sandals I am not worthy

THORN (THORN-BUSHES THORNS)

2Co 12: 7 there was given me a *t* in my flesh,

THORN-BUSHES (THORN)

Lk   6: 44 People do not pick figs from *t*,

THORNS (THORN)

Ge   3: 18 It will produce *t* and thistles
Nu   33: 55 in your eyes and *t* in your sides.
Mt   13: 7 fell among *t*, which grew up
     27: 29 and then twisted together a crown of *t*
Heb   6: 8 But land that produces *t*

THOUGHT (THINK)

Pr   14: 15 a prudent man gives *t* to his steps.
     21: 29 an upright man gives *t* to his ways.
1Co 13: 11 I talked like a child, I *t* like a child,

THOUGHTS (THINK)

1Ch 28: 9 every motive behind the *t*.
Ps   94: 11 The LORD knows the *t* of man;
    139: 23 test me and know my anxious *t*.
Isa 55: 8 "For my *t* are not your *t*,
Mt   15: 19 For out of the heart come evil *t*,
1Co   2: 11 among men knows the *t* of a man
Heb   4: 12 it judges the *t* and attitudes

THREE

Ge   6: 10 Noah had *t* sons: Shem, Ham
Ex   23: 14 "*T* times a year you are
Dt   19: 15 the testimony of two or *t* witnesses.
2Sa 23: 8 a Tahkemonite, was chief of the *T*;
Pr   30: 15 "There are *t* things that are never
     30: 18 "There are *t* things that are too
     30: 21 "Under *t* things the earth trembles,
     30: 29 "There are *t* things that are stately
Ecc   4: 12 of *t* strands is not quickly broken.
Da   3: 24 "Wasn't it *t* men that we tied up
Am   1: 3 "For *t* sins of Damascus,
Jnh   1: 17 inside the fish *t* days and *t* nights.
Mt   12: 40 so the Son of Man will be *t* days
     12: 40 *t* nights in the belly of a huge fish,
     12: 40 *t* nights in the heart of the earth.
     17: 4 I will put up *t* shelters—one
     18: 20 or *t* come together in my name,
     26: 34 you will disown me *t* times."
     26: 75 you will disown me *t* times."
     27: 63 'After *t* days I will rise again.'
Mk   8: 31 and after *t* days rise again.
      9: 5 Let us put up *t* shelters—one
     14: 30 yourself will disown me *t* times."
Jn   2: 19 and I will raise it again in *t* days."
1Co 13: 13 And now these *t* remain: faith,
     14: 27 or at the most *t*—should speak,
2Co 13: 1 testimony of two or *t* witnesses."
1Jn   5: 7 For there are *t* that testify:

THRESHER* (THRESHING-FLOOR)

1Co   9: 10 ploughman ploughs and the *t* threshes,

THRESHING-FLOOR (THRESHER)

Ru   3: 6 So she went down to the *t*
2Sa 24: 18 an altar to the LORD on the *t*
Lk   3: 17 is in his hand to clear his *t*

THREW (THROW)

Da   6: 16 and *t* him into the lions' den.
Jnh   1: 15 took Jonah and *t* him overboard,

THRIVE

Pr   29: 2 When the righteous *t*, the people

THROAT (THROATS)

Ps   5: 9 Their *t* is an open grave;
Pr   23: 2 and put a knife to your *t*

THROATS (THROAT)

Ro   3: 13 "Their *t* are open graves;

THROB*

Isa 60: 5 your heart will *t* and swell with joy;

THRONE (ENTHRONED ENTHRONES THRONES)

2Sa   7: 16 your *t* will be established for ever
1Ch 17: 12 and I will establish his *t* for ever.
Ps   11: 4 the LORD is on his heavenly *t*.
     45: 6 Your *t*, O God, will last for ever
     47: 8 God is seated on his holy *t*.
     89: 14 justice are the foundation of your *t*;
Isa   6: 1 I saw the Lord seated on a *t*,
     66: 1 "Heaven is my *t*
Eze 28: 2 I sit on the *t* of a god
Da   7: 9 His *t* was flaming with fire,
Mt   19: 28 Son of Man sits on his glorious *t*,
Ac   7: 49 prophet says: " 'Heaven is my *t*,
Heb   1: 8 "Your *t*, O God, will last for ever
      4: 16 Let us then approach the *t* of grace
     12: 2 at the right hand of the *t* of God.
Rev   3: 21 sat down with my Father on his *t*.
      3: 21 the right to sit with me on my *t*,
      4: 2 there before me was a *t* in heaven
      4: 10 They lay their crowns before the *t*
     20: 11 Then I saw a great white *t*
     22: 3 *t* of God and of the Lamb will be

THRONES (THRONE)

Mt   19: 28 me will also sit on twelve *t*,
Rev   4: 4 throne were twenty-four other *t*,

THROW (THREW)

Jn   8: 7 the first to *t* a stone at her."
Heb 10: 35 So do not *t* away your confidence;
     12: 1 Let us *t* off everything that hinders

THUNDER (THUNDERS)

Ps   93: 4 Mightier than the *t*
Mk   3: 17 which means Sons of *T*); Andrew,

THUNDERS (THUNDER)

Job 37: 5 God's voice *t* in marvellous ways;
Ps   29: 3 the God of glory *t*,
Rev 10: 3 the voices of the seven *t* spoke.

THWART* (THWARTED)

Isa 14: 27 has purposed, and who can *t* him?

THWARTED (THWART)

Job 42: 2 no plan of yours can be *t*.

THYATIRA

Rev   2: 18 the angel of the church in *T* write:

TIBNI

King of Israel (1Ki 16:21-22).

TIDINGS

Isa 40: 9 You who bring good *t* to Jerusalem
     52: 7 who bring good *t*,

TIES

Hos 11: 4 with *t* of love;
Mt 12: 29 unless he first *t* up the strong man?

TIGHT*

Jas 1: 26 and yet does not keep a *t* rein

TIGHT-FISTED*

Dt 15: 7 or *t* towards your poor brother.

TIME (TIMES)

Est 4: 14 come to royal position for such a *t*
Ecc 3: 1 There is a *t* for everything,
8: 5 wise heart will know the proper *t*
Da 7: 25 to him for a *t*, times and half a *t*.
12: 7 "It will be for a *t*, times and half a *t*.
Hos 10: 12 for it is *t* to seek the LORD,
Jn 2: 4 Jesus replied, "My *t* has not yet
17: 1 prayed: "Father, the *t* has come.
Ro 9: 9 "At the appointed *t* I will return,
13: 11 understanding the present *t*.
1Co 7: 29 brothers, is that the *t* is short.
2Co 6: 2 now is the *t* of God's favour,
2Ti 1: 9 Jesus before the beginning of *t*,
Tit 1: 2 promised before the beginning of *t*,
Heb 9: 28 and he will appear a second *t*,
10: 12 for all *t* one sacrifice for sins,
1Pe 4: 17 For it is *t* for judgment to begin

TIMES (TIME)

Ps 9: 9 a stronghold in *t* of trouble.
31: 15 My *t* are in your hands;
62: 8 Trust in him at all *t*, O people;
Pr 17: 17 A friend loves at all *t*,
Isa 46: 10 from ancient *t*, what is still to come
Am 5: 13 for the *t* are evil.
Mt 16: 3 cannot interpret the signs of the *t*.
18: 21 how many *t* shall I forgive my
Ac 1: 7 "It is not for you to know the *t*
Rev 12: 14 *t* and half a time, out

TIMID (TIMIDITY)

1Th 5: 14 encourage the *t*, help the weak,

TIMIDITY* (TIMID)

2Ti 1: 7 For God did not give us a spirit of *t*

TIMOTHY

Believer from Lystra (Ac 16:1). Joined Paul on second missionary journey (Ac 16-20). Sent to settle problems at Corinth (1Co 4:17; 16:10). Led church at Ephesus (1Ti 1:3). Co-writer with Paul (1Th 1:1; 2Th 1:1; Phm 1).

TIP

Job 33: 2 my words are on the *t* of my tongue

TIRE (TIRED)

2Th 3: 13 never *t* of doing what is right.

TIRED (TIRE)

Ex 17: 12 When Moses' hands grew *t*,
Isa 40: 28 He will not grow *t* or weary,

TITHE (TEN)

Lev 27: 30 "'A *t* of everything from the land,
Dt 12: 17 eat in your own towns the *t*
Mal 3: 10 the whole *t* into the storehouse,

TITHES (TEN)

Nu 18: 21 give to the Levites all the *t* in Israel
Mal 3: 8 'How do we rob you?' "In *t*

TITUS*

Gentile co-worker of Paul (Gal 2:1-3; 2Ti 4:10); sent to Corinth (2Co 2:13; 7-8; 12:18), Crete (Tit 1:4-5).

TODAY

Ps 2: 7 *t* I have become your Father.
95: 7 *T*, if you hear his voice,
Mt 6: 11 Give us *t* our daily bread.
Lk 2: 11 *T* in the town of David a Saviour has
23: 43 *t* you will be with me in paradise."
Ac 13: 33 *t* I have become your Father.'
Heb 1: 5 *t* I have become your Father"?
3: 7 "*T*, if you hear his voice,
3: 13 daily, as long as it is called *T*,
5: 5 *t* I have become your Father."
13: 8 Christ is the same yesterday and *t*

TOIL (TOILED TOILING)

Ge 3: 17 through painful *t* you will eat of it

TOILED (TOIL)

2Co 11: 27 and *t* and have often gone

TOILING (TOIL)

2Th 3: 8 *t* so that we would not be a burden

TOLERANCE* (TOLERATE)

Ro 2: 4 for the riches of his kindness, *t*,

TOLERATE (TOLERANCE)

Hab 1: 13 you cannot *t* wrong.
Rev 2: 2 that you cannot *t* wicked men,

TOMB

Mt 27: 65 make the *t* as secure as you know
Lk 24: 2 the stone rolled away from the *t*,

TOMORROW

Pr 27: 1 Do not boast about *t*,
Isa 22: 13 "for *t* we die!"
Mt 6: 34 Therefore do not worry about *t*,
1Co 15: 32 for *t* we die."
Jas 4: 13 "Today or *t* we will go to this

TONGUE (TONGUES)

Ex 4: 10 I am slow of speech and *t*."
Job 33: 2 my words are on the tip of my *t*.
Ps 5: 9 with their *t* they speak deceit.
34: 13 keep your *t* from evil
37: 30 and his *t* speaks what is just.
39: 1 and keep my *t* from sin;
51: 14 my *t* will sing of your righteousness
52: 4 O you deceitful *t*!
71: 24 My *t* will tell of your righteous acts
119: 172 May my *t* sing of your word,
137: 6 May my *t* cling to the roof
139: 4 Before a word is on my *t*
Pr 6: 17 a lying *t*,
10: 19 but he who holds his *t* is wise.
12: 18 but the *t* of the wise brings healing.
15: 4 The *t* that brings healing is a tree

Pr 17: 20 he whose *t* is deceitful falls
21: 23 He who guards his mouth and his *t*
25: 15 and a gentle *t* can break a bone.
26: 28 A lying *t* hates those it hurts,
28: 23 than he who has a flattering *t*.
31: 26 and faithful instruction is on her *t*.
SS 4: 11 milk and honey are under your *t*.
Isa 32: 4 and the stammering *t* will be fluent
45: 23 by me every *t* will swear.
50: 4 has given me an instructed *t*,
59: 3 and your *t* mutters wicked things.
Lk 16: 24 of his finger in water and cool my *t*,
Ro 14: 11 every *t* will confess to God.'"
1Co 14: 2 speaks in a *t* does not speak to men
14: 4 He who speaks in a *t* edifies himself
14: 9 intelligible words with your *t*,
14: 13 in a *t* should pray that he may
14: 19 than ten thousand words in a *t*.
14: 26 revelation, a *t* or an interpretation.
14: 27 If anyone speaks in a *t*, two—
Php 2: 11 every *t* confess that Jesus Christ is
Jas 1: 26 does not keep a tight rein on his *t*,
3: 5 Likewise the *t* is a small part
3: 8 but no man can tame the *t*.
1Jn 3: 18 or *t* but with actions and in truth.

TONGUES (TONGUE)

Ps 12: 4 "We will triumph with our *t*;
126: 2 our *t* with songs of joy.
Isa 28: 11 with foreign lips and strange *t*
66: 18 and gather all nations and *t*,
Jer 23: 31 the prophets who wag their own *t*
Mk 16: 17 in new *t*; they will pick up snakes
Ac 2: 3 to be *t* of fire that separated
2: 4 and began to speak in other *t*
10: 46 For they heard them speaking in *t*
19: 6 and they spoke in *t* and prophesied
Ro 3: 13 their *t* practise deceit."
1Co 12: 10 still another the interpretation of *t*.
12: 28 speaking in different kinds of *t*.
12: 30 Do all speak in *t*? Do all interpret?
13: 1 If I speak in the *t* of men
13: 8 where there are *t*, they will be
14: 5 greater than one who speaks in *t*,
14: 18 speak in *t* more than all of you.
14: 21 "Through men of strange *t*
14: 39 and do not forbid speaking in *t*.

TOOK (TAKE)

Isa 53: 4 Surely he *t* up our infirmities
Mt 8: 17 "He *t* up our infirmities
26: 26 they were eating, Jesus *t* bread,
26: 27 Then he *t* the cup, gave thanks
1Co 11: 23 the night he was betrayed, *t* bread,
11: 25 after supper he *t* the cup, saying,
Php 3: 12 for which Christ Jesus *t* hold of me.

TOOTH (TEETH)

Ex 21: 24 eye for eye, *t* for *t*, hand for hand,
Mt 5: 38 "Eye for eye, and *t* for *t*."

TOP

Dt 28: 13 you will always be at the *t*,
Isa 1: 6 of your foot to the *t* of your head
Mt 27: 51 torn in two from *t* to bottom.

TORMENT (TORMENTED TORMENTORS)

Lk 16: 28 also come to this place of *t*.'
2Co 12: 7 a messenger of Satan, to *t* me.

TORMENTED (TORMENT)

Rev 20: 10 They will be *t* day and night

TORMENTORS (TORMENT)

Ps 137: 3 our *t* demanded songs of joy;

TORN

Gal 4: 15 you would have *t* out your eyes
Php 1: 23 I do not know! I am *t*

TORTURED*

Heb 11: 35 Others were *t* and refused

TOSSED (TOSSING)

Eph 4: 14 *t* back and forth by the waves,
Jas 1: 6 of the sea, blown and *t* by the wind.

TOSSING (TOSSED)

Isa 57: 20 But the wicked are like the *t* sea,

TOUCH (TOUCHED TOUCHES)

Ge 3: 3 you must not *t* it, or you will die.'"
Ex 19: 12 go up the mountain or *t* the foot
Ps 105: 15 "Do not *t* my anointed ones;
Mt 9: 21 If I only *t* his cloak, I will be healed
Lk 18: 15 babies to Jesus to have him *t* them.
24: 39 It is I myself! *T* me and see;
2Co 6: 17 *T* no unclean thing,
Col 2: 21 Do not taste! Do not *t*!"?

TOUCHED (TOUCH)

1Sa 10: 26 men whose hearts God had *t*.
Isa 6: 7 With it he *t* my mouth and said,
Mt 14: 36 and all who *t* him were healed.
Lk 8: 45 "Who *t* me?" Jesus asked.
1Jn 1: 1 looked at and our hands have *t*—

TOUCHES (TOUCH)

Ex 19: 12 Whoever *t* the mountain shall
Zec 2: 8 for whoever *t* you *t* the apple

TOWER

Ge 11: 4 with a *t* that reaches to the heavens
Pr 18: 10 of the LORD is a strong *t*;

TOWN (TOWNS)

Mt 2: 23 and lived in a *t* called Nazareth.
Lk 4: 24 prophet is accepted in his home *t*.

TOWNS (TOWN)

Nu 35: 2 to give the Levites *t* to live
35: 15 These six *t* will be a place of refuge
Jer 11: 13 as many gods as you have *t*,
Mt 9: 35 Jesus went through all the *t*

TRACING*

Ro 11: 33 and his paths beyond *t* out!

TRACK

Job 14: 16 but not keep *t* of my sin.

TRADERS (TRADING)

1Ti 1: 10 for slave *t* and liars and perjurers—

TRADING (TRADERS)

1Ki 10: 22 The king had a fleet of *t* ships at sea
Pr 31: 18 She sees that her *t* is profitable,

TRADITION (TRADITIONS)

Mt 15: 2 "Why do your disciples break the *t*

Mt   15: 6 word of God for the sake of your *t*.
Mk   7: 13 by your *t* that you have handed
Col   2: 8 which depends on human *t*

TRADITIONS (TRADITION)

Mk   7: 8 are holding on to the *t* of men."
Gal   1: 14 zealous for the *t* of my fathers.

TRAIL

1Ti   5: 24 the sins of others *t* behind them.

TRAIN [1]*

Ps   68: 18 you led captives in your *t*;
Isa   6: 1 the *t* of his robe filled the temple.
Eph   4: 8 he led captives in his *t*

TRAIN [2]* (TRAINED TRAINING)

Pr   22: 6 *T* a child in the way he should go,
Isa   2: 4 nor will they *t* for war any more.
Mic   4: 3 nor will they *t* for war any more.
1Ti   4: 7 rather, *t* yourself to be godly.
Tit   2: 4 they can *t* the younger women

TRAINED (TRAIN [2])

Lk   6: 40 everyone who is fully *t* will be like
Ac   22: 3 Under Gamaliel I was thoroughly *t*
2Co   11: 6 I may not be a *t* speaker,
Heb   5: 14 by constant use have *t* themselves
      12: 11 for those who have been *t* by it.

TRAINING* (TRAIN [2])

1Co   9: 25 in the games goes into strict *t*.
Eph   6: 4 up in the *t* and instruction
1Ti   4: 8 For physical *t* is of some value,
2Ti   3: 16 correcting and *t* in righteousness,

TRAITOR (TRAITORS)

Lk   6: 16 and Judas Iscariot, who became a *t*.
Jn   18: 5 Judas the *t* was standing there

TRAITORS (TRAITOR)

Ps   59: 5 show no mercy to wicked *t*.

TRAMPLE (TRAMPLED)

Joel   3: 13 Come, *t* the grapes,
Am   2: 7 They *t* on the heads of the poor
       5: 11 You *t* on the poor
       8: 4 Hear this, you who *t* the needy
Mt   7: 6 they may *t* them under their feet,
Lk   10: 19 I have given you authority to *t*

TRAMPLED (TRAMPLE)

Isa   63: 6 I *t* the nations in my anger;
Lk   21: 24 Jerusalem will be *t*
Heb   10: 29 to be punished who has *t* the Son
Rev   14: 20 They were *t* in the winepress

TRANCE*

Ac   10: 10 was being prepared, he fell into a *t*.
      11: 5 and in a *t* I saw a vision.
      22: 17 into a *t* and saw the Lord speaking.

TRANQUILLITY*

Ecc   4: 6 Better one handful with *t*

TRANSACTIONS*

Ru   4: 7 method of legalising *t* in Israel.)

TRANSCENDS*

Php   4: 7 which *t* all understanding,

TRANSFIGURED*

Mt   17: 2 There he was *t* before them.
Mk   9: 2 There he was *t* before them.

TRANSFORM* (TRANSFORMED)

Php   3: 21 will *t* our lowly bodies

TRANSFORMED (TRANSFORM)

Ro   12: 2 be *t* by the renewing of your mind.
2Co   3: 18 are being *t* into his likeness

TRANSGRESSED* (TRANSGRESSION)

Da   9: 11 All Israel has *t* your law

TRANSGRESSION* (TRANSGRESSED TRANSGRESSIONS TRANSGRESSORS)

Ps   19: 13 innocent of great *t*.
Isa   53: 8 for the *t* of my people he was
Da   9: 24 and your holy city to finish *t*,
Mic   1: 5 All this is because of Jacob's *t*,
       1: 5 What is Jacob's *t*?
       3: 8 to declare to Jacob his *t*,
       6: 7 Shall I offer my firstborn for my *t*.
       7: 18 who pardons sin and forgives the *t*
Ro   4: 15 where there is no law there is no *t*.
      11: 11 Rather, because of their *t*,
      11: 12 if their *t* means riches for the world

TRANSGRESSIONS* (TRANSGRESSION)

Ps   32: 1 whose *t* are forgiven,
      32: 5 my *t* to the LORD"—
      39: 8 Save me from all my *t*;
      51: 1 blot out my *t*.
      51: 3 For I know my *t*,
      65: 3 you forgave our *t*.
     103: 12 so far has he removed our *t* from us
Isa   43: 25 your *t*, for my own sake,
      50: 1 of your *t* your mother was sent
      53: 5 But he was pierced for our *t*,
Mic   1: 13 for the *t* of Israel
Ro   4: 7 whose *t* are forgiven,
Gal   3: 19 because of *t* until the Seed to whom
Eph   2: 1 you were dead in your *t* and sins,
       2: 5 even when we were dead in *t*—

TRANSGRESSORS* (TRANSGRESSION)

Ps   51: 13 Then I will teach *t* your ways,
Isa   53: 12 and made intercession for the *t*.
      53: 12 and was numbered with the *t*.
Lk   22: 37 'And he was numbered with the *t*';

TRAP (TRAPPED TRAPS)

Ps   69: 22 may it become retribution and a *t*.
Pr   20: 25 a *t* for a man to dedicate something
      28: 10 will fall into his own *t*,
Isa   8: 14 a *t* and a snare.
Mt   22: 15 and laid plans to *t* him in his words.
Lk   21: 34 close on you unexpectedly like a *t*.
Ro   11: 9 their table become a snare and a *t*.
1Ti   3: 7 into disgrace and into the devil's *t*.
       6: 9 and a *t* and into many foolish
2Ti   2: 26 and escape from the *t* of the devil,

TRAPPED (TRAP)

Pr   6: 2 if you have been *t* by what you said
      12: 13 An evil man is *t* by his sinful talk,

TRAPS (TRAP)

Jos   23: 13 they will become snares and *t*
La   4: 20 was caught in their *t*.

TRAVEL (TRAVELLER)

Pr   4: 15   Avoid it, do not *t* on it;
Mt 23: 15   You *t* over land and sea

TRAVELLER (TRAVEL)

Job 31: 32   door was always open to the *t—*
Jer 14: 8   like a *t* who stays only a night?

TREACHEROUS (TREACHERY)

Ps   25: 3   who are *t* without excuse.
2Ti   3: 4   not lovers of the good, *t*, rash,

TREACHERY (TREACHEROUS)

Isa 59: 13   rebellion and *t* against the LORD,

TREAD (TREADING TREADS)

Ps 91: 13   You will *t* upon the lion

TREADING (TREAD)

Dt   25: 4   an ox while it is *t* out the grain.
1Co   9: 9   an ox while it is *t* out the grain."
1Ti   5: 18   the ox while it is *t* out the grain,"

TREADS (TREAD)

Rev 19: 15   He *t* the winepress of the fury

TREASURE (TREASURED TREASURES TREASURY)

Pr   2: 4   and search for it as for hidden *t*,
Isa 33: 6   of the LORD is the key to this *t*.
Mt   6: 21   For where your *t* is, there your
    13: 44   of heaven is like *t* hidden in a field.
Lk 12: 33   a *t* in heaven that will not be
2Co   4: 7   But we have this *t* in jars of clay
1Ti   6: 19   In this way they will lay up *t*

TREASURED (TREASURE)

Ex 19: 5   you will be my *t* possession.
Dt   7: 6   to be his people, his *t* possession.
    26: 18   his *t* possession as he promised,
Job 23: 12   I have *t* the words
Mal   3: 17   when I make up my *t* possession.
Lk   2: 19   But Mary *t* up all these things
    2: 51   But his mother *t* all these things

TREASURES (TREASURE)

1Ch 29: 3   my God I now give my personal *t*
Pr 10: 2   Ill-gotten *t* are of no value,
Mt   6: 19   up for yourselves *t* on earth,
    13: 52   out of his storeroom new *t*
Col   2: 3   in whom are hidden all the *t*
Heb 11: 26   of greater value than the *t* of Egypt,

TREASURY (TREASURE)

Mk 12: 43   more into the *t* than all the others.

TREAT (TREATED TREATING TREATMENT)

Lev 22: 2   sons to *t* with respect the sacred
Ps 103: 10   he does not *t* us as our sins deserve
Mt 18: 17   *t* him as you would a pagan
    18: 35   my heavenly Father will *t* each
Eph   6: 9   *t* your slaves in the same way.
1Th   5: 20   do not *t* prophecies with contempt.
1Ti   5: 1   *T* younger men as brothers,
1Pe   3: 7   and *t* them with respect

TREATED (TREAT)

Lev 19: 34   The alien living with you must be *t*
    25: 40   He is to be *t* as a hired worker

1Sa 24: 17   "You have *t* me well, but I have
Heb 10: 29   who has *t* as an unholy thing

TREATING (TREAT)

Ge 18: 25   *t* the righteous and the wicked
Heb 12: 7   as discipline; God is *t* you as sons.

TREATMENT (TREAT)

Col   2: 23   and their harsh *t* of the body,

TREATY

Ex 34: 12   not to make a *t* with those who live
Dt   7: 2   Make no *t* with them, and show

TREE (FIG-TREE TREES)

Ge   2: 9   and the *t* of the knowledge of good
    2: 9   of the garden were the *t* of life
Dt 21: 23   hung on a *t* is under God's curse.
2Sa 18: 9   Absalom's head got caught in the *t*.
1Ki 14: 23   and under every spreading *t*.
Ps   1: 3   He is like a *t* planted by streams
    52: 8   But I am like an olive *t*
    92: 12   righteous will flourish like a palm *t*,
Pr   3: 18   She is a *t* of life to those who
    11: 30   of the righteous is a *t* of life,
Isa 65: 22   For as the days of a *t*,
Jer 17: 8   He will be like a *t* planted
Eze 17: 24   I the LORD bring down the tall *t*
Da   4: 10   before me stood a *t* in the middle
Mt   3: 10   every *t* that does not produce good
    12: 33   for a *t* is recognised by its fruit.
Lk 19: 4   climbed a sycamore-fig *t* to see him
Ac   5: 30   killed by hanging him on a *t*.
Ro 11: 24   be grafted into their own olive *t*!
Gal   3: 13   is everyone who is hung on a *t*."
1Pe   2: 24   sins in his body on the *t*,
Rev   2: 7   the right to eat from the *t* of life,
    22: 2   side of the river stood the *t* of life,
    22: 14   they may have the right to the *t*
    22: 19   from him his share in the *t* of life

TREES (TREE)

Jdg   9: 8   One day the *t* went out
Ps 96: 12   Then all the *t* of the forest will sing
Isa 55: 12   and all the *t* of the field
Mt   3: 10   The axe is already at the root of the *t*
Mk   8: 24   they look like *t* walking around."
Jude   : 12   autumn *t*, without fruit

TREMBLE (TREMBLED TREMBLES TREMBLING)

Ex 15: 14   The nations will hear and *t*;
1Ch 16: 30   *T* before him, all the earth!
Ps 114: 7   *T*, O earth, at the presence
Jer   5: 22   "Should you not *t* in my presence?
Eze 38: 20   of the earth will *t* at my presence.
Joel   2: 1   Let all who live in the land *t*,
Hab   3: 6   he looked, and made the nations *t*.

TREMBLED (TREMBLE)

Ex 19: 16   Everyone in the camp *t*.
    20: 18   in smoke, they *t* with fear.
2Sa 22: 8   "The earth *t* and quaked,
Ac   7: 32   Moses *t* with fear and did not dare

TREMBLES (TREMBLE)

Ps 97: 4   the earth sees and *t*.
    104: 32   He looks at the earth, and it *t*;
Isa 66: 2   and *t* at my word.
Jer 10: 10   When he is angry, the earth *t*;

Na   1: 5 The earth *t* at his presence,

TREMBLING (TREMBLE)

Ps   2: 11 and rejoice with *t*.
Da   10: 10 set me *t* on my hands and knees.
Php   2: 12 out your salvation with fear and *t*,
Heb   12: 21 terrifying that Moses said, "I am *t*

TRESPASS* (TRESPASSES)

Ro   5: 15 But the gift is not like the *t*.
      5: 15 died by the *t* of the one man,
      5: 17 For if, by the *t* of the one man,
      5: 18 result of one *t* was condemnation
      5: 20 added so that the *t* might increase.

TRESPASSES* (TRESPASS)

Ro   5: 16 but the gift followed many *t*

TRIAL (TRIALS)

Ps   37: 33 condemned when brought to *t*.
Mk   13: 11 you are arrested and brought to *t*,
2Co   8: 2 most severe *t*, their overflowing
Jas   1: 12 is the man who perseveres under *t*,
1Pe   4: 12 at the painful *t* you are suffering,
Rev   3: 10 you from the hour of *t* that is going

TRIALS* (TRIAL)

Dt   7: 19 saw with your own eyes the great *t*,
      29: 3 own eyes you saw those great *t*,
Lk   22: 28 who have stood by me in my *t*.
1Th   3: 3 one would be unsettled by these *t*.
2Th   1: 4 the persecutions and *t* you are
Jas   1: 2 whenever you face *t* of many kinds,
1Pe   1: 6 had to suffer grief in all kinds of *t*.
2Pe   2: 9 how to rescue godly men from *t*

TRIBE (HALF-TRIBE TRIBES)

Heb   7: 13 no-one from that *t* has ever served
Rev   5: 5 See, the Lion of the *t* of Judah,
      5: 9 God from every *t* and language
      11: 9 men from every people, *t*,
      14: 6 to every nation, *t*, language

TRIBES (TRIBE)

Ge   49: 28 All these are the twelve *t* of Israel,
Mt   19: 28 judging the twelve *t* of Israel.

TRIBULATION*

Rev   7: 14 who have come out of the great *t*;

TRICKERY*

Ac   13: 10 full of all kinds of deceit and *t*.
2Co   12: 16 fellow that I am, I caught you by *t*!

TRIED (TRY)

Ps   73: 16 When I *t* to understand all this,
      95: 9 where your fathers tested and *t* me,
Heb   3: 9 where your fathers tested and *t* me

TRIES (TRY)

Lk   17: 33 Whoever *t* to keep his life will lose

TRIMMED

Mt   25: 7 virgins woke up and *t* their lamps.

TRIUMPH (TRIUMPHAL TRIUMPHED TRIUMPHING TRIUMPHS)

Ps   25: 2 nor let my enemies *t* over me.
      54: 7 my eyes have looked in *t*
      112: 8 in the end he will look in *t*

Ps   118: 7 I will look in *t* on my enemies.
Pr   28: 12 When the righteous *t*, there is great
Isa   42: 13 and will *t* over his enemies.

TRIUMPHAL* (TRIUMPH)

Isa   60: 11 their kings led in *t* procession.
2Co   2: 14 us in *t* procession in Christ

TRIUMPHED (TRIUMPH)

Rev   5: 5 of Judah, the Root of David, has *t*.

TRIUMPHING* (TRIUMPH)

Col   2: 15 of them, *t* over them by the cross.

TRIUMPHS* (TRIUMPH)

Jas   2: 13 Mercy *t* over judgment! What

TROUBLE (TROUBLED TROUBLES)

Ge   41: 51 God has made me forget all my *t*
Jos   7: 25 Why have you brought this *t* on us?
Job   2: 10 good from God, and not *t*?"
      5: 7 Yet man is born to *t*
      14: 1 is of few days and full of *t*.
      42: 11 him over all the *t* the LORD had
Ps   7: 14 conceives *t* gives birth
      7: 16 The *t* he causes recoils on himself;
      9: 9 a stronghold in times of *t*.
      10: 14 But you, O God, do see *t* and grief;
      22: 11 for *t* is near
      27: 5 For in the day of *t*
      32: 7 you will protect me from *t*
      37: 39 he is their stronghold in time of *t*.
      41: 1 LORD delivers him in times of *t*.
      46: 1 an ever-present help in *t*.
      50: 15 and call upon me in the day of *t*;
      59: 16 my refuge in times of *t*.
      66: 14 spoke when I was in *t*.
      86: 7 In the day of my *t* I will call to you,
      91: 15 I will be with him in *t*,
      107: 6 to the LORD in their *t*,
      107: 13 they cried to the LORD in their *t*,
      116: 3 I was overcome by *t* and sorrow.
      119: 143 *T* and distress have come upon me,
      138: 7 Though I walk in the midst of *t*,
      143: 11 righteousness, bring me out of *t*.
Pr   11: 8 righteous man is rescued from *t*,
      11: 17 a cruel man brings *t* on himself.
      11: 29 He who brings *t* on his family will
      12: 13 but a righteous man escapes *t*.
      12: 21 but the wicked have their fill of *t*.
      15: 27 A greedy man brings *t* to his family
      19: 23 one rests content, untouched by *t*.
      22: 8 He who sows wickedness reaps *t*,
      24: 10 If you falter in times of *t*,
      25: 19 on the unfaithful in times of *t*.
      28: 14 he who hardens his heart falls into *t*
Jer   30: 7 It will be a time of *t* for Jacob,
Na   1: 7 a refuge in times of *t*.
Zep   1: 15 a day of *t* and ruin,
Mt   6: 34 Each day has enough *t* of its own.
      13: 21 When *t* or persecution comes
Jn   16: 33 In this world you will have *t*.
Ro   8: 35 Shall *t* or hardship or persecution
2Co   1: 4 those in any *t* with the comfort we
2Th   1: 6 *t* to those who *t* you
Jas   5: 13 one of you in *t*? He should pray.

TROUBLED (TROUBLE)

Ps   38: 18 I am *t* by my sin.
Isa   38: 14 I am *t*; O Lord, come to my aid!"

Mk	14:33	began to be deeply distressed and *t*.
Jn	14: 1	"Do not let your hearts be *t*.
	14:27	Do not let your hearts be *t*
2Th	1: 7	and give relief to you who are *t*,

TROUBLES (TROUBLE)

Ps	34: 6	he saved him out of all his *t*.
	34:17	he delivers them from all their *t*.
	34:19	A righteous man may have many *t*,
	40:12	For *t* without number surround me
	54: 7	he has delivered me from all my *t*,
1Co	7:28	those who marry will face many *t*
2Co	1: 4	who comforts us in all our *t*,
	4:17	and momentary *t* are achieving
	6: 4	in *t*, hardships and distresses;
	7: 4	in all our *t* my joy knows no bounds
Php	4:14	good of you to share in my *t*.

TRUE (TRUTH)

Nu	11:23	not what I say will come *t* for you."
	12: 7	this is not *t* of my servant Moses;
Dt	18:22	does not take place or come *t*,
Jos	23:15	of the LORD your God has come *t*
1Sa	9: 6	and everything he says comes *t*.
1Ki	10: 6	and your wisdom is *t*.
2Ch	6:17	your servant David come *t*.
	15: 3	was without the *t* God,
Ps	33: 4	of the LORD is right and *t*;
	119:142	and your law is *t*.
	119:151	and all your commands are *t*.
	119:160	All your words are *t*;
Pr	8: 7	My mouth speaks what is *t*,
	22:21	teaching you *t* and reliable words,
Jer	10:10	But the LORD is the *t* God;
	28: 9	only if his prediction comes *t*."
Eze	33:33	"When all this comes *t*—
Lk	16:11	who will trust you with *t* riches?
Jn	1: 9	The *t* light that gives light
	4:23	when the *t* worshippers will worship
	6:32	Father who gives you the *t* bread
	7:28	on my own, but he who sent me is *t*
	15: 1	"I am the *t* vine and my Father is
	17: 3	the only *t* God, and Jesus Christ,
	19:35	testimony, and his testimony is *t*.
	21:24	We know that his testimony is *t*.
Ac	10:34	"I now realise how *t* it is that God
	11:23	all to remain *t* to the Lord
	14:22	them to remain *t* to the faith.
	17:11	day to see if what Paul said was *t*.
Ro	3: 4	Let God be *t*, and every man a liar.
Php	4: 8	whatever is *t*, whatever is noble,
1Jn	2: 8	and the *t* light is already shining.
	5:20	He is the *t* God and eternal life.
Rev	19: 9	"These are the *t* words of God."
	22: 6	These words are trustworthy and *t*.

TRUMPET (TRUMPETS)

Isa	27:13	And in that day a great *t* will sound
Eze	33: 5	Since he heard the sound of the *t*
Zec	9:14	Sovereign LORD will sound the *t*;
Mt	24:31	send his angels with a loud *t* call,
1Co	14: 8	if the *t* does not sound a clear call,
	15:52	for the *t* will sound, the dead will
1Th	4:16	and with the *t* call of God,
Rev	8: 7	The first angel sounded his *t*,

TRUMPETS (TRUMPET)

Jdg	7:19	They blew their *t* and broke the jars
Rev	8: 2	and to them were given seven *t*.

Ex	14:31	put their *t* in him and in Moses his
	19: 9	and will always put their *t* in you."
Nu	20:12	"Because you did not *t*
Dt	1:32	you did not *t* in the LORD your
	9:23	You did not *t* him or obey him.
	28:52	walls in which you *t* fall down.
Jdg	11:20	did not *t* Israel to pass
2Ki	17:14	who did not *t* in the LORD their
1Ch	9:22	to their positions of *t* by David
Job	4:18	If God places no *t* in his servants,
	15:15	If God places no *t* in his holy ones,
	31:24	"If I have put my *t* in gold
	39:12	Can you *t* him to bring
Ps	4: 5	and *t* in the LORD.
	9:10	Those who know your name will *t*
	13: 5	But I *t* in your unfailing love;
	20: 7	Some *t* in chariots and some
	20: 7	we *t* in the name of the LORD our
	22: 4	In you our fathers put their *t*;
	22: 9	you made me *t* in you
	25: 2	I lift up my soul; in you I *t*,
	31: 6	I *t* in the LORD.
	31:14	But I *t* in you, O LORD;
	33:21	for we *t* in his holy name.
	37: 3	*T* in the LORD and do good;
	37: 5	*t* in him and he will do this:
	40: 3	and put their *t* in the LORD.
	40: 4	who makes the LORD his *t*,
	44: 6	I do not *t* in my bow,
	49: 6	those who *t* in their wealth
	49:13	of those who *t* in themselves,
	52: 8	I *t* in God's unfailing love
	55:23	But as for me, I *t* in you.
	56: 3	I will *t* in you.
	56: 4	in God I *t*; I will not be afraid.
	56:11	in God I *t*; I will not be afraid.
	62: 8	*T* in him at all times, O people;
	62:10	Do not *t* in extortion
	78: 7	Then they would put their *t* in God
	78:22	or *t* in his deliverance.
	91: 2	my God, in whom I *t*."
	115: 8	and so will all who *t* in them.
	115: 9	O house of Israel, *t* in the LORD—
	115:10	O house of Aaron, *t* in the LORD
	115:11	You who fear him, *t* in the LORD
	118: 8	than to *t* in man.
	118: 9	than to *t* in princes.
	119:42	for I *t* in your word.
	125: 1	Those who *t* in the LORD are like
	135:18	and so will all who *t* in them.
	143: 8	for I have put my *t* in you.
	146: 3	Do not put your *t* in princes,
Pr	3: 5	*T* in the LORD with all your heart
	21:22	the stronghold in which they *t*.
	22:19	So that your *t* may be in the LORD
Isa	8:17	I will put my *t* in him.
	12: 2	I will *t* and not be afraid.
	26: 4	*T* in the LORD for ever,
	30:15	in quietness and *t* is your strength,
	31: 1	who *t* in the multitude
	36:15	to *t* in the LORD when he says,
	42:17	But those who *t* in idols,
	50:10	*t* in the name of the LORD
Jer	2:37	LORD has rejected those you *t*;
	5:17	the fortified cities in which you *t*.
	7: 4	Do not *t* in deceptive words

Jer 7:14 the temple you *t* in, the place I gave
9: 4 do not *t* your brothers.
12: 6 Do not *t* them,
28:15 you have persuaded this nation to *t*
39:18 you *t* in me, declares the LORD.'"
48: 7 Since you *t* in your deeds
49: 4 you *t* in your riches and say,
49:11 Your widows too can *t* in me."
Mic 7: 5 Do not *t* a neighbour;
Na 1: 7 He cares for those who *t* in him,
Zep 3: 2 She does not *t* in the LORD,
3:12 who *t* in the name of the LORD.
Lk 16:11 who will *t* you with true riches?
Jn 12:36 Put your *t* in the light
14: 1 *T* in God; *t* also in me.
Ac 14:23 Lord in whom they had put their *t*.
Ro 15:13 you with all joy and peace as you *t*
1Co 4: 2 been given a *t* must prove faithful.
9:17 discharging the *t* committed
2Co 13: 6 I *t* that you will discover that we
Heb 2:13 "I will put my *t* in him."

TRUSTED* (TRUST)

1Sa 27:12 Achish *t* David and said to himself,
2Ki 18: 5 Hezekiah *t* in the LORD, the God
1Ch 5:20 their prayers, because they *t*
Job 12:20 He silences the lips of *t* advisers
Ps 5: 9 from their mouth can be *t*;
22: 4 they *t* and you delivered them.
22: 5 in you they *t* and were not
26: 1 I have *t* in the LORD
41: 9 Even my close friend, whom I *t*,
52: 7 but *t* in his great wealth
Isa 20: 5 Those who *t* in Cush and boasted
25: 9 This is the LORD, we *t* in him;
25: 9 we *t* in him, and he saved us.
47:10 You have *t* in your wickedness
Jer 13:25 and *t* in false gods.
38:22 those *t* friends of yours.
48:13 ashamed when they *t* in Bethel.
Eze 16:15 "'But you *t* in your beauty
Da 3:28 They *t* in him and defied the king's
6:23 because he had *t* in his God.
Lk 11:22 the armour in which the man *t*
16:10 *t* with very little can also be *t*
Ac 12:20 a *t* personal servant of the king,
Tit 2:10 but to show that they can be fully *t*,
3: 8 so that those who have *t*

TRUSTFULLY* (TRUST)

Pr 3:29 who lives *t* near you.

TRUSTING* (TRUST)

Job 15:31 by *t* what is worthless,
Ps 112: 7 his heart is steadfast, *t*
Isa 2:22 Stop *t* in man,
Jer 7: 8 you are *t* in deceptive words that

TRUSTS* (TRUST)

Job 8:14 What he *t* in is fragile;
Ps 21: 7 For the king *t* in the LORD;
22: 8 "He *t* in the LORD;
28: 7 my heart *t* in him, and I am helped.
32:10 surrounds the man who *t* in him.
84:12 blessed is the man who *t* in you.
86: 2 who *t* in you.
Pr 11:28 Whoever *t* in his riches will fall,
16:20 blessed is he who *t* in the LORD.
28:25 he who *t* in the LORD will prosper.
28:26 He who *t* in himself is a fool,

Pr 29:25 whoever *t* in the LORD is kept safe
Isa 26: 3 because he *t* in you.
28:16 one who *t* will never be dismayed.
Jer 17: 5 "Cursed is the one who *t* in man,
17: 7 blessed is the man who *t*
Eze 33:13 but then he *t* in his righteousness
Hab 2:18 For he who makes it *t*
Mt 27:43 He *t* in God.
Ro 4: 5 but *t* God who justifies the wicked,
9:33 one who *t* in him will never be put
10:11 "Anyone who *t* in him will never
1Co 13: 7 always protects, always *t*,
1Pe 2: 6 and the one who *t* in him

TRUSTWORTHY* (TRUST)

Ex 18:21 *t* men who hate dishonest gain—
2Sa 7:28 you are God! Your words are *t*,
Ne 13:13 these men were considered *t*.
Ps 19: 7 The statutes of the LORD are *t*,
111: 7 all his precepts are *t*.
119:86 All your commands are *t*;
119:138 they are fully *t*.
Pr 11:13 but a *t* man keeps a secret.
13:17 but a *t* envoy brings healing.
25:13 is a *t* messenger to those who send
Da 2:45 and the interpretation is *t*."
6: 4 he was *t* and neither corrupt
Lk 16:11 So if you have not been *t*
16:12 And if you have not been *t*
19:17 'Because you have been *t*
1Co 7:25 one who by the Lord's mercy is *t*.
1Ti 1:15 Here is a *t* saying that deserves full
3: 1 Here is a *t* saying: If anyone sets his
3:11 but temperate and *t* in everything.
4: 9 This is a *t* saying that deserves full
2Ti 2:11 Here is a *t* saying:
Tit 1: 9 must hold firmly to the *t* message
3: 8 This is a *t* saying.
Rev 21: 5 for these words are *t* and true."
22: 6 "These words are *t* and true.

TRUTH* (TRUE TRUTHFUL TRUTHFULNESS TRUTHS)

Ge 42:16 tested to see if you are telling the *t*.
1Ki 17:24 LORD from your mouth is the *t*."
22:16 the *t* in the name of the LORD?"
2Ch 18:15 the *t* in the name of the LORD?"
Ps 15: 2 who speaks the *t* from his heart
25: 5 guide me in your *t* and teach me,
26: 3 and I walk continually in your *t*.
31: 5 redeem me, O LORD, the God of *t*
40:10 do not conceal your love and your *t*
40:11 your *t* always protect me.
43: 3 Send forth your light and your *t*,
45: 4 victoriously on behalf of *t*, humility
51: 6 Surely you desire *t*
52: 3 than speaking the *t*.
86:11 and I will walk in your *t*;
96:13 and the peoples in his *t*.
119:30 I have chosen the way of *t*;
119:43 of *t* from my mouth,
145:18 to all who call on him in *t*.
Pr 16:13 they value a man who speaks the *t*.
23:23 Buy the *t* and do not sell it;
Isa 45:19 I, the LORD, speak the *t*;
48: 1 but not in *t* or righteousness—
59:14 *t* has stumbled in the streets,
59:15 *T* is nowhere to be found,
65:16 will do so by the God of *t*;
65:16 will swear by the God of *t*.

Jer	5: 1	who deals honestly and seeks the *t*,
	5: 3	do not your eyes look for *t*?
	7: 28	*T* has perished; it has vanished
	9: 3	it is not by *t*
	9: 5	and no-one speaks the *t*.
	26: 15	for in *t* the Lord has sent me
Da	8: 12	and *t* was thrown to the ground.
	9: 13	and giving attention to your *t*.
	10: 21	what is written in the Book of *T*.
	11: 2	"Now then, I tell you the *t*:
Am	5: 10	and despise him who tells the *t*.
Zec	8: 3	will be called The City of *T*,
	8: 16	are to do: Speak the *t* to each other.
	8: 19	Therefore love *t* and peace."
Mt	5: 18	I tell you the *t*, until heaven
	5: 26	I tell you the *t*, you will not get out
	6: 2	I tell you the *t*, they have received
	6: 5	I tell you the *t*, they have received
	6: 16	I tell you the *t*, they have received
	8: 10	"I tell you the *t*, I have not found
	10: 15	I tell you the *t*, it will be more
	10: 23	I tell you the *t*, you will not finish
	10: 42	I tell you the *t*, he will certainly not
	11: 11	I tell you the *t*: Among those born
	13: 17	For I tell you the *t*, many prophets
	16: 28	I tell you the *t*, some who are
	17: 20	I tell you the *t*, if you have faith
	18: 3	And he said: "I tell you the *t*,
	18: 13	And if he finds it, I tell you the *t*,
	18: 18	"I tell you the *t*, whatever you bind
	19: 23	to his disciples, "I tell you the *t*,
	19: 28	"I tell you the *t*, at the renewal
	21: 21	Jesus replied, "I tell you the *t*,
	21: 31	Jesus said to them, "I tell you the *t*,
	22: 16	of God in accordance with the *t*.
	23: 36	I tell you the *t*, all this will come
	24: 2	"I tell you the *t*, not one stone here
	24: 34	I tell you the *t*, this generation will
	24: 47	I tell you the *t*, he will put him
	25: 12	"I tell you the *t*, I don't know you.'
	25: 40	The King will reply, 'I tell you the *t*
	25: 45	"He will reply, 'I tell you the *t*,
	26: 13	tell you the *t*, wherever this gospel
	26: 21	"I tell you the *t*, one
	26: 34	"I tell you the *t*," Jesus answered,
Mk	3: 28	I tell you the *t*, all the sins
	5: 33	with fear, told him the whole *t*.
	8: 12	I tell you the *t*, no sign will be given
	9: 1	he said to them, "I tell you the *t*,
	9: 41	I tell you the *t*, anyone who gives
	10: 15	I tell you the *t*, anyone who will not
	10: 29	"I tell you the *t*," Jesus replied,
	11: 23	I tell you the *t*, if anyone says
	12: 14	of God in accordance with the *t*.
	12: 43	Jesus said, "I tell you the *t*,
	13: 30	I tell you the *t*, this generation will
	14: 9	I tell you the *t*, wherever the gospel
	14: 18	"I tell you the *t*, one
	14: 25	"I tell you the *t*, I will not drink
	14: 30	"I tell you the *t*," Jesus answered,
Lk	4: 24	"I tell you the *t*," he continued,
	9: 27	I tell you the *t*, some who are
	12: 37	I tell you the *t*, he will dress himself
	12: 44	I tell you the *t*, he will put him
	18: 17	I tell you the *t*, anyone who will not
	18: 29	I tell you the *t*," Jesus said to them,
	20: 21	of God in accordance with the *t*.
	21: 3	"I tell you the *t*," he said, "this
	21: 32	tell you the *t*, this generation will
	23: 43	answered him, "I tell you the *t*,

Jn	1: 14	from the Father, full of grace and *t*.
	1: 17	and *t* came through Jesus Christ.
	1: 51	"I tell you the *t*, you shall see
	3: 3	"I tell you the *t*, unless a man is
	3: 5	Jesus answered, "I tell you the *t*,
	3: 11	I tell you the *t*, we speak
	3: 21	But whoever lives by the *t* comes
	4: 23	worship the Father in spirit and *t*,
	4: 24	must worship in spirit and in *t*."
	5: 19	"I tell you the *t*, the Son can do
	5: 24	"I tell you the *t*, whoever hears my
	5: 25	I tell you the *t*, a time is coming
	5: 33	and he has testified to the *t*.
	6: 26	"I tell you the *t*, you are looking
	6: 32	Jesus said to them, "I tell you the *t*,
	6: 47	I tell you the *t*, he who believes has
	6: 53	Jesus said to them, "I tell you the *t*,
	7: 18	the one who sent him is a man of *t*;
	8: 32	Then you will know the *t*,
	8: 32	and the *t* will set you free."
	8: 34	Jesus replied, "I tell you the *t*,
	8: 40	who has told you the *t* that I heard
	8: 44	to the *t*, for there is no *t* in him.
	8: 45	I tell the *t*, you do not believe me!
	8: 46	I am telling the *t*, why don't you
	8: 51	I tell you the *t*, if a man keeps my
	8: 58	"I tell you the *t*," Jesus answered,
	10: 1	"I tell you the *t*, the man who does
	10: 7	"I tell you the *t*, I am the gate
	12: 24	I tell you the *t*, unless a grain
	13: 16	I tell you the *t*, no servant is greater
	13: 20	tell you the *t*, whoever accepts
	13: 21	"I tell you the *t*, one of you is going
	13: 38	I tell you the *t*, before the cock
	14: 6	I am the way and the *t* and the life.
	14: 12	I tell you the *t*, anyone who has
	14: 17	with you for ever—the Spirit of *t*.
	15: 26	the Spirit of *t* who goes out
	16: 7	But I tell you the *t*: It is
	16: 13	But when he, the Spirit of *t*, comes,
	16: 13	comes, he will guide you into all *t*.
	16: 20	I tell you the *t*, you will weep
	16: 23	I tell you the *t*, my Father will give
	17: 17	them by the *t*; your word is *t*.
	18: 23	if I spoke the *t*, why did you strike
	18: 37	into the world, to testify to the *t*.
	18: 37	on the side of *t* listens to me."
	18: 38	"What is *t*?" Pilate asked.
	19: 35	He knows that he tells the *t*,
	21: 18	I tell you the *t*, when you were
Ac	20: 30	and distort the *t* in order
	21: 24	everybody will know there is no *t*
	21: 34	commander could not get at the *t*
	24: 8	able to learn the *t* about all these
	28: 25	"The Holy Spirit spoke the *t*
Ro	1: 18	of men who suppress the *t*
	1: 25	They exchanged the *t* of God
	2: 2	who do such things is based on *t*.
	2: 8	who reject the *t* and follow evil,
	2: 20	embodiment of knowledge and *t*—
	9: 1	I speak the *t* in Christ—I am not
	15: 8	of the Jews on behalf of God's *t*,
1Co	5: 8	the bread of sincerity and *t*.
	13: 6	in evil but rejoices with the *t*.
2Co	4: 2	setting forth the *t* plainly we
	11: 10	As surely as the *t* of Christ is in me,
	12: 6	because I would be speaking the *t*.
	13: 8	against the *t*, but only for the *t*.
Gal	2: 5	so that the *t* of the gospel might
	2: 14	in line with the *t* of the gospel,

Gal	4: 16	enemy by telling you the *t*?
	5: 7	and kept you from obeying the *t*?
Eph	1: 13	when you heard the word of *t*,
	4: 15	Instead, speaking the *t* in love,
	4: 21	him in accordance with the *t* that is
	5: 9	and *t*) and find out what pleases
	6: 14	with the belt of *t* buckled
Col	1: 5	heard about in the word of *t*.
	1: 6	understood God's grace in all its *t*.
2Th	2: 10	because they refused to love the *t*
	2: 12	who have not believed the *t*
	2: 13	and through belief in the *t*.
1Ti	2: 4	to come to a knowledge of the *t*.
	2: 7	I am telling the *t*, I am not lying—
	3: 15	the pillar and foundation of the *t*.
	4: 3	who believe and who know the *t*.
	6: 5	who have been robbed of the *t*
2Ti	2: 15	correctly handles the word of *t*.
	2: 18	have wandered away from the *t*.
	2: 25	them to a knowledge of the *t*,
	3: 7	never able to acknowledge the *t*.
	3: 8	so also these men oppose the *t*—
	4: 4	will turn their ears away from the *t*
Tit	1: 1	the knowledge of the *t* that leads
	1: 14	of those who reject the *t*.
Heb	10: 26	received the knowledge of the *t*,
Jas	1: 18	birth through the word of *t*,
	3: 14	do not boast about it or deny the *t*.
	5: 19	of you should wander from the *t*
1Pe	1: 22	by obeying the *t* so that you have
2Pe	1: 12	established in the *t* you now have.
	2: 2	the way of *t* into disrepute.
1Jn	1: 6	we lie and do not live by the *t*.
	1: 8	deceive ourselves and the *t* is not
	2: 4	commands is a liar, and the *t* is not
	2: 8	its *t* is seen in him and you,
	2: 20	and all of you know the *t*.
	2: 21	because no lie comes from the *t*.
	2: 21	because you do not know the *t*,
	3: 18	or tongue but with actions and in *t*.
	3: 19	we know that we belong to the *t*,
	4: 6	is how we recognise the Spirit of *t*
	5: 6	testifies, because the Spirit is the *t*.
2Jn	: 1	whom I love in the *t*—
	: 2	who know the *t*—because of the *t*,
	: 3	will be with us in *t* and love.
	: 4	of your children walking in the *t*,
3Jn	: 1	friend Gaius, whom I love in the *t*.
	: 3	how you continue to walk in the *t*.
	: 3	tell about your faithfulness to the *t*
	: 4	my children are walking in the *t*.
	: 8	we may work together for the *t*.
	: 12	everyone—and even by the *t* itself.

TRUTHFUL* (TRUTH)

Pr	12: 17	A *t* witness gives honest testimony,
	12: 19	*T* lips endure for ever,
	12: 22	but he delights in men who are *t*.
	14: 5	A *t* witness does not deceive,
	14: 25	A *t* witness saves lives,
Jer	4: 2	and if in a *t*, just and righteous way
Jn	3: 33	it has certified that God is *t*.
2Co	6: 7	in *t* speech and in the power

TRUTHFULNESS* (TRUTH)

Ro	3: 7	"If my falsehood enhances God's *t*

TRUTHS* (TRUTH)

1Co	2: 13	expressing spiritual *t*
1Ti	3: 9	hold of the deep *t* of the faith

1Ti	4: 6	brought up in the *t* of the faith
Heb	5: 12	to teach you the elementary *t*

TRY (TRIED TRIES TRYING)

Ps	26: 2	Test me, O LORD, and *t* me,
Isa	7: 13	enough to *t* the patience of men?
Lk	12: 58	*t* hard to be reconciled to him
	13: 24	will *t* to enter and will not be able
1Co	10: 33	even as I *t* to please everybody
	14: 12	*t* to excel in gifts that build up
2Co	5: 11	is to fear the Lord, we *t*
1Th	5: 15	always *t* to be kind to each other
Tit	2: 9	to *t* to please them, not to talk back

TRYING (TRY)

2Co	5: 12	We are not *t* to commend ourselves
Gal	1: 10	If I were still *t* to please men,
1Th	2: 4	We are not *t* to please men but God
1Pe	1: 11	*t* to find out the time
1Jn	2: 26	things to you about those who are *t*

TUMOURS

1Sa	5: 6	them and afflicted them with *t*.

TUNE

1Co	14: 7	anyone know what *t* is being

TUNIC (TUNICS)

Lk	6: 29	do not stop him from taking your *t*.

TUNICS (TUNIC)

Lk	3: 11	"The man with two *t* should share

TURMOIL

Ps	65: 7	and the *t* of the nations.
Pr	15: 16	than great wealth with *t*.

TURN (TURNED TURNING TURNS)

Ex	32: 12	*T* from your fierce anger; relent
Nu	32: 15	If you *t* away from following him,
Dt	5: 32	do not *t* aside to the right
	28: 14	Do not *t* aside from any
	30: 10	and *t* to the LORD your God
Jos	1: 7	do not *t* from it to the right
1Ki	8: 58	May he *t* our hearts to him,
2Ch	7: 14	and *t* from their wicked ways,
	30: 9	He will not *t* his face from you
Job	33: 30	to *t* back his soul from the pit,
Ps	28: 1	do not *t* a deaf ear to me.
	34: 14	*T* from evil and do good;
	51: 13	and sinners will *t* back to you.
	78: 6	they in *t* would tell their children.
	119: 36	*T* my heart towards your statutes
	119: 132	*T* to me and have mercy on me,
Pr	22: 6	when he is old he will not *t* from it.
Isa	17: 7	*t* their eyes to the Holy One
	28: 6	to those who *t* back the battle
	29: 16	You *t* things upside down,
	30: 21	Whether you *t* to the right
	45: 22	"*T* to me and be saved,
	55: 7	Let him *t* to the LORD,
Jer	31: 13	I will *t* their mourning
Eze	33: 9	if you do warn the wicked man to *t*
	33: 11	*T*! *T* from your evil ways!
Jnh	3: 9	and with compassion *t*
Mal	4: 6	He will *t* the hearts of the fathers
Mt	5: 39	you on the right cheek, *t*
	10: 35	For I have come to *t*
Lk	1: 17	to *t* the hearts of the fathers
Jn	12: 40	nor *t*—and I would heal them."

Jn 16: 20 but your grief will *t* to joy.
Ac 3: 19 Repent, then, and *t* to God,
26: 18 and *t* them from darkness to light,
1Co 14: 31 For you can all prophesy in *t*
15: 23 But each in his own *t*; Christ,
1Ti 6: 20 *T* away from godless chatter
1Pe 3: 11 He must *t* from evil and do good;

TURNED (TURN)

Dt 23: 5 *t* the curse into a blessing for you,
1Ki 11: 4 his wives *t* his heart
2Ch 15: 4 But in their distress they *t*
Est 9: 1 but now the tables were *t*
9: 22 when their sorrow was *t* into joy
Ps 14: 3 All have *t* aside,
30: 11 You *t* my wailing into dancing;
40: 1 he *t* to me and heard my cry.
Isa 9: 12 for all this, his anger is not *t* away,
53: 6 each of us has *t* to his own way;
Hos 7: 8 Ephraim is a flat cake not *t* over.
Joel 2: 31 The sun will be *t* to darkness
Lk 22: 32 And when you have *t* back,
Ro 3: 12 All have *t* away,

TURNING (TURN)

2Ki 21: 13 wiping it and *t* it upside down.
Pr 2: 2 *t* your ear to wisdom
14: 27 *t* a man from the snares of death.

TURNS (TURN)

2Sa 22: 29 the LORD *t* my darkness into light
Pr 15: 1 A gentle answer *t* away wrath,
Isa 44: 25 and *t* it into nonsense,
Jas 5: 20 Whoever *t* a sinner from the error

TWELVE

Ge 35: 22 Jacob had *t* sons: The sons of Leah:
49: 28 All these are the *t* tribes of Israel,
Mt 10: 1 He called his *t* disciples to him
Lk 9: 17 the disciples picked up *t* basketfuls
Rev 21: 12 the names of the *t* tribes of Israel.
21: 14 of the *t* apostles of the Lamb.

TWIN (TWINS)

Ge 25: 24 there were *t* boys in her womb.

TWINKLING*

1Co 15: 52 in a flash, in the *t* of an eye,

TWINS (TWIN)

Ro 9: 11 before the *t* were born

TWISTING* (TWISTS)

Pr 30: 33 and as *t* the nose produces blood,

TWISTS (TWISTING)

Ex 23: 8 and *t* the words of the righteous.

TYRANNICAL*

Pr 28: 16 A *t* ruler lacks judgment,

TYRE

Eze 28: 12 a lament concerning the king of *T*
Mt 11: 22 it will be more bearable for *T*

UNAPPROACHABLE*

1Ti 6: 16 immortal and who lives in *u* light,

UNASHAMED*

1Jn 2: 28 and *u* before him at his coming.

UNBELIEF* (UNBELIEVER UNBELIEVERS UNBELIEVING)

Mk 9: 24 help me overcome my *u*!"
Ro 4: 20 through *u* regarding the promise
11: 20 they were broken off because of *u*,
11: 23 And if they do not persist in *u*,
1Ti 1: 13 because I acted in ignorance and *u*.
Heb 3: 19 able to enter, because of their *u*.

UNBELIEVER* (UNBELIEF)

1Co 7: 15 But if the *u* leaves, let him do so.
10: 27 If some *u* invites you to a meal
14: 24 if an *u* or someone who does not
2Co 6: 15 have in common with an *u*?
1Ti 5: 8 the faith and is worse than an *u*.

UNBELIEVERS* (UNBELIEF)

Lk 12: 46 and assign him a place with the *u*.
Ro 15: 31 rescued from the *u* in Judea
1Co 6: 6 another—and this in front of *u*!
14: 22 however, is for believers, not for *u*.
14: 22 not for believers but for *u*;
14: 23 do not understand or some *u* come
2Co 4: 4 this age has blinded the minds of *u*,
6: 14 Do not be yoked together with *u*.

UNBELIEVING* (UNBELIEF)

Mt 17: 17 "O *u* and perverse generation,"
Mk 9: 19 "O *u* generation," Jesus replied,
Lk 9: 41 "O *u* and perverse generation,"
1Co 7: 14 For the *u* husband has been
7: 14 and the *u* wife has been sanctified
Heb 3: 12 *u* heart that turns away
Rev 21: 8 But the cowardly, the *u*, the vile,

UNBLEMISHED*

Heb 9: 14 the eternal Spirit offered himself *u*

UNCEASING

Ro 9: 2 and *u* anguish in my heart.

UNCERTAIN*

1Ti 6: 17 which is so *u*, but to put their hope

UNCHANGEABLE* (UNCHANGING)

Heb 6: 18 by two *u* things in which it is

UNCHANGING* (UNCHANGEABLE)

Heb 6: 17 wanted to make the *u* nature

UNCIRCUMCISED

Lev 26: 41 when their *u* hearts are humbled
1Sa 17: 26 Who is this *u* Philistine that he
Jer 9: 26 house of Israel is *u* in heart."
Ac 7: 51 stiff-necked people, with *u* hearts
Ro 4: 11 had by faith while he was still *u*.
1Co 7: 18 Was a man *u* when he was called?
Col 3: 11 circumcised or *u*, barbarian,

UNCIRCUMCISION

1Co 7: 19 is nothing and *u* is nothing.
Gal 5: 6 neither circumcision nor *u* has any

UNCLEAN

Ge 7: 2 and two of every kind of *u* animal,
Lev 10: 10 between the *u* and the clean,
11: 4 it is ceremonially *u* for you.
Isa 6: 5 ruined! For I am a man of *u* lips,
52: 11 Touch no *u* thing!
Mt 15: 11 mouth does not make him '*u*',

Ac   10: 14 never eaten anything impure or *u*."
Ro   14: 14 fully convinced that no food is *u*
2Co   6: 17 Touch no *u* thing,

UNCLOTHED*

2Co   5: 4 because we do not wish to be *u*

UNCONCERNED*

Eze   16: 49 were arrogant, overfed and *u*;

UNCOVERED

Ru   3: 7 Ruth approached quietly, *u* his feet
1Co   11: 5 with her head *u* dishonours her head
      11: 13 to pray to God with her head *u*?
Heb   4: 13 Everything is *u* and laid bare

UNDERGOES* (UNDERGOING)

Heb   12: 8 (and everyone *u* discipline),

UNDERGOING* (UNDERGOES)

1Pe   5: 9 the world are *u* the same kind

**UNDERSTAND (UNDERSTANDING
UNDERSTANDS UNDERSTOOD)**

Ne   8: 8 the people could *u* what was being
Job   38: 4 Tell me, if you *u*.
      42: 3 Surely I spoke of things I did not *u*,
Ps   14: 2 men to see if there are any who *u*,
      73: 16 When I tried to *u* all this,
      119: 27 Let me *u* the teaching
      119: 125 that I may *u* your statutes.
Pr   2: 5 then you will *u* the fear
       2: 9 Then you will *u* what is right
      30: 18 four that I do not *u*:
Ecc   7: 25 to *u* the stupidity of wickedness
      11: 5 so you cannot *u* the work of God,
Isa   6: 10 *u* with their hearts,
      44: 18 know nothing, they *u* nothing;
      52: 15 they have not heard, they will *u*.
Jer   17: 9 Who can *u* it?
      31: 19 after I came to *u*,
Da   9: 25 and *u* this: From the issuing
Hos   14: 9 Who is discerning? He will *u* them.
Mt   13: 15 *u* with their hearts
      24: 15 Daniel—let the reader *u*—
Lk   24: 45 so they could *u* the Scriptures.
Ac   8: 30 "Do you *u* what you are reading?"
Ro   7: 15 I do not *u* what I do.
      15: 21 those who have not heard will *u*."
1Co   2: 12 that we may *u* what God has freely
       2: 14 and he cannot *u* them,
      14: 16 those who do not *u* say "Amen"
Eph   5: 17 but *u* what the Lord's will is.
Heb   11: 3 By faith we *u* that the universe was
2Pe   1: 20 you must *u* that no prophecy
       3: 3 you must *u* that in the last days
       3: 16 some things that are hard to *u*,

UNDERSTANDING (UNDERSTAND)

1Ki   4: 29 and a breadth of *u* as measureless
Job   12: 12 Does not long life bring *u*?
      28: 12 Where does *u* dwell?
      28: 28 and to shun evil is *u*.'"
      32: 8 of the Almighty, that gives him *u*.
      36: 26 How great is God—beyond our *u*!
      37: 5 he does great things beyond our *u*.
Ps   111: 10 follow his precepts have good *u*.
      119: 34 Give me *u*, and I will keep your law
      119: 100 I have more *u* than the elders,
      119: 104 I gain *u* from your precepts;

Ps   119: 130 it gives *u* to the simple.
      136: 5 who by his *u* made the heavens,
      147: 5 his *u* has no limit.
Pr   2: 2 and applying your heart to *u*,
       2: 6 his mouth come knowledge and *u*.
       3: 5 and lean not on your own *u*;
       3: 13 the man who gains *u*,
       4: 5 Get wisdom, get *u*;
       4: 7 Though it cost all you have, get *u*.
       7: 4 and call *u* your kinsman,
       9: 10 knowledge of the Holy One is *u*.
      10: 23 but a man of *u* delights in wisdom.
      11: 12 but a man of *u* holds his tongue.
      14: 29 A patient man has great *u*,
      15: 21 a man of *u* keeps a straight course.
      15: 32 whoever heeds correction gains *u*.
      16: 16 to choose *u* rather than silver!
      16: 22 *U* is a fountain of life
      17: 27 and a man of *u* is even-tempered.
      18: 2 A fool finds no pleasure in *u*
      19: 8 he who cherishes *u* prospers.
      20: 5 but a man of *u* draws them out.
      23: 23 get wisdom, discipline and *u*.
Isa   11: 2 the Spirit of wisdom and of *u*,
      40: 28 and his *u* no-one can fathom.
      56: 11 They are shepherds who lack *u*;
Jer   3: 15 you with knowledge and *u*.
      10: 12 stretched out the heavens by his *u*.
Da   5: 12 a keen mind and knowledge and *u*,
      10: 12 that you set your mind to gain *u*
Hos   4: 11 which take away the *u*
Mk   4: 12 and ever hearing but never *u*;
      12: 33 with all your *u* and with all your
Lk   2: 47 who heard him was amazed at his *u*
2Co   6: 6 in purity, *u*, patience and kindness;
Eph   1: 8 on us with all wisdom and *u*.
Php   4: 7 of God, which transcends all *u*,
Col   1: 9 through all spiritual wisdom and *u*.
       2: 2 have the full riches of complete *u*,
1Jn   5: 20 God has come and has given us *u*,

UNDERSTANDS (UNDERSTAND)

1Ch   28: 9 and *u* every motive
Jer   9: 24 that he *u* and knows me,
Mt   13: 23 man who hears the word and *u* it.
Ro   3: 11 there is no-one who *u*,
1Ti   6: 4 he is conceited and *u* nothing.

UNDERSTOOD (UNDERSTAND)

Ne   8: 12 they now *u* the words that had
Ps   73: 17 then I *u* their final destiny.
Isa   40: 13 Who has *u* the mind of the Lord,
      40: 21 Have you not *u* since the earth was
Jn   1: 5 but the darkness has not *u* it.
Ro   1: 20 being *u* from what has been made,

UNDESIRABLE*

Jos   24: 15 But if serving the Lord seems *u*

UNDIVIDED*

1Ch   12: 33 to help David with *u* loyalty—
Ps   86: 11 give me an *u* heart,
Eze   11: 19 I will give them an *u* heart
1Co   7: 35 way in *u* devotion to the Lord.

UNDOING

Pr   18: 7 A fool's mouth is his *u*,

UNDYING*

Eph   6: 24 Lord Jesus Christ with an *u* love.

UNEQUALLED*

Mt 24: 21 *u* from the beginning of the world
Mk 13: 19 of distress *u* from the beginning,

UNFADING*

1Pe 3: 4 the *u* beauty of a gentle

UNFAILING*

Ex 15: 13 "In your *u* love you will lead
1Sa 20: 14 But show me *u* kindness like that
2Sa 22: 51 he shows *u* kindness
Ps 6: 4 save us because of your *u* love.
13: 5 But I trust in your *u* love;
18: 50 he shows *u* kindness
21: 7 through the *u* love
31: 16 save me in your *u* love.
32: 10 but the LORD's *u* love
33: 5 the earth is full of his *u* love.
33: 18 those whose hope is in his *u* love,
33: 22 May your *u* love rest upon us,
36: 7 How priceless is your *u* love!
44: 26 redeem us because of your *u* love.
48: 9 we meditate on your *u* love.
51: 1 according to your *u* love;
52: 8 I trust in God's *u* love
77: 8 Has his *u* love vanished for ever?
85: 7 Show us your *u* love, O LORD,
90: 14 in the morning with your *u* love,
107: 8 thanks to the LORD for his *u* love
107: 15 thanks to the LORD for his *u* love
107: 21 to the LORD for his *u* love
107: 31 to the LORD for his *u* love
119: 41 May your *u* love come to me,
119: 76 May your *u* love be my comfort,
130: 7 for with the LORD is *u* love
143: 8 bring me word of your *u* love,
143: 12 In your *u* love, silence my enemies;
147: 11 who put their hope in his *u* love.
Pr 19: 22 What a man desires is *u* love;
20: 6 Many a man claims to have *u* love,
Isa 54: 10 yet my *u* love for you will not be
La 3: 32 so great is his *u* love.
Hos 10: 12 reap the fruit of *u* love,

UNFAITHFUL (UNFAITHFULNESS)

Lev 6: 2 is *u* to the LORD by deceiving his
Nu 5: 6 and so is *u* to the LORD,
1Ch 10: 13 because he was *u* to the LORD;
Pr 11: 16 the *u* are trapped by evil desires.
13: 2 the *u* have a craving for violence.
13: 15 but the way of the *u* is hard.
22: 12 but he frustrates the words of the *u*.
23: 28 and multiplies the *u* among men.
25: 19 is reliance on the *u* in times
Jer 3: 20 But like a woman *u* to her husband,

UNFAITHFULNESS (UNFAITHFUL)

1Ch 9: 1 to Babylon because of their *u*.
Mt 5: 32 except for marital *u*, causes her
19: 9 for marital *u*, and marries another

UNFIT*

Tit 1: 16 and *u* for doing anything good.

UNFORGIVING*

2Ti 3: 3 unholy, without love, *u*, slanderous

UNFRIENDLY*

Pr 18: 1 An *u* man pursues selfish ends;

UNFRUITFUL

1Co 14: 14 my spirit prays, but my mind is *u*.

UNGODLINESS (UNGODLY)

Tit 2: 12 It teaches us to say "No" to *u*

UNGODLY (UNGODLINESS)

Ro 5: 6 powerless, Christ died for the *u*.
1Ti 1: 9 the *u* and sinful, the unholy
2Ti 2: 16 in it will become more and more *u*.
2Pe 2: 6 of what is going to happen to the *u*;
Jude : 15 and to convict all the *u*

UNGRATEFUL*

Lk 6: 35 he is kind to the *u* and wicked.
2Ti 3: 2 disobedient to their parents, *u*,

UNHOLY*

1Ti 1: 9 and sinful, the *u* and irreligious;
2Ti 3: 2 ungrateful, *u*, without love,
Heb 10: 29 as an *u* thing the blood

UNINTENTIONALLY

Lev 4: 2 'When anyone sins *u* and does
Nu 15: 22 "'Now if you *u* fail to keep any
Dt 4: 42 flee if he had *u* killed his neighbour

UNIT

1Co 12: 12 body is a *u*, though it is made up

UNITE (UNITED UNITY)

1Co 6: 15 and *u* them with a prostitute?

UNITED (UNITE)

Ge 2: 24 and mother and be *u* to his wife,
Mt 19: 5 and mother and be *u* to his wife,
Ro 6: 5 If we have been *u* with him
Eph 5: 31 and mother and be *u* to his wife,
Php 2: 1 from being *u* with Christ,
Col 2: 2 encouraged in heart and *u* in love,

UNITY* (UNITE)

2Ch 30: 12 the people to give them *u* of mind
Ps 133: 1 is when brothers live together in *u*!
Jn 17: 23 May they be brought to complete *u*
Ro 15: 5 a spirit of *u* among yourselves
Eph 4: 3 effort to keep the *u* of the Spirit
4: 13 up until we all reach *u* in the faith
Col 3: 14 them all together in perfect *u*.

UNIVERSE*

1Co 4: 9 made a spectacle to the whole *u*,
Eph 4: 10 in order to fill the whole *u*.)
Php 2: 15 which you shine like stars in the *u*
Heb 1: 2 and through whom he made the *u*.
11: 3 understand that the *u* was formed

UNJUST

Ro 3: 5 That God is *u* in bringing his wrath
9: 14 What then shall we say? Is God *u*?
1Pe 2: 19 up under the pain of *u* suffering

UNKNOWN

Ac 17: 23 TO AN *U* GOD.

UNLEAVENED

Ex 12: 17 "Celebrate the Feast of *U* Bread,
Dt 16: 16 at the Feast of *U* Bread, the Feast

UNLIMITED*

1Ti 1: 16 Jesus might display his *u* patience

UNLOVED

Pr 30: 23 an *u* woman who is married,

UNMARRIED

1Co 7: 8 It is good for them to stay *u*,
7: 27 Are you *u*? Do not look for a wife.
7: 32 An *u* man is concerned about

UNPLOUGHED

Ex 23: 11 the seventh year let the land lie *u*
Hos 10: 12 and break up your *u* ground;

UNPRODUCTIVE

Tit 3: 14 necessities and not live *u* lives.
2Pe 1: 8 and *u* in your knowledge

UNPROFITABLE

Tit 3: 9 because these are *u* and useless.

UNPUNISHED

Ex 34: 7 Yet he does not leave the guilty *u*;
Pr 6: 29 no-one who touches her will go *u*.
11: 21 of this: The wicked will not go *u*,
19: 5 A false witness will not go *u*,

UNQUENCHABLE

Lk 3: 17 he will burn up the chaff with *u* fire

UNREPENTANT*

Ro 2: 5 stubbornness and your *u* heart,

UNRIGHTEOUS*

Zep 3: 5 yet the *u* know no shame.
Mt 5: 45 rain on the righteous and the *u*.
1Pe 3: 18 the righteous for the *u*, to bring you
2Pe 2: 9 and to hold the *u* for the day

UNSEARCHABLE

Ro 11: 33 How *u* his judgments,
Eph 3: 8 preach to the Gentiles the *u* riches

UNSEEN*

Mt 6: 6 and pray to your Father, who is *u*.
6: 18 who is *u*; and your Father,
2Co 4: 18 on what is seen, but on what is *u*.
4: 18 temporary, but what is *u* is eternal.

UNSETTLED*

1Th 3: 3 so that no-one would be *u*
2Th 2: 2 not to become easily *u*

UNSHRUNK

Mt 9: 16 patch of *u* cloth on an old garment,

UNSPIRITUAL*

Ro 7: 14 but I am *u*, sold as a slave to sin.
Col 2: 18 and his *u* mind puffs him up
Jas 3: 15 down from heaven but is earthly, *u*,

UNSTABLE*

Jas 1: 8 he is a double-minded man, *u*
2Pe 2: 14 they seduce the *u*; they are experts
3: 16 ignorant and *u* people distort,

UNTHINKABLE*

Job 34: 12 It is *u* that God would do wrong,

UNTIE

Mk 1: 7 worthy to stoop down and *u*.
Lk 13: 15 each of you on the Sabbath *u* his ox

UNVEILED*

2Co 3: 18 with *u* faces all reflect the Lord's

UNWHOLESOME*

Eph 4: 29 Do not let any *u* talk come out

UNWISE

Eph 5: 15 how you live—not as *u* but as wise,

UNWORTHY*

Ge 32: 10 I am *u* of all the kindness
Job 40: 4 "I am *u*—how can I reply to you?
Lk 17: 10 should say, 'We are *u* servants;
1Co 11: 27 Lord in an *u* manner will be guilty

UPHOLD (UPHOLDS)

Isa 41: 10 I will *u* you with my righteous right
Ro 3: 31 Not at all! Rather, we *u* the law.

UPHOLDS* **(UPHOLD)**

Ps 37: 17 but the LORD *u* the righteous.
37: 24 for the LORD *u* him with his hand.
63: 8 your right hand *u* me.
140: 12 and *u* the cause of the needy.
145: 14 The LORD *u* all those who fall
146: 7 He *u* the cause of the oppressed

UPRIGHT

Dt 32: 4 *u* and just is he.
Job 1: 1 This man was blameless and *u*;
Ps 7: 10 who saves the *u* in heart.
11: 7 and the *u* will see his face.
25: 8 Good and *u* is the LORD;
33: 1 it is fitting for the *u* to praise him.
64: 10 let all the *u* in heart praise him!
92: 15 proclaiming, "The LORD is *u*;
97: 11 and joy on the *u* in heart.
119: 7 I will praise you with an *u* heart
Pr 2: 7 He holds victory in store for the *u*,
3: 32 but takes the *u* into his confidence.
14: 2 whose walk is *u* fears the LORD,
15: 8 but the prayer of the *u* pleases him.
21: 29 an *u* man gives thought to his ways.
Isa 26: 7 O *u* One, you make the way
Tit 1: 8 who is self-controlled, *u*, holy
2: 12 *u* and godly lives in this present

UPROOTED

Dt 28: 63 You will be *u* from the land you are
Jer 31: 40 The city will never again be *u*
Jude : 12 without fruit and *u*—twice dead.

UPSET

Lk 10: 41 are worried and *u* about many

URIAH

Hittite husband of Bathsheba, killed by David's order (2Sa 11).

USEFUL

Eph 4: 28 doing something *u*
2Ti 2: 21 *u* to the Master and prepared
3: 16 Scripture is God-breathed and is *u*
Phm : 11 now he has become *u* both to you

USELESS

1Co 15:14 our preaching is *u*
Tit 3: 9 these are unprofitable and *u*.
Phm :11 Formerly he was *u* to you,
Heb 7:18 *u* (for the law made nothing perfect
Jas 2:20 faith without deeds is *u*?

USURY

Ne 5:10 But let the exacting of *u* stop!
Ps 15: 5 who lends his money without *u*

UTMOST

Job 34:36 that Job might be tested to the *u*

UTTER (UTTERS)

Ps 78: 2 I will *u* things hidden from of old—
Mt 13:35 I will *u* things hidden

UTTERS (UTTER)

1Co 14: 2 he *u* mysteries with his spirit.

UZZIAH

Son of Amaziah; king of Judah also known as Azariah (2Ki 15:1-7; 1Ch 6:24; 2Ch 26). Struck with leprosy because of pride (2Ch 26:16-23).

VAIN

Ps 33:17 A horse is a *v* hope for deliverance;
73:13 in *v* have I kept my heart pure;
127: 1 its builders labour in *v*.
Isa 65:23 They will not toil in *v*
1Co 15: 2 Otherwise, you have believed in *v*.
15:58 labour in the Lord is not in *v*.
2Co 6: 1 not to receive God's grace in *v*.
Gal 2: 2 running or had run my race in *v*.

VALIANT

1Sa 10:26 by *v* men whose hearts God had

VALID

Jn 8:14 my own behalf, my testimony is *v*,

VALLEY (VALLEYS)

Ps 23: 4 walk through the *v* of the shadow
Isa 40: 4 Every *v* shall be raised up,
Joel 3:14 multitudes in the *v* of decision!

VALLEYS (VALLEY)

SS 2: 1 a lily of the *v*.

VALUABLE (VALUE)

Lk 12:24 And how much more *v* you are

VALUE (VALUABLE VALUED)

Lev 27: 3 set the *v* of a male between the ages
Pr 16:13 they *v* a man who speaks with truth.
31:11 and lacks nothing of *v*.
Mt 13:46 When he found one of great *v*,
1Ti 4: 8 For physical training is of some *v*,
Heb 11:26 as of greater *v* than the treasures

VALUED (VALUE)

Lk 16:15 What is highly *v* among men is

VANISHES

Jas 4:14 appears for a little while and then *v*.

VASHTI*

Queen of Persia replaced by Esther (Est 1-2).

VAST

Ge 2: 1 completed in all their *v* array.
Dt 1:19 of the Amorites through all that *v*
8:15 He led you through the *v*
Ps 139:17 How *v* is the sum of them!

VEGETABLES

Pr 15:17 of *v* where there is love
Ro 14: 2 whose faith is weak, eats only *v*.

VEIL

Ex 34:33 to them, he put a *v* over his face.
2Co 3:14 for to this day the same *v* remains

VENGEANCE (AVENGE AVENGER AVENGES AVENGING REVENGE)

Nu 31: 3 to carry out the LORD's *v* on them
Isa 34: 8 For the LORD has a day of *v*,
Na 1: 2 The LORD takes *v* on his foes

VERDICT

Jn 3:19 This is the *v*; Light has come

VICTOR'S* (VICTORY)

2Ti 2: 5 he does not receive the *v* crown

VICTORIES* (VICTORY)

2Sa 22:51 He gives his king great *v*;
Ps 18:50 He gives his king great *v*;
21: 1 great is his joy in the *v* you give!
21: 5 Through the *v* you gave, his glory is
44: 4 who decrees *v* for Jacob.

VICTORIOUS (VICTORY)

Ps 20: 5 for joy when you are *v*

VICTORIOUSLY* (VICTORY)

Ps 45: 4 In your majesty ride forth *v*

VICTORY (VICTOR'S VICTORIES VICTORIOUS VICTORIOUSLY)

2Sa 8: 6 gave David *v* everywhere he
Ps 44: 6 my sword does not bring me *v*;
60:12 With God we will gain the *v*,
129: 2 they have not gained the *v* over me.
Pr 11:14 but many advisers make *v* sure.
1Co 15:54 "Death has been swallowed up in *v*
15:57 He gives us the *v* through our Lord
1Jn 5: 4 This is the *v* that has overcome

VIEW

Pr 5:21 are in full *v* of the LORD,
2Ti 4: 1 and in *v* of his appearing

VILLAGE

Mk 6: 6 went around teaching from *v* to *v*.

VINDICATED (VINDICATION)

Job 13:18 I know I will be *v*.
1Ti 3:16 was *v* by the Spirit,

VINDICATION (VINDICATED)

Ps 24: 5 and *v* from God his Saviour.

VINE (VINEYARD)

Ps 128: 3 Your wife will be like a fruitful *v*
Isa 36:16 one of you will eat from his own *v*
Jnh 4: 6 Jonah was very happy about the *v*.
Jn 15: 1 "I am the true *v* and my Father is

VINEGAR

Pr	10: 26	As *v* to the teeth and smoke
Mk	15: 36	filled a sponge with wine *v*,

VINEYARD (VINE)

1Ki	21: 1	an incident involving a *v* belonging
Pr	31: 16	out of her earnings she plants a *v*.
SS	1: 6	my own *v* I have neglected.
Isa	5: 1	My loved one had a *v*
1Co	9: 7	Who plants a *v* and does not eat

VIOLATION

Heb	2: 2	every *v* and disobedience received

VIOLENCE (VIOLENT)

Ge	6: 11	in God's sight and was full of *v*.
Isa	53: 9	though he had done no *v*,
	60: 18	No longer will *v* be heard
Eze	45: 9	Give up your *v* and oppression
Joel	3: 19	of *v* done to the people of Judah,
Jnh	3: 8	give up their evil ways and their *v*.

VIOLENT (VIOLENCE)

Eze	18: 10	"Suppose he has a *v* son, who sheds
1Ti	1: 13	and a persecutor and a *v* man,
	3: 3	not *v* but gentle, not quarrelsome,
Tit	1: 7	not *v*, not pursuing dishonest gain.

VIPERS

Ps	140: 3	the poison of *v* is on their lips.
Lk	3: 7	"You brood of *v*! Who warned you
Ro	3: 13	"The poison of *v* is on their lips."

VIRGIN (VIRGINS)

Dt	22: 15	shall bring proof that she was a *v*
Isa	7: 14	The *v* will be with child
Mt	1: 23	The *v* will be with child
Lk	1: 34	I am a *v*?" The angel answered,
2Co	11: 2	that I might present you as a pure *v*

VIRGINS (VIRGIN)

Mt	25: 1	will be like ten *v* who took their
1Co	7: 25	Now about *v*: I have no command

VIRTUES*

Col	3: 14	And over all these *v* put on love,

VISIBLE

Eph	5: 13	exposed by the light becomes *v*,
Col	1: 16	and on earth, *v* and invisible,

VISION (VISIONS)

Da	9: 24	to seal up *v* and prophecy
Ac	26: 19	disobedient to the *v* from heaven.

VISIONS (VISION)

Nu	12: 6	I reveal myself to him in *v*,
Joel	2: 28	your young men will see *v*.
Ac	2: 17	your young men will see *v*,

VOICE

Dt	30: 20	listen to his *v*, and hold fast to him.
1Sa	15: 22	as in obeying the *v* of the LORD?
Job	40: 9	and can your *v* thunder like his?
Ps	19: 4	Their *v* goes out into all the earth,
	29: 3	The *v* of the LORD is
	66: 19	and heard my *v* in prayer.
	95: 7	Today, if you hear his *v*,
Pr	8: 1	Does not understanding raise her *v*
Isa	30: 21	your ears will hear a *v* behind you,

Isa	40: 3	A *v* of one calling:
Mk	1: 3	"a *v* of one calling in the desert,
Jn	5: 28	are in their graves will hear his *v*
	10: 3	and the sheep listen to his *v*.
Ro	10: 18	"Their *v* has gone out
Heb	3: 7	"Today, if you hear his *v*,
Rev	3: 20	If anyone hears my *v* and opens

VOMIT

Lev	18: 28	it will *v* you out as it vomited out
Pr	26: 11	As a dog returns to its *v*,
2Pe	2: 22	"A dog returns to its *v*," and,

VOW (VOWS)

Nu	6: 2	a *v* of separation to the LORD
	30: 2	When a man makes a *v*
Jdg	11: 30	Jephthah made a *v* to the LORD:

VOWS (VOW)

Ps	116: 14	I will fulfil my *v* to the LORD
Pr	20: 25	and only later to consider his *v*.

VULTURES

Mt	24: 28	is a carcass, there the *v* will gather.

WAGE (WAGES WAGING)

2Co	10: 3	we do not *w* war as the world does.

WAGES (WAGE)

Mal	3: 5	who defraud labourers of their *w*,
Lk	10: 7	for the worker deserves his *w*.
Ro	4: 4	his *w* are not credited to him
	6: 23	For the *w* of sin is death,
1Ti	5: 18	and "The worker deserves his *w*."

WAGING (WAGE)

Ro	7: 23	*w* war against the law of my mind

WAILING

Ps	30: 11	You turned my *w* into dancing;

WAIST

2Ki	1: 8	and a leather belt around his *w*."
Mt	3: 4	he had a leather belt around his *w*.

WAIT (AWAITS WAITED WAITING WAITS)

Ps	27: 14	*W* for the LORD;
	130: 5	I *w* for the LORD, my soul waits,
Isa	30: 18	Blessed are all who *w* for him!
Ac	1: 4	*w* for the gift my Father promised,
Ro	8: 23	as we *w* eagerly for our adoption
1Th	1: 10	and to *w* for his Son from heaven,
Tit	2: 13	while we *w* for the blessed hope—

WAITED (WAIT)

Ps	40: 1	I *w* patiently for the LORD;

WAITING (WAIT)

Heb	9: 28	to those who are *w* for him.

WAITS (WAIT)

Ro	8: 19	creation *w* in eager expectation

WAKE (AWAKE WAKENS)

Eph	5: 14	"*W* up, O sleeper,

WAKENS* (WAKE)

Isa	50: 4	He *w* me morning by morning,
	50: 4	*w* my ear to listen like one being

WALK (WALKED WALKING WALKS)

Lev	26: 12	I will w among you and be your
Dt	5: 33	W in all the way that the LORD
	6: 7	and when you w along the road,
	10: 12	to w in all his ways, to love him,
	11: 19	and when you w along the road,
	11: 22	to w in all his ways and to hold fast
	26: 17	and that you will w in his ways,
Jos	22: 5	to w in all his ways,
Ps	1: 1	who does not w in the counsel
	15: 2	He whose w is blameless
	23: 4	Even though I w
	84: 11	from those whose w is blameless.
	89: 15	who w in the light of your presence
	119: 45	I will w about in freedom,
Pr	4: 12	When you w, your steps will not be
	6: 22	When you w, they will guide you;
Isa	2: 3	so that we may w in his paths."
	2: 5	let us w in the light of the LORD.
	30: 21	saying, "This is the way; w in it."
	40: 31	they will w and not be faint.
	57: 2	Those who w uprightly
Jer	6: 16	ask where the good way is, and w
Da	4: 37	And those who w in pride he is able
Am	3: 3	Do two w together
Mic	4: 5	All the nations may w
	6: 8	and to w humbly with your God.
Mk	2: 9	'Get up, take your mat and w'?
Jn	8: 12	Whoever follows me will never w
1Jn	1: 6	with him yet w in the darkness,
	1: 7	But if we w in the light,
2Jn	: 6	his command is that you w in love.

WALKED (WALK)

Ge	5: 24	Enoch w with God; then he was no
Jos	14: 9	which your feet have w will be your
Mt	14: 29	and w on the water to Jesus.

WALKING (WALK)

1Ki	3: 3	love the LORD by w according
Da	3: 25	I see four men w around in the fire,
2Jn	: 4	of your children w in the truth,

WALKS (WALK)

Pr	10: 9	The man of integrity w securely,
	13: 20	He who w with the wise grows wise
Isa	33: 15	He who w righteously
Jn	11: 9	A man who w by day will not

WALL (WALLS)

Jos	6: 20	w collapsed; so every man charged
Ne	2: 17	let us rebuild the w of Jerusalem,
Eph	2: 14	the dividing w of hostility,
Rev	21: 12	It had a great, high w

WALLOWING

2Pe	2: 22	back to her w in the mud."

WALLS (WALL)

Isa	58: 12	be called Repairer of Broken W,
	60: 18	but you will call your w Salvation
Heb	11: 30	By faith the w of Jericho fell,

WANDER (WANDERED)

Nu	32: 13	he made them w in the desert forty
Jas	5: 19	one of you should w from the truth

WANDERED (WANDER)

Eze	34: 6	My sheep w over all the mountains

Mt	18: 12	go to look for the one that w off?
1Ti	6: 10	have w from the faith and pierced
2Ti	2: 18	who have w away from the truth.

WANT (WANTED WANTING WANTS)

1Sa	8: 19	"We w a king over us.
Mt	19: 21	Jesus answered, "If you w
Lk	19: 14	'We don't w this man to be our king
Ro	7: 15	For what I w to do I do not do,
	13: 3	Do you w to be free from fear
2Co	12: 14	what I w is not your possessions
Php	3: 10	I w to know Christ and the power

WANTED (WANT)

1Co	12: 18	of them, just as he w them to be.
Heb	6: 17	Because God w to make

WANTING (WANT)

Da	5: 27	weighed on the scales and found w.
2Pe	3: 9	with you, not w anyone to perish,

WANTS (WANT)

Mt	5: 42	from the one who w to borrow
	20: 26	whoever w to become great
Mk	8: 35	For whoever w to save his life will
	10: 43	whoever w to become great
Ro	9: 18	he hardens whom he w to harden.
1Ti	2: 4	who w all men to be saved
1Pe	5: 2	you are willing, as God w you to be;

WAR (WARRIOR WARS)

Jos	11: 23	Then the land had rest from w,
1Sa	15: 18	make w on them until you have
Ps	68: 30	the nations who delight in w.
	120: 7	but when I speak, they are for w.
	144: 1	who trains my hands for w,
Isa	2: 4	nor will they train for w any more.
Da	9: 26	W will continue until the end,
Ro	7: 23	waging w against the law
2Co	10: 3	we do not wage w as the world does
1Pe	2: 11	which w against your soul.
Rev	12: 7	And there was w in heaven.
	19: 11	With justice he judges and makes w

WARN* (WARNED WARNING WARNINGS)

Ex	19: 21	w the people so they do not force
Nu	24: 14	let me w you of what this people
1Sa	8: 9	but w them solemnly and let them
1Ki	2: 42	swear by the LORD and w you,
2Ch	19: 10	you are to w them not to sin
Ps	81: 8	O my people, and I will w you—
Jer	42: 19	I w you today that you made a fatal
Eze	3: 18	and you do not w him or speak out
	3: 19	But if you do w the wicked man
	3: 20	Since you did not w him, he will die
	3: 21	if you do w the righteous man not
	33: 3	blows the trumpet to w the people,
	33: 6	blow the trumpet to w the people
	33: 9	if you do w the wicked man to turn
Lk	16: 28	Let him w them, so that they will
Ac	4: 17	we must w these men
1Co	4: 14	but to w you, as my dear children.
Gal	5: 21	I w you, as I did before, that those
1Th	5: 14	brothers, w those who are idle,
2Th	3: 15	an enemy, but w him as a brother.
2Ti	2: 14	W them before God
Tit	3: 10	and then w him a second time.
	3: 10	W a divisive person once,
Rev	22: 18	I w everyone who hears the words

WARNED (WARN)

2Ki 17: 13 The LORD w Israel and Judah
Ps 19: 11 By them is your servant w;
Jer 22: 21 I w you when you felt secure,
Mt 3: 7 Who w you to flee
1Th 4: 6 have already told you and w you.
Heb 11: 7 when w about things not yet seen,
12: 25 they refused him who w them

WARNING (WARN)

Jer 6: 8 Take w, O Jerusalem,
1Ti 5: 20 so that the others may take w.

WARNINGS (WARN)

1Co 10: 11 and were written down as w for us,

WARRIOR (WAR)

Ex 15: 3 The LORD is a w;
1Ch 28: 3 you are a w and have shed blood.'
Pr 16: 32 Better a patient man than a w,

WARS (WAR)

Ps 46: 9 He makes w cease to the ends
Mt 24: 6 You will hear of w and rumours of w,

WASH (WASHED WASHING)

Ps 51: 7 w me, and I will be whiter
Jer 4: 14 w the evil from your heart
Jn 13: 5 and began to w his disciples' feet,
Ac 22: 16 be baptised and w your sins away,
Jas 4: 8 W your hands, you sinners,
Rev 22: 14 Blessed are those who w their robes

WASHED (WASH)

Ps 73: 13 in vain have I w my hands
1Co 6: 11 you were w, you were sanctified,
Heb 10: 22 and having our bodies w
2Pe 2: 22 and, "A sow that is w goes back
Rev 7: 14 they have w their robes

WASHING (WASH)

Eph 5: 26 cleansing her by the w with water
1Ti 5: 10 showing hospitality, w the feet
Tit 3: 5 us through the w of rebirth

WASTED (WASTING)

Jn 6: 12 Let nothing be w."

WASTING (WASTED)

2Co 4: 16 Though outwardly we are w away,

WATCH (WATCHER WATCHES WATCHING WATCHMAN)

Ge 31: 49 "May the LORD keep w
Ps 90: 4 or like a w in the night.
141: 3 keep w over the door of my lips.
Pr 4: 6 love her, and she will w over you.
6: 22 when you sleep, they will w
Jer 31: 10 will w over his flock like a shepherd
Mic 7: 7 I w in hope for the LORD,
Mt 24: 42 "Therefore keep w, because you do
26: 41 W and pray so that you will not fall
Mk 13: 35 "Therefore keep w because you do
Lk 2: 8 keeping w over their flocks at night
1Ti 4: 16 W your life and doctrine closely.
Heb 13: 17 They keep w over you

WATCHER* (WATCH)

Job 7: 20 O w of men?

WATCHES* (WATCH)

Nu 19: 5 While he w, the heifer is
Job 24: 15 The eye of the adulterer w for dusk;
Ps 1: 6 For the LORD w over the way
33: 14 from his dwelling-place he w
63: 6 of you through the w of the night.
119: 148 through the w of the night,
121: 3 he who w over you will not slumber
121: 4 indeed, he who w over Israel
121: 5 The LORD w over you—
127: 1 Unless the LORD w over the city,
145: 20 LORD w over all who love him,
146: 9 The LORD w over the alien
Pr 31: 27 She w over the affairs
Ecc 11: 4 Whoever w the wind will not plant;
La 2: 19 as the w of the night begin;
4: 16 he no longer w over them.

WATCHING (WATCH)

Lk 12: 37 whose master finds them w

WATCHMAN (WATCH)

Eze 3: 17 I have made you a w for the house
33: 6 but I will hold the w accountable

WATER (WATERED WATERING WATERS WELL-WATERED)

Ex 7: 20 all the w was changed into blood.
17: 1 but there was no w for the people
Nu 20: 2 there was no w for the community,
Ps 1: 3 like a tree planted by streams of w,
22: 14 I am poured out like w,
42: 1 As the deer pants for streams of w,
Pr 25: 21 if he is thirsty, give him w to drink.
Isa 12: 3 With joy you will draw w
30: 20 of adversity and the w of affliction,
32: 2 like streams of w in the desert
49: 10 and lead them beside springs of w.
Jer 2: 13 broken cisterns that cannot hold w.
17: 8 will be like a tree planted by the w
31: 9 I will lead them beside streams of w
Eze 36: 25 I will sprinkle clean w on you,
Zec 14: 8 On that day living w will flow out
Mt 14: 29 and walked on the w to Jesus.
Mk 9: 41 anyone who gives you a cup of w
Lk 5: 4 to Simon, "Put into deep w,
Jn 3: 5 a man is born of w and the Spirit,
4: 10 he would have given you living w."
7: 38 streams of living w will flow
Eph 5: 26 washing with w through the word,
Heb 10: 22 our bodies washed with pure w
1Pe 3: 21 this w symbolises baptism that now
2Pe 2: 17 These men are springs without w
1Jn 5: 6 This is the one who came by w
5: 6 come by w only, but by w
5: 8 the Spirit, the w and the blood;
Rev 7: 17 to springs of living w.
21: 6 cost from the spring of the w of life.

WATERED (WATER)

1Co 3: 6 I planted the seed, Apollos w it,

WATERING (WATER)

Isa 55: 10 it without w the earth

WATERS (WATER)

Ps 23: 2 he leads me beside quiet w,
Ecc 11: 1 Cast your bread upon the w,
SS 8: 7 Many w cannot quench love;
Isa 11: 9 as the w cover the sea.

Isa   43: 2 When you pass through the w,
      55: 1 come to the w;
      58:11 like a spring whose w never fail.
Hab   2:14 as the w cover the sea.
1Co   3: 7 plants nor he who w is anything,

WAVE (WAVES)

Lev   23:11 He is to w the sheaf
Jas   1: 6 he who doubts is like a w of the sea,

WAVER*

1Ki   18:21 "How long will you w
Ro   4:20 Yet he did not w through unbelief

WAVES (WAVE)

Isa   57:20 whose w cast up mire and mud.
Mt   8:27 Even the winds and the w obey him
Eph   4:14 tossed back and forth by the w,

WAY (WAYS)

Ex   13:21 of cloud to guide them on their w
      18:20 and show them the w to live
Dt   1:33 to show you the w you should go.
      32: 6 Is this the w you repay the LORD,
1Sa   12:23 I will teach you the w that is good
2Sa   22:31 "As for God, his w is perfect;
1Ki   8:23 wholeheartedly in your w,
       8:36 Teach them the right w to live,
Job   23:10 But he knows the w that I take;
Ps   1: 1 or stand in the w of sinners
      32: 8 teach you in the w you should go;
      37: 5 Commit your w to the LORD;
      86:11 Teach me your w, O LORD,
     119: 9 can a young man keep his w pure?
     139:24 See if there is any offensive w in me
Pr   4:11 I guide you in the w of wisdom
      12:15 The w of a fool seems right to him,
      14:12 There is a w that seems right
      16:17 he who guards his w guards his life
      19: 2 nor to be hasty and miss the w.
      22: 6 Train a child in the w he should go,
      30:19 and the w of a man with a maiden.
Isa   30:21 saying, "This is the w; walk in it."
      35: 8 it will be called the W of Holiness.
      40: 3 the w for the LORD;
      48:17 you in the w you should go.
      53: 6 each of us has turned to his own w;
      55: 7 Let the wicked forsake his w
Jer   5:31 and my people love it this w.
Mal   3: 1 who will prepare the w before me.
Mt   3: 3 'Prepare the w for the Lord,
Lk   7:27 who will prepare your w before you
Jn   14: 6 "I am the w and the truth
Ac   1:11 in the same w you have seen him go
       9: 2 any there who belonged to the W,
      24:14 of the W, which they call a sect.
1Co   10:13 also provide a w out so that you can
      12:31 will show you the most excellent w.
      14: 1 Follow the w of love and eagerly
Col   1:10 and may please him in every w:
Tit   2:10 that in every w they will make
Heb   4:15 who has been tempted in every w,
       9: 8 was showing by this that the w
      10:20 and living w opened for us
      13:18 desire to live honourably in every w.

WAYS (WAY)

Ex   33:13 teach me your w so I may know
Dt   10:12 to walk in all his w, to love him,
      26:17 and that you will walk in his w,

Dt   30:16 in his w, and to keep his commands
      32: 4 and all his w are just.
Jos   22: 5 in all his w, to obey his commands,
2Ch   11:17 walking in the w of David
Job   34:21 "His eyes are on the w of men;
Ps   25: 4 Show me your w, O LORD,
      25:10 All the w of the LORD are loving
      37: 7 fret when men succeed in their w,
      51:13 I will teach transgressors your w,
      77:13 Your w, O God, are holy.
     119:59 I have considered my w
     139: 3 you are familiar with all my w.
     145:17 The LORD is righteous in all his w
Pr   3: 6 in all your w acknowledge him,
       4:26 and take only w that are firm.
       5:21 For a man's w are in full view
      16: 2 All a man's w seem innocent
      16: 7 When a man's w are pleasing
Isa   2: 3 He will teach us his w,
      55: 8 neither are your w my w,"
Eze   28:15 You were blameless in your w
      33: 8 out to dissuade him from his w,
Hos   14: 9 The w of the LORD are right;
Ro   1:30 they invent w of doing evil;
Jas   3: 2 We all stumble in many w.

WEAK (WEAKER WEAKNESS WEAKNESSES

Ps   41: 1 is he who has regard for the w;
      72:13 He will take pity on the w
      82: 3 Defend the cause of the w
Eze   34: 4 You have not strengthened the w
Mt   26:41 spirit is willing, but the body is w."
Ac   20:35 of hard work we must help the w,
Ro   14: 1 Accept him whose faith is w,
      15: 1 to bear with the failings of the w
1Co   1:27 God chose the w things
       8: 9 become a stumbling-block to the w.
       9:22 To the w I became w, to win the w.
      11:30 That is why many among you are w
2Co   12:10 For when I am w, then I am strong.
1Th   5:14 help the w, be patient
Heb   12:12 your feeble arms and w knees.

WEAK-WILLED (WILL)

2Ti   3: 6 and gain control over w women,

WEAKER* (WEAK)

2Sa   3: 1 the house of Saul grew w and w.
1Co   12:22 seem to be w are indispensable,
1Pe   3: 7 them with respect as the w partner

WEAKNESS* (WEAK)

La   1: 6 in w they have fled
Ro   8:26 the Spirit helps us in our w.
1Co   1:25 and the w of God is stronger
       2: 3 I came to you in w and fear,
      15:43 it is sown in w, it is raised in power;
2Co   11:30 boast of the things that show my w.
      12: 9 for my power is made perfect in w
      13: 4 he was crucified in w, yet he lives
Heb   5: 2 since he himself is subject to w.
      11:34 whose w was turned to strength;

WEAKNESSES* (WEAK)

2Co   12: 5 about myself, except about my w.
      12: 9 all the more gladly about my w,
      12:10 I delight in w, in insults,
Heb   4:15 unable to sympathise with our w,

WEALTH

Dt	8:18	gives you the ability to produce w,
2Ch	1:11	and you have not asked for w,
Ps	39: 6	he heaps up w, not knowing who
Pr	3: 9	Honour the LORD with your w,
	10: 4	but diligent hands bring w.
	11: 4	W is worthless in the day of wrath,
	13: 7	to be poor, yet has great w.
	15:16	than great w with turmoil.
	22: 4	bring w and honour and life.
Ecc	5:10	whoever loves w is never satisfied
	5:13	w hoarded to the harm of its owner,
SS	8: 7	all the w of his house for love,
Mt	13:22	and the deceitfulness of w choke it,
Mk	10:22	away sad, because he had great w.
	12:44	They all gave out of their w; but she
Lk	15:13	and there squandered his w
1Ti	6:17	nor to put their hope in w,
Jas	5: 2	Your w has rotted, and moths have
	5: 3	You have hoarded w

WEAPON (WEAPONS)

Ne	4:17	work with one hand and held a w

WEAPONS (WEAPON)

Ecc	9:18	Wisdom is better than w of war,
2Co	6: 7	with w of righteousness
	10: 4	The w we fight with are not

WEAR (WEARING)

Dt	8: 4	Your clothes did not w out
	22: 5	nor a man w women's clothing,
Ps	102:26	they will all w out like a garment.
Pr	23: 4	Do not w yourself out to get rich;
Isa	51: 6	the earth will w out like a garment.
Heb	1:11	they will all w out like a garment.
Rev	3:18	and white clothes to w,

WEARIES (WEARY)

Ecc	12:12	and much study w the body.

WEARING (WEAR)

Jn	19: 5	When Jesus came out w the crown
Jas	2: 3	attention to the man w fine clothes
1Pe	3: 3	as braided hair and the w
Rev	7: 9	They were w white robes

WEARY (WEARIES)

Isa	40:28	He will not grow tired or w,
	40:31	they will run and not grow w,
	50: 4	know the word that sustains the w.
Mt	11:28	all you who are w and burdened,
Gal	6: 9	Let us not become w in doing good,
Heb	12: 3	so that you will not grow w
Rev	2: 3	my name, and have not grown w.

WEDDING

Mt	22:11	who was not wearing w clothes.
Rev	19: 7	For the w of the Lamb has come,

WEEDS

Mt	13:25	and sowed w among the wheat,

WEEK

Mt	28: 1	at dawn on the first day of the w,
1Co	16: 2	On the first day of every w,

WEEP (WEEPING WEPT)

Ecc	3: 4	a time to w and a time to laugh,
Lk	6:21	Blessed are you who w now,

Lk	23:28	w for yourselves and for your

WEEPING (WEEP)

Ps	30: 5	w may remain for a night,
	126: 6	He who goes out w,
Jer	31:15	Rachel w for her children
Mt	2:18	Rachel w for her children
	8:12	where there will be w and gnashing

WEIGH (OUTWEIGHS WEIGHED WEIGHS WEIGHTIER WEIGHTS)

1Co	14:29	others should w carefully what is

WEIGHED (WEIGH)

Job	28:15	nor can its price be w in silver.
Da	5:27	You have been w on the scales
Lk	21:34	or your hearts will be w

WEIGHS (WEIGH)

Pr	12:25	An anxious heart w a man down,
	15:28	of the righteous w its answers,
	21: 2	but the LORD w the heart.
	24:12	not he who w the heart perceive

WEIGHTIER* (WEIGH)

Jn	5:36	"I have testimony w than that

WEIGHTS (WEIGH)

Lev	19:36	Use honest scales and honest w,
Dt	25:13	Do not have two differing w
Pr	11: 1	but accurate w are his delight.

WELCOME (WELCOMES)

Mk	9:37	welcomes me does not w me
2Pe	1:11	and you will receive a rich w

WELCOMES (WELCOME)

Mt	18: 5	whoever w a little child like this
2Jn	: 11	Anyone who w him shares

WELL [1] (WELLED WELLING WELLS)

Lk	14: 5	falls into a w on the Sabbath day,

WELL [2]

Mt	15:31	crippled made w, the lame walking
Lk	17:19	your faith has made you w."
Jas	5:15	in faith will make the sick person w

WELL-WATERED (WATER)

Isa	58:11	You will be like a w garden,

WELLED* (WELL)

2Co	8: 2	and their extreme poverty w up

WELLING* (WELL)

Jn	4:14	of water w up to eternal life."

WELLS (WELL)

Isa	12: 3	from the w of salvation.

WELLSPRING *(SPRING)

Pr	4:23	for it is the w of life.

WEPT (WEEP)

Ps	137: 1	of Babylon we sat and w
Lk	22:62	And he went outside and w bitterly
Jn	11:35	Jesus w.

WEST

Ps	103:12	as far as the east is from the w,
	107: 3	from east and w, from north

WHEAT

Mt	3: 12	gathering the *w* into his barn
	13: 25	and sowed weeds among the *w*,
Lk	22: 31	Satan has asked to sift you as *w*.
Jn	12: 24	a grain of *w* falls to the ground

WHEELS

Eze	1: 16	appearance and structure of the *w*:

WHIRLWIND (WIND)

2Ki	2: 1	to take Elijah up to heaven in a *w*,
Hos	8: 7	and reap the *w*.
Na	1: 3	His way is in the *w* and the storm,

WHISPER (WHISPERED)

1Ki	19: 12	And after the fire came a gentle *w*.
Job	26: 14	how faint the *w* we hear of him!
Ps	107: 29	He stilled the storm to a *w*;

WHISPERED (WHISPER)

Mt	10: 27	speak in the daylight; what is *w*

WHITE (WHITER)

Isa	1: 18	they shall be as *w* as snow;
Da	7: 9	His clothing was as *w* as snow;
	7: 9	the hair of his head was *w* like wool
Mt	28: 3	and his clothes were *w* as snow.
Rev	1: 14	hair were *w* like wool, as *w* as snow,
	3: 4	dressed in *w*, for they are worthy.
	6: 2	and there before me was a *w* horse!
	7: 13	"These in *w* robes—who are they,
	19: 11	and there before me was a *w* horse,
	20: 11	Then I saw a great *w* throne

WHITER (WHITE)

Ps	51: 7	and I will be *w* than snow.

WHOLE

Ge	1: 29	plant on the face of the *w* earth
	2: 6	and watered the *w* surface
	11: 1	Now the *w* world had one language
Ex	12: 47	The *w* community
	19: 5	Although the *w* earth is mine,
Lev	16: 17	and the *w* community of Israel.
Nu	14: 21	of the LORD fills the *w* earth,
	32: 13	until the *w* generation
Dt	13: 16	*w* burnt offering to the LORD your
	19: 8	gives the *w* land he promised
Jos	2: 3	come to spy out the *w* land."
1Sa	1: 28	For his *w* life he will be given
	17: 46	the *w* world will know that there is
1Ki	10: 24	The *w* world sought audience
2Ki	21: 8	and will keep the *w* Law that my
Ps	72: 19	may the *w* earth be filled
Pr	4: 22	and health to a man's *w* body.
	8: 31	rejoicing in his *w* world
Ecc	12: 13	for this is the *w* duty of man.
Isa	1: 5	Your *w* head is injured,
	6: 3	the *w* earth is full of his glory."
	14: 26	plan determined for the *w* world;
Eze	34: 6	were scattered over the *w* earth,
	37: 11	these bones are the *w* house
Da	2: 35	mountain and filled the *w* earth.
Zep	1: 18	the *w* world will be consumed,
Zec	14: 9	will be king over the *w* earth.
Mal	3: 10	the *w* tithe into the storehouse,
Mt	5: 29	than for your *w* body to be thrown
	6: 22	your *w* body will be full of light.
	16: 26	for a man if he gains the *w* world,

Mt	24: 14	will be preached in the *w* world
Lk	21: 35	live on the face of the *w* earth.
Jn	12: 19	Look how the *w* world has gone
	13: 10	to wash his feet; his *w* body is clean
	21: 25	the *w* world would not have room
Ac	17: 26	they should inhabit the *w* earth;
	20: 27	proclaim to you the *w* will of God.
Ro	1: 9	whom I serve with my *w* heart
	3: 19	and the *w* world held accountable
	8: 22	know that the *w* creation has been
1Co	4: 9	made a spectacle to the *w* universe,
	12: 17	If the *w* body were an ear,
Gal	3: 22	declares that the *w* world is
	5: 3	obligated to obey the *w* law.
Eph	4: 10	in order to fill the *w* universe.)
	4: 13	attaining to the *w* measure
1Th	5: 23	May your *w* spirit, soul
Jas	2: 10	For whoever keeps the *w* law
1Jn	2: 2	but also for the sins of the *w* world.
Rev	3: 10	going to come upon the *w* world

WHOLEHEARTED* (HEART)

2Ki	20: 3	you faithfully and with *w* devotion
1Ch	28: 9	and serve him with *w* devotion
	29: 19	my son Solomon the *w* devotion
Isa	38: 3	you faithfully and with *w* devotion

WHOLEHEARTEDLY* (HEART)

Nu	14: 24	a different spirit and follows me *w*,
	32: 11	they have not followed me *w*,
	32: 12	for they followed the LORD *w*.'
Dt	1: 36	because he followed the LORD *w*
Jos	14: 8	followed the LORD my God *w*.
	14: 9	followed the LORD my God *w*.'
	14: 14	the LORD, the God of Israel, *w*.
1Ki	8: 23	with your servants who continue *w*
1Ch	29: 9	for they had given freely and *w*
2Ch	6: 14	with your servants who continue *w*
	15: 15	oath because they had sworn it *w*.
	19: 9	and *w* in the fear of the LORD.
	25: 2	in the eyes of the LORD, but not *w*
	31: 21	he sought his God and worked *w*.
Ro	6: 17	you *w* obeyed the form of teaching
Eph	6: 7	Serve *w*, as if you were serving

WHOLESOME*

2Ki	2: 22	And the water has remained *w*
2Pe	3: 1	to stimulate you to *w* thinking.

WICK

Isa	42: 3	a smouldering *w* he will not snuff out
Mt	12: 20	a smouldering *w* he will not snuff out

WICKED (WICKEDNESS)

Ge	13: 13	Now the men of Sodom were *w*
	39: 9	How then could I do such a *w* thing
Ex	23: 1	Do not help a *w* man
Nu	14: 35	things to this whole *w* community,
Dt	15: 9	not to harbour this *w* thought:
Jdg	19: 22	some of the *w* men
1Sa	2: 12	Eli's sons were *w* men; they had no
	15: 18	completely destroy those *w* people,
	25: 17	He is such a *w* man that no-one can
2Sa	13: 12	in Israel! Don't do this *w* thing.
2Ki	17: 11	They did *w* things that provoked
2Ch	7: 14	and turn from their *w* ways,
	19: 2	"Should you help the *w*
Ne	13: 17	"What is this *w* thing you are doing

Ps	1: 1	walk in the counsel of the *w*
	1: 5	Therefore the *w* will not stand
	7: 9	to an end the violence of the *w*
	10: 13	Why does the *w* man revile God?
	11: 5	the *w* and those who love violence
	12: 8	The *w* freely strut about
	26: 5	and refuse to sit with the *w*.
	32: 10	Many are the woes of the *w*,
	36: 1	concerning the sinfulness of the *w*:
	37: 13	but the LORD laughs at the *w*,
	49: 5	when *w* deceivers surround me—
	50: 16	But to the *w*, God says:
	58: 3	Even from birth the *w* go astray;
	73: 3	when I saw the prosperity of the *w*.
	82: 2	and show partiality to the *w*? *Selah*
	112: 10	the longings of the *w* will come
	119: 61	Though the *w* bind me with ropes,
	119: 155	Salvation is far from the *w*,
	140: 8	do not grant the *w* their desires,
	141: 10	Let the *w* fall into their own nets,
	146: 9	but he frustrates the ways of the *w*.
Pr	2: 12	you from the ways of *w* men,
	4: 14	Do not set foot on the path of the *w*
	6: 18	a heart that devises *w* schemes,
	9: 7	whoever rebukes a *w* man incurs
	10: 20	the heart of the *w* is of little value.
	10: 28	the hopes of the *w* come to nothing
	11: 5	*w* are brought down by their own
	11: 10	when the *w* perish, there are shouts
	11: 21	The *w* will not go unpunished,
	12: 5	but the advice of the *w* is deceitful.
	12: 10	the kindest acts of the *w* are cruel.
	14: 19	the *w* at the gates of the righteous.
	15: 3	keeping watch on the *w*
	15: 26	detests the thoughts of the *w*,
	21: 10	The *w* man craves evil;
	21: 29	A *w* man puts up a bold front,
	28: 1	*w* man flees though no-one pursues,
	28: 4	who forsake the law praise the *w*,
	29: 7	but the *w* have no such concern.
	29: 16	When the *w* thrive, so does sin,
	29: 27	the *w* detest the upright.
Isa	11: 4	breath of his lips he will slay the *w*.
	13: 11	the *w* for their sins.
	26: 10	Though grace is shown to the *w*,
	48: 22	says the LORD, "for the *w*."
	53: 9	He was assigned a grave with the *w*
	55: 7	Let the *w* forsake his way
	57: 20	But the *w* are like the tossing sea,
Jer	35: 15	of you must turn from your *w* ways
Eze	3: 18	that *w* man will die for his sin,
	13: 22	you encouraged the *w* not to turn
	14: 7	and puts a *w* stumbling-block
	18: 21	"But if a *w* man turns away
	18: 23	pleasure in the death of the *w*?
	21: 25	"'O profane and *w* prince of Israel,
	33: 8	When I say to the *w*, 'O *w* man,
	33: 11	pleasure in the death of the *w*,
	33: 14	to the *w* man, 'You will surely die,'
	33: 19	And if a *w* man turns away
Da	12: 10	but the *w* will continue to be *w*.
Mt	12: 39	*w* and adulterous generation asks
	12: 45	be with this *w* generation."
	12: 45	with it seven other spirits more *w*
Lk	6: 35	he is kind to the ungrateful and *w*.
Ac	2: 23	and you, with the help of *w* men,
Ro	4: 5	but trusts God who justifies the *w*,
1Co	5: 13	"Expel the *w* man from among you
	6: 9	not know that the *w* will not inherit
Rev	2: 2	that you cannot tolerate *w* men,

WICKEDNESS (WICKED)

Ge	6: 5	The LORD saw how great man's *w*
Ex	34: 7	and forgiving *w*, rebellion and sin.
Lev	16: 21	and confess over it all the *w*
	19: 29	to prostitution and be filled with *w*.
Dt	9: 4	it is on account of the *w*
Ne	9: 2	and confessed their sins and the *w*
Ps	45: 7	You love righteousness and hate *w*;
	92: 15	he is my Rock, and there is no *w*
Pr	13: 6	but *w* overthrows the sinner.
Jer	3: 2	land with your prostitution and *w*.
	8: 6	No one repents of his *w*,
	14: 20	O LORD, we acknowledge our *w*
Eze	18: 20	the *w* of the wicked will be charged
	28: 15	created till *w* was found in you.
	33: 19	wicked man turns away from his *w*
Da	4: 27	and your *w* by being kind
	9: 24	to atone for *w*, to bring
Jnh	1: 2	its *w* has come up before me."
Mt	24: 12	Because of the increase of *w*,
Lk	11: 39	inside you are full of greed and *w*.
Ac	1: 18	(With the reward he got for his *w*,
Ro	1: 18	who suppress the truth by their *w*,
1Co	5: 8	the yeast of malice and *w*,
2Co	6: 14	what do righteousness and *w* have
2Ti	2: 19	of the Lord must turn away from *w*
Tit	2: 14	for us to redeem us from all *w*
Heb	1: 9	loved righteousness and hated *w*;
	8: 12	For I will forgive their *w*
2Pe	2: 15	who loved the wages of *w*.

WIDE

Ps	81: 10	Open *w* your mouth and I will fill it
Isa	54: 2	stretch your tent curtains *w*,
Mt	7: 13	For *w* is the gate and broad is
2Co	6: 13	my children—open *w* your hearts
Eph	3: 18	to grasp how *w* and long and high

WIDOW (WIDOWS)

Ex	22: 22	"Do not take advantage of a *w*
Dt	10: 18	cause of the fatherless and the *w*,
Ps	146: 9	sustains the fatherless and the *w*,
Isa	1: 17	plead the case of the *w*.
Lk	21: 2	saw a poor *w* put in two very small
1Ti	5: 4	But if a *w* has children

WIDOWS (WIDOW)

Ps	68: 5	to the fatherless, a defender of *w*,
Ac	6: 1	their *w* were being overlooked
1Co	7: 8	to the unmarried and the *w* I say:
1Ti	5: 3	to those *w* who are really
Jas	1: 27	look after orphans and *w*

WIFE (WIVES WIVES')

Ge	2: 24	and mother and be united to his *w*,
	19: 26	But Lot's *w* looked back
	24: 67	she became his *w*, and he loved her;
Ex	20: 17	shall not covet your neighbour's *w*,
Lev	20: 10	adultery with another man's *w*—
Dt	5: 21	shall not covet your neighbour's *w*.
	24: 5	happiness to the *w* he has married.
Ru	4: 13	took Ruth and she became his *w*.
Pr	5: 18	in the *w* of your youth.
	12: 4	*w* of noble character is her
	18: 22	He who finds a *w* finds what is
	19: 13	quarrelsome *w* is like a constant
	31: 10	*w* of whole character who can find?
Hos	1: 2	take to yourself an adulterous *w*
Mal	2: 14	the witness between you and the *w*
Mt	1: 20	to take Mary home as your *w*,

WILD

Mt	19: 3	for a man to divorce his *w* for any
Lk	17:32	Remember Lot's *w*! Whoever tries
	18:29	or *w* or brothers or parents
1Co	7: 2	each man should have his own *w*,
	7:33	how he can please his *w*—
Eph	5:23	the husband is the head of the *w*
	5:33	must love his *w* as he loves himself,
1Ti	3: 2	husband of but one *w*, temperate,
Rev	21: 9	I will show you the bride, the *w*

WILD

Ge	1:25	God made the *w* animals according
	8: 1	Noah and all the *w* animals
Lk	15:13	squandered his wealth in *w* living.
Ro	11:17	and you, though a *w* olive shoot,

WILFUL (WILL)

Pr	19:13	Keep your servant also from *w* sins;

WILL (WEAK-WILLED WILFUL WILLING WILLINGNESS)

Ps	40: 8	I desire to do your *w*, O my God;
	143:10	Teach me to do your *w*,
Isa	53:10	Yet it was the LORD's *w*
Mt	6:10	your *w* be done
	7:21	who does the *w* of my Father
	10:29	apart from the *w* of your Father.
	12:50	does the *w* of my Father
	26:39	Yet not as I *w*, but as you *w*."
	26:42	I drink it, may your *w* be done."
Jn	6:38	but to do the *w* of him who sent me.
	7:17	If anyone chooses to do God's *w*,
Ac	20:27	to you the whole *w* of God.
Ro	12: 2	and approve what God's *w* is—
1Co	7:37	but has control over his own *w*,
Eph	5:17	understand what the Lord's *w* is.
Php	2:13	for it is God who works in you to *w*
1Th	4: 3	God's *w* that you should be sanctified:
	5:18	for this is God's *w* for you
2Ti	2:26	has taken them captive to do his *w*.
Heb	2: 4	distributed according to his *w*.
	9:16	In the case of a *w*, it is necessary
	10: 7	I have come to do your *w*, O God
	13:21	everything good for doing his *w*,
Jas	4:15	"If it is the Lord's *w*,
1Pe	3:17	It is better, if it is God's *w*,
	4: 2	but rather for the *w* of God.
2Pe	1:21	never had its origin in the *w*
1Jn	5:14	we ask anything according to his *w*,
Rev	4:11	and by your *w* they were created

WILLING (WILL)

1Ch	28: 9	devotion and with a *w* mind,
	29: 5	who is *w* to consecrate himself
Ps	51:12	grant me a *w* spirit, to sustain me.
Da	3:28	were *w* to give up their lives rather
Mt	18:14	Father in heaven is not *w* that any
	23:37	her wings, but you were not *w*.
	26:41	The spirit is *w*, but the body is weak
1Ti	6:18	and to be generous and *w* to share.
1Pe	5: 2	but because you are *w*,

WILLINGNESS° (WILL)

2Co	8:11	so that your eager *w*
	8:12	For if the *w* is there, the gift is

WIN (WINS WON)

1Co	9:19	myself a slave to everyone, to *w*
Php	3:14	on towards the goal to *w* the prize
1Th	4:12	your daily life may *w* the respect

WIND (WHIRLWIND WINDS)

Ps	1: 4	that the *w* blows away.
Ecc	2:11	meaningless, a chasing after the *w*;
Hos	8: 7	"They sow the *w*
Mk	4:41	Even the *w* and the waves obey
Jn	3: 8	The *w* blows wherever it pleases.
Eph	4:14	and there by every *w* of teaching
Jas	1: 6	blown and tossed by the *w*.

WINDOW

Jos	2:21	she tied the scarlet cord in the *w*.
Ac	20: 9	in a *w* was a young man named
2Co	11:33	in a basket from a *w* in the wall

WINDS (WIND)

Ps	104: 4	He makes *w* his messengers,
Mt	24:31	gather his elect from the four *w*,
Heb	1: 7	"He makes his angels *w*,

WINE

Ps	104:15	*w* that gladdens the heart of man,
Pr	20: 1	*W* is a mocker and beer a brawler;
	23:20	join those who drink too much *w*
	23:31	Do not gaze at *w* when it is red,
	31: 6	*w* to those who are in anguish;
SS	1: 2	your love is more delightful than *w*.
Isa	28: 7	And these also stagger from *w*
	55: 1	Come, buy *w* and milk
Mt	9:17	Neither do men pour new *w*
Lk	23:36	They offered him *w* vinegar
Jn	2: 3	When the *w* was gone, Jesus'
Ro	14:21	not to eat meat or drink *w*
Eph	5:18	on *w*, which leads to debauchery.
1Ti	5:23	a little *w* because of your stomach
Rev	16:19	with the *w* of the fury of his wrath.

WINEPRESS

Isa	63: 2	like those of one treading the *w*?
Rev	19:15	He treads the *w* of the fury

WINESKINS

Mt	9:17	do men pour new wine into old *w*.

WINGS

Ex	19: 4	and how I carried you on eagles' *w*
Ru	2:12	under whose *w* you have come
Ps	17: 8	hide me in the shadow of your *w*
	91: 4	under his *w* you will find refuge;
Isa	6: 2	him were seraphs, each with six *w*
	40:31	They will soar on *w* like eagles;
Eze	1: 6	of them had four faces and four *w*.
Zec	5: 9	in their *w*! They had *w* like those
Mal	4: 2	rise with healing in its *w*.
Lk	13:34	hen gathers her chicks under her *w*,
Rev	4: 8	the four living creatures had six *w*

WINS (WIN)

Pr	11:30	and he who *w* souls is wise.

WINTER

Mk	13:18	that this will not take place in *w*,

WIPE (WIPED)

Isa	25: 8	The Sovereign LORD will *w* away
Rev	7:17	God will *w* away every tear
	21: 4	He will *w* every tear

WIPED (WIPE)

Lk	7:38	Then she *w* them with her hair,
Ac	3:19	so that your sins may be *w* out,

WISDOM (WISE)

Ge	3: 6	and also desirable for gaining *w*,
1Ki	4: 29	God gave Solomon *w* and very
2Ch	1: 10	Give me *w* and knowledge,
Ps	51: 6	you teach me *w* in the inmost place
	111: 10	of the LORD is the beginning of *w*;
Pr	2: 6	For the LORD gives *w*,
	3: 13	Blessed is the man who finds *w*,
	4: 7	*W* is supreme; therefore get
	8: 11	for *w* is more precious than rubies,
	11: 2	but with humility comes *w*.
	13: 10	*w* is found in those who take advice
	23: 23	get *w*, discipline and understanding
	29: 3	A man who loves *w* brings joy
	29: 15	The rod of correction imparts *w*,
	31: 26	She speaks with *w*,
Isa	11: 2	Spirit of *w* and of understanding,
	28: 29	in counsel and magnificent in *w*.
Jer	10: 12	he founded the world by his *w*
Mic	6: 9	and to fear your name is *w*—
Mt	11: 19	But *w* is proved right by her actions
Lk	2: 52	And Jesus grew in *w* and stature,
Ac	6: 3	known to be full of the Spirit and *w*.
Ro	11: 33	the depth of the riches of the *w*
1Co	1: 17	not with words of human *w*,
	1: 30	who has become for us *w* from God
	12: 8	through the Spirit the message of *w*
Eph	1: 17	may give you the Spirit of *w*
Col	2: 3	are hidden all the treasures of *w*,
	2: 23	indeed have an appearance of *w*,
Jas	1: 5	of you lacks *w*, he should ask God,
	3: 13	in the humility that comes from *w*.
Rev	5: 12	and wealth and *w* and strength

WISE (WISDOM WISER)

1Ki	3: 12	give you a *w* and discerning heart,
Job	5: 13	He catches the *w* in their craftiness
Ps	19: 7	making *w* the simple.
Pr	3: 7	Do not be *w* in your own eyes;
	9: 8	rebuke a *w* man and he will love
	10: 1	A *w* son brings joy to his father,
	11: 30	and he who wins souls is *w*.
	13: 1	A *w* son heeds his father's
	13: 20	He who walks with the *w* grows *w*,
	16: 23	A *w* man's heart guides his mouth,
	17: 28	Even a fool is thought *w*
Ecc	9: 17	The quiet words of the *w* are more
Jer	9: 23	"Let not the *w* man boast
Eze	28: 6	"'Because you think you are *w*,
Da	2: 21	He gives wisdom to the *w*
	12: 3	Those who are *w* will shine like
Mt	11: 25	hidden these things from the *w*
	25: 2	them were foolish and five were *w*.
1Co	1: 19	I will destroy the wisdom of the *w*;
	1: 27	things of the world to shame the *w*;
	3: 19	He catches the *w* in their craftiness
Eph	5: 15	but as *w*, making the most
2Ti	3: 15	able to make you *w* for salvation
Jas	3: 13	Who is *w* and understanding

WISER (WISE)

Pr	9: 9	a wise man and he will be *w* still;
1Co	1: 25	of God is *w* than man's wisdom,

WISH (WISHES)

Jn	15: 7	ask whatever you *w*, and it will be
Ro	9: 3	For I could *w* that I myself were
Rev	3: 15	I *w* you were either one

WISHES (WISH)

Rev	22: 17	let him come; and whoever *w*,

WITCHCRAFT

Dt	18: 10	engages in *w*, or casts spells,
Gal	5: 20	idolatry and *w*; hatred, discord,

WITHDREW

Lk	5: 16	But Jesus often *w* to lonely places

WITHER (WITHERS)

Ps	1: 3	and whose leaf does not *w*.
	37: 19	In times of disaster they will not *w*;

WITHERS (WITHER)

Isa	40: 7	The grass *w* and the flowers fall,
1Pe	1: 24	the grass *w* and the flowers fall,

WITHHELD (WITHHOLD)

Ge	22: 12	you have not *w* from me your son,

WITHHOLD (WITHHELD WITHHOLDS)

Ps	84: 11	no good things does he *w*
Pr	23: 13	Do not *w* discipline from a child;

WITHHOLDS (WITHHOLD)

Dt	27: 19	"Cursed is the man who *w* justice

WITNESS (EYE-WITNESSES WITNESSES)

Pr	12: 17	truthful *w* gives honest testimony,
	19: 9	A false *w* will not go unpunished,
Jn	1: 8	he came only as a *w* to the light.

WITNESSES (WITNESS)

Dt	19: 15	by the testimony of two or three *w*.
Mt	18: 16	by the testimony of two or three *w*.'
Ac	1: 8	and you will be my *w* in Jerusalem,

WIVES (WIFE)

Eph	5: 22	*W*, submit to your husbands
	5: 25	love your *w*, just as Christ loved
1Pe	3: 1	talk by the behaviour of their *w*,

WIVES' (WIFE)

1Ti	4: 7	with godless myths and old *w* tales

WOE

Isa	6: 5	"*W* to me!" I cried.
Eze	34: 2	*W* to the shepherds
Mt	18: 7	*W* to the world
	23: 13	"*W* to you, teachers of the law
Jude	: 11	*W* to them! They have taken

WOLF (WOLVES)

Isa	65: 25	*w* and the lamb will feed together,

WOLVES (WOLF)

Mt	10: 16	you out like sheep among *w*.

WOMAN (MAN)

Ge	2: 22	God made a *w* from
	2: 23	she shall be called '*w*,'
	3: 6	*w* saw that the fruit
	3: 12	The *w* you put here with
	3: 15	between you and the *w*,
	3: 16	To the *w* he said,
	12: 11	a beautiful *w* you are.
	20: 3	because of the *w* you have
	24: 5	if the *w* is unwilling
Ex	2: 1	married a Levite *w*

Ex	3: 22	Every w is to ask her
	21: 10	If he marries another w
	21: 22	hit a pregnant w
Lev	12: 2	w who becomes pregnant
	15: 19	w has her regular flow
	15: 25	a w has a discharge
	18: 17	sexual relations with both a w
	20: 13	as one lies with a w,
Nu	5: 29	when a w goes astray
	30: 3	young w still living in
	30: 9	by a widow or divorced w
	30: 10	w living with her husband
Dt	20: 7	become pledged to a w
	21: 11	the captives a beautiful w
	22: 5	w must not wear men's
	22: 13	married this w but when
Jdg	4: 9	hand Sisera over to a w.
	13: 6	the w went to her husband
	14: 2	have seen a Philistine w
	16: 4	he fell in love with a w
	20: 4	husband of the murdered w
Ru	3: 11	a w of noble character
1Sa	1: 15	a w who is deeply troubled
	25: 3	intelligent and beautiful w,
	28: 7	a w who is a medium,
2Sa	11: 2	he saw a w bathing
	13: 17	"Get this w out of here
	14: 2	had a wise w brought
	20: 16	a wise w called from
1Ki	3: 18	this w also had a baby.
	17: 24	the w said to Elijah,
2Ki	4: 8	a well-to-do w was there,
	8: 1	Elisha had said to the w
	9: 34	"Take care of that cursed w,"
Job	14: 1	Man born of w is of few
Pr	11: 16	A kind-hearted w gains respect,
	11: 22	a beautiful w who shows no
	14: 1	a wise w builds her house,
	30: 23	unloved w who is married,
	31: 30	a w who fears the LORD
Isa	54: 1	O barren w, you who never
Mt	5: 28	looks at a w lustfully
	9: 20	a w who had been subject
	15: 28	W you have great faith!
	26: 7	a w came to him with
Mk	5: 25	a w was there who had
	7: 25	a w whose little daughter
Lk	7: 39	what kind of a w she is
	10: 38	a w named Martha opened
	13: 12	"W, you are set free
	15: 8	suppose a w has ten silver
Jn	2: 4	w, why do you involve
	4: 7	a Samaritan w came
	8: 3	a w caught in adultery.
	19: 26	w, here is your son,"
	20: 15	W, 'he said, "why are you crying?
Ac	9: 40	Turning towards the dead w,
	16: 14	was a w named Lydia,
Ro	7: 2	a married w is bound to
1Co	7: 2	each w her own husband
	7: 15	a believing man or w is
	7: 34	an unmarried w or virgin
	7: 39	w is bound to her husband
	11: 3	the head of the w is man,
	11: 7	the w is the glory of man
	11: 13	a w to pray to God with
Gal	4: 4	his Son, born of a w,
	4: 31	not children of the slave w,
1Ti	2: 11	A w should learn in
	5: 16	any w who is a believer

Rev	2: 20	You tolerate that w Jezebel,
	12: 1	a w clothed with the sun
	12: 13	he pursued the w who had
	17: 3	a w sitting on a scarlet

WOMB

Job	1: 21	Naked I came from my mother's w,
Ps	139: 13	in my mother's w.
Pr	31: 2	"O my son, O son of my w,
Jer	1: 5	you in the w I knew you,
Lk	1: 44	the baby in my w leaped for joy.
Jn	3: 4	into his mother's w to be born!"

WOMEN (MAN)

Mt	11: 11	among those born of w,
	28: 5	The angel said to the w,
Mk	15: 41	Many other w who had come
Lk	1: 42	Blessed are you among w,
	8: 2	also some w who had been
	23: 27	w who mourned and wailed
	24: 11	they did not believe the w,
Ac	1: 14	along with the w and Mary
	16: 13	speak to the w who had
	17: 4	not a few prominent w.
Ro	1: 26	w exchanged natural relations
1Co	14: 34	w should remain silent in
Php	4: 3	help these w who have
1Ti	2: 9	want w to dress modestly
	5: 2	older w as mothers,
Tit	2: 3	teach the older w to be
	2: 4	train the younger w to love
Heb	11: 35	W received back their dead
1Pe	3: 5	the holy w of the past

WON (WIN)

1Pe	3: 1	they may be w over without words

WONDER (WONDERFUL WONDERS)

Ps	17: 7	Show the w of your great love,
SS	1: 3	No w the maidens love you!

WONDERFUL* (WONDER)

2Sa	1: 26	Your love for me was w,
	1: 26	more w than that of women.
1Ch	16: 9	tell of all his w acts.
Job	42: 3	things too w for me to know.
Ps	26: 7	and telling of all your w deeds.
	31: 21	for he showed his w love to me
	75: 1	men tell of your w deeds.
	105: 2	tell of all his w acts.
	107: 8	and his w deeds for men,
	107: 15	and his w deeds for men.
	107: 21	and his w deeds for men.
	107: 24	his w deeds in the deep.
	107: 31	and his w deeds for men.
	119: 18	w things in your law.
	119: 129	Your statutes are w;
	131: 1	or things too w for me.
	139: 6	Such knowledge is too w for me,
	139: 14	your works are w,
	145: 5	I will meditate on your w works.
Isa	9: 6	W Counsellor, Mighty God,
	28: 29	w in counsel and magnificent
Mt	21: 15	of the law saw the w things he did
Lk	13: 17	with all the w things he was doing.
1Pe	2: 9	out of darkness into his w light.

WONDERS (WONDER)

Ex	3: 20	with all the w that I will perform
Dt	10: 21	and awesome w you saw

2Sa	7: 23	awesome *w* by driving out nations
Job	37: 14	stop and consider God's *w*.
Ps	9: 1	I will tell of all your *w*.
	89: 5	The heavens praise your *w*,
	119: 27	then I will meditate on your *w*.
Joel	2: 30	I will show *w* in the heavens
Ac	2: 11	we hear them declaring the *w*
	2: 19	I will show *w* in the heaven above
	5: 12	many miraculous signs and *w*
2Co	12: 12	that mark an apostle—signs, *w*
2Th	2: 9	and *w*, and in every sort
Heb	2: 4	also testified to it by signs, *w*

WOOD

| Isa | 44: 19 | Shall I bow down to a block of *w*?" |
| 1Co | 3: 12 | costly stones, *w*, hay or straw, |

WOOL

Pr	31: 13	She selects *w* and flax
Isa	1: 18	they shall be like *w*.
Da	7: 9	hair of his head was white like *w*.
Rev	1: 14	and hair were white like *w*,

WORD (BYWORD WORDS)

Nu	30: 2	he must not break his *w*
Dt	8: 3	but on every *w* that comes
2Sa	22: 31	the *w* of the LORD is flawless.
Ps	56: 4	In God, whose *w* I praise,
	119: 9	By living according to your *w*.
	119: 11	I have hidden your *w* in my heart
	119: 105	Your *w* is a lamp to my feet
Pr	12: 25	but a kind *w* cheers him up.
	15: 1	but a harsh *w* stirs up anger.
	25: 11	A *w* aptly spoken
	30: 5	"Every *w* of God is flawless;
Isa	55: 11	so is my *w* that goes out
Jer	23: 29	"Is not my *w* like fire," declares
Mt	4: 4	but on every *w* that comes
	12: 36	for every careless *w* they have
	15: 6	Thus you nullify the *w* of God
Mk	4: 14	parable? The farmer sows the *w*.
Jn	1: 1	was the *W*, and the *W* was
	1: 14	The *W* became flesh and made
	17: 17	them by the truth; your *w* is truth.
Ac	6: 4	and the ministry of the *w*."
2Co	2: 17	we do not peddle the *w* of God
	4: 2	nor do we distort the *w* of God.
Eph	6: 17	of the Spirit, which is the *w* of God.
Php	2: 16	as you hold out the *w* of life—
Col	3: 16	Let the *w* of Christ dwell
2Ti	2: 15	and who correctly handles the *w*
Heb	4: 12	For the *w* of God is living
Jas	1: 22	Do not merely listen to the *w*,
2Pe	1: 19	And we have the *w* of the prophets

WORDS

Dt	11: 18	Fix these *w* of mine in your hearts
Ps	12: 6	the *w* of the LORD are flawless,
	119: 103	How sweet are your *w* to my taste,
	119: 130	The unfolding of your *w* gives light,
	119: 160	All your *w* are true;
Pr	2: 1	My son, if you accept my *w*
	10: 19	When *w* are many, sin is not absent
	16: 24	Pleasant *w* are a honeycomb,
	30: 6	Do not add to his *w*,
Ecc	12: 11	The *w* of the wise are like goads,
Jer	15: 16	When your *w* came, I ate them;
Mt	24: 35	but my *w* will never pass away.
Lk	6: 47	and hears my *w* and puts them
Jn	6: 68	You have the *w* of eternal life.

Jn	15: 7	in me and my *w* remain in you,
1Co	2: 13	but in *w* taught by the Spirit,
	14: 19	rather speak five intelligible *w*
Rev	22: 19	And if anyone takes *w* away

**WORK (FELLOW-WORKERS WORKED
WORKER WORKERS WORKING WORKMAN
WORKMANSHIP WORKS)**

Ge	2: 2	day he rested from all his *w*.
Ex	23: 12	"Six days do your *w*,
Nu	8: 11	ready to do the *w* of the LORD.
Dt	5: 14	On it you shall not do any *w*,
Ps	19: 1	the skies proclaim the *w*
Pr	8: 22	me at the beginning of his *w*,
Ecc	5: 19	his lot and be happy in his *w*—
Jer	48: 10	lax in doing the LORD's *w*!
Mt	20: 1	to hire men to *w* in his vineyard.
Jn	6: 27	Do not *w* for food that spoils,
	9: 4	we must do the *w* of him who sent
Ac	13: 2	for the *w* to which I have called
1Co	3: 13	test the quality of each man's *w*.
	4: 12	We *w* hard with our own hands.
Eph	4: 16	up in love, as each part does its *w*.
Php	1: 6	that he who began a good *w*
	2: 12	continue to *w* out your salvation
Col	3: 23	Whatever you do, *w* at it
1Th	4: 11	and to *w* with your hands,
	5: 12	to respect those who *w* hard
2Th	3: 10	If a man will not *w*, he shall not eat
2Ti	3: 17	equipped for every good *w*.
Heb	6: 10	he will not forget your *w*
2Jn	: 11	him shares in his wicked *w*.
3Jn	: 8	men so that we may *w* together

WORKED (WORK)

| 1Co | 15: 10 | No, I *w* harder than all of them— |
| 2Th | 3: 8 | On the contrary, we *w* night |

WORKER (WORK)

| Lk | 10: 7 | for the *w* deserves his wages. |
| 1Ti | 5: 18 | and "The *w* deserves his wages." |

WORKERS (WORK)

| Mt | 9: 37 | is plentiful but the *w* are few. |

WORKING (WORK)

| Col | 3: 23 | as *w* for the Lord, not for men, |

WORKMAN (WORK)

| 2Ti | 2: 15 | a *w* who does not need |

WORKMANSHIP* (WORK)

| Eph | 2: 10 | For we are God's *w*, created |

WORKS (WORK)

Ps	66: 5	how awesome his *w* on man's behalf
	145: 6	of the power of your awesome *w*,
Pr	31: 31	let her *w* bring her praise
Ro	4: 2	in fact, Abraham was justified by *w*
	8: 28	in all things God *w* for the good
Eph	2: 9	not by *w*, so that no one can boast.
	4: 12	to prepare God's people for *w*

WORLD (WORLDLY)

Ps	9: 8	He will judge the *w*
	50: 12	for the *w* is mine, and all that is in it
	96: 13	He will judge the *w*
Pr	8: 23	before the *w* began.
Isa	13: 11	I will punish the *w* for its evil,
Zep	1: 18	the whole *w* will be consumed,

Mt	5: 14	"You are the light of the w.
	16: 26	for a man if he gains the whole w,
Mk	16: 15	into all the w and preach the good
Jn	1: 29	who takes away the sin of the w!
	3: 16	so loved the w that he gave his one
	8: 12	he said, "I am the light of the w.
	15: 19	As it is, you do not belong to the w,
	16: 33	In this w you will have trouble.
	17: 5	had with you before the w began.
	17: 14	not of the w any more than I am
	18: 36	"My kingdom is not of this w.
Ac	17: 24	"The God who made the w
Ro	3: 19	and the whole w held accountable
	10: 18	their words to the ends of the w."
1Co	1: 27	things of the w to shame the strong.
	3: 19	the wisdom of this w is foolishness
	6: 2	that the saints will judge the w?
2Co	5: 19	that God was reconciling the w
	10: 3	For though we live in the w,
1Ti	6: 7	For we brought nothing into the w,
Heb	11: 38	the w was not worthy of them.
Jas	2: 5	poor in the eyes of the w to be rich
	4: 4	with the w is hatred towards God?
1Pe	1: 20	before the creation of the w,
1Jn	2: 2	but also for the sins of the whole w.
	2: 15	not love the w or anything in the w.
	5: 4	born of God overcomes the w.
Rev	13: 8	slain from the creation of the w.

WORLDLY (WORLD)

1Co	3: 1	address you as spiritual but as w—
Tit	2: 12	to ungodliness and w passions,

WORM

Mk	9: 48	"'their w does not die,

WORRY (WORRYING)

Mt	6: 25	I tell you, do not w about your life,
	10: 19	do not w about what to say

WORRYING (WORRY)

Mt	6: 27	of you by w can add a single hour

WORSHIP (WORSHIPPED WORSHIPS)

Jos	22: 27	that we will w the LORD
2Ki	17: 36	arm, is the one you must w.
1Ch	16: 29	w the LORD in the splendour
Ps	95: 6	Come, let us bow down in w,
	100: 2	W the LORD with gladness;
Zec	14: 17	up to Jerusalem to w the King,
Mt	2: 2	and have come to w him."
	4: 9	"if you will bow down and w me."
Jn	4: 24	and his worshippers must w in spirit
Ro	12: 1	this is your spiritual act of w.
Heb	10: 1	perfect those who draw near to w.

WORSHIPPED (WORSHIP)

2Ch	29: 30	and bowed their heads and w.
Mt	28: 9	clasped his feet and w him.

WORSHIPS (WORSHIP)

Isa	44: 15	But he also fashions a god and w it;

WORTH (WORTHY)

Job	28: 13	Man does not comprehend its w;
Pr	31: 10	She is w far more than rubies.
Mt	10: 31	are w more than many sparrows.
Ro	8: 18	sufferings are not w comparing
1Pe	1: 7	of greater w than gold,
	3: 4	which is of great w in God's sight.

WORTHLESS

Pr	11: 4	Wealth is w in the day of wrath,
Jas	1: 26	himself and his religion is w.

WORTHY (WORTH)

1Ch	16: 25	For great is the LORD and most w
Mt	10: 37	more than me is not w of me;
Lk	15: 19	I am no longer w to be called your
Eph	4: 1	to live a life w of the calling you
Php	1: 27	in a manner w of the gospel
Col	1: 10	in order that you may live a life w
1Ti	3: 8	are to be men w of respect, sincere,
Heb	3: 3	Jesus has been found w
3Jn	: 6	on their way in a manner w of God.
Rev	5: 2	"Who is w to break the seals

WOUND (WOUNDS)

1Co	8: 12	and w their weak conscience,

WOUNDS (WOUND)

Pr	27: 6	w from a friend can be trusted,
Isa	53: 5	and by his w we are healed.
Zec	13: 6	'What are these w on your body?'
1Pe	2: 24	by his w you have been healed.

WRAPS

Ps	104: 2	He w himself in light

WRATH

2Ch	36: 16	scoffed at his prophets, until the w
Ps	2: 5	and terrifies them in his w, saying,
	76: 10	Surely your w against men brings
Pr	15: 1	A gentle answer turns away w,
Isa	13: 13	at the w of the LORD Almighty,
	51: 17	the cup of his w,
Jer	25: 15	filled with the wine of my w
Eze	5: 13	my w against them will subside,
	20: 8	So I said I would pour out my w
Am	1: 3	I will not turn back my w,
Na	1: 2	maintains his w against his enemies
Zep	1: 15	That day will be a day of w,
Jn	3: 36	for God's w remains on him."
Ro	1: 18	The w of God is being revealed
	2: 5	you are storing up w
	5: 9	saved from God's w through him!
	9: 22	choosing to show his w
1Th	5: 9	God did not appoint us to suffer w
Rev	6: 16	and from the w of the Lamb!
	19: 15	the fury of the w of God Almighty.

WRESTLED

Ge	32: 24	and a man w with him till daybreak

WRITE (WRITER WRITING WRITTEN WROTE)

Dt	6: 9	W them on the door-frames
	10: 2	I will w on the tablets the words
Pr	7: 3	w them on the tablet of your heart.
Jer	31: 33	and w it on their hearts.
Heb	8: 10	and w them on their hearts.
Rev	3: 12	I will also w on him my new name.

WRITER* (WRITE)

Ps	45: 1	my tongue is the pen of a skilful w.

WRITING (WRITE)

1Co	14: 37	him acknowledge that what I am w

WRITTEN (WRITE)

Dt	28: 58	which are w in this book,

Jos	1: 8	careful to do everything *w* in it.
	23: 6	to obey all that is *w* in the Book
Ps	40: 7	it is *w* about me in the scroll.
Da	12: 1	everyone whose name is found *w*
Mal	3: 16	A scroll of remembrance was *w*
Lk	10: 20	but rejoice that your names are *w*
	24: 44	must be fulfilled that is *w* about me
Jn	20: 31	these are *w* that you may believe
	21: 25	for the books that would be *w*.
Ro	2: 15	of the law are *w* on their hearts,
1Co	4: 6	"Do not go beyond what is *w*."
	10: 11	as examples and were *w* down
2Co	3: 3	*w* not with ink but with the Spirit
Col	2: 14	having cancelled the *w* code,
Heb	10: 7	it is *w* about me in the scroll—
	12: 23	whose names are *w* in heaven.
Rev	21: 27	but only those whose names are *w*

WRONG (WRONGDOING WRONGED WRONGS)

Ex	23: 2	Do not follow the crowd in doing *w*
Nu	5: 7	must make full restitution for his *w*,
Dt	32: 4	A faithful God who does no *w*,
Job	34: 12	unthinkable that God would do *w*,
Ps	5: 5	you hate all who do *w*.
Gal	2: 11	to his face, because he was in the *w*.
1Th	5: 15	that nobody pays back *w* for *w*,

WRONGDOING (WRONG)

Job	1: 22	sin by charging God with *w*.
1Jn	5: 17	All *w* is sin, and there is sin that

WRONGED (WRONG)

1Co	6: 7	not rather be *w*? Why not rather

WRONGS (WRONG)

Pr	10: 12	but love covers over all *w*.
1Co	13: 5	angered, it keeps no record of *w*.

WROTE (WRITE)

Ex	34: 28	And he *w* on the tablets the words
Jn	5: 46	for he *w* about me.
	8: 8	down and *w* on the ground.

XERXES

King of Persia, husband of Esther. Deposed Vashti; replaced her with Esther (Est 1-2). Sealed Haman's edict to annihilate the Jews (Est 3). Received Esther without having called her (Est 5:1-8). Honoured Mordecai (Est 6). Hanged Haman (Est 7). Issued edict allowing Jews to defend themselves (Est 8). Exalted Mordecai (Est 8:1-2, 15; 9:4; 10).

YEAR (YEARS)

Ex	34: 23	Three times a *y* all your men are
Lev	16: 34	to be made once a *y* for all the sins
	25: 4	But in the seventh *y* the land is
	25: 11	The fiftieth *y* shall be a jubilee
Heb	10: 1	repeated endlessly *y* after *y*,

YEARS (YEAR)

Ge	1: 14	to mark seasons and days and *y*,
Ex	12: 40	lived in Egypt was 430 *y*.
	16: 35	The Israelites ate manna forty *y*,
Job	36: 26	of his *y* is past finding out.
Ps	90: 4	For a thousand *y* in your sight
	90: 10	The length of our days is seventy *y*
Pr	3: 2	they will prolong your life many *y*
Lk	3: 23	Jesus himself was about thirty *y* old

2Pe	3: 8	the Lord a day is like a thousand *y*,
Rev	20: 2	and bound him for a thousand *y*.

YEAST

Ex	12: 15	are to eat bread made without *y*.
Mt	16: 6	guard against the *y* of the Pharisees
1Co	5: 6	you know that a little *y* works

YESTERDAY

Heb	13: 8	Jesus Christ is the same *y*

YOKE (YOKED)

1Ki	12: 4	and the heavy *y* he put on us,
Mt	11: 29	Take my *y* upon you and learn
Gal	5: 1	be burdened again by a *y*

YOKED (YOKE)

2Co	6: 14	Do not be *y* together

YOUNG (YOUNGER YOUTH)

2Ch	10: 14	he followed the advice of the *y* men
Ps	37: 25	I was *y* and now I am old,
	119: 9	How can a *y* man keep his way
Pr	20: 29	The glory of *y* men is their strength
Isa	40: 11	he gently leads those that have *y*.
Joel	2: 28	your *y* men will see visions.
Ac	2: 17	your *y* men will see visions,
	7: 58	at the feet of a *y* man named Saul.
1Ti	4: 12	down on you because you are *y*,
Tit	2: 6	encourage the *y* men
1Pe	5: 5	*Y* men, in the same way be
1Jn	2: 13	I write to you, *y* men,

YOUNGER (YOUNG)

1Ti	5: 1	Treat *y* men as brothers, older
Tit	2: 4	Then they can train the *y* women

YOUTH (YOUNG)

Ps	103: 5	so that my *y* is renewed like
Ecc	12: 1	Creator in the days of your *y*,
2Ti	2: 22	Flee the evil desires of *y*,

ZACCHAEUS

Lk	19: 2	A man was there by the name of *Z*;

ZEAL (ZEALOUS)

Ps	69: 9	for *z* for your house consumes me,
Pr	19: 2	to have *z* without knowledge,
Isa	59: 17	and wrapped himself in *z*
Jn	2: 17	"*Z* for your house will consume me
Ro	10: 2	their *z* is not based on knowledge.
	12: 11	Never be lacking in *z*,

ZEALOUS (ZEAL)

Nu	25: 13	he was *z* for the honour of his God
Pr	23: 17	always be *z* for the fear
Eze	39: 25	and I will be *z* for my holy name.
Gal	4: 18	fine to be *z*, provided the purpose is

ZEBULUN

Son of Jacob by Leah (Ge 30:20; 35:23; 1Ch 2:1). Tribe of blessed (Ge 49:13; Dt 33:18-19), numbered (Nu 1:31; 26:27), allotted land (Jos 19:10-16; Eze 48:26), failed to fully possess (Jdg 1:30), supported Deborah (Jdg 4:6-10; 5:14, 18), David (1Ch 12:33), 12,000 from (Rev 7:8).

ZECHARIAH

1. Son of Jeroboam II; king of Israel (2Ki 15:8-12).

2. Post-exilic prophet who encouraged rebuilding of temple (Ezr 5:1; 6:14; Zec 1:1).

ZEDEKIAH

1. False prophet (1Ki 22:11-24; 2Ch 18:10-23).
2. Mattaniah, son of Josiah (1Ch 3:15), made king of Judah by Nebuchadnezzar (2Ki 24:17-25:7; 2Ch 36:10-14; Jer 37-39; 52:1-11).

ZEPHANIAH

Prophet; descendant of Hezekiah (Zep 1:1).

ZERUBBABEL

Descendant of David (1Ch 3:19; Mt 1:3). Led return from exile (Ezr 2:2; Ne 7:7). Governor of Israel; helped rebuild altar and temple (Ezr 3; Hag 1-2; Zec 4).

ZILPAH

Servant of Leah, mother of Jacob's sons Gad and Asher (Ge 30:9-12; 35:26, 46:16-18).

ZIMRI

King of Israel (1Ki 16:9-20).

ZION

2Sa 5: 7 David captured the fortress of Z,

Ps	2: 6	King on Z, my holy hill."
	9: 11	to the LORD, enthroned in Z;
	74: 2	Mount Z, where you dwelt.
	87: 2	the LORD loves the gates of Z
	102: 13	and have compassion on Z,
	137: 3	"Sing us one of the songs of Z!"
Isa	2: 3	The law will go out from Z,
	28: 16	"See, I lay a stone in Z,
	51: 11	They will enter Z with singing;
	52: 8	when the LORD returns to Z,
Jer	50: 5	They will ask the way to Z
Joel	3: 21	The LORD dwells in Z!
Am	6: 1	to you who are complacent in Z,
Mic	4: 2	The law will go out from Z,
Zec	9: 9	Rejoice greatly, O Daughter of Z!
Ro	9: 33	I lay in Z a stone that causes men
	11: 26	"The deliverer will come from Z;
Heb	12: 22	But you have come to Mount Z,
Rev	14: 1	standing on Mount Z,

ZIPPORAH*

Daughter of Reuel; wife of Moses (Ex 2:21-22; 4:20-26; 18:1-6).

ZOPHAR

One of Job's friends (Job 11; 20).

NIV Bible Commentary

Edited by Alister McGrath

The highly acclaimed one-volume guide to God's Word.

A one-volume commentary written in a clear, accessible style with the minimum of theological jargon. Ideal for those just starting out on serious Bible study and wanting to gain a firmly established understanding of Scripture. Clearly introduces leading Bible themes, offering succinct and informative comment for your everyday reading of the Bible. Based on the New International Version but can also be used with other translations. Features maps and charts throughout.

Paperback   ISBN 0 340 66142 9

NIV Thematic Study Bible

General Editor: Alister McGrath

The best commentary on Scripture is Scripture itself.

A unique study Bible providing a method of reading and studying which enables the Bible to comment on and clarify itself. Rather than taking the more usual lexical approach, the *NIV Thematic Study Bible* lists theme-based references alongside the text, which point the reader to appropriate theme outlines in a separate back section. This Thematic Section contains over 2,000 themes which include a brief explanation and key Bible references for each theme, as well as cross-references to related themes.

This way of studying the Bible encourages an understanding of the unity of Scripture, as the reader engages with the text. Reading through familiar passages, while using the margin references, will immediately present the wider picture. Carefully researching a theme from the Thematic Section offers a comprehensive biblical perspective from Genesis to Revelation. Instead of using an array of commentary or study materials, the reader can benefit from this self-contained volume while reading the Bible in a truly biblical way.

USING THE NIV THEMATIC STUDY BIBLE, READERS CAN:

Identify and explore the leading themes of Scripture
See how themes interweave and develop through the Bible
Read the Bible with the minimum of subjective comment

ALSO INCLUDED:

Book Introductions emphasising the themes developed in each book of the Bible
Almost 200 explanatory panels giving more detailed descriptions of each theme
An alphabetical index of themes, panels and book introductions

Cased, blue   ISBN 0 340 56708 2
Calfskin, black   ISBN 0 340 65660 3

The Bible in One Year

New International Version

An excellent way to read through the Bible methodically in one year.

The full text of the NIV divided into 365 daily readings. Each day's selection includes text from both the Old and New Testament, as well as a reading from either Psalms or Proverbs.

Enables a structured but varied reading of the full Bible text in one year. Features the NIV Bible Guide: including an explanation of the Bible in its current form, a brief outline of each book, quick reference listing to well known people and events, five maps and a time chart.

Pocket flexi-bind   ISBN 0 340 51060 9
Standard cased   ISBN 0 340 41917 2